"Even for the most seasoned of preachers, the thought of expositing the Gospel of Matthew could be overwhelming. Thanks to Doug O'Donnell's newest commentary, chock-full of impressive insights and engaging wit, the first and perhaps greatest Gospel has suddenly become much less daunting. When Kent Hughes called on O'Donnell to write this volume, he knew exactly what he was doing."

Nicholas Perrin, Dean, Wheaton College Graduate School

"This commentary grows out of wide reading and solid learning—the footnotes alone are a gold mine. O'Donnell writes with a zest for real life, wit, and (controlled) whimsy. The outcome: sermons that both *revel in Christ* and *reveal Christ* in fresh and striking ways. The author proves to be a hard-working and natural expositor of Scripture. This book goes to the top of my list of sterling homiletical commentaries on the first Gospel."

Robert W. Yarbrough, Professor of New Testament, Covenant Theological Seminary

"The market is full of critical commentaries, but not many actually deal with what is 'critical'—the centrality of the gospel, the mission of the Church, and the life of the Christian. Doug O'Donnell's commentary on Matthew is a clear exception. With sensitivity to all the important narrative and exegetical details, O'Donnell offers an interpretation of the first Gospel that is pastoral throughout, and in some instances, truly profound. Relevant illustrations are used in almost every passage, and numerous issues are addressed with theological vigor and often from the pastoral heritage of the Church. There are times when the critical commentaries are useful, even necessary, but I cannot imagine a pastor preaching through Matthew that would not want to use this commentary as a significant resource."

Edward W. Klink III, Associate Professor of New Testament, Talbot School of Theology, Biola University

MATTHEW

PREACHING THE WORD
Edited by R. Kent Hughes

Genesis | R. Kent Hughes
Exodus | Philip Graham Ryken
Leviticus | Kenneth A. Mathews
Numbers | Iain M. Duguid
Deuteronomy | Ajith Fernando
1 Samuel | John Woodhouse
Proverbs | Raymond C. Ortlund Jr.
Ecclesiastes | Philip Graham Ryken
Song of Solomon | Douglas Sean O'Donnell
Isaiah | Raymond C. Ortlund Jr.
Jeremiah and Lamentations | Philip Graham Ryken
Daniel | Rodney D. Stortz
Mark | R. Kent Hughes
Luke | R. Kent Hughes
John | R. Kent Hughes
Acts | R. Kent Hughes
Romans | R. Kent Hughes
2 Corinthians | R. Kent Hughes
Galatians | Todd Wilson
Ephesians | R. Kent Hughes
Philippians, Colossians, and Philemon | R. Kent Hughes
1–2 Thessalonians | James H. Grant Jr.
1–2 Timothy and Titus | R. Kent Hughes and Bryan Chapell
Hebrews | R. Kent Hughes
James | R. Kent Hughes
1–2 Peter and Jude | David R. Helm
1–3 John | David L. Allen
Revelation | James M. Hamilton Jr.
The Sermon on the Mount | R. Kent Hughes

PREACHING *the* WORD

MATTHEW

ALL AUTHORITY *in* HEAVEN *and on* EARTH

DOUGLAS SEAN O'DONNELL

R. Kent Hughes
Series Editor

CROSSWAY
WHEATON, ILLINOIS

Matthew

Published by Crossway
1300 Crescent Street
Wheaton, Illinois 60187

Cover design: Jon McGrath, Simplicated Studio

Cover image: Adam Greene, illustrator

First printing 2013

Printed in the United States of America

ISBN-13: 978-1-4335-0365-8
ISBN-10: 1-4335-0365-4
ePub ISBN: 978-1-4335-3966-4
PDF ISBN: 978-1-4335-3964-0
Mobipocket ISBN: 978-1-4335-3965-7

Library of Congress Cataloging-in-Publication Data

O'Donnell, Douglas Sean, 1972-
Matthew : all authority in heaven and on earth / Douglas S. O'Donnell.
pages cm.—(Preaching the word)
Includes bibliographical references and index.
ISBN 978-1-4335-0365-8 (hc)
1. Bible. Matthew—Commentaries. I. Title.
BS2575.53.O36 2013
226.2'07—dc23 2013002796

Crossway is a publishing ministry of Good News Publishers.

VP 23 22 21 20 19 18 17 16 15 14 13
15 14 13 12 11 10 9 8 7 6 5 4 3 2 1

To Sean Michael O'Donnell,
my firstborn son,
whose birth,
by God's redemptive providence,
brought me new birth

And Jesus came and said to them, "All authority in heaven and on earth has been given to me. Go therefore and make disciples of all nations, baptizing them in the name of the Father and of the Son and of the Holy Spirit, teaching them to observe all that I have commanded you. And behold, I am with you always, to the end of the age."

MATTHEW 28:18–20

Contents

A Word to Those Who Preach the Word

There are times when I am preaching that I have especially sensed the pleasure of God. I usually become aware of it through the unnatural silence. The ever-present coughing ceases, and the pews stop creaking, bringing an almost physical quiet to the sanctuary—through which my words sail like arrows. I experience a heightened eloquence, so that the cadence and volume of my voice intensify the truth I am preaching.

There is nothing quite like it—the Holy Spirit filling one's sails, the sense of his pleasure, and the awareness that something is happening among one's hearers. This experience is, of course, not unique, for thousands of preachers have similar experiences, even greater ones.

What has happened when this takes place? How do we account for this sense of his smile? The answer for me has come from the ancient rhetorical categories of *logos*, *ethos*, and *pathos*.

The first reason for his smile is the *logos*—in terms of preaching, God's Word. This means that as we stand before God's people to proclaim his Word, we have done our homework. We have exegeted the passage, mined the significance of its words in their context, and applied sound hermeneutical principles in interpreting the text so that we understand what its words meant to its hearers. And it means that we have labored long until we can express in a sentence what the theme of the text is—so that our outline springs from the text. Then our preparation will be such that as we preach, we will not be preaching our own thoughts about God's Word, but God's actual Word, his *logos*. This is fundamental to pleasing him in preaching.

The second element in knowing God's smile in preaching is *ethos*—what you are as a person. There is a danger endemic to preaching, which is having your hands and heart cauterized by holy things. Phillips Brooks illustrated it by the analogy of a train conductor who comes to believe that he has been to the places he announces because of his long and loud heralding of them. And that is why Brooks insisted that preaching must be "the bringing of truth through personality." Though we can never perfectly embody the truth we preach, we must be subject to it, long for it, and make it as much a part of our ethos as possible. As the Puritan William Ames said, "Next to the Scriptures, nothing makes a sermon more to pierce, than when it comes out of the inward affection of the heart without any affectation." When a preacher's *ethos* backs up his *logos*, there will be the pleasure of God.

Last, there is *pathos*—personal passion and conviction. David Hume, the Scottish philosopher and skeptic, was once challenged as he was seen going to hear George Whitefield preach: "I thought you do not believe in the gospel." Hume replied, "I don't, but he does." Just so! When a preacher believes what he preaches, there will be passion. And this belief and requisite passion will know the smile of God.

The pleasure of God is a matter of *logos* (the Word), *ethos* (what you are), and *pathos* (your passion). As you preach the Word may you experience his smile—the Holy Spirit in your sails!

R. Kent Hughes

Preface

The unique feature of this commentary—as opposed to all others in the history of the church—is that I wrote it. I don't mean that arrogantly or humorously, although I hope you thought the second and are still laughing. I mean it in this sense.

I like Bible commentaries, particularly ones on my favorite book of the Bible (both before and after I was commissioned to do this)—the Gospel of Matthew. Sitting beside me as I write, I have as many commentaries on this Gospel as I have had birthdays. Many of them I have read. Some of them I have used. One of them I enjoyed so much I wish I wrote it. But this commentary is not like them. It's a pastor's commentary for pastors, written by a tall pastor from a small church in a large Chicago suburb to other pastors—tall and short, large and small—in America and around the world. It is written to those who will use it as an aid to preach sermons that would make Matthew smile with approval.

And I do mean smile. Matthew didn't write his Gospel so we'd merely write voluminous tomes that begin "Recent studies on the nature of written documents . . ." or "As in the commentary's various analytical sections, here in the introduction I will first discuss problems of synchronic analysis before turning to those of diachronic analysis." He wrote it, as the church has long and rightly assumed, as an evangelist. Irenaeus, Jerome, and those medieval monastic artists got it right: the Gospel of Matthew is the face of man.[1] This Gospel was written by a man for men about the Man. Matthew wants all people everywhere to bow down before that Man, the one to whom all authority in Heaven and on earth has been given. He wants Gentiles and Jews to submit to their King, trusting Jesus to be Savior from sins and Lord of life. He wants us to know Jesus, worship him, obey his teachings, and tell others to do the same.

Thus, my purpose is as close to Matthew's as possible. Like the Gospel, this commentary was written "to gospel."[2] I'm appealing to real people ("let the reader understand," cf. 24:15) who need a real King. This is not to say I don't deal with doctrines and difficulties in some depth. Nor is it to say I'm not concerned about getting it right. But it is to say, I am more concerned about practical theology than theoretical. To borrow from J. C. Ryle's methodology, I have endeavored "to dwell chiefly on the things needful to salvation."[3]

I shall say lastly but least importantly, the language of this commentary is reflective of this evangelistic and pastoral purpose. You see, therefore, my brothers and sisters, I've occasionally used real phrases we use in everyday ecclesial talk—like "my brothers and sisters" and "you see"—to make you see what you're supposed to see. At times I've also included "look there" because I assume you have your Bible open, either as a pastor preparing a sermon or a layperson doing daily devotions. *And* I've even disregarded those old rules of grammar (based on proper Latin, not proper English) about not starting a sentence with a conjunction. I want the language of these now dead sermons to be as alive as Christ. I hope you find that to be the case. Enjoy!

I acknowledge my heartfelt gratitude to Kent Hughes for the privilege of contributing to the Preaching the Word series. Kent left a phone message five years ago asking me to contribute a volume and to think about what book of the Bible that might be. The Gospel of Matthew is what first came to mind. However, I was young and didn't want be so presumptuous as to ask for that. So I called Kent back and left a message that I'd love to contribute and that I'd be happy to take whatever book he assigned. He called back and left another message—asking me to do Matthew!

I am indebted to the careful editing and proofreading of the Crossway staff. Thank you. I'd also like to thank Matt Newkirk, as well as Alexandra Bloom and Emily Gerdts for their various editorial tasks. Finally, I thank God for my family (Emily, Lily, Evelyn, Simeon, and Charlotte), and notably my oldest son—Sean Michael O'Donnell—to whom I dedicate this book. Sean, I am thankful to God for you more than you can know or imagine.

Douglas Sean O'Donnell
New Covenant Church, Naperville, Illinois

1

The Melodic Line of Matthew

AN INTRODUCTION AND OVERVIEW OF THE GOSPEL OF MATTHEW

WHEN VAN HALEN'S album *1984* hit the record stores, many a young lad, myself included, signed up for piano lessons. This was because the great guitarist, Eddie Van Halen, learned to play piano and proceeded to compose the hit single of that album—one still played at many NBA tip-offs—"Jump." In six short lessons I learned how to master this melody, which in those days was enough to impress friends, woo girls, and justify the expense of ten-dollar lessons. My performance at the junior high talent show was enough to bestow upon me that prestigious adjective-noun combination—rock star. I entered the stage. The spotlight moved across my face and fingers. Cameras flashed. A sixth grade girl fainted. Wearing black dress pants, a white shirt, one glove, cool sunglasses, and (yes!) a skinny piano tie, I sat on my poorly padded bench and bum before my Korg 500 digital synthesizer and played perfectly the rudimentary bass line and monotonous melody of Van Halen's masterpiece.

I'm not certain if such an introduction to a Gospel is sacrilegious or just silly. I intended neither. I actually intended to get your attention in order to make a basic point about music and to show how such a point can and does relate to our study of any piece of literature, notably Matthew's Gospel. The point is this: just as every good song has a melodic line (a tune that brings unity to the whole by its recurrence)—think of the chorus of "Jump" or "Ode to Joy" of Beethoven's Ninth Symphony, Fourth Movement—so too does every book of the Bible.

I'll put it this way. The four Gospels—Matthew, Mark, Luke, and John—all sound the same. That is, they all have a similar bass line. It's as simple as the two C notes I learned for that Van Halen song. They focus on the same person (Jesus), and they were written for the same primary purpose (conversion to Christ; see John 20:31). In all four we hear those same deep, steady notes of Jesus as the Son, Savior, and Christ. We behold him as a miracle-worker. We hear his teaching and his call to faith and repentance. We encounter his passion, death, and resurrection. In these ways, all four sound the same. They have the same bass line. Yet each Gospel has a distinct melody of its own. And just as we can recognize the melody of "Ode to Joy" each time we hear the first four notes or "Jump" when we hear the first four chords, so can we recognize Matthew's melody if we hear the recurring themes.

In Beethoven's Fourth Movement of the Ninth Symphony, the beginning and the end are important. Matthew's Gospel is the same. We hear the melody most clearly at the top and tail. Look at the first words with which Matthew begins: "The book of the genealogy of Jesus Christ, the son of David" (1:1). Notice the first two titles applied to Jesus. The first is "Christ." That is not a last name. That is a title. It means "anointed one" or "king." This is a book about King Jesus. That point is reiterated with the next title, "the son of David." David was the great king of Israel, the one to whom a great promise was made. In 2 Samuel 7 we are told that through his offspring God would establish a forever kingdom. So with those first two titles you can hear the first note of the melodic line: Jesus, the King. Jesus is a sovereign who will be sovereign over an everlasting kingdom!

From that note of kingly authority Matthew subtly drops a half-step to the next note. He does this by moving from Jesus being "the son of David" to also being "the son of Abraham."

Who was Abraham and why does he matter? Abraham was the non-Israelite Father of Israel. That is the point Paul will make in Romans 4, that Abraham *of Ur* wasn't a "Hebrew" (Genesis 14:13) until he became one (you'll have to think about that to get it). And why is he important? Abraham is important because he too received a great promise from God. In Genesis 12:1–3 God explained how through him and his offspring all "nations" would be blessed (cf. 17:4; 18:18; 22:18).

So, the point of these two persons and promises is this: Jesus will be that Davidic King who will reign over that eternal kingdom that will be a blessing to all peoples of the earth.

Jesus is King. That's the first note. Jesus is the King of Jews and Gentiles. That's the second. The third is a necessary admonition: Therefore, this King Jesus is to be worshipped. Read 2:1–11. This is perhaps the best summary picture of Matthew's Gospel. Here we find very non-Jewish people—"wise men from the east" (2:1). What have they come to do? They have come to finish the melodic line. They have come to worship the newborn king—to give their allegiance to him.

That's how this Gospel begins. That's the top.

Next let's turn to the tail. Like a fine symphony, Matthew's melodic line resurfaces time and again through each chapter, oftentimes like a cello quietly playing in the background, until finally we come to the finale, where the whole orchestra, chorus, and even the audience stand up, play, and sing in one voice! This happens in the last three verses—the Great Commission. Listen for yourself. Listen for the culmination of all the subtle and strong sounds.

> And Jesus came and said to them, "All authority in heaven and on earth has been given to me. Go therefore and make disciples of all nations, baptizing them in the name of the Father and of the Son and of the Holy Spirit, teaching them to observe all that I have commanded you. And behold, I am with you always, to the end of the age." (28:18–20)

Underline all the *all* phrases: "all authority," "all nations," "observe all" (cf. "always" in v. 20). Those are the same three notes found in 1:1—2:11 and found, as we will see throughout our study, everywhere in this Gospel. If it helps, you can think of it like this. Here's my prosaic summary: *Jesus has all authority so that all nations might obey all he has commanded,* or more simply and poetically, like this:

All authority

All nations

All allegiance

I don't like to say any one passage in the Bible is more important than another, for they are all divinely inspired, but I will say that if you understand the Great Commission in its context, you will very well understand the Gospel of Matthew.

This chapter will not be an exposition on the Great Commission per se. I will do that later in chapter 89. This is only a preparation for it. That is, at the start of our exploration of Matthew, I want to show you these three notes—this melodic line—so you might better hear them when we come to them.

All Authority

So listen to the first note of this Gospel—*all authority*. After his sacrificial death and glorious resurrection, Jesus says, "All authority in heaven and on earth has been given to me" (28:18).

That is not a statement you hear every day, is it? Yet, it is so familiar to us that we don't recognize how bizarre it is. Think of the most famous and powerful man alive today. Let's say, for the sake of argument, it's Barack Obama (the President of the United States at the time of this writing). If he said what Jesus said, what would you say of him? If he called a press conference and said, "I have all authority in Chicago," what would you think of him? How about if he said, "I have all authority in America"? What if he said, "I have all authority over the world"? If he said any of those, you'd think he was (to borrow from C. S. Lewis) either a liar or a lunatic, or more precisely an unrealistic egoist or an overly ambitious idiot.

Nobody talks the way Jesus talked. Those today who have great authority, even if they overestimate their power and over-esteem themselves, do not talk like Jesus talked. They do not claim to be the king of Heaven and earth. They do not claim, as they sit on their glorious throne no less(!), that every person from every time and everywhere will one day come before them to be judged. They do not claim to have authority to forgive sins. They do not claim to be greater than the temple and the Torah or to be the fulfillment and embodiment of the Hebrew Scriptures. They do not claim that their rule will spread to every corner of the world. They do not claim to establish an unconquerable church and institute new sacraments that have themselves as the foundation and focus. They do not claim that all their commandments are to be obeyed.

Yet with that said, as striking as such statements are, the more striking fact about Jesus is not only that he made such claims, but that somehow such claims are believable. Jesus is believable! Right? You believe him. I believe him. Maybe we're just extremely gullible. Maybe we were all just brainwashed as children. That might explain some of us, but it doesn't explain all of us. It doesn't explain how for so many centuries very sensible, non-superstitious people have taken Jesus at his word. There is something very believable about Jesus, about the testimony of him that a fisherman,[1] doctor, and tax collector put together.

And as I come to this tax collector's testimony, I compare it to the preaching of Martyn Lloyd-Jones, which can be called "logic on fire."[2] Matthew has a certain logic about him. He gives us various reasonable proofs for Jesus' crazy claims. But such proofs are not like a mathematical equation. Rather, they are like the burning bush that Moses encountered, a bush that burns but never burns out. You have to come close enough to feel its heat to know it's true. Logic on fire!

Think of it like this. I won't go too far from the burning bush analogy. I'll just update and extend the metaphor. Think of Matthew's case for Christ and his absolute authority like one of those metal fire pits. In the fire pit itself are these burning but not burning-out claims of Christ—"I have authority over all things," etc. Then there are those four sturdy, cast-iron legs that hold the pit up and in place. Each leg by itself would not necessarily hold up the claims, but together they make a pretty solid base.

Let's briefly examine the legs that hold up his claims.

The first leg is *fulfillment*. Matthew will repeatedly use the word "fulfilled" and phrases like "This was to fulfill what was spoken by the prophet" to show that what was promised in the Old Testament is now being fulfilled in Jesus. He highlights general characteristics of what to expect in the Messiah as well as specific prophecies—e.g., "Behold, the virgin shall conceive and bear a son" (1:23) or "Behold, your king is coming to you, humble, and mounted on a donkey" (21:5). Near the beginning of the Sermon on the Mount, Jesus will say of himself, "Do not think that I have come to abolish the Law or the Prophets; I have not come to abolish them but to fulfill them" (5:17). The idea is this: check what the Old Testament says. Check what Jesus does and says. Then you might very well say, "By golly, the shoe fits!"

The second leg is *teaching*. If you have one of those Bibles that has all the words of Jesus in red, in Matthew you will see a lot of red. But the point is not simply that Jesus taught a lot. It is that he taught with authority. That is what the crowds noticed. He taught them "as one who had authority" (7:29). This will be the constant criticism of his critics, who will ask, "By what authority" he does this or says that (cf. 21:23–27).

Jesus taught with authority, but an authority unlike any other. It's nice to say, as so many today do, "I like Jesus—the good moral teacher." But that is to listen to only half the story. That is to read only half the red. Jesus once said, "Heaven and earth will pass away, but my words will not pass away" (24:35). That is a remarkable statement. How can he say that and get away with it? I think he can do so because so far he has been right! It has been nearly 2,000 years since he first said those words, and we are still talking about them today. I am quoting from Jesus' teachings to people who still read commentaries on Jesus' teachings and who have, in fact, experienced the life-changing power of his words.

The third leg is *character*. A wise person can say some wise things, and some of those wise things can be remembered, even many years later. We still quote Socrates. But nobody worships Socrates. Why? Well, because he never claimed to be God, and because his character never had to fit his claims. As John Stott says, "There is no dichotomy between [Jesus'] character and his claims."[3]

I am a student of church history. And there is a certain sadness to such study, for whenever I study popular figures in Christian history, I am always left with a bittersweet taste. I admire them. But I also don't aspire to be like them (at least not precisely). I recognize their flaws. However, I've been looking and listening to Jesus and reading about him for two decades now, and I haven't yet found the flaw. Even what seems like a flaw—like his anger over the fruitless fig tree or his overturning the tables—when I understand what he was doing, all makes marvelous sense. I like Jesus more. I love Jesus more. I want to be like Jesus more. Jesus' character is so compelling. It supports his claims. And it is his humility, ironically, that I and many other Christians have found to be Christ's most compelling characteristic. John Stott puts it this way,

> [Jesus'] claims for himself are very disturbing because they are so self-centered; yet in his behavior he was clothed with humility. His claims sound proud, but he was humble. I see this paradox at its sharpest when he was with his disciples in the upper room before he died. He said he was their Lord, their teacher and their judge, but he took a towel, got on his hands and knees, and washed their feet like a common slave. Is this not unique in the history of the world? There have been lots of arrogant people, but they have all behaved like it. There have also been humble people, but they have not made great claims for themselves. It is the combination of egocentricity and humility that is so startling—the egocentricity of his teaching and the humility of his behavior.[4]

The fourth leg is his *miracles*. By themselves, the miracles are not what is unique about him. But as the last and final leg, his miracles hold everything in place perfectly. The healing of the blind men, the lepers, the multiplication of the fishes and loaves, and the resurrection itself all point beyond themselves to Jesus' identity. They point to his authority—his authority to forgive sins, his authority over disease, and his authority to conquer even death, of which there is nothing so powerful and prevalent in this world. If you can conquer death, you have a lot of power!

All authority is the first and key note in Matthew's Gospel. Tragically it is the most disregarded thought in the world today. Non-Christians don't mind if we sing to them of Jesus' compassion or humility—just don't sing of his exclusive authority. Do you hear how people talk today? They staunchly and arrogantly hold their doctrine—"doctrines do not matter"—and with a tinge of moral superiority and intellectual enlightenment (as if able to look over all the cosmos and overlook all religions), they say to us dogmatically, "All belief systems are morally equal and should thus coexist."

We are to *coexist*. Perhaps you have heard that spiritual slogan or seen it written across a bumper sticker. I actually saw it carved into a pumpkin sitting outside a church one Halloween. Do you know what I'm talking about? It is the word "coexist" with each letter a symbol of one of seven world religions or philosophies. It's a popular slogan because it's a popular sentiment.

Now I assure you, I don't have a problem with coexisting. I don't have a problem with tolerance if tolerance means what it should mean. I will tolerate you; that is, I won't persecute you for your beliefs. I will coexist with you. Christianity, Islam, and Judaism can and do coexist in most places. But I will not put my brain under a bushel basket. Since I am convicted by Matthew's logic on fire that Jesus has all authority in Heaven and on earth I'm not going to say, "Your god is as true or as real as my God." Jesus either has all authority or he does not. And if he does not, then let's move on. Let's close up shop. Let's stop calling ourselves Christians. But if he does have all authority, then we can certainly coexist with our fellow human beings who believe differently than we do, as long as we know that we won't coexist forever, for as Jesus said in Matthew 25:31–34, 41 (quite strikingly and offensively):

> When the Son of Man comes in his glory . . . then he will sit on his glorious throne. Before him will be gathered all the nations, and he will separate people one from another as a shepherd separates the sheep from the goats. . . . Then the king [King Jesus] will say to those on his right, "Come, you who are blessed by my Father, inherit the kingdom prepared for you from the foundation of the world. . . ." Then he will say to those on his left, "Depart from me, you cursed, into the eternal fire prepared for the devil and his angels."

All authority is the first note of Matthew's melodic line.[5] And I know, as you know, that note doesn't resonate with our culture. Which either means the note is off or our ears are bad. Jesus will tell everyone who rejects his claim that it is the latter.

All Nations

Whatever we might think of the first note, thankfully the second note does appeal to our American ears. It is right, and it sounds right. That note is *all nations*. In the Great Commission, Jesus commissions his followers to take the gospel to the world, to "every tribe and language and people and nation," as the book of Revelation repeatedly describes (5:9; cf. 13:7; 14:6).

This might not sound like a radical concept because we know Christianity is the largest religion in the world and the fastest growing and that it has spread to nearly every nook and cranny of this "terrestrial ball," to borrow from that very applicable hymn, "All Hail the Power of Jesus' Name." Yet I want you to know that this idea—to "go and make disciples of all nations" not by the sword but by the Word—is a concept as revolutionary as Copernicus's claim that the earth revolves around the sun.

Some people think Christianity is a Western religion, and thus assert that it is culturally rigid. That belief (to put it in a very sophisticated way) is the biggest bunch of bunk! Jesus said his kingdom would start as small as a mustard seed and grow slowly but surely into a big and beautiful tree, engrafting people from east and west, north and south, from Jerusalem, Samaria, and the ends of the earth (8:11; 13:31, 47; cf. Acts 1:8). Has he been right about that? Oh yes! As Tim Keller notes,

> The pattern of Christian expansion differs from that of every other world religion. The center and majority of Islam's population is still in the place of its origin—the Middle East. The original lands that have been the demographic centers of Hinduism, Buddhism, and Confucianism have remained so. By contrast, Christianity was first dominated by Jews and centered in Jerusalem. Later it was dominated by Hellenists and centered in the Mediterranean. Later the faith was received by the barbarians of Northern Europe and Christianity came to be dominated by western Europeans and then North Americans. Today most Christians in the world live in Africa, Latin America, and Asia. Christianity soon will be centered in the southern and eastern hemispheres.[6]

Let me ask you a trivia question: What country has or soon will have the most Christians? Missiologists estimate that China—a Communist, officially anti-Christian country—has the most Christians in the world. So, when you think of the future face of Christianity think not of an American girl but a Chinese boy.

Jesus is the King of the Jews. Matthew will make this point directly and indirectly. But he will also show us that this King of the Jews is also King of the Gentiles—"He will proclaim justice to the Gentiles . . . and in his name the Gentiles will hope" (12:18, 21; cf. Romans 15:9–12).

Above the cross was written, sarcastically, "This is Jesus, the King of the Jews" (27:37). It was written in Aramaic, Greek, and Latin—the languages of that world (see John 19:20). But today it reads, realistically, "This is Jesus, the King of the Jews and the Gentiles." And it is written in Aramaic, Greek, Latin, Mandarin, Hindi, Spanish, English, Arabic, Portuguese, Bengali, Russian, Japanese, German, and nearly every other language imaginable.

In the Synoptic Gospels, when Jesus dies, something significant and symbolic happens. The curtain of the temple is torn in two. This shows God's power and his approval of the cross. But it also symbolizes that the wall of hostility between Jews and Gentiles has been forever torn down. Now whoever believes in Immanuel can have access to God. In Matthew's Gospel, as the curtain is tearing, the ground at the foot of the cross is shaking, and the centurion upon that ground as well. Filled with fear and faith, this Gentile Roman soldier announces, "Truly this was the Son of God!" (27:54).

John the Baptist said, "God is able from these stones to raise up children for Abraham" (3:9). In Matthew's Gospel that is exactly what we see—stones being turned into children of God—a Canaanite woman, a ceremonially unclean Jewish woman, lepers, tax collectors, and even two Roman soldiers.

If you love paradox and irony, you will love this Gospel, for the rulers of the earth—Herod and Pilate—will reject Jesus. The most devoutly religious—the scribes, the Pharisees, and temple authorities—will reject Jesus. But the rejects will not reject him. Those from the wrong race or class or sex find Jesus just alright. The kids picked last for the team are picked up by Jesus. Jesus loves the losers. And the losers love him.

In the first chapter of Romans, after Paul summarizes "the gospel of God" in verses 1–5 as being good news about Jesus for the nations, he makes that memorable statement in 1:16, "For I am not ashamed of the gospel, for it is the power of God for salvation to *everyone* who believes, to the Jew first and also to the Greek [i.e., Gentile]." So yes, the gospel is exclusive—it is exclusively about Jesus and his kingdom. But it is also inclusive—it includes all who will believe.

My brothers and sisters, we must not be ashamed of this exclusive/inclusive gospel. The inclusivity of Christianity is today one of our greatest appeals. The social progressives didn't get to this first. Jesus got to it. No, Jesus created it! That's what so astonishing. It is not astonishing that Oprah or Desmond Tutu would say, "We should embrace people of different ethnicities." But for a Jewish man, twenty centuries ago, to say it and live it out in a culture where the opposite was absolutely normative . . . I can't think of anything more astonishing. It had the earliest Jewish converts to Christianity scratching their heads. But we should not be scratching ours.

All Allegiance

All authority—that's the first note; all nations, the second; now finally, *all allegiance*, the third.

As many have noticed, Matthew's Gospel is a gospel of discipleship. It speaks of the call, cost, and content of discipleship. Time and time again Jesus will say, "Follow me." Each time an individual will be met with the same choice we have before us today: Jesus above money? Jesus above power? Jesus above reputation? Jesus above comfort? Jesus above tradition? Jesus above family? Jesus above life and breath? Those are the choices put before both great governors and lowly lepers. Jesus will say:

> Whoever loves father or mother more than me is not worthy of me . . . whoever does not take his cross and follow me is not worthy of me. Whoever finds his life will lose it, and whoever loses his life for my sake will find it. (10:37–39)

Matthew's Gospel has this beautiful balance between forgiveness, faith, and obedience. At the center of the Sermon on the Mount is the petition "forgive us our debts" (6:12), and at the end of the Lord's Supper is the pronouncement, "This is my blood of the covenant, which is poured out for many for the forgiveness of sins" (26:28). And it is this blood that is poured out for the forgiveness of sins that flows into us through faith, giving our dry bones new flesh—new ears and eyes and hearts and hands, giving us all that we need for life and godliness.

Following Jesus means absolute allegiance—trust in him and obedience to him. In the Great Commission Jesus will put it this way: we are "to observe all" that he has "commanded" (28:20). Do I mean his teachings on sin and Scripture, idolatry and adultery, money and marriage, slander and suffering, anger and evangelism, purity and prayer, alms and anxiety, fasting and forgiveness, luxury and love? Yes! Everything he commanded.

Christianity is not a pick-n-save religion: you pick whatever teachings you like and you still get saved. Oh no! If that's how you think, you have it all wrong. Just listen to Jesus if you won't listen to me. He stated it straightforwardly: "Not everyone who says to me, 'Lord, Lord,' will enter the kingdom of heaven, but *the one who does the will of my Father* who is in heaven" (7:21). To be a follower of Jesus is to be someone who does "the will of [his] Father in heaven" (cf. 12:50)—not perfectly as Jesus did, but consistently and repentantly. It's a matter of allegiance: Jesus first, everyone and everything else second.

You see, all authority demands all allegiance from everybody . . . even me and even you.

Welcome to the Gospel of Matthew!

2

Perfect Aim

MATTHEW 1:1–17

RECENTLY I LISTENED to a fascinating talk by Marvin Rosenthal, a Jewish convert to Christianity. He shared how Matthew's genealogy was one of the proofs that persuaded him that Jesus is the Messiah. To explain what he meant Rosenthal used a helpful analogy from his experience as a U.S. Marine many decades ago. At the rifle range, he and his fellow soldiers would practice their aim by shooting at a target from three distances—200, 300, and 500 yards. From that distance they couldn't always tell by the naked eye if their bullets hit the target or not. So, in order to determine their accuracy, one of the soldiers would hide down in a nine-foot ravine behind the target until he heard ten shots. Then he would get up and check the sharpness of the shooter. He would add up the score and relay the results by slipping a colored disk onto the end of a pole and raising it up high. The color of the disk would communicate the shooter's accuracy. If you missed the target completely, a big flag would be waved, a military way of saying, "You ought to be embarrassed!" Yet, for each bull's-eye a red disk would be secured to the pole and the pole would go up and down. So if you were six out of ten, the pole would go up and down six times. Now, if you hit the bull's-eye ten times out of ten, that same pole and red disk would simply be spun around once. Rosenthal goes on to say that, especially for a Jewish audience (who understands the significance and the necessity of genealogical records), Matthew's genealogy hits the bull's-eye ten times out of ten.[1]

As we explore this genealogy, I'm going to utilize Rosenthal's analogy with some slight modifications. I want you to think of this text like a target set before us. Let's make it three targets. And I want you to think of God, not with a rifle in his hand (I'll tame the imagery just a bit, in fact, I'll make it more Biblical) but as an archer with a bow and three arrows (e.g., Psalm 64:7). Now watch what he'll do. With this genealogy he will take three shots at three targets, each time hitting them dead center. God can see that he has hit the bull's-eyes, but he wants us to see it as well. He wants us, if you will, to insert the red disk, raise up the pole, and turn it once, showing we know and appreciate his perfect aim.

Right Line—Jesus Is from the Line of Abraham and David

We will call the first target "God hits *the right line*." (Let's say this one is 200 yards away.) Jesus is from the right bloodline, as Matthew will say from the start. Jesus is "the son of David, the son of Abraham" (v. 1). Abraham and David are two key names in this genealogy. If you miss seeing them (at the top and tail, in v. 1 and v. 17, and also in v. 2 and v. 6), you miss everything.

Now, what's so important about these two men? Two promises! God gave each a specific promise. In Genesis 12:1–3 God says to Abraham:

> Go from your country and your kindred and your father's house to the land that I will show you. And I will make of you a great nation, and I will bless you and make your name great, so that you will be a blessing. I will bless those who bless you, and him who dishonors you I will curse, and in you all the families of the earth shall be blessed.

Through Abraham and his offspring God will raise up a people (Israel) who will be a blessing to the entire world (the Gentiles). This is the beginning of the Abrahamic Covenant. Paul also called it, in a broad sense, "the gospel" (Galatians 3:8). This "gospel" is further specified by the Davidic Covenant, the promise made in 2 Samuel 7:12, 13 (cf. 1 Chronicles 17), where David is promised that one of his descendants would establish a forever kingdom:

> When your days are fulfilled and you lie down with your fathers, I will raise up your offspring after you, who shall come from your body, and I will establish his kingdom. He shall build a house for my name, and I will establish the throne of his kingdom forever.

Throughout his Gospel, Matthew brings these promises together in the person of Christ, with what Jesus calls "the gospel of the kingdom" (4:23; 9:35; 24:14—this phrase is only used in Matthew). However, this is not the point of the genealogy. Here, the Evangelist is simply showing how God hits the lineage target—i.e., how Jesus is a descendant of both Abraham and David. Jesus comes from the right line. As Craig Blomberg summarizes, he has "the correct scriptural pedigree to be the Messiah."[2] The Messiah must be a Jew (a son of Abraham, v. 2), but he also must be from the tribe of Judah (vv. 2, 3; cf. Genesis 49:8–10), and from one specific member of that tribe (David, v. 6). Jesus has all of this going for him.

But Jesus wasn't the only person in world history to have such a lineage. All those listed in verses 6–16 shared his lineage, as well as others who were his contemporaries, like his four brothers (13:55) or the famous rabbi Hillel. So in some ways it's like the time my mother did our family genealogy in which she traced the O'Donnells back to a line of Irish kings. I come from nobility, which is no surprise to me. But it was a surprise when I learned that all of Ireland was once run by various nobles, thus indicating that anyone with Irish ancestry was descended from some Irish "king." Well, you'll be glad to know that Jewish genealogies aren't the same as Irish ones. Only a select group of men in the history of the world came from Abraham and David. The select group, however, was larger than one man. Jesus wasn't the only Jew who could claim lineage from this patriarch and that king. And that's why two more targets are set in place.

Yet, before we move on to them, I want us here and now to stop and think about the obvious, which we so often fail to do. In Matthew 1:18–25, which we will look at in the next chapter, an angel appears to Joseph and tells him what is happening with Mary, his betrothed. He is told about this son who is to come, whom he is to name, "Jesus," which means "Yahweh saves." After he is told the details of the divine plan, we read in verses 22, 23:

> All this took place to fulfill what the Lord had spoken by the prophet [Isaiah]: "Behold, the virgin shall conceive and bear a son, and they shall call his name Immanuel" (which means, God with us).

Jesus is Immanuel. The man Jesus is "God with us." Now, while "Immanuel" can refer *merely* to God's presence through Jesus, as John Nolland argues,[3] I believe an additional complementary truth can be embraced, which in no way diminishes Matthew's emphasis. That truth is that the one who brings to humankind the divine presence (Jesus) is also fully divine. Matthew stresses equally that Jesus is the presence of God in the world (cf. 18:20; 28:20),[4] while being the fleshly embodiment of the deity. Thus I say that what Paul said in Colossians 2:9 is a fitting summary of Matthew 1:23: "For in him the whole fullness of deity dwells bodily."

That's so easy to forget, isn't it? I forgot the awesomeness of it until I opened Charles Spurgeon's commentary on Matthew and saw how he pauses in his second paragraph on the genealogy. He ceases making observations and for a time simply engages in pure adoration. "Marvelous condescension," he writes, "that [God] should be a man, and have a genealogy, even He who 'was in the beginning with God,' and 'thought it not robbery to be equal to God'!"[5] Marvelous condescension!

We think it is such a wonderful thing when a queen from another country comes to visit and offers her greetings and love. We think it is such a wonderful thing when a rich businessman volunteers for a night to help at a homeless shelter, providing food and comfort to the poor. We think it is such a wonderful thing when a professional athlete gives of her time to conduct a free clinic for inner-city kids. Such are wonderful things, all of which we recognize, appreciate, and applaud—the humility and condescension. But what marvelous, unfathomable humility and condescension it was when God became man. When you read 1:1, "the book of the genealogy of Jesus Christ" alongside 1:23, "and they shall call his name Immanuel," it ought to be enough for us to stop and think, to pause and praise, and to join in the angelic chorus, singing,

> Veiled in flesh, the Godhead see,
> Hail th' incarnate Deity!
> Pleased as man with men to dwell,
> Jesus our Emmanuel.
> Hark! The herald angels sing,
> "Glory to the newborn King."[6]

Right Time—Jesus Came at the Right Time

Jesus is from the right line. That's important and necessary. Without it we stop the target practice. We look for a Messiah elsewhere.

In addition, Jesus was born at the *right time*. That's the second target we'll take a look at, and we'll see that God's arrow here likewise goes straight into the middle. Look at verse 17. Matthew wants to make sure we see this. So he ends the genealogy like this:

> So all the generations from Abraham to David were fourteen generations, and from David to the deportation to Babylon fourteen generations, and from the deportation to Babylon to the Christ fourteen generations.

Matthew is saying that there are three key periods thus far in salvation history. Frederick Dale Bruner helpfully suggests that we think of the history here like the capital letter N. The first fourteen generations head upward from Abraham to David, the second fourteen downward from Solomon to the Babylonian exile, and then the final fourteen "move upward again in hope and fulfillment from the exile to Christ."[7]

Scholars disagree as to why Matthew structures the genealogy this way. Some say the number fourteen is a literary device called a *gemetria*. In Hebrew each letter has numerical value. *Aleph*, the first letter, is worth one; *dalet*, the fourth letter, is worth four; *vav*, the sixth letter, is worth six, etc. The word "David" in Hebrew is comprised of three letters (*dalet/vav/dalet*—four/six/four) which equal fourteen. So perhaps Matthew is telling us prosaically as well as poetically, "Jesus is the son of David" (underline David).

Others theorize that the three fourteens are just a structural way of aiding our weak memories.[8] The argument is that Matthew limits all the names he could have had so we would remember the genealogy itself and the necessary and important names within it.

Beyond the numerical or mnemonic value, Matthew's structure has theological value. He has intentionally selected names (real historical people who are really part of Joseph and Mary's line) and arranged them to make the same theological point that Paul made in Galatians 4:4a: "But when the fullness of time had come, God sent forth his Son" (cf. Hebrews 9:26). In other words, God has designed history around the birth of Jesus.

On paper we agree. Christmas is the center of history. But so often this head knowledge has yet to make it to our hearts. We might write BC ("Before Christ") or AD ("*Anno Domini*," "in the year of our Lord"), but we are often far removed theologically and emotionally from the importance of this reality.

Have you ever wondered why Jesus didn't come to earth as a man in the modern age rather than in the first century? Why didn't he come to earth during the era of television, video, and the Internet, when nearly all that he said and did could be precisely documented? Can't you just picture CNN reporters and paparazzi camped a few feet away from Jesus and the Twelve for three years straight? Can't you imagine a streaming video of his each and every movement? Can't you imagine the ten o'clock news starting every night with something from the life of Christ—"Today Jesus healed ten lepers. We interviewed nine of them. One refused an interview in order to return to Jesus for a word of thanks." And can't you imagine years from now, when some rebellious teen started to doubt the claims of Christ, how the teachers of the times would just pull out their computerized contraptions and say, "Now, son, look here, it's all on video." And then this teacher would proceed to show the clip, the most famous one played on YouTube—Jesus' resurrection. Everyone has seen it. The reporter is outside the tomb, giving a play-by-play of Jesus' life, and while he's saying something about Christ's claim to rise again, lo and behold, the stone is rolled away. There it is on film! They take a close-up and out comes the Son of God, just as he said he would. Who wouldn't believe?

Sometimes we wish God's timing were different. And sometimes we wish God took out the "faith" part of our faith. What I mean is, some of us think like Carl Sagan thought. Sagan, the brilliant scientist but foolish man, once said he'd believe there was a God if God had written the Ten Commandments on the moon. Well sure, everyone would believe if that were the case. But that would take the faith out of faith, which would as be as bad as taking the mystery out of romance, the curiosity out of the cat, or the oxygen out of the air.

When Scripture says that Jesus came at "the fullness of time," it means it. God designed history—with the rise of this empire and the fall of that one, with this person born here and that person born there, with this event happening now and that one then—to prepare us for Jesus and to give room for faith. God values us too much to treat us like robots, and I'll add (and maybe I'm bold to do so) that only unimaginative atheists want the Ten Commandments painted on the moon or Jesus captured on videotape.

The Bible tells us that while God's ways are hidden to some extent (e.g., Deuteronomy 29:29; cf. 2 Corinthians 4:3–6), nevertheless "his invisible attributes, namely his eternal power and divine nature," as Romans 1:20 puts it, are as obvious as the North Star on a clear night. When we die, we will find this reality to be as real as oxygen, which we cannot see or taste or touch, but we know it's there, keeping us alive every second of the day.

God is real, and he is faithful, and we can see such attributes in creation and in Scripture. Yet God has not made himself so self-evident that no faith whatsoever is required. How boring that would be. How dull. How lifeless. How robotic. How so *not* like he who created this unbelievably complex, mysterious, beautiful universe. How so *not* like he who glories in bestowing the gift of faith to undeserving and rebellious sinners (see Matthew 16:17).

There is enough evidence for my children—whether it's facial features, lanky limbs, or personality characteristics—to recognize me as their father. But if each one of them demanded a DNA test before they would acknowledge and appreciate me as such, then they would be very ungrateful and overly demanding children. God has given us *creation*—what Calvin called the theatre of his glory—and *Scripture*, what I'll call the evidence of his faithfulness, and yet how many humans want a DNA test before they will call him, "Abba, Father." Thankless little brats, aren't they?

Let's not be thankless little brats. Let's look at the arrow in the middle of this target. Let's have faith, more than we had when we read the last page. Let's recognize that Jesus came at the right time, which is one of the many marks that he's the right one. He is the Messiah with whom we can trust our very lives.

Right Design—Jesus Came Even for Gentile Sinners

So here we are, sitting and waiting in the nine-foot ravine. We've come up once to see God hit that first target right in the middle—Jesus, the Son of David and Abraham. We are in awe of the incarnation. Then we've come up again to see God hit that second target dead-on—Jesus came at the right time (fourteen/fourteen/fourteen). Our faith in his faithfulness and in his sovereign rule of this world and its history is elevated. Finally we hear the third arrow strike. We jump up and see that, sure enough, God is three for three.

The first target is the right line, the second is the right time, and the third is (oh yes, I've made it rhyme with line and time) *the right design*. It is not simply that Jesus came as a Jew from a lineage of kings and at the perfect time in history, but it is also the design of it all—why he came and for whom he came. That's what we'll explore last but not least. In fact, this last point likely is the *least* least. This is the 500-yard shot that strikes with such accuracy and force that it goes through the bull's-eye and out the back of the target! It's the shot we are to see, stand up, and applaud!

So, what's the design? It is a strange design, but it's a Scriptural one.

Matthew's genealogy is unparalleled. While it appeals to a Jewish audience because it is a genealogy, it has at least three peculiarities that would have offended a pharisaical Jew who, for example, valued racial, moral, and patriarchal purity.

The first peculiarity is that Matthew includes five women: Tamar (v. 3), Rahab (v. 5), Ruth (v. 5), the wife of Uriah, whom we know to be Bathsheba (v. 6), and Mary (v. 16), the mother of our Lord. This mention of women here is as strange as having "Mary Magdalene and the other Mary" as the first two official eyewitnesses of the resurrection, which Matthew records in 28:1–10. This is peculiar because a woman's testimony was not valid in a court of law, and a woman's name in a Jewish genealogy was of little legal significance. (Note the word "father," repeated thirty-nine times!) This is why in other Biblical genealogies, such as the first nine chapters of 1 Chronicles, very few women are mentioned, and the ones who are named are likely added to show "the purity of the line or enhance its dignity."[9] But here in Matthew, the great Hebrew matriarchs are missing.[10] Where is Sarah, Rebekah, or Leah?

Matthew records five women in this genealogy. This is peculiar. But it's a peculiarity with a purpose. It's part of the plan. It's in the divine design. With the coming of Jesus, women do not gain new status within God's covenant people. However, they do take on key roles in the drama of Jesus' life, death, and resurrection. Matthew sees fit to note this at the beginning and end of his Gospel.

Now, if it's not bad enough that there are so many women in this genealogy, it is even worse (to continue my sarcasm) that four out of five are not even Jewish. Besides Mary, who was likely herself from the kingly line of David,[11] Jesus' genealogy is full of a bunch of *Gentile* women! Tamar and Rahab were Canaanites (a race of people with which the Israelites were forbidden to intermarry). Ruth was a Moabite. The Moabites trace their lineage back to incestuous Lot. Remember the story of Genesis 19? It's a true but terrible story. Moreover, we're told in Deuteronomy 23:3–5 that the Moabites were excluded from Israel's assembly because they refused to give them food and drink after they left Egypt. So, for Naomi's son to marry Ruth in the first place would have been as scandalous as a Swedish-American in the 1920s marrying an African-American. "You want to marry a Moabite?" We can almost hear Naomi cringe. Then we have Bathsheba. She was the wife of Uriah before she was the wife of David. Uriah, we are told in 2 Samuel 11:3, was a Hittite. He was a Gentile. While Bathsheba was likely an Israelite, as she was the daughter of Eliam, the son of Ahithophel the Gilonite (2 Samuel 11:3; 23:34),[12] through marriage she legally become a Hittite.

So am I saying that King David's great-grandmother was a Moabite and his wife, the mother of great King Solomon, a Hittite of sorts? I'm afraid so. The bloodline is impure. It's as bad as Prince Charles marrying that woman of non-royal stock. Ah, but again, it's all part of the plan, a plan that Paul explains most plainly in Galatians 3:27–29: "For as many of you as were baptized into Christ have put on Christ. There is neither *Jew nor Greek*, there is neither slave nor free, there is *no male and female*, for you are all one in Christ Jesus. And if you are Christ's, then you are Abraham's offspring, heirs according to promise." Even Canaanites, as we shall see in 15:21–28, can come into the kingdom; even Gentile dogs can eat the crumbs that fall from the King's table.

The first peculiarity of this genealogy is the mention of five women. The second is that at least three are Gentiles. The third is that most of them were involved in (how shall I put this?) irregular sexual liaisons. Tamar dressed as a prostitute in order to get her father-in-law, Judah, to give her lawful offspring. This plan worked, for that's how Perez and Zerah (the twins mentioned in v. 3) came into this world. Forget the soap opera tomorrow morning or *Desperate Housewives* reruns. Just give good old Genesis 38 a read. That's Tamar. Then we have Rahab, who didn't disguise herself as a prostitute but actually was a prostitute in Jericho, that wicked town where the walls came tumbling down. She became—as the books of Joshua (2), Hebrews (11) and James (2) point out—a woman of faith. However, the scandal of her past is what it is. Finally, we have Bathsheba, who was certainly taken advantage of by King David. But she was, in my estimation, not perfectly innocent. She was after all taking an indiscreet bath out in the open, in the king's view, and she didn't say no to his advances when the Law said that a woman should in such a situation. Either way, even if she was only 2 percent to blame, she was involved in an adulterous affair, one that cost the life of her first husband and her first son and one that certainly marred her reputation.

Yet even the sexual irregularities of these women are part of the design. For they prepare us for the most irregular sexual or *non-sexual* encounter of all time. They prepare us for the virgin conception and birth.[13] For those who doubt that God would work through an unmarried, teenage girl to bring about the Messiah, Matthew is saying, "Well, take a look at Grandma Tamar and Bathsheba. Look at the line. Notice the design!" If David and Solomon could come from where they came from, then the King of kings could come, as Isaiah said he would, from *a virgin*, this pure girl of marred reputation named Mary.

Now as I said, that's one of the things that Matthew is up to. The other is this: Jesus comes from the right stock, but it is bad stock. As one commentator says, there is "no pattern of righteousness in the lineage of Jesus."[14] Jesus comes from a bunch of sinners. I don't just mean Tamar and Rahab. Look at the list of wicked kings here—e.g., Rehoboam, Abijah, and Ahaz. Ahaz!

Moreover, look at the so-called "righteous" men of old—like Abraham (who lied) or Judah (whose idea it was to sell his brother Joseph into slavery and who was, after his own admission, worse than Tamar) or David (with his adultery and murder, two permanent marks on his background check) or Solomon (with his polygamy and idolatry) or even good Hezekiah (with his pride in being good). And you thought your family tree is a mess. It's as if Matthew puts a criminal lineup before us.

But why? What's the moral of this method? Why inform us that "Jesus did not belong to the nice clean world of middle-class respectability, but rather he 'belonged to a family of murderers, cheats, cowards, adulterers and liars'"?[15] The point is "almost too obvious to belabor."[16] Matthew wants to show us what Paul will teach us in 1 Timothy 1:15: "The saying is trustworthy and deserving of full acceptance, that Christ Jesus came into the world to save sinners." Jesus came not for the righteous but the unrighteous (cf. 9:13), for sinners—like Matthew the tax collector and Rahab the prostitute. He came for sinners like you and like me.

Conclusion: The Genesis of Jesus

In the Greek the word "genealogy" can be rendered "genesis"—"The book of the 'Genesis' of Jesus Christ."[17] This is important to note, for with Jesus we have a "New Genesis,"[18] a new beginning, one far greater than the first. For whereas God in the first Genesis fashioned the deepest oceans and the highest heavens, now in his Son he has poured into those places grace upon grace.

> Grace, grace, God's grace,
> Grace that will pardon and cleanse within;
> Grace, grace, God's grace,
> Grace that is greater than all our sin.[19]

Grace—that's not the poison but the potion on the tip of this last arrow, the one that has gone through the target but should now be stuck in your heart.

Jesus came from the right line at the right time. And it was indeed the right design—designed for sinners like you and me.

3

Conceiving Christ

MATTHEW 1:18–25

WHEN MY SON Simeon was three,[1] he liked to look at the moon. We could be walking through our neighborhood on a partially cloudy night or driving along the highway at the break of dawn, and instead of first noticing the colored Christmas lights on the trees or the cool sports car passing on the left, Simeon would spot the moon. "I see the moon!" he'd belt out from his car seat. "I see the moon," he'd say, squeezing my hand as we walked.

One night at home his gift for observing the obvious was especially memorable. He turned to the window, and there it was again. "Dad, the moon," he said softly and with astonishment, as if he had never seen it before. "I know, Simeon," I replied mildly and with less astonishment. I added playfully, "Do you think you can touch it?" Without hesitation he turned to the window, climbed up the arm of a chair, crossed over onto the windowsill, and reached his right hand up to the sky. He was only 384,403 kilometers shy of it. Discouraged but not dissuaded, he jumped down and ran to the front room, once again finding the moon. "There's another one," he yelled. Then he backed up. He ran. He leapt. He reached. This time I swear he almost touched it.

To Simeon the moon's movements were mysterious, its light lovely, and its texture close enough to touch. Sometimes when we come to passages like Matthew's condensed Christmas story, we don't come with that childlike curiosity and wonder—looking at the everyday with awe, perceiving the familiar as fascinating. But we should. We should become like little children, which Jesus said is the only way to get into the kingdom. Here's how we'll do it with Matthew 1:18–25. I'll show you in this text three important yet oftentimes unobserved observations—ones that when seen afresh, I hope will cause you to see the passage afresh. And perhaps for the first time in a long time, what has become ordinary will once again be extraordinary, as extraordinary as the moon in the eyes of an inquisitive boy.

The Scandal

Let's begin our spiritual coming of age. The first observation is *the scandal surrounding Christ's conception*. Look with me at verses 18, 19. For now I will take out the phrase that de-scandalizes the scene—"from the Holy Spirit." I'll take that out so you can feel some of what Mary and Joseph must have felt. So verses 18, 19 now read:

> Now the birth of Jesus Christ took place in this way. When his mother Mary had been betrothed to Joseph, before they came together she was found to be with child. . . . And her husband Joseph, being a just man and unwilling to put her to shame, resolved to divorce her quietly.

What's going on here? Two facts are clear: Mary is "with child," and consequently Joseph doesn't want to be with her. What is not clear, however (at least not to some modern readers), is how Joseph can be called Mary's "husband" when they are not yet married, and how they are not yet married, but Joseph can divorce her.

The key to solving these riddles is grasping the cultural context. At this time and place in history, "marriage was held to be," as William Barclay somewhat smugly suggests, "far too serious a step to be left to the dictates of the human heart."[2] As it was for most couples in this culture, Mary and Joseph's parents had likely arranged their marriage. Here's how it worked. First, the fathers of the two families would *engage* the couple. This would usually happen in childhood. Second, later in life, this couple would be *betrothed*. The girl was usually a teenager, and the man was usually older. So to be clear, their *betrothal* is not the same as our *engagement*. Rather, betrothal was the nearest step to marriage. It was the process of ratifying the engagement into which the couple had previously entered.

During the engagement period, the young woman could break the agreement if she was unwilling to marry the man. Conversely, the man could break off the engagement if the woman had not kept her virginity. But once they entered betrothal (which lasted one year), it was absolutely binding. During that year, although they didn't live together or sleep together, the couple was actually known as "husband and wife." This explains why Joseph in our text is called Mary's "husband" (v. 19; cf. Deuteronomy 22:24).[3] Now here's the final point of clarification: the only way a betrothal could be broken was through a legal divorce, which explains what Joseph was up to in verse 19.

So then, do you see the scandal of it all? Mary is pregnant. Yet she is betrothed to Joseph. Joseph is not the father of this baby. Now, if this scenario is still scandalous in our anything-goes, play-by-your-own-rules culture, imagine how it would have been in their anything-does-not-go, abide-by-God's-rules culture.

Mary was in a tough spot. But Matthew reminds us that Joseph's spot wasn't any softer. Mary was the woman whom he agreed to love, the woman who was to have his children and to nurture and teach them. Mary was the woman who was going to manage his household. And she was found out! She was found to be with child, and thus (apparently) with the stain of sexual sin. Worse than that, this baby was not his, biologically speaking. He had not touched her. He knew that. This could only mean that somebody else had.

Stop and think about this. Walk a moment in his shoes. Breathe the air he was breathing. How would you feel if you were in his situation? Would you be humiliated or angry or jealous? Matthew doesn't tell us how Joseph felt. But it is difficult to imagine him so stoic that these emotions never entered his heart.

So what did he do? What could he do? What would you do?

He thought seriously and patiently about the matter,[4] and then he "resolved" to do what was best for both persons: "And . . . Joseph, being a just man and unwilling to put her to shame, resolved to divorce her quietly."

Being a just man, he could not simply disregard God's Law (see Deuteronomy 22:23–27), and to marry Mary would have been to do just that. It would have been to overlook an offense that God's Word says should not be overlooked. In fact, it would have been to admit guilt when he was not guilty. In a sense, it would be to lie—"Yes, it's my child; shame on us."

I envision the weight of this decision in this way. On one shoulder Joseph has the righteous requirements of God's Law whispering in his ear, "You have to expose her error. This sin cannot go unpunished." On the other shoulder is the compassion and mercy of God's Law (cf. 23:23). (And note here that it's not a devil and an angel on his shoulders; these are two angels, if you will; two angels wrestling with his heart.) Compassion counsels him, "Joseph, a private divorce is the way to proceed. Dismiss her quietly. In this way you show both the justice and the love of God."

The Spirit

Thankfully, for Joseph, Mary, and Jesus (and us!), God promptly provided an alternative plan. He whisked away these two imaginary angels and sent a real one. Look with me at verse 20 and we'll fill in the blank that earlier we left in the text: "But as [Joseph] considered these things, behold, an angel of the Lord appeared to him in a dream, saying, 'Joseph, son of David, do not fear to take Mary as your wife, for that which is conceived in her is from the Holy Spirit.'" *From the Holy Spirit* is the second observation I want us to see. We move now from the scandal to the Spirit.

What Joseph was missing was this bit of information, the important information given to us in verse 18 and to Mary during *the annunciation.* After the angel Gabriel gave the news and after Mary said in essence, "How can this be? How can I, a virgin, have a baby?" do you remember how Gabriel responded? He said, "*The Holy Spirit* will come upon you" (Luke 1:35). Now notice in Matthew that this truth is twice emphasized. In verse 18 and here in verse 20 we find the phrase "from the Holy Spirit."

Have you ever thought about the role of the Spirit in the conception of Christ? I'll admit I hadn't until Matthew made me. And now I'm making you. Rest assured I'm not going to delve into the mystery of it all. That is, I'm not going to attempt to describe (for the first time ever!) the supernatural/biological process by which the Spirit worked in the virgin's womb. I am still waiting to be taken up into the third heaven for that revelation. For now I will simply point out the obvious—something as obvious as the moon, something so obvious you will wonder why I'm paid to do this. Here it is: *The Holy Spirit made the preexistent second person of the Trinity into a human being.*

The Spirit genesis-ed Jesus!

Why do I say it that way? Well, because that's how our text actually says it. Verse 18 reads in the original Greek: "Now the *genesis* of Jesus Christ . . ." (cf. 1:1). It is not "the genesis," of course, in the sense of the birth of God's preexistent Son, but rather "the genesis" of the Spirit's work to take the preexistent Son and form his inward parts—to knit him together in his mother's womb, to make him "fearfully and wonderfully" human (cf. Psalm 139:13, 14).

Look how the creed of the First Council of Constantinople (the Nicene Creed of AD 381) summarizes what Scripture teaches here:

> We believe . . . in one Lord Jesus Christ, the only-begotten Son of God . . . who for us men and for our salvation, came down from heaven, and was incarnate *by the Holy Spirit* [*ek pneumatos hagiou*—the same as in our Bible text] of the Virgin Mary, and was made man.

It was the work of the Holy Spirit to genesis Jesus. Just as the Spirit "was hovering over the face of the waters" at creation (Genesis 1:2), so here for our salvation the Spirit "overshadowed" Mary's womb (Luke 1:35), making God's Son into one of us—with bones and brains and blood, with lungs and lips and lymph nodes, with head and heart and hands.

Here I plea for awe and understanding. We ought to be (again and again!) in awe of the incarnation. But we also ought to understand better the person and doctrine of the Holy Spirit. We ought to grasp not only the necessity of the Spirit's work in the birth of Christ (i.e., "The Son is not the Son without the Spirit," as Wolfhart Pannenburg nicely phrases it),[5] but also that this work of the Holy Spirit in the conception of Christ is a *fleshly* work.[6] The Spirit's work is material, tangible, and visible. Ironically, the Spirit's work is fleshly!

A few years ago, a non-charismatic woman shared with me, a non-charismatic pastor, an interesting episode from a charismatic friend who had just returned from a charismatic retreat. On the retreat there was, as expected, much emphasis on and expression of the spiritual gifts, especially speaking in tongues. Now, when these two ladies conversed about this—talking about the Holy Spirit—near the end of the conversation, the charismatic Christian said with great astonishment, "Oh, I didn't know that you even believed in the Holy Spirit!" The assumption behind that remark (I assume) was this: people don't believe in the Holy Spirit if they don't talk about him often and if they don't regularly manifest the *outward* gifts.

I don't deny in any way that the spiritual gifts mentioned in 1 Corinthians 12—14 are real manifestations of the Holy Spirit. However, I do want to say that *the primary work* of the Holy Spirit is not found in the spiritual gifts. The primary work—or I suppose we should say the primary *works*—of the Holy Spirit are found in creation and in re-creation (i.e., regeneration). And here in our text, as it is often in Scripture, the focus is on the Spirit's work in creation, this time the creation of God in the flesh.

You see, one of the problems in the church today is that the work of the Holy Spirit is over-spiritualized. Does that sound strange? I suppose it should. But here's what I mean: where the Holy *Spirit* is present in the world, we see the *humanity* of Jesus believed and even emphasized. Conversely, where other spirits, false or demonic spirits, are at work, we find a Jesus without flesh—a super-spiritualized Jesus, a kind of cosmic Christ.

This was one of the issues the Apostle John dealt with in his three epistles. It was the main theological controversy of his day. To put it plainly, the false teachers forgot about Christmas. They so emphasized Christ's divinity that they neglected his humanity. And what did John say to that? Here is the apostolic acid test of orthodoxy: "By this you know the Spirit of God: every spirit that confesses that Jesus Christ has come in the flesh is from God" (1 John 4:2).

How do you know if your church is Spirit-filled? One way you can know is if Jesus—in all his heavenly divinity and in all his earthly humanity—is the focus! Frederick Dale Bruner calls this "the Christocentricity of the Spirit." He explains:

> It is my impression from a study of the Holy Spirit in the New Testament (cf. *The Holy Spirit: Shy Member of the Trinity*)[7] that the true *humanity* of Jesus Christ is one of the two major "lectures" of the Holy Spirit. (The other lecture is, in Paul's words, the Spirit's teaching us to say that "Jesus is Lord" (i.e., divine, 1 Cor 12:3). To put this in another way, the Holy Spirit does two major works: first, the Spirit brings Christ *down* to earth and makes him human; second, the Spirit lifts Christ *up* and shows Jesus' divinity. In other words, the Holy Spirit is a good theologian and gives two main courses: The True Humanity of Jesus Christ the first semester and The True Divinity of Jesus Christ the second. . . . It is the work of the Holy Spirit, in either course, to bring Jesus Christ *into* human lives.[8]

The Holy Spirit has been called the *shy* and *humble* member of the Trinity because it is his divine task to help us exalt the Father and the Son.[9] So yes, I believe in the Holy Spirit! I say that with some conviction, even charisma. I hope you can say the same.

The role of the Holy Spirit in the conception of Christ—what a wonderful truth to think about on Christmas! It is as obvious as the moon but so often unobserved and undervalued.

The Surrogate

Let's review. Thus far, we have *the scandal* (the scandal of Christ's conception) and *the Spirit* (the Spirit's significant role in Christ's conception). Finally, we have *the surrogate*, referring to Jesus' surrogate, earthly father, Joseph.[10]

If the Holy Spirit is the shy member of the Holy Trinity, Joseph is the shy member of the holy family. But shy or not, his importance ought to animate our minds.

Look again at this passage before us and see how Matthew writes this story. He starts, quite plainly and straightforwardly, "Now the birth of Jesus Christ took place in this way" (1:18). But notice he does not immediately describe *the birth*. There is no nativity. There is no mention of Mary's labor and delivery. Moreover, unlike Luke's Gospel, where the reader sees the unfolding events through Mary's eyes, here in Matthew it is through Joseph's eyes. Verse 18 introduces the situation. Then the rest of our passage focuses on Joseph and his conception, if you will, of the conception of Christ.

In church tradition Joseph has earned the nickname not "Shy Joseph" but "Quiet Joseph." That is because he never speaks. That is, in the Gospels we have no record of him uttering a word. But here, while Joseph may indeed be quiet (so to speak), we see how his actions—his "prompt, simple, and unspectacular" obedient actions—speak louder than words (cf. his actions in chapter 2 as well).[11] Look again with me, starting in verse 19, and pay attention to Joseph:

> And her husband Joseph, being a just man and unwilling to put her to shame, resolved to divorce her quietly. But as he considered these things, behold, an angel of the Lord appeared to him in a dream, saying, "Joseph, son of David, do not fear to take Mary as your wife. . . . She will bear a son, and you [singular] shall call his name Jesus. . . ." When Joseph woke from sleep, he did as the angel of the Lord commanded him: he took his wife, but knew her not until she had given birth to a son. And he called [the child's] name Jesus. (vv. 19–25)

Joseph is the subject of most of the sentences above.

One of the first sermons I ever preached was on Genesis 39, which is the story of Joseph, the son of the patriarch Jacob (cf. 1:2b, 16). In that sermon I showed how the context surrounding the story of Joseph and Potiphar's wife (Genesis 39) was key to understanding the beginning of salvation history.

You know the story of Joseph, right? The world is still making musicals about it. The story of Joseph starts in Genesis 37, and it is quickly and apparently interrupted in Genesis 38 by the story of Judah and his illicit relationship with Tamar, his widowed daughter-in-law. I mentioned that relationship in the previous chapter. Recall that Judah and Tamar got together when they shouldn't have and out came the twins—Perez and Zerah.

The question I asked in my Genesis 39 sermon was this: what does Judah have to do with Joseph? What does faithless Judah have to do with faithful Joseph? Why even mention Judah at the start of the grand drama of Joseph? Well, one reason is that he is a foil. Judah's impurity highlights Joseph's purity. Judah propositioned his daughter-in-law, who he mistakenly thought was a shrine prostitute. Joseph, on the other hand, was repeatedly propositioned by a powerful (and beautiful?) Egyptian woman and yet resisted each time. The other reason (and the more important one) is this: Joseph, who will come to power in Egypt, will save his brothers' lives, including Judah's. This is crucial, we learn at the end of Genesis (Genesis 49:10), because it is through Judah's offspring that the Christ will come (Hebrews 7:14)—the lion of the tribe of Judah, the ultimate King of God's people.

Matthew knows the importance of this story (the interweaving of these Genesis stories), and that's why he starts his Gospel about Jesus with a genealogy. Matthew 1:2, 3 states, "Abraham was the father of Isaac, and Isaac the father of Jacob, and Jacob the father of *Judah* and his brothers, and Judah the father of Perez and Zerah by Tamar." Now, keep your eyes on those names (as we are following Judah's line) and look ahead to verse 6, which leads us to David—"and Jesse the father of David the king." Now we are getting somewhere! But where? Is this the king we are looking for? Let's keep following Judah's line that has become David's line. Where does this line lead? Look at verse 16. Take your pencil and write next to this verse the word, "Wow!" "And Jacob [not the patriarch] the father *of Joseph* [Joseph who?] the husband of Mary, of whom Jesus was born."

So why is Joseph, the husband of Mary, so important to Jesus? What does this Joseph have to do with our Jesus? That's the question for this text. Well, you say, he functions as a competent and reliable witness to Mary's virginity (which is so important for the fulfillment of Isaiah's prophecy, mentioned in v. 23).[12] Yes, that's true. But he is much more than that. Look at verse 20. The angel gives away the answer. "Behold, an angel of the Lord appeared to Joseph in a dream, saying, 'Joseph, son of David . . .'"[13] There it is! You can also put a "Wow!" next to "son of David." Did you know that other than this reference only Jesus in all the Gospels is called "Son of David"? Which means what? It means that Joseph has royal blood. It means that this humble carpenter (13:55) is from "the house of David" (Luke 1:27). And God promised long ago that a king would come from the line of Judah and from the line of David to reign forevermore. In the annunciation, Mary hears this about her son:

> He will be great and will be called the Son of the Most High. And the Lord God will give to him the throne of his father David, and he will reign over the house of Jacob forever, and of his kingdom there will be no end. (Luke 1:32, 33)

Jesus has the right lineage, Scripturally speaking. He is the son of Abraham and the son of David. But how does he get to be the son of David? Is it through Mary? Maybe. Maybe not. Nowhere is that the point, either in Luke or Matthew. Rather, and more certainly, it is through Joseph, his surrogate father![14]

Why is this narrative before us so important? It is important because it shows us how Joseph made Mary's son his own son. That is, he made Jesus his legally. How? Two ways. First, "he took [Mary as] his wife" (v. 24). Second,

"And he [Joseph] called his name Jesus" (v. 25). By accepting Mary as his wife and by naming her child, he officially bestowed upon Jesus "the status of a descendant of David."[15]

Think of the first chapter of Matthew's Gospel in this way. The first seventeen verses—the genealogy—confirm to us that Jesus is the promised one, and then the last eight verses (with their focus on Joseph) confirm to us that Jesus is truly from the line of David, or as Paul writes, Jesus "was descended from David according to the flesh" (Romans 1:3). The camera lens is wide in verses 1–17 focusing on the big picture of salvation history. It narrows its focus in verses 18–25 upon the holy family—Mary, Jesus, and (don't forget!) Joseph.

I don't want to overdo this point, but I should mention (it would be wrong for me not to mention just briefly) how this fits with verses 22, 23.

> All this took place to fulfill what the Lord had spoken by the prophet: "Behold, the virgin shall conceive and bear a son, and they shall call his name Immanuel" (which means, God with us).

That is a quotation of Isaiah 7:14. It speaks of a sign—a virgin conception and birth—that would be given to the "house of David" (Isaiah 7:13). Now, while there is a child born in Isaiah 8, this child is not the full fulfillment of this prophecy. As we read on in Isaiah, especially in Isaiah 9 and 11, we learn of a unique child still to come. There will be a "super-fulfillment" of the prophecy, as Daniel Harrington words it.[16] Isaiah 9:6, 7 reads:

> For unto us a child is born, to us a son is given; and the government shall be upon his shoulder, and his name shall be called Wonderful Counselor, Mighty God, Everlasting Father, Prince of Peace. Of the increase of his government and of peace there will be no end, on the throne of David and over his kingdom, to establish it and to uphold it with justice and with righteousness from this time forth and forevermore.

So what does Joseph have to do with Jesus? Joseph adopts Jesus into the house of David.

Don't underestimate the unique role of quiet Joseph. Quiet Joseph quietly bestows upon Jesus this kingly inheritance and right. Joseph the surrogate—might we say that he is as important as the Spirit in this Christmas story?

Seeing like Simeon

Most nights, when my family gathers at the dinner table, we pray before the meal. When one year old Charlotte had already mastered the ritual.[17] Often she would pull herself up onto her chair and say the word "pray." Then she would fold her chubby, soft hands together, close her eyes, bow her head, and wait reverently, angelically.

My son Simeon is quite different. He performs no sinless Charlottean ceremony of his own. Instead he squirms into and in his spot, grabs his food with his fingers, shoving some in his mouth, and prays with his mouth full and his eyes wide open. I have never found such boyish behavior acceptable. Yet I will say, looking at this from the broadest and most generous perspective, perhaps the last part of his routine is justifiable and even commendable; perhaps Simeon struggles to close his eyes because he fears he'll miss seeing something spectacular, like a ladybug dancing on the floor or a new moon rising in the sky. And if that is the case, then we can learn something from him. Perhaps each Christmas we should pray with our eyes wide open—open to the creation around us, open to the wonders of God's Word, open to the heavens, never knowing when the One who came in humility will come again in glory, with the stars in his hands and the moon bright beneath his feet.

4

Fulfillments and Fulfillment

MATTHEW 1:18—2:23

IN 1893 CHICAGO HOSTED the World's Columbian Exposition, also called the Chicago World's Fair. Daniel Burnham, later responsible for *The Plan of Chicago*, was one of the distinguished architects called upon to design this event. At that time Burnham lived in Evanston. The Fair was to be in Jackson Park on the south lakefront, about twenty miles away. In those days, with poorly paved roads and inefficient means of transportation, for Burnham to commute daily from Sheridan Road down to S. Stony Island Avenue was unfeasible. So as he planned for the Fair, he actually worked and *lived* on the South Side. This time away from family in Evanston was very difficult for him, as attested by the many letters he wrote to his wife, speaking of how he missed her and longed to be home.

Now think of this. If it took Burnham in the late nineteenth century about half a day to travel from Evanston to Jackson Park, imagine how long it would have taken "the wise men" and their entourage in the first century to travel "from the east"—which could have been what is today Jordan, Iraq, Iran, Saudi Arabia, or even as far east as Afghanistan. From Baghdad to Bethlehem is 547 miles of extremely inhospitable terrain. But even if it wasn't that far—if it was only 200 miles or twenty miles—why would anyone desire to do this? Why leave friends and family (maybe wife and children) for likely a year or two? What's at stake? What's the need? What's the driving impulse?

Precise Fulfillments

Our discovery begins with our grasping what Matthew is doing here in the first part of his Gospel. Like a good architect, he has structured his narrative of the life of Jesus in a certain way. He begins with Jesus' genealogy in 1:1–17 in order to show that Jesus comes from the right line at the right time and how it is just the right design. That's the groundwork he puts in place. From there he erects five pillars. Starting in 1:18 and ending in 2:23, Matthew gives us five fulfillments of what has been said through the prophets—1:22, 23; 2:6, 15, 17, 18, and 23.[1] The first two are what I'll call *precise* fulfillments; the latter three are *patterned fulfillments*.

By precise I mean: *This is that*. I borrow this phrase from Acts 2:16 in the King James Version or Young's Literal Translation, where Peter uses it in his first sermon. *This* (what is happening now) is *that* (what was said would happen). Thus, in Acts 2 the coming of the Holy Spirit is *this*, and the prophecy of Joel is *that*. Patterned fulfillments (i.e., typology) work differently. Here is my description of them: *this is THIS*. Something that happened in the past is a pattern for something that happens in the life and ministry of Jesus. I'll explain *this is THIS* when we get to it. For now we'll look at the precise fulfillments, at *this is that*.

We start with Isaiah. In Isaiah 7—11 we read that there will be a king from the line of David who will be called such titles as "Mighty God" and "Prince of Peace" and that this king will be born in a most unusual way—of a virgin. In Matthew 1:18–25 the Evangelist is saying: Listen, *this is that*. This Mary is that virgin, and this Jesus is that God-child, that prince upon whose shoulders the whole world's governance will rest.

The second involves the place of this child's birth. The wise men know enough about Israel's prophets to know the Messiah will be born. They believe this star testifies to his birth.[2] But they don't know the Bible well enough to know where the Messiah will be born. So they travel to Jerusalem perhaps thinking, "If the king of the Jews is to be born, he will be born in the capital city." However, when they arrive and start asking around—"Where is he who has been born king of the Jews?"—the current jealous and malicious king, Herod, naturally wants to help. Herod's wise men—the scribes—inform Herod, who in turn informs the magi, about the prophet Micah's prophecy, which said in essence: "And you, O Bethlehem, in the land of Judah, are by no means least among the rulers of Judah; for from you shall come a ruler who will shepherd my people Israel" (Micah 5:2, 4). When the Messiah comes, he'll be from Bethlehem, a small town about five miles south of Jerusalem, the same place where King David was born. So again *this is that*. Jesus was born in *this* particular town. Micah predicted that the Messiah would be born in *that* same town.[3]

Those are the two precise fulfillments. And when I think about the precise fulfillments, not just the ones *about* Jesus but the ones *by* Jesus—i.e., that the gospel would spread to all the nations of the world, that his words as well as his church would last the test of time (see 28:16–20; Luke 21:33; Matthew 16:17, 18)—they are for me the closest thing to touching the wounds of Christ. When Thomas felt the hands and side and feet of Jesus, he believed. As I touch, so to speak, these fulfillments, they are almost tangible reminders that God's Word and Son can be trusted.

Patterned Fulfillments

If the precise fulfillments are like touching the hands of Christ, the patterned fulfillments here (and ironically for typology) are even more tangible. They are like holding the hand of Christ. They are not only like a momentary touching of the hand, but holding it and feeling your hand fit in his because his hand fits these Old Testament patterns so perfectly. Let me show you what I mean as we look now at 2:13–23.

A few months ago a young man from my church who is currently earning his Master's degree in Biblical Exegesis asked me when I was going to start preaching on Matthew. I replied, "Very soon." He said, with a sigh of relief, "Good, because I can't wait to hear what you have to say about chapter 2. I don't know what Matthew is doing with Scripture."

Yeah, what is Matthew doing here? At first glance it seems like he is randomly taking Old Testament verses and trying to squeeze them into the life of Jesus, much like the husband whose waistline has grown two inches since Thanksgiving trying on the new jeans his wife bought him for Christmas, sucking in his stomach, and saying, "Look, honey, they fit great!"

At a first reading I can see how you might think that's the case. You might think like William Barclay did when he wrote, "Matthew is doing what he so often did. In his eagerness he is finding a prophecy where no prophecy is."[4] Or with equal skepticism you might think as Ulrich Luz does. The distinguished Swiss scholar wrote:

> Thus at our text one can speak no longer of a fulfillment of Old Testament predictions by God but only of the early Christian belief in this fulfillment. Instead of God's activity in history leading to Jesus, there is—to overstate the case—the belief in that activity.[5]

The problem with this kind of reading is that it views these Old Testament texts (back to my analogy) as a pair of jeans that must fit a certain size body perfectly, rather than a puzzle that has seemingly random pieces that, when pieced together, fit just as they are supposed to. In fact, what we have here is a double-sided puzzle with the pieces fitted together and lying on a glass table. When you look at it faceup, sitting on top of the table, the pattern is of two key Old Testament events and what I think is the combination of two key Old Testament ideas. But when you look underneath, beneath the glass, facedown, you'll see the face of Jesus Christ, or as Paul put it, "the light of the knowledge of the glory of God in the face of Jesus Christ" (2 Corinthians 4:6).

If it helps, think of what Matthew is doing here as being similar to what the author of Hebrews does. In Hebrews we have laid on the glass table the pieces that comprise the temple, the priesthood, and the sacrifice. Once those are nicely fitted together, we look under the table and see Jesus. Jesus is the fulfillment of the whole sacrificial system. In a similar manner (although he'll deal more with history than typology), Matthew is not thumbing through his Bible looking for random proof texts that Jesus might somehow fulfill. Rather, he is reading through the whole story of Israel and noticing, under the inspiration of the Holy Spirit, how *this* story is like *THIS* one.

Out of Egypt

Here is the first similarity Matthew sees:

> Now when they had departed, behold, an angel of the Lord appeared to Joseph in a dream and said, "Rise, take the child and his mother, and flee to Egypt, and remain there until I tell you, for Herod is about to search for the child, to destroy him." And he rose and took the child and his mother by night and departed to Egypt and remained there until the death of Herod. This was to fulfill what the Lord had spoken by the prophet, "Out of Egypt I called my son." (vv. 13–15)

"The prophet" referred to here is Hosea. This is a quote from Hosea 11:1. In the original context Hosea is recalling how God through Moses called Israel out of Egypt. So as Matthew looks through Hosea 11:1 back to the exodus (and the beginning of Israel as a nation) he sees a similar pattern in Jesus' early years. As Rudolf Schnackenburg said, Matthew sees that "The old Mosaic exodus is repeated and fulfilled in a new way."[6] But it's not just that Jesus is like Moses, a new and better deliverer (see Hebrews 3:3; cf. Matthew 1:21). Rather, Jesus is the embodiment of Israel itself, a new and better "son." As we move on to the next five chapters, this will become especially clear. John Stott summarizes:

> As Israel was oppressed in Egypt under the despotic rule of Pharaoh, so the infant Jesus became a refugee in Egypt under the despotic rule of Herod. As Israel passed through the waters of the Red Sea, so Jesus passed through

> the waters of John's baptism in the River Jordan. As Israel was tested in the wilderness of Zin for forty years, so Jesus was tested in the wilderness of Judea for forty days. And as Moses from Mount Sinai gave Israel the law, so Jesus from the Mount of Beatitudes gave his disciples the true interpretation and amplification of the law.[7]

So here, at the start of this providential pattern, Matthew is saying: picture the exodus; picture Jesus. Picture Israel whom God calls in Hosea at the start of this plan of salvation "my son," and picture Jesus, whom God calls in Matthew "my beloved Son" (3:17; 17:5). And just as Israel went down to Egypt and then came out of Egypt into the promised land, so God's Son will make that same journey. *This* story is *THIS* story.

Return from the Exile

So that's the first patterned fulfillment: the exodus and Jesus. The second is the exile and Jesus, or more specifically the return from the Babylonian exile and the restoration that Jesus' coming brings to the world.

Let's say you ran into me at the grocery store and you pulled me aside and said, "Pastor, I have a very important question for you. Can you quickly name the seven most important events in Israel's history?" I would reply, "Of course I can. That's what I'm here for." I would stop squeezing the lettuce and begin without further adieu: "(1) The call and covenant of Abraham, (2) the conquest of Canaan, (3) the exodus, (4) David and the Davidic covenant, (5) Israel's exile to Assyria, (6) Judah's exile to Babylon, and (7) the return and restoration from exile."

Now if you followed that up by saying, "Nice job, Pastor. How about your top two? What would those be?" I would scratch my head (only momentarily) and say, "(1) The exodus and (2) the return from the exile." I honestly would have said this before reading Matthew 2. But now having studied Matthew 2, I'm really proud of myself that I landed exactly where he did. For Matthew says, "Look at the exodus; look at Jesus." Then he says next, in verses 16–18, "Look at the exile and the return from it, and look again at Jesus. You'll find another similarity of sorts."

Listen again to this tragic text (and I'll explain soon what I'm specifically getting at):

> Then Herod, when he saw that he had been tricked by the wise men, became furious, and he sent and killed all the male children in Bethlehem and in all that region who were two years old or under, according to the time that he had ascertained from the wise men. Then was fulfilled what was

> spoken by the prophet Jeremiah: "A voice was heard in Ramah, weeping and loud lamentation, Rachel weeping for her children; she refused to be comforted, because they are no more."

What Herod does here (usually called the slaughter of the innocents) is horrific. I don't want to downplay the evil of that event, but having said that, our focus in this sermon is more on verses 17, 18 (the prophecy) than on verse 16 (the tragedy). In the next chapter we will return to this text and will look at this event from a slightly different angle. Then we will focus more on Herod and on this atrocity. But for now we're focusing on how this tragedy fits with this prophecy and how both of them fit with Jesus.

This prophecy comes from Jeremiah 31:15. When Jeremiah speaks of Rachel he is referring to the matriarch, the wife of Jacob, the mother of Joseph and Benjamin. Rachel died, if you'll recall, giving birth to Benjamin. Because of this she took on a symbolic role for God's people. She was known as the *mater dolorosa* (sorrowful mother) of the Old Testament as well as "the mother of Israel for all time," as the rabbis called her.[8]

At one point the prophet Jeremiah, like many Judean prisoners, was held prisoner in Ramah (Jeremiah 40:1), a town about five miles north of Jerusalem. This was the town where Rachel was likely buried (Genesis 35:16–19). It was also a town through which God's people were marched, having been captured by the Babylonian army in the early sixth century BC as they traveled north from Jerusalem. Concerning this event, Jeremiah envisioned in chapter 31 the mother of Israel, as if alive in her tomb, weeping for her children as they walked to captivity right before her eyes.

You say, "Okay, but what does Jeremiah 31 have to do with Jesus? Why quote from that chapter and relate it to the slaughter of these children?" Here is the relationship between the two. In Jeremiah 31 Rachel's tears—the tears of the exile—have reached their climax in the tears of the mothers of Bethlehem.[9] In other words, with Jesus the trail of tears is finally coming to an end. That is the message of the whole chapter of Jeremiah 31. Unlike most of the book of Jeremiah, this chapter is not one of sorrow but hope. The verse right after what Matthew quotes starts, "Keep your voice from weeping, and your eyes from tears" (Jeremiah 31:16). Now, why should God's people refrain from crying? Because God's people finally "shall come back from the land of the enemy" (Jeremiah 31:16), and they shall "serve the LORD their God and [the ultimate] David their king" (30:9). The exile is over. The reign of a new king under a *new covenant* (Jeremiah 31:33, 34) is at hand.

Matthew is saying that with the coming of Jesus, the time of the exile is coming to a close! He hinted at it in the last verse of the genealogy (1:17). Now he alludes to it through the prophets. The tears shed by the mothers in Bethlehem inaugurate the reign of the one who will shed tears of blood for the forgiveness of sin and who will eventually, in the restoration of all things, wipe every tear away (Revelation 21:4).

So, can you feel your hand fitting nicely into Christ's, saying to yourself, "Yes, these patterned prophecies have helped me to grasp Jesus and to hold on to him even more tightly"?

The Branch for the Nations

Jesus and the exodus, that's the first pattern; Jesus and the return from exile, that's the second. Finally we come to the third patterned prophecy, which is the hardest puzzle of all. Take a look again at verses 19–23:

> But when Herod died, behold, an angel of the Lord appeared in a dream to Joseph in Egypt, saying, "Rise, take the child and his mother and go to the land of Israel, for those who sought the child's life are dead." And he rose and took the child and his mother and went to the land of Israel. But when he heard that Archelaus was reigning over Judea in place of his father Herod, he was afraid to go there, and being warned in a dream he withdrew to the district of Galilee. *And he went and lived in a city called Nazareth, so that what was spoken by the prophets might be fulfilled, that he would be called a Nazarene.*

What makes verse 23 (italicized above) difficult is that there is not a prophecy like this anywhere in the Bible. In fact, Nazareth is not even mentioned in the Old Testament or any ancient Jewish writing. So, what is Matthew up to? Is he using his apostolic authority to pull a white bunny out of a trick hat?

The key to beginning to understand this complex allusion is Matthew's use of the plural word "prophets." Instead of saying, as he has done thus far, "this was to fulfill what was spoken by the prophet," here he writes "prophets," using the word in the same way Peter does in his sermon at Solomon's Portico (see Acts 3:18, 24; cf. 10:43). What specifically does Matthew have in mind? "The prophets" is a big category. I think he has in mind an amalgamation or a blending together of two messianic ideas. From the time of David onward, the prophets talk a lot about the ultimate Davidic king, often called "the Son of David." They also talk about a seemingly contrary idea—at least unfathomable to the Pharisees of Jesus' day—of the Gentiles becoming part of God's people under the rule of God's king.

When Matthew says of Jesus in verse 23, "he would be called a Nazarene," he is bringing these two ideas together. Here is why I say that. In Hebrew the word for "branch" is *neser*. Isaiah 11:1, an important messianic text, uses this word. Isaiah writes, "There shall come forth a shoot from the stump of Jesse, and a branch [*neser*] from his roots shall bear fruit." From David's royal line shall come a branch (i.e., the Messiah).

> Lo, how a rose e'er blooming
> From tender stem hath sprung!
> Of Jesse's lineage coming
> As seers of old have sung.[10]

The town of Nazareth was likely named after Isaiah 11:1. It was originally settled by a remnant of Israel who returned from the exile, were from David's line, and who thus consciously gave their new settlement a messianic name.[11] They called the town *neser*/eth. I imagine under the town name something like, "Welcome to the City of the Branch." So, Matthew is saying that Jesus came from the city of David (Bethlehem) as well as from the people of David (Nazareth). Jesus is "the branch." Jesus is "the Son of David." The fact that he grew up in Nazareth as a Nazarene puts an exclamation point on this!

The other interesting fact about Nazareth is its location in the region called Galilee, a region that had a mix of Jews and Gentiles. This is why Isaiah called it (and Matthew will quote this in 4:15) "Galilee of the nations [footnote: Gentiles]" (Isaiah 9:1). Due to this ethnic diversity, Galilee (and Nazareth in particular) was looked down upon. What Nathaniel says when he first learned Jesus was from that town was the sentiment of many—"Can anything good come out of Nazareth?" (John 1:46). Nathaniel was looking for the *Jewish* Messiah, who he assumed wouldn't come from that region of the world. "Ah," Matthew says here in verse 23, "think again." Think about the prophets! Think about this vision they had of the Davidic King who would rule all the nations. Think of Isaiah 11:1—"There shall come forth a shoot from the stump of Jesse," and think of Isaiah 11:10—"of him shall the nations inquire." Think of wise men from the east traveling perhaps farther than the queen of Sheba to see a King greater than Solomon.

Finding Fulfillment

Here we have two precise and three patterned prophecies that find their fulfillment in Jesus. But that's only part of what's going on here. It is one thing to see what is being taught—"Oh, I see." But it's quite another thing to *see* it—

"Oh . . . I see!" That is, to find intellectual, emotional, spiritual *fulfillment* in what is seen here, in Jesus who fulfills these five prophecies.

There are the fulfillments, and then there is our fulfillment in the one who fulfills. I'm not just doing a cute play on words here. I actually believe part of Matthew's intention here, with the wise men in verses 1–12, is to show us that the long journey from Baghdad to Bethlehem was worth it, that Jesus filled the hollow of their hearts. Look at the second half of verse 2. The wise men say, "We saw his star when it rose and have come to *worship* him." And then the first half of verse 11, "going into the house they saw the child with Mary his mother, and they fell down and *worshiped* him."[12]

What is Matthew saying with this? He is not giving us the life story of the wise men. We don't know what happened to them. We don't know if this first act of worship was their only act or if they continued on with lives of love and service to Jesus. But he is telling us what wise men (then and now) do. Wise men and women and children—from the south and north, west and *east*—come to Jesus,[13] and wise men find fulfillment through worshipping the newborn and forever-born King of kings.

5

We *Two* Kings

MATTHEW 2:1–12

THERE ARE AT LEAST TWO historical inaccuracies in John Henry Hopkins's otherwise wonderful Christmas carol "We Three Kings." First is the number three. How many wise men were there? Were there three? Matthew doesn't provide such a detail. He just says "wise men from the east came to Jerusalem" (2:1). The plural subject of that sentence tells us there were more than one. Were there two? Were there twenty? We don't know. Well then, where do we get three? This tradition comes from the three gifts mentioned in verse 11, the logic being that if there were three gifts there must have been three men. But such logic is flawed, for if I told you I received a Rolex, a diamond-studded pinky ring, and a body-length mink coat for Christmas, these three gifts would not necessitate three givers, would they? If I told you that my wife gave me these three gifts this Christmas you might be surprised if you knew how frugal she is and that such gifts don't precisely fit my style. But you wouldn't be surprised if my wife gave me three gifts, would you? In fact, she did give me three gifts this year—a novel, a used theology book, and a stainless-steel coffee mug—all fitting gifts for my sanctified obsessions.

So the "three" in "We Three Kings" is not necessarily accurate. Neither is the description "kings." Again the gifts are to blame for this misunderstanding. Gold, frankincense, and myrrh were very expensive. Such gifts tell us that these men had abundant resources. They had money that allowed them to travel and to give Jesus what they gave him. But such wealth does not necessitate royalty.

I'm sorry to ruin what might be your favorite Christmas carol, but here in 2:1–12 there are not likely three kings. However, there are two! Matthew wants us to take note of two kings—King Herod and King Jesus. Look at verse 1, "Now after Jesus was born in Bethlehem of Judea in the days of Herod *the king* . . ." Look also at verses 3 and 9. Verse 3 begins, "When Herod *the king*. . . ," and verse 9, "After listening to *the king*. . . ." The first king is Herod.

The second king is obviously Jesus. Look at verse 2, where the wise men say of him, "Where is he who has been born *king* of the Jews?" Then, also in verse 2, they speak of "his star"—which most scholars believe is a reference to the oracle of Balaam, "a star shall come out of Jacob, and a scepter shall rise out of Israel" (Numbers 24:17). This "star" in the sky symbolizes to them this "star"—the coming of the ideal king, from the Jews, for the world.[1] Look also at verse 4, where Herod inquires about "where *the Christ* was to be born." The Greek word for "Christ" means "anointed one" or "king." Also peek at the prophecy in verse 6 that speaks of "the *rulers* of Judah" and "a *ruler*" who is to come. So we have "his star," "the Christ," and "a ruler." These are all different words than "king," but are obviously on the same theme and about the same person.[2]

This kingly theme as it relates to Jesus also fits the immediate context. It fits with the five fulfillments we examined in the last sermon, all of which have to do with Jesus being the King. The prophets—Isaiah, Jeremiah, Micah, and Hosea—all speak of a king to come. It also fits the genealogy (1:1–17) and birth narrative (1:18–25), both of which emphasize Jesus' official relationship with King David. Finally, it fits what follows in chapters 3, 4, where King Jesus is introduced nearly three decades later by John the Baptist whose message is, "Repent, for the *kingdom* of heaven is at hand" (3:2), the same words Jesus will use in 4:17 as he begins his public ministry.

So, *we two kings* is what we have here—Herod and Jesus. As readers of this Gospel, our task now is to figure out (which won't be too difficult) which king is the true king, and thus the king to whom we should submit.

Two Kings—Herod and Jesus

Matthew makes our decision rather easy, doesn't he? Do you want a madman or the Messiah? Do you want a man who would order the massacre of innocent children (v. 16) or a man who would open his arms to children and lay down his life for the less-than-innocent of the world? Do you want a ruler who rules by force, aggression, and cruelty or a ruler who rules by love, compassion, and the cross of his own sufferings? Do you want a man who slaughtered the last remnants of the dynasty that ruled before him, put to death half of the Sanhedrin, killed 300 court officers, executed his wife and mother-in-law and three sons, and as he lay dying arranged for all the notable men of Jerusalem to be assembled in the Hippodrome and killed as soon as his own death was announced, so the people might weep instead of rejoice on the day of his death?[3] Do you want him for king? Or do you want the One who when reviled did not revile in return, who when he suffered did not threaten but rather bore our sins in his body on the tree (see 1 Peter 2:21–25)? Whom do you want? Do you want the Big Bad Wolf or the Good Shepherd—a "shepherd king" like David, one who would finally and perfectly, as verse 6b puts it, "shepherd my people Israel" (cf. 2 Samuel 5:2; Ezekiel 34)?

The other day I was looking at what I think is one of Rembrandt's greatest paintings, *Belshazzar's Feast* (1635). This work is a depiction of the fifth chapter of Daniel. King Belshazzar of Babylon was throwing a grand feast, where he was surrounded by his lords and ladies. You may recall from Daniel 5:1–6 that in the midst of his drunkenness and idolatry (as he drinks wine from the temple vessels while he praises the gods of gold, silver, bronze, iron, wood, and stone), suddenly fingers of a human hand appear, which proceed to write something on the plaster of the palace wall, a message that Daniel would later decipher (5:24–28). God's Word to that king was basically this: your kingdom is coming to an end!

In his painting, Rembrandt uses light to highlight that on which he wants us to focus: the script on the wall, which is the brightest point, as well as the face of the king as he turns toward the wall in absolute shock and fear. Belshazzar is standing with his right hand on an overturned dinner plate, and his left hand is in the air, motioning as if to block the light. His head is tilted back toward the table, and his crown is slowly edging off his head. His kingdom is about to fall.

What happened to Belshazzar also happens to Herod. Herod the Great, as he was called, loses his greatness, and Jesus, the King of Heaven, of whom Daniel and the prophets prophesied, increases in his. Psalm 2, which I slightly paraphrase and reorder for emphasis, summarizes this theme:

> Why do the nations rage and the peoples plot in vain? Why do the kings of the earth set themselves . . . against the LORD and against his Anointed [i.e., the Christ]? Our God in heaven laughs, and he says to such rulers [kings like Herod], "As for me, I have set my King on Zion . . . and I have said of him, 'You are my Son'"—the king who will judge the nations, the king for whom I will make the ends of the earth his possession. . . . Be wise, O kings; be warned, O rulers of the earth. Serve the LORD with fear, and rejoice with trembling. Kiss the Son! Do homage to the King of God's kingdom.

Three Choices

So here in 2:1–12 there are not three kings but two. There is Herod, the Roman appointed "king of the Jews," and there is Jesus, *the God-appointed King of all kings*. Yet as it pertains to the second king, our Lord Jesus and our relationship to him, there are *three* choices—indifference, hostility, or worship.[4]

Indifference

First, we can choose *indifference*. This is the choice made by the Jewish religious leaders. The wise men come to town and say in effect, "Where is he? Where is the Christ-child?" Herod gets wind of their question, and in his jealousy he is "troubled" (v. 3). While he gladly accepts the title "the King of the Jews," his knowledge of the Hebrew Bible is insufficient. So he calls in the experts—the chief priests and the scribes. The scribes or "teachers of the law" especially knew their stuff. They spent all day meticulously copying the Holy Scriptures, word by word, line by line. They were professional Bible scholars and teachers. They didn't have to open to Micah to know in which town the Messiah would be born. For them, Herod's dilemma was "Bible Trivia for 100." I envision them standing side by side before Herod, like contestants on the game show *Jeopardy*, and as soon as Herod is done asking his question all of them simultaneously place their hands on the buzzer—"What is Bethlehem of Judea?"

It is not surprising that they knew the answer. It would be "shame on them" if they didn't. What is surprising is that they did nothing with the answer. Unlike these foreigners who "traversed afar" over "field and fountain, moor and mountain,"[5] these religious experts pushed their buzzer, won their prize, and went back to bury their heads in the Word of God. As Paul put it, they were "always learning and never able to arrive at a knowledge of the truth" (2 Timothy 3:7). They weren't even curious—"Could this be the one of whom the Scriptures testify?" They were as indifferent to Jesus as the priest and Levite were to the bruised and battered man in the Parable of the Good Samaritan.

The religious leaders weren't alone in their indifference. Matthew gives the impression that the whole city of Jerusalem knew, yet not one person went to the nearby town to see if these wise men were truly wise, to see if indeed the "star . . . out of Jacob" (Numbers 24:17) had come into the world. What gross indifference to Jesus! "He came unto his own, and his own received him not" (John 1:11, KJV).

The church is full of people like this. The church, you say? Don't you mean the world? No, I mean the church. Sure, there are people in the world who are indifferent to Jesus. They know he was born in Bethlehem, his mother's name was Mary, he did miracles, he died on the cross, he rose from the dead. They know all this, and they just don't care. There are lots of people like that in the world. But there are also lots of people like that in the church. If you quizzed them on Bible trivia, they'd do just fine. But if you informed them, "God in the flesh is just five miles down the street. Would you care to join me to meet him?" they would shake their heads and say, "Oh, not this time. You know the NFL playoffs start today," or "I'm sorry, it's the last day of this unbelievable New Year's sale," or "I'd hate to miss my Sunday afternoon nap. Maybe next time."

What indifference! We live in a world—a church world—of indifference. People pack the pews each Sunday but live as though there is no King upon the throne but them. They are each their own king, and they do whatever is fitting in their own eyes. But rest assured, King Jesus is not indifferent toward such false, puny, self-appointed royalty. John the Baptist (see the next chapter) will tell us this in quite vivid, nonpolitically-correct language. He will say of Jesus, "His winnowing fork is in his hand, and he will clear his threshing floor and gather his wheat into the barn, but the chaff he will burn with unquenchable fire" (3:12).

Hostility

We can choose indifference, as the scribes, chief priests, and all Jerusalem did. Or, secondly, we can choose *hostility*, as Herod did. We can choose to hate Jesus and be hostile to him and everything associated with him—his followers, teachings, church, and kingdom.

I don't know if you've noticed this, but recently there has been a sudden increase of such hostility in our country. Some of the best-selling books in the last few years are from these new atheists, self-professed "Brights" as Daniel Dennett and Richard Dawkins call themselves, who are supposedly bringing light into our dark world, yet who are in reality seeking to suffocate the true Light of the World under the bushel basket of a social, quasi-scientific Darwinism.

For example, I read Christopher Hitchens's book, *god Is not Great* (the "g" in "god" is purposefully not capitalized). His subtitle is *How Religion Poisons Everything*. Chapter 7, where he begins to talk specifically about the Bible, he entitles "Revelation: The Nightmare of the 'Old' Testament," and Chapter 8 he calls "The 'New' Testament Exceeds the Evil of the 'Old' One."

In this book this intelligent man makes some surprisingly foolish statements. For instance, concerning the four Gospels he says, "Their multiple authors—none of whom published anything until many decades after the Crucifixion—cannot agree on anything of importance."[6] However, Hitchens's own statement disproves itself, for all four Gospel writers were certainly agreed on the centrality and importance of the crucifixion! In addition to such self-contradictory statements, many of his assertions seem to be driven by ungrounded hostility. Hitchens writes, "The doings and 'sayings' of Moses and Abraham and Jesus [are] so ill-founded and so inconsistent, as well as so often immoral."[7] He refers to the Christian practice of teaching our children the truths of our faith as "child abuse" (he has a whole chapter on this).

At first I was surprised by such hostility. I thought to myself, *If God doesn't exist or if Jesus wasn't the Son of God, why make a big fuss? Why write a book against religion? People believe in far crazier things than our religion. Why attack Christianity? Why do these scientists, as many of them are, attack the faith that has thus far produced the world's greatest scientists and mathematicians, the likes of Newton and Pascal?* But then I remembered that an intelligent person only attacks what he knows to be a real threat to his way of thinking and, more importantly, his way of living. And Jesus is such a threat.

Jesus was a real threat to Herod because, as Lawrence W. Farris writes, Herod grasped what was "at stake in the birth of Jesus."[8] If Herod didn't think Jesus was actually born, if he didn't think Jesus might indeed be a king—*the* king—if he didn't think this new king, though now just a child, could in fact dethrone him, rule over him, take allegiance from him, he would not have done what he did.

You see, Jesus is a real threat to anyone and everyone who thinks seriously about him. If Jesus is king—and you can almost hear in Herod's dungeon the prophetic voice of John the Baptist before his beheading (cf. 14:4)—it means you're not. It means your dethronement. It means your submission. It means you can't lead your life any longer, as Herod did and as I suggest these new atheists do, by the dictates of your unrepresented immoral desires.[9] If Jesus is who he says he is, you either love him or you hate him! Which is exactly what Jesus said: "Do not think that I have come to bring peace to the earth.[10] I have not come to bring peace, but a sword" (10:34). This is no nice Christmas story. This is a nasty conflict of kingdoms.

Indifference, to me, is illogical. It is to ignore the facts. Hostility, however, is quite reasonable, given that we are naturally inclined to oppose God and his ways and his Son, and given the very controversial claims of Christ. If he is King, you and I are not.

Worship

We can respond to Jesus with indifference or with hostility (both equally reject his rule) or with *worship*. We can worship him as the wise men wisely did.

> Frankincense to offer have I;
> Incense owns a Deity nigh:
> Prayer and praising, all men raising,
> Worship him, God Most High.[11]

Matthew 2:11 reads: "And going into the house they saw the child with Mary his mother, and they fell down and worshiped him. Then, opening their treasures, they offered him gifts, gold and frankincense and myrrh." When read in the context of all that has come before (the long months of travel, the persistence in finding the child, etc.), I am very close to agreeing with J. C. Ryle who said concerning this verse, "We read of no greater faith than this in the whole volume of the Bible."[12]

What makes it so "great" is not merely *what* they did, which T. S. Eliot labeled a "death" to themselves,[13] since "they fell down and worshiped him."[14] What makes it so great is *who* did what. Who worships the King of the Jews? Does Herod, the earthly king of the Jews? No. How about the Jewish scribes and chief priests? No. Do all the Jews in all Jerusalem? No. But how about those Gentiles who are not from the promised land? Do they bow down in homage? Do they in essence "kiss the Son" (Psalm 2:12)? Yes, they do.

What is Matthew doing with this fact? What is the importance of who received Jesus? With the wise men, Matthew is echoing what the angel of the Lord said to the shepherds in Luke 2:10, 11: "Fear not, for behold, I bring you good news of great joy that will be *for all the people*. For unto *you* is born this day in the city of David a Savior, who is Christ the Lord." The kingdom of heaven is wide enough to accept Jews and Gentiles,[15] rich and poor, the seemingly righteousness and knowingly unrighteous. This King is for "you"—you lowly Jewish shepherds, you wealthy Gentile pilgrims.

The wise men were Gentiles, no doubt about it. They were either from Arabia, Persia, or Babylon. Following Origen of Alexandria, I think that they were from Babylon. I say this because we know from the book of Daniel that the Chaldeans or Babylonians had "wise men" (Daniel 2:12–14, 24, 27, 48; 4:6, 18; 5:6–8, 15) and also because of the theological significance attached to Babylon. Matthew is possibly saying that the pilgrimage of the nations to the holy city, the flood of Gentiles entering into the people of God, has begun, as the prophets predicted (Isaiah 2:2, 3; cf. Isaiah 60:1–5; Micah 4:1, 2). But

I also think he is giving an ironic twist. The twist is this: the return from the Babylonian exile is certainly over if the Babylonians themselves are bowing before Zion's King!

So the wise men were Gentiles, possibly Babylonian Gentiles. But more than that, they were "Gentile sinners," to borrow a phrase from Paul in Galatians 2:15. Why do I emphasize "sinners"? It is because of their occupation. The word that the ESV translates "wise men" in verses 1, 7 is *magos* in Greek, sometimes translated, "magi." Now, what English word does that remind you of? It sounds like and looks like *magic* or *magicians*. In John Milton's "On the Morning of Christ's Nativity," he calls them "the Star-led Wisards." And I think that is quite close to the truth.

In Daniel 2:2, 10 LXX, the term *magos* is used of the wise men Nebuchadnezzar asks to tell and interpret his dream. Also in Daniel 5, which I referred to earlier, after Belshazzar sees the writing on the wall, he "called loudly to bring in the enchanters . . . and the astrologers. The king declared to *the wise men* of Babylon, 'Whoever reads this writing, and shows me its interpretation . . .'" and on he goes. So his "wise men" (although note the Greek word used is *epaoidos* instead of *magos*) are likely ours—astrologers, enchanters, magicians, wizards of sorts. I picture them as a mix between Gandalf, David Copperfield, and Jeane Dixon. While I doubt they wrote "the daily horoscopes for the *Baghdad Gazette*," I don't doubt that they were stargazers who thought present and future events were to be found in the stars.[16] And while I don't think that they were quacks or charlatans as are most astrologers today—for example, Sylvia Browne or Miss Cleo—I do think they believed in and practiced magic of sorts, the same kind as Pharaoh's wise men ("Then Pharaoh summoned the wise men and the sorcerers, and they, the magicians of Egypt . . ." [Exodus 7:11; cf. Genesis 41:8]) and as Simon *Magus* or Simon the Sorcerer, as he is known in Acts 8:9–24 (cf. Acts 13:6, 8).

In our Harry Potter world we tend to think of magic not only as "cool" but spiritually neutral. The Biblical authors never thought so. That is why magic and magicians were condemned. The Old Testament forbade playing with such stuff. Don't toy with such people. What a Jewish rabbi wrote shortly before the birth of Christ summarizes well the Biblical attitude: "He who learns from a magus is worthy of death."[17] So these men were Babylonian magi—not the most spiritually-pristine class of people. They were Gentile sinners.

On Tuesday, January 6, twelve days after Christmas, the Western church celebrates Epiphany. The word *epiphany* comes from a Greek word that means "to manifest" or "to show," and on this date the church has traditionally commemorated the visit of the magi and the "epiphany." What epiphany?

God's manifestation to the Gentiles. God showed himself in the person of Christ to the Gentiles. That's what that holiday is all about. So go ahead and tell your boss that you'll take Epiphany off because it is an important religious holiday for you. And on that day, before you pack away your Nativity set, celebrate by looking closely at this passage again and noticing how the whole scene is filled with scandal. We have a teenage mother, a child conceived out of wedlock, lowly and dirty and usually irreligious shepherds (as well as lowly and dirty and certainly irreligious animals) and then . . . the magi—a bunch of "Star-led Wisards," magicians of sorts, Gentile sinners.

What a scandalous scene! Ah, but what a beautiful one as well. This scene depicts so perfectly the good news of the gospel of the kingdom. This good news is for all people, even the "least likely candidates for God's love."[18] Like scrap metal to a magnet, this good news draws "a hodgepodge" of fallen humanity—Samaritan adulterers, immoral prostitutes, greasy tax collectors on the take, despised Roman soldiers, ostracized lepers, me (the son of a poor man from Connemara on the west shore of the Emerald Isle), and even you (the son or daughter of whomever and wherever you are from).[19] Are you a Gentile? Are you a sinner? If so, I have some good news for you! The grasp of the King of the kingdom of heaven can reach even you and even now.

Is Jesus Your King?

When our Lord Jesus was on trial before Pontius Pilate, that Roman governor asked him, "Are you the King of the Jews?" Jesus answered,

> "My kingdom is not of this world. If my kingdom were of this world, my servants would have been fighting, that I might not be delivered over to the Jews. But my kingdom is not from the world." Then Pilate said to him, "So you are a king?" Jesus answered, "You say that I am a king. For this purpose I was born and for this purpose I have come into the world—to bear witness to the truth. Everyone who is of the truth listens to my voice." (John 18:33–37)

We all have a choice to make. Who is the King of the Jews? Who is your king? Whose voice are you going to heed? Will you be indifferent to Jesus? Will you be hostile? Or will you bow low, with whatever gifts you have in hand, adoringly worshipping him?

> Look there at the star!
> I, among the least,
> Will arise and take
> A journey to the East.
> *But what shall I bring*

As a present for the King?
What shall I bring to the Manger?

I will bring a song,
A song that I will sing,
A song for the King
In the Manager.

Watch out for my flocks,
Do not let them stray.
I am going on a journey
Far, far away.
But what shall I bring
As a present for the Child?
What shall I bring to the Manger?

I will bring a lamb,
Gentle, meek, and mild,
A lamb for the Child
In the Manager.

I'm just a shepherd boy,
Very poor I am—
But I know there is
A King in Bethlehem.
But what shall I bring
As a present for him?
What shall I bring to the Manger?

I will bring my heart
And give my heart to him.
I will bring my heart
To the Manger.[20]

6

Baptism of Repentance

MATTHEW 3:1–17

WHEN MY WIFE AND I lived in Hyde Park in Chicago, near the University of Chicago, a chemistry professor was part of our congregation. Every Sunday night he and his wife would invite college students and other young adults over for a nice informal dinner. When you walked through their front door there was a small, decorative sign that had one simple word written in large block letters: REPENT.

I have often thought about that sign, and I have been tempted from time to time to duplicate it, or maybe even expand upon it, in our home—perhaps to have in the entranceway, "REPENT," and then in the living room "FROM THE WRATH TO COME," and finally in the dining room, "I REALLY MEAN IT!" But I have not yet gained the courage to do so, for such a message is so at odds with our culture. I can't think of a word—other than perhaps *wrath* or *Hell*—that has such a negative connotation. And I can't think of a word, of all the ones we find often in our Bibles, that is so seldom found on our lips. Maybe this quiet and quirky chemistry professor, with his Ivy League education and his years of scientific study, was like most accomplished scientists, a bit mad. Or maybe we're the ones who are off our rockers because we are afraid of what the world might think of us. We are afraid that if we were to have on our doorposts, walls, or lips the message of John the Baptist the world might call us crazy.

However, this message of repentance—turning from self and sin to God and grace—is what the world needs. And this is why each time the gospel is preached by the apostles (and here I'm thinking specifically of the sermons we find in Acts), the one application made in every message is "repent" (e.g., Acts 2:38; 3:19; 5:31; 8:22; 17:30; 26:20; cf. 11:18; 20:21). From Peter's message to the Jews in Jerusalem to Paul's before the Greeks in Athens, the message is the same: God "commands all people everywhere to repent" (Acts 17:30).

This is the message the world needs, but it is also the message the church needs. This is why we find this theme of repentance in all the letters of the New Testament. Christians who have repented must continue to live lives of repentance (e.g., 2 Corinthians 7:9, 10; 12:21; 2 Peter 3:9). Do you remember the seven letters to the seven churches in Revelation 2, 3? Each church gets a unique message dealing with its specific issue, yet one message that is given to five of the seven is "repent" (2:5, 16, 21, 22; 3:3, 19). So, what John the Baptist says in verse 8, "Bear fruit in keeping with *repentance*," and in verse 11, "I baptize you with water for *repentance*," and verse 2, "*Repent*, for the kingdom of heaven is at hand" is a relevant message for the world and for the church today.

So that's what we will now study. With our Bibles open again to the third chapter of this great Gospel of Matthew we will talk about repentance. First, we'll explore our need for it. Isn't it amazing that all these people came out to the desert to be washed in a dirty river by a man dressed in camel hair? If I dressed in my cleanest suit and handed out free vacation passes to Palm Springs where folks could take a nice bath in their own hotel room Jacuzzi, if only they would repent, I would be glad to get one taker. So, first our need: why should we repent? Second, the means: how should we repent?

Why Repent?

Why should we repent? Our text gives us two reasons. First, we should repent because God's heavenly kingdom has arrived ("is at hand"). Look at verses 1–4.

> In those days John the Baptist came preaching in the wilderness of Judea, "Repent, for the kingdom of heaven is at hand." For this is he who was spoken of by the prophet Isaiah when he said, "The voice of one crying in the wilderness: 'Prepare the way of the Lord; make his paths straight.'" Now John wore a garment of camel's hair and a leather belt around his waist, and his food was locusts and wild honey.

We are reminded here, by his rigorist location, wardrobe, and diet, as well as by his rigorist message ("repent"), that John is cut from the same cloth (literally) as the Old Testament prophets, most notably Elijah (see 11:14; cf. 2 Kings 1:8; Malachi 4:5). I don't know about you, but I like the prophets. I mean I truly enjoy reading them. But I'm not sure how comfortable I'd feel having them over for a cup of tea. Can you imagine Ezekiel, Hosea, and John sitting in your living room, and you reaching across to them, offering them their nice cup of tea (for John with a touch of wild honey), asking, "Can I get you anything else?" John is a prophet, and as such he doesn't fit (he's not supposed to fit) perfectly into our living rooms or into our world.

But John is more than a prophet. He is, in Jesus' own estimation, the greatest man to live under the old covenant. In 11:11 Jesus said, "Truly, I say to you, among those born of women there has arisen no one greater than John the Baptist." Part of John's greatness comes from his humility. In 3:14, when Jesus comes to him for baptism, John says, "I need to be baptized by you, and do you come to *me*?" In 3:11 when John speaks of Jesus he declares not only that Jesus is "mightier" than he, but that he (John) is not even "worthy to carry" Jesus' dirty sandals. A slave would wash and carry a master's sandals. John says in effect, "His sandals are too holy for my dirty hands." Jeremiah called himself a slave of the Lord (Jeremiah 7:25; 29:19). John says in essence, "I'm not even good enough to be Jesus' slave." What humility—humility of attitude and speech, but also of action! Look at his lifestyle. Think of the sacrifices he had to make to live where and how he did. He modeled in the extreme his message of repentance—turning from self to the will of God. What sacrifice! What submission! What surrender! What *great* humility!

Now, I don't think that God calls us to emulate John exactly, as the Desert Fathers in the early church did or as some Franciscans and other monastic orders still do today. Asceticism for asceticism's sake is not found in the Bible. In fact, it is rebuked (see Colossians 2:23). John had a unique role. He was to fulfill the prophecy of Isaiah, to be the "voice . . . crying in the wilderness," preparing the way for Jesus (3:3). But with that said, he does, nevertheless, offer a corrective to our materialism, consumerism, and certainly our selfishness. Jesus said that if we want to follow him we must deny ourselves. No one better embodied such self-denial than John.

Some of us have been forced by the bad economy to give up certain luxuries. Maybe you can't eat out as often as you used to or can't afford the vacation you wanted to take or you've had to put off getting the Ferrari winterized. I don't know what you've had to sacrifice. But such forcible reductions of certain luxuries may perhaps be God's corrective providence, his spiritual surgery of sorts, removing what you don't need or what is a hindrance to your spiritual growth. But why do we always wait for such providences? Why not do some corrective cutting out and cutting off of our own? Why wait for the economy to sour before you let the Spirit lead you into the desert of dependence on God and his provision? John chose wilderness living because he chose absolute reliance upon the Father in Heaven. In lesser but similar ways we must choose to do the same.

But enough said about the person of John. It is his message that provides us the first reason why we should repent. We should repent *because* "the kingdom of heaven is at hand" (v. 2). We should repent, in other words, because the kingdom that has long been anticipated has finally arrived.

So too has the King! The first reason to repent is because the kingdom is at hand; the second reason (tied right to it) is because the King of that kingdom is also at hand. This is the focus of verses 13–17 (and also of verses 11, 12, where John first speaks of Jesus), and it is why I have included them here. Instead of dividing verses 1–12 and verses 13–17 as most commentators do, I put them together because I think they give a fuller picture of our need for repentance, a picture quite similar to Isaiah's vision in Isaiah 6:1–5. What I mean is, to say *the kingdom* is at hand is like seeing the six winged seraphim who with two wings cover their feet and with two cover their faces and hearing them call to one another, "Holy, holy, holy is the LORD of hosts; the whole earth is full of his glory!" However, to say *the King of the kingdom* is at hand is to see, as Isaiah did, "the Lord sitting upon a throne." To see just the kingdom, you would say, "Woe is me." But to see the King of the kingdom, you would say, "*Woe is me!* For I am lost; for I am a man of unclean lips."

Look with me at 3:13–17. I want you to see Jesus' absolute holy-holy-holy-holiness, or as Jesus will phrase it, "righteousness" (v. 15). All the Gospels record the baptism of Jesus (for its importance to the early church, see Acts 1:21, 22), but only Matthew has the conversation recorded in verses 13–15. I'll summarize it. Jesus comes to John for baptism (v. 13). John says in essence (v. 14), "No way. If one of us is to be baptized for the forgiveness of sins, it's me!" How does Jesus respond to that? Does he say, "John, what are you talking about? I'm the sinful one. You are the great prophet. You have lived the holiest life in the history of the world." No. Jesus says, "Let it be so now, for thus it is fitting for us to fulfill all righteousness" (v. 15).

What is going on here? A baptism of repentance (vv. 1–6) we can understand. But what's this baptism of righteousness? In the Bible the word "righteousness" is used two different ways, and both are in use here. "Righteousness" can refer to an exterior and an interior quality of life. Exterior righteousness refers to how one behaves in society; interior righteousness refers to how one thinks and believes. One can have the former without the latter, but the latter has its natural outflow in the former. Consider, for example, the statement that Job was a righteous man. We would say, "So-and-so is a good man or a godly man." In God's sight and our sight, he lives rightly. Now, it is one thing to say "Job is righteous" in this way, and another to say "Jesus is righteous." This is because we know, even from this text as well as many others, about Jesus' impeccable character (e.g., Hebrew 4:15; 9:14; 1 Peter 2:22). He was without sin—original or actual.

Think of it this way: if righteous John the Baptist can and does say of Jesus, "I'm not worthy to touch his sandals," we know Jesus is very righteous. However, it is not just John's word that we have. What does Heaven have to say? The Holy Spirit descends like a dove upon our Lord (v. 16), and the Father speaks directly to him: "This is my beloved Son, *with whom I am well pleased*" (v. 17; cf. Colossians 1:10). Jesus has sufficient character-reference—the greatest man on earth (John) and two members of the Holy Trinity (the Father and the Spirit).[1]

Beyond being righteous in character, Jesus is also righteous ontologically. The idea here is that Jesus, in his very being (ontology), became our substitute, really and truly. This idea moves us beyond the obvious theme of a second exodus in Matthew 1—4 (i.e., just as Israel was brought out of Egypt through the Red Sea and into the desert, so Jesus is brought out of Egypt, baptized in the waters, and led into the desert). Unlike unrighteous Israel, Jesus as "true Israel" does fulfill all righteousness in this three-part act (out of Egypt, through the water, into the desert). However and moreover, through his baptism he takes his unrighteous but repentant people through the new, final, and ultimate exodus—out of the slavery of sin! Put plainly, Jesus was baptized not for his sake but for ours (cf. Galatians 3:13; 2 Corinthians 5:21). I'll explain.

When the voice of God says, "This is my beloved Son, with whom I am well pleased" (3:17), what we have is a fusion of two key Old Testament texts—Psalm 2:7 and Isaiah 42:1. Psalm 2 is about the Son, the Davidic King of God's eternal kingdom. Isaiah 42 is about the Suffering Servant who would be stricken for our transgressions and would make his soul an offering for sin, even though "he had done no violence, and there was no deceit in his mouth" (see Isaiah 53:4–9). Isaiah 53:11 is crucial here as it is in the passion narratives. In that verse the Father says of the Servant, "Out of anguish of his soul he shall see and be satisfied; by his knowledge shall the *righteous one*, my servant [Jesus], make many to be *accounted righteous*, and he shall bear their iniquities." In sum, you might think of John the Baptist's baptism of Jesus in this way: John has moved God's people away from Jerusalem's temple to grant the forgiveness of sins in Jesus![2]

Thus, ontologically-speaking, when we go down into the waters of baptism, it is a symbol of the cleansing of our sins—as the water pours over our heads, we are made clean in the sight of God. When Jesus went down into the water of the Jordan River, the opposite happened—he began to take on our sin, our dirt, all the scum of all the baptized. Whatever drop of water might have entered into his mouth was his first taste of the cup of God's wrath, which he would drink in full measure on the cross. Jesus, the Son and the Servant, was baptized to "fulfill all righteousness"—to carry out God's plan of sin substitution. And if and when you and I understand that, we then should understand there is only one response to such a King and such a kingdom—repentance. As we look at Jesus' holiness and yet his humility (that he would be baptized for us), our posture should be humility and holiness or what could be called (since we are naturally neither humble nor holy) repentance.

How to Repent?

That is *why* we should repent. But the next question is, *how?* You might say, "Okay, I see now the King and his kingdom, and I want to repent, but I don't know where to begin." Thankfully, as we look at what those who came to John did, we have a universal model for us. We center now on the center of this text (verses 5–12) where I've discovered what I'll call *the three steps of repentance.*

Confess Our Sins

The first two steps we see modeled in verses 5, 6. "Then Jerusalem and all Judea and all the region about the Jordan were going out to him, and they were baptized by him in the river Jordan, confessing their sins." Baptism and the confession of sins are the first two steps. While those steps are usually found together in the New Testament, I'll separate them now for the sake of clarity. First, we'll focus on the confession of sin.

Note that a corporate renewal is occurring here. Verse 5 doesn't say, "And Tom and Tina and Bill and Betty—this individual and that individual—went out to see John," but rather, "Jerusalem and all Judea and all the region about the Jordan were going out to him." Now, while we will see that most of Israel will not listen to the voice from Heaven about Jesus, they will, at least now, heed the voice of the one calling in the wilderness. They waited 400 years to hear from God. There had been no prophetic voice until John. So like Israel of old, they journey to the wilderness to listen and obey. This renewal of repentance or mass baptism is of a corporate nature. Yet, as it is with any baptism then and now, it is also individual, and certainly personal. The text tells us they didn't confess the sins of others but "their sins" (v. 6). Each person personally confessed his or her sins.

In Psalm 32:5 David says to God, "I acknowledged my sin to you, and I did not cover my iniquity; I said, 'I will confess my transgressions to the Lord,' and you forgave the iniquity of my sin." In Proverbs 28:13 Solomon says, "Whoever conceals his transgressions will not prosper, but he who confesses and forsakes them will obtain mercy." In 1 John 1:8, 9 we read, "If we say we have no sin, we deceive ourselves, and the truth is not in us. If we confess our sins, he is faithful and just to forgive us our sins and to cleanse us from all unrighteousness." Jesus, whom John the Baptist calls "the Lamb of God, who takes away the sin of the world" (John 1:29), will take away our sins if we confess them to him.

The Parable of the Prodigal Son is an excellent illustration of this. The son asks his rich and generous father for his inheritance early. He takes the money and wastes it on "reckless living" (Luke 15:13), devouring the father's "property with prostitutes" (Luke 15:30). He comes to the end of his money quickly and the beginning of his senses eventually. "What am I doing with my life?" he says as he now finds himself not only feeding pigs for a living (not the most kosher occupation for a good Jewish boy) but longing for the same food. An idea comes into his head. "I know," he says in essence, "I'll return to Dad, and I'll confess my sins."

You know the story. On the journey home he rehearses his long confession (Luke 15:18, 19). Yet when he arrives he can only get out the first part of what he rehearsed: "Father, I have sinned against heaven and before you. I am no longer worthy to be called your son" (Luke 15:21). He can only get this out because his father is smothering him with compassion and interrupting him with a command to celebrate. The father beckons his servants, "Bring quickly the best robe, and put it on him, and put a ring on his hand, and shoes on his feet. And bring the fattened calf and kill it, and let us eat and celebrate. For this my son was dead, and is alive again; he was lost, and is found" (Luke 15:22–24).

When I came to Christ as a nineteen-year-old, I came home from work, went down into my basement apartment, fell upon my knees, and *confessed my sins*. "Lord Jesus," I said, "I know you are real. I have never doubted your existence. I have never doubted you are the Son of God. But I have never asked you to forgive me. Will you please forgive me? Clean me up on the inside, for I am full of lust and pride." Have you ever prayed like that? Have you prayed the sinner's prayer? I've prayed it—once for my salvation and a thousand times for my perseverance in the faith. Stop reading and pray it now!

Be Baptized

The first step of repentance is confession. The second step, which is directly and inseparably connected to it, is baptism.

Let me start by saying that the water baptism of Jesus was a onetime event. It was a unique baptism in the history of salvation. So also was the baptism by John the Baptist.[3] Yet one sure way both baptisms relate to Christian baptism is the use of water (vv. 6, 11, 16). The washing of water is symbolic, of course, of the washing away of our sins, which we have just confessed. Like the leprous Naaman, the commander of the Syrian army, who in 2 Kings 5:13, 14 followed Elisha's instructions and "went down and dipped himself seven times in the Jordan . . . and his flesh was restored like the flesh of a little child, and he was clean," so too the outward washing of water reminds us of the inward washing of the soul, God's cleansing us of our sins (see Acts 22:16). But confession and water baptism without the Spirit is like a lamp without oil. You might be able to light the wick once, but the flame won't last long.

Notice how John notes this. John has a baptism with water. Then there is Jesus' baptism. With what? Water? No. With the Holy Spirit! In verse 11 John says of Jesus, "He will baptize you with the Holy Spirit and fire"—that wind and fire that came down at Pentecost (Acts 2:2, 3) but that also comes down spiritually every time someone comes to Christ (see Acts 2:38).

Once I received a call from Wendell Hawley, a pastor at College Church in Wheaton. The church had just recited the Nicene Creed during the Advent season, and someone called him with the question, "Is it Biblical to say, as the Creed does, 'We believe in one baptism for the forgiveness of sins'?" Wendell wanted to know how I'd reply. After some thought I said something like the following. (I'll slightly change it to relate it to our text at hand.)

First, it is important to understand that the early church saw no disconnect, as we so often do, with water baptism and the forgiveness of sins. We see this in some of the early creeds and confessions, but also in the New Testament. In this same scene in Mark's Gospel, Mark adds, "John appeared, baptizing in the wilderness and proclaiming a baptism of repentance for the forgiveness of sins" (1:4; cf. 16:16), and the Apostle Peter, in a very clear reference to water baptism, speaks of "baptism, which . . . now saves you" (1 Peter 3:21). The idea here is that faith/repentance/baptism/forgiveness can be thought of as one continuous act of God's saving grace. So when the authors of the Nicene Creed spoke of "one baptism for the forgiveness of sins" they could have meant that, or they could have meant what John is talking about in verse 11—spirit baptism. From Romans to Revelation there are only three certain references to water baptism (1 Corinthians 1:13–17; Hebrews 6:2; 1 Peter 3:21). Moreover, the 1 Corinthian text ends with "Christ did not send me to baptize but to preach the gospel." I'll paraphrase it: "Christ didn't send me for water baptism (although that's important), but for spirit baptism, which comes when people hear the gospel preached and repent and believe."

Baptism in the Holy Spirit—which simply means conversion[4]—in contrast to water baptism is referenced often in the New Testament (only seven times explicitly—Matthew 3:11; Mark 1:8; Luke 3:16; John 1:33; Acts 1:5; 11:16; 1 Corinthians 12:13, but many times implicitly, e.g., John 3:5, 6). This Spirit baptism is the life-changing work of God wrought in one's heart. Consequently, it appears to be this baptism to which Paul refers in Ephesians 4:5, where he writes of "one Lord, one faith, one baptism."[5] Perhaps, this is what the Nicene Creed means as well.

The Fruit of Repentance

Water baptism is important. So too is Spirit baptism. And both baptisms should lead to the final step of genuine repentance—fruit.

> But when he saw many of the Pharisees and Sadducees coming for baptism, he said to them, "You brood of vipers! Who warned you to flee from the wrath to come? Bear fruit in keeping with repentance." (vv. 7, 8)

Here John is talking about the necessity of fruit, what Paul will term the fruit of the Spirit.

> Step One: The Spirit convicts us of our sins, which we must confess.
> Step Two: We are baptized in the Spirit.
> Step Three: The Spirit abides in us so that we bear fruit.

Our Spirit-wrought confession and conversion leads to the fruits of repentance—"love, joy, peace, patience, kindness, goodness, faithfulness, gentleness, self-control" (Galatians 5:22, 23a).

Having come from a Roman Catholic upbringing into the evangelical world, if you were to ask me, "In your opinion and from your experience, what is the biggest problem with the Catholic Church?" I would say, "The Bible is little taught, and it is even less understood." But do you know what I'd say for the evangelical church? I'd say, "The sin of presumption." This is the very sin that causes John to use some of the harshest language found in the Bible for these religious leaders.

We think presumptuously, *If I just half-heartedly did the first step of re-*

pentance, if I once in my life, maybe at some summer camp or Billy Graham Crusade, confessed my sins, then I'm okay. I'm going to Heaven, even if I live like Hell. These religious leaders thought presumptuously. They thought they could live like Hell because their father, Abraham, sat at the gates of Gehenna turning "back any Israelite who might by chance have been consigned to its terrors."[6] They believed that Abraham, by his goodness and favor with God, built up a "treasury of merit" for all his blood descendants, the Jews.[7] So if you couldn't merit Heaven on your own, don't worry—good old Abe has enough merit for you to inherit eternal life. His goodness will get you in (cf. John 8:33).

Look at what John has to say to such scoundrels. After he calls them a "brood of vipers" in verse 7 (cf. Jesus' use of this phrase in 12:34 and 23:33)—not the offspring of a saint but a snake, the devil himself—he next states in verse 9 that the dead stones have a better chance of being God's children than they do. John says to them there, "And do not *presume* to say to yourselves, 'We have Abraham as our father,' for I tell you, God is able from these stones to raise up children for Abraham." Then he returns to the fruit analogy in verse 10: "Even now the axe is laid to the root of the trees. Every tree therefore that does not bear good fruit is cut down and thrown into the fire."

If you see fruit on a tree, you know the tree is alive; if you see good fruit, you know it is alive and well. Repentant people, who have truly heard and understood the gospel, bear fruit (13:23; cf. 21:43); that is, they love God and love others and show this love by how they live (see Luke 3:10–14; Acts 26:20).[8] And in so doing and not doing, such people prove (cf. John 15:8) to be Jesus' disciples;[9] they prove that the Holy Spirit resides within.[10] They prove that they have touched their feet upon the third step—Spirit-wrought conviction and confession, Spirit baptism, and spiritual fruit.

Read and Heed the Sign

Above, around, and within us, whether we acknowledge it or not, God has placed his sign. It reads "REPENT." Creation points to this sign; it is as if it hangs around the sun's head and is daily carried to us upon its beams. Our own consciences point to this sign; it is as if it hangs around our heads, and each time we sin, it pricks us in the side. And then, of course, we have the Word of God, which teaches us specifically about repentance—why and how we should repent.

I trust that God's Word has done its work on you, helping you to understand afresh why you and I should repent. We should repent because we are in the presence of a holy King—Jesus, who has fulfilled all righteousness—and so we say, "Woe is me! My lips are unclean. My heart is unclean. My hands are unclean!" The kingdom of God is at hand, and so my hands need some spiritual scrubbing—they need to get cleaned up. I also trust that God's Word has helped you better understand how to repent, how to walk Jacob's ladder up to God—confessing your sins, being baptized in water but also by the Holy Spirit, and producing fruit by living a life of repentance.

Repent, for the kingdom of heaven is very much still at hand.

7

The Tempted Son

MATTHEW 4:1–11

I USED TO CHEAT IN ALGEBRA. Math has always been difficult for me. So when I was assigned to the honors algebra class, which was very much over my head, I adjusted this discrepancy by "borrowing" some answers from the best mathematician in the school and a fellow starter on the varsity basketball team.

I wasn't a Christian at the time, but I had a strong conscience, which initially burned within me each time I broke the school's law, God's law, and my own moral law. But after a while, as the teacher himself turned a blind eye to what was going on, and as my heart hardened toward this sin, the fire of conscience cooled. The guilt subsided. The teacher didn't care. My friend didn't care. I didn't care. I passed the class.

When I became a Christian a year after graduating from high school everything changed on the inside, and eventually on the outside. So when I transferred to Wheaton College to major in Bible/theology, I vowed never again to cheat.

This vow, however, was quickly tested. In my second semester of New Testament Greek (which I'm convinced uses the same mental muscles as math) I missed the midterm exam due to the flu. My professor graciously allowed me to take the test on my own time. He told me he would leave a copy of it in his mailbox outside of his office. I could pick it up and take it whenever I felt better.

A few days later, in good health, I stood before his mailbox. I saw the test and grabbed it. Yet, as I looked down in the mailbox again, I noticed another exam, completed by one of the class's best students. I looked around. The hallway was empty. I cautiously lifted the other exam. It felt heavy as if a thousand fat devils were dancing on it. Yet as heavy as it felt, it was as if a calm, reasonable voice whispered from it, "Take and copy. Take and copy." I heeded that advice. I placed both exams in my backpack and hurried across the street to the library. I opened the backpack, placed the blank test on the right, and then slowly lifted the other exam.

Then . . . I stopped. I didn't place it down on the left. Instead, convicted by the Spirit that God sees all, that cheating is a sin, and that such a sin would be offensive to God, my teacher, and my classmate, I placed the completed exam in my backpack again. I walked back across the street and placed it back in the professor's mailbox. I returned to the library and took the test on my own. I passed the test—both the Greek test and the temptation test! What a victory for me, one among many, for by God's grace I never cheated in college, graduate school, or seminary. But I certainly was, from time to time, tempted to do so.

We all struggle with various temptations. Maybe you're tempted to cheat, lie, steal, or lust. Maybe you're tempted to look the other way when wrongdoing is done around you. Maybe you're tempted to indulge in sexual sin—when you're on a business trip, when you're all alone and no one's looking. Maybe you're tempted to indulge sinful anger, and that tongue of yours is like a wildfire that once one spark hits the surface, you let rage consume you and anyone in your way. Maybe you're tempted to engage in pride—to think you're better than everyone else, especially the weak-willed and ill-willed, those who cheat, lie, steal, lust, and rage.

In 4:1–11 we come again to our Lord Jesus Christ. We come to look at his victory over temptation. And as we do so, we'll see how his victory reinforces his *identity*—"Truly this is the Son of God"—and how it gives us an *example*, the ultimate example, of resisting the devil. Jesus was tempted in order to show us that we have a Savior who "is able to help" us when we "are being tempted" (Hebrews 2:18), a Savior who is able to "sympathize with our weaknesses," because, as Hebrews 4:15 says, he was tempted in every respect as we are, "yet without sin."

A Common but False Objection

A common objection to Hebrews 2:18 and 4:15 sounds something like this: "How can Jesus, if he was without sin—if he never thought, said, or did anything wrong—sympathize with me?" It's like looking at whoever you might think is the most morally pure person in your church and saying, "How could he or she possibly sympathize with my struggles? They've never done what I've done."

This common objection is, however, ungrounded. Sure, when you share with fellow sinners, perhaps as I just did with you—that I cheated on a few math exams in high school—some who have never been tempted to do the same thing might react, "What kind of man is this?" They might think they are morally superior. But that is never how Jesus reacts. He never reacts with self-righteousness, for Jesus understands the weight of every particular temptation, even that particular temptation that so easily entangles you, because he was tempted to cheat God, to follow his own agenda, to take the detour to glory. Furthermore, just because Jesus never gave in to a particular temptation that you or I always seem to give in to does not mean he has never felt the tug of such a temptation.

For example, picture a tug-of-war. What usually happens? At first both teams try their darnedest. But soon the weaker team discovers who they are, and instead of pulling harder to try to overcome the stronger team, they usually give in, fall backward or forward, and collapse. Now, let me ask you, who felt the tug more—the winners or the losers? The winners did.

Or think of two weightlifters. Let's say both athletes are trying to lift 500 pounds over their head. The first pulls the bar off the ground, then quickly up to his knees, but then he drops it after a two-second struggle. The second lifter also pulls the bar off the ground, up to his knees, but then he lifts it up to his waist and finally, with two great thrusts, up and over his head. Who knows better the heaviness of those weights? The point is this: those who resist temptation are those who feel the weight of it most.[1]

Jesus was (and is!) a real human being who knew the weight of sin and the heaviness of temptation. He was not shadowboxing with the devil. He was vulnerable. Like Adam (perfect in nature), he could have been hit.[2] He could have fallen. But he didn't. He is the undefeated champion of the world. He won! As such, he shows us what to expect in the ring and how to jab and how to land the winning right hook.

In this chapter we will look at Jesus' identity and example, and we will briefly examine five characteristics of his temptation. We do so not merely to admire the great fighter but to become great fighters ourselves, to learn the nature of temptation so that we might win the victory.

God-Ordained but Not God-Inflicted

The first characteristic is that *Jesus' temptation was God-ordained but not God-inflicted.* In verse 1 we read of this subtle but important distinction: "Then Jesus was led up by the Spirit into the wilderness to be tempted by the devil." Notice the "by" and "by." The first "by"—"by the Spirit"—tells us this temptation was God-ordained (cf. Deuteronomy 8:2). Then once Jesus is in the desert or wilderness, Satan slithers upon the scene. Here is our second "by." God ordained the temptation, but the tempting comes not from God (cf. James 1:13) but from the accuser.[3] Jesus was tempted "by the devil." So, quite similar to the story of Job, Satan is allowed to have his way with God's man. Satan is allowed to put God's righteous "servant" (cf. Job 1:8) to the test. And it is a test here. Perhaps "test" is a better word than "temptation." Both terms/ translations are fitting. Jesus is certainly *tested*: Is he the true Son of God? Will he hold fast to God's plan of salvation? But he is also *tempted*: He is tempted to exalt himself, to avoid the pain of the cross, and to bow down to Satan's rule.

Now, what is the lesson of this "by" and "by" for us? The lesson is this: if you want to follow Jesus, know that the road to Heaven is not paved with gold and lined with daisies. Jesus, who is loved by God, was sent into the wilderness to be tested. If you are his follower, you can expect the same. Baptism into Christ does not mean health and wealth and a shallow happiness. Baptism into Christ means self-denial, suffering, trials, and temptations. This is not because God doesn't like us or love us. Rather, it is because he does. Gold is refined through fire, not by being thrown into a pile of marshmallows. We move, like our Lord did, from our baptisms into a battle that will prove and refine our character.

In the baptismal ceremony of the 1662 Prayer Book of the Anglican Church, the minister, after the baptism, does the sign of the cross over the baptized as a symbol that thereafter he or she will "not be ashamed to confess the faith of Christ crucified, and to fight manfully under his banner against sin, the world, and the Devil."[4] This old ceremony is our rite as well. We must be willing to "fight manfully"—do battle against sin, the world, and the devil, for our flesh, this world, and the devil will fight against us. We can run and hide. We can lie down and give in. Or we can fight, and in doing so, use our trials and temptations for the purposes for which God has ordained them—to make us stronger and purer.

When His Flesh Was Most Weak

Thus, the first characteristic of Jesus' temptation was that it was God-ordained but not God-inflicted. The second characteristic is that *Jesus was tempted when his flesh was most weak*. "Then Jesus was led up by the Spirit into the wilderness to be tempted by the devil"—that's verse 1. Look at verse 2 and the beginning of verse 3: "And after fasting forty days and forty nights, he was hungry. And [then!] the tempter came. . . ."

In Pablo Neruda's poem "Solitude," the great Chilean poet speaks of solitude as a beautiful word and ideal but a terrible reality. Among other things, he compares solitude to fool's gold, a counterfeit coin, and a desert.

> The desert
> is the earth's solitude, and mankind's
> solitude
> is sterile.[5]

As I currently have a house full of children I cannot readily resonate with Neruda's realism. "Oh, give me such solitude!" I often cry out. Yet, when it comes to temptation solitude can be my greatest enemy. Along with the saying, "Idleness is the workshop of the devil," I would add, so too is solitude. In addition to solitude, if my body is weak (especially due to hunger), I find that it is then that the devil so often comes around like a roaring lion seeking whom he may devour (1 Peter 5:8).

Jesus was tempted in the wilderness.[6] Jesus was tempted after eating nothing for forty days, not even locusts and wild honey. Nothing! He was alone. He was hungry. He was physically weak. He was the perfect victim for a roaring, roaming, hungry lion. And yet how strong he was!

Think of Peter, the leader of the apostles. When Peter's flesh was weak, what did he do? He gave in to temptation. He slept when his Lord most needed him to pray (26:40, 43, 45), and he lied when his Lord most needed his support (26:69–75). Or think about Israel in the wilderness. If they missed a meal, boy, would they grumble. You would think they grew up in some posh neighborhood. If they got a little thirsty, they would try to blackmail God—"If you don't do something, we're getting rid of Moses and you, and we're going back to Egypt!" Or think about Adam and Eve. Read what James Montgomery Boice says about them in contrast to Jesus:

> Adam and Eve were in paradise; Jesus was in the vast, desolate wilderness of Judah. Adam and Eve were physically content and satisfied. They were free to eat from any of the trees of the garden, save the tree of the knowledge of good and evil; Jesus was hungry, having fasted for forty days and forty nights. Adam and Eve were together. They had each other for company and mutual support; Jesus was alone. Yet Adam and Eve rapidly succumbed to Satan's wiles, carrying the entire human race into sin, misery, destruction, and both physical and spiritual death, while Jesus stood firm as the Savior who was to bring life and salvation to the race.[7]

What Adam didn't do, Jesus did. What Israel couldn't accomplish, Jesus accomplished.[8] And in doing so, he left us an example of sober-mindedness, watchfulness, and firmness of faith (1 Peter 5:8, 9), as well as an example of preparedness. We should be prepared to fight when we are most weak.

If you journeyed today to the Castle of Wartburg in Germany, the place where Martin Luther hid for a time from those who were seeking his life, you would see on the wall of the room in which he stayed a dark ink stain. It is from his temptations. In Luther's solitude, loneliness, and spiritual hunger, when the devil would tempt him, Luther would resist by throwing his inkpot at his archenemy. Now, I'm not suggesting that we throw our inkpots or our computers against the wall (although I'm not completely opposed to it), but I do suggest that we take the evil one seriously and that we face our foe as a reality. When we are weak, we do not feign. Rather, we trust in the Lord and the strength of his might (Ephesians 6:10).

Unique Yet Universal

The first characteristic of Jesus' temptation was that it was God-ordained but not God-inflicted. The second was that these temptations occurred when our Lord's flesh was most weak. The third characteristic is that *Jesus' temptation was unique yet universal.*

His temptation was unique. This is obvious. Most people aren't tempted *where* he was (in the wilderness), *when* he was (after forty days of fasting), or *by whom* he was tempted (by a clear manifestation of the devil). So where, when, and by whom Jesus was tempted are unique, as well as *how* or *with what* he was tempted.

I have been tempted in a great many ways, but I have never been tempted to turn stones into bread. Neither have I been whisked away to the top of the temple (or any significant structure for that matter) to be tempted to throw myself off, testing to see if God really loves me and would save me. And I most certainly have not been tempted by the devil to rule the world in exchange for my soul. I have not even been asked to sell my soul in order to be a rock star. I trust my experience is similar to yours.

Jesus' temptations were unique because he is unique. The divine comment in 3:17 is an apt summary of his uniqueness: "This is my beloved Son, with whom I am well pleased." Jesus is the beloved Son of God, *and* he is the Suffering Servant of God. In the last chapter I explained how this verse is a mix of two important Old Testament themes—about the Son (Psalm 2) and the Servant (Isaiah 42). Jesus is the Son of God, the promised King, who has come to be the Servant, to suffer and die so as to make atonement for our sins (1:21).

The temptations here, unique to Jesus, were all temptations to rely on his divine sonship to the neglect of his servanthood (the suffering he was called to take upon himself).[9] This is why the devil twice says, "If you are the *Son* of God . . ." (vv. 3, 6).[10] All the temptations were to grab the crown without first enduring the cross. The Father promised that Jesus will be King, and we see this clearly in Psalm 2 ("I will make the nations your heritage," v. 8) as well at the end of Matthew ("All authority in heaven and on earth has been given to me," 28:18) , but only if he follows the road to Calvary. The tempter tempts him to take the shortcut to glory by bypassing Gethsemane and Golgotha. That's what all these temptations are about.

Just look at the least obvious—verses 3, 4. Here it's as if Satan says,

> Look, Jesus, you're hungry. The whole world is hungry. If you can turn these stones into bread, which I know you can—because you're God's Son!—then feed yourself, and feed the world. Use your power for what people most need and want—their bellies to be filled—and then watch the whole world "run after you like sheep, grateful and obedient."[11] You will have the world literally eating from your hand. Give people what they really want—not the Word of God but food from God.

Now, Jesus is not opposed to feeding the hungry. We shall see him twice in Mathew feed the multitudes (14:13–21; 15:32–39). Nor is he opposed to food. Jesus feasted on earth—at a wedding, with friends, in sinners' houses—and because of this he was even called (falsely) a glutton and a winebibber (11:19). Moreover, at the end of all history, the messianic banquet will be the feast of all feasts. It will make the Presidential inaugural ball look like toddlers' birthday parties at Chuck-E-Cheese's.

Jesus is not opposed to food or providing food. What Jesus is opposed to is bribing someone into the kingdom with his miraculous powers—turning stones into bread. If someone wants to come to him and into his kingdom, they must come spiritually hungry—"Blessed are those who hunger and thirst for righteousness" (5:6a).

Jesus doesn't want to bribe anyone into the kingdom. Nor does he want to "remove the symptoms without dealing with the disease."[12] This is why Jesus quotes from Deuteronomy 8:3, where it is written, "[M]an does not live by bread alone, but man livesby every word that comes from the mouth of the Lord." There is more to life than what is "visible and edible, tangible and collectible, bankable and investable."[13] To die hungry with the gospel in your heart is to die with the hope of everlasting life. But to die with your mouth stuffed, your belly filled, but your heart cold to the gospel is to die everlastingly. Better to die with an empty belly and a full soul than with an empty soul but a full belly. Do you remember the Parable of Lazarus and the Rich Man?

Jesus makes this very point. Lazarus dies hungry but goes to Heaven; the rich man dies full but goes to Hell.

So Jesus' temptations are unique. But they are also universal. What I mean is this: aren't we all tempted to grab the crown without the cross? Aren't we all tempted to think that the physical is more important than the spiritual? Aren't we all tempted to sell out the gospel through gimmicks, entertainment, and worldly means—our own version of turning stones into bread? Aren't we tempted, as Jesus was (and as Adam and Eve were), with "the desires of the flesh and the desires of the eyes and pride of life" (1 John 2:16)? Aren't we all tempted to move away from "holy reliance upon the Father to an unholy independence"?[14] Jesus' temptations were unique but also universal. We are all tempted in similar ways. That's the third characteristic.

The Shield of the Spirit Shields the Savior

The fourth characteristic is that *Jesus resisted these temptations with the Word of God*. On this point the early church father Jerome says of Jesus, "He breaks the false arrows of the devil drawn from the Scriptures upon the true shields of the Scriptures."[15]

I like this *shield* analogy. At first I thought I'd go, quite naturally, with Paul's *sword* analogy from Ephesians 6, that great passage on the armor of God, where the apostle writes of taking up "the sword of the Spirit, which is the word of God" (6:17). Yet here Jesus is more on the defensive than on the offensive, and I think it is his trust in his heavenly Father, which includes believing in the promises of his Word, that Jesus best demonstrates. So he holds up "the shield of faith," as Ephesians 6:16 says, with which he extinguishes "the flaming darts [or arrows] of the evil one."

The devil tempts our Lord with what must have been most tempting to him. That's why he toys with and twists the promises of God in each and every temptation.[16] That's why he tempts Jesus, not with "obvious evils"—steal this, lie about that, lust after her—but with what is normally good.[17] He tempts Jesus with God's good creation—bread. He takes Jesus to the temple pinnacle (God's holy place), he quotes the Bible (God's Holy Word), and he says, "Beloved Son, does God really love you?" (God's holy provision). Yet with each "false arrow" the Son of God puts up his shield of faith. "It is written . . . it is written . . . it is written" (vv. 4, 7, 10).

Paul writes in Romans 10:17, "So faith comes from hearing, and hearing through the word of Christ" (cf. Galatians 3:2, 5). Do you know the Word—its content? Do you know how to interpret it correctly? And do you trust what God has written? After forty days of hunger—or whatever the equivalent would be for you—do you still believe that we do not live on bread alone but by every word that comes from the mouth of God?

Tough but Temporary

I have one final word on this Word. The fifth and final characteristic of Jesus' temptations is this: The temptations were certainly *tough but also temporary*. This is taught in verses 10, 11. After the final temptation to worship Satan, Jesus says to him, "Be gone, Satan! For it is written, 'You shall worship the Lord your God and him only shall you serve'" (v. 10; cf. Deuteronomy 6:13). Then what happened? "Then the devil left him, and behold, angels came and were ministering to him" (v. 11).[18]

Jesus says, "Be gone," and Satan leaves him. Temptations are always temporary. This is a grace of God. If you can "[r]esist the devil . . . he will flee from you" (see James 4:7). Our God only allows Satan to tempt us for our good, to try and test and refine our faith. And as 1 Corinthians 10:13 makes clear, there is no temptation (1) that is not common to everyone—don't think your particular temptation is so tough that no one else struggles with it, (2) that is not beyond your ability to resist with our Lord's help—Jesus is "able to help those who are being tempted" (Hebrews 2:18), and (3) from which God does not provide a way of escape—if you say, "No," the devil will go.

Temptations are tough, but they are temporary. Remember that. Say to yourself, "If I can just get through this, if I can just say 'be gone' like Jesus did, or run out of the room as Joseph did with Potiphar's wife, then the devil will gain no foothold." But if you give him an inch, stay in the room longer than you should, or toy with the temptation, then watch out. He'll have you by the heel, then the leg, then the heart.

Temptations are tough but always temporary. Resist the devil, and he *will* flee from you.

Closing Thought

Our Lord Jesus was tempted in every respect as we are, yet was without sin. He never sinned. We sinners must learn from our Lord and cling to him, that we might by faith win the victory for his glory and our good.

8

A Great Light in Galilee

MATTHEW 4:12–25

"THAT VERSE FITS PERFECTLY!" is what I thought one morning when I stopped at Romans 1:16 in my devotional reading: "For I am not ashamed of the gospel, for it is the power of God for salvation to everyone who believes, to the Jew first and also to the Greek." Paul's summary application of the gospel in Romans perfectly describes what is illustrated in 4:12–25—the story of Jesus preaching the kingdom, calling his first followers, and healing the crowds. Thus, without apology, reservation, or further explanation I bring you—in Paul's language—*my* two points on Matthew's text.

Don't Be Ashamed . . . for the Gospel Brings Light to the World

Point one: *Don't be ashamed of the gospel because it brings salvation* (or "light" as Isaiah and Matthew say) *to the world—to both Jews and Gentiles.*

Did you notice all the geography? Oftentimes when reading through the Gospels I pay little attention to what region or town Jesus is in. I focus more on what he is saying or doing. But here even I couldn't miss all the place names. In verses 12, 13 five places are mentioned: "Now when he [Jesus] heard that John had been arrested, he withdrew into *Galilee*. And leaving *Nazareth* he went and lived in *Capernaum* by the sea, in the territory of *Zebulun and Naphtali*." And in verses 23–25 six places are mentioned: "And he [Jesus] went throughout all *Galilee*. . . . So his fame spread throughout all *Syria*. . . . And great crowds followed him from *Galilee* and the *Decapolis*, and from *Jerusalem and Judea*, and from beyond the *Jordan* [River]."

If you open to the map in the back of your Bible and look at what is described here, you'll see that Matthew is doing something very interesting. Here the whole land of Israel is covered. We have Galilee in the northwest, the Decapolis in the northeast, Jerusalem and Judea in the southwest, and finally "beyond the Jordan," in the southeast.[1] I don't want to make too much of this. However, since Matthew's mind is so saturated with the Old Testament, especially in the first four chapters of his Gospel, I deduce that he is using all this geography to depict Jesus as a new Joshua. It's as if he wants us to picture a new Joshua ("Jesus" is Greek for the Hebrew name "Joshua") coming to reconquer the promised land and to rule it, to usher in a new and better kingdom, a heavenly kingdom (v. 17), drawing Jews from the north and south and east and west.

So the geography here is important. Jesus has come into the promised land for the salvation of the promised people. However, what should jump out at us geographically (and theologically) is Matthew's mention of *Galilee.* If you look in your Bibles and trace your finger along our text, you will find Galilee mentioned in four verses—12, 15, 23, and 25 (five, if we count "the Sea of Galilee" in verse 18). The most significant of these references is verse 15, where Matthew calls Galilee "Galilee of the Gentiles." Remember that the gospel is for Jews first (and we will see that first in the calling of four Jews—Peter, Andrew, James, and John), but also for Gentiles (we have seen that already with the magi in 2:1–12, and we will see that next in 8:5–13 with the extraordinary faith of the Roman centurion). The seed for the Great Commission, which was planted in 1:1–17, is watered here. So Jesus starts his ministry in Galilee of the Gentiles.

"But wait a minute," a Jew in Jesus' day might have objected, "what is the Messiah doing in Galilee? Shouldn't he be in Bethlehem and then Jerusalem? And shouldn't he be ministering among the political and spiritual elites—the priests, scribes, and Pharisees? What is he doing with a bunch of 'country bumpkins' and 'hicks'[2] in this despised, Gentile-filled region of Israel?"[3]

Matthew provides an answer. He tells us to open our Bibles to Isaiah 9:1, 2, which he quotes to explain Jesus' actions:[4]

> The land of Zebulun and the land of Naphtali,
> the way of the sea, beyond the Jordan, Galilee of the Gentiles—
> the people dwelling in darkness
> have seen a great light,
> and for those dwelling in the region and shadow of death,
> on them a light has dawned. (vv. 15, 16)

"Jesus is in Galilee, this I know, because the Bible tells me so." That's my summary of the above citation. The Bible says that Galilee was where the

Messiah would minister and where he would inaugurate the kingdom. This same chapter of Isaiah describes the coming of this messianic kingdom just a few verses later:

> For to us a child is born, to us a son is given;
>   and the government shall be upon his shoulder. . . .
> Of the increase of his government and of peace
>   there will be no end,
> on the throne of David and over his kingdom,
>   to establish it and to uphold it
> with justice and with righteousness
>   from this time forth and forevermore. (Isaiah 9:6, 7)

This kingdom is to be inaugurated in an unexpected place—Galilee of the Gentiles. That is where the Lord's "salvation" shall come, in the words of Simeon, as "a light for revelation to the Gentiles" (Luke 2:30, 32).[5]

So Jesus is in Galilee to fulfill Scripture, "so that what was spoken by the prophet Isaiah might be fulfilled" (v. 14). Here again, for the sixth time, the fulfillment formula is used (cf. 1:22; 2:15, 17, 23; 3:15).[6] However, Jesus is also in Galilee because he is fishing for followers. He is fishing, surprisingly, not from the religious or political elite (e.g., Nicodemus, Caiaphas, Herod) but rather from the average Joes of this world—Peter, James, and John.

So I am not ashamed of the gospel, and you ought not to be ashamed of the gospel, because it brings salvation/light to the world—to Jews first but also to Gentiles.[7] Why should we Christians ever be ashamed of the message that Jesus has come even for the lowly, *and* that Jesus has come for people from every tongue and tribe and nation? As *exclusive* as Christianity is—there is only one way to the one God, and it is through the one and only Son of God—it is far and away the most *inclusive* religion in the history of the world. Jesus welcomes Galilean fishermen, Samaritan women, and Roman soldiers, and his church welcomes Irishmen and Indonesians, Indians and Americans, and so many others. Tell me another religion in the first century that did that. Tell me another religion in the world today that does that. It's part of our history. It's part of our theology. It's part of our gospel!

So don't be ashamed of the gospel (especially in this day and age as our culture is finally catching up with Christianity) because the gospel brings salvation to all kinds of people in all kinds of places. It brings light to the world. Red and yellow, black and white, they're all precious in his sight; Jesus loves the lowly Gentile sinners of the world. That's the first point.

Don't Be Ashamed . . . for the Gospel Is God's Power for Salvation

Point two: Don't be ashamed of the gospel because it is the *power of God* for salvation for *everyone who believes*. In the middle section of our passage, Matthew highlights the theological tension between God's sovereign call and people's willful belief.

First, we see the *power of God*. The sovereign power of God in salvation (cf. 1 Thessalonians 1:5) is on display. Look again at verses 18–22. Starting in verse 18 we read, "While walking by the Sea of Galilee, he [Jesus] saw two brothers, Simon (who is called Peter) and Andrew his brother, casting a net into the sea, for they were fishermen." And then what does Jesus do? He gives them not some polite or reasoned invitation but a seemingly unconditional command.[8] He says to them, "Follow me, and I will make you fishers of men" (v. 19). And what happens? Do they say, "Oh, well, ah, let me check with a few of my best customers first," or "Let me make sure my wife can manage without me for a few days, months, three years"? No. What do we read in verse 20? "Immediately they left their nets and followed him."

Matthew doesn't stop there. He continues on with a second nearly identical example of Jesus' power: "And going on from there he [Jesus] saw two other brothers, James the son of Zebedee and John his brother, in the boat with Zebedee their father, mending their nets, and he called them" (v. 21).[9] And they said . . . well, they didn't say anything. "Immediately [there's that word again] they left the boat and their father and followed him" (v. 22). They left both finances and family!

Sovereign command and immediate obedience is the twofold pattern in these two stories. Now that's power, isn't it? It's almost as powerful as the Creator of our universe, saying, "Let there be light, and there was light; let there be stars and there were stars; let there be fish; and there were fish." This powerful calling reflects the power of God for salvation. If you miss Jesus' power here, you miss what's going on. He is the Lord. He has all authority. Matthew is going to say that and show that repeatedly.

However, if you miss or underplay the fact that these four men actually "followed" (a word used four times here), then you miss the other side of the message. The gospel is the power of God for "everyone who believes."

Jesus calls; we must come.

This is actually the emphasis, according to the word order, in Jesus' first recorded message in Matthew: "Repent, for the kingdom of heaven is at hand" (v. 17; cf. 3:2). Jesus announces that the *eschatological reality* of the future reign of God's King is now here and that the *ethical imperative* that naturally follows that reality is repentance.[10] "Repent" is the first word out of our Lord's mouth to his would-be disciples. They are to repent and follow. To summarize, we see:

> The necessity of *repentance*.
> The necessity of *following*.
> The necessity of *faith*.

I want us to pause here and dwell on this human side of things—on our responsibility to repent and follow,[11] or in a more generic and more popular New Testament term, our need and delightful duty to believe.

Matthew doesn't use the word "believe," as Mark does in his version of this story (Mark 1:15), but *faith* is what Matthew is getting at. Matthew is saying to his readers, "I'll show you what Jesus' first four followers did, and then you tell me if you would do likewise. Here in the mirror are Peter, Andrew, James, and John. Does your faith in any way reflect theirs?"

Well, does it? Let's take a look.

Let me ask you a few personal and perhaps penetrating questions. Is Jesus Lord? If so, is he Lord over your life so much that in his presence you recognize the spiritual difference that exists between you and him—he is holy, you are not? In light of this difference, do you repent of your sins? And more than understanding and embracing repentance in this first sense—repenting of sin—do you also repent from following anyone or anything more than Jesus?

That is the real point pressed on us here, and it will be pressed on us again and again in Matthew, especially at the end of chapter 10.[12] Who or what is first in your life—the fish, the nets, the boat, the career, the income, the brother, the father, the family? Are you willing to break from any or all "former loyalties"[13]—occupation, friends, family, religion, etc.—in order to wholeheartedly serve one Master? Moreover, are you willing to do what this Master says? To go where he wants you to go? To give away what must now be given away?

We won't all be leaving the fishing profession to be called "apostles" or to be martyred for the faith. I know that. But I also know that when Christ calls you to repent and follow him, you better expect to be disrupted from your ordinary life.[14] You better expect a sword to sever relationships, pierce your bank account, and cut off all those sins that so easily entangle you. You better expect such changes and many more.

The prophet Isaiah envisioned a time (oh, he longed for it) when God would break into history in the most remarkable way; the time would come when God would begin to establish his heavenly rule on earth. Well, praise be to God, for the King has come and the kingdom of heaven has been brought into our world through Jesus. So repent, believe, and follow. *Turn away from* sin and idolatry and *turn to* Jesus—the Savior and King—offering yourself to him and him alone, which is your spiritual worship (Romans 12:1).

Point two is, don't be ashamed of the gospel because it is the power of God for salvation for *everyone who believes*—everyone who says, like the disciples did, "Yes, Lord, I trust your sovereign call enough to freely and completely follow you."

Three Reasons to Believe

I can surmise that some of you, as you look in this mirror, know quite well how poorly you reflect the faith of these four fishermen, because you are still holding on to some of your "nets." Perhaps when you come to church, you zip your "nets" up in your purse or stuff them down your socks, but you still have them. You are still a bit caught up in them. But you honestly don't want to be. You want to repent more fully. You want to follow Jesus better. So you're thinking, "I do believe, help my unbelief."

Well, I will do my best. You see, my job, with the blessing of the Holy Spirit, is to crack hard hearts so they might be softened to receive the gospel, but it's also to take soft hearts and strengthen them. If your heart is soft to God right now—if you genuinely want to have more faith—I want you to consider with me *why* these four fishermen first believed. I think that as we grasp why they believed, it will help us believe as well. It will strengthen our faith.

First, Peter, Andrew, James, and John believed because of the *truth of the message*. While they obviously had less information here than they would have three years later, what they saw and heard regarding Jesus made sense. It made the best sense of the world and of the predictions of Scripture. There was something believable about Jesus and his teaching. Here with Jesus' message (summarized in v. 17), they were apparently as awestruck as the crowd would be at the end of the Sermon on the Mount.

Second, they believed because of the *value of the mission*. They were fishermen, and when Jesus approached them he offered them what I'll call a promotion. "Follow me," he said, "and I will make you fishers of men" (v. 19). Don't fish for salmon when you can fish for souls; don't catch minnows when you can capture men. Christ's call is more than our own salvation; it is a call for the salvation of others. And because of this selflessness, it is ironically self-rewarding. Christian ministry—the work of spreading the gospel like a net to each corner of the world—is exhilarating. It is life-giving, more life-giving than anything I know or have done. People are always looking to find meaning and purpose in life. Well, nothing is more fulfilling and purposeful than joining the school of Christ and being sent out to capture a school of souls! This is why the kingdom, if you find it, and the King, if you will follow him, is like a treasure hidden in a field—it's worth giving everything to get it.

Third, they believed because of *the reality of the miracles*. Message, mission, miracles—those are the three reasons they believed, reasons that should help us believe as well. When I first think of Matthew's Gospel in comparison with the other Gospels, what first comes to mind is Jesus' teaching ministry—the parables, the Olivet Discourse, and most notably the Sermon on the Mount. However, it's interesting to note that Matthew is just as interested in miracles,[15] some might argue even more so, as Mark, Luke, and John. This is true especially in 4:23—9:35. Look at 4:23. Now turn to 9:35. Notice that Matthew writes a very similar sentence:

> 4:23: "And he went throughout all Galilee, teaching in their synagogues and proclaiming the gospel of the kingdom and healing every disease and every affliction among the people."
>
> 9:35: "And Jesus went throughout all the cities and villages, teaching in their synagogues and proclaiming the gospel of the kingdom and healing every disease and every affliction."

This is called an *inclusio*. Surrounding the Sermon on the Mount—Jesus' words—are stories and summaries about his miracles—Jesus' deeds. The point in the *inclusio* is that "Jesus not only talks; he heals."[16] More specifically, his miraculous healings testify to his identity. Later, in 11:3, some of John the Baptist's followers will approach Jesus and ask him, "Are you the Messiah, or should we expect someone else?" (my paraphrase). And how did Jesus reply? He said, "Go and tell John what you hear and see: the blind receive their sight and the lame walk, lepers are cleansed and the deaf hear, and the dead are raised up" (11:4, 5).

When we see that Jesus does miracles that no one has ever done before, and when we see that Jesus healed all who came to him—"all the sick . . . those oppressed by demons" (v. 24), we are to see that Jesus is no Tanzanian witch doctor. He is no Orlando televangelist. This is no reenactment of the magic of Egypt. Rather, in the words of Pharaoh's magicians, "This is the finger of God" (Exodus 8:19). With Jesus' healings, the eschatological inbreaking of the kingdom of heaven has come to earth. Heaven's lack of death, mourning, crying, or pain is at hand! The curse is being buried in the sweat-soaked ground; Satan's head is slowly being crushed under Christ's heel (we might say, under his heal).

Who Jesus heals, how Jesus heals, and what he is able to heal—all of this points to him as God's Son come in the flesh. It's not only "Who can forgive sins but God alone?" but who can walk on water, who can still the wind and waves, who can expel a thousand demons with one word, who can take a lifelong illness away with one touch, who can turn seven loaves into 7,000, and who can catch 100 fish at one command?

Even at the start of Jesus' ministry Peter, Andrew, James, and John understood this. They understood the faith-drawing, faith-building power of Jesus' miracles.[17] While we have not seen or touched him as they did, we should nevertheless believe as we read the apostolic reports of him. The miracles by themselves don't close the case. But along with the claims, commands, and character of Christ, they build a fairly strong one.

So the truth of the message, the value of the mission, and the reality of the miracles—those are the three reasons they believed. These same reasons should help us who have not seen and yet believe to trust in Jesus for everything and follow him anywhere and everywhere.

No Shame

> For I am not ashamed of the gospel, for it is the power of God for salvation to everyone who believes, to the Jew first and also to the Greek. (Romans 1:16)

As we look afresh at 4:12–25, let us be reminded and encouraged that there is no reason to be ashamed of the good news of Jesus Christ, for this gospel brings salvation to all kinds of people in all kinds of places. It is the *power of God* for salvation for *everyone*—I've experienced it; you've experienced it—*who believes*.

9

A Sermon on *the* Sermon

MATTHEW 5—7

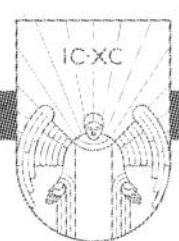

JESUS MADE A NUMBER of remarkable statements, but perhaps none as remarkable as when he said, "Heaven and earth will pass away, but my words will not pass away" (24:35). Think about that claim. If I told you today that what I am about to say in the next few pages, each and every word that is mine, will be remembered when we're all dead and gone, in fact, when the whole world is dead and gone, what would you think of me? If I was to claim, as Jesus did, that there is lasting value to each sentence I speak, what would you think of me? Well, those who know me well might think I was making a joke, and those who don't know me might think I was one. You see, no one in the history of the world, who had his head on straight, talked like Jesus talked, claiming that his words have eternal value.

I make my living by speaking, and yet I am self-aware enough to know that when words fall from my mouth, it's as if they fade into the wind, or it's as if they are swallowed up by time. And this is not true of only my words or your words—it's true of everybody's words.

After President Obama's inaugural speech in 2008, I remember how some in the media claimed that America's new President's words would be "chiseled in stone"; in other words, what he said would be long remembered. Now, certainly I would agree that such a speech by our first African-American president has historical value to it, but I had to laugh at such a claim (and this may offend some of you; I don't mean to be offensive, and I promise I'll be far more offensive later in this chapter, so please wait until then to be offended)—only because I know from history that even presidential speeches—the best of them, the most historically significant of them—are easily and usually forgotten.

What about George Washington's Farewell Address or FDR's War Message or Lincoln's Gettysburg Address? Yes, all those are famous presidential speeches, but even the Gettysburg Address, the most famous of the three, though we might remember how it starts ("Four score and seven years ago our fathers brought forth, upon this continent, a new nation . . .") is forgettable. Let's be honest, most Americans have forgotten the precise contents of that speech, and some of us can't even remember what "four score" means.

Important words might be written down or even "chiseled in stone," but like the chiseled script on most monuments in your city's downtown as well as downtown Washington, DC, we have forgotten when and who and what was said.

But not so with the words of Jesus! Isn't that remarkable? Have you ever thought about that? Have you ever stopped to think, "How is it that this carpenter's son, born out of wedlock [wasn't he?], this poor Jew from the nowhere town of Nazareth, who lived 2,000 years ago and who lived fewer years than what is required to be the President of our country—how is it that his words are as *alive* today as the oxygen in this air, as the blood that pulses through our veins?" I don't care how long you have gone to church or how much or how little you have studied the Bible, you have likely heard Jesus' teachings from the Sermon on the Mount.

> Blessed are the pure in heart, for they shall see God. (5:8)
>
> [I]f anyone slaps you on the right cheek, turn to him the other also. (5:39)
>
> No one can serve two masters, for either he will hate the one and love the other, or he will be devoted to the one and despise the other. You cannot serve God and money. (6:24)
>
> Judge not that you be not judged. . . . Why do you see the speck that is in your brother's eye, but do not notice the log that is in your own eye? (7:1, 3)
>
> Ask, and it will be given to you; seek, and you will find; knock, and it will be opened to you. (7:7)
>
> So whatever you wish that others would do to you, do also to them. (7:12)
>
> Our Father in heaven, hallowed be your name. Your kingdom come, your will be done, on earth as it is in heaven. Give us this day our daily bread, and forgive us our debts, as we also have forgiven our debtors. And lead us not into temptation, but deliver us from evil. (6:9–13)

Those words aren't chiseled in stone. Rather, they are words sown into the fabric of the civilized (and uncivilized) world, as Christianity has spread from the Middle East to North Africa and Europe, then over to North America, then south to Latin America, Africa, and India, and finally to Asia, where it is currently spreading like wildfire. You see, it's not just that he has the whole world in his hands, but also that now the whole world has his words in its mouth.

So, as skeptical as someone might be about Christ and Christianity, I cannot grasp how anyone can disprove Jesus' own prophecy about the longevity of his words. Was Jesus right? Well, yes! He was right, right? Whatever you think of him, so far so good; he said his words would be around, and sure enough and writing about them now, and you're reading my words about them now. And we're not alone. In every continent and in every major city around the world Jesus' name is being praised and his words are being explained and applied.

But why is this so? That's what I'm trying to get us to think about. "Well," you might respond, "that's simple. It's indoctrination. In the Western world, since the time of Constantine, we have indoctrinated our children with this religious rubbish." Yeah, maybe you're right. But I don't think so. Each and every culture indoctrinates their children with stuff that's really rubbish, and like rubbish it easily or eventually dissolves. Truths, however, have a way of rising to the surface. If one culture or country seeks to bury them in the sand—like atheistic Russia did a few decades ago or Communist China does today—strangely, oddly, almost inexplicably (some might call it miraculously) Christianity flourishes. It grows like a thousand wildflowers through the cracks of a city sidewalk. I don't think it's indoctrination. Rather, I think there is *something* inherently truthful and powerful in Jesus' words because *someone* inherently truthful and powerful said them.

What is the Sermon on the Mount all about? That's what we will look at in this chapter. What's the Sermon on the Mount—Jesus' most remembered words of his well-remembered words—all about? The short answer is, JESUS. It's about Jesus. The long answer is, it's about Jesus' authority. The longer answer is, it's about Jesus' truthful and powerful authority and why you and I should submit to him.

It's about Ethics, Right?

"But wait a minute," you say. "The Sermon on the Mount is about ethics, isn't it? It's not about Jesus; it's about the moral teachings of Jesus, right?"[1] Well, to be sure Jesus makes ethical statements. In fact, he gives fifty imperatives:[2]

do this, don't do that; be like this, don't be like that. And yes, he deals with ethical issues that affect family and society, such as adultery and divorce and the taking of oaths. He speaks on religion—true religion and religious hypocrisy—and he instructs us on prayer and fasting and almsgiving. He teaches on doing good works and doing God's will. He speaks on virtues—being merciful, peaceful, humble, loving our neighbors and even our enemies. And he speaks on vices—lust, anger, anxiety, undue and ungrounded and unexamined criticism.

So, yes, his teachings are ethical. But, no, he is not just some moral teacher, as is so often claimed. Many people today like to "befriend" Jesus only to domesticate or update or revise his words to fit their own politics or philosophy or lifestyle. And many, because of this, just pick and choose from the sayings of this Sermon, like a three-year-old boy picks at his dinner plate, pushing the broccoli aside for the Jell-O. They say, "I like the stuff about love, but not divorce; about feeding the poor, but not poverty of spirit; about the dangers of materialism but not of idolatry; about God being good but not about me being evil; about those who are judgmental, but not about me having to stand before Jesus as Judge."

Ah, but you see, Jesus' ethical teachings are like the relationship between our bones and our bodies. If you took all that surrounds our bones—our organs, veins, muscles, flab, and whatever else there is—we'd die. The "bones" of Jesus' teaching cannot be separated from the body of the Teacher or from his life, death, and resurrection as well as his theology—his view of God, humankind, and the necessity of new birth, repentance, and faith for one to enter into a saving relationship with God.

It's about Authority

What we have here are not moral platitudes for the masses, especially that ever so popular one-size-fits-all morality. These are ethics of the kingdom for those who call Jesus King—for those who have come, so to speak, to the feet of Jesus, listening to him on the Mount as he opens his mouth (5:1, 2).[3] This Sermon is not about ethics so much as it is about the Ethicist! It's about *Jesus*. So it's about Jesus' *authority* and why you and I should submit to him and his words.[4]

Let me show you from this text, quickly and convincingly (I hope), this central theme.

To set the broader context, we'll start with the bookends of the Gospel of Matthew (chapters 1 and 28). Then we'll look at the bookends of the Sermon on the Mount (5:1–12 and 7:21–29).

The Gospel of Matthew begins with Jesus' genealogy. Now, what's the point of this long list of names (so and so was the father of so and so . . . and so on)? The point is to say, as Matthew does say in the first verse, that Jesus is the son of Abraham and the son of David (1:1), that is, he is the Messiah, the King of the Jews.

That's how Matthew's Gospel begins. But how does it end? Turn again to Matthew 28. It ends with the Great Commission, where Jesus tells his disciples to spread the gospel throughout the world. But what does he say before that? Before the *commission* he makes an *admission*. He says in verses 18 and 19, "All authority in heaven and on earth has been given to me. Go therefore and make disciples of all nations." "All authority"—those are the two key words of this Gospel!

> Matthew 1—he's the King of the Jews.
> Matthew 28—he's the King of the universe!

Those are the bookends to the book.

Next let's turn our attention to chapters 5, 6, and 7. What's at the start and stop of the Sermon on the Mount? Again we find this theme of authority! In 7:28, 29 we read, "And when Jesus finished these sayings, the crowds were astonished at his teaching, for he was teaching them as one who had *authority*, and not as their scribes." The first reaction from the first hearers was, "Wow! What authority! Who is this teacher? He has a weight to him that even our best Bible authorities don't have."

This same note of authority is found in the Sermon's setting, 5:1, 2. Here we learn that Jesus "went up on the mountain," there "sat down," and then "opened his mouth and taught them." Each of these actions—going atop a mountain, sitting, and opening his mouth—actually relates to his authority. Here's why I say that.

In Matthew mountains are important. Seven times we find Jesus on one—at his temptation (4:8), when he went away to pray (14:23), when he healed and fed the multitudes (15:29–38), during the transfiguration (17:1), when he gave the Olivet Discourse (24:3) and the Great Commission (28:16), and here in the Sermon on the Mount (5:1).

Mountains are also important elsewhere in the Bible. We think especially of Moses and *Mount* Sinai where God speaks to him and gives him the Ten Commandments. So the mountain is a hint to us that something important is going on here and someone important is at hand. But so too is the posture of sitting. Sitting in the ancient world and sometimes today is a symbol of authority. Kings sit when you come into their presence. The Pope, when he has something authoritative to say, speaks *ex cathedra*, which is Latin for "out of the chair." He's sitting. Jewish rabbis in Jesus' day would sit to speak from or about the Scriptures (cf. Luke 4:20, 21). So Jesus sat to teach. He opened his mouth, but not merely to speak from or about the Scriptures, but in fact to claim authority of interpretation and application over them, and even fulfillment of them.[5] "Do not think," Jesus says, "that I have come to abolish the Law or the Prophets; I have not come to abolish them but to fulfill them" (5:17). Now that's authority! In the past when God had something to say, he spoke through Moses or Samuel or Isaiah or Jeremiah. He spoke through the prophets. But now, with Jesus, we have the direct and authoritative voice of God's beloved Son, of "Immanuel" ("God with us"), as Matthew calls him (1:23).[6]

> Matthew 5:1–2—authority
> Matthew 7:28–29—authority

Let us look at something else related to this theme of authority in the Beatitudes. Look afresh (5:2ff.) to what Jesus says here, and concentrate especially on the end of the first and last beatitudes. The first says: "Blessed are the poor in spirit, for theirs is the kingdom of heaven" (5:3). Now ask this question to that beatitude: Says who? What authority do you have, Jesus, to say who gets into Heaven and how? Now note the last beatitude: "Blessed are you when others revile you and persecute you and utter all kinds of evil against you falsely *on my account*. Rejoice and be glad, for your reward is great in heaven" (5:11, 12a; cf. 24:9). Again, says who? On your account? You, Jesus, know and determine what kind of faithful perseverance will be rewarded in the afterlife?[7]

Now, if you thought or you now think that the Beatitudes have a bite to them, let me show you Jesus' final words, the tail of this text (7:21–27), which, like that of a scorpion, has quite a sting of its own. And here look again for those penetrating first-person personal pronouns—every "I" and "me" and "my" and "mine." Note also the phrase "your name." Jesus says:

> Not everyone who says to *me*, "Lord, Lord," will enter the kingdom of heaven, but the one who does the will of *my* Father who is in heaven. On that day many will say to *me*, "Lord, Lord, did we not prophesy in *your* name, and cast out demons in *your* name, and do many mighty works in *your* name?" And then will *I* declare to them, "*I* never knew you; depart from *me*, you workers of lawlessness."

Keep looking. We're in the middle of the potentially offensive part of the chapter.

> Everyone then who hears these words of *mine* and does them will be like a wise man who built his house on the rock. And the rain fell, and the floods came, and the winds blew and beat on that house, but it did not fall, because it had been founded on the rock. And everyone who hears these words of *mine* and does not do them will be like a foolish man who built his house on the sand. And the rain fell, and the floods came, and the winds blew and beat against that house, and it fell, and great was the fall of it.

End of sermon. Wow! What authority! Who preaches like that?

I'd like to say, here at the end of the Sermon, that Jesus gives a gracious invitation—"Come to me," as he'll later say, "and I will give you rest" (11:28). But here our Lord gives not so much an invitation as an assessment. He says in essence, "Listen, I will be the Judge of everyone. And your final destiny will be determined by our relationship or lack thereof, whether you know me or not, whether I know you or not, and along with that, whether you listened to my words or not."

I know this is not politically correct. Jesus is not PC. I'm not PC by saying he's not PC. And I know (trust me I know) that the biggest mental and moral issue in our culture today is exclusivity. I know that I can say to you just about anything about Jesus—that he's my personal Savior, that he loves little children, that he once walked on water. I can say all that—I just can't say, "He is the only way to God." I can't say what he said: "If you don't know me, then you don't know my Father in Heaven." Yes, that sounds arrogant, but it is not any more or less arrogant or exclusive than the person who says, "I think all religions are the same," "I think each religion has some of the truth but not all of it," or "I think everyone is going to Heaven."

Why do I say that? Because says who? Says you! And who are you to say such things? I'm serious. As I see it I have three choices: (1) I can believe you or someone just like you—another mere human being, (2) I can believe myself (and whatever I want to think and claim about such matters), or (3) I can believe Jesus and what he said.

You see, it's a matter of authority. Who is your Lord? Self, society, freedom of choice (the great idol of our age)? Who is Lord? Jesus is my Lord because I believe he is the Lord! I believe he has authority over Heaven and earth, which includes me and my itty-bitty mind, me and my unholy heart, and me and my dirty hands. He is Lord! And I don't claim that for him—I simply acknowledge it and live by it.

I became a Christian when I was nearly twenty years old, after I had lived exactly how Jesus says here in the Sermon on the Mount not to live. I was like a whitewashed tomb—clean on the outside, but full of dead bones on the inside. I would pray each day—mumble, mumble, mumble to God, thinking the more prayers, the greater the likelihood he would hear and love me; I would do religious acts to be seen and esteemed by others; *and* I was no adulterer, but I was full of lust; no murderer, but full of hate; no perjurer but full of lies. But Jesus got ahold of my heart. He showed me its blackness; then he cleaned it up. He made it white as snow. And he made it beat, beat, beat to the rhythm of his voice.

When I tell people about my conversion to Christ, some say, sometimes in a patronizing voice, "Well, that's nice. I guess that's what you needed. You know, I think religion has some value to it. It brings comfort and joy, a sense of belonging." Well, yes, all those things are true. As a Christian I have found comfort and joy and a sense of belonging, much more than when I was not a Christian. I have felt fulfillment and happiness and hope. But, you know, I'm not primarily or foundationally a Christian because of these benefits, as real as they are. I'm a Christian not because it's nice or even because it's helpful, but because it's true.[8] You see, it's a matter of authority, and then of allegiance. Since Jesus is Lord (*the Lord*), then I acknowledge that—I believe, I submit, I love the Lord my God with all my heart and mind and strength and soul.

Fall at His Feet

Jesus made a number of remarkable statements, didn't he? He predicted that the gospel would reach the ends of the earth and that someone from every nation would know him and accept the good news about him. He claimed that his church—first comprised of former fisherman (4:18–22), lepers (8:2–4), Roman soldiers (8:5–13), demon-possessed men (8:28–34), cripples (9:1–8), tax collectors (9:9–13), those who were blind and mute (9:27–34), thieves, murderers, and prostitutes—would remain, even if all Hell fought against her (16:18). And he said that Heaven and earth would pass away but his words would last and last and last (24:35). And so far he has been right about all of these. It is not a matter of opinion or belief; it's a matter of history!

And if he has been right about those things, might he also be right about who he is and why he came? He is the Lord, as he says here in 7:21, who "came," as he says in 9:13, "not to call the righteous [those who think they are not morally sick, cf. 9:12], but sinners [those who know they need a Savior]." And might he be right about how such "sinners" enter the kingdom of heaven? We enter (1) through poverty of spirit—the first beatitude, (2) through the asking of forgiveness for our trespasses—the center petition of the Lord's Prayer, and (3) through faith[9]—which underlies every word here in chapters 5, 6, and 7 and is as obvious as a red cross on a white shield in chapters 8, 9.

C. S. Lewis became an atheist when he was fifteen because, in his own words, he was "very angry with God for not existing."[10] But then later in life, at the age of thirty-three, while a professor at Oxford, he came like an unwilling child "kicking and screaming" into the kingdom of God. He was, in his own words, a "reluctant convert" to Christ, but a real one. He didn't want to become a Christian, but as he looked at the person and teachings of Jesus, he just didn't see another viable alternative. "In the Trinity Term of 1929," he writes, "I gave in, and admitted that God was God, and knelt and prayed."

Later Lewis would write in *Mere Christianity* these now famous but always thought-provoking words:

> A man who was merely a man and said the sort of things Jesus said would not be a great moral teacher. He would either be a lunatic—on the level with the man who says he is a poached egg—or else he would be the Devil of Hell. You can shut Him up for a fool, you can spit at Him and kill Him as a demon; or . . . you can fall at His feet and call Him Lord and God.[11]

My prayer today is that you and I do (and continue to do) the latter—that we admit that God is God and that Jesus is indeed Lord.

10

A Broken Blessedness

MATTHEW 5:3–10

MY FATHER, in his lyrical Irish brogue, ends many conversations with a gracious, "God bless." I sometimes finish a letter or an e-mail with one simple, all-encompassing, religious yet inoffensive word, "blessings." Many people, Christians and non-Christians alike, invoke God's blessing after someone sneezes—"God bless you." Moreover, politicians often close important political speeches with the benediction, "God bless you. God bless the United States of America."

But what does it mean to be blessed? What does it mean to be blessed by God? Does it mean good health—I hope that sneeze, by divine intervention, doesn't turn into something worse? Does it mean much wealth—I hope God prospers you and this country economically, bringing security and comfort? It can mean those things. Health and wealth can be great blessings from God. The Wisdom Literature of the Bible, especially Proverbs, speaks of such blessings. The Prophets also add their voices, as they predicted that when God's kingdom finally arrived there would be a reign of peace and plenty (see Isaiah 65:16–25; Haggai 2:6–9). Even as we look at the start of Jesus' earthly ministry, we get the impression that this "blessed" kingdom has arrived. What is Jesus doing in 4:17–25, right before the Sermon on the Mount? He is "proclaiming the gospel of the kingdom," *and* he is "healing every disease and every affliction among the people" (4:23). Jesus is teaching about God's kingdom and showing via healing that it was beginning to come.

If you lived back then, heard this message, and saw such healings (or were healed), wouldn't you do what the crowd did in 4:25? You would crowd around Jesus, wondering, *What's he going to do next? What's he going to say next?*

Well, what does he say? He talks about blessing. But he doesn't say what they likely thought he would say. Instead he says what seems like one contradiction after another.

Blessed are the poor in spirit.
Blessed are those who mourn.
Blessed are the meek.
Blessed are those who hunger and thirst for righteousness.
Blessed are those who are persecuted.

According to Jesus, who is "blessed"? Is it the courageous, the wise, the temperate, or the just?[1] No. How about the agreeable, the funny, the intelligent, the attractive, the sensitive, and the fit?[2] No. According to Jesus, the one who is poor, sad, lowly, hungry, and mistreated is blessed.

Ladies and gentlemen, welcome to the strange world and wisdom of Jesus. Welcome to Jesus' narrow-gate theology, teaching that separates the "crowds" who want health and wealth in the here and now and the "disciples" who are willing to deny themselves, pick up their crosses, and follow Jesus (cf. 5:1). Welcome not to "the few, the proud, the Marines," but "the few, the humble, the followers of Jesus." Welcome to what it means to be a "blessed" disciple of Jesus Christ.

A Broken Blessedness

In the last chapter we asked, what's the Sermon on the Mount all about? Our answer was, Jesus! It's about Jesus, his authority, and why we should submit to him. In this chapter we ask, what are the Beatitudes all about? Our answer is threefold, the first of which is: the Beatitudes are about *a broken blessedness*.

In 1888 Friedrich Nietzsche wrote a very anti-Christian book quite creatively titled *The Anti-Christ*. In it he asks and answers questions such as this:

Question: "What is more harmful than any vice?"
Answer: "Active sympathy for the ill-constituted and weak—Christianity."

Nietzsche defined *good* as "all that heightens the feeling of power, the will to power, power itself in man," and he defined *bad* as "all that proceeds from weakness."[3] As wrong as this philosopher was about what constitutes good and bad, he was right about the unique feature of Jesus Christ and his teachings. What the first four beatitudes have in common is that they all point out our spiritual *weakness*.

Jesus teaches that you know that God's blessing is upon you if you are "poor in spirit," that is, if you acknowledge your "spiritual bankruptcy," as D. A. Carson summarizes.[4] Put differently, you are poor in spirit if you know there is nothing in you—not family ties, respect in the community, occupation, or so-called "good" works or personal "holiness"—that is valuable enough to commend you to God. Put illustratively, you are blessed when you see you're just a beggar coming to the door of the kingdom without anything to give to get you in, and so you are pounding on the door, appealing to the King, "O Lord, let me in; O Lord, give me what is needed for entrance—your grace and mercy."

Tied to poverty of spirit, Jesus next announces the emotional counterpart to that first beatitude[5]—"Blessed are those who mourn" (5:4a). Here Jesus does not mean merely mourning over the losses of this life (e.g., a job or a spouse), but also mourning over your own sins, the sins of others, and the sins that pervade our world. We are to grieve over various injustices, but also indifference to the gospel (cf. Psalm 119:36; Romans 9:1–3; 2 Corinthians 12:21).[6]

Jesus teaches that you know you are blessed if you are "poor in spirit," if you "mourn" over sin, and if you are "meek," a disposition that naturally follows the first two. For if you understand and feel your need for God, you will not be bold, brash, and self-assertive. You wouldn't be a macho man but a meek man, which is not someone who says, "Walk all over me," but rather "Let me walk a mile or two for you." Meekness describes someone who is gentle, humble, unassuming, and willing to serve.[7]

How blessed it is to be poor in spirit, to mourn, to be meek, and fourthly to "hunger and thirst for righteousness," a righteousness that comes through faith alone in Christ alone (justification) through the work of the Holy Spirit in our lives (sanctification),[8] knowing you are unholy.

So how "blessed" are you? I can tell how truly blessed you are based on your attitude toward yourself. Do you believe what Jesus teaches here or have you believed the most prevailing lie of our times—*express yourself, believe in yourself, realize the powers that are innate in yourself, be self-confident, self-reliant, self-assured?*[9] *Be like God. Reach out, take, and eat the fruit of that forbidden tree!*

Jesus once told a parable that I think perfectly visualizes these first four beatitudes.

> Two men went up into the temple to pray, one a Pharisee and the other a tax collector. The Pharisee, standing by himself, prayed thus: "God, I thank you that I am not like other men, extortioners, unjust, adulterers, or even like this tax collector. I fast twice a week; I give tithes of all that I get." But the tax collector, standing far off, would not even lift up his eyes

to heaven, but beat his breast, saying, "God, be merciful to me, a sinner!" (Luke 18:10–13)

What is the moral of that story? Why did Jesus tell it? Luke says that he told it because there were some "who trusted in themselves that they were righteous" (Luke 18:9a). The point of that parable is the same point as in these first four beatitudes: no one gets into the kingdom of heaven unless one recognizes his need for God. No one squeezes through the eye of the needle unless she gives up all the baggage that fattens and weighs down her soul—whether it's possessions or pride, self-love or self-righteousness.

Nothing in my hand I bring,
Simply to thy cross I cling;
Naked, come to thee for dress;
Helpless, look to thee for grace;
Foul, I to the fountain fly;
Wash me, Savior, or I die.[10]

A Future Blessedness

Second, the Beatitudes are about *a future blessedness*.

Notice the structure here. There are eight beatitudes. Some claim there are only seven, since seven is the perfect number. Others claim there are nine because verse 11 also starts with another "blessed." I think verses 11, 12 are both a continuation of the last beatitude and the start of a new section. I say this because Jesus changes his grammar. In verses 3–10 he says, "Blessed are *those*," but in verse 11 he says, "Blessed are *you*." This grammatical shift supports viewing these eight beatitudes as a unit, followed by a series of teachings in the second-person plural.

In addition, the first and the eighth beatitudes (and only these) end the same way: "for theirs *is* the kingdom of heaven" (vv. 3, 10). Now, despite what a former President said about this word's complexities,[11] "is" means "is." Whoever *is* poor in spirit and whoever *is* persecuted for righteousness' sake *is* (right now) part of the kingdom of heaven.[12]

So there is this "is-ness" to the Beatitudes. We *are* presently part of the kingdom.[13] However, the stress falls on the *future*,[14] which is made clear in the second halves of verses 4–9. Notice the repetition of "they shall"—they shall be comforted, they shall inherit, they shall be satisfied, they shall see God, they shall be called sons of God. For believers parts of these promises are true in the here and now. We have some grasp that we are sons and daughters of God, some comfort over the forgiveness of our sins, some sense of satisfaction that comes from living holy lives, and some vision of God. But we have not yet inherited the earth or actually seen God or, as verse 12 puts it, experienced our reward "in heaven" (not a heavenly reward now, but a reward "in heaven").[15] So there is an already/not yet component to the Beatitudes, but the emphasis falls on the *not yet*. It falls on the future. Such an emphasis, I think, is a real challenge to us.

Have you ever heard the term *delayed gratification*? I'm sure most of us have. Yet I cannot think of a concept more foreign to our culture and, sadly, more and more foreign to the church. "I want it now!" That is how most people talk and think. If I ever run for political office that will be the platform I'll run on. Do you want it now? Then vote for me.

"I don't want to work for my retirement; I'll take a huge pension now." Okay, you have it. "I only make $30,000 a year, but I want a half a million-dollar house now." Okay, you have it. "I hate eating healthy food. I just want to eat jellybeans all day." Okay, you have it. "I want complete sexual freedom to be with whomever, whenever, however; no strings attached, no marriage bed." Okay, you have it.

Do I exaggerate?—only slightly.

Henry David Thoreau, the famous transcendentalist, best known for his works *Walden* and *Civil Disobedience*, supposedly had the following discussion with his aunt on his deathbed.

Aunt: *Have you made your peace with your God?*
Thoreau: I never quarreled with my God.
Aunt: *But aren't you concerned about the next world?*
Thoreau: One world at a time.[16]

One world at a time; I want it now—those are our slogans, aren't they? They'd win a political campaign, attract a following, and even grow a church. *Do you want the perfect marriage, perfect kids, perfect health, perfect spirituality, all right now? Come to our church. We guarantee immediate satisfaction or your money back.*

Christian, do you believe in delayed gratification? Do you hold out in faith for the promises of God? Do you join in Paul's elation for the future, longing for that "crown of righteousness" that is laid up for you, "which the Lord . . . will award" to you on the Day of Judgment (2 Timothy 4:8)? Can you say with the apostle, in his radical heavenly-mindedness, "For to me to live is Christ, and to die is gain" (Philippians 1:21)? Death is gain because only Heaven (as Paul talks about it in Philippians) and the new heaven (as John talks about it in Revelation; cf. 1 John 3:2) offers full comfort and satisfaction and salvation and sonship and inheritance.

> Then I saw a new heaven and a new earth [for theirs is the kingdom of heaven; for they shall inherit the earth]. . . . And I saw the . . . new Jerusalem, coming down out of heaven from God, prepared as a bride adorned for her husband. And I heard a loud voice from the throne saying, "Behold, the dwelling place of God is with man. He will dwell with them, and they will be his people [for they shall be called sons of God], and God himself will be with them as their God. He will wipe away every tear from their eyes, and death shall be no more, neither shall there be mourning, nor crying, nor pain anymore [for they shall be comforted], for the former things have passed away. . . . No longer will there be anything accursed [for they shall receive mercy], but the throne of God and of the Lamb will be in it, and his servants will worship him [for they shall be satisfied]. They will see his face [for they shall see God]. . . . (Revelation 21:1a, 2–4; 22:3, 4a)

A Selfless Blessedness

Third, the Beatitudes are about *a selfless blessedness*. What I mean is this: the Beatitudes do appeal to us because they promise real rewards both now and in the future. However, none of them focus on self. There is no "Blessed are those who look out for number one." Rather, each beatitude focuses either on God, others, or a combination of both.

The first four beatitudes (vv. 3–6) basically say, "Blessed is the one who thinks little of himself or thinks enough of himself that he knows he shouldn't think much of himself. Blessed are those who know they are spiritually poor and thus are meek before God and others. Blessed are those who know their sins, mourn over them, and long for a time when they won't be weighed down by them."

Those are the first four beatitudes, what one scholar calls "beatitudes of need."[17] We need God. The last four beatitudes are "beatitudes of action,"[18] actions that are pleasing to God because they are lovingly helpful to others (cf. 7:12).

When I was studying to become a pastor, I took a theology class on John Calvin, the great Protestant Reformer. In that class we only had a single two-volume textbook, Calvin's *Institutes of the Christian Religion*. As a class we read the volumes and talked and wrote about their content. Now, if you were to ask me, "Pastor, what were the most influential books you ever read?" I would reply, "Well, besides the Bible and Augustine's *Confessions*, I would say Calvin's *Institutes*." If you followed that question up, saying, "Isn't that just a boring 1,734-page theological textbook?" I would say, "No, my dear confused friend. This book is so Scriptural, so insightful, so pastoral, and so relevant." Then if I convinced you of its importance, if you next and finally asked me, "What was your favorite section?" I would answer, "Book III, Chapter VII, 'The Sum of the Christian Life: The Denial of Self.'"[19]

Self-denial! That is what we find in verses 7–10. Take a fresh look: "Blessed are the merciful," that is, those who forgive others their trespasses as theirs have already been forgiven by God. "Blessed are the pure in heart," that is, those who aren't motivated by self-love or man's approval (cf. 6:1ff), but those who serve God and others with an undivided heart.[20] "Blessed are the peacemakers," that is, those who bring reconciliation between this person and that one, or between this nation and that one, or most importantly, between God and man through the gospel of peace.[21] Finally, "blessed are those who are persecuted," that is, those who are reviled and rejected for preaching true peace and living the way of peace, which is the cross (see Colossians 1:19, 20; Romans 5:1, 10). A selfless blessedness!

I know this is contrary to the way we are wired, but not necessarily to our own experience. Have you ever selflessly helped somebody? Let's say you saw someone stranded by the side of the road. You stopped and helped. How did you feel? Depressed? No. Upset? No. Blessed? Yes! God has actually designed us to find fulfillment and blessing when and *only when* we stop living for self—only when we stop hungering and thirsting for wealth, position, status, fame, or whatever else our world thinks matters most.

The Embodiment of the Beatitudes

A broken blessedness, a future blessedness, a selfless blessedness—that's what the Beatitudes are all about!

Let me end with a simple question with a very obvious answer, but perhaps a question and answer you have never thought about before: can you think of anyone you know who has perfectly embodied these beatitudes? Well, you might say, every Christian I know—who is filled with the power of the Holy Spirit—to some extent or another embodies these beatitudes. Yes, that's true.[22] But it's true only to an extent, which we all know. We all know that only Jesus embodies the Beatitudes perfectly! Right?

Jesus was poor in spirit, though not the same way we are (due to our sin). But he did, while on earth, daily depend on God the Father and Spirit for everything. That's why he prayed. That's why he did and said nothing that was not in accordance with the Father's will. That's why in greatest humility he became a human and was crucified. And Jesus mourned, didn't he? He mourned not over his own sin, for he had none, but over our sin—the sins of the world. He wept over Jerusalem and her rejection of the good news. And wasn't our Lord the mightiest but also the meekest man, who offered a gentle yoke to all who would call him "Lord"? And didn't he hunger and thirst for God's righteous rule to come, which is why, on the one hand, he overturned the tables and, on the other hand, received sinners in table fellowship? And didn't he show mercy in healing and feeding the multitudes and in forgiving sins? And who was more pure in heart, undivided in his commitment to God's will? And wasn't (and isn't) Jesus the ultimate peacemaker as he brought peace through his own outstretched arms—peace between Jew and Gentile, peace between God and man? And finally, who better embodied the last beatitude? From the moment of his first breath to his last, more than any figure in human history, Jesus was persecuted for righteousness' sake.

Jesus embodied this broken blessedness!

> And they stripped him and put a scarlet robe on him, and twisting together a crown of thorns, they put it on his head and put a reed in his right hand. And kneeling before him, they mocked him, saying, "Hail, King of the Jews!" And they spit on him and took the reed and struck him on the head. And when they had mocked him, they stripped him of the robe . . . and led him away to crucify him. (27:28–31)

Jesus embodied this future blessedness.

> Consider him [Jesus] who endured from sinners such hostility against himself . . . looking to Jesus, the founder and perfecter of our faith, who for the joy that was set before him endured the cross . . . and is [now] seated at the right hand of the throne of God. (Hebrews 12:3, 2)

And Jesus embodied this selfless blessedness.

> . . . though he was in the form of God, [he] did not count equality with God a thing to be grasped, but emptied himself, by taking the form of a servant. . . . And . . . he humbled himself by becoming obedient to the point of death, even death on a cross. (Philippians 2:6–8)

I don't mean to put down other world religions or people's faith in other gods, but seriously, who is like Jesus, and what is like Christianity? We serve a Lord who does not ask his followers to follow any road he himself has not traveled, a Lord who *selflessly* entered into the *brokenness* of this world to give all who would believe in him a *future*, the blessings of the kingdom of heaven.

11

Unworldly for the World

MATTHEW 5:11–16

MARTYN LLOYD-JONES ONCE SAID, "The glory of the gospel is that when the Church is absolutely different from the world, she invariably attracts it. It is then that the world is made to listen to her message, though it may hate it at first."[1] That is a wonderful summary of what we learn from Jesus here in 5:11–16. If we embody the Beatitudes and model the Sermon on the Mount, the world takes notice and takes action. The world will either hate us for being holy, or, by means of our godliness, it will taste and see that God is good and thus worthy of praise.

Being Salt and Light

Coming out of the Beatitudes, Jesus summarizes Christian character and its relationship to the unbelieving world (this "absolute difference" Lloyd-Jones is talking about) by using two domestic metaphors, the first of which is "salt."

Salt: No Diluted Disciples

In verse 13 Jesus says to his disciples:

> You are the salt of the earth, but if salt has lost its taste, how shall its saltiness be restored? It is no longer good for anything except to be thrown out and trampled under people's feet.

What does Jesus mean by "salt"? I turned to W. D. Davies and Dale C. Allison Jr.'s voluminous three-volume commentary on Matthew to see what these scholars had to say about the subject. Using the Bible and other ancient writings as their sources, they listed eleven options for what "salt" could refer to here, including preservation (salt preserves meat), sacrifice (salt was added to Old Testament ritual sacrifices), peace, friendship, and wisdom.[2]

I am grateful for such thorough research, and I enjoy expanding my mind on the subject of salt. However, it seems that Jesus is quite clear about what he means by salt, for when he speaks of "salt" he speaks of tasting it: "but if salt has lost its *taste*." Therefore, this refers to the salt that we put on the food that we eat, as it also does elsewhere in Scripture (cf. Job 6:6; Colossians 4:5).

So with that in mind, here's how I envision Jesus' teaching. I think of it as a bowl of soup. One time I had lunch with Charleen and Sam, an older couple from my church. Charleen made us some wonderful soup. After I said, "This is very *tasty* soup," she said, "Yeah, it has lots of salt!" Now, I know that salt is bad for high blood pressure, etc., but I also know that soup without salt doesn't taste very good.

So, Christians (bear with my analogy) are like a bowl of salty soup. If we trust in Christ, the world notices a distinct flavor to our lives. But if we stop acting salty (i.e., if we lose our distinctiveness), we become worthless. It's as if there is no salt in the soup.

I know that salt is a very stable chemical compound. So, strictly speaking, sodium chloride remains sodium chloride. But salt can lose its saltiness if it is "contaminated by mixture with impurities"[3] or if it is oversaturated with other substances. So think of a bowl of soup that at first has just the right amount of ingredients. It has some broth and carrots, meat and potatoes, noodles and garlic, oregano and basil, and *salt*. What would happen to the taste of the salt if you added too many carrots or potatoes or too much water? Let's say you had a perfect pint of soup that you dumped into a six-quart stockpot. Then you added four quarts of water. Now, if you proceeded to plunge your wooden kitchen spoon into this batch for a taste, you wouldn't be able to taste the sodium chloride. The salt in that soup would lose its saltiness.

The point is simple: there should be no diluted disciples! "You are the salt," Jesus says. This is not an imperative (a command—"be salt") but an indicative (a statement of fact—"you are salt"). But if you start adding all the ingredients the world loves—a dash of the love of money, a pinch of the fleeing pleasures of sexual immorality, and so on—then you start to water down your witness and taste just like every other bland, unsalted, or under-salted soup. There is to be a distinct taste to Christians. But if we, for example, spend three weeks picking out expensive drapes for our third lake house, five minutes laughing at a dirty joke at the watercooler, or all day Sunday glued to the television set watching our politicians spin and athletes run and jump, don't think the world doesn't notice, and don't think a heap of water isn't being poured into our once salty soup. "Oh, he says he believes in Jesus, he says Jesus will come to judge us, he says there is a world to come, but he sure doesn't live like any of that is true."

Light: No Invisible Christians

Second, in verses 14–16 Jesus calls us "light."

> You are the light of the world. A city set on a hill cannot be hidden. Nor do people light a lamp and put it under a basket, but on a stand, and it gives light to all in the house. In the same way, let your light shine before others, so that they may see your good works and give glory to your Father who is in heaven.

There are many fascinating details here. I find the range of the brightness interesting. Jesus doesn't say, "You are the light of Nazareth or Judea or even the Roman Empire," but rather "You are the light of the [whole] world" (i.e., "the earth," as in v. 13).[4] Also, considering Jesus is addressing a Jewish audience, I find it interesting that he doesn't say what the Old Testament says—that the nation of Israel is light, or that the Torah or the temple or even the holy city of Jerusalem is light. Instead, he labels his followers (and them alone) "the light" (and not merely and more modestly, "a" light). I find that interesting and provocative because I understand what is implied by it. The implication is that those who aren't Christians, those who are part of "the world"—whether they tout themselves as "enlightened" or not—are in fact in darkness, spiritually speaking.[5]

All those facts are interesting and important. However, the main point of interest and importance, according to Jesus, is visibility. Christians are to be visible! This is not what we might have expected coming out of the Beatitudes, for those eight blessings are so countercultural that we might have thought Jesus would follow them by saying something like, "Now, I want all those who are going to follow me to build a monastery in the Egyptian desert or to start a secluded settlement in the barren fields of Eastern Pennsylvania." But here Jesus says just the opposite. We are not to hide ourselves from the world, but rather to permeate and penetrate the darkness of it. We are to be in the world, but not of the world. We are to be "in the world for the world."[6] Like Christ, who called himself "the light of the world" (John 9:5), we are to be as visible as a lamp on a table in a once dark house or as visible as a fully lit skyscraper in an otherwise blacked-out urban sky.

But how so? How do I make this little light of mine shine? Is it through political involvement? That's good and fine, but that's not what is said here.

How about through oral proclamation of the gospel? Well, of course, we are to witness through words.[7] But again that is not the emphasis here.[8] Well, what then? What's the light? Answer: good works! Jesus puts it this way in verse 16: "In the same way, let *your light* shine before others, so that they may see *your good works* and give glory to your Father who is in heaven." Do you see the connection between "your light" and "your good works"? Christianity is made most visible, Jesus teaches here and the apostles teach elsewhere, through good works.

A few years ago a bold and aggressive Christian friend of mine told me about a time he was witnessing to someone on the train. The person who was being witnessed to wanted nothing to do with the gospel, my friend, or the combination of both. So, in frustration but confidence my friend put his face right in the face of this uninterested and now growingly indignant man, and he said to him, "Look me in my eyes! Can't you see Jesus?" Now, what is the answer to that silly question? The answer is no. The world is not to look *into our eyes* in order to see Jesus, but they are to look *at our hands*, if you will. They will look there to see if we have anything to show. If we do good works, they'll see them!

Before I exhort you to do "good works," it would help to define the term. Here's a definition: good works are actions that God has commanded us to do in his holy Word that are fruit and evidence of a true and lively faith.[9] So, first, faith is the stimulus or catalyst for truly *good* or God-pleasing works.[10] "Without faith it is impossible to please him [God]" (Hebrews 11:6). Second, good works are "good" only if they are actions taught by God in his Word. That doesn't negate something good and honorable like caring for grandparents, recycling plastic, and eating healthy foods. There are many potently "good works" that can be deduced from Scripture. However, knowing and heeding the explicit ethical commands in the Bible is the place to start and stand. When Christians live out the living Word of God—whether it is a command from the Sermon on the Mount, elsewhere in the Gospels, or anything taught by the apostles in the rest of the New Testament (also including the moral laws of the Old Testament)—non-Christians start to see the beauty, attractiveness, and truthfulness of Jesus Christ.

When Christians love others (even their enemies), the world tastes the salt and sees the light of the gospel. When we pray for and respect those in authority, the world tastes the salt and sees the light of the gospel. When we give generously to those in need, the world tastes the salt and sees the light of the gospel. When we control our anger, lust, and lies, the world tastes the salt and sees the light of the gospel. When we trust in God to provide in trying economic times, the world tastes the salt and sees the light of the gospel. When we feed the hungry, clothe the naked, welcome the stranger, or visit the sick and those in prison, it is as though we become like Moses when he descended from Mount Sinai—our faces (and our hands) show to this dark world something of the Father's glory!

The Two Results

To sum up: Christians are to be salt, that is, we are to have a distinct and favorable taste to us. If we want to reach the world, we can't be diluted disciples. We are also to be light, that is, we are to light the path to God by daily lighting up the thousand candles of our good works.

If we are salt and if we are light, the world will take notice and take action, usually in two opposite extremes. One result is repentance. The salt and the light bring to life the spiritually dead. This is what Jesus teaches at the end of verse 16: "In the same way, let your light shine before others, so that they may see your good works and *give glory* to your Father who is in heaven."

In this verse, to "give glory" can simply mean a sincere but generic praise of God, as given, for example, after one of Jesus' mighty miracles (e.g., 9:8; 15:31). Or it could be shorthand for saving faith. Illustrative of this second view is 1 Peter 2:9–12. Borrowing heavily from the Sermon on the Mount, Peter reiterates Jesus' teaching when he writes of Christians,

> But you are a chosen race, a royal priesthood, a holy nation, a people for his own possession, that you may proclaim the excellencies of him who called you out of darkness into his marvelous light. Once you were not a people, but now you are God's people; once you had not received mercy, but now you have received mercy. Beloved, I urge you as sojourners and exiles to abstain from the passions of the flesh, which wage war against your soul. Keep your conduct among the Gentiles [i.e., unbelievers] honorable, so that when they speak against you as evildoers, they may see your good deeds and glorify God on the day of visitation.

Certainly someone can glorify God by showing forth God's justice—i.e., being judged for disbelief and disobedience (Romans 9:22, 23). Yet in both 1 Peter 2 and Matthew 5 the tone is positive. Someone sees our good works and then that person desires to give God glory. How so? By believing,[11] and then also by loving and serving God.

Whatever the precise meaning of "give glory," Jesus certainly has in mind a connection between ethics and evangelism. Based on the two texts above, perhaps we can define evangelism as *declaring and demonstrating the excellencies of Christ for the glory of God.* We are to declare or, as Peter says, "proclaim the excellencies of him who called you [us] out of darkness into his marvelous light" (1 Peter 2:9). Yet we are also to demonstrate this gospel by abstaining from sinful behaviors, conducting ourselves honorably, and doing good works.

Peter illustrates such evangelism, particularly the second part of the definition, in chapter 3. It is no evangelistic anomaly when a wife married to an unbelieving husband wins him to Christ "without a word" (1 Peter 3:1). Certainly people must know the content of the gospel in order to believe the gospel, but most people are not attracted to the gospel purely by *hearing* it, but so often by *seeing* the good deeds that spring from it.[12]

Let me put this to the test. How were you converted? Was it through encountering a street evangelist or through a personal relationship with a Christian? Most of us were converted to Christ due to a relationship with a Christian—a coworker, parents, uncle, or a friend. We were converted in part because we saw the Christian faith in action before we believed in it.

That is certainly part of my testimony. I grew up hearing some of the truths of Christianity, but it wasn't until I saw them lived out that I wanted to believe and that I desired to glorify God with my life.

It was the summer of 1990. I had just graduated from high school, and I was selected to play basketball in the Prairie State Games, which is kind of an Olympics for Illinois. Most of the guys on the team were typical guys. We swore a lot, talked disrespectfully and immorally about girls, and (as superstar athletes!) were full of ourselves. But one guy on the team was noticeably different. His name was Marc Davidson. Marc never swore on or off the court. He only talked and acted respectfully toward girls. He treated everyone on the team, even the water boy, with dignity and kindness. And he was humble, even though he was the best player on the team. In fact, he was voted the best player in the state of Illinois. Marc was a Christian. I knew this by the Bible he kept next to his dorm room bed and from the openness of his conversation, but also and most importantly by his godly behavior and good works. I became a Christian about a year and a half after tasting the salt and seeing the light of Marc Davidson. His behavior made it clear to me, as it settled during those months upon my conscience, what it meant to follow Jesus.

William Barclay once wrote, "A man's Christianity should be perfectly visible to all men."[13] Let me ask you, are you invisible? Are you a closet Christian?[14] If it were against the law to be a Christian, would you be arrested? And if so, if you were put on trial, would there be enough evidence to convict you? Do you do good works, not to bring praise to self, but to bring others to Christ and thereby glory to God?

Salvation or Persecution

One reaction to Christians being salt and light to the world is salvation. Another opposite reaction is persecution. This is what Jesus teaches in verses 11, 12 and also in the eighth beatitude in verse 10.

> Blessed are those who are persecuted for righteousness' sake, for theirs is the kingdom of heaven. Blessed are you when others revile you and persecute you and utter all kinds of evil against you falsely on my account. Rejoice and be glad, for your reward is great in heaven, for so they persecuted the prophets who were before you. (vv. 10–12)

Note the word "persecute" in verse 11 and the word "persecuted" in verses 10, 12. Christians will be persecuted. But persecuted for what? Is it for doing something evil or wrong (see 1 Peter 4:15)? No. Is it for being difficult, obnoxious, fanatical, overzealous, or foolish? No. How about for fighting for a cause, even a good one, a religious-political one? No. What about for just being good, noble, or self-sacrificing?[15] No, certainly not that. In fact, the world generally praises and esteems and even loves people like that—the Nelson Mandelas and Mother Theresas. In these verses the reason is clear: Christians are persecuted for *identifying with* Christ and *acting like* him, that is, they are persecuted "on . . . account" of him (v. 11) and "for righteousness' sake" (v. 10).

I know this is highly ironic. It is ironic that someone who embodies the Beatitudes (who is humble, meek, merciful, and a peacemaker) is persecuted. I know it's ironic, but it's also realistic. Read the end of Matthew's Gospel. Read the Book of Acts. Read every New Testament epistle. Read Revelation. Read the whole history of the church.

In the Upper Room Jesus said to his disciples,

> If you were of the world, the world would love you as its own; but because you are not of the world, but I chose you out of the world, therefore the world hates you. Remember the word that I said to you: "A servant is not greater than his master." If they persecuted me, they will also persecute you. (John 15:19, 20a)

The picture of a Christian as the gullible nice guy—as the good neighbor who always lends a helping hand but never offers any offense—is not the picture of a Christian presented in our Bibles. Jesus said, "Woe to you, when all people speak well of you" (Luke 6:26). Consider that statement. If everybody likes you, chances are you're not a Christian. Paul states this truth quite plainly: "Indeed, all who desire to live a godly life in Christ Jesus will be persecuted" (2 Timothy 3:12).

"Well," you might say, "this isn't true in America." I disagree. You couldn't be more wrong. I don't care how Christianized your culture is—if you live like Jesus and for Jesus and stand up for what Jesus taught, people aren't going to like it. They aren't going to like you any more than the runaway convict likes the prison watchtower light when it beams across his face.

Now certainly here in our country, as opposed to many other places in the world, no one is going to lock you up for your beliefs or physically torture you. Yet. But that is not even the emphasis here. Jesus says, "Blessed are you when others revile you . . . and utter all kinds of evil against you falsely." We've all heard, "Sticks and stones may break my bones, but words will never hurt me." Phooey! Nothing hurts as much as slander and gossip. Nothing hurts as much as your mother, father, sister, or brother wanting nothing to do with you because you now have everything to do with Jesus. Reviling is really a form of persecution. It is not as dramatic as a solider putting a pistol to your head, but it is real persecution nonetheless.

If you have never encountered persecution in your life due to your faith, then test and see if you really are of the faith. For whoever identifies with and acts like Jesus will be persecuted. We are not to seek it, but we are to expect it. "For it *has been granted* to you," Paul writes in Philippians 1:29, "that for the sake of Christ you should not only believe in him but also suffer for his sake." The verb emphasized above has God as its subject and Christians as the object!

Please don't fret or be anxious. Certainly don't be downcast. For in that same epistle, prisoner Paul writes about the theme of joy! While in chains, he commands Christians, "Rejoice in the Lord always" (Philippians 4:4). Where did Paul get these crazy ideas? He got them from Jesus in the Beatitudes. In 5:12 Jesus says, "Rejoice and be glad [when you are persecuted], for your reward is great in heaven, for so they persecuted the prophets who were before you."

It's natural to rejoice if someone comes to saving faith because they taste the salt and see the light and come to the Light. But it's supernatural to rejoice when our salt is spit out and our light snuffed out. But that's what we're called to do. Here's the imperative: "Rejoice."

But why rejoice in persecution? Our suffering Savior gives us two reasons: First, we can rejoice because this world is not our home, and it is not the place where we will be rewarded for righteousness. "Rejoice and be glad, for your reward is great *in heaven*" (5:12a), Jesus says. This brings us back to the principle of delayed gratification that we talked about in the last chapter. Second, we can rejoice because we know that we are in good company. How does Jesus put it? He ends this verse by saying, "for so they persecuted the prophets who were before you" (5:12b). Look forward to Heaven, but also look back to the prophets and note how they suffered.[16] Read about Daniel, Jeremiah, Ezekiel, Amos, or Zechariah. Read about the heroes of the faith listed in Hebrews 11, none of whom found reward in this life, and yet all of whom found meaning, hope, and even joy in the eternal promises of God. Suffering is like a seal of our salvation. That's why we can and should rejoice in it, rejoicing that we "were counted worthy to suffer dishonor for the name [of Jesus]" (Acts 5:41).

Unworldly for the World

Again, Lloyd-Jones said it well: "The glory of the gospel is that when the Church is absolutely different from the world, she invariably attracts it. It is then that the world is made to listen to her message, though it may hate it at first."

How do we win the world to Christ? We win the world by being different from it—by rejoicing in suffering because we live not for this world but for the one to come, by flavoring those godless, drab philosophies and moralities with the saltiness of the gospel, and by showing forth the oftentimes irresistible light of our lives, our good works that grow from the implanted word. We win the world by being unworldly.

12

"I Say to You," Part 1

MATTHEW 5:17–48

TAKE A PENCIL AND A BLANK NOTEBOOK. *Walk across to the campus and find a place to sit. Then for the next half hour just look around and write down everything you see.* That was the command given years ago to a group of ministry interns that included me. Our pastor-mentor wanted us to learn how to read the Bible better by first simply learning how to sit and see.

That short exercise in observation changed my life. As I observed the beautiful detail and design of the old limestone hall, the play and pursuits of wild squirrels (as well as the play and pursuits of college couples), and leaves softly falling to the ground while quietly bending the blades of grass on which they landed, I came to see how little I usually see and how much there is to be seen. Since that day, when it comes to sermon preparation I embrace what the Germans call *sitzfleisch* ("sitting flesh")—the ability to sit on my flesh for long periods of time in order to see what is so obvious, yet so often missed.

So as I sit with my pencil in hand and paper on lap and with my Bible opened to this text, one of the first things I see is the phrase Jesus used repeatedly, "I say to you." ("I [emphatic by initial position] say to you [plural].")[1] It first occurs in verse 18, "For truly, I say to you." Then it's in verse 20. The ESV translates it, "For I *tell* you," but in Greek it is the same as verse 18, "I say to you." We also find it in verses 22, 26, 28, 32, 34, 39 and 44. Nine times!

This is not only the most repeated phrase of our text, but it is also the key phrase because it embodies perfectly and succinctly its two main themes. The "I say" speaks of Jesus' authority and the "to you" of our ethics. Jesus' authority and our ethics will be what we look at now as we explore what all these "I say to you" statements say to us.

I Say

First, we have Jesus' authority. Look at verses 17–19:

> Do not think that I have come to abolish the Law or the Prophets; I have not come to abolish them but to fulfill them. For truly, I say to you, until heaven and earth pass away, not an iota, not a dot, will pass from the Law until all is accomplished. Therefore whoever relaxes one of the least of these commandments and teaches others to do the same will be called least in the kingdom of heaven, but whoever does them and teaches them will be called great in the kingdom of heaven.

What is Jesus saying here? First notice the first three words—"do not think." This tells us that there must have been people, perhaps "the scribes and Pharisees" mentioned in verse 20, who thought and perhaps taught that Jesus—this new, self-appointed rabbi—doesn't uphold the Law and the Prophets.

Here Jesus sets the record straight. He pledges his "full and unswerving loyalty to the law" (cf. Romans 3:31).[2] He is pro-Old Testament. In fact, to Jesus the smallest letter (i.e., the Hebrew letter *yod*) and the least stroke of a pen (i.e., a *horn*—the ornamental marks customarily added to certain Hebrew letters) matter to Jesus. None of what Jesus is saying and doing is abolishing any word, letter, or mark that has been written. He is not relaxing or teaching anyone to relax any of God's commands. Rather, he is living out and teaching others to live out those very rules. And while he has been or will be dining with sinners, talking with women,[3] healing on the Sabbath, and even overturning the greedy and racist moneychangers' tables in the temple, none of those things are aberrations of God's Word, as the scribes and Pharisees think. Instead those actions accord with the Law's highest principles.

So here in verses 17–19 Jesus teaches: "I am not against the Bible. I am absolutely for it!" But that's not all he says. He also adds, "And the Bible is for me." Look again at verse 17. Here we should all fall to the ground like the soldiers who arrested Jesus did. Our Lord said, "Do not think that I have come to abolish the Law or the Prophets; I have not come to abolish them *but to fulfill them*."

It would have been bold if Jesus said, "I have come to adhere perfectly, as no man has ever done, to the Law," or if he said, "I have come to give the best and final authoritative teaching on the Law." Both of those would have been enough for the religious crowd first to scratch their heads and then to rend their garments. But to say what Jesus actually said will get one crucified.

Now we should acknowledge and appreciate that Matthew has done his best to prepare us for 5:17. The language in chapters 1—4 is full of fulfillment. Various things were done "to fulfil" what was written in the Law or the Prophets. Yet, try as he did, there is really nothing that can dull the pointed edge of this pronouncement.

Who does Jesus think he is? It is one thing to claim, as he does in verse 18, that the Law will pass away once "all is accomplished," but it's quite another thing to say, as he does here in verse 17, "I have . . . come . . . to *fulfill* them." Jesus is saying, "All the promises of God—like my passion and death, the engrafting of the Gentiles, etc.—find their yes," to borrow from Paul's language, "in me" (cf. 2 Corinthians 1:20). What a stupendous claim![4] For Jesus to claim to be the inerrant expositor of the Word who has come to tell everyone what the Law really teaches is one highly controversial claim. But to also claim to be the absolute embodiment of God's greatest promises is more than a bit blasphemous if it's not true.

One of the most fascinating and ironically faith-building books I have ever read was Jacob Neusner's *A Rabbi Talks with Jesus*. Neusner is a Jewish rabbi, one of the world's preeminent authorities on Judaism in the first centuries of the Christian era, and a prolific writer. Prolific is an understatement, as he has authored or edited more than 950 books. Now that's *sitzfleisch!*

In *A Rabbi Talks with Jesus* Neusner pretends to have an intermillennial, interfaith exchange with Jesus. He writes of his honest and open debate with Jesus over some of our Lord's claims and teachings. The book begins,

> Imagine walking on a dusty road in Galilee some summer, meeting up with a small band of youngsters, led by a young man. The man's presence catches your attention: he talks, the others listen, respond, argue, obey—care what he says, follow him. You don't know who the man is, but you do know he makes a difference to the people with him and to nearly everybody he meets. People respond, some with anger, some with admiration, a few with genuine faith. But no one walks away uninterested in the man and the things he says and does.[5]

The dialogue between Neusner and Jesus starts after Jesus delivers the Sermon on the Mount. After hearing what Jesus taught, Neusner notes how he would have responded just as the original crowd did, with astonishment. "Here is a Torah-teacher," the rabbi says, "who says in his own name what the Torah says in God's name." He notes how the prophets and sages, how Moses, for example, never said, "I say to you," but rather "the LORD says to you." "At Sinai, God spoke through Moses. On this Galilean hill, Jesus speaks for himself." The rabbi is taken aback by this teacher who stands seemingly above the Torah. And it is here, at their first encounter, that Neusner admits that it is not Jesus' teachings so much as the figure of Jesus "that is at issue." He says, "I am troubled not so much by the message, though I might take exception to this or that, as I am by the messenger."[6]

When you clear away all the clichés and platitudes that have developed like ten-inch plaque on the teeth of Jesus' teachings, and when you listen as this rabbi did, with fresh and unclogged ears, there is really only one of two conclusions to make. If Jesus claims to be the Lord of the Law—to transcend the Torah without violating even the tiniest word and the smallest ethic, to be the final, authoritative, and infallible interpreter of God's Word, *and* to personify its promises—he is either right or wrong. We cannot remain neutral before him.

If we think he is wrong, then we openly reject him, as Neusner does with refreshing honesty. "I would follow the Pharisees," he writes in one of his final chapters, "and I do that even now."[7] But if we think Jesus is right about himself, then we come not to some ingenious Torah teacher but to God himself, and there is no difference between the voice of God on Mount Sinai and the words of this Man on this Mount. There is no difference between "Thus says the LORD" and "I say to you."

To You

I say. This first point is foundational. If Jesus is not the Son of God, why listen to what he has to say *to us* in verse 20ff.? Why listen to his kingdom ethics about anger, adultery, or anything else? Who is he to tell me how to live or not live my life? If he didn't make this world, why in the world would I listen to what he has to say about the world and my relation to others in it? Wouldn't it be better if I just did what most people do today—look within my black heart and let it color my convictions, or perhaps just reach out into that "free-floating morality"[8] that hangs with airy intangibility above us, grabbing what I think is good and bad, taking advice from this guru and that bartender?

You can look within, you can look without, or you can look to Jesus. If he is indeed God's beloved Son, then we should do as the Father instructed the disciples to do on the Mount of Transfiguration—we should "listen to him" (17:5). We should listen to what he says to be right and wrong, holy and unholy, righteous and unrighteous.

Therefore, turn with me toward him as we turn now to his words recorded in verses 20–48. We'll look at this passage again in the next chapter, where I'll do another whole sermon on those "to you" verses. For now, however, I want us simply to see the forest before we climb the trees. To do this, we'll focus just on the first and final verses—verses 20 and 48.

In verse 20 Jesus gives his "thesis statement" for all that follows in the Sermon on the Mount:[9] "For I say to you [literal translation], unless your righteousness exceeds that of the scribes and Pharisees, you will never enter the kingdom of heaven." Then in verse 48 he ends this section by saying, "You therefore must be perfect, as your heavenly Father is perfect."

I know these verses are a bit tricky, but not as tricky as you might think. The basic message of verses 20–48 is: don't act like the scribes and Pharisees, but instead act like God.

Perfect Love

I'll explain the last part first. When Jesus says, "be perfect, as your heavenly Father is perfect" (v. 48), what is the perfection about which Jesus is talking? Is it some kind of absolute moral perfection, as the medieval monks were fond of teaching? They thought the Sermon on the Mount was only for the super-spiritual and that only a few (namely themselves) ever climbed these stairs to perfection.[10] However, this is the absolute opposite of what Jesus is talking about. If that notion is in your head (monastic spirituality has become quite popular today), put it under your foot like a cigarette butt and crush it into the ground. For in context the meaning of the word "perfect" is perfectly clear. In verses 43–47 Jesus teaches how God the Father shows indiscriminate love by making the sun rise and the rain fall on both the good and the bad. He doesn't hide the sun from immoral people. He doesn't fail to water the fields of the wicked. In the same way, Jesus says, we are to love all people—our brothers (those who love us) and even our enemies (those who don't love us). That is perfect love.[11]

Think of it like a triangle. We are to love God. This is the greatest commandment and the tip of the triangle. But we are also to love our neighbors, the nice ones. They are, let's say, the right point of the triangle. But if we stop there, it is imperfect love. We must also love those at the left point of the triangle, who we'd naturally like to leave for the lions.

Everybody, the worst of people, love their own. You won't find an Italian mobster who doesn't love the family or a brutal inner-city gangbanger who won't take a bullet for his grandmother. But what kind of love is that? It is lopsided love. It's a one-pointed triangle! We are to love with perfect, complete, or whole love, as the Father daily demonstrates, and as the Father most fully demonstrated in the cross of Christ. ". . . while we were *enemies* we were reconciled to God by the death of his Son" (Romans 5:10). That's perfect love. That's the love we are to emulate. It's the love of God the Father for us in Christ.

If you are born of God, you are to act like God in his perfect love—loving even the unlovely. Of course, love is not what gets you into the kingdom, but love is what you will show if you are already part of it. John's epistles make this clear. For example, in 2 John 5 the apostle says that we are to "love *one another*," and then he continues in verse 6, saying, "And this is love, that we walk according to *his commandments*." That is precisely what Jesus teaches here in verses 20–48. We are to love others. How? We love by obeying Christ's commandments, which relate to ethics and affect others—for example, the commands that prohibit murder, adultery, divorce, perjury, and retaliation.

Have you ever wondered why Jesus selected these Old Testament commands out of the hundreds he could have selected on which to comment? It is because of what binds them all together—love toward others! These are all relational commands. If you murder someone, it is obviously unloving, but so too is having a sexual relationship outside of marriage, getting a quick and easy divorce, making false oaths, or wronging someone every time he or she wrongs you. Kingdom righteousness puts on love, which "covers a multitude of sins" (1 Peter 4:8).

The love of others—that is the Law and the Prophets (7:12),[12] and that is kingdom righteousness.

Unrighteous "Righteousness"

In verse 48 Jesus teaches that we are to have God-emulating, perfect love. We are to act like God. In verse 20, the other crucial verse, Jesus gives the counter-example. We are *not* to act like the scribes and Pharisees with their unrighteous "righteousness."

As I said earlier, Jesus' audience would have been astonished by his claim in verse 17. While the astonishment may have subsided slightly during verses 18, 19, verse 20 would have brought it right back again: "[U]nless your righteousness exceeds that of the scribes and Pharisees, you will never enter the kingdom of heaven." The closest equivalent today would be for the average Roman Catholic to hear the divine pronouncement, "Unless you are holier than His Holiness [a common title for the Pope], you're not getting into Heaven!" For you see, the scribes and the Pharisees were the super-spiritual in Jesus' day. They were the ethically elite. The scribes were the Bible experts. They devoted their whole lives to reading, studying, and teaching the Bible. And the Pharisees, a word meaning "separatists," were known for being separate from the common Jew. They not only knew God's Law and sought to obey it, but they went overboard in obedience to it. For example, if the Law decreed to fast once a year, they fasted twice a week, or if the Law commanded resting on the Sabbath, they excluded every kind of work on Saturday.

Thus, the average Jew in Jesus' day couldn't imagine being more "righteous" than these two characters. However, what Jesus is teaching here is not that one needs to be more spiritually stringent or that one needs to improve their Bible IQ. Instead what Jesus says is that one's righteousness needs to be, in fact, quite the opposite of these pretentious pretenders.

What Jesus will do in verses 21–48, the rest of the Sermon on the Mount, and throughout much of the Gospel of Matthew, especially with the woes in chapter 23, is call their bluff. He will expose their unethical ethics. He will display *their* disloyalty to the Law. He will lovingly hate their hypocrisy. He will denounce their "righteousness" as unrighteous.

First, what is unrighteous about their righteousness is their adherence to the letter rather than the spirit of the Law. The letter of the Law is "don't take a knife and stab somebody to death." The spirit of the Law is "don't even lose your cool and then curse someone out." The letter of the Law is "don't sleep with someone who is not your spouse." The spirit of the Law is "keep from lusting." They loved the letter of the Law (which is so much easier to keep) but not the spirit. But obedience to the letter and the spirit of the Law is true fulfillment of it, and that Law, as Paul and James will put it, and as Jesus puts it here, is the law of loving others (see Romans 13:8–10; Galatians 5:14; James 2:8).

Second, what was unrighteous about their righteousness was that they "neglected the weightier matters of the law" and focused on the nitpicky (23:23b). For example, they would teach (and I'll modernize their thought), "If you're going to make a proper oath, make sure you have a black leather King James Bible to put your hand on; otherwise the oath doesn't count." To this Jesus says, "If you're going to tell the whole truth and nothing but the truth, there is no need to place your hand on any Bible; just say whatever you're going to say."

I don't think it mattered (and few people who live in Illinois as I do would think it mattered) if former (now convicted to fourteen years in jail) Governor Rod Blagojevich "swears to God" or not in his official testimony. It shouldn't matter if you are talking to a late-night talk show host or a Chief Justice of the United States Supreme Court. Your yes should be yes and your no no.

The Pharisees loved the nitpicky, but they neglected what was the obvious *loving* thing to do. The Law allows you to divorce your wife for certain reasons, but why not forgive her and have compassion on her instead? The

Law says there is proper retribution, but why not let mercy forgive that debt, why not turn the other cheek or go the extra mile?

In their neglect of the spirit of the Law and the weightier matters of the Law, the scribes and Pharisees' "righteousness" was unrighteous.

My brothers and sisters, we are to act like God, showing perfect love (even to those who have wronged us) and not be like the scribes and Pharisees with their unrighteous "righteousness" (taking this law of love and squeezing "the love of others" out of it).

Jesus before the High Priest

In the famous seventeenth-century painting *Christ before the High Priest,* our Lord is depicted standing on trial with his hands bound before the high priest, Caiaphas. A Bible is opened before Caiaphas. He looks up at Jesus angrily and accusingly, leaning on the Bible and pointing his finger at him. There is a candle on the table, yet interestingly (if I've understood the shading correctly) the light on Jesus is somehow brighter than the glow that falls on the pages of the Bible, and in fact it is somehow brighter than the candle flame itself.

The artist, Gerrit van Honthorst, has perfectly captured the irony of the situation. Jesus, who has come to fulfill what is in that Bible, is on trial for disregarding its teachings. And Jesus, who alone is the Light of *the Word*, and who alone has lived out the ethics of the Law (perfect love!), is being judged a criminal. But such is the story, isn't it—the true and marvelous story of the gospel of our Lord Jesus Christ. He is Lord over the Law, and his law is love.

13

"I Say *to You*," Part 2

MATTHEW 5:21–48

IN THE LAST CHAPTER I mentioned Jacob Neusner's fascinating book, *A Rabbi Talks with Jesus*. To me the most fascinating section of that book is when Neusner is pretending to explain Jesus and his teachings to one of the great rabbis of the Jewish faith. In order to instruct but also understand Jesus, this master rabbi turns to *Makkot* 24A-B of the Babylonian Talmud, which provides various summaries of the Torah.

> Rabbi Simelai expounded, "Six hundred and thirteen commandments were given to Moses. . . . David came and reduced them to eleven [Psalm 15]. . . . Isaiah came and reduced them to six [Isaiah 33:25–26]. . . . Micah came and reduced them to three [Micah 6:8]. . . . Isaiah again came and reduced them to two [Isaiah 56:1]. . . . Amos came and reduced them to one, as it is said, 'For thus says the Lord to the house of Israel. Seek Me and live' [Amos 5:4]. Habakkuk further came and based them on one, as it is said, 'But the righteous shall live by his faith' (Hab 2:4)."

After the master rabbi completes this quotation, he turns to Neusner and says, "So, is this what the sage, Jesus, had to say?" Neusner replies, "Not exactly, but close." "What did he leave out?" asks the rabbi. "Nothing," says Neusner. "Then what did he add?" "Himself," admits Neusner.[1]

That's right! Jesus didn't remove anything from God's Law, and he didn't add anything to it—except himself. "Come follow me," Jesus will say again and again to all who want entrance into God's kingdom. "All authority in heaven and on earth has been given to me," he will announce to his apostles as he commissions them to teach all nations "to observe all" that he has commanded (28:18, 19). Jesus holds to the Law in its fullness. It is what he adds—namely himself—that changes everything. Because of this addition, like most of the scribes and Pharisees in the Gospels, Neusner rejects him. But it is also because of this addition (or what we would call "fulfillment") that you and I receive him, as the Apostle Thomas did, as our Lord and our God (John 20:28).

In the last chapter, as we looked at 5:17–48, I showed you how the phrase "I say to you" was the key phrase of that text. This is not only because it is repeated nine times, but also because it nicely summarizes the two main themes of this section—divine authority ("I say") and kingdom ethics ("to you"). If Jesus is the King, what is to be our kingdom behavior?

In the last chapter we touched on this second theme as we looked at verses 20 and 48. I shared how we are *not* to act like the Pharisees with their unrighteous "righteousness," but rather to act like God in his perfect love—loving others, even our enemies. I also shared how the six Old Testament commands on murder, adultery, divorce, vows, retaliation, and love of neighbor, as interpreted and applied by Jesus, put on this perfect love.

Now we come to Part Two, "to you." As we focus on verses 21–48, we will give two answers to the question, why these six? Besides using them as illustrations of this theme of perfect love, of the 613 commands in the Torah why did Jesus choose to teach on these six?

The First Reason

The first reason is to *expose the unlawfulness of the scribes' and Pharisees' interpretation of the Law*. Six of those nine "I say to you" statements are antithetical. Look, for example, at the beginnings of verses 21 and 22: "You have heard that it was said to those of old . . ." (v. 21); "But I say to you . . ." (v. 22). Note that these antitheses do not start, "It is written" (cf. 2:5; 4:4, 7, 10). Neither do they start with "what the Lord had spoken by the prophet" (cf. 1:22; 2:15, 17, 23; 3:3). Here the stress is not on reading what is written but rather on hearing what has been said: "You have heard that it was said" (cf. v. 31, "It was also said"). Jesus speaks this way because he is addressing their oral traditions, those man-made *additions to* or *subtractions from* the Word of God. Remember that he has just told us in verses 17–19 that he did not come to abolish the Law, not even the smallest letters of it. Nor did he come to relax any of its commands or to condone anyone who does. However, in verse 20 he does tell us in a sense that he has come to abolish something. He has come to abolish the unrighteous traditions of the self-righteous scribes and Pharisees—to show that their take on the Law is lawless and thus antithetical to kingdom entrance.

When I was first learning how to read, study, and teach the Bible, one of the lessons I learned from Dick Lucas, former rector of St. Helen's Church in

London, is something he calls *the line of Scripture*. Lucas taught that we are to hold to the line of Scripture, which means that we are not to go below the line (that is, subtract from Scripture) because this leads to liberalism, nor are we to go above the line (that is, add to Scripture) because this leads to legalism. So, for example, to teach that Jesus did not rise bodily from the dead, but he has arisen spiritually in the hearts of those who believe in him—that's liberalism. That's not what the Gospel texts teach. Or to teach that since Jesus rose from the dead on Sunday (i.e., the Christian Sabbath), we should "celebrate" the reality of the resurrection by being dour all day—no dancing, playing cards, or smiles on Sunday—that's legalism. It is adding to what those Gospel texts teach.

All of us, even the best Christians, are prone to these errors—of going above or below the line of Scripture. I remember the story of the great American evangelist Peter Cartwright. Cartwright is known for losing the U. S. Congress seat to Abraham Lincoln, but is better known for being a Methodist circuit rider. A circuit rider rode a horse from town to town throughout the Wild West—then Tennessee and Kentucky—preaching the gospel. Cartwright was a very rugged man, as one had to be in order to do this job. And for who he was and what he did—he baptized 12,000 people—I honestly admire him.

Yet he had his flaws. As the story goes, one day after he preached, a man came up to him and, to test the sincerity of Cartwright's Christianity, struck him on the right cheek and then again on the left. Through both blows Cartwright stood his ground. He did not retaliate. Yet when the man struck him a third time, this strong evangelist landed a nice upper cut on that chap's face. And as he did so he said, "My Lord said nothing about a third slap." As deserving as the punch may have been, that is getting off the line of Scripture! Or it is at least an example of misapplying the spirit of the text.

Well, the scribes and Pharisees were masters of manipulating the Bible like that. Much of Jesus' conflict with them was due to their legalism—e.g., make sure you don't carry that load of laundry on Saturday, or make sure you twist that sacred curl of your hair from right to left and not left to right. Here, however, his conflict is with their liberalism.

Look first at verse 21. Here we have the sixth commandment from the Ten Commandments: "You shall not murder" (Exodus 20:13). To this they added, "And whoever murders will be liable to judgment." What's wrong with that? That sounds good. It even sounds like what is written in Numbers 35:30, 31. What's wrong with it is that the "judgment" referenced here is only the judgment of the civil courts[2] (not a judgment from God), *and* as such it is a judgment only based on what man can see.

Thus, in his initial correction of their liberalism in verse 22, Jesus says that there are fuller implications to the sixth commandment. He teaches that we should worry about the civil court and their judgment for murder, but we should also concern ourselves with God, who looks deep within our hearts and sees all its secret intentions (Romans 2:16). We should concern ourselves with him and his X-ray vision and his *eternal* judgment ("the hell of fire"). The root of the crime of murder is in the human heart, yet physical murder is not the only bad fruit of that heart—our tongues can kill as well as our hands! Saying what we ought not to say and doing what we ought not to do are both damnable offenses, not always in the civil courts but certainly in the Final Court—for we will all stand before God's throne of judgment and give an account for every deed and every *word* (Matthew 12:36).

Jesus continues his correction in verses 23–26. Here he takes the negative command—"You shall not murder"—and he gives it a positive thrust. He basically says:

> Don't you dare come to worship God—to bring your sacrifice of thanksgiving to the altar in the temple—and yet hold hatred in your heart toward your brother. If you can't forgive your brother (i.e., fellow believer), don't think God will forgive you [see 6:15]. Those who are friends with God are friendly with others. Those truly reconciled to God are reconciled to others.

You see, the Pharisees loved to live below the line of Scripture. What can I get away with? What are the minimum requirements of the Law?

Sometimes pastors are asked by engaged couples who are trying hard to remain sexually pure before marriage, "How far is too far?" That is a normal question, but it is also a pharisaical one. The sentiment is, how close can I get to breaking God's Word without technically breaking it? We are all prone to think this way. But who naturally asks what Jesus is encouraging us to ask: "How far can I extend the commands of God? How can I expand a negative command to every imaginable positive application?"

This is in fact what we see in verses 27–32 on the commands about adultery and divorce.

In "the good old days" of the first century there wasn't much *good* about the popular divorce proceedings. In Greco-Roman circles divorce required no formal or legal procedure. A man (and it was usually the man) could just write a certificate of divorce, or he could just say to his wife, "Hey, honey, you're not my 'honey' anymore." And that was it. Divorce was more common then than it is now in America. In Jewish circles there was certainly a higher view of marriage due to God's Law concerning adultery and divorce. According to

Deuteronomy 24:1, divorce was only permissible if a man found "some indecency" in his wife. That phrase "some indecency," which is clearly defined in the text's context, became a blanket statement that covered up a husband's unlawfulness.

Here is what happened. Some of the religiously elite made this "some indecency" clause as wide as the ocean. According to the Mishnah, a record of these oral traditions that Jesus is combating, a man could divorce his wife if she burned his toast. I'm not kidding. It is laughable to us. But it was no laughing matter to Jesus or to the thousands of poor women such divorce laws crushed.

What the so-called "righteous" in Jesus' day would do was get married, then for some small reason find a legal way to have many sex partners. How? Divorce and remarriage! Divorce and remarriage! Divorce and remarriage!

This still happens today, doesn't it? The Roman Catholics call it an annulment. We Protestants need to find a clever term like that to save our spiritual skin. Oh, these scribes and Pharisees would turn their noses down upon the pagan for his sexual liaisons, but their behavior was much the same—legally pure (only sex within marriage), yet sexually impure (with eight different wives).

Our Lord will have none of this liberal but anti-liberating interpretation. "No easy divorces," he says. What is written in Deuteronomy was not intended to "facilitate divorce but to restrict it."[3] Divorce destroys the original intent of marriage—it separates what God, in his providence and for his purposes, "has joined together" (see 19:6). It divides families, leaves women and children at risk, and can cut the core out of a culture or country.

Adultery is the one reason given here for divorce. This is because that sin alone breaks the covenant bond. Sex in marriage is like superglue. It binds a couple together. It makes two one—physically and metaphysically! But if that bond is severed, it is so difficult to re-glue these two pieces. Yet, by God's grace it can be done and in most cases should be done (God models this in the Prophets; see especially Jeremiah 3).

This is one reason why, I think, before Jesus speaks about divorce and a wife's adultery, he speaks *to the men* about their adultery—the private parties they throw with their eyes and their minds. "Listen, guys," Jesus essentially says in verse 28, "before you throw your wife out on the street and marry another, take a good look at your own eyes. See if you might first find . . . oh I don't know . . . a gigantic log! For if you so as much look at a woman with lust in your heart you are guilty of adultery." Jesus turns the tables on the men of his culture, the men of all cultures! *He* who is without sin, let *him* cast the first stone (John 8:7).

From there Jesus moves on to the sin of breaking oaths. The Old Testament Law is not opposed to vows or oaths per se (Numbers 30:2; Deuteronomy 23:21–23). But what the scribes and Pharisees did with the Numbers and Deuteronomy texts was devise a number of "escape clauses from binding oaths."[4] If you made an oath by Jerusalem or Heaven and earth or even the hairs on your head, you could break that commitment. It was only if you said, "I swear to God" that the oath was binding.

Joe: Hey, you promised to pay me by Tuesday.
John: Now, wait a minute, pal. I never said, "I swear to God." I only said, "Cross my heart and hope to die."

Ah, such trickery with the Torah![5] Are you starting to see how, with a hammer in hand, Jesus is chiseling away the scribes' and Pharisees' spiritual façade, exposing their outward lawfulness as inward lawlessness?

Next we come to verses 38–42, his second to last hit. Here our Lord is dealing with the famous law from Exodus 21:24 (cf. Leviticus 24:20; Deuteronomy 19:21), "an eye for an eye and a tooth for a tooth."

What the religious scholars did with this command, which was designed not for private revenge but legal justice and "not to justify retaliation but to limit it,"[6] was twist it to say (I paraphrase), "Hey, if you toucha me, I breaka your face." They twisted God's Word so as to condone the unloving attitude and action of "I'm gettin' even."

Jesus will untwist their twisting and teach that Exodus 21:24 is a righteous law that is for the protective good of the individual and community alike. Imagine a world where the government doesn't punish people for crimes. What an awful world that would be. But also imagine a world where there was no personal retaliation. Imagine that. It's not easy if you try. Imagine the day when a slap on the cheek doesn't lead to a lawsuit, fistfight, or war. Imagine a world in which God's will is done on earth as it is in Heaven, where selflessly walking the extra mile and giving to those in need are practices as common as raindrops in Ireland. Such is and *will be* the kingdom of God.

Finally, we come to the sixth antithesis (say that phrase six times), verses 43–48. The command to love one's neighbor comes from Leviticus 19:18. The addition "and hate your enemy" comes from (let me see . . .) nowhere in the Bible.[7] But it does come, quite naturally, from the human heart. There is nothing as natural, easy, and *sinful* as only loving those who love us and hating those who don't. Yet perfect love, the kind of love to which Christ is calling us, loves like God the Father does daily. In his gracious provision for daily needs,

God loves indiscriminately both the good and the evil, both those who love him and those who don't. That is the kind of love we are to show to all, and that is the kind of love that runs like a river through these twenty-eight verses.

So do you see, with these six antitheses, how Jesus shows the Pharisaic interpretation of the Law to be utterly unlawful? With some subtractions and additions, they went below the line of Scripture. They were liberal in the worst sense of the word. I'm a liberal. I love freedom (that's what the word means), the freedom that comes from obedience to the gospel and walking in the way of the Spirit. They were liberals who used their freedom for lawless living, all under the guise of perfect adherence to God's Law.

The Second Reason

The second reason Jesus chose to comment on these six particular Old Testament commands was to allow the richness of God's Word to make us—what's the first beatitude?—"poor in spirit," or, I'll put it this way, *to allow the holy heaviness of the Law to make us wholly humble before God.*

What do I mean by this? Well, picture a clean-cut kid. He's eighteen, gets good grades, obeys his parents, loves his brothers and sisters, and visits Grandma from time to time. He doesn't party, doesn't stay out too late, doesn't fool around with girls, *and* he goes to church each week and even prays each night before he goes to bed. This is a good kid. This is the boy most parents want their daughter to bring home someday.

With his handling of the Law, Jesus tells this good kid to sit down and hold out his hands. Then our Lord proceeds to place this heavy command and that heavy command upon this young man (YM).

Jesus: Have you ever murdered somebody?

YM: No, sir, of course not.

Jesus: What I mean is, have you ever lost your temper? Have you ever let a careless, biting, hurtful word fly from your mouth—like "You blockhead" or "You foolish idiot"?

YM: Yes, sir.

Jesus: Alright, here's a 200-pound weight. Hold that in your right hand. Are you ready for the next question? Here it is. Have you ever committed adultery?

YM: No, sir. I'm not even married.

Jesus: Oh no, no, my question for you has nothing to do with marriage. Let me put it this way—have you ever thought any impure thoughts about any girl?

YM: Yes, sir, of course, sir.

Jesus: Ah, I thought so. Well, here you go—another 200-pound weight. Put this in your left hand.

At this point Jesus looks at this poor soul and, noticing his discomfort, says, "Shall I go on?" The young man answers, "No, sir, please stop. I get the point." Jesus replies, "But I haven't gotten to the 500-pound question, the one I planned to place on your head. Don't you want to hear my 'perfect love' question? Have you loved everybody, even your enemies, at all times?" "No, sir. I'm done, sir. I get the point."

He gets the point. Do you get the point? What's the point? The point is that we have a very inadequate anthropology and thus *theo*logy. We don't feel the weight of God's glory, the heaviness of his holiness. One of our favorite questions gives the game away. We love to ask, "How could a good and loving God send anyone to Hell?" Why doesn't anyone ask, "How can a good and holy God bring anyone to Heaven?" Or "How can an absolutely good, pure, sinless, utterly transcendent God redeem rebels, save sinners, take 'worm[s]' like us (as Isaiah calls Judah in Isaiah 41:14), and metamorphose us into worshippers?" Who asks questions like those these days? Or who even asks the psalmist's question, "[W]hat is man that you are mindful of him?" (Psalm 8:4).

Recall the time in the Gospels when that rich young ruler (that clean-cut kid) came up to Jesus and said, "Good Teacher, what must I do to inherit eternal life?" Before our Lord went to God's Law—to some of these very commands here in Matthew—what did he do first? He said, "Why do you call me good? No one is good except God alone" (Mark 10:17, 18).[8] Only God is good. We don't really think that. We're fine with "God is good." We just don't like the adverb "only." *Only* God is perfectly good.

Here in Matthew 5 Jesus explains the full and rich implications of God's perfect Law so that we might embrace poverty of spirit—recognizing our unrighteousness and thus our need for God's perfect righteousness. We must know that the road to Heaven is not paved with good intentions, good works, or even keeping the works of the Law (as if that could be done), but it has been paved already by the Man of Sorrows, who bled for our sins, carried the cross of our condemnation, and died so we might live. Draw a straight line from these *commands* to the *cross*, from 5:21–48 to 27:50—"And Jesus cried out again with a loud voice and yielded up his spirit."

I'm not saying that kingdom ethics here are not important for those who already believe in Jesus. What I am saying is that such ethics are significant for those who don't believe but should. Sure, what we have here teaches us something about what John Owen called "the mortification of sin" and what Calvin called "the third use of the Law." For those who believe, the Law is our guide, showing us the way to please God. That is here. Jesus speaks of true worship in verses 23, 24—you can't worship God unless you love and forgive others. He speaks of doing battle with our flesh in verses 29, 30—he calls (interestingly) for external actions to deal with internal issues. We are to cut out an eye and cut off a hand—even what is most precious and seemingly necessary—for the sake of our souls. That is all here, the third use of the Law indeed. But more than that and beneath that is *the first use of the Law*—the Law as our schoolmaster or guardian, to use Paul's terminology in Galatians 3:24. The Law guides us to a true understanding of ourselves so that we might recognize the depth of our sin and the love that God offers to sinners in the person of our Savior, Jesus Christ. The holy heaviness of the Law ought to make us wholly humble before God.

14

God-Rewarded Righteousness

MATTHEW 6:1–18

SADDAM HUSSEIN was a very religious man, or so it seems. During his twenty-four years of dictatorship in Iraq, he brought about many religious "advances." He built, for example, the largest mosque in the region, which supposedly contained a copy of the Quran written in his own blood. During his reign, he also added an inscription in his own hand on the Iraqi flag: *Allahu Akbar* ("God is Great").

Shortly after Saddam's death the British journalist Christopher Hitchens wrote a book using this Iraqi motto sarcastically for his title: *god Is Not Great*. In that book, which is critical of both Christianity and Islam, Hitchens argues *How Religion Poisons Everything*, as his less than subtle subtitle says. His hatred for religion comes from his intellectual convictions (he is an atheist, Darwinist, and materialist) but also from his experience as a journalist in which he saw firsthand so much religious hypocrisy.

For example, he writes about his visit to Iran, which like Iraq is an Islamic nation and thus stringently upholds the teachings of the Quran. Therefore, premarital intercourse and prostitution are outlawed. However, what happens is that the mullahs (the Islamic religious leaders) profit monetarily by licensing something they call "temporary marriages." That is, a man comes to the mullah, often in a specially designated house, and receives a temporary marriage license to be the temporary husband of a girl he has never met. Then he can have a temporary union with her and just a few minutes later conveniently and lawfully receive a permanent divorce declaration. Some might call this legalized prostitution. Hitchens writes about how he was offered "such a bargain," of all places, outside the shrine to the Ayatollah Khomeini in south Tehran.[1]

As we have been learning from the Sermon on the Mount, our Lord Jesus Christ is just as hard on hypocrisy, though with a different result. He obviously doesn't think hypocrisy negates holiness or that disingenuous religion nullifies true religion. But he does think that *man-made* religion indeed poisons everything.

As we studied the second half of Matthew 5, we saw him point out such poisoning when he spoke of those who held to the letter of the Law but neglected its spirit. In our current text Jesus is still on the attack. He warns us, "Beware of practicing your righteousness before other people in order to be seen by them" (v. 1).

In 5:20–48 Jesus taught us about *right righteousness*, a righteousness that is not like the scribes' and Pharisees', but a righteousness that puts on love—love for others—as its chief and foundational ethic. Moreover, in 5:14–16 he taught how this righteousness ought to make a difference in the world. People ought to see our good works. However, here in 6:1–18 he warns that this light that others will notice needs to point in the right direction—not to ourselves but to our Father in Heaven (cf. 5:16b).

Therefore, here in our text Jesus is going to talk about motives. He is going to test us to make sure our natural disposition is not overruling our supernatural one. It is natural to hide our righteousness when we should show it and to show it when we should hide it.[2] It is natural to do good in order to be seen and praised by others. But Jesus says that we shouldn't practice our piety in order to been seen and rewarded by *people*, but rather to be seen and rewarded by *God* (cf. John 12:43).

House of Holiness

Before we look at almsgiving, prayer, and fasting, I want us first to see the importance of *God's sight* and *God's rewards* and how these two realities should be part of our motives for holy living.

First, we have *God's sight*. Hebrews 4:13 says, "And no creature is hidden from his sight, but all are naked and exposed to the eyes of him to whom we must give account." In Psalm 139:7, 8 David writes, "Where shall I go from your Spirit? Or where shall I flee from your presence? If I ascend to heaven, you are there! If I make my bed in Sheol, you are there!"

Sometimes in a counseling situation, I might ask a man who is struggling with a particular sin, "Would you do such a thing if your wife was present?" He answers, "Oh no, of course not." I follow up, "How about if your boss was around?" Again he replies, "Oh no, certainly not." I conclude, "Well then, why do you do this thing when you know that God is always present?"

God is always present! He knows all and sees all. Martyn Lloyd-Jones speaks of this reality as being "a fundamental principle for the whole of our life." He writes,

> I sometimes feel that there is no better way of living, and trying to live, the holy and sanctified life than just to be constantly reminding ourselves of that. When we wake up in the morning we should immediately remind ourselves and recollect that we are in the presence of God. It is not a bad thing to say to ourselves before we go any further: 'Throughout the whole of this day, everything I do, and say, and attempt, and think, and imagine, is going to be done under the eye of God. He is going to be with me; he sees everything; he knows everything. There is nothing I can do or attempt but God is fully aware of it all. "Thou God seest me."' It would revolutionize our lives if we always did that.[3]

Our holiness is not so much waiting for God to do a work in us, although it can be that. Rather, it is recognizing that he is present even now and that his presence is power when it comes to our fight against sin, the flesh, and the Devil. I'll put it this way: we will only be as sanctified as we are aware of God's ever-seeing sight.

If you think of our holiness as a house—let's call it our House of Holiness—this concept of God's sight is like the roof. It is always over us, and without it we are in serious trouble. The house is thus left unprotected and easy to destroy, both from internal as well as external forces.

However, the foundation to this House of Holiness, at least in this text, is very different than what we may have expected. As we go down to the basement and look at what holds this house up, we first see the cornerstone, and engraved in that stone is JESUS CHRIST AND HIS RIGHTEOUSNESS. Then we find in the rest of the foundation's stone walls what look like little safes. Written across all of them are REWARDS, and on many of them beneath that word are the words *treasures in Heaven.*

As little as we think about God's sight mattering to our everyday Christian lives, I fear that *God's rewards*—both present and future—mean even less to us. In fact, most of us, when we see how Jesus uses this language of rewards (seven times!), we do with it what we are not to do with our good works. We shove it under a bushel. But Jesus says, "Oh no, rewards are good and necessary. Without them your House of Holiness would fall."

Nowhere does Jesus teach that we must be good for the sake of being good. That sounds noble, but it is not Biblical thinking. Throughout Matthew—think of the end of each beatitude or the parables on the last judgment (cf. 10:42; 25:14–30)—Jesus persistently uses the motive of God-given rewards to help believers live for God.

The problem, however, is that some of us view God like some stingy old boss who only reluctantly gives a raise, bonus, or praise. But God is not like that at all. Jesus will later teach that even earthly fathers, even the worst fathers, give good things to their children—they don't give their son a snake when he asks for a fish (7:10). Our gracious, kind, and benevolent heavenly Father is quite happy to give us rewards for good behavior. Why wouldn't he? A good government rewards righteousness; a good teacher or parent does as well. Why wouldn't a good God?

The rewards mentioned here might include present benefits. If you live according to God's ways, then blessings will follow—sometimes material blessings, sometimes emotional blessings, but always spiritual blessings—the closeness of God's presence in the here and now (cf. James 4:8).

However, it seems most likely that the rewards Jesus refers to here are eternal blessings—"treasures in heaven" (6:19–21; cf. Luke 14:14). I say this because our Lord will repeatedly stress that following him here and now will bring about trials and tribulations, sufferings and persecutions. If you want to follow him, you must deny yourself and pick up your cross. So the reward is very much like Jesus' own "reward"—if I can use that word—for his work. We are told in Hebrews 12:2 that it was for "the joy that was set before him" that he "endured the cross." It is also like the reward to which the heroes of the faith listed in Hebrews 11 looked forward: they had their eyes on the ultimate prize—the city of God.

Therefore, Christian, when the rains and winds of this world beat against you, think about the roof and the foundation of this House of Holiness. As you seek to live not for self but for the glory of God, recognize that God gives you motives for perseverance—his sight and his rewards. Live before him and for him, knowing that the narrow way leads to life—to the final and eternal vision of God and to those unfading pleasures that he holds in his right hand (Psalm 16:11).

Almsgiving

Now that we have seen what is above and beneath the house, let's see next what is to come out of the house—almsgiving, prayer, and fasting. Jesus doesn't use these three examples because they are the most important good works, but rather because they were the most important to the scribes and Pharisees. I'll put it this way: as he is building up our house, he is also leveling theirs.

After Jesus' thesis—"Beware of practicing your righteousness before other people in order to be seen by them, for then you will have no reward from your Father who is in heaven" (v. 1)—he gives his application:

> Thus, when you give to the needy, sound no trumpet before you, as the hypocrites do in the synagogues and in the streets, that they may be praised by others. Truly, I say to you, they have received their reward. But when you give to the needy, do not let your left hand know what your right hand is doing, so that your giving may be in secret. And your Father who sees in secret will reward you. (vv. 2–4)

Throughout Scripture—e.g., in the Law,[4] the prophets,[5] the Gospels,[6] and the Epistles[7]—God exhorts his people to care for those in need. Jesus modeled this in his own earthly ministry. He and the Twelve kept a money bag, partly to provide for themselves and partly to provide for the poor (John 13:29). Moreover, he modeled this in his very being: "For you know the grace of our Lord Jesus Christ, that though he was rich, yet for your sake he became poor, so that you by his poverty might become rich" (2 Corinthians 8:9). In our richness—our spiritual richness—we should care for the materially and oftentimes spiritually poor.

Yet, in Jesus' day the act of almsgiving "had been carried to absurd [and un-Biblical] extremes by rabbinic tradition."[8] For example, according to the apocryphal book of Tobit, "It is better to give to charity than to lay up gold. For charity will save a man from death; it will expiate any sin" (12:8; cf. Sirach 3:14, 15, 30). Why give? According to second temple Judaism, it was to atone for sin. This tainted theology explains why, when Jesus taught that "only with difficulty will a rich person enter the kingdom of heaven" (19:23), his disciples were baffled (19:25). In their minds, it was *easy* for a rich man to enter the kingdom because such a man could essentially buy his way in by simply giving to the poor.

Such a perspective is not far removed from many of today's donors. Why do people give? Some are motivated by religious guilt. They give in order to get into Heaven. But people today aren't all that religious, and most people's motives are actually much closer, oddly enough, to what Jesus says of the super-religious of his day. People give in order to get a reward (not from God, but from others). The reward could be something tangible like a nice plaque or the wing of a building named in their honor. It could be the reward of a tax deduction. I find tax deductions so ironic. No one today wants to admit that people are basically sinful, yet why would any government offer tax deductions if people are basically good? Won't people give from the goodness of their heart or simply based on the size of the need? Our government smartly says, "I doubt it." People give to get—to get publicity, to earn the esteem of others, to save on taxes, etc.

What does our Lord Jesus say to this give-to-get scam? He says, "Don't blow your own horn." That now common saying comes from right here in verse 2. Don't blow your own horn, that is, don't give in order to get notice, praise, love, an appeased conscience, or whatever your wrong motive may be. Instead, give (a) because you should—it is God's Law, (b) because you love others, which goes back to our Lord's teaching in the previous chapter, and (c) because of God's reward, which is far better than the praise of man. You give because you have faith in the future promises of God.

Now, Jesus knows we are going to struggle with all this, so in verses 3, 4a he helps us out. He says, "But when you give to the needy, do not let your left hand know what your right hand is doing, so that your giving may be in secret." Here Jesus counsels us to "seek secrecy."[9] We are not to announce our generosity to others. In fact, we are not even to announce it to ourselves.[10]

Jesus gives this apparently absurd illustration about the two hands "to emphasize the intense privacy that should be present when we give to help others."[11] I say "apparently absurd" because any athlete knows that if you train your muscles—say to swing a bat when a ball is coming eighty miles per hour over home plate—you do not stop to think about what you are doing. You just do it. The same is true of a musician whose fingers, because of much practice, have remembered exactly what notes to play and when. It becomes second nature.[12] Similarly, our giving is to be second nature, like a trained moral muscle.

So, do you see how it works? Ah, the genius of Jesus! It is hard to be praised by others (that's the temptation) when nobody knows what you have given *and* when you don't even remember what you yourself have done. It's just part of who you are.

Do you recall the teaching of our Lord in 25:31–40, where he speaks of his second coming, when he will gather all the nations and separate people, some on his right and others on his left? Those on the right—the "righteous" or "the sheep" as he calls them—will enter into eternal life. These are the ones who fed the hungry, welcomed the stranger, clothed the naked, and visited the sick and imprisoned. Do you remember their reaction when Jesus welcomes them into his kingdom, telling them of their good works? What do they say? They answer him:

> Lord, when did we see you hungry and feed you, or thirsty and give you drink? And when did we see you a stranger and welcome you, or naked

> and clothe you? And when did we see you sick or in prison and visit you? (25:37–39)

They didn't see what their hands were up to. They had a self-forgetfulness about what they did. And I'll tell you, God loves such forgetfulness![13] The King replies in essence, "What you did for the least was, in fact, done for me" (25:40). "Enter into the joy of your master" (25:21). That is how to give to charity—Jesus-style.

Fasting

From almsgiving, which for the Jews was "the most sacred of all religious duties,"[14] our Lord turns his attention to prayer, which was a close second. Since he talks most about prayer in this section, I thought I'd do the same. So I will give you two chapters on prayer, based on verses 5–15. For now, let's jump over these middle verses to the final three. Look with me at verses 16–18 and this topic of fasting. Here Jesus teaches:

> And when you fast, do not look gloomy like the hypocrites, for they disfigure their faces that their fasting may be seen by others. Truly, I say to you, they have received their reward. But when you fast, anoint your head and wash your face, that your fasting may not be seen by others but by your Father who is in secret. And your Father who sees in secret will reward you.

Again we hear the language of sight and reward. We also have the idea of secrecy as a measure against wrong motives. But those central facts aside, do you know what word I find most fascinating here? It's the word "when." "And *when* you fast . . ." What's with the "when"? It implies that Christians fast.

I grew up as a devout Roman Catholic, and as such I most certainly fasted when and how I was told to. During the season of Lent, I ate no meat on Fridays, and on Good Friday (this was more of my own extreme tradition) I fasted completely from food. When I became a Protestant evangelical—a tradition with comparatively little emphasis on fasting—I remember my first Good Friday with my Christian college housemates. When Good Friday came around, I planned on keeping my usual tradition—not only fasting from meat, but fasting from all food. However, my housemates, with their freedom in Christ, planned (and executed quite well) a pig roast. On the morning of Good Friday a pit was dug in the ground, the fire lit, and the pig set in place. Well, on that day I joined the dark side. At the time of Jesus' death (3:00 p.m.), I skipped both church and my prayer time in order to stuff myself with pork.

Since that very un-kosher Good Friday, I have thought a bit about fasting as it is laid out in God's Word. Here is my summary: from a Biblical perspective, fasting lies somewhere between a roasted pig and fried fish—that is, between unbridled license and man-made rules.

Let me explain. In the Old Testament there was only one time per year when God's people were called to fast—the Day of Atonement (Leviticus 16:29–34; cf. Acts 27:9). Since that Day has been fulfilled in Christ's death (Colossians 2:14), there is no longer any command for us to fast. You won't find one in all the New Testament. Note that. It's important. If you don't want to fast, it is no fat off my skin (it might, however, be fat under yours). I mean that seriously (the first part). For the moment we start commanding what God himself does not command, we fall into the danger I talked about in the last chapter—going above the line of Scripture. So, fast if you'd like. And fast when you'd like. In 6:16, the word "when" or "whenever" is key. Jesus never said, "Fast on Good Friday," "Fast on the day before Christmas," or "Fast during Lent." Nor did he ever say, "Fast from meat but not from fish." As an aside, the fasting done by some during Lent can be a mockery and reproach to God. To abstain from a hamburger and Coke for the market value catch of the day and a glass of expensive Merlot—how ridiculous! Why fast from dark chocolate but not from one's darkest sins?

Jesus doesn't command us to fast, but he assumes—with this "when"—that after his death and resurrection, his disciples will fast. He says so in 9:15b: "The days will come when the bridegroom is taken away from them, and then they will fast." I like very much what Martin Luther—the first Protestant—had to teach on this matter. While he acknowledges that fasting is "not confined to any rule or measure, to any time or place,"[15] he nevertheless says:

> I would also be glad if at certain times, once a week or as often as might seem best, there were no evening meal, except a piece of bread and something to drink, to keep everything from being used up with the kind of incessant guzzling and gobbling that we Germans do, and to teach people to live a little more moderately, especially those who are young, sturdy, and strong.[16]

Here Luther touches on one of the important reasons for fasting—to temper our appetites. Now, we know that the gobbling and guzzling of Germans is not an exclusive nationalistic trait. We obese or anorexic Americans have our share of troubles with food as well. We so often live between two equally obsessive and idolatrous extremes—either stuffing our faces or starving ourselves.

Have you ever been to one of our supermarkets with someone from a Third World country? Can you imagine trying to explain the plenty, to navigate through the raised eyebrows and dropped jaw when standing before the fresh fruit and vegetables and fish and meat and bread? Then after explaining that, as well as the cereal aisle and the apparent "need" for 150 brands—can you imagine turning to this impoverished friend and explaining why you are intentionally starving yourself so as to fit into a certain size jeans? It is no exaggeration to say that for too many Americans, to use Paul's words, "Their god is their belly" (Philippians 3:19; cf. Titus 1:12). Who do you think about more throughout the day—the God of Heaven or the god of your gut? Are you counting your blessings or are you counting your calories?

Fasting is what we need, for in fasting we essentially say, "I do not live for my appetites—my physical appetites, my sexual appetites, my material appetites.[17] Therefore, with self-control, which is a fruit of the Holy Spirit, I'm going to stop all this incessant 'nibbling at the table of the world.'[18] I do not live for my appetites. But much more than that, I live for God and for his blessing." That's what we say when we fast.

The Bible provides a number of reasons for fasting—it might be an expression of humiliation and sorrow over one's sin (Leviticus 16:29–34; Jonah 3:5) or of bereavement over a great loss (1 Samuel 31:13; 2 Samuel 1:12). As we see in Acts, fasting occurs in conjunction with the appointment of elders (14:23) or the commissioning of missionaries (13:2, 3). But the main reason we fast is "to nourish our hunger for God and to reduce our hunger for the world."[19] I think that is in part the "reward" Jesus talks about in verse 18. Our "reward" for fasting is ironically but wonderfully a hunger and thirst for God, for he who hungers and thirsts for God shall be spiritually satisfied. Fasting can give you a larger appetite for God. This is why the Puritans, who fasted often, called it "soul-fattening."[20] Do you want a fatter soul? Then take seriously this word *when*—"when you fast . . ."

Rearranging the Ashes

There is a story about a so-called "holy man" who in a far eastern city, as a sign of his great humility, covered himself with ashes. However, every day he would situate himself on the most prominent street corner in the city and sit there all day. As the story goes, when a tourist would come up to him and ask for his picture, he would take his ashes and rearrange them so as "to give the best image of destitution and humility."[21]

In commenting on this story, Pastor John MacArthur notes:

> A great deal of religion amounts to nothing more than rearranging religious "ashes" to impress the world with one's supposed humility and devotion.

> The problem, of course, is that the humility is a sham, and the devotion is to self, not to God.[22]

In our passage Jesus says, "Beware" (v. 1). Beware when we give, pray, fast, or do anything good. We must beware of practicing our righteousness before other people in order to be seen and praised by them. Instead we must live holy lives because we love God and love others, and also because we know that God's eyes are always on us and his rewards are for those who seek first the kingdom of God and his righteousness (6:33).

15

How *Not* to Pray

MATTHEW 6:5–8

IT WAS LIKE THOSE TIMES when you are lying in bed with your eyes half-closed, not knowing if you are dreaming or awake. But there I was, sitting behind a table with my associate pastor, Andrew Fulton, at my side. We were guest panelists over at the local college, where our job was to defend the claims of Christianity. One student after another would come up to the microphone and politely ask his or her questions. We gave our answers. So far, so good; it was all going quite well. But then a young man approached the microphone, and with some venom in his voice he said, "Jesus said a lot of things that are just plain wrong." Then he went on to cite some supposed examples from Jesus' teachings. When he was done with his accusations, he swaggered back to his seat and sat down quite satisfied.

Here is what I did in the dream. (I don't know about your dreams, but in mine, I am much bolder than I am in reality.) I stood up, leaned over the table, looked him dead in the eyes, and said, "You don't know what you are talking about. Have you ever read the Bible? Do you know anything of Western literature or philosophy or religion or history?" Andrew looked up at me with a worried expression on his face. But on I went. "Listen, kid, there was and is nobody like Jesus. Don't tell me what Jesus said was wrong. Are you kidding me? Who are you? What do you know?" And then, just as I was ready to throw my folding chair at him and simultaneously shout, "Get out of here," Andrew grabbed my shoulder, pulled me down, and whispered, "I'll take this one."

There is usually something true about our dreams. So perhaps I could use a class on anger management. But I also do have great zeal for Jesus and the Book about him. In John 7:46, as the Jews are debating over Jesus and his claims, the temple officers defend the fact that they have not brought Jesus into custody for some crime, saying, "No one ever spoke like this man!" That is exactly how I feel, at a much deeper level. I have read the great writers. I have listened to the great speakers. I know my history, philosophy, literature, religion, and theology, and I can tell you that no one in the history of the world ever spoke like Jesus. No one!

And just one of the ways Jesus demonstrates his awesome uniqueness is, interestingly and perhaps unexpectedly, in his teaching on prayer. What he says on prayer is certainly different than what is taught in any of the world's great religions or by any popular New Age mystic. It is also different than anything in the whole of Scripture! It is different in the sense that from Genesis to Revelation, this is the only place where we have direct instruction on prayer.[1]

So as we come again to the Sermon on the Mount, we come to the pinnacle of prayer, the most unique and important teaching on prayer in the history of the world. My hope now, as we look at this pinnacle, is that we will begin not only to see this mountain but to move it, if you will, into the plain of our lives.

When You Pray

In verse 5 Jesus begins, "And when you pray, you must not be like the hypocrites."

Jesus' audience was surely struck by the last part of that sentence, "you must not be like the hypocrites." For many of us, however, the first part is the cause for concern and/or consternation. "When you pray . . ." You see, Jesus assumes his audience prays—both his closest disciples and even those who would eventually become his enemies.

But surely that same assumption cannot be made today, not only outside the church, but also within it. Just as an avowed atheist will only resort to prayer (in whatever form and to whatever god) as his last resort, sadly I fear that many Christians today likewise resort to prayer only in times of great need or when they desire the fulfillment of some bigheaded dream. For many of us, prayer is not a habit in our lives. We do not emulate Daniel who prayed three times a day (Daniel 6:10), nor the psalmist who praised God "seven times a day" (Psalm 119:164). And the example of Anna, who "worship[ed] with fasting and prayer night and day" (Luke 2:37), or Jesus, who spent the whole night in prayer (Luke 6:12), is unreal or surreal to us.[2] The plot in H. G. Wells's *War of the Worlds* is more likely to occur. Martians from Mars attacking the earth is more probable than you and I praying a whole day and night. Let's be perfectly honest. We live in a prayerless world and in a prayerless church. I can say with confidence that the good majority of us are not disciplined when it comes to prayer.

We can blame our negligence on the recent advances in science and technology, which seek to unveil all mysteries and free us from dependence on supernatural forces beyond our control. Or we can blame the great influence of entertainment, which takes our attention from the sublime and the divine and focuses it on the trite and the trivial. But the real blame must fall on us. We don't pray because we don't understand God. Or worse, we don't pray because we don't love, trust, or need God. Since God doesn't matter to us as much as we think or say, prayer doesn't matter much either.

So in this chapter I start where Jesus saw no need to start. I start with a plea for prayer. And I plead with you to pray, not solely on the basis of the Scriptural commands do so,[3] but also because you believe God actually exists, cares, and is powerful to help. I plead with you to pray as a sincere expression of your trust and your desire to commune with the true and living God.[4]

But how are we to pray? That is a real question for many of us. We may desire to pray, but we don't know where to begin. If that is where you find yourself, you are in good company, for that is the precise place we find Jesus' first followers. In Luke's version of the Lord's Prayer, Jesus' instructions are in response to a disciple's request, "Lord, teach us to pray" (Luke 11:1). Let that disposition be ours now as we go through 6:5–8 and see what Jesus has to say.

How Not to Pray

Over the years I have been criticized for being too critical in my preaching. And I'm sure from time to time such accusations have some truth to them. There is a temptation for young preachers to shock and exaggerate. Yet I must say, in defense of continuing the practice of preaching the negatives, I am but a poor copy of the original. Jesus' teaching style, which was the same as the prophets and apostles, was usually to present the true in light of the false. He would teach what we should believe or do by first showing what we should not believe or do. This is certainly what he does throughout the Sermon on the Mount. The most repeated phrase in this grand exhortation is, "You have heard it said, but I say to you . . ." In other words, "You have heard such and such a doctrine or practice as meaning this or that, but now I say to you that such thinking or doing is wrong, and what I now have to teach you is right."

This is precisely what Jesus does in this passage on prayer. He starts with a short sermon on *how not to pray*. Just look at how positively negative Jesus is! Look with me at verses 5–8, and notice all the *nots*.

> And when you pray, you must *not* be like the hypocrites. . . . And when you pray, do *not* heap up empty phrases as the Gentiles do. . . . Do *not* be like them. . . .

Before Jesus presents the positives on prayer, he starts with the negatives. We are *not* to be like the hypocrites. We are *not* to be like the Gentiles. We are *not* to pray like them!

Not like the Hypocrites

First, we are *not* to pray like the hypocrites. To pray like a hypocrite is to play-act or pray-act in order to "be seen by others" (v. 5b).[5] So again, as it was with giving and fasting, the goal of being seen by others is the problem.

Since Jesus says that "they love to stand and pray in the synagogues and at the street corners" (v. 5b), it is tempting to take issue with the posture and places of these hypocrites. They are standing when they pray and are praying both indoors and outdoors,[6] in religious and secular places—in "the synagogues and at the street corners." However, their posture is not the essential problem, although it is perhaps a symptom. I say it is not the posture because the Bible shows that one can pray standing, sitting, kneeling, or prostrate (facedown),[7] and that our Lord modeled most of these postures himself.[8] Nor is the place the basic problem. It was more than appropriate to pray in the synagogue (a place of prayer) as well as to pray in the streets if it was the time for prayer. Of course, the fact that these hypocrites were praying on the "street corners" or more literally at "the corners of the wide streets" (in other words, the busy intersections) does sound a sour note, like the note of a loud trumpet played off-key. Yet, it is crucial for us to know that the ancient Jews, similar to modern Muslims, would pray at set times. There is no reason to believe Jesus rejected this tradition, and there is positive evidence that the apostles practiced it. In Acts 3:1, for example, Peter and John went to the temple at "the hour of prayer, the ninth hour."

So the problem was neither posture nor place but people![9] These hypocrites were praying to receive the praise of people, which was "their reward" (v. 5c), as Jesus says sarcastically. "Their reward" was the praise of men but not of God, the approval and applause of earth but not of Heaven. Who is our audience in prayer, and what is our motive? That's what Jesus is getting at.

In one of his classic books on prayer, R. A. Torrey says, "We should never utter one syllable of prayer either in public or in private until we are definitely conscious that we have come into the presence of God and are actually praying to Him."[10] That is precisely what Jesus teaches in verse 6, where he gives the corrective to this oxymoronic notion of man-centered devotion.[11] Jesus says, "But when you pray, go into your room and shut the door and pray to your Father who is in secret. And your Father who sees in secret will reward you."

The secret to understanding this verse is the word "secret." The secret to sincere prayer, prayer that is "rewarded" (perhaps with an answer or certainly with divine approval), is making sure that the only eyes open to us during times of prayer are those of this secret-seeing or universally-present God. "Thou God seest me" (Genesis 16:13, KJV). You see me when I give and fast, and also when I pray.

That said, it is not as though Jesus is opposed to public prayer. He himself prayed publicly (see John 11:41, 42; Matthew 14:19), as did Solomon (2 Chronicles 6:1–42), the Levites (Nehemiah 9:5–38), and many other notable figures in the Bible. Rather, being acutely aware of the human tendency to pray in order to gain the praise of others, our Lord provides a helpful remedy: find a room and lock the door. Find even a storeroom (which Jesus is possibly referring to here), the least sanctified place in the house—where food, tools, and other supplies were stored, but where privacy is most likely assured.[12] Of course, a locked room does not guarantee sincerity and humility before God, but it is a safe solution against insincerity and pride—against hypocrisy. As John MacArthur notes, "the word hypocrite originally referred to actors who used large masks to portray the roles they were playing."[13] It is hard to be a hypocrite—to play-act before God—if you are alone in a closet with the door shut. It can be done, but it is less likely to be done.[14]

At this point don't make the mistake of thinking that Jesus' primary emphasis is on location (that we must have a prayer closet). Rather, his emphasis is on attitude. "Don't show off when you pray!"—that's his point. And since most of us are show-offs by nature, a quiet, secluded place will help us meet our proper objective. So it is essential that we find a time and place where we can pray unobserved, undisturbed, and unheard by people, but not by God,[15] for God alone is always to be "before our eyes when we engage in prayer."[16]

I know this can be a real challenge for many of us. It used to be quite a challenge for me. I am an early riser, so I get up at least an hour before everyone else in my home. This allows me some time for prayer and reading. Yet just a few years ago finding such a time and place for unobserved, undisturbed devotion to God was nearly impossible. This was due mostly to my second daughter (who will remain unnamed) who would awake as early as I did. Yet at that season of my life, I did learn to resign myself to a pattern of prayer that I have found to be not only more practical but also (perhaps?) more Biblical.

Based on this passage, Martin Luther said prayers should be "brief, frequent, and intense."[17] I like that, for the brevity of prayer can naturally lead to the frequency of prayer, and more frequent prayer might lead to more fervent prayer.[18] And that's what we want. It is of no value to pray for prayer's sake. How far better to pray when you really mean it and when your attention is focused where it should be—namely, on God.

Ecclesiastes 5:1, 2 provides a wonderful word on prayer:

> Guard your steps when you go to the house of God. To draw near to listen is better than to offer the sacrifice of fools, for they do not know that they are doing evil. Be not rash with your mouth, nor let your heart be hasty to utter a word before God, for God is in heaven and you are on earth. Therefore *let your words be few.*

When we come before our great and holy God, let our words be few.[19] Augustine put it this way: "Remove from prayer much speaking, not much praying."[20]

Not like the Gentiles

Having scattered the proud, Jesus next quiets the babblers: "And when you pray, do not heap up empty phrases as the Gentiles do, for they think that they will be heard for their many words. Do not be like them, for your Father knows what you need before you ask him" (vv. 7, 8).

It appears from the Gospels that the public prayers of the scribes and Pharisees were "ritualistic, mechanical, long, repetitious, and above all ostentatious."[21] But it is not the Jews Jesus criticizes here, but the "Gentiles," a term that simply means "non-Jews." In other words, Jesus is talking about how pagans pray. And at the heart of pagan prayer is the heaping up of many empty phrases or what earlier translators called "vain repetition."

Jesus does not condemn all long prayers or all repetition here, for as I mentioned earlier, he prayed all night (Luke 6:12) and repeated his prayer at Gethsemane (26:36–46). Rather, it is *vain* repetitions, where "many words" are thought to mediate between God and man.[22]

There is a decent example of this indecent act in Acts 19 where we read that the silversmiths of Ephesus aroused a crowd against Paul and his companions, chanting for two hours to their god, "Great is Artemis of the Ephesians!" (v. 34). For two hours—can you imagine? With this Acts text, however, it is difficult to discern whether the mob is merely shouting or if their shouting is based on prayer patterns. Another and clearer example of this phenomenon is the conflict between Elijah and the priests of Baal on Mount Carmel. Do you remember the absurdity of the pagans' prayers? First Kings

18:26 tells us that from morning till noon these pagan priests were hard at it, repeating over and over again, "O Baal, answer us!" "But there was no voice, and no one answered" (surprise, surprise!). At noon Elijah, the fun-loving prophet of the true God, mocked them: "Cry aloud, for he is a god [right?]. Either he is musing, or he is relieving himself, or he is on a journey, or perhaps he is asleep and must be awakened" (v. 27). To this the priests of Baal

> cried aloud and cut themselves after their custom with swords and lances, until the blood gushed out upon them. And as midday passed, they *raved on* until the time of the offering of the oblation, but there was no voice. No one answered; no one paid attention. (vv. 28, 29)

In contrast, how did Elijah act? He modeled perfectly Jesus' point with his composed frame of mind and his concise, faith-filled petition. But the point here is that this episode is quite typical of pagan prayer. The rule of pagan or "Gentile" prayer (and I include in this group Muslims, Hindus, Buddhists, and any other world religion save Christianity) is "much avails much," that is, the more I talk to god, the more likely he is to listen.

Sadly Christianity, with its long and at times sordid history, has not been immune to the practice of pagan prayer or the influence of Gentile babbling. For example, in *The Way of a Pilgrim*, a classic work on Russian Orthodox spirituality, the author combines the tax collector's prayer ("Lord, have mercy on me a sinner") with Paul's admonition to "pray without ceasing" and calls this combination "the Jesus Prayer." If you have ever read J. D. Salinger's novel *Franny and Zooey*, this is modeled by Franny. "The Jesus Prayer" consists of repeating over and over again, "Lord Jesus Christ, Son of God, have mercy on me." Although this is called "the Jesus Prayer," in reality it is far from how Jesus taught us to pray. In fact if you turn up the speed and number of repetitions, it resembles a pagan mantra more than a Christian prayer.[23]

Having grown up Roman Catholic I remember "praying" my rosary (which, by the way, came to Catholicism from Buddhism by way of Spanish Muslims during the Middle Ages)[24] with devotion and sincerity but with a quickness of repetition that eclipsed my brain waves. One month out of the year I would pray the rosary every day, and since the rosary consists of fifty-three Hail Mary's, six Our Father's and six Glory Be's (i.e., the *Gloria Patri*), here is how I would pray to get through it in a reasonable amount of time. Fingering each bead, I would pray:

> *hailmaryfullofgracethelordiswiththeeblessedarethouamongwomen andblessedisthefruitofthywombJesusholymarymotherofgodprayforus*

> *sinnersnowandatthehourofourdeathamenourfatherwhoartinheaven hallowedbethynamethykingdomcomethywillbedoneonearthasitisinheaven giveusthisdayourdailybreadandforgiveusourtrespassesasweforgivethose whohavetrespassedagainstusandleadusnotintotemptationbutdeliverus fromevilglorybetothefatherandtothesonandtotheholyspiritasitwasinthe beginningisnowandevermoreshallbeworldwithoutendamen.*

Not bad, huh? How sad, huh? A bunch of "Christian" prayers prayed like a pagan.

It is this kind of mindless prayer that Jesus has in mind.[25] Lip-labor that is not in service to the soul and not connected to the mind is reproved and condemned.

Of course, all of us (even we Protestants) have been guilty of this kind of mindlessness in prayer, of letting our tongues run ahead of our heads, whether it is while praying before a meal or during a prayer meeting. Our lips are moving, but our hearts and minds stand still. They are deaf to what is being said. This is not very different, Jesus is teaching us, from a pagan uttering nonsense syllables or magical incantations.

Earlier I mentioned what Luther said about prayer—that it is to be "brief, frequent, and intense." Here is another bit of practical advice from him. Full of his usual blend of humor and sobriety, Luther writes concerning verse 7:

> The Gentile delusion [is] that prayer meant making both God and oneself tired with yelling and murmuring. . . . But the Christian's prayer is easy [!], and it does not cause hard work. . . . It presents its need from the heart. Faith quickly gets through telling what it wants. . . . God has no need of such everlasting twaddle.[26]

Interestingly, Luther goes on to say that "the ancient fathers [i.e., the church fathers] have said correctly that many long prayers are not the way. They recommend short, fervent prayers, where one sighs toward Heaven with a word or two, as is often quite possible in the midst of reading, writing, or doing some other task."[27] Jesus gives us great liberty and latitude! Don't put yourself in a straitjacket when Jesus has given you wings to fly.

Pagan prayer requires much because it has a wrong view of God, a view that he is a grudging giver, reluctant to act unless prayers are long and usually hard-fought.[28] But Jesus teaches that this attitude is all wrong. Look again at our final verse. Here Jesus teaches that our "Father" has no need of long prayers because he has no lack of information. He "knows what you need before you ask him" (v. 8). Isn't that a relief? If God already knows what you need, there is no need to fill his ears with a lot of drivel or—what did Luther call it?—"everlasting twaddle." Get to the point—that's the point. God is not a mortal man who needs to be informed and then solicited.[29] Our God can discern, as is taught in Romans 8:26, "groanings too deep for words." So pray to God with reverence, like a servant addressing a king. But pray also with "simplicity, directness, and sincerity,"[30] like a child asking something of his loving father.

The Light Yoke of Prayer

I have prayed my whole life. There is not a day in my post-toddler days when I cannot remember offering up some sort of prayer. But most of my prayer life has been a farce. I can say for certain during the first half of my life, although I prayed and prayed and prayed, most often I heaped up empty phrases to God and thus treated him more like an idol than the supreme maker and sustainer of this universe.

But when I came to Christ, the first prayer I offered to God was perhaps the best and the purest prayer I have ever given or will ever give. It was short and simple. And it was sincere. It was like a naughty, guilty little child asking his father for the forgiveness and reconciliation he so desperately needed.

Jesus gave an example of the perfect prayer (what we now call the Lord's Prayer), and it too was *short* (it might take twenty seconds to pray) and *simple* (even a two-year-old can say and memorize the words), and if prayed *sincerely* it is a most pleasing prayer.

My brothers and sisters, whether I am dreaming about defending my Lord Jesus, as I did a few days ago, or teaching his words, as I am doing right now, I must tell you I only grow in my conviction that "No one ever spoke like this man!" No one is like Jesus—so humble, powerful, and wise. And what wisdom he has here for us—a yoke that is light. If we rest in him, this yoke of prayer is surprisingly light.

16

How to Pray

MATTHEW 6:9–15

ONE WAY YOU KNOW that a work of art is a masterpiece is that you cannot exhaust it with observations. You can stare at it for hours and still miss important facets. And then each time you return to stare at it again you find new and wonderful aspects you never saw before, components that continue to reveal the true genius of its creator. At the center of the Sermon on the Mount (almost exactly the center, as there are 116 lines before and 114 after it)[1] is a perfect masterpiece on prayer—the Lord's Prayer—which is perfect in both structure and substance.

Structurally Jesus gives six petitions in two symmetrical parts.[2] The first part, with its three petitions, focuses on God, and thus all the petitions contain the word "your" (referring to God)—"hallowed be *your* name," "*your* kingdom come," "*your* will be done." These are what we might call the *divine petitions*. The second part, with its three petitions, focuses on human needs, hence the "our" and "us" in each petition—"give *us* this day *our* daily bread," "forgive *us our* debts," and "lead *us* not into temptation, but deliver *us* from evil." These are the *human petitions*.

For the rest of this chapter, we will focus on the substance of this prayer, or *some* of the substance, for as I said, this masterpiece on prayer is inexhaustible in its genius.

Our Father in Heaven

We start with the divine petitions, the first of which we find in verse 9: "Our Father in heaven, hallowed be your name." Here Jesus emphasizes that God and his glory ought to be *first* in our prayers. That is not to say that the "our" is lost, certainly not. It is important as well, for the word "our" shows that this is a corporate prayer. It reminds us that we are not praying alone. We are praying with and for each other.

Beyond this community solidarity, the "our" reveals to us the often overlooked (or taken for granted) reality that God is *ours*—not, of course, in the sense that we own or possess him, but in the sense that we are in a relationship with him. The fact that we can call God "our Father" informs us that Jesus is bestowing upon us "something of his own priceless [relationship with] God."[3] Throughout the Gospels Jesus talks about God being his "Father." For the first and only time in the Gospels, here he speaks of his disciples as sharing in this fellowship.[4] God is not only Jesus' Father but also "our Father" (cf. Romans 8:15).

But lest we get too cozy and chummy with God as "our Father," Jesus adds some balance with the phrase "in heaven."[5] While this phrase might merely "designate the difference from the earthly father,"[6] it might also reflect something of God's infinite greatness and righteous transcendence[7]—i.e., that "our Father" is in some sense "in the heaven*s* or the skies." God is "in all the skies over *every single creature* on the planet."[8] Psalm 33:13–15 makes the point this way: "The Lord looks down from heaven; he sees all the children of man; from where he sits enthroned he looks out on all the inhabitants of the earth, he who fashions the hearts of them all and observes all their deeds." If this is the sense of the phrase "in heaven," then the added point is that God in Christ may be as intimate as a father to us, but he still remains almighty. He is, as we say in the creeds, God the Father *Almighty*! Therefore, when we approach him in prayer we ought to recognize that there is a great distance between him and us, a difference at least as vast as that between Heaven and earth.

Hallowed Be Your Name

This thought and precondition naturally moves us into the actual petition, which is, "Hallowed be your name." That is, "May your name or reputation—who you are and what you have done—be thought of and acknowledged as holy."

In the earliest known Christian book on prayer, Origen's *Treatise on Prayer*, the author divides prayer into four parts: adoration, contrition, thanksgiving, and supplication. Adoration comes first, and that is precisely how Jesus starts. Jesus teaches us that we are to pray, first and foremost (what we so often don't pray), that God's name would be regarded by all people as holy.

Recently I learned of a church that for the purpose of reaching out to their community turned its "sanctuary" into a movie theater and its narthex into a box office. They offered free popcorn upon entrance, and I'm sure a brief candy-coated message before departure. What is taught here in this passage is a corrective to that. In the Bible what happened to people who came into the presence of God? They were struck with fear. They fell to the ground. They took off their shoes rather than putting them on the table. Even when a human encountered an angel we often find these same reactions. The purity of an angel was overpowering to them. But in our contemporary churches, with their come-as-you-are and worship-as-you-want "praise" services, the hallowedness of God's name is not a priority. With little or no regard for what honors God, we design church around the whims of man, and thus we are met with the oddity of a worship leader calling God's people into God's presence with buttered popcorn in their mouths. What flippancy! What arrogance! What blasphemy!

Just because the distinction between holy and common space has been abolished in the death of Christ (thus it is okay to meet in the basement of a children's museum, as my church did, or a Roman catacomb, as some early Christians did), that does not mean we can approach God in private prayer or in corporate worship with carelessness and with a carefree attitude. The end of Hebrews 12 talks about this. After explaining how we have come into a new covenant through Christ's blood, the author does not then say, "Therefore let us offer to God causal and lighthearted worship because you know God is so like way cool." Rather he writes, "[T]hus let us offer to God acceptable worship [which means that some worship is not acceptable], with reverence and awe, for our God is a consuming fire"—completely holy (12:28, 29). He is holy, holy, holy, and we ought never to treat him otherwise.

A few years ago my wife and I attended "Shakespeare in the Park." We saw, *The Complete Works of William Shakespeare Abridged*, which is a comically condensed version of all of Shakespeare's plays. We noticed on the first page of the program a warning label. It said that this show contained "adult material." We enquired as to the content of this adult material. To our satisfaction the director informed us that the label was mostly due to a spoof they were doing on one of Shakespeare's early and extremely violent plays. Yet we quickly learned that the director's sensibilities were different than our own, for as this play went on, what bothered us most was not the joking at senseless and excessive violence but the toying with God's name. God's name was mentioned in nearly every scene, never once with homage or in prayer. Their warning sticker should have read: "Warning: God's name will be taken in vain. This play is thus not suitable for children *or* adults. This play is not suitable for anyone who hallows God's name."

God's name is holy, and we are to regard him as holy when we come to pray, gather to worship, attend the theater, ballpark, or restaurant, watch TV, or talk in the shopping mall with our friends.[9] "Our Father in heaven, hallowed be your name"—that is the first petition, the first and foremost of the divine petitions.

Your Kingdom Come, Your Will Be Done

Look with me next at the second and third petitions, which I have grouped together because they naturally flow into one another. Look at verse 10: "Your kingdom come, your will be done, on earth as it is in heaven." Think of this petition in this way. God is in Heaven. While God is omnipresent, God dwells in some places in a certain, special way. Thus, his space, if you will, is up there in the unseen heavens, a place where perfect purity is observed, where his will is impeccably heeded. Our space is the earth—a place where impurity and immorality are everyday realities, where, in other words, God's will (in the prescriptive sense) is not perfectly observed. But long ago God promised he would send a King who would establish a kingdom—a kingdom on earth in which righteousness would dwell. Matthew tells us that that King is Jesus. And when Jesus, the Son of God, took on flesh and came to earth, "the kingdom of *heaven*," as he announced at the beginning of his ministry, was "at hand" (4:17). The day will come, so the prophets and apostles have foretold, when God's space will become our space. And surprisingly this will happen in a way that is counterintuitive. In the book of Revelation the picture is this: we are not taken from earth to Heaven, but rather Heaven comes to earth; the holy city, the New Jerusalem, comes down from Heaven to earth. "God's space and ours are finally married, integrated at last."[10] That picture of the new heavens and new earth is at the very heart of this petition. We are pleading with God to give us Jesus—"Amen. Come, Lord Jesus!" (Revelation 22:20)—that he as the King of kings would come again to reign supremely so that "[his] will" might conquer all once and for all.

In the fourth century the Emperor Julian (later known as Julian the Apostate) abandoned the Christian faith and sought to abolish Christianity, replacing it with the worship of the ancient gods of Rome and Greece. At the very height of his power, and as it looked as though the abolishment of Christianity could become a real possibility, he was mortally wounded in battle. "The historians tell how, when he lay bleeding to death, he took a handful of his blood and tossed it in the air, saying: 'You have conquered, O man of Galilee!'"[11] Christ's "conquering" of the Emperor Julian, as Julian viewed it, was but one small step away for the "man of Galilee" from the throne of Heaven and earth.

For when Christ returns in glory he will have the heads of all evil rulers and all disobedient people under his foot. Then, finally and absolutely, the will of Heaven will become the way of earth.[12]

So "Your kingdom come, your will be done, on earth as it is in heaven" is an extraordinary thing to ask for. And its extraordinariness is why I think we don't ordinarily ask for it. Of all the petitions in the Lord's Prayer, this one is the hardest for most of us to pray. It is hard because we fail to understand it or its full implications, but also hard because we are so concerned with ourselves and our little kingdoms. Further, we are concerned with our own name and reputation, more than with God's name and reputation. But here Jesus corrects our self-centered prayers with his God-centered one, reminding us of what we ought to ask for first.

Give Us Our Daily Bread

From such lofty heights—the high heavens—Jesus next takes us down to earth and, almost oddly, to the amber waves of grain. He takes us from these grand spiritual concerns (about God's name, kingdom, and will) to our everyday physical and spiritual concerns (our needs for ongoing food, forgiveness, and protection from evil).

The first of these human petitions is for daily bread—"Give us this day our daily bread" (v. 11). Some notable figures in church history (e.g., Augustine, Jerome, and Erasmus) rejected the plain interpretation that "bread" here means "bread" (or more broadly, provisions for our bodily health), and they spiritualized this petition to mean Communion bread or "the invisible bread of the Word of God."[13] Erasmus, for example, "reckons it impossible that, when we come into the presence of God, Christ should enjoin us to make mention of food."[14] Asking God for food is not spiritual enough, so he thought.

I'm not poking fun at these great men. I admire them. I read their works to learn and often emulate their otherworldly perspective. Much better than we often do, they lived in light of eternal values and realities. But here their interpretation is more otherworldly than Jesus, which is not the most spiritual place to be.

So while we are not to pray here for "our daily cake," as one commentator humorously puts it,[15] or "for riches [or] delicate living [or] costly raiment," as another phrases it,[16] we are to pray for bread, for daily provisions. I'll put it this way: We are not to pray for our greeds but for our needs, for every physical and material need.[17] "[G]ive me neither poverty nor riches; feed me [only] with the food that is *needful* for me, lest I be full and deny you and say, 'Who is the Lord?' or lest I be poor and steal and profane the name of my

God" (Proverbs 30:8, 9). That's how Proverbs puts it. "Give us this day our daily bread" is how Jesus puts it. "Lord, give us what we need to live, so that we might live a life of gratitude toward you and generosity towards others."[18]

Forgive Us Our Debts

If we stopped here with this petition, we would miss what is even more necessary than bread for our bodies—salvation for our souls. For if we are *not* pardoned of our daily sins, then all the daily bread we have filled our bellies with throughout our whole lives only fattens us for the slaughter. So the next petition is most necessary: "forgive us our debts" (v. 12a). The sense of the petition is this: "Lord, we continually depend on you for all things—for daily food but also for daily forgiveness. So give us this day our daily bread, and forgive us this day our daily debts." Or "trespasses,"[19] if you prefer that word, or even "sins." It is literally the word "sins" in Luke's version of this prayer (Luke 11:4).[20] That is the basic idea here in Matthew as well. We are asking God to forgive our sins.

Yet this concept of indebtedness or "debts," which is the word Matthew uses, sheds some light on the nature of our sins. The idea is this: we owe God our complete obedience. When we fail to give our complete obedience, we become debtors, and God becomes our creditor. Now, when you think of how many times we have sinned against God, you will realize that we live "in the land of debts," that "we are up to our ears" in debt.[21]

You thought our national economy is bad. Our spiritual economy has been in a depression for thousands of years. Our debt is astronomical (see 18:24). We should all be embarrassed—red in the face because of how much we are in the red—personally and corporately!

For very reason I want you to recognize the apparent audacity of this petition to God to "forgive us our debts." Think of it this way. Let's say you owe the government $100,000 for school loans. You are well aware of the severity of the hole you are in financially. What we are asking God to do here is like you asking the government to cancel what is owed. If you have any personal pride or honor, it seems like a shameless thing to do. But that is precisely what Jesus calls us to do. We are to put aside our pride and ask our Father for what we need—our debt forgiven.

Here Jesus does not fill in the big picture. But he knows where this Gospel of Matthew is going to end. And he knows where he is going—the cross. Our past, present, and future indebtedness can be forgiven *only* because Jesus came "to give his life as a *ransom*"—a full payment (20:28). He paid our infinite debt through his death. Jesus paid the price. Jesus paid it all.

If Jesus paid it all, there would be nothing so profane as to accept forgiveness for our sins but to leave unpardoned the sins of others. That is why Jesus includes an important condition, "And forgive us our debts, as we also have forgiven our debtors" (v. 12b). Jesus assumes that if we are asking for divine forgiveness, we have already been in the business of forgiving the little debts of even our biggest debtors.

John Wesley was once approached by a man who was well known for his unbending nature. In a particularly prideful moment, this man boasted to Wesley, "I never forgive." Wesley replied, "Then I hope, sir, you never sin."[22] That's funny. But, of course, there is nothing funny about the forgiven being unforgiving.

Whenever I conduct interviews for church membership, I always ask, "Is there anyone in your life you have not forgiven?" This is just as important a question as asking, "Do you believe in the Trinity?" or "Do you believe Jesus is the Son of God?" or "Do you believe Jesus died for your sins?"

The Puritan Thomas Watson said, "A man can as well go to hell for not forgiving as for not believing."[23] That's a strong but appropriate and memorable way of putting it, for that is what is taught later in 18:21–35 in the Parable of the Unforgiving Servant, but also here in 6:12b as well as in 6:14, 15, where Jesus reiterates this point (and this is the only petition he reemphasizes): "For if you forgive others their trespasses, your heavenly Father will also forgive you, but if you do not forgive others their trespasses, neither will your Father forgive your trespasses." You see, *the forgiven must be forgiving*—not forgiving in order to be justified before God but because we are justified before God.[24] In Ephesians 4:32 Paul expresses it this way: "Be kind to one another, tenderhearted, forgiving one other, as God in Christ forgave you."

Lead Us Not . . . but Deliver Us

We need forgiveness of all past sins, but we also and finally need assistance in overcoming any and all future sins. This is why Jesus teaches us next to pray, "And lead us not into temptation, but deliver us from evil" (v. 13).

The idea here is *not*, "Lord, please don't bring us to the place of temptation," or "don't allow us to be tempted."[25] We know from 4:1 that God's Spirit brought Jesus into the wilderness to be tempted. So what is being asked here is rather, "Lord, don't let us succumb to temptation," or "don't abandon us to temptation."[26] Here we find a petition for utter dependence on God's providence, protection, and power. It is a prayer of a weak person to a strong God.

In Foxe's *Book of Martyrs* the story is told of the fate of two men under the reign of Bloody Mary. Both of these men were condemned to burn at the stake for their religious convictions. One of them boasted loudly to the other prisoners that he would be a "man" when he approached his doom, that he was so grounded in the gospel that he could not imagine denying Christ if and when he was given the opportunity. Even on the day of his execution, he spoke of his imminent death in the most pious terms, saying that he was like a bride made ready for the wedding day.

Next to this man was a man of another disposition. Although he too was determined not to deny Christ, he admitted that he was terribly fearful of fire. He shared that he had always been very sensitive to suffering, and he was in great dread that when that first flame came near his body, he would cry out and recant, thus denying his Lord. So he urged this other man to pray for him, and he spent his time weeping over his weakness and crying out to God for strength. Befuddled by this blubbering, the other man rebuked and chided him for being so cowardly.

When they came to the stake, he who had been so bold recanted at first sight of the fire and thus was released, never to return to Christ. The other man, the trembling one, whose prayer at that moment had been, "Father, lead me not into temptation," stood firm as a rock, praising and magnifying God as he died a cruel but courageous death.[27]

All of us must undergo various trials and temptations in order that God might test the authenticity of our faith. We are all tested as if by fire. So, our prayer should be that though tested, we are not consumed.

Temptation is one thing, but evil another. So Jesus teaches that we are to pray not only "lead us not into temptation," but also "deliver us from evil" and/or "the evil one" (v. 13). The word here for "deliver" can be rendered "snatch." It is a most aggressive word.[28] So here we are asking God, with his divine hand, to snatch us from Satan. "Lord, grab us from the grip of the evil one and his evil ways" is the sense of the prayer. The parallelism plays out as follows: Lead us not into temptation (i.e., lead us not into Satan's temptations), but deliver us from the evil one (i.e., deliver us from Satan).

That is how the Lord's Prayer ends. It ends quite abruptly and seemingly oddly, with the word "evil" or "evil one." This abrupt and seemingly odd ending was what likely prodded a scribe somewhere down the line to tack on a doxology, "For yours is the kingdom and the power and the glory forever. Amen." It is a beautiful doxology, and the words are Biblical, for similar words are found in 1 Chronicles 29:11. However, such words are not found in the earliest and most reliable Greek manuscripts of the New Testament. Thus, the "evil" ending, if you will, is the original ending. And the purpose of that original ending may be to convey the grand contrast with the original opening. In Greek the first word of the Lord's Prayer is "Father," and the last words are "evil one." The structural point then is something like: As children of Jesus' Father, who live our daily lives between God and the devil, we must recognize the warning here and therefore offer up in this last petition a real and "raw cry for help"[29]—"Help me, Lord, to remain faithful to you."

We are not spiritual superheroes, but we must be prayer warriors, warring for our very souls. So we don't pray, "Bring on the temptations and the tempter." We don't go looking for tests of strength. We realize, as Jesus said, that "sufficient for the day is its own trouble" (6:34), and may I add also "temptations" and "evils." *O Lord, lead us not into temptation, but deliver us from evil.*

A Masterpiece on Prayer

Matthew 6:5–15 is a masterpiece on prayer. And although we have seen only part of its genius, hopefully it has been enough for us to appreciate that prayer. We should appreciate the genius of the prayer, but more importantly the greatness of Jesus, for there indeed was and is no one who spoke like this man, no one who lived like this man, no one who died like this man, and no one who lived again like this man. Can you say amen to that? Amen, indeed!

17

Treasure and Trust

MATTHEW 6:19–34

IN THE SECOND BOOK of *The Divine Comedy*, Dante and Virgil emerge from Hell at the foot of Mount Purgatory. There they find seven cornices on which penitent sinners are graciously cleansed from the seven sinful tendencies that hinder them from full harmony with God. On the first cornice those guilty of pride circle the mountain, crawling low to the ground, bearing heavy burdens on their backs, and praying the Lord's Prayer.

While I do not believe purgatory to be an actual place, I do agree with Dante's creative mind that the Lord's Prayer teaches us humility. When we cry out to God that *his name be holy, that his kingdom come, that his will be done*, we declare that we desire him be supreme in our lives and in this world and that we are dependent on him to bring all this about. Then when we pray even for ourselves and our needs—*give us this day our daily bread, forgive us our sins, and lead us away from temptation and the tempter*, we likewise in humility ask God to be our protector and provider.

This theme of God as our provider summarizes well 6:19–34.[1] For here Jesus argues that if you treasure God more than anyone or anything else, especially money (vv. 19–24), then you will trust that "your heavenly Father" (vv. 26, 32) will provide for you (vv. 25–34). Put succinctly, this is a text about treasure and trust.

Treasure God

Jesus teaches this lesson about treasure and trust by giving us two central commands, followed by two corrective commands.

The first central command is found in verse 19: "Do not lay up for yourselves treasures on earth," and then its corrective in verse 20, "but lay up for yourselves treasures in heaven." Let's start by asking: what does Jesus mean by "treasures on earth"? I think he means *things money can buy*. Like what? Here it is not those "things" that might naturally come to mind—the big house, the nice car, or the expensive jewels. Interestingly, the only "things" Jesus mentions in our text (in v. 25ff.) are food, drink, and clothing. So treasures on earth can actually be things we need. The issue here is bigger than whether or not you live luxuriously. Rather, the question is, do you trust in money more than you trust in God to provide? Or put differently, is money the middle man or the main man?

Jesus asks, how do you *see* this matter? How is your eye (vv. 22, 23)? Is it "healthy" (v. 22)? That is, do you see God as Master and money as slave? Or is your eye "bad" (v. 23)? That is, is your whole view of who provides for you darkened by "covetousness, which is idolatry" (Colossians 3:5)? So then, to "lay up . . . treasures on earth" is the selfish love and hoarding of material things, which is based upon the "bad" view that money, rather than God, is what ultimately provides.

Treasures in Heaven

To "lay up . . . treasures in heaven" is just the opposite (v. 20). Instead of viewing money as the source of provision, you see God as the source. Instead of getting things—food, clothing, houses, cars, etc.—because you are worried about not having what you need, you selflessly love others with the things you have. You get in order to give. You beat money into submission.[2] You sit money down and say to it, "Thank you for coming today. Listen, I just wanted to make sure the rules are clear. You shall serve me, not I you!"

Some time ago my then teenage son Sean sat in my office and asked, "Dad, if I had a million dollars, what car would you want me to buy you?" I replied, "I'd rather you buy land for the church." He smiled and said, "No, come on. What would it be? A Jaguar?" (He said this because he knows I like Jaguars.) I said, "No, son, honestly, if you really think you need to buy me something, get me a new mini-van." This time he didn't smile, because sadly he knew I was serious. "Dad," he said in frustration, "what car?" I gave in. "Okay, son, you can buy me a Bentley. Shaquille O'Neal had a nice one of those made for him. You can get the same model for me."

Since I sensed that what was behind such questioning was materialism, I said to him, "Hey, Sean, do you know what Bible passage I'm preaching on this week?" He said, "No. What?" I said, "'You cannot serve God and money.'" Without missing a beat he replied to my confidently-stated Bible verse, "Yeah, but you can serve God with money."

Do you know what? He's right. You cannot serve God *and* money, but you can serve God *with* money. That is very much the point of these first six verses. Of course, Jesus did not exactly teach, "Buy your father a Bentley." But he did teach, "Think about others first when you think about your money. Think about how you can give away what you get."

What did Jesus say to the rich young ruler, who was so blind to his sin of coveting, so blind to his love and adoration and submission to money? Jesus said, "[G]o, sell what you possess and give to the poor, and you will have treasure in heaven; and come, follow me" (19:21). Do you want to be rich toward God (Luke 12:21)? If you do, then be rich toward others. Jesus has given us not the golden goose but the Golden Rule. And heeding it will make you rich. Love others who have greater need than you by giving what you have been given. That is what it means to store up treasures in Heaven.

> Riches I heed not, nor man's empty praise,
> Thou mine Inheritance, now and always:
> Thou and Thou only, first in my heart,
> High King of Heaven, my Treasure Thou art.[3]

Trust God

In this chapter we are talking about *treasure* and *trust*. Do you treasure God more than you do money? That's the question raised in verses 19–24. Now in verses 25–34 we have what I'll call our Savior's treasure test. Because of the word "therefore" (or it can be translated, "for this reason") in verse 25 we should note that our Lord gives a logical exhortation based on what has preceded. He has added this treasure test, which is also a stress test.

Someone might say, "Oh yes, I treasure God." Jesus says, "Well then, why are you so worried about everything? If you treasure God you will trust him." In verse 25 Jesus says, "Therefore [in light of the fact that God, not money, should be your treasure] I tell you, do not be anxious about your life, what you will eat or what you will drink, nor about your body, what you will put on." Do not be anxious about necessary provisions.

Jesus is not here teaching anything that would contradict what is said elsewhere in God's Word. So he is not anti-private property. He assumes, like the Ten Commandments do, that people do and will own things. Nor is he anti-labor. He is not saying there is no need to get a job, no need to work, no need to provide for your family (cf. 1 Timothy 5:8). He is not he anti-banking, anti-savings, or anti-investment. Moreover, he is not even anti-enjoyment. He does not contradict Ecclesiastes, for example, which teaches we should enjoy the work of our hands and what it brings (e.g., 2:24, 25).

Of course, beyond all these money matters, Jesus is not discounting common concern for our own welfare or the welfare of others. When my son Simeon ran into the street when he was one year old and starting booking around the corner, you better believe I was *concerned* for his life. If a car came around that corner, I knew he would be hit. He would die. "Lord," I cried out, "don't take my son."

Jesus is not talking about a Hawaiian hang-loose or Californian chill-out mentality. And he most certainly is not telling you to be a spiritual sloth. He is not telling you to sit back on your sofa with the remote control in one hand, a bottle of beer in the other, and your mouth wide open waiting for God to drop potato chips into it periodically.

But he is saying, "Don't let the trinity of the world's cares [the three 'do not's' in this passage] make you distrust the Trinity." He is saying, "Atheistic anxiety—that is, worry that thinks God cannot see, does not care, and will not give—is ungodly." It is an affront to the person and providence and provision of God.[4] So cut it out. "Do not be anxious" (v. 25). "Do not be anxious" (v. 31). "Do not be anxious" (v. 34).

Anxiety Is Unproductive

But why does Jesus say this? He gives us three reasonable reasons.[5] The first of these is: *anxiety is unproductive.*

We see this reason given in question form in verse 27: "And which of you by being anxious can add a single hour to his span of life?" Now that's a good question. Many teachings in the health industry advocate remedies and regimens to live an active and long life. However, I have yet to hear anyone advocate anxiety: "What you need every day is to wake up first thing in the morning and stress yourself out. It will really help you get through your day. And it will add years, possibly decades, to your life."

Smoking is no longer an acceptable behavior in our society. So we tax cigarettes with a "sin tax" and outlaw puffing in our pubs. But what about worry? That's still far too acceptable a sin. "I'm such a worrier," people say often, as if it's an innocent statement. Why are you such a worrier? Don't you know there is nothing acceptable about it? To Jesus it smells like secondhand smoke. He outlaws it. He bans it in his kingdom. Why worry? You can't add an hour to your life; in fact, you might take a few away.

Anxiety Is Unnecessary

The second reason to avoid anxiety is that *anxiety is unnecessary*. Look at verse 26ff. Look at the birds, and look at the lilies.

> Look at the birds of the air: they neither sow nor reap nor gather into barns, and yet your heavenly Father feeds them. Are you not of more value than they? . . . And why are you anxious about clothing? Consider the lilies of the field [wildflowers], how they grow: they neither toil nor spin, yet I tell you, even Solomon in all his glory was not arrayed like one of these. But if God so clothes the grass of the field, which today is alive and tomorrow is thrown into the oven, will he not much more clothe you, O you of little faith? Therefore do not be anxious, saying, "What shall we eat?" or "What shall we drink?" or "What shall we wear?" For the Gentiles seek after all these things, and your heavenly Father knows that you need them all.

Here Jesus gives what philosophers would call an argument *a minore ad maius* (from the lesser to the greater).[6] That is, he says, "Look at God's lesser creatures and creation. Have you ever seen a bird begging for food on the street corner? Have you ever seen a lily pulling its petals out over a bad color job? God provides for them; he will provide for you. Trust him. Have faith in your heavenly Father. Let the lilies preach to you. Let the sparrows sing to you of God's sovereign sustenance."

Now you might reply, "That's easy for you to advocate, pastor. You have a job," or "Your job is not in jeopardy," or "You haven't taken a pay cut in this terrible economy. And, hey, now that I think about it, your job is kind of cushy. What do you do all day? What do you know of hardship?"

I know quite a bit. Sometime in a later chapter I will give you a fuller testimony of how I came to Christ. For now I will simply share with you that when I was eighteen years old I learned that my girlfriend was pregnant. Now here's what I did (what I felt I had to do). I quit college, moved home, and started to work full-time. Eventually I would return to school. But from six months before my son's birth to this present moment, I have always worked a full-time job. I worked a few years for a carpet and tile company. I worked for three years as a janitor. I worked over four years as an overnight security guard. I worked a few more selling used theological books. I worked full-time to support myself, my son, and my schooling. I worked full-time, I went to school full-time, and I trusted in God for provision full-time.

I still trust in God for provision, for my "daily bread." One of my constant prayers is, "God, please provide for my family." And you know what? He always does. So I'm not telling you to do something that I have never had to do. I certainly have had and do have to trust God for provision.

Nor is Jesus telling us to do something that he never had to do. Jesus' "life on earth was anything but birdlike and lilylike."[7] He was a man with few possessions and "nowhere to lay his head" (8:20). He was someone who knew quite well "the pinch of near-starvation,"[8] who, as he spoke these very words in the Sermon on the Mount, stood with the Mount of Calvary in the distance, looming over him like a deadly storm cloud. Jesus said that each day has troubles of its own (v. 34). He knew and experienced those troubles and much more. Since he could trust his heavenly Father for provision—from his birth in a lowly manger to his death on a cruel cross—we can and should trust him as well.

Anxiety Is Unworthy

Finally, *anxiety is unworthy*. This is the most important reason Jesus gives. Look at the question our Lord asks at the end of verse 25: "Is not life more than food, and the body more than clothing?" That's another good question, and it is one that, I think, most people would answer, "Yeah, sure."

But most people don't live that answer, do they? Go over to the local bookstore. Stand before the magazine rack and randomly pick a magazine. Open it. There you will find ad after ad about food, drink, and clothing. "Is not life more than food, and the body more than clothing?" "Yeah, sure," we say to ourselves, "but I sure could use those new jeans or that pair of shoes or that expensive meal at that nice restaurant. And (when I'm not eating out) I sure could use that granite countertop for those new dishes, which I sure could use with my freshly polished antique silverware." On and on and on we go.

Life is more than food and clothing. Do you get that? Do you believe that? Do you live like you believe that? If you don't it is probably because you don't know what Jesus meant by the word "more." Life is "*more*" than food and clothing. Okay, I agree. But what is the "more"?

Thankfully, in verse 33 Jesus gives us the answer: the "more" is God's kingdom and his righteousness. Don't seek after what every distrusting and dis-treasuring unbeliever in the world seeks after—money and the things money can buy. Rather, "seek first the kingdom of God and his righteousness" (v. 33). Do you see the big picture in verses 25–34? Don't worry about things money can buy, but rather "worry" about God's kingdom and righteousness!

Jesus is very logical here. Why would you seek after stuff that (think about it) has no lasting value to it? You finally get that dream job so you can finally get that dream car that will someday rust. At my grandfather's wake I recall talking to my father's boss. We had a brief but good discussion about traditional Irish wakes. He shared the story of a friend who, at his wake, was propped up in his beloved Corvette. My dad's boss thought it was a fun way to go. I thought that it might just be the stupidest thing I've ever heard. Can you imagine the scene? "Oh, he loved that car," Aunt Irene said. "Oh, it's so nice that we could celebrate his life in this way," added Uncle Seamus. What a joke! What a waste! What a waste of a life! When I die you can bury me in my expensive black suit if that makes you feel nice. You can bury me with a shamrock in my mouth if you think that would appease my Irish family. But please don't bury me in my sporty 2003 Dodge Caravan.

The other day I was reading an encyclopedia article about pyramids. (If you wonder what I do for fun, there it is.) Did you know that many civilizations, not just the Egyptians, built these elaborate tombs for their kings and queens? There are pyramids in China, France, Greece, India, Italy, Cambodia, and the Americas. The oldest and largest of the Egyptian pyramids, the Great Pyramid of Giza, is one of the Seven Wonders of the Ancient World. And yes, architecturally, it is indeed a wonder. But theologically it is quite a blunder. One will never find a footnote in these articles saying, "And by the way, these people were utterly foolish, weren't they?" However, such a footnote would be quite accurate. For what an absolute waste of thought, strength, and time it was to build an elaborate tomb and fill it with priceless treasures that (guess what?) never made it into the afterlife. The only purpose the pyramids serve would be centuries later when they were excavated by overly educated explorers, only to be displayed in some museum where day after day cranky schoolchildren are pulled along by their teachers to help them gain an appreciation for history and civilization. The pyramids are just big illustrations of how right Jesus was and how foolish people can be.

Why die a fool? Why live for the god of money? As Luther asks, "What sort of god is it that is not even capable of defending himself against moths and rust?"[9] Furthermore, what sort of kingdom is so worth living and dying for that it can't even keep out thieves? Don't seek after treasures on earth that have no lasting value, that are so corruptible that a little moth can nibble through them, that water mixed with a slice of sunlight and a touch of time can corrode. Rather seek after God. Seek after his kingdom. Seek after his righteousness.

Which means what? It means that you live for "the spread of the reign of Christ" throughout the world.[10] It means that you declare with your mouth and demonstrate with your life that you believe in Jesus, that you embrace the eternal King and his everlasting reign, and that you passionately "desire that His name should receive from [all people everywhere] the honour which is due to it."[11]

Don't seek after what money can buy. Rather, seek after what neither money nor power can acquire and what no moths, rust, or thieves can ever take away: the gospel that gives everlasting life to those who believe, to those who treasure and trust God.

Who Is Your God?

Who is your God? Is it money or the Lord? Test yourself. Whom do you treasure? Whom do you trust? What do you think about all day? What would upset you most if you lost it? How do you measure other people? What can't you seemingly be happy without?[12] What do you worry about? If you truly *treasure* God, you will *trust* him to provide.

18

The Loving Art of Speck Removal

MATTHEW 7:1–12

MANY FAMOUS PHRASES that we in the Western world use in our common vocabulary come from the Sermon on the Mount. Some examples include *go the extra mile, pay the last penny, don't blow your own horn, a city on a hill, the light of the world, the salt of the earth, the narrow gate*. However, no phrase from the Sermon (and perhaps from the whole Bible) is more popular today than that found in 7:1, "Judge not, that ye be not judged" (KJV). (People even say it in the King James Version.)

Yet what I find ironic about our culture's abundant use of this verse is that when quoted it is almost always used by a non-Christian to a Christian after that Christian has advocated some Christian belief or ethic. I can be sitting with a group of men in a pub on a Sunday morning watching the English Premier League, and if I say, "Argh, when is Manchester United going to trade so and so? He is so lazy and overpaid," no one will turn to me and say, "Judge not, that ye be not judged." We all expect to make and hear judgments on professional athletes, coaches, and teams. Or if I am with my non-Christian neighbors in their family room watching a political debate and I say something like, "You know, I think the senator's foreign policy is uniformed and naïve," my neighbor will not likely turn to me and say, "Judge not, that ye be not judged." Again, we all expect to make and hear judgments on politics and politicians.

However, if in these same two contexts I say, "I think that Joe Athlete (who we know from the news media lavishly spends his unjustified salary on all sorts of luxuries) spends his money not only irresponsibly but immorally," what response would I get? Or if I said, "I think Islamic terrorism is based on some fundamental theological flaws in Islam's holy book, the Quran," what response would I get? It is then (and often only then) that the world's new favorite Bible verse rears its head: "Judge not, that ye be not judged."

However, here our culture is confused. When the Lord Jesus said, "Judge not, that you be not judged," he did not mean what our culture means when people presume to borrow this phrase. Jesus' command does not mean that we are never to make an exclusive theological judgment or offer a moral corrective that is based on God's Word.

I say this first and most obviously because of the words and actions of our Lord himself. Throughout the Sermon on the Mount, Jesus makes one theological and ethical judgment after another. If you took out all the verses in chapters 5, 6 where Jesus says in essence, "Think this way, not that way; live this way, not that way," you wouldn't have many verses left. Or simply look in our text. Look at verse 5. It starts with a judgment, with Jesus' favorite term for the person who turns God's Law on its head—"You hypocrite" (cf. Matthew 23). Our Lord calls a spade a spade and a sinner a sinner.

Moreover, look at the next verse. In verse 6, as we shall see, Jesus commands us to discern who acts like a Christian—a "brother," vv. 3–5—and who acts like an animal—a "dog" or a "pig." These are not only harsh terms, but they are terms of judgment. Chapter 7, in fact, ends in verses 13–27 with us having to make one judgment after another: enter this narrow gate, not that wide one. Build your house on the rock, not on the sand. Listen to true teachers, not false ones.[1]

Therefore, the verse "Judge not, that you be not judged" is not the end of Jesus' discussion on judgment; rather it is just the beginning. In 7:1–12 our Lord Jesus is not teaching us not to judge (period), but rather how to make true, wise, and (most importantly) *loving* judgments. He will teach us *the loving art of speck-removal.*

Asking Our Father for What?

The first question often asked as one reads through this passage is, what is Jesus' train of thought? For, first, Jesus talks about judging, next he gives this proverb about a dog and a pig, then he talks about prayer, and finally he tacks on the Golden Rule. So what's the ordering here? What is the progression of thought? What is Jesus getting at?

The first thing to notice is what John Stott calls the "connecting thread"[2] of relationships between Christians and (1) God, (2) other Christians, and (3) hostile unbelievers. Once we see this thread, the next thing to do is to start with what Jesus says about our relationship with God (in other words, vv. 7–11). For if we start there (and understand what is taught there), then what comes after it in verse 12 and before it in verses 1–6 starts to unfold like petals of a flower on a lovely spring day.

So let's start our study on speck removal with verses 7–11. Notice the word "ask" or "asks." We are to ask (v. 7) and then ask (v. 8) and then ask (v. 9) and then ask (v. 10) and finally ask (v. 11). We are to ask God. We are also to "seek" and even "knock" (vv. 7, 8). We are not to stay put. We are to urgently and continuously call upon the Lord. Confident that our loving Lord will give us good things, we are to stand at his door and knock until he lets our petitions in. That's the picture here.

But for what are we to pray? For what are we to ask God? The only answer found in verses 7–11 is a rather vague one—"good gifts" or "good things." Look at verse 11. Jesus says, "If you then, who are evil, know how to *give good gifts* to your children, how much more will your Father who is in heaven *give good things* to those who ask him!"

So we are asking God, our Father, for "good things." Such as? Well, I don't know. Is this a blank check? How about a ton of money for all the things money can buy? I doubt that considering what we learned in Matthew 6. So what are these good gifts from God? Perhaps we are asking for forgiveness, strength to resist temptation, deliverance from Satan, power to proclaim the gospel, or all of the above and more. Luke's version reads, "[H]ow much more will the heavenly Father give *the Holy Spirit* to those who ask him!" (Luke 11:13). Whether the Holy Spirit is in Matthew's mind when he penned "good things" we cannot be certain. We can, however, be certain of our need for the Spirit to understand and live out all that Jesus has taught thus far in the Sermon on the Mount (5:2—7:6)! More directly related to this context, we need the Spirit to help us heed the Golden Rule (v. 12), especially in the most difficult circumstances, such as rightly judging ourselves and others. We need God's gifts of the Holy Spirit, discernment, and love—these "good gifts"—so that we might "see clearly," as Jesus puts it in the middle of verse 5—see ourselves clearly and then see others clearly.

Seeing Ourselves Clearly

So that's the gist of verses 7–11, of what is to be our relationship through prayer with God. Next look at verse 12, just the first part, as we move from our relationship with God to others: "So whatever you wish that others would do to you . . ." Do you see how the first part focuses on self? What would you want done to you? Well, no one would want what happens in verses 3, 4 done to them. No one would want some self-righteous, oblivious, uncaring, and condemning hypocrite to judge him from a distance, "Hey you. Yeah, you over there. I see a speck in your eye." You think to yourself, "What? He sees a what?" And then here he comes, proudly parading over to you, condescendingly coaching you along the way. "Now you stay put. I'll get that for you." Who would want that done to them?

So first we are to ask God's help to see ourselves clearly, which involves seeing two things. First, we are to see the scales; second, we are to see the log. By "seeing the scales" I refer to what Jesus teaches in verse 2, where he says (starting in v. 1), "Judge not, that you be not judged. For with the judgment you pronounce you will be judged, and with the measure you use it will be measured to you."

Throughout chapter 7 Jesus emphasizes the judgment of God.[3] Here the scale of God's judgment on the last day is to be in our sight (cf. Romans 2:1–3; 1 Corinthians 4:4, 5). Jesus is telling us to remember before we pass judgment on someone else that we too will one day stand before the throne of God to give an account for everything. So, with what scale would you like God to weigh you? The *scale of mercy* that is very forgiving, or the *scale of justice* that is very exacting, which weighs each and every sinful thought, word, and action with the proper punishment? Jesus calls you to consider the scale of your forgiving heavenly Father before you judge your earthly brother.

So, first, see the scale; then second, see the log.

> Why do you see the speck that is in your brother's eye, but do not notice the log that is in your own eye? Or how can you say to your brother, "Let me take the speck out of your eye," when there is a log in your own eye? You hypocrite, first take the log out of your own eye, and then you will see clearly . . . (vv. 3–5a)

Stop there. Here Jesus is making a very serious point with a very funny illustration. Picture a guy with a speck in his eye. He really does have a problem. Like a sliver in a lion's paw, a speck in the eye is not easy to live with. You want someone to remove it. So here comes help. Here comes Mr. Log-in-the-Eye. He has in his eye one of those main beams that holds up a house, which in Jesus' day were about forty feet long and five feet around.[4] There is no way he could possibly get close enough or see clearly enough to remove the speck. To remove a speck you need to get face-to-face with someone and look closely and carefully.

If the point of the analogy of the scales is, don't be unmerciful in your judgment of others, the point of this log analogy is, don't be a hypocrite. However, being a hypocrite consists of more than meets the eye (pun intended). Most of us don't intentionally act like hypocrites. Hypocrisy is usually like that small splash of spaghetti sauce on your left check. In order to see it you need someone else to say something to you, or you need to see it for yourself in the mirror. It is like David who needed Nathan to show him the log of his sin (2 Samuel 12). Or it is like those men who were ready to stone that woman caught in adultery who needed Jesus to open their eyes in order to look first at themselves: "Let him who is without sin among you be the first to throw a stone at her" (John 8:7).[5] We all need a prophet or a friend or Jesus, as it is here, to help us see ourselves clearly and (taught here) to see clearly that we are quite dirty not only on the outside but also on the inside.

It is no slip of the tongue when Jesus, almost in passing, calls his followers "evil" in verse 11—"If you then, who are evil, know how to give good gifts to your children . . ." That is a profoundly true theological statement. We might do "good things." We might "give good gifts" to our children. But at the root of everything we are and do, we still have our fallen human nature, which is fundamentally "evil."

It is this evil within that makes it so easy to gossip, tell tales, find faults in others, make rash and hasty and ill-informed judgments, think the worst of others' motives and actions, or take minor offenses and turn them into grand jury indictments,[6] all the while missing the spaghetti sauce on our own face. Here Jesus says, "None of this in my kingdom. Put away all anger, wrath, malice, slander, and put on compassion, kindness, humility, meekness, and patience; put away complaining and criticizing others, and put on love, thus bearing with one another and forgiving one another" (cf. Colossians 3:7, 12–14).

See the scales. See the log. See yourself clearly before you start removing specks.

Seeing Others Clearly

Back again to verse 12. The first part reads, "So whatever you wish that others would do to you . . ."—what I have titled, *seeing ourselves clearly*. The second half continues, "do also to them. . . ."

We need to see ourselves clearly. However, if we stop there we miss this full command of love. We also need to see others clearly, so that we might act in appropriate ways toward them, and especially (in this context) so that we might judge others rightly and lovingly.

Thus we will now focus on verses 5b, 6. Look first at verse 6. Jesus has moved from the birds in chapter 6 to the dogs and the pigs: "Do not give dogs what is holy, and do not throw your pearls before pigs, lest they trample them underfoot and turn to attack you." Here Jesus says we must be able to discern between who is a "brother," as in verses 3–5a (the word "brother" is used three times there) and who is a "dog" or a "pig."

"Dog" is a term Jesus uses elsewhere to refer to "Gentiles" or more generically "unbelievers" (cf. 15:26, 27 and Revelation 22:15). Now I know that some of you are dog lovers, so prepare yourselves emotionally for what I have to say, for our gracious Lord Jesus does not speak well of man's best friend. This is because in his day dogs were despised creatures. They roamed freely. They were dangerous. They were scavengers who ate whatever scraps they could find. Therefore, unlike our culture, it was uncommon in Jesus' culture to have a dog as a companion. The only time the Bible mentions dogs hanging out with humans is when the dogs kept homeless Lazarus company by licking his sores (Luke 16:21).

Dogs were disgusting. And pigs . . . well, pigs were pigs. To a Jew, a pig was the "epitome of uncleanness"—both literally and spiritually.[7] Unlike the pigs we might think of—like Wilbur in *Charlotte's Web*—they were not kind. (And they didn't talk!) They were more like wild boars. These unkosher creatures had a reputation for being not only filthy but also greedy and vicious.

Do you see what Jesus is saying? A "brother" is a believer and a "dog/pig" an unbeliever, though not just your average unbeliever but an antagonistic one (cf. 2 Peter 2:22). Our Lord says in essence, "Now listen, Christian, you need to be discerning here. Don't take the gospel of the kingdom (what he labels 'pearls') and present it to those who are overly antagonistic toward it. Not only will they not appreciate it, they will be upset at you for throwing them a jewel when all they want is slop. Rather than the gospel that brings life, all they want is their own autonomous, foolish philosophy."

What Jesus teaches here accords with what is taught in places like Proverbs 9:7, 8a: "Whoever corrects a scoffer gets himself abuse, and he who reproves a wicked man incurs injury. Do not reprove a scoffer, or he will hate you." Furthermore, what Jesus teaches here is illustrated throughout the Scriptures in places like 10:14, where the disciples are told to shake the dust off their feet if they are not welcomed, or Acts 19:9, where we read that Paul "withdrew" from teaching in the synagogue in Ephesus because "some became stubborn and continued in unbelief, speaking evil of the Way before the congregation." They rejected the gospel, so Paul moved on.

As Christians, once we see ourselves rightly, we also must see others rightly. We are to "judge with right judgment," as Jesus puts it in John 7:24b (cf. 1 John 4:1; Titus 3:10, 11). We are not to feed the dogs. We are not to play with pigs. We are to see that some people want nothing to do with us and our gospel. And so, with sorrow in our hearts and tears in our eyes, like our Lord himself (see Luke 19:41, 42), we are to leave them to themselves, and ultimately to the hands of God.

That is the first judgment we are to make. We are to discern the dogs from the disciples, the boars from the brothers. However, what are we to do with our brothers if we see that they have a speck in their eye? Are we to say, "Oh, that must be painful, but you know, I'm too busy to do anything about it"? No. Look at the second half of verse 5—the often forgotten aspect of the "judge not, that you be not judged" passage. After you have removed that log from your own eye, Jesus says, "then you will see clearly to take the speck out of your brother's eye.'" Am I reading that right? Yes. There it is! "Take the speck out of your brother's eye."

> Step One: See the log in your own eye.
> Step Two: Remove it. Repent of your sin.
> Step Three: See the speck in your brother's eye.
> Step Four: Remove it. Take the speck out!

Some people think that the teachings in the Sermon on the Mount are too lofty, too otherworldly, and thus too unrealistic.[8] On the contrary, they are not. Certainly the kingdom ethics of the Sermon on the Mount are high and difficult; they are as challenging and rewarding as climbing a mountain. But they are also as tangible as that mountain, for throughout this Sermon Jesus is repeatedly realistic. In chapter 5 he teaches that entrance into the kingdom doesn't require absolute keeping of the Law, but humility before God and sorrow over our sins. In chapter 6 he teaches us a prayer, the center of which petitions, "And forgive us our debts." Jesus knows that we will have debts to ask forgiveness for daily. Here in chapter 7 Jesus says that the Christian community will be filled with sinful brothers, some with specks and others with logs. According to Jesus, even those with logs—bigger or more obvious sins—have not only the right but also the obligation to help those with specks—those with little or less obvious sins. Isn't that fascinating? Isn't that beautiful?

Ligon Duncan describes this as the call for Christians to mutually discipline each other in the Lord.[9] In the same vein Jesus calls Leviticus 19:18b ("You shall love your neighbor as yourself") the second greatest commandment. But do you know what comes right before that? Leviticus 19:17, 18a reads:

> You shall not hate your brother in your heart, but you shall reason frankly with your neighbor [i.e., "brother"], lest you incur sin because of him. You

> shall not take vengeance or bear a grudge against the sons of your own people [i.e., your brothers], but you shall love your neighbor as yourself.

This "reasoning frankly with your neighbor" is the difficult and delicate procedure of speck removal. The loving thing to do is to rebuke and remove sin. This involves (1) seeing your brother's sin, (2) helping your brother see his sin, and (3) having him lie down, open wide his eyelids, and trust you—even you with the one-time log in your eye—to remove it carefully and caringly.

Jesus teaches in 18:15,

> If your brother sins against you, go and tell him his fault, between you and him alone. If he listens to you, you have gained your brother.

Jesus goes on to say what should happen if he won't listen, which eventually ends in excommunication, treating him "as a Gentile," like a dog (see vv. 16, 17). The ideal, however, is corrective eye surgery.

John Chrysostom once said, "Correct your brother, not as a foe, nor as an adversary, exacting a penalty, but as a physician."[10] That is the perfect analogy. Brothers and sisters in Christ, we are all physicians (ah! the physicianhood of all believers!), and just as we should not be taken aback if a doctor were to tell us that something is wrong with our eye and that the cure "might hurt a bit," so we should not be surprised by the sins our brothers and sisters see in us—specks that need to be seen and removed for our own spiritual health.

> Love is patient and kind; love does not envy or boast; it is not arrogant or rude. It does not insist on its own way; it is not irritable or resentful; it does not rejoice at wrongdoing, but rejoices with the truth. Love bears all things, believes all things, hopes all things, endures all things. (1 Corinthians 13:4–7)

And may I add, love judges all things rightly, wisely, with others' best interests in mind.

It is unloving to judge your brother when you have a log in your own eye. *But* it is also unloving to leave a speck in your brother's eye.

Asking for Wisdom

When I was a young Christian, I started reading through the New Testament. When I came to that wonderful book of James, I read these words:

> If any of you lacks wisdom, let him ask God, who gives generously to all without reproach, and it will be given him. But let him ask in faith . . . (1:5, 6a)

Do you know what I did right after I read those verses? I took God at his word. I put down my Bible and prayed, "God, give me wisdom."

At the time I didn't know exactly what wisdom was or what I was asking for, but now I know. I was asking God, like Solomon did, to help me *judge* matters rightly, to distinguish between right and wrong thinking and living. I was asking God for what Jesus is instructing all his followers here to ask for: to help me make true, right, and (most importantly) loving judgments—those that are in the best interests of others and that I would like others to do for me.

When you pray, for what do you pray? When you knock on Heaven's door . . . when you seek earnestly after God . . . when you pray to your Father in Heaven . . . for what do you *ask*? Here in 7:1–12 our Lord Jesus teaches us to pray that we might see ourselves clearly and thus see others clearly—to pray for wisdom so that we might judge one another lovingly.

19

The Narrow Gate to Life

MATTHEW 7:13–29

HASN'T SCIENCE DISPROVED most of the basic claims of Christianity, including God's being the Creator of the universe? If God is so great, explain why the history of organized religion is so terrible. Isn't religion to blame for most wars, hatred, and terrorism in the world? How could an all-loving and all-powerful God allow senseless suffering? Isn't the Bible full of contradictions as well as historical, scientific, and moral errors? How can anyone believe that faith in Jesus is the only way to God?

Those are some of the questions people are asking today. As I traveled to various small groups in my church, asking which of the questions above are most often asked, the overwhelming majority said that the last question is first. Theological exclusivity is the issue of the day! When we read Jesus' words, "Enter by the narrow gate" (v. 13a), an array of questions might come to mind, such as: What is this narrow gate? How does one enter in? Why is it narrow in the first place? Why do so many people not enter it? How can anyone believe that faith in Jesus Christ is the only way to God?

In our examination of 7:13–29 we'll look at some answers to these tough questions of theological exclusivity. We will start with the shortest and easiest one: What is the narrow gate?

What Is the Narrow Gate?

The narrow gate is more of a who than a what. The narrow gate is Jesus. I say this because of what Jesus himself teaches in John 10:9, where he calls himself "the door" (cf. v. 3 "gatekeeper") or "the gate" (NIV). In a context similar to what we have here in Matthew (as Jesus is talking about false teachers who try to steal and harm the sheep), he says in John 10:9, "I am the door [i.e., the gate through which the sheep enter safely]. If anyone enters by me, he will be saved." This same sort of imagery and language in John 10:9 is used in 7:21, where Jesus says, "Not everyone who says to me, 'Lord, Lord,' will enter the kingdom of heaven." Enter what? The kingdom of heaven. How? Through the narrow gate (i.e., Jesus). Jesus teaches, "Not everyone who says *to me* . . ." He is the gate into Heaven, the way into life, the way into eternal fellowship with God (cf. John 14:6).

How Does One Enter In?

So if Jesus is "the gate," how does one enter in? That's our second question. To find the answer we can stay in verse 21, where Jesus again instructs, "Not everyone who says to me, 'Lord, Lord,' will enter the kingdom of heaven, but *the one who does the will of my Father* who is in heaven."

In Scripture, the concept of *God's will* covers much territory—from his providence over every detail of this universe (not a sparrow falls to the ground unless he wills it) to ethics (it is God's will that you avoid sexual immorality) even to Jesus' death on the cross (Jesus gave himself for our sins according to the will of God). Also included in *God's will* is faith in Christ. Listen to what Jesus says in John 6:38, 40: "I have come down from heaven, not to do my own will but the will of him who sent me. . . . For this is the will of my Father, that everyone who looks on the Son and *believes in him* should have eternal life." It is God's will that we believe in Jesus.

So, getting through the gate here in Matthew 7 is what one commentator calls our "evangelical decision" (that is, trusting in Jesus), and then *walking on the way* (down this hard path) is our "ethical endurance."[1] So although one is saved by faith alone in Christ alone, that saving faith is never alone. It works. It loves. It obeys. It endures. It perseveres, not perfectly but persistently. What is taught in James 2 is likewise taught here. It is not enough to say "I believe in God" or even "I believe in Jesus" (the "Lord, Lord" talk of our text). We must walk the talk.[2] A saving faith is a doing faith. Therefore, the word "does" does matter![3] "The one who *does* the will of my Father . . ."[4] Our Lord is not separating our evangelical decision (faith alone) from our ethical endurance (the perseverance of the saints).

Why Is the Gate Narrow?

So, according to Jesus, there is this narrow gate and there is this way of getting through. That claim then raises another question: why is the gate narrow in the first place? Put differently, why is it that faith alone in Jesus alone is the only way?

Let me start by saying that while we are all opposed to narrow-mindedness, we are not as opposed to exclusivity as we might at first think. For example, no one is opposed to a supermarket or a restaurant—a place where food is handled and sold and consumed—having an exclusive sign on the front glass that reads, "No Shoes, No Shirt, No Service." No one is opposed to the Spanish Club at your local high school being comprised only of members who have an interest in and a basic knowledge of the Spanish language. No one is opposed to Woman's Workout World having a policy that men are not allowed to work out there. And nobody thinks that if there is only one vaccine that will cure polio, that is too narrow, that we should be able to take whatever drug we want to cure polio.

Thus intellectually we are not completely opposed to the concept of narrowness, except (nowadays) when it comes to religion. "There can't be only one way to God" or "There shouldn't be only one way to God" are views frequently expressed. However, can you hear what is beneath such questions? The questioners assume that God is unjust. They also assume that we somehow see things better than God does.[5] But those are absolutely wrong assumptions. Perhaps for this reason this question of exclusivity is not found in our text. It does not arise from this text, and it is not answered in this text.

We wouldn't question the justice and goodness of the scientist who found *the one* cure for the Great Plague. So why do we question God when he has provided only one cure for our Great Plague? Thus, the question "why so narrow?" is a question of ingratitude and insubordination. It is as contemptible as putting Sir Alexander Fleming on trial for *only* giving us penicillin. Therefore, in this courtroom I throw out this case against God. Instead I do what God does here in his Word. He puts us on trial. We must stand before him and give an account for our choices.

Why Do So Many People Not Enter It?

The question raised and answered here in the text is not, why is God's gate so narrow? but rather, why do people go so wide? Expressed differently, why does the majority of humanity not look for the narrow gate, not find it, and not walk through it? We now turn our attention to that important inquiry.

Chapter 7 gives us three answers. The first answer is that we are all *evil* by nature. This is taught in many places in Scripture, including verse 11, which we discussed in the last chapter. Note that in verse 11 Jesus is talking not to the scribes and Pharisees, the Roman officials and soldiers, or the pagans and blasphemers, but to his followers. He says, "If you then, who are evil, know how to give good gifts to your children . . ." Stop there. Rewind the tape. He says, "If you then, who are evil . . ." What a claim!

Can you imagine someone making that claim today the way Jesus does? Let's say you are serving on the local school board, and you're in a meeting, discussing new curriculum, and one of the ladies on the board says, "Well, since we are all evil and our children are all evil, I advocate that we . . ." What would happen? All the heads in the room would quickly turn and stare at this woman whom they are now quite certain is an alien.

But how out of this world is that claim? The doctrine of original sin is the most verifiable doctrine of the Christian faith. Gather a toddler from every country in the world, put them in a room together, and tell them, "Only one of you gets this piece of candy." See then if they are naturally selfish or not. I'm sure you can think of a better example. Why? It is because we all have experienced regularly the truth of our fallen nature. In the United States our very form of government is based on the assumption of inherent evil—that all people, even the best of us, if given too much power for too long, will act corruptly. So the claim that people are fundamentally evil is not unthinkable. Rather, it is simply not thought about today. It is not that it's not true. Rather, it is not thought about, and thus it's not taught.

However, everything in the Christian faith hinges on this reality. If people are not evil, fallen, and rebels against God, then Jesus is not necessary, and God's plan of salvation makes no sense. But if you take a careful look at your own inclinations, attitudes, and actions, you might just see that Jesus' accusation is accurate.

The Russian novelist Ivan Turgenev wrote, "I do not know what the heart of a bad man is like, but I do know what the heart of a good man is like, and it is terrible."[6] In some professions seeing evil is an everyday reality. Being a pastor is one such profession. I often see people at their worst. But I'm not talking about my parishioners at their worse; I'm talking about me at my best. If you looked at me from a distance, it all looks nice enough. Here is a man who spends his whole week studying the Bible and preparing to teach it; look at him up there, teaching away. But what you don't see is that in this heart there is always (at least) a touch of pride, ambition, and worry. I care too much about what the congregation thinks of me. So, although the satellite view can't detect anything wrong, the microscopic camera picks it all up.

God has that little lens on us all the time. You don't fool him. I don't fool him. I know that the heart of that bad man and this fairly good man are both terrible! I agree with verse 11. I'm evil, and so are you. That is the first and most foundational reason people choose the wide gate. Due to the fall, we are naturally inclined to do so.

The second reason is closely related to the first. Evil is the first. *Ease* is the second. Look at verses 13, 14, where again we read, "Enter by the narrow gate. For the gate is wide and the way is *easy* that leads to destruction, and those who enter by it are many. For the gate is narrow and the way is *hard* that leads to life, and those who find it are few."[7]

Why go wide? It's the same reason why Division 1 college athletes major in general studies rather than astrophysics. It's easy. And it's easy to live under the lordship of our own rules, like the made-up legislation in our head that says, "It doesn't matter what you believe so long as you're sincere" or "How can it be wrong if it feels so right?"

Here's how I picture what's going on in verses 13, 14. You are on a journey, and you have some luggage with you—holding all the stuff of earth that you like and want to take with you forever. You have your suitcases packed full of vices and a huge mountain backpack filled with money and all the things money can buy. You come up to this big, wide, and beautiful gate. Behind the gate you see what looks like a lovely and easy road to travel. On the posts of the gate are engraved in gold the words FREEDOM and FUN.

You notice off to the side, however, a little sign stuck in the ground that reads, "This way to find the narrow gate to life." You think, "Hmm . . . I wonder what that is." But a fellow comes along and says, "Oh, you don't want that gate. Trust me, it is *so* narrow. You have to give up freedom and fun, and you wouldn't be able to carry that backpack and those suitcases through. It's far too narrow. And do you know what is written *in blood* on its gateposts? On one is written 'DEATH—death to self' and on the other 'SORROW—sorrow over sin.' You have to die to self, and if you want to go through there, you have to repent of sin."

"Well," you say to yourself, "let's see. Do I choose this narrow gate, which I have to go and find, and which I can't go through with all this stuff, and which speaks of death and sorrow? Or do I choose this other gate?" Easy decision, isn't it? You choose ease along with so many others. So many have chosen the highway to Hell where on the back of these golden gateposts, which no one can read until it's too late, are not the words FREEDOM and FUN but DEATH and SORROW (eternal death, eternal sorrow).

Why do people go wide? Why does the majority of humanity make the wrong choice? Evil and ease are the first two answers our Lord provides. The third and final answer is false prophets, mentioned much in verses 15–23.

In the last chapter I described 7:1 as the world's new favorite verse. Anytime we make a distinctive Christian judgment about theology or ethics, that verse is thrown in our faces. Yet, Christians too have taken up the un-Biblical notion that anytime a Christian leader talks against other so-called "Christian" leaders, churches, or ministries he is being judgmental. But that is the absolute opposite of what Jesus is saying here. He says, "Beware." Beware of whom? Beware of those new atheists who attack Christianity? No, we can recognize them for who they are. Beware of bizarre cult leaders? No, they are obvious also. Rather, we are to beware of men and women who look like Christians (who come to you in sheep's clothing), who talk like Christians ("Lord, Lord"), and who act like super-Christians (preaching and casting out demons and doing mighty miracles).

So if I tell you from the pulpit or in private that a certain person is a false teacher, do not think I'm acting un-Christlike. On the contrary, I am never more like the Good Shepherd than when I'm protecting you from wolves (see Titus 1:9)—when I'm looking for and pointing out to you diseased trees and their poisonous fruit. A good tree will produce good fruit, and a bad tree will produce bad fruit (vv. 16–20). Therefore, we are to do a fruit check with every tree that comes along, looking for "anyone [who] teaches a different doctrine and does not agree with the sound words of our Lord Jesus Christ and the teaching that accords with godliness" (1 Timothy 6:3; cf. Titus 1:16). We are to look for ungodliness or "lawlessness," which according to verse 23 is Christ's accusation against these false prophets, his reason for turning them away. We are to look for lawless teaching and living.

Thus, to contemporize our Lord's teaching, it's as if Jesus says, "I teach self-denial; they teach *look great, feel great*. I teach the dangers of materialism; they teach *live your best life now*. I teach that there is only one way to God; they teach *love wins*—that the *wideness of God's mercy* is so wide that everyone is eventually included in his kingdom. I teach humility and dependence upon God; they teach *if it's to be, it's up to me*."

Look carefully at verse 22. Look at what these false speakers will say on Judgment Day. "On that day many will say to me . . ." Say what? They will say with great devotion and correct Christology, "'Lord, Lord, did we not prophesy in your name, and cast out demons in your name, and do many mighty works in your name?' Lord, don't you have my spiritual resumé?" Indeed he does, and he views it as being as impressive as Judas's.

Do you see how they give their "christocentric-charismatic credentials"?[8] They list the gifts of the Spirit but not the fruit of the Spirit. They boast of great religion but not true religion (James 1:27). How very different than the unwittingly (or unpresumptuous) "righteous" of 25:37–39, who say:

> Lord, when did we see you hungry and feed you, or thirsty and give you drink? And when did we see you a stranger and welcome you, or naked and clothe you? And when did we see you sick or in prison and visit you?

Do not underestimate the influence of bad theology and false teaching. So many people choose the wide way to destruction because of these clanging cymbals, these showy charlatans who teach "'Peace, peace,' when there is no peace" (Jeremiah 6:14; 8:11), who deliver moving sermons and work wonders (24:11; 2 Thessalonians 2:8, 9; cf. Deuteronomy 13:1–3), yet who preach a "different gospel" that is no gospel at all (Galatians 1:6, 7)—the gospel of "a God without wrath [who] brought men without sin into a kingdom without judgment through the ministrations of a Christ without a cross."[9]

Take Him at His Word

Having laid that groundwork, finally, we come to THE BIG question: how can anyone believe that faith in Jesus Christ is the only way to God? What is our answer to that? Based on this text, our answer is quite straightforward. We can believe that Jesus is the only way because we *take Jesus at his word.* In other words, because he says so!

Basically this is an issue of authority. We all make judgments about who is an authority on certain matters. Then if we believe that someone is an authority, we trust his or her view on that particular issue. If the world's most renowned heart surgeon tells us we need heart surgery as soon as possible, we take her at her word. If our company's top computer guru tells us the problem with our computer is related to a certain virus and he explains how to remove it, we heed his advice. The argument that the Bible gives for theological exclusivity uses the same line of logic. If Jesus is the unique Son of God, who created and sustains the universe, who came to earth as a man, who performed miracles (especially rising from the dead), and if what he taught and did was predicted by the prophets and attested to by apostolic eyewitnesses, then what he says about entrance into the kingdom of heaven is trustworthy.

So taking him at his word and saying, "I believe Jesus is the only way because he says so" is not a trite or superficial answer. The issue of theological exclusivity is an issue of authority. The ultimate question of the Sermon on the Mount from Jesus is not just "What do you think of my teaching?" but "What do you think of me?"[10] "[W]ho do you say that I am?" (16:15). Do we recognize Jesus as his first audience did, "as one who had authority" (7:29),[11] or do we recognize him as that and much more, as the one who has all authority over Heaven and earth (28:18)?

Jesus says, "Everyone . . . who hears *these words of mine* and does them will be like a wise man. . . . And everyone who hears *these words of mine* and does not do them will be like a foolish man" (vv. 24a, 26a). Jesus claims that human wisdom and human folly will be assessed based on one's reception or rejection of the Sermon on the Mount![12] What a staggering claim!

But that's not all he claims. Listen afresh to verses 21–23 and notice Jesus' self-focus:

- "Not everyone who says to me, 'Lord, Lord,' will enter the kingdom of heaven" (v. 21a).
- "On that day many will say to me . . ." (v. 22a).
- "And then will I declare to them, 'I never knew you; depart from me'" (v. 23a).

Me, me, I, I, me! Just who does he think he is? There is nothing indirect or modest about the final verses of the Sermon on the Mount. Here Jesus gives what might just be the boldest claims in the history of the world. The prophet Isaiah writes, "For the LORD is our judge; the LORD is our lawgiver; the LORD is our king; he will save us" (Isaiah 33:22). That is what Jesus claims here of himself. He is judge. He is lawgiver. He is king. He is the only one who can save us. Ultimately salvation is in his hands. He will judge whether we come into his presence or not based on how we respond to his words—"these words of mine" (7:24, 26). He will decide and declare our destinies.[13]

Think about what Jesus says. Let me put it into perspective. If today I ran into a young man who had no job or formal education and who after he gave a short lecture on the top of some hill came up to me and said, "You, my friend, will one day stand before me, and I will determine your eternal destiny based on your response to what you have just heard," I would say, "Oh that's nice" and dismiss him as a self-deceived lunatic. How is it then that when Jesus claims that he will be the judge before whom we all will stand and that whether or not we get into the kingdom of heaven will be judged based on what we did with his words, I find him so very believable? And why I am not alone in my assessment? Millions of others from every imaginable country and culture believe the same.

Why is this? Is it that his message is so universally applicable? Is it that he, unlike any other teacher ever, seems to know intimately the mind of God and yet intimately the ways and needs and desires of man, touching every possible line of relationship with which you and I deal on a daily basis—everything from whom we should worship to what we shouldn't worry about?[14] Is it that his claims—as lofty and seemingly egocentric as they are—

somehow come across as the words of the humblest man ever to walk the face of the earth? Yes, I suppose it is those three reasons and more! His message is otherworldly but down-to-earth. His claims and character collide in a most convicting way. Whatever it is, he has me (and I'm not a gullible person) by the heart and won't let go. He demands my life, my soul, my all. And I say, "You have it. Here it all is. Into your hands I commit my spirit. You are the Lawgiver. You are the Judge. You are the King. You are my Savior."

But what about you? Where are your feet today? Are they sifting through sand or are they solidly placed upon the Rock? Our loving Lord is warning you today. Beware of false prophets. Beware of the wide gate and easy path. Beware of building your house on the wrong foundation. Beware of the coming judgment. Beware lest your house crumble and fall to the ground (v. 27), and your seemingly carefree walk through this world ends in destruction (v. 13), and your very body and soul are banished from Christ's presence (v. 23) and are thrown into the fire (v. 19). "Beware," Jesus warns.

However, he also graciously invites you to "Choose life,"[15] to "enter by the narrow gate." It doesn't look like it leads to much of anything, but believe Jesus (take him at his word) that it actually does lead to true life, freedom, and joy . . . both now and forevermore!

20

Pictures of Power

MATTHEW 8:1–17

MY WIFE HAS THE GIFT of finding bargains. Just the other day she put this gift to use for my benefit. At a neighbor's garage sale Emily found four antique picture frames for the bare wall in my home office. My guess, if the frames are as old as the prints inside them, is that these perfectly scuffed, slightly ornate frames are over a hundred years old. We bought the four frames for fifteen dollars.

What I did first with these finds was pry open the backs of them (they had a thin layer of wood nailed to the back). Then I pulled out the glass and the old prints, took a knife, and carefully cut through the glue that held the prints to the matting. The prints are black-and-white pencil sketches of famous scientists and writers of the nineteenth century. I put on top of the faces of these four important men (I hope they do forgive me for this) pictures I cut out from a book on church architecture. These are all prints from early Christian art found on the walls of catacombs and churches—portraits of Jesus as king, warrior, teacher, and shepherd.

In 8:1–17 we also see portraits of Jesus. The Gospel writer gives us three portraits of Jesus' divine power as healer. Beneath each portrait are parts of an older portrait drawn long ago by the prophet Isaiah—that of the Suffering Servant. What lies beneath, if you will bear with the analogy, Jesus' power to heal any and everything from leprosy to demon possession is the prophecy of Isaiah 53:4, "He took our illnesses and bore our diseases" (quoted in 8:17).[1]

You see, the end is the end (*telos*). That is, the last verse of this pericope (v. 17) is the reason Matthew—from all the miracle stories about Jesus he could tell—tells these three. Ironically, they are portraits of power from the one who has come to bear in his own body on the cross all the disease, sickness, and ugliness of our sin (cf. 1 Peter 2:24).[2] They are portraits of power for the powerless—an unclean leper, a Gentile's servant, and a Jewish woman.

Picture One: The Leper

We start with the leper. "When he [Jesus] came down from the mountain, great crowds followed him. And behold, a leper came to him . . ." (vv. 1, 2).

Like HIV/AIDS today, leprosy in ancient Israel was the most dreaded disease. Leprosy is a contagious skin disease that not only affects the skin (its color, texture, and odor) and throat (it creates a raspy voice), but also slowly destroys nerves that sense pain in our bodies. Thus, lepers often lost the tips of fingers and toes and broke limbs because they couldn't feel the weight of something heavy or the heat of the fire or the cut of a knife.

For a Jew, however, the worst part of this disease was the necessary *separateness* that went along with it. According to Leviticus 13:45, 46, a leper had to wear torn clothes, keep his hair unkempt, cover his mouth, and cry out "Unclean! Unclean!" in order to prevent spreading his disease to others. Moreover, this uncleanness meant that lepers could not reside within the community of Israel; they were banished from God's people (cf. Numbers 5:2) and temple presence.

This reality about leprosy—from the disease itself to the social and cultic separateness that went with it—is what makes verse 2 and following so remarkable: "And behold, a leper came to him [Jesus] and knelt before him, saying, 'Lord, if you will, you can make me clean.'"

His condition was so deplorable, but his faith so commendable! Look again at verses 1, 2. The leper somehow made his way through a large crowd and then jumped right into the front of the line so he might speak face-to-face with Jesus. Well, maybe not face-to-face, but face-to-foot, for notice his reverent posture: "[He] knelt before him" (v. 2). Then notice the first word out of his mouth, "Lord." You can call Jesus "Lord" without having saving faith in him. Jesus teaches that at the end of the Sermon on the Mount. However, consistently throughout Matthew's Gospel this title is only found on the lips of Jesus' disciples or those who, like this leper, are sick and in desperate need of him.

It seems most likely that the title "Lord" is more than a polite or respectable "Sir" because of what the leper says next.[3] He invokes Jesus' Lordship. He doesn't say, "Lord, *if you can*, make me clean." Rather he says, "Lord, if you will, *you can* make me clean." This is more of a statement than a question. If it is a question, however, it's something like, "Jesus, I recognize you have the power to make me clean. So, will you?" (cf. Daniel 3:17, 18). Notice the balance of the leper's faith. He has confidence in Jesus ("you can heal me") mixed with humility ("only if you will"). Now that's faith—absolute trust in Jesus and absolute poverty of spirit before him.

What does Jesus do? He doesn't say, "Whoa, now wait a minute . . . ah, why the kneeling? And what's with the calling me 'Lord'? And leprosy . . . umm . . . that's a tough one. I'm not a leprosy specialist." He doesn't say anything like that. In fact, he doesn't say anything at first. Although he can heal just by the power of his word (as we'll see in vv. 5–13), he doesn't simply respond by speaking. Instead he does something remarkable. He "touched him." He touched a leper! "And Jesus stretched out his hand and touched him" (v. 3a). What compassion (cf. Mark 1:41)![4] What love!

How long was this man a leper? We don't know. How long had it been since someone had touched him? One year, two years, ten years? Can you imagine no one touching you for a month—no handshake, no hug, no holding your hand, no playful rub of the head, no hand on your shoulder? "[He] touched him." Jesus reached out his hand and touched him. This touch is the gospel![5] For on one hand it's the tangible demonstration of God's love for us in Christ, and on the other hand it's Jesus' taking on all our infirmities—all our sickness and sin. It's Isaiah 53.

According to Leviticus 5:3, Jesus becomes unclean the moment he touches this leper. Yet by means of his healing touch it's as if he transcends the Law without abolishing it. Jesus' touch doesn't make Jesus unclean; rather it cleanses the unclean.[6] But in another sense, by touching this leper Jesus is showing us that he is willing to take on his impurities and is foreshadowing his taking all of ours as well (2 Corinthians 5:21). Put differently, his mission is the cross.

So, he touches him (tenderly like a mother touches the forehead of her sick child), and then (like a foreman yelling out orders to the wrecking crew) he gives a command to that leprous body: "Be clean!" (v. 3). And what happened? The walls of sin and sickness and separation came tumbling down: "And immediately his leprosy was cleansed" (v. 4). I don't know if scales fell off his skin, if bruises and wounds were instantaneously healed, if the tips of toes and fingers grew back, or if his face, hair, and breath were suddenly fresh and clean. But whatever it looked like, it must have been something to see.

I think that if you or I were there and were commissioned to write something about this miracle, we would have written about that detail next. Instead Matthew ends this miracle story in an odd and unspectacular way: "And Jesus said to him, 'See that you say nothing to anyone, but go, show yourself to the priest and offer the gift that Moses commanded, for a proof to them'" (v. 4). There is a proper timing to Jesus' ministry. He doesn't want word about him getting out too soon or in a way that is misinformed about his purposes.

So Jesus says to him, as he says to all of us, "You've shown faith in me. Now I want you to obey me. And to obey me is to obey God's Word. Yes, I've come to establish a new kingdom, but not a novel kingdom. I'm playing by the Book. And if you want to follow me, so are you. Thus, do what the Old Testament says (see Leviticus 14). After the cross and resurrection, we'll do away with Mosaic cleansing rituals, but for now even those rituals testify to me. They witness that someone greater than Moses is here. They witness that the kingdom of heaven is breaking into the world. They witness that the Christ has come." As Bruner notes, "Jesus will not storm Israel with his messianic claim"; instead he will "knock quietly at its door, leper by leper, little by little."[7] Well said.

Picture Two: The Centurion's Servant

The second picture is in verses 5–13. Comprising this picture we find no less than seven surprises.

The first surprise is that "a centurion" approached Jesus (v. 5). Being a centurion meant two things, both very off-putting for Jews. First, he was a Gentile. He was not of the people of God. Second, he was part of the Roman military. He was oppressing the people of God. Thus, according to Jewish thinking, he was the wrong race and wore the wrong uniform.

The second surprise is that this centurion, who is under the lordship of Caesar, twice calls Jesus "Lord." "Lord" is the first word of his request (v. 6), and "Lord" is the first word of his reply (v. 8). Even if he is speaking better than he knows (which I don't think he is based on what he asks), again this word "Lord" in Matthew is significant symbolically. Believers call Jesus "Lord," while non-believers call him "teacher," "rabbi," etc.

The third surprise is that this centurion makes an appeal on behalf of his servant, who according to the word Matthew uses in verse 6 is a "young servant" (NLT) or "young man" (YLT), perhaps a boy who was born to one of his household slaves. You say, "What's the big deal? What's the surprise in that?" The big deal is that in the Greco-Roman world "the average slave owner . . . had no more regard for his slave than for an animal."[8] In his *Ethics*, Aristotle said there should be no friendship and no justice toward inanimate things, as well as a horse, ox, or slave.[9] Roman writers like Varro and Cato "maintained that the only difference between a slave, a beast, and a cart was that the slave talked."[10] So do you see the surprise? Why does this high-powered soldier's solider care for this slave? Let him die and buy another one. Don't humiliate yourself by begging before this beggar, Jesus.

The fourth surprise is that Jesus responds to this request, saying, "I will come and heal him" (v. 7). It is surprising that Jesus doesn't say, "Well, let me first take a look at him and see if I can do anything for him." Rather he says, "I will come and *heal him*." It is also surprising (and this surprises the centurion) that Jesus is willing to enter a Gentile's house. Jews were prohibited from doing so. It was a cultural no-no. It would be similar to a white man sitting in the back of the bus or drinking from a "black only" drinking fountain in pre-civil rights America. Jesus was willing to cross over that line.

The fifth surprise, however, is that this Gentile won't let him. "Lord," he says, "I am not worthy to have you come under my roof" (v. 8). In our next passage Jesus will say that he "has nowhere to lay his head" (8:20); he has no roof over his head, or at least none that he can call his own. What is so worthy about this homeless Jew?

Do you see the humility here? A Gentile, a military leader in the world's greatest army, a free Roman citizen, a man who has a household of slaves (which means he has some money) thinks Jesus is so worthy that it's unthinkable that our Lord should come over and just let himself in. It's like the Queen of England coming to town, meeting you on the street, and saying, "Oh, I'll just stay at your house tonight." What would you say to that? At first you would be honored. But then you'd come to your senses. And I don't care how upscale your house might be, you would suddenly recognize what a dump it is. "Oh, she can't stay here." That is this man's disposition. He is unworthy to have royalty—the Lord—into his house.

From there we come to *the sixth surprise*, found in verse 8–10: "Lord, I am not worthy to have you come under my roof, but only *say the word*, and my servant will be healed. For I too am a man under authority, with soldiers under me. And I say to one, 'Go,' and he goes, and to another, 'Come,' and he comes, and to my servant, 'Do this,' and he does it" (vv. 8. 9). "Just say a word, Jesus. I believe it will travel far enough, quickly enough, and powerfully enough to restore my servant."

"When Jesus heard this, he marveled and said to those who followed him, 'Truly, I tell you, with no one in Israel have I found such faith'" (v. 10). This sixth surprise—this man's faith—is what *surprises* Jesus. Jesus marveled that someone who didn't grow up like Paul, for example, learning the Torah, or even like Timothy with a Jewish mother and grandmother to teach him the Scriptures, knew enough to believe in Jesus and his word. This man expressed an "unlimited confidence in the authority of Jesus."[11] You see, what Jesus is highlighting to his disciples, who were then all Jews, is that not even they "had shown the sincerity, sensitivity, humility, love, and depth of faith of this Gentile soldier."[12]

The seventh surprise follows quite naturally. It is Jesus' provocative statements in verses 11, 12:

> I tell you, many will come from east and west [i.e., believing Gentiles] and recline at table with Abraham, Isaac, and Jacob in the kingdom of heaven, while the sons of the kingdom [i.e., unbelieving Jews] will be thrown into the outer darkness. In that place there will be weeping and gnashing of teeth.

It may be surprising to some that Jesus compares Heaven to a feast, the best banquet ever thrown (cf. Isaiah 25:6–9; 65:13, 14; Revelation 19:9). It may be surprising to others that Jesus talks about Hell as a real place. Hell is a place of great pain and regret, a place where no one would want to be. But the greatest surprise (if I can rightly call the Scripture's predicted inclusion of the Gentiles a surprise), especially to the Jews of Jesus' day, is who's in and who's out. Even the super-religious—a Jewish Pharisee, for example—is out if he won't bow the knee to Jesus and call him Lord. However, the Gentile military man working for the bad guys, due to his childlike faith, is in. The greatest surprise is that those who are in will become "a great multitude that no one could number, from every nation, from all tribes and peoples and languages" (Revelation 7:9). Or the greatest surprise is, in the words of Isaiah 54:1–3 (yes, from the section on the Suffering Servant; cf. Psalm 22:27, 28):

> "Sing, O barren one, who did not bear; break forth into singing and cry aloud, you who have not been in labor! For the children of the desolate one will be more than the children of her who is married," says the LORD. "Enlarge the place of your tent, and let the curtains of your habitations be stretched out; do not hold back; lengthen your cords and strengthen your stakes. For you will spread abroad to the right and to the left [the east and the west], and your offspring will possess the nations. . . ."[13]

This second picture is full of surprises. The only thing that isn't a surprise is the miracle itself in verse 13. It's as though Matthew just tacks it on at the end. Oh, by the way, Jesus simply said, "Let it be done," and it was done. "And the servant was healed at that very moment."

Picture Three: The Woman

Now we come to our final picture—how (again with divine power) Jesus heals Peter's mother-in-law.

> And when Jesus entered Peter's house, he saw his [Peter's] mother-in-law lying sick with a fever. He touched her hand, and the fever left her, and she rose and began to serve him. (vv. 14, 15)

What is Matthew doing here? Why tell us of this third apparently minor miracle? Is he perhaps reminding Roman Catholics that Peter, the so-called first Pope, was married? I think that's the best way to read the fact that Peter had a mother-in-law. Jerome did as well. He conceded that all the apostles except John were married (cf. 1 Corinthians 9:5).[14] But I doubt that Matthew had that in mind. Was it to show that no health issue (even a fever) is too small for Jesus? I don't think so. Was it to show that when women get healed it is then their duty to stay at home and serve men, since that's what this woman did? I highly doubt that.[15] Well then, was it to show that Jesus, on his own initiative (note: in this miracle he is not asked to help) can help and likes to help (he is eager to help) whomever and whenever he wants? Now we are getting somewhere. Was it to show that despite his harsh words toward the Jews in verses 11, 12 Jesus had not forsaken his chosen people like this Jew?[16] Yes, certainly that is part of the picture.

But the main reason Matthew includes this miracle is to show that Jesus has come, in the words of Psalm 147:2, to gather "the outcasts of Israel" (a leper and a woman) and of the world (a Roman slave) to the true Israel, Jesus. You might ask, "A woman is an outcast?" In those days women were viewed as second-class citizens. In the Jewish synagogue, for example, "women were placed behind screens, to the rear, as in modern Muslim mosques."[17] Furthermore, "in some Jewish traditions, touching a woman [or even a woman's hand like Jesus did here] would make [you] unclean or unholy. Jewish Halakah forbade touching persons with many kinds of fever (SBK, 1:479f.)."[18] Along the same lines, one of the Eighteen Benedictions prayed each day by any devout Jewish man was, "Lord, I thank Thee that I was not born *a slave, a Gentile, or a woman*" (emphasis mine).

So, do you see what's going on here? Oh, it's so beautiful. Jesus' first three recorded miracles in Matthew are of three groups of religious outcasts. In other words, Jesus is letting outsiders in. With his death the veil of the temple will be split in two. What will happen then—the substitutionary benefits of the Suffering Servant—is foreshadowed here.

The temple in Jerusalem was comprised of the Holy of Holies (for the high priest) and then the Holy Place (for the priests), then the Court of Men (for Jewish men), the Court of Women (for Jewish women), then the Court of the Gentiles (for Gentile converts to Judaism), and then the outer wall of the temple complex. With these three miracles the walls to the Court of the Women are broken down, then beyond that the walls of the Court of the Gentiles, and then beyond that, the walls of the temple itself are leveled, so that even the lepers of this world can wander in. Behold, with Jesus the gates to the kingdom of heaven are open to all who believe, to all who will call him Lord and get up and serve him.

The Big Picture

I told you at the start of this sermon that on my home office wall there are four ancient portraits of Jesus. In the last few pages I've shared with you how Matthew presents three pictures of Jesus and how all three display his power to the powerless.

On my office wall I arranged the pictures in a straight line, one next to the other. Here in Matthew the pictures are arranged in a different way. I envision the picture of Jesus and the centurion as the longest picture. It spreads out from east to west. Above it is the picture of the leper, and below it is the picture of the woman. It forms the shape of a cross, which fits nicely with the old portraits of Isaiah 53.[19] Then I imagine beneath this pictorial cross an inscription from Galatians 3:28: "There is neither Jew nor Greek, there is neither slave nor free, there is no male and female, for you are all one in Christ Jesus." This is the big picture of Matthew's three portraits—all people united by faith under the cross.

21

Even the Wind Obeys Him

MATTHEW 8:18–27

THE OTHER DAY I WAS at a park pushing my youngest daughter on the big-girl swing and listening to her laugh. Between the laughs she would say again and again, "Underdog, Daddy"—asking me to run under her as I'm pushing the swing so as to give her optimal height and velocity. As my daughter was flying through the air, enjoying herself thoroughly, I noticed a little girl, about three years old, who had climbed onto the swing next to us. She settled herself in place and then called back to her father, "Daddy, come push me." Her father immediately got up from the park bench and started to walk toward her. I noticed that he was struggling just to walk to the swing. If I were to guess, I would say he was suffering from MS or MD (muscular dystrophy). Other than the obvious weakness of his legs, arms, and back, he looked very healthy. He hobbled over to the swing, placed his hand on her back, and gave the best push he could give. She went just a little bit forward and just a little bit back, hardly a push at all.

Have you ever felt helpless? I felt completely helpless as I watched him. On the one hand, I felt helpless since I couldn't very well say, "Oh, move over, let me give her a real push," although I wanted to for her sake. On the other hand, I felt helpless because I couldn't heal him. I wanted to walk over, put my hand on his back, and say, "Disease, be gone," and then see his body straighten up and his back and arms and legs gain strength and see, with one push, his daughter fly through the air, laughing and smiling on that swing.

I believe in healing. I have prayed for healing for members of my congregation. All of us at some point in our lives will need such prayer. I have also seen and heard of real, miraculous healings. But it has never been under my control. I have never had the power to say, "Walk" and watch a paralyzed man get up and walk, or to say, "See" and see a child blind from birth open her eyes for the first time to see blue birds and brown trees and orange sunsets. Imagine if I was able to do that. Imagine—no matter what the illness or ailment—if, with but a word or a touch or even a glance, I could cure whomever and whenever. What would the response be? It would be the same as it was for Jesus. I would draw a crowd.

That's how our passage begins. After giving the greatest sermon in the history of the world (the Sermon on the Mount), and after healing the untouchables with a touch—a leper, a servant, a woman—Jesus drew "a crowd" (v. 18).

But, so different than most celebrities today, Jesus is not interested in drawing a crowd. He is not interested in having people *follow* him; he is interested in having *followers*. He is interested in people like the leper, the centurion, and Peter's mother-in-law—those who call him Lord and get up and serve him. In other words, he is interested in making disciples. Now, the passage before us is very much a passage on discipleship. What does and doesn't a true disciple of Jesus look like? However, the focus here is really on three negative examples. It reminds me of the teaching Jesus gives right before the Lord's Prayer, where he teaches how not to pray: do not pray like the hypocrites, and do not pray like the Gentiles. Here he "teaches" *how not to follow him.*

Without Airs

The first example of how not to follow Jesus is the scribe who is described in verses 19, 20: "And a scribe came up [to Jesus] and said to him, 'Teacher, I will follow you wherever you go.' And Jesus said to him, 'Foxes have holes, and birds of the air have nests, but the Son of Man has nowhere to lay his head.'" I'll make sense of Jesus' apparently nonsensical reply in a minute. First, let's make sense of this scribe and his statement.

A scribe was a Bible scholar and teacher, an expert in the Scriptures. In Jesus' day, to be a scribe was a respectable occupation, like a brain surgeon today. It took intellect and skill. As a result, such a man was highly esteemed by his society. This scribe in our story knows that and, as we shall see, relishes in that.

The first word out of this man's mouth sounds fairly noble. He calls Jesus "Teacher." And he is even willing to follow this teacher—Jesus. But in Matthew's Gospel the five times Jesus is called "teacher" (8:19; 12:38; 19:16;

22:16, 36), it is always on the lips of someone who isn't or won't become a disciple. So there is already a hint, with this title "teacher," however much of a concession it might be, that something is amiss with this man's "faith."

Yet, we might ask, what is amiss with what he actually says? What could be wrong with saying, "Teacher, I will follow you wherever you go"? Even today it's hard to find people—let alone academics—who are willing to state publicly their willingness to follow Jesus. However, Jesus sees beneath the surface to this man's pride and obliviousness, both of which our Lord brings to the surface. The title Jesus gives himself—"the Son of Man" (v. 20)—hits at the pride issue, and the talk about poverty—"nowhere to lay his head"—strikes at this man's obliviousness to the cost of discipleship.

What this scribe says could be said with humility: "Teacher, I will follow you wherever you go." Or it could be said with a high sense of self and confusion about the nature of the kingdom, something like:

> *Teacher*,[1] as one Bible expert to another, *I* have noticed who is on your team thus far—fishermen, lepers, soldiers, and middle-aged women. Perhaps you could use someone with a head on his shoulders and with some religious respectability. Say . . . someone like me! This is your lucky day, for *I will follow you wherever you go*. I hope it's into battle. It is far time those blasted Romans met their match. I'm with you 110 percent. Let's do it. You and I can bring about this kingdom you've been talking about.

Perhaps my self-loving, power-monger reading above is wrong or exaggerated. I do, however, think there is something negative about the manner in which he addresses Jesus. For note who the subject of verse 19 is, and compare that to what the leper and the centurion say to Jesus.[2] This man talks about what he will do; they talk about what Jesus can do. Moreover, I favor the less charitable reading due to Jesus' response. In verse 20 Jesus basically says, "You don't know *who* you are talking to, and you don't know *what* you're talking about." His actual words are these: "Foxes have holes, and birds of the air have nests, but the Son of Man has nowhere to lay his head." The sense of Jesus' subtle rebuke is something like this:

> Listen, I'm the Son of Man,[3] not merely some scribe like you. I'm not just a better Bible teacher. I'm the king Daniel wrote about, the one who will be given absolute dominion over Heaven and earth. Read Daniel 7:13, 14 when you get home. You don't know who I am. And you certainly don't know where I'm going. I'm going to Calvary. Are you willing to follow me there? Are you willing to deny yourself, pick up your cross, and follow me? Homelessness is the least of your worries. You may or may not have a roof over your head if you follow me. There is more than a house to leave behind!

You see, Jesus had no faith in this man's "faith" because he knew that at the heart of this scribe's bold declaration was self-love, not self-denial, and a desire for power, not a willingness to be powerless—without a home, esteem, and possibly a life.

Jesus wants disciples. But here he teaches us that he will not accept just anyone! He will not even accept a scribe who comes with airs, who comes without humility and recognition that the road to the cross lies ahead.

So this "eager scribe" or "hasty scholar" or "Mr. Bighead," as one commentator calls him,[4] apparently (we aren't told) retracts his bold declaration. It's as if his big head has been deflated, and like a popped balloon I imagine him chaotically scurrying away.

Without Compromise

Ah, but the story isn't over. Here comes another man. Shall we call him "the reluctant disciple" or "the hesitant son"? How about "Mr. Faintheart"[5] or "Mr. Family-First"? Oh, I know. Let's call him "Mr. Moneybags." Exit Mr. Bighead; enter Mr. Moneybags. I'll explain that name in a minute. For now just look at verses 21, 22:

> Another of the disciples said to him, "Lord, let me first go and bury my father." And Jesus said to him, "Follow me, and leave the dead to bury their own dead."

Now wait a minute. What happened to "Jesus meek and mild"? Where's that nice blue-eyed, blond-haired, hanging-on-your-nursery-wall, wouldn't-hurt-a-fly Jesus? Matthew must have skipped Sunday school as a child, for his Jesus gives a left hook, then a right, and down goes Mr. Bighead and down goes Mr. Moneybags. 1, 2, 3, 4, 5, 6, 7, 8, 9, 10. They're knocked out!

What is going on here? If Mr. Bighead's issues were pride and obliviousness to the cost of discipleship, what is Mr. Moneybag's problem? Let me give you a hint. It has something to do with money. You might say, "Money? What are you talking about? All he wants to do is bury his dear old dad. What could be wrong with that? And what does that have to do with money?"

Well, there is certainly nothing wrong with a proper Jewish burial. If anything the Bible goes out of its way to say, with the burials of Sarah (Genesis 23:8–20), Jacob (Genesis 50:5, 6), and even Jesus himself (John 19:38–42), that care and priority should be given to the deceased. However, the Jews of Jesus' day took this obligation to exaggerated, perhaps even idolatrous heights (some viewed burial as the supreme duty, even above saying the Shema).[6] Yet here Jesus is not attacking Jewish or Hellenistic burial rites or the common and necessary concern one should have for one's parents,[7] even and especially upon their death. He is not doing away with the fifth commandment. Just read his scolding of the Pharisees for not properly caring for their parents in 15:1–9 (cf. 1 Timothy 5:8). The key to understanding Jesus' seemingly insensitive reply is grasping precisely what the man is asking.[8]

If his father had just died, he wouldn't have been following Jesus, at least not on that day, for "in Israel the dead were required to be buried on the same day they died."[9] So what's going on? The most positive (but I don't think accurate) reading of verse 21 is to say that this man is just asking permission "to remain at home during his father's last [days or] years and follow Jesus only after that phrase of his life is over."[10] Yet if that is the case, what Jesus says in verse 22 is no less shocking and difficult for us to get our heads around. He is then cutting at the root of idolatry, saying something like, to borrow from Augustine, "*Amandus est generator, sed praeponendus est Creator*" ("One should love the begetter but prefer the creator").[11] That is, put God first and family second.

Jesus is not opposed to this kind of rebuke. We'll hear it from him soon enough in 10:28–30, 34–39. Although there might be some of that here, I do not think the issue is idolatry—family and not God being this man's first love. Note the word "first": "Lord, let me *first* go and bury my father" (v. 21). Rather, I think it primarily has to do with money, or really the love of money, which is "a root of all kinds of evils" (1 Timothy 6:10) and most notably the root of unbelief. It can and often does choke trust (13:22).[12]

I say it is the love of money because the phrase this man uses—"Let me . . . go and bury my father"—was a Near-Eastern figure of speech. We use figures of speech all the time, like "It's raining cats and dogs" or "break a leg" or "I'll give you a piece of my mind." We don't take any of those literally. Summarizing the work of K. E. Bailey (*Through Peasant Eyes*, pp. 25–27], R. T. France explains the idiom to "bury one's father" as follows:

> If the father had just died, the son could hardly be out at the roadside with Jesus; his place was to be keeping vigil and preparing for the funeral. Rather, to "bury one's father" is standard idiom for fulfilling one's filial responsibilities for the remainder of the father's lifetime, with no prospect of his imminent death. This then would be a request for indefinite postponement of discipleship, likely to be for years rather than days.[13]

Thus, to contemporize the conversation, the man said to Jesus, "I'll follow you soon. However, I first have an obligation as a son to help my father in the family business, and if I don't, when he dies (whenever that is) I might not get the inheritance.[14] So, Jesus, I can't afford to follow you right now. But I will in time. Once dear old dad is dead and gone and once the money has come in, then I'm all yours. You see, Jesus, financial security is the issue. You understand, right?"

"Wrong," Jesus says. "The first guy was too fast, but you're too slow.[15] I turned the first guy away. I don't want anything to do with pride. It repels me. My kingdom will do just fine with fishermen and tax collectors [cf. 1 Corinthians 1:26]. I don't need kings, intellectuals, or celebrities. I knew what was in the first guy's heart, and I know what is in your heart too. But with you I see potential. So I'm inviting you to love God, not money. 'Discipleship is always a present obligation.'[16] Right now you need to make a choice. Let me help you make the right choice. Here's my free financial advice (JESUS CFO): 'Leave the dead to bury their own dead'" (8:22).

Jesus doesn't have a flattering view of the world. He doesn't think that if only we educate everyone, things will all work out. He pictures the world as a bunch of dead men walking. He talks about what cannot literally happen: corpses burying corpses. What he means is that the spiritually dead will take care of business. They'll make sure all worldly matters are taken care of, but we must put the kingdom of God and his righteousness first, knowing that all these things will be added. So if we choose this world we've chosen death; if we choose Jesus we've chosen life.

Now, again we don't know what happened to Mr. Moneybags. But I imagine, like the rich young ruler we'll meet in chapter 19, he walked away sad and that he walked away with his money in hand (or at least still in heart).[17]

Without Fear

After these encounters with Mr. Bighead and Mr. Moneybags, in verses 23–27 Jesus' disciples follow him into a boat to journey to the other side of the lake. Have you ever seen the play (or movie) *Twelve Angry Men*? Here I envision Twelve Anxious Men, or even better Twelve Chicken Chickens.

Look with me at verses 23–27. We won't look at the whole story in this chapter. We'll revisit it, along with verses 28–34, in the next chapter. For now I just want to point out their fear and Jesus' strong rebuke of it.

> And when he [Jesus] got into the boat, his disciples followed him. And behold, there arose a great storm on the sea, so that the boat was being swamped by the waves; but he was asleep. And they went and woke him, saying, "Save us, Lord; we are perishing." And he said to them [I love this—he doesn't deal with the unsettled sea first; instead first he deals with

> their unsettled faith],[18] "Why are you afraid, O you of little faith?" Then he rose and rebuked the winds and the sea, and there was a great calm. And the men marveled, saying, "What sort of man is this, that even winds and sea obey him?"

There is a lot here, and in the next sermon we will flesh it all out. For now we'll focus on verse 26—their lack of faith. We'll keep focusing on what we've been focusing on—in a sense, *how not to follow Jesus*. That is, how not to follow Jesus in three lessons: lesson one—*without airs* (in humility), lesson two—*without compromise* (Jesus above family, occupation, and fortune), and finally lesson three—*without fear*.

When you think about this situation in verses 24, 25—the boat and the storm—who of us wouldn't be afraid? Have you ever been walking, driving, or sailing in really dangerous weather? In such situations it would be less than human not to be a bit chicken. It is important to say that Jesus is not addressing fear as such (fear in the ordinary or necessary sense), but rather their "excessive fear."[19] Fear that pushes faith in God out the back door. Fear that doesn't recognize who's in control. Fear that doesn't acknowledge who's onboard the boat.

I think it is too much to claim, as a number of commentators do, that these disciples should have known that if Jesus died with them in this storm, the kingdom of God would die, which couldn't happen. I think that is too much to claim because who would think about such things—make these theological commitments and logical connections—when waves are crashing over your head? It's easy for us at a safe distance to say, "Oh they should have known better," or "They should have known what the wind and waves knew."

That seems too much to claim. But I don't think it's too much to claim, as Jesus claims in verse 26 with his sharp rebuke, that they should have known something of his divine authority, enough of it to trust him even in this situation. That seems to be what is behind his question, "Why are you afraid, O you of little faith?" Although I don't think they should have seen the big picture, they should have seen who was sleeping onboard and why he was able to sleep through such a storm. But instead here they show "no faith" (Mark 4:40) in Jesus, other than faith in his ability to save them from drowning (the "little faith" of Matthew's version). For they do eventually wake him and cry out to him, "Lord! Save! We are being destroyed!"—that's the sense of it in the Greek.[20] Jesus takes them where they are—weak faith and all. He doesn't say to them, "You want me to do what? I'm not stopping this storm until I see some real faith. Wake me up again when your faith is stronger. What a bunch of wimps you are. Twelve Chicken Chickens."[21] Jesus doesn't say that. He hears their prayer. He stops the seas. He stills the storm. This shows us that "even little faith is faith still" and that "Jesus helps us however we come to him"—so just come as you are.[22] Jesus will save "even weak-in-faith disciples."[23]

But the point here is not to think that Jesus is flattered with weak faith. I think sometimes we think he is. But I ask you to find me a place in the Gospels where such is the case. Think of all his encounters with Peter. When Peter says something bold and brave (when he knows what he's talking about), Jesus commends him. But when Peter cowers or compromises, Jesus never says (and I think we sometimes wish he did), "O Simon, you poor soul. Faith is hard, I know. That's okay. Just try again." Sure, Jesus understands weak faith, but he never commends it. Never!

That is the lesson here. Faith is to be without fear, or put positively, faith "*is* a form of bravery."[24] Do you ever think about faith like that? The Bible consistently does. In the New Testament faith is not simply "a passive acceptance of truths, a weak resignation that 'just believes.'"[25] Rather, faith is often depicted as "courageous confidence" that believes "Jesus is [always] equal to the occasion,"[26] he is always up to the issue at hand.

Think about the leper and the centurion's faith in 8:1–13. What absolute confidence in Jesus. As I said in the last chapter concerning the leper, his faith is the perfect blend of confidence and humility. "Lord, you can heal me; will you?" Or think about the heroes of faith who surround us as a great cloud of witnesses in Hebrews 11, a whole chapter on faith. What are the examples of faith in that chapter? "[T]hrough faith," we are told, some "conquered kingdoms . . . stopped the mouths of lions, quenched . . . fire, escaped the edge of the sword . . ." (vv. 33, 34); others "suffered mocking and flogging . . . chains and imprisonment" (v. 36); "they were stoned . . . sawn in two . . . killed with the sword" (v. 37a), "destitute, afflicted, mistreated" (v. 37b); "some were tortured, refusing to accept release, so that they might rise again to a better life" (v. 35). Courageous confidence!

Or think about the heroic acts recorded in the Acts of the Apostles, stories of some of the men on that boat. Think of Peter and John boldly declaring the gospel in the temple and suffering persecution because of it. Think about Paul. What an example of fearless faith (or you can take the adjective "fearless" out because it's redundant). What an example of faith! "To live is Christ, and to die is gain" (Philippians 1:21). Right before that famous verse, he speaks of not being "at all ashamed" but having "full courage" (Philippians 1:20). Do you have faith? Do you have full courage?

Perpetual Perpetuas

In the first three centuries of the church, if Christians were known for anything it was their courageous faith. The accounts of the early Christian martyrs tell the stories of many followers of Jesus who demonstrated this courageous faith even unto death. One such martyr was Perpetua.

Perpetua was twenty-two years old. She was married and the mother of an infant boy whom she nursed from her jail cell. She was in prison for being a Christian. All she had to do was recant her belief in Jesus, offer a simple sacrifice to Caesar, and call him, "Lord." Her father begged her to do this, but she refused time and again. Finally, as she was led out into the Roman Colosseum to be killed by beast or gladiator, she was singing hymns to Jesus. Can you imagine that kind of courage? Twenty-two years old! Her last words, spoken to her brother, also a Christian, were, "Stand in the faith."[27]

Do you want to follow Jesus? Great. Go for it. But know that if you are to follow him, you must do it *without airs* (humbly come to him and serve him as Lord), *without compromise* (he is first; everyone and everything else is a far second), and *without fear* (courageously trust him).

22

Christus Victor

MATTHEW 8:23–34

IN 1942, DURING WORLD WAR II, C. S. Lewis published his book *The Screwtape Letters*. The book, as you likely know, is an inverted allegory. It's a group of letters by Screwtape, a high-ranking demon, to Wormwood, an under-devil, about how to cunningly lead someone to Hell. When the book first came to America, it was a great success. It sold well and received great reviews. For example, in the 1948 edition I have, there is a review from *The Atlantic Monthly* that reads, "This witty and sincere book has been deservedly popular here."

The same popular acclaim has come to director Jeffery Fiske and actor Max McLean for their stage rendition of Lewis's book. The play sold out quickly and consistently in New York, Washington, and Chicago, and critics described it as entertaining but also thought-provoking. Jayne Blanchard of the *Washington Times* wrote, "No matter what your religion, 'The Screwtape Letters' may set you to thinking about your own eternal soul" (April 25, 2008). Chris Jones of the *Chicago Tribune* wrote, "The main takeaway: remember the devil really exists" (October 14, 2008).

Yet I have found that such critics, readers, and playgoers (whatever they may think about their eternal souls or the devil) fall prey ironically to precisely what Lewis exhorts us not to—complacency with spiritual realities and with the very active but subtle activity of the demonic realm. Max McLean, who played Screwtape and who is a Christian, when asked what he wanted the audience to walk away with, hoped that people would "take Satan very seriously."[1]

But we don't. Our culture certainly doesn't. We might say something like, "It brings the devil out in him" when talking about the effects of an addiction, but we are more prone to look for a scientific (often psychological) explanation for compulsions, obsessions, disorders, and sin. In his 2002 State of the Union Address, President George W. Bush was strongly criticized by some for referring to Iran, Iraq, and North Korea as "the axis of evil" because the term "evil" implies there are moral categories to reality and perhaps there is something or someone evil behind the evil. Imagine if he were to call the work of 9/11 "satanic," or the tsunami not "an act of God" but a "deed of the devil." Few people talk that way today—not even religious Presidents. Few people give credit where credit might very well be due. This is because most people today, whether they liked Lewis's clever book or not, miss the point of it. The belief of many is not that God is dead in our society (most people today believe in God), but it is that the devil is apparently as frozen as a finally-frozen-over Hell.

However, in this passage we are reminded that the devil and his minions are very much alive. But so is Jesus. What we'll see with these two miracle stories is more than just Jesus' control of chaos but his defeat of evil. We will witness the beginnings of his crushing the serpent's head, to borrow the image from Genesis 3:15. We will see *Christus Victor*, which is the famous Latin theological phrase for our theme—Christ's victory over the forces of evil in this world.

Two Exorcisms

Matthew 8:23–34 records two miracle stories—Jesus calms the sea, and Jesus controls the demons. "Jesus stills storm of sea and soul," we might say.[2] But there are also two exorcisms. The obvious one is the deal with the pigs. The other exorcism is Jesus' rebuke of the storm.

There are three reasons I advocate this second exorcism. First, in Matthew, Mark, and Luke these stories are told together as a pair. This is the Synoptics' way of saying, "Read these together." This then raises the question, why? This leads to my second reason. I think there is a linguistic link. The word Matthew uses for the storm, *seismos*, which literally means "earthquake," is a term used elsewhere in Matthew only for "apocalyptic upheavals (cf. 24:7; 27:54; 28:2)."[3] The idea is that there is something preternatural or supernatural about this particular storm, a storm that, remember, has experienced fisherman scared to death. This is the perfect storm, a perfectly devilish storm. That's the idea. It's as if "Satan is attacking."[4] It's as if the devil himself is holding the sea and shaking it like a giant would a glass of water.[5]

So this word for the storm has satanic overtones. But there is also the word Jesus used for Jesus' commanding the sea: "rebuked." "Then he rose and rebuked the winds and the sea" (v. 26). This is the common term *epitemaō*, used in exorcism stories such as in Mark 1:25, where Jesus "rebuked" the demon-possessed man, and "the unclean spirit . . . came out of him" (v. 26; cf. Mark 9:25; Luke 4:41).

So, first, there is the fact that these two stories are together in the Synoptic Gospels; second, the terms Matthew employs are related to supernatural, otherworld, demonic activity. Third, the stilling of the storm is an exorcism story (of sorts) due to how the Jews perceived the sea.

In Jewish writings, most notably the Bible, the sea is often represented as wild or chaotic and thus threatening. This is why you won't find many stories about the sea in the Old Testament, and the ones you do find usually have dark connotations. When Israel first comes to the Red Sea, this sea is extremely unwelcoming. It meets them like a dragon's mouth. The same is true of the sea in the story of Jonah. The sea would have swallowed up Jonah if the big fish didn't first. However, God provides in both instances. He controls the sea to save his people. But note that the sea needs controlling. It's the force, if you will, with which he's doing battle.

This is also how "the sea" is talked about in Revelation. We find in 13:1, "And I saw a beast rising *out of the sea*" (cf. Isaiah 27:1). Then at the end, when we get the picture of the New Jerusalem, did you ever notice what is missing? "Then I saw a new heaven and a new earth, for the first heaven and the first earth had passed away, *and the sea was no more*" (Revelation 21:1). There is a river, but no sea. After the defeat of all evil, the sea is dried up. God has finally conquered all chaos.

The first exorcism is of the sea; the second is of the demons first mentioned in verse 28, which Jesus and the disciples encounter the moment they step out of the boat on "the other side."

Below, our text (vv. 28–34) is on the left, my short running commentary on the right.

And when he came to the other side,	The other side of the Sea of Galilee
to the country of the Gadarenes,	This is the northeast shore of the Sea of Galilee, about six miles from Capernaum, where they were previously. It is very likely Gentile territory, which explains the pigs.[6]
two demon-possessed men met him, coming out of the tombs	Or the "burial caves"—the abode of the dead, and, in this situation, devils. This is one spiritually unclean place—there are pigs, tombs, and demons, and if you thought a leper was an "outsider," these demon-possessed men are "the outsiders of the outsiders," and they didn't want to let anyone in.

so fierce that no one could pass that way. And behold, they cried out, "What have you to do with us, O Son of God?"	We'll come back to that title in a minute.
"Have you come here to torment us before the time?"	We'll come back to that as well.
Now a herd of many pigs was feeding at some distance from them. And the demons begged him, saying, "If you cast us out, send us away into the herd of pigs."	Mark tells us there were 2,000 (Mark 5:13).
And he said to them, "Go."	He gave them permission.
So they came out and went into the pigs, and behold, the whole herd rushed down the steep bank into the sea and drowned in the waters.	Whatever we make of the pigs' death, this is "visible proof" of Jesus' miracle.[7]
The herdsmen fled, and going into the city they told everything, especially what had happened to the demon-possessed men.	Mark and Luke tell us more about the positive status of the "men."[8]
And behold,	Matthew will focus some on the negative status of the men of that region.
all the city came out to meet Jesus, and when they saw him, they begged him	The last time the word "begged" was used, it was from the demons. That's a bad connotation, but an appropriate one, for these townspeople act quite devilish themselves.[9] They ask Jesus "to leave their region."
to leave their region.	The most likely reason is that of Mr. Moneybags from the last chapter: they think Jesus is a drain on their business. "A few more exorcisms like this will wipe out the city's economy."[10]

The Main Lesson

That is a brief summary of what's going on in this passage. But if you are like me, you might say, "Well, that's all nice. But what does this ancient exorcism have to do with me? What is the main lesson we are to derive from this?"

Are we to realize that demons are real, and, as Paul writes in Ephesians 6:12, that "we do not wrestle against flesh and blood, but against the rulers, against the authorities, against the cosmic powers over this present darkness, against the spiritual forces of evil in the heavenly places"? That is indeed a lesson for us.[11] But it's not the main lesson.

Does the main lesson have to do with discipleship? Instead of being thanked, Jesus is "unwelcomed by those whose religious or economic security is threatened."[12] Is the lesson therefore that as we bring the gospel to hostile regions of the world, we should likewise expect rejection and possibly persecution?[13] Yes, that is a lesson as well. But here, unlike the previous passage, discipleship is not the main emphasis.

Well then, what about the pigs? Is the main lesson something as simple and catchy as (here's a good sermon title)—people before pigs? Unlike the townspeople are we to care more about the fate of people (those two men who were demon-possessed) than what happens to the poor pigs?[14] Is that the lesson? Again there is a real lesson in that. We should value people over pigs and any of our possessions, even our most prized ones. On this point Daniel Doriani writes:

> There are people who don't want toddlers to enter their homes because they don't want them to drool on the table or touch the antiques. They have not learned the lesson of the pigs. There are people who will not spend their money or use their property to meet human needs because they are afraid of depleting their assets. They have not learned the lesson of the pigs. People are more important than possessions.[15]

That is indeed a lesson, and so it's good if you resolve today to take the plastic off the couches and let the grandkids drool on them if they must. That's good. That's what church and sermons are for—real life change. "People before pigs" is an important lesson.

These lessons that we have surveyed are all good lessons, but they all focus on the wrong character in the story. This is not a story about the townspeople or the disciples or the pigs or the demons or even the demon-possessed men and their restoration (notice how little is said about them and about their response).[16] This story is about Jesus. He is the central character on which we are to center. This story is about Jesus' identity.

What Kind of Man?

Look at verse 27. After Jesus rose and rebuked the wind and waves, the men on the boat "marveled, saying, 'What sort of a man is this, that even winds and sea obey him?'" In other words, "Who is this?"

In 14:33, the next time the disciples are on a boat[17]—the time when they see Jesus walking on the water—they will answer their own question, saying, "Truly you are the Son of God." Peter will also answer this question in 16:15, 16. To Jesus' question, "[W]ho do you say that I am?" Peter gives his "blessed" reply, "You are the Christ, the Son of the living God" (v. 17). Another time this question is answered is by Jesus himself. When Jesus is on trial, the high priest asks, "Tell us if you are . . . the Son of God," to which our Lord said, "It is as you have said" (my slight paraphrase of 26:64). The final time Jesus' identity is straightforwardly revealed comes ironically from the lips of the centurion at the cross. After witnessing Jesus' sufferings and death, a centurion and those who were with him "were filled with awe and said, 'Truly this was the Son of God!'" (27:54).

However, before all those confessions of faith, it is ironically the demons who first announce to the disciples just who Jesus is.[18] Theophylact said it this way: "While the men in the boat are doubting what manner of man this is . . . the demons come to tell them."[19] The demons cried out, "What have you to do with us, O Son of God?" (8:29a).[20] There it is—the main lesson for us today: Jesus is indeed the Son of God!

The demons believe that Jesus is the Son of God, but as James 2:19 claims, they shudder. "Have you come here to torment us before the time?" (8:29b). They shudder because "their belief is that of recognition but not acceptance, and they fully realize the consequence of rejecting God."[21]

When I was in college, once a week I would go over to the local community college and ask students to take a religious survey. One of the questions I asked was, "Who do you think Jesus is?" Now, this survey was done maybe sixteen years ago, so I don't know if students today would answer they same way as they did then. But back then at least half would actually say, "Jesus . . . umm . . . he's the Son of God." Most of them answered like they were answering a trivia question. The tone in their reply was an interrogative—"The Son of God, right?" Their tone was also sadly disinterested. Whether he was or is the Son of God meant little to them personally.

But it's no little thing to say, "Jesus is the Son of God." This is not merely a matter of intellectual adherence. It's a matter of allegiance. If I acknowledge that he is the Son of God in my head, then that information needs to travel to my heart, hands, and feet. I need to love him, serve him, and walk in his ways. I need to count the cost and follow him (remember 8:18–22). The disciples saw these two exorcisms with their own eyes, and their eventual admission that Jesus is God's Son meant their total allegiance and their commitment to Christ unto death. Thus in this passage the demons *say* Jesus is the Son of God, but the disciples *see* it. I want us to see it as well. I want us to see in verses 23–34 that Jesus *is the Son of God* because he acts as only God can act. He rules over creation. He judges evil. He saves his people.

Son of God—He Rules Creation

First, Jesus rules over creation.

Some have pointed out that Jesus' sleeping in the boat shows us his humanity. He was a real man. He got tired, so he fell asleep just as real human beings fall asleep. While I think Jesus was and is truly and fully human, and while I think in some sense this first exorcism shows the two cardinal doctrines of the person of Christ—"his true humanity (he sleeps) and his true deity (he commands wind and sea)"[22]—here, as throughout our text, it is Jesus' full deity that is on display. Even the sleeping "indicates not powerlessness but the fullness of absolute rule."[23] The idea is that only someone who has everything under control could sleep during a storm like this. But whatever we do with the sleeping, we'll let that sleep, for the rest of the passage is up and at 'em! It's alive and in our face regarding Jesus' divine power.

In the Bible only God controls the sea. Consider Psalm 89:8, 9: "O LORD God of hosts, who is mighty as you are, O LORD . . . ? You rule the raging of the sea; when its waves rise, you still them" (cf. Psalm 107:23–30; 65:5–8), or Job 38:8–11, where God speaks about the "prescribed limits" he has put on the sea: "Thus far shall you come, and no farther, and here shall your proud waves be stayed."

In our text, notice that Jesus doesn't pray to God to stop the storm. He addresses the storm directly. Jesus says to the waves, "Play dead," and they, like an obedient dog, lie flat. It's as if creation recognizes its Creator's voice. It's as if "all things hold together . . . by the word of his power" (Colossians 1:17; Hebrews 1:3). Stilling a storm—have you ever seen anyone do that? That's power! That's authority! That's something that only God could do.

Son of God—He Judges Evil

Only God can rule over creation. Jesus, as God's Son, does just that. But also, as only God can do, he judges. He judges evil. The demons know and fear this, which is why they cry out in terror, "Have you come here to torment us before the time?" (8:29b). They know that Jesus is the appointed judge who will judge at the appointed time. One day "He will come to judge the living and dead," as we say in the Apostles' Creed. According to D. A. Carson, this judicial role "confirms the fullest meaning of 'Son of God.'"[24] But I think that Jesus' answer to their question, "Have you come here to torment us before the time?" is actually, "Yes." (Here we have some realized eschatology.) While it might look like an act of mercy, it is truly an act of judgment. They ask to be sent into those dirty pigs, and Jesus allows it. But notice what happens. The pigs don't just go about their business, doing what pigs do. Rather, they stampede off the cliff into the sea! Yes, that same sea that almost swallowed up Jesus and his disciples. But unlike the disciples, these demons go into the sea and disappear into the depths.[25] I see this drowning in the sea to be Jesus' present judgment of them. Jesus' one word—"Go"—stands out, especially if you have a red-lettered Bible. With one little word, the demons are judged by God's Son.

And though this world with devils filled,
Should threaten to undo us,
We will not fear, for God hath willed
His truth to triumph through us.
The prince of darkness grim,
We tremble not for him;
His rage we can endure,
For lo! His doom is sure;
One little word shall fell him.[26]

Son of God—He Saves People

Jesus proves to be God's Son in that he (1) rules creation, (2) judges evil, and finally (3) saves his people.[27] In chapter 8 our Lord saves the leper, the slave, the woman, and many others from their illnesses. He saves the disciples from drowning. He saves the demon-possessed men from their demons. He thus shows himself to be the Savior.

However there is more to Jesus' mission than these smaller salvations in chapter 8. There's also the cross of chapter 27. When Mary, the mother of our Lord, learned that she would bear a son, the angel Gabriel announced the nature of her Son's mission: "and you shall call his name Jesus, for he will save his people from their sins" (1:21). That salvation from sins happens not when Jesus stretches out his arms to still the sea, but when he stretched them out on the cross to die for you and me.

The title "Son of God" is used of Jesus nine times in Matthew's Gospel. I have talked about all of them but one in this chapter. The one other time is while he is on the cross and those who passed by him derided him, saying, "If you are the *Son of God*, come down from the cross" (27:40). Just like the devil when he tempted our Lord in 4:1–11, here those who pass by think that if Jesus is the Son of God he will come down off the cross, he will manifest his identity through worldly power. On the contrary, since he is the Son of God he will stay on that cross, for on the cross he will save his people from their sin.

Here's the beauty of the Christian faith: "The reason the Son of God appeared was to destroy the works of the devil" (1 John 3:8b). That is what's happening on the cross. It's the ultimate exorcism! The chaos of creation, the powers of evil, and the sins of you and me have been rebuked and exorcised on the cross. *Christus Victor*! Christ victorious over evil—the evils of sickness, sin, death, and Hell.

So, yes, we must take Satan seriously. But we must also take Jesus seriously. For what sort of a man is this? This is the Son of God who rules creation, judges evil, and saves his people, and thus the one to whom all allegiance and adoration is due.

> "Worthy is the Lamb who was slain, to receive power and wealth and wisdom and might and honor and glory and blessing! . . . To him who sits on the throne and to the Lamb be blessing and honor and glory and might forever and ever!" And the four living creatures said, "Amen!" (Revelation 5:12–14)

23

Authority to Forgive

MATTHEW 9:1–8

HORACE BUSHNELL WAS WELL KNOWN in the nineteenth century as the pioneer of liberal theology in New England. Characteristic of his liberalism was his dismissal of the classic definition of the Trinity, his denial of Christ's substitutionary atonement, and his view of Christ's miracles as natural phenomena that were all explainable within the boundaries of scientific law.[1]

Bushnell often spoke foolishly concerning God and his Word, yet occasionally he spoke better than he usually thought. One such instance was when he said the beautiful and memorable words, "Forgiveness is man's deepest need and God's highest achievement." That is not only a good summary of the effects of Jesus' gospel, but it is also a good summary of what we read here in the first eight verses of the ninth chapter of Matthew's Gospel. For here we will indeed see both that *forgiveness is man's deepest need* and also *God's highest achievement.*

And Behold—Their Faith

Our text takes us from "the other side" (8:28)—the region of the Gadarenes where Jesus exorcised the demons. Jesus is now back to "his own city," as verse 1 says. This was not Jesus' birth city (Bethlehem) or his boyhood city (Nazareth) but his adopted city, the city at the center of his Galilean ministry, Capernaum. In his retelling of this miracle, Mark confirms this as the setting and fills in some details. Jesus is in a house preaching the Word to a standing-room-only crowd. Meanwhile, four men who are unable to enter the room through the front door carry their paralyzed friend atop the house (Jewish houses in those days had outside staircases and flat roofs) and enter in an unconventional way. They tear open the roof and let their friend down through it (see Mark 2:1–4). Matthew leaves out the de-roofing and other such details and gets right to the heart of the miracle: "And behold some people brought to him a paralytic, lying on a bed. And when Jesus saw their faith, he said to the paralytic, 'Take heart, my son; your sins are forgiven'" (9:2). "Faith" and "forgive[ness]" are the two key concepts here.

First, Jesus takes note of and commends their faith. Like the leper and the centurion of chapter 8, these five men (the paralytic included)[2] didn't question in their hearts whether Jesus *could* heal, only if he *would* heal. Thus, they took a bold step of faith, no matter the social or material cost, to see what would happen. Jesus saw this faith, and he liked what he saw. As we will see throughout this Gospel, faith manifests itself not so much by what one knows or feels, but by what one does in response to Jesus. These men wholeheartedly trusted that Jesus was sufficient. That's why they did what they did. "[O]nly say the word, and my servant will be healed" (8:8) was their faithful disposition,[3] the type of faith in the Gospels that "invites the Lord's miraculous powers."[4]

Secondly, we see forgiveness. Instead of an immediate miracle, as was Jesus' practice thus far—he immediately healed the leper, servant, and woman; he immediately stilled the sea and cast out the demons—here he immediately forgives sins. "Take heart, my son," he says with fatherly care to this poor crippled man; "your sins are forgiven" (v. 2). Imagine the shock! Imagine the disappointment! Why didn't he heal the man physically? Imagine what people thought.

Many Christian leaders today tell us that the church and its message need to be relevant. We need to meet people where they are. We need to discover people's felt needs (e.g., loneliness, feelings of inadequacy, etc.) and use those needs to bring such people into a saving relationship with Jesus. Such talk makes some sense, and it certainly sounds kind and understanding. However, it does not reflect Jesus' philosophy of ministry here. His approach was quite different.

I'm sure this poor paralytic had more than a few felt needs. In ancient times the disabled were social outcasts. There were no mandatory building codes for wheelchair accessibility. There were no special care centers. There was no group therapy. In general, paralytics were lonely, helpless, and hurting people. So, can you imagine all his felt needs? Can you imagine all his real physical needs? This was a desperate man.

So here comes Jesus to the rescue. We can count on Christ's sympathy for this man, stuck to a mat, barely able to raise his head, longing for a cure, right? But what do we get? Our Lord has the apparent audacity and cruelty to gloss over the most obvious need. Jesus does not first say to him, "Rise, pick up your bed and go home" (v. 6). Rather he first says, "Take heart, my son; your sins are forgiven" (v. 2). How irrelevant! How inappropriate! It is an outrageous statement but "a calculatedly outrageous statement,"[5] for which Jesus is well-known.

It is possible that what Jesus says to the paralytic reflects his knowledge of this man's particular sins and their relationship to his paralysis (it is not uncommon for Scripture to speak of illness and misfortunes as being the result of sin). This man's sin or sins may have brought about this sickness. Yet it's also possible (and I think this is the case) that Jesus addresses this man in this way because this man, like any naturally sinful human being, needed his sins to be forgiven.[6] That's what he (like we) needed most.

Think of what our Lord says here in this way. Imagine being in a car accident and rushed to the ER. If the doctor there treated your broken toe before your internal brain hemorrhage, you would not think him to be especially compassionate or levelheaded. Here Jesus, the Great Physician, shows both his compassion and his levelheadedness by treating this man's greatest need first. Jesus stops the spiritual bleeding of the soul caused by sin. He does this because he knows that to cure this man's body would have been an immediate but impermanent solution. To restore his health would perhaps save him from decades of suffering, but to restore his soul would save him (whatever becomes of his body) from an eternity of suffering. So in verse 2 Jesus' authoritative declaration of the forgiveness of sins may not have been what the paralytic and his friends wanted to hear (it certainly wasn't what the scribes wanted to hear), but it was what they needed to hear. It is what we need to hear as well.

Our felt needs or physical needs may be great, but they will never be as great as our need for forgiveness.

And Behold—Their Doubt

Forgiveness is man's deepest need and God's highest achievement. That's why Jesus first says, "Take heart, my son; your sins are forgiven" (v. 2). However, the story doesn't stop there. Jesus' declaration in verse 2 creates a most unexpected twist in the story in verses 3, 4. The action abruptly shifts from the needs of the paralytic to the thoughts of the religious authorities. It shifts, we may say, from the physical paralytic to the spiritual paralytics—"the scribes"—some of whom said to themselves, "This man is blaspheming" (v. 3).[7]

Now, before we are overly accusatory toward the scribes, I want us to sit in their seats for a minute. Often we come down too hard on these religious leaders simply because we fail to understand their perspective. Here we must understand that in Jewish theology one thing was clear: sin could be forgiven by bringing an offering to God in the temple. Yet, what do we find here? There is no sin offering, no priest, and no temple. Thus it is no wonder these men who were schooled in the Law "question[ed] in their hearts, 'Why does this man speak like that? He is blaspheming! Who can forgive sins but God alone?'" (Mark 2:6, 7). If only God can forgive sins, which the Hebrew Bible everywhere attests,[8] then what is this man Jesus up to? Who on earth does he think he is? Does he think he is God (cf. John 10:33)?

The Jewish scribes are no keystone cops. They are no three stooges. They are not bumbling idiots. The scribes were thinking rightly about this "teacher," Jesus, for if God alone can forgive sins, Jesus is either claiming to be God or is guilty of blasphemy. And looking at him—this man of real flesh and bones and blood—they naturally concluded the second option to be more likely. In their view Jesus is guilty of claiming to stand in the very place of God and to exercise God's power to forgive. Only God can forgive sins; Jesus claimed to forgive sins; he is only a man; he is thus guilty of blasphemy, which according to Leviticus 24:10–16 is a capital offense; therefore Jesus must die! This is their logic, for this is precisely what unfolds in the Gospel narrative. Months later, when Jesus was standing before the Jewish Council, comprised of the high priest, the chief priests, the elders, and *the scribes* (see 26:57), the high priest declared concerning Jesus, "'You have now heard his blasphemy. What is your judgment?' They answered, 'He deserves death'" (26:65b, 66).

I'm sure you have seen a movie where a bank robbery has gone awry and the robber is holding someone hostage, and the police captain or FBI agent is told in his earpiece, "Our sharpshooters have the man in range." Trained to hit a target with absolute precision, the sharpshooters are just waiting for the command to pull the trigger. Similarly, the scribes, Bible sharpshooters if you will, are eyeing the target. As the story unfolds, they will take the shot and tragically kill the most innocent man ever to live. Their judgment was good, but not good enough. Here Jesus warns them not to be so trigger-happy, and he reprimands them for the slight inaccuracy of their aim.

> But Jesus, knowing their thoughts, said, "Why do you think evil in your hearts? For which is easier, to say, 'Your sins are forgiven,' or to say, 'Rise and walk'? But that you may know that the Son of Man has authority on earth to forgive sins"—he then said to the paralytic—"Rise, pick up your bed and go home." And he rose and went home. (vv. 4–7)

I doubt that Jesus had any formal education in philosophy, but he certainly demonstrated a mastery of the art of argument. Here our Lord gives what philosophers call an *a fortiori* argument, which goes like this: if something more difficult can be achieved, then this guarantees the validity of the claim of something less difficult. This is the precise logic Jesus uses in his clever counter-question: "Which is easier to say, 'Your sins are forgiven,' or to say, 'Rise, and walk?'" Well, "it is surely easier to say that the man's sins are forgiven (for which there is no empirical verification) than to say that the paralytic should get up and walk (for which there would be an immediate empirical verification)."[9] Therefore, since there was no way to test the reality of forgiveness, but an easy way to test the reality of healing, Jesus proved he had the power to forgive sin by healing the paralyzed man. Demonstrating his divine power in both word and deed, he commanded the paralytic to rise, pick up his bed, and go home. And what happened? "And he rose and went home" (v. 7).

Think about this miracle for a moment. Out of this mob of people gathered in this house, how many of these people did Jesus heal? We don't know. Matthew highlights only one. Why only one? Only one was needed to make the point. Jesus' point, given in verse 6, is, "the Son of Man has authority on earth to forgive sins."

Be careful when you read the miracle stories of Jesus not to miss the point. In this passage, just when we may think we have our finger on its message, Jesus says, "Look carefully at it again." We may point to this passage and say it is primarily about how Jesus can heal (v. 7). "No," Jesus says, "it's not about that." We point again and say it is primarily about the type of faith necessary to bring about such healing (v. 2). But Jesus says, "No, it's not about that either." What it is about is Jesus' authority and ability to forgive sins! Note verse 6: "the Son of Man has authority on earth to forgive sins." That's what this passage is about. If you've missed that message, you've missed everything.

Jesus is "the Son of Man"—that is, he is the king prophesied in Daniel who has come into the world with all divine authority. He is "the Son of Man [who] has authority on earth," which means no more need for a temple *on earth*, a sacrificial system *on earth*, or a priesthood *on earth* to make those sacrifices in the temple. The Son of Man now has authority on earth to forgive sins.[10]

What can wash away all my sin?

The temple? The priests? The blood of bulls and goats?

Nothing but the blood of Jesus.[11]

The forgiveness of sin is our deepest need, and *through Christ* it is God's highest achievement.

Following the Crowd

Some years ago I used to commute to work. Seven minutes there and seven minutes back home. During this commute I would always listen to a book on tape. "Redeeming the time because the days are evil," Paul said (Ephesians 5:16 KJV). You'd be amazed how many books you can get through in just fourteen minutes a day. I listened to *Moby Dick*, *The Iliad*, *The Odyssey*, *Tom Sawyer*, and dozens of other great books.

One month I listened to H. G. Wells's famous novel *The Invisible Man*. Throughout this brilliant work of fiction, Wells describes the story of a scientist who discovered a way to make the appearance but not the matter of his body disappear. In one scene the invisible man encounters the skeptical Professor Kemp, who just that morning had repudiated the newspaper's claim that an invisible man was on the loose. Using the best scientific information available, this professor claimed the whole thing a hoax—until the invisible man paid him a visit. Once Professor Kemp recognized the movements and heard the voice of this invisible man, it was only a matter of seconds before he changed his opinion and believed in this absurd reality.

In a similar way Jesus' healing of the paralytic proved his invisible miracle of forgiving this man's sins. As Professor Kemp's doubt changed to faith when he experienced undisputable evidence, so too did Jesus desire that these scribes and this crowd would "know" (v. 6) this invisible reality for themselves. Jesus wanted them to know and experience firsthand both the right and the authority by which he forgives sins, as well as the forgiveness of sins itself. But it appears, as usual, that the crowd and the scribes missed the point.

However, this is not so obvious from the text itself. At first glance verse 8 seems to be a positive conclusion: "When the crowds saw it [the miracle], they were afraid ["filled with awe" is the sense, NIV; NASB, "awestruck"], and they glorified God, who had given such authority to men." This sounds positive enough until we realize that this glorification of God is somewhat superficial. That they "glorified God" does not mean that they recognized Jesus' true identity or that they recognized that Jesus' "physical miracle verified his moral miracle."[12] Remember that this was a small religious community and as such no one doubted when this paralytic took up his bed and paraded home. They knew something miraculous and amazing had just happened. They rightly and naturally responded with terror or amazement, saying essentially, "Wow, God, this is truly awesome. In all our lives we have never seen anything like this!"

Yet similar to the declaration at the end of other miracle stories, this seemingly positive declaration contains everything except the one thing that is necessary (the only thing Jesus is looking for)—faith. Their response lacked faith *in* Jesus as the Christ, the Son of God, the Son of Man, the one to whom we now go to receive forgiveness of sin.

The older I get, the more I appreciate my mother's common sense in not allowing me as a child to do something simply because everyone else was doing it. The plea of "everyone else is doing it" rarely worked with my mother. She turned a deaf ear to the notion of following the crowd, I suppose because she knew that the crowd was not a valid indication of whether or not an activity was wise or profitable. As in real life, in the Bible we often find that the crowd rarely knows what they're saying or doing. In Matthew's Gospel particularly we know for certain that the crowd is not to be followed.

The word "crowds" in Greek is *oxlos*. I don't know why, but I love saying the word *oxlos*. Matthew must have liked it just as much, for he used it fifty times in his Gospel. But for Matthew the word *oxlos* was far more than an interesting-sounding word. To him there is a whole theology behind this two-syllable noun.

At the beginning of Jesus' ministry he is rarely without a large crowd surrounding him. The crowd forms the audience for his teaching, and the crowds are often the object of his miraculous compassion. Yet it is this same crowd whom Matthew never once describes as corporately turning to Jesus in repentance and faith. They may be amazed. They may give generic worship or lip service to God. But the crowd never turns to Jesus for the forgiveness of their sins.

If you think I'm being too hard on them (I'm stretching verse 8 beyond how it can or should be stretched)—"Leave this poor crowd in Capernaum alone!"—you ought to hear what Jesus will say of this crowd later in 11:23, 24:

> And you, Capernaum, will you be exalted to heaven? You will be brought down to Hades. For if the mighty works done in you had been done in Sodom, it would have remained until this day. But I tell you that it will be more tolerable on the day of judgment for the land of Sodom than for you.

This crowd in Capernaum saw Jesus in the flesh more than any group in history. Our Lord considered their city "his own city" (9:1). This crowd heard his sermons live and in person. This crowd witnessed with their own eyes his miracles. Yes, they were amazed. Yes, they were astonished. Yes, they were filled with awe. But they were never filled with faith. The crowd was never converted. The crowd never came to Jesus for the forgiveness of their sins.

The point of all this is that *amazement is not enough!* Don't follow the crowd, or at least not this crowd. If you want to follow a crowd, follow the one at Pentecost, who was "cut to the heart" after hearing Peter's powerful sermon about "this Jesus whom you crucified," this Jesus whom "God has made . . . both Lord and Christ" (Acts 2:36b, 37a). This crowd said to Peter and the rest of the apostles, "'Brothers, what shall we do?' And Peter said to them, 'Repent and be baptized every one of you in the name of Jesus Christ for *the forgiveness of your sins*'" (Acts 2:37b, 38a). Then what happened? They did just that, "and there were added that day about three thousand souls" (Acts 2:41b). Do you want to join a crowd? That's fine, but don't join the one in Capernaum. Join the one in Jerusalem. Repent, believe, and be baptized in the name of Jesus for the forgiveness of your sins.

God's Highest Achievement

If you have leprosy or some other terrible skin disease, I can't promise you that Jesus will heal your leprosy. If you have a child or someone you love who is dying, I can't promise you that Jesus will cure him or her. If you have a fever, I can't promise you that Jesus will cool it. If you're paralyzed, I can't promise you that Jesus will heal you. But if you are a sinner who knows that you are as helpless as a crippled man lowered through a ceiling on a mat, I can promise you that if you have faith in Jesus and his death and resurrection—the ultimate display of his power and authority and compassion—he will forgive your sins.

It's not that Jesus can't deal with whatever physical issues with which you and I are dealing. He certainly has the power and at times the willingness, as clearly shown in Matthew 8, 9. It's not that Jesus can't or won't deal with all that ails us on the outside. Rather, it's that his priority is dealing with what ails us on the inside. For you see, "forgiveness is our deepest need"—this world needs forgiveness more than we need a cure for cancer, and such forgiveness is what God offers to us in the gospel, which is truly his "highest achievement"—the forgiveness of sins through the life, death, and resurrection of our Lord Jesus Christ.

24

Supper with Sinners

MATTHEW 9:9–13

IN THE APOSTLES' CREED a few statements are slightly controversial. Some Christians debate its theology (did Christ really "descend into *hell*"?). Others argue about its terminology (is it right to say, "the holy *catholic* church"?). Yet, whatever minor divisions there may be over these statements and others, there is no division whatsoever over the statement, "I believe . . . in the forgiveness of sins." No Christian cringes at that because every Christian recognizes that this *small* affirmation is a *large* part of our Christian faith.

This is as it should be, for near the beginning of our Lord's ministry, when he teaches his disciples to pray "the Lord's Prayer," forgiveness is at the center. And at the end of his earthly life, during the Last Supper, Jesus takes the cup and says to his disciples, "this is my blood of the covenant, which is poured out for many for the forgiveness of sins" (26:28). Even while shedding his own precious blood, Jesus cried out, "Father, forgive them, for they know not what they do" (Luke 23:34). After the resurrection, Jesus appeared to his disciples, and opening "their minds to understand the Scriptures," he said to them, "Thus it is written, that the Christ should suffer and on the third day rise from the dead, and that repentance and forgiveness of sins should be proclaimed in his name to all nations, beginning from Jerusalem" (Luke 24:45–47).[1]

So, yes, I believe (and I hope you believe) in the forgiveness of sins, for this is the heart and soul of Jesus' lifesaving mission.

In the last chapter we learned that Jesus has the authority to forgive sins. In this chapter we will learn how he uses that authority. We will learn how he uses that authority to *sovereignly* call *sinners*. With the conversion of Matthew we will learn two truths—first, that Christ's call is sovereign, and second, that Christ's call is for sinners.

Christ's Call Is Sovereign

For better or for worse, my wife and I are in the habit of watching murder mysteries. On the negative side, I have learned all sorts of diabolical ways to take the life of another human being. On the positive side, I have also learned, through watching these great detectives solve their cases, the fine art of observation. When Sherlock Holmes, Hercule Poirot, or Adrian Monk arrive at the scene of the crime, they always observe what is most obvious because they know that is often what can and will be used to solve the mystery. In a similar manner, when we arrive at this first verse of our text, we should make some careful observations of the obvious, recognizing that what is ordinary may in fact be extraordinary.

So look again carefully and observantly at verse 9: "As Jesus passed on from there, he saw a man called Matthew sitting at the tax booth, and he said to him, 'Follow me.' And he rose and followed him." Question: Why Matthew? Why did Jesus approach and call this man? In Mark's version we are told that "all the crowd was coming to him [Jesus]" (Mark 2:13), which is then followed by, "he saw Levi . . . sitting at the tax booth." As I envision this scene, the one thing that strikes me as being most peculiar is that Jesus, who is mobbed by a crowd that is showing great interest in him, approaches the one man in town who seems to show no interest in him.

It is not that Matthew didn't know anything about Jesus. As a tax collector whose booth was likely set up on the shore of the Sea of Galilee,[2] he knew more than most people about what was going on in town. And if he hadn't already met Jesus face-to-face, he most certainly had heard about him. Everybody in Capernaum had at least heard about him. And still Matthew *sits*. He is apparently uninterested in Christ and his ministry. He is not even curious like the crowd or the scribes, some of whom traveled a great distance to see Jesus in action and to judge for themselves.

As Jesus passes by, with a large crowd following him, Matthew doesn't even budge to see this great rabbi, this new prophet, this miracle-worker. Matthew may be Jewish in name. His given name is Levi, named after one of Jacob's sons. But he shows no interest in this "King of the Jews." Why? I surmise it is because, like most tax collectors of his time, he bows the knee to the god of money. He is the ancient equivalent to today's Wall Street workaholic who regardless of the uproar around him is busy at work, "sitting" behind his desk, convinced in his mind that time is money. So of all the men, women, and children that day surrounding Jesus, you would think Jesus would show interest in someone in the crowd. But instead what does he do? He goes to Matthew, the one man who is not going to him.

It is strange enough that Jesus goes to Matthew and that he specifically says to Matthew and to no one else in the crowd, "Follow me" (9:9a). But surely it is more striking that Matthew actually responds positively! In one brief sentence we are told, "And he [Matthew] rose and followed him" (v. 9b). Luke 5:28 adds that Matthew "left everything behind" (NASB.) We know the story. But imagine if you didn't. Imagine reading this for the first time. Wouldn't you be surprised when you read that this too-busy tax collector, with one simple call, leaves his lucrative occupation to follow this controversial itinerant preacher who has nowhere to lay his head?

So, why did Jesus call Matthew, and why did Matthew follow Jesus? What do these odd occurrences teach us? What are we to learn from Jesus' unpredictable selection of Matthew and Matthew's unexpected response? *We are to learn that Christ's call unto salvation is completely sovereign!* How else can we explain what happened?[3]

While it is not explicitly stated here, if we shine the full light of the rest of Scripture upon this one verse, we must recognize that Matthew was called by God's irresistible grace (cf. Galatians 1:15). What happed to Matthew is what happened to James, John, Peter, Andrew, you, me, and every Christian who has ever come to follow Christ. It is what Paul speaks of in 2 Corinthians 4:6: "For God, who said, 'Let light shine out of darkness' [at creation], has shone in our hearts [at re-creation] to give the light of the knowledge of the glory of God in the face of Jesus Christ." As Matthew looked into the face of Jesus Christ and heard Christ's command, he experienced the powerful call of God, a God who "saved us and called us to a holy calling, not because of our works but because of his own purpose and grace, which he gave us in Christ Jesus before the ages began" (2 Timothy 1:9).

Christ's call unto salvation is sovereign—it is specific and effectual. Thus, Jesus' call is far different than the man who is all dressed and ready to go, yelling up the stairs to his family, "Come on. Let's go. We're going to be late." Jesus' call here is met with immediate obedience. We are not told that Jesus said, "Come on, Levi, let's go," and Matthew replied, "Hold on, I'm coming, I'm coming. I'll be there in a minute; first let me take care of this transaction," or "First let me pack my bags," or "First let me grab a bite to eat, comb my hair, and brush my teeth." No. To the leper Jesus says, "Be clean," and he is immediately clean. To the paralytic he says, "Rise," and he immediately rises. And to Matthew Jesus says, "Follow me," and he immediately follows. Is this not as much of a miracle as any miracle we have seen in chapters 8, 9? Jonathan Edwards said it well: "I am bold to say, that the work of God in the conversion of one soul . . . is a more glorious work of God than the creation of the whole material world."[4] Amen to that.

However, such obvious sovereignty does not discount Matthew's genuine response.[5] Matthew is not some kind of robot whom Christ reprograms and then flips on the power switch. As much as this is a perfect illustration of Christ's sovereign calling, God does not do our believing for us. It is no little statement that Matthew "rose and followed him" (v. 9). That showed a converted heart, mind, and will. It demonstrated a genuine faith.[6] In Matthew's *following*, his *faith* is evident.

Yet, with that said, we miss the point here if we see Matthew's conversion as an act of self-will or as if his conversion happened as an act of random kindness—that he was just the right guy in the right place at the right time. Verse 9 does not allow for such an understanding. Instead it displays to us "the radical character of Jesus' call"[7]—a call that, like a king summoning a servant to become an heir, is graciously sovereign.

Think about this truth as it relates to us and to those in our lives. If Christ can and does call an uninterested and undeserved sinner like Matthew,[8] then there is hope that no one we know is too far removed from the sovereign call of Christ. If Christ sovereignly calls a person, we can trust that individual will respond. This truth should bring us great encouragement and hope. When we read this passage of Scripture—when we hear the wonderful news that Matthew gets up and follows Jesus—we should never despair over those people in our lives who seem farthest from the kingdom of God. Their disinterest in God is not a valid indication of God's disinterest in them. Every soul you know, no matter his or her reputation for unrighteousness and a refusal of religion, is only one call away from following Jesus. So pray to the Lord of the Harvest. Pray for Christ's call upon their lives.

Years ago I traveled to Malawi, Africa, where every night for nearly two weeks I gave evangelistic talks to college students. In one of the universities I was preaching to a packed and for the most part compliant crowd. But to my right in the balcony was a group of rowdy college girls who, I believe, had had a bit too much to drink.

Throughout most of my talk one girl in particular was an annoyance. Sometimes she yelled; other times she taunted me. One time she even got up and sang and danced. After a while I simply got used to her and virtually forgot she was there. That night I was preaching on the Gospel story of the rich young ruler. I walked through the way Jesus dealt with this self-righteous and sinful man, and I talked about the impossibility of salvation by works and the possibility of salvation through faith in Christ. At the end of the talk, instead of giving a traditional invitation to come forward, I reversed the call of commitment. I said, "If you are interested in giving your life to Christ, simply stay where you are. Stay in your seat, and someone will come to talk to you."

Nearly everyone left rather quickly, except for a few, most notably this girl. Sometime during my sermon this drunken soul was sobered by the Spirit. She sat there in that balcony all alone, repented, and received forgiveness. Now that's power! Not my power, but God's power. That's inexplicable power. You explain it to me. I can't figure it out. She sat there with tears of sorrow and joy. That night I witnessed a fat camel being pushed through the eye of a needle!

Matthew received the gospel for the same reason this girl received the gospel and the same reason that we received the gospel—because God worked sovereignly and powerfully through his Word and through his Spirit, calling all of us to Christ.

Christ's Call Is for Sinners

For some years now some Christians have had red-letter Bibles that conveniently highlight the words of Christ in red. Perhaps soon, when these Christian publishers get their acts together, we'll have an electronic Bible that lights up the main point of the text when you open to the passage being studied. However, until that heroic day arrives you have my permission to underline, star, circle, or highlight the end of verse 13, where Christ says, "I came not to call the righteous, but sinners." Jesus "came . . . to call . . . sinners." That is the main point of this passage. That is what should be flashing before your eyes!

Matthew was a tax collector, which may mean little to us. We may think of him as working for the Roman Empire's equivalent of the IRS, that he had a kind of respectable but slightly reviled occupation. But that certainly was not the case. To most first-century Jews, tax collectors "were easily the most hated men in Hebrew society."[9] They were viewed as religious and political traitors, trained extortionists, and thugs among the highest criminal element.[10] The Mishnah and the Talmud, two ancient rabbinical documents, "register scathing judgments of tax collectors, lumping them together with thieves and murderers."[11]

So Matthew was a tax collector,[12] officially excommunicated from the synagogue and unofficially from respectable society. But don't feel sorry for him, for he freely chose this seedy occupation, likely compelled (as I said earlier) by greed. Like today's casino boss, perhaps he accepted his somewhat socially and morally exiled (but government-approved) occupation because the paycheck was nice.

As Matthew is retelling his own story, he wants us to know that the type of person he was—a tax collector—is the type of person Jesus approached and called.[13] The story we have here is not so much about *how* Matthew was converted, but *who* was converted. This casino boss, mobster, thug got saved!

Use your imagination. Picture Jesus gathering his first four disciples—James and John, Peter and Andrew—and saying to them, "Now, fellas, I have decided to increase our number." Excitedly they respond, "Who, Lord? Who's it going to be? One of the scribes visiting from Jerusalem? That would be nice. Some worthy candidate from the crowd?" "Ah, no, no, I've decided to call Matthew to join us, you know the greedy, godless guy down at the tax office."

Stunned silence follows.

Peter, presumably unable to stop himself from talking, pulls Jesus aside and says quite frankly, "Lord, if you choose that man you will alienate everybody in this area. It is bad enough that you only have a bunch of fishermen to call your closest associates. But if you pick Matthew, you will wreck your cause. I don't yet know what your cause is, but I do know that if you choose him you'll wreck it."[14]

Assuming Peter said or thought something like that, like so many evangelicals today he was just being pragmatic. How often at our evangelistic campaigns do we think that if we just have some famous Christian athlete, musician, or intellectual share his or her testimony, our culture will be won to Christ? Thankfully Jesus was never pragmatic in his ministry, for if he wanted to impress others, especially the movers and shakers of his society, he never would have shown interest in Matthew, a most unfavorable candidate for his cause. But our Lord was not interested in the big names or the religious elite. He was *and is* interested in sinners from every walk of life, especially those sinners with whom no self-righteous person would dare associate.

That's what we see with Jesus calling Matthew (v. 9), and that's what we see with Jesus attending a banquet in verses 10–13:

> And as Jesus reclined at table in the house, behold, many tax collectors and sinners came and were reclining with Jesus and his disciples. And when the Pharisees saw this, they said to his disciples, "Why does your teacher eat with tax collectors and sinners?" But when he heard it, he said, "Those who are well have no need of a physician, but those who are sick. Go and learn what this means, 'I desire mercy, and not sacrifice' [Hosea 6:6]. For I came not to call the righteous [those who already think they are good enough], but sinners [those who know, or at least others know, they're not good at all]."

The great missionary C. T. Studd (I suppose if you are to be a great missionary you should have a name like that) once wrote, "Some want to live within the sound of Church or Chapel bell; I want to run a rescue shop within a yard of hell."[15] I think Jesus would have liked that missionary *motto*, for it seems to be the precise missionary *model* he employs.

The word "sinners" occurs three times in these four verses. Jesus is running a rescue shop one foot away from Matthew's dinner table. He is at a tax collector's house eating with tax collectors and sinners. He is reclining and eating with the outcasts (cf. 11:19; 22:1–10), with those who were known for flagrantly breaking the moral law of God as well as being unobservant of scribal traditions.[16]

Just as we normally sit at a table to eat meals, so did ancient Jews share this same posture for most of their meals. They sat at a table. Yet for formal dinners and special banquets they usually reclined on couches or carpets. They would lie down with their heads facing the table and their feet extending outward from it.[17] So here is Jesus, the holy Lord God of the universe, reclining with the reprehensible, dining with the detestable, communicating with the unclean, supping with the scum of society. Here is Jesus, the Messiah of Israel sharing meal fellowship (the most intimate social custom in Jewish society) with unclean Jews and Gentiles, extending "to them fellowship with God."[18] And according to Mark's Gospel, it appears that Jesus' message of mercy and forgiveness was well received that night—"there were many who followed him" (Mark 2:15).

While in graduate school I went on a weekend evangelistic outreach to Cook County Jail, where I was assigned to witness to the inmates of the First Division, the division reserved for the worst of Chicago's convicted criminals. Everyone I spoke with was a murderer.

At this time in my life I was regularly doing college ministry at a local community college (as I shared a few chapters ago), a place where I rarely found a student who would acknowledge that he or she was a sinner. They didn't like the label or the idea. They might say "Jesus is the Son of God" but not that they were "sinners."

What a difference it was with the inmates of the First Division! Of the men I talked with (even the ones who weren't interested in the gospel), all of them admitted to being a sinner. They took that label and stuck it right on their chests. Not because they were proud of it, but because they were realistic about it. The worst sinners often make the ripest candidates for God's mercy because, unlike the "righteous"—the religious person with no blemishes on his background check—the sinner knows his need and longs for a cure.

Christ stands (or even reclines) close to those who know they are far from him. Why? Because that's why he came to earth. He "came . . . to call . . . sinners," not after they have shown interest in him or cleaned up their act, but while they are still ten feet deep in their sins.

If I had to pick a favorite Bible verse, I would pick 1 Timothy 1:15: "The saying is trustworthy and deserving of full acceptance, that Christ Jesus came into the world to save sinners." Sinners! *Christ Jesus came into the world to save sinners!* Yes, Jesus was a teacher. Yes, he was a miracle-worker. Yes, he was a King. Yes, he was the perfect moral example of how we should live our lives. But if that were all he was, there would be no hope for us fallen creatures suffering from a fatal disease, dying physically and spiritually from the plague of sin. Jesus was and is a Savior for sinners. He is a Savior who so loved us that he came down to give us God's medicine for our eternal relief—the forgiveness of our sins.

Open up now and take it in.

A Line from the Creed

I began this chapter talking about the Apostles' Creed. As you may know, this creed is one of the earliest known Christian creeds, and legend has it (underscore "legend") that each of the twelve apostles wrote one of its twelve articles of faith.[19] In part that is why, according to this legend, it is called the Apostles' Creed.

I think this story is fanciful, but it is very creative nevertheless. Going along with such creativity, I like to imagine Peter telling each man to write down a line as part of this creed. And so they all write their line. Peter collects them and then gathers the Twelve together to read each line aloud. He reads his own line: "I believe in Jesus Christ, his only Son, our Lord." And he reads Thomas's line: "I believe in the resurrection of the body." Finally, after going through the others, he gets to Matthew's: "I believe in the forgiveness of sins." He did. They did. I do. Do you?

25

A Critique of "Pure" Religion

MATTHEW 9:14–17

IN HIS BOOK *The End of Faith*, outspoken atheist Sam Harris writes:

> Tell a devout Christian . . . that frozen yogurt can make a man invisible, and he is likely to require as much evidence as anyone else, and to be persuaded only to the extent that you give it. Tell him that the book he keeps by his bed was written by an invisible deity who will punish him with fire for eternity if he fails to accept its every incredible claim about the universe, and he seems to require no evidence whatsoever.[1]

Today's Christian is bombarded with accusations like Harris's, which are based upon the philosophical presupposition that human reason is "the best—indeed the only—way to comprehend reality."[2] But what evidence is there for the reliability of reason? What evidence is there that there is only one reality to this world—that which we can sense with our five senses?

Oddly enough, the great Enlightenment philosopher Immanuel Kant wrote a book against such "enlightened" thinking, entitled *A Critique of Pure Reason*. In this famous work, Kant argued that "there is a much greater limit to what human beings can know."[3] He showed that human reason and science cannot "gain access to and eventually comprehend the whole of reality."[4] In other words, there is no such thing as "pure" reason. What we perceive as reality may or may not be reality itself, or it may not be all there is to reality. Therefore, the man who keeps a Bible by his bed and believes what it teaches may not be as unrealistic about this universe as many *unbelievers* today would like to *believe*.

Another reason I bring up Immanuel Kant is to get us to the man he is named after: Jesus—"'Immanuel' (which means, God with us)" (1:23). Of course, Jesus wrote no treatise on the value and limits of human reason. (We have no record of anything he wrote.) But we do have a record of what he said and did in the Gospels. In the Gospel of Matthew we have a record of what I'll call our Lord's *Critique of "Pure" Religion*. Just as Kant critiqued his Enlightenment culture, saying, "You're not as bright as you think," similarly Jesus critiqued his religious culture, saying, "You're not as righteous as you think."

Critiquing the Pharisaical Religion

From the very start of his ministry, in his teachings, miracles, and outreach to the outcasts, Jesus is critiquing pharisaical religion.[5] That is, he is tearing down any man-made, religious traditions that had come to overshadow, supersede, or contradict the Old Testament and the gospel of the kingdom.[6]

In verse 17 Jesus talks about new wine, new wineskins, and old wineskins.[7] The *new wine* symbolizes the good news of the kingdom that has come in Christ (i.e., "the newness of the gospel [cf. John 2:1–11], personified in Jesus").[8] The *new wineskins*, as I understand them, are whatever teaching and conduct points to or holds up the gospel of Messiah Jesus. Then the *old wineskins*—which if you pour the new wine of the gospel into them will swell and burst as it ferments—represents Judaism, both teachings in the Torah that are fulfilled in Christ (e.g., the temple cultic) as well as, and more to the point, any un-Biblical traditions such as those of the Pharisees.

In his critique of "pure" religion, Jesus doesn't critique all Jewish religious practices. He doesn't say anything negative about the tradition of the synagogue that developed during the Exile, and he doesn't say anything negative about the many traditions surrounding the Passover meal. Rather, he seems to embrace such man-made traditions. But he does critique any and all religious views and practices that can't hold the new wine of the gospel.

If you put the new wine of the gospel into the right skin—the fresh wineskin—it will hold it. In fact, both the wine and the wineskin will be "preserved." Remember that Jesus did not come to abolish the Law but to fulfill it (5:17; cf. 13:52). Or to use the analogy here, he came to fill it! Jesus is not at odds with the Old Testament. Matthew makes this evident in 1:1—9:13 with his minefield of Old Testament quotations and allusions. Everywhere you go you step on one. We stepped on Hosea 6:6 in the previous chapter.

Put the new wine of the gospel into the new wineskins of Holy Scripture and it will hold. But put the new wine of the gospel into the old wineskins of Judaism and the new wine will show the imperfections of this "pure" religion—the weakness of the wineskins.[9] It will stretch and crack them. To use Jesus' other analogy in verse 16, it is like taking a new piece of cloth that has never been washed and dried (never shrunk) and sewing it on your old blue jeans. Good luck with that. You might as well throw them out.

So, just as Immanuel Kant critiqued the notion of "pure" reason (that our experience of reality is all there is to reality), so our Immanuel critiqued "pure" religion (religion that cannot hold up and hold onto the gospel).

Three Religious Questions

In the immediate context of our passage, three religious groups ask Jesus three old wineskins questions. The first group is the scribes. After Jesus tells the paralytic that his sins are forgiven, the scribes equate such a statement with blasphemy, for they thought in essence, "Who can forgive sins but God alone?" (9:3). The old wineskin answer to that question is, no one. God alone can forgive sins, and he alone can forgive sins *through* the priest offering an animal sacrifice at the temple in Jerusalem. However, the new wine answer—Jesus' answer—is, "The times are changing. I'm the priest. I'm the sacrifice. I'm the temple. The Son of Man has authority to forgive sins." So in 9:1–8 (the miracle of the paralytic) the old wineskin of the scribes bursts.

Then comes the second religious group, the Pharisees. In 9:9–13, when Jesus offers mercy to Matthew the tax collector and his friends, a bunch of "sinners," the Pharisees raise the question, "Why is Jesus eating with these types of people?" The old wineskin answer to that question is, "There is no good reason. He should be separate from them. Holiness means separateness: you don't eat this food or that food, and you don't fellowship with those irreligious Jews or any of those godless Gentiles." But the new wine answer is, "The times are changing. Holiness does at times mean separation. We must be careful with whom we associate so as not to fall into sinners' sins and idolaters' idolatries.[10] Yet, for the sake of the gospel we are to become all things to all people—to sup even with sinners for the sake of their salvation." So, in verses 9–13 (the meal at Matthew's house) the old wineskin of the Pharisees bursts.

Finally, we have one last religious group—the disciples of John the Baptist. We pick up their old wineskin question in verse 14: "Then the disciples of John came to him [Jesus], saying, 'Why do we and the Pharisees fast, but your disciples [and perhaps implied, 'you too, Jesus'] do not fast?'"

As far as we know, the scene hasn't changed. Jesus is still reclining at table at Matthew's house. First, the Pharisees interrupt, "Why is Jesus eating with them?" Then the disciples of John interrupt, "Why is he eating at all?" Later in 11:18, 19a Jesus will say:

> For John came neither eating nor drinking, and they say, "He has a demon." The Son of Man came eating and drinking, and they say, "Look at him! A glutton and a drunkard, a friend of tax collectors and sinners!"

You're darned if you do; you're darned if you don't. If you fast too much, they'll think this; if you eat too much (or eat at all), they'll think that. Here Jesus finds himself stuck between these two religious extremes.

To understand the mind-set of John's followers we need to recognize something of John's ministry. John the Baptist was an ascetic. His ministry was to embody repentance in how he lived, what he looked like, and what he did or did not eat. So when Jesus came on the scene preaching the same message as John did—"Repent, for the kingdom of heaven is at hand" (cf. 3:2; 4:17)—John's followers expected Jesus to embody in his body this same repentance.[11] Now, to some extent he did. He was poor. He did fast (once for forty days!). And in the Sermon on the Mount he taught about the top three Jewish spiritual disciplines—prayer, almsgiving, and *fasting* (6:16–18). Moreover, I would doubt if Jesus and his disciples would have broken God's Law in Leviticus 16:1–34 and Numbers 29:7–11 and not fasted on the Day of Atonement, the one time of year, Biblically-speaking, that God's people as a people were to fast.

Yet, what Jesus and his disciples were likely not doing was holding to the pharisaical custom of the first century, which was to fast twice a week—on Mondays and Thursdays. So I like to imagine that Jesus and the boys were eating at this banquet on Thursday evening, which would explain why all the lawless in town could make it to Matthew's that night to eat (they weren't ever fasting), and also explain why the Pharisees and John's disciples were likewise free to watch (they were fasting).[12]

A Fast from Fasting

Regardless of what night it was or whether or nor John's disciples held precisely to pharisaical fasting practices, I hope you understand a little better where this question in verse 14 was coming from. This was a sincere question from a group who would be willing to listen to what Jesus has to say. This is why our Lord doesn't rebuke them, as he does the other two religious groups. Instead he teaches them that his disciples are taking a *fast from fasting* because there is a wedding in town—a messianic jubilee! *Here comes the bridegroom!* Look at verse 15. Look at his "times are changing/new wine" answer, an answer that will burst their old wineskin. Jesus said to them:

> Can the wedding guests mourn as long as the bridegroom is with them? The days will come when the bridegroom is taken away from them, and then they will fast.

There are many things I love about the Gospels. But perhaps what I love most is the question/answer times with Jesus. In the Gospels whenever our Lord is confronted with tough theological questions, his answers are always brilliant. They are usually short, simple, and easy enough to understand, but they are like a mountain made of gold. You dig into it some and you say, "Wow! Look at this—gold!" You dig a bit more. "More gold!" Eight hours later you realize there is more gold here than you could have ever imagined. "This whole mountain is full of gold!"

Look again at verse 15. The first half of this golden mountain is Jesus' return question: "Can the wedding guests mourn as long as the bridegroom is with them?" Jesus often answered a question with a question (a marvelous strategy) for the purpose of getting the questioners to think. They basically asked, "Why aren't you all fasting like any normal religious person would do?" Jesus takes their serve and volleys it back to them. "You first tell me—would you fast if you were at a wedding?" Of course not! Fasting at a wedding? What could be more inappropriate? In Jesus' day the typical Jewish wedding lasted seven days. Everyone who was invited would take time off from work so they could work hard at having a good time. Jesus' first miracle, when he "manifested his glory" (John 2:11), was at a wedding where he turned water into wine.

In this passage, as we dig into this side of the mountain, Jesus equates his earthly ministry with a wedding party. He claims that just as it would be unnatural, rude, selfish, and insulting[13] to fast at someone's wedding—"no thanks: no soup, no bread, no meat, no drink, no cake for me"—so it would be morally wrong and irreligious for Jesus' disciples not to celebrate the appearance of "the bridegroom."

This passage is full of analogies—the unshrunk cloth, the new wine, and so on. Is this term "the bridegroom" merely another analogy? I don't think so. I think that Jesus is instructing John's disciples to think back on something John the Baptist once said. In John 3:28–30, when they asked John about Jesus, John said,

> I am not the Christ, but I have been sent before him. The one who has the bride is the bridegroom. The friend of the bridegroom [i.e., John], who stands and hears him [Jesus, the bridegroom], rejoices greatly at the bridegroom's voice. Therefore this joy of mine is now complete. He must increase, but I must decrease.

Why did John equate Jesus with the bridegroom? That is strong language for a prophet to use, for in the prophets such language is reserved for God.[14] To see this, turn to Ezekiel 16:7, 8 or Jeremiah 2:2, or Isaiah 54:5–8, where we read:

> For your Maker is your *husband*,
> the LORD of Hosts is his name;
> and the Holy One of Israel is your Redeemer. . . .
> For the LORD has called you
> like *a wife deserted and grieved in spirit*. . . .
> For a brief moment I deserted you,
> but with great compassion I will gather you.
> In overflowing anger for a moment
> I hid my face from you,
> but with everlasting love I will have compassion on you.
> (cf. Isaiah 62:4)

Or you could turn to the book of Hosea. Remember that Jesus just quoted from Hosea 6:6 in verse 13 when he answered the Pharisees' question. Might Jesus here, in his answer to John's disciples, have another passage in Hosea in mind—perhaps 2:14–20?

> Therefore, behold, I will allure her,
> and bring her into the wilderness,
> and speak tenderly to her.
> And there I will give her her vineyards. . . .

> And in that day, declares the LORD, you will call me "My Husband"... And I will make for them a covenant. . . . And I will betroth you to me forever. I will betroth you to me in righteousness and in justice, in steadfast love and in mercy. I will betroth you to me in faithfulness. And you shall know the LORD.

Do you see what Jesus is saying here? Are you looking carefully at the purity of this gold? In verse 15a Jesus is making (thus far in Matthew) the "highest christological claim."[15] Jesus has called himself or been called "the Son of God" (4:3; 8:29) and "the Son of Man" (8:20; 9:6), and now he calls himself "the bridegroom," which can either mean he is using an inappropriate analogy or he is claiming equality with God.

I think this claim went right over the heads of everyone there that day when he said it. But I don't think it went over Matthew's head as he was retelling it in this Gospel, and I don't think it went over the early church's head either. Paul in Ephesians 5:23 and 2 Corinthians 11:2 and John in Revelation 19:7 and 22:17 had no trouble getting the point that Christ is the bridegroom and that the church is united to him through faith.

So the first part of Jesus' answer to their question (why no fasting?) is something like this: we ought not to be upset or uptight. The kingdom of God is at hand! So, yes, we should repent. But we should also rejoice and be glad, for this kingdom is like a wedding, and Jesus is the bridegroom. So, pull up a seat. Sit down for the meal. Join in the celebration.

Freedom to Fast

For the second part of his answer (see v. 15b), our Lord says in essence, "Listen, I'm not against fasting. It's an issue of appropriate timing. For the days will come when I am taken away from these disciples of mine, and then they will fast."

When Jesus speaks of himself being "taken away from them," he is likely referring in part to his death and burial. I say "in part" because I believe Jesus' ascension is also included. Perhaps the ascension is the preferred referent (i.e., Jesus being "taken away" refers to when he was "lifted up . . . into heaven" [Acts 1:9, 10]). Once Jesus ascends, the church will be left without his physical presence as we long for the consummation of our marriage to Christ, what John calls "the marriage of the Lamb" (Revelation 19:7). We have his spiritual presence through the Holy Spirit ("I am with you always *spiritually*"), but we long for the day when we will see him face-to-face.

We live in the time between the ascension and the second coming. Therefore, the way Jesus ends verse 15 is directly applicable to us today. How so? We have the freedom to fast. I word it that way intentionally, for notice that Jesus does not say that Christians *must* fast. That is important; this is not a command. Nor does Jesus say that Christians *ought* to fast (shame on you if you don't). Rather he says they *will* fast.

We will fast when we are trying to develop and practice self-control, telling our flesh who is in control of our bodies when it comes to resisting temptation and sin. *We will* fast to grow our moral muscles—if we can resist tasty food that is not good for us, we can resist those sensual pleasures that are also not good for us. *We will* fast when we are repenting of sin (the times when we have failed to control ourselves). *We will* fast to say, "I'm sorry, Lord. Please help me, Lord." *We will* fast, as the early church did, when we are calling upon the Lord to know his will, make a wise judgment, or ask him to open a door for the gospel. *We will* fast simply because we long for the wedding of the Lamb. *We will* fast because we long for the day when God will let justice roll like a mighty river, the day when "the earth will be filled with the knowledge of the glory of the LORD as the waters cover the sea" (Habakkuk 2:14).

So, yes, *we will* fast. However, if you don't fast or haven't yet fasted, don't worry. The last thing I'm going to do with this text is place some man-made burden on your back. This passage is not so much about fasting as it is about freedom.

So much foolish, un-Biblical fasting has gone on in the church for hundreds of years—fasting from meat on Fridays during Lent, fasting to gain God's approval, fasting to show others just how holy you are and how unholy others are. If the only fasting we witness is legalistic, ritualistic, ostentatious, or for the purpose of works-righteousness, it is no wonder that true, Biblical, God-honoring fasting is not in vogue today. It is no wonder that Protestants run from it like we would from a grenade. That kind of fasting is destructive to the body and *the soul.*

The "pure" religion that Jesus is critiquing here and everywhere in the Gospels always equates the rigor of fasting with the level of spirituality: the more you fast, the more acceptable you are in the sight of God. But Jesus is tearing down all such religious rubbish and calling us to leave "pure" religion for a personal relationship: "Come to me," he invites, ". . . and I will give you rest. Take my yoke upon you. . . . For my yoke is easy, and my burden is light" (11:28–30). Put differently, submission to Jesus is freeing![16]

This is the paradox of the Christian faith. Through faith and faith alone are we united to Christ in a personal relationship that compels us to love, serve, sacrifice, follow, obey, and yes, even fast if and when it is in our interest or the interest of others. Christ gives no command that compels us to fast. Paul, the Pharisee of Pharisees, gives no command to fast (he doesn't even write about it, except negatively).[17] It is rather the love of God that controls us and even compels us (see 2 Corinthians 5:14) to do what is right and pleasing in the sight of God. Our freedom in Christ gives us the freedom to fast without fear as we wait patiently but expectantly, with oil burning in our lamps, longing for the bridegroom to come. Oh, *we will* fast as we long for his return, as "The Spirit and the Bride" together call out, "Come" (Revelation 22:17a). Indeed, "Come, Lord Jesus!" (Revelation 22:20b).

26

Two Touches

MATTHEW 9:18–26

ON FRIDAY, OCTOBER 23, 2009 I received a phone call from Randy Gruendyke, the chaplain of Taylor University and a longtime friend and mentor. Randy asked me if I could come to Taylor on Monday to give the chapel talk. The reason for this last-minute invitation was because Kent Hughes, who was scheduled to speak, just moments before he boarded a plane from Spokane learned that his granddaughter, Caroline, had been tragically struck by a car. He naturally rushed from the airport to the hospital to see her before she died. She was nineteen years old.

On Sunday afternoon as I was making the four-hour drive from Naperville, Illinois to Taylor University I came to the two-lane country road from Lafayette to Upland, Indiana, where I turned off the radio, rolled down the widows, and began to enjoy the fresh air and quiet countryside. But thoughts of death quickly began to disquiet my mind.

I first thought about my own death. Caroline's accident seemed so not "accidental"—a man had a heart attack and died while driving, obviously lost control of his car, and ran right into her as she was waiting at a bus stop with music playing in her earphones. She literally didn't know what hit her. How easy it would be for me, I thought as I was driving on that country road, to take a curve too fast, to misjudge when passing a slow truck, to get hit by an oncoming car. How easy it would be to be just another name painted on a white wooden cross on the side of the road. With my eyes firmly fixed on the pavement in front of me and my mind alert as ever, I still recognized afresh how little I was in control and how quickly my life could end—a flat tire, bad brakes, a worn-out bridge, a drunk driver, a foolish driver, a dead driver killed by a heart attack two seconds before our paths would cross.

I thought about my own death. I also thought about my children and especially the death of my daughters. How emotionally difficult it would be for me to lose Lily, Evelyn, or Charlotte, one of my beautiful little girls.

One More Guest at Table

The Apostle Matthew begins this next section with a father who has just lost his daughter, his little twelve-year-old daughter, as Mark tells us (Mark 5:23, 41, 42), his "only daughter," Luke adds (Luke 8:42).

Can you feel the emotional weight of verse 18?

> While he [Jesus] was saying these things to them, behold, a ruler [a man named Jairus, who was "one of the rulers of the synagogue," Mark 5:22; Luke 8:41], came in and knelt before him, saying, "My daughter has just died, but come and lay your hand on her, and she will live."

When some Biblical scholars and commentators, even the ones I most respect, look at Jairus and his plea for help from Jesus, they see a desperate faith. For example, one commentator writes,

> We must not mistakenly think Jairus had become a [follower] of Jesus or that he was a man of great faith. The simple fact was he was desperate. He had heard of Jesus' miracles (maybe had even seen some) and possibly had talked to some who had been healed. He was not sure about Jesus, but Jesus was his only chance.[1]

Another commentator adds, "If you compare the ruler of the synagogue with the centurion you will say that the full brightness of faith shone in the centurion, while scarcely the smallest portion of it was visible in the ruler."[2]

I agree that if we compare the faith of the centurion with the faith of Jairus, the latter would fall short. In 8:10 Jesus unreservedly says of the centurion, "Truly, I tell you, with no one in Israel have I found such faith." But to say that the light of Jairus's faith was less luminous because he asked Jesus to come and lay his hands on his daughter instead of merely asking our Lord to speak the word is a bit much. Moreover, to say that his faith was completely erroneous—that it was only his utter desperation that brought him to Christ—is to miss the whole point. What is wrong with saying that this man had a desperate faith or that the woman we will encounter in verses 20–22 had the same or that we, when we came to Christ, came in some sense or in every sense in utter desperation and complete dependence? I came to Christ only after I had lost everything, including my pride.

In Matthew 19 Jesus finds himself bombarded with little children. His disciples don't like this and want to put a stop to this spectacle. But Jesus sternly rebukes them, saying, "Let the little children come to me and do not hinder them, for to such belongs the kingdom of heaven" (v. 14). What I find most interesting is that Jesus makes this comment right before another "ruler"—a rich young ruler—refuses to become childlike in faith. He refuses to come to Jesus in desperation and complete dependence. But here, along with the ruler of chapter 9, a very different picture emerges. It is a beautiful picture of dependent faith. Here an old synagogue ruler becomes like a little child.

This childlike faith is apparent in many ways. First, his faith is demonstrated in that he came to Jesus, and as far as we know, to Jesus alone. He didn't run to the doctors in town or to the religious leaders who were in Matthew's house, though the scribes, the Pharisees, and the disciples of John the Baptist were all there. He came to Jesus. Second, his faith is demonstrated in his posture. He came to Jesus like the magi and the leper (and the seraphim and cherubim in Revelation 5:8, 14). That is, he "knelt" before Jesus (v. 18). He "fell at his feet" is how Mark phrases it (Mark 5:22).

Picture the scene. I like to imagine the reaction of the religious crowd who are gathered outside Matthew's front door, throwing their questions at Jesus and murmuring their accusations against him. And then here comes Jairus. They know Jairus. He's one of the rulers of the local synagogue. They think, "Ah, he must have a question for Jesus too. Just line up behind us." But no, there is no question, only a bended knee and a confession, a statement full of faith in Jesus. The sense of his plea is this:

> My daughter has died. But I have faith in you. I may not know who you are—a prophet, the Messiah, God in the flesh? What I do know is that God is with you in a unique way, an extraordinary way, that he is with you as he was with Elijah (1 Kings 17:17–24) and Elisha (2 Kings 4:32–37).[3] And just as they raised the dead, I believe you, Jesus, if you would just come to my house and simply lay your hand on her (not stretch your body over the child like Elijah did, and not even hand-to-hand or mouth-to-mouth or eyes-to-eyes as Elisha did),[4] I believe that she will be brought back to life.

Can you imagine this scene? What did the scribes and Pharisees think of this—this posture, this request? *Has the whole world gone mad? What is our Jairus doing? How can it be that our colleague, one of the pillars of the Jewish community, is groveling at the feet of some unordained popular preacher, some demon-empowered miracle-worker from the lowly town of Nazareth?*

This ruler's faith was not perfect (whose faith is?), but it was pleasing to God. I say that because Jesus accepted his offer. When we read verse 19, "And

Jesus rose and followed him, with his disciples," we see our Lord's positive reply to Jairus's humble and faithful plea for help.

Jesus is not afraid to tell people that their faith is misplaced or lacking. But here he doesn't. Here there is no rebuke, no correction, no "O ye of little faith." Here Jesus arises to raise this girl from the dead. Here Jesus gets up from the table with sinners to show that just as he has the authority to forgive sins, so he has the authority to conquer the curse. He has the power to raise the dead, to breathe life into dead bones and bodies.

The First Touch

So Jesus journeys to Jairus's home. But on the way he is interrupted by the silent plea of another desperate soul, a woman whose prospects were little better than the little girl our Lord was going to save. Verses 20–22 describe this woman, her reason for coming to Jesus, and her faith in him.

> And behold, a woman who had suffered from a discharge of blood for twelve years came up behind him and touched the fringe of his garment, for she said to herself, "If I only touch his garment, I will be made well." Jesus turned, and seeing her he said, "Take heart, daughter [that's an interesting word];[5] your faith has made you well." And instantly the woman was made well.

Certainly this ruler's situation was desperate, but so too was this woman's situation, perhaps even more so. If Jairus loses his daughter, it would indeed be a personal tragedy, but he still has a job, house, money, servants, and a wife. But this woman has nothing. Due to her persistent discharge of blood she has been "discharged" of her health *and* of her wealth, and likely this poor woman has also been discharged from any marital relationship she may have enjoyed.[6] Furthermore, she was discharged from normal interaction within her culture, especially from the Jewish religion.[7] According to Leviticus 15:19–33, a woman was "unclean" for seven days after her monthly period. Therefore, this woman has been "unclean" not for seven days but for twelve years. Due to her bleeding she had been unable to participate in any of the public rituals of worship for over a decade.

However, you have to understand that this woman, as bad off as she was, was not like some of the homeless who walk our city streets because they have consciously walked down the path of destruction. She wasn't a drug addict. She wasn't a runaway. And she hadn't given up on life. She was restless in her pursuit of help. According to Mark, she had "spent all that she had" on physicians, and yet to no avail (Mark 5:26). Despite getting treatments, she nevertheless "grew worse" (Mark 5:26).

But one day she spots Jesus, the Great Physician. "She had heard the reports about Jesus" (Mark 5:27). At this point in Capernaum, who hadn't? So she came up with a plan. "I will sneak up behind him, hide myself in the crowd, and then touch his tassel." Every Jewish man in Jesus' day had four tassels sewn upon the four corners of his cloak, the fringe of the "garment." These tassels were visible reminders to obey God's covenant commands (Numbers 15:37–41; Deuteronomy 22:12).[8] Touch one tassel. Just one! That was her plan.

Now again we look at this and say, "Hmm, what's up with this?" At first it makes sense why some would argue that this woman's "faith" is merely or mostly superstitious. Just touch the tassel? Some scholars don't give her the benefit of the doubt. Some suggest that her faith resembles the type of person who would touch the television screen when the televangelist promises a healing by doing so.

But this is not the impression we get from the Gospel writers. Matthew, Mark, and Luke (and Matthew especially)[9] tell us that she hears about Jesus and responds to him. This is one of the genuine and basic characteristics of discipleship. Like the synagogue ruler's faith, her faith in Christ comes *prior* to her healing. That's significant. The timing is important.

I have an old friend, who is now serving as a missionary in the Middle East, who came to faith in Jesus Christ because when a teenager she was healed of a deadly disease. After the doctors had told her there was no hope for recovery, she was healed when a group of young, faith-filled Christians laid their hands on her dying body and prayed. Before this happened, she had been very rebellious. She had no faith in God or Jesus. She wanted nothing to do with Christianity. Yet through that gracious miracle God softened her hard heart to the gospel.

That seems natural enough. You are dying. God heals you. In gratitude you respond in faith and serve him the rest of your life. That's wonderful! However, that's not the picture of faith here. We can rightly say that this woman has greater faith than my friend because this woman's faith is not a response to a miracle but a faithful expectation of one. Her faith may be imperfect (yes, mixed with "sin and error"),[10] but it is bold and brave and strong enough to pick up a mountain and throw it into the sea. As we discover in verse 22, such faith is pleasing to God. We know it is pleasing to God because Jesus healed her. The flow of blood dried up. Immediately she was made well. Moreover, Jesus explicitly commended her, not saying, "I have made you well," but "[Y]our faith has made you well" (v. 22). Only one comment is made regarding the nature of her faith, and it is positive, not negative. Jerome put it this way: "Her touch on the hem of his garment was the cry of a believing heart."[11] Her faith is childish, perhaps, but also childlike.

From this, I want you to know that you don't need to have all your theological ducks in a row to come to Jesus. Nor do you have to have all your commandment-keeping ducks in a row to come to Jesus. You just need to come to him. You need to push through the crowd and come to him, the more empty-handed the better.

The Second Touch

I think this miracle—this interruption in the drama that keeps the first-time reader in suspense concerning the dead girl—would only strengthen Jairus's confidence in Christ. I think as he is walking home stride by stride with our Lord, his faith builds with each step. However, when he finally arrives home, we come to another interruption in the drama, an expected but disheartening one. At the very least it's a stark reminder to him of reality. His daughter is still dead. This woman's flow of blood might have stopped finally—and for her that was life again, but his daughter's flow of blood had also stopped finally. It stopped because her heart stopped. So when he arrived home the only life there is the noise of sad-sounding flutes and the sadder-sounding cries of the crowd (v. 23).

Many years ago when I was a teenager I attended the wake of a close friend of mine, a boy who was two years younger than I. Like Caroline, he was struck by a car. This happened at an intersection that was less than two blocks away from my childhood home. I will never forget standing in line with hundreds of other people steadily walking toward his casket to pay respects and offer a prayer and seeing and hearing his mother in the front row weeping and wailing. Her youngest son lay lifeless before her, and she had no compulsion other than to cry out at the top of her lungs, calling out her son's name.

It may be that is precisely the type of scene Jairus and Jesus came upon—a mother, family members, and neighbors sincerely weeping and wailing. But it is more likely that those causing such a "commotion" were professional mourners, as strange as that may sound to us. In ancient Israel, as even today in some non-Christian cultures, professional mourners were hired at the time of death. In the Mishnah it is said that for burial "even the poorest in Israel should hire not less than two flutes and one wailing woman."[12] Since this ruler was likely a rich man, the combination of the mournful music, the wailing of the many women, the hand-clapping, the beating of the breast, the tearing of hair, and the rending of garments ripped to the heart must have created quite a "commotion," awakening everybody in town but the one body that mattered most. This reality of professional grievers makes better sense of Jesus' directness and their response to his directness. "[H]e said, 'Go away, for the girl is not dead but sleeping.' And they laughed at him" (v. 24).

Of course, Jesus is not here denying her death. He is not a brilliant medical specialist arriving at the house with a correct second opinion: "Oh, no, she is only in a coma. You fools, if I hadn't arrived as soon as I did, this poor girl would have been buried alive." Jesus is not denying her death; he is redefining it. Her death is not the end. It is not the grim reality it seems. It is nothing worse than deep sleep. In due course she will be getting up again. In due course Jesus will be dying and getting up again, and because of this you and I will likewise be dying and getting up again. She was only sleeping.

They wouldn't hear a word of it—"they laughed at him" (v. 24). They laughed him to scorn. Their tears were quickly changed to laughter, which is a clear indication of the superficiality of their grief. From a human perspective their laughter makes sense, for, of course, this poor girl is really dead! But they don't know with whom they are dealing—the Son of the *living* God who can calm a deadly storm with one word of rebuke, tame a thousand untamable demons with one command, and surely tell a "sleeping" body to wake up!

And so, as verse 25 records—*here's the miracle!*—with complete authority over the situation, after "the crowd had been put outside," our Lord "went in and took her by the hand, and the girl arose." The weeping, wailing, and great commotion pulsing all around her could not renew the pulse of this deceased child.[13] Yet the powerful *touch* of Christ literally woke the dead,[14] a touch that spread to others as "the report of this went through all that district" (v. 26). It spread from Capernaum to Jerusalem to Damascus to Rome to London to New York to Chicago to wherever you are now, and it's still traveling, giving hope to all who trust in Christ and his resurrection power.

Hammer Away

Martin Luther lost his beloved fourteen-year-old daughter, Magdalena, to the Great Plague that swept through Europe in the sixteenth century. Those who knew Luther later recalled the event:[15]

> Brokenhearted Luther knelt beside her bed and begged God to release her from the pain. Then when she had finally died, and the carpenters were nailing down the lid of the coffin, Luther screamed out, "Hammer away! Hammer away . . . for on the last day she shall rise again."[16]

That is our hope for Kent's granddaughter, Caroline. That is our hope for all who die in Christ. Our ultimate hope is not to escape death. Who escapes death? This twelve-year-old girl would one day die again, just as Lazarus, who was also raised from the dead, also eventually died again. This miracle story is not about how we should trust that Jesus will save us from an early death or from death itself. Jesus is not some mystical, magical, mythical Fountain of Youth. No. He is our resurrected Savior!

This story before us is really just a miniature version of the great story of our salvation:[17] in the death of Christ is the death of death. He takes on the curse of death that Adam brought into the world. Specifically, in the death of Christ is the death of our *spiritual* death (we will be forgiven our sin), and in the resurrection of Christ is the death of our *physical* death (we will rise again bodily). Since Christ died and rose again, we who are united to him, though we may die, will also rise again to a better life. In the words of Horatio Spafford, the hymn-writer who lost his four daughters at sea, we will rise to a life where Satan does not buffet, where trials do not come, where sea billows do not roll, and where all is finally well with our souls.[18]

That is our hope. It is a hope based on the reality of the resurrection and a hope that I hope brings encouragement to you today. Hammer away! Hammer away . . . for on the last day *we shall rise again*.

27

Too Blind Men

MATTHEW 9:27–34

IF YOU WERE TO RUN INTO ME at a restaurant, bookstore, football game, or dark alley at midnight and ask me, "Hey, Pastor, why do you believe Jesus is the Messiah?" I would show you my right hand, spread wide my five fingers, and say, "There are five reasons."

First, I believe Jesus is the Messiah because of his words. What he said, when he said it, and how he said it—with such authority, authenticity, and insight into both the mind of God and the human heart—has convinced me that "No one ever spoke like this man" (John 7:46). In a poem I wrote when I was twenty, I have a line about my conversion that goes like this:

> But Jesus spoke those silly words that gods like me twist and turn
> Until they turned and twist'd me, like Winter does to Autumn's leaves. . . .

Once God's Spirit began to work on my hard heart, those "silly words" of Jesus—those seemingly ridiculous commands and those crazy claims about himself—"turned and twist'd me." They had the power to soften my heart, renew my mind, and free my will to know and love and follow him.

So, first, I believe Jesus is the Messiah because of his words. Second, and closely related to the first, I believe because of his verifiable predictions. I wrote about a few of these predictions in my chapter on the Sermon on the Mount (chapter 9). For example, Jesus said, "Heaven and earth will pass away, but my words will not pass away" (24:35). Now, if ten, fifty, or 500 years after Jesus said something like that, nobody spoke or heard of his words—e.g., the Golden Rule or the Lord's Prayer—then I would say, "Hey, this Christianity thing is bogus." If 2,000 years after he said something like "Judge not, that you be not judged" (7:1) only 2,000 people in the world knew who said that or had even heard that phrase, then also I'd think, "Ah, this Christianity thing is bogus." But when millions of people, even those who don't go to church, use Jesus' words in their own regular conversations, sometimes without knowing it, that gets my attention.

Another prediction Jesus made that gets my attention concerns the church. He spoke of the permanence of the church—"the gates of hell shall not prevail against it" (16:18b), and he spoke of the scope of the church's mission—that the gospel would spread "east to west" and be believed by people from every nation (see 8:11; 28:19). Think about that claim, especially in the context of the first century. If we lived in the first century and Caesar Augustus predicted, "Roman rule will last for 2,000 years, and our way of life will have dominion over people from every little corner of the world," we likely would have agreed. But we know now that is not what happened. Rome didn't fall in a day, but it fell. And that is what is so remarkable. How could the Roman Empire crumble to the ground? How could the Egyptian, Assyrian, and British empires all crumble to the ground while this tiny religion from this insignificant Middle-Eastern people—this "kingdom," as Jesus calls it—keeps growing?

The third reason I believe Jesus is the Messiah (and forgive the long introduction; we will get to the blind men in just a minute) is because he fulfills Old Testament prophecies and patterns. In Luke 24:44 Jesus said that what was written in the Law of Moses, the Prophets, and the Psalms was all "fulfilled" in him. He claims there is a unity to the Bible and that he is the unifying figure.

The more I read the Bible with Christ-centered spectacles, the more I am amazed at how it all fits together. It's not just the predictive prophecies—the Messiah will be born of a virgin (Isaiah 7:14), in the town of Bethlehem (Micah 5:2), or a Suffering Servant will atone for our sins (Isaiah 53)—it's also the patterns. For example, the three key Old Testament offices—prophet, priest, and king—are but shadows of the real thing—Jesus!

Fourth, I believe Jesus is the Messiah because of his miracles. Now we are getting closer to our text and closer to what we have looked at for the last few sermons in the eight miracles thus far in Matthew 8, 9. Other religions might believe in miracles or allow for miracles, but Christianity depends on them.[1] Most notably we depend on the miracle of Christ's resurrection. If Jesus did not miraculously rise from the dead, then our faith is null and void. But it's not just that great miracle, for which I think there is ample evidence, that helps me believe. It's also all the less spectacular miracles scattered throughout the Gospels. If we look at the summary sections of Jesus' miracles (we have one coming up in 9:35), we get the picture that Jesus healed thousands of people from "every disease and every affliction." The fact that our Lord performed many miracles was not denied by the Roman rulers or Jewish leaders of the day. Even the notable Jewish historian Josephus admits that Jesus was a miracle-worker. No other explanation accounts for all the eyewitness testimony and all the interest in him.

But it is not just that Jesus was a miracle-worker—it is *how* he performed his miracles. He never showed off like so-called miracle-workers today do (he got rid of the crowd whenever he could). Moreover, he touched the untouchables—a leper, a dead body, the eyes of the blind. Why touch them? Why not just bark out some command from a safe distance? How he healed is significant, but also *when* he healed. He healed on the Sabbath, for example. He did this to make a theological point for sure, but also to show he had the power to heal however and whenever he wanted. It's how he healed, it's when he healed, and it's *what* he healed—leprosy, demon-possession, paralysis, blindness, even death. His resumé is pretty impressive. He wasn't healing sprained ankles, pimples, or runny noses, was he? *What* he did, *when* he did it, and *how* he did it not only was never seen in the history of Israel (v. 33), but never seen in the history of the world. Jesus' miracles help me believe.

The fifth reason I believe Jesus is the Messiah is tied to this reality of Jesus as miracle-worker. It's *whom* Jesus healed. However, it's broader than simply physical healing; it's whom Jesus healed spiritually. It's whom Jesus welcomed into the kingdom of heaven. It's the Lord of the Harvest harvesting lepers and Roman centurions and women and demon-possessed men and tax collectors and the blind and deaf and dumb. Put differently, it is Jesus' compassion for both the materially and religiously poor—the social and religious outcasts of his society.

We are so familiar with Jesus' compassion (a compassion mentioned in 9:36: "He had compassion for them"), and we have been so Christianized in the Western world with basic Christian ethics, that we don't think twice about helping the hungry, caring for the sick, loving the loveless, forgiving those who trespass against us, or welcoming ethnic and economic diversity within the Body of Christ. We take the compassion of Christ and Christianity for granted. But what he did, not only in his death on the cross (which was the ultimate show of compassion for outcasts) but also what he did here in Matthew 8, 9, is unparalleled. No one in the history of the world showed compassion how he did and to whom he did. And it's that compassion that makes me exclaim with great joy and with conviction from the heart, "Truly this is God's Son. Truly this is the Messiah. Truly Christianity is true."

Two Blind Men

With that long and thick foundation poured and now hardening beneath our feet, finally we come to the two blind men (9:27–31), our ninth miracle story in Matthew.

What does this story teach us? I'll put it this way: what color do these two blind men add to Matthew 8, 9, this already colorful picture of Christ? They certainly add another bullet point to Jesus' impressive miracle-worker resumé. They show forth again our Lord's authority over the effects of the curse in this world—everything from blindness to death. However, I want us to see that before they ever receive their sight, these two men add to our perception of *faith*.

You see, this miracle focuses on faith: "Do you believe?" (v. 28) and "[a]ccording to your faith" (v. 29). To the confident but humble faith of the leper and the centurion, the immediate and obedient faith of Matthew, and the desperate but childlike faith of Jairus and the woman with the issue of blood,[2] these two blind men add *clarity* to our definition of faith. Specifically, they bring clarity to three questions: (1) In whom are we to have faith? (2) For what are we to ask? (3) How are we to come to Christ?

First, *In whom are we to have faith?* Their answer to that question is that faith is *in Jesus*.

> And as Jesus passed on from there, two blind men followed him, crying aloud, "Have mercy on us, Son of David." When he entered the house [likely Peter's house], the blind men came to him, and Jesus said to them, "Do you believe that I am able to do this?" They said to him, "Yes, Lord." Then he touched their eyes, saying, "According to your faith be it done to you." And their eyes were opened. (vv. 27–30a)

Notice a few details here. First, the topic of faith is at the center of their conversation. In faith they call out to Jesus because they want to be healed. Jesus then asks them if they believe that he is able to do this. Note that he doesn't ask, "Do you believe that I can ask my Father in Heaven for the power to heal?" Rather, he says, "Do you believe that I can heal?" And they say, "Yes, Lord." The sense is, "Yes, Lord, we do believe in you and in your own power to do this."

Jesus is the object of their faith. Jesus as the "Son of David" (v. 27) is the object of their faith. They are the first to use this important messianic term for Jesus. They are the first to *see* both Jesus' royalty and also his fulfillment[3]—that he is the fulfillment of the Davidic covenant. The first words of Matthew's Gospel are, "The book of the genealogy of Jesus Christ, the son of David . . ."

(1:1). Well, hooray! Finally someone has caught up with Matthew's line of thinking. This Jesus is the Son of David, the promised King (cf. 2 Timothy 2:8). That is the one in whom they have faith.

Despite what many people today think, faith is not some nebulous thing—"I have faith." Rather, faith is *in* something or someone. If you tell me you have faith in the philosophical notion that all faiths are the same, I'll say, "Fine. You're wrong. You're not thinking historically or logically about things. But at least you're admitting you have faith in something." But don't give me this "I have faith in faith" nonsense, for whether we admit it or not each of us has faith in something. As Christians we have faith in Jesus. Like these blind men, we look to him alone as the object of saving faith, for he alone is "the Son of David," and he alone is "Lord" (cf. Romans 10:9).

So the first question these blind men answer is: *In whom are we to have faith?* Their answer is, Jesus, the Lord, the Son of David. The second question they help us answer is: *For what?* We are to have faith in Jesus, but for what? Answer: mercy. We read in verse 27 that "two blind men followed him, crying aloud, 'Have mercy on us.'"

Obviously they wanted Jesus to have compassion on their condition. Blindness then (and even today) led to obvious hardships and usually poverty. The blind in Jesus' day were almost always beggars (e.g., Mark 10:46). But more than that, blindness also had a religious stigma attached to it. In Old Testament times, while God's people were to be considerate and compassionate to the blind (e.g., Leviticus 19:14), nevertheless, every example of someone becoming blind is in the context of their being judged/punished for sin (cf. Deuteronomy 28:28). Think of the Sodomites knocking on Lot's door. They were "struck with blindness" (Genesis 19:11). Or think of the Syrians who were attacking God's people. Elisha prayed to the Lord, "Please strike this people with blindness. So he [the Lord] struck them with blindness" (2 Kings 6:18). Or think of Samson and how his eyes, due to his sin, were gouged out (Judges 16:21). He died blind.

In the New Testament, although Jesus' healing of the blind man in John 9 shows that blindness is not always related to sin, other texts like Acts 9:8 (cf. 13:11)—Paul's temporary blindness—reminds us that sometimes it is. Sin always has consequences. Sometimes those consequences manifest themselves physically.

All that to say, there *might* be more to this plea for mercy than a cure for blindness. They *might* be confessing their sin and repenting of a sin or series of sins that has caused their blindness. "Jesus, have mercy on us—body and soul." Now, if that's not right—if it is only physical blindness on their minds—Matthew nevertheless wants us to think more spiritually. For like the paralytic brought to Jesus at the beginning of chapter 9, their biggest need and our biggest need—blind or not blind—is God's merciful forgiveness of sins. Jesus didn't die to make nice people even nicer. He didn't die just to show us how to sacrifice for others. Jesus died to demonstrate God's hatred toward sin and mercy toward sinners, sin-blinded sinners like you and me . . . and them.

So, who are we to have faith in? Jesus. And for what? Mercy. And finally: *How are we to come in faith to Jesus for mercy?* What should our posture be? We should come with a "hungering humility."[4]

Jesus passes by. They follow him, and they cry out loudly, "Have mercy on us, Son of David" (v. 27). And then what does Jesus do? For the first time in this Gospel, when asked for something he just keeps on walking. What's he doing? Is he testing their faith? Or perhaps he is concerned that what they said—they called him "Son of David" (they are the first to call him the Messiah), while true, might be misinterpreted by the crowd—that he is some political messiah (cf. vv. 30, 31). Whatever the reason, he goes into the house, and they go in right after him. They sure are hungry, aren't they?—hungry for healing. Like the father of the dead girl, the bleeding woman, and the four guys who tore off the roof of the house to save their buddy, these two blind men are "absolutely determined to get into the presence of Jesus."[5] That's hungering humility! That's gospel faith![6]

Having finally gotten Jesus' attention, like the others before them in this chapter, they show faith in Jesus before he performs any miracle. Jesus makes sure of it. He asks them point-blank, "Do you believe that I am able to do this?" (v. 28)—that is, to heal their blindness/to have mercy on them. They reply, "Amen. Yes, Lord. Let it be so. Truly we believe." And Jesus just eats up this hungering humility. In his own humility, he *touches* (!) their unclean, diseased, sin-infected, curse-laden eyes. "'According to your faith be it done to you.' And their eyes were opened" (v. 30). And they saw (can you imagine it?) the light of the sun, the flight of the sparrow, the color of Jesus' blue (?), green (?), probably brown eyes.

The "Disobedience" of Faith

Their eyes were opened.

The irony here, which will only build as we move to the next miracle, is that once these blind men see, the first thing they do is disobey Jesus (v. 31). In Romans Paul calls us to "the obedience of faith" (Romans 1:5; 16:26). These men show what I'll label humorously, although it's no laughing matter, "the disobedience of faith." Just look at verses 30, 31. Here is how their story ends:

> And their eyes were opened. And Jesus sternly warned[7] them, "See that no one knows about it." But they went away and spread his fame through all that district.

I don't want to spend too much time on what scholars call the "messianic secret"[8]—why Jesus sometimes told people to be quiet about a miracle (and sometimes didn't, cf. John 4). I think the reason for the command to be silent here involves what I hinted at earlier—Jesus is not looking for the fanfare that comes with the power to heal and, more importantly, he does not want the crowds and his disciples to misunderstand the nature of his kingship. He is the Son of David, but unlike David (and nobody will get this until after the resurrection) he has not come as a military warrior but as a sacrificial lamb. He is the Son of David, but also the Suffering Servant.

We can be sympathetic that what happens in verse 31 is natural enough. It was wrong because it was disobedience to a direct command. But come on, they were just helplessly happy, gleefully grateful. We'd all do the same thing. Right?

I actually think Matthew includes this verse as a subtle rebuke. For when blind they see. They see in whom they are to have faith, what they are to ask for, and how they are to approach Jesus. But once they see, they stop living by faith, which is always manifested by obedience to Christ's commands (cf. 1 John 2:3), however countercultural and counterintuitive some of those commands may be. So, perhaps the point of verse 31 is that it is better to be blind and obedient than to see and disobey.

Too Blind Men

Whether I have that right or not, I'm not sure. I am sure, however, that I have this next part right—the purpose of the second miracle. Read with me again verses 32–34:

> As they were going away, behold, a demon-oppressed man who was mute was brought to him. And when the demon had been cast out, the mute man spoke. And the crowds marveled, saying, "Never was anything like this seen in Israel." But the Pharisees said, "He casts out demons by the prince of demons."

After preaching seven sermons on the miracle stories of chapters 8, 9, I began to pick up on how these stories work. All of the miracles highlight both Jesus' divine authority and power. "Only God could do that" is what we should think. And most of them demonstrate the nature of authentic faith.

This is how we are to respond to Jesus. But two of the miracles—the healing of Peter's mother-in-law and the exorcism of this deaf-mute—are noticeably different than the rest. Faith is not mentioned in either account. Furthermore, in the other miracles the dialogue between Jesus and whomever he heals is central. But when Jesus heals Peter's mother-in-law, there's no recorded dialogue. The same is true here with this deaf-mute. Well, you might say, "Umm, Pastor, it's because this guy is deaf and mute. He can't hear, and he can't talk. That's why there is no dialogue." That's true, but there is more to it than that.

Here is my theory: when there is *no* conversation between Jesus and the person healed, Matthew is making some important theological point. That's why that particular miracle is included. Now it is true that Matthew is always making theological points. But I mean that he is making some really strong theological point. You might say, "Okay, nice theory, but what's the point then? What's the purpose of this miracle?" The Pharisees' blindness—that's what this miracle shows. Here the focus is not on the faith of the mute or on the miracle itself. Little or no ink is spilt there. Rather, the focus is on *the reactions* to the miracle. The crowd marvels—"Never was anything like this seen in Israel" (v. 33).[9] But what do the Pharisees do? They do something almost unbelievable. They don't marvel. That's for sure. They don't believe. That's for sure. Instead, having seen with their own eyes Jesus heal the leper, the lame, the blind, *this mute man*, and also having seen a demon cast out of this man, they accuse Jesus of demonic activity, of working for the devil (cf. 12:24). Instead of remembering their Holy Scriptures—like Isaiah 35:5, 6 (cf. 11:3–5),[10] which "predicts the healing of the blind and deaf mutes in the messianic age"[11] and thus recognizing Jesus as the Messiah—they are blind to God's Word and thus blind to God's Son. Do you *see* that?

The centurion shows that Gentiles can see Jesus for who he is. The tax collector Matthew shows that sinners can also see him. And then, irony of ironies, even blind men see Jesus as Lord and Christ. But these Jewish religious elites are completely blind. *The blind see, the mute speak, but the Pharisees speak out of their blindness.*

This is why I've entitled this chapter "Too Blind Men." That's not a misspelling. The idea here is this: verses 27–31 describe *two* blind men who, although they cannot see, do see. They see who Jesus is! Then verses 32–34 describe another group of men, the Pharisees. They too are blind. They are *too* blind. Not blind physically but spiritually. Although they can see and have seen, they cannot see and will not see Jesus for who he is. They are *too* blind to see Jesus. And this is why Jesus will say of them in Matthew 23, "Woe to you, *blind* guides . . ." (vv. 16, 24), woe to "[y]ou *blind* fools" (v. 17), woe to "you *blind* men" (v. 19), woe to "[y]ou *blind* Pharisee[s]" (v. 26). And this is why he will say, after he heals the blind man in John 9:39, "For judgment I came into this world, that those who do not see may see, and those who see may become *blind*."

Do You See?

What do you see today? Do you see anything? Are you blind (John 12:39, 40; 2 Corinthians 4:4)? Or do you see Jesus as the Son of David, as Lord and Christ? And do you see him as full of mercy, willing to be merciful even to you, to all who come to him with hungering humility?

> The LORD opens the eyes of the blind.
> The LORD lifts up those who are bowed down;
> the LORD loves the righteous. (Psalm 146:8)

28

The Motive and Means of Mission

MATTHEW 9:35—10:4

I DON'T GET OUT MUCH. And when I do, I don't go to electronics stores. I especially don't go to electronics stores two days before Christmas. But there I was at 1:00 on December 23rd, along with the whole wide world. I was there to get a new car radio for my hip Dodge Caravan, as our radio had died a sudden death a few weeks prior.

After I selected my Sony, I followed the young blue-shirted sales associate to the front of the store as he held my new radio (I was not allowed to touch it until I bought it). There he placed it on checkout #8, turned to me, and said, "Please go to the back of the line." And off I went—to infinity and beyond. As I waited in line, I formed a few critical and condescending thoughts. I looked at the guy who escorted me to the front. There he was two aisles away, flirting with some coworker. He was probably thirty years old, had greased-back black hair, and was kind of frumpy looking. I thought to myself, "What's he living for? I bet he lives at home, takes a class or two at the local community college to pacify his worried mother, works part-time at this store, and then spends most of his paycheck on video games, the latest electronic gadgets, fast food, and Friday night drinking binges with his buddies."

Then I looked at the people in line with me. We were all roped in together—like sheep being led to slaughter. A woman was doing her best to corral us, prodding us to move along. Now remember, I had nothing in my hand. My radio—too valuable for my potently thieving hands to touch—was waiting patiently for me. But everyone around me had carts full of stuff—expensive electronic stuff. So I began to think, *What is this world coming to?*

And what are these people living for? Do they have enough money to buy all this (from the looks of them, they don't)? And if they do, "What does it profit a man to gain a big-screen TV but to lose his soul?" How long, O Lord, must the righteous wait for your deliverance? But then my pseudo-Christian thoughts of disgust turned into compassion. I now looked at them and thought, *Has anyone ever taught you how to handle money? Has anyone ever taught you what to live for? Has anyone ever taught you the way of salvation?* Out of compassion I wanted to round them all up, bring them to church, and preach to them the meaning of Christmas—that Christ Jesus came into the world to save sinners, that Jesus came to seek and save lost sheep.

Compassion for the Helpless

As we have been making our way through Matthew's Gospel, we have seen in Jesus' teaching ministry (especially in the Sermon on the Mount) and in his healing ministry, notably in chapters 8, 9, how our Lord has been like a good shepherd to Israel. He has healed and protected and led his flock in the way they should go. And yet as our Lord steadily marches toward his crucifixion, he knows that he will lay down his life for the sheep, the ultimate act of compassion. He also knows that he must first provide for the flock, leaving under-shepherds to continue to care, protect, and heal. However, before Jesus provides the Twelve with the *means* of mission (9:37—11:1), he first demonstrates *the motive* for mission. Christ's compassion, described explicitly in 9:36, is not only the door that takes us from the last section (4:23—9:35) to the next section (9:37—11:1),[1] it is also the cornerstone of the mission of the church.

> And Jesus went throughout all the cities and villages, *teaching* in their synagogues and *proclaiming* the gospel of the kingdom and *healing* every disease and every affliction. When he saw the crowds, he had compassion for them, because they were harassed and helpless, like sheep without a shepherd. (9:35, 36)

The Greek verb *splanchnizomai*—"to have compassion"—means literally, "to feel in the viscera" or bowels or entrails, if you prefer. We usually speak of feeling with our hearts: "She broke my heart." Yet we are not completely unaccustomed to speaking of our emotions, especially those of hatred or disgust, as coming from our guts: "I hate him with all my guts!" Many years ago when I unintentionally (I assure you) drove over a raccoon and her five babies (true story; I was young; it was late; the road was dark; I swear I didn't see them until I saw them), I felt not only nauseous in my stomach but also deeply sad. At times our emotions—hatred, disgust, but also pity, love, and compassion—make their way down to our viscera.

So here in verse 36 Jesus *feels for* (the Greek sense of the word) and he *suffers with* (if I can add the Latin sense of it) the crowd. He has compassion because they were "harassed and helpless." They were "harassed" physically perhaps—some in that crowd were surely poor and sick and hungry (cf. 15:32)—but also spiritually. Here Jesus gives a subtle indictment on the Jewish religious leaders who were not only not properly feeding and protecting the flock, but these so-called spiritual shepherds were actually harassing or oppressing the flock. They were acting like wolves (cf. 7:15; Acts 20:29). In the words of Ezekiel, they were ruling "with force and harshness" (Ezekiel 34:4b), or in the words of Jesus, they "tie up heavy burdens . . . and lay them on people's shoulders" (23:4).

Jesus also saw that they were "helpless." They couldn't lift or didn't know how to lift this scribal and pharisaical yoke, all these un-Biblical burdens, from their backs—the ones Jesus attacked in the Sermon on the Mount and would attack throughout his ministry, and the ones Jesus promised to rid them of if they would come to him for rest (11:28). As the ultimate shepherd who has sought the lost, brought in those who have strayed, bound up the injured, and strengthened the weak, Jesus here feels (deep down) for this crowd.

Now, there are times in Jesus' ministry when he is grieved and upset with what he sees. Just a few chapters from now he will speak of that generation as "evil and adulterous" (12:39). But here in 9:36 there is no loathing, but only loving. Here he doesn't look out at the crowd and say, "What a lot you are! You are so sinful it makes me sick. You put the 'total' in 'total depravity.'" Instead (I imagine whatever emotions stirred within him when he wept at Lazarus's tomb, see John 11:33–38), here our Lord longs to roll away the stone that was rolled over the souls of these sheep.[2]

So, what is the motive for mission? Compassion. Compassion is the cornerstone.[3] Christian mission starts with compassion, the compassion of Christ seen and hopefully felt here.

I think we sometimes take this cornerstone for granted, like we can just kick it out and the whole edifice won't crumble, or we think that other religions share the same stone, the same basic structure. But that is simply not true. It is normal for us to say, as Scripture says, that "God is love" (1 John 4:8, 16) and that we "love God" (Romans 8:28; 1 John 5:2)—for us to speak as Paul speaks in Galatians 2:20 of the Son of God "who loved me." But ask a Muslim cleric if "God is love" in any kind of personal way. Then ask him if the second greatest commandment is "to love your neighbor as yourself," which includes loving your enemies (those infidels!) as much as you love yourself. Or tell a Buddhist that benevolence has nothing to do with merit, and then watch him pretend not to have a desire to get mad at you. Or tell a Brahmin, a priest from the highest Hindu caste, to care for the sick and dying in Calcutta, those of a much lower, untouchable caste. Tell him to love the lowly the way that old European nun Mother Theresa did for decades, dressed in white and blue, dressed with Christian (not Hindu) compassion, with incarnational compassion, with loving-the-least compassion.

That "God is love" and that such a God of love, "because of the great love with which he loved us" (Ephesians 2:4), would so love the world that he would send his one and only Son to live, suffer, die and then take lowly fishermen, sinful tax collectors, adulterous women, even Gentiles and spread his compassion *through them* to the world is remarkable. That's uniquely Christian compassion. Don't take such compassion for granted.

Don't take *the root* of Christian compassion (Christ's compassion) for granted, and don't take *the fruit* of it for granted. In verse 35 Jesus taught and preached and healed. Following his lead, Christianity gave birth to universities (teaching) and churches (preaching) and hospitals (healing).

The next time you find yourself in the emergency room at a local hospital thank God for Christ, and thank God for Christ's compassion, and thank God for the Christian doctors and donors who years ago took that call to compassion quite seriously. And the next time there is a local or international disaster (earthquake, famine, flood, genocide), notice the many Christian organizations that run to the rescue—Samaritan's Purse, Operation Blessing, World Vision, and the Salvation Army, and perhaps more importantly, notice who doesn't run to the rescue. Which religions stay at home? And the next time you think fondly on the glory days of a world-class American education or on our world-class Ivy League schools such as Harvard, Yale, Brown, or Columbia, thank God for Christ's compassion and for the Christians who took that call to *teach and preach* compassion quite seriously. Harvard, Yale, and Princeton and other universities began as seminaries that trained young men to preach the gospel. And do you know what the mottos of these schools still are? Columbia: "In Thy light shall we see the light." Brown: "In God We Hope." Princeton: "Under God's power she flourishes." Yale: "Light and truth."

Harvard's motto today is simply *Veritas*, which means "truth." It's the perfect postmodern motto—just "truth" with nothing qualifying it. But Harvard's original motto was *Veritas Christo et Ecclesiae*—"Truth for Christ and the Church." And do you know what the original purpose of a Harvard education was? "Let every Student be plainly instructed, and earnestly pressed to consider well, the maine end of his life and studies is, *to know God and which is eternall life*, John 17. 3 and therefore to lay *Christ* in the bottome, as the only foundation of all sound knowledge and Learning."[4]

We take Christian compassion for granted—the root of it and the fruit of it—our schools, our hospitals, and our churches. But like Paul, who was compelled by "the love of Christ" (2 Corinthians 5:14) to reach the world, let us never forget our motive for mission, that the force pushing us forward and undergirding the feet that bring good news (through preaching/teaching/healing) is compassion. Without compassion, we do not have Christianity; without compassion we do not have authentic Christian mission.

Prayer for Helpers

The motive for our mission is compassion. The means are prayer and people, as taught in verses 37, 38: "Then he said to his disciples, 'The harvest is plentiful, but the laborers are few; therefore *pray* earnestly to the Lord of the harvest to send out laborers [*people*] into his harvest." We see here the need for prayer and the need for people, or the need for the Lord of the Harvest through our prayers to send out people—laborers, missionaries, gospel-workers.

When I taught on the book of Acts, I came up with an equation for church growth. The equation is this: prayer + preaching + persecution = growth! That's what we see in Acts, and that's what we see in the first three centuries of the church. That's what we see throughout church history, wherever the church is genuinely growing. That's what we see today in places like the Ukraine, Albania, and China. And that's what we will see in the next chapter in our study of Matthew 10. The kingdom of God advances through persecution, preaching, and prayer.

When I was in college I took a class on the history of revivals. The class was primarily about American revivals, notably the First and Second Great Awakenings. But my professor began with "revivals" recorded in the Old and New Testaments, and he argued that most of the public manifestations of God's renewal and revival—in both the Bible and Christian history—began with prayer. In the Bible you can think of Acts 1:14; 4:24–31; and 13:1–3 where Christian mission sprang from prayer meetings. In Christian history the most obvious and perhaps famous example would be the 1857 Prayer Revival.

In September 1857 Jeremiah Lamphier, a New York City businessman, decided to invite people to pray during the lunch hour one day a week. The first day he prayed alone for half an hour, but then was joined by six other men. The next week there were nearly forty people. With such a good turnout, they decided to pray daily. Soon there were 100 people. In less than six months, 6,000 people in 150 different locations throughout Brooklyn and Manhattan met daily to pray. Within the year these one hour lunchtime prayer meetings were being held in many cities, including Boston, Baltimore, Washington, DC, Pittsburgh, Chicago, St. Louis, Memphis, Savannah, and New Orleans. In June 1858 it was estimated that nearly 100,000 people had been converted, not through preaching or works of charity, but solely by listening to these Christians pray.

Oh, that we would see the day when every day at noon office cafeterias and break rooms are filled with Christians praying for gospel revival. Perhaps there is too much singing in our churches today. Perhaps there is too much doing. Perhaps there is too much eating. Perhaps there is even too much preaching and not enough praying—corporate and private—as Jesus taught us to pray: "Lord, raise up workers for the harvest . . . and Lord, even me."

The Lord of the Harvest Helps

So the motive for Christian mission is compassion, and the means are (first) prayer and (second) people: "The harvest is plentiful, but the laborers are few; therefore *pray* earnestly to the Lord of the harvest to send out laborers [*people*] into his harvest." Prayer and people.

One of my favorite compliments I sometimes receive is when someone from my church will come up to me after the sermon and say, "I have known that Bible passage my whole life, but I never saw what you taught me today." Implied in that word of encouragement is, "What you saw, Pastor, is right, and it is right there to be seen." In other words, I wasn't teaching something novel or heretical. This person just needed someone to point it out to him or her. And I merely pointed it out.

As I looked afresh at these famous verses (vv. 37, 38), I saw a few things I'd never seen before. As I read them, I said to myself, "Okay, so there's this big harvest. Ah, but there's a problem—not enough harvesters. Jesus' solution is to pray for more people." But I thought (perhaps cynically), *Wait a minute, Lord. In chapters 8, 9 we have just watched you have authority over everything visible and invisible—demons, diseases, sin. You name it, you have power over it. So why not cut out the middleman? Why ask people to pray for more people to reach all these people? Why don't you as the Lord of the Harvest just do all the harvesting?*

I have three answers to the above questions. First, God is a God of means. Because he is transcendent from us and yet compassionate (he desires to be near to us) he uses people and prayers. He uses even his own Son. God does not sit behind a thundercloud and zap all our sins and infirmities away. He sends his Son, in our very flesh, to touch blind eyes, crippled legs, dead bodies, and sin-stained souls. So, it's an attribute-of-God issue. It is part of who God is and how he has decided to work in this world.

Second, the plan of God involves means. Jesus' mission is to live, suffer, die, rise again, ascend into Heaven, give the Holy Spirit, and rule from Heaven until he returns. In the meantime he will build his church "on the foundation of the apostles" (Ephesians 2:20). Think of it this way: Jesus needs to build a bridge from his ministry to the ministry that will continue after him in his name, and right here in 10:1–4 we find the first plank on that necessary overpass.[5] Those disciples who have been sitting on the sidelines watching the first string do his thing now get some playing time, because in time they will teach and heal and lead God's sheep.

Third, the work of God involves means. Whenever I hear this harvest text talked about, the message usually has either a self-aggrandizing feel to it ("If it's going to be, it's up to me!") or negative, guilt-ridden weight attached to it ("If you won't pray for missionaries, if you won't go yourself, then God's hands are tied, and guess who's responsible for this huge harvest that's gonna spoil and rot? You!").

This passage is preached like it's all about the church. It's about us getting our missionary act together. But look afresh at the text. Who is doing the work here? The first laborers will get out into the field in chapter 10, but in our text it is "the Lord of the harvest." Following John Chrysostom,[6] I take this as a reference to Jesus, the one who will call himself "lord of the Sabbath" in 12:8 and who will describe himself as the one in charge of the gathering angels in the Parable of the Soils (13:41; cf. 24:31), in a similar manner in which John the Baptist describes him "winnowing" in 3:12.[7] Isn't it the Lord of the Harvest, the one who has "[a]ll authority in heaven and on earth" (28:18) and the one who will commission the Twelve at the end of our gospel and the beginning of Acts, who is the main worker here in our text?

In 9:38 Jesus says, "pray." But before anyone has lifted a prayer, *he* gets to work. He calls and commissions the Twelve: "And he [Jesus] called to him his twelve disciples and gave them authority over unclean spirits, to cast them out, and to heal every disease and every affliction" (10:1), which is what he just asked to be done and prayed for. Then it is Jesus who sends, instructs, and commands: "These twelve Jesus sent out, instructing them, 'Go . . .'" (10:5). I'll put it this way: Jesus was already at work before they were at work or at prayer. That's the case here, and that's the case always. This is why John Stott suggests we perhaps retitle Acts of the Apostles as "The Continuing Words and Deeds of Jesus by His Spirit through His Apostles."[8]

Often this text is preached as if Jesus wasn't at work and as if we were in the same position as these twelve men (i.e., we have yet to harvest anything). But I think it is fair to say that the mustard seed has grown into a tree, the pearl has been found, the good fish caught, and the fields with hidden treasures bought many times over. The harvest is huge indeed! In the last 2,000 years Jesus through his church has harvested millions of people. This prayer has been answered, is being answered, and will continue to be answered until the last hour.

In the apostles' day there was a huge mission field and hardly any workers (twelve guys to bring in the harvest). By the end of the book of Acts there was still a huge mission field, but a few thousand workers had spread out their harvesting hands from Jerusalem to Judea and Samaria and even all the way to Rome. Today there is still a huge mission field, but perhaps a million workers and counting, reaching the ends of the earth. Jesus has been quite busy, hasn't he?

To me the parables of chapter 13, which we will look at in a few chapters, are the key that unlocks this theme. Those parables teach us that (a) the church will grow despite serious opposition from the world, and (b) harvesting doesn't mean everyone everywhere at all times becomes a Christian. The harvest is huge and universal, but it's not universalistic.[9] There will be wheat and weeds, good soil and bad soil (more bad soil than good). But from the good soil there will be fruit worth harvesting!

Even though the Lord of the Harvest has harvested, is harvesting, and will continue to harvest, this doesn't mean that prayer and people aren't the means by which he harvests. The Lord of the Harvest has chosen to use prayer and people to harvest the fields. So, are you feeling overwhelmed by the prospect that the harvest is too hard, too big, and too impossible for us? Don't fret. Trust in the Lord and in the power of his might. But if you are feeling guilty about not praying and not being a gospel worker in this world, then you should feel that way. (Our mission is to pray and go!) So feel guilty, confess, then start praying or starting going or start praying as you start going.

Jesus has built his church, is building his church, and will build his church, and all the powers of Hell shall not prevail against it. Jesus is at work. You might as well join the winning team, for the full and final harvest celebration is at hand. The jars of new wine are being filled, the fattened calf is being prepared, and the daughters of Miriam are ready and waiting to pound and shake their tambourines for one final, eternal victory dance.

29

Jesus' Sermon on Suffering Mission

MATTHEW 9:35—11:1

VICTOR KULIGIN, one of my church's missionaries, wrote a book provocatively entitled *Ten Things I Wish Jesus Never Said*. In his preface Kuligin writes:

> With the rise of the health-and-wealth gospel and prosperity preaching, we have become accustomed to a comfortable, "What a Friend We Have in Jesus" Messiah. It is a picture of Jesus I call "Jesus-lite." Great taste, less demanding. Jesus is just interested in my happiness and nothing more. He wants me to be financially comfortable, physically fit, mentally and emotionally stable. He never demands of me anything that would cause these basic goals to be missed. . . . Difficulties, trials, and hardships in my life are only there because of a lack of faith on my part to believe that Jesus truly wants me to be happy.

Later he writes: "The teaching of Jesus was often harsh. He was not a preacher of convenience, but hardship; not a preacher of comfort, but suffering."[1]

In 9:35–11:1 it is hard to miss this theme of suffering or, more precisely, the theme of persecution, "suffering that derives from the world's *no* to Jesus."[2] In 10:14 Jesus speaks of the possibility of an unfavorable reception and in verse 23 of the reality of persecution: "[w]hen they persecute you in one town." In verse 16 Jesus speaks of being sent out "as sheep in the midst of wolves" and in verses 17–19 of being brought before the wolves—before the Jewish synagogue court—to be flogged[3] and then dragged before the Gentile rulers to be sentenced to jail or death. In this section our Lord speaks of even one's family becoming one's enemy, to the point where a brother is turned against his brother, a father his child, a child his parents, delivering the Christian over to the authorities (vv. 21, 22, 35, 36). Jesus also speaks of being maligned (v. 25), of being "hated by all" (v. 22), and of martyrdom (vv. 21, 28, 38, 39).

In his commentary, Frederick Dale Bruner writes of our text, "I was sorely tempted to entitle this chapter 'Jesus' Sermon on Suffering Mission' because of Jesus' main emphasis in it."[4] Well, I have succumbed to that temptation, and thus I have no problem with borrowing the title of my sermon from Bruner's rough draft. The main emphasis here is suffering—Jesus' call for his disciples to pick up their crosses (more literally than we might imagine) and follow him.

In the last sermon, as we looked at 9:35–38, I addressed our motive for mission (compassion) and the means (prayer and people). In this sermon I'll address the actual mission. What is the church called to do? However, before we take this text and apply it to ourselves, I first want us to walk a mile in the shoes (or lack of shoes) of the apostles, for if we don't understand first what he was saying *to them* then, we will miss what God is saying *to us* now.

He's Not Talking to You, Stupid!

Perhaps my favorite preacher, certainly one of the two most influential preachers in my life, is Dick Lucas, now retired rector of St. Helen's Church Bishopsgate in London. Dick has a number of basic lessons on how to read and teach the Bible properly, which have come to be known as "Lucas Lessons." One of those lessons he labels "He's Not Talking to You, Stupid." I'll change "stupid" to "silly" because "stupid" is not a word Emily and I allow to be spoken in our home, though as a family we certainly recognize the world is filled with very many "stupid" ideas and people.

The "He's Not Talking to You, Silly" lesson is a corrective against our tendency to read the Bible existentially (what is God saying to me?) rather than historically (what did God say to them?). It is a corrective against, in the extreme, just flipping through our Bibles looking for a word from the Lord: "Lord, what do you have to say to me today?" Flip and read: "[G]o, sell what you possess and give to the poor" (19:21). Hmm, perhaps there is a different word from the Lord today. Flip and read: "[D]estroy the survivors of [the] cities" (Numbers 24:19). No, Lord, I'm looking for something less militaristic. Flip and read: "Let him kiss me with the kisses of his mouth! For your love is better than wine" (Song of Solomon 1:2). No, no, no, Lord, something less erotic and alcohol-free. Flip and read: "For I know the plans I have for you . . . plans for welfare . . . to give you a future and a hope" (Jeremiah 29:11). Ah, there it is. I like that. God has spoken to me through his Word.

So you see, in this Lucas Lesson, Dick simply teaches that we need to understand first and foremost that there are passages in the Bible that we will misunderstand and misapply if we don't first understand who the original author and audience were. So when Paul writes to Titus and tells him to "appoint elders in every town" around Crete (Titus 1:5), we are not to read that as God saying directly to us that we are to do precisely the same—i.e., appoint elders in various Greek cities. And as we come to our text, once we realize who is doing the talking (Jesus) and to whom (the apostles), then we can try to determine if what is descriptive is prescriptive—in other words, if what Jesus said to the Twelve applies indirectly to us today.

First, note to whom Jesus is talking: "his disciples" (9:37). That term appears six times in our text—at the beginning (9:37; 10:1), middle (10:24, 25), and end (10:42; 11:1).[5] In 10:1 those "disciples" are defined further as being "his twelve disciples," and in verse 2 as the "apostles." The word "apostles" is used here for the first and only time in Matthew (compare that to twenty-nine times in Acts), and then those said apostles are named in verses 2–4.

Those names are given to us—listed here, as they are three other places in the New Testament (Mark 3:16–19; Luke 6:12–16; Acts 1:13)—not merely to help us name our children and churches and hospitals, but so we might know whom Jesus is addressing *and* their significance. That is, Jesus is (a) replacing Israel's present, ungodly leaders with "[the] twelve" (10:1; 11:1)[6]—the number "twelve" corresponding to the twelve tribes of Israel;[7] and he is (b) beginning to build his church, as Paul wrote in Ephesians 2:20, "on the foundation of the apostles."

Two Major Differences

So, do you see to whom Jesus is talking? In our text he's not talking to you, silly![8] He's talking to the Twelve. But what (if anything) did he say to the Twelve that is not said to us? Or what is different about their mission and ours? I think there are two major differences.

The first is what I'll call *apostolic authority*. In 10:1 Jesus calls "his twelve disciples" and gives them "authority." Later this authority—and remember in my reading of Matthew "all authority" is the key note of the melodic line—will enable them to bind and loose sins (16:19) and in Acts to preach the gospel boldly through the power of the Spirit. But here the emphasis is on healing powers—authority over demons and diseases.

It is especially interesting to note that the Great Commission doesn't mention healing at all, and yet here in their commission we find, "Heal the sick, raise the dead, cleanse lepers, cast out demons" (10:8). We can safely say that Christians, other than the apostles, have done all four actions mentioned here. But it is not normative like it was for the apostles. Have you read the Acts of the Apostles and noticed all the miracles? And have you ever noticed who is doing all those miracles? Nearly all the miracles are performed by an apostle. *Acts of the Apostles* is an apt title, for it is about the *acts*—the works and words—of the *apostles* as acted out through the power of the Holy Spirit given to them by Jesus.

There is a difference between the apostolic age of Christianity and our age, a difference between the apostles' powers and ours, a difference between "the signs of a true apostle"—mighty works of healing, signs, and wonders (2 Corinthians 12:12)—and the permanent qualifications for Christian leadership (those listed in the Pastoral Epistles for elders and deacons).

So the first difference between them and us is that they had unique *apostolic authority*—power to preach and heal. The second difference is perhaps more obvious: *the scope and severity of their mission.* Here in 10:5, 6 they were commissioned to take the gospel *only* to "the lost sheep of the house of Israel," not to Gentiles or Samaritans. In obedience to the Great Commission, we are to take the gospel to "all nations" (28:19)—both Jews and Gentiles. Even the apostles will do this (their mission expands after Pentecost). But here their scope is specific: Israel must hear the good news first. The apostles must go "through all the towns of Israel before the Son of Man comes" (10:23; that last part likely refers not to Christ's second coming but to his death and resurrection).[9]

So the scope and *the severity* of their mission are different. I'm not saying there have never been Christians who took Jesus' call of "no gold [money] . . . no bag . . . no clothes . . . no sandals . . . no staff" (see 10:9, 10) literally (read the life of St. Francis and the rule of St. Francis, or take George Mueller as a more modern example). Nor am I saying that other Christians haven't been persecuted, tortured, and killed for their faith. But you'll have to admit that there is a greater intensity here. Jesus warns these twelve (as he will in his High-Priestly Prayer in John 17) that slander, suffering, and death await them, and according to Christian history all but Judas (who would hang himself) and John (who would be exiled to the island of Patmos) died a martyr's death:[10] Bartholomew and James, the son of Zebedee, and Matthias (Judas's replacement) were beheaded; Thomas and Matthew were speared to death; Peter, Andrew, Philip, Jude, Simon the Zealot, and James, the son of Alphaeus, were crucified.

So, yes, we are called to share in the sufferings of Christ—"Indeed, all who desire to live a godly life in Christ Jesus will be persecuted" (2 Timothy

3:12)—but not always to suffer unto death. We must pick up our crosses, but such crosses don't always lead to Roman execution.

He's Talking to Us . . . Seriously

Those are the two major differences between them and us. What then is the same, if anything? No if. There *is* application for us. Matthew has not written his Gospel simply as a history book. This evangelist has written an evangelistic tract and a manual for Christian discipleship. The call and commission of the Twelve provides the church with some timeless truths, what I'll call *Six Principles for Gospel Mission Today.*

One: The first principle is a summary of what we learned in the last chapter in our study of 9:35–38: *Our motive for mission is compassion, and the basic means of harvesting are prayer and people.* We are to be compassionate. We are to pray. We are to work.

Two: We don't have to be great to reach the least. The apostles' mission is to "the lost sheep" of Israel (10:6), a term used in Jeremiah 50:6 to refer to the people who were under the leadership of ungodly "shepherds." Here we might say that "the crowds" (9:36) were similarly under the scribes and Pharisees. Or, put differently and more precisely, the apostles' mission was to those to whom Jesus has thus far been ministering—the crowds but also and especially (reread Matthew 4—9) the social and religious outcasts.

The mission is to the least, and by the world's standards the missionaries aren't exactly the greatest. Look at the twelve names of these ordinary men in 10:2–4. And look at the slight additions, those extra long nametags on a few of them. Judas, the last listed (quite intentionally), gets that diabolical addition, "who betrayed him." A few other tags are added to those who share the same first name, so as to distinguish this James from that James or this Simon—the Zealot—from the other Simon—Peter—who is intentionally listed first (v. 1). But only one man gets his occupation added. It's not Andrew the fishermen, Thomas the dental hygienist, or Philip the used car salesman. It's "Matthew the tax collector" (v. 3).

I don't want to make too much of this addition other than the point I'm making. God chose outcasts to reach outcasts. Here we find not Peter the Great, or Dr. John von Thunder of the Tübingen Institute of Theology, or St. Thaddeus of the Holiest Order of Most Holy Hermits. Rather we find common and uncouth men. And it is this ignoble group of twelve who take the noble message of the gospel to the ignoble of the world (see 1 Corinthians 1:25–29).

You don't need money; you don't need an elite education; you don't need worldly power and prestige; you don't need an acclaimed reputation (we know about the lives of only a few of these men); you don't need all that to be an effective minister of the gospel of Jesus Christ. The church was built upon the faithful testimony of a bunch of rustics, as Jerome called them.[11] God delighted in and still delights in building his church with such seemingly insufficient and slightly contorted building materials.

Three: Gospel goers depend on gospel givers. Put more fully, gospel goers depend on God's providential provision through Christian giving and hospitality. Notice here the two groups involved in the mission. There are the goers (here the apostles, who are to bring nothing with them, vv. 8–10) and the givers (whom Jesus describes as "worthy" in v. 11), those who welcome the goers into their homes, providing food and lodging and perhaps travel expenses.

Some of you are in full-time gospel ministry or will be in full-time gospel ministry, but the majority of you are givers, not goers. And the beautiful thing here is that Jesus essentially says to the givers, "Keep your head up; without you the mission fails." In verse 40 Jesus equates receiving the goers as receiving him and the Father. Then he speaks of the givers getting a reward (v. 41), even for the seemingly insignificant act of hospitality, giving "a cup of cold water" (v. 42). How lovely. Simple sustenance for working in and getting back to the harvest field gets rewarded!

Thus, as much as this passage commands that the goers can't be greedy and must sacrifice much, it also commands sacrifice for the givers. I know a Christian man, a retired millionaire, who chose to live in a trailer park so he could pay for the college educations of all his relatives and give generously and sacrificially to Christian missions. If you're not going to go, you must give, and if you're not going to give generously, then you're going to go where the Sodomites went. With the closed-doored and close-fisted, God will shake off the dust from his feet (v. 14). The world is at war with Christ. This is no time for cowards and half-hearted hospitality. Either we go or we give to the goers . . . or else.

Four: Our character commends Christ. Verses 8b–10 teach that the goers must not be greedy for gain. We better not preach the gospel for money. Disciples are not to be beggars or mendicants,[12] but we better not be well-to-do or economically ostentatious, since "going green" in that way is a contradiction of the message of the gospel.[13] In fact it is an offense and affront to it. Further, we must be dependent on God's provision of givers. Moreover, our simplicity, urgency, and even austerity should embody the gospel since the gospel is not about worldly wealth, power, or security. We well commend Christ when we have "nothing to commend other than Jesus himself."[14]

In verse 16 we find further character commands—what we might call the crest of Christian character.[15] School crests or family coat-of-arms often have pictures of animals, perhaps a lion, bear, eagle, or some other powerful creature. Sticking with the animal theme, here the Christian coat-of-arms has a sheep (surrounded by wolves) and then a snake and a dove. "Behold," Jesus says, "I am sending you out as sheep in the midst of wolves, so be wise as serpents and innocent as doves" (10:16). A sheep, snake, and dove. Seemingly not very impressive, I'll admit.

In terms of character, we are not to be like tigers—preying on the weak, strutting our bold and beautiful colors, showing our teeth, if needed, to coerce people to believe or else. We are to be as sheep—peaceful, nonviolent, vulnerable, fully dependent on the shepherd to lead, provide, care for, and protect. But we are not to be as sheep in their sheepishness or in their foolishness. That is why Jesus adds the bit about the snake and the dove. We are to be shrewd but innocent, a rare combination of characteristics that we usually put backwards. It is easy to be as "guilty as serpents and as stupid as doves."[16] Instead we are to be godly but not gullible—snake smart, but not snake sneaky. For our character commends Christ; our godliness proclaims the gospel.

Five: Like the apostles, *we are to give the same gospel announcement*: "The kingdom of heaven is at hand" (10:7). I say gospel *announcement* intentionally, because both here and in Acts the Christian message is not so much a suggestion or even an offer—"God loves you and has a wonderful plan for your life, if you'll welcome him into your heart." Rather it's an announcement of the good news of the kingdom!

The good news is that God, in the person of Christ, has sent from Heaven his own Son as King. God has demonstrated Jesus to be the King through his life, teachings, miracles, sufferings, death, and resurrection—all in fulfillment of Scripture and all witnessed in history. Therefore, the time of ignorance is over, and the time for repentance (cf. Mark 6:12) and faith is here, for God has "fixed a day on which he will judge the world in righteousness by a man whom he has appointed; and of this he has given assurance to all by raising him from the dead" (Acts 17:31). Either you submit to Christ and receive eternal life, or you do not submit and thus incur his just judgment.

It is often preached in churches today that God can change your life—God can help you find yourself—God can help you love yourself—God can bring you peace of mind—God can save your marriage or get you a new job or help you be a success in this world. Such messages will not cause persecution, will they? The world loves those messages. They'll buy your book and watch your TV show. But if you preach what Jesus said and what the apostles preached—that Jesus is the only way to God because he is from God (v. 40) and therefore we must have allegiance to him above even our closest family members (v. 37) and that judgment is a reality, since God "can destroy both soul and body in hell" (v. 28)—you can expect persecution. You can expect persecution for heeding Jesus' commands on how to think, live, and witness to the world. Preach the gospel of the kingdom and what happens? Exactly what Jesus said would happen—persecution!

Six: Our mission is dangerous and divisive, but it's worth giving our very lives. The mission is dangerous—there is nothing as obvious in our text as that. Are you looking to be maligned, hated, and possibly put to death? If so, sign up today for Christian Missions 101.

Moreover, our mission is not only dangerous but also divisive. It is divisive not just in society but in our own homes. Christianity can renew a home. I have seen a wife converted to Christianity and then soon after her husband, and the aroma of that house went from the smell of death (fighting, hatred, disunity, even abuse) to an aroma of life (love, consideration, hospitality, forgiveness). But I have also seen households torn asunder because a husband or wife or child or parent hates the gospel and does everything in his or her power to destroy it and banish it from that home.

In verse 34 Jesus says, "Do not think that I have come to bring peace to the earth. I have not come to bring peace, but a sword."

I'm sure you are familiar with the peace symbol. This symbol was originally designed for the British nuclear disarmament movement. But the first time I heard an explanation of its symbolism, which was a historically inaccurate explanation, was at a Christian summer camp, where the director told us counselors that the peace symbol was a broken cross and thus anti-Christian. Even though that explanation is inaccurate, I have often thought there is something to the anti-Christianness of how the world views the notion of peace. To most people, peace means merely a lack of hostility between all people.

Christianity is not opposed to such peace, but for the Christian the means of obtaining it and the timing is different. True peace between God and man—and also between man and man—comes only through "the blood of [the] cross" (Colossians 1:20) and is to be seen in the church. Eventually there will be such peace that even lions lie down with lambs, children play with asps, and Calvinists will hug Arminians and enjoy it. But that final eschatological peace will only come with the second coming of Christ.

Now, however, those who do not believe view the cross as a sword. God's peace sign is not a broken cross but the cross of Christ, and yet, as Dietrich Bonhoeffer rightly said, "The cross is God's sword on earth."[17] The cross is a sword because its message is not the message that insurrectionists want to hear.[18] Who wants to hear that he is sinful at the core of his being? And who wants to hear that in Jesus' death God has opened the gates of freedom and peace for all insurrectionists, if and only if they stop their insurrection? And who then wants to hear that God won't permit such insurrection to go unchallenged forever—that judgment awaits those who will not accept this peace treaty from the Prince of Peace?

Let me be clear here: if you come home after being born again, and you tell your dear mother how foolish she is for not believing in Jesus and that you see the light and she doesn't . . . it is not the cross that is offensive, but you. Many Christians today are needlessly offensive, committing great blunders and stirring up much opposition "which might have been avoided by the little prudence and exercise of judgment."[19] But if your heart has indeed been changed, and your actions follow, and in time you begin to demonstrate Christian humility and witness in words and in deeds to your dear mother, and then, if she rejects the gospel, the cross of peace for her has, as Jesus predicted, become a sword of division between you and her.

So our mission is dangerous and divisive, but *it's worth giving our very lives*. Did you notice in our text all the motives Jesus gives for missionary perseverance? Jesus teaches that we must expect persecution, endure persecution, and not fear persecution. But why? Why not fear? There are four reasons: (1) this was the way Jesus went—he suffered; we will suffer. Through suffering for the gospel, we identify with Christ.[20] (2) Such persecutions will not impede the advance of the gospel but actually promote it.[21] (3) God knows how many hairs are on your head and knows when a sparrow falls to the ground dead, and with fatherly love God is with you even through your sufferings. (4) Following Jesus, according to Jesus, is worth it: "Whoever finds his life will lose it, and whoever loses his life for my sake will find it" (v. 39).

If you are doing everything in your power "to make it"—to get the perfect spouse, the lucrative job, the big house, and all the right connections, guess what? You lose. The biggest gainers are the biggest losers. But if you are willing to come to Jesus as King and give him your life—"Here's my life, Lord. It's all yours. I'll go where you would have me go, do what you would have me do, give what you would have me give, suffer what you would have me suffer"—then (and this is the beautiful irony of the kingdom life) you will find life, true life in this life and true life (and reward) in the life to come.

In summary:

1. Our motive for mission is compassion, and the basic means of harvesting are prayer and people.
2. We don't have to be great to reach the least.
3. Gospel goers must depend on gospel givers (and gospel givers must give).
4. Our character commends Christ.
5. We are to give the same gospel announcement that the apostles did.
6. Our mission is dangerous and divisive, but it's worth giving our very lives.

30

His Mighty Works

MATTHEW 11:2–24

EXPECTATIONS. EXPECTATIONS. Have you ever gone to a dinner party, thinking it was casual attire, and everyone but you was dressed to a T—the men in suits and ties, the ladies in evening gowns and high heels? Or perhaps you were set up by a friend on a blind date, and this friend raved about this cousin of hers, so you expected the date to go well. But instead this date, if you could call her that, was neither attractive nor interesting. Or perhaps you attended a particular church service for the first time, and you expected a Chris Tomlin song and not a Charles Wesley hymn, or a laid-back, with-it, speak-off-the-cuff pastor and instead you got me. Expectations. Expectations.

John's Doubt (vv. 2–6)

In the early first century, the time when Jesus lived, everyone in Israel had expectations. They had expectations about the Messiah, the One who would come into the world. Some had a highly militant portrait in their minds. They expected a Caesar of sorts, someone who through military might and political revolution would bring a new exodus for God's people from the bondage of Roman rule. Others expected that the Messiah—whether he was a military man or not—would act a like a holy man and in righteousness proclaim God's judgment upon evildoers—Romans, Greeks, barbarians, and even unrighteous Jews, like Matthew the tax collector.

John the Baptist and his disciples fell into this second camp. Matthew's Gospel includes three passages that focus on John (cf. 16:14; 17:13). There is our present passage, chapter 14 (his gruesome murder), and also chapter 3, where we are first introduced to John as he is baptizing in the wilderness and preaching repentance. From all these texts, especially chapter 3, we learn that

John, a preacher of fire and brimstone, expected that same heat from our Lord. He expected that, as the Messiah, Jesus would judge lawbreakers like Herod (14:4), who actually would have John's head (and not the other way around, as it should have been).

John was likely fine with Jesus the healer and Jesus the Savior. He was fine with Jesus showing he had the power to conquer demons and diseases and sin. But in 11:2, 3, it seems, he began to wonder where the justice and judgment were. John warned those who wouldn't bear fruit with repentance that "the axe is laid to the root of the trees" (3:10a). But now "in prison" (11:2) and soon to die for proclaiming God's righteousness and the coming Messiah, John wondered where this axe was and when Jesus was going to start swinging it.[1]

Pretend you are John for a moment. As the prophets foretold, you expect not just a Year of Jubilee but an era of full and final jubilee—when all the wrongs would be righted and all the prisoners set free (Isaiah 61:1). Yet here you are—the most righteous of righteous men—imprisoned for months in the fortress of a scoundrel, the least righteous of unrighteous men.[2] And while you are imprisoned, out there Jesus is befriending Torah-breakers. Jesus is not acting like God's "Son" (remember what the heavenly voice said about Jesus at his baptism, 3:17, which John perhaps heard?), but like the "rebellious . . . son" of Deuteronomy 21:20—a boozer and a glutton.[3] It's bad enough that Jesus is eating and drinking so much (what holy man would do that?); it's even worse with whom he is eating and drinking (tax collectors and sinners, political and moral traitors).

So pretend you are John. Your mind begins to flood with thoughts. *Why did Jesus need to be baptized in the first place if he wasn't a sinner? That still doesn't make sense. Why, when Jesus was tempted in the wilderness (given the opportunity to have earthly power), didn't he take it? That could have helped our cause. And then, what's with him asking four fishermen (of all people) into his inner circle and then telling them their mission is to catch men for salvation, not to judge men for rebellion? And in that Sermon on the Mount, as it's now being called, what's with the opening monologue, the bit about "Blessed are the peacemakers, for they shall be called sons of God" (5:9)? And what's with the idea of loving our enemies and praying for those who persecute us (5:44)? And now that I think about it, why isn't Jesus in Jerusalem, the Holy City, the capital city? What's the Messiah doing in "northern Idaho"*[4] *[i.e., Galilee] when he should be in Washington, DC? What's Jesus doing in the backwoods of the world with the backwards of the world? It's fine to heal people, but why those people? Why be a do-gooder to the done-bad? Heal a leper, fine, but not a centurion's servant. Save a cripple from his sin, but not a prostitute from hers.*

Of course, we don't know what specific misgivings John had about Jesus as the Messiah. But we do know he had misgivings or even doubts. And we know this from verses 2, 3:

> Now when John heard in prison about the deeds of the Christ, he sent word by his disciples and said to him, "Are you the one who is to come [i.e., the Messiah], or shall we look for another?"

This is a fairly straightforward question. (Jesus likes such questions.) It's a question that shows John's honest confusion and reservations. It seems that like other prophets who have gone before him—Elijah despairing of his life after the victory of Mount Carmel as Jezebel pursued him (1 Kings 19:4), Jeremiah cursing the day he was born as he was grieved by the impending doom to come upon God's people (Jeremiah 20:14–18)—John, the "super-prophet," has a kryptonite moment, a moment of misery and misunderstanding that has led to honest misgivings.

So with a loving correction Jesus graciously answered him:

> Go and tell John what you hear and see: the blind receive their sight and the lame walk, lepers are cleansed and the deaf hear, and the dead are raised up, and the poor have good news preached to them. (vv. 4, 5)

Jesus also said in essence, "And tell him not to feel slighted by what I'm up to, for 'blessed is the one who is not offended by me' [v. 6]. He can trust me. I'm the one. I'm the right guy."

Here Jesus speaks insider Bible-talk. Without directly quoting the Bible, Jesus relays a message that John would understand. He asks John to "see" and "hear" what the Word says about the Messiah and then, based on that word, to change his expectations. If John could grasp that what Isaiah's Messiah was to do, it would fit what Jesus has been doing.

John asks in effect, "Ask Jesus if he is the coming one," which is likely a reference to Isaiah 35:4, where Isaiah speaks of God coming "with vengeance" to judge. Jesus answered in essence, "Yes, I am coming to judge [in fact that's how Jesus will end our text—with judgment], but first I'm coming to save." Listen to Isaiah 35:4–6a (this is where Jesus is directing John to go):

> Say to those who have an anxious heart [like John],
> "Be strong; fear not!
> Behold, your God
> will come with vengeance,
> with the recompense of God.
> He will come and save you."

> Then the eyes of the blind shall be opened,
> and the ears of the deaf unstopped;
> then shall the lame man leap like a deer,
> and the tongue of the mute sing for joy.

Jesus is not simply saying, "John, who can raise the dead?[5] Who can give the blind sight? Look and listen—I'm so powerful I must be the Messiah." He is saying, "Scripture says that when Messiah comes, these miracles will happen, and so will judgment. I haven't forgotten about the judgment part of the promise. In fact, I'll start with a bit of judgment the moment I'm done disquieting your doubts."

"So tell John," Jesus says to John's disciples, in effect, "to reread Isaiah 35:4–6—the blind receive their sight and the lame walk, and so on—and then to reread Isaiah 61:1, 2" (the text about himself that Jesus would read in the synagogue; see Luke 4:18):

> The Spirit of the Lord GOD is upon me,
> because the LORD has anointed me
> to bring good news to the poor;
> he has sent me to bind up the brokenhearted,
> to proclaim liberty to the captives [the spiritual exile is over;
> the kingdom of heaven is at hand],
> and the opening of the prison to those who are bound;
> to proclaim the year of the LORD's favor,
> and the day of vengeance of our God;
> to comfort all who mourn.

The day of vengeance is coming. God's enemies will get theirs. But first Christ must bring the gospel to the poor. The poor must "have good news preached to them" (11:5b). That's Jesus' answer to John.

Stop and think here for a second. As I look at John's doubt and how Jesus alleviates it, two thoughts come to mind. First, if it's okay for the best-born-of-woman man in the world (see v. 11) to have a period of doubt concerning Jesus, then it's okay if you or I have our bouts with doubts. Second, if we are to doubt, perhaps because like John we are experiencing hardship, we should doubt as John did—a faithful doubt, an I'll-give-Jesus-the-benefit-of-the-doubt doubt. You see, John sent his disciples *to Jesus* to ask John's question because his expectations about Jesus were not aligning with his experience. But the fact that he went to Jesus for answers shows he knew where to go, and in faith he did go.

We often think it is fine to doubt like most agnostics doubt: "Well, you know, this world is a pretty big place. There are lots of ideas about God, and hasn't science confirmed that we evolved from algae? And doesn't that then mean there isn't a God? There are too many world religions for there to be one true religion. And isn't morality relative? Why can't I do whatever I feel is right for me to do?" That's not intelligent doubt. That's lazy doubt. That's self-centered doubt. That's I-want-to-do-whatever-I-want-to-do doubt. Rather, when we doubt, we must doubt like John doubted and go to Jesus and God's Word for answers.

For we believe, don't we? Lord, help our unbelief.

Tri-Cities of Disbelief (vv. 7–24)

In verses 2–6 we have John's doubt and Jesus' cure for that doubt. And I surmise, mostly because of Jesus' extremely positive comments about John in verses 7ff., that John listened to the word. He saw afresh that Jesus' works were in accordance with the Word, and though he never got out of the depths of that dungeon, he did get out of the depths of his doubt.

Next we come to verses 7–24. Here Jesus turns his attention from John and John's disciples to the crowds. "As they [John's disciples] went away, Jesus began to speak to the crowds" (v. 7). What would he have to say to them? He speaks words of judgment! John will not stay long offended by Jesus, but the crowd, which I take in part to be those people from the towns mentioned in verses 21–24, would. Like spoiled children, they would accept nothing God put before them. John came through town, sang his sad song of repentance, and they said, "Oh, he's a madman!" Jesus came through town and sang his happy song of salvation, and they said, "Oh, he's immoral!" God gave them John, and they did not repent. God gave them Jesus, and again they "did not repent" (v. 20). Fascination? Yes. Faith? No. Curiosity? Yes. Contrition? No.

Thus in verses 20–24, following the pattern of the oracles against the nations in Isaiah 13—20, Jeremiah 46—51, Ezekiel 25—32, and Amos 1:3—2:3,[6] Jesus pronounces the coming woe of judgment upon these Jewish (!) cities. He pronounces God's woe upon God's "holy" people (the Jews) in God's Holy Land (Israel). Here Jesus makes these seemingly exaggerated claims that Tyre and Sidon, two cities that epitomized Israel's enemies in the Old Testament (cf. Isaiah 23; Ezekiel 26—28; Amos 1:9, 10),[7] had they seen Jesus do what he did in Chorazin and Bethsaida, "would have repented long ago in sackcloth and ashes" (11:21). Then he claims that on judgment day Sodom (that's code for "the worst city ever!") will get off with a slap on the hand compared to Capernaum.

But why such woes for Capernaum, which had been Jesus' base for missions thus far and even his adopted hometown? What had they done that deserved this? They were guilty of what Stanley Hauerwas calls "perverse normality."[8] Like most normal people in the world, they were not guilty of any notorious crime or of "anything particularly offensive or inhumane."[9] Here we find no abnormal atrocities—genocide, ethnic cleansing, or the sodomy of the Sodomites. Here we simply have the normal perversity of disbelief in Jesus.

Disbelief? Is that the worst sin in the world? Everyone ranks sins differently—murder, adultery, stealing, parking in a handicap space without a sticker, eating trans fats. But disbelief—failure to trust in Jesus? That's not even on some people's lists. Well, it's on Jesus' list, at the very top!

We struggle with disbelief being so diabolical because today's media "ethicists," if I can call them that (whether they are religious or secular personalities), say the opposite. To believe in Jesus—that he is the only way to God, that his commandments are authoritative for all nations, and that every knee should bow before him in worship (themes that will come up in Matthew repeatedly)—is seen as unethical. Moreover, to take it all a step further, to proselytize—to preach this good news to others (as Jesus suggests in chapter 10)—is seen by many today as being as unethical as stealing a lollipop from a three-year-old girl on her birthday. The strong sentiment is that disbelief is not a sin, and further that belief in Jesus, as he is presented in the Bible, is on the top of society's sin list. The fundamentalist's faith in *this* Jesus is viewed as fundamentally wrong.

Whose voice will you listen to? Who's the universal ethicist? Who's the boss? Who has authority in Heaven and on earth to tell you what to think and do? Is disbelief in Jesus contemptible or is it intellectual? Is it condemnable or commendable? Jesus says it's contemptible and condemnable, and especially so for those so close to the action.

When you haven't seen and heard Jesus, as John the Baptist hadn't for a while, and doubt sets in, that's one thing. Such doubt can be dealt with in a correctively loving manner. But when you have seen and heard Jesus, as the people in these three cities had, and disbelief sets in, that's another thing altogether. Such hardness of heart cannot so readily be softened; such calloused stones cannot be easily smoothed. It's better to tie the whole bundle up and throw them into the bottom of the sea.

Jesus judges the disbelief of the people of these three cities so strongly because they saw the mighty works of the Messiah the most, *and yet* they did not repent and believe. Notice the phrase used in verses 21 and 23: "[I]f the mighty works done in you had been done" in . . . Tokyo, Cairo, Amsterdam,

Las Vegas—even people from those secular cities would have believed. Jesus denounced the cities "where most of his mighty works had been done, because they did not repent" and believe (v. 20).

A contemporary comparison would be a person who grows up in a country where Christianity is prominent or at least normative (e.g., the USA), has been surrounded by the gospel taught and lived out at church and home by Christian parents and others, and yet rejects the saving grace of God. Perhaps this describes you. Be warned. It is no trivial matter to know so much and not believe.

So, why the woes? Why is Jesus so upset at these people? First, the powerful miracles should have produced faith. Second, the person of John should have likewise produced faith. Look with me at verses 7–15, and I'll explain what I mean. Starting in verse 7 Jesus gives what we might call his "Sermon on John." But think of it this way: for every point Jesus makes about John, he also makes a point about himself.

In verse 7b–9, speaking about John, Jesus said,

> What did you go out into the wilderness to see? A reed shaken by the wind? [No.] What then did you go out to see? A man dressed in soft clothing? [No.] Behold, those who wear soft clothing are in kings' houses. What then did you go out to see? A prophet? Yes, I tell you, and more than a prophet. This is he of whom it is written, "Behold, I send my messenger before your face, who will prepare your way before you." (see Malachi 3:1)

As Frederick Dale Bruner explains, John was more than a prophet because "he was prophe*sied.* He is more than a bearer of prophecy; he is an *object* of prophecy (Klostermann, 97). John is the prophet promised as the advance man *for the Messiah.*"[10]

"If that is John," says Jesus, "then who am I?" Malachi 3:1 reads, "Behold, I [the Lord] send my messenger, and he will prepare the way before me." In Matthew, Jesus changes the pronouns: "Behold, I send my messenger before *your face* who will prepare *your* way before *you.*" These second person singular pronouns—"you" and "your"—refer not to God but to Jesus. What is Jesus doing with these pronoun changes and additions? Does he think he is the Lord? Does he think he is "God with us"? Does he think he is the Lord *and* the Messiah? Absolutely. Both with his earlier allusion to Isaiah 35 and now with this quotation from Malachi 3, the point being made is that the coming of Christ is the coming of God himself! It is not as explicit as John 1:1, 14a ("In the beginning was the Word, and the Word was with God, and the Word was God. . . . And the Word became flesh and dwelt among us"), but it is close.

Now back to Jesus' "Sermon on John." Next point: "Truly, I say to you, among those born of women there has arisen no one greater than John the Baptist. Yet the one who is least in the kingdom of heaven is greater than he" (v. 11). What is Jesus doing here? Here's the argument: as great as John was, his ministry was old school. He is the last and greatest Old Testament prophet. *Now* even the littlest newborn in the kingdom of heaven, someone who has come to faith in Jesus, is greater—not greater in stature or holiness—but truly greater (because the new covenant is a "better covenant" than the old, Hebrews 7:22; 8:6) than the greatest old era man, John. And with that thought in mind, here is what we're to dwell on, to "hear" as Jesus would put it in verse 15. Here is the *a fortiori* argument: "If John is the greatest man ever born, and if the most insignificant person in the coming kingdom of heaven is greater than John, what does this make *Jesus*, who is the *bringer* of that kingdom?"[11] Let's think about it. How high can your Christology go?

So in verses 7–15 we have Jesus' three-point sermon on John.

- Point 1: If John is the super-prophet, what does that make Jesus?
- Point 2: If John is the greatest pre-kingdom man, what does that make Jesus as the King of the kingdom?
- Point 3: If John is "Elijah"—not some reincarnation of Elijah (see John 1:21), but the one who has come, as the Jews expected, in the "spirit and power" of Elijah (Luke 1:17; cf. Matthew 17:12), as the "Elijah" of Malachi 4:5, the one who would prepare the way, not for the Messiah, but for God[12]—who then is Jesus?

Based on those points, I'll paraphrase some of verses 12–15 quite dramatically. Jesus says:

> Listen, from the days of John the Baptist until now the kingdom of heaven has suffered violence because violent people—like Herod and Caiaphas, the political and religious establishment—are always trying to destroy it, take it by force, and step on it [read chapter 10 again: the kingdom will be victim before it is victor].[13] For all the prophets (like Elijah) and the Law (Moses) prophesied until John, and if you are willing to accept what I'm getting at, John is that Elijah-figure who is to come, who has come. He is the one who each Passover you set a place for hoping he'll show up. He has shown up because I am the Lord. That empty chair has been filled, for behold the Lamb of God who takes away the sins of the world. Do you hear what I'm saying?

Bruner summarizes Jesus' sermon this way: "Matthew, I'm convinced, believes that we cannot think too highly of Jesus. Jesus is talking about John;

Matthew is talking about Jesus; readers are to think about God. That's the point."[14] Yes, that's the point of verses 7–15: Jesus is God in the flesh!

Expectations, Expectations

Back to our question: why the woes? Why does Jesus judge so severely? First, the powerful miracles should have produced faith in him (vv. 20–24). Second, the person of John should have produced faith in the person of Jesus (vv. 7–15).

I began talking about expectations. We all have expectations when it comes to a dinner party, a blind date, a church service, and even when it comes to God. Some might expect that if there is a God, he should write his name and message in the stars—"God exists, Yahweh is my name, and Jesus is my Son." Then they would repent and believe. But God has expectations too. He expects human beings to repent and believe because he has done something greater than writing something up there.

First he sent his prophets—from Moses to John—to prepare the way for the Lord. Many of these prophets wrote down what we should expect God to do in history. Then, in the fullness of time, God sent his own Son to teach, perform miracles, be lifted up on the cross, and rise again from the dead (all before eyewitnesses). And yet we ask for more. We want God to scribble signs with the stars when he has plainly given his word in Scripture and his word in the flesh, in his Son. What spoiled children we are! What wedding jig do you want God to play before you will dance, what dirge to sing before you'll cry? The Word of God and the Son of God—that should be enough (see Luke 16:29–31). That should be enough to get all of us to repent and believe, to follow the Lord Jesus in faith.

31

Resting in the Son

MATTHEW 11:25–30

HE WHO HAS PRIDE as his mother cannot have God as his Father. That's the first point I derive from Matthew 11:25–30. I borrow the language from Cyprian, the early church leader, who said, "He cannot have God for his father, who has not the Church for his mother."[1]

Here the thought is that pride is the greatest obstacle to a saving relationship with God, whom Jesus refers to five times as "Father" in these verses: "I thank you, Father" (v. 25), "yes, Father" (v. 26), "All things have been handed over to me by my Father, and no one knows the Son except the Father, and no one knows the Father . . ." (v. 27). If you want God as your Father, pride cannot be your mother. Pride cannot be the ruling principle in your life. Pride cannot be the authority over all your actions. Pride cannot be the voice telling you what to do.

As we look at this *thanksgiving* (an odd place for a thanksgiving—following those terrible woes upon Chorazin, Bethsaida, and Capernaum) that Jesus gives, we will see that his focus is not on us (our pride or humility) but on God—God who is called "Father," but also "Lord of heaven and earth," a God who shows his absolute sovereignty over creation and over all creatures, even and especially human beings, by hiding the gospel from some and mercifully revealing it to others, "for such was your gracious will" (v. 26).

I know God is the focus here, his sovereign justice and grace. But I can't help but get to the point of why Jesus says this prayer out loud "[a]t that time" (v. 25) to those people (his disciples and the crowd [11:1–24]). Jesus praises God out loud so that they and we might apply such praise. And the application is, as I have stated, he who has pride as his mother cannot have God as his Father.

There is a deep unfathomable mystery here. Why does God hide the gospel from anyone, no matter how proud they are? Why doesn't he, through his providence, humble everyone? He humbled Nebuchadnezzar, why not a Donald Trump? He humbled Naaman, why not a Rush Limbaugh? Why not take all the Muhammad Alis of the world—"I am the greatest"—and show them, by whatever means, just how great they are not? I don't know. God's sovereign election is indeed a deep and unfathomable mystery to me. But I believe God's Word. And I know myself. I know that I was not so good that God should save me, be gracious to me, and open my heart as he did Lydia's (Acts 16:14). Why choose me from this rubble of humanity? And I know that God would be just in damning all and saving none, and thus is gracious (as v. 26 powerfully asserts) in saving some, revealing himself, revealing his Son to those who come to him for rest, who come to him in humility.

Why do some people come to Christ and others don't? One side of the coin is God's sovereignty: "I . . . will show mercy on whom I will show mercy" (see Exodus 33:19; cf. Romans 9:15). The other side of the coin is human responsibility. Humility opens the door to the kingdom, and pride keeps it closed. And in 11:23, 25 the door-slamming sin of pride is addressed by our Lord.

In verse 23, where Jesus denounces the people of Capernaum for their disbelief, he echoes Isaiah 14:13–15 (on the pride of the king of Babylon), adding, "And you, Capernaum, will you be exalted to heaven? [No.] You will be brought down to Hades." The idea is this: this city that witnessed more of Jesus' miracles than any other city (Capernaum) did not humble itself and accept Jesus and his kingdom, but they sure liked the dog and pony show. Jesus was quite a boom for their little town. After Jesus came through town and did all he did, they didn't believe, but they did change the city sign from "Welcome to Capernaum: Fishing Capital of the Northeast" to "Welcome to Capernaum: The City Lifted to Heaven—Home of Jesus the Wonder Worker."[2] You can't have pride as your mother if you want God as your Father.

Then, in 11:25, Jesus speaks of "the wise and understanding" versus "little children." "The wise and understanding" have the gospel "hidden" from them, while it is "revealed . . . to little children." Here the contrast is not against the smart and the dumb or the adults and the kids, but rather between "those who are self-sufficient and deem themselves wise and those who are dependent and love to be taught."[3]

It is the contrast in the Gospels between "the entire religious aristocracy" and the twelve ordinary men,[4] between the Scriptural-savvy scribes and the seemingly gullible fishermen. It's the difference between the Pharisee who lifts his eyes to Heaven ("O Lord, I'm glad I'm not like them") and the tax collector who pounds his chest ("O Lord, have mercy upon me, a sinner") (see Luke 18:10–14). It's the difference between Caiaphas, who points at our Lord and demands in effect, "Are you the Son of God?" (cf. 26:63) and the Roman centurion who points to Christ crucified and says, "Truly this was the Son of God!" (27:54). It's the difference between the rich young ruler who walked away distraught, with his camel-sized pockets still heavy with gold, and little Zacchaeus, who climbed up a big sycamore tree and after he came down opened his heart to Jesus and his pockets to the poor. It's the difference between the proud in heart and the poor in spirit. It's the difference between conceited self-reliance and meek dependence upon God through Christ.

So, if you find yourself interested enough in the person of Christ, thinking, "Yes, this Jesus is quite the fellow. I'll admit that much," here's my advice to you: turn the lens you have on him back on yourself and ask, are you little enough in your own eyes to see him for who he is? You see, God is not looking for big shots. He is not interested in the somebodies of this world. He is interested in the nobodies (see 1 Corinthians 1:26–31). Are you enough of a nobody for him to be interested in you? That is, before him do you humbly confess your unworthiness, emptiness, and helplessness? Do you acknowledge that you are not good enough for God? Or has your education, wealth, power, position, talent, or knowledge puffed you up (cf. 1 Corinthians 8:1) and made you like a proud peacock, with your feathers spread too wide to walk through the narrow gate to freedom?

"God opposes the proud, but gives grace to the humble" (Proverbs 3:34 LXX; James 4:6; 1 Peter 5:5). "There are six things that the LORD hates, seven that are an abomination to him . . . [number one!] haughty eyes" (Proverbs 6:16, 17). "Whoever exalts himself will be humbled, and whoever humbles himself will be exalted" (23:12). Do you want to become a son or daughter of the heavenly Father? You must become childlike in faith, trust, and dependence (cf. 18:3). You must become like a newborn; yes, you must become, as it were, born again.[5]

He Who Knows Not the Son Knows Not God

He who has pride as his mother cannot have God as his Father. That's the first point of this passage. The second is this: *he who knows not the Son knows not God*. This point comes from verse 27, where Jesus says, "All things have been handed over to me by my Father, and no one knows the Son except the Father, and no one knows the Father except the Son and anyone to whom the Son chooses to reveal him."

In verses 25, 26 Jesus says that the only way into the kingdom is through humility, and in verse 27 he gives perhaps the four most seemingly arrogant claims in the history of humanity! He claims the following:

1. He has all authority over "all things," which I take to mean "everything"[6]—all "power" and all "wisdom" as Paul wrote in 1 Corinthians 1:24 (cf. 15:24–28)[7] and "all authority in heaven and on earth," as Jesus says later in 28:18.
2. He alone, as God's Son, really "knows" God as Father—"*my* Father."[8]
3. We can't know God except through knowing the Son.
4. We can't know God unless he chooses to reveal him to us.

Aren't those the lofty claims made here by the one who calls himself "lowly in heart" (v. 29)? I'm not reading this wrong, am I? And aren't these claims very offensive today? In one verse Jesus manages to offend the whole world. Jesus claims he has all authority and that he, from God and *like God*, has lordship over Heaven and earth (v. 25), etc. That's a bit much, isn't it? Claim to be a carpenter but not the Creator, a wise teacher but not Wisdom embodied, lowly of heart but not equal with the Father. How offensive!

Then there is Jesus' claim that he is the Son of God.[9] That claim is considered blasphemous by Muslims (how can God have a Son?). And it is considered irrelevant to Buddhists and atheists because the existence of God—let alone some son of his—is unnecessary for moral behavior and meaningful life.[10] How offensive! Then there's his claim that knowledge of God comes only through knowledge of him. That notion certainly attacks the multifaceted belief system of Hinduism and many other religions and leaves the postmodernist speechless, for it undermines the agnostic notion that we cannot "know" God. How offensive! Then he even claims that we can't know God unless Jesus chooses to reveal him to us. That is a fatal stab wound in the heart of self-autonomy. Don't I determine my own destiny? Isn't all of life in my hands? Don't I freely will all I do? How offensive!

All these claims are very offensive and arrogant—unless they are true. What then is it that has convinced millions of people from different countries and cultures and centuries that these claims are true? For me the trust comes not in the lofty claims themselves—these claims aren't dangling in midair—but when I see that the claims fit the character. Jesus says he is humble, and I believe him. I believe him because I've watched him in Matthew's Gospel. I've watched his birth. I've watched his temptation. I've watched him reach out to the lowly, preach good news to the poor, heal the suffering, welcome the outcasts, and have compassion on sinners. And I've watched him walk the road to Calvary. I've seen the crown of thorns upon his brow, the whip upon his back, the nails through his skin, the cry of agony, and his head drop in death. The character fits the claims.

People can be quite sincere about their beliefs, but God was just as sincere when he sent forth his one and only Son to live and teach and heal and suffer and die. And in return some mock God, assuming they can believe whatever they want to think about God and Jesus.

In his lectures on Galatians, Martin Luther said to the divinity students under his tutelage, "Stop speculating about the Godhead and climbing into heaven to see who or what or how God is; hold on to this man Jesus, he is the only God we've got!"[11] Yes, in Jesus, we have "the knowledge of the glory of God" (2 Corinthians 4:6; cf. John 1:18; 14:9).

He who knows not the Son knows not God.

He Who Has the Son Has Rest

The third point is: *he who has the Son has rest.* Matthew 11:21–24 records Jesus' denunciation, verses 28–30 his invitation:[12]

> Come to me, all who labor and are heavy laden, and I will give you rest. Take my yoke upon you, and learn from me, for I am gentle and lowly in heart, and you will find rest for your souls. For my yoke is easy, and my burden is light.

Before we get to the point of the third point—finding rest in Jesus—two details leap off the page at me from the world's most famous invitation. First, the fact that Jesus chooses us does not negate our choice. Right after Jesus says, "No one knows the Father except the Son and anyone to whom the Son *chooses* to reveal him," we find two imperatives: "*Come* to me . . . *Take* my yoke upon you." Which is it, Jesus? Make up your mind. Do you choose or do we come? He chooses, and we come.[13]

Call it a paradox if you'd like. The better word is antinomy. An antinomy is the appearance of a contradiction. J. I. Packer notes, "It is an *apparent* incompatibility between two apparent truths."[14] In physics, for example, Huygens first discovered that light consists of waves, but then Newton discovered that it consists of particles. Later scientists—Planck, Einstein, de Broglie, and Compton—discovered "wave-particle duality," the theory that light consists of both waves and particles. How can it be both? In our tiny and tidy little minds, we don't know. It just is. We cannot comprehend how light can be both waves and particles, but neither can we deny it. It is incomprehensible but undeniable.

So too is Jesus' sovereign choice and our choice to come to him. He chooses; we come. You can try to deny the facts based only on your experience, saying to yourself, "I chose Christ; I came to him in faith first." But to do so is as immature as a first-year physics student denying the dual properties of light. Perhaps this analogy will help: Jesus has thrown a lasso around us, and we are running toward his pull. He chooses us. He pulls us along. But we do also run toward him, happily and gratefully.

That's the first detail that jumps off the page at me. The second is that Jesus does not say, "Come to *God*, all who labor and are heavy laden, and *he* will give you rest." Instead he replaces "God"—as it would be in Old Testament invitations similar to this one (as well as ones we find in the Apocrypha)—with "me"—himself:

> Come to *me*, all who labor and are heavy laden, and *I* will give you rest. Take *my* yoke upon you, and learn from *me*, for *I* am gentle and lowly in heart, and you will find rest for your souls. For *my* yoke is easy, and *my* burden is light.

Have "all things . . . been handed over" to Jesus, even salvation? It sure seems like it. Remember, for Matthew you cannot think too highly of Christ. And just wait until the next passage! Jesus is not going to stop bombarding us with his identity.

Those two "little" details aside, we come to the point at hand: *he who has the Son has rest.*

If there is one thing every human being longs for, it is rest. We all long to rest in peace not only after we die but also while we are alive. Who doesn't want the inward and outward peace that comes from being in a right relationship? Have you ever been in a wrong relationship? It is the least restful state of being. But a right relationship brings rest. Jesus claims that the ultimate rest—the longing of every human heart for the most right of all relationships—comes only through being in a relationship with him. That's quite a claim. Not only does he replace his name for God's, but in essence he says, "You want rest? I'm the Rest-Maker. I'm the one you must embrace."

What I love about Jesus' invitation here is (a) whom he invites and (b) to what he invites them. Jesus does not invite those who have found their self-worth. He does not invite the self-satisfied. He does not invite the self-righteous.[15] He does not invite those living the life of ease, with their legs outstretched and their feet pushing through the soft sand of the beach. Here Jesus invites "all who labor and are heavy laden" (v. 28). He invites the tired, the poor, the tempest-tossed, the wretched refuse, those huddled masses yearning to be free.[16]

I love *whom* Jesus invites, but also *to what* he invites them. After verse 28, "and I will give you rest," perhaps you expected to read something about a vacation destination, a new recliner, a relaxing massage, or a sleeping pill. Instead you find a work order: "Take my yoke upon you" (v. 29). Do you know what a yoke is? It's an instrument for *work*. It is a wooden frame that is placed upon the shoulders in order to make a load or burden easier to carry. It is designed to distribute the weight in equal proportions to both sides of the body.[17] Do you see the paradox here? "What yoke is comfortable, what burden light?"[18]

Jesus doesn't promise *escape* from reality, but he promises the right *equipment* to deal with it.[19] He promises a yoke. A yoke! But what is his yoke? "Take *my* yoke upon you." His yoke has something to do with his teachings, because he adds "and learn from me" (v. 29). So, it is not the heavy yoke of the scribes and Pharisees. It is not those "heavy burdens," as Jesus calls them in 23:4 (cf. 15:1–9), that Israel's rulers have laid upon "people's shoulders" (23:4). Biblical burdens, if we can call them that, have a lightness to them because they have been graciously given by God as gifts to help us, given from the mouth of a man who is indeed, in every way, "gentle and lowly in heart," one who has carried them himself (5:17)—our Lord Jesus!

Now, compared with the hundreds of Jewish laws, there are fewer commands from Christ to carry. True. But there is something to carry. Let's not push the Sermon on the Mount, the parables, and the Great Commission off our backs. Those teachings bring rest. Rest comes from working. Rest comes from laboring. Rest comes from obedience. Rest comes in seeking first the kingdom of God and his righteousness. Rest comes from God's will being done on earth as it is in Heaven.

Jesus did not say, "Take my chair"[20] or "Take my mattress." That's equipment for sitting and sleeping. There's no sitting. There's no sleeping. He said, "Take my yoke. You'll be working, walking, moving forward, carrying what I tell you to carry, even your own cross. Life might be uncomfortable, hard, and trying, but (irony of ironies) walk my way and you'll find rest—the refreshment that comes with forgiveness, the renewal that comes with purposeful living, the rest that comes from working for me!" (See 2 Corinthians 4:16–18; cf. Romans 8:18; Matthew 5:10–12).[21]

So, what I love about Jesus' invitation here is (a) whom he invites and (b) to what he invites them (and us): "Are you tired of working for whomever and whatever? Come work for me." Furthermore, I love that Jesus' invitation here provides an easy way to prove him wrong. Take him up on it. Put his yoke over your shoulders and give it a try. See if learning from him, walking forward with him at the lead (or is he next to us, helping carry the weight?),[22] trusting him as an infant trusts a parent for everything, brings rest. See if he brings the *shalom* of right relationship, satisfaction of salvation.[23]

"The Voice of Experience"[24]

When I was a freshman in college, I was full of myself. I don't think anyone at the time would have said so, and I didn't think so, but now in retrospect I know it was so. Every choice I made revolved around pleasing me. Pride was my mother, if you will, and I did whatever she said to do.

I had reasons to be proud. I was an honors student, straight A's, Mr. Smarty-Pants. I had a nice-looking girlfriend. She was tall, blonde, and athletic. And I was athletic myself. I was one of two freshmen playing on the varsity basketball team (Division III), on a team that was so good it would finish second in the nation. The other freshman on varsity was so skilled he would transfer a year later to start for the University of Iowa.

I had all that going for me. I had the grades, the girl, and the prowess. And I believed Jesus was who the church said he was. That's just how I was raised—religiously. He is the Son of God, sure; rose from the dead, fine; died for my sins, very good. I believed in my brain, but not in my heart. And because I didn't believe down there, I played by my own rules. No need to put some yoke on this boy's back. I wanted freedom, the freedom that comes with me deciding what is right and wrong. But do you know what my yokeless and Christless living never brought? It never brought rest.

However, when Christ chose to befriend me by his gracious will, by first destroying all my idols and then pressing down my peacock feathers (I lost everything that made me proud)—when he made me humble enough to see straight—I was then willing to put Jesus' yoke on my back. There was a new yoke and a new burden I had to carry, but do you know what? For the first time in my life I felt restful. There were all these new ways of thinking and speaking and living. But each time I walked forward in faith it felt surprisingly light and even easy (cf. 1 John 5:4). Even today it is still like my body and soul are designed to carry this.

So take him up on it. I'm serious. Come on, how heavy is all that junk you are carrying on your back? Has sexual immorality brought you rest? Has partying every weekend brought you rest? Has that perfect girl or guy brought you rest? Has your education brought you rest? Has climbing the corporate ladder brought you rest? Has any of that stuff you keep buying—the house, the car, the vintage sports car, the vacation home, the home entertainment center, the hot tub, the box of Twinkies—brought you rest? Has any of that really brought you rest?

Following Christ is the hardest thing you will ever do. There's a yoke—you must follow his rules. And there's a burden—this stuff you must carry (persecutions, trials, testings). But I tell you, it works. This Jesus is right. He brings the rest every human being longs for, the rest that comes only by being in the right relationship.

So get rid of the pride, come to the Son, and find that rest you've been longing for—both now and in the life to come.

32

Lord of the Sabbath

MATTHEW 12:1–8

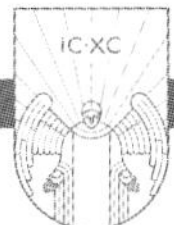

> Remember the Sabbath day, to keep it holy. Six days you shall labor, and do all your work, but the seventh day is a Sabbath to the LORD your God. On it you shall not do any work, you, or your son, or your daughter, your male servant, or your female servant, or your livestock, or the sojourner who is within your gates. For in six days the LORD made heaven and earth, the sea, and all that is in them, and rested the seventh day. Therefore the LORD blessed the Sabbath day and made it holy. (Exodus 20:8–11; cf. Exodus 31:12–17)

From the founding of our country until today, our government has written, passed, and enforced what are disparagingly called "blue laws," laws based originally on the Biblical injunction against working on the Sabbath. The first blue law was enacted in the Virginia colony. It required that every citizen attend church on Sunday. Currently, in thirteen states, including Illinois, car dealerships are closed on Sundays. That's a blue law. Hunting is prohibited on Sundays in Massachusetts, Connecticut, and Pennsylvania. That's a blue law. Many states prohibit selling alcohol on Sunday before noon (another blue law). The original rationale is that Sunday morning is for attending church, not the tavern. But in most states all the laws you could find in the books even just sixty years ago—laws that banned various business, leisure, and sporting activities on Sunday, such as barbering, clam digging, and even cockfighting—have been repealed. And aren't we glad? My goodness, what would we all do without the pleasure of a good Sunday afternoon cockfight?

In all seriousness, I bring up blue laws to say that such laws, while ridiculous at times, nevertheless exemplified the conviction not only that the Bible matters, but also that time matters. This sacredness of time was expressed every weekend as the stores closed their doors and the churches opened theirs. And it was epitomized, for example, in the actions of Eric Liddell, the Scottish sprinter who refused to run on a Sunday race during the 1924 Paris Olympic Games. The movie *Chariots of Fire* is based on his story. It was also epitomized in the courageous decision of the Wright brothers, who saved their historic first flight for Monday morning, even when the weather on Sunday was far more ideal. They wouldn't fly on Sunday!

For an athlete to give up running for an Olympic gold medal and for two great inventors to risk their lives all because of their shared conviction about the sacredness of a day of the week is difficult for us to understand, for in our fast-paced society the concept of sacred time has long been consumed by consumerism.

Most of us are indifferent toward time, especially toward setting aside one day a week and viewing it is holy, set apart from the rest in order to rest. And such indifference, of course, is to our disadvantage in many ways. But concerning our text, this is to our disadvantage as we try to understand why the Pharisees were so upset by the actions of Christ's disciples. It may require some deep thinking and creative re-imagining for us to get into the minds of the typical ancient Jew.

So, with your Bible open, picture again the scene set in 12:1. It is a happy *Saturday* morning in early spring. Jesus, his disciples, and the entourage following him get up at dawn and start into the city, heading for the synagogue. There they will catch the first service. Christ's disciples are from this region, so they lead the way, walking a few paces ahead of Jesus, who apparently (at least this is how I envision this scene) is striding side by side with the Pharisees. As they walk, the disciples decide to partake of the original breakfast of champions, so they grab a few grains and begin to nibble.

In their minds what they are doing is completely innocent and legal, for according to Leviticus 19:9 and Deuteronomy 23:25 a farmer is to leave the edges of his fields unharvested so some of the crops could be picked by the poor or by travelers. Just as walking on a sidewalk in our culture is not trespassing on private property, in their culture picking heads of grain at the edge of a field was not considered stealing. Stealing is not the issue.

The Pharisees also knew this law. After all they were experts in the Law of Moses. So when they made their statement to Jesus, "Look, your disciples are doing what is not lawful to do on the Sabbath" (v. 2), the focus falls on the final prepositional phrase, "on the Sabbath." To the Pharisees it was not so much *what* these disciples were doing, but *when* they were doing it. They were "pluck[ing] heads of grain . . . *on the Sabbath*." They were breaking the bluest of blue laws.

Where are the Pharisees coming from? What are they thinking here? The fourth commandment, with which I started this chapter, talks about not working on the Sabbath. However, it does not define "not working," although it certainly implies not doing your six-day-a-week work (i.e., what you do for a living). In fact, in the whole of the Torah, the first five books of the Bible, only one "work" activity was forbidden—kindling fires (Exodus 35:3; cf. the condemnation in Numbers 15:32–36 for gathering sticks [for a fire?]).

Even if you went beyond the first five books, to Nehemiah and the prophets, there you would find only a few more details regarding what constitutes "work." There you'd find regulations about not carrying burdens (Jeremiah 17:21–27), not buying or selling (see Nehemiah 10:31; 13:15–17; Amos 8:4, 5), and not talking idly and seeking your own pleasure but instead delighting in God (Isaiah 58:13). But that's it. In the whole of the Old Testament, that's it.

This vagueness was problematic for legalists. Their thought was, "Well, if God is not going to give more specification than that, we must add our own specifications, careful clarifications of what constitutes 'work.'" Thus, over time, like blue laws in our country, many additional commandments were created *by man* to answer every conceivable Sabbath question. And with these invented and uninspired additions, the Sabbath, which was intended to bring freedom and rest to men, "was hedged around with literally thousands of petty rules and regulations"[1] that ironically made much work of not working. What was originally intended to serve as a sign of Israel's unique role in the history of redemption and honor the absolute holiness of Yahweh (as their God and Creator) mutated into something wholly un-Scriptural. What started as an amoeba of devotion centered on one's use of time in relation to one's worship of God evolved, especially during the exile when Israel was deprived of the temple and Jerusalem, into this monstrous mutation of Jewish political pride.

The Mishnah (which is a compilation of these oral traditions) lists thirty-nine classes of work that profane the Sabbath, "including those we might expect, such as plowing, hunting, and butchering, and those we would not such as tying or loosing knots, sewing more than one stitch, or writing more than one letter"[2] (*m. Sabb.* 7:2). Some of these novel rulings bordered on the ridiculous. For example, one rule stated, "If a building fell down on the Sabbath enough rubble could be removed to discover if any victims were dead or alive. If alive, they could be rescued, but if dead, the corpses must be left until sunset."[3]

The disciples were not touching a dead body, which would surely make them unclean. To the Pharisees, however, their touch of these "heads of grain" was just as damning. Of these thirty-nine different classes of work, four of these were reaping, winnowing, threshing, and preparing a meal. And perhaps in the minds of the Pharisees the disciples' actions broke all four of these rules, and thus it was obvious to them (as they thought it should have been to Jesus) that these men were blatantly breaking God's commandment. According to the Old Testament law and Jewish tradition, breaking the Sabbath was a serious offense demanding the same sentence as first-degree murder (see Exodus 31:14, 15; 35:2). While it seems fantastic to us, to a devout Jew of the first century one's behavior on the Sabbath was a matter of life and death.

Have You Not Read . . . about David?

As a good Jew, in some ways Jesus couldn't agree more. He viewed the Sabbath as a holy day, and how one understood and practiced the Sabbath was likewise to him a matter of life and death. That is why he sought to correct their perception and practice of the Sabbath by answering their accusation in the way he did, highlighting the *spirit* of the Law and the original and *ultimate* intention of the fourth commandment.

To their statement regarding his disciples—"Look, your disciples are doing what is not lawful to do on the Sabbath"—Jesus gives three replies. To these "hypercritical formalists" (as Charles Spurgeon calls them),[4] Jesus goes to the Bible. First, he gives an example from the former prophets (1 Samuel 21:1–6) about King David, then from the Law (Numbers 28:9, 10) about the priests, and finally he cites the latter prophets (from Hosea 6:6, one of his favorite verses). Jesus brings the Old Testament to his defense. He brings the sword of the Spirit out to cut off all the ungodly traditions that have attached themselves to God's holy Law.

The first cut comes in verses 3, 4, where he says, "Have you not read what David did when he was hungry, and those who were with him: how he entered the house of God and ate the bread of the Presence, which it was not lawful for him to eat nor for those who were with him, but only for the priests?" The first phrase of Christ's reply is quite sharp. To the Pharisees, Jesus starts by saying, "Have you not read . . ." and then goes on to give an Old Testament story that would have been as familiar to them as the narrative of Christ's birth is to us. Jesus' question "Have you not read . . . ?" suggests an ironic criticism of their supposed knowledge of Scripture. Our Lord's remark is in a sense as disrespectful as you or I walking up to a Shakespeare scholar and asking her if she has ever read *Macbeth*.

Jesus is quite bold. And I admire his boldness, for it reminds me with whom we are dealing. We are not dealing with some average carpenter's son from some obscure village in ancient Palestine, but the Son of God (remember 11:27), the one audacious enough to surround this tiny earthly sphere in which we live with the inexplicable splendor of a thousand unknown galaxies.

So Jesus is bold, strategically bold. In verses 3, 4 he basically says to the Pharisees, "Gentlemen, let us see if the Bible can shed some light on your accusation. I assume that you have read 1 Samuel 21, where it records what King David did when he and his companions were extremely hungry?"

The story is this: David went into the tabernacle, the house of God, *on the Sabbath* and asked for food. (Saul was the actual king; David was the anointed but not yet enthroned king.) The high priest Ahimelech first replied that he couldn't help because the only food in the house was the Bread of the Presence, the twelve consecrated loaves that were placed on a table in the tabernacle each Sabbath, a meal only eaten by the priests. David begged to partake even of this holy meal. The priest had a choice to make: should he let common mercy (these people are hungry) *and* this king's authority (this is after all David) override sacred ritual? What did he do? Seeing David's need and recognizing David's authority (did Ahimelech take David, not Saul, to be God's true king?), the priest broke the letter of the Law so as to uphold its spirit. He gave David and his men the consecrated bread. And they gladly ate it.

Jesus is asking the Pharisees, "What does Scripture say about this action? Does it say, 'Shame on David and Ahimelech—they shouldn't have done that'? No. It says nothing." It neither condemns nor approves the action. Does this silence sanction this otherwise condemnable occurrence? Jesus' gloss on the 1 Samuel text certainly leans that way. To him, by implication that silence equals evaluative approval.

What then are the implications of this divinely inspired story? Jesus proceeds. First Samuel 21:1–6 gives legal precedence, the implication being that if "the great king David had committed a far greater breach of Sabbath laws when he was in need, and he was not blamed [or punished] for it,"[5] then the disciples are not to be blamed or punished for acting in the manner in which they did. That's Jesus' argument in verses 3, 4.

Now, if you are a Pharisee listening to this line of reasoning, you might very well agree that round one goes to Jesus. You might concede that Scripture does not berate Ahimelech and David for their inappropriate actions and thus that in a life and death situation God understands and overlooks breaking a commandment. But that would be as far as you would go. "Not so fast, Jesus!" you might say next. "Your disciples were in no danger of starving to death. And besides, David is David—who are you?"[6]

Have You Not Read . . . about the Priests?

You see, Jesus' legal precedent argument only works "if Jesus is at least as special as David."[7] "So Jesus, are you as special as David? Is that what you're claiming? Are you claiming to be king—a new David?"

"Ah," Jesus says, "I'll get to that." (Just wait for verses 6, 8!) But first Jesus wields his sword again. This time he goes to Numbers 28:9, 10 for his second slash (or is it a stab?): "Or have you not read in the Law how on the Sabbath the priests in the temple profane the Sabbath and [yet] are guiltless?" (v. 5).

I'll explain Jesus' argument here via illustration. I'm not an Old Testament priest. I'm proudly a humble New Testament pastor. But like a priest, my workweek is the opposite of most people. For many their workweek ends on Friday afternoon. However, my work intensifies into the weekend, with Sunday often being the busiest day for me. Jesus is saying here, "Look, priests 'work' on Saturdays, right? They work on the Sabbath. They get all dressed up in their priestly attire, walk over to the temple, light a few candles, gather wood, and build a fire to bake some loaves of showbread. Is their 'work' wrong? No. Why? They are not guilty of breaking the Sabbath because *temple work trumps Sabbath rest*." That's Jesus' Biblical argument here.

Now, if the Pharisees had a chance to interject between verses 5, 6 they could have said, "Okay, Jesus. True enough. Temple work trumps Sabbath rest. Your second use of Scripture is correct. But what's your point?" But then it dawns on them. "Whoa. Now what? Do you think you are equal not just to a king but also to a priest?" And to that Jesus says, "Oh no, I'm not equal to a priest. I'm greater than a priest. I'm greater than the priesthood. Hold on to your phylacteries! 'I tell you, something greater than the temple is here'" (v. 6). Jesus is not merely greater that the priesthood; he is greater than the place where they "work"!

Can you hear the robes start to tear? Can you hear the word "blasphemy" being breathed throughout the crowd? Do you get what Jesus is getting at here? Do you see how the whole argument holds together? If what King David did trumps the temple, and if the temple trumps Sabbath rest, then it follows logically that if someone greater than David (cf. 1:1) *and* greater than the temple is here—embodied in the person of Jesus—then Jesus' disciples can have a little wheat snack on the Sabbath.

Jesus claims to be the fulfillment and embodiment of the Sabbath day, the sanctuary temple, and even the Scriptural Law, the three realities dearest to the people of God. And thus salvation comes not through keeping the Sabbath, perfect obedience to the Law, or temple sacrifice, but only through faith in Christ. Salvation comes (do you remember the last chapter?) only to those who rest in Jesus, who come to him, weary and heavy laden, for final Sabbath rest (see Hebrews 4).[8]

Have You Not Read . . . about Mercy?

You would think that with such claims Jesus would close his case and let the jury decide what it would decide. But no, Jesus is not finished. He takes the Bible again from these Bible-thumpers and thumps them one more time: "And if you had known [from what's in this book of yours] what this means, 'I desire mercy, and not sacrifice' [Hosea 6:6], you would not have condemned the guiltless [i.e., my disciples]" (12:7). In other words, love for people (no matter what day it is) is love for God. Even if you bring 10,000 firstborn bulls to the temple to be sacrificed, if you walk over the poor beggar on your way in, don't think God is pleased with your abundant devotion. Divine devotion without human sympathy is irreligious. It's ungodly. It's un-Biblical. Above all God desires mercy. The Sabbath is made for man. The Sabbath is made for man to show mercy to men.

Finally Jesus is done. He rubs his hands. He nods to the jury. He takes his seat. He rests his case. Wait. What's this? He's up again. He thunders in essence, "And one final point of clarification—let me be absolutely clear: I can say all I'm saying about the Sabbath (correcting you with those three Scriptures) because 'the Son of Man is lord of the Sabbath'" (v. 8). Wow!

Jesus is equal with David? Yes. Well, no. He is *greater than David*. Jesus is equal with the temple? Yes. Well, no. He is *greater than the temple*. Well, then who is he? Here is who he thinks he is: "the Son of Man."

The term "the Son of Man" does not mean "Jesus is human, a man." Rather, it's a reference to the divine king prophesied in the seventh chapter of the book of Daniel.[9] In his vision Daniel saw "one like a son of man" (Daniel 7:13). This "son of man" was presented before God, "the Ancient of Days." Similar to the Davidic covenant (2 Samuel 7:12, 13) and the beginning of the Great Commission (28:18), Daniel 7:14 reads:

> And to him [the Son of Man] was given dominion
> and glory and a kingdom,
> that all peoples, nations, and languages
> should serve him;
> his dominion is an everlasting dominion,
> which shall not pass away,
> and his kingdom one
> that shall not be destroyed.

As "the Son of Man" Jesus possesses the same lordship over the Sabbath possessed by God at creation, an authority that gives him the right and power to render all poisonous pharisaic superstitions null and void and to dictate whether or not his disciples' actions were lawful or unlawful, permissible or impermissible.[10] Having been given all authority over everything (11:27), being Lord of Heaven and earth (28:18), Jesus as the Son of Man has Lordship even over the Sabbath!

Enough to Get a Man Killed

Greater than David. Greater than the temple. The Son of Man. Lord of the Sabbath. Those are Jesus' claims in 12:1–8. And yes, such claims in such a culture are enough to get a man killed.

In the record of Jesus' trial in Matthew 26, after our Lord has been accused of claiming to destroy the temple (an interesting charge in light of our text), the high priest asks Jesus if he is "the Christ, the Son of God" (26:63). Jesus responds, "You have said so" (i.e., "I am the Christ, the Son of God"). But he doesn't stop there. He adds, "But I tell you, from now on you will see the Son of Man seated at the right hand of Power and coming on the clouds of heaven" (26:64). And how will the council react to all this—that he will destroy the temple, that he is the Son of Man? Verses 65, 66 of Matthew 26 tell us:

> Then the high priest tore his robes and said, "He has uttered blasphemy. What further witnesses do we need? You have now heard his blasphemy. What is your judgment?" They answered, "He deserves death."

This little Sabbath controversy here in Matthew 12 is no little matter. It is a matter of life and death, Jesus' life and death.

If you came to this text expecting me to write about whether Christians should keep the Sabbath or not, whether you should feel guilty or not about watching sports on Sunday, I won't tell you what I think because this passage is not about that. Here we are not to ask, are we as Christians to keep the Sabbath, or if so, how do we? Rather we are to ask, who is Jesus? What authority does he have? And what does it matter? Who is Jesus and what authority does he have over the days of the week, over kingdoms and nations, over me and my heart?

33

Lord of Mercy and Justice

MATTHEW 12:9–21

WHEN I SAY THE WORDS "POWERFUL KING," what sort of a man do you envision? For me, kings like Henry VIII of England and Leopold II of Belgium come to mind, and also other world leaders like Alexander the Great, Caesar Augustus, Attila the Hun, Genghis Khan, Ivan the Terrible, Napoleon, Hirohito, Adolf Hitler, Pol Pot, and Mao Tse-tung—mighty men who had absolute rule over a certain country or region or empire, and who all just happened be notoriously wicked. When I think "powerful king" I think of men infamous for their injustices and lack of mercy.

Perhaps your mind is more edified than mine. So when I wrote "powerful king" you thought of good kings, like Solomon (really?) or Hezekiah (are you sure?) or Uzziah (nice try). You thought of someone. There had to be good kings, right? And whoever they are, you are thinking of them right now.

But for me, with my unedified imagination, the only men I could think of as "powerful kings" all fit well the famous dictum, "Power corrupts; absolute power corrupts absolutely." That saying comes from Lord Acton (1834–1902) in a letter he wrote to Bishop Mandell Creighton in 1887. The full saying is: "Power tends to corrupt, and absolute power corrupts absolutely. Great men are almost always bad men."[1] Shakespeare's Macbeth, Hamlet, and Richard III are not merely historical fictions. They represent men who still make the front page of the world's daily newspapers. Powerful kings tend to be or become unjust and merciless.

Ah, but then there is Jesus!

Throughout his Gospel, Matthew has been arguing that Jesus is *the* absolute sovereign, *the* most powerful king. We saw this in the last sermon. Jesus is greater than King David. Jesus is greater than the temple. Jesus is the Son of

Man. Jesus is Lord of the Sabbath. And we are moving toward the climax of the Gospel where we will read that Jesus is Lord of Heaven and earth (28:18). Yet here in 12:9–21 we learn that this powerful king is unlike other powerful kings in that he is merciful (vv. 9–14) and just (vv. 15–21).

Jesus, the Merciful King

First, Jesus is the merciful king. Verses 9, 10a say, "[Jesus] went on from there and entered their synagogue. And a man was there with a withered hand." It sounds like a title to an Alfred Hitchcock movie, *The Man with the Withered Hand*. Anyway, we move on to verse 10b, where the Pharisees asked Jesus, "Is it lawful to heal on the Sabbath?" They asked this question because they knew the answer. According to their law it was unlawful "to set a broken limb or straighten a deformed body"[2] on the Sabbath.

They asked this question "so that they might accuse him" (v. 10c). They thought the odds were good that Jesus might be at odds with them, and if so they would have grounds to accuse him of breaking Sabbath law. But Jesus replied by switching from the Scriptural defense of verses 1–8 to common sense and shared human experience and sympathy. He exhorts them to use their heads and hearts: "Which one of you who has a sheep, if it falls into a pit on the Sabbath, will not take hold of it and lift it out?" (v. 11). The answer to Jesus' question is obvious. Of course the Pharisees would do that. In fact, according to one of their laws, it was permissible to rescue an animal on the Sabbath (see *b. Sabb.* 128b).[3] Perhaps that's why Jesus uses this illustration.

After establishing that a sheep is worthy of saving on the Sabbath, in verse 12 Jesus gives the argumentative punch: "Of how much more value is a man than a sheep!" Notice the exclamation point. It could be an exclamation point or a question mark. I like the translator's exclamation point. However, with the forces of animal equality pushing in on us, we might be forced to turn that exclamation point into a question mark: "Of how much more value is a man than a sheep?" Biologically speaking all creatures are equal, right? Save the whales, save the sheep, and so on. Jesus says, "No, they're not" (cf. 6:26; 10:31). Come on, even the most biologically-sensitive person would save a drowning child before a drowning sheep (cf. Luke 14:5). We'll leave the exclamation point as is. You see, even Jesus' analogies tackle some of the tough issues of our day. People are more important than animals.

Back to the argument. If a human being is more valuable than a sheep, and if any normal human being would save a sheep that has fallen into a pit (i.e., "work" on the Sabbath), then "it is lawful to do good [to people] on the Sabbath" (v. 12). God is best worshipped on the Sabbath—who could think otherwise?[4]—when love for animals *and* people are extended. One is reminded of 1 John 4:20, 21. How can you love God whom you've not seen if you can't love your brother whom you have seen? Love of one's neighbor trumps Sabbath law. No, that's not right. Love of one's neighbor *is* Sabbath law. It is lawful to love. Healing another person on Saturday or Sunday or any day of the week is an act of love. It's okay. It's worshipful.

That is our Lord's brief lecture on mercy. (Remember, he is the merciful King.) Next he demonstrates mercy: "Then he said to the man, 'Stretch out your hand.' [Luke 6:6 tells us it was his right hand; it was hard to make a living in those days, and even today, with a bad right hand.] And the man stretched it out, and it was restored, healthy like the other" (v. 13). Amen! Praise God! What a miracle! This is not something you see every day, is it?

Notice that with this miracle Jesus didn't move. He didn't lift a finger. He didn't touch the man. One wonders if he even blinked. He just spoke a few words. That's power, sure enough. But that's also hard to categorize as work—just saying four words. The Pharisees said eight words in verse 10.[5] With such talk, were they *working* on the Sabbath?

But Jesus knows what he's doing here. He is intentionally provoking the Pharisees. Think about it. This man was not in mortal danger. This withered hand wasn't going to kill him on this day or anytime soon. Perhaps he had lived with this withered hand for years. This man's restoration could have waited for Sunday or Monday. So why not wait until then? Or why not wait until the synagogue service was over and then heal the man quietly and secretly?

Furthermore, why perform this miracle when Jesus wasn't even asked to perform a miracle? The man with the withered hand didn't beg him for divine physical therapy. No one asked Jesus to heal anybody. No stretcher came through the open tiles of the ceiling. No desperate voice pleaded for help. Did you know there are only three miracle stories (by my count) in all the Gospels when Jesus took the initiative? Jesus is the one, in Mark's version of the story, who asked the man to stand up and to stand front and center. And here in Matthew, as well as in Mark, Jesus is the one who with one simple command—"Stretch out your hand" (v. 13)—restored a useless and shriveled limb. But why? Why did Jesus do this *then* and *there*?

He did it because *his mission was the cross*![6] And we see the shadow of his own stretched-out hands begin to form in verse 14 with the Pharisees' response to Jesus' miraculous mercy: "But the Pharisees went out and conspired against him, how to destroy him" (v. 14). Here the conversation of the cross starts to form in the back room, and now in Matthew's Gospel the action intensifies as the clash of authorities gets louder and louder. Soon even the crowds, who now stand amazed at Jesus, will join in the cleric-stirred chant, "Let him be crucified!" (27:22, 23).

Verses 9–14 don't merely record another Sabbath controversy. This text is not primarily about Jesus' interpretation of the Sabbath—the Pharisees have it wrong, and he has it right, so he corrects them, first in word and then in deed. There is more to it than that. This is a passage about Jesus as the merciful King. He is Lord of the Sabbath, and he uses that Lordship to do good, to show God's mercy in healing a man's withered hand, *and* he shows mercy by taking the sins of the world upon his own hands and feet and side ("with his wounds we are healed," Isaiah 53:5).

Jesus, the Just King

This is precisely what comes to Matthew's mind. As he is writing his Gospel, deciding what stories to include and where to put them, right after he recalls and writes about the Pharisees' response to Jesus' miracle, he thinks about the "servant" in Isaiah (42—53). Isaiah 42:1–4 is quoted in verses 18–21.

So from verse 14 to verses 15–21 there is a natural progression. You can think of it this way: Jesus demonstrates mercy (vv. 9–14); Jesus embodies mercy (vv. 15–21). Or you can think of it more specifically, as I have outlined the whole passage:

1. Jesus is the powerful King.
2. But unlike most powerful kings he brings mercy (vv. 9–14), and in his merciful life and death he brings justice (vv. 15–21).

Look again at verses 15–21, and note the word "justice."

> Jesus, aware of this [their growing hostility], withdrew from there. And many followed him, and he healed them all and ordered them not to make him known. This was to fulfill what was spoken by the prophet Isaiah:
>
> Behold, my servant whom I have chosen,
> my beloved with whom my soul is well pleased.
> I will put my Spirit upon him,
> and he will proclaim *justice to the Gentiles* [what an interesting concept to come after a Jewish Sabbath squabble].
> He will not quarrel or cry aloud,
> nor will anyone hear his voice in the streets;
> a bruised reed he will not break,
> and a smoldering wick he will not quench,
> until he brings justice to victory;
> and in his name the Gentiles will hope.

What's going on here? Jesus withdraws from the heated debate. The Pharisees want him dead. But it's not the right time for him to be captured and killed. Timing is everything in Jesus' mission and in God's plan. In "the fullness of time" (Galatians 4:4) Jesus came into the world, and at the right time ("my time has not yet come," see John 7:6–8) he would leave it. This explains why he leaves that situation in the synagogue and why he commands those he healed "not to make him known" (12:16).

Jesus' behavior here reminds Matthew of Isaiah. Matthew is often reminded of the book of Isaiah. He has already quoted it four times (see 1:23; 3:3; 4:15, 16; 8:17). Matthew is reminded of the Suffering Servant of Isaiah. And so, one third through his Gospel, Matthew now quotes Isaiah 42:1–4, 9 (this is his longest Old Testament quotation). And in this Old Testament text, Matthew sees that Jesus is the powerful King (spoken of earlier in Isaiah 7, 9). But Jesus has not come to start a political war. Nor has he come to make a big deal of himself—"Here I am, King Jesus. Look at me! Quick, someone call CNN." Rather Jesus will retreat behind the cameras. He'll do his work, as important as it is, but he'll do it without dramatic flair, but with purpose and perfect timing.

And with God's love within him (this is God's "beloved son," 3:17; 17:5) and God's Spirit upon him, God's servant will serve. He will serve the weak, those people who are like bruised reeds. A reed is a symbol of weakness. Nobody names a sports team the Rumbling Reeds or something like that, right? Also a bruised reed is a picture of something utterly useless, something that looks beyond repair.[7] He will serve people who are like bruised reeds and smoldering wicks (picture a candle about to go out, something that has very little life left in it).

The servant will serve people who look like they are about to be snapped off or snuffed out—the "good for nothing," we might call them, "the losers," "the marginalized."[8] To those sorts of people from among the "nations" or "Gentiles"[9] (non-religious elite Jews—shall I put it that way?) and from those who keep breaking pharisaical Sabbath laws (because such laws are too heavy, too burdensome), Jesus comes not only with rest but also with justice. He comes to judge those who will not believe, but also those who will believe or, put differently, who place their hope in the saving name of the Suffering Servant and the King of kings. You see, Jesus is Lord—not just Lord of the Sabbath or Lord of the nations but *Lord*, period. The noun in 12:8, "Lord," tells us "*who* Jesus is," and the other noun here in verse 18, "servant," tells us "*how* he is" or how he rules—he rules in humility for the humble.[10]

"Are you the king of the Jews?" "Yes, it is as you say—King of the

Jews"—written in Aramaic, Greek, and Latin (John 19:20), that all the world might read it and know it. Jesus is a king, a king who rules in humility for the humble. He enlists in his army a bunch of weaklings.[11] Have you ever heard of such strange behavior? Would Alexander the Great have allowed bruised reeds and smoldering wicks as soldiers? Would Hitler have allowed his troops to lack rigorous training, discipline, skill, and courage? And yet the kingdoms of this world—whether great Greece or great Germany—have all come to an end, and other kingdoms will soon come to an end, but the kingdom of God, with its weaklings, marches on. "Glory! Glory! Halleluiah! His truth is marching on."[12] The truth is that Jesus came to bring justice to nobodies who could find it nowhere else, a justice that will come finally, ultimately, eschatologically with the final judgment.

Although Matthew's quote of Isaiah 42 emphasizes what the servant does not do, it ends with the one thing he will do—bring justice. One commentator puts it this way:

> This Servant will never rest in his nonviolent zeal until he brings God's great verdict of *perfect justice* and *righteous judgment* to earth. The Servant is quiet but not quietistic, nonviolent but not noninvolved, gentle but passionate for God's truth—a truth, we are promised, that he shall one day bring successfully to victory. This victory is won at Jesus' awful cross, is proclaimed at his triumphant resurrection, is worked out in history in his reign at God's right hand, and will be consummated at his glorious judgment.[13]

Yes! Yes indeed.

So coming out of the dark cloud of verse 14, these verses from Isaiah are like gentle warm rain. Jesus will die, but in his death justice begins to "roll down like waters" (Amos 5:24), the earth is slowly being "filled with the knowledge of the glory of the LORD" (Habakkuk 2:14), and soon the whole earth will be flooded with hope.

The Bottom Line

When the small group I lead gets together on Sunday nights to discuss the passage that was preached on Sunday morning, I usually start by asking the group a simple yes or no question. The question is this: "Wasn't that sermon awesome—yes or no?" Just kidding. I usually start by asking, "What was the main point of the sermon (which should be the main point of the Bible text)?" Or put differently, "What is the bottom line?"

Suppose a man in my group says, "I think this passage is about religious hypocrisy." I say, "Yes, true, but how so?"

"Well," this man replies, "it is as the great mathematician and physicist Blaise Pascal once wrote [you'll have to forgive me, my group is very heady], 'Men never do evil so completely and cheerfully as when they do it from religious conviction.'"[14]

I say, "That's a good quote. I could have used it in my sermon this morning."

"You see, Pastor," he goes on to say, "with their stubborn resistance, blind jealousy, and hatred, the Pharisees' priorities became so twisted that they accused Jesus of breaking the Sabbath for healing a man, while they, on the Sabbath, are plotting to murder an innocent man (Jesus), thus breaking the great commandment to love one's neighbor (Leviticus 19:18). We Christians must be careful that we don't let man-made traditions blind us to love, or to true religion, as James put it."[15]

"True," I say, "an excellent point and a good application, but do you think that is really the bottom line?"

Another brave soul raises her voice and shares her opinion. "This text is about the Sabbath. As you said last week, the church has lost the sense of the sacredness of time. We need to stop wasting time, especially on the Lord's Day, watching football, basketball, or the Olympics, whatever we watch, and use that time—redeem the time—for worship and works of mercy. We have to give God our Sundays! Isn't that our church's motto, Pastor?"

"It is," I say. "It's one of our many mottos. And yes, I agree that it is great on Sundays to take a break from whatever you do for a living and gather in the morning and evening for worship with God's people—to stir one another up toward love and good deeds. And it's good to spend time with family and take a long walk with your spouse, visit someone in the hospital or in a retirement home, volunteer at a charity, or bake brownies for our poor famished college students. Yes, spend yourself on others. Yes, yes, yes—that is resting in Christ, working for him on the Sabbath. But I think the Sabbath issue here is not the bottom line. Neither this text nor the one before it is about the Sabbath. The Sabbath is merely the setting. It's a dramatic setting. It's like all the characters are balancing on a tightrope talking theology. But this passage is not about the tightrope, is it? So, nice try, but you too are wrong. [Don't you wish you were part of my growth group? I have a very inviting personality.] Any other thoughts?"

"Okay . . ." Someone else works up the courage to give it a try. "The bottom line—that's what you want, right?"

"Yes, it is," I say.

"The bottom line is not the inward focus but the outward focus. It's not about religious hypocrisy—Christians shouldn't be like the Pharisees—and it's not about what we should or should not do on Sundays, but it's about the church's mission to the world."

He stops and looks at me.

I nod encouragingly and curiously. "There is so much," this man goes on to say, "we can learn about missions and evangelism from Jesus' method and his target. Listen, his method (and it's not just here, it's everywhere in the Gospels) was not some big PR campaign—'Come see Jesus, the mighty miracle-worker.' We evangelicals are so concerned about power and publicity—voting in the right politicians, making sure Jesus gets some face-time on the news or in our public schools. But Jesus' own method was always calculatedly quiet, and Jesus' power was perfected in weakness . . . and yet look at the results: millions of people still to this day, and for 2,000 years, call him 'Lord' and 'God' and 'Savior.' It's time the church stopped looking to be so fashionable and started acting like Jesus."

Silence.

"So what I'm saying," he goes on, "is that Jesus' method has to be ours, and his target needs to be ours as well. He went after the broken reeds and smoldering wicks, not the rich, not the famous, not the religiously pristine. It's time we as a church go out and bring in the lowlifes and losers. Amen?"

He gets a few amens, but then I turn to the group and say, "I'll admit he's preached a better sermon than I did, but I'm glad to say that he too is wrong. No, no, no, my friends. These are all excellent thoughts and perfect applications of this passage, but they are not *the* bottom line. The bottom line is not inward or outward but upward. This passage is about Jesus and his identity."

Identity, identity, identity. Every passage in every Gospel—Matthew, Mark, Luke, and John—is primarily about Jesus' identity. (It's not only that, but it's primarily that.) And here again in our passage Matthew is telling us in story form who Jesus is. He is the powerful King. He is the powerful *but merciful* King! He is the powerful but *just* King!

He is the powerful, merciful, just King who says, "I don't care how wretched or unremarkable you are or may seem,[16] I've come to bring even you life and rest and hope. So come to me. Trust me with your life. I'm a servant and yet a king. I'm a powerful king and yet full of mercy and justice. So line up, broken reeds and smoldering wicks; come unto me. 'All ye nations rise, join the triumph of the skies.'"[17]

Jesus is the bottom line. Jesus. Jesus. Jesus.

34

Two Kingdoms, One Choice

MATTHEW 12:22–37

AFTER THE DEVASTATING EARTHQUAKE IN HAITI, Pat Robertson blamed the tragedy on a pact the Haitian people made with the devil, a pact supposedly made over 200 years ago, during the days of French colonialism. I didn't watch the whole segment on CBN, so I don't know if Robertson was quoted out of context—if we only got a sound bite from an otherwise carefully reasoned systematic theology of the problem of evil—or if he ended his interview saying, "And yet, with all I've said, like Jesus I weep over the grim reality of death, and like Job, I cover my mouth, for I cannot fathom all there is to fathom of this inexplicable tragedy." But I do know that our media and comedians had a field day with what he said. His devil-talk became the butt of their jokes.

But why? Why is it that when a popular Christian figure like Robertson speaks about a powerful God and also powerful demonic forces at work in this world and about past sins having present consequences he is first lambasted and then laughed at? In a culture whose best-selling books and most popular TV shows and movies are about wizards, witches, and vampires, are we too scientifically sophisticated for Satan?

Sure, there is a danger in overemphasizing the demonic (and that seems to be what Pat Robertson did). But there is a greater danger in underemphasizing and underestimating it—not to take seriously what Paul says in Ephesians 2:1–4 about the devil, that he is "the prince of the power of the air . . . [who] is now at work in the sons of disobedience" and that we fight not merely "against flesh and blood," but against "the schemes of the devil . . . against the cosmic powers . . . against the spiritual forces of evil" (Ephesians 6:10–12).

Our Lord Jesus took the devil seriously. In John 12:31 and 14:30, Jesus labeled him "the ruler of this world." That is, the devil is the ruler of those who dismiss the rule of Christ. He is the ruler of this fallen world. And here in our text Jesus states plainly that there is a devil, that he has a kingdom, and that such a kingdom has power and influence in this world. And he affirms the belief that diseases and decisions (and perhaps disasters) can be influenced by demons. And he believes, so it seems from his illustration in verse 29, that the world is not merely lost—on some deserted desert island with little hope of rescue—but is held as a *prisoner of war*[1] and that apart from the rescue mission of Christ all human beings are bound by the supernatural strong man, Satan.

So before we come to our text, as I invite you to open your Bible again to Matthew 12, I want us to open our minds to the Biblical worldview—a way of looking at the world that might just be closer (or spot-on) to the way the world really is.

One Miracle, Three Motifs

Let's begin our exploration of this exorcism. "Then a *demon-oppressed* [or possessed] man who was blind and mute was brought to him [Jesus], and he healed him, so that the man spoke and saw" (v. 22).

Compared to other miracles, this one is told with "admirable brevity."[2] That is, it's short but significant. It's significant for a number of reasons. First, it again shows Jesus' power. Just think about this. Perhaps you know someone who is blind or mute. I have a neighbor whose daughter, when she was four years old, was diagnosed with a disease that would slowly take away her vision. I remember the day my wife told me this sad news and how distraught I was to think of this terrible thing happening to this sweet little girl. Today, over a decade later, she is nearly blind. And every time I see her I wish I had *the power* to heal her. Jesus has such power. That's what these people, including the Pharisees, witnessed.

Verse 15 says that Jesus performed many miracles—"*many* followed him, and he healed them *all*." But this particular miracle of healing of this blind, mute, demon-possessed man makes it into Matthew's Gospel. And perhaps it makes it in because it was the most spectacular of the day, or perhaps because it is the perfect parable for the discussion that follows. I think it's both. It's a real, powerful miracle, but it's also a symbolic miracle.

In verses 23–37 there are three main motifs—sight, speech, and supernatural spiritual powers. Sight is the most subtle motif. The crowd sees Jesus for who he is. Or they are at least open to the possibility that he is the Messiah—"Can this be the Son of David?" (v. 23). But the Pharisees are blind to Jesus, so they say in effect, "Might this be the sidekick or subordinate of Satan?"

Beyond the motif of sight and blindness, we also have the motifs of speech and supernatural spirits. My original title for this chapter was "A Word on Words" because I noticed how much *talking* is talked about. Including words like "spoke," "said," "tell," "speak" and "speaks," "word" and "words," "blasphemy," and "mute," I counted seventeen words that talk about talking. And this theme of speech builds as Jesus speaks, especially in verses 31–37, which ends with these words on words, "by your words you will be justified, and by your words you will be condemned."

The man who was cured by Jesus was blind and mute—he lacked sight and speech. But the root of those problems was that he was demon-possessed. That is the third and most important motif. Here two kingdoms are depicted. On one side we have "Satan" or "Beelzebul" (slang for Satan; the word "Beelzebul" is literally "Lord of the flies"), his "demons" (mentioned five times), "evil" (mentioned four times), and even "vipers"—"you brood of vipers" (a subtle reference to the snake of Genesis?). On the other side we have the "the Son of Man" (Jesus) and "the kingdom of God" (the Father) and most critical to this text, "the Holy Spirit." The Trinity! The Trinity—Father, Son, and Spirit—is mentioned at Jesus' baptism (3:16, 17), mentioned here, and then mentioned again and finally at the Great Commission (28:19). So here we have, in one corner, the devil and his many minions and in the other corner the Trinity—one God in three persons. The power of our good God versus all the powers of evil.

So, is this is a supernatural miracle? For sure. But is it also a symbolic miracle? Absolutely! Do you see that?

Two Reponses

If the Bible's theology and history do not invite you to praise Christ, let its artistry. The first Gospel is artistically first-rate. This miracle—this one miracle (short but significant)—sets everything in motion.

Let's look now at that motion. Verse 22 describes Jesus' miracle. Verse 23 describes the people's reaction: "Can this be the Son of David?" They wonder if Jesus is the King who would fulfill the Davidic covenant. The Pharisees heard verse 23, and they essentially said in verse 24, "Oh no! No way!" I imagine them then scrambling for a quick answer.

They don't doubt the exorcism. Isn't that interesting? N. T. Wright sees their reaction as attesting to the historicity of Jesus' miracles.[3] Jesus was no amateur magician struggling to pull a rabbit out of a hat, or they would have said so. Rather, he was doing inexplicable miracles that no one had even seen before—raising the dead, giving sight to the blind, etc. The Pharisees knew that Jesus had power. They saw the hand of God. But they hardened their hearts to that hand. They refused to let that hand nudge or push (or punch) them into the kingdom.

And they refused because to them, other than some of the miracles, Jesus was doing everything opposite of what they expected the Son of David to do. Not only did Jesus not offer or "endorse a program of national liberation,"[4] but he was associating with the enemy (a Roman centurion) and with the social and religious outcasts (tax collectors and sinners). And not only was he violating (blatantly so it seemed) long-held rabbinic ethical codes, but he was making preposterous claims. He claimed to be greater than David, greater than the temple, having the authority to forgive sins and calling people to have Sabbath rest in him.

They could not and did not deny the power. This Jesus has supernatural authority. But, they did not believe it could be the supernatural power of Yahweh (cf. Deuteronomy 13:1–5). Thus it had to be the supernatural power of Satan: "It is only by Beelzebul, the prince of demons, that this man casts out demons" (v. 24).

Two Logical Rebuttals

In verses 22–24 we have the miracle and two reactions—one reaction positive and on the mark, the other negative and off the mark. Then in verses 25–27 we have Jesus' rebuttal of the Pharisees' false accusation. In those verses our Lord gives two logical rebuttals, one choice, and two gracious warnings.

First we'll look at the two logical rebuttals. I say *logical* because here Jesus doesn't use Scripture as he did in verses 3–7 or shared human sympathy as he did in verses 11, 12. Here he uses logic, what is called a *reductio ad absurdum.* Look at verses 25, 26. Knowing their thoughts by either divine intuition or human observation, Jesus basically said, "Don't be absurd," or as Matthew records it:

> Every kingdom divided against itself is laid waste, and no city or house divided against itself will stand. And if Satan casts out Satan, he is divided against himself. How then will his kingdom stand?

Do you get the logic here? Jesus gives three scenarios, moving from kingdom to city to house. If it helps you can think of any organized entity like a government, a company, and even my church. If I said the vision of my church is, "By God's grace we hope to see love extended unto the church, the city, and the world," and the associate pastor said, "No, the vision is that we, by the magic of Tinker Bell, hope to see pixie dust scattered onto the church, the city, and the world," needless to say, we'd have a problem. It wouldn't be long before our whole experiment in church planting imploded and then exploded.

So here Jesus says in essence, "Use your head. What sense would it make for the devil to empower me to deliver people from devils? What sense would it make to make them healthy in body, mind, and spirit?"[5] That is the logical response Jesus gives in verses 25, 26. His reply in verse 27 is only slightly different. In verses 25, 26 Jesus says in effect, "Use your head," and in verse 27 he says, "Come on now, will you please use your head!" The actual words in verse 27 are these: "And if I cast out demons by Beelzebul, by whom do your sons [the Pharisees' followers—the Pharisees were known for their exorcisms] cast them out? Therefore they will be your judges." The idea here is that if your underlings can perform little exorcisms and no one doubts it is of God, then when Jesus performs his super-exorcisms, you better believe that he's playing for God's team. Thus, in verse 28 Jesus says, "But if it is by the Spirit of God that I cast out demons, then the kingdom of God has come upon you." Guess what? The Son of David is here. So guess what? The eternal kingdom of the eternal God is now present.

That's Jesus first logical rebuttal. Here is his second.[6] It's in more parabolic form: "Or how can someone enter a strong man's house and plunder his goods, unless he first binds the strong man? Then indeed he may plunder his house" (v. 29). The "strong man" represents Satan; his "house" is his kingdom, and his "goods" are those people under his influence. As the parable proceeds, Jesus is the one who breaks down the front door, ties up the strong man—"His craft and power are great, and armed with cruel hate, on earth is not his equal"[7]—and then delivers the hostages. He plunders the house of the devil's goods.

You see, Jesus is not sitting on his heavenly throne being entertained by angels as they do somersaults in the sky. Rather, he is on the front line kicking down the devil's door and setting the captives free! This incarnational attack, we might say, began at his birth. His first victory was won in the wilderness, his most decisive victory was on the cross, and his final victory is still to come with the second coming. So, "far from belonging to Satan's kingdom and using Satan's power, Jesus has attacked [and will attack] that kingdom and overcome its power."[8]

One Choice

Verses 25–29 provide us with Jesus' two logical rebuttals. Then, in the middle of our text—the theological and structural center—we have the choice, our one choice. Jesus says, "Whoever is not with me is against me, and whoever does not gather with me scatters" (v. 30).

I thought about entitling this chapter "Two Kingdoms, Two Choices." But here it is really two kingdoms, one choice. You either *see* Jesus to be the Son of David (the promised earthly king) and the Son of Man (the promised divine King) and thus choose him as King or you don't. And if you don't, you are not on neutral ground. You are in hostile, enemy territory. There are only two kingdoms and one choice. Stay where you are, call it your own kingdom if you like (if that makes you feel better or safer), and think of yourself as Mr. Middle-of-the Road or Mrs. Broadminded, but in reality you are teeter-tottering on the devil's playground. Jesus dispels the myth of religious neutrality.

With the rise of the scientific worldview it is difficult for many to believe in demons and demonic activity without being able to test it in a laboratory. With the rise of pluralism it is difficult for many to believe that Jesus is the only way to God. We do not live in a religious bubble. Not only can we learn about other religions by reading, traveling, or surfing the Web, but also by sitting down at the school cafeteria or coffee shop and listening to our coworkers or fellow students, who come from different parts of the world and believe very different things about the world.

But as Christians we must not let such information make us intelligently impotent. The claims of Jesus are the claims of Jesus. We either believe them or we don't. What he said in verse 30 is either true or false. We can re-imagine Jesus into our own image, twisting and turning his words to sound a lot like our own. This has been done in many Christian denominations, hasn't it? Such behavior I find intellectually dishonest. Don't call yourself a Christian if you don't believe Jesus ever existed. Don't call yourself a Christian if you believe only half of the red letters in your Bible have any connection to the historical Jesus. Don't call yourself a Christian if you think Jesus didn't die for your sins and rise for your justification. Don't call yourself a Christian if you think obeying Christ's commands are optional. And don't call yourself a Christian if you think there are many ways to God. To be a Christian is, at the very least, to take Jesus at his word. "Whoever is not with me is against me, and whoever does not gather with me scatters" (v. 30). Thus saith the Lord.

So "Those who hedge about devotion to Jesus . . . or about the importance of a clear decision for him . . . who question Jesus' exclusivity . . . and who disdain his gathering work of evangelism . . . are in trouble."[9] That's what Jesus teaches here. They are "against" God's kingdom. They might think they are standing safe and still, but in fact they are busy scattering seeds of sedition.

Two Gracious Warnings

We have looked at two logical rebuttals (vv. 25–29) and the one choice (v. 30). Finally, we have two gracious warnings (vv. 31–37), which serve to help us make the choice we should make about Jesus.

The first warning is found in verses 31, 32, the second in verses 33–37. Note that both warnings involve *words*, and both end by speaking of *the final judgment*: "on *the day of judgment* people will give account for every careless *word* they *speak*."

We'll look at the first warning first:

> Therefore I tell you, every sin and blasphemy will be forgiven people, but the blasphemy against the Spirit will not be forgiven. And whoever speaks a word against the Son of Man will be forgiven, but whoever speaks against the Holy Spirit will not be forgiven, either in this age or in the age to come. (vv. 31, 32)

After hearing those words, you might say, "Okay, I'm hearing loud and clear the warning part. This is a severe warning! Jesus is talking about committing some sin that cannot be forgiven. I get that. What then is *gracious* about this warning?" I'll get to that shortly. Let me first define, for those who are curious or concerned (I hope you are at least curious), "the blasphemy against the Holy Spirit."

Walford's concise definition of the blasphemy of the Holy Spirit is "attributing to Satan what is accomplished by the power of God,"[10] basically doing what the Pharisees are doing here. And it involves, if we flesh out that basic definition a bit, the "combination of clear knowledge and deliberate rejection of Christ."[11] So there's a certain amount of light in the head—one can see clearly who Jesus is, as plainly as the Pharisees saw his miracles—and yet there is hatred of that light in the heart. Therefore, blasphemy of the Holy Spirit is a knowledge of the light, a hatred of it, and I'll add (and this addition is key) that there is also an earnest and *persistent* effort to put out the light.

With that definition in place, I can safely say that Matthew Henry's long-standing pastoral counsel on these verses is still appropriate. He wrote, "Those who fear they have committed this sin give a good sign that they have not."[12] That is, if you are someone who has committed the blasphemy of the Holy Spirit, you won't care about the state of your soul because you've passed the point of no return (cf. Hebrews 12:17). You are so self-deceived that you've not only stopped believing in Jesus and some Holy Spirit ("that's like fairy tale stories, stuff for little children and ignorant old ladies"), but you have actually thought yourself so wise, so beyond others that you're now earning a nice living writing best-selling books about why Jesus' miracles never happened and how Jesus never said what we once thought he said. Such a person, who at one point may have tasted the truth of the gospel, has now spit it out (cf. Hebrews 6:4–6), and he or she wants others to spit it out as well. For such a person as this there is no chance of forgiveness because there is no chance of a change of heart. That person's heart is so hard it cannot soften. It cannot and will not repent no matter how obvious the evidence, even if a dead man would rise again on the third day. That's the blasphemy of the Holy Spirit and Jesus' warning about it.

So, what is gracious about this warning? First, Jesus is essentially saying to the Pharisees, as hard as they are, and others—perhaps you, as hard or soft as you might be—"Now is the time to recognize the work of the Holy Spirit in me." He is saying, "Listen, I'm 'patient toward you, not wishing that any should perish, but that all should reach repentance'" (2 Peter 3:9). Here Jesus warns the Pharisees about the unpardonable sin. He doesn't accuse them of having committed it. That's what is gracious about this warning.

What is also extremely gracious is just how many sins can be forgiven. Skim through these two verses again and notice twice the phrase "will not be forgiven"—that refers to the blasphemy of the Holy Spirit. But then also notice the phrase "will be forgiven" (also repeated twice), and then notice the word "every" in verse 31. "Every" is the loveliest word in the world. "Therefore I tell you, *every* sin and blasphemy will be forgiven."

What about driving under the influence? Every sin will be forgiven. What about cheating on that history test? Every sin will be forgiven. What about getting your teenage girlfriend pregnant? Every sin will be forgiven. What about having an abortion? Every sin will be forgiven. What about lying under oath? Every sin will be forgiven. What about all the backbiting? Every sin will be forgiven. What about cheating on your husband? Every sin will be forgiven. What about loving money more than God? Every sin will be forgiven. What about experimenting with homosexuality? Every sin will be forgiven. What about murder? Every sin will be forgiven.

Yes, every sin will be forgiven, for "The saying is trustworthy and deserving all acceptance, that Christ Jesus came into the world to save sinners" like us (1 Timothy 1:15). Do you know who wrote that? A guy name Saul of Tarsus. Do you remember his story? He was a Pharisee. He called himself "a Pharisee, a son of Pharisees" (Acts 23:6). He was so zealous for the traditions of the elders—Jewish traditions, the ones that got the Pharisees here so mad—that he persecuted the church. He pursued and captured Christians and had them killed. And yet we all know what happened to him. Jesus captured and killed Saul and turned him into a new man named Paul. Paul would take the good news of the forgiveness of sins to Greece and Italy, and Paul would write the words, "The saying is trustworthy and deserving of full acceptance, that Christ Jesus came into the world to save sinners, of whom I am the foremost." Are you a worse sinner than Paul? I highly doubt it. Every sin can be forgiven. That's grace. And that's what I call a gracious warning.

Here is the second gracious warning. In verse 33–37 Jesus says,

> Either make the tree good and its fruit good, or make the tree bad and its fruit bad, for the tree is known by its fruit. You brood of vipers! How can you speak good, when you are evil? For out of the abundance of the heart the mouth speaks. The good person out of his good treasure brings forth good, and the evil person out of his evil treasure brings forth evil. I tell you, on the day of judgment people will give account for every careless word they speak, for by your words you will be justified, and by your words you will be condemned.

After Jesus says to the Pharisees, "You brood of vipers" (i.e., "you sons of snakes") you might be saying, "Okay, again I hear the warning. In fact, I hear more than a warning—I hear an announcement of judgment." And yes, I'll admit Jesus is giving them a prophetic judgment. Like the prophets of old, he is pronouncing woe. He is saying that God is fed up with such talk about him. It's devilish to deny Jesus. It's Garden of Eden snake talk. "You shouldn't be saying what you are saying, and no one should be tempted to listen to what you say."

The announcement here is severe. But it is an announcement mixed with admonishment. That's why I call it a gracious warning. Later in chapter 23—with Jesus' seven woes to the Pharisees—there is no admonition (note 23:33). But here, verse 33 begins with a call for change: "Either make the tree good and its fruit good, or make the tree bad and its fruit bad, for the tree is known by its fruit." In other words, "You guys speak evil about me because you are evil. You are like a bad tree. Bad trees produce bad, rotten, inedible fruit. Good trees produce good, fresh, tasty fruit."

We often underestimate the connection between the heart and the tongue. We might admit the notion of "Freudian slips" (sometimes our tongues reveal our subconscious), but we deny that such slips of the tongue, words that escape in casual conversation, are a "reliable indicator of . . . the state of the heart."[13] We say things like "I didn't mean what I said." However, as Jesus has taught in the Sermon on the Mount (5:22–26, 33–37; 6:7; 7:4, 5, 21–23), here he again teaches that our words are reliable indicators of who we are, so reliable that on Judgment Day Jesus will know we are Christians by our tongues. What is in the heart—good or bad—comes out of the mouth.

So, what's the solution for bad mouths? New hearts. You must be born again, born of the Spirit. Verse 33 is a call to be converted. This is a gracious warning. The tongue is such a small part of our body (James 3:5), and yet it shows the heart. Most people think their heart is okay, but they struggle a bit with their tongue. Jesus says you struggle with the tongue because your heart is not okay. You haven't yet moved from the dominion of the devil into the kingdom of God. So repent and believe. Cut down that old bad tree, and let the Lord Jesus plant a new one. Abide in him and watch the good fruit grow.

Proverbs 18:21 says, "Death and life are in the power of the tongue." In Matthew 25 it is by our works that we are acknowledged to be righteous; here it's our words. Our works (what we actually do) and our words (what we actually say) show whether we have faith in Christ or not. We are justified by faith alone, but true faith is never alone—it comes out in our words and in our works.

35

Easter and the Evil Generation

MATTHEW 12:38–45

This chapter was originally preached as a sermon Easter 2010, and is dedicated to Anne Hoffner (January 6, 1976—March 29, 2010).

GIVE ME A SIGN, *and then I'll believe. Give me some sign that Jesus is the Son of God, and then I will gladly become a Christian. I'll go to church, say my prayers, read my Bible, and do the other things Christians are supposed to do. Just give me a sign.*

The request of the scribes and Pharisees in verse 38, said nearly 2,000 years ago, is an everyday, every-generation request. But it is not so much a request as it is an excuse. People want signs that God exists and that Jesus is Lord, but they always want *their* signs rather than the ones God provides.

Some people today want a scientific sign. "I would believe in God if engraved upon the first moon rock picked up by Neil Armstrong were the words, 'In the beginning God created the heavens and the earth.' And if the genetic instructions of the complete DNA sequence somehow formed the sentence, 'The Bible is inerrant in its original manuscripts,' then I'd take this book as holy and authoritative. And if the cloud formation from the first atomic bomb spelled out, 'Repent and believe in Jesus,' I would gladly do so."

Others want a political power sign. We might call this the Constantinian sign. When the Emperor Constantine was marching to war, he looked up to the sun and saw a cross of light above it, with the Greek words *en toutō nika*,

"In this [sign], you shall conquer."[1] And conquer he did (through the cross, so he thought). Some people today assert, "I will hold to the truths of the Christian faith if the Christian church holds worldly power and prestige. I want a St. Peter's Basilica on every Main Street in every town in every country. Show me the political power. Show me the institutional presence. Show me the worldly glory, and then I will believe."

Still others just want miraculous signs. "I will trust in Jesus if God cures this cancer . . . if he saves this unsalvageable marriage . . . if he right now turns my hair blonde, now black, now back to brown. Show me something miraculous. Just give me a sign."

In our text the Jewish religious leaders fall somewhere into this third camp—the "show me something miraculous" camp. You might say, "But why are they in this camp? Haven't they seen Jesus heal the sick, raise the dead, cleanse the leper, and drive out demons?" Yes, they have. And from Matthew's perspective we get the impression that those signs and wonders should have been enough to persuade them (cf. Acts 2:22). However, here they are not looking for another earthly miracle. They don't ask for a miracle but for a sign, the idea being "a heavenly miracle," a sign in the sky (not one on earth).[2] I'll put it this way: not something an Egyptian magician could duplicate; something that would show them that the Lord *in Heaven* is for Jesus *on earth*.

So they ask, we might say, not for Jesus to multiply seven loaves of bread into 7,000, but for manna to fall from Heaven. They ask not for the Red Sea to part but for a cloud of smoke and a pillar of fire. If this Jesus is, as he has been claiming, greater than the temple and the Torah, the one who has come to deliver his people Israel, then let him do something greater than Moses. Order hail from Heaven (Exodus 9:13–35) or send darkness over the whole land (Exodus 10:21–29). Do something like that.

The Only Sign

And to that Jesus says to them, as much as he says to us today,

> An evil and adulterous generation seeks for a sign,[3] but no sign will be given to it except the sign of the prophet Jonah. For just as Jonah was three days and three nights in the belly of the great fish, so will the Son of Man be three days and three nights in the heart of the earth. (vv. 39, 40)

The only sign that has been given to every generation is Good Friday and Easter, the death and resurrection of Jesus.[4] Just as Jonah was in the belly of that big fish and then vomited up alive, so Jesus will be buried and rise again on the third day.

Now let's stop here, and let me make two simple observations, for I don't want anyone to misunderstand some of the details of verses 39, 40.

First, the Jesus/Jonah comparison is not intended to be a perfect parallel. Jonah was a prophet, Jesus much more than a prophet. Jonah was disobedient up until the point he prayed that beautiful prayer of salvation in the fish. Jesus was perfectly obedient from the womb to the tomb. Jonah did not die when he was buried in the belly of the fish. Jesus died and was buried. The main similarity between Jesus and Jonah was that they were both delivered alive after three days from a deadly situation in which there was no normal hope for life afterward.

Second, don't get bogged down by the mathematics of verse 40, where Jesus speaks of the three days and three nights. Perhaps when you read that you might think, "Wait, wasn't Jesus buried for just one and a half days? He died at 'the ninth hour' (3:00 p.m.) on Friday, and then he was buried later that evening. So he was in the tomb some of Friday, all of Saturday, and then part of Sunday. That is not three days and nights."

The key to understanding the potential discrepancy of days here is first of all to understand how ancient Jews calculated time. A new day began after sunset (not at midnight), and part of a day was often counted as a whole day. I can give you five different examples from the Bible where this was the case.[5] Matthew obviously knew the time line. Read the end of his Gospel. He knows how long Jesus was actually in the tomb. But to him and to his first readers, the count goes like this: Jesus was in the tomb—Friday, Saturday, and Sunday—one, two, three.[6]

However, this explanation does not explain the "three *nights*." This explains "three days" fine, but it does not explain the "three nights" part. Even if you count a new day beginning at sunset and a partial day as a whole day, Friday afternoon to Sunday morning does not make three nights. Perhaps then it is best to follow Vincent Taylor's understanding that the three days and nights means "in the shortest possible time."[7]

Whatever the best clarification, let's please understand that the main idea here is not precision of time but similarity of sign: as Jonah went down and came up, so Jesus will die and rise again. So, yes, there is a time correlation, but more so a sign relation. And the whole point of verses 39, 40 is that only one sign will be given to that generation, and only one sign has been given from the time of Jesus' resurrection until his return—the death and resurrection of Jesus.

In Jesus' life and ministry, God has delivered one proof after another, but in Jesus' death and resurrection he has pulled out all the stops, giving us all that is necessary to believe.[8] The resurrection of the crucified Christ—that is the sign. Period. Exclamation point. One sign. Take it or leave it.

Gather one, gather all for the greatest show on earth—the greatest sign you will ever see, God's "once-for-all and perpetual" sign.[9] Behold the man! Behold your King! Behold the Lamb of God slain and yet he lives! Behold the sign of Jonah!

The Sufficient Sign

Wait. What is so great about that sign? Wouldn't the scientific sign or the political power sign or some sign in the sky (some remarkable, unprecedented heavenly miracle) be a more sufficient sign? I don't think so. And Jesus certainly doesn't think so.

The sign of the death and resurrection of Christ is a fully sufficient sign for at least two reasons: (1) it is historically viable and, I'll argue, historically verifiable, and (2) it allows room for faith, and it is faith that allows room for anyone and everyone who will believe.

I'll touch on that second reason first. If a saving relationship with God were based on human strength, then only those who could bench-press at least 300 pounds would get into Heaven. If it was based on human intelligence, "getting into heaven would be like getting into Harvard,"[10] and only a very few elite academics could do it. If it were based on beauty, only a few people like my wife would experience divine glory. But if salvation is obtained by faith alone (you see, there are an "infinite number of things which surpass" reason[11] and strength and beauty, including faith), then even humble folk like fishermen and weak people like little children can gain entrance into the kingdom of heaven. That is one reason the sign of Jonah is sufficient—faith is democratic, available to the masses. Faith allows all kinds of people (strong/weak, pretty/ugly, smart/dumb, black/white, male/female, Jew/Gentile, and so on) to enter the kingdom.

The other reason that this sign is sufficient is the historical validity of Jesus' resurrection. Oftentimes skeptics think that the burden of proof for the resurrection is on Christians: "You have to dig up the historical facts and prove that Jesus really rose from the dead." But I think the burden of proof is on the skeptics. They have to find the corpse of Christ. The early Christians claimed he rose from the dead, and there were over 500 eyewitnesses (1 Corinthians 15:3–6), including Roman soldiers paid to guard the tomb and paid off when they couldn't find the body. So you tell me, what happened to Jesus?

Surely someone somewhere (back then especially—the Romans, the Jews, the enemies of the church) had the body or bones of Jesus. So where are they?

And then explain, I would urge skeptics, why Christianity emerged so rapidly and with such force in a culture more skeptical about bodily resurrections than ours. What on earth could have happened that would make a bunch of Jews—Simon Peter, James, John, Paul, and the others—not only start preaching that Jesus rose from the dead (new worldviews like that, and it was new for the time, don't formulate overnight) but then worship him as God? Have you read the New Testament lately? How do you explain Revelation 5, Philippians 2, or Colossians 1? These monotheistic Jews were worshipping Jesus! Explain that. Call him a prophet as Muhammad's followers called Muhammad or enlightened as the Buddha's followers called Buddha, but not "My Lord and my God" (John 20:28), like once-doubting Thomas did of Jesus.

Furthermore, what would make these same followers sacrifice their very lives for a lie? Pascal once wrote, "I [believe] those witnesses that get their throats cut."[12] Perhaps one man would die for a hoax, but not an honest man, only a deranged man. But for virtually all the apostles and many of the first eyewitnesses to die for some corporate hoax or hallucination, some made-up myth, some dead guy whose strange teachings they liked so much they were willing to be hanged, crucified, thrown to the lions, or tortured to death—that's more far-fetched than if I claimed I could grow wings and fly home. It really is.

The problem is not with the sign. The sign is sufficient. Eyewitness testimony is still the most valid and reliable form of witness in our courts today. If people don't believe, the problem is with them.

Many people who don't believe in Jesus and his resurrection suffer from what I'll call the rich man's syndrome. Do you remember the Parable of the Rich Man and Lazarus in Luke 16:19–31? It was told to the Pharisees, who knew their Bibles but were "lovers of money" and full of pride (they thought their own righteousness justified them, see Luke 16:14–17). I won't go through the whole parable. I'll just touch on the end. Toward the end, the rich man is suffering in Hell, while the poor man, Lazarus, is in heavenly luxury. The rich man says something quite telling. He asks Abraham to send someone to warn his five brothers, who obviously were living as hellishly as he did. To that request Abraham basically replies, "They have the Bible—Moses and the prophets—let them listen to that voice." The rich man replies, "No, Father Abraham, send someone back from the dead, then they will repent." Abraham concludes, "No, they won't. If they won't listen to what the Bible says, they won't listen to anyone, even someone who rises from the dead" (see Luke 16:29–31).

The point of that parable concerns the sufficiency of the Scriptures as a testimony to Christ and a fitting testimony against the self-righteous, self-indulgent Pharisees. Applied to our text in Matthew, this parable addresses those people who make up any and all excuses not to believe in Jesus. "Oh, I will believe in Jesus if . . ." Then they lay out their demands. If this, if that. "If someone visited me from the dead and told me what to believe, then I'd believe." Like Abraham, I respond, "I doubt it." The problem is not the sign God has given—the problem is unbelieving individuals. They won't accept the sign. They want God's sign to be their sign. God has shown them A, B, and C, but they ask for X, Y, and Z. It is a pride issue. It is rebellion. They refuse to submit. They won't cast their crowns before God. They continue to steady their puny little crown upon their big oversized head. Pride is the problem. The sign is sufficient—the death and resurrection of Jesus is enough. But it's not enough for those who refuse to see and hear.

The Right Responses

That is what Jesus will address in the coming parables in chapter 13, and it is what he addresses next in verses 41–45.

Let's look first at verses 41, 42, what I'll label the damning witness of two right responses. After Jesus says, "For just as Jonah was three days and three nights in the belly of the great fish, so will the Son of Man be three days and three nights in the heart of the earth" (v. 40), he follows with, "The men of Nineveh will rise up at the judgment with this generation and condemn it, for they repented at the preaching of Jonah [not the miracles of Jonah, just from hearing his message; so little evidence, and yet so much repentance],[13] and behold, something greater than Jonah is here" (v. 41). That's the first right response. Then comes the second: "The queen of the South will rise up at the judgment with this generation and condemn it, for she came from the ends of the earth to hear the wisdom of Solomon, and behold, something greater than Solomon is here" (v. 42).

Do you see the picture here? Jesus envisions this trial scene on the last day or "at the judgment," as he puts it. There on trial stand the scribes, Pharisees, and those like them who have refused to believe in Jesus despite what they have seen and heard, despite having front row seats to the greatest show on earth. The first witness is called. Will it be Abraham or Moses? No; here come the Ninevites. What? The awful Assyrians?[14] Yes, even the awful Assyrians are valid witnesses because they repented when Jonah (aka Unmerciful

Prophet of the Century) came to town. So the men of Nineveh stand up, walk over to the accused, point a finger, and say, "Guilty as charged."

Then the second witness is called. It is Elijah or Isaiah? No. It's not a man. It's not even a Jew. It's a Gentile woman, "the queen of the South." Jesus loves to use the most unlikely characters to rile up the religious snobs of his day. Do you remember her story? It's recorded in 1 Kings 10. The queen of the South—"the queen of Sheba" as she is called there—heard about Solomon's wisdom but doubted the accuracy of the reports. "No one can be that wise," she thought. "I have to see and hear this man for myself." So she journeyed from Ethiopia. Addis Ababa to Jerusalem is 1,588 miles! And remember Henry Ford wasn't around back then. She traveled all that way, 1 Kings 10:1 tells us, "to test him[Solomon] with hard questions." In this way she was just like the Jewish religious leaders of Jesus' day. They came to test Jesus' wisdom, to ask him tough questions. But once the queen listened to Solomon's words of wisdom, she believed. "There was no more breath in her" is how 1 Kings 10:5 puts it. What a beautiful way to say "she believed." For her, seeing and *hearing* was believing. And then, after she had seen and heard Solomon, like the magi (Matthew 2:1–11), she emptied her pockets and gave some of her treasures to him. Then she worshipped. She said to Solomon, "Blessed be the LORD your God" (1 Kings 10:9). So the good old queen of Sheba, with her awe at and acceptance of Solomon's wisdom, stands up, walks over to the accused, points a finger, and says, "Guilty as charged."

These two right responses provide a damning witness. But so too does Jesus himself. Three times in chapter 12 Jesus has used this phrase of himself—"greater than." In 12:6 he said, I'm "greater than the temple" (i.e., greater than the priesthood and sacrificial system). In 12:41 he said, I'm "greater than Jonah" (i.e., greater than the prophets). And finally in 12:42 he said, I'm "greater than Solomon" (i.e., greater than the kings). In other words, he claims to be *the* prophet, priest, and king.[15] And as such he stands also as *the* judge, saying to the Pharisees and all like them, "Guilty as charged." For while pagans understood the truth when it reached their ears, the teachers of the Torah refused to come, refused to repent, refused to stop their mouths, quiet their questions, step back, and look and listen and admit, "Truly this must be the Messiah, the Son of the living God." Guilty. Guilty. Guilty.

A Warning about Neutralism

But what is Jesus getting at in verses 43–45, with this bit about the eight spirits? Let's take a step back and follow the flow of the whole text. I'll put it in question/answer form.

First, in verses 38–40 we have the question, what's the sign? Answer: God's sign is the sign of Jonah (Jesus' death and resurrection).

Second, in verses 41, 42 we have the question, how should we respond to this sign? Answer: Be like the men of Nineveh and that woman from the south. Repent and come to Christ. Unless you want to stand guilty at the judgment, journey to Jesus.

Third and finally, in verses 43–45 we have the question, what if I don't repent and believe? What if I just stay where I am? To this our Lord replies in essence, "Religion won't save you from the final judgment. Outward reform will not do. And neutrality toward me is not neutral. The choice is this: (a) stay with this evil generation or (b) embrace Easter."

Just listen to what our Lord says in verses 43–45. Listen to how he illustrates his answer:

> When the unclean spirit has gone out of a person, it passes through waterless places seeking rest, but finds none. Then it says, "I will return to my house from which I came." And when it comes, it finds the house empty, swept, and put in order. Then it goes and brings with it seven other spirits more evil than itself, and they enter and dwell there, and the last state of that person is worse than the first. So also will it be with this evil generation.

It took me a while to get my head around what Jesus is saying here. While he is talking about a person and a generation (a group of persons from one time period), it helped me to envision "the house" here as the temple, and then that house being "swept" clean and "put in order" as the time when Jesus cleansed the temple. For at least one day or moment, the demon, if you will, had been expelled. The house was empty of evil. But will it be filled with faith in Christ? If not, the demon will soon return, and that demon won't be alone; seven others will be with him—a perfection of evil, so to speak. And "the last state" will be "worse than the first" (cf. 2 Peter 2:20). There is nothing worse than a Pharisee—an outwardly clean/inwardly unclean person.

Here Jesus calls those who won't repent an "evil generation," which serves as an inclusio to this text (in v. 39 and v. 49). Those who, after hearing and seeing sufficient evidence, refuse to repent and commit to Christ are guilty. Neutrality is not neutral. Neutrality toward Jesus is disbelief, and as we have seen in Matthew, disbelief is treason, the worst evil of all.

A Harmless Holiday?

This text teaches about Easter and the evil generation. We have Easter—the sign of Jesus' death and *resurrection*, and we have the "evil generation"—that is, any group of people at any time who will not repent as the Ninevites did and will not come to the King like the queen of Sheba did, any group that will not recognize, acknowledge, and live like Jesus is Lord.

Easter is indeed a happy holiday—a day filled with pastel colors, sweet smells, lovely lilies, and cute little girls dressed so prettily. But it's not a harmless holiday. It may not have any betrayal or blood, no cross or nails, but it still has some teeth to it (see Acts 17:30, 31). Easter is not as harmless as a cute, fluffy, big-eyed bunny. It's as dangerous as a tiger. To a world looking for signs for and from God, God has given his sign to the world—the one and only, sufficient sign, the sign of Jonah. And for those who are willing and able to see it and believe it, Easter is a day to repent and rejoice that Christ the Lord is risen.

36

Focus on the Family

MATTHEW 12:46–50

USUALLY WHEN I AM STUDYING A TEXT for a sermon I look first for what Martyn Lloyd-Jones called "the great theme." The great theme is just the main theme, but I prefer the word "great" because it reminds me that the theological truth emphasized in a particular portion of Scripture is great, eminent, extraordinary, and important!

With such a short and straightforward text as we have here, it didn't take me long to find the great theme. The great theme is that *a relationship with Jesus takes priority over every other relationship, even the relationship with one's family.* We might say that what Jesus said in 10:37a is illustrated here—"Whoever loves father or mother more than me is not worthy of me." The abbreviated version is, *Jesus first.*

Matthew has slowly been building to this pivotal point of calling the readers of this Gospel to make a decision to put Christ first in their lives. We've seen the push to this point of decision especially in the most recent context where Jesus claimed to be greater than the temple and Solomon. So although other voices swirl in the air—the negative voices of the Pharisees, the confused voices of the crowd, and even the concerned voices of Jesus' mother and brothers—we need to listen to the beloved Son. We need to listen to what Jesus has to say about our relationship with him being of preeminent importance.

Even the "Holy Family" Was outside the Household of Faith

In this passage we will see two seemingly roundabout ways that Jesus gets to this great theme. First, in verses 46–48 he teaches that at this point in his ministry even his family is *outside* the household of faith.

We read in verse 46, "While he was still speaking to the people, behold, his mother and his brothers stood outside, asking to speak to him." Then we come to verse 47. Wait a minute—there is no verse 47! This verse is not included in the ESV because some of the more reliable Greek manuscripts of the New Testament do not contain it. We have over 5,000 Greek manuscripts of the New Testament from different times and places, and there are relatively few variants.[1] However, from time to time there is a slight mistake in the copying process—someone forgot to copy a letter, a word, or something small like that. Other times, like our verse 47, someone decided to add a sentence. (This doesn't happen very often.) Some scribe copying these verses thought the words "he replied to the man who told him" didn't make sense unless this "man" was first introduced, so he inserted, "Someone told him, 'Your mother and your brothers are standing outside, asking to speak to you.'" Now, whatever you think of this insertion, please note that whether this verse is inserted or not makes absolutely no theological difference. It basically repeats the action of verse 46. It is also quite close to Mark 3:32b.

These sorts of differences (called textual variants) are what some unbelievers today make a big deal about—"The Bible is full of errors." Not so. The next time you hear that, say, "Really, what kind of errors? Can you show me these errors?" And if they take you to 12:47 walk them through what I just walked you through and explain to them that the manuscript evidence for the New Testament is the most reliable of any ancient document.[2]

Anyway, let's get back to verse 46 and then on to verses 48–50:

> While he was still speaking to the people, behold, his mother and his brothers stood outside, asking to speak to him. But he replied to the man who told him, "Who is my mother, and who are my brothers?" And stretching out his hand toward his disciples, he said, "Here are my mother and my brothers! For whoever does the will of my Father in heaven is my brother and sister and mother."

Jesus' family comes up to the house that Jesus is apparently in (see 13:1; cf. Mark 3:20), they inquire of him, someone goes into the house and tells him, and then Jesus responds not to his family directly, but to "the man" and (most importantly) to his disciples who are within arm's reach. He wants them especially to listen to what he has to say. His reply is, "Who is my mother, and who are my brothers?" (v. 48).

With this reply, he is not being cute or ignorant. He knows he wasn't dropped from Heaven into the manger at Bethlehem. He knows that Mary is his mother. He knows that Joseph, his earthly father, has died (that's what most scholars surmise). And he knows he has sisters (13:56), who are not named in Matthew, and brothers, who are named—James, Joseph, Simon, and Judas (13:55). Jesus knew he had half-sisters and half-brothers.

I say as an aside that the mention of "brothers" here does not fare well for the Roman Catholic dogma of the perpetual virginity of Mary—that after Jesus' birth she remained a virgin for her whole life. Sure, "brothers" can have a broader meaning. In Acts 22:1 Paul addresses his Jewish brethren as "brothers and fathers." Such terms of Jewish fellowship were transferred to Christian fellowship, which we see not only in the New Testament epistles but throughout Matthew, and "brother" or "brothers" is used a number of places in this way,[3] including verses 49, 50. But the word "brothers" in verse 48, as it is used in eleven other places in Matthew,[4] means blood brothers. This is evident to most who look into the matter.[5] Even the distinguished Roman Catholic Biblical scholar Daniel Harrington notes in his commentary on Matthew (and he mentions nothing about this Catholic dogma except this), "It is doubtful that Matthew knew the tradition of the perpetual virginity of Mary."[6] Indeed.

I was a devout Roman Catholic for much of my life. I don't have an axe to grind, but I'm addressing this now because that's my background and I notice these things. When I read "brothers," I say, "What? Jesus had brothers?" But I've included it here to say that the exegesis of Scripture must determine doctrine, and thus if Jesus had brothers, then Mary was not a perpetual virgin, which means earlier in Matthew when we read that Joseph "took his wife, but knew her not *until* she had given birth to a son" (1:24b, 25a), the word "until" means what it always means.

Let's return our focus to verses 46–49. Why is Jesus' family there in the first place? Matthew does not explain. He just tells us they are "outside." That's an important spatial and theological position. Jesus and his disciples are inside. Mary and Jesus' brothers are still outside. They are likely outside because they haven't been following him like the disciples have.

While Matthew seems to indicate their indecision, Mark and John tell us that at this point Jesus' family was not "in complete sympathy" with Jesus' ministry.[7] In fact, in John 7:1–5, which comes after Jesus has fed the 5,000, walked on water, and done many other miracles, we learn that his brothers wanted Jesus to leave town because they feared for his life. John then interprets their actions: "For not even his brothers believed in him."[8] In Mark 3:20, 21 we find a similar disposition of disbelief. Jesus' family wants to seize him before the authorities do. Perhaps they know of the Pharisees' plot to destroy him (12:14), and they want to put a stop to it. That is why they are knocking on the door.

So when Matthew says they are "outside," he means they are outsiders. That is, they don't understand that Jesus' mission is the cross. Even Mary, as faithful as she was thirty years ago in the story, like John the Baptist in prison (see 11:1–24), struggles to make sense of the Suffering Servant, that the Messiah's mission is the cross, that her own flesh and blood would die. She didn't want him to die.

And so when Jesus says, "Who is my mother?" as harsh as that might sound to us, it is a far tamer sentence than he will use for Peter: "Get behind me, Satan!" (16:23a). But both Peter then and Mary have their minds set not "on the things of God, but on the things of man" (16:23b); both were on rescue missions to save Jesus from the ultimate rescue mission.

The great theme of this whole passage is *Jesus first*. However, the first sub-point is this ironic bit about the "holy family"—Mary and the brothers—being outside the household of faith. Sure, they are not as far outside as the Pharisees or even the crowd, but they are outside.

There are three applications of that.

First, if Jesus' family showed confusion and concern and perhaps even hostility toward Jesus and the gospel, we Christians today should not be surprised if unbelievers in our families think we are out of minds, or as Jesus made clear in his "Sermon on Suffering Mission" (9:35—11:1), if mother or brother rise up against us to persecute us (10:21), if "a person's enemies [become] those of his own household" (10:36). We might express this first application as, don't be surprised by family division and derision. (Or, more visual than that, with Christ at the center, don't be surprised if the nuclear family explodes!)

The second application is this: give it time. If you have a family member who does not believe in Jesus right now, give it time. For this isn't the last time we see Jesus' family, is it? Michelangelo's famous *Pieta* pictures Mary holding her son, Jesus, after his death. And while the Gospels don't portray that, John does say she was present at the crucifixion: "When Jesus saw his mother . . . standing nearby, he said to his mother, 'Woman, behold, your son! [John]' . . . '[John], behold, your mother!'" (John 19:26, 27). John is commanded to take care of her. You see, Mary would look to the cross of Christ literally. She was right there looking. And spiritually, on that day or soon after, she would rejoice in God her Savior.

After the resurrection and on the Day of Pentecost, when the Holy Spirit came in power upon the church, who do we find *inside* the upper room, with Jesus' disciples? "All these [the twelve apostles minus Judas] with one accord were devoting themselves to prayer, together with the women and *Mary the mother of Jesus, and his brothers*" (Acts 1:14). Isn't that wonderful? Through faith in their resurrected Lord, these outsiders in Matthew 12 have become insiders in Acts 1. Through faith they became part of the true family of God. Jesus' mother became his "mother," his brothers his "brothers."

What happened when the wind of God breathed upon that room? That family preached Jesus as Lord, Jesus' brother James most notably becoming the head of the church in Jerusalem (see Acts 15:13–21) and writing the epistle that bears his name[9] and begins, "James, a servant of God and of the Lord Jesus Christ" (James 1:1a). That is a humble admission for a brother.

The third application is this: putting Jesus first is incompatible with an overly high veneration of Mary, James, Peter, John the Baptist, or anyone else.

I hear the ecumenical mumblings and grumblings. "Oh, Pastor, give it a rest. You've already debunked the perpetual virginity of Mary. Please leave the poor papists alone." No, I won't. I'm not beating a dead horse. I'm merely trying to kick a running one, a horse very much alive and well and galloping quite fast, even through my own town.

The Protestant Reformation was first and foremost a reform of worship. What should be the forms of worship? But more importantly, whom should we worship? To whom should we pray? Should we pray to Mary and the saints, or only to God through Jesus? The Protestant Reformers were willing to die over the issue of right worship. But have you heard any Catholic-Protestant debate lately? The debaters don't debate these days. They play theological patty-cake. We'll give a little room here, you give a little room there, and by the end of the evening everyone is holding hands. This happens while poor Truth has been dropped to the floor, kicking and screaming, pleading for someone to pick her up.

The Protestant Reformers were willing to die over the issue of idolatry. But we Protestants today offer no protest when the devout Catholic down the street offers up a rosary, praying, "Holy Mary, Mother of God, pray for us sinners," or when someone prays the popular *Memorare*:

> Remember, O most gracious Virgin Mary that never was it known that anyone who fled to your protection, implored your help, or sought Your intercession was left unaided. Inspired with this confidence, we fly to you, O Virgin of virgins, our Mother. To you we come; before you we stand, sinful and sorrowful. O Mother of the Word Incarnate, despise not our petitions, but in your mercy, hear and answer us.[10]

That is not mere veneration, as would be proper veneration for certain men or women of God. This prayer *to God-like Mary* is idolatry.

Do we find any such prayer in the Bible? Most certainly not! No one prays to Moses or David or Abraham. No one prays to Peter or Paul or Mary. We are to praise God and pray only to God. Read the whole New Testament. Read the apostolic fathers. Even read the church fathers carefully on this issue.[11]

The Mary of the New Testament is a woman to be emulated, not adored. As Matthew is pointing out, she shared the same flaws as Peter, John the Baptist, and James, and yet like them and the heroes of faith listed in Hebrews 11 she ran the race. She has opened the running lane for us so we might run the race set before us, looking to Christ Jesus, the author and perfecter of our faith.

So Jesus first means we are to worship God alone. That's a real modern-day implication and application of this text.

Blood Is Not Thicker Than Water

The first thing we have heard from Jesus here is that even his family was *outside* the household of faith. That is the first sub-point of the main point—*Jesus first*. The second sub-point I'll rephrase in this way: blood might be thicker than ordinary water, but the water Jesus has to offer—the water welling up to eternal life, the waters of baptism—is thicker than blood.

We naturally think, "My family is made of up those who are related to me by blood or some legal document. I had no choice in the matter, and I have to stick with them because they are well . . . blood. There is thus a thickness to our relationship." But Jesus is saying, "That is true. You are related to certain people by blood, and there is a certain bond to that. However, the unity of Spirit through faith and baptism is thicker than that. That is, it is more substantial, permanent, strong, and sure."

"Who is my mother, and who are my brothers?" Look again at verses 49, 50. "And stretching out his hand toward his disciples, he said, 'Here are my mother and my brothers! For whoever does the will of my Father in heaven is my brother and sister and mother.'"

With this bold statement Jesus is not breaking family ties but is loosening them. He is not dissolving natural family bonds but is showing the strength of the supernatural family bond. And what is beautiful is that Jesus puts no spiritual value in blood relations or religious heritage. Did you notice that? He doesn't care if your father was the high priest or the Grand Poobah. The kingdom of God is not open to the who's who but to "whoever" (v. 50). Isn't that a refreshing word for a tax collector like Matthew? "Whoever"—Jew/Gentile, man/woman, slave/free, saint/sinner.

Whoever what? Whoever believes? That's what we would expect, right? Does Jesus mean, "whoever believes in him may have eternal life" (John

3:15)? Not here. What is emphasized here, as it is everywhere in Matthew, is *doing*. "Whoever does the will of my Father in heaven"—that's who is in the church, in family fellowship with the Father, "brothers and sisters" in Christ. Whoever *does* God's will.

Matthew is not redefining the Pauline doctrine of justification by faith. He is merely illustrating what that faith alone looks like: it is never alone. Those who are in fellowship with God through faith in Christ *talk* a certain way (12:36, 37), and they *walk* a certain way (5:3—7:27). Their words and works show they are right with God. There may be no *do* in the word *disciple*, but there should be. We somehow need to cram it in there, for *do* or *does* is the disciple's distinctive. So, how is your *doing* doing?

You see, one is not a Christian by a mere profession of faith, church attendance, generous tithing, or baptismal rite. One is a Christian by being a "doing disciple." So, as Paul perfectly exhorts, "Examine yourselves, to see whether you are in the faith" (2 Corinthians 13:5). Michael Green summarizes this concept well when he writes of Matthew here bringing

> the importance of decision about Jesus to a climax. It is possible to be religious like the Pharisees, and still not be part of the kingdom of God. It is possible to be physically related to the Messiah himself, and still not be part of the kingdom of God. Religious practices and religious pedigree are utterly inadequate to bring anybody into the kingdom. There needs to be an acknowledgment of who Jesus is, and a determined decision to follow him.[12]

That's good. And I'll add to that—not merely a determined decision to follow Jesus, but a disciplined doing of God's will. For as Pierre Bonnard writes, "The essence of discipleship is not mere profession, right doctrine, or even charismatic phenomena, but doing the will of God (7:21–23)."[13]

But what is "the will" of God? It is the will of God to believe in Christ. And it is the will of God to "rejoice always, pray without ceasing, give thanks in all circumstances" (1 Thessalonians 5:16–18), to love not the lusts of the world (1 John 2:15–17; cf. 1 Peter 4:1–5), to "abstain from sexual immorality" (1 Thessalonians 4:3), and to "be subject . . . to every human institution" (1 Peter 2:13–15). Furthermore, it is the will of God (I'll throw in a few family-related ones) to "provide . . . for . . . relatives" in need (1 Timothy 5:8), for elders within the church to "manage [their] own households well" (1 Timothy 3:4; cf. Titus 1:6), for fathers and mothers to raise their children in "the discipline and instruction of the Lord" (Ephesians 6:4), and for children to honor and "obey [their] parents in the Lord" (Ephesians 6:1).

Also, in the context of Matthew 8–12, it is the will of God to follow Jesus, listen to him, rest in him, be in awe of him, and acknowledge him as a king greater than Solomon in all his glory. Putting him first—that is the will of God, and that is what a disciple does.

Our Prayer

When I was wondrously converted to Christ over two decades ago, my sinner's prayer was this: "Jesus, I know you are real. I have never doubted your existence or that you are the Son of God. But I have never asked you to forgive me. Will you please forgive me of my sin and clean me up on the inside, for I am so full of lust and pride. And I promise you that from this day forward I will put you first in my life. I've put you second or third or tenth. But I promise now to put you first."

First above my girlfriend.
First above ambition.
First above school.
First above sports.
First above money.
First above family . . . yes, even above family!

Jesus first. That is what this text teaches. And that is what my prayer was then and what our prayer should be today.

37

The Purpose of Parables

MATTHEW 13:10–17, 34, 35, 51, 52

LET'S PLAY A GAME I'll call "an exercise in ignorance." Sounds like fun, doesn't it? Let's pretend we all live in a remote region of the world where we have never heard any of Jesus' parables before. Let's also pretend that we have recently discovered an ancient parchment in an underground cave that contains what other less remote folks would call the Parable of the Sower. We don't yet know what to call it or what to make of it. However, we sure are curious. So we get one of our language scholars to decipher the text and read it to us. For the first time ever, with fresh eyes and open ears, we hear these words:

> A sower went out to sow. And as he sowed, some seeds fell along the path, and the birds came and devoured them. Other seeds fell on rocky ground, where they did not have much soil, and immediately they sprang up, since they had no depth of soil, but when the sun rose they were scorched. And since they had no root, they withered away. Other seeds fell among thorns, and the thorns grew up and choked them. Other seeds fell on good soil and produced grain, some a hundredfold, some sixty, some thirty. (13:3–8)

That's it. That's the entire text we have.

What would we think about it? A few of us might think it is just a story, a rather short and dull one. The majority might argue that it is part of an ancient instruction manual on gardening, for from the text itself we have a farmer scattering seed on four different surfaces, only one of which produces any kind of grain. We kind of chuckle at the technique, because even though we live far from civilization our modern methods of farming are more advanced.[1] We wouldn't waste seed on rocky surfaces. And we certainly would plow before we sow. But with our lack of chronological snobbery, we surmise that for these ancient unsophisticated people there is some kind of agricultural wisdom here, such as, when sowing seed, avoid hard surfaces, hungry birds, overexposure to the sun, and thorn-infested dirt. That, or something like that, is the lesson, right?

I told you you'd have fun. Well, fun or no fun I hope that through this "exercise in ignorance" you are ignorant no more. I hope you understand that we are so familiar with this parable *and its interpretation* that we often fail to realize that these words of Jesus hold little meaning in and of themselves and neither reflect distinct religious language nor promote any theological conceptions whatsoever. And I hope you also get why it was necessary for Jesus' disciples to gather around him and ask, "What are you talking about? Why don't you speak simply and straightforwardly?" (v. 10, my paraphrase).

In verses 11–17 Jesus tells them why he is talking that way. Parables have two primary purposes: parables conceal and reveal. First, parables *conceal* the truth from those who will not submit to Christ and his rule; and second, parables *reveal* the truth to those who by God's grace will submit to Christ and his rule.

Parables Conceal the Truth

We begin with how parables *conceal the truth* (vv. 11–15).

One of the key words in the last chapter was the word "outside." Jesus' family was standing "outside" (12:46). They did not yet believe. In verse 11 of this passage, Jesus tells his closest disciples, to those who are in a sense "inside," that "the secrets of the kingdom of heaven" have been given or revealed to them, "but to them [the crowds and the Jewish religious leaders, 'those *outside*' is how Mark phrases it (Mark 4:11)] it has not been given." Then Jesus goes on to say:

> For to the one who has, more will be given,[2] and he will have an abundance, but from the one who has not, even what he has will be taken away. *This is why I speak to them in parables*, because seeing they do not see, and hearing they do not hear, nor do they understand. Indeed, in their case the prophecy of Isaiah is fulfilled that says:
>
> "'You will indeed hear but never understand,
> and you will indeed see but never perceive.'
> For this people's heart has grown dull,
> and with their ears they can barely hear,
> and their eyes they have closed,
> lest they should see with their eyes
> and hear with their ears

> and understand with their heart
> and turn, and I would heal them."[3] (13:12–15)

That is quite a statement, isn't it? Jesus catches us off guard here—"Wait, Lord, what are you saying here? Really?" It would have been fine if Jesus clarified that he did not tell parables for the same reason that modern preachers tell stories, to attract our attention or to make abstract ideas more concrete.[4] And it would have been fine if Jesus explained that parables, like miracles, will not produce faith by themselves. It would have been real nice if Jesus just said something like that. But for him to state that his parables were told in order to hide the truth, to conceal the mystery of the kingdom in order to prevent "outsiders" from coming in to find spiritual healing, seems to undermine his merciful mission to bring restoration for all who repent of their sins.

So what are we to make of these startling, almost contradictory statements? Are we to see these lovely anecdotes of Jesus that we enjoy reading to our children as somehow a means of predetermined divine judgment? Are we to see the parables as a means of punishment for those who persistently refuse to believe? Well, yes, this is precisely how we are to understand one important purpose of Christ's parables.[5] In these verses we are unashamedly presented with the tension, often given in Scripture, between divine sovereignty regarding *election* and human responsibility regarding *rejection*.

It does not matter with what theological grid you come to this text. We all have to admit that the disciples are freely and graciously "given . . . the secrets of the kingdom," while others are not (that's divine sovereignty in election). Yet, in the middle section (vv. 13–17)—with its quotation of Isaiah 6:9, 10—and especially in Christ's forthcoming interpretation of the Parable of the Sower in verses 18–23, the emphasis falls on human responsibility or culpability.[6]

What I mean is this: if the saving message of God has been freely offered to all who have come in contact with Christ (the "whoever" of 12:50), and if the gospel has been scattered like seed as Jesus traveled throughout the region of Galilee preaching the gospel of the kingdom, then the Parable of the Sower is perfectly positioned in Matthew's Gospel to explain why only a few people respond and enter, while many others do not. Although neither the parable nor its interpretation explain why people respond the way they do, the parable as explained by Jesus does "identify the source of the problem [which is bad soil]—human hardness, shallowness, and self-indulgence."[7] It is like Romans 1:24, 26, 28, where three times we are told "God gave them up"—that is, God gave them over to their sin. He let them do what they wanted to do.

As C. S. Lewis memorably put it, "There are only two kinds of people in the end: those who say to God, 'Thy will be done,' and those to whom God says . . . 'Thy will be done.'"[8]

The chilling truth of verses 13–15 is that, like those in Isaiah's day who repeatedly rebelled against their Creator and Redeemer (see Isaiah 1–5),[9] those in Jesus' day who have "seen" Jesus and "heard" his message, yet unrelentingly reject him, are punished by only "seeing" and "hearing" enough to find God's revelation in these parables to be nothing more than unsolvable riddles.[10] For those "spiritually calcified" by persistent disbelief and disobedience, God's Word in Isaiah's prophecies and Christ's parables serves only to increase their blindness and deafness.[11] Instead of being windows through which unbelievers could see the light of salvation in the face of Jesus (2 Corinthians 4:6), these parables become closed doors that seal the entrance into the eternal kingdom of heaven.[12]

The Two Sides of Stained-Glass Windows

When I pastored a church in Batavia, Illinois, for our Sunday morning services we rented an old Roman Catholic church building, now owned by the Park District. It was a beautiful limestone building with spectacular Christ-centered stained-glass windows.

Every Sunday morning as we worshipped together and as the sun would strike the glass, one glass pane depicted Christ's death, another pane his resurrection and ascension, and then in the back, over the choir loft, there was a picture of Jesus surrounded by angels, portraying his glorious heavenly reign and also his eminent return. Each detail of every window—whether subtle like the three conjoining circles representing the Trinity or the striking details of a bloodied white lamb sitting atop a book with seven seals—shared a gospel story or depicted a deep theological truth.

On the inside of the building, when that bright sun shone through, we could see these creative depictions of the person and work of Christ. But at the same time of day if you were standing outside and looked up at the glass it was dull, gray, and lifeless. You might be able to make out some of the shapes, but you would see nothing of the brilliant color and the artistry and intricacy of the images. You have to be inside to see that.

So too with the parables of Jesus: the secrets of the kingdom have been revealed to those on the inside, but for those on the outside they are still concealed. Like the outside of those stained-glass windows, Christ's parables conceal facts about his identity and mission from those who refuse to believe, and like the inside of those same windows, Christ's parables reveal aspects of the kingdom to those who seek to know him and to submit to his Lordship over their lives.

Parables Reveal the Truth

So parables conceal and reveal. We turn now to their revelation, the second purpose of the parables: they *reveal* the truth to those who by God's grace will submit to Christ and his rule.

Jesus says to his disciples, "[B]lessed are your eyes, for they see, and your ears, for they hear. For truly, I say to you, many prophets and righteous people longed to see what you see, and did not see it, and to hear what you hear, and did not hear it" (vv. 16, 17).

To those on the inside, so to speak, those who are part of the new family of God—Jesus' brothers and sisters by faith—parables reveal once-hidden truths. Parables unveil what Jesus calls "the secrets of the kingdom of heaven" (v. 11).

To most of us secrets are a precious commodity. If someone comes up to you and whispers in your ear, "I want to tell you a secret," I assume that you are immediately engaged with this person and almost instantaneously feel a sense of intimacy that may not have existed before the notion of sharing some secret was communicated. If someone wants to share a secret with me, I recognize that this person is likely going to share with me something he or she is unwilling to share with others, something special that he or she trusts me to keep. So most of the time, secrets are special to us.

As a special gift Jesus shares certain secrets with his closest followers, what he calls "the secrets of the kingdom of heaven." To them and *only* to them he says, "To you it has been *given* to know the secrets of the kingdom of heaven." Although we are not told specifically the nature of the secret, from what these disciples have "seen" and "heard" we can safely assume that "the secrets of the kingdom of heaven" concern the rule of God revealed in the person, works, and words of Jesus. And from what Jesus says in verses 34, 35, "the secrets of the kingdom of heaven" are similar to Paul's term in Ephesians, "the mystery of the gospel" (Ephesians 6:19; cf. 1:9; 3:1–10; 5:32; Romans 16:25–27). That which has been "hidden since the foundation of the world" (13:35) is slowly coming to light, this gospel about Jesus—the one who comes to suffer, die, rise again, and commission his church to take the good news to all the world, breaking down the walls of hostility between Jews and Gentiles.

In Jesus "the plan of the mystery hidden for ages in God" (Ephesians 3:9) comes to light. It is a riddle no more. The secret is out.

> In him [Christ] we have redemption through his blood, the forgiveness of our trespasses, according to the riches of his [God's] grace, which he lavished upon us, in all wisdom and insight *making known to us the mystery* [the secret] *of his will*, according to his purpose, which he set forth in Christ as a plan for the fullness of time, to unite all things in him, things in heaven and things on earth. (Ephesians 1:7–10)

That sounds a lot like 28:19, doesn't it? It echoes and expands it.

What was once hidden to the world, and still remains hidden to the crowd and the Jewish religious leaders and to any who follow in their faithless footsteps, God has now revealed to a former tax collector, a few former fishermen, and anyone who is humble enough to heed the call of Christ and put on his gentle yoke. Parables conceal, but they also *reveal*.

So What? Implications and Applications

So parables conceal and parables reveal—so what? If you are not seeing or hearing correctly, as you hear these parables explained in the following chapters, let them not be a means of God's punishment, but rather a way in which he penetrates your hard heart. When you hear the words of warnings that end many of the parables, warnings like "In that place there will be weeping and gnashing of teeth" (13:42b, 50; cf. vv. 30, 40), take it as a challenge and not a conclusion, an invitation to life and not a sentence of death.

Let these parables be the trumpet sound and the glaring light that wake you from your spiritual slumber and push you out of your comfortable bed and say, "Time to get up. Wake up. Smell the espresso. See and hear that the kingdom of heaven is at hand."

Gratitude for Grace

That's my application for those who don't believe in Jesus. But for those of us who do believe, our first application is simply *gratitude for grace*. We should be grateful for the gift mentioned in verses 11, 12—that we can see and hear and believe. We should be grateful that though we were once deaf to the gospel, now we hear, and though we were once blind to the kingdom, now we see. Gratitude for grace!

We could spend a lifetime trying to answer a question Scripture does not fully answer and that I think may never be answered (even when we are glorified in Heaven): "Why doesn't God save everyone?[13] Why has this gift of salvation been given to me but not to ____________?" We could spend an eternity on that tough question. But here we are to dwell not on the privation of the gift, but on the gift itself that should bring wonder, awe, and gratitude.

Listen and remember: by nature we are all "children of wrath" (Ephesians 2:3). So, what kind of a gift does a child of wrath get to open on Christmas? Any gift? What do those who have been naughty get in their stockings? Nothing. Not even black coal. Who of us deserves to know the secrets of the kingdom of heaven? Who of us deserves to open the gift of the gospel of grace?

And yet the gift has been given—"while we were still sinners, Christ died for us" (Romans 5:8). For this reason the fact that we can hear the parables and understand them should lead us to doxology.

> Oh, the depth of the riches and wisdom and knowledge of God! How unsearchable are his judgments and how inscrutable his ways!
>
> "For who has known the mind of the Lord,
> or who has been his counselor?"
> "Or who has given a gift to him
> that he might be repaid?"
>
> For from him and through him and to him are all things. To him be glory forever. Amen. (Romans 11:33–36)

Amen! The parables should lead us to praise (cf. Ephesians 1:11, 12).

After Thomas saw Christ's wounds and heard his voice, Jesus said, "Blessed are those who have not seen and yet have believed" (John 20:29b). Do you feel blessed today? Can you say to Jesus with awe and gratitude, "My Lord and my God!" (John 20:28b). Abel and Abraham, Sarah and Samuel, Jacob and Jephthah, and thousands of others (Hebrews 11; cf. John 8:56; 1 Peter 1:10, 11) longed to know Christ the way we know him, to hear his words read and explained each Sunday, and to sense his presence and power through the Holy Spirit. We are a privileged people.

Given to Give

"The hearing ear and the seeing eye, the Lord has made them both" (Proverbs 20:12). For that we ought to be grateful. That's one application. The other application is this: we have been blessed to bless, or perhaps said better, we have been *given to give*. We have been given God's grace as a gift, a gift to be given to others.

I get this application from verses 51, 52. In verse 51, after he finished his parables, Jesus asked, "Have you understood all these things?" They replied in essence, "Yes, somehow. We see. We hear. We understand." Jesus then replied that school is still in session: "Therefore every scribe who has been trained for the kingdom of heaven is like a master of a house, who brings out of his treasure [who brings out the gospel of the kingdom, cf. v. 44] what is new and what is old" (v. 52). Here Jesus says not only, "Have you been given?" but "Are you giving?" If you have been given understanding (if you grasp the secrets of the kingdom), if you have become a "scribe" trained in the truths of the kingdom, then you must share your treasures with others. You must bring the treasures out and share them. For "to whom much was given . . . much [is] required" (Luke 12:48).

We have been given much indeed! We have been given the gospel; thus it is required of us freely to give this good news to others.[14] We are to act like Stephen in Acts 7. Before he was martyred, Stephen spoke from the old revelation about the new revelation in Jesus—the good news, but also the new news that in the man Jesus Christ the temple has been replaced. We now come to God through Christ. Our sins are forgiven through faith in him. Like Stephen, like the Twelve, and like all who call themselves disciples of Jesus, we have been given the gift of salvation so we might give to others.

Let us not grow weary in doing so. Let us not grow weary in our gratitude for the gift. And let us not grow weary in giving the gift, in sharing the treasure of Jesus, for that is part of the purpose of these parables.

38

Three Ways of Disaster, Three Grades of Glory

MATTHEW 13:1–9, 18–23 (WITH 57, 58)

> Earth's crammed with heaven,
> And every common bush afire with God:
> But only he who sees, takes off his shoes,
> The rest sit round it, and pluck blackberries. . . .

Those are a few lines from Elizabeth Barrett Browning's lengthy poem "Aurora Leigh" (1857).[1]

I begin with those words because they remind me of Jesus' parables, in which he took what was of earth and crammed it with Heaven. That is, he used ordinary, everyday, earthly things like lamps, doors, fig trees, vines, wheat, sheep, goats, pearls, and even seeds and soil to explain that every common bush was "afire with God." To him common characters—a prodigal son, an unjust judge, a foolish builder, a bridegroom, a watchman, a thief that comes in the night—could be used to explain the mystery of the kingdom of heaven. And yet that mystery, as we saw in the last sermon, was revealed to some and concealed from others. Some people—the crowds in Jesus' day and the crowds in our today—don't see Jesus for who he is. So instead of taking off their shoes, as Moses did before the burning presence of God, they just sit around and "pluck blackberries." Seeing they do not see.

In this chapter, with the Parable of the Sower before us, there will be no plucking of blackberries allowed. Instead we will stand with shoes to the side, ears open, and eyes focused, to listen as Jesus brings Heaven down to earth so we might be brought to God. Below is our Lord's explanation of the parable he gave in verses 1–9:

> Hear then the parable of the sower: When anyone hears the word of the kingdom and does not understand it, the evil one comes and snatches away what has been sown in his heart. This is what was sown along the path. As for what was sown on rocky ground, this is the one who hears the word and immediately receives it with joy, yet he has no root in himself, but endures for a while, and when tribulation or persecution arises on account of the word, immediately he falls away. As for what was sown among thorns, this is the one who hears the word, but the cares of the world and the deceitfulness of riches choke the word, and it proves unfruitful. As for what was sown on good soil, this is the one who hears the word and understands it. He indeed bears fruit and yields, in one case a hundredfold, in another sixty, and in another thirty. (vv. 18–23)

The Sower, the Seeds, and the Soils

When I sat down to study this passage, I first made a simple chart with two columns. In the left column I listed the main details in the parable as given in verses 3–9. I listed *the sower*, *the seeds*, and the *four soils*. Then, in the right column, looking at verses 18–23, I listed how Jesus interpreted these various details.

In doing this I first discovered that the "sower" mentioned in verse 3 is not identified. Having noticed this omission, and believing there was some purpose for it, I concluded the "sower" must symbolize one or all of the following. It could be that the "sower" refers to God, for at times this language is used of him in the Old Testament. Or it could be that the "sower" refers to Jesus, for when Jesus explains the Parable of the Weeds he says in 13:37, "The one who sows the good seed is the Son of Man." Or it could be that the "sower" represents any preacher, parent, or Sunday school teacher—that is, anyone and everyone who sows the word. Our Lord's lack of interpretation regarding the "sower," which I think is intentional, allows for an expanded application. The "sower" could include or does include God, his Son, and any and all gospel workers.

As I worked my way down this chart, I noticed next that the "seeds" (cf. Isaiah 55:10, 11) mentioned in this parable symbolized "the word" (six times) and more specifically "the word of the kingdom" (v. 19). This is just Jesus' way of saying "the gospel"—the good news to the nations of the establishment of Jesus' sovereign rule by means of his death and resurrection. The "seed" is the gospel.

So we have the "sower" and the "seeds." Next we come to the "soils."

This parable is often called the Parable of the Sower and the Seeds or the Parable of the Sower. This title obviously comes from Jesus himself in verse 18. However, verse 18 really just sets the stage for what follows. While the sower and the seeds are mentioned first, it is the four different *soils* and their receptivity or lack thereof that dominates the rest of the parable. And this is why some have relabeled this text the Parable of the Soils (although I think the title the Parable of the Surfaces might be even better).

Obviously there are four soils, or four types of surfaces, and three are bad and one is good. Because of that three-to-one division, many people have taught this parable pessimistically, dividing it into four parts, spending equal time on each soil (so three-fourths negative, one-fourth positive). However, because I'm convinced that the last soil in our text is the pinnacle of the parable[2]—the ultimate reason for the parable, the point of the parable—I want to give the first three soils half our time, so we can give the last soil the other half of the chapter as well.

Long, long ago in a land far, far away there was another Christian preacher who thought the way I thought, or perhaps I'm thinking the way he thought. Anyway, in the fifth century Cyril of Alexandria spoke of this parable in this way: "Christ has recounted the three ways of disaster, and . . . the three grades of glory."[3] (I don't know if the three grades of glory is exactly right, but at the very least you see the balance.) Soils one through three represent the "three ways of disaster," and soil four (getting equal emphasis) represents "the three grades of glory."

Three Ways of Disaster

With that division in mind, we'll start where Jesus does, with *the three ways of disaster* (vv. 19–22).

Before we look at the three ways of disaster represented by these three sorry soils, I want us to grasp that there are two different perspectives to take in interpreting Jesus' interpretation, both of which are necessary. One perspective is to view *the three ways of disaster* from an internal perspective, from the soils' point of view, so to speak. That is, identifying the problem in the soil's hardness, shallowness, and self-indulgence,[4] what James Montgomery Boice called the hard heart, the shallow heart, and the strangled heart.[5] Another perspective is to view *the three ways of disaster* from an external perspective, identifying the problem from the outside—in terms of Satan (the birds of v. 4), persecutions, trials, and temptations.

With that in mind, in looking then at the first soil, the soil "along the path" (v. 4), if we are looking from both perspectives, we should see that both demonic warfare and human hardheartedness are the reasons why the seed is swiftly gobbled up. On the one hand, Satan is to blame, for like a hungry bird he "comes and snatches away what has been sown" (v. 19). On the other hand, the only reason Satan can consume such seed is because the seed never went below the surface; it stayed atop the hard ground.

Now, who in the Gospel of Matthew represents this soil? Of course, we think of the Pharisees. They certainly fit nicely into this soil sample. At first they are curious about Jesus. Along with the crowd, at the beginning they think, "Can this be the Christ? Let's give him a good look." But it doesn't take long for their hearts to harden. When they hear Jesus say that he has the authority to forgive sins, their hearts begin to tighten; and when they see him welcome sinners to table fellowship, their hearts start to slowly freeze; and finally, once he breaks their sacred laws by healing a man on the Sabbath, their small, cold hearts become calcified, as hard as a floor. And the seed still sitting there right atop their hard hearts is an easy swallow for Satan.

However, the Pharisees are not alone in this category. Many others fit in as well, even those people of Jesus' own hometown: "And when Jesus had finished these parables, he went away from there, and coming to his hometown [Nazareth] he taught them in their synagogue, so that they were astonished, and said, 'Where did this man get this wisdom and these mighty works?'" (vv. 53, 54). Here the seed of the gospel is planted, but listen to the hardness of heart, watch the arteries start to clog.

Wait a minute, they say.

> "Is not this the carpenter's son? Is not his mother called Mary? And are not his brothers James and Joseph and Simon and Judas? And are not all his sisters with us? Where then did this [ordinary and familiar] man get all these things [this power and wisdom]?" (vv. 55, 56)

Their mind-set was, "Jesus sure acts like the Messiah, and he sure speaks like the Messiah, but he can't possibly be the Messiah because he's one of us. He is a poor boy from the backstreets of the Bronx. 'Can anything good come out of Nazareth?'" (John 1:46).

Then look at verse 57. Here that devilish bird grabs the seed, gives it one shake, and down it goes. "And they took offense at him" (v. 57). What's going on here? They go from awe to offense and "unbelief" (v. 58). "He came to his own [his own town], and his own [towns]people did not receive him" (John 1:11). So I want you to see in 12:46–50, which comes right before the seven parables, and here in 13:53–58, which comes right after them, that we find this unpleasant inclusio: Jesus is rejected by house and home, by his own household (his mother and brothers) and also by his own hometown (his fellow townspeople).[6]

That's the first soil—human hard-heartedness and satanic swooping.

The second soil is the "rocky ground." "This is the one," as Jesus explains in verses 20, 21, "who hears the word and immediately receives it with joy, yet he has no root in himself, but endures for a while, and when tribulation or persecution arises on account of the word, immediately he falls away." Here we have represented those people whose inward shallowness (they are not hard but shallow) is exposed the moment outward trouble arises. They reject the gospel due to *rootlessness*: "he has no root in himself" (v. 21). When tribulations and persecutions—various sufferings of sorts—arise like the scorching sun (that's the image Jesus gives in v. 6), this shallow "faith" sadly withers away. The same person who "immediately" received the gospel with joy also "immediately . . . falls away" (v. 21).

Years ago I remember hearing a story about Martyn Lloyd-Jones, one of the great preachers of the last century. One day after Lloyd-Jones preached a powerful sermon, an unbeliever came up to him and said, "Dr. Lloyd-Jones, I must tell you that if you would have given an altar call at the end of your message I certainly would have come forward. I would have believed." Lloyd-Jones replied, "If you don't want Jesus five minutes after the service is over, then I assure you that you didn't truly want him at any point during my sermon." Now perhaps that is stronger than you would put it. But the point is a good one.

The true test of discipleship is not whether or not one received the gospel with joy at some datable moment in history. The true test of discipleship is whether or not one picks up his cross and follows Jesus, not for one day or two weeks or three months or four years, but until Jesus calls him home. The true Christian is not like a cut flower that a husband gives to his wife, a flower quite beautiful and alive for a week, but quite repulsive and dead after the unrelenting sun has beaten down upon it for a month.

Have you ever known someone who has fallen away from the faith? I would imagine most of us have. And why in America, where there is so little persecution, is this true? Right now as you read this chapter, Christians in Sudan, China, and Iran are meeting secretly in homes, hotel rooms, and backrooms of businesses, and other Christians throughout the world are being beaten, tortured, and killed because they will not renounce Jesus Christ. As Blomberg notes, "In the twentieth century there were more martyrs for the Christian faith worldwide than in all nineteen previous centuries of church history combined."[7] So why in America, where there is so little persecution, do so many people fall away from the faith?

Part of the reason comes with the next bad surface—the love of this world (and especially the love of money). However, another part of the blame must be laid on those sloppy, sappy sowers—Christian evangelists who preach a half-seeded gospel, evangelists who never tell their disciples what Jesus repeatedly has been telling us in Matthew—that if you follow him, suffering will follow you. Today's evangelist says, "I need a thousand raised hands as a sign of success and God's blessing," but Jesus says, "Just give me twelve men who are willing to suffer and endure until the end, and I'll change the world." Perseverance through persecutions and triumphing through trials is what is necessary, through the power of God's might. Endurance is part of the basics of Christianity: "But the one who endures to the end will be saved" (10:22; 24:13).[8]

So the first bad surface is "the path" (the person who cannot hold on to the gospel because he is inwardly hard and thus outwardly easy prey). The second bad surface is the "rocky ground" (the person who is so inwardly shallow that he outwardly cannot withstand the testing of his faith). The third bad surface is the thorn-infested soil. Concerning this soil Jesus says, "As for what was sown among thorns, this is the one who hears the word, but the cares of the world and the deceitfulness of riches choke the word, and it proves unfruitful" (v. 22).

The person described is inwardly self-indulgent and thus outwardly choked by worldly concerns. Put differently, this person cares too little about his soul because he cares too much about the world. For him the good seed never grows, but the thorns, which represent his worldly attachments, certainly do. Two thorns in particular grow, and they grow from the same root system. One thorn is "the cares of the world," and the other is "the deceitfulness of riches."

Both have at their root the love of money. Both have to do with not trusting God always and ultimately. You cannot serve both God and money. If you trust and treasure money above all, when you don't have enough of it your heart will be flooded with all sorts of anxieties. But if you trust and treasure money above all and you have a lot of it, then your problems are solved, right? Wrong! Then you have a bigger problem: you won't see your need for God and his grace, provision, and salvation.

I can count on my fingers and toes, with ten fingers and ten toes left, how many money-lovers live like the lilies—that is, in carefree joy, trusting in their heavenly Father for everything! Money, money, money, money . . . MONEY. It can choke your spiritual life.

At the end of the last century, historian Martin Marty called evangelicals "the most worldly people in America."[9] What a condemnation! But he's right. Listen to this statistic. Each Sunday evangelicals around American sing songs like "I Surrender All," but 80 percent of us give on average only between 2 and 3 percent of our income, and 20 percent don't give anything at all.

Let's do the math. The average household income (usually two incomes) in the city where I live is $120,000 a year. Two to 3 percent is somewhere around $3,000 out of pocket given to others. These are people who claim to be Christians. Where on earth is the rest of the money going? I'll tell you where it's going—it's lining their (your?) coffins. You can't take it with you to Heaven, but you sure will take it with you to Hell. Don't think you can trust money and get into Heaven. Don't think you can treasure earthly treasures and still inherit the eternal pleasures of God. "Friendship with the world is enmity with God" (James 4:4). If money is your best friend, God is not.

I know riches are not the problem.[10] The heart is the problem. I know a rich man can get into the kingdom of heaven, but I also know how hard it is. Watch out for riches; they can be deceitful. They will love you one day and leave you the next. No, they will love you one day and choke you the next. Money, money, money, money . . . MONEY. You wouldn't sell Jesus for thirty silver coins, would you? Or would you?

Three Grades of Glory

Satan. Suffering. Stuff. The hard heart. The shallow heart. The strangled heart. There are three ways of disaster. But (praise be to God!) there are also three grades of glory. Take off your shoes. Finally we've come to verse 23. Let's feel the holy heat of this verse. "As for what was sown on good soil," our Lord explains, "this is the one who hears the word and understands it. He indeed bears fruit and yields, in one case a hundredfold, in another sixty, and in another thirty."

It is true, as Jesus said about the wide road to destruction (7:13), that the majority of people who have indeed heard the gospel have rejected it, due in part, as this parable tells us, to human weakness and wickedness. Yet it is interesting that here Jesus makes no strong statement of judgment upon these three groups of apostates and unbelievers; instead he refers only to the great fruitfulness of the number who will be saved. Here Jesus ignores judgment (which he won't do at the end of the other parables) and focuses instead on this "superabundant harvest."[11]

I say "superabundant" because the average harvest at that time in history in that barren, desert region of the world (Palestine is no Nebraska) was probably "no more than seven or eight times the amount of seed sown."[12] So, to produce tenfold the amount of seed was considered a good harvest, twentyfold an exceptional harvest, and a thirtyfold or sixtyfold or (my goodness) a hundredfold, well, such a harvest was almost unthinkable.

Here we have this unthinkable harvest, which would have stunned the original audience. As Jesus spoke from the boat and his voice carried up the hillside (vv. 1, 2), these words would have hit them like an unexpected tsunami. So in using this shocking language of thirtyfold, sixtyfold, and a hundredfold, Jesus is ending on a very positive note. And he is not saying, "All Christians will bear fruit, some a little and some a lot." Rather he is saying, "All Christians will bear fruit, some a lot, some a lot more, and some a whole lot more."

If we could return to my chart and visualize the four soils in the left column and their interpretation in the right, what I found to be most remarkable was that for each soil or type of response Jesus essentially begins with the words "the one who hears the word" (vv. 20, 22, 23), or as it is in verse 19, "When anyone hears the word . . ." The difference between the soils is not hearing. They all hear. All four soils hear the word and to some extent or for some period of time accept it. Even the first soil is for a time on "the path" (v. 4)—i.e., the seed is "sown in his heart" (v. 19). The one difference between the three bad soils and the one good soil is that the latter "bears fruit" (v. 23; cf. v. 8).

There are vital differences between the first three bad surfaces and the last good soil, between the three bad hearers and the good hearer. The good hearer, who is neither hard nor shallow nor self-indulgent, welcomes the word *immediately* so it cannot be snatched away by Satan, welcomes it *deeply* so it is not withered by persecution, and welcomes it *exclusively* so other concerns do not strangle it.[13] Then he bears fruit! He is not just a "hearer of the word" but a "doer" of the word (James 1:23). He bears fruit, a harvest of "love, joy, peace, patience, kindness, goodness, faithfulness, gentleness, self-control" (Galatians 5:22, 23), as well as a harvest of humility, prayerfulness, heavenly-mindedness. He lives a life of consistent obedience to the commands of Christ, a steadfast commitment to the will of God in Heaven on earth.

In 3:8, 10 John the Baptist said, "Bear fruit in keeping with repentance. . . . Even now the axe is laid to the root of the trees. Every tree therefore that does not bear good fruit is cut down and thrown into the fire." Our Lord Jesus, in John 15:5–8, adds:

> I am the vine; you are the branches. Whoever abides in me and I in him, he it is that *bears much fruit*. . . . If anyone does not abide in me he is thrown away like a branch and withers; and the branches are gathered, thrown into

> the fire, and burned. . . . By this my Father is glorified, that you *bear much fruit* and so *prove* to be my disciples.

What a statement! You prove yourself to be a disciple of Jesus if you [do what? Say you are, work miracles, speak like an angel? No, if you bear much fruit—thirtyfold, sixtyfold, a hundredfold. The true work of Christ in the believer is as obvious as red delicious apples on an apple tree! Don't tell me you are a Christian if there is no fruit (cf. 7:16–21; 12:33; 21:43). As another great poet once wrote:

> Blessed is the man
> who walks not in the counsel of the wicked,
> nor stands in the way of sinners,
> nor sits in the seat of scoffers [he doesn't let such outside influences get to his heart, to harden it or strangle it];
> but his delight is in the law of the LORD,
> and on his law he meditates day and night.
> [He takes the seed of God's Word immediately and
> deeply and exclusively. And so what happens?]
>
> He is like a tree
> planted by streams of water
> that yields its fruit in its season. (Psalm 1:1–3a)

Are you abiding in Christ? If so, there will be fruit one season after another.

39

Seven Parables; Three Themes

MATTHEW 13:24–33, 36–50

WHY DOES THE GOSPEL have so little impact on the world? Why isn't Christianity the one world religion that is embraced and lived out by all? Why does anyone reject Jesus? And why do some of those who don't reject him but call him "Lord" live so little under his Lordship? In other words, why is there so much sin and evil and hypocrisy in the church? And for that matter, why is there so much sin and evil and hypocrisy in the world, especially after Jesus has lived, died, and risen again and now reigns in glory, ruling over all with all authority? Sure, Jesus sits enthroned in Heaven, but when is he going to bring heavenly justice down to earth? Doesn't he see what's going on? Isn't he aware of the daily crimes and injustices? Why is the Jesus who speaks so much in Matthew now so silent? And if such evils exist and if God and his gospel seem so powerless against them, then of what value is the gospel? Why should I follow Jesus? Why should I sacrifice for him, be persecuted for him, lose my life for him?

Those were some of the questions being asked by the first Christians. And those are often our questions as well, questions that keep rising to the surface unless we have God's Word—Jesus' parables here—to lift them up, look them dead in the eye, and answer them.

Jesus' seven parables in Matthew 13 are God's perfect providential provision for the imperfections we experience daily.[1] Here, as we shall see, Jesus is not silent. Our Lord teaches that if you understand *gospel growth* and *gospel judgment*, you will understand *gospel gain*—why fully embracing Jesus and his kingdom is like finding a hidden treasure or a priceless pearl, something of such great value that it is worth selling all you have, or even giving your very life, to get.

Gospel growth, gospel judgment, and gospel gain are the three themes that will make sense of the seven parables. And those are the themes, Lord willing, that will make sense of this world and our calling as Christians in it.

Gospel Growth

First we have *gospel growth.* Imagine you lived when Matthew wrote his Gospel, let's say thirty or forty years after Jesus uttered the words, "All authority in heaven and on earth has been given to me. Go therefore and make disciples of all nations . . ." (28:18, 19a).

In your lifetime you have seen some remarkable things. You have seen thousands of people, many of them Gentiles, come to faith in the Jewish Messiah, Jesus. You have seen the gospel spread to regions of the world you have never even heard about. In hundreds of towns throughout the Roman Empire there are house churches, one here, one there, one seemingly everywhere! The gospel has certainly spread.

But other than the Day of Pentecost, when the Holy Spirit came down upon Jerusalem in power, the seed of the gospel has grown in very subtle ways—a convert here and a household there, fifty people meeting in Lydia's house in Philippi, ten in Paul's jail cell in Rome. And compared to the Roman Empire the church still seems small and insignificant. From outward appearances it is Caesar, not Jesus, who is Lord. In law, the marketplace, culture, and art, Caesar appears omnipotent and omnipresent. As a humble Christian you are conflicted. You wonder, *Is Jesus going to win? It sure seems like Rome is winning. Yes, we are growing. But they are fully grown.* So with your head down, you mosey over to the assembly of the saints gathered on the Lord's Day, and there you pray and sing songs to Jesus, and you are reminded of his sufferings and his love for you. You also hear from the Bible. First someone reads from the Old Testament, then perhaps through one of Paul's epistles that the church had just received. Finally the Gospel is read. There are four Gospels—Matthew, Mark, Luke, and John. But your church only has a copy of Matthew. And the pastor or the bishop or the president (as he was sometimes called) opens to Matthew 13 and says, "Listen now to the words of our Lord Jesus," and he reads:

> The kingdom of heaven is like a grain of mustard seed that a man took and sowed in his field. It is the smallest of all seeds, but when it has grown it is larger than all the garden plants and becomes a tree, so that the birds of the

> air come and make nests in its branches. . . . The kingdom of heaven is like leaven that a woman took and hid in three measures of flour, till it was all leavened. (vv. 31–33)

He closes the sacred scroll or parchment, and he then gives some simple words of exhortation. He says, "Brothers and sisters, let us remember what our Lord has taught us about his kingdom. What seems to be the smallest of seeds (a mustard seed) will one day grow into a large tree, a tree so large that all kinds of birds—birds from Jerusalem, birds from Damascus, birds from Macedonia, birds from every corner of the world—will make their nest upon it.[2]

"So let us trust this promise. And let us wait with patience and hope and expectation that what is now humble will be glorious, what is now unseen will be seen, what is now hidden will be revealed, what is now only whispered in our gatherings will one day be shouted upon every housetop. For Christ's words and his ways, like leaven, at first imperceptible, will soon pervade and permeate the whole world.[3] The whole earth shall be filled with his glory and the glorious good news of the kingdom!

"Despite opposition, setback, loss, rejection, heresies, and defections, we have seen growth in our own individual lives—the thirtyfold, sixtyfold, hundredfold fruit of faith. In the same way we must wait in faith to see such growth in the church universal, trusting the gospel will indeed spread to Jerusalem, Judea, Samaria, and to the ends of the earth. The seed of the Sower that has landed on good soil will grow. God's Word will not fail. It will not return void."

End of exhortation. And that once discouraged first-century Christian heads home with his head up.

Fast forward 1,950 years to today and good old me about to explain to you this theme of growth in the parables of Matthew 13. What would I first do? Well, I'd point out to you how this theme of growth permeates this passage. We find "growth" talked about in verses 8, 12, 23, and arguably 47 and 48 with the kingdom being compared to a huge net thrown into the sea (I envision the Atlantic Ocean) and there being a "full" (v. 48) catch.[4] Sure, some of those fish are bad and will be disposed of, but the net is full. Growth! And then of course we have the parables of the mustard seed and the leaven in verses 31–33.

What would I say to us about these two short parables? I would explain what a mustard seed is since I've never seen one and presume that you most likely have not either. And because we want to be botanically accurate, I'd explain that such a seed is not the smallest seed in the world but the smallest seed "commonly planted in Palestinian fields"[5] and that around the Sea of Galilee it grows eight to ten feet tall. And perhaps for some of you I'd have to explain what leaven is—it is used in baking bread, for example. (I hope not, but you never know these days when Home Economics is often replaced with Sex Education.) I would also mention that Jesus used leaven—usually used in Scripture in a negative way—positively, with perhaps ironic intention, the ironic idea being that Jesus will use less than respectable sorts (uneducated fishermen and farmers, carpenters and women, tax collectors and dastardly characters) to transform society.[6] That's just a guess.

Listen, brothers and sisters, Jesus has been remarkably accurate, hasn't he? The Roman Empire no longer exists. It hasn't existed for over 1,500 years! Ah, but the kingdom of heaven, that little mustard seed Jesus planted in Galilee two millennia ago, has grown into a tree—the biggest, longest-living kingdom in history! The Egyptian Empire? The Assyrian Empire? The Babylonian Empire? The Aztec Empire? The Ottoman Empire? The Mongol Empire? Christianity has beat them all by persisting for 2,000 years and counting. And look at the branches of this tree. There are branches (and birds on those branches) in North Carolina and South Korea, East Timor and the West Indies (Caribbean).

Think about this for a moment. How did Jesus know this would happen? How could he possibly predict such a thing? Let's be honest. If he predicted such growth, but Christianity only spread to one region of the world, then Jesus' parabolic predictions failed. But Christianity grows in the most hostile environments. You wouldn't think it could grow in Communist China, but that is one place where it is growing the fastest. Christianity has spread all over this earth. It started in the Middle East, then spread to Southern Europe, West Asia, India, and North Africa, then Northern Europe, and then over to America. From America it spread over to Africa, Latin America, and then East Asia. Christianity is not a localized religion. It's a world religion.

Run out today, buy a globe, give it a good spin, randomly point your finger to stop the spinning, and I'll bet you my lunch there's a bird on the branch, if you know what I mean. From the first follower, "Simon (who is called Peter)" (4:18), to the millions today who say of Jesus, "You are the Christ, the Son of the living God" (16:16), Christianity has grown like a mustard seed and like a loaf of bread with lots of leaven in it. Gospel growth! That's what I'm talking about. Amen?

But listen, our "Amen" can only be so loud, for although there has been growth (Jesus' prophecy has come true), there are still unreached people groups, and there are still regions of the world where the gospel is not growing extensively and intensively. Where is the growth in Japan or Jordan or even in Italy or Ireland of all places?

Every week as I preach the good news of Jesus Christ, I wonder why every seat in the building is not filled. I'm sure we could pack the place if U2 sang at a Good Friday service or the Jonas Brothers at Easter. But why aren't people knocking down church doors to hear Christ preached from all the Scriptures? Why is it like pulling teeth when I invite my friends or neighbors to come? I'm not selling them some overpriced lemon. I'm freely offering them freedom, the sweetness of knowing and serving Jesus.

Until the day when we see "a great multitude that no one could number" (Revelation 7:9) we will be tempted toward discouragement, just as the early church was, and also tempted to sell out, to compromise the message by using methods that do not befit it. But the parables of Matthew 13 teach us: Don't. Don't sell out, and don't give up. Keep on sowing the seed. Others will water. And God will continue to grow his gospel.

Gospel Judgment

Gospel growth is the first theme of these parables. The second theme is *gospel judgment*. The gospel brings joy to those who believe, but judgment to those who do not.

If you read through the seven parables carefully, this theme is hard to miss. In fact, this theme of judgment is prevalent almost everywhere in Matthew where Jesus speaks in parables. This fits the idea I wrote about earlier—that parables reveal or conceal, or we might say, reward or judge.

Three of the seven parables in chapter 13 have this judgment theme. In the Parable of the Sower, the theme of judgment is subtle. It is God's judgment that those who are hard, shallow, or self-indulgent have the seed of the gospel "devoured" (v. 4), "withered away" (v. 6), or "choked" (v. 7). Because they heard but didn't heed and saw but didn't strive (see vv. 13–15), what they had is "taken away" (v. 12). That's judgment. Human responsibility? Yes. Divine judgment? Yes also.

But that is just the subtle stuff. There is nothing subtle about the endings of the Parable of the Weeds and the Parable of the Net. Both parables end with these same words, "and throw them into the fiery furnace. In that place, there will be weeping and gnashing of teeth" (vv. 42, 50). The weeds represent "the sons of the evil one" (v. 38). But then, quite interestingly, these weeds are defined as being within the kingdom (v. 41). They are gathered out of Christ's kingdom. Thus, they appear to be those who profess faith in Christ but don't walk their talk. This is why they are defined as "law-breakers"

(v. 41) and, even worse, as not merely sinners but those who cause others to sin. These weeds will be gathered, bound, and burned (vv. 30, 40–42). That is judgment, isn't it?

A similar judgment happens with the fish. In the final parable (vv. 47–50) we read of a great catch. The net that was thrown into the sea "gathered fish of every kind" (perhaps a reference to every tongue and tribe and nation). When this net was "full," the fishermen brought it ashore and sorted through the catch. They put the good fish "into containers" to preserve, but they "threw away the bad" (v. 48). Now, being thrown away doesn't sound as bad as being thrown into a fiery furnace. But Jesus isn't finished. Sure enough we see in verses 49, 50 that the throwing out of the bad fish is just an analogy for when the angels on behalf of the Son of Man[7] throw the unrighteous "into the fiery furnace" (yes, another reference to Daniel). Is this simply a moment of extinction or annihilation? No, it is not a period of time but a *place* of punishment—a place where "there will be weeping and gnashing of teeth [sorrow and regret]" (vv. 42, 50).

Now that's judgment, and there is no way around it. But why are we always looking for a way around it? What is wrong with judgment? Why does judgment, when found on the lips of Jesus, get a bad rap? Think about it. We call judges in our country from the Supreme Court to the lowest court "justices." The idea is that their rulings are just and bring about justice. Nobody complains if a justice punishes a lawbreaker for breaking one of our nation's laws. The Bible depicts Jesus as the ultimate Justice. Why then do people complain all the time about God punishing someone for breaking his laws? Our laws are imperfect. His are perfect. Our justices are imperfect. His Son is perfect. Jesus is the ultimate just Justice.

This is why I have labeled this section "gospel" judgment. It is *good news* that one day Jesus will come and judge the living and the dead. That reality is as good as when Jesus cried out on the cross, "My God, my God, why have you forsaken me?" (27:46)—when Jesus took on our sin, taking on himself the heat of the fiery furnace and the unbearable separation from his Father. It is good news that in the death of Christ we have the death of death, the death of our spiritual death. He died for our sins. He took on the full wrath of God so we might be fully right with God. Hallelujah!

That is the gospel—Jesus is Savior! But "Jesus is Judge" is also the gospel. When you wake up in the morning and open the newspaper and read what it reports—everything from terrorism to murder to sex scandals to kidnappings—don't you long for justice? Don't you long for a world made right? Don't you long for the kingdom of heaven to reign on earth?

Jesus will judge the world in righteousness. Jesus will also judge the church in righteousness.[8] The weeds will be weeded out and the bad fish and bad soils and bad apples disposed of. They will be sent to eternal destruction at "the end of the age" (vv. 39, 40, 49) when the Son of Man comes upon the clouds of Heaven with his angels in power to save and to judge (cf. 16:27; 24:30; 26:64).

Just as people balk at the concept of God as judge, they also balk at the timing of his judgment. I am amazed that the question raised in the Apostle Peter's day is the number one question raised today. It goes something like this: why does God continue to allow evil in the world? Why doesn't he put a stop to it right now? The answer of 2 Peter 3:8, 9 is this:

> But do not overlook this one fact, beloved, that with the Lord one day is as a thousand years, and a thousand years as one day. The Lord is not slow to fulfill his promise as some count slowness, but is patient toward you, not wishing that any should perish, but that all should reach repentance.

This theme of judgment[9]—gospel judgment—is what believers are to hope for—the day when we will "shine like the sun" (v. 43) as we are finally delivered from evil, even from our sins and failings. What a glorious image. But for the unbeliever this theme of judgment is a gracious warning and invitation. God is still lavishly offering salvation to all. He is scattering the seed of the gospel everywhere. Take hold of it. Plant it deeply and safely within the good soil, and watch it grow like wheat waiting to be harvested. Why stay a weed? As charitable Augustine wrote, "Those who are weeds today may be wheat tomorrow."[10] Why stay a weed? Repent. Turn from your sin, and turn to Christ. Trust in him alone to save you from the judgment to come.

Gospel Gain

We have looked at gospel growth and gospel judgment. Lastly we come to gospel gain. This theme is found in parables five and six.

> The kingdom of heaven is like treasure hidden in a field, which a man found and covered up. Then in his joy he goes and sells all that he has and buys that field. Again, the kingdom of heaven is like a merchant in search of fine pearls, who, on finding one pearl of great value, went and sold all that he had and bought it. (vv. 44–46)

Notice the parallels between these two parables. They both begin, "The kingdom of heaven is like . . ." (vv. 44a, 45a), and they both end with precisely the same action described with slightly different words. In verse 44c the man goes and sells all he has and buys the field, and in verse 46b he went and sold all he had and bought the pearl that was found. The element of joy is mentioned in the first parable and implied in the second.

So two parables make the same point. And what is the point? That God wants me to be rich? No. That it's okay to spend one's life looking for hidden treasures? No. That it's ethically valid to buy someone else's land if you know there is something valuable hidden within it?[11] Again, no. That the wearing of fine pearls on Sunday for church is a sign of holiness? No. The point is "that the kingdom is so valuable that it is worth sacrificing anything to gain it."[12] The gain is worth the pain.

In Philippians 3:8 Paul says, "Indeed, I count everything as loss because of the surpassing *worth* of knowing Christ Jesus my Lord. For his sake I have suffered the loss of all things and count them as rubbish, in order that I may *gain* Christ." Underline "gain." Put a star next to it.

I want to follow Jesus even if it means persecution or poverty because it means citizenship in the kingdom of heaven. As Jesus said concerning persecution in the Sermon on the Mount, "Rejoice and be glad, for your reward is great in heaven" (5:12). Gospel gain!

To most people in the world the kingdom of heaven is hidden. But to those who recognize its value, search for it, find it, and take hold of it despite the cost, it is worth it.

Encouragement

Gospel growth, gospel judgment, and gospel gain are the three themes of these seven parables. Gospel growth says to us, "Don't be discouraged. The gospel has grown, it is growing, and it will continue to growth until harvest-time." Gospel judgment says to us, "Don't be less gracious than God. God will eradicate evil, but first he wants people to repent, find the kingdom, and embrace the King." Gospel gain says to us, "The kingdom of heaven is worth infinitely more than the cost of discipleship."[13] Such sacrifice is worth it, for it will bring eternal blessedness (shining-like-the-sun blessedness!) when the King of the kingdom comes again to gather the good fish, the fruitful wheat, and all those beautiful birds nesting on the branches of that once tiny mustard seed.

40

The Headless Prophet and the Heartless King, Part 1

MATTHEW 14:1–12

AT THE BEGINNING OF MATTHEW 14, we are presented with two characters who are spiritually worlds apart. To use the language of Psalm 1, we have "the wicked" man and "the righteous" man. The wicked man is Herod the tetrarch (or Herod Antipas as he is also called), and the righteous man is John the Baptist.

In almost every passage thus far in Matthew's Gospel Jesus has been the subject.[1] That is, he is the one speaking or doing. But here in 14:1–12, which is a flashback to John's death that also foreshadows the fate of Christ,[2] Herod is the subject. He is the one acting in nearly every sentence. It is Herod who hears about Jesus, Herod who seized John, Herod who desired to put John to death, Herod who feared the people, Herod who promised an oath, Herod who was sorry after he promised that oath, yet who nevertheless acted out that oath: Herod commanded; Herod sent for John's head.

So, in a Gospel about Jesus this is one place where the camera lens shifts from the hero to a villain. We see something of Herod's sad saga. Due to this, in this chapter and the next we will look not directly at Christ but at two responses to him. In this chapter we will look at Herod and his vices that blinded him both to his sin and to the person of Jesus. For as our text begins, Herod thought that Jesus was John raised from the dead, a response thus far in Matthew's Gospel not only furthest from the truth but furthest from reality.[3]

Sigmund Freud's Analysis of Herod

One of God's greatest gifts to me is the gift of an inquisitive mind. My areas of formal study are the Bible, Christian theology, and history. While never bored by these subjects, I am always intrigued by other subjects, usually subjects about which I know little.

For example, last year I wanted to know more about science. So I picked up our *Children's Science Encyclopedia* and read it through. After that I was intrigued by the infamous Charles Darwin, so I read his *Autobiography*, then a scholarly book on his theory of evolution, and finally his famous and controversial *Origin of the Species*. Just a few years before my study of Darwin, I wanted to know something about Sigmund Freud. So guess what I did? I read him, and I read about him. And let me tell you that Freud is as fascinating, controversial, and influential as Darwin.

I bring up Darwin only to get to Freud, and I bring up Freud only to tackle this text in an intriguing way. Knowing what I know about Freud and Herod, I thought, "How interesting it would be to have Freud psychoanalyze Herod!" In a moment, God's Word will analyze Herod. But first I thought to myself, *What would Sigmund Freud make of Herod Antipas?*

Play along with me. Just imagine Herod, after all he has done in our text, and his obvious paranoia in verses 1, 2, lying down on Freud's couch, staring up at the ceiling, ready for therapy session number one. Then imagine Freud's first question. What do you think it might be? Knowing what I know of Freud, I think it would be something like, "So, Herod, tell me about your father."

What a question that would be for Herod Antipas to answer! His father was Herod the Great, whom we have already met in Matthew 2, which describes the slaughter of the innocents, the Herod who put to death all the boys under the age of two in Bethlehem. That small window is a clear window into his life, for Herod the Great was anything but great. They should have called him Herod the Less or Herod the Small or Herod the Envious Egotistical Tyrant.

Herod Antipas' mother (Freud would want to know about her too) was Herod the Great's fourth wife out of ten. With all his wives and fourteen children, Herod grew insanely suspicious of whoever had claim to his throne. He grew so insanely suspicious that he had many who were closest to him murdered, executed, assassinated. At this time there was a popular saying: "It is safer to be Herod's pig than Herod's son."[4] If you thought your dad was bad, imagine having Herod the Great for your dysfunctional father.

So Herod Antipas' answer to Freud's question—"Tell me about your father"—would be of great interest to the doctor.

If that were the first question Freud would ask, what would be the second? Perhaps something like, "Why are you here?"

If you thought Herod's first answer was of interest, the second is even juicier. Do you like day-time dramas? Are prime-time soap operas your thing? Well, Herod's life is more intriguing and evil than anyone on *The Young and the Restless*, *Sex in the City*, or whatever other comparable shows are on television today.

Let me tell you some of his story. Herod Antipas was first married to an Arabian princess, Phasaelis, the daughter of King Aretas IV of Nabatea.[5] This was a political marriage, which is intriguing because Herod the Great was Jewish. The Roman Senate elected him as "King of the Jews."[6] But in reality, like Freud, his Jewishness did not affect his moral views and choices.

Herod Antipas had a brother named Aristobulus, who was murdered by Herod the Great. Aristobulus had a daughter named Herodias, who is mentioned in verse 3. (Guess who she was named after?) Herodias married Herod Philip, Herod Antipas' half-brother. So, technically Herodias was Herod Antipas' niece as well as his sister-in-law.[7] Are you following the genealogy here? And are you seeing a scandal brewing?

Well, Herod Antipas fell out of love with his wife and in love with his brother's wife, and she fell in love with him. And one day while Herod Antipas was visiting Philip, he proposed marriage to Herodias. He, a married man, proposed to her, a married woman. She accepted, and on they went to sever their previous nuptial commitments. Their *oaths!* She got a divorce. He got a divorce. She and her daughter moved in with Herod. This was common knowledge, as we see in verse 4, since even camping-in-the-desert John the Baptist knows what happened. So what do we have here? Hollywood, eat your heart out! Adultery, divorce, backstabbing, deceit, high-handed political maneuverings, *and* the voice of one crying in this wilderness of debauchery.

That is only half of the story. (Imagine all the notes Freud would have to scribble down.) Then we have Herod's infamous birthday party.

Do you like birthday parties? Who doesn't? Well, the Jews didn't because only pagans celebrated birthdays.[8] There are only two birthday celebrations mentioned in the Bible. The first is Pharaoh's birthday in Genesis 40:20, and the second is right here.

Anyway, Herod has this birthday party, which is more like a crude bachelor party. All the leading men of Galilee are gathered—the prestigious and powerful. And when it is time for the entertainment, which usually meant the slave girls would come in and dance, instead Herodias's daughter Salome dances.[9] She "danced before the company," we are told.[10] We are also told that all this "pleased" Herod (v. 6), a very tame way of speaking of his lust.

Like any man in that state of idiocy driven by sexual fantasy, he "promised with an oath to give her [Salome] whatever she might ask" (v. 7). In Mark's version, Herod says to her (with words nearly identical to what King Ahasuerus said to Queen Esther),[11] "Whatever you ask me, I will give you, up to half of my kingdom" (Mark 6:23). He is boasting. Herod is just a minor "king." He is a tetrarch; that is, he rules a quarter of his father's territory. And his father works for Rome. So Herod technically has no kingdom to give away. What territory he rules (Galilee and Peraea) he rules only by the will of his father and as confirmed by Emperor Augustus.[12]

"Whatever you ask me . . . up to half of my kingdom" (Mark 6:23). You can almost feel the thickness of his vices in the air—his lust, his pride. He thinks he is walking on air. But little does he know that his new wife has set a trap through his stepdaughter. And into it he falls. Salome says, "Give me the head of John the Baptist here on a platter" (14:8). Can you imagine? For a moment a teenage girl wields such wicked weight over the "king" (v. 9). Herod was caught. He could either keep his oath or John could keep his head—that was his choice.[13] Her seductive dance, his foolish oath, her gruesome request, and five minutes later John is dead. His head is served. Everyone gasps. But then the music starts again, the drinks flow, and Herod's birthday party marches on.

What would Freud make of all this? Freud would surely speak of *paranoia* and *repression*—how Herod's present problems are a result of his childhood. He could blame Herod's dad for his issues, perhaps also suggesting that Herod suffers from some sort of Oedipus complex, which would explain why the two women in his life dominate his decisions.[14] However, because of Freud's humanistic philosophy that undergirded his psychoanalysis, one thing he would never do is make any moral judgments. That is the first rule of psychoanalysis. If he had Herod lying on his couch, he would never blame Herod's wicked behavior on wicked Herod. Freud taught that every action could be accounted for by two basic instincts: *eros* (the sexual or erotic instinct that causes someone to lust or covet someone or something else) and *thanatos* (the death instinct that causes someone to be aggressive, self-destructive, and at times cruel). This fits Herod pretty well. But the Bible's analysis is that lust and death are fruits of sin. Herod's lust after Herodias and her daughter and his cruelty toward John are only symptoms of a heartless king, a sinner,[15] a man who refused to hear the word of God, first from John and then also from Jesus (see Luke 23:7–16).

So Freud's analysis would only get us so far (if it gets us anywhere). There is secular analysis, and there is Scriptural analysis. Here is what the Bible has to say about Herod.

The Bible's Analysis

To determine the Bible's analysis, we could turn to the Sermon on the Mount and see how Herod fared with Jesus' teachings on lust, adultery, oaths, hatred, murder, revenge, and so on. Instead we will turn to Proverbs 6:16–19, where I have found a very interesting correlation to our text. That portion of God's Word says, "There are six things that the Lord hates, seven that are an abomination to him: haughty eyes, a lying tongue, and hands that shed innocent blood, a heart that devises wicked plans, feet that make haste to run to evil, a false witness who breathes out lies, and one who sows discord among brothers."

What I found so interesting about this text as it relates to our passage is that it sheds tremendous light on *God's analysis* of Herod as well as his wife and stepdaughter. For Herod, by marrying his brother Philip's wife (Philip still being alive) surely sowed "discord among brothers" (abomination 7, according to Proverbs 6). The actions of Herodias, with her carefully crafted manipulation of both her daughter and her husband, make up one of the best examples in the Bible of abomination 4, "a heart that devises wicked plans." In the rash vow Herod made we have highlighted abomination 2, "a lying tongue" (when he offers Salome up to half of his kingdom when he doesn't really have a kingdom to give). Then in fulfilling this vow we have abominations 1 and 5. It is Herod's pride, his "haughty eyes" as Proverbs describes it, that compels him to hastily "run to evil" to save face instead of saving the prophet's head. Finally, in their triangle of transgression, Herod, Herodias, and Salome are all guilty of abomination 3, "shed[ding] innocent blood," the innocent blood of John the Baptist.

Isn't that remarkable? Here in this story we have illustrated at least six, if not all seven, "things that the Lord hates," according to Proverbs 6. How is that for judgment! You see, the Lord would only need one brief session of analysis to diagnose Herod's problem (sin) and offer a one-word answer as his solution (repent).

What is the purpose of all this? The purpose is not merely to prove that the three villains in this text are indeed villainous. Rather, the primary purpose of identifying such abominations is to serve as a mirror to our souls. That is, when we look at this wicked man in our text, in what ways do we see ourselves? If we are to recognize Jesus' true identity and live under his divine

Lordship, there are at least two aspects of Herod's life that we must be careful to avoid: (1) repeatedly acting against our conscience, and (2) repeatedly refusing to lay aside the sins that so easy entangle us.

Clarity about Our Consciences

Let's look at our consciences first. In my old office I had pictures of three of the most prominent Protestant Reformers—Martin Luther, John Calvin, and Thomas Cranmer. Throughout the day those three dour faces would stare down upon me, making sure I was not slacking off (and making sure I'm still protesting).

Thomas Cranmer was the key theological figure of the English Protestant Reformation. From the reign of King Henry VIII to the reign of Queen Mary ("Bloody Mary" as she was to be remembered), Cranmer served as the Archbishop of Canterbury. When Mary came to power, as a devout Catholic she demanded that all Protestant bishops reconvert to Roman Catholicism on pain of death. For a time Cranmer refused to recant. He stayed Protestant. Yet, after being forced to watch his good friends Hugh Latimer and Nicholas Ridley burn at the stake, Cranmer agreed to sign a number of recantations. In doing so he officially renounced his faith. But on the eve of what would turn out to be his execution "his courage returned to him as he stood in St. Mary's Church in Oxford. Instead of repeating his recantations, he repudiated them."[16] This is what he said:

> And now I come to the great thing which so much troubleth my conscience, more than any thing that ever I did or said in my whole life, and that is the setting abroad of a writing contrary to the truth, which now here I renounce and refuse as things written with my hand contrary to the truth which I thought in my heart, and written for fear of death, and to save my life. . . . And forasmuch as my hand offendeth, writing contrary to my heart, therefore my hand shall first be punished; for when I come to the fire [to be burned at the stake], it shall first be burned.[17]

According to John Foxe, in his *Book of Martyrs*, that is precisely what happened. Thomas Cranmer, when tied to the stake and surrounded by flames, in good conscience placed his right hand in the consuming fire, allowing his body rather than his soul to burn.

Herod Antipas' actions were the opposite of Cranmer's. In Mark's version of this same story, Mark tells us that Herod thought John was "a righteous and holy man" (Mark 6:20). Herod knew the difference between righteous and unrighteous, between good and bad, right and wrong. That is why Herod, again in Mark's version, "kept him [John] safe" (6:20) and why he would actually go and listen to the prophet. He "heard him [John] gladly" (Mark 6:20), we are told, and yet with great perplexity and fear. In other words, something about John and John's message pricked Herod's conscience.

Herod's conscience was alive and well, working within him, inwardly testifying along with the words of the prophet to the truth and the necessity of John's message, "Repent, for the kingdom of heaven is at hand" (4:17). However, though hearing, Herod would not hear. And by refusing to accept the word of God that aligned perfectly with the word in his soul, he only seared his conscience each time he listened to John and severed his own head, we might say, when he complied with Salome's wish. Oh, he felt "sorry," as verse 9 says ("exceedingly sorry," Mark 6:26), about the choice he'd made regarding the life of John the Baptist and his ignorant oath. But he felt the kind of sorrow that Judas did. He was filled with remorse but not repentance. There is a world of difference between the two.

To murder a man you know is right and righteous and to show no remorse—we call such people psychopaths. But Herod was no psychopath. He was just an ordinary guy who made one small foolish step after another—a small step toward a woman who was not his wife, another step behind his brother's back, a momentary fit of passion at a birthday party, and next thing you know there's John's head staring at you, so to speak, served on a royal platter.

In 14:5 we read that Herod "feared the people." I also think he feared God. He feared God in the sense that he was frightened of the revenging justice of God, for verse 2 tells us Herod thought that Jesus' miracles were best explained as some kind of reincarnation/resurrection of John. What do you make of that? William Barclay called it the "verdict of a guilty conscience."[18] I agree, for after John's murder Herod was like a defendant who got off the hook legally but was haunted by the accusations of his own conscience.

In 1 Timothy 1:18, 19 Paul says to Timothy, "This charge I entrust to you, Timothy, my child, in accordance with the prophecies previously made about you, that by them you may wage the good warfare, holding faith and *a good conscience*. By rejecting this, some have made shipwreck of their faith." To go against the better judgment of your conscience repeatedly, as Herod did, is to poke holes in the vessel of your soul. Sinning against one's conscience is the first step in shipwrecking one's faith, or, in Herod's case, never having faith in the first place. Sinning against his conscience kept him from Christ.

So, in looking at the flawed character of Herod, we should be exhorted to hold on to "faith and *a good conscience*" and "always take pains," as Paul says in Acts 24:16, "to have a clear conscience toward both God and man."

Little Sins, Big Sins, Big Problem

Along with a clear conscience it is important that we rid ourselves of any known sin, especially sin, as Hebrews 12:1 says, that "so easily entangles" (NIV).

Sir Walter Scott wrote, "Oh what a tangled web we weave when first we practice to deceive."[19] In the case of Herod, we might better say it this way: "Oh, what a tangled web we weave when by our sinful pleasures we're deceived." Herod was entangled by sinful pleasures. He was vise-gripped by his vices. When he first met Herodias, as a married man he should never have entertained the idea of a possible marital relationship with her. Yet, as the historian Josephus tells us, it was Herod who sought this sinful relationship, and as our text portrays, once he obtained it he refused to let it go. Proverbs 9:17, 18 says, "Stolen water is sweet, and bread eaten in secret is pleasant. But he does not know [by drinking of this water and eating of this bread] that the dead are there, that her guests are in the depths of Sheol."

In Mark's account four times we read of Herod "hearing." Herod heard John's message well enough. In fact, the truth was enticing to him. He must have contemplated submitting to it. But as preacher Mark Connelly has noted, "in the end Herod loved his sinful pleasures more than God's truth."[20] Thus instead of severing his immoral relationship with Herodias (which John was calling him to do), he severed (literally) his relationship with John. "Off with John's head, and on with my sin."

In this way Herod is the perfect illustration of the third soil in Jesus' Parable of the Sower, where the seed is sown among thorns. Herod hears the word, but "the cares of the world" (he has a "kingdom" to run and important people to impress), "the deceitfulness of riches" (he's not about to give up his position and the wealth that goes with it to follow some hermit from an obscure little town in Judea or some traveling peasant from Nazareth), and lusts for other things (women, power, you name it) enter in and choke the word, and it proves unfruitful (13:22). So it never grows.

That was Herod. Yes, he had an awful father. Yes, he was surrounded by temptations. However, he is not a man who so easily gets off the hook. Matthew puts Herod's story here because Herod heard the prophet and heard of the Lord, and yet he refused to listen. That was Herod.

What about you? Are you, like Herod, entangled by some sin? Maybe it's a sinful relationship. Maybe it's a sinful thought life. Maybe it's a sinful indulgence, a hobby or a habit that you refuse to stop. Maybe it's one of those deadly vices that receives little attention today because they are no longer thought to be lethal—the sin of greed or sloth or gluttony. Whatever it is, we know why we won't get rid of it. We allow it to take up residency in our lives because we like the temporal pleasure it provides. And when we're confronted, like Herod was, with Biblical truths that challenge us to forfeit our pleasure, our temptation is to come up with some middle ground where we feel like we've made some effort to follow Christ without really having to give up our favorite sin. I know this from experience, and I assume you do too. We try to negotiate the sin in our lives rather than eradicate it. However, what happens, whether we are conscious of it or not, is that the web of self-deception encircles us until we are helpless (caught like a bug).[21] Oh, what a tangled web we weave when by our sinful pleasures we're deceived!

A Simple Lesson

From having Herod psychoanalyzed and then Scripture-analyzed, we learn a simple lesson. We learn *not* to be like him (cf. 1 Corinthians 10:6). If we want to see Jesus for who he is, we must not be like Herod. We must be careful to cultivate a good conscience and to be proactive in cutting ourselves free, by the power of the Spirit, from any and all sinful pleasures that entangle our souls.

The headless prophet and the heartless king. To be continued.

41

The Headless Prophet and the Heartless King, Part 2

MATTHEW 14:1–12

JAMES 5:10, 11a SAYS, "As an example of suffering and patience, brothers, take the prophets who spoke in the name of the Lord. Behold, we consider those blessed who remained steadfast." In this sermon we will behold the greatest of the prophets—John the Baptist—and will consider the blessed example of his life and especially his last hours.

One of Thomas Cranmer's "collects" was written to be recited at the Nativity of John the Baptist, a feast day celebrated on June 24 on the Anglican Church calendar. The prayer begins with a short summary of John's life and ministry: "Almighty God, by whose providence thy servant, John the Baptist, was wonderfully born, and sent to prepare the way of thy Son our Savior, by preaching of repentance . . ." The prayer starts by reminding us of John's unique birth, of his important mission as the forerunner of Jesus, and of the content of his preaching. Then the prayer shifts from God's work in John's life to a petition for God's work in our lives: "Make us so to follow his doctrine and holy life, that *we may truly repent* according to his preaching; and after his example *constantly speak the truth, boldly rebuke vice,* and *patiently suffer* for the truth's sake" (emphasis mine).[1]

I don't know if Cranmer had his Bible open to 14:1–12 when he wrote this prayer, but I would guess that he did, for this prayer serves as an excellent outline for this passage. This text reminds us:

1. Unlike Herod, we are to "repent according to [John's] preaching."
2. Following John's example, we are exhorted to "constantly speak the truth," which includes "boldly rebuking vice."
3. Finally, and again following John's example, we are called to "patiently suffer for the truth's sake."

That We May Truly Repent

First we must practice repentance. If you remember anything from the last chapter (besides all you learned about Sigmund Freud), I hope you remembered the two applications I gave in response to Herod's two vices—not to be like Herod in acting against your conscience, and not to be like Herod in not repenting—letting sin so easily entangle you so that you cannot or will not see Jesus for who he is.

In this chapter, while we have shifted our focus from Herod the heartless king to John the headless prophet, we nevertheless begin where we left off—with repentance. The message of repentance was at the heart of John's ministry, and it was the primary reason he was killed.

In 3:1, 2 we learn of John and of his message: "In those days John the Baptist came preaching in the wilderness of Judea, 'Repent, for the kingdom of heaven is at hand.'" The next time Matthew mentions John he is in prison (11:2). As we learn from our current passage, he is in prison for playing again that broken record of repentance: "For Herod had seized John and bound him and put him in prison for the sake of Herodias, his brother Philip's wife, *because* John had been saying to him, 'It is not lawful for you to have her'" (11:3, 4). In other words, "Herod, repent of your sin of marrying your brother's wife while your brother is still alive (and your rightful wife is still alive as well). Sever this immoral, unlawful (it is directly against the laws of Leviticus),[2] polygamous relationship.[3] You can't have an unlawfully divorced wife *and* an unlawfully wedded wife. Leave the second, and re-cleave to the first!"

The first time I led a call to worship in a church service was when I was a pastoral intern at Holy Trinity Church in Chicago. I walked up to the pulpit, opened my Bible, and read, "Repent, for the kingdom of God is at hand." I closed my Bible and sat down. The music played, "Softly and tenderly, Jesus is calling" or whatever song was sung. What a way to start a service!

Afterward the senior pastor took me aside and gently reminded me of the purpose of a call to worship and what is usually said and done. I appreciated that, and I learned from that. But three years later a college student who had attended that service told me that my call to worship was the reason he started attending Holy Trinity. When I got up and read what I read, at that moment he said to himself, "Wow. What kind of a church starts its service like this? What kind of a church takes sin and the need for repentance so seriously? This is the church for me!"

John began his ministry with the words, "Repent, for the kingdom of heaven is at hand," and Jesus did the same. In fact, the Reformation was birthed through the same words. The first thesis of the 95 Theses is, "Our Lord and Master Jesus Christ, when he said 'Repent' [*poenitentiam agite*], willed that the whole life of believers should be repentance." So that is our call to worship, not only in a church service, but in all of the Christian life!

That's point one. In looking at the character and example of John, it is crucial that we first heed his message of repentance and that we get in the practice of constantly asking ourselves, "Are we continuing to bring our sin to our Savior?" We will indeed sin. So are we continually confessing our sins? And are we asking Jesus to deeply transform us by the power of his gospel? We should pray, "Jesus, help me to abide in you (that's where the sin-breaking power of grace comes from) and rejoice in you. Help me to be grateful for all that you have given and continue to give—life, breath, salvation—for gratitude can squelch the surge of sin; it can flatten the fires of our flesh. Help me to come to you daily in dependence, like a little child clinging to his father's strong, tall leg. Here am I, Lord, cleanse me, save me, sanctify me, and send me! I repent. I repent again. My whole earthly life is a life of perpetual repentance."

That We May Constantly Speak the Truth

The first application we should take from the totality of John's life is to *repent*. The second is to *rebuke*. In looking at the example of John the Baptist, we should ask God to help us to "constantly speak the truth," as John did, especially in regard to "boldly rebuking vice."

Years ago I took a class on British Church History with Dr. Mark Noll. When the class discussed Henry VIII, Dr. Noll, who is known for being refined and levelheaded in his judgments regarding historical figures, in an uncanny outburst said to the class, "Henry VIII was a monster!"

The same could be said of Herod. He was a monster. He was the epitome of "the doubled-minded man" James addressed in the first chapter of his epistle. While Herod had a conscience and possessed some good impulses, he was nevertheless an extremely evil man, unstable in all he did (James 1:8). In the last chapter, when I pretended to have Sigmund Freud psychoanalyze Herod, I was not embellishing on the historical facts regarding Herod or his family. Commentator James Edwards agrees that the family affairs of Herod Antipas "could supply the script for a long soap opera series"[4] or a HBO mini-series. And everyone in John's day knew this. They knew of the widespread decadence of Herod Antipas. Through gossip, Herod's indiscretions were as publicized as England's royal family's indiscretions have been through the tabloids. Everyone in John's day had the dirt on Herod.

This being the case, what I find so incredibly courageous is that John the Baptist bothered to challenge Palestine's earthly king and the accepted reality of his wickedness. Why rock the boat? Why fight the establishment? Why, of all people, go after "king" Herod, a man who very well could have your head on a platter? Why? Because John was a true prophet!

In Ezekiel 13 we read of the many false prophets who "misled" God's people (Ezekiel 13:10), prophesying "from their own hearts" (Ezekiel 13:2) the message "'Peace,' when there is no peace" (Ezekiel 13:10); rather only divine judgment was to come. Like Ezekiel and all the faithful Old Testament prophets, John the Baptist obeyed his divine orders to offend even the king and all who refuse to heed the truth.

Because he was faithful to his calling, John spoke truthfully to Herod concerning his bad behavior. As J. C. Ryle put it, John didn't flatter "the king's ungodliness by using soft words to describe his offense. He told his royal hearer the plain truth regardless of all consequences,"[5] regardless of how untimely, imprudent, and politically incorrect his words were.

In light of John's bold witness to the truth, it struck me like a rock being thrown at my head that many of us don't experience much persecution or we don't have many (or any) enemies because we are cowards. We have mastered the fine art of biting our tongue all the time—not just when we should, but also when we shouldn't. But think about this: what is one of our Lord's most famous commands? Love your enemies. Right? Okay, so Christ calls us to love our enemies, but who in the church has enemies to love? Although it is a terrible thing to have enemies because you have been cruel to someone, it is a blessed thing to have enemies if they have been created through "speaking the truth in love" (Ephesians 4:15).

We often define the godly person as someone who never stirs up controversy or makes his or her opinions public, especially moral judgments. But the Bible does not. Just read the Psalms and look for the word "enemies." The psalmists seem unable to lift a prayer without mentioning an enemy. We can try to write this off as some old-covenant mentality, some false ancient prejudice. Or we can take seriously the clear portrait of every single godly person in the Bible as one who had enemies because, like John, they constantly spoke the truth and boldly rebuked vices. I'll put it this way: the more you are like Christ in his holiness, the more you will be like Christ in his sufferings.

Let's bring this idea straight into our world. So, should we protest immoralities—abortion, same-sex marriages, promiscuity? Yes. So picket a clinic, write a letter, sign a petition, and elect a candidate. But more than that we should open our mouths to the immoralities around us, especially in the church. There is enough immorality in the church to keep us quite busy. You see, it is easier to do something about immorality from a distance (to throw stones from Fargo to Washington, Duluth to Hollywood), but what about bending down and pushing a doorstop against the sins crouching at your front door? My point is, it is not easy to confront people we know (church members, family members, friends, neighbors, etc.) who are disobeying the commands of Christ, especially if they profess to be Christians.

It is certainly easy for me (and I would imagine for you as well) to stand in front of an abortion clinic and hold up a sign that reads, "Abortion stops a beating heart." But it is far more difficult to confront someone I know and love who is in a sexually immoral relationship and say to him or her, "You must break off this engagement" or "You must move out of this living situation; you must stop what you are doing." That takes the bravery of a John the Baptist.

During my junior and senior years of college I lived in a campus-owned house with five other guys. Five of the six are now full-time pastors. The one who is not worked as a youth pastor until something happened in his life. He flew into Chicago one day to tell me about it. Over a cup of coffee and a slice of pie he announced to me (not gleefully but somewhat remorsefully) that he had rejected God and had begun experimenting with homosexuality. He told me to pray for him because he didn't feel like he was in a good place.

Before I responded to this shocking news, I asked him how many Christian friends and leaders had responded to him, and he replied, "Everyone has been very understanding and loving about this whole situation." When he said that, my heart broke, for I thought to myself, *No! They have been neither understanding nor loving, for this is love, my friend: "Repent, for the kingdom of heaven is at hand."* Those were not the words I used in my response, but they well expressed the sentiment of my message to him. I told him he had upset me and that he had certainly angered God.

What a freedom there is in speaking the truth in love rather than speaking so-called love without truth. He wasn't angry with my anger, but if he had been, it wouldn't have fazed me because more and more I have come to expect that the ungodly will become upset, like Herod was, when they are told the truth. And if this close friend of mine became my enemy (which he didn't), so be it. I am called to love him even if he hates me.

That was a time I boldly spoke the truth, but there have been a thousand other times when I have cowardly bitten my tongue. Why? Because I'm afraid of what others might think. I'm afraid of making enemies! But do you know what Jesus once said about that fear? In Luke 6:26 he said to his disciples, "Woe to you, when all people speak well of you, for so their fathers did to the false prophets." You see, if one is faithfully proclaiming and living out the gospel, then it is no disgrace to have enemies. When we faithfully bear witness in word and deed against sin, the world, and the devil, it is no disgrace to give offense. Rather, according to our Lord, it is a disgrace to be thought well of by everybody because we have never taken a stand on anything.

So through the testimony of John the Baptist (v. 4) God reminds us in his Word that with humility, gentleness, and love, and through careful attention to the situation and to the person we are addressing, we are called to "constantly speak the truth," as we saw earlier from Thomas Cranmer's words.

That We May Patiently Suffer for the Truth's Sake

We are to truly repent of our unrighteousness (point one). We are to boldly rebuke unrighteousness in others (point two). Finally, because of points one and two, we are to *patiently suffer*, as John did, *for the sake of the truth* (point three).

John the Baptist was a living beatitude. He was poor in spirit, meek, merciful, and pure in heart, and he mourned over the sins of God's people. He brought the message of peace and reconciliation with God for those who repent. He hungered and thirsted for righteousness. He was persecuted for righteousness' sake.

In his final beatitude our Lord Jesus said, "Blessed are you when others revile you and persecute you and utter all kinds of evil against you falsely on my account. Rejoice and be glad, for your reward is great in heaven, for so they persecuted the prophets who were before you" (5:11, 12). Throughout John's ministry he was treated just like the prophets who went before him. He was reviled and persecuted in his life and mocked in the manner of his death. The one whom Jesus called the greatest man "born of women" (11:11) had his head chopped off and served on a platter because some foolish tetrarch made a rash vow at a lewd birthday party. Think about that. What a way to go. The only more humiliating death would be to hang upon a Roman cross.

Surely in John's death, as promised by Jesus, we are to recognize the reality of his heavenly reward. It is a glorious thing that John died the way he did. Yet here in Matthew we are not given this heavenly perspective. There is no mention of angels rejoicing, no singing of Psalm 116:15, "Precious in the sight of the LORD is the death of his saints." There are no apostolic words of comfort: "He received his crown in heaven though he had lost his head on earth."[6] There is none of that. In fact, "the only act of decency in the account of John's martyrdom is the arrival of his disciples to give his body a proper burial"[7] (see v. 12).

In the terrible fate of John we see only the grim face of death. We see the picture of the cross John bore that foreshadows, as I mentioned, the cross of Christ. It is no coincidence that there are parallels between the two passions.[8] As John was seized and bound, so Jesus will be seized and bound (the same words are used), and as John stands before Herod, so Jesus will stand before Pontus Pilate (both leaders wavered in moral courage and both washed their hands of the crime or tried to), and so on.

John's martyrdom prefigures Jesus' death; John's "cross" points to Jesus' cross. But it also points to the cross of Christians. That is, John's death prefigures the death of anyone who would follow Christ. In other words, discipleship and death is our calling in Christ. "If *anyone* would come after me," Jesus says, "let him deny himself and take up his cross and follow me" (16:24). We are to patiently suffer for the sake of the truth.

The slogan for a popular Christian radio station is "Positive, encouraging, and safe for the whole family." There are some very positive things we should glean from this otherwise negative passage. For example, we should be positively encouraged that Herod Antipas, though severing John's head, could not and did not silence his message; while Herod fades into the oblivion of history, the gospel of the kingdom of heaven that John preached continues to grow to this day! Tertullian's famous dictum is true in the case of John: "the blood of the martyrs is the seed of the church."[9] So too is Søren Kierkegaard's axiom, "The tyrant dies and his rule ends, the martyr dies and his rule begins."[10] It is true that the death of John the Baptist is both positive and encouraging in that it reminds us that the kingdom advances in spite of the evil and cruelty of the world. Yet it is also true that this message of the gospel is not "safe for the whole family" or for the individual Christian. Just as there is nothing safe about befriending a lion, so there is nothing safe about befriending the Lion of Judah.

A brave Chinese Christian by the name of Watchman Nee wrote the famous book *The Normal Christian Life*. The book is not so much about suffering as it is about living the so-called "victorious Christian life." Yet, to borrow his title, I will say this about how the apostles defined the normal Christian life. Peter said:

> Beloved, do not be surprised at the fiery trial when it comes upon you to test you, as though something strange were happening to you [suffering is the normal Christian life]. But rejoice insofar as you *share Christ's sufferings* [cf. Romans 8:17], that you may also rejoice and be glad when his glory is revealed [at his return]. If you are insulted for the name of Christ, you are blessed, because the Spirit of glory and of God rests upon you. (1 Peter 4:12–14)

That is what Peter has to say about the normal Christian life, and Paul says in 2 Timothy 3:12, "Indeed, *all* who desire to live a godly life in Christ Jesus will be persecuted"—not *might* be persecuted, but *will be* persecuted. They will not necessarily have their heads cut off, but their words will be laughed at, their moral values spit upon, their ideologies scorned.

I don't care what that radio station says; the Bible says that Christianity is not safe for the whole family! It is not safe for those who seek truly to follow Christ. Rather, the call of Christ, as Cranmer's prayer rightly puts it, is the call to "patiently suffer for the truth's sake."

Two Sermons in Sum

So that's my take on 14:1–12. We should not be like Herod, but we should be like John. We should repent, as John preached. When needed and appropriate, we should rebuke others and constantly speak the truth, even and especially boldly rebuking vice. Then, because we are willing to repent and rebuke, we should bear the weight of the consequences—suffering patiently for the truth's sake.

Years ago I preached on Mark 6:14–29, Mark's version on this Matthew text. When I was ready to print the sermon, my printer broke. I walked down the street and asked a neighbor, who happens to be a Christian, if I could use her printer to print out my sermon. She said that would be fine. Now, as she saw the top of the first page of the sermon with its unusual title (I think I used the same title as in this book), "The Headless Prophet and the Heartless King," she turned to me and asked in a very curious tone of voice, "What topic are you preaching on this Sunday?" I smiled and said, "The beheading of John the Baptist." She paused, and with a confused expression on her face she said, "Who picks the sermon topics for your church?"

While that was a humorous moment, it was also a telling moment in some ways of the standard mentality most Christians have regarding what topics or texts are good or normal. In most churches Christians have become accustomed to hearing sermons on important topics, Biblical topics, often revolving around salvation, marriage, family, children, work, evangelism, etc. But the topic of suffering for righteousness' sake is rarely addressed. Yet, in the Gospels and in the Epistles the topic of suffering is far more normative than the topic of how a husband should treat his wife. The topic of how a husband should treat his wife is an important topic, and that is why it is addressed at least three times in the New Testament. However, the topic of suffering is also important, and that is why it is addressed on nearly every other page of the New Testament.

The suffering of the righteous may not be a popular sermon series, but it is an appropriate and important one. It is the sum of what this chapter on John the prophet says to us.

42

Contemplation and Compassion

MATTHEW 14:13–23

JESUS IS HUMAN. Sometimes I have a hard time getting my head around that. I have a hard time grasping that he has ascended bodily into Heaven and that this person to whom I pray, whom I have never seen, heard, or touched, is human.

He was in his mother's womb for nine months. He was a messy, mucous baby when he came out of that womb. He was a little boy. Can you imagine Jesus being like my son Simeon, who skipped across the sanctuary platform one Sunday as he returned from children's church? Can you imagine Jesus jumping or falling, scraping his knee? He was a boy who grew physically and mentally and perhaps in some incomprehensible way spiritually. He learned to walk, talk, read, write, and pray.

He was a human baby and boy. And, of course, he was a man. And as a man we don't know if he was tall or short or had blue or brown eyes. We don't know if he liked folk music or if he had a good singing voice. We don't know if he had a sweet tooth or bad teeth. There is a lot we don't know about his humanness. But from the Gospels we do know that he walked, sat, sailed, and got hungry (Mark 11:12) and thirsty (John 19:28). We know he felt tired (John 4:6), and so he slept (Mark 4:38). And we know he spoke, sang, and prayed (cf. Hebrews 5:7), grieved, and wept (John 11:33–35), and he did the most fallen human activity—he died (27:50).[1]

Jesus is human. Sometimes I have a hard time getting my head around that. And our text—which is so much about Jesus' divine power (what a supernatural miracle the feeding of the 5,000 is)—begins and ends with a very human Jesus. Fully divine, yet fully human.

Christ's Contemplation

As we look at this text, we will look at Christ's humanity first, starting with an *inclusio* of Christ's contemplation in verses 13, 14 and 22, 23. Here he desires to get away from the crowd and his disciples in order to "linger in prayer" (v. 13), as Hagner says (cf. v. 23).[2] Starting in verse 12 we read, "And his disciples came and took the body [of John the Baptist] and buried it, and they went and told Jesus." They likely told Jesus everything we read of in verses 1–11, the horrid details of John's death.

"Now when," verse 13a reads, "Jesus heard this, he withdrew from there in a boat to a desolate [*eremon* = desert or wilderness] place by himself." We are not told where he went, likely somewhere on the northwestern shore of the Sea of Galilee (e.g., "Bethsaida," Luke 9:10b). We know, however, what happens once he gets there. The paparazzi are waiting for him. "But when the crowds heard it, they followed him on foot from the towns. When he went ashore he saw a great crowd" (vv. 13b, 14a). Jesus saw a crowd that killed his contemplation, or at least paused it.

Then verses 14b–21 record the miracles of healing and feeding, which I will discuss in just a moment. But as we are still contemplating Christ's contemplation, look at verses 22. There we read, "Immediately he [Jesus] made the disciples get into the boat and go before him to the other side, while he dismissed the crowds."

So plan A was: "I'll get in the boat to get away."[3] That didn't work. So he went to plan B: "You disciples get in the boat. Off you go. Bye-bye. See you on the other side." How on earth Jesus is going to get to the other side? They have no idea.

He dismissed the crowd (v. 23a), and off they go because the sick were cured and the hungry fed (vv. 14, 19, 20). Then finally comes verse 23b: "[H]e went up on the mountain by himself to pray. When evening came [at last], he was there alone. . . ."

Do you see all this? Jesus hears of John's death and wants some solitude. Plan A: The great boat escape. Plan B: Feed 'em, heal 'em, send 'em all away happy in Jesus. Then, once the coast is clear (literally) up the mountain he goes for some alone time—a time to pray and contemplate.

What was on his mind?

We can only speculate, but speculate I will. Here is my sanctified-by-Scripture speculation (read the endnote for my defense).[4] I think he thought about John's death.[5] Not only did he grieve over that death and perhaps weep as he did when Lazarus his dear friend died, but I think he thought of John's death in light of his own death.

As we saw earlier, John's passion in verses 1–11 foreshadows Jesus' passion. Like John, innocent Jesus would suffer and die for the truth at the hands of the political powers of the day. Jesus knew that. Jesus also knew that with John down, he was soon to fall as well. That was God's will for him.

So I think he thought about what human beings think about when they lose a loved one. I also think he thought about what he thought about at the Garden of Gethsemane—the thirty-nine lashes, the crown of thorns, the falling on the road to Golgotha, the nails, the thirst, the laughter at the foot of the cross, the rejection, and the loneliness—"My God, my God, why have you forsaken me" (27:46). He thought of the loneliness of the atonement—of becoming sin so we might become the righteousness of God through faith in him (2 Corinthians 5:21). I think he thought about the cross of Calvary. On this mountain he thought of that mountain. On a hill far, far away he thought of that hill that was no longer so far, far away from him, a hill that was closing in on him.

Christ's Compassion

And it's that thought (if I've thought rightly about his thought) that makes what happens between this *inclusio* so remarkable, but also so predictable. The one who wants to contemplate his crucifixion—the ultimate act of selfless love—here (in the middle of our text) has compassion on (selflessly loves) the tired, the poor, the huddled masses, those longing to be free and longing to be fed.

Look again at verse 14. Jesus got on the boat to get away, but when he steps off the boat, a sea of people crash against him. Ah, the crowd, mentioned four times in our text. The crowd crashes against him. So much for solitude.

When I'm writing a sermon, contemplating some important idea, or praying and I'm interrupted by a sheep from my flock or an arrow from my quiver, my gut reaction is not compassion but *consternation*.

But look at verse 14b. It's so beautiful! It tells us so much about the heart of our Great Shepherd. Here the heart of God is laid open before us. When Jesus "saw a great crowd, and he had compassion on them and healed their sick," and then he fed their bellies. He had compassion. "His heart went out to them" (14:14; cf. 9:36; 15:32; 20:34). I like that rendering of the word "compassion." His heart went out to them, and his hands healed and fed them. Jesus demonstrates not just an *attitude* of compassion but *acts* of compassion. What

Moses *heard* from God about God on Mount Sinai—"The Lord, the Lord, a God merciful and gracious, slow to anger, and abounding in steadfast love and faithfulness" (Exodus 34:6b)—is what we *see* here in Jesus.

This is also something that can be seen throughout the history of the Christian church—an attitude of compassion accompanied by actions of compassion. That's the one-two punch of Christian activism! Jesus cared about the physical needs of people. Here he doesn't hand out gospel tracts on how to get in touch with God. Here he feeds. Here he heals.

Our churches and charities follow in his footsteps. Look at the needs of the world today—people who are sick, hungry, and hurting. Close the camera in on who is there helping, and you will find Christians. A man in my church, Dr. Vadim Gaponenko, is a professor of biochemistry at the University of Illinois at Chicago. He works on cancer research, developing ways to fight and kill cancer. When I interviewed him for membership, I asked him if his work environment—being surrounded by biologists—was hostile to his faith. He replied that when he did his PhD work there was some hostility. But since he has gone into the area of cancer research—first at the National Cancer Institute in Maryland and now in Chicago—he has found little persecution because many of the doctors and professors in this field are Christians or share Christian values. Isn't that interesting?

I'll put his experience differently, in my own slightly exaggerated words: Christian biologists flock to cancer research because they are motivated not by money or power or prestige but by the compassion of Christ. Because of Christ's compassion, Christians want to heal dying people. And because of Christ's compassion, Christians want to feed starving people.

In my house we do not have a television, but we do have a computer and the Internet. So my wife and I watch shows via the Internet site hulu.com. Hulu has short commercials, and in early 2010 many were about Haiti relief. World Vision is one of the organizations that bought some commercial time, and this evangelical Christian organization said something like this in their twenty-second slot: "World Vision—we were there before the earthquake, we have been there afterwards, and we will be there in the future."

The key is the beginning and the end. We were already there, helping in this poor country, and we will be there after the whole world (and its cameras) have moved on to the next high-TV-ratings natural disaster. I thought to myself, *That's Christianity—Christ's compassion in the world. When nobody's looking, Christians are breaking down protein molecules in a university lab and breaking bread in some impoverished region of the world.*

So the compassion of Christ is to be the compassion of the church. We love the world in attitude and action because God in Christ first loved us.

But as we look back at our text let me ask you, is this miracle recorded only to serve as a perpetual motivation for Christian charity—to keep us going in leading the world in healing the sick and feeding the poor? No; there is a greater reason.

Interestingly, this is the only miracle recorded in all four Gospels. Why? What is its importance? What's the point of it? That Jesus is really nice? That he loves people? That he puts people first? That he shares his food? That we should do all of the above?

No. The point is power—compassionate power—compassionate power that points to personhood—who Jesus is. Jesus' authority over creation points to its Creator's identity.

Let me point out how this power points to Jesus' person. Look again at the miracles. After Jesus put on a half-day messianic medical clinic for likely hundreds of people, we read:

> Now when it was evening the disciples came to him and said, "This is a desolate place, and the day is now over; send the crowds away to go into the villages and buy food for themselves." But Jesus said, "They need not go away; you give them something to eat." They said to him, "We have only five loaves here and two fish." And he said, "Bring them here to me." (vv. 15–18)

Then what happened? "Then he ordered the crowds to sit down on the grass" (v. 19). He laid them down in green pastures, "and taking the five loaves and the two fish, he looked up to heaven and said a blessing [possibly the traditional Jewish blessing—"Blessed art Thou, O Lord our God, King of the world, who bringest forth bread from the earth"].[6] Then he broke the loaves and gave them to the disciples, and the disciples gave them to the crowds. And they all ate and were satisfied. And they took up twelve baskets full of the broken pieces left over. And those who ate were about five thousand men, besides women and children."

So what do we have here? With most men having wives and (let's say) "two and a half children" per suburbanite (as pollsters like to put it), that's nearly 24,000 people. That's a lot of mouths to feed. That's a lot of bread. That's a lot of fish. That's a lot of supernatural spontaneous regeneration. That's a lot of holy mackerel.

At the beginning of this chapter I talked about Jesus' humanity. I hope you saw his humanity at the top and tail of our text. But here in the center we see his divinity. Don't miss it. Here we are to see, in the language of Isaiah 7:14, "Immanuel"—God with us.

Ulrich Luz writes this statement in disbelief: "We must give up all attempts for a historical kernel of something that once happened here, if one doesn't simply want to assert oneself against all verifiable experience."[7] In other words, this couldn't have happened in history because we've never experienced something like this—one loaf turning into thousands of loaves . . . one fish, two fish, new fish, true fish! We haven't seen it, so how can we believe it? It goes against—like the resurrection—verifiable experience.

That type of attitude is unfortunate, but it really gets to the heart of the issue. Unbelievable! That should be our first reaction to this miracle. Not, "Oh, this miracle again; I know it like the back of my hand; yeah, Jesus takes five loaves, two fish, 5,000 are fed, twelve baskets of scraps." Rather, we should react like this: "He took what? Just five loaves and two fish and fed 5,000, 10,000, 20,000, 30,000 people!? And there were doggie bags for everyone?" You see, Matthew wants us to see this miracle and say of it, "This must be the hand of God. This must be the Son of God!" Jesus' power reveals his identity.

Think carefully about this miracle and what is so unique about it. No first-rate faith healer could do this, and no world-class magician could duplicate this. The greatest tricks our greatest magicians do are just that—tricks. They are illusions. You might think that the Statue of Liberty has disappeared, but it has not. It is a very carefully crafted illusion, and magicians like David Copperfield know that and boast in that. They know how the whole thing works. It is scientific to them, not magical.

Or think of charismatic faith healers. Have you ever watched one of them do the miracles Jesus did—cure a leper, give sight to the blind, walk on water, stop the wind, raise a little girl from the dead? I doubt you have, for his "miracles" are all stuff that *can't* be verified. Oh, he'll "heal" a bad back, a bum leg, ringing in the ears, a sinus infection. But here Jesus takes seven pieces of food and does a perfectly unduplicatable miracle. Oh, the magician can do it, but he knows and his staff knows that bread and frozen fish trucks delivered the secret stash the day before. And the faith healer, well, he's not fooling anyone. He wouldn't dare try this one. He would rather sink in the water as he attempts to walk on it than gather 24,000 hungry people in some superdome and have them all leave with their bellies empty, their fists in the air, and their 100-dollar checks still in their back pockets.

This supernatural multiplication is just that—supernatural! One person could be fooled by someone somehow turning one fish into two. Maybe the second fish, as sick as it sounds, was literally up his sleeve. But 24,000 people could not be fooled by someone when two fish turn into 10,000. Do you know what I'm getting at? This is a visible, tangible, verifiable, *edible* attestation of Jesus' identity. This is no cheat, no imposter, no false prophet. This miracle screams, "This is God in the flesh!" Who else can this be? You see, the power shows the person; the authority (over the elements of this world) reveal his identity.

If you miss that in this miracle, you miss its meaning. Yes, feed the hungry, heal the sick. Jesus is compassionate, and you should be compassionate too. Yes, that's here. But that's not all that is here. Here Jesus is the sovereign Lord of creation. The one who spun the stars into existence and has speedily—not in one day or seven days, not in one second or seven seconds, but in point seven seconds—changed the immaterial into material, the nonexistent to the existing. With the blink of an eye, the passing of a loaf, one turns to two to three to four to five. This is the bread of God from the hand of God. That's what we are to see.

In case we miss that—seeing the miracle for what it is and thus Jesus for who he is—Matthew provides some other subtle details. Think back to the Old Testament. (I'll do this quickly. This chapter is making me hungry.) Think back to divine food provisions in the Old Testament. What are the two key stories? The most obvious one is the provision of manna (and meat) during Israel's wilderness wanderings (see Exodus 16; Numbers 11). Similarly, here in 14:13 the setting is "a desolate place," which is wilderness-like (see especially John 6:31).[8] And that's the first important story for understanding this story.[9]

The other one comes from 2 Kings 4:42–44,[10] the story about the prophet Elisha feeding 100 men with twenty loaves. Several details in the 2 Kings text coincide with our text. First, there is a crowd. Second, a man brings to the prophet an insufficient amount of food to feed the crowd. Third, Elisha says in essence, "Great. That's all we need. Give these loaves to the men so they may eat." Fourth, the man says, "Hey, Elisha, do the math—twenty here/100 there." Fifth, Elisha says, "Let God do the math. You just do what I say." Sixth, he does it. Seventh, "And they ate and had some left" (v. 44).

The point of the parallels with Moses and Elisha is to say: Behold, Jesus is greater than Moses and Elisha! The words said of Jesus at his baptism and at the transfiguration are reiterated figuratively here: "This is God's beloved Son." That's what we are to see. This is God with us! Do you see that? Do you believe that? This was written so you'd see that and believe that.

Count to Eight

In 14:13–23 we learn about contemplation (Jesus sought solitude, a time and place to get away to stop and think and pray, and we should do the same). We also learn about compassion (as Christ was compassionate in attitude and action, so should we be). We learn about contemplation and compassion and even about provision. As Bruner says, "Disciples should always count to eight."[11] That is, in this passage there are seemingly only seven things available to provide for the people—five loaves and two fish—but we should always count to eight. We should always count on Jesus, the *one* factor we can count on to provide our daily bread.

However, while we learn about contemplation, compassion, and provision, the main lesson here is that Jesus is "God with us," God's "beloved Son," or as Jesus describes himself elsewhere, "the bread of life" (John 6:35), "the bread that came down from heaven" (John 6:58a), and "whoever comes to [him] shall not hunger" (John 6:35), and "whoever feeds on this bread will live forever" (John 6:58b). That's the point of this passage. We are to contemplate the power of Christ. We are to contemplate the compassion of Christ. We are to contemplate the humanity of Christ. We are to contemplate the divinity of Christ. We are to contemplate the powerful compassion of the God-man and how we find everlasting sustenance and satisfaction in him alone.

43

It is I AM

MATTHEW 14:22–33

HE HEALED ALL THE SICK (4:24). He cleansed a leper (8:1–4). He cured a Roman centurion's servant (8:5–13). He cooled a fever (8:14, 15). He stilled the wind (8:23–27). He exorcised demons (8:28–32). He restored a paralytic (9:1–8). He stopped a desperate woman's twelve-year discharge of blood (9:20–23). He raised a little girl from the dead (9:18, 23–26). He opened the eyes of the blind (9:27–30; cf. 12:22). He made the mute speak (9:32, 33; cf. 12:22). He healed a man with a withered hand *on the Sabbath* (12:9–13). And he took five loaves and two fishes and fed over 5,000 people (14:19)!

These are the miracles of Jesus thus far in Matthew's Gospel. These miracles—by *how* they are done, *when* they are done, *where* they are done, and *to whom* they are done—show us something of the nature of the kingdom. What is the kingdom of heaven like? Look to the parables of Matthew 13, but look also to the miracles of Matthew 4—14. The kingdom of heaven is for rich and poor, religious and non-religious, Jew and Gentile, male and female, adult and child. The kingdom is for all who recognize their spiritual sickness and come to Christ in faith for rest, satisfaction, and the forgiveness of sin.

The miracles teach us about the nature of the kingdom. But they also reveal to us the identity of the King. In the miracles we are to see Jesus as the one prophesied in the Old Testament, the one whose very miracles—the blind receiving their sight, the lame walking, the lepers cleansed, the deaf hearing, and the dead raised to life (11:4, 5)—attest to his identity. This is the promised Christ.

And we are to see in these miracles that the one who has authority over every disease and every affliction (4:23, 24; 8:16; 9:35; 14:34–36; 15:29–31) also has authority over our greatest illness (sin) and what sin leads to (death).

We are to see that the one who has authority to heal has the authority to forgive sins (9:2, 6) and that such forgiveness ultimately comes on the cross, when "He took our illnesses and bore our diseases" (8:17, quoting Isaiah 53:4). We are to see that this is "Jesus," the name that means Savior, "for he will save his people from their sins" (1:21).

So in the miracles of our Lord we are to see him as *the Christ* (the Messiah) and as *Jesus* (the Savior). Moreover, as I explained in the last sermon, we are to see him as God's Son, "'Immanuel' (which means, God with us)" (1:23). Jesus Christ is God in the flesh. Now, if you zoned out in the last chapter when I was making this point—the point of the passage—Matthew mercifully follows the miracle of the feeding of the 5,000 with Jesus Christ walking on water, the miracle above all miracles where Jesus *shows* he is God and *says* he is God.

Christology: Jesus Is I Am

First, let me show you what he *says*.

Whenever I am studying a section of Scripture, I first look for structure. Is there structure to this miracle story? And if so, what is it? Here there certainly is structure. Matthew has divided his retelling of this miracle into two parts or acts. Act 1 is verses 22–27, Act 2 verses 28–33. Act 1 is about Jesus walking on water. Act 2 is about the disciples' response to Jesus' walking on water.

Notice that Act 2 ends with the words, "And those in the boat worshiped him, saying, 'Truly you are the Son of God'" (v. 33). Worship? That's a very odd thing for pious Jews to do to another human being. Then, stranger still, these monotheistic Jews call Jesus God's Son! It's the first time they say that. God the Father has said it of Jesus in 3:17. The demons have said it of him in 8:29. But now and finally the disciples say it as well. And by their saying it Matthew is saying to us that we should say it as well.

So that's the end of the miracle story and the end of Act 2. We have adoration and confession. Truly this is God's Son. How does Act 1 end? It ends with Jesus *saying*—perhaps screaming (that's how I envision it)—these words through the howling wind and rising waves:[1] "Take heart; it is I. Do not be afraid" (v. 27).

Here is where the original language and structure is helpful and interesting. In the original language of our text, after Jesus says, "Take heart" (it is one word in Greek and can mean "take heart" or "be of good courage"), he tells the disciples, "Do not be afraid." Between those words—fear not/fear not—we find the words, *ego eimi*. The ESV translates it, "it is I." But in Greek it is a very straightforward formula that means "I am." "Don't fear—I AM is here." The phrase *ego eimi* is the name God used for himself in the Old Testament, most famously at the burning bush. God tells Moses to tell the Israelites his name. "Say this to the people of Israel, 'I AM has sent me to you'" (Exodus 3:14 LXX).

Even more interestingly, this divine "self-identification formula" (I AM) is combined in a few places in Isaiah with the phrase, "fear not."[2] The most striking example comes from near the beginning of the first Servant section. In Isaiah 43:1–3 we read (I've cited for emphasis just the beginning of the verses):

> But now thus says the LORD,
> he who created you . . .
> "*Fear not*, for I have redeemed you . . .
> When you pass through the waters, I will be with you . . .
> For *I am* the LORD your God,
> the Holy One of Israel, your Savior."

If you think I'm making too much of these two little Greek words and this combination of "I am" and "fear not" in Isaiah, here's where the structure comes in to support the suspected significance. I told you the overall structure here. Act 1 ends at verse 27 and Act 2 at verse 33, and both acts end with a resounding Christological note: "Truly you are the Son of God" (v. 33), "It is I am" (v. 27). But both before and after that phrase in the middle—"saying, 'Take heart; it is I am,'" or "saying to them, 'Take courage; I am'"—are ninety-one words in Greek. In other words, structurally that phrase is dead center.

Is it merely a coincidence that in the middle of the one miracle that crystallized in the disciples' minds or at least verbalized on the disciples' lips the deity of Jesus we have the words "I am"? I don't think so, and neither do a host of other Bible commentators. For example, one commentator wrote, "The center of the story is Jesus' imperial '*I am*.' The feeder of the hungry in the preceding story is now identified as the divine Lord who walks on water."[3] Yes, Jesus is "the divine Lord who walks on water." Jesus says as much, and he shows as much. He *says* his identity (that's the bit about the "I am"), but he also *shows* his identity, obviously by walking on "the water" or "the sea."

In Scripture "the sea" often represented the forces of evil because it's powerful, uncontrollable, and deadly. You may remember in my chapter on the demonic exorcisms in 8:23–34 how it was significant that Jesus cast the demons out of the men into the pigs (unclean animals according to Old Testament law) and then the pigs fled into "the sea" (the sea representing the evil underworld, all that is unruly in this fallen cosmos). The sea often represented the forces of evil. Thus in Scripture, "the sea" is a power over which only God has power. Think of the crossing and closing of the Red Sea. Think of Jonah—of the storm, the calming of the storm, and that huge sea-creature rescuing the prophet by opening and closing its God-directed mouth.

Jesus walks on the sea! Jesus controls the sea!

When we read that we are not only to say, "Wow, what a miracle!" but also, "Wait, only God can control the sea!" As the psalmist says, "O Lord God of hosts, who is mighty as you are, O Lord . . . ? You rule the raging of the sea; when its waves rise, you still them" (Psalm 89:8, 9; cf. Psalm 65:5–8; 107:23–32). And as Job says of God, ". . . who commands the sun . . . who seals up the stars; who alone stretched out the heavens and trampled [or walked upon] the waves of the sea" (Job 9:7, 8; cf. Job 38:16; Psalm 77:19). Only God controls the sea and walks upon the waves—metaphorically or literally. Jesus controls the sea and walks upon the waves. Therefore, draw this line to that one and that one to this. This is God's Son (v. 33). This is "I am" (v. 27).[4] Jesus *says* he is God incarnate, and Jesus *shows* he is God incarnate.

Think of this miracle afresh. One day Jesus decided not to take a boat to the other side. He wasn't opposed to rowing or sailing a boat. We saw him do that in the last sermon (v. 13). However, this day he decided not to walk to the other side (and the crowd did likewise, see John 6:24, 25). Instead Jesus decided on this particular day (and only this day as far as we know) to walk on water from this side of the sea to the disciples' tossed-about boat *because* he wanted to make something clear before he would journey to Jerusalem to be the Passover sacrifice for our sins. He wanted to make clear to them and to us that it was "Immanuel" on that cross, that God incarnate was the one who took on in his flesh all of our iniquities.

Is that clear? Is it also clear why there is only one right response to this reality? Worship! Glory be to the Father and to the Son and to the Holy Ghost; as it was in the beginning, is now, and ever shall be, world without end. Amen and Amen.

Discipleship: Our Response to I Am

As with the last miracle story, this miracle story is about identity. More specifically, it's about Christology. Jesus Christ's supernatural authority over the sea and his claim while walking upon the sea shows and says to us that he is God's Son, "God with us" in the flesh, and he is thus worthy of our worship.

But that's only one side of the story. The other side has to do with discipleship—what it means to follow Jesus.

I'm sure (as I hope you're sure) that this passage before us records a real historical event. But I think, as many ancient and modern commentators have thought, that this event functions or can function (is intended to function) like "a little parable" on Christian discipleship.[5] This is what a Christian disciple looks like. With that in mind, before we get to the main lesson, here are two lesser lessons of Christian discipleship.

Lesser lesson 1: If you follow Christ's commands, it does not mean you will be spared adversity. Jesus "made the disciples get into the boat" (v. 22). Those disciples started to sail to the other side. Now Jesus knew what was going to happen when they were "a long way from the land" (v. 24)—the middle of the sea ("about three or four miles" out, John 6:19). He knew then that "the wind [would be] against them" (14:24). He knew the storm was coming. Obedience to Jesus' word does not mean no stormy seas ahead. In fact, as we have learned throughout our study of Matthew, quite the opposite is true. If you want to follow Jesus, watch out. Watch out for the temptations and troubles and trials that will arise and crash upon you like waves crashing against a boat in the middle of rough waters.

Lesser lesson 2: Nevertheless, Jesus knows the trouble we are in, and he knows how to rescue his disciples from such troubles, and we can count on him to do so. One miracle is Jesus' walking on water; a second miracle is Peter walking on water, but a third miracle (the one most often ignored) is the sea actually settling down once Jesus gets on board. If the sea didn't stop, nobody would be rescued. These men still have to deal with this deadly storm. They are still on that boat in those waters. Jesus' stilling the storm (we are not told how, but I envision a one-word whisper, "Quiet") is an act of divine rescue. So the lesser lesson is this: Jesus will not abandon his own. He comes to save us. He comes to deliver us from evil.

With this in mind, verses 22–33 record a smaller version of the story of our salvation. Jesus is up on a mountain, praying. He is communing with God the Father. Meanwhile, God's people are in need of rescue. So Jesus descends. He comes down from his communion with the Father. He walks straight into the thick of evil, into the darkness ("the fourth watch of the night"—3 a.m. to 6 a.m.). He walks on the sea. Then at dawn while it is still partly dark—like Easter morning (John 20:1)—he rescues those who cry out as Peter did, "Lord, save me" (14:30). That is lesser lesson 2: Jesus knows how to rescue his people.

Those are the two lesser lessons, or potential lessons. I say "potential" only because I'm not absolutely sure it's appropriate to turn this text into a little parable and see certain historical actions as symbolic. But the one lesson I'm certain we should learn from this passage is the lesson of faith. The theme is, what is the nature of Christian discipleship? But under that umbrella is another question: what is the nature of a disciple's faith?

Here is where Peter comes into play. Look with me at verses 28–31.

John records Jesus' walking on water. Mark records Jesus' walking on water. But only Matthew adds this bit about Peter walking on water and sinking into the water. Why? I think there may be a few reasons for this. One reason might simply be to validate the miracle—the idea being that not only did Jesus have the power to make another person walk on water (J. C. Ryle calls that "a mightier miracle still"),[6] but that Jesus is not a "ghost" as the disciples first thought, if sinking Peter was rescued by Jesus' physical hand. Another reason might be to flash back to chapter 10 and flash forward to chapter 28, where Jesus shares his power with his church: "All authority . . . has been given to me. Go therefore [you—through my presence and my power] and make disciples."

Peter's walking on water might be for one of those two reasons. But the final and best reason, I think, is to teach us about the nature of Christian faith. Look again at verses 28–31, and I'll explain what I mean by the nature of Christian faith.

After Jesus said, "Take heart; it is I [*I am*]. Do not be afraid," we read that Peter answers, "Lord, if it is you, command me to come to you on the water" (v. 28). Jesus said, "'Come.' So Peter got out of the boat and walked on the water and came to Jesus. But when he saw [the effects of] the wind, he was afraid, and beginning to sink . . ." (vv. 28–30a). Petras sinks like a rock. But then he cried out in faith, "Lord, save me" (v. 30b). And Jesus did. He "immediately reached out his hand and took hold of him." He didn't next say, "Good try. Way to go. Peter, you're the first human (besides me) to walk on water." Rather he said, "O you of little faith, why did you doubt?" (v. 31).

What do we do with this? What does this teach us about faith? Some view Jesus' rebuke (and it is a rebuke—we might be glad, as I'm sure Peter was glad, our Lord saves before he scolds)[7] as a rebuke against Peter's arrogance. For example, Calvin thinks Peter should have stayed on the boat. It was not for him to walk on water. To do so was to overreach his bounds. Calvin writes that "by [Peter's] example believers are taught to beware of over-much rashness . . . of transgressing . . . [our] limits."[8] We're not God; let's not pretend for a moment that we are. In a similar vein Matthew Henry writes of Jesus allowing Peter to walk and *sink* so as to have Peter "check his [self]-confidence."[9]

As much as I respect Calvin and Henry, I don't think either of those readings is right. Peter is no "faultless hero" in this Gospel, and in some ways this scene foreshadows the drama of his denial—his "overconfident confession (26.30–36), his denial of the Lord (26.69–75), and his final restoration (cf. 28.16–17)."[10] However, I don't see Jesus' invitation "Come" (v. 29) to be inauthentic or some kind of trick to show Peter how proud or weak or in need of Jesus' salvation he is. I think Peter knows all that already.

Peter is to be scolded, if I can use that hard a word for what Jesus says in verse 31, not for leaving the boat but for not abiding in the faith, for not persevering, for losing his focus. You see, the nature of faith here (with this vivid picture) seems to be not just "I'm a proud, weak, desperate sinner, save me"—that we only need to reach our hand up to Jesus as Savior. Rather the picture here is of walking toward Jesus as Lord. Yes, we need him as Savior (we all come to him with our bodies so to speak beneath the waters), but once we are pulled up out of those waters, we must also walk. We must walk toward him as Lord, trusting in his divine power each step of the way.

What is the nature of Christian faith? Here I think we are taught that faith is *confidence* not in self or self-righteousness but in Christ. We may doubt, but there is no need to doubt. Jesus isn't high on doubt here, is he? "O you of little faith, why did you doubt?" (v. 31). You see, doubt equals little faith—not no faith, but less faith than you should have.

Faith is *confidence* in Christ. Faith is also *courage* through Christ.[11] Faith is courage through or by means of the power of Christ. Jesus said, "[W]hy did you doubt?" (v. 31). Faith is confidence in Christ. But he also said, "Do not be afraid" or "fear not" (v. 27). As doubt is contrary to faith (21:21), so fear is contrary to faith. Do you see that? In verse 26 the disciples are "terrified . . . they cried out in fear." In verse 27 Jesus said, "Do not be afraid." In verse 30, "when he [Peter] saw the wind, he was afraid, and [guess what happened? He began] to sink." Fear or faith? Fear that God can't provide and can't save is contrary to faith (see especially Habakkuk 3:17–19).

"The LORD is my shepherd; I shall not want" (Psalm 23:1), but also I shall not fear. I will not fear famine (you make "me lie down in green pastures," you lead "me beside still waters"),[13] enemies (you prepare me "a table . . . in the presence of my enemies"), or death ("even though I walk through the valley of the shadow of death . . . you are with me. . . . I shall dwell in the house of the LORD forever"). What is the nature of a disciple's faith? Doubt not; fear not. Confidence in Christ; courage by means of Christ.

Hebrews 11:1 defines faith as "the *conviction* of things not seen." Hebrews 11:2ff. then illustrates that definition with the heroes of the faith who were all looking forward confidently in faith (see esp. v. 26). Faith is conviction. It's confidence. And faith is, as Hebrews 12:2 phrases it, "looking to Jesus, the founder and perfecter of our faith." Looking to Jesus, as Peter was and then wasn't. Looking to Jesus not once but every step of the way. Considering him (Hebrews 12:3) and walking toward him, with eyes fixed on him, not growing weary no matter how high or heavy the waves of this world crash against us. Doubt not. Fear not. Confidence in Christ; courage by means of Christ—that's faith.

So yes, faith means assenting to certain truths—"Jesus is the Son of God," etc. And yes, faith means understanding those truths—"Jesus, fully God, became fully man, so that I (a fully sinful man) might be fully reconciled to God." Faith means assent and understanding. But faith also means trust—getting out of the boat into the evil waters and walking forward to Jesus, by the power of Jesus, until we get to Jesus.[14]

Christology and discipleship—that's 14:22–33. That's the miracle of Jesus walking on water. That's the sum of Christianity (when you think about it) in twelve short verses. Not bad, Matthew. Not bad at all.

44

The Damning Effects of Spiritual Blindness

MATTHEW 14:34—15:20

IN SEVENTH GRADE Kevin Koplowski had the coolest science fair project ever. His project earned him a place in the State Fair, where he did not place. It was not for lack of genius of mind or coolness of project that it didn't place, but rather because he didn't carefully follow directions. His project was technically not an experiment. Unlike my experiment, which proved through carefully, rigorous, repeated testing which paper towel was the most absorbent, Kevin's display, report, or whatever it should be called merely showed the existence of blind spots in the human eye.

Here's how it worked. You would come up to his booth, stand on a certain X on the floor in front of it, place your head wherever you were supposed to place your head, and then try to view certain objects at various points around you. The fact that you couldn't see all the points proved the existence of blind spots.

Blood Spots

It is one thing to be blind physically. We all are blind to a certain extent. We all have blind spots. But it is quite another thing to be blind spiritually. The disciples had spiritual blind spots. They couldn't perfectly see who Jesus was and understand what he was up to. But overall they could see, and their sight, as the life of Jesus unfolded before their eyes, sharpened and broadened. However, the scribes and Pharisees, those Jewish religious leaders we encounter here again in 15:1, were completely blind spiritually. And it's not just that they were blind, but they were attempting to lead other blind people.

This is what Jesus says of them in verse 14: "[T]hey are blind guides." Then he addresses their dark, dangerous, *damning* activity: "And if the blind lead the blind, both will fall into a pit."

In this chapter we are going to look at the damning effects of spiritual blindness. I say "damning" because spiritual blindness has consequences, which Jesus speaks of metaphorically in verse 13, 14: "Every plant that my heavenly Father has not planted will be rooted up. Let them alone. . . ." It is not a good thing to be "let alone" from hearing/understanding the gospel (cf. 25:41). And it is certainly not a good thing to be rooted up and (if the metaphor is connected to what is said earlier in 3:10–12) to be thrown into the fire—i.e., to be judged eternally.

In this chapter we will look at the scribes and Pharisees and the effects of their spiritual blindness. We will do so for two reasons. First, so we might recognize them as false teachers and thus not follow their lead. Second, so we might correct, if necessary, our own vision.

What I see in them are three big blind spots. Collectively these blind spots are large enough to blind them completely. And I see these three blind spots to be characteristic of every spiritually blind person—then (in the days of Jesus) and now (in our day).

The Spiritually Blind Ask the Wrong Religious Questions

First, the spiritually blind always ask the wrong religious questions. Their question to Jesus comes in 15:2: "Why do your disciples break the tradition of the elders?"

What comes before that question in Matthew's Gospel? As we saw in the last two chapters, we have Jesus' look-at-me-I'm-God-in-the-flesh miracles—the feeding of the 5,000 and the walking on the sea. Those two miracles scream to us, "This must be God!" And that's what the disciples on the boat finally saw. The previous sermon's miracle centers on Jesus' claim, "Don't fear; I AM is here," and it ends and culminates with the disciples' adoration and confession, with worship and then those words, "Truly you are the Son of God" (14:33).[1]

So before the scribes and Pharisees ask their question, we have the disciples' eyes widening to the person of Jesus through the miracles of Jesus. But we also have a group from Gennesaret and how they react to Jesus. Just run your eyes through 14:34–36. What is significant about this seemingly insignificant summary section?

Two things are significant. First, Gennesaret is no Jerusalem. Jerusalem is the religious center of the Jewish world. It's where these important Jewish religious leaders come from (15:1). In our Christian context, it's no Rome, Geneva, or Canterbury. It's as significant a city as Evaz, Iran is to Christianity. Where? Exactly. Second, look at how this town responds to Jesus. The verbs tell the story. "And when the men of that place *recognized* him, they *sent* around to all that region and brought to him all who were sick and *implored* him that they might only touch the fringe of his garment. And as many as touched it [just the fringe!] were made well" (14:35, 36).

That's the context. That's what comes before the scribes and Pharisees' question. Jesus is a man who can feed thousands of people with five loaves and two fishes. Jesus is a man who can walk on water and calm the sea. Jesus is a man who has such power that if you just touch the fringe of his garment in faith you can be cured of whatever ails you. Completely cured! So what kind of a question should you ask such a man? How about "Who are you?" How about "What must I do to follow you?"

But what do they ask? They ask nothing about Jesus. Instead they ask, "Why do your disciples [not even Jesus] break the tradition of the elders? For they do not wash their hands when they eat" (15:2). They ask a very serious and seemingly important religious question. However, it is the wrong question. It's like a reporter asking a firefighter just after he has rescued a baby from a burning building, "Now, sir, I've heard that your brother eats meat on Fridays during Lent. Is that true?" What? Meat? Lent? My brother? What kind of a question is that? Considering all Jesus has done and taught, they could have (should have) come up with a better question than that. But that's just part of the disease. Spiritually blind people—then and now—are always asking the wrong questions.

Have you ever had this happen to you? You're sharing the gospel with someone, thinking they are listening quite intently, and when you are done, they ask a question that has nothing to do with the death and resurrection of Christ, sin and forgiveness, Heaven and Hell. They don't ask, "Is it true that Jesus rose from the dead?" or "How can I be sure that what you've shared with me is true?" Instead they want to know if Jesus was married to Mary Magdalene. They want to know if you're pro-choice. They want to know if you think we evolved from monkeys. They want to know how many angels can dance on the head of a needle.

The scribes and Pharisees come all the way from Jerusalem. They are on some top-level official business. They have heard and seen Jesus. Surely now they will ask him an important question. Instead they come to ask Jesus about his disciples and their new eating habits. What "blind fools" (23:17)!

The Spiritually Blind Trust in Un-Scriptural Traditions

The second blind spot is that the spiritually blind trust in un-Scriptural traditions. Before we examine verses 3 to 9—Jesus' right response to their wrong question—let me first make clear that I know that Jesus knows where these men are coming from with their question. He knows that they are not the Jewish germ police, out to serve and protect Israel from poor hygiene. He knows this is an issue of ritual purity to them. He knows that before they reclined to eat they first washed themselves and everything else—the cups and pots and copper vessels and even their dining couches (see Mark 7:3, 4). He also knows that their rules and regulations concerning ceremonial cleanliness don't come from Scripture. According to the *written law*[2] (in Exodus 30 and Leviticus 22) only Aaron, his sons, and their offspring (the priests), in or before their temple service, are to make themselves clean, not everybody before every meal. Jesus also knows that their rules and regulations come from *oral tradition*, the oral tradition of the elders that prescribed the precise way to wash, when to wash, how often to wash, with what to wash, and why if you don't wash when and where and with what you are terribly offensive to God.

Knowing all that, how does Jesus respond? The one who has been breaking one oral tradition of theirs after another—touching lepers, dead bodies, and menstruating woman (yikes!), associating with tax collectors and Gentile sinners (double yikes!), and breaking bread in public without any mention of washing hands (triple yikes!) answers with a one-two punch from the *written* Word of God. First, he gives an upper cut from the Law (from Moses) that makes them stagger and stumble backwards. Then he lands a short, quick jab, the knock-out punch from the prophets (from Isaiah). A one-two punch: It is written; it is written. And down they go.

Let's start with the knockout punch, the quick jab from Isaiah 29:13. Our Lord says:

> You hypocrites, well did Isaiah prophesy of you, when he said:
>
> "This people honors me with their lips,
> but their heart is far from me;
> in vain do they worship me,
> teaching as doctrines the commandments of men." (15:7, 8)

Three times in Jesus' answer he charges them with supplanting the Scriptures. In verse 3 he says, "you break the commandment of God for the sake of your tradition." In verse 6 he says, "So for the sake of your tradition you have made void the word of God." Finally in verse 9 he speaks of them as "teaching as doctrines the commandments of men." Jesus accuses them of holding hostage the divine commandment. He accuses them of gagging God's voice with the tattered rag of their traditions. He says, in essence, that the spiritually blind trust in un-Scriptural traditions.

He doesn't just say this. He substantiates it with an illustration from but one of their many lawless traditions. Jesus answered them:

> And why do you break the commandment of God for the sake of your tradition? For God commanded, "Honor your father and your mother" [Exodus 20:12], and, "Whoever reviles father or mother must surely die" [Exodus 21:17]. But you say, "If anyone tells his father or his mother, 'What you would have gained from me is given to God,' he need not honor his father." So for the sake of your tradition you have made void the word of God. (15:3–6)

Jesus sets up what they say ("[b]ut you say," v. 5) against what God said ("[f]or God commanded," v. 4), showing how they set aside even one of the Ten Commandments (the fifth commandment) for the man-made and man-centered tradition of "Corban" (Mark 7:11).

Let me explain this tradition, so you feel the sting of Jesus' hit. Corban was the practice of pledging money to the temple to be paid upon one's death.[3] That sounds fine, right? It's like willing some resources to a church or charity. Well, here's where the religious tomfoolery and trickery comes in. These funds, since they were set aside for "religious" purposes, could not be used or given to one's parents in their hour of need. So here is what happened in Jesus' day. If you wanted to get out of helping your parents in their old age, you could simply declare your goods "given to God." The sanctified selfishness would be excusable: "Sorry, Mom and Dad, I'd love to help you out. But, you know, all this money I have is 'Corban.' I can use it for myself, but whatever is left is going to God. You understand."

Oh, Jesus understood. To him Corban broke the law of love. It broke not just the fifth commandment. It broke both tables of the Law—the love of God and the love of neighbor. To him Corban killed compassion. Only someone spiritually blind wouldn't see this. Only someone very spiritually blind would practice this and teach others to practice it.

The spiritually blind trust in un-Scriptural traditions and trusting in un-Scriptural traditions is dangerous. It harms real people. It's dangerous, and it's damning. It has real effects upon those who practice it.

Now, to clarify this section (15:3–9) Jesus does not demonize tradition. Jesus is not saying to the Pharisees, "The reason I disagree with you is because

I don't believe in tradition. In fact, I have never believed in tradition. Why? Well, because the founders of our faith—Abraham, Isaac, and Jacob—didn't believe in tradition. And Moses didn't believe in tradition. So we can't start following some tradition now, especially in light of the history of our rich tradition of not following any tradition whatsoever."[4] Jesus was not saying here that it is his tradition not to follow tradition. Human experience and history tell us that society cannot function without some set traditions in place. The church is no different, for every Christian "community has to apply the word of God to situations in real life, and [thus] traditions inevitably develop from this undertaking."[5]

My church, as is true of every church, has its traditions. Here are some traditions from our regular Sunday morning service. We say the Apostle's Creed. We take a public offering with silky crimson bags. We sometimes sing the Doxology. We have a benediction at the end of the service. The pastors wear suit jackets as part of our holy vestments. We offer something called Sunday school for both adults and children. We sing hymns almost exclusively written by dead Englishmen. We sing choruses composed by mostly living Caucasians. We have a Christmas Eve service. We celebrate Easter on a certain day. These are all traditions that are not found in the Word of God. However, there is a significant difference between our traditions and the Pharisees' traditions. Our traditions are traditions (Lord willing, they must always be tested) that have been put in place as servants of the Word—that is, traditions that do not nullify the Word of God but uplift, clarify, or apply it.

The question for us is not, does this church hold to certain traditions or not? Rather, the question is, does this church hold to certain traditions that contradict Scripture or depose the authority of the Word of God? Does our church, and do we as individuals, hold certain faulty and misleading traditions that are far removed from God's original intention?

Here Jesus is teaching against the enthronement of tradition and the dethronement of the Word of God. He is addressing traditions that immediately or inevitably force God's people to *leave*, *reject*, or *nullify* the written Scriptures. Thus we are taught here that those very traditions—if we are to see as we should see—are to be left, rejected, and nullified. The spiritually blind trust in un-Scriptural traditions, but those with spiritual sight trust in the Word of God for the proper worship of God.

The Spiritually Blind Don't See That Spiritual Defilement Is a Matter of the Heart

The first blind spot is that the spiritually blind ask the wrong religious questions. The second blind spot is that the spiritually blind trust in un-Scriptural traditions. The third and final blind spot is that the spiritually blind underestimate, in Jeremiah's words, how desperately wicked the human heart is, or in Jesus' words, how unclean it is. The spiritually blind don't see that spiritual defilement is first, foremost, and foundationally a matter of the heart.

In 15:10ff. our Lord calls the crowd and gives his own Shema, "Hear and understand." He says, "[I]t is not what goes into the mouth that defiles a person, but what comes out of the mouth [which comes out of the heart, v. 18]; this defiles a person."

That (vv. 10, 11) is Jesus' little "parable" as Peter calls it in verse 15. And what does this parable mean? Jesus explains it in verses 17–20:

> Do you not see that whatever goes into the mouth passes into the stomach and is expelled? But what comes out of the mouth proceeds from the heart, and this defiles a person. For out of the heart come evil thoughts, murder, adultery, sexual immorality, theft, false witness, slander. These are what defile a person. But to eat with unwashed hands does not defile anyone.

Jesus teaches there are two places to look for spiritual purity or impurity—the heart and the mouth (not the hands or stomach). But notice that Jesus isn't high on either. He doesn't speak of "the good things that come up out of human hearts"[6]—sympathy, kindness, artistry, creativity, love. Instead he speaks only of the bad things—"evil thoughts, murder, adultery, sexual immorality, theft, false witness, slander." Here he actually uses the second table of the Ten Commandments. He used the fifth commandment earlier. Now he brings out commandments six, seven, eight, nine, and maybe ten. Here he takes God's perfect Law and uses it as a spotlight on the human heart. It's similar to what he did in the Sermon on the Mount. "Let's look at the human heart," Jesus says in essence. "Oh, let's look very carefully and closely. Now, what do we see? It is beating but diseased." The human heart is indeed diseased. We all suffer from heart disease. Our heart pumps evil through our arteries—go ahead and hate, go ahead and lust, go ahead and curse and covet and lie and steal.

Here our Lord gives no optimistic anthropology. According to Jesus, as Bruner notes, "The filth of the [toilet] is not so great as that of a human heart *not yet cleansed*" (emphasis mine). Bruner continues with this question: ". . . who thoroughly weighs this?"[7] Good question.

"How's your heart?" is how I might phrase it. And you might say, "How do I know? Listen, I get all that about washing hands, cups, and pots, eating kosher food, keeping the Sabbath, and so on. I get that all that stuff doesn't get me right with God, but this old ticker, how do I know what's in it? How do I know if Jesus is shooting straight here or just exaggerating to make a point?"

Jesus solves the riddle. He is shooting straight. He is telling the truth about the human heart. How do you know what's in your heart? Easy; just look at what comes out of your mouth: "What comes out of the mouth proceeds from the heart" (v. 18).

We all know that how you talk to and about your spouse tells you (and everyone in earshot) about the quality of your marriage. The same is true of father-son, boss-employee, pastor-congregation relationships. The same is true of every relationship. The same is true of our relationship with God. "I tell you," Jesus told us already in 12:36, 37, "on the day of judgment people will give account for every careless word they speak, for by your words you will be justified, and by your words you will be condemned." Our words speak volumes. Our words are the window to our hearts.

How clean is your heart? It's as clean as your tongue. And who of us has never sworn or gossiped or spoken in unholy anger or given unjust criticism or taken the name of the Lord our God in vain? Lay down your stone, O sinner. Cover your mouths, for we are a people with unclean lips. Yes, the world is full of dirty words. And it will take a lot more than the efforts of the EPA to clean it up. Our world is filthy, and the world's "major pollutant" is words.[8] Words are the great human impurity. Words are the toxin of today. Our bad words show our bad hearts.

Jesus' "Parable of the Mouth"[9] teaches that we are not clean enough on the inside to be right with God through washing our hands before we eat. Put differently, clean hands are not the mediator between God and man. Jesus is. Through the Holy Spirit we need Jesus to give us broken and contrite hearts (Psalm 51:17), circumcised hearts (Romans 2:29), clean hearts (Hebrews 10:22), pure hearts (1 Peter 1:22), new hearts (Ezekiel 36:26), sincere hearts (Ephesians 6:5), so that we might believe from the heart (Ephesians 3:17) and obey from the heart (Deuteronomy 11:13), so we might have Christ dwell in our hearts through faith (Ephesians 3:17).[10]

Yes, "The filth of the [toilet] is not so great as that of a human heart *not yet cleansed*."[11] But Christ—his righteousness, his purity, his perfectly clean hands and head and heart—dwelling in our hearts through faith changes everything. What can cure a sin-diseased heart? Faith. Faith in Jesus. What can wash away all those unclean words? Faith. Faith in Jesus. Faith in Christ and him crucified, dying upon the cross for all our sins—the blasphemies, the backtalk, every careless thought and deed and *word*.

The scribes and the Pharisees were blind to this. They were blind to Jesus.

That's why they asked the wrong question, trusted in their un-Scriptural traditions, and thought purity was just an outside, not an inside, deal. But here Jesus has taught us, as he tried to teach them, that "the kingdom of God is not a matter of eating and drinking but of righteousness and peace and joy in the Holy Spirit" (Romans 14:17), that the Father is seeking "true worshippers" who will worship him "in spirit and truth" (John 4:23), and that only the pure in heart shall see God (5:8).

That is what is he has taught here—that only the pure in heart shall see God. So how's your heart? How's your mouth? How's your sight? Are you seeing as you should see? Or are you still blind?

45

Feeding the "Dogs"

MATTHEW 15:21–39

WHEN GOD WANTS TO EXPRESS his love for his people, he often does so with food. Eden was filled with fruit; the promised land with milk and honey; the wilderness with quail and manna; the Feast of Booths with its food, drink, oils, etc.; and the Lord's Supper with bread and wine, and at the end of all history there will be the feast of all feasts—the wedding supper of the Lamb. "Blessed are those who are invited" (Revelation 19:9).

In Jesus' day, God's people longed for this messianic banquet. They knew, believed, and trusted that when Messiah comes, God's people would sit at table with him and feast. Our text is but a foretaste of that. When we read these two stories placed side by side in Matthew's Gospel, we are to say, "Here is the Messiah, the Master of God's house and God's people, the one who has set a table in the wilderness, a table filled with food so abundant that there are leftovers and crumbs scattered everywhere—enough food to feed the world, enough food to feed all who have faith in Jesus."

Look with me now at 15:21–39. I divide this text not by the two stories but by the two themes, themes that we'll get at by asking and answering two questions. The first question is, who's invited to the master's table? The second question is, how does one get into the banquet?

Who's Invited to the Master's Table?

The answer to the first question—who is invited to the master's table?—is, everyone! It's an open invitation.

Matthew's Gospel, which is rightly understood as being the most Jewish of the Gospels,[1] is arguably the most Gentile as well.[2] Think of Matthew's genealogy, which includes Gentiles. Think of the visit of the magi. Think of the healing of the Roman centurion's slave. Think of another Roman centurion's confession at the foot of the cross. Think of the Great Commission. Think of Jesus' words in 8:11, "I tell you, many will come from east and west and recline at table with Abraham, Isaac, and Jacob in the kingdom of heaven." Matthew's Gospel says the door to the kingdom of heaven is open to all—to the Jew first (Abraham, Isaac, and Jacob), *but also to the Gentile* (Romans 1:16).

What we have seen throughout Matthew is how those with gold star invitations—the Jewish religious and political leaders—have come up with one excuse after another why they can't make the party. However, here in our text we find people from the highways and byways—the poor, the crippled, the lame, the blind (v. 30), the demon-possessed (v. 22)—willing to dine in the desert, willing to eat even the crumbs that fall from the master's table (see v. 27; cf. Luke 14:12–24).[3]

The house of David will be filled by the Son of David. That is, our Lord Jesus will fill his messianic banquet table with all who are willing to come to him for sustenance. What he said in John 6:37b ("whoever comes to me I will never cast out"), here he acts out. "Whoever" denotes an open invitation—male/female, master/slave, Jew and even Gentile (cf. Galatians 3:28). Gentiles? Yes, even Gentiles.

In case this *Gentile inclusion idea* isn't plain to you, let me show you it to you in the verses before us. First, we have verse 21: "And Jesus went away from there [Gennesaret] and withdrew to the district of Tyre and Sidon." Why would Jesus walk from Gennesaret to Tyre and then from Tyre up to Sidon? It is thirty-five miles from Gennesaret to Tyre and twenty-five miles from Tyre to Sidon. That's a long way to walk. Why walk? And why walk *there*?

The distance is not as shocking as the destination itself. Tyre and Sidon? That's Gentile territory. What's Jesus doing out there and up there? Why is Jesus leaving the promised land for "paganland"?[4] What is the Son of Abraham/the Son of David (the Jewish Messiah) doing there? Craig Blomberg summarizes the move perfectly: "Jesus has obviously withdrawn from Israel ideologically in vv. 1–20; now he . . . withdraws geographically."[5] I'll take Blomberg's thought a step further. Jesus is on a short-term missions trip. He is *showing* the Great Commission before he *commands* it.

So that's verse 21—Jesus' journey to Gentileville. Then look at verse 22, and note who Jesus meets there. Why, it's a Gentile! "And behold, a Canaanite woman from that region came out . . ." Not a "Syrophoenician" woman, as Mark would call her in his version of the story (Mark 7:26) and as she would have been called in Jesus' day, but "a Canaanite woman" is how Matthew puts it, an Old Testament way of describing her race and religion. And, my well-read Old Testament readers, what does the word "Canaanite" conjure up in your minds? They're the bad guys. These guys and gals are Israel's enemies!

There are the Egyptians, the Babylonians, the Canaanites—all Israel's archenemies. But here is Jesus (who came out of Egypt) bringing (so it seems) even Israel's enemies out of exile. Yes, Jesus is extending grace to a Canaanite woman. Both descriptions are striking. This is a Canaanite. That's pretty bad. Stay away from her, Jesus. Ah, but she's a woman too. Jewish men were not to associate with women, any woman who was not their wife or mother. And Jewish rabbis were never to associate with Gentile sinners. Remember how flabbergasted the disciples were when Jesus talked with the woman at the well, a Samaritan woman (John 4). Well, this is a *Canaanite* woman! Tattoo "Gentile sinner" across her forehead.

So in 15:21, 22 we see where Jesus is (Gentileville) and who he is talking to (a Gentile) and who he will minister to (Gentiles). In the following verses we will see three other, less subtle details that show Jesus is extending grace to Gentiles.

First, we have the reference to "dogs" in verses 26, 27. I will say more about their dog dialogue in a moment. For now we have the following scenario: the woman begs Jesus for help. She begs again. And then Jesus replies with his "dog" comment: "It is not right to take the children's bread and throw it to the dogs" (v. 26). What is he talking about? Well, she knows what he's talking about. Here "the children" (the children of God) symbolizes "Israel" and the "dogs" the Gentiles. Just as someone might call my Irish father a paddy (in fact his name is Patrick or Padraic in Gaelic), and someone might (even still today) call those big police vans paddy wagons (for those troublesome Irishmen), so the Jews of Jesus' day, as a ethnic/racial slur, called Gentiles "dogs."

So Jesus is dealing with a Gentile "dog." But interestingly here he doesn't use the common slur word "dog," referring to those "wild, homeless scavenger" dogs one would have found on the streets of Palestine.[6] Instead he uses the word for "house dog."

Well, you might say, "Big deal. That's not much better. Messiah or no Messiah, he shouldn't go around calling women 'dogs' or any other animal. Most women don't appreciate that." But he is not name-calling. And she gets that. She gets the reference to her. And she gets his point. It's a loaded theological point. She'll stick around, as we'll revisit their dialogue in a few pages, to debate him about it.

For now, however, the point I want us to see (as we are answering the question, who's invited?) is Jesus' willingness to let the dogs into the house.

He is willing to call Gentiles "house dogs." He is willing to let these dogs eat from the messianic table in the house of David. He is willing to let Jews and Gentiles live and dine under the same roof.[7]

All this is quite revolutionary, and she knows it. So when Jesus opens that door just a crack, she pushes her way in. She will beg like a dog and even eat like a dog. But the Master of the house, by the end of the story, is very willing to accept her—a Canaanite woman!—as a daughter of Abraham, as a "child" of God. What is taught in Galatians 3:26–29 is illustrated here, or better, acted out here:

> For in Christ Jesus you are all sons [children] of God, through faith. . . . There is neither Jew nor Greek . . . no male and female, for you are all one in Christ Jesus. And if you are Christ's, then you are Abraham's offspring [his children], heirs according to promise.

Who's invited to the table? Everyone is; both Jew and Gentile.

More Food for More "Dogs"

Let's review. Jesus is in Tyre and Sidon (Gentile cities), and he encounters and accepts a Gentile woman. When our Lord leaves this region, he returns to somewhere (v. 29) "beside the Sea of Galilee," somewhere where he would feed 4,000 people. Now, who were these people? Jews or Gentiles or some mix of both? I think they were mostly Gentiles. I say this for three reasons.

First, I say this because in Mark's version of the story he tells us where the feeding of the 4,000 took place—"the region of the Decapolis" (Mark 7:31); that is, ten cities that were known for being inhabited by mostly Gentiles. Second, I say this because of how these people responded to the healings. At the end of verse 31 we read, "And they glorified the God of Israel." "God of Israel" is a unique response in the Gospels. It is used in Isaiah 45:15 in the context of the one, true God's dealing with the nations. So maybe their reply is what a Gentile would say. Not just, "And they glorified God," but "And they glorified the God of Israel." A final possible reason those fed were mostly Gentiles has to do with numerology. Yes, numerology!

Since the fourth century, if not earlier, Christian commentators have understood the feeding of the 5,000 to symbolize "Jesus' provision for the Jews" and the feeding of the 4,000 as his "provision for the Gentiles."[8] So, what I'm suggesting here isn't something novel. In fact, some of the earliest Christian commentators, the majority of whom were Gentiles, were so deeply moved by this glorious illustration of Jesus' inclusion of the Gentiles that they perceived the particular numbers used in this text (numbers like "seven" and "four thousand") to symbolize certain theological truths.

Some of the church fathers, for example, believed that the number "four thousand" symbolized "the four corners of the earth from which the Gentiles came."[9] Also the number "seven" (interestingly mentioned three times in our text, 777) they saw to symbolize the perfect and "the worldwide scope of Jesus' message."[10] In Scripture the number "seven" often signifies perfection or completeness, as in the seven days of creation (Genesis 1, 2). Further the numbers "seven" and "seventy" are also representative of the Gentile population (according to the list of nations provided in Genesis 10 there are or were "seventy" nations in the world).[11]

While such an understanding of Scripture may rightly be too extravagant for our modern sensibilities, it nevertheless forcefully makes an important, in fact necessary, point that we overly sophisticated people often miss or neglect. Unlike John in the book of Revelation, Matthew "doesn't major in symbolic meanings," and thus in general it is unwise to overanalyze or over-symbolize his details, and particularly his use of numbers.[12] (So I don't see the "three days" in verse 32 to represent the Trinity.) Yet it would be shortsighted, in my estimation, to miss the likely symbolism of these two miracles, a symbolism not generated or made by Matthew, the artistic author, but made or created in real history solely by the sovereign providence of God.

So, modern exegete that I am, I say the symbolism stands. Yes, I say what I think Matthew was saying: when the 5,000 Jews were fed and there were twelve baskets left, it was emblematic of God's full provision for the twelve tribes of Israel. And when the 4,000 Gentiles were fed and there were seven large baskets of leftovers, it symbolized the completion and fullness of Christ's mission, the overabundance of God's love and mercy in the gospel of our Lord Jesus Christ that extends still today throughout the world to every tongue and tribe and nation.[13]

How Does One Get into the Banquet?

In this sermon we are answering two questions from this text. First: who's invited to the master's table? Answer: everyone—Jews and Gentiles. The second question is: how does one get into this banquet? What's the ticket to the table? Answer: faith in Jesus as Lord.

I have argued previously (chapter 1) that the melodic line of Matthew's Gospel is found in the Great Commission and can be summarized as follows:

All authority

All nations

All allegiance

Here we see (as we do in nearly every passage) *all authority*. Again Jesus shows his amazing authority. Look at these miracles—a demon-possessed daughter instantly healed when Jesus says so (v. 28), another long list of healings (v. 30), and then the second grand multiplication of loaves and fish (vv. 36, 37). Jesus shows his authority. Also, we find here *all nations*. That's what the first half of this chapter was all about. The gospel of the kingdom is for Jews and Gentiles. It's a universal, global, transcultural, not-of-this-world-but-for-this-world message. All authority, all nations, and *all allegiance*. In other words, the crucial point is faith in Jesus as King/the one in charge/the one from whom you beg, submit to, and even worship as Lord.

So, who's invited? Everyone. The gospel is inclusive. But how does one get in? Well, one must be properly dressed for such an important occasion. A bride doesn't wear a mechanic's jumpsuit to her wedding; a groom doesn't wear orange corduroy shorts. One must be properly dressed, dressed in the righteousness of Christ through faith in him. So how does one get in? Faith alone in Christ alone—*sola fide; sola Christus*. That's not only a Protestant Reformation slogan—it's illustrated right here in our Bibles! The gospel is inclusive and yet exclusive. The gospel is beautifully (necessarily) inclusively exclusive. One must come through the gate that God has provided—Jesus alone—and one must unlock that gate with the just the right key—faith alone. As even Alexander Sand, a distinguished Roman Catholic Bible scholar, writes of verses 21–28: "The theme of this whole story is this—it is not belonging to Israel that guarantees salvation, 'but faith alone' (*sondern allein der Glaube*)."[14]

Now you might say, "Okay. Faith alone in Christ alone. But what does such faith look like?" Verses 21–28—that's what it looks like.

I don't know about you, but I'm glad that the Bible rarely defines theological terms. To my knowledge there is no definition of the Trinity, only the workings of the Trinity, and only one definition of faith (Hebrews 11:1), but hundreds of examples of it. The Bible is not like a doctoral dissertation: "Let's start by defining our terms." Rather it is like a motion picture: "Let me show you how it looks."

And what does faith look like? Look at Abraham. Look at Job. Look at Habakkuk—"the righteous shall live by his faith." And in Matthew's Gospel at whom are we to look? The scribes and Pharisees? Oh, no. They have no faith. How about the disciples? Well, they do have faith, "little faith" (14:31; 16:8; cf. 6:30; 17:20). Look at 15:33. Look at what they ask. After seeing Jesus walk on water, raise the dead, multiply the loaves and fishes, they said to him, "Where are we to get enough bread in such a desolate place to feed so great a crowd?" Little faith.

So, the scribes and Pharisees—no faith; the disciples—little faith. Who then is left? All who are left are a bunch of Gentiles who have great faith—the magi, that Roman centurion, and this Canaanite woman. Look at verse 28. Underline it in your heart. "Then Jesus answered her, 'O woman, great is your faith!'" In Greek the word for "great" is *megalē* (mega, as in Mega Mart or mega-drive or mega-millions). Disciples—little faith; Canaanite—big faith. Mega. Great. Here "Jesus marvels at her faith and gives her his Great Faith Oscar."[15]

What's so great about her great faith? Here's what's so great—person and persistence. Those are the two essential aspects of her faith, two aspects that we should check ourselves on, to see where we fall on the spiritual spectrum—no faith, little faith, or great faith.

First, her faith acknowledges certain truths about the *person* of Jesus. You see, faith is not merely intellectual assent (James tells us as much—even the demons acknowledge who Jesus is, James 2:19), but it is not less than that. Look at what she says about Jesus to Jesus. Three times she calls him "Lord."

Jesus is called "Lord" some twenty times in Matthew's Gospel, and such a term all but once or twice is used in faith. When the disciples stop believing, the title "Lord" ceases to come from their lips. For example, you won't find the word "Lord" on their lips in verses 32–34. Yet three times (vv. 22, 25, 27) she calls Jesus "Lord."

That's not all. Look also at verse 22. She says, "Have mercy on me, O Lord, Son of David." Wow. Not just "Lord" but "Son of David." Matthew's Gospel begins, "The book of the genealogy of Jesus Christ, the son of David" (1:1). Then in 12:23 the crowd, after witnessing Jesus' power, says, "Can this be the Son of David?" Now finally in 15:22 we hear in effect, "Oh, let me answer that question: Yes, He is the Son of David"—that is, Jesus is the Messiah or the Christ (cf. 22:42). That's what she (of all people) believes. That's what she publicly confesses! She's the opening band for Peter's great rock show in chapter 16!

God's covenant with Abraham promised blessing to all the nations. God's covenant with David promised an everlasting king and kingdom. Jesus is the fulfillment of those two covenants. And (here's the kicker) this Canaanite women gets it. She (of all people) believes. In the language of 2 Corinthians 1:20, she believes that "all of the promises of God find their Yes in him [Jesus]."

The promise to Abraham? Yes!

The promise to David? Yes!

The Old Testament teaches that when the Christ comes he will bring blessing to the nations. But this blessing won't come (and this is what Jesus is getting at in vv. 23–26) until after his death and resurrection. Good Friday comes before the Great Commission. So he says to her, "Woman, you'll have to wait." But she says, "Oh no, Jesus, feed me now. Jew or not, my daughter needs healing." She is insisting on Easter. That's how N. T. Wright writes about it.[16] And he's right! So Jesus says, "Okay. But listen—I can only give scraps now." And she says, "Scraps? I'll take 'em." Scraps? Some scraps! The child is "healed instantly" (v. 28) and completely.

The person of Christ is everything. She acknowledges Jesus as Lord, the Son of David, and she in faith begs for his mercy. She shouts to the heavens because her daughter is living in torment. And Jesus comes to fill the gap—the gap between Heaven and Hell. He comes to break down the wall of hostility between Jews and Gentiles.

Kyrie Eleison
Lord, have mercy.
Lord, have mercy.
Christ, have mercy.
Christ, have mercy.
Lord, have mercy.
Lord, have mercy.

The church still says her prayer. Shouldn't we? Indeed.

What does faith look like? First, faith acknowledges who Jesus is—the Lord, the Messiah, the one who has come to conquer the devil and bring mercy to those who trust in him. First, person; second, persistence.

I could have added another *p*—posture, but I'll include that in her persistence. First she stands before him (v. 22). When that's not working, she kneels (v. 25). Not a bad way to get through to Jesus in prayer—on your knees. That shows a lot about what you think about the person of Jesus and about how persistent you are.

This is a story of persistence. In verse 22 she comes to Jesus, crying out, "Help!" In verse 23a Jesus is silent (the silence of God doesn't mean he is uncaring or unconcerned; ask Job). In verse 23b the disciples are indignant and/or annoyed—"Will you get rid of her? Stop all this screaming!" In verse 24 Jesus speaks to her: "I can't help you. Sorry, it's just not in the plan. You're right—I'm the Son of David. I'm the king of the Jews, not the Gentiles. I was sent only to the lost sheep of Israel." In verse 25 she persists. She fights through the disciples' annoyance and Jesus' seeming reluctance. Down she goes on her knees, on all fours, and she looks up at the Master and begs. In verse 26 Jesus says, "Sorry, it's just not right to give you the food that's only for them. I can't take the Jewish messianic feast and give it to Gentiles." Here Jesus seems firm in his theological position. You can hear the disciples saying, "Amen. Preach it, Lord. What are we doing here with her? Let's go home."

But she won't give up. She'll wrestle with the angel of the Lord until he blesses her. She'll knock on that door until the owner gets up and lets her in. "Yes, Lord," she says, "yet even the dogs eat the crumbs that fall from their masters' table" (v. 27). What a response! Luz says she's turned the tables on him. I don't think she's done that. But I do think she has slid her way to the table and is at least now under that table. Martin Luther says of her response, "Isn't this a masterpiece? She traps Christ in his own words. How can Christ get out of this?"[17] Well, he can't. He doesn't want to. He never really wanted to. He came to Paganland for pagans. He'll not feed her crumbs. He'll push the whole fatted calf onto the floor. "O woman, feast! It's all yours! Great is your faith! Be it done for you as you desire."

What does great faith look like? It looks like this woman's faith. Faith is in the person of Jesus (Jesus is Lord; Jesus is Christ), and faith is persistent ("Lord, have mercy on me. Lord, do something about this. Lord, have mercy on me, on them, on us"). That's faith. That's how one gets into the kingdom and how one stays in the kingdom.

A Catholic Evangelicalism

In 15:21–39 we learn who is invited to the table (everyone), and we learn how one gets in through the front door of the house to get to that table (faith). We learn about, if I can say it this way, catholic evangelicalism.[18] The gospel of Jesus Christ is catholic (it's universal—an open invitation to all the peoples of the world) but also evangelical (one enters into and receives the benefits of the gospel only through faith and only through faith in Jesus). Catholic evangelicalism!

Here we learn what is so clearly taught in Romans 1:16, 17:

> For I am not ashamed of the gospel, for it is the power of God for salvation to everyone [it's catholic] who believes [it's also evangelical], to the Jew first and also to the Greek [it's catholic]. For in it the righteousness of God is revealed from faith for faith [catholic/evangelical], as it is written, "The righteous shall live [or walk or persevere or persist] by faith."

46

Dual Dangers

MATTHEW 16:1–12

THERE IS AN OLD AND WISE SAYING about prayer: God always answers prayer. Sometimes God says "yes," sometimes he says "no," and sometimes he says "wait." We have all had God say "no" (for our own good). We have all had God say "wait" (you might be waiting right now). We have also (I would imagine if you've been a Christian for any length of time) had God say "yes." You have asked for something in faith and according to his will, and God gave it to you.

In a sermon on 1 Kings 17 at our church, Dr. Nick Perrin shared a story of how God provided for him. When he was working for InterVarsity and was short on financial support, he laid out (literally on the floor) all his needs (the bills/the costs) before the Lord, crying out to him for help. Almost immediately after that prayer, the phone rang. It was nearly midnight. It was an old friend who wanted to support the ministry. God said, "Yes." Now all of us have heard stories like that—wonderful stories of God's provision in times of great need. And many of us, I hope, have experienced God's provision, answers to prayer, in ways that only the word *miraculous* is properly attached to them.

Have you ever had God say "yes" to a specific prayer? Yes, you have. (At least I hope you have.) But have you ever had God say "yes" one day and then the next day or week or month you are confronted with a new crisis and you doubt God's care and competence? Or, even more common with me, a need arises, I have *not* yet prayed for what I need, and God provides miraculously anyway. He knows what I need before I ask, and he gives what I need before I ask. And then (here's the sad part of the story) the next time a crisis comes, I open my mouth to God in prayer (if it can be called that) only to grumble, complain, doubt. "God, how am I possibly to deal with this?"

As we begin Matthew 16, we are warned about dual dangers. One is false teaching, what Jesus calls "the leaven of the Pharisees and Sadducees"; the other is spiritual amnesia or forgetfulness. We will start with forgetfulness.

The First Danger: Forgetfulness

The first danger is forgetfulness, forgetting what God has done in the past, or here specifically in our text, *forgetting Jesus' mighty works*. The middle of our text records,

> When the disciples reached the other side, they had forgotten to bring any bread. Jesus said to them, "Watch and beware of the leaven of the Pharisees and Sadducees." And they began discussing it among themselves, saying, "We brought no bread." (vv. 5–7)

I envision the scene like this. It's like a husband and wife driving, taking a needed getaway, and the husband crosses onto a drawbridge, and suddenly he feels and he sees that the bridge is rising. So he turns to his wife and shouts, "We have to do something; we're going to plunge into the river!" And she replies, "You know what, I forgot to pack my swimsuit and the suntan lotion." His warning went in one ear and out the other. There is real danger ahead, but she's heard only enough of his warning to think of some temporal need.

I will give another illustration, to prove I'm not chauvinistic. This same couple is in that same car again on that same vacation, and the man is driving (I still think the man should drive) and they whiz by a sign that reads, "Warning: Bridge Out!" The wife immediately turns to him and exclaims, "Honey, stop! The bridge is out!" But he, too oblivious to look at the obvious, checks his GPS and says, "Oh, don't worry, this says that the road goes right through." Whoosh. Down they go.

Have you ever been oblivious when it comes to God like these disciples were? One moment you touch and taste and see the Lord is good, and the next moment you're wondering about Wonder Bread. "Hey, Jesus, we forgot the bread. Are you listening? We forgot the bread!"

What does Jesus say to this lack-of-manna mantra? "I know you forgot the bread, you knuckleheads." That's my paraphrase of verse 8. "I don't care if you forgot the bread. You forgot me! You forgot what I just did twice in the past two months." The real version reads like this:

> But Jesus, aware of this, said, "O you of little faith, why are you discussing among yourselves the fact that you have no bread? Do you not yet perceive? Do you not remember [ah, forgetfulness!] the five loaves for the five

> thousand, and how many baskets you gathered? Or the seven loaves for the four thousand, and how many baskets you gathered?" (vv. 8–10)

Faithless Forgetfulness. Spiritual Amnesia.

I'm not a very mathematical man. But I'm proud to say that even I can do the math here. Even I can do the messianic math of verses 9, 10!

One day Jesus took five loaves and fed 5,000. Then, what seemed like the next day, he took seven loaves and fed 4,000. Now, I can count to five and to seven, with eight toes left. I can add them together (the answer is twelve). I can even add 4,000 and 5,000 (that's 9,000). I can do the math. But isn't this strange math, unmathematical math, when it comes to the multiplication? Why five for 5,000 and seven for 4,000? Shouldn't it be the other way around? The more the disciples had, the more Jesus could do? No. That's just Jesus' point. The less the disciples have to work with, the more Jesus can do![1]

Here I think Jesus is not merely saying, "Remember the leftovers—twelve baskets, then seven baskets full of scraps." I think he is also saying, "Remember what I had to work with." With seven loaves, he fed 4,000. With five loaves, he fed 5,000. Imagine what he could do with zero! "We brought no bread." No bread, no problem. *Ex nihilo*; *no es problema*. "Don't forget what I've done. Don't forget who I am. Don't forget how I work." That's what Jesus is saying here.

How easy it is for us to forget what God has done in our lives *and* in salvation history! Our generation so little values two essential components of the Christian faith—history and eschatology. That is, instead of looking backwards at what God has done in history and looking forward to what God will do in due time (that's eschatology, having a longing for the last things, the culmination of God's kingdom), we live instead in the ahistorical/existential *now*.

There is nothing wrong with a now faith (I hope you trust in Christ right now). But it limits the growth of our faith if we don't also, in the now, look back to then and look forward to that.

In my book *God's Lyrics*, I talk about how the songs we find in both the Old and New Testaments recall God's mighty acts in history.[2] In the Old Testament songs, God's people sang of the creation of the world, Israel's election, the exodus, the giving of the Law, the establishment of David's kingdom, exilic judgment, restoration, and so on. In the New Testament God's people sing of Jesus' incarnation, life, death, resurrection, and return. In both Testaments they sing (as we should sing) of God's works in history.

In the song of Habakkuk, the last song I study in that book, I write about Habakkuk's faith, which is the model for faith in the New Testament—"the righteous shall live by his faith" (Habakkuk 2:4). Here's how Habakkuk lived by faith. It's all spelled out in chapter 3 of his little book. He first remembers God's redemptive history, notably what God did in the exodus and the conquest (those two important events meld together into one memory in his mind). Then, based on God's righteous judgments in the past, Habakkuk, in the present, trusts that God will judge and save again in the future. He had this historical/eschatological faith, the faith we all need if we want to grow, a faith that looks to the future—trusting God will work again—because it looks back into history, *remembering* (not forgetting) what God has already done.

The Second Danger: False Teaching

The first danger is forgetfulness, forgetting what God has done in the past or here specifically in our text forgetting Jesus' mighty works—who he is, what he has done, how he works, what he likes to work with. The second danger is false teaching, a specific false teaching (v. 12), what Jesus labels "the leaven of the Pharisees and Sadducees" (vv. 6, 11, 12).

A few years ago I read through the New Testament quickly—five to fifteen chapters a day. I did it that way because I wanted to get a feel for the flow of the whole. I also wanted to see what themes were most often repeated (the ones I might miss from reading just a chapter or two a day). By doing this I noticed three themes I previously relegated to "insignificant." First, I noticed the call to persevere in the faith. Second, I noticed Jew/Gentile relations—the newness of that relationship in the gospel, the necessity of it, the theological and cultural tensions with it, and the way forward in unity. Third, I noticed how much attention is given to false teachers and false teaching. Have you ever noticed those themes?

Sometimes we have this existential faith (a now and now only faith), and sometimes we read the Bible existentially (what topics, themes, verses can I relate to, understand, apply to me right now?). But false teaching is in there. Don't miss it.

The apostles hit on that theme and Jesus hits on that theme so often because false teachers and their false teaching (even more so than the teachers themselves) are so dangerous. This is one of the great flaws in today's everybody-is-entitled-to-one's-own-opinion opinion. That idea is one of the most thoughtless thoughts in the history of the world, in my opinion. Listen, ideas have consequences. My opinion is not necessarily equal to yours, and vice versa.

We can see, in retrospect, that ideas have consequences with, for example, someone like Adolf Hitler. In 1925–1926 Hitler wrote a book called *Mein Kampf* ("My Struggle" in English), and he writes about his struggle. His struggle with what? The Jews, of course. He details how and why he became growingly anti-Semitic, concluding that one cannot be both a German and a Jew. What a political ideology! He was nuts, right? What impact would this two-volume work have on the world? Ideas have consequences. Those two volumes led to World War II. Evil ideas are the most dangerous powers in the world—now, then, always.

First Jesus warns us about forgetfulness, but second, he warns about evil ideas or false teaching. So "beware"—that's the word he uses. And notice he doesn't say, "Beware of the huge red dragon with six heads that looks and sounds dangerous and breathes out fiery false teachings." Rather he says, "Look out for leaven!" Not even, "Watch out for burnt crust on the bread" or "mold around the edges." No, he warns of leaven, a substance you can't see well, a substance that is hard to perceive is there. But something unseen has subtle but sure effects, like drops of an odorless, colorless poison in a glass of champagne—one sip doesn't kill, but drinking the glass dry will. Not immediately but eventually you're dead. This is why the word "understand" (or "understood" or "perceive") is used several times in our text. Watch out for the leaven. See what is hard to see, but you need to see.

So, what then does deadly "leaven" look like? What are we to watch out for? Let's look back at our text and see what we can see. In verse 1 we read, "And the Pharisees and Sadducees came, and to test him they asked him to show them a sign from heaven."

Notice several facts here. First, this is the first time the Sadducees are mentioned in reference to Jesus' ministry. (They are referenced in 3:7 in relation to John the Baptist.) We've gotten to know the scribes and Pharisees, but who are the Sadducees? What you need to know about them is what Scripture says about them. This is how Matthew describes them: "Sadducees . . . say that there is no resurrection" (22:23; cf. Acts 23:6–8). This was a different theological position from Jesus, but also from the Pharisees.

So first notice the Sadducees have entered the drama. Second, notice they approach Jesus with the Pharisees. This is a very "unlikely alliance."[3] It would be like the Israeli national soccer team getting together with the Iranian team to eat pig's feet while they cheer for the U.S. in the World Cup. What are these two doing together—the overly ritualistic with the overly rationalistic, the super-serious with the super-sophisticated, the legalist with the modernist? They are together because Jesus threatens them—their religious power—individually, and so they come together corporately to deal with him. It's a diabolical, not a theological alliance.

Third, notice that they came to "test him." The word "test" here is the same word used in 4:1 of Jesus' temptation in the wilderness. They come to tempt him. How? The same way the devil tempted Adam and Eve—"be like God"—and the same way the devil tempted Jesus in the wilderness—"act like God." They say, "Give us a heavenly sign. Yes, we've seen the earthly signs. You turned bread into more bread, but we want to see you turn the moon into blood. Enough with healing the sick, feeding the poor, and dealing with those of a lesser spiritual caste; show us something spectacular in the sky! You've made some God-sized claims for yourself [see 7:21–23; 9:2; 11:4–6, 27; 12:28], so we want a God-sized sign. We'll take the sun standing still, a starless night sky, lightning that strikes a few trees that then fall and spell out M for Messiah. Hey, we'll even take a voice from Heaven. Just give us a voice, somebody up there saying, 'This is my beloved Son, listen to him.'"

Ah, but what they ask for in verse 1 flies in the face of Jesus' person and mission. He has not come to show off his superpowers, but to demonstrate the power and justice and love of God through his weakness, even his death on a cross. And while he lives he will never perform just to prove himself. Do you want to see from God and hear from God? Here's how it works, according to chapters 8–15: you must come in faith first. And then let the fireworks begin. No faith, no fireworks (cf. 13:56)! No faith, no heavenly voice. No faith, no manna in the wilderness. No faith, no sky-filled wonders for you from this Messiah.

He answered them, "You want to talk about signs; let's talk about signs."

> When it is evening, you say, "It will be fair weather, for the sky is red." And in the morning, "It will be stormy today, for the sky is red and threatening." You know how to interpret the appearance of the sky, but you cannot interpret the signs of the times [what you see down here on earth, before your very eyes]. An evil and adulterous generation seeks for a [heavenly] sign, but no sign will be given to it except the [earthly] sign of Jonah." (vv. 2–4)

Madeleine L'Engle, in her poem "The Irrational Season," writes:

> As I grow older
> I get surer
> Man's heart is colder
> His life no purer.[4]

That is I think how Jesus felt here. He felt the coldness of these men's hearts. He saw the charcoal impurities of these purity freaks.

Oh, they could tell the weather—isn't that still the world's preoccupation?—but they couldn't tell time. They knew if it was going to storm or not, but they couldn't tell that the fullness of time was upon them, that the King of the kingdom of the heavens was here. And in this way they are so like some of our friends, coworkers, and neighbors. They worry about whether or not it's going to rain tomorrow, but they don't give a single serious thought about Jesus[5] and his death and resurrection.

Do you want a sign, Pharisees and Sadducees? Do you want a sign, weather-watchers of our world? Here's a sign—the sign of Jonah (cf. 12:39).[6] That's the sign to look for! Remember Jonah—his self-sacrifice ("throw me overboard"), his burial in the waters (he's as good as dead), but then his deliverance from death (the big fish—salvation!), and then remember his proclamation to the Gentiles, the Ninevites (the Gentiles of the Gentiles). "Remember Jonah. Now look at me. What he did, I'm doing and will do. Just watch and see! Watch what I do. Listen to what I teach. See if it fits with Moses and the Prophets. See if it fits with the promises of God. See if it fits with the pattern of the prophet Jonah. For if you won't watch and listen now, you won't believe even if I rise from the dead (cf. Luke 16:31). You want a heavenly sign. You're looking at him—the heavenly Son of God come down to earth!"

So, those are verses 1–4. Question/answer time with Jesus is always invigorating! But now on to the second point I'm making—the second dual danger is the leaven of these leaders. What then is this leaven? What are we looking to avoid? What does this leaven look like?

If you take the whole Gospel of Matthew into account, what J. C. Ryle wrote is most fitting:

> Let us remember that we live in a world where Pharisaism and Sadduceeism are continually striving for the mastery in the church of Christ. Some want to add to the Gospel, and some want to take away from it; some would bury it, and some would pare it down to nothing; some would stifle it by heaping on additions, and some would bleed it to death by subtraction from its truths. Both parties agree only in one respect: both would kill and destroy the life of Christianity if they succeeded in having their own way. Against both errors let us watch and pray, and stand on guard. Let us not add to the Gospel, to please the modern Pharisee; let us not subtract from the Gospel, to please the modern Sadducee. Let our principle be "the truth, the whole truth, and nothing but the truth": nothing added to it, and nothing taken away.[7]

So Bishop Ryle sees the leaven here as adding to or subtracting from the gospel, or more broadly, adding to or subtracting from Scripture. And that is very true when you look, for example, at 15:1–9 and how the Pharisees by their oral traditions (ceremonial hand-washing for all people always) added to the Word of God, and if you look at 22:23–33, for example, where the Sadducees, by their denial of the resurrection, subtracted from Scripture.

Ryle is right. We must watch out for this. We must watch others, watch ourselves. Are we staying on the line of Scripture, or are we straying above it (legalism) or below it (liberalism), above it (perfectionism) or below it (antinomianism), above it (traditionalism) or below it (pragmatism)?

So, yes, there is something to the leaven of the Pharisees and Sadducees being adding to and/or subtracting from Scripture. *But* in the immediate context—these leaders looking for a heavenly sign, and Jesus telling them, "I'm only giving you one sign"—I think Jesus is warning about "*one* doctrinal tendency" found in both groups, and found too often in us or desired by us, and that is "wanting more than Jesus"[8] and wanting more from Jesus than what he has offered to give, or in our case more than he has given. It's the attitude, for example, so prevalent in the world and sadly so prevalent in the church that says, "Give me something more lively than the life of Christ. Give me something more powerful than the passion of Christ. Give me something more dynamic than the death of Christ. Give me something more relevant than the resurrection of Christ."

Do you know what my first word as a child was? It was "more." Not "mommy" or "daddy," but "more," said in the context of wanting more applesauce or something sweet to eat. Well, spiritually immature people always want "more" of the wrong thing. They are not satisfied with the Bread from Heaven. They are "not satisfied with the sufficiency of the suffering and resurrected Jesus."[9] They consider "simple faith in the crucified and risen Lord himself to be . . . merely milk; not meat; appetizers, not the meal."[10] But oh, how wrong they are. The person of Jesus and his work—his death and resurrection especially—that's the milk, water, bread, wine, filet mignon, and a big slice of apple pie. That's the full substance of our faith. No more saying "more" when you have that.

So, watch out for the leaven of the Pharisees and Sadducees. This leaven is alive and rising still today, working its way through the church. Beware of going above or below the line of Scripture, and beware of wanting more from God than Jesus and his death and resurrection.

These dual dangers are what God's Word urges us to think about and apply to our lives. The first danger is forgetfulness, forgetting what God has done in the past, especially *forgetting Jesus' mighty works*. The second danger is false teaching (yet very much related to the first danger), particularly the false teaching that says, "I won't believe in Jesus until you show me more than Jesus."

May God protect us from such dangers. May he deliver us from these two evils. Amen.

47

The Great Confession

MATTHEW 16:13–20

THIS TEXT TACKLES three important questions: (1) Who is Jesus? (2) How does someone come to the right answer to that question? (3) Why does having the right answer matter? The first question is as popular as a picture of Jesus on the front cover of *Time* or *Newsweek* or many other news periodicals in the last decade. The identity of Jesus is still newsworthy.

Who Is Jesus?

In verses 13–16 Jesus raises the issue.

> Now when Jesus came into the district of Caesarea Philippi, he asked his disciples, "Who do people say that the Son of Man is?" And they said, "Some say John the Baptist, others say Elijah, and others Jeremiah or one of the prophets." He said to them, "But who do you say that I am?" Simon Peter replied, "You are the Christ, the Son of the living God."

Then in verse 17 Jesus basically says, "That's right, Peter. Good answer. Right answer."

The disciples tell Jesus that the common people (*hoi anthropoi*), the regular Jewish Joe and Jane, think Jesus is a prophet. They come to this conclusion likely because Jesus has acted much like an Old Testament prophet. He *speaks* God's words, and he *works* God's wonders. This Jesus must be a prophet! That's a natural enough conclusion. However, I find it odd that they think he is a resurrected or a reincarnated prophet. They don't say, "We think he is a new prophet like the prophets of old," but rather "He is an old prophet in new flesh."

Whatever they think about Jesus, they are partly right and partly wrong. They are partly wrong: he is not "the reappearance of the executed John the

Baptist, or the past and expected Elijah, or the venerated Jeremiah."[1] But they are partly right: he is a prophet, as Calvin first rightly labeled him, and Christians have done so ever since—Jesus is our *Prophet*, Priest, and King. He holds all three offices simultaneously. He speaks for God as Prophet, intercedes on our behalf as Priest, and rules over all as King.

This kingship of Jesus is of special interest to Matthew. His Gospel starts and ends with it, and each chapter is about it. So when Peter says of Jesus, "You are the Christ" (i.e., King), Jesus says, "Yes. That's it!" And Matthew says, "Amen. Amen. This is so important, I'm putting it in the middle of my Gospel." It's the centerpiece, and from here we will journey from this confession—"You are the Christ"—to the cross—"Let him be crucified!" (27:22, 23).

Yes, Jesus is the King. He is a prophet (sure), but also and most importantly, he is "the Christ."

Like most people today, the people here have good thoughts about Jesus, just not precisely right thoughts. These people saw Jesus as a prophet. To them he was like a lion. All prophets have a roar about them. Jesus roared against injustices. Jesus turned over the tables of hypocrisy. To them he was a lion. That is, partly true. To people today he is the opposite, a lamb. Jesus is viewed as a meek social reformer, a gentle moralist, a wise teacher, or a sympathetic healer. He was all that, but not only that. He was a lamb but also a lion. He was a prophet but also "the Christ"—the lamb slain, the lion-like ruling King!

Or he is—if you want to fill in the picture here with the two other titles used of him—"the Son of Man" (v. 13), Jesus' favorite title for himself, and "the Son of the living God" (v. 16). In the Greek the word order for the latter is, "The Son of God, the living one." He is the Son of Man and the Son of God, the Christ. He is the earthly Christ, "the expected anointed king of the House of David who would rule over God's people" (2 Samuel 7).[2] He is the heavenly Son of Man, whose universal rule—over all peoples, all nations—will be without end, an "everlasting dominion," an indestructible "kingdom" (Daniel 7:14). And he is the Son of God, that Son in whom we must take refuge through faith or else (Psalm 2).

He is the Son of Man, the Son of God, and the Christ. Those are three different melodies that resolve into one trumpet-like blast from the choir: "King of kings and Lord of lords, and he shall reign forever and forever."

So, who is Jesus? "[W]ho do you say that I am?" Jesus still asks his church that question today. How we answer it turns our lives, ministries, and destinies in one direction or another. Peter might not fully know, but we ought to know, much more fully than he did. Peter certainly didn't fully understand what he was saying. Just look at the following verses, when he can't accept Jesus as the Christ *crucified.* This explains why Jesus strictly charges (v. 20) the group not to tell the world who he is until they better understand the man and the message. But we ought to say today with fuller clarity and conviction, "Jesus, you are *the* Son of Man, *the* Christ, *the* Son of God, *the* living One."[3]

How Does One Arrive at the Right Answer?

The second question is, how does one come to the right answer to the first question? Verse 17 gives us Jesus' answer: "Blessed are you, Simon Bar-Jonah! For flesh and blood has not revealed this to you, but my Father who is in heaven."

Notice how Jesus contrasts Simon Peter's earthly father with his heavenly Father. Jesus calls Peter by his given name, "Simon," and then he tags on, "Bar-Jonah," son of a guy named Jonah. What Jesus says here to him is this: "Simon, you didn't come to understand who I am through your dad's teaching you about me. In fact, this is not a flesh-and-blood thing. No earthly father or mother or rabbi or teacher could have opened your heart to understand my identity. It's a God thing. It's a heavenly Father thing. It's a work of God. It's a revelation of God. It's a blessing of God." "Blessed are you, Simon Bar-Jonah! For flesh and blood has not revealed this to you, but my Father who is in heaven."

Certainly from a human perspective, and certainly from Peter's perspective, we must recognize that there is a mix of means. God didn't zap him into the kingdom. Peter saw Jesus do this, and heard Jesus say that, and eventually the pieces of the messianic puzzle fit into place. But here Jesus emphasizes that *ultimately*, while there are many means in place and involved in the process, there is only one gift-giver, and that is God. "Praise God from whom *all* blessings flow"—even and especially the blessing of faith.[4]

Jonathan Edwards summarizes this concept in two of my favorite quotes from him. First, "To take on yourself to work out redemption, is a greater thing than if you had taken it upon you to create a world."[5] Second, "I am bold to say, that the work of God in the conversion of one soul . . . is a more glorious work of God than the creation of the whole material world."[6] The great confession, which always follows the great conversion, is a great work of God.

If you haven't figured that out yet, you need to now (I'm dead serious). You need to grasp that it was not your impeccable character or your bubbly personality or your sincere seeking or your open and affirming attitude or your nice niceness that made the difference. It wasn't anything inside you that opened the door to the kingdom of heaven to see Jesus as Messiah. It was

God; it was all his gracious and merciful work. It was he who predestined, elected, and loved (interchangeable words for the same Scriptural idea) you.

The one thing I've learned about human beings, being one for forty years, living with other human beings for forty years, married to another human being for thirteen years, having five children who are human beings, and pastoring human beings for over a dozen years, is that human beings love to glory in themselves, to take credit where credit is not due. But the gospel won't let us.

"It is, and always is, the Father who gives saving faith."[7] As Jesus taught his disciples in 13:11, "To you it has been given to know the secrets of the kingdom of heaven." Or as the beloved apostle wrote in John 1:11–13:

> He came to his own, and his own people did not receive him [there's culpability for unbelief]. But to all who did receive him, who believed in his name [we really and truly receive and believe], he gave the right to become children of God, who were born, not of blood nor of the will of the flesh nor of the will of man, but of God.

Who is Jesus? He's the Christ. How does one arrive at this right answer? Ultimately it's a work of God. God's blessing is bestowed upon the believer, as it was here bestowed upon Peter.

What Does It Matter?

We have answered questions one and two. Now we come to question three: So what? Why does it all matter? What does it matter if I know or don't know the answer to Jesus' question? What does it matter if I know or don't know who opens eyes to see? Why does having the right answer to the question of who Jesus is matter? Verses 18, 19 answer that question.

Before I explain how those verses answer the question, I would be remiss if I didn't tell you that verse 18 is the most debated verse in the Bible, and I would also be remiss if I didn't tell you something of the debate and how my authoritative, absolutely right, no-questions-asked-after-this-section-please perspective will finally, once for all time, settle the debate.

The debate centers on the identity of "this rock." "And I tell you, you are Peter, and on *this rock* I will build my church." The Roman Catholic Church argues (and so much of their theology lives or dies on this hill) that Peter—not just his person but also his office (the perpetual office of the papacy)—is described here. The Protestant and Eastern Orthodox churches agree that the Catholics are wrong and that "this rock" refers not to Peter himself but to Peter's faith and confession, which was, up until the Council of Trent (1545–

1563), the "almost unanimously" position held by the church,[8] both in the East and in the West.[9] Even Augustine, in his *Retractions*, espoused this view.[10]

Yet today, interestingly, there is a growing trend among evangelicals to admit that the Roman Catholics are right—that Peter is "this rock"—while maintaining the Catholics are wrong that this text has anything whatsoever to say about the perpetual office of the papacy. Due to the pun here—"You are *Petros* and upon this *petra*"—Peter is seen as the *primus inter pares* (first among equals). In this view this primacy is chronological, pointing not to some papal office but to the apostolic office (the apostolate). In other words, here he speaks as the symbolic head of the Twelve, upon whose testimony Jesus will build the church. D. A. Carson, R. T. France, and Craig Blomberg, to name a few, hold to this view.

However, I think all these readings are wrong. I take a minority position, a position that has no historical consensus to support it, a position that is not supported by prominent New Testament scholars (although Gundry comes close). I even take the minority opinion and argue differently than those in the minority camp. I am a minority among minorities. Yet here I stand. I can do no other. My conscience is captive to the Word of God. May God help me.

I think "this rock" refers to Christ, not to Peter or Peter's faith and confession. *Jesus is the rock!* Whether he rolls your blues away or not, Jesus is the rock. That old ditty (out of context) gets it right.

Here is why I think so.

Let me just say, as I begin my infallible defense, that what I'm about to argue for may be wrong, but the beautiful thing is that my whole theological system doesn't fall to the ground if I am wrong. Whatever I make of this verse, it is clear (in this otherwise ambiguous verse) that this verse has something to do with Peter and everything to do with Jesus, but it certainly has nothing to do with sacerdotalism, hierarchy, the papacy, apostolic succession, or Petrine infallibility. To get there you have to climb far above the line of Scripture. Such thinking is far from the mind of Christ and far from the whole tenor of Matthew's Gospel, a Gospel that exalts Jesus and does not exalt Peter. The last words we hear from Peter in this Gospel are his "confession" of denial—that he does not know Jesus (see 26:69–75)—e.g., "I do not know the man" (26:74). And yet in this same Gospel we hear those last words of Jesus, "All authority in heaven and on earth has been given to me" (28:18).[11] Jesus or Peter—who is the church built upon in Matthew? The answer is obvious.

Actually that's not part of my argument. Here's my "argument," which is really just three simple observations as to why I say Jesus is "this rock."

First, I am aware of the wordplay here on Peter's name in Greek[12]—"You are *Petros*, and upon this *petra*." But when I was reading through this verse in English and also in Greek what jumped out at me was not the obvious *Petros/ petra* pun but the less obvious, easy to overlook word, "this." "*This* rock"—why did Jesus say "this"? It seemed out of place to me. What I mean about "this" is this: in verses 17–19 Jesus uses the word "you" to refer to Peter: "Blessed are you" (v. 17), "I will give you the keys . . . whatever you bind . . . whatever you loose" (v. 19). So why then, if Jesus has been using the word "you," didn't he say in verse 18, "And I tell you, you are Peter, and upon you, the rock, I will build my church" and so on? If Jesus said it this way you would still have the wordplay. Jesus' meaning would just be a whole lot clearer.

Second, this "this" instead of the more natural "you" got me thinking and seeing. It helped focus my attention away from Peter—who is addressed as "you" throughout verses 17–19—to Jesus, the one speaking and the one saying he will act. So I noticed words like "my" and "I"—"my church" and "I tell you" and "I will build" and "I will give you" and, implied, "I will make sure this church is protected and preserved." I noticed that the focus here, as is true of the whole passage, as is true of the whole Gospel, is not on Peter but on Jesus!

From there, third, I did a word study on the words "rock" and "stone" in the Gospel of Matthew. The word "rock" is used only four times, once here, once of the tomb, and twice in the Sermon on the Mount, referencing Jesus' teaching, and perhaps in some ways (as the two are fairly interchangeable in Matthew) Jesus himself: "Everyone then who hears these words of mine and does them will be like a wise man who built his house on the rock" (7:24).

In the whole of the New Testament the word "rock" is used only twelve times, *and* it is *never* used of any person other than Jesus. Consider, for example, 1 Corinthians 10:4, where Paul writes about the water from the rock in the wilderness, saying, "and the Rock was Christ." Similarly the word "stone," when it does not refer to a literal stone, refers to Jesus. We read in Matthew 21:42, 44, "Jesus said to them, 'Have you never read in the Scriptures: "The stone that the builders rejected has become the cornerstone?"... And the one who falls on *this stone* will be broken to pieces." In Romans 9:33 Paul calls Jesus (quoting Isaiah 28:16) "a stone of stumbling, and a rock of offense," and then he adds, "and whoever believes in him [stands upon this rock/this stone] will not be put to shame." Furthermore, Peter (no less) preaches about Jesus. Filled with the Holy Spirit, Peter preached at Pentecost:

> [L]et it be known to all of you and to all the people of Israel that by the name of Jesus Christ of Nazareth, whom you crucified, whom God raised from the dead . . . This Jesus is *the stone* that was rejected by you, the build-

> ers, which has become *the cornerstone*. And there is salvation in no one else, for there is no other name under heaven given among men by which we must be saved. (Acts 4:10–12)

So, what did the earliest church do with the rock/stone language? They never applied it to Peter and always applied it to Christ. Read 1 *Peter* 2:4–8, or listen to Paul:

> So then you are no longer strangers and aliens, but you are fellow citizens with the saints and members of the household of God, built on the foundation of the apostles and prophets, Christ Jesus himself being the cornerstone, in whom the whole structure, being joined together, grows into a holy temple in the Lord. In him you also are being built together into a dwelling place for God by the Spirit. (Ephesians 2:19–22)

Note that Paul does not say that the household of God is built upon the foundation of *Peter* and the apostles. Note also that he writes of Jesus, not Peter, as being the cornerstone, the most foundational stone of the foundation. It is in Jesus, not Peter, the apostles, or the prophets, that Christians are "being built together." Who is the rock in Peter and Paul's letters? Jesus!

Furthermore, no one in the whole Bible is called "rock" except God,[13] who is so often called "the rock" or "my rock" (it appears to be a divine name of sorts, which is why it is capitalized in most translations).[14]

Thus, with the above evidence in mind, I say Jesus is "this rock" of Matthew 16:18. Here's my paraphrase with pointers on verses 18, 19. Jesus says:

> And I tell you, you are Peter, and on this rock [visualize Jesus pointing to himself if that helps; you are Peter (*Petros*), but I am *petra*] I [yes me, Peter, not you] will build my [not your] church, and the gates of hell shall not prevail against it. I will give [Jesus is still the subject of the sentence] you [now let's talk about your role] the keys of the kingdom of heaven, and whatever you bind on earth shall be bound in heaven, and whatever you loose on earth shall be loosed in heaven.

Now, putting that to the side, what does all that have to do with our question? How does it answer the question, what does it matter what one makes of Jesus? Well, here (finally) are two reasons it matters.

First, it matters for church unity.

The Roman Catholic Church claims that there cannot be any full communion until every church and every Christian submits to the magisterium. Now I know as an ex-Catholic that I'm biased, but I refuse to take as the foundational point of unity something like the papacy, a doctrine so far above the line of Scripture. Rather, if various churches under the umbrella of Christendom are to come to the ecumenical table, we must start by acknowledging Jesus as the Christ. Then from there we can build a Scriptural ecclesiology.

Evangelicals are talked down to from our high-church brethren: "They don't have a vibrant ecclesiology like us; it's a shallow, sloppy doctrine of the church." And to that I say, "What absolute rubbish." What is a higher ecclesiology—making sure the priest or minister wears the right-colored vestments for Lent or emphasizing that the church is composed of all who are washed in the blood of the Lamb, those of every color who through faith are clothed in Christ's righteousness? What is a higher ecclesiology—having an intuitional presence that is as wealthy, powerful, and overly glamorous as anything this world has ever seen or to acknowledge that Jesus "is the head of the . . . church" (Colossians 1:18), and wherever two or more are gathered in his name, there he is present? If you focus first on Christology and soteriology, you will then get right ecclesiology.

You see, the church is comprised of everyone who has been baptized by, in, and with the Holy Spirit, those who with one heart and mind believe the same basic doctrines and live out the gospel. Outside of that church there is no salvation, and outside of Christ as the rock there is no foundation for unity.

Second, the question matters in regard to salvation and damnation. Look again at verse 18b. Jesus says, "I will build my church, and the gates of hell shall not prevail against it." He claims that he will build an eternal, invincible assembly against which even the powers of the devil and of death are powerless. And to Peter he grants "the keys" to this heavenly kingdom (v. 19). What Peter then must do, and those who follow after him (note that the command of 18:18 is also given to all disciples, 18:1), is as follows: "whatever you bind on earth shall be bound in heaven, and whatever you loose on earth shall be loosed in heaven" (16:19b).

Which means what? What's the mission? What's this bit about the keys? Well, as we look at the Acts of the Apostles, our best source on this (cf. Matthew 23:13), I think that "the keys" have to do with preaching the gospel of the kingdom. Zwingli summarizes the Protestant consensus like this:

> The keys are nothing else than this: the preaching of the pure, unfalsified Word of the gospel. Whoever believes this [gospel] will be free of his sins and be saved. Whoever does not believe this will be damned (Mark 16:16).[15]

J. C. Ryle puts it like this: "As the Old Testament priest declared authoritatively whose leprosy was cleansed, so the apostles were appointed to 'declare and pronounce' authoritatively whose sins were forgiven."[16] Craig Blomberg comments, "[T]he imagery of keys that close and open, lock and unlock (based on Isa 22:22) . . . take the binding and loosing as referring to Christians' making entrance to God's kingdom available or unavailable to people through their witness, preaching, and ministry."

So the idea of St. Peter standing in Heaven at the pearly gates with the keys tied around his waist comes from this text but is far removed from it. Peter's duty is entirely earthly. *Here on earth* he is to preach the gospel—repentance, faith, obedience to the commands of Christ, the cost of discipleship—and those who receive that apostolic message receive Jesus, and the door to life opens wide (cf. 10:40). And *here on earth* those who refuse the gospel are judged (they already stand in judgment). The door remains locked and shut. No joke. Gray-haired St. Peter standing at the pearly gates is a joke. But verse 19 is no joke. It's a matter of life and death, eternal life and eternal death, to accept what Peter preached.

Every Tongue Confess

Two thousand years ago Jesus took his disciples to a town called Caesarea Philippi, a city located at the northernmost border of Israel (some have thought of it as the boundary between Israel and the world), a city bestowed to Herod the Great by Emperor Augustus Caesar. Herod's son Philip rebuilt this city and then renamed it after the Roman Emperor and (in the Herod family tradition) after himself, thus Caesarea Philippi.

In this city, towering above Jesus as he spoke, was a massive, resplendent, white marble temple built in honor of the Emperor. Also in this city of great religious diversity was the temple to the Syrian god Baal and the Greek god Pan. Here, in this "perfectly astounding setting"[17]—in this global village, this city of syncretism, this pantheon of world religions—Jesus asks, "Who do you say that I am?" And here Peter, with firmness of conviction, calls Jesus "the Christ." Jesus Christ! But not, of course, as a swear word (as so many, too many, do today), but as a title of absolute lordship: "You and you alone are King!" Not Caesar. Not Baal. Not Pan. Not any other so-called gods of this world. Those gods are dead. "You are *the* Christ, *the* Son of God, *the* living One," the one and only living God, the one to whom all authority has been given and all allegiance is due. Jesus Christ!

48

No Cross; No Crown

MATTHEW 16:21–28

I RECENTLY READ LEWIS CARROLL'S CLASSICS *Alice's Adventures in Wonderland* (the abbreviated title is *Alice in Wonderland*) and its sequel, *Alice through the Looking Glass, and What Alice Found There*. The two books are often printed together and blended together in movie form. In *Alice through the Looking Glass*, Carroll created a mirror image of the world, where in order to get somewhere in that world you need to think inside out. For example, if you want to walk toward something you must walk away from it.[1]

Throughout Matthew's Gospel, our Lord Jesus has been looking at reality in a very different way than everyone else around him, kind of backwards or upside-down or inside-out. For example, he has been teaching these strange paradoxes: those who thirst, mourn, and are persecuted are blessed; the first shall be last and the last first; the greatest is the most humble, and so on. And here he teaches that to save one's life one must lose it, and he teaches that the Son of Man, who will come in glory, must first suffer and die, that the Christ (i.e., the King) must be crucified. These are all very upside-down, backwards, inside-out ways of looking at things, or so it seems.

When I was in college, the Bible study I was a part of had a way of getting at this looking-glass perspective, seeing things the way God wants us to see them. Each week as we studied a passage of Scripture we asked five questions, one of which was, what's surprising in this text? This question wasn't merely dealing with something surprising in the experiential realm like "The short skinny man got stuck in the tall wide door. Isn't that surprising? How did that happen?" Rather, the question deals with what we wouldn't know—about God, Jesus, this world, ourselves, reality, etc.—unless the Bible taught it to us.

Here in 16:21–28, with this looking-glass/what's-surprising mentality in mind, I want to show three concepts that are surprising, ideas that we never would have come to see unless God showed us his ways, showed us the way things really work in his world. In summary, if we want to reach Heaven, if we want to receive a crown of glory upon our heads, we must first robe ourselves with self-denial and suffering.

Christ Crucified: The Christ Would Suffer and Die

The first surprising concept is Christ crucified. That is, "the Christ" (16:16) would suffer and die in Jerusalem at the hands of the Jewish religious leaders: "From that time[2] Jesus began to show his disciples that he must go to Jerusalem and suffer many things from the elders and chief priests and scribes, and be killed, and on the third day be raised" (v. 21).

Here the context is king. And the context (vv. 13–20) tells us that Jesus is the King. "You are the Christ" (16:16) is Peter's great confession. Jesus is the Christ, the Messiah, the anointed one, the King. Right. Got it. What's next? Here's what's next: Christ crucified. Christ what? Crucified? No, it should be, Christ conquering. Now that we have the King, how do we get the kingdom? It's time to take over. Let's sit down and figure out our strategy. How do we get rid of the present political powers, the ruling religious authorities? How shall we crusade against the infidels and retake the holy city?

Or how do we win them to our side? Imagine Jesus coming into Jerusalem on a white horse, with the scribes and elders laying palm branches down before him, and Pilate and Herod striding with him, not side by side but a bit behind him, on smaller, darker horses. And then imagine the high priest, who has led the parade, shouting a chant that spreads throughout the crowd: "Hosanna, Hosanna. Hosanna to God in the highest. Blessed is he who comes in the name of the Lord. Hosanna to the Son of David, the King."

Christ crucified? No! God forbid. But Christ conquering! Yes! Christ marching into Jerusalem for holy war and holy victory. Amen and Amen.

But Jesus says, "No! The Christ—yes, but the Christ crucified—also yes." Here is God's plan. It's not a mere prediction, like making a weather forecast based on observing certain previous trends and existing conditions. No, here's the predetermined, "definite" divine plan (see Acts 2:22, 23). "[I]t was the will of the LORD to crush him" (Isaiah 53:10a), and "The LORD has laid on him the iniquity of us all" (Isaiah 53:6)—that is how Isaiah puts it. Here's how Jesus puts it: "I *must* go," not "I *will* go." "[I] must be delivered into the hands of sinful men and be crucified" (Luke 24:7). "I must go to Jerusalem, that city where all those millions of atoning sacrifices have been offered, to sacrifice myself, once and for all, for millions, for the sins of my people. I must go to Jerusalem, not to gather its leaders to my side, but to watch them pierce my side and crown my head with thorns and mock me and spit on me and cry out to me, 'If you are the Son of God, come down from the cross'" (Matthew 27:40).

Christ crucified—to human wisdom this is nonsense!

Christ crucified—Jerusalem wouldn't get it. Christ crucified—the first disciples wouldn't get it either. You see, they are moving forward when they should be moving backwards. They are right-side-up when they need to be upside-down. They are missing what's in the mirror because the idea of the Messiah being put to death as "a public menace," as a religious and political traitor, is too shocking, too surprising for them there to comprehend.[3]

We will get to what Peter thinks of all this in a minute. It's so important, importantly wrong, that I've made it into a separate point. For now let's just get into our heads that from that day to our day almost nothing has changed in the minds of men. While the edge of the idea of the Christ crucified has been dulled by the countless crosses atop church steeples or the incalculable golden crosses hung around our necks, the concept is still crazy to the spiritually sane and is still anti-academic to the intelligentsia. How did Paul put it?

> For Jews demand signs and Greeks seek wisdom, but we preach Christ crucified, a stumbling block to Jews and folly to Gentiles. . . . For the word of the cross is folly to those who are perishing. (1 Corinthians 1:22–24, 18a)

Oddly enough, "Jesus Christ and him crucified" (1 Corinthians 2:2) is what the religious leaders of our day oppose, and not just religious leaders in general, but those who gladly check the box for "Christian" when filling out a religious survey. Here I mean not only liberal Protestants who deny the deity of Christ, his substitutionary death, his bodily resurrection, and the exclusivity of salvation—that there is only one mediator between God and man, the man Jesus Christ. Yes, I mean them. But I also mean evangelicals who have declawed the lion of Judah and pulled the bloody cross out of the side of the Lamb of God.

"Christians" have done remarkably well in writing books that have sold well, even making the *New York Times* bestsellers list. But find me a best-selling Christian book in the past ten years that has made such a list that is exclusively about the cross of Christ. Or find me ten books right now in the top 100 best-selling Christian books in Christian bookstores that mention the cross of Christ. Or, easier still, just find me ten churches in 10,000 that preach two times a year on the cross. Nearly every evangelical church today has on its website or sign "Christ-centered," but how many are cross-centered?

But listen, you can't be Christ-centered without being cross-centered. Christ crucified is the crux of Christianity. The summary symbol of our faith is not a fish or a shepherd or a dove or a shamrock but a cross—"that old rugged cross, so despised by the world. . . . that old rugged cross, stained with blood so divine."[4]

Simon the Stumbling Stone

The first surprise is Christ crucified, that the King must suffer and die, that Jesus' passion and death must precede his resurrection and return, that the cross must come before the crown. The second surprise is Simon the stumbling stone. That is, right after Simon Peter gives the most important confession in the history of the world—"You [Jesus] are the Christ"—the very next time he opens his mouth he shoves his left foot and his right hand and his elbows and his other foot—everything he can—into his mouth.

Amazing! Verse 15: Jesus "said to them, 'But who do you say that I am?'" Verse 16: Simon Peter replied in essence, "Everyone clear out. Put your hands down. I'll answer this one. 'You are the Christ, the Son of the living God.'" A+. Peter moves to the head of the class. Twenty seconds later, verse 21: "From that time Jesus began to show his disciples that he must go to Jerusalem and suffer many things . . . and be killed." Verse 22: "And Peter," thinking he has moved from star pupil to the Chair of the Bible Department, "took him aside and began to rebuke him, saying, 'Far be it from you, Lord!'" Here Peter literally says, "May God be merciful to you, Lord," or, my paraphrase, "God loves you and has a wonderful plan for your life, which doesn't include suffering and death. This shall never happen to you." And then verse 23: "But he [Jesus] turned and said to Peter, 'Get behind me, Satan! You are a hindrance to me. For you are not setting your mind on the things of God, but on the things of man.'" He sends Peter to the very back of the class. "Here's a hat," he says. "Put it on." The hat has a D on it. The D however is not for "dunce" but "devil."

What a surprising change. From "you are Peter" (v. 18) to you are Satan (v. 23), from Saint Peter to Simon Sinner, from Rock Star to Stumbling Stone. It's surprising that Peter can get "you are the Christ" but not get "and you are the Christ crucified." Well, at least it's surprising to us, who can look back on the finished puzzle and see how each piece fits perfectly in place. But we must remember that just as the Old Testament prophets "had difficulty reconciling the sufferings and glory of the Messiah (1 Pet 1:10–12),"[5] so too did Peter. He would eventually get it; he writes in 1 Peter 2:24, "He himself bore our sins in his body on the tree, that we might die to sin and live to righteousness. By his wounds you have been healed." But here he's looking at it all backwards. The garment Jesus is wearing reads "Conquering Christ" in the mirror, but in reality it says, "Christ Crucified."

Three Applications from the Second Surprise

Let me draw out three applications from this second surprise. First, *we are not called to pastor Jesus but follow him.*

As I look at these verses, I get the sense that from verse 16 to verse 21 (or at least v. 20) Peter is feeling pretty good about himself. I mean, who wouldn't? He got the answer right. And he got a pretty big pat on the back for it. However, it all seems to go to his head. Here Peter thinks he is Pope Petrus I, already sitting in his golden throne at the Vatican about to speak *ex cathedra*. So he speaks, like the perfect pontiff should speak, with gentle authority and merciful moral exhortation! "Jesus, let me pastor you. God will be merciful to you, and God's mercy never means pain." He sounds a bit like Job's friends, doesn't he?

However, Jesus sounds a bit like God from the whirlwind. "Oh, Peter, shut your mouth. Your first encyclical is entirely fallible.[6] It's worse than fallible—it's diabolical! You are acting devilishly. Just as Satan tempted me in the wilderness—'Turn stones into bread! Jump! I'll give you the world; avoid suffering, stand above the crowd, show off your superpowers, win now!'[7]—Peter, you are tempting me. You are tempting me to take the easy road—to skip Gethsemane and Golgotha and go directly to Glory. And not only are you tempting me, you are offending me. Get behind me, Satan. The cross is offensive to the world, but the things contrary to the cross are offensive to me."[8]

The moment we think we think better than Christ we're not thinking right. The moment we pull Jesus aside for a spiritual lesson or two—instructing him about the cross, human sexuality, exclusivity, etc.—is the moment we are not seeing straight (see 1 Timothy 6:3, 4).

We are not to be like Peter when he pastors Jesus. We are only to be like Peter when he follows Jesus. That's the first application. Here's the second: *don't be satanic*. No satanic spiritually allowed in the church! What do I mean by satanic spirituality? I mean letting the world's ways (not God's way) dictate your decisions.

I'll give two examples and let the Holy Spirit give you a thousand more. First, it is satanic if your twenty-one year old daughter wants to go to the mission field to a dangerous region of the world and you oppose that decision, wanting her instead to stay safely at home. (The key word there being "safely" [i.e., no cross].) Second example: It is satanic if you oppose the breadwinner in your family who wants to follow John Wesley's wealth dictum (to "gain all you can, save all you can, give all you can"[9]) and who thus when he makes $65,000 a year gives away $5,000, when he makes $80,000 gives away $20,000, when he makes $300,000 gives away $240,000. Each year, as he makes more, he decides to live on less so he can give more—more to missions, more to the church, more to the poor, more to the gospel of Jesus Christ. No opposing gospel generosity or gospel sacrifice! No satanic spirituality please!

My third application is this: *God is patient with Peters*, not wishing that anyone like him should perish but rather come to repentance (2 Peter 3:9). Return to Jesus after dumb denials ("you can't die like that") and even after devious denials ("I do not know the man"). God is patient with Peters.

What I like about Peter (what I think we all like about Peter) is that he never seems to arrive. Not just in the Gospels, but also in Galatians. In Galatians 2:11–14 we learn that Peter has gone off course in his teaching. He has taken the B out of the A, B, C's of the gospel. So Paul opposes him to his face. Peter never seems to arrive. But through the ups and downs we do see him slowly moving up, not perfectly sanctified, but steadily sanctified—ethically, theologically.

God was patient with Peter as he is patient with all of us. Let that gracious patience encourage you. Let it encourage you, in Peter's own words, to "grow in the grace and knowledge of our Lord and Savior Jesus Christ" (2 Peter 3:18).

Passion Pattern: We Must Follow the Pattern of Cross, Then Crown

With this text we are looking into Looking Glass Land, where everything is inside-out, upside-down, backwards. Surprising. And we've seen the first surprise (Christ crucified) and the second surprise (Simon the stumbling stone), and finally we come to the third surprise, what I call a passion pattern. What Jesus clearly teaches in verses 24–28 is the pattern we must follow—*cross, then crown.*

This pattern is surprising because after Jesus speaks of the basic content of the gospel (his death and resurrection—the resurrection part went over Peter's head), he next speaks of our work. It's astonishing that after he essentially says, "Listen, here's the work I have to do *for you* to save your souls," he doesn't next say, "So sit back and just enjoy my finished work." Instead he says, "Get to work."

Further, it's surprising that that this work (our work) is cross-work. Jesus says, "I have my cross, and you have yours." And we say, "Why so, Lord? After all you have done, why our cross too? Why not your cross and our crown? Why not reward now, suffering never? For you see, Lord, avoiding suffering is a high priority to us. The pursuit of happiness is a constitutional right. A comfortable lifestyle is a suburban necessity. William Penn's famous book title of 1682—*No Cross, No Crown*—doesn't read right to us today. No cross, no crown, oh no—that slogan won't stick to the backs of our new Porsche SUVs or even our old Dodge mini-vans."

It's surprising that *we* have cross-work to do too! There is his cross *and* our cross: "If anyone would come after me, let him deny himself and take up his cross and follow me" (v. 24). Write that verse on your doorpost, bind it on your forehead, tuck it deep into the recesses of your heart.

Let me ask you: what makes a Christian a Christian or a church a church? What are the marks of the church? What are the characteristics of a Christian? I like how Frederick Dale Bruner answers that question, based on his study of Matthew 16. He says there are two qualifications:

1. Confessing Jesus as Christ (Christo-centricity)
2. Following Jesus as the suffering Christ (Crucio-christocentricity)[10]

What a perfect summary! We must confess, "Jesus, you are the Christ." And we must follow him as the suffering Christ. So all theologies of glory in the here and now must be tossed out the window. "When Christ calls a man he bids him come and die" (Bonhoeffer).[11] Die to self and live for Christ—that's what Jesus is teaching here.

Yes, he teaches us that we must carry a cross. He teaches us what that cross is. And (thankfully) he gives us good reasons why cross-carrying is worth it.

So, what is this cross we must carry? Is it enduring suffering—those trials and tribulations of life (the death of a loved one, economic hardship, poor health, a tyrannical boss, a nagging wife, a lazy husband, a rebellious child, and so on)? Or is it persecutions—suffering for believing, preaching, and living out the gospel? I think it can be both. (Job in Uz carried as much of a cross as John in Patmos or Paul in prison.) But whatever it is, cross-carrying centers on *self-denial*. I say that because of what Jesus says and *how* he says it: "If anyone would come after me, let him deny himself and take up his cross and follow me" (v. 24). Notice the poetic symmetry here:

Come after me
    Deny himself
    Take up his cross
Follow me

What does it mean to "come after" or to "follow" Jesus? Metaphorically it means "take up your cross"; literally it means "deny yourself." To follow Jesus means to deny self.

In his *Institutes of the Christian Religion*, John Calvin taught that "the sum of the Christian life" is self-denial.[12] What do you think about that? Is that how you summarize your Christian life, what it means to follow Jesus? It's how Jesus summarized it! To *come to Christ* is to deny self—to admit that we're sinful, that we need a Savior. And to *live for Christ* is to deny self—to abide in him, pray to him, walk in his power. God's plan of salvation and sanctification has one summary command: deny yourself!

Therefore, Christ-follower, how's the self-denial going? Are you saying no to sin, those sins that so easily entangle you? And are you saying yes to Christ, doing something difficult for Jesus' sake?[13] Do you sacrifice time, money, convenience, comfort, safety to do those things that Jesus especially sees—that list he gives at judgment day (in 25:31–46)—feeding the hungry, giving drink to the thirsty, receiving the stranger, clothing the naked, caring for the sick, and visiting the imprisoned?[14]

Yes, self-denial is the sum of the Christian life. Or let me put it more positively. Following Jesus as Lord—that's the sum of the Christian life. Not following self-loves and self-rules but Jesus as your first love and his rules as the best rules for living.

In fact, we must be willing to risk our life "on the dare that Jesus is It."[15] And as "It" he knows what he's talking about, and he knows the way to glory—that it passes through the city of suffering, down the road of rejection, and up the valley of death. Self-denial, the self-denial Jesus is talking about here, is not giving up steak sandwiches and chocolate bon bons for Lent. Rather, it is giving up our own selves as lord. It is saying, "Jesus is Lord" and living like you mean it. Perhaps the four clauses in verse 24 all say the same thing, and the key word is not "cross" or "deny" or "follow" but "me." "Come after *me*/follow *me*." Who's king? You or Jesus? Perhaps the answer to the opening question of the *Heidelberg Confession* (1563) is the answer here:

Question: What is your only comfort in life and death?
Answer: That I belong, body and soul, in life and in death, not to myself but to my faithful Savior Jesus Christ.

Now, if Jesus is commanding his church to live Lord-centered, cruciformed lives, what's the motive for such a seemingly morbid mission? In verses 25–28 Jesus provides the motive: "For whoever . . ." (v. 25), "for what will it profit . . ." (v. 26), "for the Son of Man is going to come . . ." (v. 27). The overarching or all-embodying reason is that Jesus' wins and those with him win, and those not with him lose. If you choose the cross now, you get the crown then; if you choose the crown now, you get the cross then.

Verse 28 is a difficult verse: "Truly, I say to you, there are some standing here who will not taste death until they see the Son of Man coming in his kingdom." This verse could refer to the fall of Jerusalem in AD 70 or to the giving of the Spirit at Pentecost or to both Jesus' resurrection and return, two events of one final coming.[16] Or it could refer to a general prediction of Christ's future glory, encompassing the resurrection, ascension, Pentecost, and his present heavenly session.[17] I think it simply refers to the transfiguration, where "some"—Peter, James, and John—see "the Son of Man" (Jesus) in his kingdom glory. Verse 28 is a difficult verse, but verse 27 is the key verse: "For the Son of Man is going to come with his angels in the glory of his Father, and then he will repay each person according to what he has done." Then the righteous are rewarded and the unrighteous are undone.

In our text Jesus has talked about his passion, death, resurrection, and now his return as world judge. That's clear. And when Jesus comes as judge, those who didn't deny self and follow him—those who tried to hold on to life as if it was the most important entity, and those who lived to gain the world and touch and taste all the pleasures it has to offer—forfeit the game of life. Only doing for Jesus, and doing for others in the name of Jesus, matters. He who dies with the most toys most certainly does not win.

Let me be clear—Jesus isn't just saying what weight lifters coax each other with: no pain; no gain. He's not teaching what my ex-Marine basketball coach had printed on our practice jerseys: "Whatever doesn't kill you makes you stronger." Those sayings might very well be true. But what Jesus is here saying is far more serious. It's not no pain, no gain, but no pain, much more pain. This is Heaven and Hell stuff Jesus is talking about. Discipleship is not teatime.[18] It's not a casual coffeehouse conversation. It's life or death, eternal life or eternal death. At the last judgment Jesus will not slap the wrists of those professing Christians who toyed with his teachings, who moonlighted with power and possessions, who chose self-indulgence over self-denial, who thought orthodoxy had nothing to do with orthopraxis.[19] He won't say, "What a shame. Now you've lost the big city mansion by the River of Life. You're stuck with a refurbished farmhouse far out in the country." No, he will say, "You've lost everything. Not just your life, but eternal life with God!"

And there is no wheeling and dealing at that point. There is no members' fee you can pay to get in. There is no bargain to strike with the holy Son of Man. When he comes again in glory to judge, then "it's too late. You made the wrong choices, you sought false goals, you had other gods,"[20] and now you will pay for your whoring after success and status and self.

At the last judgment all looking glasses shall be shattered, and everyone shall see as they should have seen. We shall see that the first shall be last and the last first, that to live for self is to die and to die to self is to live, and that the crucified Christ shall rise again and soon return in glory with his angels, and with them (upon their wings I imagine) a hundred thousand blessings, crowns of righteousness for "all who have loved his appearing" (2 Timothy 4:8).

Alice in Wonderland and *Alice through the Looking Glass* are "two beloved masterpieces of the nonsensical."[21] But the Bible, as much as its Author turns things on their heads, is a masterpiece of the "sensical," a book designed to make sense of the world we live in, and to bring us, like the prodigal son, to our senses, to Jesus, the perfectly righteous King who served sinners, the everlasting God who died so that we who now live to serve and die to self might reign with him as kings and queens forever and ever.

49

This High Mountain . . . That Lowly Hill

MATTHEW 17:1–13, 22, 23

THE SUMMER OF MY junior year of high school, I attended the prestigious Five Star basketball camp. Each morning at the coach's session, a particular coach taught a new drill to all the campers. The first day of camp Coach Dave Odom, then the assistant coach at the University of Virginia, asked a camper named Bobby to demonstrate the drill. When Bobby got up and walked onto the court, I was surprised by Coach Odom's selection. Unlike many athletes around me who were tall and strong, Bobby was short and scrawny. Also he had on runner's shorts—those tight, kind-of girlish shorts worn high above the thigh muscles (trust me, we all wore our shorts high in those days, but not that high). Anyway, little Bobby with his little shorts did a fine job with the drill. In fact, a very fine job! I remember thinking to myself as he made 80 percent of his shots, "Not bad for a short, scrawny kid."

That afternoon I was reading the local newspaper. As I rifled through the sports page, I stopped to read the list of the top high school boys basketball players in the country. And as I looked at the First Team All-Americans, one name and picture jumped out at me. The best point guard in the nation was a boy named Bobby—Bobby Hurley—the short, scrawny kid I had just seen an hour ago. Of course, if you know anything about basketball, you know that Bobby Hurley lived up to the expectations—a four-year starter for Duke University, three Final Four appearances, two national championships, in one of which he was named MVP, a first-team All-American his senior year, NCAA all-time assists leader, seventh overall pick in the NBA draft.

In our text I want you to see that as it relates to the person of Jesus, *ap-*

pearances can be deceiving, and to see this truth both in his transfiguration on this high mountain and also in his death on that lowly hill.

This High Mountain

First we will look at this "high mountain"—the transfiguration—recorded for us in 17:1–8. Here I want you to see, as I walk you through many of the details of it, how the transfiguration shows us, as it showed Peter, James, and John originally, that Jesus is more than a teacher, healer, exorcist, and king. He is the glorious, holy, sovereign, preeminent, beloved Son of God, indwelt with all the fullness of God.

But first we start with the seemingly simple setting: "And after six days Jesus took with him Peter and James, and John his brother, and led them up a high mountain by themselves" (v. 1). Note three important details. First, Matthew starts by saying, "And after six days." Why add that detail? Matthew usually starts a transition text like this by mentioning something of the geographical location—"Now when Jesus came into the district of Caesarea Philippi" (16:13) or "When they came to Capernaum" (17:24). He rarely mentions time—"Then four days later" or something like that. So the mention of "six days" strikes us as odd and thus is potentially significant. Does Matthew want us to relate what happens here with the days of creation (Genesis 1, 2)? Does he want us to make some connection with *Moses* on *the mountain*, where the *cloud* of God's glory covered it, and *after six days* the *Lord's voice* called out to Moses (Exodus 24:15, 16)? Does he want us to see Jesus as the new Moses, the new exodus, the new lawgiver, the old Creator, all of the above? (He does.)

"And after six days"—that's significant. Also significant are the three men. "Jesus took with him Peter and James, and John." Why three? There were *three* because both Old Testament law (Deuteronomy 17:6) and New Testament law state that official testimony is "established by the evidence of two or three witnesses" (18:16). So here we have three eyewitnesses. In fact, in 2 Peter 1:16 Peter writes about the transfiguration, saying "we were *eyewitnesses* of his majesty." So, that's likely why three.

But why these three? Why elect them from the elect? It could be that they just needed to be put in their place—consider Peter's rebuke of Jesus in 16:22 and James's and John's thoughts about being the greatest in the kingdom, which will surface in 20:21. Or it could be, and I think it is, that they were chosen because they mattered. Not only did they matter to Jesus personally (he loved them), but they mattered missionally. They mattered to the Messiah's mission to the world. You see, these three would become the three pillars of the church (see Galatians 2:9), not perfect pillars, but pillars nonetheless.

I don't know about you, but I can't imagine Christianity without them—their leadership, their missionary work, their writings. And this seems to be the focus Peter takes in 2 Peter 1:12–21 when he talks about this event—*they* have been given the sure "prophetic word," a word on equal inspirational plane with the prophets (cf. 2 Peter 3:1, 2; Ephesians 2:20).[1] Jesus chose them because these three (along with Paul later) would become most instrumental in building, sustaining, and growing the church.

So the setting is significant: first six days, second three men, and finally a high mountain. "[Jesus] led them up a high mountain" (v. 1c). I've said this before, and it's worth saying again: mountains matter in Matthew. In chapters 5—7 we have the Sermon on the Mount. In 14:23 Jesus prayed on the mountain; in 15:29–38 he healed and fed the multitudes on the mountain; in chapters 24, 25 he taught on the mountain (the Mount of Olives) about the sign of his coming and the close of the age; and in 28:16–20, the Great Commission (the final word from Jesus in Matthew), we are told that the disciples went "to the mountain to which Jesus had directed them" (v. 16). Then we also have, in chapter 4, the temptation of Christ, where "the devil took him [Jesus] to a very *high mountain* and showed him all the kingdoms and of the world and their glory" (v. 8). Some scholars surmise that the high mount of transfiguration is the antithesis of the high mount of temptation—true glory versus false glory. I like that.

Mountains matter in Matthew. They matter in Matthew because they matter in the Old Testament, most significantly for our text—Moses on the mountain, where Lord spoke to him (Exodus 19, 20), and Elijah on the mountain (1 Kings 19, the same mountain), where God's reassuring voice came in "a low whisper" (v. 12).

So six days, three men, and a high mountain—a good name for a sitcom, an even better name for a setting. That's the setting (v. 1), an awesome setting! And here's the even more awesome story, starting in verses 2, 3.

> And [on this high mountain] he was transfigured before them, and his face shone like the sun, and his clothes became white as light. And behold, there appeared to them Moses and Elijah, talking with him.

The Greek word here for "he was transfigured" is *metemorphōthē*, from which we get the word "metamorphosed," which means to change in constitution or physical form (like a caterpillar into a butterfly). But here the emphasis is not on a change of form. Jesus doesn't turn into a dove or an angel or his pre-incarnate being. He remains fully human, at least so it seems from Peter talking to him in verse 4, as well as from Jesus' touching and then talking to all three of them in verse 7. Here the emphasis is on the change in his complexion, if I can put it that way. Jesus lights up.

Jesus' face gets as bright as that bright star in our solar system—the sun. (John's vision of Jesus in Revelation gets a similar description: "his face was like the sun shining in full strength" [Revelation 1:16]). That's a lot of light! And that abundant light that is on Jesus' skin and seemingly coming from within radiates out, bleaching his clothes. There's a poetic parallelism here (see below): his face is *hōs ho heōliōs* ("like the sun") and his clothes *hōs to phōs* ("white as [the] light").

and his face	shone	like the sun,
and his clothes	became white	as [the] light (v. 2bc).

Face/clothes; sun/light. He's all very bright! That's what we are to see here.

Now, what's with Jesus looking like this self-producing, self-sustaining, and self-projecting light? What's all the brightness about? It's about divine glory—"Christ's heavenly or divine nature, a revelation of Jesus as he always was and is."[2] I say that because in verse 5 God the Father shows up with or within "a *bright* cloud." I italicize "bright" for a reason. The Son (Jesus) is bright; the Father (God) is bright. They are both bright, and they are both bright because they are both "one substance," to use the later language of the church. The Shekinah glory that led Israel in the wilderness (Exodus 13:21), came upon Moses at Sinai (Exodus 24:15–18), and filled the tabernacle (Exodus 40:34, 35) and temple (2 Chronicles 7:1–3) is here. Jesus' brightness is about Jesus' divine glory:

> Glory be to the Father and the Son and to the Holy Spirit.
> As it was in the beginning, is now, and ever shall be, world without end.
> Amen.

So there is Jesus Christ superstar (in the brightness sense of that word—he is like a super *star*), and then next to him, stars in their own right, but seemingly not shining (unless you take "glory" to equal "light" in Luke 9:31, which I do not) are Moses and Elijah (v. 3).

We know who they are. But how did the disciples know who they were?[3] And, more basic than that, how did these two prophets get there? Are they real and resurrected or what? We don't know the answers to those questions. But we do know (or can take an educated guess at) why these two were there at this moment.

They were there as representatives of the Law and the Prophets,[4] the whole of the Old Testament. I say that because of what Peter says in 2 Peter 3:1–2. There he connects the New Testament apostolic ministry to the Old Testament prophets' ministry by means of Jesus. I also say that because Jesus, as he relates to the Law and Prophets, is never far from Matthew's mind. Four times in Matthew's Gospel the apostle speaks of Jesus' relation to the "the Law" and "the Prophets" (5:17; 7:12; 11:13; 22:40).

Therefore, here's how I see it. I see Law (Moses) and Prophets (Elijah) showing up and both shaking hands with Gospel (Jesus). "Hello," they say. "Nice to finally meet you." I take 17:3 as a visual of 5:17, where Jesus said, "Do not think that I have come to abolish the Law or the Prophets; I have not come to abolish them but to fulfill them."

So, if you put the transfigured brightness of Jesus alongside the *living* testimony (note that somehow Moses and Elijah, in whatever form they took here, are as alive as Jesus and Peter and James and John) of these two Old Testament saints, what do you get? The picture is worth a thousand words, or at least sixteen words. Here are my sixteen words: The radiant Son of God, who enlightens all of Scripture, is the light of the world (see John 8:12; 9:5; cf. 4:16).[5] That's what I think we're to see in verses 2, 3.

The Problems with Pious Peter

Having looked at the setting of the transfiguration, the actual transfiguring (and figuring that out), we next come to Peter's reaction (v. 4). Notice here that we only get Peter's reaction. Why? What are the other two up to? We don't know. Not talking? Yes, they are not talking. But look who *is* talking. It's Peter. No surprise here. And Peter talked to Jesus and said, "Lord"—that's a good way to start a sentence. "It is good that we are here"—that's a good way to finish a sentence and a speech. "If you wish"—oh, Peter, now is the time to stop talking—"I will make three tents here, one for you and one for Moses and one for Elijah."

Luke and Mark, in their versions of this event, tell us that Peter didn't know what he was saying (see Luke 9:33; Mark says it more tamely: "he did not know what to say," Mark 9:6). Matthew, however, thinks such a clarification is unnecessary. It is obvious that Peter has goofed.

But how so? What's wrong with his pious short speech? There are at least two problems. First, Peter misunderstands the temporary nature of this glorious vision. One almost has to wonder, has he forgotten the cross (what Jesus said in 16:21–23)? That cross thing hasn't happened yet, has it? Remember, Peter, that it goes first death, then resurrection; first cross, then crown. But here Peter wants to build tents, mini-dwellings (reminiscent of the Feast of Tabernacles), mini-temples for these three holy people, two of whom, I would surmise, would prefer to go back to where they have come from—"the glory of heaven and the angels,"[6] and another of whom most certainly needs no temple, for he himself is the living, walking, talking, healing, dying, and rising temple of the living God. Do you think Immanuel needs a pup tent from Peter? It's a pious gesture, but an ill-informed one. By wanting to hold on to the glory of the transfiguration Peter has no place for the glory of that gory cross.

That's the first problem with Peter's three-tent theology. The second problem follows. Peter, why the *three* tents? What's he thinking? Is he implying an equality of personhood? I can't imagine that he would, but it seems like he is. Even after confessing to Jesus, "You are the Christ, the Son of the living God" (16:16), has Peter now been swayed by the popular opinion of the day, that Jesus is just a prophet? Is he seeing this vision and thinking like Muhammad would six centuries later—"One tent for the prophet Moses, one for the prophet Elijah, and one for the prophet Jesus, the greatest prophet of all"? I don't know. I don't know what he's thinking. I don't know if he knows what he's thinking. But whatever he is thinking, God thinks little of it. And so comes the heavenly corrective, the lesson for Peter (and for us) about this grand event:

> He was still speaking [I love that—it tells us he is interrupted from his no-end-in-sight blabbering] when, behold, a bright cloud overshadowed them, and a voice from the cloud [cuts in and] said, "This is my beloved Son, with whom I am well pleased; listen to him." When the disciples heard this, they fell on their faces and were terrified [ah, the holiness of God]. But Jesus came and touched them [ah, the incarnational grace of God], saying, "Rise, and have no fear." And when they lifted up their eyes, they saw no one but Jesus only. (vv. 5–8)

Do you see the corrective here? God cuts into Peter to do some brain surgery using two key concepts, summarized well in two key phrases. The first phrase is the last phrase in verse 8, "And when they lifted up their eyes, they saw no one but Jesus only." In the Greek it ends, "him [emphatic] Jesus only." Jesus alone! You see (Matthew wants us to see), Jesus was the last man standing, the only man standing. Where did Moses and Elijah go? Who knows? Who cares? The point has been made, quite visually. Look up. Who do you see? Jesus! Jesus only. Right. Look neither to Moses nor to Elijah (they have done their job), but *now* look to Jesus and to *him alone*.

The second key phrase is, "listen to him," (v. 7) which is at the very center of this story structurally (vv. 1–8).[7] In Matthew, God the Father only speaks twice—once at Jesus' baptism and the other time here. And on those two occasions he only has one line: "This is my beloved Son, with whom I am well pleased" (3:17; 17:5). Even that one line is unoriginal, if I can be so bold as to put it that way. It comes from Psalm 2:7 (about the anointed king, "You are my Son") and from Isaiah 42:1 (about the Suffering Servant, "in whom my soul delights"). "You are my Son in whom I delight."

But notice what is added here to that line: "Listen to him," and perhaps implied, as Moses and Elijah have gone bye-bye, "Listen to him *only*," or "Listen to him as the supreme interpreter of Scripture and authority over Scripture." Moses is a prophet, Elijah a prophet, but Jesus is the "prophet" of Deuteronomy 18:15 (exclamation point) and moreover and more importantly "the beloved Son of God" (triple exclamation point). Listen to him! Yes, listen to his commandments in the Sermon on the Mount—his "but I say to you's." And listen to his talk about the cross to come—his "here is what I'll do for you."

Jesus only.

Listen to him.

Those are the lessons from verses 5–8. Now let me build on those two lessons with five more.

Five More Lessons

Lesson One: Jesus is glorious! John 1:14 (written by the John in our Matthew text) says, "And the Word became flesh and dwelt among us, and we have seen his glory, glory as of the only Son from the Father, full of grace and truth." As they saw Jesus, so let us (as best we can, in the power of the Spirit) see him too. Let us see him as the glorious Son of God.

Lesson Two: Jesus was not merely a great leader (Heavenly CEO) or a profound moralist (What Would Jesus Do?), but he was/is the glorious Son of God, *and thus* he deserves our acknowledgment ("You are our Lord and God"), our adoration ("We fall before you and worship you"), and our obedience ("We will listen to what you have to say").

Lesson Three: God uses not-so-bright people (and I mean not-so-bright both in the sense of a lack of holiness and of intellect) to bring to this dark world "the light of the knowledge of the glory of God in the face of Jesus Christ" (2 Corinthians 4:6).

Lesson Four: Christians who revere holy places (e.g., Matthew's *unnamed* mountain) and holy people (Moses, Elijah, et al) more than they revere the holy Son of God are wholly mistaken, if not wholly unholy (i.e., idolatrous). Here you have arguably the top six heroes of the Old and New Testaments in one place and one time, and God the Father acknowledges and honors Jesus exclusively (it couldn't be plainer), and then he rebukes Peter for the first building project in church history—wanting to build holy shrines for holy people in the Holy Land. What would Peter now think of St. Peter's Basilica?

Lesson Five: Doing something seemingly good for Jesus can be very bad for the church and the world. If Peter had his way, with his first two encyclicals—the first *De Crucis Vitatione* ("Concerning the Avoidance of the Cross") in 16:22 and the second *De Tabernaculis Statuendis* ("Concerning Tents to be Pitched") in 17:4—we would not have a Christless Christianity, but a crossless one. But the gospel is Christ *and him crucified*. That's how Paul would put it in 1 Corinthians 2:2, and that's how Peter himself would preach it at Pentecost: "Let all the house of Israel therefore know for certain that God has made him both Lord and *Christ*, this Jesus whom you *crucified*" (Acts 2:36). *Christ and him crucified*—woe to us if we don't preach that gospel! Doing something seemingly good for Jesus can be very bad for the church and the world. The world needs to hear the message of the cross.

That Lowly Hill

Keep that final lesson at the front of your minds because Jesus has it at the front of his as he travels down this high mountain heading for that lowly hill—that little hill outside Jerusalem (it's called Golgotha or Calvary) where he will die for the sins of the world.

We come now to verses 9–13. As we looked at verses 1–8, I've shown you (what this actual historical event shows us) that Jesus is more than a mere man. Oh, he looks like a man, he sounds like a man, he feels like a man (yes, he is truly flesh of our flesh), but he is more than a man. Appearances can be deceiving. He is the divine Son of God. And for a brief moment we see that. The curtain is pulled aside, the veil removed, and we witness the pure light (or as pure as human eyes are permitted to see). And Lord willing, we are permanently transformed by this momentary transfiguration.

That is all one part of the picture here. The other part comes in verses 9–13 and is later supplemented with verses 22, 23. We start in verse 9 with an important topological/theological shift: "And as they were coming down the mountain, Jesus commanded them, 'Tell no one the vision, until the Son of Man is raised from the dead.'" In other words, "Peter and James and John, don't open your mouths to tell the story of salvation until the story is done." And the story is not done at the transfiguration. There's the resurrection. And before that, there's the cross. The last word of verse 9 is crucial—"dead." The Son of Man . . . dead.

You see, appearances can be deceiving. What Peter, James, and John had just witnessed—the glorious Son of God on this high mountain—is only half of the vision. The other half involves the glorious Son of Man (vv. 9, 22) dead on that lowly hill. This is what Jesus clearly teaches not only right before the transfiguration (16:21ff.) but also right after it:[8]

> As they were gathering in Galilee, Jesus said to them, "The Son of Man is about to be delivered into the hands of men, and they will kill him, and he will be raised on the third day." And they [heard, it seems, only the first two phrases, because they] were greatly distressed. (vv. 22, 23)

In verse 23 they are distressed about Jesus' death. In verse 10, however, they are confused by it. That is why they ask their question about Elijah, which is even more confusing to us. Their question to Jesus is this: "Then why do the scribes say that first Elijah must come?" This question seems out of place coming just after Jesus' talking about getting killed. But it's not. I'll explain.

Here they refer to Malachi 4:5, 6, the last word of the Old Testament. (Malachi 4:5, 6 is immediately followed by Matthew 1:1.) In Malachi, God speaks of sending Elijah before "the great and awesome day of the Lord" (v. 5), when Elijah will bring relational restoration, turning "the hearts of fathers to their children and the hearts of children to their fathers" (v. 6).

Now, why would that prophecy pop into their heads? Because the "scribes" of their day (the expert Bible teachers) were talking about it (cf. 27:47–49).[9] Also because (obviously) they had just seen Elijah standing right next to Jesus and Moses. (Interestingly, Moses is mentioned in Malachi 4:4—"Remember the law of my servant *Moses*, the statutes and rules that I commanded him at Horeb for all Israel.") That's why Elijah comes to mind.

Malachi said: Elijah first; the coming of the Lord (the Messiah) second. They are thinking to themselves, *We just saw Elijah, but he didn't stay and didn't do anything. If he's not doing what he's supposed to be doing, then despite what we just saw and heard, Jesus can't be the Messiah, the one who is to bring about the day of the Lord*. That's their riddle.

And here's how Jesus solves that riddle. He answered:

> Elijah does come, and he will restore all things. But I tell you that Elijah has already come, and they did not recognize him, but did to him whatever they pleased. (vv. 11, 12a)

The Jewish religious and political establishment killed him (see 14:1–11). "Then the disciples understood [rightly so] that he was speaking to them of John the Baptist" (v. 13).

So here is how it all comes together. To Jesus, this Elijah-type figure (cf. Luke 1:17) has come in the person of John, and through the message of John, the preaching of repentance, and the true Israelites who responded to that message, the promised restoration has taken place. But this Elijah—here's the shock of it, and the connection with the end of 17:9—suffered and died (he was rejected), just as the Messiah is about to suffer and die (be rejected).

Thus, the point is: as the three disciples are walking down the mountain, perhaps hoping all that talk about suffering is finally over, Jesus teaches them that the fate of his forerunner foreshadows his cross. "*So also* the Son of Man will certainly suffer at their hands" (v. 12b).

Paradoxical Parallels

Before Peter, James, and John get to Gethsemane (and yes, it will be these three who witness that wrestling agony), Jesus wants them to see (not yet taste from) the cup that he is about to drink. With the high mountain behind them and that lowly hill ahead, he wants them to understand both Colossians 1:19 *and* 20:

> For in him all the fullness of God was pleased to dwell [the transfiguration—"this is my beloved Son"], and through him to reconcile to himself all things, whether on earth or in heaven, making peace by the blood of his cross [the crucifixion—"the Son of Man will certainly suffer"].

He wants them to hold those tensions together. The exalted Jesus, with garments glistening, standing on a high mountain, flanked by two religious giants from the past, where all is light, *is also* the humiliated Jesus whose clothes have been torn from him and divided, the one lifted upon the cross, flanked by two common, convicted criminals as darkness settles over the land.[10] What paradoxical parallels we see between the transfiguration (17:1–8) and the crucifixion (27:33–54)! We have light and darkness, two saints and two sinners, and between all this is *him*—"This is my beloved Son" (17:5) (God's voice from Heaven) and "Truly this was the Son of God" (27:54) (that pagan soldier's voice moments after the crucifixion).[11]

Jesus wants us to make the same connections Matthew does. He wants us to see, as Chrysostom nicely phrased it, that Jesus was "transfigured to manifest the glory of the cross."[12] He wants us to see that you can't have the high mountain without the lowly hill. The mountaintop explains the hilltop, and the hilltop the mountaintop.[13] And the mountaintop teaches us Jesus' last word in this Gospel—that he has been given "[a]ll authority in heaven and on earth" (28:18). So fear not, get up, and move out, for there is a world to be won and a glorious inheritance ahead to be had. But the hilltop teaches us Jesus' last word in chapter 16: "If anyone would come after me, let him deny himself and take up his cross and follow me" (v. 24). Christians, it's a cross now and a crown then.

Appearances can be deceiving.

And here in 17:1–13 we have seen just that. As we've looked at verses 1–8 we've seen that Jesus is more than a mere man. He is the glorious Son of God on this high mountain. But as we've looked at verses 9–13 and verses 22, 23 and beyond to 27:33–54, we've seen that Jesus is also the glorious Son of Man who came to die not on some high mountain—that of Sinai or Zion or wherever—but on the lowly hill outside the holy city for our unholy souls.

And so, for the condescension, the humility, the humiliation, and the sufferings—for the cross, to him be the glory forever and ever. Amen.

50

Visualize Mustard-Seed Faith

MATTHEW 17:14–20

THE SCREWTAPE LETTERS is C. S. Lewis's little book on the big problem of demons in our modern world. It consists of a series of letters written by Screwtape, an important official in the devil's hierarchy (or "Lowerarchy" as Lewis phrases it), to Wormwood, his nephew, a junior devil residing on earth. These letters are all instructions on how to corrupt the beliefs of Wormwood's "patient," a young man is who is in danger of becoming a Christian.

In Screwtape's seventh letter he gives this instruction on how to avoid detection:

> My Dear Wormwood, I wonder you should ask me whether it is essential to keep the patient in ignorance of your own existence. That question, at least for the present phase of the struggle, has been answered for us by the High Command [the Devil]. Our policy, for the moment, is to conceal ourselves. Of course this has not always been so. We are really faced with a cruel dilemma. When humans disbelieve in our existence we lose all the pleasing results of direct terrorism and we make no magicians. On the other hand, when they believe in us, we cannot make them materialists and skeptics. At least, not yet.

Screwtape continues,

> I have great hopes that we shall learn in due time how to emotionalize and mythologize their science to such an extent that what is, in effect, a belief in us (though not under that name) will creep in while the human mind remains closed to belief in the Enemy [God]. . . . If once we can produce our

> perfect work, the Materialist Magician, the man, not using, but veritably worshipping, what he vaguely calls 'forces' while denying the existence of 'spirits'—then the end of the war will be in sight.

"But in the meantime," Screwtape concludes, "We must obey our orders. I do not think you will have much difficulty in keeping the patient in the dark. The fact that 'devils' are predominantly *comic* figures in the modern imagination will help you. If any faint suspicion of your existence begins to arise in his mind, suggest to him a picture of something in red tights, and persuade him that since he cannot believe in that (it is an old textbook method of confusing them) he therefore cannot believe in you."[1]

Today's text records an exorcism! That's easy to overlook because there is so much talk here about faith (the exorcism easily gets buried under all the conversation surrounding it), and it's easy to overlook because we are in the practice of overlooking such things. You see, we have a category for what is said in verse 15, where the father says of his son, "he is an epileptic,"[2] but we don't know what to do with what is done in verse 18, "And Jesus rebuked *the demon*, and it came out of him." The demon?

For us, the Screwtapes and Wormwoods of this world, who are unapologetically presented to us in Scripture, need an apologetic. Yes, in a culture where *unseen* demons are *seen* as funny, fluffy team mascots—the Blue Demons of DePaul or the Red Devils of Manchester United, to name two of 200 examples—the idea of a demon so controlling a little boy that he is out of control is far from our mind's eye. But it ought not to be!

If we are to get into this text we need to move from our modern worldview into the Biblical worldview. We need to move from the culture we live in, which is made up of "Materialist Magicians"—people who, on one hand, won't believe in anything unless there is scientific data to support it, and who yet, on the other hand, believe in almost anything that has the ring of "magic" to it. Today it strikes us as perfectly normal that the FBI would hire a psychic to solve a case and that a computer programmer is a witch on the weekends. We need to move from that into believing that *reality* includes the existence and the effects of unseen spirits. For you see, as Jesus comes down from the mount of transfiguration, he walks into the valley of "a demon-infested world."[3] And as we come now to study *him*, we must walk with him into the same world—our world. There is not far to walk. Here we are. And we are to *see* the unseen demon (that's a given). But we are also (and more importantly) to *see* (1) the nature and power of Jesus and (2) the nature and power of faith.

The Nature and Power of Jesus

Let me start with Jesus—his person and power. In all the commentaries I read on this text, not one of them focused on Jesus.[4] They didn't ignore him, but he wasn't their main focus. Faith was the focus—that is, the disciples' lack of faith, Jesus' teaching on faith, and so on. Now, that is here. That's my second point. But it's not my only point, and it's not my first and *foremost* point. Listen, Jesus is the center of the gospel and of the Gospels—Matthew, Mark, Luke, and John. And in Matthew's Gospel, as is true of all four, Jesus is not a minor character. Each and every scene is a spotlight on him. And as easy as it is for us to miss the demon hiding in the boy, so it's easy for us to miss the person who is talking and acting the most in this passage—namely, Jesus.

So let's look at him first.

As Christians we believe that Jesus is fully God and fully man, yet one person. That theology is played out perfectly in the whole of chapter 17, especially in the contrast between Jesus' divine light on the mountain (he's as bright as God) and his coming death on the hill (he's as human as you and me). "God is Dead" is not an appropriate title for this chapter, but "God Will Die" might be. Jesus, the divine Son of God, will die. This theology—that Jesus is fully God and fully man, yet one person—is also played out in nearly every verse of our text. Now, to prove this point more dramatically (and to have more fun), I'm going to walk backwards through our passage, moving us from verse 20 to 19, 18, 17, 16, 15, 14.

Here we go. In verse 20, coming off the disciples' question in verse 19, Jesus talks about moving mountains through mustard-seed faith. He says:

> For truly, I say to you, if you have faith like a grain of mustard seed, you will say to this mountain, "Move from here to there," and it will move, and nothing will be impossible for you.

Think about that statement for a moment. Think about *what* he says and *how* he says it. Here he makes a claim to his disciples that if they have faith "nothing will be impossible" for them. That claim is as crazy as the claim that he is the fulfillment of the Law, his words will last forever, and he will judge the world by separating the sheep from the goats. Yes, it's a crazy claim unless he has divine authority. Or more than that, unless he is divine himself.

What he says here has that I-am-God ring to it, and so too does *how* he says it. Here Jesus doesn't say, "Thus says the Lord." In fact, he never talks that way. He doesn't talk like a prophet. He talks like someone far greater than a prophet, far greater than Moses and Elijah and all the prophets thrown together into one pot and stirred. Here he says, "For truly, I say to you . . ."

(v. 20b). He sounds like he sounded in the Sermon on the Mount. He sounds like he knows what he's talking about. He sounds like God would sound . . . *does sound like* . . . in the Old Testament. *Jesus, by what authority do you talk with such authority?*

Now as we move from verses 20 and 19 to verse 18, it reminds me of the healing of the paralytic in chapter 9, where Jesus proves his authority to forgive sins—only God can forgive sins!—by instantly healing the paralytic. Here Jesus proves that he can say *what* he says about moving mountains—doing the impossible—and *how* he wants to say it because he instantly, with one word, heals the boy: "And Jesus rebuked the demon, and it came out of him, and the boy was healed instantly," or more literally "from that hour" (v. 18).

Matthew gives us a great setup to this miracle. In verse 16 we read that the nine disciples (remember, three went up the mountain with Jesus) each gave it their best shot with this tough devil. The results? Verse 16: "they could not heal him." Verse 19b: they "could not . . . cast it out." In both places the word used for "they could" (in their case, add "not") comes from the word we use for dynamite. The root word in Greek is *dynamis*. They were unable. They didn't have the power. Their best dynamite didn't work. One guy tries, then another, and another and another. Nine tries, no success. It is impossible. But then comes Jesus to move this mountain. And he does! Nothing is impossible (v. 20; the word "impossible" here has the same root word for "unable," that dynamite word). Nothing is impossible for him.

So what do we have here? You can almost hear the music to "A Mighty Fortress Is Our God" begin in the background, and the host of angels starts to sing. They sing verse 1. They sing verse 2. They sing verse 3:

> And though this world, with devils filled,
> Should threaten to undo us,
> We will not fear, for God hath willed
> His truth to triumph through us;
> The Prince of Darkness grim,
> We tremble not for him;
> His rage we can endure,
> For lo, his doom is sure;
> One little word shall fell him.[5]

Jesus rebuked him, and the demon came out instantly. One little word brought that demon down and out. The point is, Jesus is the powerful Son of God. Where there is inability, he is more than able. He's dynamite!

We are not done walking backwards. (I told you this would be fun.) We have two more steps to take. We will look at the nature and power of faith in a moment, but now we are looking at the nature and power of Jesus. Next we step back to verse 17, a verse that to me summarizes what I've been saying about Jesus being fully God and fully man and yet one person.

Here we have the humanity of Jesus. Jesus is not a Buddhist, emptying himself of all feelings. Jesus felt emotions. In G. Walter Hansen's excellent article "The Emotions of Jesus and Why We Need to Experience Them," he begins:

> The gospel writers paint their portraits of Jesus using a kaleidoscope of brilliant "emotional" colors. Jesus felt *compassion;* he was *angry, indignant,* and *consumed with zeal;* he was *troubled, greatly distressed, very sorrowful, depressed, deeply moved,* and *grieved;* he *sighed;* he *wept* and *sobbed;* he *groaned;* he was *in agony;* he was *surprised* and *amazed;* he *rejoiced very greatly* and was *full of joy;* he *greatly desired,* and he *loved.*[6]

Yes, Jesus felt love for his disciples. He felt compassion for the blind, the crippled, and the hungry. He felt sadness for Mary and Martha at Lazarus's tomb. He felt fear (of death and of God's wrath for our sin) at Gethsemane. He felt anger toward hypocrisy. And here he felt "righteous exasperation."[7] He felt frustrated with the faithless: "O faithless and twisted generation, how long am I to be with you? How long am I to bear with you? Bring him here to me" (v. 17).

"At the top of the mountain," Frederick Dale Bruner writes, "Jesus had shone and glowed; at the foot of the mountain he moans and groans. There we saw his deity; here his humanity."[8] True. Here Jesus is fully human. But is he not also here, with his moaning and groaning, fully divine? For doesn't he sound like Yahweh in the Old Testament Scriptures? Note Numbers 14:11: "And the LORD said to Moses, 'How long will this people despise me? And how long will they not believe in me, in spite of all the signs that I have done among them?'"[9] Or Numbers 14:26, 27: "And the LORD spoke to Moses and to Aaron, saying, 'How long shall this wicked congregation grumble against me?'" Or Isaiah 46:12a: "Listen to me, you stubborn of heart." Or that God-dictated song—God said to Moses "write this song and teach it to the people of Israel" (Deuteronomy 31:19)—that we call the Song of Moses, which has lines like, "they are a crooked and twisted generation" (Deuteronomy 32:5), and "they are a perverse generation, children in whom is no faithfulness" (v. 20).[10]

Yes, our Lord Jesus sounds like the Lord God. And notice also, in Jesus' language, that he has an otherworldly consciousness "of his heavenly origin and destiny,"[11] mixed with this otherworldly authority: "[H]ow long *am I* to be with you? How long *am I* to bear with you? Bring him here to *me*" (17:17b). Who is he to talk this way? Does he come from Heaven? Does his "am I?" point to him as "I Am"? I think it does.

Verse 17 is a Christology class: Jesus is fully God and fully man, yet one person. Now step over verse 16. We'll come back to it in a bit; in fact we'll come back to most of these verses again. And next time, for the next point, we'll walk forward instead of backwards. But for now we're still walking backwards, back to where the story starts, where I end my first point on the person and power of Jesus. In verses 14, 15 we have the father's posture and prayer. This father kneels before Jesus (v. 14b), and he says, "Lord, have mercy on my son" (v. 15a). I'll revisit this man's posture and prayer when I talk about faith, but for now I just want you to see how this scene opens.

I don't know what's in the man's mind, but I have a good guess what's in Matthew's mind—a picture of the doctrine of the deity of Jesus Christ, the beloved Son of God on the high mountain and the Son of Man on the lowly hill. This desperate father genuflects before Jesus, calls him "Lord," and begs for mercy. If that's not a summary of what the worship of Yahweh looks like in the Old Testament, I'm not sure what is. Jesus is the merciful Lord! What's the walk-away from this walk backwards? That's it. Jesus is the merciful *Lord*!

The Nature and Power of Faith

So, point one (I'm done with it) is about Jesus—his person and power. He is the divine/human Son of God sent down to deal with the devil (the devil's stranglehold on the world and the people and powers within the world).

Before we get to point two, let me insert here that if I spend too much time talking about us to the exclusion or neglect of talking about Jesus, I'm sorry. It is my job as a preacher to preach Christ—to lift him up. I say that not only because Matthew's Gospel is about him but also because when he is lifted up we are drawn to him. In other words, we followers of Christ want to follow him.

One Sunday night before the college group I host in my home, the college pastor of my church said to me, "That sermon made me want to follow Jesus." When I lift up Christ, you should want to love him, trust him, and follow him because there is nobody like him. Right?

So, having lifted him up in the glory of the transfiguration, and having lifted him up in the glory of the cross, and having lifted him up in the glory of his person, and having lifted him up in the glory of his power (what a miracle we have here), now we come to the nature and power of faith.

Three "Faiths"

Three times in our text Jesus talks about faith. In verse 17 he speaks of a "faithless . . . generation," in verse 20a of his "little faith" disciples, and then in verse 20b of "faith" again—"faith like a grain of mustard seed"—small faith that can move big mountains. So in sum we have (1) no faith, (2) small faith, and (3) mustard-seed faith.

We know what no faith looks like. It looks like the self-satisfied scribes and Pharisees leering in the distance ("Some great rabbi. Ha, his followers are failures!") and in the crowd ("When's the next sign? My interest in Jesus lasts as long as the entertainment value"). And we know what Jesus thinks about such faithlessness. He thunders against it. In verse 17 he says, "O faithless and twisted generation, how long am I to be with you? How long am I to bear with you? Bring him here to me." Do you hear the roar of thunder, the crash of lightning? Here our Savior storms!

He gives this prophetic pronouncement that I think goes into the disciples' ears (no doubt) but is intended to go over them into the crowd, especially to those in the crowd who will plot his crucifixion and those in the crowd who will cheer it on. The disciples are to be corrected here, but the crowd condemned. Verse 17 is the beginning of Jesus' judgment on apostate Israel. This "generation"—in Matthew's Gospel you don't want to be counted part of this "generation" (see 11:16; 12:39–45; 16:4; 23:36; 24:34)—will not fare well at the final judgment. Why? They have no faith in Jesus as Lord.

So we know what no faith looks like and what Jesus thinks about it. But what's the difference here between little faith and mustard-seed faith? A mustard seed is the smallest seed where Jesus comes from. So, where is he coming from? What is he talking about? Little faith versus super-small-seed-faith? One bad, the other good? One powerless, the other all the dynamite you need? Neither Matthew nor Jesus defines the difference, but Matthew does clearly show the difference: little faith looks like the nine disciples' failure, mustard-seed faith like the father's successful plea.

First, we see the nine disciples' failure. What was their problem? Was it inexperience? True enough, they were new at this miracle stuff. It was only a few months ago that Jesus gave them the authority and the ability to heal the sick, raise the dead, cleanse lepers, and cast out demons (10:1, 8). Maybe they just needed a few more demons under their belt? No, that wasn't it. It wasn't inexperience. How about technique? Were they using the right stance—arms out, head up, back straight, stand on one leg, now kick with the other? No, that wasn't it either. How about their words? Were they using the correct exorcism incantation? Where they saying "hocus-pocus" when they should have been saying "*hasta la vista*, baby"? No, it wasn't that either. How about lack of leadership? With Peter, James, and John up on the mountain with Jesus, was it impossible to win this battle without their boldest and best warriors? No, not even that was their problem.

Their problem was a lack of power. But why didn't they possess the power needed? No power because no prayer? (That's how verse 21 of the King James reads: "Howbeit this kind goeth not out but by prayer and fasting.") We don't have this verse in our more modern editions of the Bible because the earliest and best Greek manuscripts discovered in the last 400 years do not have it. But be not dismayed by textual variants. It is likely that some pious monk, while copying Matthew, inserted this phrase on prayer because that's how Mark's version ends—"This kind cannot be driven out by anything but prayer" (Mark 9:29)—and that monk inserted the bit about fasting because . . . well, medieval monks liked to fast and thought everyone should join them (no joke).

So, is it no power because no prayer? Well, yes, it is, in Mark's Gospel for sure.[12] But I like what Matthew does. We'll stick with him. He doesn't mention prayer; rather he shows it. He shows it in verses 14b, 15a: "A man came up to him [Jesus] and, kneeling before him, said, 'Lord, have mercy on my son.'" This is found only in Matthew. Only in Matthew do we have this father on his knees (that's the right posture) calling Jesus "Lord" (that's the right title) and asking for "mercy" (that's the right prayer).

In verse 16 we get the frustrated father's report to Jesus. "My son has life-threatening seizures—sometimes when he gets them he 'falls into the fire' (perhaps the fire in the home, which would have been used to heat it), and sometimes, more often, my son falls 'into the water' (perhaps the outside well in the courtyard used for drinking water, imagine that).[13] And your disciples did not have the power to heal him."

Luke's version adds that the boy was this man's "only child" (Luke 9:38) and that the father could "hardly leave" his son for a moment because when seized by the spirit the boy convulsed and foamed at the mouth (Luke 9:39). This is a desperate situation. This is (if I may) a mountainous problem! It's one of thing to move "this mountain" (the mount of transfiguration), but how is "this mountain" (this boy's difficult demonic dilemma) to be moved "from here to there" (v. 20)? I'll tell you it is not by the push of little faith but by the power of prayer. "Prayer," one theologian wrote, "is simply faith breathing."[14] Isn't that great? Prayer is simply faith breathing. And here can you feel this father's breath. And do you see on *whom* he is breathing? Jesus!

Notice here (if you notice anything) that this is not just prayer ("Let us have a moment of silence, and if you'd like, please pray to the god of your personal preference"). No, here it's prayer *to Jesus*! Back to *Christology 101*. It's humble prayer to Jesus.

What's the difference between little faith and mustard-seed faith? Here it is. We are starting to see it. The picture is coming into focus. It's humble prayer to Jesus. Little faith is not directed *to Jesus*, and little faith is *not humble before Jesus*. Little faith is big on self. It's do-it-yourself faith. It believes in itself (have you ever heard that slogan before?), just as these nine disciples believed in themselves—their own ability, power, dynamite.

Come along with me, and let's revisit this scene with some rhetorical embellishment. I imagine these nine disciples one after the other coming up to the poor man and saying something like, "Step aside, step aside, everyone step aside. Here's my resumé. You'll see that I've been commanded and commissioned by Jesus—mountaintop Jesus—light-up-the-sky Jesus. What's the issue? Epilepsy? No problem. Spirit-induced seizures? Not a big deal. You have a demon? I'm your man. I'm ten for ten since chapter 10." At this point each time the father interjects, "But, sir, don't you think we should first pray?" And each time he gets the reply, "Who needs prayer when I'm here."

I am exaggerating the disciples' attitude. But I am not exaggerating the point that they had a lot of faith in themselves ("Why could *we* not cast it out?," v. 19), a faith that always means "little faith" in Jesus (v. 20). They were proud, not humble. They believed in themselves, not in Jesus.

Little faith is not directed *to Jesus*, and little faith is *not humble before Jesus*. But mustard-seed faith is the opposite. It's big on Jesus and not too big on self. It's humble prayer to Jesus. Just look at this man. This father's faith is mustard-seed faith. He's kneeling. Kneeling is not the posture of self-worth. He's begging. Begging someone else to help you because you're helpless doesn't strengthen one's inner ego. And begging someone on behalf of someone else is far removed from the natural necessity of looking out for number one. So, yes, he's kneeling and begging Jesus, and as he is doing so the mountain is girding its loins, and up and off it goes down the road, into the abyss, as far away as Heaven is from Hell.

You see, it's not the amount of faith that matters; it's the posture and object of faith. (Little faith is small; mustard-seed faith is small.) The posture here is kneeling, and the object here is certainly not self and not merely God but Jesus—Jesus as "Lord."

Do you want to move mountains? I'm not talking about commanding Mount Kilimanjaro to skip into the Indian Ocean. And neither is Jesus. I'm not talking about getting that new Rolls-Royce you've been eying in that magazine. And neither is Jesus. God is not your personal pleasure genie. Your wish is not his command. But do you want to move mountains—the mountains God wants you to move?[15] You don't need the world's biggest backhoe; you just need a bit of faith in the right mountain-mover, *Jesus*. You don't need more self-reliance. You don't need more gumption. You don't need more faith in faith. You need humble faith in Jesus. For apart from him, in his own words, "you can do nothing" (John 15:5), but if you abide in him and his words (and his power) abide in you, "ask whatever you wish"—according to God's will and for his glory—and Jesus promises, "and it will be done for you" (v. 7).

It's not the amount of faith—it's the posture and object of faith. Mustard-seed faith is humble prayer to Jesus for power over evil—the evil we see and the evil we don't see in this demon-infested world.

Believe In

Some of you are familiar with the brave missionary John Paton. If not, here's a slice of his story. In 1858 he traveled from his native Scotland to serve the natives of the South Seas in New Hebrides (now Vanuatu). After he had learned enough of the local language, he began to translate the Gospel of John into their tongue. However, he puzzled over how to translate one of the Apostle John's favorite expressions, *pisteuo eis* ("believe in").

He puzzled over this important expression because (a) the natives had no specific word in their language for trust, which made sense because (b) they were a group of cannibals, a group that knew little or nothing about such a concept. Paton was relieved when his servant, who was a converted native, arrived on the scene and came to his assistance. Sitting at his desk, Paton asked him, "What am I doing?" The man replied, "You are sitting at a desk." Paton then raised both his feet off the floor and sat back on his chair. "Tell me, what am I doing now?" The servant, in his native tongue, used a verb that means "to lean your whole weight upon." That was the precise expression Paton was looking for and the one he used throughout his Gospel translation for the all-important verb "believe in."[16]

"To lean with your whole weight upon"—isn't that what we see here with this desperate but dependent father? By expecting everything from Jesus and nothing from his "own piety or power,"[17] and by yielding his insufficiency to the "true sufficiency" of Christ,[18] this faithful father "leans with his whole weight upon" Jesus, and in doing so he becomes for us a great model of genuine faith—a faith that is aware of inadequacies, a faith that takes no confidence in itself, a faith that does not judge Jesus by the weakness of his followers, a faith that looks to the powerful Son of God and to him alone,[19] and a faith (quite simply) that kneels and prays, "Lord, have mercy."

Do you have that faith? It's not big faith! It's just a faith that humbly prays to Jesus for the dynamite to do the difficult, for the power to overcome the impossible. Do you have that faith? It can be yours. Just get down on your knees before him whom I have tried to lift up in this chapter.

51

Death and Taxes

MATTHEW 17:24–27

I BEGAN THE LAST SERMON by reading part of a letter from C. S. Lewis's *Screwtape Letters*, and I did so to free us from the modern framework of anti-supernaturalism, both in the case of the existence of demons and in the exorcism of them. I then talked about how it is easy for us to read a passage that talks about the nature and power of faith but miss the person and power of Jesus, who is the object of faith. With this text I give the same cautions. Let's not come to these four verses with an anti-supernatural framework ("this stuff about a coin in a fish's mouth is not credible!"), and let's not miss the person and power of Jesus ("he's incredible!"). Well, so we won't be tempted to do either, let's start with Jesus' miracle.

Jesus' Miracle

As in the last sermon we begin at the end. (I promise you I will not always go backwards in my preaching. But here we go again.) That ending reads, "[Peter], go to the sea and cast a hook and take the first fish that comes up, and when you open its mouth you will find a shekel. Take that and give it to them for me and for yourself" (v. 27).

I'll give the context quickly, and then less quickly I'll give two observations about the oddity of this "miracle." The context is this: Jesus and Peter (and assuming also the Twelve) journey back to Capernaum, the town Peter is from, and which Jesus also calls home (4:13). When they arrive, the tax collectors are there to say, "Hello, welcome home." Capernaum is on the Sea of Galilee, so perhaps the collectors collected for this tax when people came to shore. Perhaps this is what Matthew once did, and perhaps that is why he alone records this event.

Whatever the specifics, these "collectors of the two-drachma tax" are there, and they ask Peter, "Does your teacher not pay the tax?" referring to the half-shekel or temple tax. With their question they assume Jesus does pay the tax. They assume this because every pious Jewish man would attend the synagogue on the Sabbath (Jesus did that), keep the yearly feasts (Jesus did that), pilgrimage to Jerusalem (Jesus did that), and pay the temple tax (as Peter says, Jesus did that too, v. 25). So they say, "Does he pay?" Peter says, "He does." And then Jesus affirms Peter's affirmation by saying, "Peter, go fish."

Now we come to the miracle. There are two oddities about it. First, no miracle is recorded. The story ends with the command, "Peter, go fish," and then three assumptions—(a) that Peter did fish, (b) that Peter caught that one fish with that one coin, and (c) that Peter used that coin to pay the tax. But Matthew doesn't record what we assume. And this is different than any of the other miracles in Matthew thus far. Here there is no "And Jesus stretched out his hand and touched him, saying, '. . . be clean.' And immediately his [the man's] leprosy was cleansed" (8:3), or "Then he [Jesus] rose and rebuked the winds and the sea, and there was a great calm" (8:26), or "And he [Jesus] said to the man [with the withered hand] 'Stretch out your hand,' . . . and it [the hand] was restored" (12:13), or "And Jesus rebuked the demon, and it came out" (17:18). Here we just get what Jesus commanded, but we don't get what follows. We wonder, did it all work?

The second oddity is that if it did work, it sure sounds like a tall tale. There is this folklore feel to this assumed miracle.[1] Jesus produced what (a coin?) from what (a fish?)? That sounds too much like a Greek or Roman myth to be credible. What is this, the coin to pay Charon to ferry the soul across the River Styx?

These two oddities might lead you to think that (a) no miracle occurred or (b) if it did, it mattered little to Matthew—his focus is on the message, not the miracle. But I disagree with both thoughts. I think a miracle occurred and that it mattered much to Matthew.

I see the faulty logic (held by some notable scholars) behind the notion that since no miracle is recorded, no miracle occurred. Let's say I told you that the Bears played the Seahawks, and the Packers played the Falcons, and then said that the winners of those two games will play each other today. Then I said, "Today the Bears play the Falcons," and that's all I said. Wouldn't you make the connection that the Bears must have beaten the Seahawks and the Falcons must have beaten the Packers? You wouldn't say, "Well, unless you tell me the Bears and Packers won, they must not have won."

The miracle is assumed, and that's okay. That's enough. It should be enough. Do we have any reason, after reading Matthew 4—16, to think that Jesus doesn't possess the power to do something like this? What's a shekel in a grey mullet's mouth compared to a expelling a demon, curing a leper, raising the dead, or giving sight to the blind? And do we have any reason to doubt the power and truthfulness of Jesus' word? Is he teasing Peter or lying to him? And does it make any sense to say what Jesus said about paying the tax if he didn't pay the tax? His whole message in verses 25, 26 is based on the assumption that the command in verse 27 will work—that Peter will pay the tax by these miraculous means.

Matthew simply omits the obvious. I think he omits the obvious for obvious reasons. Two plus two makes four; if you have four at the end and two at the beginning, you do the math. But I also think he omits the obvious (the actual coin was in the fish's mouth) because he understood the folklore feel to this miracle, and thus he was careful in his description of it (or lack thereof) not to put it in that category. If he wanted to, he would have not only recorded the details of it but embellished upon them.

Have you ever read medieval hagiography—like *The Lives of the Saints*? (I grew up on the stuff.) Matthew could have done it up like those stories are done up. He could have added twenty verses after verse 27.

> And St. Peter dropped his hook into the sea. It was the Dead Sea. (Fish don't swim in the Dead Sea!) A large fish was immediately caught. It was a king salmon. (Salmon don't swim in Palestinian waters!) St. Peter grabbed it with his bare hand, took the hook out, opened its mouth, and forced that fish to cough up the coin. The coin was silver, and the silver shone in his holy hand. A dove flew overhead and winked. St. Peter gave the coin to Jesus. The moment our Lord touched it the imprint of Caesar's head melted and molded into a picture of the Ark of the Covenant. And as Jesus gave it to the tax collectors, their bodies were immediately plagued with tumors.

That is *not* how Matthew does it. Rather, he is careful here to separate history from legend. In speaking of this miracle—knowing its truth sounds stranger than fiction—he wants to separate it from a facetious telling of it. The best way to do that is the way he did it. And to that I say, "Well done, brother Mathew. I appreciate your modesty."

This is an odd miracle. I acknowledge that, as perhaps does Matthew. But odd does not equal inauthentic.[2] The oddities argue for its authenticity.

So I think a real miracle occurred—precisely as Jesus outlined in verse 27, *and* I also think this miracle mattered much to Matthew. Listen, the whole story hangs on it. As I just said, if there is no miracle there is no message.

Jesus ends by saying, "Take that [shekel] and give it to them for me and for yourself." If there is no miracle—take what and give what? The message hangs on the miracle.

Thus, take the miracle seriously. Look at it with neither a critical nor a cautious eye. Believe it. See it as authentic *and* see it as awesome!

In the last two chapters I have hit on the theme that Jesus is the divine Son of God. He is fully human but also *fully God*. And this miracle, this "very remarkable . . . providence,"[3] this act of "unutterable power"[4]—what sovereign control of the sea (think of the parting of the Red Sea; think of Jonah and the big fish)—falls under the category that I label in very technical terms, "Hey, this guy is God!" Think about what needs to happen in this miracle for it to work. Jesus needs divine power, and Jesus needs divine foreknowledge.[5] He needs to know there is a coin in the sea. He needs to know that some fish swallowed it or is actually holding it in its mouth (hasn't swallowed it). He needs to know that this fish is near the shore. He needs to know that it will be the first fish Peter catches. He needs to know it will have a shekel in its mouth, which is precisely the amount of the tax for two people.

This miracle is awesome! Transferred to the person of Jesus, we see that this man is awesome![6] This man is God. This God-man is awesome. What then is this God-man's message about taxes?

The miracle, like the transfiguration, is designed to make you listen up. "This is my beloved Son . . . listen to him" (17:5). Listen to him as he speaks about his death. Listen to him as he talks about taxes. Death and taxes—there you have it. There's my chapter title. But that chapter title is not as contrived as you might first think.

Jesus' Message

The message here is very simple and very Jesus, we might say. The message is, *you are free to love*. You are *free* (from the temple tax) to *love* (so pay the tax). This apparent paradox comes at the end of verse 26 and the beginning of verse 27. At the end of verse 26 Jesus says, "Then the sons are free" (from the tax). At the beginning of verse 27 he continues, "However, not to give offense," please pay it.

You Are Free

Let me divide these concepts (freedom and love), explain them separately, and then bring them back together. First we have freedom. The tax collectors ask their tax question, "Jesus pays taxes, right?" Peter assures them, "Yes, he does." Then Jesus and the Twelve go into "the house" (v. 25)—likely Peter's house since they are in Peter's hometown (see 8:14). Maybe it's the tax booth. It doesn't matter. What matters is Jesus' lesson.

Singling out Simon Peter as representative of the Twelve, Jesus says:

> "What do you think, Simon? From whom do kings of the earth take toll or tax? From their sons or from others?" And when he said, "From others," Jesus said to him, "Then the sons are free." (vv. 25b, 26)

"Peter, you are *free* from such temple taxes due to the fact that you are a son of the kingdom, a child of the King." Here I don't think Jesus is rebuking Peter, saying, "You were a bit hasty with your quick 'yes, Jesus pays the tax,' because I don't and neither should you" (see v. 27). They will pay the tax. Rather, I think Jesus is quite comforting here. With his analogy Jesus places Peter in the "son" camp, which I'm sure was reassuring to Peter. Jesus had called him "Satan" in 16:23—"Get behind me, Satan! You are a hindrance to me." And here our Lord calls him "son." Going from Satan to son must have been reassuring to him. I know that is reassuring to me. I don't always think rightly or act rightly (my mind is sometimes set on the things of man and not of God), but God doesn't disown his sons. Our sometimes satanic behavior is covered by our sonship. God be praised!

But back to the point: Peter, as a son of the King, doesn't have to pay the tax. Why? First, what king collects taxes from his children? Part of a king's taxes is taken to provide for the royal family. It would make no sense to take taxes from a king's son only to give the same money back to that son. Peter gets the royal family's exemption.

The other reason Peter need not pay is because Jesus paid it all. I don't mean that lightly, and I'm not importing the theology of an old hymn title into our ancient text. But Jesus alludes to his death here. There is indeed death and taxes. No joke. I'll explain.

My explanation begins with the tax itself. This half-shekel tax was called the temple tax. It was based on the command in Exodus 30:12–14—"each shall give a ransom for his life" by giving "half a shekel according to the shekel of the sanctuary [tabernacle/temple] . . . as an offering to the Lord."[7] This tax, which was only collected once a year, usually in one's hometown, would cost every Jewish man over the age of twenty two day's wages. One shekel equals four drachmas. A drachma was nearly equivalent to a Roman denarius, which was "the standard wage for a day laborer."[8] And this temple tax was, naturally, for the temple. That didn't mean that the tax collectors—in the exchange of currency—didn't make a profit (they did), but it did mean that most of the money went for the upkeep of Herod's temple, the temple in Jerusalem in Jesus' day. Included in that upkeep, in fact central to it, was the support of the sacrificial system. It went to pay for the priests (their salaries and sacred attire) and for their sacrificial materials (wood, wine, oil, flour, candles, knives, and so on). Put more succinctly, it went to pay for their sins. So you see paying this tax was more than supporting Herod's good standing with Rome. It was paying for the life and blood (literally) of the Jewish faith—the temple and the sacrificial system.[9]

Can you start to see how this passage is loaded with theological tension? What does Jesus think of Judaism? What does Jesus think of the Torah—the command from Exodus 30? What does Jesus, the one who predicts the destruction of the temple (24:2), the one who cleanses the temple (21:12, 13), and the one who claims to be "greater than the temple" (12:6), think about the temple? What does "the Lamb of God, who takes away the sin of the world" (see John 1:29) through his blood sacrifice, think of paying for all those priests to sacrifice all those lambs in the temple?

Our Lord gives two answers. Publicly to the tax collectors he says in essence, "Sure, I support the temple. Here's the money. Have a nice day." Privately to Peter, however, he hints at a time when the tax will be null and void. He speaks of a time when there will be no taxation *due to* representation. That is, he as our representative will pay the price. Not the price of the temple tax, but the price of all the temple sacrifices from day one to the day he dies. His death will cut the temple curtain in two. It will push down stone upon stone until no stone stands. He will become (of course, he is now for us) the very temple of the living God—Immanuel incarnate—"the divinely authorized meeting place" between God and man.[10] He will become (of course, he has become for us) the last and final sacrifice for sin.

> Jesus paid it all,
> All to Him I owe;
> Sin had left a crimson stain,
> He washed it white as snow.[11]

Who needs a temple when "Jesus is God's temple in person," and who needs a temple tax when Jesus paid the temple tax "with his own blood"?[12]

Death and taxes. His death; no taxes. His death means no more temple taxes for me and you, and even for Peter.[13] But there's a timing issue here, isn't there? History is about to change, to dramatically shift, to move not from BC to AD, but from BCD to ACD—from Before Christ's Death to After Christ's Death.

But that shift hasn't happened yet for the characters in Matthew 17. And so, while free—free as sons, freed by the Son of God—they are free to love. And love here means paying taxes. That's how you would define love, isn't it? Yes, they are *free* (from such temple taxes) to *love* (so pay those taxes).

You Are Free to Love

But why pay the tax? Is it because Jesus supports the tax collectors' union? No. Is it because he is fully on board with Herod and all he has done for Judaism? No. Is it because he thinks the high priest and chief priests are holy men and he is worried that their families will starve? No. Is it because he's an old-school dispensationalist and he thinks the church should start raising money for the next temple in Jerusalem? Sorry to offend some, but no. He tells us why we should pay the tax—"not to give offense to them." To whom? Well, to the tax collectors, but also everyone involved in the whole system—from the high priest to the guy who just turned twenty and gets to write his first check.

Jesus is not anti-Torah, and he is not anti-temple. But the Torah has its place (to point to him), and the temple has its place (also to point to him). Jesus is pro-Judaism, the Judaism that points to him as true Israel, the Messiah, the fulfillment of Torah and temple. But he knows for such profound and revolutionary and shocking truths to be heard, he needs to pay his temple tax. He wasn't about to die on this hill (that less than 2 percent tax hill in Capernaum) when he knew he was soon to die on that other hill (the hill outside Jerusalem), where he would give 100 percent of himself to set us free—free from the temple tax, free from sin, free from Hell and eternal damnation. Peter, you are free to love.

Our Text for This Study

That is what is going on here. But how do we bridge the gap between their time and our time? How do we apply this text for today? What first came to my mind, and perhaps yours as well (as we live in just as politically charged a time as Jesus did), was the application to American politics. Some of our taxes will go to people and programs that we think unnecessary or even anti-Christian, but we pay our taxes anyway because (a) we know God rules over all the rulers of the earth, and (b) our leaders would be more open to accepting and promoting, or at least not suppressing, the gospel if Christians were known for praying and giving. Some Christians (the Religious Right?) are known for protesting and griping. How much better for the spread of the gospel if Christians gained a reputation for prayer—"Those Christians are always praying for our President, our Senate, our House, our governor, our state and town officials." And how much better for the spread of the gospel if we were always the first to rush in time of trouble to give our government our time, treasures, and talents.

But with this controversial point aired, I retract it. I'm not sure that is a perfect application of this text because the tax here is religious, not secular. It was a tax for the priests in the temple, not for Caesar in his palace.

So then I thought perhaps the application is something more like this: you tithe to your church even though you don't fully support each and every program or even each and every person on staff. You do so because (a) you trust that God's hand is on your church—despite its leaders' inadequacies and sins, and (b) you have committed to support your church through thick and thin.

The problem with that application is that it doesn't fit with this idea of not offending outsiders. That is so much of the thrust of Jesus' message here. If you want to get outsiders in, don't offend them in trivial matters.

So here is what I have arrived at: there is not a direct proposition to take from this passage but rather an indirect principle. And the principle is this: *be willing to compromise for the sake of conversion.* Compromise is not a dirty word, and it's not a dirty deed. In politics, law, business, marriage, and any number of relationships at times one has to compromise for a greater good. And that's what Jesus does here and teaches his disciples to do. The greater good is the gospel. He refuses to put a little stumbling stone—like the temple tax—in front of the cross, the great stumbling stone.

We conservative Christians often fail to apply this principle. Sometimes we would rather stand up for our personal rights than see the wrong person get right with God.[14] Sometimes we would rather have a young man dress appropriately in church than come to church at all. Sometimes we would rather that our neighbor stop drinking alcohol than come in faith to the table of our Lord. Yes, sometimes, I fear, we still snicker outside the door to Matthew's house, whispering to one another, "What's Jesus doing with *those* people?"

Listen, as children of God we have been freed, freed to love. And love means paying your taxes. Love means sacrificing the small for the greater good. Love means removing every unnecessary barrier to our friends, family, neighbors, coworkers, high and low government officials hearing and responding to the good news of Jesus Christ, the good news that Jesus is now the only place/person where we can find the forgiveness of sins.

Martin Luther, in his excellent treatise *The Freedom of a Christian*, phrased it this way:

> A Christian is a perfectly free lord of all, subject to none.
> A Christian is a perfectly dutiful servant of all, subject to all.[15]

Precisely. Later in that treatise Luther writes:

> Who then can comprehend the riches and the glory of the Christian life? It can do all things and has all things and lacks nothing. It is lord over sin, death, and hell, and yet at the same time it serves, ministers to, and benefits all men.[16]

Having been given "the freedom of the glory of the children of God" (Romans 8:21), we freely serve all in the hope that people from all nations and all walks of life will be drawn to our all-loving Lord. *Be willing to compromise for the sake of conversion.*

This principle Jesus laid out in Matthew 17 was the foundation of Paul's entire evangelistic efforts. Think about how he preached differently to Jews versus Gentiles, to those in the marketplace and those on Mars Hill. Before Paul brought the offense of the gospel—he always brought that, and the cross is offensive to those who are perishing—he first tried not to offend. He quoted their poets. He bowed before their authorities. He conceded to their traditions. He spoke in their native tongue. He was, in his own words, "all things to all people, that by all means I might save some."

That's what he wrote in 1 Corinthians 9:22. And here's what he wrote before that. In verse 12 he writes, "[W]e endure anything rather than put an obstacle in the way of the gospel of Christ." (Isn't that a perfect summary of our passage?) Then in verses 19–22 he writes:

> For though I am free from all, I have made myself a servant to all, that I might win more of them. To the Jews I became as a Jew, in order to win Jews. To those under the law I became as one under the law (though not being myself under the law [he's free!]) that I might win those under the law. To those outside the law I became as one outside the law (not being outside the law of God but under the law of Christ [the law of love]) that I might win those outside the law. To the weak I became weak, that I might win the weak. I have become all things to all people, that by all means I might save some.

You see, there is the delicate balance between Christian compromise and Christian noncompliance.[17] We are not to comply when our government or our church (God forbid) or our best friend tells us to stop preaching that Jesus is the only way to God (see, e.g., Acts 4:8–12, 18–20). It is okay to offend with the stumbling stone of the cross. But we are to compromise—to not give "unnecessary offense on secondary issues"[18]—if those little stumbling stones make a person stumble on their way to the cross. Does that make sense? We are become all things to all people so by all means we might save some, *and* we are to preach Christ and him crucified. We are to balance both. We are to "[o]we no one anything, except to love each other" (Romans 13:8), but love means "Pay . . . taxes to whom taxes are owed" (Romans 13:7).

There you have it—death and taxes. Christ's death has freed us to love. And love means putting up with trivial matters and pushing aside any and every obstacle to get people to the gospel, the lifesaving message of our Lord Jesus Christ.

52

Little Ones

MATTHEW 18:1–14

WHO IS THE GREATEST basketball player of all time? Those of us in Chicago know the answer to that question. Michael Jordan, of course. Who is the greatest criminal of all time? Chicagoans also know the answer to that question. But who is the greatest preacher of all time? Once again those of us in Chicago know the answer to that. (It was D. L. Moody, not me.) Then again in my sermons I do kind of float like a butterfly and sting like a bee. Perhaps I am the greatest!

Ah, the sin of pride. If I may quote myself (and who else is worth quoting?), "Pride is the mother of all sins, and there is a bit of her DNA in all of us."[1] And perhaps (if I may correct myself) there is a bit more than "a bit." Pride rears its ugly head in everyone everywhere. I have seen it in the kindergarten girls' soccer team I coached, when one girl kicks the ball farther than the rest of the team in a practice drill and she thinks she has scored the winning goal in the World Cup finals. I have seen it in prisoners in the First Division of the Cook Country Jail, where one inmate thinks he rules the world because he rules the cellblock. I have seen it in myself, and if you would let me close enough to your heart, I will see it in you as well.

Pride rears its ugly head in everyone everywhere. And it rears its ugly head here in 18:1: "At that time [seemingly right after the tax question and lesson] the disciples came to Jesus, saying, 'Who is the greatest in the kingdom of heaven?'"

Questioning Their Question

What a question! Had they forgotten the first beatitude—"Blessed are the poor in spirit" (5:3)? Had they forgotten the faith-filled Roman centurion's humility—"Lord, I am not worthy to have you come under my roof, but only say the word, and my servant will be healed" (8:8)? Had they forgotten that father's mustard-seed faith—"a man came up to him [Jesus] and, kneeling before him, said, 'Lord, have mercy on my son'" (17:14, 15)? Yes. Yes. Yes. It seems they had forgotten.[2]

In 18:4 Jesus tells us that the motive behind his disciples' question was pride, for he begins that verse, "Whoever humbles himself . . ." Jesus' response in verse 4 and following indicates there was not a pure motive here, or even mere curiosity—"Oh, Jesus, out of curiosity, how does one become great in the kingdom?" The sense is more like, "Jesus, in your expert estimation, which one of us is now the greatest?"

Their question was so out-of-line. It was as out-of-line as my introduction to this chapter. Who do these guys think they are or have become? Half of them are fishermen. And the most educated and wealthy of the dirty dozen is likely Matthew, a former tax collector, which in Jewish culture was worse than having to wear an embroidered "A" on one's chest for "Adulterer" (cf. 18:17).

When and why did these nobodies start thinking they were somebodies? I'm sure pride subtly set in due to all they had seen Jesus do and what they themselves had done—miracles! Peter, for example, had walked on water. He witnessed the transfiguration. Just that day he'd caught a fish with a shekel in its mouth, just the right amount of the temple tax. One can respond to such things in one of two extremes—humility or pride. Pious Peter got proud, as did the rest of them, so it seems. In fact, with Peter's highs and lows in the last month or so, perhaps the eleven got to thinking, "Well, now is as good a time as ever not only to make the starting lineup but to become the go-to guy." So they collectively ask, "Who among us is presently the greatest? Line us up and rank us."

Entrance and Elevation

Our Lord Jesus, however, will have none of their presumption. In verses 2–4 he gives a visual and verbal rebuke:

> And calling to him a child, he put him in the midst of them and said, "Truly, I say to you, unless you turn and become like children, you will never enter the kingdom of heaven. Whoever humbles himself like this child is the greatest in the kingdom of heaven."

Knowing human nature as I hope we do, the disciples' question shouldn't surprise us. However, Jesus' answer is almost as surprising today as it was then! First, it's surprising that he answers their question about elevation (whose the greatest?) with a comment about entrance (who says you're even in?).

They assumed they were in "the kingdom" (i.e., the saved community under Christ's kingship), and thus their only concern was greatness—how many diadems will be on my crown compared to his and his and his and his? But Jesus turns the tables on them. He says in essence, "What you should be worried about—with such an attitude as expressed in your question—is whether you are in the kingdom or not. Big-headed people can't fit through the narrow gate. Fat camels can't squeeze through the eye of the needle." To quote him exactly, "Truly, I say to you" (v. 3)—when Jesus uses that language you better listen up—"unless you *turn* and *become* like children, you will never *enter* the kingdom of heaven." Never mind whose first among the Twelve; make sure you are one of the Twelve. "Forget greatness; get in!"[3] That's the first surprise.

The second surprise is that Jesus calls for a re-conversion to childlikeness. In John 3:3 he says, "Truly, truly, I say to you, unless one is born again he cannot see the kingdom of God," and here in 18:3 he says similarly, "Truly, I say to you, unless you turn and become like children, you will never enter the kingdom of heaven." Where we might expect Jesus to say, as would be typical of a rabbi of his day, "If you want to get in you must have an Olympic-sized righteousness—abounding in good works, martyr-like in self-sacrifice, skilled in reading and teaching the Torah," he says nearly the opposite: "You must become like a child."

What is so surprising or shocking about that is that children were the lowest of the low in the ancient world. That might be hard for us to imagine since children today have TV shows and movies and video games and amusement parks and toys and cell phones and even restaurants designed for their pleasure and in their honor. That is the world we live in, but that was not the world in which Jesus lived. Some scholars are convinced that this is the first and only time in ancient Jewish literature (perhaps all ancient literature) where a child is used as a positive example. What Jesus does here is original and radical. And did you know that in Koine Greek the word for "child" is neither masculine nor feminine? It's neuter. Here is a wooden translation of the Greek of verse 2: "And having called a child he [Jesus] set *it* in [the] midst of them." It?

So, what's surprising here—our second surprise—is that "*It* is in, and *it* is up." If you want to get in the kingdom you must be like *it*, and if you to move up in the kingdom you must move down like *it*. *It* is in, and *it* is up. And *it* is everything in the Christian life. There is no stage before it and none after it. It is a constant state of being. It is a rule of life. It is being re-converted each and every day after the day of your conversion.[4] It is being born again and again and again.[5]

With a lot hanging on what *it* is, let me define *it* (i.e., what it means to be "like children"). My definition comes solely from our text. In this text being "like children" does not mean being innocent, simple-minded, easily amused, or possessing the uncanny ability to throw temper tantrums. Rather, it means humility—"whoever *humbles* himself like this child" (v. 4).

But humility then is defined by "this" particular child's attitude and action toward Jesus. Jesus calls this child to himself, and she (let's make "it" a "she" to be even more radical for Jesus' day) comes to Jesus (a) because she must trust (cf. "*believe in* [him]," v. 6) that he's okay to come to,[6] and (b) because she listens to him, like a child is supposed to listen to an adult, but also like all believers are supposed to—remember the transfiguration?—"listen to him" (17:5).[7] So she is humble, and that humility expresses itself as mustard-seed faith expressed itself in 17:14, 15 by trusting in Jesus and listening to (i.e., obeying) him. That's what it means to "turn and become like children."

We didn't literally see this visual parable (a little girl [or boy] coming to Jesus) as the disciples did, but hopefully we can see it. Hopefully we can get at what Jesus is getting at—to *get in* the kingdom and to *move up* in it (so to speak) requires humility. "Humble yourselves before the Lord, and he will exalt you" (James 4:10).

Actions toward the Little Ones

In his book *What Is Christianity?* Adolf von Harnack wrote:

> Humility is not a virtue by itself; but it is pure receptivity, the expression of inner need, the prayer for God's grace and forgiveness, in a word, the opening up of the heart to God. This, then, is the source and origin of the love of one's neighbor.[8]

Note the transition Harnack made from humility before God to love toward neighbor. Humility is the source of a right relationship with God, and it is the source of a right relationship with others. Coming out of verse 4 into verses 5–14, Jesus makes that same transition. In verses 5–9 our Lord teaches them and us about *our actions toward little ones* and in verses 10–14 about *our attitude toward little ones*.

First, we have our actions toward little ones (vv. 5–9). I say "little ones" instead of "children" because Jesus makes this linguistic shift in verses 5, 6. He starts (v. 5), "Whoever receives one such *child* in my name receives me," then continues (v. 6), "but whoever causes one of these *little ones* . . ." and only uses the term "little ones" from that point on. This might just be a parallelism (child = little one), and that seems to be the case in verses 5, 6. But in what follows (vv. 7–14) we learn that Jesus subtly shifts from talking about literal children to certain children of God, those he labels "little ones."

By "little ones" Jesus could mean everyone in the kingdom of heaven regardless of age, or he could mean, as I think he means,[9] "the least of these my brothers" as he would phrase it in 25:40. That is, "little ones" are those Christians who are most often marginalized or whom we'd be tempted to marginalize due to lack of wealth, health, giftedness, or spiritual maturity. They are those with little resources, little social standing, and perhaps little faith (i.e., the weaker brethren of Romans 14:13; 1 Corinthians 8:13). They are those prone to wander like that one lost sheep of verse 12.

So then, regarding these "little ones" within the church, Jesus calls his church (especially the more mature or less "little") to action. And the primary action here is guarding oneself as a means of guarding them. You see, we are not only to "receive" these little ones into our fellowship because Christ receives such into his fellowship—we open the church door to them "in [his] name" (v. 5)—but we are also to protect them once they're in. Jesus teaches:

> Whoever receives one such child in my name receives me, but whoever causes one of these little ones who believe in me to sin, it would be better for him to have a great millstone fastened around his neck and to be drowned in the depth of the sea. Woe to the world for temptations to sin! For it is necessary that temptations come, but woe to the one by whom the temptation comes! And [note the connection] if your hand or your foot causes you to sin, cut it off and throw it away. It is better for you to enter life [eternal life] crippled or lame than with two hands or two feet to be thrown into the eternal fire. And if your eye causes you to sin, tear it out and throw it away. It is better for you to enter life with one eye than with two eyes to be thrown into the hell of fire. (vv. 5–9)

Here Jesus uses two graphic and grotesque images to wake up *Christians*. Yes, these are warnings for believers, not unbelievers.[10] Christian, if you think your little sins are not a big deal to Christ and his church, you couldn't be farther from the mind of Christ. To our Savior, personal holiness is a matter of life and death, Heaven and Hell for you and others.

The two judgment images here involve water and fire. First fire. Imagine being thrown into a pit that's on fire—"the hell of fire." You are engulfed by flames. Eternal fire is everywhere!

Then water. Imagine a great millstone—a two-ton slab of circular stone so huge and heavy that it needs a donkey to move it—fastened around your neck. There you are wearing this heavy and horrific concrete collar. Then imagine being taken out to the middle of the sea and left to yourself. Bye-bye. Down you go. You'll hit the bottom pretty fast. And you'll hit the bottom and stay there. There is no means of escape from this "dark, eternal grave,"[11] or this "black Gehenna,"[12] as Milton put it. Death by fire or death by water; burning or drowning—what will it be? Neither option sounds all that pleasant.

Christian, wake up. Shape up. Grow up. Your personal holiness matters. Christian, "be killing sin or it will be killing you"[13] and potentially killing others, these "little ones" in the Lord. What we do privately—with our hand or our foot or our eye (those are private or personal parts)—actually can affect other believers. That's what Jesus is teaching here. How you see things (the eye) affects how others see, what you do (the hand) affects what others will do, and how you walk (the foot) affects how others will walk (cf. Ephesians 4:25). You see, the church, especially the local church, is like a thousand dominoes perfectly spaced apart, standing together. We are all equal in God's sight, and we all can potentially affect one another equally. But we know that if the first domino falls, all fall. We should also know that even if the five hundredth domino tips and touches this way and then tips and touches that way, it would affect us all equally. We would all fall down as well.

So the action here is guarding oneself as a means of guarding all, but especially "the little ones" (dominos 1–100). And note that the action here is not half-repentant ("Lord, take these three fingers, but leave the thumb and pinky"), and it's not gradual ("Lord, this week I will give up my right hand, and next week my left"). The action here is immediate, decisive, and absolute, and it's going hurt (have you ever broken a sinful habit?). "If your hand . . . causes you to sin, cut it off and throw it away" (18:8; cf. 5:30). Ouch!

Jesus has talked this way about sexual sin in the Sermon on the Mount (5:29, 30). But here he expands it to every imaginable sin. Do you grasp for worldly power? Do you rush to judgment? Do you easily lose your temper? Do you overstuff your stomach? Do you gossip? Do you hoard money? Do you overlook the unimportant? Do you think yourself so very important? Cut it off and cut it out. Cut off pride. Cut off lust. Cut off sloth. Cut off anger. Cut off greed. Cut off envy. Cut off gluttony. Cut off those seven deadly sins and seventy more because they will kill you—"It is better for you to enter life with one eye than with two eyes to be thrown into the hell of fire" (v. 9b)—*and* because they endanger the lives of the "little ones," some of your dear brothers and sisters in Christ. This is serious stuff. So take it seriously.

Attitude toward the Little Ones

But also take seriously verses 10–14, where our Lord transitions from teaching about our *actions* toward little ones to our *attitude* toward them.

Look at verse 10a. Here Jesus teaches, "See that you do not despise one of these little ones." Attitude check! Why should we not "despise" or look down on them, as would be natural? Or, put positively, why should we value them? Jesus gives one reason (they matter much to God) and two illustrations.

The first illustration is about "their angels": "For I tell you that in heaven their angels always see the face of my Father who is in heaven" (v. 10b). There is no need for us to get bogged down on whether or not every child or every "little one" has a guardian angel. It seems they do—if not *a* guardian angel (cf. Acts 12:15), guardian *angels* (cf. Luke 16:22)—that is, in the words of Hebrews 1:14, "ministering spirits sent out to serve . . . those who are to inherit salvation." (Note, however, that the guardian angel or angels here are in Heaven, not on earth as popularly depicted.) But the point is not that some or all Christians have angels who protect them. Rather, the point is, if these beings ("angels") who serve these "little ones" (they are "*their* angels") are "in heaven" (that's an important place to be) and they there are directly looking upon God (these must be angels of "the very highest order"[14]), how much more valuable are "the little ones" they serve and protect? Does that make sense? If your bodyguards are Moses and Elijah, you must be fairly important. And if your angel stands perpetually before the face of God, your stock has substantially gone up. God values these little ones.

The second illustration of this divine value is the Parable of the Lost Sheep. Our Lord says:

> What do you think? If a man has a hundred sheep, and one of them has gone astray, does he not leave the ninety-nine on the mountains and go in search of the one that went astray? And if he finds it, truly, I say to you, he rejoices over it more than over the ninety-nine that never went astray. So it is not the will of my Father who is in heaven that one of these little ones should perish. (vv. 12–14)

I will identify the characters in this parable and then highlight two points. There are three characters: (1) the ninety-nine sheep, (2) the strayed sheep, and (3) the man, who is obviously a good shepherd.

The shepherd represents Jesus Christ.[15] I say that because (a) Jesus is often called a shepherd,[16] (b) this shepherd is called "a man," and (c) what the shepherd does here fits the purpose of the incarnation: "[F]or he [Jesus] will save his people from their sins" (1:21).

But also look at the footnote in our text: "Some [Greek] manuscripts add verse 11 [taken from Luke 19:10]: 'For the Son of Man came to save the lost.'" That's not a bad insertion at all. The shepherd represents any good shepherd, but especially the Great Shepherd, our Lord Jesus Christ.

The hundred sheep represent the church or the community of the kingdom of heaven. The ninety-nine are either the spiritually mature or more likely those not currently backsliding. Presently they are doing a good job of sticking near Christ and Christians and are cutting off sin. The strayed sheep then is the backsliding Christian, or more specifically the Christian who is so proud he doesn't think he needs the shepherd or the other sheep to guard him and so foolish or sinful that he thinks he can wander off into various sins without any real danger.

Those are the characters of the parable. But what is the point? As parables are flexible entities (sometimes you can find a point for each character or a point for each phrase), let me give you one point before I give you the primary point. *God is joyously gracious to each Christian.*

By *God* I mean Father, Son, and, Holy Spirit, but here especially the Father (vv. 10, 14) and the Son as shepherd (vv. 12, 13). The *joyous* part comes from God's great joy in finding the estranged sheep—"I say to you, he rejoices over it" (v. 13). The *gracious* part comes from God pursing the estranged sheep.

Look how gracious God is here! Coming out of the warning in verses 5–9 about not straying into sin or else, I find it refreshing, uplifting, and encouraging that if and when I do stray verses 10–14 teach that God pursues, finds, and returns straying sheep. Now don't misread me here. I think eternal judgment awaits the "*unrepentant* lost"—even those within the church whose lifestyle is characterized by unrepentant behavior. But the "*wandering* lost"—the lapsed little one who didn't know better or didn't know how to return once he did know better—God goes after with the same passion and (if you'll allow me) frantic effort as a loving father who has his lost three-year-old daughter in a 600,000 square-feet supermarket.[17]

God is joyously gracious . . . to each Christian. Yes, to each Christian. Notice the word "one" (eight times) and "ones" (three times) and the emphasis on the individual in this otherwise very communal passage.[18] Our passage begins with Jesus calling "a child" to himself, and it ends with Jesus saying that it is God's will that not "one of these little ones should perish" (v. 14). Again, coming out of verses 5–9 (which speak so much of life together/church community/the necessity of many to make it) I find it refreshing and uplifting and encouraging that God cares for each individual Christian equally. The "statistically unimportant"—one out of one hundred—is important to him.[20] One matters (you matter) so much to the Father that he sends out his Shepherd on the ultimate search and rescue mission. "Of those whom you [the Father] gave me," Jesus says in John 18:9, "I have not lost *one*." Not one.

That is the *other* point to this parable: *God is joyously gracious to each Christian*. But here is the primary point. It's simple, and it's short. The primary point goes back to verse 10a: "See that you do not despise one of these little ones." It's about our attitude. "Let not earth despise those whom heaven respects" is how Matthew Henry summarizes it.[21] I put it this way: we are to value each and every little one as God does. That's the primary point of this parable.

Humility before God (vv. 1–4) leads to love of the least—in attitude and action (vv. 5–14). Humility is the source both of a right relationship with God and with others. That's what our Lord teaches here.

Kitchen Shelf Proverbs

My wife and I have gotten in the good habit of praying before bed, and also in the good habit of asking each other some accountability questions, and if needed confessing our sins to each other and to God. One day—the day after I had confessed a sin to Emily—I saw on the kitchen shelf over our sink a 4x6 postcard with two handwritten verses from Proverbs.

> A man without self-control is like a city broken into and left without walls. (25:28)
>
> It is not good to eat much honey, nor is it glorious to seek one's own glory. (25:27)

When my beloved wife got up that morning, I said to her, "Thanks for the stinging rebuke." She said, "What do you mean?" I said, "The two Proverbs in the kitchen." "Proverbs?" she said, "Oh, I wouldn't be that cruel. Those weren't for you. They were for me and for the kids, for us to memorize." And I said, "Then they're for us all, aren't they?"

Yes, pride and self-control and loving others—what God's Word teaches about those topics in Proverbs and Matthew and other places—that's for the whole family—the whole O'Donnell family, the whole local church family, and the whole, holy, catholic church—east to west, north to south, first century to the very last.

53

Immanuel's *Ecclesia*

MATTHEW 18:15–20

WHEN I WAS IN FOURTH GRADE, Sister Mary Bernard, the principal of St. Philip the Apostle's Grade School, called me into her office. There she sat uncomfortably behind her big brown uncomforting desk. I sat obediently in front of it. Sister leaned forward and asked quietly, "How was your time in the library yesterday?" I said, "Fine." (The day before, I was volunteered during my recess to shelve new books.) She then asked, a little less quietly, "Young man, did you deface library property?" Not knowing what the word *deface* meant and honestly not remembering doing anything wrong, I replied, "I don't think so."

This response was the wrong response. She stood up, left the room, and quickly came back with two armloads of books. She said, "Open that one." She continued, "And open that one." And on and on I went opening the books. Then it dawned on me what the word *deface* meant. She stared at me in astonishment with that "save your lies" expression on her face. And I did save my lies, for there lying before my eyes were dozens of books with my full Christian name on each nameplate in fluorescent orange permanent marker. *Douglas*—I was the only Douglas in the school; *Sean*—I was the only Douglas Sean; and *O'Donnell*—I wasn't the only O'Donnell, but I was the only Douglas Sean O'Donnell.

Have you ever been confronted? I have a few times, and sadly all but once it was perfectly appropriate. And every time I have been confronted it has been a humbling experience. It makes you feel small. But small, as we learned in the last chapter, is the appropriate size to get into the kingdom as well as to move up in it. Thus, if confrontation can lead to that kind of smallness, it is something we all, from time to time, very well need.

Why Confront?

This text is the Magna Carta of church confrontation.[1] It is about *how* the church confronts the church. But before we look at *how* such confrontation is to be done, I feel it necessary to start with *why*. Why confront? Christian confrontation (or more broadly, church discipline) is as popular today in the church as public spanking is at the local supermarket.

Hypothetically speaking, I can imagine a pastor of a certain church in Naperville, Illinois taking his four hungry children to the Super Target and hearing these children, one after another, ask for various products they were told not to ask for before they went into the store, and I can imagine after ten consecutive whining complaints from one particular child, this said pastor whispering, "You are getting a spanking." Then as soon as the word "spanking" enters the air, I can imagine shocked mothers dropping their grocery lists, concerned teenagers cautiously dialing 9-1-1, and soon hearing over the intercom that thundering voice, "Everyone please clear aisle 7. Code Red. We have a report of a spanking."

Church discipline is as popular as a public spanking, and church discipline to some is as repulsive as a public hanging. For our generation to hear the verdict "Pat Smith has been excommunicated from the church" sounds harsh, judgmental, unloving, so against the spirit of the age. And because that is the case (the sad case of our society and church), I feel the need to begin where Jesus felt no need to begin, to answer the question "why?" before I answer the question "how?"

So, why? Why should one Christian confront another? There are four reasons, one of which is drawn from our text and three of which are drawn from the surrounding context.

The first reason for Christian confrontation is *the value of one straying sheep*. If you have a red-lettered Bible as I do (the words of Christ are in red), you will notice that there are no black letters in verses 3–14 or in verses 15–20. It's all red. It's all Jesus. Jesus moves from the Parable of the Lost Sheep, which is about how God values each individual Christian, even and especially the strayed sheep (vv. 12–14), to this proclamation (vv. 15–20). And he moves directly from one to the other because they are thematically linked. The Father's concern for sinners and the Shepherd's rescue of those who have wandered from the fold are now to be the church's concern. The church confronts because we value each and every sheep, even and especially the straying sheep.

The second reason for Christian confrontation is *the hope of forgiveness and family reconciliation*. Again we look to the immediate context. The theme of 18:15–35 is the forgiveness of a brother's sin. You'll note that the word "brother" is found in both verses 15 and 35. Now, "brother," as you know, is generic for "Christian"—that is, men, women, and children in Christ. But the term "brother" rather than "disciple" or "Christian" or "Jesus People" or whatever other term we might use for ourselves is significant. It is significant in that it highlights a family relationship.

There is nothing more beautiful and joyous for a family than a son or daughter who has wandered from home returning home. Consider the Parable of the Prodigal Son. When that boy journeyed away from his father's house, all that father wanted was for his son to return. That is why when his son did return, the father responded the way he did. He didn't reluctantly (after twenty-five knocks on the front door) meet his son with his arms folded in disgust and say, "Well, boy, wasn't that stupid of you? Are you done wasting your life and my money?" Rather he was waiting (so it seems) at the door for his son to return, and when he saw him far off he ran to him, embraced him, kissed him, forgave him, and then, filled with immense joy, threw a big party. That's why we confront (that joyous hope is before our eyes). We confront because the church wants to throw a family forgiveness party! We want to celebrate God's forgiveness of our sins by forgiving our brother who has sinned against the family of God.

The third reason for Christian confrontation is, *a little laxity leads to a lot of lapsing*. That's my version of Paul's "a little leaven leavens the whole lump" (1 Corinthians 5:6). This is just the way things work in a sinful world. A little leaven (neglected sin in the church) leavens the whole lump (affects the whole church); a little laxity (let this or that sin go unchecked) leads to a lot of lapsing (I guess if he does that, I can do this). One domino hits the next.

We talked about this idea in the last chapter with Jesus' teaching on cutting off sin—that by guarding our own personal holiness we guard others, especially those weaker in the faith. If a newly baptized Christian sees an elder in the church sinning, and that elder is not confronted and corrected by the church, then the younger Christian will likely be tempted to similarly sin. In verse 7 Jesus notes that temptation isn't going away anytime soon—"Woe to the world for temptations to sin! For it is *necessary* that temptations come." But he warns mature Christians not to let such temptations come from them: "but woe to the one by whom the temptation comes!" And earlier he said, "whoever causes one of these little ones who believe in me to sin, it would be better for him to have a great millstone fastened around his neck and to be drowned in the depth of the sea" (v. 6). Christian confrontation helps protect and purify the church, and it helps prevent the spread of sin throughout the Body of Christ.

I think you all get the idea. Suppose you say to one of your children, "Please go clean your room, and when you have finished you will get a brownie." If this child does not clean her room and you say, "Oh, well, don't worry about it. I love you so much I'll give you the brownie anyway," what happens the next time she is told to do something? And what then happens to the behavior of the other children in the home? You see, a little laxity leads to a lot of lapsing. You'll have a very messy house and dirty chocolate-crumbed faces.

The fourth reason for Christian confrontation is that *it is a command of Christ*. We are told to do so. It is a command of Christ, and Christians are to keep Christ's commands.[2] That is the emphasis Jesus gives in the Great Commission. The church is to be "teaching them [newly baptized disciples] to observe all that [he has] commanded" (28:20a). Thus, if he commands confrontation for sin, we do it because Jesus is Lord.

I'm so sick of people saying, "Oh, I'm a Christian, but I have a different understanding than Jesus did on race (I think it's okay to have a black-only church and a white-only church in the same small town), on divorce (I think it's okay to divorce if you feel you have become incompatible), or on money (I think it's okay to stockpile money even if there's a need in the church or the world)." Christians do what Christ commands because he is Lord! And we do it because Jesus is the *loving* Lord of the church.

The source of Jesus' teaching here is likely Leviticus 19:17, 18 (cf. Leviticus 19:1–16, 19–37), where "[r]eproof and love belong together."[3] After a brother has sinned against you, we read this instruction on attitude and action:

> You shall not hate your brother in your heart, but you shall reason frankly with [him], lest you incur sin because of him. You shall not take vengeance or bear a grudge against . . . [him], but you shall love your neighbor as yourself: [Why?] I am the LORD. (Leviticus 19:17, 18)

Today we have torn asunder what God has joined together—love of the sinner and hatred of their sin. We think *love* means toleration of sin. We think *open and affirming* means anything goes. But in Scripture love and holiness and discipline walk hand in hand. Care and confrontation skip along together. Because God loves us, he disciplines us (see Proverbs 3:11, 12; cf. Hebrews 12:5–11). It's the loving (not the unloving!) shepherd who goes after the lost sheep. The unloving shepherd stays at home; he is either indifferent ("What's one sheep out of 100?") or he is lenient ("Oh, sheep will be sheep").

So, Christians are to confront sinning Christians because we value one straying sheep, we hope for forgiveness and family reconciliation, we know that a little laxity leads to a lot of lapsing (we care about the unity and purity of the church, and the glory of God's holy name and gospel), and because Christian confrontation is a loving command from the most loving man who ever lived.

How to Confront

With those four reasons for Christian confrontation in place, let's get to the substance of our text. This text is not so much about *why* but *how*. How are we to confront? Our Lord gives us three steps.

Step One: Go and Gain

Step one is, *go and gain*.

> If your brother sins against you, *go* and tell him his fault, between you and him alone. If he listens to you, you have *gained* your brother. (v. 15)

Before I get to the actual step—the going and gaining—I want us to notice three important details found in the first half of that verse. First, notice *who is confronting whom*—it is brother to brother. These are not directions for the church's confrontation of the world. There is a time and place for confronting a non-believing neighbor and the non-believing world, but verse 15 isn't describing that time and place.

Second, notice *when* this Christian confrontation is to occur—only "*if* your brother sins against you." The "if" is important. Here Jesus is not calling us to take a spotlight and look through everyone's closet until we find some dirt. Rather, he is calling us to confront only *if* a sin has occurred, and a sin against you personally, if we are to leave in the phrase "against you" as the ESV does.[4] That is why the first step in the confrontation is a conversation "between you and him alone" (v. 15). Now this doesn't mean that if you see a brother publicly disgracing Christ you wouldn't say or do something, but it does mean that the emphasis here falls on two brothers whose relationship has been severed by some (serious? obvious?) sin.

And it is "sin," behavior that is "clearly and consistently contrary" to Christ's commands; in other words, "what Scripture calls sin is sin; nothing else."[5] Evil actions such as murder, adultery, stealing, lying, swindling, and drunkenness, for example, are "sins," as are false beliefs and teachings, such as "Jesus is *not* the only way to God," or "Jesus was fully human but not fully divine." It is sin (not bad personality traits or poor hygiene) that is to be confronted, and a wide variety of it—"*whatever* you bind . . . *whatever* you loose" (v. 18).

Third, notice (speaking of sin) that Jesus assumes Christians will sin. True, he doesn't say "*when*" but "*if* a brother sins," but the "when" is assumed. That's why Jesus is not surprised by Peter's question in verse 21: "Lord, how often will my brother sin against me, and I forgive him?" Jesus doesn't reply, "A brother sin? A brother sin repeatedly? A brother sin repeatedly against another brother? I can't fathom that, Peter. What are you talking about?" Our Lord assumes his church will be full of sinners—saved sinners, trying-to-be-more-sanctified sinners, but sinners nonetheless. This is why the church can pray every Sunday and every day the prayer our Lord taught us to pray: "Father, . . . forgive us our sins, as we forgive those who sin against us" (see 6:9–13, NLT; Luke 11:4).

With all that said, finally we come to step one. When sin occurs we are to go in order to gain: "*Go* and tell him [your brother] his fault, between you and him alone. If he listens to you, you have *gained* your brother" (v. 15b). So step one is not to wait: "I'm not making the first move. He has to make the first move. He has to come to me to ask for forgiveness." And step one is not to sit and sulk: "I can't believe he would do that to me." And step one is not to give the cold shoulder: "Hey, what's wrong with you?" "I don't know. You tell me. What's wrong with me?" And step one is not indifference: "Live and let live. Who cares what he did. Let bygones be bygones." And step one is not tit for tat: "He stole my dog, so I'm stealing his." And step one is not to gossip: "Do you know what so-and-so did to me? Can I share it with you confidentially as a prayer request?" And step one is not public slander: "Welcome to New Covenant Church. Let's begin our time of worship by letting everyone know that on Wednesday night Andrew Johnston nicked Sam Anderson's car, and I'm fairly sure he didn't tell Sam he did it. I have seen it! The dent is deeper than it looks. Now I haven't had a chance to ask Andrew, but based on their parking proximity that night and what I know about Andrew, trust me, it's the type of thing he'd do. Now . . . let us quiet our hearts before the Lord."[6] Rather, step one is a private conversation—underline "you and him alone."

And this private conversation, depending on the certainty of the evidence and your relationship with the person, can be done with gentleness and/or with holy harshness. The prophet Nathan when he confronted David modeled this balance (see 2 Samuel 12:1–7), as did Paul throughout his ministry. Regarding false teachers within the church, Paul tells Titus to "rebuke them sharply, that they may be sound in the faith" (Titus 1:13; see also John's reply concerning Diotrephes in 3 John 9, 10), and regarding Peter's false actions regarding Gentiles, Paul says in Galatians 2:11, "I opposed him to his face, because he stood condemned." (I think that confrontation had some holy harshness to it.) But later in Galatians Paul tells the church, "Brothers, if anyone is caught in any transgression, you who are spiritual should restore him in a spirit of gentleness" (6:1a). There is a time and place for gentleness and a time and a place for holy harshness, the holy harshness Jesus himself employs in 18:8, 9.

Whatever the demeanor (and each case and person will be different), the spirit is that of humility and love, a solemn concern for your brother's soul. "My brothers," James writes, "if anyone among you wanders from the truth and someone brings him back, let him know that whoever brings back a sinner from his wandering will *save his soul* from death and will cover a multitude of sins" (James 5:19, 20).

So we are to "go," but to go hoping to "gain," that is, to restore our brother to God and to fellowship with the church. In our conversation we are attempting to bring to light this person's darkness. If that person *sees* this darkness, if you will, and confesses it and asks for forgiveness, then you have "gained" your brother. You have reestablished real spiritual intimacy, as seemingly happened between Peter and Paul after Paul's confrontation of Peter. Years after that face-to-face showdown, Peter called Paul his "beloved brother" (2 Peter 3:15), the brother whom he loves.

In his classic book on Christian community, *Life Together*, Dietrich Bonheoffer summarizes step one so well. He writes,

> Sin demands to have a man by himself. It withdraws him from the community. The more isolated a person is, the more destructive will be the power of sin over him, and the more deeply he becomes involved in it, the more disastrous is his isolation. Sin wants to remain unknown. It shuns the light. . . . [But] In confession, the light of the gospel breaks into the darkness and seclusion of the heart. The sin must be brought to the light. . . . Since the confession of sin is made in the presence of a Christian brother, the last stronghold of self-justification is abandoned. The sinner surrenders; he gives up all his evil. He gives his heart to God, and he finds the forgiveness of all his sin in the fellowship of Jesus Christ and his brother. The expressed, acknowledged sin has lost all its power. It has been revealed for he has cast off his sin from him. Now he stands in the fellowship of sinners who live by the grace of God and the cross of Christ.[7]

Step Two: Establish Evidence

If necessary (Lord willing, it is not), step two is to *establish evidence*. Again I get this from the language of our text. In verse 16 our Lord says, "But if he does not listen, take one or two others along with you, that every charge may be *established* by the *evidence* of two or three witnesses."

In this passage Jesus is immensely practical, but he is also realistic. Most of us when confronted get defensive. We get defensive because we are proud. Instead of melting like butter before the light of truth, we harden like clay. So Jesus' lesson on becoming like little children applies here as well. Humility is needed! And such humility is helped along by bringing others to hear the case.

What Jesus teaches here is based on Deuteronomy 19:15. (He has been in Leviticus; now he moves to Deuteronomy.) The "two or three" brothers join the first two brothers for two or possibly three reasons: (1) to protect against a false accusation—brother B is exaggerating or lying about brother A's offense, (2) to help brother A, if he has been rightly accused, to see his sin as sin, or in other words, to add their voice of reproof so he might repent, and (3) to be public witnesses, if needed, if the matter comes to the attention of the whole church (cf. 2 Corinthians 13:1; 1 Timothy 5:19).

Notice here with step two that the accused brother is not treated like a criminal. He is given time. He is walked through a careful and caring process. He is innocent until proven guilty. And he is treated as an equal. It is brothers to brother, or even sisters to brother. Here Jesus doesn't say, "And when the elders and deacons come to hear the matter . . ." Our Lord makes no mention of the bishop, his two inquisitors, and the local jailer knocking on the front door. Here it is democratic discipline, disciples disciplining disciples. Jesus, if I may put it this way, is "low" church. He has what high churchmen today would call "a low ecclesiology." He must not have read John Henry Newman.

Step Three: Church Censure

Finally, we have step three, what I'm calling *church censure*. A censure is an official reprimand and judgment. Here it is the church saying, "Three strikes and you're out—you have been excommunicated from the fellowship."

Before I explain excommunication, let's be clear on who is to blame here. It is the unrepentant brother. He has refused to listen—"If he listens to you" (v. 15), "If he does not listen . . . [to] two or three witnesses" (v. 16), "if he refuses to listen to them" (v. 17a), and "if he refuses to listen even to the church" (v. 17b). The key word here is "listen." He's not listening. (And this tells us that this is not just a text about how to confront but also *how to respond to confrontation* if true: do not "not listen"!) If you do "not listen," it is all on your head. Three strikes and you're out. If a sinner won't cut off his sin, the church cuts him off, as our Lord makes clear in verse 17:

> If he refuses to listen to them [the two or three], tell it to [all] the church. And if he refuses to listen even to the church [seemingly everyone in

> the body], let him be to you [plural—the church] as a Gentile and a tax collector.

That is, treat him like someone who has betrayed the covenant (a traitorous tax collector, for example) and someone who does not currently believe in the covenant (a Gentile or pagan). It's not that tax collectors or Gentiles can't become part of the church. They did, and they do. But they can't remain in their unbelief and sin.[8]

Both the Old Testament (see Genesis 17:14; Exodus 12:15, 19; 30:33, 38) and the New Testament make clear what this excommunication or "disfellowship" looked like (and should look like).[9] In the New Testament it meant not allowing this unrepentant "brother" to participate in the public gatherings—a worship service, the Lord's Supper, a prayer meeting, and a judicial meeting of some sorts (where a vote was taken on something). For some this shunning was limited only to that. It was okay to say hello in the market or at a wedding, for example. But for others it was unlimited. Here's where you get language like this: If any false teacher "comes to you . . . do not receive him into your house or give him any greeting" (2 John 10), or again "As for a person who stirs up division, after warning him once and then twice [what we have taught here], have nothing more to do with him" (Titus 3:10), and "[Do] not . . . associate with anyone who bears the name of brother if he is guilty of sexual immorality or greed, or is an idolater, reviler, drunkard, or swindler—[do] not even . . . eat with such a one" (1 Corinthians 5:11).

Yet for both—with limited and unlimited shunning—the hope was held out that this "severe measure" would make the sinner come to his senses,[10] that this "brother" would act like a brother should—repent and return. As Paul put it, "You are to deliver this man to Satan for the destruction of the flesh, *so that* his spirit may be saved in the day of the Lord" (1 Corinthians 5:5), and in such discipline, "Do not regard him as an enemy, but warn him as a brother" (2 Thessalonians 3:15). That is, "have nothing to do with him, that he may be ashamed" (2 Thessalonians 3:14), and that shame might turn to sorrow, sorrow to repentance, and repentance to renewed life and fellowship and joy—a church potluck for the prodigal returned home!

Objection Sustained

Coming out of verses 15–17 (steps one to three), our Lord masterfully assumes an objection that would come in time when he was no longer physically present with his church. The objection is simply this: "Says who?" You see, when a brother or sister is excommunicated, before they leave (and/or sue) the disciplining church and go to another, they will nearly always reply to the disciplining church, "You're not God. Who gives you the right?" And to that objection our Lord leaves his church verses 18–20, his gentle way of saying to us, "Tell that unrepentant brother to shut it."

> Truly, I say to you, whatever you [plural—as the church][11] bind on earth shall be bound in heaven, and whatever you loose on earth shall be loosed in heaven. Again I say to you, if two of you agree on earth about anything they ask, it will be done for them by my Father in heaven. For where two or three are gathered in my name, there am I among them.

These verses are not about the value of prayer meetings ("You should come on Wednesday night because Jesus shows up"). And these are not verses about getting the indwelling presence of the risen Christ into a building on a Sunday morning (Jesus indwells each believer always—"And behold, I am with you [singular] always" [28:20a]; "Abide in me, and I in you" [John 15:4a]). Rather, these verses are about Jesus giving his divine authority to forgive sins (to loose) or not forgive sins (to bind) into the hands of the church. He gives the keys of the kingdom not just to Peter (16:19), but to the local assembly assembled to judge.

If the local church gathers together in the name of Christ—even two or three—to judge another brother (that's the context, v. 17 especially), then what these brothers decide on earth is decided in Heaven. Why? Jesus' answer is, "Because I say so. If you follow my guidelines, if you bend your will to God's holy, loving, and reproving will, you then get God's endorsement and empowerment." It's a matter of transference of authority.

Due to Christ's *divine* authority—divine because only God is omnipresent, and only God can claim that sins on earth are forgiven in Heaven, and only in God's name (Jesus says it's in his name, v. 20) are his people to gather[12]—the church has been given the authority to forgive (receive back into fellowship) or excommunicate (remove from fellowship). Yes, Immanuel's (Jesus'—"God with us," 1:23) *ecclesia* (Greek for "church") has the Father's authority to forgive—to keep closed the door to life or to open it. Jesus' lowly *ecclesia* has been given such high authority.

Rejoicing over One

A few years ago, a sister in my church committed a grave sin. When a brother confronted her, she denied it. When he confronted her repeatedly, she finally admitted her sin, but she refused to abandon it. When two other "brothers" (my wife and I) were brought in to confront her, she began to soften, and in time she repented and was restored to fellowship. She came back to the fold and found the shelter and protection and forgiveness she needed.

I know I'm not to have favorites when I distribute the elements for Communion, but she's my favorite because she comes to the table (we walk forward at my church) with a rare mixture of hunger and joy. She still needs Jesus' forgiveness, and she still delights in getting it.

You see, holiness and love and reproof and repentance and humility and authority are all necessary for the life of the church, and the life of the church is life for the world. There is no better witness to the world than Christians acting Christianly. So let us be faithful to Christ's command to confront.

54

The Heart of Perfect Forgiveness

MATTHEW 18:21–35

WHO NEEDS A good opening illustration when the Master storyteller has given his own? But before we get to Jesus' parable, we will start with Peter's question: "Then Peter came up and said to him, 'Lord, how often will my brother sin against me, and I forgive him? As many as seven times?'" (v. 21).

Ah, Peter is so Peter—always pious but often imprecise. In chapter 16 he said to Jesus, "You are the Christ" (16:16) but then added in essence, "But don't go to the cross" (see 16:22). In chapter 17 he said to the transfigured Jesus, "Lord, it is good that we are here" (17:4) but then added in effect, "What this mountain sure could use is three new tents" (17:4). And here in chapter 18 Peter is once again (and not for the last time) quite himself. He asks a pious question but an imprecise one.

What is pious about Peter's question is that (a) he calls Jesus "Lord," which is the right title for the divine King; (b) he understands human nature well enough to know that even Christians need forgiveness, and oftentimes repeated forgiveness for repeat offenses; (c) he is seemingly eager to personally apply what Jesus just taught in verses 15–20 about forgiveness; and (d) he is willing to double the then-normal Jewish forgiveness limit. The rabbis of Jesus' day recommended—based on some verses in Amos 1, 2 about God revoking punishment for three offenses but not four (see Amos 1:3, 6, 9, 11, 13; 2:1, 4, 6)—limiting forgiveness to three times (e.g., *b. Yoma* 86b-87a).[1] Peter was being generous. They say three; he says seven![2] "Lord, will seven times do?"

This is a very pious question. But it is sadly imprecise. What is imprecise is what Jesus points out in verse 22: "I do not say to you seven times, but seventy times seven."[3] Here Jesus gives a loving redirection. Doubling plus one, he says, is not enough. Forgiveness is limitless. That is what Jesus means by "seventy times seven." He doesn't mean, have a forgiveness checklist on your refrigerator, then check a box each time your brother sins against you and you forgive him, *until* you get to box 491, and then forgiveness stops. Then burn the list and bind your brother. Then vengeance is yours![4] No, here our Lord is commanding Peter (and us) to stop counting and starting forgiving.[5]

To be clear (verse 22 can be and has been stretched beyond its intention), here Jesus is not dismissing the government's role and rule—that a good government should never catch and punish those who break the law. And here Jesus is not dismissing what he just said in verses 17–20 about the church rendering the judgment of excommunication on the unrepentant.[6] The church as the church can and should sometimes bind (not forgive). And here Jesus is not dismissing what he teaches in verses 31–35 about God's justice, that God as God has the right and duty to hold sinners accountable. God is not blind or indifferent to unrepentant sinners. Those who break the golden rule God shall break with an iron rod. And here Jesus is not saying that sin, while fully forgiven, doesn't have consequences. In 19:9 he will teach that it is permissible to divorce one's spouse due to "sexual immorality," but he does not permit holding a grudge and not forgiving the sinner for his or her sin. One must forgive, but forgiveness doesn't necessarily mean the marriage lasts.

What Jesus says in 18:22 is that Christians must forgive other Christians who ask for forgiveness and must forgive them (if needed) over and over. Now, will another Christian actually sin against you 490 times? Perhaps. I don't know about you, but I think it's safe to say that I sin (intentionally or unintentionally) at least once a day. So let's do the math. There are 365 days in the year. I'm forty. That's over 14,000 sins. Well then, just imagine if my wife, my children, my church kept count. Just imagine if God kept count of my sins (not to mention yours). Through Christ, God doesn't keep count. So don't you keep count! That's the point. Got it? As God in Christ forgives us again and again and again, so we are to forgive our brothers and sisters in Christ again and again and again.

That principle brings us to the parable. It's often called the Parable of the Unforgiving Servant. I call it the Parable of the New Covenant. I base this on our Lord's words of institution during the Last Supper:

> And he took a cup, and when he had given thanks he gave it to them, saying, "Drink of it, all of you, for this is my blood of the covenant [the new

> covenant; see Hebrews 8:8–13; 9:15; 12:24], which is poured out for many for *the forgiveness of sins*." (26:27, 28)

This parable is about forgiveness,[7] and it's about (this chapter title) "The Heart of Perfect Forgiveness." Note that this parable is not so much about our action—what Peter is asking about, "How many times shall I forgive?"—but about our attitude.[8] It is about getting our hearts in the right place to forgive.

Look with me now at verses 23–35, and let me explain this parable to you. For the sake of clarity, and to follow the three scenes here, I've divided the parable into three points.

1. Just as God in Christ forgave your zillion-dollar debt
2. so you ought to forgive, from the heart, your brother's smaller but significant debt
3. or else face God's eternal judgment!

Scene One

First we will look at God's infinite forgiveness—*Just as God in Christ forgave your zillion-dollar debt* . . . Read again verses 23–27, where our Lord says:

> Therefore the kingdom of heaven may be compared to a king who wished to settle accounts with his servants. When he began to settle, one was brought to him who owed him ten thousand talents. And since he could not pay, his master ordered him to be sold, with his wife and children and all that he had, and payment to be made. So the servant fell on his knees, imploring him, "Have patience with me, and I will pay you everything." And out of pity for him, the master of that servant released him and forgave him the debt.

First things first. This is a parable, which means when Jesus says, "the kingdom of heaven *may be compared to*," he does not mean the kingdom is precisely like this. Embellishment and exaggeration are allowed in a parable just as they are in children's fables to make a point. And so, while true that the "king" or "master" does represent the "heavenly Father," as Jesus says in verse 35, not all of this lord's actions follow the Lord's actions. For example, it was against Jewish law to sell people into slavery,[9] as is threatened in verse 25. Thus in this verse Jesus is not teaching us that the character of God is such that, like an Assyrian despot, he will sell children into slavery to pay for their father's sin. No! Think parable. Think exaggeration is acceptable.

You have to think this way because every major detail here is an exaggeration: no servant or slave could ever amass such a debt; no king (a Gentile king no less) would ever unconditionally forgive such an immense debt; no freshly forgiven debtor would treat another less indebted debtor with such cruelty (choking him); and no king would sentence this cruel servant to debtor's prison for a debt that he couldn't ever pay. Jesus is exaggerating to make his points. And his first point is that just as this Gentile king forgave his servant's astronomical debt, so the God of Israel in Christ has forgiven us our sins.

This first servant's debt was "ten thousand talents" (v. 24). A talent was the highest unit of currency, and ten thousand was then the highest Greek numeral. So how much was "ten thousand talents"? It was the highest or largest imaginable amount. Robert Gundry says "zillions."[10] Zillions of dollars would be the modern equivalent. The lesson then drawn from this largest number is this: like this servant we are in the deepest possible debt to God, and like this servant we can't come close to paying our debt, and therefore like this servant the only choice we have is to plead for mercy from the king.

Before I get to what the servant does and how the king responds, let's take note of Jesus' anthropology (his view of people) and then, tightly and necessarily connected with his anthropology, his soteriology (his view of salvation). Here Jesus depicts human beings, due to their sin, not as being $10,000 in debt or $40,000,000 in debt or even $75,000,000,000,000 in debt, but rather as being zillions of dollars in debt to God. Which means what? It means Jesus thinks deep down (and not so deep down) people are really, really bad. Perhaps more visual than debt, think of a zillion-mile chasm between God's goodness and our badness. Or think both.

With Jesus' calculation, the implications are obvious. He puts to rest any notion of works-righteousness. It's a zillion-mile chasm! It's a zillion-dollar debt! Good luck with the climb. Good luck with a bank loan. You won't balance that budget or bridge that chasm by yourself. You'll only balance it and bridge it by clinging to that old, rugged, and *colossal* cross! A cross deeper and wider and vaster than you can ever fathom. For if one person's debt (one person!) is a zillion dollars, what is the debt for the sins of the whole world for which Christ pays?[11] Christ's cry on the cross, "My God, my God, why have you forsaken me?" (27:46), was the cry of a zillion times a zillion sins laid on one man. Yes, the cross of Christ is deeper and wider and vaster than you can ever fathom. And that's no exaggeration.

Now back to the parable and to the end of the first scene. When this first servant senses (somewhat) the gap, he prays the "sinner's prayer," which is, as it is here, always an imperfect plea. He fell on his knees (that's right), and he implored the king (that's right), "Have patience with me [that's right], and I will pay you everything [that's wrong]" (v. 26). He can't pay everything back, but he honestly wants to, and he recognizes that he needs to or else.

It isn't surprising that this servant, put in the situation he was put in, would reply the way he did. But what is out-of-this-world unexpected is that the king, out of compassion, would cancel the debt completely: "And out of pity for him, the master of that servant released him and forgave him the debt" (v. 27). This is *amazing grace*. The slave wanted a chance to repay, but what he got was a "complete *remission* of debt."[12] He got forgiveness that was motivated by "pity" or what can be translated "compassion." It's the same word used for Jesus' emotions and actions (see 9:36; 14:14; 15:32; 20:34).[13] What this servant wanted was a patient king. What he got was a patient *and* compassionate *and* forgiving king!

Scene Two

As the curtain closes for scene one (vv. 23–27), we all rise to our feet and give a standing ovation to grace: our anthropological dilemma—"deep debt and human inability to pay it"—has been met by God's debt cancellation program (what we know as, and what Jesus is walking towards, the cross)—a complete "forgiveness of all indebtedness by a gracious king."[14] Now as the curtain opens again for scene two, we expect to see great things from this forgiven servant. We expect a heroic man to emerge, not heroic in the sense of American cinema (Rambo) or Greek legend (Achilles) or even the book of Genesis (Lamech)[15]—men of violent vengeance. Rather we expect a hero of gentle grace—Captain Forgiveness! But instead who emerges? The Incredible Sulk, or Doctor Cruel, or Mr. Supersonic Scum, or whatever we might call this unforgiving servant. He is anything but heroic.

> But when that *same* servant went out, he found one of his *fellow* servants who owed him a hundred denarii, and seizing him, he began to choke him, saying, "Pay what you owe." So his fellow servant fell down and pleaded with him, "Have patience with me, and I will pay you." He refused and went and put him in prison until he should pay the debt. (vv. 28–30)

So scene two starts and finishes quickly, so quickly that we are still standing and clapping for the end of scene one. But one by one we stop clapping, a few of us drop to our seats, and all of us cover our mouths in awe and disbelief. What we see here is so unexpected and so irrational.

But that's just it. Sin is irrational. It's as irrational as this forgiven man's inexplicably evil behavior. Replay the scene with me. This first servant comes out of the king's chambers having just been forgiven his zillion-dollar debt.

And what is first on his mind? What is first on his mind is finding the guy who owes him some cash and getting that guy to pay it all back immediately or else. You see, his mind or "heart," as the Old Testament would put it (and as Jesus would put it in v. 35), is filled with no mercy, no patience, no forgiveness, no gratitude, no grace. His king has just forgiven his debt. If that's how a *king* treats a *slave*, then how ought a *slave* to treat another *slave*? Perhaps graciously? Forget perhaps. However, he finds his fellow servant (note the words "he found"—which means he went out looking for him), and he seizes him, chokes him, and says to him, "Pay [right now] what you owe [me]." Finding, seizing, choking! Really? Choking a fellow servant over what? This must be a huge debt. What are we talking—a million dollars, a hundred thousand dollars? No, what is owed is "a hundred denarii."

A denarius was a day's wages. So here we are talking about four months' wages. If you take home $2,000 a month, that's $8,000; if you take home $4,000, that's $16,000. That's not insubstantial. It's a real debt. But it is insubstantial when compared to 60,000,000 denarii. One talent equals 6,000 denarii; 10,000 talents is literally 60,000,000 denarii. But as I said, since 10,000 was the highest number used then, and a talent was the highest monetary unit, it's equivalent to zillions, the highest number you can think of or make up.

So, in comparison this substantial debt is insubstantial. It is a "trivial" or "trifling" or "paltry" or "piddling sum," as four different commentators describe it.[16] Think of it this way. Our debt to God is like the distance from the earth to the sun. But our debt to one another—you sin against me or I sin against you—is like the distance between Chicago and Indianapolis as viewed from the sun.[17] There's real distance, but it's not comparable. And if God can bridge the first gap, we should bridge the second.

This is what the second servant attempts to do. He replies to this true accusation (he does owe him the money) almost as precisely as the first servant did before the king. He "fell down and pleaded with him, 'Have patience with me, and I will pay you'" (v. 29). Now, you would think that action and that verbiage would jog the first slave's memory, soften his hard heart, and open his mouth to say the words, "Your debt is forgiven. Go. You're as free as I am!" Instead he said nothing. His hard heart hardened. The memory of his own forgiveness was like dust in the wind. He refused this second slave's petition and threw him into prison.

He threw him into prison perhaps hoping some sympathetic soul (a brother, a father, a rich uncle, the king[!]) would pay the other servant's debt. Or he threw him into debtor's prison, where the debt would slowly but surely be repaid by this second servant's manual labor. Or perhaps this final move is as irrational as every action that has come before it. The first slave sends the second slave to prison, where now there is no way he can generate income to pay back the debt.

Whatever the specifics, I hope you see the picture. This is what a Christian brother not forgiving a guilty but repentant brother looks like to God. It's despicable. It's disgusting. It's completely irrational. And that's Jesus' point: don't act like this irrational idiot. Rather, as the prophet Micah put it, "walk humbly before God, do justly, and *love mercy*" (my reordering of Micah 6:8 AT); or as Jesus put it, "Be merciful, even as your Father is merciful" (Luke 6:36). Putting points one and two together, just as God in Christ forgave your zillion-dollar debt, so you ought to forgive, from the heart, your brother's significant but significantly smaller debt (cf. v. 33).

I've entitled this chapter "The Heart of Perfect Forgiveness." I use the word "heart" because of Jesus' own summary of the parable (v. 35). His final word, for emphasis, in our text is "from your heart*s*" (plural), literally "from the hearts of you all." Jesus is teaching about heart-attitude here. He is teaching that "[t]rue forgiveness may not simply hang from the lips."[18] It's not the reluctant and mumbled "I frrg you" from the big sister after being ordered by mom to forgive her grouchy younger brother's, "I said I'm so . . . rrrrr . . . y!!!" Rather, here is it repentance and forgiveness *from the heart*.

"The Heart of *Perfect* Forgiveness." I use the word "perfect" because of Jesus' numerology here ("seventy times seven"), but also because of what Jesus taught about God's love in the Sermon on the Mount. In 5:20–48 our Lord said, don't act like scribes and Pharisees (see 5:20); instead act like God—"be perfect, as your heavenly father is perfect" (5:48). In context, the meaning of the word "perfect" is perfectly clear. In 5:43–47 Jesus teaches how God the Father shows indiscriminate love in that he makes the sun rise and the rain fall for the good of both the good and the bad. He doesn't hide the sun from immoral people. He doesn't fail to water the fields of the wicked. In the same way, Jesus says, we are to love all people—our brothers (those who usually love us) and even our enemies (those who usually don't love us). That's perfect love.

As I explained in chapter 12, this concept of perfect love is like a triangle. We are to love God. This is the tip of the triangle. But we are also to love our neighbors, the nice ones. They are the right point of the triangle. But if we stop there, it is imperfect love. We must also love those on the left, who we'd naturally like to kick to the curb.

Everybody, even the worst of people, loves their own. You won't find an Italian mobster who doesn't love *the family* or the most brutal inner-city gangbanger who won't take a bullet for his grandmother. But what kind of love is that? It is lopsided love. It's a one-pointed triangle. We are to love with perfect or complete or whole love, as the Father daily demonstrates, and as the Father most fully demonstrated in the cross of Christ (cf. Romans 5:8, 10). So "perfect" forgiveness is not much different than "perfect" love. If someone begs you for mercy for whatever sin and however many times a sin has been committed against you, you are to have compassion, and you are to offer forgiveness.

Scene Three

You are to offer forgiveness . . . or else. Our Lord's parable is not done. We come now to the third and final scene. There are three scenes in this parable and three points:

1. Just as God in Christ forgave your zillion- dollar debt
2. so you ought to forgive, from the heart, your brother's smaller but significant debt
3. or else face God's eternal judgment.

Look at, listen to, and tremble before Jesus' words in verses 31–35:

> When his fellow servants saw what had taken place, they were greatly distressed, and they went and reported to their master [the king] all that had taken place. Then his master summoned him and said to him, "You wicked servant! I forgave you all that debt because you pleaded with me. And should not you have had mercy on your fellow servant, as I had mercy on you?" And in anger his master delivered him to the jailers, until he should pay all his debt. So also my heavenly Father will do to every one of you, if you do not forgive your brother from your heart.

Jesus is so strong here. Jesus is so loving here (every warning is an act of love). Jesus is so relevant here. For these final five verses correct three popular views in the church today. First, that God will save all people (universalism). Second, that God never gets angry, and if he gets angry (an unlikely "if") he certainly never gets angry enough to eternally judge someone. Third, warnings about Hell don't apply to professing Christians. All of those ideas, according to Jesus, are wrong.

First, the idea that God will save all people is wrong. If there was ever a place in Jesus' teaching ministry to walk into, through the front door no less, the doctrine of universalism, it would be here. Having heard Jesus teach on seventy-times-seven forgiveness and having heard his story of "the astounding magnanimity of the king"[19] (God is so generous and gracious), we might next expect him to finish by saying, "And guess what? Everyone gets into the kingdom! End of story. Group hug." Instead (almost as if he anticipated the popularity of universalism in our day), he teaches that judgment awaits the wicked.

That leads to our second wrong view. Today you won't hear many sermons entitled, as Jonathan Edwards's most famous sermon was entitled, "Sinners in the Hands of an Angry God." You won't hear such a title because too many pastors today don't believe God ever gets angry, or if he gets "angry" (but let's not use that word, how about "disappointed"?), he certainly never would get "disappointed" enough to eternally judge someone. Today verse 34 of our Lord Jesus Christ's teaching has been lifted off the page, tossed in the air, and punted 10,000 yards out of the church sanctuary.

But for Christ's sake and our sake, I've brought it back, and I want to show it to you again now. My brothers and sisters, there is nothing antiquated or unethical about "Sinners in the Hands of an Angry God." It's just Bible language about heavenly and earthly and under-the-earth realities. God's anger shows that he is holy. It also shows that he cares about justice. In this parable, the heavenly "Father" (note that Jesus calls him "Father," not "Judge" or "King") gets angry at the guy he just forgave who went on to choke his fellow man and demand reparation.[20] If ingratitude and inhuman cruelty like that didn't upset God, we'd have a major ethical dilemma on our hands.

When we get angry we almost always sin. I get that. Anger has a negative connotation to us. But when God gets angry he never sins. We need to get that into our heads. His anger always leads to just judgment. And as much as the world today needs God's forgiveness, it also needs God's justice, what we read about in verse 34: "And in anger his master delivered him to the jailers, until he should pay all his debt."

Now that final phrase—"until he should pay all his debt"—needs some explanation. Is Jesus here teaching the Roman Catholic doctrine of purgatory? Certainly not.[21] Such a notion is so far removed from the Biblical testimony. Well then, is Jesus simply talking about punitive punishment—that God disciplines those he loves, and the discipline here is to imprison this "servant" (i.e., Christian brother, v. 30) until he forgives as he has been forgiven? Perhaps. Perhaps the "debt" here is forgiveness. Once he forgives, he gets out of jail.

The best understanding, however, is that this phrase—"until he should pay all his debt"—symbolized eternal punishment,[22] what Jesus has recently called "Hell" (18:9) and what he would later describe as "the eternal fire [and "eternal punishment," 25:46] prepared for the devil and his angels" (25:41). I hold this view based mostly on the amount of the unpaid debt. Remember this first slave's debt is zillions. Now tell me, how quickly does a man in jail pay that off? Oh, let's see—how about "Never!" That's the idea. Instead of saying, "This bad guy goes to jail for life and afterlife," Jesus instead paints a picture, as he so often does, of the reality he wants us to avoid. Picture yourself in debtor's prison *forever*.

The third and final popular misconception our Lord here dispels is that warnings about Hell don't apply to professing Christians. I am aware of only a few times in the Gospel of Matthew where Jesus uses the term "Hell" in reference to unbelievers (13:42, 50; 23:15, 33).[23] Most of the "Hell" texts and many of the judgment passages, like the one before us, are given to Christians. Look again at verse 35 with that thought in mind: "So also my heavenly Father will do to every one of *you*, if *you* do not forgive *your brother* [fellow Christian] from your heart." Who is the "you"? The disciples listening then (18:1) and the disciples reading now—yes, "you."

Jesus was not a turn-or-burn street evangelist. That's the right message, but it's the wrong crowd. Jesus *loved* unbelievers into the kingdom, but he *warned* those already in (or those who think they're already in) about what's out there or down there—Hell. So he sermonized like Jonathan Edwards sermonized. He preached sermons like "Sinners in the Hands of an Angry God" at church to the church, hoping by God's power to bring about revival and renewal—revival (waking non-Christian professing Christians from their spiritual deadness) and renewal (waking authentic but sleeping Christians from their spiritual slumber). Here Jesus warns Christians about Hell to wake them up and move them on, to push them to persevere.[24]

So, does Jesus think Christians can lose their salvation? No. I think Jesus illustrates that they can't in the Parable of the Lost Sheep and teaches that in John 18:9: "Of those whom you gave me I have lost not one." Jesus hasn't lost and isn't going to lose any of his sheep. Be confident of that. But does Jesus think a professing Christian, someone who smugly sins while he hums his false-confidence mantra—"once saved, always saved"—will be saved or ever was saved? I don't think so. Those who say to him on the last day, "Lord, Lord," after living lawlessly (see 7:21–23), will not be let in. Read the Sermon on the Mount. Read Matthew 25. Read 1 John. Read Jude. Read Revelation. Read all of Peter's and Paul's epistles!

You see, we all stand between the cross and the chair,[25] the day of God's first salvation (the cross) and God's final salvation (the chair), God's first judgment on sin (the cross) and God's final judgment upon sinners (the chair). Christians stand between this past event and that future reality, and thus our heads need to be constantly turning—looking back and looking ahead—

appreciating the King's forgiveness, yet fearing the King's judgment. Forgiveness and fear are not antithetical realities to Jesus, and thus they shouldn't be to us. In our pilgrimage to the celestial city, God uses both—forgiveness and fear—to push us along.

Now, to be clear, our forgiveness of others is not a condition of salvation, but it is a consequence of it. "There will be no forgiveness in that day [judgment day] for unforgiving people,"[26] J. C. Ryle has rightly said. I say it this way: There is no such creature as an unforgiving Christian. That being doesn't exist. Christians forgive. We forgive because we have been transformed by the power of the gospel. The last point of my church's vision statement is, "lives transformed by the power of the gospel," and Jesus readily endorses that. If the gospel of forgiveness gets in you, it comes out of you. It brings the fruit of relational transformation.

Letter from the Heart

When I came to Christ, my sinner's prayer resembled this first slave's. It wasn't perfect—I promised too much and undervalued my inability. It wasn't perfect, but it was from the heart. It was sincere, and it was reverent. God's holiness so overwhelmed me that I had, for the first time in my life, a sense of the spiritual gap between me and him. It brought me to my knees. It brought me to tears of repentance. It brought me to faith in the one meditator between God and man, the man Jesus Christ.

And soon after my conversion, forgiveness became the air I breathed. I breathed in God's forgiveness, I breathed out my own forgiveness of others, *and* I asked others to breathe in and breathe out forgiveness of me. I remember quite vividly reading afresh the Gospel of Matthew and coming to 5:21–24, near the beginning of the Sermon on the Mount. In that section on perfect love (where Jesus also warns believers about judgment [v. 21] and "Hell" [v. 22]), I read these needle-to-the-heart words:

> So if you are offering your gift at the altar and there remember that your brother has something against you, leave your gift there before the altar and go. First be reconciled to your brother, and then come and offer your gift. (5:23, 24)

I closed my Bible. I took out a pen and paper, and I wrote a letter to two people I had deeply offended with my sin. I sealed it and mailed it. I'm fairly certain they received it but am uncertain how they responded. I still don't know today. Did they trash it immediately, or it is tucked away somewhere in their “I can’t believe this guy would ask for our forgiveness” pile? I hope and think it’s the latter. But it doesn’t honestly matter to me. What matters is that God gave me a new heart, and that new heart was given this “persistent power” to receive and to give forgiveness.[27]

Our Lord’s question from this parable (related to Peter’s question) is this: do you have such a heart? Imperfect sinner as you are, do you have that God-given heart of perfect forgiveness—a heart that takes in and gives out forgiveness seventy-times-seven?

55

The Beginning and End of Marriage

MATTHEW 19:1–12

I. HOWARD MARSHALL is a prominent New Testament scholar. He is also, on the issues of election and predestination, an Arminian. That is, he is not a Calvinist like I am and like John Calvin was and Martin Luther and Augustine and Paul and John and Jesus. Anyway, when I was in college Dr. Marshall came to my New Testament Criticism class and gave a guest lecture on the pseudepigraphy of 2 Peter. He answered the question, "Did the Apostle Peter write 2 Peter?"

After the class, as he was walking down the hall with his scholarly entourage, I pushed through the crowd, came up to him, and asked, "Dr. Marshall, is it true you are an Arminian?" That was my question. It obviously had nothing to do with the class lecture, but everything to do with what was most important to me at the time. I don't remember precisely how he answered my question, but he said something to the effect that he admitted his guilt. He was an Arminian of sorts. "Well," I thought to myself, "now I've got him." I had two more prepared questions. My first question was, "Have you ever read Jonathan Edwards?" Jonathan Edwards, the great American theologian, is a convicting advocate for Calvinism. I had just read Edwards and thought I'd have the advantage. He replied, "I have read Edwards." That's it. That's all he said.

Okay, that was a minor setback. I couldn't then send him home with Edwards's *Freedom of the Will* and say, "Read this, you ignoramus." Ah, but I had another loaded question. I wasn't done. I fired away. "Have you ever read Romans 9?" Honestly, that was my got-ya question. Now remember that this guy is a prominent New Testament scholar, and also remember that Romans is in the New Testament. Startled by the question, he turned to me, smiled, and said politely in his dear British accent, "Yes, I have read Romans 9." Then he went on to explain the whole book of Romans and how, in his view, Romans 9—11 fits into Paul's overall argument.

I start this way, as you may have guessed, because my encounter with I. Howard Marshall reminds me of the Pharisees' encounter with Jesus in 19:1–12. Not only did they ignore what he had come to say and do (they didn't want to talk about that), but they even tried to test and trap a man who was so far their superior in everything and, as we shall see, even and especially in his knowledge of Scripture. I tried to test and trap the Professor Emeritus of New Testament Exegesis and honorary research professor at the University of Aberdeen. They tried to test and trap the Son of God, wisdom incarnate.

We know how I fared (or you can guess). I made a fool of myself. Let's see how the Pharisees shall fare, perhaps no different than I did.

Question One

The Pharisees ask Jesus two questions. The first is, "Is it lawful to divorce one's wife for any cause?" (v. 3). Let's talk about the *nerve* and the *nature* of their question.

First, we have the nerve of it. In verses 1, 2 Matthew gives us a concise setting. He talks about Jesus' geographical movement and messianic miracles. After Jesus finished teaching what he taught in chapter 18 about forgiveness, he moved on from Galilee (this marks the end of his significant Galilean ministry, which began in 4:12) to "the region of Judea beyond the Jordan." Where is he going? He is moving toward Jerusalem (16:21; cf. 20:17). He is moving toward the cross. He is moving deliberately toward the final and ultimate act of forgiveness.

But before he gets to Jerusalem he stops to heal the crowds. Don't overlook verse 2: "And large crowds followed him, and he healed them there." How large? We don't know. How many were healed? We don't know. Matthew leaves his description vague, I think intentionally in order to say that Jesus didn't just heal one crippled man or one leprous woman; rather, it was as if he healed whole "crowds," plural. He healed this large crowd, and that large crowd, as he moved toward Jerusalem. *And then*, after all that healing, *then* came the Pharisees, these blind men with their deaf and dumb question.

Do you see the nerve of it? The setting highlights it. Instead of asking, "Where do your miraculous powers come from?" they ask about divorce. Instead of asking, "Tell us more about this death and resurrection business.

Help us to understand," they ask about divorce. Instead of asking, "Are you the Messiah, the promised one?" they ask about divorce.

My questions to I. Howard Marshall were sophomoric, but their questions were audacious and devilish. I say devilish because of how Matthew says it. He speaks not only of the nerve but also of the *nature* of their question, and he does so in this manner: "And the Pharisees came up to him and tested him" (v. 3a) or "tempted him" ("tested" can be translated "tempted"). In the same way the devil tempted Adam and Eve in the garden and Jesus in the wilderness. So these super-spiritual men slither up to Jesus. They set their trap beneath his feet, step back, and ask, "Is it lawful to divorce one's wife for any cause?" (v. 3b).

What a tricky, tricky question. If Jesus moves this way a bit ("ah, he doesn't revere Moses") or that way a bit ("oh, so men can indulge in any and every lust"), the trap springs, he's caught, and down he goes. Or so they think.

What they are doing here is inviting Jesus to take a side on one of the hot debates of the day. The debate centered on the interpretation of Deuteronomy 24:1, which they will reference next in their second question (v. 7), and particularly the phrase in that verse, "some indecency" or "anything indecent." In Judaism there was the conservative school of thought and the liberal school of thought. The conservative school, represented by Rabbi Shammai, focused on the word "indecency" in the phrase "anything indecent," teaching that God required divorce for sexual unfaithfulness (adultery). The liberal school, represented by Rabbi Hillel, focused on the word "anything" in the phrase "anything indecent," teaching that God required divorce for "anything" the man deemed indecent in his wife.[1] This could include trivial offenses such as burning a meal. The famous Rabbi Akiba taught that a man can divorce his wife "even if he found someone else prettier than she."[2] How very modern. How very wicked! Yes, just as wicked as the Pharisees here. "Jesus, what's your view on the matter? Are you liberal or conservative?"

I think they know he will be conservative, as he was in 5:31, 32 (where he taught that lust constitutes spiritual adultery), and that is what they want. They want that because then they've got him. The best case scenario is this: if he sides with the conservatives perhaps he will suffer the fate of John the Baptist. Remember what Herod did to John when he voiced his conservative views on divorce. Maybe now Herod and Pontius Pilate would like to hear what this Jesus says about divorce. The worst case scenario (which was still good for them) is that he falls into their next trap, their follow-up question about Deuteronomy. *Ah, he's a lawbreaker then! He disregards Moses.* Either way they think they have him. He either angers the powerful or the pious, or both the powerful and the pious. It's perfect. They've trapped the great teacher with one trick question.

Answer One

Ah, but not so fast. Jesus will silence them yet. Look below at our Lord's reply. Here I imagine him turning toward them, smiling, and saying politely, in his Galilean accent:

> Have you not read that he who created them from the beginning made them male and female, and said, "Therefore a man shall leave his father and his mother and hold fast to his wife, and the two shall become one flesh"? So they are no longer two but one flesh. What therefore God has joined together, let not man separate. (vv. 4–6)

This answer is brilliant and beautiful. All of Jesus' answers to these types of trick questions in the Gospels are like inexhaustible works of art. You can look at them all day, listen to them hour after hour, and still not exhaust their brilliance and beauty. And because that is true, I have limited my 2,259 observations to just two.

First, Jesus goes to the Bible for his answer. This shouldn't surprise us, for when tempted by the devil he answered with his threefold refrain, "It is written . . . it is written . . . it is written" (4:4, 6, 7). Here he answers their question with a question, "Have you not read . . . ?" (v. 4a), referring to the first book in the Bible, which is not the last word on marriage but the most foundational. Well, of course, they had read Genesis 1, 2, just as surely as Dr. Marshall had read Romans 9.

Our Lord is not mocking them with his simple question, but he's close. He is questioning his questioners. "Are you so fluent in the language that you have somehow forgotten how to sing the alphabet song?" He challenges their basic Bible knowledge, the A of the A, B, C's of marriage. Letter A: God intended marriage between a man and woman for life.[3] There was no provision for divorce in paradise. Jesus can't find it in Genesis 1:27, which he alludes to in verse 4, or Genesis 2:24, which he quotes almost verbatim (from the LXX) in verse 5.

> Therefore a man shall leave his father and his mother and hold fast to his wife, and "the two shall become one flesh."

Then in verse 6 he gives his gloss—his brief commentary on those two

Genesis texts, emphasizing God-ordained unity: "So they are no longer two but one flesh. What therefore God has joined together, let not man separate."

In verses 4–6 Jesus could have emphasized the equal image of the sexes, that both man and woman are made in the image of God. That's true, but that's not the issue at hand. Or he could have emphasized the concept of heterosexual monogamy (one man and one woman)—that these texts teach against both polygamy and homosexuality. That's true, but again that's not the issue at hand here. (Homosexuality is, of course, the issue at hand in the church and culture today, so we'd better find ourselves looking in Genesis for the right answers. You don't go to Romans first but to Genesis. Does homosexuality fit God's original intention for marriage? That is the question with which to start.)

Anyway, Jesus doesn't emphasize those two important truths. Rather he emphasizes God-ordained unity. The unity language is most obvious. It's everywhere. The man is to "hold fast to his wife," and they together then "become one flesh." That's verse 5. Then in verse 6 Jesus speaks of the married couple being "one flesh" and "joined together," and then he finishes with his unity warning, "let not man separate." Unity. Unity. Unity. Unity. Unity. Jesus gives five unity phrases. That's obvious.

What is not as obvious but will be obvious once I point it out (if you haven't already seen it yourself) is that *God* is the focus here. While the text of Genesis speaks of the man's action ("a man shall leave his father and his mother and hold fast to his wife"), Jesus speaks of God's action ("what therefore God has joined together"). Jesus gives quite a high view of providence. According to him, and he should know, it is God who brings people together in the bond of holy wedlock. This is e-harmony at its best; the *e* stands for Elohim. God brings a man and a woman together, and thus God does not then want "man"—a mere man, any mere man—to separate God's physical and metaphysical new creation—one man/one woman/one flesh.[4] That's God math: one plus one plus one equals one (the doctrine of the Trinity), and one plus one also equals one (the doctrine of marriage).

So, first, Jesus goes to the Bible for his answer (there is nothing new in his view; it's as old as creation; it's as basic as the first book of the Book). And, second, from the Bible he answers their divorce question with a divinely inspired purpose statement on marriage. His answer is brilliant. It's beautiful.

Question Two and Answer Two

Of course, the Pharisees see neither the brilliance nor the beauty. They only see that their trap has snapped and has grabbed hold of Jesus' foot. Now all they have to do is push. So they push with their second (I think prepared) question: "They said to him, 'Why then [got ya] did Moses command one to give a certificate of divorce and to send her away?'" (v. 7).

Here they push Jesus into their Torah Trap (or maybe Pentateuch Pit is better), and they say, "Here, Jesus, while you're down there, chew on this proof text." They throw him Deuteronomy 24:1, where Moses wrote:

> When a man takes a wife and marries her, if then she finds no favor in his eyes because he has found some indecency in her, and he writes her a certificate of divorce and puts it in her hand and sends her out of his house. . . . [Stop!]

They'll need to stop there to prove their point that Jesus' view of divorce is not Moses'.

Now, what Jesus does with this bone is quite brilliant and beautiful, of course. He carefully examines the bone, then adds some meat back to it—its surrounding context (Deuteronomy 24:2–4)—and says, "Here you go."

> Because of your hardness of heart Moses allowed you to divorce your wives, but from the beginning it was not so. And I say to you: whoever divorces his wife, except for sexual immorality, and marries another, commits adultery." (vv. 8, 9)

Here Jesus offers two *corrections* and one *command*. The first correction is that Moses didn't command divorce, but rather he allowed it. They said that Moses "command[ed]" (v. 7). Jesus said, "Moses allowed" (v. 8). To illustrate the crucial difference between "commanded" and "allowed," N. T. Wright offers this helpful car illustration:

> Just as a car is made to drive safely on the road, not to skid around colliding with other cars, so marriage was made to be a partnership of one woman and one man for life, not something that could be split up and reassembled whenever one person wanted it . . . . Moses didn't say, as it were, 'when you drive your car, this is how to have an accident'; rather, 'when you drive a car, take care not to have an accident; but if, tragically, an accident occurs, this is how to deal with it.'[5]

You see, Moses didn't command (my words now), "go wreck your car and get a new one." Rather, he saw all the car wrecks and felt compelled to write some rules of the road. He tried to regulate the wrecks. And the specific regulation of Deuteronomy 24:1–4 goes like this: If a man divorces his wife and she marries another man and that second husband divorces her, that woman can't then be remarried to her first husband. That's the specific law. And I think part of its intention, the gentle genius of it, is a corrective to the first husband: "Don't be so quick in getting rid of her in the first place because you might very well want her back."

Jesus' first correction is that Moses didn't command divorce, he allowed it. His second correction is that he allowed it due to hard-heartedness: "Because of your hardness of heart Moses allowed you to divorce your wives, but from the beginning it was not so" (v. 8). Do you hear the contrast there? Sometimes theologians, in a category far different than I'm talking about here, talk about the two wills of God. We can use the same language here. There are two wills—God's ideal will (the original intention of marriage advocated in Genesis—"from the beginning") and God's allowed will (the necessary regulations due to human sin), due to what Jesus labels here hard-heartedness—"because of your hardness of heart."

Note in that phrase the word "your" and then later in that sentence "you" and "your" again. Jesus doesn't say "our" like a preacher should say—"It is due to our sin." And he doesn't say "their" referring only to the men of Moses' time. He says "your," excluding himself (a subtle way of admitting his complete innocence of this sin and likely all sin) and including these Pharisees in the sins of their forefathers. Their hard-heartedness runs in the family. Marriage is not the problem. Hard-hearted men (and let's add women, to be fair) are the problem—then, now, always. *You* are the problem. Take away the disease of hard-heartedness, and you can take away all divorce laws, divorce attorneys, divorce courts, and divorce settlements.

It is as if Jesus turns to us and bemoans, "Oh, if that were only the case with my people. Oh, if my people, when they think about marriage, wouldn't think of Deuteronomy first (may we never have to go there) but rather Genesis. Go to Genesis. Go back to God's primary plan, his ideal will for marriage—one man/one woman/one flesh . . . till death."

In verses 8, 9 Jesus gives two corrections and one command. We have looked at the two corrections; now we come to the command: "And I say to you: whoever divorces his wife, except for sexual immorality, and marries another, commits adultery" (v. 9).

We are all so familiar with this command that it is easy for us to miss what is so surprising about it. I find it surprising, coming on the tail of what Jesus says in verse 8 and earlier in verses 4–6, that Jesus allows an allowance for divorce at all. He doesn't say, "If you want to follow me, you must go back to pre-fall paradise and live there. Divorce? What's that? As it was then, so it shall be now. There is to be no divorce in my house, in my kingdom, in my church." He seems to balance here the two wills of God. He hates divorce (divorce is never desirable), but he allows for it. I'll come back to that allowance in a minute.

The other surprise here is Jesus' authority. What authority! Note the ordering of Jesus argument (do you see what sticks out like a blueberry stain on a wedding dress here?). The Bible says (vv. 4, 5) . . . the Bible says (v. 8) . . ." I say to you" (v. 9).

Brothers and sisters, don't ever overlook the words "I say to you" in Matthew's Gospel. All authority in Heaven and on earth has been given to Jesus, and that authority is on display right here. Behold (we are to behold) someone greater than Moses (Deuteronomy). Behold someone present and equal with the Father and Spirit at creation (Genesis). Behold Jesus, the Son of Man and Son of God, divine wisdom and divine authority incarnate!

Let's return to the exception clause. First, however, let's read the command without the exception clause: "[W]hoever divorces his wife . . . and marries another, commits adultery" (v. 9). Jesus is clear here. To divorce your spouse (for any cause you can drum up) and marry another is to commit adultery. That behavior (so common today within our culture and the church, sadly) is clearly against Christ's command. *But*—now let's add the exception clause—if your wife (and I think it is fair to expand it to husbands as well) has been sexually immoral, you can get a divorce. That is what Jesus teaches.

Now comes the flood of a thousand questions, 996 of which I will not answer. I will answer only four and all four quite briefly.

Question 1: What is meant by "sexual immorality" (*porneia*)?

Answer: Sexual intercourse that is contrary to the moral standards of Old Testament Law—e.g., incest, bestiality, homosexually, fornication, and adultery. In our context it primarily but not exclusively refers to *adultery*—that is, having sexual relations with someone who is not your spouse.

Question 2: Why is adultery the one exception?

Answer: Because adultery is the one sin that tears apart the "one flesh" Jesus talked about in verses 5, 6. According to Old Testament Law, the punishment for adultery was death (Deuteronomy 22:22). Death—that's the end of the marriage. In Roman culture (and Jewish culture) at the time of Jesus, this punishment was not in place. So Jesus puts something similar in place: adultery equals (in some cases and in many cases) death, the death of the marriage via divorce.[6]

Question 3: Is adultery the only exception?

Answer: It is here. However, in 1 Corinthian 7:15 Paul adds another exception in a very different context. He allows divorce for abandonment, often called "willful desertion." This God-inspired addition opens the door (I say this cautiously, but with much study, thought, and prayer) for the church, especially the local church in each particular case, to use its head.

For example, should a woman who is physically abused repeatedly and brutally by her husband not seek a divorce? I think some Christians have become far too pharisaical in our application of 19:9. If he bashes your head in, you have to stay with him, but once he commits adultery, then you get God's free ticket to divorce. Where are "the weightier matters of the law," as Jesus would put it in 23:23 to the Pharisees—where's the "justice and mercy" (23:23) in that? You see (it's important to see), unlike the scribes and Pharisees, Jesus rarely gives a tightly-tied ethic. Instead he has given his Spirit to his church—the Spirit of truth and love and holiness—and he has given us prayer, wisdom, compassion, and our own two cents.

Question 4: Does the sin of adultery (or any other grave sin) necessitate divorce?

Answer: Certainly not. Why do I say that? Well, what is the lesson of chapter 18? Forgive (seventy-times-seven forgiveness!). Do you think it's a coincidence that chapters 18 and 19 back up to each other, rub shoulders, hold hands, kiss, become one flesh? If adultery occurs, you have two choices. Choice one is divorce. He or she has broken the "one flesh" covenant. It's the death penalty. Choice two (and this isn't easy) is to forgive. That is, to re-embrace the repentant, to offer anew the gospel of forgiveness—seventy-times-seven forgiveness for a zillion-dollar debt.

Have you ever seen this happen? I have on a number of occasions. This is my in-laws' story. I have seen God's reconstructive grace, this supernatural superglue at work. I have seen God glue the divided back together as one. And, you know, sometimes that cracked vase ends up looking more stunning than the original.

You see, just as excommunication for the unrepentant is a real calling for the church (we must cut off the unrepentant brother from the assembly), so divorce is a real choice for the offended party (you can cut him or her out of the marriage, especially if there is no repentance). But just as forgiveness for the repentant brother should bring full restoration within the church, so repentance of the adulterer and adulteress should bring full restoration in a marriage as well. Put on and put out forgiveness.

Those are merely four questions answered. There are, of course, many more good questions to be asked and answered. But let me just say that when you think about all the possible questions related to marriage and divorce and remarriage, I want you to think Genesis and think gospel. Think Genesis:

hold fast to one another. Think gospel: forgive one another. Think Genesis and think gospel and think the goal of both, which is the same: what God has joined together, let no one separate.

A Higher View of the Kingdom

After Jesus finishes verse 9, how do the Pharisees' respond? We don't know. It's as if . . . *poof* . . . they have disappeared, or rather they have slithered away with their two traps in hand and their tails between their legs. They won't catch Jesus this time. But in their place, Jesus' disciples give voice. And they say to Jesus, "If such is the case of a man with his wife, it is better not to marry" (v. 10).

What are they saying here? Are they being chauvinists—"If I can't get rid of this woman whenever and for whatever, then why marry in the first place?" Perhaps. Are they being realistic—"What marriage is so great that it lasts a lifetime? Come on, Jesus, lighten up." Perhaps. Or are they just misunderstanding Jesus' lofty marriage ethics? I think so. I think they just don't get it, like they won't get why Jesus wants to bless little children in 19:13 and not bless a rich man in 19:16ff. They have a fine track record of not getting it (e.g., 14:16, 17; 16:21–23).

But that's expected. At this point we have gotten used to their not getting it. But what is unexpected is that Jesus seemingly shifts the conversation from marriage to singleness. He doesn't reply to their "it is better not to marry" with an apologetic for marriage. He doesn't say, "Oh, guys, you have marriage all wrong. Marriage can be so wonderful. Imagine walking hand in hand with your sweetheart, watching the waves of the Mediterranean crash against the shore of Spain as turtledoves coo in the cliffs above and the warm sun slowly sets." For some reason Jesus doesn't give such imaginative marriage therapy. He delivers no pep talk on nuptial bliss. Instead he gives a eulogy for eunuchs, a tribute to single-minded singles:

> But he said to them, "Not everyone can receive this saying, but only those to whom it is given. For there are eunuchs who have been so from birth, and there are eunuchs who have been made eunuchs by men, and there are eunuchs who have made themselves eunuchs [metaphorically speaking; it's not self-mutilation here; cf. 18:8, 9; those who have stayed single, before marriage or after the death of a spouse, and perhaps after a divorce] for the sake of the kingdom of heaven. Let the one who is able to receive this receive it." (vv. 11, 12)

What is Jesus getting at here? Is he talking about the gift of singleness? He is talking about singleness—a "eunuch" is certainly someone who is single, someone who is single and not sexually active for one of three reasons: natural (someone born that way), unnatural (someone made that way), or this new category Jesus has introduced, which we'll called willfully or volitional (someone who desires to be that way or stay that way) for the gospel.

So, yes, Jesus is talking about singleness, and he is talking about the gift related to this last category of eunuch—"only those to whom it is given" (v. 11b) and perhaps "Let the one who is able to receive this receive it" (v. 12b). But his point is grander than "esteem and embrace the gift of singleness." His point is this: *The kingdom of heaven is so important that it should seem perfectly normal if someone would want to give up marriage for it.*

The context here is so important. In verses 4–6 and 8, 9 Jesus teaches that you can't have too high a view of marriage. It is so high the disciples are taken aback by it. But in verses 11, 12 he adds that however high your view of marriage is, your view of the kingdom ought to be far higher.

You see, verses 4–9 are not Jesus' treatise on marriage. That's only one passage on that topic (a few verses). What Jesus says in chapter 18 on forgiveness is also part of the church's marriage manual, as is what he says about self-denial and cross bearing in chapter 16. The church misses the point when we make marriage the point. And Jesus makes that point in verses 11, 12, which is not merely a treatise on singleness but an exhortation on single-minded devotion.

Our first focus is always to be on the gospel. It is not as though Jesus is against focusing on the family. He focused on the family in the first half of our text. But he is against focusing on the family or marriage or work or money or house or land or anything else ahead of the kingdom. Gospel first; everything else second—that's his motto, and that's his model. That's how he lived. He denied himself marriage and the pleasures of marriage—companionship, physical intimacy, children—for the spread of the kingdom of heaven on earth. He was a eunuch for the kingdom.

And he calls those who can to do the same. And he calls those who can't do the same (you're gifted with marriage, or you're not gifted with singleness—you want to get married) to want the same, to want to give everything "for the sake of the kingdom of heaven," or in Paul's language to have "undivided devotion to the Lord" (1 Corinthians 7:35) because you believe that it is the Christian's highest calling to "seek *first* the kingdom of God" (6:33a).

I. Howard Marshall said it this way: "To all who would follow him . . . Jesus issues the summons to be willing to say 'No' to themselves and their own ambitions and to follow him, even to the point of daily readiness for martyrdom."[7] May God grant us such willingness and readiness, I pray. Amen.

56

The Impossibility of Salvation

MATTHEW 19:13–30

Alice was close behind [the White Rabbit] when she turned the corner, but the Rabbit was no longer to be seen: she found herself in a long, low hall, which was lit up by a row of lamps hanging from the roof. There were doors all round the hall, but they were all locked; and when Alice had been all the way down one side and up the other, trying every door, she walked sadly down the middle, wondering how she was ever to get out again. Suddenly she came upon a little three-legged table, all made of solid glass; there was nothing on it except a tiny golden key, and Alice's first thought was that it might belong to one of the doors of the hall; but, alas! Either the locks were too large, or the key was too small, but at any rate it would not open any of them.

However, on the second time round, she came upon a low curtain she had not noticed before, and behind it was a little door about fifteen inches high: she tried the little golden key in the lock, and to her great delight it fitted!

Alice opened the door and found that it led into a small passage . . . she knelt down and looked along the passage into the loveliest garden you ever saw. How she longed to get out of that dark hall, and wander about among those beds of bright flowers and those cool fountains, but she could not even get her head though the doorway.

There seemed to be no use in waiting by the little door, so she went back to the table, half hoping she might find another key on it. This time she found a little bottle on it . . . and round the neck of the bottle was a paper label, with the words 'DRINK ME' beautifully printed on it in large letters. It was all very well to say 'Drink me,' but the wise little Alice was not going to do *that* in a hurry. 'No, I'll look first,' she said, 'and see whether it's marked "poison" or not' . . . for she had never forgotten that, if you drink much from a bottle marked 'poison,' it is almost certain to disagree with you, sooner or later.

> However, this bottle was *not* marked 'poison,' so Alice ventured to taste it, and finding it very nice, she very soon finished it off. 'What a curious feeling!' said Alice [as she began to shrink]; 'I must be [closing up] like a telescope.' And so she was indeed: she was now only ten inches high, and her face brightened up at the thought that she was now the right size for going through the little door into that lovely garden.

The beginning of *Alice in Wonderland* is a fitting illustration for the whole of our passage. For here in the middle of Matthew 19 we find a young man stuck (metaphorically speaking) in a long dark hallway at the edge of a lovely garden. And, like Alice, he is stuck, not because he doesn't have the right key, but rather because he is too big. This "young" (Matthew's description), "rich" (Mark's description), "ruler" (Luke's description) is too big to fit through the impossibly small door of the kingdom of heaven. He is like a giraffe or an elephant or a camel (yes, a camel!) trying to squeeze its way through the tip of a tiny sewing needle.

The Rich Man's Question

From the start of this story, however, this "camel" doesn't look too tall or too wide or too hefty. In fact, this camel is somewhat commendable in his "smallness" of appearance and action. He is to be commended for coming to the right person, Jesus. In Mark's version he "ran up and knelt before" Jesus (Mark 10:17). He is also to be commended for coming with the right (okay, half-right) question: "Teacher, what good deed must I do to have eternal life?" (Matthew 19:16). This question, despite its obvious flaws, displays his fear of God, his recognition of Jesus' authority, his genuine concern for his own soul, and his belief in life after death—the "attainment of the resurrected state."[1]

I think if most of us were honest we would admit that we think very little about life after death. It is simply not our everyday preoccupation. It is not what makes us restless. It is not what worries us. Our biggest concerns usually revolve around missing out on the benefits of *this* life. Most of the so-called important questions we ask have something or other to do with the here and now. They are earthbound questions. But this man appears to be genuinely concerned about life after death, not simply and superficially about this life. So this man's question, though he himself will prove to be full of love for the present world, is the right question in that it asks "*the* essential question."[2]

His question is a good question, but it is not the perfect question; its imperfections are found right in the middle—"what good deed must I do?" The words "deed" and "do" are problematic. By those words this man implies a piety of achievement that stands in direct contrast to Jesus' teaching in Mark

10:15 that one must "*receive* the kingdom of God like a child" and Jesus' modeling in 19:13–15 of that reception—those children brought to him for blessing. Instead of coming to Jesus helpless, dependent, as small as a child, this young ruler comes as a man, a rich man, an able man, a good man. But Jesus will attempt to show him (commendable as he may be) that he is still far too big for the wonders of Wonderland!

The Question of Goodness

This is why Jesus says to him in essence, "I see by your very question that I need to make you smaller. Take and drink of these words." Matthew records it this way: "Why do you ask me about what is good? There is only one who is good" (v. 17a). With the first half of this response, Jesus basically asks him, "Who is really good?" And the answer, Jesus reminds him, is that God alone is good (cf. Mark 10:18b). Here Jesus does not deny his deity or his own goodness; rather he spotlights the unique goodness of God in the hope that this man will recognize that the only way to obtain eternal life is to be utterly reliant not upon sinful self but upon a good and gracious God.

It follows then that after Jesus has reminded this man (in v. 17a) that God alone is "good," next (in vv. 17b–19) he specifically tests this man's so-called goodness by means of God's good law. In essence, our Lord asks him, "Are you good?"

> If you would enter life, keep the commandments. . . . You shall not murder, You shall not commit adultery, You shall not steal, You shall not bear false witness, Honor your father and mother, and, You shall love your neighbor as yourself.

Jesus gives no new spiritual insight or revolutionary teaching here; rather he takes this Jewish man back to the heart of the Jewish religion: the Ten Commandments (Exodus 20; Deuteronomy 5) and Leviticus 19:18, the most quoted verse in the New Testament from the Pentateuch. Christ understands well that if we feed on the heart of the Law—the inward and outward ethics of it—we should quickly learn how bad our life is in the sight of a truly good God. We should learn, as the Apostle Paul taught and discovered for himself, that "through the law comes knowledge of sin" (Romans 3:20; cf. Galatians 3:24).

Like a sword, Jesus here wields the Law of God to sever the plastic armor of this man's goodness and tear away his robe of self-righteousness in order to expose the reality of his not-good heart. And *how* our Lord strikes him and wounds him with the Word is most fascinating to me. Take a good look at verses 18, 19. Here Jesus does something very interesting with the Ten Commandments. He *omits from* them (if I can put it that way). He makes two omissions.

First, he left out the first four commandments, the first table of the Decalogue. Why do that? Why, to this particular man, does our Lord make this noticeable omission? Our Lord's quote from Leviticus 19:18—"You shall love your neighbor as yourself"—provides the answer. By quoting only from the second table Jesus places the mirror of *neighborly love* before this man's face, saying, "Hey, how do you look? Have you defrauded anyone to make your fortune [see Mark 10:19, where Jesus adds "Do not defraud" to the commandments]? Have you made your riches through exploiting the poor? Have you been generous and compassionate, rich man with your wealth, young man with your vigor, rich young ruler with your judgments? Have you truly loved your neighbor as much as you love yourself?"

The first intentional and ingenious omission is the first four commandments. The second omission is the last commandment, the Tenth Commandment, which is, "You shall not covet" others' possessions (Exodus 20:17). You would think that of all the commandments Jesus would have cited to this rich man, the last commandment would have been first. So why, to this particular man, does Jesus make this small but significant omission?

The reason is that the rest of Christ's response will focus exclusively on this command. This man's particular vice, his obvious moral defect (as divinely detected by Jesus), is his failure to adhere to the Tenth Commandment. This man is filled with the disease of coveting. And so after this man declares his innocence—"All these I have kept. What do I still lack?" (v. 20)—Jesus lovingly (see Mark 10:21) applies the painful remedy. Jesus asks him in effect, "Have you really kept all the commandments? All of them? Every single one of them? Ever since you were young? Well, how about, 'You shall not covet'?" He puts it this way: "If you would be perfect, go, sell what you possess and give to the poor, and you will have treasure in heaven; and come, follow me" (v. 21). Jesus calls him to perfection, "perfect" in the sense of keeping both tables of the Law. He is to love others, especially the poor (i.e., widows, orphans, blind beggars, and perhaps Christ's followers), and follow (i.e., love first) Jesus.

The rich man knew he lacked something. That is why he asked Jesus what he asked. But he thought whatever it was he *lacked* could simply be *added* to his life. But the one thing he lacked was a childlike dependence on Christ. So our Lord, seeking to bring this man to the point of such dependence, challenged this rich man to cut off his riches ("sell all that you possess and give to the poor") and challenged this rich ruler to cut off his self-rule ("come, follow me"). Here our Lord demands not almsgiving (giving something to someone) but everything (give everything to others and everything to me).[3] He demands everything.

> Give everything to others—love your neighbor.
> Give everything to Christ—love the Lord your God.

Well, such a challenge was too hard, too impossibly difficult. The arrow of Christ's command struck the young man's Achilles' heel. The weight of just the Tenth Commandment crushed him. This man who only moments ago knelt before Jesus enthusiastic and expectant now stood up, turned his back on our Lord, and "went away sorrowful" (v. 22). Why? There is only one reason given: "for he had great possessions" (v. 22), or we might rightly say, because great possessions had him.

At the very core of this man who led an exemplary but idolatrous life lay the sin of coveting. He sincerely loved things more than he loved God, more than he wanted eternal life. "Majestic mighty" money was the highest of his gods.[4] Here we see the Parable of the Soils at work. We see the "deceitfulness of riches" (13:22) grow like a thousand thorns, moving up and around this man's body until the seed planted in his heart is choked. Here we see a man strangled to death by mammon.[5] He walked away sad. He walked away bigger, taller, fatter, and deader.

The Danger of Riches

In *Teaching a Stone to Talk*, Annie Dillard recalls the tragic story of the Franklin expedition to the North Pole. In 1845 a group of English explorers died because they were ill prepared for the challenges they would face. Instead of providing room on board their two ships for storing additional coal for the steam engines, these careless adventurers used the space for a large library, a barrel organ, china place settings, and cut-glass wine goblets. Needless to say, when they ran out of coal, as they did, their books and tea cups and ornate musical instruments were not enough to warm their freezing bodies. Every member of that expedition died. Sadly, 128 men lost their lives.

Years later when the search party found the remains of the men who had set off to walk for help, they discovered one skeleton dressed in a fine blue cloth uniform edged with silk braid, sadly grasping in his hand a place setting of sterling silver flatware. What a picture of their deadly foolishness.[6]

This rich young ruler in Matthew acted as foolishly as that dead British explorer. But instead of trying to carry sterling silver through the frozen Arctic, this man was trying to carry all his possessions through the tiny entrance into the kingdom of God. And just as all those explorers had to do was make sure their ships had more coal and fewer luxuries, so too all this rich man needed to do was unhinge this huge weight from his back and walk as a small man, a poor man, a humble man, a childlike man . . . walk in faith uprightly through the small and narrow way.

However, this is easier said than done. Jesus knew that. That is why, if you look again at our passage, he turned to his disciples and said to them:

> Truly, I say to you, only with difficulty will a rich person enter the kingdom of heaven. Again I tell you ["children," Mark 10:24], it is easier for a camel to go through the eye of a needle than for a rich person to enter the kingdom of God. (vv. 23, 24)

Mark Twain once wrote, "It ain't those parts of the Bible that I can't understand that bother me, it is the parts that I do understand."[7] I think Jesus' words in verses 23, 24 are understandable but bothersome. And because they are so very bothersome it is tempting for us to make them incomprehensible. That is, to take these clear words and blur them, to convince ourselves that these words were addressed to this particular rich man and his particular sin at this particular time in history, and thus it is more than appropriate for us modern disciples to "whittle away the radical demand [and] make it more reasonable" and to create, as is necessary, "an imaginary 'riches danger line'" that we always manage to fall below, for we can always find someone who earns more and has more than we do.[8] "He's the rich man," we say, "not me!" It is tempting to make Christ's words apply to anyone other than us. But to do so would be both wrong and unwise.

We well-to-do Americans can indeed take some comfort in the fact that Jesus does not categorically condemn wealth and in the fact that our Lord never commanded every rich person he encountered to sell all of his or her possessions. In fact, this is the only incident we have of such a command. However, based on the fact that Jesus in the Gospels has nothing positive to say about money,[9] that he never speaks of wealth as a blessing, that he repeatedly uses illustrations regarding the abundance of possessions to be "toxic to the soul,"[10] it is fair to state that wealth (in and of itself) can be and often is a great barrier or roadblock on the path to paradise. In other words, nothing fattens the camel like an abundance of worldly goods!

For me, one of the great surprises of this text is that Jesus, who certainly was testing this particular rich man to see if he would covet the kingdom more than cash, turns to his disciples and says nothing at all about coveting. Instead he says, "only with difficulty will a rich person enter the kingdom of heaven" (v. 23). I expected him to say something along the lines of, "How difficult it will be for those who covet or hoard or love riches to enter the kingdom!" But that is not what he said. Our Lord here recognizes an inherent danger in having much money.

We think of the rich as privileged, but Jesus consistently saw them as underprivileged. The people of his day saw riches as a manifest sign of the blessing of God, but he saw wealth as a hindrance to spiritual progress. (And that's why it is dangerous!) In Jesus' estimation wealth naturally creates all that makes people too big, too fat, and too adult. Wealth often "deadens the instinct for self-sacrifice."[11] Wealth often fosters the ungodly notion that this world has much to offer. Wealth often numbs our minds to the reality of the joys of Heaven and the torments of Hell. There is always something more on earth to buy or look forward to when one has wealth. Wealth often lures us into believing that everything can be had for a price. In most cases with wealth comes self-indulgence, self-reliance, self-importance, and self-security. Wealth has a way of ruling one's life, ruling one's time, ruling one's vocation, ruling one's commitments, ruling one's concerns. And the whole point of Jesus' "colorful hyperbole" about the camel and the eye of the needle reinforces the truth "that those who are ruled by money cannot be ruled by God."[12]

Thus, while it is true and not to be forgotten that "it is not so much the having of money, as the trusting in it, which ruins the soul,"[13] it is likewise true that it is easier to trust in it if you have it to trust in. And what is required by Christ and his gospel is a childlike faith in the heavenly Father. What is demanded is a poverty of spirit that so often goes hand in hand with a poverty of possessions.

The Impossible becomes Possible

If you are a bit offended or perplexed or aghast, you are not alone. The disciples couldn't believe what they were hearing: "When the disciples heard this, they were greatly astonished, saying, 'Who then can be saved?'" (v. 25). In their minds, if this *good* (seemingly faithful to the Law) and *rich* (obviously blessed) man could not enter the kingdom of heaven, then who on earth could?

Jesus likes what is happening here. Finally the disciples are asking the right question. So here in verse 26 Jesus confirms their thinking. "That's right. No one qualifies!" "Jesus looked at them and said, 'With man this [salvation you speak of; this eternal life he wanted] is impossible, but with God all things are possible.'" Here Jesus answers them in these "absolute terms" in order to impress upon them "that salvation, from start to finish, is not a human achievement."[14] The great won't be let in because they are great. The good won't be let in because they are good. The rich won't be let in because they are rich.

Jonathan Edwards once wrote, "To take on yourself to work out redemption, is a greater thing than if you had taken it upon you to create a world."[15] This world is full of those who think they can enter into a saving relationship with God (and then get to Heaven) any way they like. But how foolish they are, for it would be easier to shape the mountains, to drive the winds, to fill the oceans, to spin the planets, and to scatter the stars than it would be to take upon the work of their own salvation. Salvation, my friends, is a miracle. It is completely beyond the sphere of human possibilities. For, as Paul says, "[T] he mind that is set on the flesh is hostile to God, for it does not submit to God's law; indeed, it cannot" (Romans 8:7). Salvation is impossible for man, but not for God. Here Jesus explains the possibility of the impossible. Here we discover just how Jesus plans to get a fat camel through the eye of a needle. Here is the answer to how any sinful human being is able to enter into the kingdom of God. Jesus later said:

> See, we are going up to Jerusalem. And the Son of Man will be delivered over to the chief priests and scribes, and they will condemn him to death and deliver him over to the Gentiles to be mocked and flogged and crucified, and he will be raised on the third day. (20:18, 19)

There it is! Jesus suffers. Jesus dies. Jesus rises again! And looking upon the holy one of Holy Week, we trust in him like little children trust their parents for bread and clothing and shelter and life. Jesus suffers. Jesus dies. Jesus rises again! And we believe.

Think of it this way. I'll take you back to the introduction to this chapter, where I cited part of the opening scene from *Alice in Wonderland*. The life, death, and resurrection of Jesus Christ is like that potion placed upon the table. It is a free gift given from above. "For God so loved the world, that he *gave* his only Son" (John 3:16a). Alice could choose to drink the potion or not, she could refuse it thinking it was poison or in faith take it, believing it was the remedy for her dilemma. We too are faced with a decision—to drink or not drink, to believe or not believe. "For God so loved the world, that he gave his only Son, *that whoever* believes in him should not perish but have eternal life" (John 3:16). In John 6:53, 54 Jesus puts it this way:

> Truly, truly, I say to you, unless you eat the flesh of the Son of Man and drink his blood, you have no life in you. Whoever feeds on my flesh and drinks my blood has eternal life, and I will raise him up on the last day.

Eat. Drink. Taste and see that the Lord is good. For us the impossible becomes possible when God gives to us a life of faith, a childlike faith (back to 19:13, 14; cf. 18:3, 4) that demonstrates itself in daily dependence—drinking in Christ and eating him up . . . for life. This is the kind of faith Peter expresses, interestingly enough, in Matthew 19:27. Peter said to Jesus, "See, we have left everything and followed you. What then will we have?"

At first I thought Peter's response was yet another thoughtless blunder. I might have said to Peter, "Oh, Peter, you have once again missed the whole point. The real issue here is not possessions but loyalty. It is not about whether or not one gives up one's house, family, and land; it is rather about whether one gives one's ultimate allegiance to Jesus." Yet the way Jesus responded in verses 28–30 corrects my poor perception of Peter. Our Lord saw Peter's reply not as childish but childlike. You see, the early apostles did in fact give up all earthly allegiances. They left their jobs to follow Jesus. They left their families (at least for a time, if not for a lifetime) to follow Jesus. They left their homes and property to follow Jesus. And because of such faith, a faith demonstrated with such sacrificial works, Christ gave them here a word of comfort and blessing. In verses 28–30 Jesus said to them:

> Truly, I say to you, in the new world [think "new heavens and new earth"], when the Son of Man will sit on his glorious throne, *you* who have followed me [thus excluding Judas and including Mathias] will also sit on twelve thrones, judging the twelve tribes of Israel [whatever he means by this, this is no little responsibility and reward]. And *everyone* [not just you] who has left houses or brothers or sisters or father or mother or children or lands, for my name's sake, will receive a hundredfold [in this life? Perhaps. In the next life? Certainly] and will inherit eternal life [what the rich young ruler was after]. But many who are first [like the rich man] will be last, and the last [like Peter] first.

Christian (Noun)

An early edition of *Webster's Dictionary* defined a Christian as "a decent, civilized, or presentable person." The rich man would surely qualify under that easy but faulty definition. The *Random House Dictionary* does a slightly better job with its definition. It says a Christian is one who exhibits "a spirit proper to a follower of Jesus Christ, as in having a loving regard for other persons." That's a bit incomplete, but not completely bad. But here's a better definition, one that comes from my summation of Jesus' teachings: a Christian is simply someone who is *last* who places Jesus *first*; that is, someone who is humble and trusting enough to subordinate all allegiances to Christ. That's what a Christian is.

It was nearly twenty years ago that God, in his infinite and irresistible grace, used this very story in this very Gospel as one of the means of converting me to Christ. For the first half of my life I was told and believed the most common religious lie—that I was basically a good person who occasionally sinned, but did nothing that would ultimately disqualify me from one day entering the joys of eternal life. But then the Holy Spirit taught me what should have been obvious—I was a sinner. Not a good person who occasionally sinned, but a sinner (at heart a very bad person) who was in a continual state of rebellion against a good God and his good Law. I didn't love God. I didn't love others. And I certainly loved myself.

But it wasn't just the first half of this passage but also the second half that the Lord used to change my mind and heart and will. I knew that God alone was perfectly good. I believed that Jesus was indeed the Son of God and the Savior of the world. But at that time in my life he was never my Savior. He was never my Lord, the supreme Lord of my life. And as I prayed to Christ those many years ago and asked him to forgive me and to clean me up on the inside, I also (with this passage in mind) told him (in so many words) that I would "sell everything," that I would put him first in my life—first above self, first above family, first above career, first above education, first above sports, first above every aspect and every love of my life. I told him I would be last, and he would be first!

My brothers and sisters, dear Alice may have unexpectedly entered Wonderland by drinking from that bottle. However, we are given a sure promise that if we drink of Christ we gain that which is most refreshing in the here and now (real life) and that which makes us small enough to enter the kingdom of heaven, where there is indeed (so I'm told) an ever-so-lovely garden and life everlasting. May we one day—by God's grace and goodness alone—find ourselves there.

57

The "Injustice" of a Generous God

MATTHEW 20:1–16

A FEW YEARS ago a friend loaned me a book by Dr. Kevin Leman, cleverly titled *Adolescence Isn't Terminal.* As I skimmed through the book, I came across an interesting story not about adolescence but about Einstein. Leman shares:

> In the late 1930's, a young golf instructor had the formidable task of trying to teach the game to the renowned physicist Albert Einstein. . . . Unfortunately what Einstein had in mental ability he seemed to lack in physical dexterity. His hand-eye coordination wasn't the best, and Einstein kept missing many of his shots. After each miss, the golf pro dutifully pointed out what Einstein had done wrong.
>
> "Take the club back more slowly."
>
> "Choke up on the club."
>
> "Keep your head down."
>
> "Don't open up the club face."
>
> "You're jerking the club when you transition into the downswing."
>
> Finally an obviously frustrated Einstein asked the young golf pro to hand him a few balls, which the pro did. Then, throwing four balls back to the pro at once, Einstein yelled, "Catch!"
>
> The pro dodged and weaved but failed to catch a single ball. Einstein raised his finger and offered, "Young man, if I throw you just one ball, you can catch it. If I throw four at once, you can't catch even one. So when you teach, make only one point at a time!"[1]

In this chapter on Jesus' Parable of the Workers in the Vineyard, I will give you four points—one major point, two sub-points, and one minor point—one point at a time.

A Summary of the Symbolism

In the world of parable interpretation there are a number of schools of thought, two of which I find most convincing. One school advocates that each parable has one main point; the other school advocates that there are as many main points as there are main characters. I think this parable has one main point (thus I side with the first school), but is best preached using three points (thus I side, not in theory but in practice, with the second school). I am truly all things to all people. I offend none and embrace all.

The main point of this parable, or what I'll call the "major" point so as to distinguish it from the "minor" point, is this: *God's gift of salvation is just and generous*. But I'll divide that major point into two sub-points, both of which focus, as the parable itself does, on those workers hired first but paid last.

Let me state the sub-points, unveil the symbolism of the story, and then come back to the sub-points and explain them. If that sounded confusing, welcome to the preparation for this chapter—parables are confusing, as in part they are designed to be. The first sub-point is: *God's gift of salvation is just, so don't grumble about God's undeserved grace*. The second sub-point is: *God's gift of salvation is equally gracious, so don't begrudge God's unequal generosity*.

Here's my shot at the symbolism. (We'll come back to those points in a few pages.) This parable has three main characters. The most important character (theologically) is the master—"the master of the house" (v. 11) also called "the owner of the vineyard" (v. 8). This master, or literally "lord," not "owner" as in verse 8, represents God the Father. Some think he represents the Lord Jesus. Others think this master's "foreman" in verse 8 represents Jesus because the foreman calls the laborers for the judgment, to render to each according to his work. I think the foreman is an insignificant detail to the story. He is not a major character. He is not Jesus. Take him out and the plot is still strong. Why do we have to argue about these things? Listen, the lord of the vineyard is the Lord God, our good God (compare 19:17 with the phrase "because I am good" in 20:15 [my translation]). End of discussion.

Then we have two other main characters—the two sets of laborers. Technically there are five sets—those hired in the early morning, those hired the third hour (9 a.m.), those hired the sixth hour (noon), those hired the ninth hour (3 p.m.), and those hired the eleventh hour (5 p.m.). But the way Jesus ends the story focuses on those hired first and those hired last. And as I noted, he especially draws our attention to the first. Notice we hear nothing from the lips of the last and much from the mouths of the first. Verses 10–15 are all about their attitude (begrudging) and their action (grumbling). In the study of parables there is something called "the law of end stress," which teaches that what is said at the end is most important. That is certainly the case here.

So then, who are "the first" and who are "the last"? "The first" symbolize those who arrive at church before the service starts, and "the last," well you can guess who they symbolize. You all know who you are. More accurately and seriously, "the last" (I'll start with them first) symbolize those believers least esteemed in the eyes of the world (and perhaps sometimes even in the eyes of the church), but those whom, nevertheless, God views highly due to their humility—certainly humility of heart and service ("whoever would be *first* among you must be your slave" [20:27]), but also often humility of skill and status.

What then do "the last" look like? Matthew has paraded a lineup of such people before our eyes—most recently, little children; before them, a leper, two blind men, a centurion ("the last" are not necessarily the poor or powerless), a paralytic, a Canaanite woman, and Matthew, the tax collector, to name a few. They are "the last." "The last" are those picked last in this parable because no one else wants them, no one else thinks they are worth hiring or worth investing in. They are the ignoble, the unskilled, the oldest, the weakest, the likely least productive, and thus the ignored. But the owner of the vineyard (i.e., God) values the "least of these my brothers," if I can use Jesus terminology from 25:40, as much as he values the first, the "best" of the brethren.

So then "the first" symbolize the opposite of "the last." "The first" are those believers (they are Christians as well) who due to their status, wealth, power, talent, beauty, success, fame, or any other trait deemed valuable to the world are much esteemed by the world and often also within the church. They are first in the eyes of man, but not necessarily in the eyes of God. That's my take on "the first" who are "last" (v. 16).

I should mention that some notable and respected scholars would disagree with my take.[2] They would argue that "the first" symbolize the twelve apostles, those literally first to follow Christ, and thus those who might be most tempted to think of themselves as first (as James and John do in 20:21) due to following Jesus first and due to Christ's prophecy in 19:28 about their sitting on twelve thrones and judging all of Israel. I don't have that narrow of a categorization. In fact, I think that at the beginning and in the end the Twelve (minus Judas, plus Mathias), if we are to put them in one of the two groupings, best fit with "the last." These nobodies become somebodies, but I don't think (other than a bout here and there with pride—we've seen that and will see that again) they became "first." They lived and worked and died as humble servants of Christ. This is why in the eternal kingdom they will sit highest, if it is fair to put it that way.

Let me make sense of a few other details of the drama. The master of the vineyard is God. The laborers of the vineyard are members of the kingdom of heaven (i.e., Christians). The work of the vineyard then represents Christian work—either more broadly (the specific work the Lord has given you to do) or more specifically gospel work (reaping those people God has saved through the message of his gospel). I lean toward the latter due to the earlier harvest-laborers language in 9:37, 38 (the only other place the two words "laborers" and "harvest" are used together):

> Then he said to his disciples, "The harvest is plentiful, but the laborers are few; therefore pray earnestly to the Lord of the harvest to send out laborers into his harvest."

In that context the vineyard (and the harvest of that vineyard) is Israel (cf. Isaiah 5; Jeremiah 12). But as Matthew's Gospel progresses, so does the kingdom's boundaries. In 21:39–41 Jesus' Parable of the Wicked Tenants ends with the owner of the vineyard casting out the original tenants (i.e., the unbelieving Jews) and seeking to employ new tenants (believing Jews *and* Gentiles) to pluck the ripe fruit. And then again, the final scene in Matthew is the Great Commission where Jesus teaches that the work of kingdom workers is to make disciples of the nations. Thus, in my view, the harvesting of the vineyard represents Christians working for the world harvest of other Christians.

The final detail is the denarius. In Jesus' day a denarius was simply the amount of money paid to a day laborer for a day's worth of labor. The denarius here represents the gift of final salvation (the "eternal life" the rich young ruler was wanting in the last sermon), or put differently, the eschatological judgment of the just. Notice that the money is given at the end of the day. This fits Old Testament labor laws (Leviticus 19:13; Deuteronomy 24:14, 15), but it also fits New Testament eschatology. Christians are saved now—the moment we trust in Christ—but we will be saved in the future, on the day of reckoning, when the ransom of Christ's death (20:28) will be paid out in full to those who believe. So the denarius is the gift of final salvation given for a day's work—a believer's lifetime of humble gospel service.

That's my *shot* at the symbolism. Now don't shoot me if I have a detail or two wrong. Jesus gave me no divine interpretation to work with. But that's intentional. You can actually misunderstand or misinterpret a detail or two and the point of the story still stands. That's the beauty of this parable. So let's get back to that point and its two sub-points.

Sub-Point One

The point of this parable is this: *God's gift of salvation is just and generous.* The first sub-point is: *God's gift of salvation is just, so don't grumble about God's undeserved grace.* Look again at verses 8–15 (these verses will be the focus of our study because they are the focus of the parable):

> And when evening came, the owner of the vineyard said to his foreman, "Call the laborers and pay them their wages, beginning with the last, up to the first." And when those hired about the eleventh hour came, each of them received a denarius. Now when those hired first came, they thought they would receive more, but each of them also received a denarius. And on receiving it they grumbled at the master of the house, saying, "These last worked only one hour, and you have made them equal to us who have borne the burden of the day and the scorching heat." But he replied to one of them, "Friend, I am doing you no wrong. Did you not agree with me for a denarius? Take what belongs to you and go. I choose to give to this last worker as I give to you. Am I not allowed to do what I choose with what belongs to me? Or do you begrudge my generosity?"

There are two wrong replies to grace—the attitude of begrudging and the action of grumbling. We'll deal with the grumbling first. Of course, the word "grumbled" (v. 11) might remind you of Israel's grumblings in the wilderness.[3] I think Jesus intends for us to make that connection. The point is: don't be like the exodus generation—saved from slavery, saved from the rule of Pharaoh, saved from the Red Sea, only to die without inheriting the promise. They died because they never got past their grumbling. They were never grateful for grace.

If you look at all the references to grumbling in the Bible, you will realize that to God grumbling is as deadly a sin as adultery or murder. The grumblers' camp is not a good camp in which to be.[4] That's why Paul tells Christians not to grumble (Philippians 2:14), Peter tells Christians not to grumble (1 Peter 4:9), James tells Christians not to grumble (James 5:9), and our Lord Jesus, here in this parable in his own way, teaches that same truth. Don't grumble against God.

But as we see this story unfold the way it does, when Jesus gets to verse 8, we are sympathetic with the grumblers of verses 11, 12. When the last get paid first, we cry, "Injustice," and when the last get paid the same amount, we cry out again, "Injustice." The lord of this vineyard has broken the first rule of all economics: the more work, the more pay.[5]

Let's admit this employer does not model fair labor laws. And he is a bit eccentric and irrational. Who hires someone at quitting time—5:00 o'clock? Who pays the same wages for nearly a day's difference in work?

Ah, but parables are not designed to teach business ethics or principles. Rather, parables are designed to get us to think (and act). And here we are not to think (although it is natural to think) alongside the first hired, "Hey, that's not fair." Rather, as Jesus wants (see the summary stress of v. 16), we are to think, "Wow, when it comes to grace, God's generosity transcends human conceptions of fairness." Concerning grace, R. T. France says it this way: "No one receives less than they deserve, but some receive far more."[6] We undeserving sinners are given more than we deserve. Think of it that way.

According to Scripture, everyone deserves damnation; no one deserves salvation. That's justice. If you want to appeal for justice, you'll be putting the noose around your own neck! What then is "unjust" is that some get grace. The lesson here is this: when we emotionally trip over this foundational concept of the Christian message—sinners are saved by grace—we stumble not over God's injustice (although it seems like that) but rather his generosity. Daniel Doriani expresses this idea in this way:

> God's generosity actually takes two forms. He gives gifts we do not deserve and he withholds punishments we do deserve. Sadly, many take God's generosity for granted, so that "Amazing Grace" has become boring grace. It is boring because we no longer think of ourselves as sinners, or at least not as great sinners.[7]

We should be thankful that God is "not fair"—that is, that he doesn't give us what we deserve. We should be gushing with gratitude that it is not some lackey but the Lord himself who goes out to give grace, and goes out so often (five times in our text), and goes out even for those whom no one else thinks are worth going out for. Oh, the grace and goodness and love of God! Who is the subject of most of this parable's sentences? Who's talking? Who's acting? Who takes the initiative? Who calls the workers? Who kindly—"friend" (v. 13)—but firmly corrects false perceptions? The owner of the vineyard—God!

The first sub-point is: *God's gift of salvation is just*—he will do "whatever is right" (v. 4); he will do "no wrong" (v. 13)—so *don't grumble about God's undeserved grace*. Has not the potter the right to do what he wishes with the clay (Romans 9:21)? Don't feel wronged or cheated by God if he seemingly gives more grace to others than you would. Don't be angry or envious if others are loved by God who are not as holy or as hard-working or as long-working as you. Be grateful for being chosen. Be grateful for the opportunity to work. Be grateful for getting paid anything at the end of the day. Don't grumble.

Sub-Point Two

The first sub-point is: *God's gift of salvation is just (or fair), so don't grumble about God's undeserved grace*. The second sub-point is: *God's gift of salvation is equally gracious, so don't begrudge* (look upon with disapproval) *God's unequal generosity*.

We are still studying verses 8–15, looking at them now from another angle. We have looked at the wrong action of grumbling, and now we turn to the wrong attitude of begrudging—"Or do you begrudge my generosity?" (v. 15b; ESV margin, "Is your eye bad because I am good?"). Do you see the play on *God is good* and *you are evil*, or thinking evil, or seeing evil? The focus is on the eye, the evil eye. Have you ever given anyone the evil eye? Well, these workers give it to God. They are not seeing him as good or generous. That's their problem, which is too often our problem. Self-interest, a lack of compassion for others, or a misunderstanding of the nature of grace distorts our clear vision. We see what is good as evil, compassionate as cruel, generous as tightfisted.

God's gift of salvation is equally gracious (every believer equally gets eternal life), so don't begrudge God's unequal generosity (that is, if he wants to give such life to someone who really, really, really doesn't deserve it). Like that sinful woman who wept at Jesus' feet, drying them with her hair; like Zacchaeus, the tax collector; like Cornelius, the Roman centurion; like that thief on the cross.

Fill in the blank of the sinner or sinner group you like least. Let me fill in a name for you, and let me know how it makes you feel:

Don't begrudge God's unequal generosity toward Jeffrey Dahmer.

Most of you know that name and cringe at hearing it. When I did a Google search for him, and typed in J-E-F-F-R the first suggested search was Jeffrey Dahmer. That shows me his popularity has not diminished much. For those of you who don't know Dahmer, I won't say much because his deeds were so wicked, it is hard to describe them in any setting. He killed seventeen young men, and he did so in the most gruesome and grotesque ways.

While in prison, however, Dahmer was sent books and tracts on the Christian gospel. Over time he began to meet with a local pastor. Dahmer himself writes about how he came to grips with how he was a sinner and accountable before a holy God. In a television interview with Stone Philips he said, "I've . . . come to believe that the Lord Jesus Christ is truly God, and I believe that I, as well as everyone else, will be accountable to him." In that same interview he called Jesus his "Lord and Savior." From all accounts—his own, his father's, the pastor's—he came to a saving faith in Christ. He believed and was baptized. Jeffrey Dahmer was baptized in the name of the Father, Son, and Holy Spirit!

Then, one day after attending chapel, a fellow inmate attacked him. He lived. Soon after, while working in the prison gym, he was attacked again. This time he died. Then what? Did Jeffrey Dahmer—the most horrific human being of my lifetime—go into the presence of a holy God? Did he get a denarius? He tortured and killed people, lots of people. Sure, he professed faith in Christ, but he died so shortly after, he hardly had a chance to prove himself worthy of the kingdom.

What do you think about sharing an apple from the tree of life with Jeffrey Dahmer in the new heavens and new earth? Does the thought of it make you sick? Does the thought of it shock all spiritual sensibilities? Well, my brothers and sisters, that's the shock of grace! That's the shock of the gospel. That's the shock of this parable, the parable of the shockingly, super-generous Lord.[8]

Don't begrudge God's generosity!

Minor Point

We come to the final point, what I've labeled a minor point. I label it "minor" because it is of less theological significance to *this* parable (not to the New Testament) and because I might be wrong about my observations.

Once after I preached a sermon, a visitor came up to me and made a number of nice comments about the sermon (which, by the way, I always find better than someone grumbling to me about it). He said, "You preached with great authority." I do try, by God's help, to preach with authority when and where such authority is needed and deeply and obviously grounded in the text of our study. But I want you to know that I am not the authority even if I preach and write with great authority. I may preach or write with authority and yet be absolutely unauthorized in my views. I can be saying something strongly that is not strongly said in Scripture or is not said at all. So never take my authoritative interpretations on an equal plane with the absolute authority of God's Word. That's why in my church we read the Bible aloud before I teach—to make sure my congregation heard something absolutely true.

With that in mind, and with you now likely intrigued about this potentially unauthorized and perhaps unorthodox idea, here is the minor point. I will first say it in a way I feel most fair to the language of the text and then in a second way that is more sensible to our Protestant theological sensibilities. The minor point can be said like this: God's gift of final salvation is offered to those who receive it and work for it (that's controversial). Or it can be said like this: God's grace is not antithetical to kingdom labor and reward (that's better).

In the 1980s and 1990s a debate raged in the American evangelical church over what has been called the "Lordship Controversy." One side advocated that salvation is by grace alone in Christ alone through faith alone, and thus a mere profession of faith at some point in one's life was enough to assure salvation. The other side (the lordship side) held to the traditional Protestant position that salvation is indeed by grace alone in Christ alone through faith alone, but such faith is never alone—it produces fruit. Faith loves. Faith works. Faith obeys. And if such fruit is not found, then the assurance of salvation cannot (should not) be offered. Jesus must be both Savior *and Lord.*

In the academy, the lordship side won the debate. However, outside the academy—in the pew, so to speak—the lordship side lost. Many of you will have grown up, if you grew up in the evangelical church in America, with this cheap grace version of the gospel. If you just said a prayer, raised your hand, accepted the altar call, came forward at the crusade, the deal was sealed regardless of future attitudes and actions.

Such a heresy—I'll call it that, and with authority—is deadly. It's as deadly a heresy as the Jews of Jesus' day saying the sign of circumcision was enough to guarantee salvation. It's as deadly a heresy as the churches today that say the sacrament of baptism does the same. Cheap grace is a deadly plague, and sadly many of us have breathed in too much of that poisonous air, and some of us still breathe it in. And this is why when some of us think "grace," we know there are two rules to the grace game. Rule number one: don't talk about grace and works in the same sentence. Rule number two: don't talk about grace and rewards in the next sentence.

But if your mind is saturated with Matthew's Gospel, the epistle of James, the three epistles of John, the book of Revelation—now that I think of it, the whole of the New Testament—you will see that Jesus and his earliest followers often broke both rules. Too many contemporary evangelicals think "grace" and then think, "Please don't put 'works' and 'rewards' in the same room. Don't even put them in the same zip code." But here in Jesus' *Sola Gratia* sermon, his parable on God's grace alone, he very comfortably snuggles all three in one bed. Grace is in the middle with his arms tightly around works and rewards. And our Lord doesn't find it scandalous.

Where's my evidence for such a bold claim? It's everywhere. First we have the language of grace and work. Jesus calls those in the kingdom of heaven "laborers" (vv. 1, 2, 8; cf. "worker" in v. 14) on earth who "worked" (v. 12). The one thing everyone in this parable does is work, if even for an hour.

Our Lord could have used another analogy. Do you see the word "idle"? It's used twice (vv. 3, 6). He could have worked the idle analogy (don't mind the pun). It would go something like this:

> In the marketplace, the master found some people standing idling by (doing nothing, not working). And then he approached those people and asked them to work. But they refused (stayed idle). And so he picked them up, brought them to his vineyard, and paid them a full day's wages.

Such an analogy, as bad as it sounds, would prove that we do nothing to earn God's grace. But Jesus doesn't go with the idle analogy. He doesn't call his disciples "heirs of the rich and famous," those who need not lift a finger to inherit it all. Rather he calls Christians manual "laborers," workers who do specific work—work in the vineyard, harvesting the fruit of the master's land.

So there is the language of labor. There is also the language of getting paid for one's labor. I've called it "rewards" (because that's a Jesus term used for it), but you can call it whatever you'd like, just as long as we both agree that these laborers, who are freely and graciously and generously given a job, get paid "their wages" at the end of the day.

We can debate whether there are degrees of rewards in Heaven or not (likely not).[9] But we shouldn't debate the concept of rewards—the bestowing of God's bounty of an eternal inheritance (Colossians 3:24) in accordance with a covenant. "Rejoice and be glad," Jesus said in the Beatitudes, "for your reward is great in heaven" (5:12a). What reward? At the very least (and it's very much) the "reward" of eternal life—"theirs is the kingdom of heaven" (5:3, 10).

What's the point of this minor point? Why even bring it up? The point is this: whenever Jesus teaches on grace, as exemplified even here, he teaches lordship salvation. You see, his view stands between two erroneous extremes. He does not advocate that God's grace takes idle people, keeps them idle, and still rewards them with eternal life. And he does not advocate salvation by good works, which is very pharisaical (or Talmudic),[10] or hard work alone, which is very American. Rather, he advocates that no one earns salvation or is owed salvation based on good works or hard work or much work, but those who are chosen by grace are given work to do, do that work, and are rewarded for it.

It might be a minor point here, but it has major implications for the church today.

An Endnote on Einstein

I don't know if Einstein ever improved his golf swing. And sadly I don't think that he ever understood God's grace—the forgiveness of sins offered in and through the person and work of Jesus Christ. But he did once say this theological statement, in his usual inquisitive and witty way: "I want to know God's thoughts. The rest are details." Well, here in 20:1–16, through the teaching of our Lord Jesus, we don't learn *all* of God's thoughts, but we do learn this important "detail" about his grace: *God's gift of salvation is just and generous.*

So don't grumble. Don't begrudge. Be grateful for God's amazing grace.

58

The Greatness of Going Up to Jerusalem

MATTHEW 20:17–28

FOR HIS COLLEGE APPLICATION ESSAY for New York University, Hugh Gallagher answered question 3A in this way:

> 3A. ESSAY: IN ORDER FOR THE ADMISSIONS STAFF OF OUR COLLEGE TO GET TO KNOW YOU, THE APPLICANT, BETTER, WE ASK THAT YOU ANSWER THE FOLLOWING QUESTION: ARE THERE ANY SIGNIFICANT EXPERIENCES YOU HAVE HAD, OR ACCOMPLISHMENTS YOU HAVE REALIZED, THAT HAVE HELPED TO DEFINE YOU AS A PERSON?
>
> I am a dynamic figure, often seen scaling walls and crushing ice. I have been known to remodel train stations on my lunch breaks, making them more efficient in the area of heat retention. I translate ethnic slurs for Cuban refugees, I write award-winning operas, I manage time efficiently. Occasionally, I tread water for three days in a row.
>
> . . . . I cook Thirty-Minute Brownies in twenty minutes. I am an expert in stucco, a veteran in love, and an outlaw in Peru.
>
> I play bluegrass cello, I was scouted by the Mets, I am the subject of numerous documentaries. When I'm bored, I build large suspension bridges in my yard. . . .
>
> I am an abstract artist, a concrete analyst, and a ruthless bookie. . . . I don't perspire. . . . Children trust me.
>
> I can hurl tennis rackets at small moving objects with deadly accuracy. I once read Paradise Lost, Moby Dick, and David Copperfield in one day and still had time to refurbish an entire dining room that evening. I know the exact location of every food item in the supermarket. . . . I sleep once a week; when I do sleep, I sleep in a chair. While on vacation in Canada, I successfully negotiated with a group of terrorists who had seized a small bakery. The laws of physics do not apply to me.

> I balance, I weave, I dodge, I frolic, and my bills are all paid. . . . I have won bullfights in San Juan, cliff-diving competitions in Sri Lanka, and spelling bees at the Kremlin. I have played Hamlet, I have performed open-heart surgery, and I have spoken with Elvis.
>
> But I have not yet gone to college.[1]

We laugh at that essay (and laugh quite loudly) for a number of reasons, one being that most of us, in applying to a college or for a job, have had to write that what's-so-great-about-me essay or resumé cover letter. We also laugh because such unreserved and exaggerated self-promotion is humorous. However, as we will be reminded of now, there is nothing funny about prideful ambition in those who seek to follow Christ.

Apostolic Idiocy and Indignation

In 20:17–28 prideful ambition rears its ugly head from those who should now be the least likely candidates, the twelve apostles. We'll especially see it in James and John by means of their mother. Look with me first at verses 20, 21.

Then the mother of the sons of Zebedee came up to him with her sons, and kneeling before him she asked him for something. And he said to her, "What do you want?" She said to him, "Say that these two sons of mine are to sit, one at your right hand and one at your left, in your kingdom."

> This mother's question is cowardly, commendable, and condemnable. It's cowardly in that it's not so much her question as her boys'. She's not the coward—they are. Notice that when Jesus replies in verse 22, he talks around her to them. The "you" (second-person plural) in that verse is the two boys. They're acting like bashful schoolchildren on the playground pushing their bravest friend over to the girls. "Go ask Susie if she'll go to the dance with me." They are cowering behind their mom's shirt. Does Jesus roll his eyes here? Does he think to himself, *You're getting your mother to ask your question?* What he did with his eyes and thought in his mind, we don't know. What we do know is that he brought these sons of thunder down to earth with his cup question (which we'll get to in a minute). The cup question is about courage. *Do you two cowards have it?*

This question is cowardly. It is also commendable. It's not as commendable as her posture (she humbly kneels before Jesus before she asks their less-than-humble question), but it's commendable. Its source is faith in Christ and his kingdom. To ask this question shows that they believe in the kingdom of heaven—what Jesus has been teaching about himself, his coming reign,[2] and the community that will exist under his Lordship.[3] They don't perfectly understand the concept, as shown in their question, but they do think Jesus' vision will succeed.

I glean at least two lessons for us here. First, we should recognize that true faith and real error can be mixed in the heart of the best Christians. Can a high view of Jesus coexist with a higher view of self? Yes. Can great faith and great ignorance be wed in one brain? Yes again. Thus we ought to persistently pray for purity, and we ought to gently seek to purify one another. I'll put it this way. We should be willing to push aside the crumb caught in our brother's beard and wipe off the spaghetti sauce stuck on our sister's cheek. We ought to care enough to correct obvious impurities. Second, as much as we shake our heads in dismay or wag our fingers at them in shame, nevertheless "we may," as Charles Spurgeon said, "question ourselves as to whether we think as much of our Lord as [they] did."[4] Do we believe Jesus will reign? Do we give a passing thought to the eternal kingdom? Do we hope to get a good spot in it?

The question of verse 21 is cowardly but commendable. However, it is ultimately condemnable. The context of their question makes it especially condemnable. Right after Jesus speaks of his brutal death in Jerusalem (vv. 18, 19), "then" (v. 20)—that conjunction will introduce such a great contrast—comes the ambition question. Jesus will be lifted up on a tree, and these boys want to be lifted up to thrones number two and three.

But surprisingly, with such a striking contrast in mind, Jesus is gentle with them. He says, in I think a sad but sympathetic tone, "You do not know what you are asking" (v. 22a). It has the same feel as "Father, forgive them, for they know not what they do" (Luke 23:34) and here it is not "do" but "ask." What is condemnable to Jesus is not the questioners (he loves them) but their question.

Let me add that I don't think these two (or three) are alone in their pride. Joining them are ten angry men. I'll toss them into the pride pool too. In verse 24 we read, "And when the ten heard it [the question asked], they were indignant at the two brothers." Were they upset because these brothers would ask such an awful question, or were they angry because those two got to Jesus first? I think their indignation comes from their own desire for preference and promotion.[5] I say that only because Jesus' response to all of "them" in verses 25–28 points in that direction. He tells not just the two brothers great but the ten brothers grim just how grim a view of Gentile greatness is.

So I think all twelve men stand before Jesus condemned—guilty of the vice of pride and the sin of vain ambition. And at times I think we all stand shoulder to shoulder with them. The idea of one-upmanship is in us all.

The Correction of the Cross

As I said, Jesus won't condemn them, even though their attitudes and actions are condemnable. Instead he will correct them. And he will correct them by holding out to them (and us) his cross.

In the last two sections in Matthew, Jesus has given us his last-first theology (his view of kingdom greatness), and here he relates that teaching to his own person and work. He says in effect, "Do you want to learn about greatness? Let me teach you about the greatness of going up to Jerusalem. Let me tell you why the cross is so great."

Two reasons are given. First, the cross of Christ is so great because it shows that humble servanthood and sacrificial suffering are exalted actions. Second, the cross of Christ is so great because the two-day death of one man gave eternal life to many.

Jesus' Death as an Example

The first reason—the cross of Christ is so great because it shows that humble servanthood and sacrificial suffering are exalted actions—can be found in verses 22b–28a. We'll look at humble servanthood first. Look again at verses 25–28a:

> But Jesus called them [his indignant apostles] to him and said, "[Cool down,] you know that the rulers of the Gentiles lord it over them, and their great ones exercise authority over them. It shall not be so among you. But whoever would be great among you must be your servant, and whoever would be first among you must be your slave, even as the Son of Man came not to be served but to serve, and to give his life . . ."

Jesus' corrective here is straightforward: (a) Gentile or pagan rulers rule this way because they view greatness in this way; (b) you are to rule another way because you view greatness in the opposite way; and (c) that way is the way of the cross. And the way of the cross is humble servanthood.

In verses 26, 27 Jesus gives this parallelism:

> Whoever would be *great* among you
>   Must be your **servant**.
> Whoever would be *first*
>   Must be your **slave**.

In Hebrew poetic parallelisms this would be called synonymous or "focusing" parallelism;[6] that is, the first term is nearly the same as the second, but its slight difference *focuses* on the point of it. I'll put the point this way. Do you want to be "great"? Then you need to be a "servant" (*diakonos*)—that is, wait tables, serve others. Do you want to not just be "great" but to be "first" (the first among the greats)? Then you need to be a "slave" (*doulos*)—that is, someone "who has no right or existence on his own, who lives solely for others."[7]

All of us are repulsed by the idea of American antebellum slavery (and rightly so), but few of us would mind a maid or butler around the house 24/7. We ring the bell, and Jeeves comes and says, "You rang, sir?"

"Yes, Jeeves, fetch me my smoking jacket."

"Certainly, sir. I'm at your service."

"Very well, Jeeves, thank you. That will be all for now."

Jesus says, "Christian, think Jeeves." That is, there is no need to sacrifice your brain, but there is much need to sacrifice yourself in order to serve others first and even (what Jeeves rarely does in P. G. Wodehouse's novels) consider "others more significant than" yourself (Philippians 2:3). Here Jesus is teaching his new community a new paradigm, where "the only valid ambition" is the aspiration to serve.[8]

In Plato's *Gorgias,* Callicles states, "How can anyone be happy when he is the slave of anyone else at all?" (491E). This characteristically Greek or "Gentile" assumption and ideal Jesus turns on its head. Our Lord states, if you will, "How can anyone be happy [or perhaps at peace with God, others, and self—truly happy] *unless* one is the slave of everyone else?"[9]

I doubt that I have to tell you how radically countercultural Jesus' paradigm shift was then as it is now. Our culture "ceaselessly" directs us up, up, up; we must "pray almost daily for the wisdom and courage" to go down, down, down.[10] And we go down, down, down because Jesus went down, down, down. He descended into greatness. He went down to go up. Philippians 2:9–11 reveals the last leg of the journey. Matthew 20:28 tells of the first: "even as the Son of Man came not to be served but to serve, and to give his life . . ." Jesus is the ultimate example of servant and slave made great and first. In his life and death Jesus waited on the world. He came to the table and said to all, "I'm at your service." To prove the point he washed his disciples' unclean feet (John 13)! To prove his point he died for unclean sinners. That's humble service, and that is also sacrificial suffering.

Gentile greatness equals no serving, no suffering (it sounds like the way we usually think about the good life); *Jesus greatness* equals the opposite. Look now at verses 22b, 23. Here Jesus replies to James and John:

> "Are you able to drink the cup that I am to drink?" They said to him, "We are able." [We wish they humbly added, "With your help!" but they aren't

> there yet. They knew not what they asked, and they knew not what they answered].[14] He said to them, "You will drink my cup, but to sit at my right hand and at my left is not mine to grant, but it is for those for whom it has been prepared by my Father."

Here, interestingly, Jesus doesn't deny that some people (perhaps even these two) have glory coming to them. (Shall Peter, Susan, Edmund, and Lucy be made kings and queens?) He just says the Father has not delegated that office to him.[15] But the one office he has certainly delegated is that of Suffering Servant. "And," Jesus says in essence, "if you want to follow me, let's talk servanthood and suffering. I will drink my cup of suffering, shame, and death, and you will also sip from it." Of course they would—James, "with shocking suddenness," drank the cup of martyrdom (he was beheaded by Herod, Acts 12:2), and John, "with wearisome waiting," drank the cup of exile and tribulation on the island of Patmos (Revelation 1:9).[16]

"You two (and you all)," Jesus says, "know this—before the crown comes the cross—my cross and yours." In Paul's words, Christians will share in the sufferings of Christ (Colossians 1:24), or in Augustine's words, "In His Passion we see what we ought to suffer" (*City of God*, 18:49).

They are going up to Jerusalem, and there Jesus will be mockingly but truly enthroned "King," as he ironically dies between two crucified criminals, one on his right hand, the other on his left (27:38). That's the picture of Jesus' greatness. James and John's mother didn't see it here, but she would witness it then—"And Jesus cried out again with a loud voice and yielded up his spirit. . . . There were also many women there, looking on from a distance . . . among whom were Mary Magdalene and Mary the mother of James and Joseph and *the mother of the sons of Zebedee*" (27:50, 55, 56).

So in our church era of celebrity Christianity, ecclesiastical self-aggrandizement, presumptuous power plays,[17] dumb-downed worship, truncated evangelistic witness—the removal of servanthood and suffering to make the gospel more attractive to the world (or the worldly, I should say)—let us attach the cross of Christ to our shoulders, let us sign our letters to each other (as I had a pastor in England do to me recently), "Your servant in Christ," and let us join Brother Lawrence, the famous-for-his humility, kitchen-working servant, in praying, "Lord of all pots and pans . . . make me a saint by getting meals and washing up the dishes."[18]

Jesus' Death as a Substitution

Having looked at the first reason (the cross of Christ is so great because it shows that humble servanthood and sacrificial suffering are exalted actions), we come to the second: the cross of Christ is so great because the three-day (Good Friday, Holy Saturday) death of one man gave eternal life to many. The first reason can be shortened to Jesus' death as example, the second reason to Jesus' death as substitution.

With this second reason we'll focus on the top (vv. 17–19) and the tail (v. 28) of this passage. I think the top and the tail form an *inclusio* because they share similar themes and language and can be summarized like this: the Son of Man came to die. In verse 18 Jesus calls himself "the Son of Man," and also in verse 28. He speaks of "death" (v. 18) and being "crucified" (v. 19), and then in verse 28 he speaks of dying as "to give his life."

While these two parts go together, let me divide them so you can better see their significance. Verse 28 is one of the most significant verses in the Bible. So I will save that last verse of our text for last. Let's first focus on verses 17–19.

> And as Jesus was going up to Jerusalem, he took the twelve disciples aside, and on the way he said to them, "See, we are going up to Jerusalem. And the Son of Man will be delivered over to the chief priests and scribes, and they will condemn him to death and deliver him over to the Gentiles to be mocked and flogged and crucified, and he will be raised on the third day."

This is the third Passion Week prediction (see 16:21; 17:22, 23). What is new here is "the specific references to the Gentiles and to the nature of Jesus' torment and execution—mocking, flogging, and crucifixion,"[19] facts that would become the heart of apostolic preaching. What is significant here is that Jesus assures his first disciples, and all those since, that his "violent death [was] not a meaningless accident of history" but part of God's predetermined plan and that he was "not a hapless victim but a knowing partner in the divine strategy."[20] Every possible kind of suffering the world could inflict upon a man—mental, emotional, and physical—flashed before him like a picture.[21] And still Jesus knowingly, willingly, and lovingly headed toward Calvary to gain victory. He gained victory through the full surrender of his life to those who "deliver[ed] him over" (20:19; cf. 27:2)—his earthly enemies but also his holy heavenly Father.

That's the top (vv. 17–19); here's the tail (v. 28): ". . . even as the Son of Man came not to be served but to serve, and to give his life as a ransom for many." Every word in this sentence is a theological gold mine. We will, however, have to limit ourselves to mining only a few of the best nuggets. And we'll get to these nuggets by answering two questions.

The first question is, who died? Jesus died. But who is Jesus?

We know that Jesus had predictive powers, if that's the right term to use. That is, he predicted the future, and the future came to pass. What he predicted in verses 18, 19 occurred. He entered Jerusalem (chapter 21). He was charged and condemned by the Jewish and then by the Gentile authorities (chapters 26, 27). He was mocked, whipped, and crucified (chapter 27). And he rose from the dead (chapter 28). Whoever he is, he is at least a true prophet (21:11).

But, of course, we know that he is more than a prophet. He tells us as much with his favorite self-designation, "the Son of Man." This title refers to the heavenly figure Daniel saw in his vision (Daniel 7), the one coming on the clouds and receiving dominion and glory and an everlasting kingdom.[22] Ah, the strange paradoxes here. When we read 20:28 with Daniel 7:13, 14 in mind we expect to read, "The Son of Man came to rule." We do not expect to read, "The Son of man came to serve." We expect to read, "The Son of Man came to live forever." We do not expect to read, "The Son of man came to give his life" (v. 28). But to Jesus, the Son of Man (Daniel 7) and the Suffering Servant (Isaiah 53, the one whose suffering and death "bore the sin of many," v. 12) are one person. Ah, the glorious mystery of the cross! "The Son of Man" as servant? Wow! The Son of Man as servant via suffering? Double wow!

Who died? Jesus the prophet, Jesus the Son of Man, but also and finally and most significantly, Jesus the beloved Son of God. Now we have heard the announcement, after the baptism and transfiguration, "This is my beloved Son" (3:17; 17:5). Here my view is that Jesus' divine preexistence is assumed, and it's echoed and accentuated in the simple verb "came." Jesus said, "The Son of Man came . . . to give his life." Question: Came from where? Answer: "In the beginning was the Word, and the Word was with God, and the Word was God" (John 1:1). Answer: "Before Abraham was, I am" (John 8:58). Or to use Matthew's language, Jesus is "Immanuel . . . God with us" (1:23). Jesus is the divine, preexistent Son of the living God who "came" from Heaven to earth to die for us.

Recently my church intern, John Higgins, and I got together with Dr. Duane Litfin, President Emeritus of Wheaton College. We got together with him to talk about the art of preaching (he has taught and still teaches homiletics, and his two dissertations were on rhetoric).

Of all the interesting and helpful things Dr. Litfin said, the most penetrating was when he shared that his favorite text to preach is John 17:1–5, which speaks about Christ's pre-incarnate glory. Here are verses 4, 5 of Jesus' High-Priestly Prayer:

> I glorified you on earth, having accomplished the work that you gave me to do. And now, Father, glorify me in your own presence with the glory that I had with you before the world existed.

Litfin said that's the message the church today needs to hear[23]—the Jesus of the Gospels is now glorified in the presence of the Father with the glory he had before the world began. That is the Jesus of today. That is the Jesus we are to worship. Yes, Jesus came to earth. Yes, Jesus healed the sick. Yes, Jesus fed the hungry. Yes, Jesus taught parables. Yes, Jesus suffered. Yes, Jesus died. Yes, Jesus rose again. But now Jesus is seated in Heaven in glory.

That's who died on the cross! Feel free to shout a few Amens his way.

That's who died. Consider too why he died. If you have the *who* wrong—as many cults and world religions today do—then the puzzle piece of *why* he died can't fit into place (so rightly argued Anselm in *Cur Deus Homo*).

Why did Jesus die? There are three key words (two from v. 28) that tell the whole story: (a) "cup," (b) "ransom," and (c) "for."

I'll start with the word *for*. Jesus gave "his life as a ransom *for* many." The word here could be translated "for" or, I think more clearly, "in the stead of" or "in the place of." The preposition here means substitution.[24] One commentator translates it "gift of substitution."[25]

The idea of Jesus as a substitute rubs us the wrong way both because it's something done *for us* and because it's not something done *by us*. Jesus as our example alone—that theory will sell today and always because *we* get to follow him. It's something *we* are to do and seemingly can do. But Jesus as our substitute—he dies in our place for us—that's something done by him and him alone.[26] We can't take any credit for it. We can't boast in self but only in Christ and him crucified. That puny word "for" might be one of the mightiest words in the world!

The second key word is "cup." Jesus speaks of "my cup" (v. 23), "the cup that I am to drink" (v. 22). What is Jesus' cup? Part of the drink is the hostilities that arise from faithful gospel proclamation and living—what James and John experienced. But the other part, the part Jesus alone will drink (did drink), is the cup of God's wrathful judgment upon wickedness.[27] In the Old Testament this cup is the frequent, graphic expression of God's wrath that rebellious sinners must drink.[28]

You see, the original drink from this Holy Grail is a fiery liquid. It's nothing for which you would quest. It would kill you to dip your finger in it. It's the chalice of all of God's wrath against sinners (cf. Psalm 75:8; Isaiah 51:17). Jesus knows he is to drink this and asks God in Gethsemane to take it from him—"let this cup pass from me" (26:39), and then with arms stretched out on Calvary—"My God, my God, why have you for forsaken me" (27:46)—he drinks the cup dry. This cup is more than the cup of bitter suffering; it is Jesus in his body and soul bearing God's judgment due to us upon himself.

Why did Jesus die? He died to appease God's wrath—to drink the cup—and thereby to ransom many: "the Son of Man came . . . to give his life as a ransom for many" (v. 28).

One highly-esteemed Bible scholar says "the many" is not a "fixed number" but rather is a term that "embraces the whole human race" (cf. 1 Timothy 2:6). Do you know who said that? John Calvin. Others are more Calvinistic than Calvin on this term, and they say "the many" refers to the elect or God's people.[29] I'm in this camp, not merely because I make every effort to squeeze oddly-shaped Bible verses into my squarely shaped Presbyterian framework, but because I think Jesus here is borrowing language from Isaiah 53. In Isaiah 53:12 we read that the Servant "bore the sin of *many,* and makes intercession for the transgressors," and before that in 53:8 we read that the Servant was "stricken for the transgression of *my people*." So I think in 20:28 the "many" are "God's people," or here and now "the church,"[30] those "who accept Jesus' offer of forgiveness, made possible by his death, and who commit their lives to him in discipleship."[31]

For the "many"—whether you think "many" means "all" or "some"—Jesus gave "his life as a ransom." Our final key word is "ransom." We still use the word *ransom* today, usually talking about a hostage situation. Kidnappers demand a ransom of two million dollars for the release of the dignitary's daughter or whatever. In the first century it simply referred to the price paid for the release of slaves. It also could refer to money paid in the place of capital punishment.[32] Perhaps in the case of Jesus' death it is good to keep both definitions in mind. Jesus' death paid for our sins (our zillion-dollar debt), releasing us from the servitude of and punishment due to sin.

So do you see the picture here? You are slaves to sin. Through his death, Jesus paid to set you free. You are set free from sin and made a slave to righteousness. You have been freed to serve others first. You have been freed to sacrificially live out the gospel. The answer to the Heidelberg Catechism's first question provides a good summary of all we've learned from this text:

> That I belong—body and soul, in life and in death—not to myself but to my faithful Savior, Jesus Christ, who at the cost of his own blood has fully paid for all my sins and has completely freed me from the dominion of the devil. . . . Therefore, by his Holy Spirit, he also assures me of eternal life, and makes me wholeheartedly willing and ready from now on to live for him.

Why is the cross of Christ is so great? The cross is so great because it shows that humble servanthood and sacrificial suffering are exalted actions and because the two-day death of one man gave eternal life to many.

Another Einstein Endnote

I finished the last chapter with a witty theological quote from Einstein. I thought I'd end this sermon with another. Albert Einstein once said, "Only two things are infinite, the universe and human stupidity, and I'm not sure about the former."[33]

Now, our Lord Jesus, with his significant role in the creation of the universe, would certainly deny the infinity of it (only God is infinite), and I think he would slightly tweak the stupidity statement. Instead of saying humans are infinitely stupid he would say humans are substantially sinful. That is, if the human heart were layered like an onion, and you were able to peel layer after layer until you get to the core, you would peel away layers of friendliness and generosity and compassion, then layers of greed and ingratitude and hatred and idolatry. But then, at the center, you'd find pride. You'd find self-love, self-rule, and self-glory.

This was seen in the rich young ruler, where we might have expected it, but it is also seen in the twelve men closest to our Lord Jesus, the apostles. And the message here is, let's not find it in you and me, brothers and sisters. Or when we find it, let's remove it. Let Christ and him crucified be at the core. Let the cross be the symbol we not merely have around our necks but chained to the core of our hearts.

59

Seeing with the Blind

MATTHEW 20:29–34

AFTER HEARING THE previous sermon on the greatness of the cross—humble servanthood and sacrificial suffering—someone from my congregation quoted to me a verse from a contemporary Irish "poet." He goes by the name of Bono and hangs out with three other guys; they call themselves U2. The verse is this:

> To touch is to heal,
> to hurt is to steal,
> If you want to kiss the sky,
> better learn how to kneel
> On your knees, boy.[1]

The last three lines of that verse are not a bad summary of 20:17–28. If you want to kiss the sky (to be exalted in God's heavenly kingdom), you better learn (humility) how to kneel; on your knees, boy.

With the next pericope in Matthew (20:29–34), I want you to stay there—on your knees, boy (and girl). That is, I want you to stay low to the ground because there you will see those who can't see literally help us to see spiritually. As Jesus, his disciples, and a great crowd traveled out from Jericho, heading for Jerusalem (fifteen miles away), sitting by the side of the road were two blind men. Matthew writes, "And behold [or 'look'], there were two blind men" (v. 30a). We're going to lie low with them and look at them as they look to Jesus.

Look at the Crowd

However, before we look at them and then with them to Jesus, let's look at the crowd. Jesus and the blind men are the major characters, but the minor character is the crowd. I want you to see them first.

Often in Matthew's Gospel he intentionally contrasts different reactions to Jesus. For example, earlier in 9:27–34 Jesus heals two blind men and a mute man who was demon-possessed. Then Matthew records two reactions to those two miracles. First is the crowd. They are awestruck, and they say, "Never was anything like this seen in Israel" (v. 33). That is a good response, an accurate one. Then the Pharisees respond, saying, "He casts out demons by the prince of demons" (v. 34). That's a bad response, and an inaccurate one.

The Pharisees are not found in our current text, but we know enough about them to assume their response. We have seen the veil over their eyes.[2] And we know, as the seven woes of chapter 23 are on the horizon, that Jesus will call out their spiritual blindness: "Woe to you, blind guides" (23:16), "blind fools" (23:17), "blind men" (23:19), "blind Pharisee[s]" (23:26).

But here, before and after the miracle, we have only two reactions. After the blind men "recovered their sight" (look at the end of v. 34), we read that they "followed him." And our text starts (look at the end of v. 29), "a great crowd followed him." The blind men followed Jesus, and the crowd followed him as well. In Matthew's Gospel it's a good thing to follow Jesus. "Follow me," Jesus says, and those who follow him are to be applauded.

However, there is one extra not-to-be-applauded detail about the crowd we should notice. First, they "followed" Jesus (v. 29). Bravo. Hip, hip, hurray. But, second, they "rebuked" the two blind men (v. 31), after those blind men screamed out the greatest profession of faith in Matthew's Gospel: "Lord, have mercy on us, Son of David!" (v. 30c). "The crowd rebuked them, telling them to be silent" (v. 31a).

This rebuke is a small but symbolically significant action. It's symbolic of the crowd's faith, a "faith" that likes Jesus as mighty king, but not Jesus as merciful king, a king who came not to be served but to serve, a king who came to live and die and live again for the least—the outcasts of society, even blind beggars.

Jesus here was intentionally traveling the same route of Joshua's conquest of the promised land. (Remember, in Greek the name "Jesus" is the equivalent of "Joshua" in Hebrew.) So as he is coming through and out of Jericho up to Jerusalem, this crowd likes what it sees. But the irony of the short, significant phrase "followed him" shouldn't be lost on us. We can appropriately add the word "now" to it. They followed him *now*. For we know that while Jesus entered Jerusalem with a great entourage, he would leave the holy city, a week later, dead and buried, alone in a borrowed tomb.[3]

So look here to the crowd, and see that they follow the right Jesus in the wrong way. The lesson for us is not to follow them in the way they followed him.

It's only natural and thus tempting to follow the crowd. I'm sure all of us have asked our mothers for something—can we go to this movie, stay over at that friend's house, or go to that birthday party?—and our mother said, "No, you can't." Then in response our best line of defense was "But everybody's doing it" or "Everybody's going." That line of reasoning never worked on my mother and likely not on yours either. She returned to the old cliché, "If everyone jumped in a lake, would you jump in a lake?" And in my heart I always thought, "Yes. That's why I'm asking you. I want to jump in the lake *because* everyone is jumping in the lake."

We will always be tempted to follow the crowd. And here we should learn there are plenty of people who follow the right Jesus in the wrong way. And thus when they strayed off the hard and hot narrow way to jump in that cool lake, we should not jump in with them.

Jacob Reynolds, the principal of the Irish Bible Institute in Dublin, shared a personal story that relates to this point about the crowd. He was converted to Christ as a young man, in the early 1970s in Ireland. In those days being a Catholic in the Republic of Ireland was much like being a Muslim in Saudi Arabia. It was the state religion. It was a cultural identity marker. If you're Irish, you're Catholic! Well, Jacob's Catholic "faith" was only a matter of going through the motions, as it was for nearly everyone in those days. A new archbishop was recently quoted in the *Irish Times* saying that Roman Catholics need to have a "personal relationship" with Jesus. Jacob said that that kind of talk was never heard in his days.

Jacob started attending a small faith-filled Baptist gathering. There were only about twenty to thirty people. But as a good Catholic (and so as not to offend his family and everyone in town) he would go to Mass before hanging out with the Baptists. The Mass he attended was at the Church of Our Lady of Lourdes, a large church in downtown Drogheda. These were the days when 95 percent of the Irish population went to Mass. So on a Sunday morning there were 2,000 people in attendance. One day as Jacob was there going through the motions of the Mass, he thought to himself, *How can this many people be wrong? How can twenty-five be right and 25,000 be wrong?*

The Gospel reading for that day was from Matthew 27, the story of the release of the notorious prisoner Barabbas. Pilate asked *the crowd*, "Whom do you want me to release for you: Barabbas, or Jesus who is called Christ?" (v. 17). The *crowd* said, "Barabbas" (v. 21). Then Pilate said to them, "Then what shall I do with Jesus?" The *crowd* said, "Let him be crucified!" Pilate said, "Why, what evil has he done?" And the *crowd* shouted all the more, "Let him be crucified!" (vv. 22, 23). So Pilate released Barabbas and had Jesus whipped and delivered over to be crucified (v. 26).

After the priest read that Gospel reading, Jacob thought to himself, *If the crowd was wrong then, they can be wrong now*. He never went back.

In the Gospels, as it often is in life, the crowd is usually going in the wrong direction. Don't follow them. The crowd here followed the right Jesus in the wrong way.

Look at the Blind Men

Next let's look at the blind men. I'll phrase the second point (as it relates to them) like this: *Look, the blind "see" before they see*. My cleverness will be clear in a moment. Look at verses 30–32:

> And behold, there were two blind men sitting by the roadside, and when they heard that Jesus was passing by, they cried out, "Lord, have mercy on us, Son of David!" The crowd rebuked them, telling them to be silent, but they cried out all the more, "Lord, have mercy on us, Son of David!" And stopping, Jesus . . .

Jesus does what? He doesn't rebuke them—"Hush! Be quiet. Not now. My time is not yet at hand" (cf. 9:30). No. He doesn't rebuke them this time because his time is at hand (20:18, 19). He is going up to Jerusalem to go up on a cross. And it is his reluctance to denounce such titles—Lord, Son of David, and with those, Son of Man and Son of God—that will get him where it got him.

"And stopping, Jesus called them and said, 'What do you want me to do for you?'" (v. 32). "Do you want money? Or do you want something more from me? Do you really believe that I'm the Son of David and thus able to cure blindness, your deepest need?" "They said to him, 'Lord, let our eyes be opened'" (v. 33).

These guys are blind, yet they *see* Jesus as the Davidic king and as, I think and will argue for, the Lord God. In other words, they get Jesus' identity. Of all people, they see him for who he is!

Let's see what they see. First, they see Jesus as the Davidic king. If you were to ask me, what are the five most important chapters in the Old Testament? I would say, "Genesis 1 (leading up to Genesis 2, 3—creation and the fall), Genesis 12 (God's covenant with Abraham that through Abraham the Lord would bless the nations, repeated in Genesis 15 and 17), Exodus 20 or Deuteronomy 5 (the Ten Commandments), 2 Samuel 7 (God's covenant with David), and Isaiah 53 (the Suffering Servant). Now we can argue if my top five are your top five (would you substitute Psalm 2, 110, Deuteronomy 4, or Jeremiah 31 for one or two of mine?), but I will wrestle and pin you hard to the floor over 2 Samuel 7. I am bigger than most people. Don't fight me over that one.

In 2 Samuel 7 God promised David an eternal king and kingdom through his offspring. Here are some of the key verses:

> [T]he LORD declares to you [David] that the LORD will make you a house. When your days are fulfilled and you lie down with your fathers [when you die], I will raise up your offspring after you, who shall come from your body, and I will establish his kingdom. He shall build a house for my name, and I will establish the throne of his kingdom forever. (2 Samuel 7:11b–13)

Matthew's Gospel begins, "The book of the genealogy of Jesus Christ, the son of David . . ." (1:1).[4] In 12:23, after a great miracle, the crowd asks, "Can this be the Son of David?"—that is, the Messiah, the Christ, the promised offspring of David (cf. John 7:42). Then that question is answered in faith by three unlikely candidates—children, crying out in the temple, "Hosanna to the Son of David!" (21:15); a Canaanite woman (a female Gentile): "Have mercy on me, O Lord, Son of David" (15:22); and two sets of two blind men, who share the chorus, "Have mercy on us, Son of David" (9:27; 20:30, 31). Moreover, the final and climactic time we hear the term "Son of David" comes in Jesus' dialogue with the Pharisees. In his complex question to the Pharisees he asks:

> "What do you think about the Christ? Whose son is he?" They said to him, "The son of David." He said to them, "How is it then that David, in the Spirit, calls him Lord, saying,
>
> 'The Lord said to my Lord,
> Sit at my right hand,
> until I put your enemies under your feet'?
>
> If then David calls him Lord, how is he his son?" (22:42–45)

Jesus silenced them then (22:46). But he doesn't silence us now. With those Jewish children, that Gentile woman, and these two blind men, we shout, "Jesus, you are the Son of David! You are the promised king, who came from David's line to rule an everlasting kingdom." We shout and celebrate what Paul calls the gospel—"Jesus Christ, risen from the dead, the offspring of David" (2 Timothy 2:8).

As Jesus connects the terms "Lord" and "son of David" in 22:41–45, so these blind men make the same connection. These two men give eyewitness testimony (minus the eyes) to the true identity of Jesus. He is both the human

"Son of David" and the divine Lord God. Three times they call Jesus "Lord." Each time they open their mouths, that's the first word out.

The term "Lord" (*kyrios* in Greek) could simply mean "sir," like when the waiter comes to your table and says, "Sir, can I take your order?" It's just a term of respect. But here I think it means much more than that from them, and certainly from Matthew as he has chosen to record it for the church (in his Gospel only true believers call Jesus "Lord"). They ask Jesus and him alone (they don't ask him to ask God) to do what only God does in the Old Testament[5] and what Isaiah's Servant will do when he comes[6]—open the eyes of the blind. Their "Lord" equals "Lord" in the Old Testament because it's combined with the title "Son of David," a plea for mercy, a specific request for sight.

Think of the times the prophets cured the blind. You can't think of any? Okay.[7] Think of all the times the apostles opened the eyes of the blind. You can't think of any? Okay. Think of the times today's faith healers have given sight to the blind. You can't think of any? How about Jesus? Jesus alone in the Bible and Jesus alone in world history (as far as I'm concerned) gives sight to the blind. Why? Because Jesus alone is the divine Son of God.

After church I will sometimes ask my little ones what they learned in Sunday school. Let's say, for example, the story was about the miracle of the man with the withered hand. With something like that I might start with a simple question like, "So who performed that miracle?" Charlotte, my youngest, might say, "God." And I'll say, "Well, yes, dear, God, but 'Jesus' is the better answer." Then Simeon, her slightly older brother, will correct me. "But, Dad, Jesus is God." Fair enough. Here I want all of you to repeat after my brilliant boy, "Jesus is God. He is *kyrios*, the Lord God Almighty."

Throughout the Gospel of Matthew the persistent underlining question is, who is Jesus? or perhaps better, is Jesus who Matthew says he is, especially at the top and tail of his Gospel? Is Jesus Immanuel, "God with us" (1:23) and thus with us always until the end of the age (28:20)? Is Jesus the Son of David, the King of Israel (1:1), for the nations (28:19)?

In chapter 21 (and I'll add this transition passage, 20:29–34), as one scholar puts it, "Matthew gives us what we can fairly call a *summary Christology*. Here all that Jesus is and has shown himself to be so far in this Gospel is summarized in a comprehensive way for the church."[8] This scholar divides chapter 21 like this: Jesus is:

The Merciful Lord
The Modest King
The Mighty Prophet

Whether those divisions and designations are right or not, we shall see. But what we are certainly to see here is that these blind men see. They "see" before they see. They see Jesus as the Son of David (the promised King) and Jesus as Lord (the merciful and powerful God of Israel). And we are to see him as they saw him.

Look at Jesus

First, we looked at the crowd, and we saw that they followed the right Jesus in the wrong way. Second, we looked at the blind men, and we saw that in cases like this the blind "see" before they see. Finally, we will now look upon Jesus. I'll phrase the final point this way: *Look, Jesus acts as they ask.* The two blind men ask Jesus to act as merciful Lord, and that is how he acts. Note again verses 31–34.

> The crowd rebuked them, telling them to be silent, but they cried out all the more, "Lord, have mercy on us, Son of David!" And stopping, Jesus called them and said, "What do you want me to do for you?" They said to him, "Lord, let our eyes be opened." And Jesus in pity touched their eyes, and immediately they recovered their sight and followed him.

Here Jesus acts as *Lord.* They ask for restored sight, and he restores their sight. He does it "immediately." He makes no magic incantation. He needs no mediating staff or rod. He offers no prayer to Heaven. "What do you want *me to do* for you?" Me? Jesus, do you mean to say that the powers and prerogatives God alone possesses you also possess?[9] This miracle is a divine miracle. Jesus acts as God alone would and could act. He acts as they ask. They ask for the Lord to heal their blindness, and the Lord heals their blindness.

Yes, here Jesus acts as Lord, but note also that he acts (as they ask) as *merciful* Lord. Verse 34 is a "touching" verse, in both senses of the word: "And Jesus in pity touched their eyes, and immediately they recovered their sight and followed him." Here Matthew tells us what Jesus felt and did. He felt "pity," or it can be translated "compassion," a common enough characteristic of his (cf. 9:36; 14:14; 15:32). It's that deep-down feeling of heartache for someone. One scholar translates the blind men's plea as "Have a heart for us, O Lord, Son of David!" and translates Jesus' internal reply as "Jesus' heart went out to them."[10]

His heart went out to them, as did his hand or hands. "Jesus in pity touched their eyes." Here he heals not by word but by deed and by deed alone—a mere touch. This is so very Matthew, and so very Jesus—he touches the untouchables. He has no problem curing with a word from a distance

(8:5–13). But whenever "the disease is particularly loathsome (leprosy or blindness with its running sores), Jesus *touches* it (cf. 8:3; 9:29). Jesus moves in where others usually" move out or move away or move on.[11] Look here at Jesus! What deep-hearted mercy from the merciful Lord! This Davidic king, greater than Solomon, "delivers the needy when he calls, the poor and him who has no helper" (Psalm 72:12).

Recently my wife, Emily, and I got away for two days. We went to Carmel, Indiana. All the flights to Cancun were booked. She was there for a one-day conference. I was there on vacation. On vacation I edited my old sermon manuscripts at the downtown Indianapolis Starbucks. Let's just say I know how to relax. While there, working but not working, a few homeless men came in and out of the coffeehouse.

One guy was about thirty. He came in with his ragged backpack and a plastic milk crate with his stuff stuffed in it. At first I felt sorry for him. But then he grabbed a table, took out a wad of dollar bills, and began counting them. One, two, three, four. He must have counted to forty. Well, my pity turned into indignation. I thought to myself, *You're young. You're fit. You're seemingly of a right mind. What are you doing? Stop conning people at the central city square and get a job, you bum.* Maybe I need a real vacation.

But when another man walked in, and he was old, unfit, not in his right mind, I pitied him. And if he asked me for money, I would have given him something.

In Jesus' day beggars would congregate outside the city walls to ask travelers for money, much like the homeless today hang out at the train station, near a ball park, or outside (or inside) coffeehouses. When Jesus encountered these blind beggars outside of Jericho, he encountered two men who had lost their livelihoods. Note that they "recovered their sight," which likely implies that they once could see, they once had a way of making a living. But now they join "the guiltless poor," as Jeremiah would call them (Jeremiah 2:34)—widows, orphans, the mute, the lame. That is, through no fault of their own they had to rely on the mercy of others to live. These men spent their days outside the city, without shelter, sitting on the ground, calling out to each person who passed by, "Please, can you spare some change?"

Imagine having this "livelihood." Day after day person after person ignores you or gives you a sad smile you cannot see. Someone tosses a coin in the coffer. Someone gives you a pair of old gloves or a worn, oversized, or undersized garment. But nobody stops to talk to you. Nobody stops to touch you—except the King of the Nobodies—Jesus of Nazareth! He hears their cry. He stops to talk. He stops to touch. He stops to put a stop to their suffering.

The merciful Lord stops to lift up "those who are bowed down"; the merciful Lord stops to open "the eyes of the blind" (Psalm 146:8). With one touch these blind men see. They see the beauties of Jericho, a city in the desert that is full of life—fresh water, palm trees, fruits, etc. They see each other for the first time. "Bartimaeus, son of Timaeus [Mark 10:46], so good to finally see you, friend." They see Jesus. They see Jesus spiritually and now literally. They see "the light of the knowledge of the glory of God in the face of Jesus Christ" (2 Corinthians 4:6).

My brothers and sisters, just think about the compassion here. Coming out of verses 17–28, don't you think Jesus has enough on his mind—his inhumane torture and brutal death? Crucifixion was the worst way to die.[12] And yet here he stops to put himself in their shoes and to get them out of their shoes. But why? Why, when the mission of the cross was so close at hand, did he take time to bother with these blind beggars—men "at the bottom of the social scale,"[13] the "no-accounts in Israel,"[14] and perhaps even religious outcasts? Note they are sitting, not traveling, as they should be, to Jerusalem for the Passover. Why them? Why then? The reason is that many of the "many" he would ransom (20:28) would be (and still are) from the lowliest of the low. The reason is that he is the compassionate King of everybody and of the nobodies.

Come to the Compassionate Christ

Now listen and listen carefully. Let me end not with a summary of all we have learned (points one, two, and three), but rather with a plea. Here it is.

If you're not a Christian, I don't know what you are thinking. I don't. Look at this merciful man, the Lord Jesus Christ. Look at the claims of Christ. But look also at the compassion of Christ. The compassion of Christ should be enough to soften your hard heart. Enough with your excuses. Your rebellion against the King stops here. Put down your arms, and throw up your arms in surrender. The compassionate King has come to conquer your heart. He is here today to break down the walls of your personal Jericho.

Come to him—to this compassionate Christ! Come to him as these two blind men came to him. They never saw Jesus' miracles (how could they?), and yet they believed. "Faith comes from hearing" (Romans 10:17), not from seeing. You don't need to see in order to believe; you need to believe in order to see. You need to listen to the truth of the gospel.

Come to him—to this compassionate Christ! Come to him as these two blind men came to him. Come, as they did, acknowledging your inability to help yourself and the surety that Jesus can help you, even help you with your deepest need.

Come to him—to this compassionate Christ! Come to him as these two blind men came to him. Come, as they did, with faith and faith alone, a faith alone that trusts in Christ's person and power alone and then follows Christ alone. The blind men offered Jesus nothing in return except everything—"they recovered their sight *and followed him*" (v. 34).[15] Mark adds "on the way" (Mark 10:52). Coming out of 20:18, 19, 28 we might add, "on the way to the cross." He's going up to Jerusalem, and those whose sight is restored by him follow him up there as well.[16]

So come to him—to this compassionate Christ! Come to him as these two blind men came to him. Come, as they did, unashamedly confessing before others (cf. 10:32) that Jesus is Christ and Jesus is Lord! And when any so-called disciples of Jesus tell you to quiet down, redouble your efforts. With even greater determination, shout over the noise of hypocrisy, "Lord! Lord! Lord! Son of David! Son of David! Lord, have mercy on me!"

60

The Son of God on a Child of a Donkey

MATTHEW 21:1–11

SOON AFTER WE ARE BORN into this fascinating but fallen world, a nurse takes our fingerprints and footprints. As you know, this is done to help our parents and the hospital properly identify us. Today, of course, there are other more high-tech ways of identifying individuals. Eye scanners are used in some workplaces, and surveillance cameras are now used almost everywhere. Some cameras, at airports and government buildings, even have the capability of taking a picture of a person and then making an accurate identification simply by noting a few unique facial features.

In the familiar story of the "triumphal" entry, we have a story designed, as are all of the stories in Matthew's Gospel, to help us recognize from afar some of the distinct features of Jesus, to help us recognize and respond to him as the promised King, as the one who has come in the name of the Lord.

The Theme of Fulfillment

In this sermon I want us to notice two distinct features. In verses 1–7 we are introduced to the theme of fulfillment, the first feature we are to notice. In this famous scene we see two fulfillments—the fulfillment of a *present command* and the fulfillment of a *past prophecy*.

First is the fulfillment of Christ's *present command.* In verses 1–3 Jesus describes what two of his disciples are to do and what they will encounter in doing it. These two are to go into the village. There they will immediately find a mother donkey and her foal or colt. Those animals will be tied up. These men are to untie them and bring them to Jesus. Jesus adds, "If anyone says anything to you ["Hey, what are you doing?" or "Stop, thieves!"], you shall say, 'The Lord needs them,' and he will send them at once" (v. 3).

What's going on here? Did Jesus prearrange this? Did the owner of these animals have an angelic revelation of the plan? Or was the man merely a follower of Jesus, and when these two said the code word "Lord," he gladly gave them what they wanted? We aren't told. What we are told, in verses 6, 7, is that what Jesus told the disciples to expect and do was precisely fulfilled.

Such a fulfillment (whether natural or supernatural) is, of course, not the main point of verses 1–7. There is another point, another fulfillment that demands our fuller attention. In verse 3 we read that the "Lord needs them" (i.e., these animals). It's a paradoxical statement. Does *the Lord* need anything? Does Jesus, who thus far has walked everywhere—long miles up north and now down south—need these beasts of burden for his overburdened legs? No. That is not the reason he needs them. The reason he needs these animals, and specifically the colt, is to reveal *who* he is and *what* his mission is all about. He needs them to fulfill a *past prophecy*.

In 1 Corinthians 15:3, 4 we are told that Jesus died "in accordance with the Scriptures" and that he rose again "in accordance with the Scriptures." Here in Matthew's Gospel we should notice that Jesus rode into Jerusalem on a colt, of all animals, also according to the Scriptures—in other words, to fulfill a specific Old Testament prophecy, Zechariah 9:9, which Matthew alone of the four Gospel writers quotes.

> This took place to fulfill what was spoken by the prophet, saying,
>
> "Say to the daughter of Zion,
> 'Behold, your king is coming to you,
> humble, and mounted on a donkey,
> on a colt, the foal of a beast of burden.'" (vv. 4, 5)

Zechariah is often labeled a "minor prophet," but his prophecies are of *major* importance, for he is alluded to or quoted over eighty times in the New Testament. And in his most famous prophecy (Zechariah 9:9) he exhorts God's people, whom he calls the "daughter of Zion," to celebrate their future—to rejoice in the promise of the coming King and in the establishment of his kingdom: "Rejoice greatly, O daughter of Zion! Shout aloud, O daughter of Jerusalem! Behold, your king is coming to you; righteous and having salvation is he. . . ."

As we examine the first part of the verse we might think that it is not so extraordinary to think that if God were to raise up an earthly king to bring divine victory and to inaugurate his peaceful kingdom (as v. 10 of Zechariah goes on to depict), such a ruler would be a righteous deliverer. This makes sense. In contrast to the many wicked kings who have preceded him, we would only expect that God's divinely appointed king would conform to the morality of God's Law and bring with him redemption for God's people. So when Zechariah speaks of this king as being "righteous and having salvation," we find nothing in such a description to be out of the ordinary.

Yet, when the prophet goes on to depict this great king as being "humble and mounted on a donkey," we are tempted to think something is wrong. Humble? Donkey? Is this a mistake? Is this a misprint? It should be "glorious." It should be "warhorse." But this is no mistake. This is no misprint. The prophet intentionally wrote of this king being humble.

In the context of the book of Zechariah, as well as the rest of the prophets, this word "humble" does not mean so much "gentle" as it means "lowly" or "bowed down" or even "full of suffering." The word "humble" denotes, as C. F. Keil claims, "the whole of the lowly, miserable, suffering condition, as it is elaborately depicted in Isaiah 53."[1] So, in contrast with the arrogance and violence usually associated with earthly kings, this king, we are told, will be poor and afflicted; he will be a sovereign Lord and yet a suffering servant.

This description and prediction of humility is superseded in its strangeness only by the description and prediction that this king would come "mounted on a donkey." Let's go back to the little donkey for a little while. To prophesy that a king would come in this specific manner must have sounded bizarre to Zechariah's original audience (perhaps as bizarre as it sounds to us), for since the time of King Solomon, when the breeding of horses was introduced, we are given no example in the Old Testament of any royal figure riding upon such a beast. In fact in all of antiquity we would be hard-pressed to find an example of any sort of ruler mounting a colt. The only example comes, oddly and importantly enough, in Genesis 49:11, which talks about the coming king as from the tribe of Judah.

It's laughable to think about a Roman emperor straddled over such a slow, dirty, undignified, and unpretentious beast. It would be like the President coming into Chicago and traveling down the Magnificent Mile on a tricycle. When a king comes to town, the expectation is that he will ride proudly upon a battle steed at the head of a parade of decorated troops, as Alexander the Great did when he rode into Jerusalem in 332 BC. And yet the prophet Zechariah envisions a king who will ride into Jerusalem "mounted on . . . the foal of a donkey." How interesting, to say the least.

Five hundred years passed from the time Zechariah wrote those words.

Five hundred years passed from his penning that peculiar promise. Five hundred years passed until, as all four Gospels tell us, Jesus asked for a colt, he was brought a colt, and he sat on it. The phrase "he sat on them" (v. 7) refers, I think, to the cloaks, not to the two animals at once. This is why Mark, Luke, and John all say that Jesus "sat on it" (Mark 11:7; cf. Luke 19:35), referring to "a young donkey" (John 12:14). He sat on it. The Prince of Peace who comes in peace, who will one day bring the peace of the consummated kingdom (cf. Isaiah 11:1–10),[2] sat on it. He sat and steadied this unbroken beast (an animal "so young that it had never been ridden"[3]), just as he did the winds and the waves (8:23–27; 14:22–33).

Now such words—"he sat on it"—are not as dramatic as something like "It is finished," but they are just as significant. "[H]e sat on it." That's one of my favorite Bible prophecies . . . fulfilled!

Often when I share my testimony, I close by saying *why* I became a Christian and why I remain one. My usual line is this: "I became a Christian and remain a Christian because I am convinced that what the Bible teaches about God, this world, and humanity is true." I'm a Christian, in other words, because Christianity is *true*!

In our tolerant and pluralistic world, the word *true* has fallen on hard times. Pontus Pilate's skeptical reply to Jesus—"What is truth?" (John 18:38)—has become the slogan of our postmodern culture that ironically affirms only one truth: objective and universal truths are not true. "What is truth?" That's the one absolute that underlies much of today's thinking, or lack thereof.

I'm sure every Christian reading this has experienced a conversation like this: We tell our unbelieving friends or family that we firmly believe that Jesus is "the way, the truth, and the life" and that no one can come to God the Father except through faith in Jesus. Then we are given some patronizing remark about how nice it is that we have found religion or something to get us through these tough times. I rarely encounter someone (after I have presented the gospel) who gives me an honest answer. Someone usually says something like "How can you possibly believe that? That's simply not true!" or "To me Christianity is nothing but a crutch for the feebleminded!" How refreshing such a conversation would be in this day and age. But nobody ever calls me a liar or a fool for believing in Jesus. They just say, "That's nice *for you*, but not for me." But when I became a Christian I didn't throw my mind out the door. In fact, quite the opposite happened. I discovered I actually had a mind, a mind that has been designed to love the Lord my God, a mind designed to embrace something called *truth*.

In Acts 26 when the prisoner Paul stood before King Agrippa and his royal court to present his case, the apostle appealed to what I'll call "Scriptural reason." Let me walk you through his amazing testimony to truth. Paul says to Agrippa, "To this day I have had the help that comes from God, and so I stand here testifying both to small and great, saying nothing but what the *prophets* and Moses [the Old Testament] said would come to pass: [and what did the Old Testament say? It said] that the Christ must suffer and that, by being the first to rise from the dead, he would proclaim light both to our people [i.e., Jews; Paul and Agrippa are both Jews] and to the Gentiles" (v. 22). At this point Festus, who is the procurator of the Roman province of Judea, interrupts "with a loud voice," saying, "Paul, you are out of your mind; your great learning is driving you out of your mind" (v. 24). But Paul retorts, "I am not out of my mind, most excellent Festus, but I am speaking *true* and *rational* words" (v. 25).

How can Paul make such a statement—that the gospel he is presenting is true and rational? It is true and rational when one sizes it up, as Paul has just said, with the Old Testament prophetic writings. So Paul appeals to Agrippa:

> For the king knows about these things, and to him I speak boldly. For I am persuaded that none of these things has escaped his notice, for this has not been done in a corner. King Agrippa, do you believe the prophets? I know that you believe. (vv. 26, 27)

That's the question: "Do you believe the prophets?" Implied here is that if you do believe the prophets, you should believe Jesus to be the Christ.

The king, feeling a bit pushed into a corner, feeling that he is now on trial, quickly changes the direction of the conversation. In fact he brings it to an end. He leaves his mind at the door. Agrippa said to Paul, "In a short time would you persuade me to be a Christian?" (v. 28). In other words, he says, "Do you think you can so easily and quickly change my mind? In such a short span of time do you think you can convince me that Jesus fulfills the prophets?" And Paul says to him (I love this final reply), "Whether short or long, I would to God that not only you but also all who hear me this day might become such as I am" (i.e., a Christian).

There are a number of reasons why I was "persuaded" to become a Christian. Perhaps atop the list is that the claims of Christ and his apostles are Scripturally reasonable. The Old Testament said the Messiah would fulfill A, B, C, D . . . X, Y, and Z, and sure enough Jesus fulfills A, B, C, D . . . X, Y, and Z.

Like a complex puzzle the prophet Zechariah (if you look at the whole of his prophecies) gave us two oddly shaped, seemingly contradictory pieces—

piece A and piece Z. He spoke in chapter 9 of the coming of a human king and then in chapter 14 of the coming of a divine king. And it is in the coming and revelation of Jesus Christ and him alone that these two pieces, these apparently incongruent images, integrate. Jesus is the Son of David, and Jesus is David's Lord. In our Lord's first appearance he comes, as the prophets foretold, as the humble king, the king who came to suffer and die for the sins of the world, the king who came to bring salvation. When he comes again, as the prophets also foretold, he will then consummate his kingdom and rule the earth in perfect righteousness and glory.

Why am I a Christian? Why are you a Christian? And why should all who are not Christians become Christians? Such a faith in such a person is reasonable and true. We are Christians because we know that Jesus fulfilled the Scriptures, that in him all the prophecies find their "Amen"; as Paul says in 2 Corinthians 1:20, "For all the promises of God find their Yes in him." All the puzzle pieces of the Old Testament prophecies, when rightly aligned, show us the portrait of Jesus. They identify his facial features—and his hands, feet, and side. They identify him to be just the man, just the king, just the Savior for which we have been looking.

When Jesus told the Parable of the Prodigal Son, the story about the young man who spent his early inheritance on riotous living, he said that when this boy finally hit rock bottom he "came to his senses" (Luke 15:17, NIV). That is, he repented of the behavior that went against rational thought (he repented of his riotous living) and returned (as only is sensible) to his loving and forgiving father. I know that some of us still need to come to our senses. It is my hope and prayer that in presenting Jesus as the reasonable fulfillment of Zechariah's prophecy, presenting him as the King who has come and the King who will come, that even in "a short time" I have persuaded or will persuade you to became as I am.

The Audacity of Jesus' Intentionality

The first feature is fulfillment. Now we will consider the second.

I have never met someone who doesn't have some admiration for Jesus. Sure, I have meet people who may disdain Christianity as a system of thought or the church as a religious institution, but everyone I know admires Jesus for any of a number of reasons—his fearless criticism of the establishment, his championing the cause of the poor, his friendship with the outcasts of society, his compassion for the despised and rejected, his moral teaching on loving one's neighbor, or the fact that he actually practiced what he preached.[4] To this list I will add that most people esteem Jesus for his genuine humility—his washing the disciples' feet, his death on the cross, and yes, his riding into town on a lowly, little donkey.

But however much one might admire Jesus for his attitudes and actions, one still has to come to grips with his claims, claims that appear to be quite the opposite of humility, claims that (how should I put it?) are extraordinarily self-focused. This is the second feature about Jesus I want us to notice. I'll call it "The Audacity of Jesus' Intentionality."

What is most surprising to me about 21:1–11 is not Jesus' humility but his self-promotion. His actions are premeditated. By riding into town the way he rode into town and receiving the praise he received (vv. 8, 9) with no personal protest ("Who me? No. Stop that!"), he is announcing to the world, "The King has come." So the irony of the triumphal entry, if you will, is our Lord's promotion or publication of his *humble* reign!

No matter how you look at it, by mounting that animal and riding it into Jerusalem, Jesus is making a bold statement. He is claiming to be the Messiah. He is claiming to be the fulfillment of Zechariah's prophecy. Now those who don't want to accept this claim and submit to it (or to Christ I should say) may be tempted to brush off this particular action as a mere oversight on the part of the otherwise good and humble teacher from Nazareth. Yet one only has to glance through the Gospels to find in Jesus a pattern of self-promotion.

For example, what are we to make of his "I am" statements in John's Gospel? For example, he said, "I am the bread of life; whoever comes to me shall not hunger, and whoever believes in me shall never thirst" (John 6:35). He claimed, "I am the living bread that came down from heaven. If anyone eats of this bread, he will live forever" (John 6:51). What are we to make of such claims? If we trust in Jesus we will live forever? Really? Who talks like this?

Who would dare claim, "I am the light of the world. Whoever follows me will not walk in darkness, but will have the light of life" (John 8:12)? What complete audacity to claim the world is dark, he alone is light, and one must follow him in order to get out of the darkness. Can you imagine the Dalai Lama or the Pope standing up at the United Nations and saying, "I am the resurrection and the life. Whoever believes in me, though he die, yet shall he live" (John 11:25)? Can you even fathom some preacher today asserting, "Everyone who is of the truth listens to my voice" (John 18:37) or "When I am lifted up from the earth, [I] will draw all people to myself" (John 12:32)? What do you think the media would do to Chicago Mayor Rahm Emanuel (an interesting name to say the least) if he had begun his acceptance speech after his election by saying something like, "Heaven and earth will pass away, but my words will not pass away" (Matthew 24:35)?

Think about the claims of Christ! It is one thing for a man to say, as Jesus did, that we are to love God with all our heart and soul and strength, but quite another thing to say, "Whoever loves father or mother more than me is not worthy of me, and whoever loves son or daughter more than me is not worthy of me" (10:37). In the Gospels Jesus can't stop talking about himself.

We usually disdain people who talk so much about themselves. We are repulsed by anyone who demands our love and obedience, our total allegiance. And yet what is it about Jesus that makes him not only likable but also *believable*? There is perhaps nothing so remarkable about Jesus than the fact that he advanced himself as the object of faith, love, and obedience, and yet he comes across as the most humble man to walk the face of the earth. When Muhammad Ali claimed to be the greatest, we all just rolled our eyes and smirked. But when Jesus claims to be the Savior and Judge of the world, to be "the greatest" by dying and rising again, we somehow are prone to bow our heads and agree. Why?

Deluded people usually "delude no one but themselves."[5] You only have to be in the presence of such persons for a few minutes before you recognize that their claims are bogus and they are living in a fantasy world. But with Jesus this is not the case. His first disciples didn't see in him such a delusion. Neither have the millions of people (is it billions now?) throughout history who have and do and will bow the knee to this son of a poor Jewish maiden.

John Stott calls what I'm talking about simply "the paradox of Jesus." Stott writes that Jesus' "claims sound like the ravings of a lunatic, but he shows no sign of being a fanatic, a neurotic or, still less, a psychotic. On the contrary, he comes before us in the pages of the Gospels as the most balanced and integrated of human beings."[6] That's the paradox of Jesus. He covers himself with disturbing claims (disturbing because they are so self-focused), and yet we see him clothed with utter humility. That, my friends, is the profound paradox we see in our passage. And it is one of those things that you really don't notice unless you pay careful attention.

Jesus arranges the whole scene. He determines the details. He decides to ride slightly above the crowd into Jerusalem upon a foal of a beast of burden, which is an action little different than how he started his earthly ministry in Luke's Gospel (Luke 4:16–21), taking up the scroll of Isaiah, reading it in the synagogue, sitting down to teach, and then expounding the text, saying in essence, "If you want to know to whom the prophet was referring, he was writing about me."[7] Jesus rode into Jerusalem that first Palm Sunday announcing that Israel's Messiah had arrived, just as Zechariah said he would. By mounting that beast, Jesus in essence said, "If you want to know to whom the prophet was referring, he was writing about me."

It's all quite mind-boggling.

Shake and Shout

One reason I am a Christian is because it is Scripturally reasonable. As I test the person, words, and actions of Jesus against what the Old Testament messianic prophecies say, I find the right match. Jesus fulfills the Scriptures. Another reason I am a Christian, I must admit, is because of this wonderfully alluring paradox of Jesus. (Here it's the audacity of his intentionally—to intentionally ride in on a donkey.) And it is these two distinct features in our passage that I want us all to recognize and to respond to today.

When Jesus rode into Jerusalem we read that "the whole city was stirred up, saying, 'Who is this?'" (v. 10). The city was "stirred up" or "quaked" (the literal word used here); the city quaked like it would "quake" on Good Friday (at his death) and on Easter Sunday (at his resurrection).[8] And the question that came out of this quaking was the right one: "Who is this?" (v. 10).

"And the crowds said, 'This is the prophet Jesus'" (v. 11). Yes, Jesus is a prophet like Moses, but he is more than a prophet or even *the* prophet (Deuteronomy 18:15). He is, as the crowd shouts, echoing the blind men in 20:30 and the children in 21:15, "the Son of David!" (v. 9). He is the prophet. He is the long-awaited King.

But is he not more than prophet and king? Is he not, as Bruner beautifully puts it, "the *lowly* Lord, the *human* God. . . . Emmanuel . . . the true God-with-us in a truly *human* way, at our level: God on a donkey"?[9] Is he not, as I'll put it, the Son of God on the child of a donkey, the one who came to save us (1:21)? Hosanna. Save us, Lord. And is he not also the one we still long for, to come in power at the true triumphal entry? He is! And thus we still cry out (echoing and expanding upon Psalm 118:25, 26), "Hosanna"—"save us!" "Blessed is he who comes in the name of the LORD!" Hosanna in the highest! Prophet, King, Savior, come again. The earth still shakes, and we still shout, "Come and save us."

61

A Withered Temple

MATTHEW 21:12–22

MY WIFE HAS BEEN TO St. Peter's in Rome. I have been to St. Paul's in London. Between us we have seen the two largest churches in the world. And if you have ever been in such a building, something so massive, ornate, and meticulously designed, you likely experienced what we experienced—that inexplicable architectural euphoria.

For most first-century Jews, especially those country bumpkins from Galilee we have been following for some time now, entering Herod's temple in the holy city produced that same sense of euphoria. The temple was one of the world's most magnificent structures. Its outer walls, for example, were comprised of huge double colonnades, made with hundreds of pillars of pure white marble, covered with roofs adorned with cedar painstakingly engraved and painted. Most of these columns were thirty feet high, and some of them were a hundred feet high. The columns were so massive that it would have taken three persons with hands joined together to surround one of them at the base. Those were just the boundary walls of this immense and extravagant edifice, a building that took 10,000 carpenters and masons, laboring over four decades, to build.

At the heart of the temple was the Holy of Holies; then came the Holy Place (its doors were between sixty and 100 feet high), then the Court of the Priests (where the altar was and the sacrifices were made), then the Court of Israel (for Jewish men), then the Court of the Women (for Jewish women), and then surrounding these center structures, last and certainly least, was the Court of the Gentiles (a place for non-Jewish converts to Judaism).

This Court of the Gentiles is important as it pertains to our passage, for it is there in that thirty-five acre, open-air courtyard where Jesus would have made, as everyone did, his entrance into the temple.

Worship in the Temple

With all that in mind, when we read in verse 12, "And Jesus entered the temple," we perhaps expect to read something about his euphoric experience. Perhaps he would say, as his disciples would (in Mark 13:1), "What wonderful stones and what wonderful buildings!" Or perhaps we expected something more—that something supernatural was about to happen, especially considering the history of Israel—the glory of the Lord filled the temple in the days of Solomon. Concerning the entrance of the one "greater than Solomon" (12:42), the one who is touted in verse 9 to be the coming King, "the Son of David," the triumphal entrance of the Lord who opens the eyes of the blind, we may well have expected the *shekinah* glory to fall upon this sacred place then and there.

However, if we had such expectations they were surely not met, for we read at the end of verse 12 that when Jesus got there, what he did was so shockingly unexpected: he "drove out all who sold and bought in the temple, and he overturned the tables of the money-changers and the seats of those who sold pigeons."

What Jesus saw as he entered the Court of the Gentiles was none other than "a huge religious circus!"[1] Although God had originally instructed his people to bring sacrifices from their *own* flocks (Deuteronomy 12:5–7), Jesus noticed that the religious authorities disregarded that specific law and instituted instead a convenient and profitable marketplace wherein travelers could purchase an overpriced but authorized animal. And for the sake of expediency instead of offering such a "service" outside the temple walls (as would be more proper) they authorized the use of this immense Court of the Gentiles.

The problem with this was that this was the only place where Gentile converts to Judaism could worship. So Jesus saw that these Gentiles, some of whom would have traveled long distances (think of someone like the Ethiopian eunuch), came into the temple only to find that their place of worship was crammed with livestock and loose change, that their sanctuary resembled the bizarre mix of a county fair and the pit of a stock exchange.[2]

That's what Jesus *saw*. What Jesus *did* was drive out and overturn, which are two very symbolic actions. He was *overturning* these new, unlawful, unmerciful, and anti-Abrahamic-covenant temple traditions. And he was driving out the spiritual swindlers (those who squeezed the poor), the currency exchange racketeers and the used pigeon salesmen. Out they went and in went the poor: "the blind and lame came to him *in the temple*, and he healed them" free of charge (v. 14). Jesus opens the gates of the temple—dare I say the Holy of Holies?—to those normally excluded from entrance (cf. 2 Samuel 5:8), yes, to those who "eke out their existence as beggars" outside the city gates.[3] He lets them in to him—to his presence and healing touch.

Matthew 21:12 may be as important a verse as 20:28. Don't overlook it. Don't underestimate its importance. Nearly 2,000 years ago the Lamb of God (the ultimate and final sacrifice for sin, who would bring healing to the hopeless) who is also the lion of Judah (the king who came to judge Israel and soon all the world in righteousness) walked into the temple.[4] He walked into the temple to save the poor in spirit but also to judge those who are rich in religious hypocrisy.

Here is where that good old fig tree thickens the plot. Skip over verses 15, 16 (we'll come back to them) and look ahead to verses 17–19.

> And leaving them [the indignant chief priests and the scribes], he went out of the city to Bethany and lodged there. In the morning, as he was returning to the city, he became hungry. And seeing a fig tree by the wayside, he went to it and found nothing on it but only leaves. And he said to it, "May no fruit ever come from you again!" And the fig tree withered at once.

What's with the fig tree? Certainly the fact that Jesus was "hungry" illustrates his humanity. Our *divine* Lord could get hungry and need food. However, it is not his hunger that surprises us as much as his seemingly irrational and irritable behavior. The famous philosopher Bertrand Russell, as he examined the cursing of the fig tree, accused Jesus here of what he called "vindictive fury." For him this whole episode tarnished Jesus' character. "I cannot myself feel," Russell wrote, "that either in the matter of wisdom or in the matter of virtue Christ stands quite as high as some other people known to history."[5] Russell is not alone in claiming that Jesus was in some ways "acting like a spoiled child who did not get his way."[6] That is perhaps the natural but uninformed reading.

For those of us who know enough about Scripture and a bit about botany, we recognize that Jesus here is not, with supernatural spite, taking out his frustrations on some organic object. We remember he could do without food. He went without food for forty days in the wilderness, resisting the temptation to turn stones into bread. And we remember he could surely produce fruit from this tree if he so desired. He did after all multiply the loaves and fishes. So we doubt he would be stymied by a little fruit tree. But that raises the question, if Jesus was not acting like a spoiled child endowed with supernatural powers, what was he up to?

Let me offer a short explanation that starts with a brief lesson in horticulture. Let's talk about fig trees, a topic too often neglected in churches today. In the land of Israel, during the month of March, fig trees produce small edible green buds called *paggîm* (called *taqsh* by modern Palestinian Arabs).[7] In April large green leaves sprout forth. Then in May these buds fall off and are replaced by figs. Now we know from the time in which Passover was celebrated and the mention of the "leaves" (v. 19; Mark 11:13, "in leaf") that this incident occurred in April. Thus when our Lord saw from a distance the green leaves he expected not to find figs (for as Mark tells us, "it was not the season for figs"). But he did expect to find something—*paggîm* or *taqsh*—those early but edible fruit buds. However, this particular tree was deceptive. With all its green foliage, there should have been fruit. There should have been something. But, alas there was nothing. This fruit tree, which had the signs of fruit, was found to be fruitless.

So you see, Jesus didn't curse this fig tree because he was upset at not getting food from it. Rather he cursed it to provide his disciples (those who "heard" [Mark 11:14] and "saw" [v. 20] this curse) with a visible parable or object lesson of what was happening to Israel, as Israel was often compared to a fig tree in the Old Testament (Micah 7:1–6; Jeremiah 8:13).[8] Like this green tree, Israel was fruitful in appearance alone. Spiritually they were barren. From a distance the temple looked inspiring, but upon close examination it was fruitless. Inside the activities that surrounded the Passover sacrifice were only hollow rituals offered to God neither in spirit nor in truth.

When Jesus entered the temple, the fruit he expected to see were prayers and praises offered up to God, along with the necessary fruits of righteousness—humility, kindness, and justice. Instead he discovered merciless injustices as the Gentiles were pushed out and the poor were extorted. That's why he cited Isaiah 56:7, "It is written, 'My house shall be called a house of prayer.'" Matthew stops there. That verse from Isaiah ends, however (and perhaps Matthew implies—with his emphasis on the nations—what Mark makes explicit), "for all the nations" (11:17).

The popular Jewish literature of this time informs us that the Jews expected the Messiah, when he came, to purge Jerusalem and the temple of Gentiles and foreigners. Jesus' attitude and action, however, was "exactly the reverse."[9] As the true Messiah, the one who came to fulfill the Scriptures, Jesus "does not clear the temple of Gentiles, but *for* them."[10] He clears the temple so that Gentiles might worship God! So Jesus quotes from Isaiah 56 because it is there where the prophet "speaks of the extension of God's salvation to people who formerly were excluded from it,"[11] where Isaiah speaks of how the temple is not the sole property of Israel but is a witness to the nations.

As Jesus turns over tables, he turns the Jews' attention to their prophets—first to Isaiah and second to Jeremiah. In the second half of verse 13, where Jesus says, "[B]ut you make it a den of robbers," he quotes from Jeremiah 7:11. (Here's where it really gets interesting!) Look below at Jeremiah 7:1–11. I think Jesus had this whole text in mind.

> The word that came to Jeremiah from the LORD: "Stand in the gate of the LORD's house [the temple], and proclaim there this word, and say, Hear the word of the LORD, all you men of Judah who enter these gates to worship the LORD. Thus says the LORD of hosts, the God of Israel: Amend your ways and your deeds, and I will let you dwell in this place. Do not trust in these deceptive words: 'This is the temple of the LORD, the temple of the LORD, the temple of the LORD.'
>
> For if you truly amend your ways and your deeds, if you truly execute justice one with another, if you do not oppress the sojourner, the fatherless, or the widow, or shed innocent blood in this place, and if you do not go after other gods to your own harm, then I will let you dwell in this place, in the land that I gave of old to your fathers forever. Behold, you trust in deceptive words to no avail. Will you steal, murder, commit adultery, swear falsely, make offerings to Baal, and go after other gods that you have not known, and then come and stand before me in this house, which is called by my name, and say, 'We are delivered!'—only to go on doing all these abominations? Has this house, which is called by my name, become a den of robbers in your eyes? Behold, *I myself have seen it*, declares the LORD." (Jeremiah 7:1–11)

This is precisely what Jesus *himself* has seen and now judges. The temple has become "a den of robbers."

Understand what he is saying. Thieves don't do their robbing in their den. Rather, their den is their safe hideout. So here Jesus is not merely denouncing all the buying and selling. Rather, he is denouncing the false security of those who come into the temple to offer a sacrifice for sin without the fruits of repentance. The temple, Jesus is saying, has degenerated into a hideout where people think they can find God's fellowship and forgiveness no matter how they live.

Many faithless Jews, who stole, murdered, committed adultery, lied under oath, and worshipped other gods (in other words, didn't heed the two tables of the Law—love God and neighbor) nevertheless came once a year to Jerusalem, bought their proper animal, had it sacrificed, and stood before God in the temple and said, "We are delivered!" They thought they could just walk into this oversized confessional booth, go through the motions, and walk out completely absolved of their sins, so much so that they would run right back to them and then go through the same motions the next year and the year after that and so on. Do you see what Jesus saw? What hypocrisy!

Let's stop and turn the tables on ourselves. I want to talk for just a moment to the hypocrites. And I don't mean all of us. I don't like when preachers say to the unbeliever's question about Christian hypocrisy, "Hey, we are all hypocrites. The church is full of hypocrites. Come join the hypocrites." If the church is truly full of hypocrites, as the Bible defines hypocrisy, why on earth would anyone want to join us? Our Lord Jesus never has anything good to say about hypocrisy (see especially chapter 23). Sure, as Christians we all still sin against God and against each other, but that is very different than being a hypocrite, someone who has no heart for God but will do whatever is necessary to make sure the "god" in his life is appeased and the people in his life are pleased.

So I'm talking now to the real hypocrites. I'm talking to you who rob God throughout the week by doing things you ought not to do and not doing things you should do and then go to church to find "sanctuary," a hiding place for a now guiltless conscience. There is no fear of God before your eyes! But listen, if there is anything we learn from this passage it is that the green leaves of your religious practices cannot cover a fruitless life. The leaf of baptism or the leaf of church membership or the leaf of praying the prayer—these things cannot hide your nakedness from the eye of an all-seeing God. As Jesus came closer to the fig tree and as he entered into the temple to check for fruit, so even now he enters to examine your lives, looking for the fruit of repentance and holiness of life and sincerity of faith. And if there is no fruit, then stop fooling yourself and others. There is only one thing to expect—judgment!

Isn't that what is so vividly displayed in our text? Here we see that Jesus will have none of this religious hypocrisy, this playacting in piety. Those in the temple on that Passover can say all they want. They can shout, "We are delivered. We are saved!" Like thieves after their looting, they can return to their hideout, and they can stand within the temple and profess, "We're safe! We're safe! This is the temple of the Lord, the temple of the Lord, the temple of the Lord." But, the Lord has suddenly come into his temple (see Malachi 3:1b). And there and then the *Lord* Jesus, standing in the midst of their hideout, tells them the game is over. By overturning the tables, driving out those who sold the animals *necessary for sacrifice*, our Lord was doing something radical, perhaps his most revolutionary action to date.[12] He was making a prophetic protest and pronouncement. He was not cleansing the temple; rather he was *cursing* it! He was withering Israel's fig tree.

And of course, that's the significance of what happens in verses 19, 20, where we discover that Jesus has done more than merely condemn the tree. He has killed it.

> And seeing a fig tree by the wayside, he went to it and found nothing on it but only leaves. And he said to it, "May no fruit ever come from you again!" And the fig tree withered at once. When the disciples saw it, they marveled, saying, "How did the fig tree wither at once?"

The first disciples may not have understood the symbolic significance of this day with its many strange events, but we as readers of Matthew's Gospel are able to fill in the theological gaps. Throughout his ministry we are able to see that Jesus has been subtly taking the place of the temple. He announces forgiveness. He heals the sick. He brings sinners into a saving relationship with God. He is the very presence of God in the world. He is (dare I say?) the temple!

With that in mind come back to verses 15, 16:

> But when the chief priests and the scribes saw the wonderful things that he did, and the children crying out in the temple, "Hosanna to the Son of David!" they were indignant, and they said to him, "Do you hear what these are saying?" And Jesus said to them, "Yes; have you never read, 'Out of the mouth of infants and nursing babies you have prepared praise'?"

If the religious leaders thought what Jesus did in the temple was "wonderful" (beyond belief), what he had just said is even more "wonderful." He quotes from Psalm 8:2 (8:3 LXX) verbatim, which depicts children rightly praising Yahweh, and applies it to himself. How truly wonderful—i.e., blasphemous! Or how truly wonderful—i.e., the praise of Yahweh and the praise of Jesus are inseparable! Jesus applauds the children's acclamation. He accepts the title ("Son of David") and the praise ("Hosanna"). Is this not the precursor to Revelation 4, 5? First, God is worshipped, then the Lamb:

> "To him who sits on the throne and to the Lamb
> be blessing and honor and glory and might forever and ever!"
>
> And the four living creatures said, "Amen!" and the elders fell down and worshiped. (Revelation 5:13, 14)

What the children in Matthew say will be echoed throughout eternity!

No wonder the chief priests and scribes are "indignant" (v. 15) or in Mark's version are now plotting "a way to destroy" Jesus (Mark 11:18). Ah, but we are all too aware of the irony of their indignation and the actions of that indignation. For we know from the end of this Gospel that it is this very destruction (the death of Christ) that brings an end, a destruction, to their temple.

This is deeply theological, but it is very important to understand some of the basics of Christian doctrine. According to the Gospels Jesus "cleared" the temple *two times*—once at the beginning of his ministry and once (as we have here) at the end. The first time "the Jews said to him, 'What sign do you show us for doing these things?'" (John 2:18) And Jesus replied, "Destroy this temple, and in three days I will raise it up" (John 2:19). The Jews, of course, were quite baffled by this response, so they said, "It has taken forty-six years to build this temple, and will you raise it up in three days?" (John 2:20). Thankfully John helps us by inserting his commentary, "But [Jesus] was speaking about the temple of his body" (John 2:21).

As we look at the end of Matthew's Gospel (chapters 21—28), we find this same theology at play. When the temple of Jesus' body is destroyed (i.e., he dies), at that very moment the temple in Jerusalem (the building itself that will be destroyed literally in just a few decades) is symbolically destroyed. It has theologically gone out of business.

Let me show you what I'm talking about. Let's look ahead to the crucifixion scene. Look at chapter 27, starting in verses 39, 40: "And those who passed by derided him, wagging their heads and saying, 'You who would destroy the temple and rebuild it in three days, save yourself! If you are the Son of God, come down from the cross!'" Skip down to verse 50: "And Jesus cried out again with a loud voice and yielded up his spirit." Then what happened? What happened at the moment of his death? Underline it. Circle it. Put a star by it. Write it on your forehead. "And behold, the curtain of the temple was torn in two, from top to bottom" (v. 51).

The curtain that divided the Holy of Holies from the rest of the world, from the Court of the Priests, from the Court of Israel, from the Court of the Women, from the Court of the Gentiles, was torn asunder. The point is that through Christ's sacrificial death the earthly temple completely crumbles to the ground and is replaced by the one who said of himself, "I tell you, something greater than the temple is here" (12:6). Through Jesus' death, the curtain has been torn in two, so that all people, all those who believe in Israel's Messiah ("Hosanna to the Son of David!") might be sewn together into one body, the church—slave and free, male and female, Jew and *Gentile* (Galatians 3:28).

I think this is the precise point Matthew is trying to make in 27:54. In that verse we find these remarkable words: "When the centurion and those who were with him, keeping watch over Jesus, saw the earthquake and what took place, they were filled with awe and said, 'Truly this was the Son of God!'" The Jewish children and Gentile soldiers alike praise him.

The Worship of the Temple

The onetime president of Princeton, James McCosh, once said, "The book to read is not the one which thinks for you, but the one which makes you think. No book in the world equals the Bible for that."[13] Here in Matthew the Bible has once again made us think. As we have looked at these first eight verses of our passage, we have *thought* about the temple—the purpose of the temple, Jesus' relationship to the temple, and Jesus' reaction to what was going on in the temple. But we are not done thinking just yet. As we move to verses 21, 22, we move into a section of application, a set of exhortations on faith that I want you to see are very much connected with what came before. Think of verses 12–20 as "The Worship *in* the Temple: Faithless and Fruitless." That's my title for them. Then think of verses 21, 22 as "The Worship *of* the Temple: Faithful and Fruitful." That's my title for those verses.

The phrase "the worship *of* the temple," of course, picks up on the language of the New Testament epistles, where Paul, for example, unabashedly calls Christians "God's temple." In 1 Corinthians 3:16, 17 Paul says to believers, "Do you not know you are God's temple and that God's Spirit dwells in you? . . . God's temple is holy, and you are that temple."

Such language would be sacrilegious if Herod's Temple, with its priesthood and sacrifices, was still the place of God's presence, the one and only place where one meets God and where sins are forgiven. But if this earthly temple in Jerusalem on Mount Zion, if this temple mount has been (so to speak) "thrown into the sea" (v. 21),[14] and if Christ is the new and everlasting temple, the one and only person in whom we meet God and have our sins forgiven, and if his Spirit dwells in those who now believe, then what Jesus calls his followers to in verses 21, 22 makes perfect sense. There is no awkwardness in the transition of thought then. Outside of Jerusalem and the temple, Jesus calls his church to worship. He calls us to have *faith.*

Twice the word "faith" is used in the final two verses, but the concept is in every phrase.

> And Jesus answered them, "Truly, I say to you, if you have *faith* and do not doubt, you will not only do what has been done to the fig tree, but even if you say to this mountain, 'Be taken up and thrown into the sea,' it will happen. And whatever you ask in prayer, you will receive, if you have *faith.*" (vv. 21, 22)

As followers of Christ, we are here exhorted to "have faith." Question: In whom? Answer: Follow the children's lead—in Jesus! Question: Where? Answer: Wherever Jesus is. Lo, he is with us always. In other words, there is nothing sacred about Jerusalem. There is nothing sacred about the temple, that desolate house they just abandoned and that will be laid to the ground in forty years (23:38), never to be rebuilt. Have faith in Jesus now and anywhere and everywhere. Question: For what? Answer: Whatever—"whatever you ask in prayer, you will receive, if you have faith" (v. 22).

When we first read that verse, and the one before it where Jesus speaks of tossing mountains around, we might be tempted to align ourselves with the proponents of today's health and wealth gospel—that is, to accept the teaching that all we need to do is just "name it" and then "claim it," and God then must indeed "give it." So if you want a new car, name it (make and model, year and color), claim it in faith, and let God work his magic.

A couple of years ago I heard one of these health and wealth teachers share his story of "faith." He and his wife were walking through a nice part of downtown Houston, and he said, "Oh I wish we could afford a house like that," and his wife said, "You just have to trust God." Then his church grew, and then his salary grew, and sure enough God answered their "prayer of faith." Now they live in one of those multi-million dollar houses.

We can be quite certain that is not what Jesus is talking about here. These verses indeed teach that God will answer our prayers, but not as a result of positive thinking. Jesus' statement here was not a blank check. To pray effectively, you need faith in the Lord, not faith in yourself or faith in your own faith or faith in the object of your request.

Scripture teaches that God does not grant requests that violate his own nature or will or are not in harmony with the purposes of his kingdom. So keeping in mind that there are some things Christians should not ask for and some things God will not give, we are nevertheless encouraged here to pray, to pray in faith—to pray confidently and expectantly.

So what does the worship *of* the temple look like? You might say it is praise of Jesus as the temple of the living God. We are to praise him as the children did. But it is also faith *in* him, a faith that trusts in him and prays to him for "whatever," knowing that if we abide in him, we will bear much fruit.

The Ultimate Temple

Right before I planted New Covenant Church, in my last sermon at College Church in Wheaton, Illinois (our sending church) I said something like this: As I move on to Naperville I will miss so many things about College Church. I will certainly miss my colleagues in the ministry and the staff and the people. And, being an admirer of aesthetics, I will also miss the building with its great aesthetic value—its Roman columns, its high ceiling, its circular space, its thoughtful use of natural light, its acoustic excellence, and its subtle extravagance (the massive organ tucked in behind and above the choir loft). I said I would miss all that as I went to preach in some auditorium or gym or comedy club or backstreet alleyway (you never know where you'll end up meeting in a church plant) or the children's museum basement (been there) or little theatre (done that).

But I said that the one thing I wouldn't miss is the temptation that comes with such a structure. You see, one of the beauties of church planting (not aesthetic beauties but theological beauties) is that it is easier to keep first things first. It is easier to keep faith in Jesus at the center of our everyday worship and our Sunday worship. For our church buildings are no temples, our pastors are not priests, and there is no Holy of Holies tucked behind the organ. But God's people are the temple, they are the priests, and in and through Christ all Christians have entered the Holy of Holies. So if our church building crumbles to the ground or someday its doors are closed, the Word of God exhorts us today (and always) to worship. It exhorts us to have faith, to have faith in Jesus, the ultimate temple of the living God.

62

What Authority? What Authority!

MATTHEW 21:23–46

NEAR THE BEGINNING OF James Joyce's novel *A Portrait of the Artist as a Young Man,* the main character, young Stephen Dedalus, has been dropped off at boarding school. There Stephen encountered some of his classmates. One of the boys, Wells, asked Stephen:

> "Tell, us Dedalus, do you kiss your mother before you go to bed?"
> Stephen answered: "I do."
> Wells turned to the other fellows and said: "O, I say, here's a fellow says he kisses his mother every night before he goes to bed."
> The other fellows stopped their game and turned around, laughing. Stephen blushed under their eyes and said: "I do not."
> Wells said: "O, I say, here's a fellow says he doesn't kiss his mother before he goes to bed."
> They all laughed again. Stephen tried to laugh with them. He felt his whole body hot and confused in a moment. What was the right answer to the question? . . . Was it right to kiss his mother or wrong to kiss his mother?[1]

I'd hate to compare our Lord and Savior to a trickster schoolboy, but I must say that Jesus here traps the chief priests and the elders of the people as cleverly as Wells did Stephen. He asks them a simple question about John the Baptist that will have them blushing, hot, and confused, looking to each other and saying, "What's the right answer to the question?"

The Matchup: In This Corner . . .

As we begin our study, let me set the stage for you. In 21:12 Jesus enters the temple in Jerusalem. There he cleanses (curses) it. He overturns the tables, drives out the racketeers, and lets in the needy to him and receives the children's praise of him. Next he leaves the temple and stays the night in Bethany. In the morning, as he is returning to the city, in a symbolic gesture he withers the fruitless fig tree. Then we come to our text. In 21:23 Jesus enters the temple again. And from 21:23 until 24:1 (where we read "Jesus left the temple"), there, in the temple, is a clash of authorities—the chief priests, the elders, the Pharisees, the Herodians, the Sadducees, and the scribes versus Jesus.

My friend Nick Perrin has written a book called *Jesus the Temple*. That book's front cover features Giotto's painting, *Expulsion of the Money-changers from the Temple*. (It's a depiction of the previous chapter's text.) On the left it shows the apostles shocked and confused. One is covering his face; another is raising his hands as if to say, "There must be a good explanation for this." On the right the merchants are cowering, the animals escaping, and then in the far background are the temple authorities, whispering to each other. At the center is Jesus. Behind him is the temple, and in front of him is an overturned table. Over his right shoulder Jesus holds a whip in his clenched right hand. The whip, because of its light coloring, is barely noticeable, so it looks like he is about to punch one of the merchants. (Nice cover, Nick. How very seeker-sensitive.)

I have nothing bad to say about the cover. I love it. It's about time Christians got *that* picture of Jesus into their heads. There are a lot of different pictures of Jesus in the Gospels. That's not the only one, but that's one of them.

If I were to paint a picture of today's text, it would have that same Jesus at the center with his fist still clenched, but this time paired against him would be the temple authorities, in their proper boxing stance. You see, our text is a clash of authorities. Of course, there is nothing physical or violent here (Jesus, in the greatest act of nonviolence, is about to give his life even for his enemies), but I want you to feel with disturbing angst that our Lord Jesus was in a real battle here. Theological punches are being thrown by them and *by him*.

The religious authorities' punches will come in the form of questions. In 21:23—22:46, four questions are thrown at Jesus from at least four different groups of truth squads. Jesus' defenses (that's a nicer term than "punches") will come in parables. There are three total (three in a row), and we will examine two of them now.

Their First Question

Come with me to 21:23–27. We'll start with verse 23:

> And when he entered the temple, the chief priests and the elders of the people came up to him as he was teaching, and said, "By what authority are you doing these things, and who gave you this authority?"

This question itself is not improper. Let's face it, Jesus just walked into their holy place (the chief priests had ruled the temple for centuries) and started rearranging the furniture. A touch of table-turning here and a little dusting over there as the change falls to the ground. Ah, that looks much better. Then the next day he's back. Now he is teaching in the temple. This nobody from Nazareth—not a scribe, not a Pharisee, not a Sadducee, not a priest, not an elder, not a rabbi—is teaching. And he is likely teaching stuff like "Blessed are you when others revile you and persecute you and utter all kinds of evil against you falsely *on my account.* Rejoice and be glad, for your reward is great in heaven" (5:11, 12a). Or worse, "Destroy this temple, and in three days I will raise it up" (John 2:19). So do you see where the Jewish leaders are coming from? What's this Jesus up to—tossing things out of the temple one day and teaching in the temple the next? Who does he think he is? By what authority is he doing these things?

This question itself is not improper, but their demeanor is. They weren't asking sincerely. (I think their tone here is more accusatory—"By what authority . . . !" That is, "You have no right!") They weren't open to the truth. They didn't come in faith. So Jesus turns the tables on them again, saying in essence, "If you're not capable enough to judge John the Baptist as Heaven-sent, then you are certainly not capable to judge me."[2] Look now at verses 24–27:

> Jesus answered them, "I also will ask you one question, and if you tell me the answer, then I also will tell you by what authority I do these things. The baptism of John, from where did it come? From heaven or from man?" And they discussed it among themselves, saying, "If we say, 'From heaven' [from God], he will say to us, 'Why then did you not believe him?' But if we say, 'From man' [not from God], we are afraid of the crowd, for they all hold that John was a prophet." So they answered Jesus, "We do not know." [We take the Fifth.] And he said to them, "[Me too] Neither will I tell you by what authority I do these things."

Notice a few details here. First notice (quite obviously) that authority is the issue. Some scholars think that now in Matthew the issue of authority becomes a fundamental issue. I think it has been, is now, and will continue to be *the* fundamental issue of the whole Gospel. This theme of authority I take to be part one of the three-part harmony of Matthew's melodic line: all authority, all nations, all allegiance. Jesus has been given all authority over all the nations and thus demands total allegiance from everyone. I'll return to this authority issue at the end of this chapter, with a small punch of my own.

Second, notice how worried these leaders are about the people. The polls have such a hold over their political and theological decisions. In verse 26 we read that they were "afraid of the crowd." Later in verse 46 there's an echo: "They feared the crowds." Contrast them with Jesus, of whom the Pharisees rightly say in 22:16, "Teacher, we know that you are true and teach the way of God truthfully, *and you do not care about anyone's opinion*." Sometimes godly leadership demands godly decisions even if those decisions aren't popular with the populace.

Third, notice that in Jesus' seemingly elusive or evasive answer he actually answers their question and then, with the two forthcoming parables, illustrates his answer. While these leaders didn't believe John's message (v. 32), our Lord doubted that they would say publicly that John's baptism for repentance was merely "from man" (i.e., the opposite of the idiom "from heaven"). They may have thought that John's ministry was not from God, but they would be hard-pressed to say (even to themselves) that his ministry was completely unauthorized or evil.[3]

You see, what John said about Jesus was the answer to their question. (That's what Jesus is getting at here.) And what did John say? In Matthew's Gospel his testimony was this:

> I baptize you with water for repentance, but he who is coming after me is mightier than I, whose sandals I am not worthy to carry. He will baptize you with the Holy Spirit and fire. His winnowing fork is in his hand, and he will clear his threshing floor and gather his wheat into the barn, but the chaff he will burn with unquenchable fire. (3:11, 12)

In John's Gospel, John the Baptist's testimony is even more Christologically bold:

> I am the voice of one crying out in the wilderness, "Make straight the way of *the Lord*." (John 1:23)

> Behold, *the Lamb of God*, who takes away the sin of the world! This is he of whom I said, "After me comes a man who ranks before me, *because he was before me*." (John 1:29, 30; cf. John 3:31–35)

In 21:24–27 Jesus replies to the Jewish leaders (and let us listen in carefully) that the only right response to him is to heed John's authoritative, Heaven-sent message about him—which is to repent and believe, to call Jesus the Lord, the Lamb, the before-Abraham-was I AM.

Here is where the parables come in. Again there are three parables, two of which we will examine here. All three parables share two themes—faith and judgment.

Parable "Punch" Number One

Let's look at the first parable. I'll explain it briefly and apply it forthrightly. With great authority Jesus teaches these authorities about his authority.

> "What do you think? A man had two sons. And he went to the first and said, 'Son, go and work in the vineyard today.' And he answered, 'I will not,' but afterward he changed his mind and went. And he went to the other son and said the same. And he answered, 'I go, sir,' ["Yes, sir, I will," is the sense, NLT] but did not go. Which of the two did the will of his father?" They said, "The first." Jesus said to them [the point of the parable], "Truly, *I say to you* [Jesus' favorite personal authority expression], the tax collectors and the prostitutes go into the kingdom of God before you. For John came to you in the way of righteousness, and you did not believe him, but the tax collectors and the prostitutes believed him. And even when you saw it [those repentant sinners modeled what you should do], you did not afterward change your minds [repent] and believe him." (vv. 28–32)

Needless to say, this parable is a jab at them. It's parable punch number one.

Here the father represents God the Father. The first son—the I-won't-but-did boy—symbolizes the tax collectors and prostitutes who, in the end, believed John's message (about repentance of sin and faith in Jesus). Tax collectors and prostitutes! The shock here is intentional. But it is not merely a literary shock; it is a reality shock. Both tax collectors (rightly condemned for their traitorous collaboration with Rome and greed for gain) and prostitutes (rightly condemned for their sexual immorality)—those who defiantly said to God, "We will not obey your Word"—when they heard John preaching the way of righteousness listened, thought it through, and changed their minds and actions.[4]

The second son—the I-will-but-didn't boy—symbolizes Israel's leaders, who were so verbally zealous in their obedience to God, yet failed to heed God's two highest authorized emissaries, John and Jesus. They professed allegiance to God. They called themselves his sons and servants. But when called upon by John (and later by Jesus) to repent of their pride in position and their inward gross immoralities, they refused. The "bad" sons prove to be good and the "good" to be bad.

That's my brief explanation of the parable. Here are my two lessons from it for us.

First, the gates to God's kingdom open wide to the bluntly ungodly if they repent, but not a crack for the precisely orthodox if they do not. That's the ironic reality here. God's kingdom is compromised of some pretty bad cats or dogs (Gentile dogs) or pigs (unclean swine). Jesus didn't come for the healthy. He came to cure the sick. So we shouldn't be surprised if the church is comprised of a bunch of once seemingly terminal spiritual cases.

At my last church a young couple learned of my background—what I did and got caught doing before my conversion to Christ—and they left the church because of it. They thought, *A pastor should not have any kind of sin like that in his past.* I was devastated by that. Not personally devastated (in this case and with this couple I honestly could care less what they thought of me), but devastated that these professing Christians didn't get grace. Listen, prostitutes who repent of their sins and trust in Christ get into the kingdom, just as do Pharisees who repent of their sins and trust in Christ. That's the beauty of the gospel, and that's our first big lesson from the little parable. Don't ever forget it.

The second lesson is, "show me your faith." Of course that is how James puts it in 2:18 of his letter. In Romans, Paul calls it "the obedience of faith" (1:5; 16:26). Jesus' slogan (you're all familiar with it) is, *Just do it.* To Jesus, one is not saved by talk alone—"Lord, Lord, Lord, Lord, Lord (cf. 7:21–23; 25:11, 12); yes, sir, I'll do that right away"—but by faith alone (see the word "believe" three times in verse 32), a faith that is never alone (a faith that obeys the word/will/voice of God). To Jesus, verbal faith is not saving faith; a doing faith is saving faith.

Those are the two lessons.

Parable "Punch" Number Two

Now as the chief priests and the elders are staggering after being hit with parable punch number one, without pause parable punch number two strikes them. "Hear another parable," Jesus says.

> There was a master of a house who planted a vineyard and put a fence around it and dug a winepress in it and built a tower and leased it to tenants, and went into another country. When the season for fruit drew near, he sent his servants to the tenants to get his fruit. And the tenants took his servants and beat one, killed another, and stoned another. Again he sent other servants, more than the first. And they did the same to them. Finally he sent his son to them, saying, "They will respect my son." But when the tenants saw the son, they said to themselves, "This is the heir. Come, let us kill him and have his inheritance." And they took him and threw him out of the vineyard

> and killed him. When therefore the owner of the vineyard comes, what will he do to those tenants? They said to him, "He will put those wretches to a miserable death and let out the vineyard to other tenants who will give him the fruits in their seasons." (vv. 33–41)

In this parable Jesus gives a condensed, symbolic (or allegorical) version of salvation history. The master of the house is God the Father. The vineyard is God's people, Israel.[5] The tenants are Israel's leaders—past and present in our text. The fruit (a key term here—vv. 34b, 41b, 43) represents, to borrow from John the Baptist's language, the fruit of repentance (3:8, 10), or more broadly, a righteously obedient life (7:16–20). The two sets of servants are the Old Testament prophets, perhaps the former and the latter prophets. The beatings and stonings and killings represent their persecutions.

The son is the Son of God, our Lord Jesus, a veiled reference to himself, but also to the first public unveiling of his true identity.[6] The killing of the son is the cross. The "other tenants" (v. 41) mentioned in the leaders' reply (while technically not part of the parable, they are very much part of the story Jesus is telling) symbolize "a people producing its fruits" (v. 43), that is, a new people, a "third race,"[7] as one commentator calls them, the elect of Christ's kingdom, a rightly ruled community that is not defined ethnically—as Jewish or Gentile—but spiritually, as those whose faith is fruitful.

The story is simply and sadly that God so deeply loved the world he chose Israel from among the nations to bless the nations. He tenderly brought them to life and then cared and nurtured them to health—he rescued them out of Egypt, gave them the Law, set up his city, built a temple, and prepared an altar.[8] There are eight verbs in verse 33, showing how much God worked on their behalf. Then he sent his prophets to reap what he had sown. But the leaders of his people persecuted and killed the prophets. Then, in his great patience, God sent more prophets, and the same fate met them. Finally, he so loved Israel that he sent his own son, Jesus. And yet Israel's leaders plotted (v. 38), arrested (v. 46), and killed (v. 39) even the Son of God. This beloved son was killed outside the vineyard, or as Hebrews puts it "outside the gate" (13:12, 13).

Then . . . the story is not over. Look at verse 40 and following. Here comes the punch of the parable. Jesus ends his parable with a question: "When therefore the owner of the vineyard comes, what will he do to those tenants?" The leaders reply, "He will put those wretches to a miserable death and let out the vineyard to other tenants who will give him the fruits in their seasons" (v. 41). Here, without knowing it, they have hung themselves. They have rightly discerned the judgment coming to them. The coming of the owner of the vineyard is the coming judgment upon Israel's leaders and all who follow their lead. This coming of God in judgment could refer to the final judgment (and in part I suppose it must) but also and likely to the destruction of the temple spiritually in AD 33 (or thereabouts) and physically in AD 70.

And in place of that temple (then as now) is Jesus. Jesus is the temple? Perhaps Perrin is on to something. "Jesus said to them, 'Have you never read in the Scriptures: "The stone that the builders rejected has become the cornerstone; this was the Lord's doing, and it is marvelous in our eyes"?'" (v. 42).

Here Jesus quotes from Psalm 118:22, 23, a text that originally spoke of the nation of Israel, and here, as Messiah, he appropriately and authoritatively applies it to himself. He continues:

> Therefore I tell you, the kingdom of God will be taken away from you and given to a people [*ethnos*, "a people"—a collective singular][9] producing its fruits. And the one who falls on this stone will be broken to pieces; and when it falls on anyone, it will crush him. (vv. 43, 44)[10]

From the rubble of the temple—every stone of that temple will be laid to the ground—a new and everlasting stone is put in place. That stone is Jesus, in particular Christ and him crucified, risen, and exalted—what will indeed be "the Lord's doing" and "marvelous" in the eyes of the apostles and still in our eyes today! The stone that the builders (or "tenants") or Jewish leaders rejected has become the foundational stone of the new temple. And this stone either saves or crushes. The stone either stays in place as the cornerstone on which you build your fruitful life or that stone is pushed out of place and becomes a stumbling stone that rolls over and crushes to dust all who oppose it (see Isaiah 8:14, 15; cf. Daniel 2:34, 35).

So that's it. That's the Parable of the Wicked Tenants, or perhaps a better title is the Parable of the Patient but Just Master.

What are the lessons for us? I have two. Both are big-picture gospel lessons.

First, God is patient. You could place 2 Peter 3:9 atop our text. "The Lord is . . . patient toward you, not wishing that any should perish, but that all should reach repentance." That's where Jesus starts here (vv. 33–37), and that's where the gospel starts. The Lord (or "master") is lovingly long-suffering. He plants his vineyard, cares for it, and sends servants to harvest it. And even after the first servants are hurt or destroyed, he holds back his anger and sends more servants,[11] and finally, in the greatest act of loving long-suffering, he sends his own son. In parable form it all sounds crazy. What landowner would do such a thing? But that's just the point. What defies historical realism really happened in and outside Jerusalem 2,000 years ago. God's apparent gullibility is his intentional grace! At the "dramatic center of the story" is the sending of the son[12] and the blessing extended to all who will accept him as such.

But that patience can be exhausted. This is the Parable of the Patient but *Just* Master. God is patient; God is just. The second lesson is this: God will judge those who don't accept his Son. Here Jesus does not depict people as neutral. Verse 38 embodies the cry of all who reject God's kindness and his King, Jesus. The scheming—"Come, let us kill him and have his inheritance"—is the cry of the natural rebellious heart. "We know better than God. We'd rule better than his son." Even "We want to be God!"[13]—squatter's rights on his property. The rejection *and* crucifixion of the Son of God is not merely a tragedy. It's the crime of the century. It's the greatest crime of world history! And the guilt for it hangs over all our heads.

Those (Jesus is quite strong here) who won't joyfully accept his loving authority (the authority of the sacrificial son) will feel the weight of his judging authority (the authority of the stone). "The person who trips over this stone will be smashed to pieces, and the person on whom this stone falls will be ground to powder" is one translation of verse 44.[14] That's doesn't sound nice. What a "miserable death" (v. 41) that would be. You don't want that.

God is patient; God is just. Don't try his patience; trust his Son.

What Authority!

As I was thinking over this theme of authority in Matthew's Gospel, I skimmed through this Gospel looking for places where I could (in a sense, not in reality) insert the chief priests and elders' question—"Jesus, by what authority . . . ?"

So, for example, after Jesus said, "Do not think that I have come to abolish the Law or the Prophets; I have not come to abolish them but to fulfill them" (5:17), we insert, "By what authority?" Or when he teaches, "You have heard that it was said, 'You shall love your neighbor and hate your enemy.' But I say to you, Love your enemies and pray for those who persecute you" (5:43, 44), we insert, "By what authority?" Or when he announces: "Not everyone who says to me, 'Lord, Lord,' will enter the kingdom of heaven, but the one who does the will of my Father who is in heaven" (7:21), we insert, "By what authority?" Or when he said to the paralytic, "Take heart, my son; your sins are forgiven" (9:2), we insert, "By what authority?"

Or when he claims, "All things have been handed over to me by my Father, and no one knows the Son except the Father, and no one knows the Father except the Son and anyone to whom the Son chooses to reveal him. Come to me, all who labor and are heavy laden, and I will give you rest" (11:27, 28), we insert, "By what authority?" Or when he says of himself, "I tell you, something greater than the temple is here. And if you had known what this means, 'I desire mercy, and not sacrifice,' you would not have condemned the guiltless. For the Son of Man is lord of the Sabbath" (12:6–8), we insert, "By what authority?"

Or when he announced, "The queen of the South will rise up at the judgment with this generation and condemn it, for she came from the ends of the earth to hear the wisdom of Solomon, and behold, something greater than Solomon is here" (12:42), we insert, "By what authority?" Or when he replies, "Here are my mother and my brothers! For whoever does the will of my Father in heaven is my brother and sister and mother" (12:49b, 50), we insert, "By what authority?"

Or when he said, "To eat with unwashed hands does not defile anyone" (15:20), we insert, "By what authority?" Or when he claims, "I will build my church, and the gates of hell shall not prevail against it" (16:18) or the sentence after that (to Peter and later the disciples, 18:18), "whatever you bind on earth shall be bound in heaven, and whatever you loose on earth shall be loosed in heaven" (16:19b), we insert, "By what authority?"

Shall I go on? No need to.

You see, what is asked in 21:23 is the *climactic question* that every person alive then and there and every observant reader here and now should ask: "Jesus, by what authority are you doing these things, and who gave you this authority?"

And we are to hear loud and clear Jesus' reply: "By what authority am I doing these things? Answer: by God's authority. I am the Son he sent. Who gave me this authority? Answer: God did. I am the stone he set in place. By God's authority I am the Son, and I am the stone." And to that we are to say, with bowed heads, soft hearts, and raised hands, "What authority!" Not what authority? but what authority! What Heaven-sent, God-given, sweet-to-be-under authority!

63

A Peculiar Parable with a Poignant Point

MATTHEW 22:1–14

I ONCE HAD THE PRIVILEGE AND JOY of teaching a high school class on medieval literature. We studied some beautiful but often complex pieces, such as *Beowulf* and the *Song of Roland*. We read from Thomas Aquinas, Bernard of Clairvaux, Dante, and my favorite, Geoffrey Chaucer. Chaucer's *Canterbury Tales* are quite fun, especially if you speak Middle English for fun as I do. "Virginitee is greet prefeccion, And continence eek with devocion" (105–106), I often hum around the home.

My favorite tale is the Pardoner's Tale. As these religious pilgrims are on pilgrimage to Canterbury, the Physician has finished has tragic tale. The Host then turns to the Pardoner and asks him to tell a more upbeat or happy tale. Others disagree and ask for a moral tale. The Pardoner agrees to tell a moral tale only after he has his fill of food and drink. (Chaucer was ahead of Luther on teasing the gluttonous, greedy clerics who trekked throughout Europe tricking people into buying pardons, fake relics, and the like.)

So this immoral man tells this moral story. In his drunken stupor he reveals the trick of his trade—how he cheats people of their money by preaching on money being the root of all evil. His tale is this: Three lawless young men go on a search for Death. They think if they can find Death, they will be able to kill him. As they are searching, they meet an old man who tells them that Death can be found at the foot of an oak tree. Off they go to the tree. There instead of finding Death, they find eight bushels of gold. With Death now out of mind and greed in mind, they decide to sleep there that night and sneak away with the treasure in the morning.

Meanwhile, the youngest goes into town to buy some food and drink. He also buys some rat poison and poisons the wine. He wants the gold all to himself. Ah, but the other two want the gold for themselves. So they plot to kill him when he returns. Sure enough that is what they do. When the man returns, they stab him to death. To celebrate, they lift their cups and drink the poisoned wine. They too die.

The old man was right. All three greedy men found Death under that tree.

Like the Pardoner's Tale, Jesus' parables are full of surprises, surprises that usually come (as they do in any good story) at the end. That is what we find in his Parable of the Wedding Feast. It is a wedding reception that somehow ends with "weeping and gnashing of teeth" (v. 13).

Israel's Burned City

Before we get there, let's walk through this short story. Thankfully, this anything-but-nice parable divides rather nicely. There are two parts in which two main groups are addressed during two distinct time periods. And then there is only one main point—that poignant point—to both parts, and that point is made at the very end.

The first part is verses 1–7. This part of the parable is a prophecy to and about Israel, particularly the Jews of Jesus' day. Here our Lord speaks symbolically about the time after his resurrection until the destruction of the temple in Jerusalem (so roughly AD 33 to AD 70).

I'll explain all that by explaining the characters and the story. Look with me at verses 1–7. Verse 1 simply sets the stage: "And again Jesus spoke to them in parables." This sentence introduces the genre and the original audience. The genre is parable. That tells us not to look for precise definitions and not to be worried about unrealistic actions, like a king burning a city on his son's wedding day. The original audience (the "them" here) is the Jewish religious leaders, as made clear in the context—21:23, 24, 27b, 31b, 42a, and especially 45, "When the chief priests and the Pharisees heard his parables, they perceived that he was speaking about them." As we start in 22:1, we are to perceive the same thing. He is still talking to (literally, "answering") them.

To them some of the symbolism here might *conceal* the truth, but to us—those who hear and see (and especially see from a mile-high, two-thousand-year vantage point) the symbolism *reveals* the truth. The characters, plot, and climax are not hard to decipher. Let's read it and then crack the code:

> The kingdom of heaven may be compared to a king who gave a wedding feast for his son, and sent his servants to call those who were invited to the

> wedding feast ["invite the already invited," is the sense], but they would not come. [Imagine that!] Again he sent other servants, saying, "Tell those who are invited, 'See, I have prepared my dinner, my oxen and my fat calves have been slaughtered [this king is not a vegetarian], and everything is ready. Come to the wedding feast.'" But they paid no attention and went off, one to his farm, another to his business, while the rest seized his servants, treated them shamefully, and killed them. The king was angry, and he sent his troops and destroyed those murderers and burned their city. (vv. 2–7)

Nice family-friendly story. Jesus meek and mild? Meek? Yes. Mild? My foot.

Okay, let's crack the code. Let's start with the easiest character for Christians to identify. Who is the "son," mentioned *only* in verse 2? Jesus. When in doubt, as in Sunday school, so in church, always say "Jesus." He is the answer. The bridegroom son is Jesus.[1] Who then is the king? God. God the Father,[2] if we want to be more specific. Note that the king is the central figure of this parable. He is the protagonist throughout verses 2–13. In verses 2–7 he hosts the wedding feast, he invites people to it, he sends out his servants, and he eventually sends out his troops. He is also the only one who talks (whose words are recorded, to be more accurate).[3]

So the "king" is God, the "son" is Jesus, and the "wedding feast" is the messianic banquet, a celebration centered on the Messiah (Jesus), which the prophets, John the Baptist, Jesus himself (8:11; 26:29), and later the apostles talked about. In the language of Revelation 19:9, it is "the marriage supper of the Lamb" (Jesus) and his bride (the church). "Eternal life with God in Heaven" is how we might commonly talk of it, as long as we don't view Heaven as our invisible bodies floating through the clouds as we eye harp-plucking angels. Heaven has some *meat* (and wine) to it.

The king's servants ("servants" are mentioned five times) represent those who offered the gospel invitation, including the prophets, but especially the apostles and their first ministry teammates and successors. From Jesus' resurrection to the destruction of the temple, this lot had endured quite a lot of persecution. Think of the shameful treatment of Peter and Paul. Think of the stoning of Stephen and the beheading ("killed . . . with the sword," Acts 12:2) of James.

"Those who were invited" (vv. 3, 4) symbolize Israel in general and their religious leaders in particular. Not all the Jews of Jesus' generation rejected him (for example, the Twelve were all Jewish), but many did. "He came to his own, and his own people did not receive him" (John 1:11).

Finally, the "troops" mentioned in verse 7 symbolize the Roman army under Titus, who was ultimately, like Cyrus or Nebuchadnezzar, under the sovereign control of God (it is "his" troops).[4] God the Father's troops came into "their city" (Jerusalem) and flattened it.

Those are the characters, and with their identities revealed the story is almost told. But in case you don't yet see it, the story is simply this (I'll divide it into three sections): First, God patiently and persistently invited Israel to the messianic banquet. He sent his own Son, which is not the emphasis here. Jesus did invite. Jesus did woo by word and deed. But the emphasis here is that God sent his prophets; then God sent his apostles. God sent his servants to Israel and to Israel alone. They shouted, "The feast is ready. Come to the feast." They invited Israel to a wedding, not to a wake (the word "wedding" is used eight times), a feast, not a famine.

So, first, God patiently and persistently invited Israel to the messianic banquet. But, second, most Israelites rejected the invitation. Verses 5, 6 reveal the two basic types of rude rejections. One rejection was busy indifference, and the other was violent indignation.

The first group was indifferent. They "paid no attention and went off, one to his farm, another to his business" (v. 5). Here think of the Parable of the Sower and the choking power of "the cares of the world" (13:22)—not only money but also job, family, and possessions (cf. Luke 14:18–20). Or think of the average unbeliever today. Fill in his or her name. They don't necessarily want the churches' doors or the preachers' mouths closed, they just don't want their ears opened. They pay no attention and go about their more "important" business.

They remind me of the clever Disney version of *Alice in Wonderland*. The rabbit is so busy. His mantra is "I'm late. I'm late for a very important date. No time to say 'Hello, goodbye.' I'm late, I'm late, I'm late." We live in a world where people are so busy that they simply find no time to stop and listen to the generous invitation, no time to see the Mad Hatter's tea party (I mean, the Messiah's banquet) set before them.

I thought about this recently on a flight from Calgary to Chicago. People are too busy traveling from Calgary to Chicago and Chicago to Calgary and Calgary to Chicago and Chicago to Calgary to look out the plane window in awe at the glories of the heavens and earth and he who made them. "Good" people are doing their "good" work but are ignoring the good news of their great God, and that might possibly be the most damning influence in the world today. Don't let your occupation preoccupy your soul.[5] Don't lose your life by making a living.

That's one group. The other group is hostile. Look at verse 6. This group seizes God's servants, treats them shamefully, and then kills them. Now you might say, "What an absurdly exaggerated response,"[6] and yet one that sadly corresponds with the inexplicably monstrous behavior of the scribes, the Pharisees, and the chief priests in the Gospels and Acts. Ironically, then as it has been throughout church history religious leaders are the most antagonistic toward the gospel. I don't worry when Mel Gibson or Uma Thurman come on Larry King to talk religion. I worry when Reverend So-and-So and Mr. Celebrity Evangelical do.

First, God patiently and persistently invited Israel to the messianic banquet. Second, most Israelites rejected the invitation. Third and finally, God justifiably and justly judges. That's the picture given in verse 7. God has been gracious. He is throwing a party for them. God has been patient. Twice he has invited them. But even God's patience has its limit. Reject the king, reject the king's son, reject the king's servants, reject the king's invitation to the table, and all that is left is righteous anger and wrath: "The king was angry, and he sent his troops and destroyed those murderers and burned their city" (v. 7).

Those first listening to Jesus' words in verse 7 may not have known what he was talking about, but the first readers of Matthew's Gospel certainly did. This is, as I said, only a thinly veiled allusion to the Roman Empire's destruction of the Holy City, Jerusalem.[7] You can read Josephus for a fuller account. But don't go there and miss what is here. In Jesus' short account he claims that God is the ultimate actor. God orders the destruction of the city. More shockingly, God orders the destruction of the temple and those thieves and "murderers" hiding out in it.

We live in a culture that gets so angry with the notion of an angry God, who thinks a God of justice to be unjust, who hates the idea of a loving God being wrathful. Our kinder, gentler culture (so they think—the murder capital of world is just thirty miles down the road from me [i.e., Chicago])—thinks they want, as C. S. Lewis put it, "not so much a father in Heaven as a grandfather in Heaven—a senile benevolence."[8] But let me tell you, they don't really want that God any more than they want a President who would refuse to give the orders to attack and kill an enemy like Osama Bin Laden. We didn't praise the President of the United States or the elite Navy Seals for planning and executing the murder of a man but for planning and executing the murder of a madman. We praise justice when we see it, and I'm telling you verse 7 is reason for praise. Do you think Jehovah unjust or Christ's party parable cruel? I hope not but fear so. It is high time the church stops getting squeamish around

Jesus' strong stories. It's time we put down our oversensitivity spectacles and see the Lord for who he is.

Now there are lots of lessons we might glean from verses 1–7 as we move toward the poignant point at the end of verses 11–14, but the one lesson I want us all to understand is something of the nature of God. Jesus doesn't cram the whole doctrine of God into seven verses, but he does push in quite a bit. God is a king. He is sovereign ruler. God has a son. How's that for Christology?[9] God is gracious and generous. He invites people to a wedding feast. God is patient. He sends out word again and again. Why seek rebels twice? Why seek them even once? God is so patient. But God is also holy and just, and he will mete out justice to those who reject his joyful (party-like) rule.

The Church's Unchosen

That is the first part of this two-part parable. It is a prophecy about Israel's rejection of God's invitation. The second part of the parable (vv. 8–14) is a prophecy (I think it's fair to call it that) to the church about what will happen in the last days, that is, the days from the destruction of the temple until the last or final judgment.

Verses 8–14 have a similar structure as the first half. We find:

Invitations (vv. 2, 3a; 4; 8, 9; 11, 12a)
Responses (vv. 3b; 10; 12c)
Judgments (vv. 7; 13b)

We also find similar characters and details. The king, servants, and the wedding feast represent the same persons and realities. The two new characters are "the attendants," whom the king uses to bind the guilty, and the "guests," those from the highways and byways. The "guests" represent the church (if that isn't clear now, it will be in a moment). And based on the Parable of the Weeds, "the attendants" are likely the angels: "The Son of Man will send his angels, and they will gather out of this kingdom all causes of sin and all law-breakers, and throw them into the fiery furnace. In that place there will be weeping and gnashing of teeth" (13:41, 42). The same language is used for angels in the Parable of the Nets (13:49, 50).[10]

With all that in mind, hear now the short symbolic story of the long history of world missions—the gathering of the church, but also the judgment of the church.

> Then he [the king] said to his servants [Christian missionaries or gospelers], "The wedding feast [the messianic banquet] is ready, but those invited

> [Israel, cf. 8:11, 12] were not worthy [cf. Acts 13:46]. Go therefore to the main roads [what Spurgeon calls "the heathen highways of the world"[11]] and invite to the wedding feast as many as you find." (vv. 8, 9)

This is the Great Commission! The gospelers are told to "go" out to "the main roads" or perhaps better, the "'outlets' of the city streets,"[12] that is, to the points where the highways become gravel roads. The Jewish city folk have rejected the message; perhaps the Gentile country bumpkins won't. And sure enough they won't![13] Those *outsiders* will eat up this idea of coming *in* for a free feast! Verse 10 triumphantly records the mission's success: "And those servants went out into the roads and gathered all whom they found, both bad and good [people from all walks of life?]. So the wedding hall was filled with guests."

In verses 2–7 we heard rejection, rejection. In the Gospel of Luke, it's rejection, rejection, rejection. In the Gospel of Thomas (bear with me), it's rejection, rejection, rejection, rejection.[14] Whether it is two, three, or four rejections, there is repeated rejection to the king's gracious offer. Now finally, with verse 10, someone (many someones) accept. The place is packed. Emily and I had 300 people at our wedding. Here imagine 300,000,000,000! "The wedding hall was filled with guests." And then the music starts and the choir sings:

> Glory be to the Father, and to the Son, and to the Holy Ghost,
> As it was in the beginning, is now, and ever shall be, world without end.

The end! Right? Wrong. Jesus does not end on this positive note. He does not say, "And the many were merry!" or "All the elect lived happily ever after." No, this is a parable with a poignant point. What does *poignant* mean? It could mean "piercing" or "cutting" or "moving." What do I mean by it? All of the above. We are to have this emotional prick of conscience, a cut-to-the heart heartbreak when we read the end. Like the Pardoner's Tale, this parable ends with a deadly surprise:

> But when the king came in to look at the guests, he saw there a man who had no wedding garment. And he said to him, "Friend [that's the same word Jesus used of Judas at his betrayal, 26:50], how did you get in here without a wedding garment?" And he was speechless. Then the king said to the attendants, "Bind him hand and foot and cast him into the outer darkness. In that place there will be weeping and gnashing of teeth." For many are called, but few are chosen. (vv. 11–14)

So much for the notion that parables are simply fun little stories told by the supreme, seeker-sensitive storyteller. Wow, Jesus. What a sober story!

Now let me explain a few details, and then let's let this poignant point penetrate.

What is clear is not everyone who has accepted the invitation to the wedding and shows up to eat gets to eat. What is also clear is that those who don't show up with the proper wedding attire eventually get thrown out into the darkness. But note (please note) that it is a just judgment, for the one judged (and note the individual account one must give) has no defense—"And he was speechless" (v. 12b), and he is full of shame and regret—"in that place there will be weeping and gnashing of teeth" (v. 13b).[15] The judgment of verse 7 is pictured as a city being burned; the judgment of verse 13 is of a person all alone in darkness. Which picture of Hell looks nicer to you? Pick your poison. He should have known better. (He should have dressed better.) It's his own fault he is exposed and then (eternally?) exiled.

That's what's clear.

What is not clear is what the "wedding garment" is, which is surprising since it is the hinge upon which the verdict turns. So, what is it?

If we interpret Scripture with Scripture, we find a few possibilities. Looking at Galatians 3:27, perhaps the garment represents baptism. Paul writes, "For as many of you as were baptized into Christ have put on Christ." We know from history that the early Christians wore baptismal garments or robes. Or, looking at Colossians, perhaps the "garment" here is less literal. In Colossians 3:12, 14 Paul writes:

> Put on then, as God's chosen ones, holy and beloved, compassionate hearts, kindness, humility, meekness, and patience. . . . And above all these put on love, which binds everything together in perfect harmony.

Augustine took the garment here to mean "love."[16] Perhaps he is on to something (pun intended). Is the clothing here charity—if you have faith but not love you are nothing (cf. 1 Corinthians 13:2)?

Or, looking at Revelation 19, might the "garment" symbolize good works? Look at verses 7, 8 of that passage (and note the setting):

> "Let us rejoice and exult and give him the glory, for the marriage of the Lamb has come [ah, a wedding], and his Bride has made herself ready; it was granted her to clothe herself with fine linen, bright and pure [sounds like a garment]"—for the fine linen is [drumroll please] the righteous deeds of the saints.

Most commentators, ancient and modern, cite this cross-reference and argue that the "garment" is "righteous deeds," or more clearly, "the evidential works of righteousness."[17] This man is judged by his works. And he has no works to show, so out he goes. Now that might cut against the grain of our grace sensibilities, but it certainly fits themes that arise like mountains coming out of the sea throughout Jesus' teachings, especially in his final parable, the Parable of the Sheep and the Goats (25:31–46).

A final option is faith. Not surprisingly Martin Luther writes, "The wedding garment here is faith, which many will lack at Judgment Day. Without faith no one can remain at the wedding."[18] If that sounds forced, one only has to recall the imagery of Revelation 7:9–14, where God's people from every nation, tribe, and language are "clothed in white robes" (Revelation 7:9, 13), robes that have been washed "white in the blood of the lamb" (Revelation 7:14). I think the idea is they have "the cleansing effects of [Christ's] death on their behalf" by means of a trial-steady trust,[19] or more succinctly, by faith alone. And faith alone is a theme that Matthew won't leave alone. Every person in his Gospel who demonstrates saving faith (i.e., *gets into* the kingdom) comes to Christ empty of self but full of faith. Think of the centurion. Think of the synagogue ruler. Think of the paralytic. Think of Matthew himself. They have nothing to give Jesus, certainly no righteousness of their own.

Okay, those are the options. Which one is the right one? Do the garments represent faith, good works, love, or baptism? Well, I have two rules I follow in parable interpretation (and I have patented these rules, so you can't steal them). The first rule is this: if Jesus gives you the interpretation, take it. So if he says, "And the seed represents the word of the kingdom," say, "Okay, Jesus, then the seed is the word of the kingdom." The second rule is this: if Jesus doesn't give you the interpretation, don't be afraid to let the application be more elastic.

What I mean is this: perhaps the lack of a clear definition is intentional. The point, in other words, being put to the reader involves questions like these: What do you think you need to get in and stay in? What might you lack? What must you be sure to have on? Perhaps here Jesus holds up a mirror to all Christians and says, "Take a good look. Are you properly dressed?" To those who boast in their own righteousness, he says, "Make sure you are wearing my righteous covering, not your own." To those who confidentially cover only their lips (not their lives) with a mere profession of faith, he calls for a full-body coat of many colors—"show me your faith, your love, your works, your baptism."

All that to say what Calvin said 500 years ago (why do I try to improve upon him?):

> There is no point in arguing about the marriage garment, whether it is faith or a holy and godly life; for faith cannot be separated from good works and good works proceed only from faith. All Christ wants to say here is that we are called by the Lord under the condition that we be renewed in our spirits into His image, and therefore, if we are to remain always in His house, the old man with all his blemishes is to be cast off and we are to practice the new life so that our appearance may correspond to our honourable calling.[20]

A-plus, Jean Cauvin. I'll expand on Calvin's idea, keeping his house analogy: it might not be necessary to have a wedding garment to get into the house (the good and the bad came in with no personal righteousness of their own). But it is necessary to have a wedding garment to stay in the house for the meal.[21] Does that mean personal righteousness is necessary? I suppose it does. To Jesus, grace and faith and salvation are never antithetical to repentance and holiness and obedience. Bruner, as usual, says it just right:

> True faith in God's imputed righteousness moves believers to want to *be* righteous personally—not as a basis for standing before God (only Christ can give that), but as an evidence of wanting to please the Father who was gracious enough to invite. The gift of the *Holy* Spirit, given *with* faith, moves believers to want to *be* holy.[22]
>
> But where this desire to be holy is lacking, where there is the carelessness of presumption, or where there is an immoral "once saved always saved," ostensibly in the interest of eternal security, there the church is taught by the parable's ending to fear. God wants good people. And if we don't want to be good, or don't even want to try, or don't think it is even necessary to want to try, or if we see the Christian gospel as simply a making safe, a permission to live as one pleases, "unconditionally," then this parable warns.[23]

Amen and Amen.

Called but Not Chosen

Later Bruner adds (and this quote gets my double amen again), "Failure to seek a holy life will mean failure to enter the kingdom of God."[24] Really? Says who? Says some scholar? No. Says Jesus Christ right here. Our Lord gives his summary of his parable in verse 14. It's the high point of his poignant point.

> For *many* are **called**,
> but *few* are **chosen**.

What does Jesus mean by this antithetical parallel? I'll explain, apply, and then end.

Here the word "called" (in Greek, a key word used in vv. 3, 8, 9, 14) in the context of the parable is clear. It means to accept the invitation. In our context we can think of it meaning someone who professes faith in Christ and becomes part of his visible church. So Jesus is not using the term "called" in the same way Paul sometimes does (e.g., Romans 8:29, 30), meaning "irresistible calling."[25] Jesus is also not using the word "chosen" (*eklekoi*, i.e., elect) the way Paul often does.

Here is where it gets confusing, I know. For Jesus here "chosen" means "persevering to the end (24:22, 24, 31)."[26] Note that although the king, as I said, dominates the talking and acting, here at the end it is this man's decision not to get dressed properly that gets him tossed out. Here personal responsibility comes face-to-face with divine sovereignty. So Paul uses the word "chosen" to speak of divine sovereignty (God chooses the chosen), and Jesus uses it to speak of human responsibility (the chosen choose God's way). Paul uses the word to give assurance of our already possessed salvation,[27] Jesus to warn of losing it.[28] Paul uses it as a source word (predestinarian), Jesus as a goal word (ethical action—energetic ethical effort).[29] I'll put it this way (perhaps this will help): Paul uses the word to pull us, Jesus to push us, to push us through the narrow gate and down the straight and narrow path that leads to life.

That's my explanation of verse 14. Let me now apply it. The church is a mixed body (*corpus mixtum*)[30] comprised of wheat and weeds, sheep and goats. That's what Jesus teaches in Matthew. Thus, like Israel of old (v. 7), the church of the new covenant will face judgment (cf. 16:27; 2 Corinthians 5:10). (Matthew's Gospel alone "contains detailed descriptions of the Final Judgment—for example 7:21ff.; 13:36ff.; 47ff.; 25:31ff.,"[31] all of which are given to professing Christians! Isn't that interesting?) So every disciple who openly professes Jesus as Lord ("Lord, Lord") will stand before the King and Judge. Jesus Christ will have judicial robes on. The question is, will you have the proper attire? Faith? Sure, faith! A faith that loves, works, obeys, gets baptized into Christ.

You see, as Christians we live between the *cross* (in the past) and the *chair* (in the future), under the *commands* of Christ (in the present, by the power of his sustaining presence).[32] In the meantime for the end time we must conform our lives to the gospel.[33] That's the short of it. We must conform our lives to the gospel or else!

The end.

That's the ending I'll give because that's the ending Jesus gives. The Pardoner's Tale might be a laughing matter (it's intended in part to be funny), but Jesus' Parable of the Wedding Feast is not. We must conform our lives to the gospel or else!

64

Give Back to God

MATTHEW 22:15–22

IN *THE REPUBLIC,* Plato tells a philosophical parable about a group of humans who have lived in "an underground, cavelike dwelling." They have been there "since childhood, fixed in the same place, with their necks and legs fettered, able to see only in front of them, because their bonds prevent them from turning their heads around." Behind them is an elevated area with a blazing fire. In front of that fire there are men talking and walking back and forth "carrying all kinds of artifacts . . . statues of people and other animals, made out of stone, wood, and every material." The glow from the fire casts shadows of the mobile people and objects on the wall in front of the immobile prisoners. And so, quite naturally, the prisoners hear the echoes and see the various movements and assume (wrongly) that it is the shadows themselves that both move and speak.

As the story continues, Plato (using the voice of his mentor Socrates) then asks what would happen if one of the prisoners was released and allowed to walk upright toward the fire. Socrates proposes that such a person, having been cramped for so many years, would find both the walking toward and the viewing of the fire to be so painful to his limbs and his eyes that he would prefer to return to his customary position and confine his view to the familiar shadows.[1]

That is the beginning of Plato's famous *Allegory of the Cave*, which is his illustration of the unenlightened man, his vivid picture of man trapped in the depths of ignorance and unaware of his own limited perspective. In this chapter, as we continue our study in Matthew's Gospel, we don't find an allegory or a parable but rather a historical narrative (a true story) about a group of men so enslaved to their man-made traditions—so used to hearing echoes and seeing shadows—that when they see and hear the reality of Jesus Christ, they find "the true light" that has come into the world to be unbearable (cf. John 1:9). It is so unbearable that they seek not only to return to their customary position in the dark but first to douse the cause of their discomfort, to extinguish the fire altogether.

Throughout Matthew's Gospel, Matthew has provided reasons for their desire to snuff out the Savior and the light and heat that radiates from him. Jesus has been anything but dim and cool in his claims. In 5:20 he claimed that "unless your righteousness exceeds that of the scribes and Pharisees, you will never enter the kingdom of heaven." In Matthew 9—19 he claimed that the Pharisees' views on fasting, Sabbath-keeping, and divorce were wrong. In Matthew 21, 22 he told parables about and *against* them.

And here in our text from Jesus' perspective the pot is about to boil. The seven woes of chapter 23 are soon to pour out from his mouth. From the Pharisees' perspective, however, that pot has already boiled over. In 21:46 we learn that they were ready to arrest him. Here in 22:15 they have come to gather evidence to further justify that arrest. They are plotting, as our text says, to entangle him in his talk. And the bait they will use is a tricky question.

We'll look next at that deceptive question and also at Jesus' ingenious answer.

The Question

As the Parable of the Wedding Feast divided nicely into two sections (vv. 1–7; 8–14), so the first of three questions put to Jesus (22:17, 28, 36) divides nicely as well. There is their question (vv. 15–17) and Jesus' answer (vv. 18–21). Then there is the answer to his answer (v. 22), a holding of their hats in their hands, which I'll include under Jesus' answer.

We start with the question:

> Then the Pharisees went and plotted how to entangle him in his words. And they sent their disciples to him, along with the Herodians, saying, "Teacher, we know that you are true and teach the way of God truthfully, and you do not care about anyone's opinion, for you are not swayed by appearances. Tell us, then, what you think. Is it lawful to pay taxes to Caesar, or not?" (vv. 15–17)

To get the fuller meaning of their question, let's bring in a few basic interrogatives of our own. Let's question their question with *who*, *why*, *where*, and *what*.

First, *who* is asking the question? You'll notice that two groups are mentioned—the Pharisees (v. 15) and the Herodians (v. 16).[2] This is an unlikely union, as the Pharisees were "ardent nationalists, opposed to Roman rule, while the Herodians, as their name indicates, supported the Roman rule" of Herod the Great and his dynasty.[3] Yet, as unlikely as this union might be, it's not implausible, for it is common enough for enemies to become allies when they have a common enemy. Such is the case here. Jesus is that common enemy.

Also mentioned are the Pharisees' disciples—"And they sent their disciples to him" (v. 16). So the picture here is that of the older Pharisees asking their younger pupils, along with the Herodians, to ask Jesus their premeditated question. Why they ask their disciples to do their dirty work, we don't know. Perhaps it was to give some distance. Or perhaps it was because they had been in the ring with Jesus recently and hadn't fared so well.

Our second question to their question is *why*. Why are they asking what they ask? Matthew reveals their motives. After hearing Jesus talk in parables about them, the Pharisees "plotted how to entangle him in his words" (v. 15). Jesus also reveals their evil intentions. He was, as verse 18 says, "aware of their malice" or literally "evil." He knows it's an evil temptation (cf. 4:1) or trap or test: "Why put me to the test, you hypocrites?" (v. 18). I think of it this way. They ask their question like some sly reporters today ask politicians questions, hoping the candidate puts his foot in his mouth, or here, more specifically, hoping our Savior, with some sacrilegious sound bite, will sign his own death sentence.

Our third question to their question is, *where?* Where are they when they ask Jesus this question? They are in the temple. In 21:23 we read, "And when he entered the temple," and then in 24:1 we read, "Jesus left the temple." So between those two verses we find temple talk, or talk in the temple. They are in the temple! Tuck that temple context in the back of your minds. We'll untuck it in a minute.

Our final question to their question is, *what?* What did they ask? They asked, "Is it lawful to pay taxes to Caesar, or not?" (v. 17).

If Jesus answers no to their question—"No, don't pay taxes to the Roman Emperor," he then admits not only that his lordship is lame (he has been talking about a kingdom and acting like a king), but his rule is seditious. His no to them could be construed to mean yes to the charge of insurrection. And we know what Rome does with insurrections. Rebels against Rome don't fare well. Let's remember the official crime for which Jesus died. It was written above his head: "This is Jesus, *the King* of the Jews" (27:37).[4] That was the sarcastic but serious charge. The Pharisees would love for him to freely admit that he, as the king of the Jews, will not pay taxes to a Gentile Lord.

That's if he says no. But if Jesus answers yes to their question ("Yes, pay taxes to Caesar"), then the rumor proves true—he is a friend not only of Gentile sinners but also of Roman tax-collectors. You see, this is a short question, but not a simple one.

Some scholars think the Pharisees would have answered the question no (it is not lawful) but the Herodians yes (it is lawful). Whether the Pharisees represent one horn of the dilemma and the Herodians the other, we don't know for certain.[5] What we do know is that those are the two horns of the dilemma—revolution against Rome or collaboration with it. If Jesus moves too far this way or that way, he is nicked or cut or killed.

The Answer

What does Jesus do? Does he stand quietly balanced between the two horns? No. He doesn't stand quietly or safely between them. Rather, he takes the horns by the horns and breaks them. He destroys their false dichotomy. Let me show you what I mean. Look next at Jesus' brilliant answer. I'll take you through it verse by verse.

First, we have verse 18: "But Jesus, aware of their malice, said, 'Why put me to the test, you hypocrites?'" Yes, our loving Lord calls them "hypocrites," a word he will use thirteen times in this Gospel. It's a favorite of his. Now, what's a hypocrite? The Greek word translated "hypocrite" refers to actors in the theater, those who would play a part often by putting on a mask. And that's precisely the sense here. Jesus calls them out for their playacting. They have smiles on their faces but have come with evil intentions—to trap him in their trap. Psalm 55:21 can be applied to them:

> His speech was smooth as butter,
> yet war was in his heart;
> his words were softer than oil,
> yet they were drawn swords.

Behind their soft and smooth words are warring intentions and sharp swords. That's what Jesus detects here. So the word "hypocrites" is Jesus' way of exposing them. He removes the mask from their flattering introduction to the question. Here's that introduction again. Listen. Look. Feel the butter. It's soft and smooth.

> Teacher, we know that you are true and teach the way of God truthfully, and you do not care about anyone's opinion, for you are not swayed by appearances. Tell us, then, what you think [about Roman taxes]. . . . (vv. 16b, 17a)

In other words, "Jesus, you are a straight shooter. And we really admire that about you. So shoot straight with us now. Should we pay the poll tax to Rome? Is that the right thing to do? Yes or no?"

What is so interesting here is that their buttering him up is both irrational and ironic. It's irrational because if they really believed that Jesus couldn't be moved by the opinions of others (i.e., by being buttered up), why then butter him up? Their sweet talk makes no sense. It's irrational.

It's also ironic. What's ironic is that his questioners "will soon learn to their discomfort that their praise is all too true."[6] Jesus will shoot straight with them. And the gun won't backfire. The bullet will go straight through their forked tongues. He will silence them with one shot.

What is also ironic is that their flattery is true. They're right about Jesus. He is a "teacher," in fact the greatest teacher of all time. He is also a truthful teacher and a teacher of the truth. And he himself, as they say, is "true." One might even call him "the truth"—"the way, and *the truth*, and the life" (John 14:6). You see, the irony is that their hypocrisy unmasks both their true identity and Jesus'.

In verses 19–21a Jesus continues his exposé of hypocrisy. Next he says:

> "Show me the coin for the tax." And they brought him a denarius. And Jesus said to them, "Whose likeness and inscription is this?" They said, "Caesar's."

What's the hypocrisy here? To answer that question let's go back to our *where* question. Where are they when they ask this question? The temple. What had Jesus just done in the temple? He "overturned the tables of the money-changers" (21:12). Perhaps people are still picking up Roman coins all over the Court of the Gentiles. But notice that Jesus apparently has no money on him. Or at least the pagan coin in question was not in his possession.[7] So in the temple, to the super-spiritual, he says, "How about you? Any Roman coinage on you?" And they unwittingly say, "Oh, sure. Here you go." Ah ha! The first part of *his* trap has sprung. Here comes the second. Jesus then questions his questioners. "Okay, boys, tell me, whose image and inscription is on it?" "That's easy," they say. "Caesar's." "Yes. The image [or to use Bible language, the graven image, Exodus 20:4] that you hold in your hands is that of Caesar."

We know from archeology[8] that the portrait on the denarius was likely the head of Tiberius, with a crown of bay leaves. We also have a good idea of what the inscription was. On one side was written:

> *TI CAESAR DIVI AVG F AVGVSTVS* (that is, "Ti[berius] Caesar Divi Aug[gusti] F[ilius] Augustus).[9]

Translated, we might render it, "Tiberius Caesar Augustus son of the divine Augustus."[10] On the other side was a picture of a seated woman (symbolizing peace, the *Pax Romana*), perhaps the Emperor's wife, Livia. There the inscription reads either *PONTIF MAXIM* (that is, Pontif[ex] Maxim[us]),[11] which means "High Priest," or *Divus et Pontifex Maximus,*[12] "God and High Priest." Needless to say this coin's images and inscriptions didn't fare well with the first and second commandments.

The coin itself is quite a visual aid to their hypocrisy. In this silver coin Jesus wants them to see their hypocritical reflection. "Most pious of pious Jews, what are you, most separate of the separatists, doing with pagan money in God's holy temple? How is it that you hold in your holy hands idolatrous images with blasphemous inscriptions?"

Jesus is sharp here, very sharp indeed. Psalm 9:16 reads, "the wicked are snared in the work of their own hands." Here in 22:19–21a, the wicked indeed find the snare in their own hands! Jesus caught them red-handed.

In verse 21b we come (finally) to Jesus' answer. His setup to it has been so great. Can his actual answer surpass it? Oh, yes, it can and will. "Then he said to them, 'Therefore render to Caesar the things that are Caesar's, and to God the things that are God's.'"

In the first part of his answer ("Therefore render [or literally "give back"] to Caesar the things that are Caesar's") he adds nothing to their own reply ("Caesar's") except an obvious application. If it's Caesar's coin (he, in a sense, made it and gave it to them to use), then simply give it back to Caesar when he asks for it. In verse 17 they ask, "Is it lawful to pay [or literally "give," *dote*] . . . to Caesar?" in the sense of giving a gift to him.[13] Jesus replies, "No need to give him a gift. It's not a gift. He's not a god. But you are to give back [*apodote*][14] to him what was first his." In other words, pay the tax.

But why? Why does he answer this way? Why would a pious Jew pay a pagan tax? Here's why. Let me spell out some of the practical theology (and exile theology) at work here.

Living under Roman rule—like living under Babylonian or Egyptian rule—had its ups and its downs. The big downer of the downs was Roman colonization and occupation.

Being the son of an Irishman and thus legally being an Irish citizen myself (I have an Irish passport), I know that much of Irish identity is English oppression. The slogan "700 years of English oppression" finds its way into Irish songs and slurs and jokes. I'm sure some of the Jews of Jesus' day joked about their situation, but all of them knew it was no laughing matter. None of them liked being under Rome's thumb.

In Judea in AD 6 or 7 the Roman poll tax (the tax in question here) was introduced and enforced. Not surprisingly, it was met with opposition, some of which was violent. A man by the name of Judas of Galilee (a popular name back then and a perfect name for a political zealot—named after Judas Maccabeus) led a revolt against Rome. He wanted his people to have their land back. He acknowledged only Yahweh as God and king. Thus he refused to pay the tax. And how did he and his insurrection friends fare? They were mercilessly massacred. As a warning to all the Jews, Rome crucified these men. They lined the countryside with crosses.[15] The sign was clear: "Pay this small tax or you will pay a big price."

That could be the downside of living under Roman rule.

But there was an upside, the same sort of upside to British colonization, with which we are far more familiar. When the British pulled out or were cast out of many African counties, for example, it was a victory for political freedom, but it also led to great political, social, and economic instability. Many of those countries today are the most dangerous countries to live in or travel through. Sadly, the despots of the world have filled the English void.

Being under Roman rule, as it was with British rule, had its advantages. My daughter, Evelyn, when she was in second grade, studied the history of Western civilization. Her teacher gave the class an interesting assignment just a week before I preached on this text—to write a thank you note to the Romans for all their contributions. Seriously. Here is her letter:

> Dear Romans,
> Thank you for . . .
>
> - Starting a democracy
> - Creating Roman numerals
> - Making beautiful architecture
> - Inventing concrete
> - Making bathhouses
> - Teaching us how to build roads
> - Building aqueducts
>
> Sincerely,
> Thankful Evelyn

As even Evelyn now knows, being under Roman rule had its advantages. The Roman Empire provided water, sanitation, roads, law and order, and police protection. They brought much to the world in the areas of agriculture, education, and architecture. And for all this, all they asked for was one coin a year, a denarius, which was the average day's wages (cf. 20:2). For the very poor, this could be a burden, but for most the tax in question was not a large amount but was fair for all the benefits received. Rome was not demanding an excessive tax.[16] Rome was demanding far less than my hometown (and likely yours) does, to put it in context and make us cringe.

So with all that in mind, now back to our text.

There are two parts to Jesus' answer. The first part—give Caesar's coins back to Caesar—teaches them and us that during our exile on earth (be it under Rome, England, or whatever) "respect for government is an import form of respect for God."[17]

In the New Testament epistles—written at a time when the Roman government wasn't chummy with the church—there are no Christian writings on revolution. There aren't even political gripes. Instead we find calls for prayer, subjection, and respect. Below are the key exhortations.

> First of all, then, I urge that supplications, prayers, intercessions, and thanksgivings be made for all people, for kings and all who are in high positions. (1 Timothy 2:1, 2a)

> Remind them to be submissive to rulers and authorities, to be obedient, to be ready for every good work, to speak evil of no one, to avoid quarreling, to be gentle, and to show perfect courtesy toward all people. (Titus 3:1, 2)

> Be subject for the Lord's sake to every human institution, whether it be to the emperor as supreme, or to governors as sent by him to punish those who do evil and to praise those who do good. . . . Honor everyone. Love the brotherhood. Fear God. Honor the emperor. (1 Peter 2:13, 14, 17)

Where did such an attitude come from? National Public Radio? No. Fox News? No. Jesus? Yes. I think it came from Jesus' words in 22:21.

Let me be clear: "If Caesar coins a new Gospel, he is not to be obeyed."[18] That is, if the government outlaws Christian faith and practice, we must revolt against such rules and pay the price of such revolution. Read the book of Revelation (especially chapters 13 and 18). Read the lives of the early church martyrs. Jesus, not Caesar, is Lord! We better believe that and live that out—and die for it if necessary.

I am very concerned today about Christian political animosity. We live in a republic, and living in a republic gives us greater freedoms to express our views through petitions, voting, letters, and so on. But I wonder how many evangelical Christians today pray for our government leaders, including (and especially) our President.

Some of us wrongly think that to freely serve God we must be free of the yoke of any godless government. Why? Christ was not completely opposed to Caesar. Even Rome would play its part in the Christian drama—in the spread of the gospel to Asia Minor and Southern Europe through Roman roads and through the spread of salvation to the world through that old rugged *Roman* cross. God is not opposed to government, even ungodly ones, for even ungodly governments can be used as God's servant for the church's good (Romans 13:4).

So while I agree with Douglas Hare that "we must be careful . . . not to draw from the passage more than it contains,"[19] I think it is fair and reasonable to draw at least two conclusions, or "lessons" we might better call them. The first lesson is the legitimacy of government. Whatever government God has given us to rule over us, we are to have respect for it and (as much as we can) submit to it. In this era of exile (1 Peter 1:1), as we long for the city of God (cf. Hebrews 11:10), Christians pay taxes to the glory of God and for the welfare of the city (Jeremiah 29:7).

Give Back to God

That's the first lesson. Give back to government might be the simplest way to say it. The second lesson is give back to God. Look again at verse 21b: "Therefore render to Caesar the things that are Caesar's, and to *God* the things that are God's."

Note three things here. First, Jesus gives, as he is prone to do, a common Hebrew parallelism:

Render to	Caesar	the things that are	Caesar's,
And [render] to	God	the things that are	God's.

Second, the second half of the parallel is unnecessary. That is, it is an additional answer to their question. They just ask about the tax. Jesus answers their tax question, but he also adds to it. Thus, third, this addition must be important.

I'll put it this way. "Render to Caesar the things that are Caesar's" is the lesser lesson. (Perhaps I have spent too much time on it.) "[Render] to God the things that are God's" is the major lesson. It is not that the God-point trumps the government-point, but the God-point does put the government-point in its place. If you like pictures, then picture the heel of Yahweh with Caesar Tiberius under it. The whole emphasis is not on God, but most of it is. So the idea (and application) is: if you should freely give a few denarii to Tiberius

Caesar Augustus, son of the so-called "divine" Augustus, shouldn't you then give *everything* to the Most High God?

Our application to Jesus' clever, profound, impressive, unforgettable answer is not merely admiration.[20] "Wow, what an amazing teacher Jesus was! Maybe we should obey what this guy teaches until the end of the ages." Our application is to be adoration and allegiance to God and to his Christ, King Jesus.

You see, as Jesus was likely challenging the Pharisees' loyalty to God as they held Caesar's coins in hand (and too much in heart), so he challenges us today. Do you serve money or God? You can only serve one (see 6:24). Do you seek first your own rule and ways of living or the kingdom of God and his righteousness (6:33)? Do you fervently pray, "Our Father in heaven, hallowed be your name. Your kingdom come, your will be done, on earth as it is in heaven" (6:9, 10)? *O Lord, let your rule reign . . . in this world . . . now. Free us from Egypt. Free us from Rome. Free us from sin! Free us from all sinful rulers forever.*

When the Pharisees and the Herodians heard Jesus' reply, "they marveled," but then "they left him and went away" (v. 22). That is the opposite of what we are to do. We are not to merely marvel ("wow, nice answer, Jesus!") but to worship ("wow, what a Savior, High Priest, and divine Lord!"). And we are not to leave and go away from our Lord, but to cling to him and follow him. We are to give back to God. To God, who has given us life and breath, salvation and sanctification, his Son and his Spirit, we are to give back our adoration and allegiance, our treasures and talents, our hearts and heads and bodies and souls.

65

Like Angels in Heaven

MATTHEW 22:23–33

IN FOURTH GRADE I earned the prestigious honor of becoming the first boy in my class to have a girlfriend. She wasn't nearly as attractive as her older sister who coerced me into establishing this relationship, but Miss Francesca Quantra (Franny) was a start, a start to a twenty-year quest for love. Sadly, Franny and I, due to various social, political, and economic factors, as well as the usual instability of fourth grade romances, were unable to live up to the bold inscriptions that defaced the covers of our notebooks: Doug + Franny/TLF (True Love *Forever*). Our relationship, for better or for worse, fizzled as quickly as it flamed.

Human love, as even a fourth grader can discover, is frail and impermanent. Yet to most of us this notion of "true love forever" is not merely an adolescent illusion. Rather it is a slogan ingrained upon the human heart as much as it is scribbled upon our notebooks. And that is likely why the one line from this passage that leaps from the sacred page is Jesus' brief comment on the transience of marriage—"In the resurrection they neither marry nor are given in marriage" (v. 30). However there is another claim that Jesus makes here that should be just as surprising, if not more surprising.

I think because we Christians believe in life after death, and because we live in a culture that generally assumes and accepts an afterlife in one form or another (at most funerals we hear said, "He has gone to a better place" and the like), we have the tendency to focus on Jesus' brief revelation on the status of marriage in Heaven to the neglect of the central thrust of this passage—namely, Jesus' defense of the resurrection. In Heaven, it is true, the sacred bonds of human matrimony will be forever severed, yet the more remarkable truth of this text (one that we are to marvel at, as we marvel also at our Lord Jesus) is that our dead bodies will one day rise again!

An Open Bible and an Open Mind

As you open your Bible to 22:23–33, I want you to open your mind too—especially to the mind-set of the Sadducees. That is, I want you to "go native" (a favorite phrase of my favorite church history professor). To "go native" means to try and understand how someone in history could arrive at a certain cultural or theological conviction.

With the Sadducees going native is not as hard as you might expect, for the Sadducees were like us in a number of ways. The most important similarity was that they, like historical Protestants, held that the Bible alone was to be the authority in all matters of doctrine and practice. Thus they were convinced that the Torah, the first five books of the Bible (which was their canon), gave no clear teaching on the resurrection. As Matthew points out in verse 23, this was their theological distinctive. As opposed to the Pharisees and to Jesus, they believed "that there is no resurrection."

This theological conviction (based on their ancient version of *Sola Scriptura*) explains why when they approached Jesus, these men went straight to their Bibles and (in v. 24) referenced Deuteronomy 25:5, 6. "Teacher," they said to Jesus, "Moses said, 'If a man dies having no children, his brother must marry the widow and raise up offspring for his brother'" (v. 24). This law was called the levirate law, a law graciously given by God to provide economic and social protection to widows, as well as to guarantee continuance of a family name. In other words, it gave a woman a chance of a future if her husband died young.

So, you see, the Biblical basis for the question they are about to pose (about this woman and her seven husbands) comes from Moses, from Deuteronomy, from the Bible, and (in their minds) from God. To the Sadducees, the implications of this God-given mandate were obvious. This law was the surest proof-text that the idea of a resurrection, in certain cases, was inconceivable, even ridiculous. To them, the whole notion of the resurrection was Biblically and philosophically absurd. And this is why these Sad-u-sees *happily* presented our Lord with their inquiry. In verses 25–27, they said:

> Now there were seven brothers among us. The first one married and died, and having no offspring left his wife to his brother. So too the second and third, down to the seventh. After them all, the woman died. In the resurrection, therefore, of the seven, whose wife will she be? For they all had her.

Their question, at first glance, was magnificent. It was apparently Biblically sound, logically tight, and extraordinarily clever. It was a question to which they expected no response, for it was designed more to ridicule than to obtain an answer.[1] Likely comprised of fabricated circumstances, it was intended to strike like a dagger at the heart of Jesus' predictions of his own resurrection, as well as his teachings on the reality of eternal life and the resurrection of the dead in general.

As I look at the complicated nuances of their question, it reminds me of word problems, those dreaded stories usually found lingering at the end of algebra examinations. To me, such mathematical narratives were psychologically deceptive because they always began with the plain details of an everyday event or situation (which you could get), but then concluded with a question the solution to which was not so easy to get (and especially to me, as I didn't "apply myself" to mathematics the way I should have). When we read the Sadducees' question to Jesus, we can almost picture it at the end of our final exam:

> There were seven brothers all of whom married the same woman. (Okay, I've got that.) Johnny, who was the oldest brother, was the first to marry Susie. Johnny, however, died before he and his wife had any children together. So Johnny's younger brother Tommy, under obligation to his brother, married Susie in order to perpetuate his brother's name. (Right.) Tommy also unfortunately died before having any children with her. So Billy, Tommy's younger brother, married Susie for the same reasons, but like his older brothers he widowed infertile Susie once again. Jimmy took over where Johnny and Tommy and Billy had failed, but sadly he too died before leaving Susie any offspring. So Sammy, Jimmy's younger brother, and Charlie, Sammy's younger brother, and finally Louie, Johnny's and Tommy's and Billy's and Jimmy's and Charlie's and Sammy's younger brother, married Susie. In due time they all married Susie, and one after another met the same fate. Now the question is, what is the square root of 529?

No, the question is, in Heaven of the seven whose wife will she be? You see, there's a complexity to this seemingly simple question presented to our Lord.

I don't know about you, but when I had the great misfortune of attempting to solve such word problems, I always took a separate sheet of paper and recorded all the necessary details. Then I tried to answer the question by getting a handle on these facts. My basic flaw was not in my method but in my inability to figure out how the many details provided before the question in any way related to or answered the question itself. Of course, when it comes to the "word problem" recorded in Matthew 22, it doesn't take a mathematical genius to solve this riddle. Rather it takes theological genius, a mind that possesses divine insight as well as a right understanding of the inspired Word of God.

The Mind of Christ

The Pharisees may not have had a good answer or any answer to this simple word problem offered by the Sadducees. But Jesus did. And with grace and wisdom and wit and authority, "the Son of David" and yet David's "Lord"—that's who was speaking to them (22:42–45)—opened his mouth and with a straightforward, almost effortless reply "silenced" (v. 34) their rejection of the resurrection.

Jesus answered them, "You are wrong, because you know neither the Scriptures nor the power of God" (v. 29). How's that for straightforward? "You are wrong. You are mistaken." Why? "Because you don't know your Bibles (although you think you do), and because you don't know the resurrection power of God!" Jesus continues, "For in the resurrection [or, "in the resurrected condition"][2] they [people] neither marry nor are given in marriage, but are like angels in heaven" (v. 30).

Let's stop here and look at this first part of Jesus' reply (vv. 29, 30).

The first loophole in the their argument, as Jesus saw it, was their wrong-headed notion that the institution of marriage was as central and as necessary a component of heavenly existence as it is of earthly existence. To them the afterlife could never be a reality because the relationship structures of a resurrected people would be utterly confusing, especially in regard to remarriage.

I like to imagine that when the Sadducees got together for dinner parties, and they broke out expensive bottles of wine (the Sadducees were the *rich* religious leaders; they aligned themselves with "the priestly aristocracy and other men of wealth and influence"),[3] they must have had quite the fun coming up with this prize question of theirs, this stump-Jesus question. And they must have had fun running it through various scenarios. One of them would say to another, "Do you think in the 'afterlife' (wink, wink) husband A will have to arm wrestle husband B, and husband B husband C (and so on) to find out who wins their earthly wife for eternal life?" Ha, ha, ha. They all laugh. What a hoot! Oh, these Sadducees had quite a question here. It was their top dog.

Ah, but with one simple statement Jesus puts this dog to death. Forever. It would never rise again (from them)! With one simple statement he rebukes and corrects the logic of Sadducean thought. Concerning the nature of the resurrected state, he reveals the truth that the present conditions (of marriage and remarriage) are not to be resumed in Heaven but *surpassed*.[4] The resurrected life, Jesus tells them, is not an exact counterpart or continuation of earthly life.[5] The surprise to them (and perhaps to many of us) is the fact that marriage is a temporary institution. Your marriage might be made in Heaven, but it's not made *for* Heaven.

Now, of course, the purpose of Jesus' statement on marriage here was not intended to provide a comprehensive theology of it. He only mentions marriage because he is working with and against their illustration, their story and question. He addresses the topic of marriage, in other words, only as a defense of the resurrection. Yet when we meditate on Jesus' unexpected revelation on the relationships of eternal life, many of our own perceptions of Heaven and marriage are turned upside down. This little part of this little verse has grand implications.

A few years ago College Church in Wheaton (Illinois) hosted a marriage conference. My wife and I attended it. She attended all of it, and I attended most of it (I had to work a bit on a sermon, a sermon on this text no less). So I skipped the session on Saturday morning. When I told my wife I might have to do that, she said, "Oh great, what am I to tell people when they see me sitting all alone? Oh, I know," she said with a downcast face, "I'll just tell them my husband is upstairs working on his *'there's no marriage in Heaven'* sermon." Yes, my wife can be quite funny at times; not as funny as me, but funny nevertheless.

Anyway, that conference was wonderful because it put marriage in the right perspective, teaching that the key to marital unity and love is not romance but worship.[6] It is only when we worship God as Creator, King, and Savior that we will then love others as we should. The truth that God is to be first and that our love for him is to be first is the best way to keep a marriage strong.

Christians can get so sidetracked by a kind of Hollywood perception of love—you know, the kind of powerful "love" where a man and woman accidently bump into each other at the supermarket, causing their eyes to connect, which then produces a massive shot of romantic electricity that surges down their spines and then up through their hands as they instantaneously drop their produce and unabashedly throw their arms around each other. At first sight they have found the love of their life. Christians get sidetracked by such idiocy. Sure, chemistry matters to some extent. (Read my sermons on the Song of Solomon!)[7] But gospel-centeredness and God-centeredness (God firstness) matters so much more. It matters in marriage, and it matters in all of life.

So as we come to the end of this excursus I want to ask you a delve-into-your-heart-of-hearts question. Here it is. I'm borrowing from Jesus' illustration. *Are you envious of the angels?* More than anything, would you right now like to commune with God and to serve him perfectly, without hesitation and without weariness and without sin, "like angels in heaven" (v. 30b)?[8] For singleness will be the social structure of Heaven and single-minded devotion its everyday reality. So the irony of the resurrected state will be that my marriage to my wife will be forever dissolved, but our love for each other and for God ever increasing.

"For in the resurrection they neither marry nor are given in marriage, but are like angels in heaven" (v. 30). That's the first part of Jesus' answer. Here's the second part. Look with me at verses 31, 32. With the Sadducees' assumptions of the resurrected relationship crushed by Jesus' brief declaration on the status of marriage in Heaven, he next continues his gentle assault by attacking, as he did with the devil in the wilderness, their understanding of Scripture. They have twisted Scripture one way;[9] he will twist it back into its proper place. "And as for the resurrection of the dead, *have you not read* [in your Bibles] what was said *to you* by God: 'I am the God of Abraham, and the God of Isaac, and the God of Jacob'? [Commentary:] He is not God of the dead, but of the living."

Jesus is quite remarkable here. I'd like to say he's at his best, but if you read through the Gospels enough you realize he's always at his best. Jesus always uses just the right words, and Jesus always gives just the right answer at just the right time.

Our Lord could have answered this particular question in a number of different ways. He could have given a lengthy theological treatise, beginning with the logic of Genesis 1, 2. He could have called the Sadducees' bluff by laying down the card of creation. Every Jewish man or woman, child or slave, no matter what religious group or sect they were a part of, accepted the fact that God (YHWH), with infinite power, raised the dust of the earth and breathed life into it. So Jesus could have questioned his questioners, saying, "Don't you think that a God who created man out of dust could also take the scattered dust of the dead and remold it into a resurrected body? Couldn't he take these dead bones and breathe life into them?"

Then, after presenting this theological foundation from Genesis, Jesus could have piled text upon text to further prove the validity of the doctrine of the resurrection. He could have cited, for example, Daniel 12:2 ("And many of those who sleep in the dust of the earth shall awake, some to everlasting life, and some to shame and everlasting contempt") or Isaiah 26:19 ("Your dead shall live; their bodies shall rise. You who dwell in the dust, awake and sing for joy!") or a few different verses from Job, including Job 19:25, 26 ("For I know that my Redeemer lives, and at the last [day] he will stand upon the earth. And after my skin has been thus destroyed, yet in my flesh I shall see God"), or, as the apostles did in the book of Acts, our Lord Jesus could have quoted a plethora of Psalms, like Psalms 16, 68, or 110, all of which testify to the reality of the resurrection.

Or think about this—we studied Matthew 17 a few chapters ago, and Jesus could have said, "You should have seen the transfiguration. Do you remember Moses (he died 1,480 years ago) and Elijah (he went away in that whirlwind about 900 years ago)? Well, Peter, James and John just saw and heard them. Those two prophets aren't dead!" Or—even better, in fact best of all—Jesus could have said, "Can you guys just wait a few days? Watch me die. Check the tomb. Check it again. I will rise from the grave."

Jesus could have argued his defense in this manner. But instead he took the approach of saying more by saying less. All our ingenious Lord did was recite and *briefly* comment upon the well-known and often quoted verse from the Torah, Exodus 3:6. This simple reference, which contains the words, "I am the . . . God of Abraham, the God of Isaac, and the God of Jacob," would have been as recognizable to any first-century religious and patriotic Jew as John 3:16 would be to the average evangelical today.

Every aspect of Jesus' short defense is significant. It is significant that our Lord selected a verse from the Torah because he recognized that the Torah alone was the authority used by his opposition. Furthermore, it is significant that of all the verses he could have selected from the Torah, he cited Exodus 3:6. Instead of building his case on a pile of proof-texts, through this one verse Jesus reminded the Sadducees, in the simplest terms, that at the heart of the covenant is the promise of a real and living and lasting relationship between YHWH and his people.[10] With words easy enough for a one-year-old to memorize, Jesus re-enrolls the teachers of Israel in Old Testament 101, Lesson 1: Since the Torah teaches that God is a covenantal God, it is therefore inconceivable that God's promises and blessings cease when his people die.

The Sadducees' understanding of death as extinction, without any hope of resurrection, implies that God is a "God of the dead" (cf. v. 32). Jesus reminded them that it would be foolish for God to undertake the task of protecting his people from calamity during their lives, but fail in delivering them from the supreme calamity of death. What kind of protection is that? If death has the final word, then God's covenant has been breached or broken.

So by carefully selecting Exodus 3:6 as his star witness, Jesus demonstrated beyond a shadow of a doubt how resurrection faith is attached in a profound way to the central concept of Biblical revelation (the covenant) and how the salvation promised by God to the patriarchs and their descendants, in virtue of the covenant, contains implicitly the assurance of the resurrection. So the "grievous error" of the Sadducees was their failure to recognize and appreciate the necessary link between God's covenantal faithfulness and the resurrection.[11] They had overlooked the implications of this everyday passage. They never stopped to think about the language and theology of this short but crucial verse.

I told you, Jesus is at his *best* best here.

Their Response and Ours

The Apostle Matthew tell us in verse 34 that Jesus' quotation of Exodus was so surprising and his brief interpretation of it so convincing that the Sadducees apparently found themselves muzzled by the plain truth of Scripture. When they heard Jesus' response, they had nothing more to say. Their proud riddle had been solved. Their party fun had come to an end.

The crowd, however, Matthew tells us, was "astonished at his teaching" (v. 33). Perhaps never in their whole lives had they witnessed such a spectacle, a complex religious question answered so quickly, so correctly, and so simply that even this uneducated mass of men, women, and children knew exactly who now held the religious and moral authority in Jerusalem, and perhaps over the entire world.

"They were astonished." How about you? Matthew records their response to Jesus, but what's your response to him? I would guess that you wouldn't be reading a commentary on the Gospel of Matthew if Jesus had little or no appeal to you. But I wonder how often you are astonished by him. Are you envious of the angels? Are you at all astonished by Jesus? Those are two good questions to repeatedly ask ourselves.

My Own Astonishment

It has been over twenty years since I was first overwhelmingly astonished by the Lord Jesus Christ. I had grown up learning the stories of the Gospels, learning about God, learning about Jesus, but it wasn't until I picked up this Gospel for myself, the Gospel of Matthew no less, that Jesus began to astonish me. I was astonished by his *miracles*—his healing of the paralytic and the two blind men, his raising of the dead, his calming of the storm, his feeding of the 4,000, and so on. And I was astonished by his *teachings*, his parables, and especially his claims and his callings. "Blessed are the meek, for they shall inherit the earth," (5:5). "If anyone slaps you on the right cheek, turn to him the other also" (5:39). "Whoever finds his life will lose it, and whoever loses his life for my sake will find it" (10:39). "If anyone would come after me, let him deny himself and take up his cross and follow me" (16:24). "For what will it profit a man if he gains the whole world and forfeits his soul?" (16:26). "You shall love the Lord your God with all your heart and with all your soul and with all your mind" (22:37).

Then it happened. This astonishment overtook me. I was nineteen years old. It was one o'clock in the morning. (By now you know the story.) I fell upon my knees. I cried out to Jesus (this was the essence of it), "Forgive me, save me, bring me into a relationship with you. Love me as I now truly and finally love you. You are first in my life. You and me, me and you—true love forever." I prayed this in no silly, superficial, fourth-grade way.

Human love, as even a child can discover, is frail and impermanent. But divine love is everlasting! The marriage between the Lamb and his church is eternal. So God says *to you* today, "Incline your ear, and come to me; hear, that your soul may live; and I will make with you an everlasting covenant, my steadfast, sure love" (Isaiah 55:3).

66

Out of the Eater Came Something to Eat

MATTHEW 22:34–40

OUT OF THE EATER CAME SOMETHING TO EAT. Out of the strong came something sweet." Within any Children's Bible certain Old Testament stories are sure to be found—the story of Noah and the ark, David and Goliath, Jonah and the whale, and, of course, the story of Samson and the lion.

The story of Samson and the lion comes from the fourteenth chapter of the book of Judges. There we are told that as "a young lion came toward him roaring. . . . the Spirit of the LORD rushed upon him, and . . . [with his bare hands] he tore the lion in pieces" (Judges 14:5, 6). Now, of course, our Children's Bibles (as is only appropriate, I suppose) depict Samson wrestling with the beast rather than tearing it limb from limb. And such Bibles often end the story of Samson with just that memorable scene. But in the book of Judges itself we are told that Samson returns later—"after some days" (Judges 14:8)—to see a swarm of bees in the dead lion's body, and with the swarm he finds a bit of honey. Fearless Samson then, finding this sweet treasure, puts his hand into the carcass and scrapes the bee's honey out of the lion's side. Later this event became the answer to Samson's famous riddle: "Out of the eater came something to eat. Out of the strong came something sweet" (Judges 14:14).

The story and the riddle of Samson symbolizes well what has occurred in 21:23–27 and 22:15–33. But here, instead of a lion attacking a mighty man of God, we have a den of religious predators seeking to devour the sovereign Son of God. The first attack comes from "the chief priests and the elders of the people" (21:23). In 21:23–27 they claw at Jesus' self-imposed authority. The second strike comes from the Pharisees and Herodians. In 22:15–22 the upper jaw of the Pharisees comes together with the lower jaw of the Herodians, seeking to squeeze Jesus with their question, "Is it lawful to pay taxes to Caesar, or not?" Then finally the Sadducees roar about the resurrection. In 22:23–33 this last group seeks to deface our Lord with their ingenuous question about a woman and her seven husbands.

Yet like Samson (the strongest man in the world), Jesus (the wisest man in the world) tears them to pieces, if you don't mind the less-than-tame analogy. It is out of the carcasses of his questioners' questions that we Christians find something sweet.

The Lawyer and His Question

As we come to our text for this chapter, we see there is one more challenge our Lord must face. It is the potential sting of one hovering bee. Look with me at 22:35. Here we have "a lawyer" who has been buzzing around. He is a *lawyer* in the sense that he is an expert in the written Old Testament *law* as well as its oral interpretation and application. He is a religious lawyer, a Pharisee who is "one of the scribes" (Mark 12:28).

At first, when we read in verse 35, "And one of them [a Pharisee], a lawyer, asked him a question to test him," we may rightly fear he has only come to lower his stinger, for you see the scribes, whenever mentioned in Matthew's Gospel, are fond stabbing at our Lord. Also the word "test" or "tempt" doesn't have positive connotations. Is this lawyer trying to get Jesus to indict himself with some lawless statement on the Law? "Who needs the Law? I am the Law unto myself. Follow me." Furthermore, the language of verse 34 ("they gathered together," cf. v. 41) reminds one of Psalm 2:2: "the rulers take counsel together, against the Lord and against his Anointed."

Matthew seems to add such subtle details to intensify the animosity: the scribe is here to sting! Mark's version, however, views the scribe more as someone who is scrapping for honey, if you will. He is there to learn. I think if you blend those two voices, you arrive at this man's voice here. In verse 36 he asks, with the mix of animosity (as a lawyer who is there to test the "teacher" about his "knowledge of and fidelity to the Torah")[1] and yet sincerity (as a learned man who is still willing to learn), "Teacher, which is the great commandment in the Law?"

With this question this man is not asking "which laws from the Scriptures need to be obeyed and which can safely be ignored?"[2] Instead he is asking, "Jesus, in your opinion, what is the fundamental premise of the Law on which all the individual commands depend?"[3] He is asking, "Of the 613 commands (as later rabbinic tradition would number them—248 positive and 365 prohibitive)—which command gets at the heart of them all?"

About twenty years before Jesus, the story is told of a Gentile convert to Judaism who approached Rabbi Hillel and asked him to summarize the whole Law while he stood on one leg (in other words, summarize it quickly). Hillel's answer was a negative version of the Golden Rule. He said, "What thou hatest for thyself, do not to thy neighbor. This is the whole law; the rest is commentary. Go and learn."[4] Before and after the time of Jesus, other rabbis used key Bible verses to answer this common question. One rabbi quoted Proverbs 3:6 as the heart of the Law: "In all your ways acknowledge him, and he will make straight your paths." Another rabbi quoted Habakkuk 2:4: "The righteous shall live by his faith."

Jesus' Answer: Love God

It is in this tradition that Jesus is asked, and that he answers, the question. He quotes from the Torah, as he did in the previous text with Exodus 3:6. Here he quotes from Deuteronomy 6:5 and Leviticus 19:18. Jesus answered:

> You shall love the Lord your God with all your heart and with all your soul and with all your mind [Deuteronomy 6:5]. This is the great and first commandment. And a second is like it: You shall love your neighbor as yourself [Leviticus 19:18]. On these two commandments depend all the Law and the Prophets. (22:37–39)

Here Jesus provides an interesting and helpful image. He has us envision both the Law *and the Prophets* (his canon [cf. 5:17; 7:12] is bigger than the Sadducees'), with its "commandments and covenants, prophecies and promises, types and testimonies, invitations and exhortations,"[5] as *hanging* (Young's Literal Translation renders the phrase, "on these—the two commands—all the law and the prophet do hang") on these two love-command hooks. One scholar summarizes the image like this: "The picture, then, is of two pegs at equal height from which a great bundle hangs."[6]

That image is interesting and unique because many Jews in Jesus' day viewed their Bibles as hundreds of pegs "from which hundreds of individual commands hang down in suspensions of almost equal lengths."[7] So here Jesus cut all those strings, pulled out all the pegs but two, "and suspended the whole Bible *from* its two main commandments," which are so close to each other they can rightly be called "the Double-Love Command,"[8] two separate pegs united by love—two pegs nailed or pushed into the wall and two nails through the sides of both pegs.

Let's look at these two pegs separately, and then we'll place them back together, as intended.

The first command to love comes from Deuteronomy 6. In the original Hebrew the first word of Deuteronomy 6:4 is the word "*Shema*," which means "hear." "Hear, O Israel: The LORD our God, the LORD is one." As the Apostles' Creed has long been the oral creed of Christianity, the *Shema* was "the oral creed of Judaism."[9] The synagogue service began with its recitation. While in prayer, a pious Jew wore it on his forehead and on his wrist, in a tiny leather box called a *phylactery*. At home the *Shema* hung upon their doors. And in every godly household it was repeated in the morning and again in the evening every single day of the year.

The *Shema*, of course, contains no command. It is simply a distinctive theological statement about monotheism: God is one. Yet, like all theological statements in Scripture, it has applications. Its application comes in Deuteronomy 6:5, which Jesus quotes in verse 37: "You shall love the Lord your God with all your heart and with all your soul and with all your mind."

So, to Jesus what mattered most were not the hundreds of various laws and their relative rankings. What mattered most was a loving relationship with the one true God (love for YHWH, not Baal or Allah or Vishnu), a loving relationship that requires the whole of a person—heart, soul, and "might" (Deuteronomy 6:5), or as Jesus puts it "mind."

Perhaps he substituted "mind" for "might" as a subtle rebuke to their riddles, the sense being, "Use your heads!" More likely, heart, soul, and mind are simply "overlapping categories" representing "our every faculty and capacity."[10] Love God with everything you are. That is, the mention here of "heart . . . soul and . . . mind" was not intended to give us a psychological breakdown of the various components of the human personality—the *heart* being the hub of the wheel of all our thoughts, words, and deeds, the *soul* representing the seat of our emotional activity, the center of our desires and affections, the *mind* understood as the seat and center of our intellectual life as well as dispositions and attitudes.[11] Rather these three parts were intended to give us a comprehensive picture of what is to be our total devotion.

The key to this command is observing the "alls." Three times in verse 37 the word "all" is repeated. "You shall love the Lord your God with *all* your heart and with *all* your soul and with *all* your mind." This repetition of the word "all" emphasizes "the necessity of a total response of love to the lordship of God."[12] "God's wholehearted love," as one commentator put it, "must not be answered in a halfhearted manner."[13] And as another commentator summarized, "[T]he demand is for total allegiance: one should love God with every globule of one's being."[14] All! "You shall love the Lord your God with *all* your heart and with *all* your soul and with *all* your mind," with all of everything you are. Total devotion.

In Mark's version (Mark 12:28–34) of this story the scribe's question and Jesus' answer is surrounded by what I take to be an example of what the fulfillment of this love commandment *doesn't* look like and an example of what it *does* look like. (I use the term *fulfillment* because Paul is fond of using it in relation to love.)[15] Fulfilling this love command *doesn't* look like the great mob of people who have come from every corner of the Roman Empire to use the temple like "a den of robbers" (as a hideout), those religious schizophrenics who murder and commit adultery and all sorts of other evils throughout the week but come to the temple to pray, offer a sacrifice, and receive forgiveness (see Mark 11:15–19). However, fulfilling the love command *does* look like that famous widow (Mark 12:41–44) who gave God "everything she had" (Mark 12:44)—all her heart, all her soul, all her mind (and yes, all her money, "all she had to live on"). She loved God! That's one example, I think, of what love looks like.

Now back to Matthew, but don't move far from the widow. She is an example of what our inner and outer devotion to God should be. God gives everything to us; we give everything to God—however little it looks like to the world. Loving God isn't easy, but it's not impossible. All things are possible with God. As Augustine prayed, "Grant what you command, and command what you will."[16]

Recently I met with a small group of pastors in Chicago. At one point in the conversation we were talking about good commentaries on the Gospel of Matthew. As two of us were raving about one commentator in particular, another pastor jumped in and said, "Yeah, he's good, but he's too pietistic for me." I said, "Well, I like piety." He replied, "You would." That was a jab—a friendly but intentional jab—not at my overly sentimental or emotional preaching but at my persistent preaching on the necessity of good works and holiness and a changed life. To some such preaching is too pietistic because they think it takes away from the cross of Christ.

Well, the morning after that, in my pietistic devotional time I have each morning, I prayed, "Lord, am I too pietistic in my preaching? Am I missing the gospel? Am I preaching too much about what we should do rather than what Christ has done?" This was a sincere prayer. The answer came (it would have come audibly if I was more pietistic than I am), and I think I have the mind of Christ on this. I say that mostly because the answer came to me in question form, which is very much how our Lord thought and talked.

Anyway, here's what came to mind: when did Protestant piety go out of theological fashion? It's in all the Reformed Confessions![17] How does piety distract or remove from the work of the cross? What would Paul think of that? And didn't Jesus decide to answer this scribe's question by talking about *love*? He didn't say, "The greatest commandment is to be justified by faith alone." And he didn't say, "And I really mean 'alone'!" He chose to go the pietism route and talk about love—our actions (certainly) but also our attitudes and affections. *Love* is a fairly all-encompassing word, isn't it?

Therefore, with all that said (I stand firmly upon the foundation of the founder of my religion), here's some pietistic preaching for you. My brothers and sisters in Christ, God is to be first in our lives. That's what this first great commandment teaches us. He can't be second or third or fourth of fifth or fiftieth. The sum of the whole Old Testament (and New Testament) is the command to love God and to love him before all others, more than anything and anyone else. And in a world that lacks a God-consciousness (let alone a God-centeredness), and in churches where preachers refuse to preach straightly and forthrightly the need for Christians to love God, we need to pray doubly hard to set the Lord God before our eyes and to see him (as Jesus did) towering "in sovereignty above the state (22:15–22), above death (vv. 23–33), and . . . above all other human responsibilities (vv. 34–40)."[18]

This day I say to you, with proud humility, that the purpose of my life is to live for God. I love God, not perfectly, not completely, but totally, with heart and soul and mind. I'll put it this way: I'm totally depraved. That is, I'm sinful in every part of who I am. Yet, by God's powerful grace I'm totally saved. That is, now, by God's grace I love God with every part of who I am. You see, I say, with proud humility, that I'm totally God's. And I hope you can say the same. I hope you can join me in my piety.

Jesus' Answer: Love Others

The second part of Jesus' answer follows quite naturally. Like the shape of a cross, the vertical dimension (the command to love God) connects with the horizontal dimension (the command to love others). In verse 39 Jesus says, "And a second is like it." "Like it" in the sense of flowing from it (the "motive force")[19] or "like it" in the sense of equally important (Paul seems to think so; cf. Romans 13:9; Galatians 5:14)? Can it be both? I don't know.

"And a second is like it: You shall love your neighbor as yourself." Again, Jesus quotes from Leviticus 19:18, which he quotes three times in Matthew's Gospel (cf. 5:43; 19:19), more than any other Old Testament text. I guess Jesus likes love. (He's so pietistic.)

In the context of Leviticus, loving one's neighbor means (and what a corrective the content of this command is for today's concepts of love) not harboring anger in your heart, or seeking vengeance, or bearing a grudge, and yet frankly reasoning or kindly rebuking him or her if necessary. That's love in Leviticus.

Unoriginal Originality

On one hand Jesus' answer to this scribe's question is unoriginal (he does, after all, simply quote from two popular Old Testament texts), yet on the other hand it is quite original. For you see, while this combination of these love commands is commonplace to us, it was not to them. This combination was revolutionary.[20] James Edwards writes, "Although love of God and love of humanity were occasionally affirmed separately in Israel, there is no evidence that before Jesus they were ever combined. It does not appear that any rabbi before Jesus regarded love of God and neighbor as the center and sum of the law."[21]

So while Jesus' answer was based on two well-known and often-cited texts from the Torah, he was the first in history to affirm that love for God and love for people are indivisible. He was the first to say that the *Shema* must be complemented and completed by a love for one's neighbor.[22] So there is a distinction between the two love commandments, but not a division. The first command is *greater* than the second; yet the first cannot be met unless the second is accomplished (and vice versa).

So with that said I say, away with the doctrines of humanism, which teach us to love people without any reference to God, and away with the doctrines of mysticism (I'll define that word in a minute), which teach us to love God without any reference to people. Both of these dangers, humanism prevalent in the world and mysticism prevalent in the church, are diffused by Jesus' answer.

Let me address mysticism for a moment. There is room for mystery (and piety) and even subjective communion with God in Christian devotion, but there is not room for mysticism, defined as a love for God that is detached from a love for others. Let me give you an odd but awesome example.

A few years ago I read an old and interesting book on the desert fathers. The desert fathers were hermits of the third and fourth centuries who lived in the desert (surprise, surprise). On a positive note these men resembled those faithful persons described at the end of the list of the heroes of faith in the eleventh chapter of Hebrews, those who "went about in skins of sheep and goats, destitute, afflicted, mistreated—of whom the world was not worthy—wandering about in *deserts* and mountains, and in dens and caves of the earth" (vv. 37, 38). But on a negative note, with their extreme denial of food, water, clothing, shelter, and sleep, these men resembled those false teachers whom Paul addressed in Colossians 2:16–23, where he speaks of a "self-made religion and asceticism and severity to the body" that have "an appearance of wisdom" but are "of no value in stopping the indulgence of the flesh."

In this book I read about Nathaniel, a man so focused in his devotion to God that he resolved never to cross the portal of his cell. Simply put, he wouldn't leave his humble little house. Well, one day a ten-year-old boy came to the monk's door because the boy's donkey had fallen down and was hurt. The boy cried out, "Father Nathaniel, have mercy on me and give me a hand!" Nathaniel heard the voice and opened the door. Standing inside, he asked him, "Who are you and what do you want me to do?" The boy replied, "I am So-and-so's servant, and I am bringing loaves [of bread for Communion for the church in town]. I beg you, do not neglect me, lest I be eaten by hyenas." The blessed Nathaniel, we are told, stood there surprised and stunned; filled with compassion, he debated within himself and said, "I must fail either the commandment [the commandment to love one's neighbor] or my resolution [his resolution not to leave his house]." How did this supposedly great man of faith reply? "Listen, boy!" he said. "I believe that if you are in need, the God whom I serve will send you aid." He shut the door and went back to his business of "loving" God.[23]

Now, of course, this is the type of religiosity that Jesus rebukes in the Sermon on the Mount[24] and in his famous Parable of the Good Samaritan. In Luke's account of our passage (Luke 10:25–37), it is this very parable that Jesus tells to this scribe. In the parable, if you recall, it is the religious leaders, a priest and a Levite, eager to get to Jerusalem apparently to worship God in the temple with their ritual sacrifices, who on their way walk around the body of the half-dead man. They are presumably too busy "loving God" to love others, so busy focusing on the first great commandment that they don't have time for the second, for their neighbor, the person who has been providentially placed along their path, the person in need of compassion and care.

Here in 22:39 Jesus makes clear that he will have nothing to do with this kind of "love." He teaches that a genuine love for God must express itself in genuine love for neighbor. As the Apostle John wrote in 1 John 4:20, 21, "If anyone says, 'I love God,' and hates his brother, he is a liar; for he who does not love his brother whom he has seen cannot love God whom he has not seen. And this commandment we have from him [Jesus]: whoever loves God *must* also love his brother."

God cannot be loved apart from our neighbor, and our neighbor cannot be loved apart from God. There are two pegs nailed into the wall of God's Word, and those two pegs are also nailed into each other. And those two pegs are the pegs that ought to be nailed into the heart of every Christian.

The Assumption of Self-Love

As is sadly necessary, let me make a final clarification on the condition of this command. We are told we are to love our neighbors as we *love ourselves*.

In recent decades it has become popular to advocate that Jesus teaches we must love ourselves before we can love others, that we must build up our self-esteem before we can esteem others. If you buy into this thinking, Jesus here teaches not two great commands but three: (1) Love God, (2) *love ourselves*, and then (3) love others. Barbara De Angelis represents this position when she writes, "If you aren't good at loving yourself, you will have a difficult time loving anyone, since you'll resent the time and energy you give another person that you aren't even giving to yourself."[25] Wow. Really? No. That's nonsense. Let me repeat—that's nonsense.

Years ago I remember hearing a good Christian speaker (I think it was Ravi Zacharias) claim that the downward spiral of self-love in the culture and the church was well reflected in the starting publication dates of certain popular magazines. First, there was *People Magazine*. Then there was *Us Magazine*. And now there is *Self Magazine*. We have gone from focusing on people to us to self. But, of course, the trend of the culture is the reverse of the theology of the Bible. The Bible teaches we are to move from self (me) to us (the church) to people (the world). So the magazine title for Christianity should be something like *Self-denial* (cf. 10:38, 39; 16:24–26). That word should be printed in large, bold type on the front cover of Christianity today and always. Self-denial!

When Jesus commands us to love our neighbor as we love ourselves, he assumes a healthy dose of self-love is already in place—a self-love that is natural (it is the way we were created; we naturally care for our bodies, our needs, etc.) and a self-love that is sinful (an egocentric affection that continually seeks self above and before others).

Like most people I have not had to work on loving myself. I naturally love myself more than I love my congregation, more than I love my God. That's not a good thing to say, but it is an honest thing to say. It is only by God's grace that I ever think about loving others and loving God more than I love myself. Looking out for number one will always be our number one priority. So the call here is that we take this inclination and focus it elsewhere. Instead of focusing inward, we focus outward. We must focus our self-love on loving others. The measure by which we love ourselves now becomes the measure (it's a high measure) by which we are called to love others.

So, what is the greatest commandment? Jesus says there are two. The first is to love God; the second is to love others as much as we love ourselves. That is Jesus' sweeter-than-honey answer to this buzzing-around-the-carcass scribe. And it's the answer not only to the meaning of Scripture[26] but also to the meaning of life.

Soaking My Soul

If I were to give a critique of my own preaching, it would not be that I'm too pietistic. It would rather be that I too often don't let what I'm learning and saying soak into my own soul. My friend Todd Wilson said in a sermon he gave on the topic of preaching, "My growing conviction about preaching is this: preaching exists not primarily to impart to you information from the Bible—about who God is, or about who Jesus is, or about the Christian life—preaching exists primarily to enable the people of God to encounter the living Christ."[27] Amen to that. I wish my hearers (and readers) would encounter the living Christ when I preach about Christ. I wish that *I* would encounter the living Christ when I preach about Christ.

You see, it is one thing to tell you about loving God and loving others. I can and hopefully did correctly explain all the details. But it is another thing altogether for you and me to desire Christ so much that we want to and do heed his commandments—to see him, as it were, and to like the fact that we see him and to mourn over our lack of love for the Lord and others. Why do we still so blatantly sin against God? Why do we ever, even for a moment, hold a grudge against a fellow Christian? Why can we love the poor of the world by writing a check but care so little and do even less for that poor neighbor who struggles to make ends meet?

May this text always—is this not at the heart of Christianity?—soak into your soul. And may it soak into mine too. Be transformed by the power of the gospel. Be transformed by the teachings of Jesus Christ. Love God. Love your neighbor. There is nothing greater in the whole wide world.

67

Answering to Jesus

MATTHEW 22:41–46

ON APRIL 29, 2011 the world once again was taken into Westminster Abbey. This time it was to witness the wedding of Prince William and Kate Middleton. Westminster is the usual place for British royal weddings. It is also the place for royal coronations. If a prince is being crowned as king or a princess as queen, he or she sits upon a throne housed in Westminster. The throne is called King Edward's Chair. It was built in 1296, and all but two English monarchs sat on it for their coronation. Two features are striking about the chair. First, it is a plain-looking *wooden* chair. While it was once likely gilded with gold paint and ornamented with other colors, today you see mostly the bare, aged oak, along with some carved, choir-boy graffiti. Second, it is huge! Those old enough to remember the crowning of Queen Elizabeth II in 1953 might remember how small her already small stature looked in that giant chair.

Either King Edward was a giant (ten feet high, four feet wide) or his throne was intentionally built big to make a point. Likely the latter is true. The point being that no one king or queen can ever fill that seat. No one person can fill the greatness of Great Britain's royal rule.[1]

In Scripture we learn of King David's throne. It too is a big "chair," far bigger than that of King Edward and far grander than the rule of England. In 2 Samuel 7 God promised David that he (God) would establish an eternal kingdom, a royal rule that would never end (vv. 13, 16) and that he would "establish the throne" of this kingdom (v. 13) through David's offspring (v. 12; cf. Psalm 18:49, 50).

We learn from 2 Samuel, 1 and 2 Kings, and 1 and 2 Chronicles that this "chair" is too big for David and any of his twenty-one immediate heirs to fill.

Even Solomon in his greatness looked liked a newborn, propped up in the corner of one of those huge red Santa chairs at the shopping mall. A bigger king than Solomon was needed to fill this big chair. A bigger king than David was needed to rule over this big kingdom. From Psalm 2, a psalm of David, we learn that "the nations" will be this king's heritage and "the ends of the earth" his possession (Psalm 2:8). From Psalm 72, a psalm of Solomon, we learn that this king will have "dominion from sea to sea" (Psalm 72:8) and that "all kings" will "fall down before him" and "all nations serve him!" (Psalm 72:11).

This "throne" is huge. Who could possibly sit on it and rule over that entire-earth kingdom?

In this chapter I want you to see Jesus walk up to that huge Davidic throne and sit on it. And I want you to see that there is no space left for anyone else. He fills the chair! He *alone* fills the chair. Thus I want you to see *and do* what Philippians 2 says to see and do: "God has highly exalted him and bestowed on him the name that is above every name, so that at the name of Jesus every knee should bow, in heaven and on earth and under the earth, and every tongue *confess that Jesus Christ is Lord . . .*" (Philippians 2:9–11a).

What's the Right Answer?

With that grand aim before us, we turn our eyes now to 22:41–46 and our minds to the Spirit for illumination. Starting in verse 41 we read, "Now while the Pharisees were gathered together, Jesus asked them a question." The language—"the Pharisees were gathered together"—reminds us of Peter's sermon in Acts 4:26, 27, which is based on Psalm 2:2, "and the rulers take counsel together, against the LORD and against his Anointed [i.e., the Christ, the son of David]." Moreover, with the language—"Jesus asked them a question"—we are reminded that Jesus is in the middle (actually, near the end) of a debate. It has been question/answer time with Jesus.

First the Pharisees threw him their fastball about paying taxes to Caesar (vv. 15–22). Jesus knocked it out of the park. Then the Sadducees threw him their curveball about marriage and the afterlife (vv. 23–33). Jesus again knocked it out of the park. Finally an expert in the Law lobed him a soft pitch about the greatest commandment (vv. 34–41). Jesus hit that ball to Damascus.

In our text it is Jesus' turn to throw something at them. So he takes the mound, warms up, stretches a bit, winks at the catcher, and first throws an easy ball that they bunt into play. Ah, but then he throws a pitch that is impossible for everyone (but him) to hit.[2] Verse 46 records one reporter's praise: "And no one was able to answer him a word, nor from that day did anyone dare to ask him any more questions."

Let's look at these two pitches he threw. First comes the hittable pitch in verse 42. Jesus asked, "What do you think about the Christ? Whose son is he?" They answered him, "The son of David." There is nothing unexpected or unorthodox about their answer. The messianic expectation was that the Christ would come from David's lineage.[3] (And they hoped he would act like David did in his military prowess. They longed for their Goliath—the Roman Empire—to fall.)

So the Pharisees' answer "The son of David" is true, but "only half of the truth."[4] The answer to the question "Whose son is he?" is "the Son of David,"[5] but also "the Son of God,"[6] the title ("Son") that God the Father calls Jesus at his baptism (3:17) and transfiguration (17:5). Jesus is David's son *and* God's son!

This is what Jesus is getting at in his follow-up question. Here comes the second pitch, the unhittable one. Jesus asked:

> How is it then that David, in the Spirit, calls him Lord, saying,
>
> "The Lord said to my Lord,
> Sit at my right hand,
> until I put your enemies under your feet"?
>
> If then David calls him Lord, how is he his son? (vv. 43–45)

The Pharisees asked about Roman taxes, the Sadducees about the resurrection, the lawyer about the Law, but Christ questions them about Christology! "What think ye of Christ?"[7] Is the Messiah more than a mere man?

He gets to that question by means of Psalm 110:1, which he quotes: "The Lord said to my Lord, Sit at my right hand, until I put your enemies under your feet." In this Psalm there is an apparent contradiction. How is it that David calls his "son" "Lord"? What father, especially a king, calls his son "Lord"? How can the man that King David calls "Lord," and who is somehow sitting at the right hand of God, in any way be David's "son"? Put differently, and with even more complexity, how can King David, the author of the Psalm according to the superscription (and *according to Jesus*), "in the Spirit" no less (i.e., inspired by the Spirit of God) write about the Lord-God, Yahweh (the first "Lord" mentioned) and invite someone also called "Lord" (the second "Lord," the messianic "Son of David") to sit next to him, at his right hand?[8]

The first commandment is, "You shall have no other gods *besides* me" (Exodus 20:3).[9] So what is this "Lord" doing beside the *Lord*? Who is this *kyrios* sitting next to the *kyrios* (the Septuagint's rendering of the two Hebrew words *YHWH* and *Adoni*)? What is this text doing in the "Hebrew, monotheistic, Scriptures"?[10] How is this second "Lord" David's "son"? Good question, Jesus. Very good.

The Pharisees scratch their heads with both hands, we might imagine. But we raise both our hands in praise, for we know the answer, don't we, post-resurrection church? The answer is that Jesus is David's son and David's Lord! "David's son as man, David's Lord as God"[11]—that is the only answer to the question. The second "Lord" of Psalm 110:1 must be big enough to fill the Davidic/divine throne. Only Jesus is David's son *and* God's son.[12] He is "the Word [made] flesh" (John 1:14)—David's son according to the flesh, and yet he is also the divine *logos*: "In the beginning was the Word, and the Word was with God, and the Word was God" (1:1).

Commenting on our text, John Chrysostom wrote that Jesus "is now quietly leading them to the point of confessing that he is God."[13] Exactly. Here Jesus solves the riddle *quietly* but also *clearly*. The Pharisees, having asked a question they had never asked before about David's famous messianic Psalm, and having asked it had no idea how to answer it, failed to see that the answer himself was "standing in front of them in flesh and blood."[14] What the crowd and children shouted upon Jesus' triumphal entry in Jerusalem, "Hosanna to the Son of David" (21:9, 15), Jesus now subtly accepts and expands upon. He is the King, the king David longed for, the one king big enough to fill that huge chair. As Peter confessed in 16:16, Jesus is "the Christ, the Son of the living God." Jesus is "the Christ"—i.e., the son of David, and he is "the Son of the living God"—i.e., God's Son.[15]

Following the lead of Peter's confession, the Apostle Paul adds his own. He declares that that gospel is what God

> promised beforehand through his prophets in the holy Scriptures, concerning his Son, who was *descended from David* according to the flesh and was declared to be *the Son of God* in power according to the Spirit of holiness by his resurrection from the dead, Jesus Christ our *Lord*. (Romans 1:2–4)[16]

Jesus is the son of David by birth, the Son of God as confirmed by his resurrection, and namely or thus the Lord!

What's the Right Response?

In the first part of this chapter we have explored the right answer to Jesus' question. The answer is: Jesus is Lord—David's Lord, our Lord—equal with *the Lord.* In the second part of the chapter we will explore two answers to the question, what then is the right response to Jesus?

The first right response is to confess Jesus as Lord. In Romans 10:9 Paul writes, "[I]f you confess with your mouth that Jesus is Lord and believe in your heart that God raised him from the dead, you will be saved." A few verses later he continues, saying of Jesus, "the same Lord is Lord of all, bestowing his riches on all who call on him. For 'everyone who calls on the name of the Lord will be saved'" (vv. 12, 13). In Joel 2:32, quoted in verse 13, the reference is clearly to Yahweh, the *Lord.* In Romans the reference is clearly to Jesus, the *Lord.* Precisely Paul's point!

Three Sub-Points

On this point—that we are to confess Jesus as *Lord*—let me give three sub-points. The first is the most obvious: let's not shy away from *defending the deity of Christ.*

One temptation Christians face today is to think too lightly about groups like the Jehovah's Witnesses or the Church of Latter-Day Saints (Mormons). They are nice people. They are good neighbors. They raise God-fearing children. They are often on the same side of the political issues as we are. They esteem traditional Christian morals. They believe in God and Jesus. But they don't believe what Jesus is teaching here today and what sounds forth like a trumpet in middle of the night in John 1 and Revelation 4, 5 and what has been echoed by the communion of saints throughout the ages as all true Christians happily sing the tunes affirmed at the Councils of Nicea and Chalcedon. They don't believe the Biblical testimony that Jesus, "the Word was [is] God," and they don't believe the church's testimony that Jesus is "very God of very God." And this belief in Christ as fully man and fully God is no little matter. It is the heart of the body called Christianity. Take it out, and the church shall not rise again.

The second sub-point under our confession that Jesus is Lord is *proper acknowledgment.*

In the British Museum there hangs an anonymous French miniature painting entitled "The Tree of Jesse with Musical Instruments." It pictures Jesse, King David's father, asleep in bed, and from his loins (shall we say) sprouts a tree of eleven musical kings, including David. The twelfth king is depicted twice. First, he is depicted as a baby held by his virgin mother. That is at the center of the piece. Second, he is depicted as a coronated king. That is at the very top and much smaller.[17]

Like that painting, we sometimes have the baby Jesus at the center of our vision. Matthew himself doesn't downplay the incarnation, that Jesus is "God with us," (1:23) as a baby and as a man. However, he does seem to showcase the idea of Jesus as Lord. He paints a picture of Jesus as the supreme sovereign. It's at the center of his thought, and especially at the end of his Gospel. From the end of chapter 22 until the end of the Gospel, there is an escalation of the revelation of Jesus' authority.

Let me give you three brush strokes from Matthew's portrait of Jesus. The first brush stroke comes in 25:31–34, where Jesus says of himself:

> When the Son of Man comes in his glory, and all the angels with him, then he will sit on his glorious throne. Before him will be gathered all the nations, and he will separate people one from another as a shepherd separates the sheep from the goats. And he will place the sheep on his right, but the goats on the left. Then the King will say to those on his right . . . [and on Jesus goes with his role as kingly judge of the world].

The second brush stroke comes in 26:64, when Jesus answers the high priest Caiaphas's question, "I adjure you by the living God, tell us if you are the Christ [i.e., the Son of David], the Son of God." Verse 64 reads:

> Jesus said to him, "You have said so. But I tell you, from now on you will see the Son of Man seated at the right hand of Power and coming on the clouds of heaven."

The third brush stroke comes at the Great Commission, which begins with Jesus' announcement of absolute authority: "All authority in heaven and on earth has been given to me" (28:18).

How much authority? "*All* authority"! Jesus continues:

> Go therefore and make disciples of *all nations*, baptizing them in the name of the Father and *of the Son* and of the Holy Spirit, teaching them to *observe all that I have commanded* you. And behold, *I am with you always,* to the end of the age. (28:19, 20)

Those italicized words above are important. Jesus is King over "all nations." Jesus, "the Son," is equal with "the Father . . . [and] the Spirit." Jesus, as "God with us," is "with" his church "always."

Do you see the picture Matthew paints? It is not of a baby in a mother's arms but rather of an all-powerful divine King upon an immensely large throne.

On this crucial-to-your Christianity theme, James Montgomery Boice writes:

> Most people's image of Jesus is at best that of a baby in a manger. It is a sentimental picture best reserved for Christmas and other sentimental moments. Others picture him hanging on a cross. That too is sentimental, though it is sentimentality of a different, pious sort. Jesus is not in a manger today. That is past. Nor is he hanging on a cross. That too is past. Jesus came once to die and after that to ascend to heaven to share in the fullness of God's power and great glory.[18]

Boice continues:

> When Stephen, the first martyr, had his vision of the exalted Christ, it was of Jesus "standing at the right hand of God" to receive him into heaven (Acts 7:55). When John had his vision of Jesus on the Isle of Patmos, it was of one who was as God himself. The apostle was so overcome by Jesus' heavenly splendor that he "fell at his feet as though dead" (Rev. 1:17). We need to recover this understanding of who Jesus is and where he is now.[19]

Yes, we need to recover the vision of Jesus put forth in Psalm 110—that Jesus is priest, judge, and king. He is "a priest forever after the order of Melchizedek" (Psalm 110:4). "He will execute judgment among the nations" (Psalm 110:6). And he sits at the right hand of God with a "mighty scepter" (Psalm 110:2) and with his vanquished "enemies" under his feet (Psalm 110:1). That is the vision of Jesus in the New Testament. And that is why, I would imagine, Psalm 110 is the most alluded to and quoted Psalm in the New Testament, by one count thirty-seven times.[20] The inspired apostolic-era authors wanted their readers to see Jesus as the exalted Lord. So let's see him that way! Let's see him as friend and teacher, sure. But let's also see him (acknowledge him) as cosmic Lord.[21]

The third sub-point under our confession that Jesus is Lord is that *confession never means mere profession*. This is especially clear in the Gospel of Matthew. It couldn't be clearer in Matthew 7, where Jesus says:

> Not everyone who says to me, "Lord, Lord," will enter the kingdom of heaven, but the one who does the will of my Father who is in heaven. On that day many will say to me, "Lord, Lord, did we not prophesy in your name, and cast out demons in your name, and do many mighty works in your name?" And then will I declare to them, "I never knew you; depart from me, you workers of lawlessness." (vv. 21–23)

James said, "faith without works is dead" (James 2:26, NKJV). In Matthew 7 Jesus seems to say, "Faith without fruit is condemned." Confession never means mere profession.

In John Bunyan's *Pilgrim's Progress*, one of the characters Christian encounters on his way to the Celestial City is Talkative. Talkative talks the talk. He'll talk your ear off about "the vanity of earthly things, and the benefit of things above . . . the necessity of the New-birth, the insufficiency of our works, the need of Christ's righteousness . . . [about] what it is to repent, to believe, to pray, to suffer."[22] But as Christian soon learns, Talkative's Christian confession is all talk. Christian says to his companion, Faithful, "He talketh of Prayer, of Repentance, of Faith, and of the New-birth: but he knows but only to *talk* of them. . . . Religion hath no place in his heart . . . all he hath lieth in his *tongue*."[23] To this Faithful replies, "Well, I see that Saying, and Doing are two things."[24] A few pages later Faithful speaks of the need for "an experimental confession of . . . Faith in Christ."[25] That is what we would call spiritual experience, what Jonathan Edwards called "religious affections."

"My Jesus 'Tis Now"

With that important thought in mind (and feeling in heart), let me transition to my second answer to the question, what is our right response to Jesus as Lord? First, we are to confess Jesus as "the *Lord*"—which is not a mere profession but a heartfelt confession that properly acknowledges the person and power of Jesus and readily defends his deity. Second, we are to *love the Lord Jesus*.

Let me explain and then illustrate this answer. This answer comes from the context. In 22:36 Jesus is asked, "Which is the great[est] commandment in the Law?" He replied, "You shall love the Lord your God with all your heart and with all your soul and with all your mind" (v. 37). So here is the connection I'm making. See if this makes sense. In 22:37 Jesus says that we are to love the Lord our God. Then in 22:43–45 we learn that Jesus is the Lord our God.[26] Right? Thus, the contextual connection is: we are to love the Lord Jesus as *Lord*.

That's my explanation of loving Jesus as Lord. Here now is my illustration. It too comes from the context. In my Bible it comes with a mere flip of the page. In 26:6, 7 we have a picture of such love. In contrast to the decision of the chief priests and the elders of the people to kill Jesus (26:3, 4) and Judas's decision to betray him (26:14–16), a woman comes to love the Lord Jesus as Lord. We read of her in 26:6, 7: "Now when Jesus was at Bethany in the house of Simon the leper, a woman came up to him with an alabaster flask of very expensive ointment, and she poured it on his head as he reclined at table."

What is this all about? This is an incredible act of adoration, which underscores something of the reality (necessity?) of Jesus' death (she anoints him for his burial) and perhaps something of the reality of Jesus' rule (does she anoint him as king? [cf. 1 Samuel 9:16]). Now, whether or not she knows what she is doing in relationship to the overall plan of God's kingdom, here she certainly acknowledges Jesus as Lord and loves him accordingly.

One commentator calls this action a "lived-out commentary on the double-Love commands that Jesus taught as the main commandment of the law (22:34–40),"[27] as she loves the Lord Jesus with deep emotion and sacrificial giving (the cost of the pouring out was at least a year's wages; that's the scholarly estimation of the anointment's expense). Another commentator says, "This self-giving love models what we each must feel and do as we serve Jesus."[28] A final commentator—his name is Jesus—says "she has done a beautiful thing to me" (v. 10), something so beautiful that "wherever this gospel is proclaimed in the whole world, what she has done will also be told in memory of her" (v. 13). What does loving the Lord look like? It looks like "wasting" the best of what you have on Jesus because you see the significance of his death, burial, resurrection, and rule.

At my church we always sing a hymn to Christ, which we intentionally sing to Jesus as we would to God the Father. On the morning I preached from this text we sang the hymn, "My Jesus, I Love Thee." Over the years I've heard mixed reactions to the straightforward lyrics, "If ever I loved Thee, my Jesus 'tis now." I have heard some Christians quip, "I'm forced to sing something I don't or might not in the moment feel." I have heard others retort, "I don't think it is right to use the word 'love' in relationship to Jesus. Knowing he is our Lord, not our lover, we should say 'worship' or 'exalt' or 'trust in' or something other than 'love.'" But I like the song as it is. In fact, I *love* that love song. I love it because sometimes I do feel for Jesus exactly what the song says. I also love it because when I don't feel that way I pray to God that I would. "Jesus, use this sweet melody to open my heart to you. As I sing of my love for you, let me feel it." For me the song softens and warms my sometimes cold, hard heart.

We should love the Lord Jesus through obedience to his commands. We should love the Lord Jesus through compassionate care of others. But we should also love the Lord Jesus through heartfelt devotion toward him, like the woman in Bethany—pouring everything out. We should—with mind and soul and heart—"love the Lord," and we should do so every hour of every week.

Recently, I was doing my usual late-morning treadmill workout at the YMCA. While I run to live I listen to dead languages. On Monday and Tuesday it is Koine Greek, Wednesday Ecclesiastical Latin, Thursday and Friday Classical Hebrew. Don't be too impressed. I only do this because I'm awful at getting and retaining languages, and yet I think these three are important ones for me to have some handle on.

It was Tuesday. Greek! The Greek word is pronounced. There is a slight pause. Then the English definition follows. Now as I began my mental and physical workout, the television screen twenty feet in front of me had on *Access Hollywood*. I usually avoid eying this less-than-edifying show by working out on the opposite side. However, on that day all those treadmills were taken. The image that *Access* placed in front of me was the front cover of a popular pornographic magazine. It ends with "boy" and begins with "Play." What such an image was doing on daytime television and on a screen at the Young Man's *Christian* Association, I know not. But there it was.

Here is how I responded. I first turned my glance elsewhere, where I had the choice between the Cooking Channel, with the making of some mouth-watering dessert, a commercial with someone comfortably lounging on a La-Z-Boy, or ESPN with an NFL linebacker with his shirt off. Over lust, gluttony, and sloth, I choose envy (ESPN).

Just kidding. What I chose to do (no joking matter) to resist these four vices was something new. I refocused on my Greek and on my God. Here's what I did (and I hope it becomes a holy habit). I heard the Greek word, silently gave the definition before it came, *and then* after the definition I prayed a prayer based on the word. Here's a sampling of how it sounded:

Amartia	sin	Father, forgive me of my sin.
Basileia	kingdom	For thine is the kingdom and power and the glory.
Zao	I live	I live for you, my God.
Kardia	heart	Lord, open my heart to obey your will.
Agapao	I love.	

For that final word I could have prayed Psalm 18, which begins, "I love you, O LORD, my strength" (v. 1) and ends, "For this I will praise you, O LORD, among the nations, and sing to your name. Great salvation he brings to his king, and shows steadfast love to his anointed, to David and his offspring forever" (vv. 49, 50). But since I didn't have that much time and I didn't have that Psalm memorized, what I prayed was simply, "My Jesus, I love thee."

Whenever and wherever and however you practice the presence of God through persistent prayer, I pray that your answer to Jesus' all-important question of verse 45 is more than merely academic—"Jesus is David's Lord"—but is both academic (of the mind) and affectionate (of the heart)—"Jesus is my Lord! The Lord who sits on the throne of David is the Lord who sits on the throne of my heart."

68

The Exaltation of Humility

MATTHEW 23:1–12

I ENDED THE LAST CHAPTER with five Greek vocabulary words. I begin this chapter with one Latin word, *iustitia. Iustitia* means justice or righteousness. It is used in Christian theology for the doctrine of justification by faith—*Iustitia Dei*, "the righteousness of God" (Romans 3:21) and *ex Deo est iustitia in fide*, "the righteousness from God that depends on faith [in Christ]" (Philippians 3:9).

A question raised in many of Paul's other letters is the question, how does someone who is unrighteous get right with a perfectly righteous God? The basic answer given is, *by God's grace*. More specifically, God pardons all our sins and accepts us as righteous in his sight due to the righteousness of Jesus Christ imputed to us and received by faith alone. That's how the Westminster Shorter Catechism (A. 33) defines justification. And I agree. That's what justification is. But what does this faith that justifies look like?

In *The Voyage of the Dawn Treader*, C. S. Lewis gives as good an illustration of such faith as I have ever seen. He shows us what justification looks like through the transformation of a character called Eustace.[1]

Lewis's book begins with one of the great lines in literature: "There was a boy called Eustace Clarence Scrubb, and he almost deserved it." This boy deserved such an awful name because he was an awful boy. At the heart of his overall awfulness was his pride, a pride that led to perpetual complaining and persistent disbelief. He refused to believe in Narnia even though he was sailing upon its rough seas and holding conservations with its talking animals.

Lewis shows us what justification looks like by what J. I. Packer called Eustace's "endragoning and dedragoning."[2] While on an unexplored island, Eustace wanders away from the group and finds a dragon's hoard. Soon after, he is transformed into a dragon by the "greedy, dragonish thoughts" in his heart.[3] It is then that Eustace begins to see himself for who he really is. He has been selfish, greedy, and proud because he is selfish, greedy, and proud. His dragonish actions have come from his dragonish heart. He also recognizes his inability to remove all of his dragon's skin, and thus he must and does call upon the lion Aslan (the Christ-figure) to dedragon him—to return him to human form, the same outside now with a new inside. On the final page of the book, the narrator says of Eustace, "You'd never know him for the same boy."[4]

I begin with a definition and illustration of justifying faith in Christ, not because I want to impute that theology into our text, but because I want us to read this text on the theme of "the exaltation of humility," as I've titled this sermon, through the lens of the humility of Christ, who is not only the ultimate example of the exaltation of humility, but also the only means by which anyone is put right with God. Put more directly, if there are any dragons reading these words, I want you to be dedragoned before the day is done. I want you to lose your old self in the newness of Christ.

Exposing Hypocrisy

In 23:1–12 Jesus does two things. First, he exposes hypocrisy. Second, he exalts humility. In verses 1–7 Jesus exposes hypocrisy.

Notice here that Jesus is talking "*to* the crowds and *to* his disciples" (v. 1) *about* "the scribes and the Pharisees" (vv. 2–7). In verses 13–36 he'll shift. Verse 13 begins, "But woe to you, scribes and Pharisees." There he talks directly to them or "at them."[5] But here in verses 1–12 his direct audience is *the church*, if I can put it that way. Here he is not exposing the decay and kicking down the walls of the desolate house of Judaism (we'll see that in the next sermon); rather he is building up his future church upon the present cornerstone of his own perfect humility. For "his disciples" and those from the crowd who will become his disciples, he is laying down the foundation, and he is laying down the law. Adolf Schlatter labels part of our text, "The Constitution of the Church."[6] That is a helpful analogy, for what Jesus teaches here should always govern the church.

Keeping with the analogy of a constitution, let me lay down before you one article with two sections. Article I of the Church Constitution is called "Regarding the Matter of Religious Hypocrisy." Section 1 is titled "No Big Mouths" and Section 2 "No Big Heads."

"No Big Mouths" is what Jesus talks about in verses 2–4:

> The scribes and the Pharisees sit on Moses' seat, so do and observe whatever they tell you, but not the works they do. For they preach, but do not practice.

> They tie up heavy burdens, hard to bear, and lay them on people's shoulders, but they themselves are not willing to move them with their finger.

I label this section "No Big Mouths" because of the theme of teaching/talking without doing or helping others to do. They have big mouths; that is, they talk a good talk, but they certainly do not walk a good walk. In verse 3 Jesus says they "preach, but do not practice," and in verse 4 "[t]hey tie up heavy burdens" but won't help anyone walk under their weight. These burdens, I take it, come through their teachings.

In the past in regard to Bible teaching, I have used the illustration of staying *on the line* of Scripture. We are not to add to what Scripture says (go *above the line*) or subtract from what it says (go *below the line*). Well, here the scribes and Pharisees do all three. Sometimes they stayed on the line of Scripture. They taught precisely what Moses taught. This is likely what Jesus meant by his admonition to "do and observe whatever they tell you" (v. 3) when they "sit on Moses' seat" (v. 2; i.e., when they preach the Scriptures from the synagogue "pulpit"). When they actually teach the Word of God, they truly function as successors and official interpreters of Moses, and thus their teaching is to be listened to and obeyed, even if they themselves don't listen and obey.[7]

The scribes and Pharisees sometimes taught *on the line* of Scripture. But they also taught *below the line*. They taught others to live below the line, not always in their teaching so much as in their living. (Godliness is more caught than taught.) They preached God's Law, but they didn't live out the Law. "[T]hey preach, but do not practice," as Jesus put it in verse 3, or as Paul said of the teachers of the Law in Romans 2:21–23:

> [Y]ou then who teach others, do you not teach yourself? While you preach against stealing, do you steal? You who say that one must not commit adultery, do you commit adultery? You who abhor idols, do you rob temples? You who boast in the law dishonor God by breaking the law.

The scribes and Pharisees lived (and thus taught others to live) below the line of Scripture. Moreover, they taught others to live *above the line*. Unlike Jesus who offered genuine rest for weary souls through putting on the yoke of his commandments (see 11:28–30; 28:20a; "his commandments are not burdensome" [1 John 5:3]), the scribes and Pharisees added so many man-made rules atop God's Word that the Word of God seemed stifling, tiring, and crushing. Later in chapter 23 our Lord will point out how the scribes and Pharisees have left out *the lightness* (if you will) of "*the weightier* matters" of God's

Law—"justice and mercy and faithfulness" (23:23)—and placed on people's backs instead a thousand seemingly lighter laws—cleaning cups, swearing oaths, and tithing "mint and dill and cumin" (23:23), a thousand little laws that weigh just a pound each. There is a one-pound law here, another there, and soon a thousand pounds on one's back. A thousand pounds that they have placed there with their big mouths and that they refuse (Jesus doesn't say "they are not able" but rather "they . . . are not willing," v. 4) to lift ("move") even one finger to remove.

What a picture of hypocrisy! And, from this picture of hypocrisy we gain a word to the wise. The call to the Christian church is Christ's call in verse 3: "do . . . not the works they do." Do not teach below the line. Do not teach above the line.

"No Big Mouths" is Article 1, section 1 of the Church Constitution. Section 2 is "No Big Heads." Pride is the issue Jesus hammers on in verses 5–7:

> They do all their deeds to be seen by others. For they make their phylacteries broad and their fringes long, and they love the place of honor at feasts and the best seats in the synagogues and greetings in the marketplaces and being called rabbi by others.

With these very Jewish verses—with words like "phylacteries," "fringes," "feasts," "synagogues," and "rabbi"—Jesus again exposes the hypocrisy of the Jewish leaders of his day. Two key verbs summarize his critique: "They do" (v. 5), and "they love" (v. 6). What do they do? What do they love?

Here is what they do: "They do *all* their deeds to be seen by others" (v. 5a). The word "all" should jump off the page. "All" their actions are polluted with pride. Two small examples of their bigheadedness should suffice. "[T]hey make their phylacteries broad and their fringes long" (v. 5b).

First, let's consider their phylacteries. In order to be seen as being super-pious, the scribes and Pharisees took the words of Exodus 13:9 literally (overly so, in my estimation), which speak of wearing God's Word between your eyes and on your hand. Every day but the Sabbath and holy days, they wore, as some Jews still do today, little leather boxes strapped around their wrist and forehead, filled with Torah texts.[8] Jesus' problem here was not that they took their Bibles literally (although that might be part of the issue he is getting at). Rather, the big issue was size: "broad" boxes for big heads.

That is what was wrong with their phylacteries. What was wrong with their "fringes" was similar. The "fringes" Jesus referenced were those blue or white strings that you might see on a Jewish prayer shawl today. In Jesus' day they were sewn onto the four corners of the hem of the outer robe. This was in keeping with Numbers 15:37–41 (cf. Deuteronomy 22:12). Again the issue wasn't so much that they had such adornment (Jesus himself wore a robe with fringes, 9:20; 14:36). The issue was ostentatious adornment, with the three key words of Jesus' critique being "long" and "broad" and "to be seen" (v. 5).

If the picture of a modern-day bishop—with his red hat on his head, silver shepherd's staff in his hand, large golden cross on his chest, and fifty-nine nickel-sized rosary beads around his waist—comes to mind, your mind is not far from the matter at hand. I think if Jesus witnessed the pomp of Vatican II, he would tear his peasant robe in two. But you might also want to think beyond high churchmen to low churchmen. I think of the contemporary worship leader who calls attention to himself by wearing skinny jeans, canvas shoes that look like they cost two dollars but actually cost two hundred dollars, and a winter scarf below his hairsprayed "bed-head" when it is 100 degrees outside.[9] How many levels lower on the ostentatious scale is his rock-star showmanship than the coronation of Pope Leo XIII—entering the Sistine Chapel of the Vatican Palace on his pontifical chair under a white canopy borne by eight clerics to be crowned with the traditional three-tiered Papal Tiara as a Cardinal says, "Receive the tiara adorned with three crowns and know that thou art the father of princes and kings, the ruler of the world, the vicar on earth of Our Savior, Jesus Christ. . . ."?[10] The rock star worship leader and the kingly pope are both outrageous pictures.

Anyway, back to first-century Judea. (I'll step down from my Protestant soapbox for the moment.) In verses 5–7 Jesus exposes the hypocrisy of Jewish leaders of his day. We looked at what "[t]hey do" (v. 5). Next let's look at what "they love" (v. 6). They love bigheaded seats (v. 6) and bigheaded greetings (v. 7). When they come over for dinner, what they crave more than the food, hospitality, and conversation is the seat next to the host. They love being the guest of honor. And what is true when they enter a house is also true when they enter God's house. They would love this idea of special pastors' chairs (or are they thrones?) facing the congregation. They would love the idea of buying pews in colonial Boston. They would love the mega-church's speaker's spotlight. For when they enter into the synagogue, it's showtime, *Saturday Morning Live*! Their pious theatrics are on full display for all to see and admire.

They love the first and best seats. They also love getting greetings that match their self-perceived greatness. Whether they walk through the temple or the marketplace, the repeated greeting "rabbi" or "father" or "instructor" adds to their already big heads.

That is what they do, and that is what they love.

Now, what should be our application from what Jesus said about their arrogant attitudes and actions? It shouldn't be too difficult for us to figure it out. As our application to verses 2–4 was "do . . . not the works they do," so here we hear that note again: in essence, "do not do what they do." We add to that, "do not love what they love." "Greatnessism," as one scholar labels what Jesus exposes in verses 1–7, "is a major social-spiritual disease,"[11] and if it is not cured it will not only plague the church but will destroy the individual soul. For you see, the door to the kingdom of heaven is only small enough for a child to enter in—i.e., those with childlike (humble) faith in Jesus. There is no way a big dragon is getting through, huff and puff as he might. This is what Jesus teaches in verses 8–12. If we want to be big, we must grow small. If we want to move up, we must go down. If we are to get in at all, we must lay flat on the floor.

Exalting Humility

"But you," Jesus says to *his disciples* (the "you" here are them, and let me add "us"),

> are not to be called rabbi, for you have one teacher, and you are all brothers. And call no man your father on earth, for you have one Father, who is in heaven. Neither be called instructors, for you have one instructor, the Christ. The greatest among you shall be your servant. Whoever exalts himself will be humbled, and whoever humbles himself will be exalted.

We move now from Jesus' exposing hypocrisy to his exalting humility, from his diagnoses of religious sickness (vv. 1–7) to its cure (vv. 8–12). The medicine for big mouths and big heads is small talk and small thoughts (of self). Sticking with our church constitution analogy, we'll explore now Article II, "Regarding the Matter of Religious Humility." Section 1 is entitled "Small Talk" and Section 2 "Small Thoughts."

If you have read much Victorian and pre-Victorian literature (or seen it these days, as the genre has gained much popularity in the movies in the past twenty years), you have in your mind some picture of what Jesus saw. Think of Mr. Elton in Jane Austen's *Emma* or Dr. Thomas Proudie in Anthony Trollope's *Barchester Towers,* proud clergymen who snub those beneath them and try to impress those above them. With men like them in mind, how do you shrink such big heads and close such big mouths? Jesus says that you first stop feeding them ecclesial titles.

Notice the word "call" in verses 8–10.

> But you are not to be *called* rabbi, for you have one teacher, and you are all brothers. And *call* no man your father on earth, for you have one Father, who is in heaven. Neither be *called* instructors, for you have one instructor, the Christ.

The calling of Christian leaders, if I can put it that way, is *not to be called anything special.* A nice dose of small talk goes a long way. Jesus outlaws three titles—"rabbi" (v. 8), "father" (v. 9), and "instructor" (v. 10). Here Jesus uses what is called in poetry an ABA pattern. It looks like this:

A. Rabbi
    B. Father
A'. Instructor

Thus the titles "rabbi" and "instructor" are synonymous. While the name "rabbi" etymologically means "my great one," I don't think Jesus is using it that way. In fact, I think all three titles focus on the role of the teacher, the Bible teacher. They are all synonymous. The point is that there is no need for lofty titles like "rabbi," "father," or "instructor" for Bible teachers.

Why is there no need? Two reasons are given—"all" and "one." First, "you are *all* brothers." Second, there is only "*one*" Father (God) and "*one*" instructor (the Christ, Jesus).

Let me explain the second reason first. There is no need for lofty teacher titles because "you have one Father, who is in heaven" and "one instructor, the Christ" (v. 10). We must be careful about calling anyone in the church "father"—be it the local parish priest ("Good morning, "*Father* Brown") or an early church father ("As the church *father* Ambrose once said . . .")—because such a title might communicate an unorthodox equality with the one and only heavenly Father.

In Matthew's Gospel Jesus uses the term "father" nearly exclusively in reference to his heavenly Father. For example, in the Sermon on the Mount Jesus uses the word "Father" seventeen times, and in each case he references his heavenly Father. His point here, however, is not that we should never call our earthly dads "father," but rather that we shouldn't call our earthly Bible teachers "father." Why the Church (capital C) has chosen to ignore or disobey this teaching, I'm uncertain. Furthermore, why—of all titles we could use for church leaders (should we use any?)[12]—the Roman Catholic Church has chosen "father" as its most prominent title honestly boggles the mind.

There is only "*one*" Father (God), and there is only "*one*" instructor (Jesus Christ). In his *Institutes of the Christian Religion*, Calvin claims that

Christ "alone is the schoolmaster of the church."[13] In his commentary on the Gospels he writes, "The sum of this teaching is that all should depend on the lips of Christ alone."[14] That captures the idea here. There is one top teacher in the church, and that top teacher is Jesus. In John 13:13 Jesus said, "You call me Teacher and Lord, and you are right, for so I am."[15]

Yet, this is not to say that the Teacher hasn't made teachers. Let's remember that the Gospel of Matthew ends with Christ's commissioning his disciples to teach. And what are they to teach? All that Christ commanded (28:20).[16] So when Jesus says there is to be "one instructor, the Christ," he is instructing his church to do away with all personality cults in the church—"I follow Dr. Bible." "Oh, really? I follow Super-Apostle Sam" (cf. 1 Corinthians 1:12). Don't follow anyone but Christ! The only voice we are to hear is that of Jesus, and we hear that voice today only when teachers (small t) teach what the Teacher (capital T) taught. All faithful Christian preachers are to preach Christ. That is what it means (if I may) to preach from the *chair of Christ*.

So one reason there is no need for lofty teacher titles in the church is because there is only "*one*" Father (God) and "*one*" instructor (Jesus Christ). The other reason is that "you are *all* brothers." While there are different roles in the church, there is an equality of status. So Jesus' counsel is that we go public with that status. If you don't say to the usher, "Good morning, Usher Bradley," is there really a need to say, "Good morning, Pastor Doug"? Might it be better to say, "Good morning, Brother Bradley," and "Good morning, Brother Doug"?

I don't want to get too nitpicky here. I think the title *pastor* is a good title, for it means *shepherd*. (There's nothing lofty about that.) I think the title *senior minister* is fine too, if we understand what we are saying. *Senior minister* is another way of saying *top servant*. It reminds me of Gregory the Great's title for the Bishop of Rome—"The Servant of the Servants of God." That's a long title, but not a lofty one. The issue is not so much whether we give certain people titles within the church. It is more whether such titles are used to confer special privilege or status.[17]

When I am called "pastor" it doesn't go to my head (because these days being a pastor is not an esteemed profession in our culture). The other day a neighbor came up to me and said, "So, I hear you are a writer?" I said, "No, I'm a pastor, and I've written a couple of books." "Oh," he replied (not as interested in me as before), and on he went to ask me about being a writer. Being called "pastor" doesn't and won't go to my head, but being called a "writer" or better "doctor" (I have mistakenly been called "Doctor O'Donnell") might.

I could get used to such titillating titles. It's not the title's problem. It's my problem. But that's just the problem. *Pastor* is a humble title; *His Eminence* is not. *Bondservant* is a humble title; *Very Reverend* is not. And titles like *Mother Superior* and *His Holiness* ought to make us nauseous.[18] Let's vomit them out of the church's mouth! If we are to bestow titles upon those who teach the Word of God, let's stick with humble titles. Small talk is what is called for. It's the first cure for big heads and big mouths.

The second cure is "Small Thoughts." This is what Jesus teaches in verses 11, 12. Here's your medicine. Plug your nose. Open up. Gulp it down. "The greatest among you shall be your servant. Whoever exalts himself will be humbled, and whoever humbles himself will be exalted."

In our study of the parables I have talked about something called "the law of end stress," when Jesus stresses his main point at the very end. That is precisely what we have here. What are verses 1–12 all about? Humility! As the church *father*, I mean *early church servant-leader*, John Chrysostom said, "In this passage [Jesus] plucks up pride by the roots."[19] And the uprooting here starts in the brain, with small thoughts about the self. We must all renew our minds. We must

> *[h]ave this mind* among [ourselves], which is [ours] in Christ Jesus, who, though he was in the form of God, did not count equality with God a thing to be grasped, but emptied himself, by taking the form of a servant, being born in the likeness of men. And being found in human form, he humbled himself by becoming obedient to the point of death, even death on a cross. *Therefore* God has highly exalted him. . . . (Philippians 2:5–9a)

We must think, "Those up must go down, for those down will go up." Jesus makes a statement (or is it a command? so Hagner):[20] "the greatest among you shall be ["must be"?] your servant" (v. 11). Those up must go down. Then he adds two motives: "Whoever exalts himself will be humbled, and whoever humbles himself will be exalted" (v. 12). Put differently, those now down will then go up, and those now up will then go down.

Jesus intentionally ends on this eschatological note. He pushes the future into the present. He takes the last day and sets it in the present day. Listen *now*, for when you stand before your Judge and Maker, you will "either be promoted and called to high office or demoted and sentenced to condemnation."[21] Jesus is very black and white here, isn't he?

The Methodist church in my town did a sermon series entitled "Seeing Gray in a World of Black and White." I don't know what the precise topic was (so I won't say a bad word about it), but I will say that I think we need the opposite today. We need to see, as Jesus does here, "Black and White in a World of Gray." Our Lord does not blur the colors in verse 12. Black is black, and white is white. There is nothing gray. You will either be exalted because you were humble, or you will be humbled because you were proud. Let me rephrase that through the filter of the gospel and what Jesus will further explain about himself in Matthew 24—28: if you do not humble yourself before him as King, then you will remain in your proud, deadly, and ultimately damning disbelief.

Pride is the deadliest of the seven (or is it seven hundred?) deadly sins. It's deadly because it so often lies deep beneath the surface of everything we think and say and do. When Eustace (to return to him here at the end) shares with Edmund about his transformative encounter with Aslan, he begins with the lion's command for him to undress before bathing in the healing waters. So Eustace, eager to change back into a human being, removes his dragon's skin. But then, to his dismay, he finds another layer of skin beneath, and then another. "Oh dear," he thought to himself, "how ever many skins have I got to take off?" "So I scratched away," he says, "for the third time and got off a third skin, just like the two others, and stepped out of it. But as soon as I looked at myself in the water I knew it had been no good." Finally Aslan offered a suggestion. "Then the lion said . . . 'You will have to let me undress you.'"[22]

When Eustace changed into a dragon, he realized for the first time in his life the existence of self-love, self-admiration, and self-will. But the besetting sin of pride still lingered under his dragonish skin, for he actually thought he could just remove all the layers of sin himself. He thought some self-improvement would cure self-love. But as he learned, it is one thing to remove a layer of scaly skin, but quite another thing to turn a dragon back into a boy. So Eustace had a choice to make—to continue trying to peel off layer after layer, or to surrender and let the lion tear it all off. Eustace choose wisely. "I just lay flat down on my back," he tells Edmund, "to *let* him do it"—to let the Lion of Judah tear away at his dragonish nature. And the lion began to claw. "The very first tear he made," said the boy, "was so deep that I thought it had gone right into my heart."[23]

How does a sinful boy (or girl or man or woman) get right with a perfectly righteous God? He lies down (what a picture of humility and trust, i.e., justifying faith) and lets the lion do his work. He lies down and lets the one who "came not to be served but to serve" (20:28) serve him by scraping away layer after layer until he is finally ready to bathe in the waters, letting the Spirit of God pour over his body and into his soul.

69

"Is He Quite Safe?"

MATTHEW 23:13–39

I PROMISE NOT TO USE C. S. Lewis's *Chronicles of Narnia* for all my introductions from here on out, but I am compelled to start this chapter with another Narnian dialogue. In *The Lion, the Witch and the Wardrobe,* when Mr. and Mrs. Beaver tell the four children that Aslan (the Christ-figure) is a lion, Susan replies, "Ooh! . . . Is he—quite safe? I shall feel rather nervous about meeting a lion."

> "That you will, dearie, and make no mistake," said Mrs. Beaver; "if there is anyone who can appear before Aslan without their knees knocking, they're either braver than most or else just silly."
>
> "Then he isn't safe?" said Lucy.
>
> "Safe?" said Mrs. Beaver . . ."Who said anything about safe? 'Course he isn't safe. But he's good. He's the King, I tell you."[1]

In those few lines Lewis hits on a theme that is sadly far from the church's thought today. We may believe in the goodness of Jesus—"He's good" all the time! We may believe in the Lordship of Jesus—"He's the king, I tell you." But I'm not sure we have it in our heads (and hearts) that a good king doesn't always mean a safe king. Think—when is the last time you came before Jesus in private prayer or public praise with your knees knocking?

Well, if there is ever a text to get our knees knocking before the fearful but gentle presence of King Jesus it is 23:13–39. I say fearful for obvious reasons. A. T. Robertson called this sustained denunciation of the scribes and Pharisees "the rolling thunder of Christ's wrath." Alfred Plummer spoke of these seven woes as being "like thunder in their unanswerable severity, and like lightning in their unsparing exposure. . . . They illuminate while they strike."[2] Here Jesus rolls like thunder and strikes like lightning. And yet the one and only image that he gives us of himself in this terrible text is not that of a storm or a lion, but rather that of a mother hen, an earthly feminine image for the heavenly Son.

> O Jerusalem, Jerusalem, the city that kills the prophets and stones those who are sent to it! How often would I have gathered your children together as *a hen* gathers her brood under her wings. . . . (v. 37)

Jesus is the Lion King. Jesus is the Mother Hen. Those two images—thundering judgment and gentle, patient (motherly) love—blend perfectly together in the God-man Jesus Christ. If we miss that mixture, we will misread and misapply this heart-pounding, knee-knocking, anything-but-safe passage.

A Right Reading

In Matthew 23 it is obvious that Jesus is judging the *scribes* and the *Pharisees*. At the time of Jesus, the Jewish religious authorities could be divided into four major groups: the priesthood (comprised of the priests, chief priests, and high priest), the religious parties (the Pharisees, Sadducees, and Herodians), the scholars (the scribes), and the Councils (the local synagogue councils and the supreme council, called the Sanhedrin).[3] In our study of Matthew we have already met many of these men; by the time we are done with Matthew, we will have met them all. Here Jesus singles out the two most influential groups upon the populace—the scribes (the expert Bible teachers) and the Pharisees (the super-spiritual Bible keepers). They are the "you" in verse 13 and throughout. Every "you" and "your" is about or includes them.[4]

Because the "you" of our text is not directly you and me, this text has been abused by many self-professed "Christians" throughout Christian history. The "you" here has been over-applied and ill-applied against the Jews. For example, in Munich on April 12, 1922 Adolf Hitler said this in his speech:

> My feelings as a Christian point me to my Lord and Savior as a fighter. It points me to the man who once in loneliness, surrounded only by a few followers, recognized these Jews for what they were and summoned men to fight against them. . . . In boundless love as a Christian and as a man I read through the passage which tells us how the Lord at last rose in His might and seized the courage to drive out of the Temple the brood of vipers and of adders. How terrific was His fight for the world against the Jewish poison![5]

God forbid that we read the Gospels with the poison of Nazi racism. Jesus was a Jew. Jesus was not against the Jews. He came to fulfill their law, not abolish it. He came for them and for their salvation. And like Paul, who was also a Jew through and through, Jesus' "heart's desire . . . for them" was that they would "be saved" (Romans 10:1). That's what comes out clearly in verse 37 of our text. However, what also comes out is his judgment, judgment that is not based on their race but on their unbelief and violent rejection of God's servants and God's Son.

Needless to say, we won't read Matthew's Gospel like Hitler did. Rather, we will read these woes in an almost opposite way. We will read these woes self-critically. That is, we will examine ourselves in the light of the scribes and Pharisees' hypocrisy. We will read this word to them as a "living and active" word to us (Hebrews 4:12). Think of it this way. Jesus is facing the scribes and Pharisees. We are standing behind Jesus. They are in front of Jesus. Behind them is a mirror. So we see the face of Jesus looking at them and beyond them, through the mirror, to us, his church. Less visual but more simply, we will use Jesus' woes to them as warnings to us.

There are four warnings I want us to see. If I'm allowed to have a subtitle for this chapter, it's "Four Warnings to Every Christian from Jesus' Seven Woes to the Jewish Religious Leaders."

The First Warning

The first warning is against *zeal without knowledge*. In Romans 10:2, 3 Paul writes of his fellow Jews—those who have rejected Jesus, "I bear them witness that they have a zeal for God, but not according to knowledge. For, being ignorant of the righteousness of God, and seeking to establish their own, they did not submit to God's righteousness." Paul goes on to say that righteousness comes through faith in Jesus as Christ and Lord.

In 23:13–15 Jesus starts with a similar assessment, adding a more severe judgment. In the Old Testament the phrase "woe to you" is almost always used of *divine* judgment. So here Jesus speaks not merely like the prophets of old—railing against Israel's hypocrisy[6]—but like God himself, pronouncing a judgment upon apostasy. Thus says the Son of God:

> But woe to you, scribes and Pharisees, hypocrites! For you shut the kingdom of heaven in people's faces. For you neither enter yourselves nor allow those who would enter to go in. . . . Woe to you, scribes and Pharisees, hypocrites! For you travel across sea and land to make a single proselyte, and when he becomes a proselyte, you make him twice as much a child of hell as yourselves. (vv. 13, 15)

With each woe Jesus paints a picture. (The language throughout is so vivid!) Envision a door. It is the door to the kingdom of heaven. The scribes and Pharisees stand at this door. They themselves won't go through. What is worse, when people are about to walk through it, these self-appointed doormen close the door in people's faces. They do these two evil actions because they *think* they are doing something good. They are protecting wandering souls from this would-be Messiah, Jesus of Nazareth.

In Jesus' second woe he further exposes their zeal without knowledge. Instead of entering into the kingdom and opening wider the door to *Heaven* for *all the people* to enter in, they "travel across sea and land to make a *single* proselyte," and they make this one convert "twice as much a child of *hell*" as they are (v. 15). They shut the people out of Heaven. They open the trapdoor to Hell. And their followers fall further into their false teaching. Their followers double the zeal and thus double the lack of true knowledge. You see, the scribes and Pharisees are "not simply wrong but contagiously wrong."[7] They are like the English doctors during the early phase of the bubonic plague who told the sick to leave London for the fresh air of the countryside and who, in doing so, spread the disease throughout the nation.

In Hosea 4:6a the Lord says, "My people are destroyed for lack of knowledge." Don't underestimate the importance of right knowledge in the church, and don't underestimate the danger of uniformed enthusiasm. Matthew has made his Gospel clear on who Jesus is and what he has done. If we run to the mission field without first bowing before Jesus as Lord and without knowing what his commandments are that we are to teach others, we are in danger of falling into the same pit as the scribes and Pharisees did.

How zealous are Muslim jihadists? How zealous are Mormon missionaries? Religious zeal is not an indication of truth. Woe to us if we have zeal without knowledge. Woe also to us if we have knowledge without zeal. We need both. But one comes before the other—knowledge first; zeal second. We are to be light and heat—light (full of the right knowledge of God) and heat (full of high devotion for God).

The Second Warning

The second warning is against *majoring in minors*. This warning is found in verses 16–24. Jesus says:

> Woe to you, blind guides, who say, "If anyone swears by the temple, it is nothing, but if anyone swears by the gold of the temple, he is bound by his oath." You blind fools! For which is greater, the gold or the temple that has made the gold sacred? And you say, "If anyone swears by the altar, it is nothing, but if anyone swears by the gift that is on the altar, he is bound by his oath." You blind men! For which is greater, the gift or the altar that

> makes the gift sacred? So whoever swears by the altar swears by it and by everything on it. And whoever swears by the temple swears by it and by him who dwells in it. And whoever swears by heaven swears by the throne of God and by him who sits upon it. Woe to you, scribes and Pharisees, hypocrites! For you tithe mint and dill and cumin, and have neglected the weightier matters of the law: justice and mercy and faithfulness. These you ought to have done, without neglecting the others. You blind guides, straining out a gnat and swallowing a camel!

Four times in these nine verses Jesus calls the scribes and Pharisees "blind." Twice he calls them "blind guides." While Jesus is making a very serious point here, this image of blind guides is the first of two (maybe three) humorous images in his three-image mosaic on majoring in minors. Think of it this way: if you went on a sightseeing tour of the Grand Canyon and you discovered your guide was blind, you might think that is strange and dangerous. Indeed! That's what Jesus wants us to see. These blind guides are a strange sight. These blind guides are a dangerous sight. Don't follow them.

What these build guides don't see is our second image, that of a scale, the scale God uses to weigh our actions and hearts. The scale is called his Law. What God values the most (it's heavy like gold) is "justice and mercy and faithfulness" (v. 23). What he still values, but less so (something light like the leaves from a small garden plant) is tithing and the swearing of oaths. Both the light and the heavy are found in his Law (i.e., on his scale) but one is "greater" (vv. 17, 19) than the other in his eyes.

As in the last chapter, their big mouths come into play. The word "swears" is used seven times here (Jesus is talking about their talking), and the word "say" is used twice. While they are so busy talking about which oaths are valid and invalid before God, they not only disvalue plain talk and true talk (let your yes be yes and your no be no, cf. 5:33–37), but they neglect doing what God most wants done—loving God and neighbor.

The third image of this not-so-funny mosaic is the funniest: "You blind guides," Jesus says in verse 24 as he summarizes verses 16–23, "straining out a gnat and swallowing a camel!" Both a gnat (a small insect) and a camel (a large animal) were considered unclean (cf. Leviticus 11:4, 23, 24, 41). So, as William Barclay explains, "In order to avoid the risk of drinking anything unclean, wine was strained through muslin gauze so that any possible impurity might be strained *out* of it."[8] The picture then that Jesus gives is this: imagine these blind, unbalanced religious leaders one moment straining their wine through a thin cloth to avoid swallowing a microscopic bug and the next moment grabbing a camel and swallowing that big beast whole. It's a picture of people who have "completely lost [their] sense of proportion."[9] It is a funny/not-so-funny picture of majoring in minors.

As the church, we are to major in the majors, without neglecting the minors.[10] Tithing matters. Truth-talking matters. What you do with your money and your mouth matters. But what matters even more is "the weightier matters of the law"—what Jesus lived out and calls his followers to embody—"justice and mercy and faithfulness" (v. 23; cf. Micah 6:8; Zechariah 7:9). The love of neighbor: be fair and merciful toward all. The love of God: be faithful to him and his commandments. The world will not know we are Christians by the color of the church carpeting, the height of the steeple, or the glorious sound of the choir, but by our love. They will know we are Christians—Christ-followers—by our love.

The Third Warning

The third warning is against *outward appearances*. In verses 25–28 Jesus again thunders and strikes.

> Woe to you, scribes and Pharisees, hypocrites! For you *clean* the **outside** of the cup and the plate, but inside they are full of greed and self-indulgence. You blind Pharisee! First *clean* the inside of the cup and the plate, that the **outside** also may be *clean*.
>
> Woe to you, scribes and Pharisees, hypocrites! For you are like *white-washed* tombs [i.e., clean-looking], which **outwardly** appear beautiful, but within are full of dead people's bones and all *uncleanness*. So you also **outwardly** appear righteous to others, but within you are full of hypocrisy and lawlessness. (vv. 25–28)

The word "hypocrites" is used only fourteen times in the New Testament,[11] twelve of those times in Matthew, six of those times in our text, two of those times in verses 25–28 (notice also "hypocrisy" in v. 28). These verses show the height of hypocrisy. A hypocrite is someone who "puts on a false face" (a mask) and pretends to be what he or she is not.[12] In Matthew's theology this hypocrisy especially plays its way out in someone who wants the applause of the crowd more than the approval of God.

Here, as it was in the Sermon on the Mount, our Lord shows the awful dichotomy between outward appearance and inward reality—outward cleanness but inward "uncleanness" (v. 27), outward allegiance to the Law but inward "lawlessness" (v. 28, the last word in this section). Again Jesus is into images. Two images of their outward "righteousness" (cf. v. 28a) but inward rot are given.

The first image is their spotless outer dinnerware. On the outside they eat only from clean cups and plates, or better visually "bowls and mugs."[13] These religious fanatics are meticulous in keeping the ritual purity laws. But they neglect ever cleaning up what's inside these vessels. For example, they spend half the afternoon cleaning the outside of their soup bowl, and then they sit down for dinner and spoon out a fresh spoonful of soup that has been sitting atop month-old minestrone. Again it is a humorous and grotesque picture. We might laugh for the moment, but soon we should feel sick to our stomach.

What is also sick to the stomach is the second image Jesus gives. They are "like whitewashed tombs, which outwardly appear beautiful, but within are full of dead people's bones and all uncleanness" (v. 27). In the springtime before the Passover, it was the custom to whitewash the roadside tombstones so no pilgrim to Jerusalem would mistakenly touch a tomb and thus be rendered unclean for the seven days of the feast (Numbers 19:16). The scribes and Pharisees looked like those tombs. Outwardly they looked so beautifully clean. Inwardly they were unclean—dead, decaying, putrid.

The point of both images is obvious. As Jesus summarizes in verse 28, they "outwardly appear righteous to others, but within [they] are full of hypocrisy and lawlessness." They put on a fabulous façade!

The warning to us should be as obvious as the images: watch out for keeping up outward appearances and yet neglecting inward holiness. It's not that our outward appearance doesn't matter; it's that it matters less than inward holiness. I'll put it this way: may your Sunday best be your Monday best! Christians are to be Christians 24/7. Christians are to be Christians when only God knows what they're up to. We are to be outwardly and inwardly righteous, holy, pure.

The Fourth Warning

The fourth warning is against the *inexcusable excuse of unbelief*. In verses 29–36 we come to the final woe for them, which is also a warning for us. I have included verses 37–39 because it gives a fuller picture of Jesus' final judgment. Before we read verses 29–39, I want you to notice that this is the *seventh* woe. The numerology might be intentional, as the number seven does symbolize completeness or fullness, and it often appears in judgment texts—think of Genesis 4:24, Leviticus 26:18, Proverbs 6:31, and the book of Revelation (with its seven seals, seven plagues, seven golden bowls).[14] Certainly the picture here is the pot of God's patience boiling over. It's more than complete or full.

The other detail to notice here before you read the text is the judicial language. I will highlight it at the start. Starting in verse 29, Jesus announces:

> Woe to you, scribes and Pharisees, hypocrites! For you build the tombs of the prophets and decorate the monuments of the righteous, saying [here is part of their defense], "If we had lived in the days of our fathers, we would not have taken part with them in shedding the blood of the prophets." Thus you *witness against yourselves* that you are sons of those who murdered [a crime!] the prophets. Fill up, then, the measure of your fathers. You serpents, you brood of vipers, how are you to escape being *sentenced* to hell? Therefore I send you prophets and wise men and scribes, some of whom you will kill and crucify, and some you will flog in your synagogues and persecute from town to town, so that on you may come all the righteous blood shed on earth, from the blood of righteous Abel to the blood of Zechariah the son of Barachiah, whom you murdered between the sanctuary and the altar. Truly, I say to you, all these things will come upon this generation.

Then we read in verses 37—39:

> O Jerusalem, Jerusalem, the city that kills the prophets and stones those who are sent to it! How often would I have gathered your children together as a hen gathers her brood under her wings, and you were not willing! See, your [not his or his Father's house anymore, 21:13] house is left to you desolate. For I tell you, you will not see me again, until you say, "Blessed is he who comes in the name of the Lord."

Due to this judicial language, I think the best and easiest way to remember this final woe and warning is with the image of a courtroom. The scene is this: Jesus is the divine judge. I say *divine* because Jesus speaks here only as God would speak in the Old Testament. The four "I" statements show his hand. "Therefore *I* send you prophets and wise men and scribes . . ." (v. 34). Who does he think he is—God? "Truly, *I* say to you, all these things will come upon this generation" (v. 36). Who does he think he is—God? "How often would *I* have gathered your children together as a hen gathers her brood under her wings . . ." (v. 37). Who does he think he is—God? "For *I* tell you, you will not see me again, until you say, 'Blessed is he who comes in the name of the Lord'" (v. 39). Who does he think he is—God? Does the Lord Jesus think he is the Lord God? Yes!

The scribes and Pharisees are the defendants. They are on trial for the crimes of unbelief and murder. They did not come to Jesus for life (v. 37; cf. John 5:40); instead they put him to death, along with the prophets before him and the servants sent after them. Their actions are inexcusable. Thus Judge

Jesus renders his sentence (guilty as charged) and punishment (a razed city [Jerusalem] and ever-rising flames [Hell]). That's the sad, scary scene.

I don't have space to go into how they could be guilty for killing everyone from Abel (the first "martyr" in the Bible) to Zechariah (the last martyr in the Hebrew canon).[15] I also won't tackle the nature of the punishment—(a) that Jesus predicts the temporal punishment of the destruction of the temple in AD 70 (vv. 36, 38), as well as (b) the eternal punishment of hellfire (v. 33, cf. v. 13). I will simply focus on the serious nature of the crime of unbelief, for that is the most pertinent warning to us.

Three days before I preached on this text, my agnostic neighbor shouted from his front porch, "Come over. I have a Bible question." This man is an investment banker. Two of his wealthiest clients are Baptists. From time to time those good Baptists send him an e-mail with a Bible verse attached. One of those verses was James 2:14: "What good is it, my brothers, if someone says he has faith but does not have works? Can that faith save him?" My neighbor's question from James's rhetorical question was, "So can I just be a good person and not believe in Jesus (I don't like the believing in Jesus stuff) and still get into Heaven? Is that what James is saying?" I said, "No." I then explained to him that James is not against faith in Jesus; he is against faith without works. I also explained that I don't think faith in Jesus matters because *I think* it matters, but rather because *Jesus says* it matters.

I am a Christian. If Jesus Christ said that he is "the way, and the truth, and the life" and that "no one comes to the Father [God] except through" belief in him (John 14:6), I hold that statement to be true. I also hold it to be self-evident. I know by faith that Jesus alone satisfies the inquiring mind and heart because he alone—as the dominant theme of all revelation, the key to all of world history, the ultimate interpreter of God to men, and the final judge of the living and the dead—is the only remedy to the tragedy of sin and death. How is it that even in the harshest twenty-seven verses in the Bible (23:13–39) I find Jesus so compelling?[16]

"The genius of the Gospels," Merrill Tenney writes in his book by that title,

> lies not in their rhetorical or philosophical qualities, but lies rather in their presentation of Christ who is unparalleled in all other literature. His supernatural origin, His sinless life, His penetrative teaching, His triumphant death and resurrection might seem to belong to fiction; and if the Gospels were fiction, they would rank among the world's greatest stories. They are, however, sober history, and are consequently all the greater. The Gospels did not make Jesus; He made them. Because of Him they are distinctive, and through their individual emphases and peculiarities He bids the successive generations of men to come to Him.[17]

The world around us hates the exclusive claims of Christ and Christianity. Some say, "A good God should let everyone into Heaven whether or not they believe in Jesus." Others say, "A just God will at least let good religious people into Heaven." But tell me, who exactly is Jesus judging here? He is judging men who regularly attended worship services, were overseas missionaries, made religious vows, tithed their income, meticulously tried every hour of every day to observe God's Law, and even built magnificent monuments to the heroes of the faith. Surely such people get into the kingdom of heaven. Jesus says, no, they don't. Why? The answer is their crime of hypocrisy. The answer is their murder of the Messiah. The answer is their rejection of Jesus as Christ—"you were not willing" (v. 37). They would not come to Christ. They would not believe in Jesus. They would not bow to this Lord as *the Lord*.

Matthew didn't include chapter 23 in his Gospel so we would be appalled at how un-Christian Christ acts. He wrote it so the church would listen afresh to her Lord's woes as warnings, *and* so we might see Jesus for who he really is.

Is he safe? Who said anything about safe? Of course he isn't safe. But he's good. He's the King, I tell you. He's the good King who lovingly accepts and protects all who come under his wings for refuge. He is, in the words of Exodus 34:6, 7a, "The Lord, the Lord, a God merciful and gracious, slow to anger, and abounding in steadfast love and faithfulness, keeping steadfast love for thousands, forgiving iniquity and transgression and sin, but who will by no means clear the guilty."

70

Our Heads inside the Heavens

MATTHEW 24:1–14

ON THIS TEXT J. C. RYLE WROTE, "All portions of Scripture like this ought to be approached with deep humility and earnest prayer for the teaching of the Spirit."[1] Let's begin where he suggested. Let's pray for the Spirit's help.

> *Our great God, we do ask for your wisdom today, wisdom that comes from your Word, and wisdom that comes through your Holy Spirit. So we ask that the Spirit, through his divinely inspired Word, would teach us about the teachings of Christ. We ask this in Jesus' name. Amen.*

In a healthy marriage it is crucial that a husband and a wife be in the regular habit of admitting mistakes, asking for forgiveness, and receiving pardon. Apologies like "I'm sorry, I was wrong" and absolutions like "I forgive you" are often to be on our lips. Now while the relationship between a pastor's sermons and his congregation wouldn't serve either party well if the pastor was constantly offering an apology for his teaching, nevertheless I must say in the case of Matthew 24 and the chapters you are about to read on it that I thought it necessary to start with a word of apology. I won't go so far as to say at this point, "I'm sorry" (for you haven't yet read my interpretation of this passage). But I do think it is fair to confess from the beginning, "I may be wrong."

This chapter and the next, which records what is often called "The Olivet Discourse" because Jesus speaks "on the Mount of Olives" (v. 3), is likely the most difficult section in Matthew. It is difficult for at least three reasons. First, it is difficult because Jesus uses somewhat unfamiliar language, a mix of prophetic and apocalyptic utterances. Second, it is difficult because Jesus makes few clear chronological distinctions. As we read we wonder, about what time in history is he talking? Finally, it is difficult because there is not a consensus among Christian commentators as to its interpretation. In fact, the more one studies the history of its interpretation,[2] including the current debates and perspectives, more questions arise than answers.

I have no desire to draw you into the immensely complex maze I have walked through in studying this passage. Instead in these next few chapters I want to walk you straight through what Jesus said, why he said it, and what difference it should make in our lives.

First notice all the imperatives in Matthew 24, 25. There are twelve imperatives (vv. 4, 6, 16, 17, 18, 20, 23, 26 [two], 32, 42, 44), such as the first "see that no one leads you astray" (v. 4) and the last, "be ready" (v. 44). I mention those imperatives from the start because whatever we make of the chronology, we must first and foremost recognize that Jesus' primary aim was to exhort and encourage his disciples to think and feel and do. To Jesus "the eschatological imagination does not displace practical moral concern"[3]—personal readiness, perseverance, discernment. So it is both necessary that we start with a proper humility and a willingness to admit we do not know everything about this passage and that we understand that these imperatives are of great importance.

However, before we jump to these easy-to-find but hard-to-do imperatives, we do need to do some mental grunt work. We do need to come to some understanding of the chronology of the days and times that Jesus was specifically addressing.

There are three major schools of thought on how to understand the time period or periods represented in this passage. The first school is called *preterism.* These folks view the whole of Matthew 24 as saying nothing about the return of Christ or the events of the last days of history. To them Jesus here predicts what will happen from the time of his resurrection to the time of the destruction of the temple in Jerusalem in AD 70.[4] If you are curious, R. C. Sproul provides a version of this position in his book *The Last Days According to Jesus.*

A second school of thought is called *futurism.* This view is nearly the opposite of the preterist perspective. A futurist sees most (or all) of the Olivet Discourse as relating to the future, particularly end-times prophecies. While a few from this school admit that some of the events in Matthew 24, 25 speak of the fall of Jerusalem, they see the majority of the discourse as addressing a future tribulation. To them this text, combined with a few others, depicts the following scenario: "The nation of Israel will be back in the land of Palestine with a rebuilt temple, only to suffer great persecution from the antichrist after the secret rapture and the removal of Gentile believers."[5] Many of us are familiar with this perspective due in part to the overwhelming success of Bible prophecy writers such as Hal Lindsey as well as Tim LaHaye and Jerry Jenkins, the authors of the Left Behind series. That series has sold a mere 65 million more than my first three books.

There is a third school, and I have happily enrolled in this one. I don't know if we yet have a label attached to our beliefs. I simply and *humbly* call us the "everyone-is-wrong-and-we-are-right school." Perhaps you can come up with a better name. The gist of our thought is this: we view this discourse as describing both the events before and during the destruction of the temple as well as the last days before and during Christ's return.[6] So, for example, in verses 15–28 Jesus speaks primarily *but not exclusively* (see Doriani's helpful table below)[7] about what will occur before and during the destruction of Jerusalem in AD 70. Then in verses 29–31 he shifts his focus and addresses primarily what will occur before and during his second coming. Scholars call his prophecy foreshortening, "the idea being that events in the near future and those much further ahead, are spoken of as if they are very close together, because they have common characteristics."[8] The analogy of a mountain range is often used to explain this concept. If we stood on a mountaintop staring across to another mountaintop, it might appear that the peaks are close to each other when in fact they are miles apart. Likewise, Jesus spoke of two mountaintops (AD 70 and the *parousia*) as if they were close together when in reality they are thousands of years apart.[9]

The following chart summarizes Jesus' prophecies, their fulfillment in AD 70, and the way they may be fulfilled in the last days:

Predictions and Texts	Fulfillment by AD 70	Final Fulfillment
False christs will come (24:5, 23, 24).	Jewish prophets predict God will deliver Jews from Rome.	The great Antichrist deceives many by his words and deeds.
Wars, famines, and earthquakes will strike (24:7, 8).	Rome is often at war; there is famine in the reign of Claudius (AD 41–54).	The troubles of this life intensify near the end.
The gospel will be preached in the whole world (24:14).	The gospel is proclaimed through the *known* world.	The gospel is preached to *every* people.
The abomination that causes desolation will stand in the holy place (24:15).	Idolatrous Roman armies invade Jerusalem and fight and kill many, even in the temple.	Final rebellion against God brings religious abomination and desolation.
The sun and moon will be darkened when Jesus comes (24:29–31).	Jerusalem's fall foreshadows the end of earth's powers.	This world order ends when Christ returns.
The sign of the Son of Man will appear in Heaven (24:30).	Fulfillment of prophecy shows Jesus reigns in Heaven.	Jesus returns on clouds of the sky with angels.

The appeal of this position (and it is now the majority view among conservative scholars of every millennial perspective)[10] is that it is the view that best does justice to the actual situation (spoken of in vv. 1, 2) as well as to the precise questions put to Jesus (in v. 3) by his disciples.

The Disciples' Questions

Let me show you what I mean. Look with me at verses 1–3. Let's start with the actual situation of Jesus' famous discourse. The first part of the first verse records that "Jesus left the temple and was going away." That is, he was climbing down from Jerusalem and then up the Mount of Olives (v. 3). Jesus' movement reminds one of what is written in Ezekiel 11:23: "the glory of the LORD went up from the midst of the city [Jerusalem] and stood on the mountain that is on the east side of the city [the mount called Olivet]." Here we are to see geographical theology at play: the "Holiest of the Holies"[11] has left the desolate house (23:38), and with that move the presence and glory and protective power of God has walked away with him. Jesus knows the fate about to fall upon that den of robbers—the eschatological judgment of God's enemies (cf. Zechariah 14:4).

But the disciples don't. Thus Jesus' geographical shift concerns them. In the second half of verse 1, the disciples seek to turn Jesus' attention back to the temple. We read that "his disciples came to point out to him the buildings of the temple." In Mark's version one of the disciples says, "Look, Teacher, what wonderful stones and what wonderful buildings!" (Mark 13:1; cf. Luke 21:5). That disciple, likely representative of the Twelve, understood the historical, theological, and national significance of the temple, and therefore he wanted to return Jesus' focus to it. "Don't walk away from it—walk back to it" is the sense of what that disciple says and what they all likely think. They are hoping that the awe of the architecture will draw Jesus back. You see, Herod's temple, as G. R. Beasley-Murray put it, "was probably the most awesome building in the ancient world."[12] And to pious Jews such as Jesus' disciples that building complex represented not only the beauty of Israel's culture and the glory of God's presence but also the *permanence* of Israel's religion.

Yet to this certainly beautiful and seemingly permanent edifice, Jesus replies to his disciples' caution and enthusiasm with no word of admiration. Jesus doesn't say, "Oh, sorry, you're right. Those massive pillars, stunning stones, and roofs of gold are awe-inspiring! What are we doing here when we should be there?" Instead he said to them, "You see all these 'great buildings' [Mark 13:2], do you not? 'Truly, I say to you, there will not be left here one stone upon another that will not be thrown down'" (24:2). It is one thing to say, as Jesus did of himself, that "something greater than the temple is here" (12:6); it is quite another thing to predict that the temple will be irreversibly flattened, that God is about to hang an eternally-out-of-order sign on its remaining ruins.

What an incredible prophecy! It was as incredible as everything Jesus said and did that pre-Passover week. Yet, however stunned the disciples were at first, we are given the impression that they actually took Jesus' word as credible. They actually believed him. And they believed him because this is what they thought: for every stone of that temple to be "thrown down" would be as incredible as trying to lasso the sun and pull it to earth. So if Jesus said this is going to happen, they reasoned, he must be talking about the end of the world.

Because we have witnessed in modern times great buildings and even cities leveled to the ground due to atomic bombs and airplanes used as missiles, we can to some extent view a prediction of such utter destruction as being unrelated to the end of the world. The Twin Towers may have crumbled to the ground, but few of us thought that one event was a sign that the end of the world was at hand. From an ancient perspective, however, to say that Herod's solid stone temple,[13] a building that took "forty-six years to build" (John 2:20), would be completely leveled only made sense in light of the end of the world, when God, as the prophets foretold, would destroy Jerusalem (Jeremiah 9:11; Micah 3:12). In the disciples' minds the destruction of the temple would be such a cataclysmic event that it could scarcely occur without the curtain on the world's story closing at the same time.

We know this is the disciples' assumption from their private question posed in verse 3. As Jesus "sat on the Mount of Olives" (thus, he was likely looking down on the temple below), "the disciples came to him privately, saying, 'Tell us, *when* will these things be, and *what* will be the sign of your coming and of the end of the age?'"

Jesus' Answer

Jesus answers their two questions—"when" and "what"—by explaining that the coming destruction of Jerusalem's sacred mount will not be the end of the world. What the disciples thought to be one event, Jesus taught to be two separate events. There will be two judgments at two different times in history. There will be a local judgment in AD 70, and then (after an unspecified period of time) there will be another judgment, a final worldwide judgment on the last day.

What makes this prophecy difficult is determining which details belong to the destruction of the temple and which belong to the return of Christ. My view is that verses 15–26 and 32–35 speak of the events before and/or during AD 70 (the destruction of the temple); verses 29–31, 36–41 (cf. vv. 3c, 6c, 14b) speak of the second coming; verses 4–14, 27, 28, 42–44 speak of what will transpire from the time of Christ's resurrection until his return. George Eldon Ladd called this intertwining or overlapping of eras "prophetic foreshortening."[14] The closer event—the destruction of the temple—symbolizes the coming event—the end of the world.

With that said, let's explore Jesus' two answers to his disciples' two questions. (Put your thinking caps on.) The disciples first ask: *When will "these things" happen? When will the temple be destroyed?* Answer: When you witness false Christs and prophets, great apostasy, and wars and rumor of wars, famines and earthquakes (vv. 5–8), "the end" of the world "is not yet" at hand (v. 6b). In fact, "these are but the beginning of the birth pains" (v. 8). "I won't tell you when the temple will be destroyed, only that it will occur. When you see all these things taking place, know that the Son of Man 'is near'" (will soon return, v. 27). You can count on my words (v. 35). These birth pains will happen in your lifetime (v. 34). In the meantime, here is what going to happen, and here is how you are to respond . . ."

Before the temple is destroyed, Jesus says, there will be false Christs. Don't be led astray. There will be wars, earthquakes, and famines. Don't be alarmed. There will be persecutions. Endure to the end. Then, when the temple is being destroyed, when you see "the abomination of desolation" (v. 15), quickly flee from the region. And while you are fleeing, again you might be tempted to think this is the end of the world. But don't be fooled. If someone says to you, "Look, the Christ has returned," do not believe him. Even if you see these false Christs and false prophets performing "great signs and wonders" (v. 24), don't be led astray.

Next, we come to the disciples' second question: *What will be the sign that the world is coming to an end and that Christ is returning?* Jesus has told us in verses 4–28 what are *not* signs of the end. Then in verses 29–31 our Lord says that *the sign* that the world is coming to an end will be obvious (there won't be any secret signs that only Christians or certain Christians know):[15]

> Immediately after the tribulation of those days the sun will be darkened, and the moon will not give its light, and the stars will fall from heaven, and the powers of the heavens will be shaken. Then will appear in heaven *the sign* of the Son of Man, and then all the tribes of the earth will mourn, and they will see the Son of Man coming on the clouds of heaven with power and great glory. And he will send out his angels with a loud trumpet call,

> and they will gather his elect from the four winds, from one end of heaven to the other.

Christ will return suddenly, publicly, unmistakably. Therefore, "stay awake" (v. 42), "be ready" (v. 44), and do the work you have been called to do (24:45—25:46). Keep the faith and you'll be eternally saved (v. 13)! Don't keep the faith and you'll be eternally judged (24:39, 40, 41, 51; 25:12, 28–30, 32, 41–46).

Well, there you have it. But we still have a little more mental grunt work to do.

Making Imperative the Imperatives

Having looked at verses 1–3 (and an overview of it all), let's next turn our attention to verses 4–14. We'll do this quickly—too quickly. Here Jesus addresses how his disciples are to respond to the various troubles that will precede the destruction of the temple. "The disciples—and believers since—want to know the future, but Jesus directs them unflinchingly to the present."[16] Look first at verses 4–8.

> And Jesus answered them, "See that no one leads you astray. For many will come in my name, saying, 'I am the Christ,' and they will lead many astray. And you will hear of wars and rumors of wars. See that you are not alarmed, for this must take place, but the end is not yet. For nation will rise against nation, and kingdom against kingdom, and there will be famines and earthquakes in various places. All these are but the beginning of the birth pains."

It is extraordinary to note the accuracy of Christ's predictions. In the years preceding the Jewish Revolt in AD 66 there arose several messianic pretenders. You can go to any good library today and browse through Gnostic literature written in the first century that testifies to the fact that there were groups and leaders that, using the name of Jesus of Nazareth, espoused views contrary to apostolic Christianity and sadly led many professing Christians astray. You can also find in Roman and Jewish histories of this same time period that there were "rumors of wars." For example, there was a rumor of a war in AD 40 when Caligula, who was the Roman Emperor AD 37–41, attempted to erect a statue of himself in the temple in Jerusalem. And, of course, there were not only "rumors of wars," but there were actual wars, which isn't all that strange since war has been one of the constants of history. In their book *The Lessons of History* (published in 1968), Will and Ariel

Durant note that war "has not diminished with civilization and democracy. In the last 3,421 years of recorded history only 268 have seen no war."[17] Finally, we have records of famines and earthquakes. There was a famine during the reign of Claudius (see Acts 11:28). Claudius was Emperor AD 41–54. A major earthquake struck Phrygia in AD 61 and one that was ultimately responsible for leveling the city of Pompeii in AD 63. Also Antioch, the city in which perhaps Matthew wrote his Gospel, experienced large earthquakes in AD 37, 42, and 115.[18]

While it is extremely interesting to note that the events Jesus prophesied here happened, we miss the point if we think Jesus is more concerned with prophecy than *perseverance*. In verses 4–8 we have but the beginning of Jesus' many admonitions "against future speculations at the expense of present obedience."[19] So as much as Jesus speaks prophetically here, he likewise speaks pastorally. In these verses Jesus tells his followers to expect earthly groanings—earthquakes, famines, wars—in this fallen world. But he cautions them not to see these events as signs. They will seem like signs, but they are *not* signs.

In verses 9–12 Jesus moves on to inform his disciples to further expect troubles from unbelievers—outside and inside the church.

> Then they [outsiders] will deliver you up to tribulation and put you to death, and you will be hated by all nations for my name's sake. And then many [insiders] will fall away and betray one another and hate one another. And many false prophets [insiders] will arise and lead many astray. And because lawlessness will be increased, the love of many [insiders] will grow cold.

The disciples may have naturally expected that after Jesus' glorious resurrection they would enter a time of triumph, but Jesus reminds them it will instead be a prolonged period of persecution. From outside the church they can expect hatred and even martyrdom. From inside the church they can expect false teachers, apostasy, immorality, and the "chief characteristic of spiritual death"—loveless hearts.[20]

We know the history of early Christianity—the stoning of Stephen, the beheading of James, the many persecutions of Peter and Paul. There was a steady wave of persecutions under the Roman rule of Nero, Domitian, Trajan, Marcus Aurelius, Septimus Severus, Decius, Valerian, Maximus the Thracian, Aurelian, Diocletian, and Galerius (c. 64–324). And we should know from the rest of Christian history that the true church has so often been a persecuted church. Let me give you a brief overview of Christian history. (I'll put my M.A. in Church History to work.) You might find this helpful:

- First century: Labor pains.
- Second century: Labor pains.
- Third century: Labor pains.
- Fourth century: Labor pains.
- Fifth century: Labor pains.
- Sixth century: Labor pains.

Do you get the idea?

- Twentieth century: Labor pains.
- Twenty-first century: Labor pains.

Herein lies the labor lesson for us. We ought to rid ourselves of the utopian dream that someday before Christ's return the church will be free from such sufferings—these labor pains. Jesus tells us, as he told them, that the normal Christian life between his resurrection and return is filled with adversity, suffering, and pain. Wasn't Jesus clear on this when he said, "If anyone would come after me, let him deny himself and *take up his cross* and follow me" (16:24; cf. Colossians 1:24)? It's cross now, crown then. It is labor now, delivery then. So be patient. Endure. Breathe in; breathe out. Trust that God will work everything for your good. That baby is soon to be born. And the hard and long labor will then all seem worth it.

Joy at the End of the Tether

Coming to 24:13, 14 we learn that the story here is not all bad. It was the worst of times; it was the best of times. After listing eight negatives (vv. 4–12),[21] Jesus ends with two positives (vv. 13, 14). You see, as much as these verses tell us to expect troubles—from the fallen world and from fallen people—we find in our two final verses two comforting and encouraging promises. Despite the trials, Jesus tells his followers to keep their heads up. First, we can be encouraged because "the one who endures to the end will be saved" (v. 13).

If we are faithful to Jesus, we will be "hated by all" who oppose him (v. 9), but (here's the great hope and promise) those who "endure to the end will be saved." Final deliverance! Final salvation! In Revelation 1:9 the Apostle John identifies himself as "your brother and partner in the tribulation and the kingdom and the patient endurance that are in Jesus." What a way to identify oneself! In Acts 14:22, when Paul and Barnabas returned to the congregations they had founded, they exhorted them to continue in the faith, saying, "through many tribulations we must enter the kingdom of God." Jesus told us in the Parable of the Soils that the reality of "tribulation or persecution . . . on account of the word" (Matthew 13:21) will sift out the false Christians from the true.

The Christian life is not a ten-yard dash—such a short sprint that we can get the prize after the first five steps. Rather it is a grueling marathon that we must run all the way to the finish line. The gospel demands distance runners, those who run toward Heaven with hardship burning on our heels, those who patiently pace themselves, knowing that "momentary affliction is preparing for us an eternal weight of glory beyond all comparison" (2 Corinthians 4:17).

"The one who endures to the end will be saved" (v. 13)—this is not salvation by endurance; rather it is salvation by faith, a faith that endures. Perseverance marks the already saved. Perseverance marks true saints.

A second word of comfort comes in verse 14: "this gospel of the kingdom will be proclaimed throughout the whole world as a testimony to all nations, and then the end will come." This verse, along with verse 13, is a bright spot in an otherwise dark section. God promises that these troubles—from the fallen world and from fallen people—will not disrupt or obstruct the progress of the kingdom. In fact, they will provide unique opportunities for gospel growth.

This is precisely what the book of Acts depicts. Today's church growth experts tell us that the church grows through trimming the Word and adding worldly trimmings, but the inspired book of Acts illustrates the church growing through proclamation and persecution.

Let me give you one example. In Acts 4 Peter and John are arrested and jailed, put on trial, beaten, and finally released. In Acts 5:41, 42 we are told, "Then they left the presence of the council, rejoicing that they were counted worthy to suffer dishonor for *the name* [of Christ]. And every day, in the temple and from house to house, they did not cease teaching and preaching that the Christ is Jesus." The next verse, Acts 6:1, tells us of remarkable church growth: "Now in these days . . . the disciples were *increasing* in number." There is much truth in Tertullian's famous words, "The more we are cut down by you, the more in number we grow; the blood of Christians is seed,"[22] often paraphrased as "the blood of the martyrs is the seed of the church."

Jesus promised that "this gospel of the kingdom"—what Jesus taught and what is taught about him—would be "proclaimed . . . to all nations," that the word of God would increase and multiply (v. 14; Acts 12:24). There will be *many* false teachers and *many* who fall away and *many* who then betray you and hate you, but there will also be *many* who come to faith in Christ. The church will not only survive, she will thrive.[23] After the bad news of "wars, persecutions, martyrdoms, apostasies, false teachings, lawlessness," finally there is some good news—the one great good news, "this wonderful news of the kingdom."[24]

Therefore, instead of Christians wasting their time trying to decipher current events (whether a famine in Somalia or an earthquake in Japan is some sort of sign of the second coming), here it is implied that we are first and foremost to heed the Great Commission to "go . . . and make disciples of all nations" (28:19). When Jesus returns, I assure you that he will not commend those who have accurately predicted the date of his coming (someone is bound to be right someday), but he will say, "Well done, good and faithful servant" (25:21) to those who have been busy heralding the good news of Heaven throughout the bad-news earth. For Christians, "the purpose of time is *mission.*"[25] The interim between Pentecost and the *parousia* is "filled with one great task—mission."[26]

And what's the scope of our mission? The globe is the grand goal. Okay then, let's be realistic. Can a crucified (but now risen) Messiah with his persecuted, purged, minority church reach the "world"?[27] Yes. In John 16:33 Jesus said, "In the world you will have tribulation. But take heart; I have overcome the world." Indeed he has. The apostles, in a sense, reached their world for Christ as the gospel spread in their generation from Jerusalem to the four corners of the Roman Empire (Acts 1:8; cf. 2:5; Romans 1:8). It is our turn to reach the four corners of our world, a seemingly ever-expanding one. Christian, please believe me when I say, we are not raptured out of the world, we are called into it. We are called to proclaim the good news throughout the whole world. The time between Christ's resurrection and return is *missions time!* Fasten your seatbelts. Hit the Go button. It's time to "Lift high the Cross, the love of Christ proclaim, Till all the world adore His sacred name."[28]

The Wise Man

G. K. Chesterton wrote, "It is only the fool who tries to get the heavens inside his head, and not unnaturally his head bursts. The wise man is content to get his head inside the heavens."[29] In this chapter we have attempted to do the latter, to poke our heads into this heavenly revelation in order to wrap our minds around the meaning and proper application of our Lord's teaching.

And what have we seen in the first fourteen verses of the twenty-fourth chapter of Matthew? We have seen in verse 3 that the disciples, with their questions, desired to be in on some fairly confidential information. They wanted to know when the world would come to an end. We have seen in verses 4–14 that Jesus, with his answers, gives them not what they want but what they need. He gives them instructions on "how to discern the signs of the times so they will not be disheartened by persecution, panicked by wars, fooled by appearances, or led to apostasy by false prophets during uncertain and trying days"[30] and so find hope in the growth and saving power of the kingdom.

Then, as we have applied what Jesus said to them, we have found that Jesus' words still have much to say to us about how to live the Christian life in these troublesome days before his return. How are we to respond to false messiahs and false prophets, those who spout out unsound teaching? We are to reject them, however spectacular they might be or seem. We are to watch out so that we are not led astray. How are we to respond to calamities—be it wars, famines, earthquakes, or all of the above? We are not to be alarmed. These occurrences will happen in a fallen world. Finally, what are we to do when we are persecuted for our faith by religious authorities or secular rulers? We are called to finish the race (cf. 2 Timothy 4:7). We are called to "endure suffering" and "do the work of an evangelist" (2 Timothy 4:5). We are called to preach the Word to the world.

71

Apocalypse Then

MATTHEW 24:15–28, 32–35

NEAR THE END OF World War II downtown Warsaw was almost completely leveled. According to one witness, the only skeletal structure remaining on the main street was the Polish headquarters of the British and Foreign Bible Society. The words engraved upon the only wall standing, which were clearly legible from the street, were the words, "Heaven and earth will pass away, but my words will never pass away."[1]

Again we return to that thorny text we call the Olivet Discourse. Yet it is a text, however thorny, that is quite smooth and straight (clear) on the matters that should matter most to us. For example, it is clear on Jesus' identity. Jesus is a true prophet (cf. Deuteronomy 18:15). The text we will explore has come true. But of course Jesus is so much more than a prophet. He is the Son of David, the Son of Man, and the Son of God. He is the *divine* Son of God, who came to earth from Heaven as "Immanuel (. . . God with us)" (1:23) and who now reigns in Heaven, having been granted "all authority in heaven and on earth" (28:18). And as such we take notice of how he talks.

He speaks with divine authority, language like "*Truly, I say to you*, this generation will not pass away until all these things take place" (v. 34) and "Heaven and earth will pass away, but *my words* will not pass away" (v. 35).[2] Those are not just bold claims; they are claims that can be tested by history. Jesus predicted the destruction of the temple, and it happened. He predicted that his words would stick around longer than all created matter (the heavens and the earth), and so far so good. He has been right about his linguistic longevity.

The Olivet Discourse is clear on Jesus' identity. Furthermore, it is clear on the importance of the imperatives. Christians in all times and places are to "stay awake" (v. 42), "not [be] alarmed" (v. 6), not be led "astray" (v. 4), and so on.

In this sermon we will keep, as we always should, an eye on the person of Jesus (he is not just some moral teacher or accurate prophet), but our main focus will be on the truth of what he *said* would happen (and did happen) to Jerusalem.

In the last sermon I explained that there are three different schools of thought on how to read this Discourse and that I enlisted in the *already/not yet school*, if you will. That is, I think some of Matthew 24 describes the events before and/or during the destruction of the temple in AD 70, some describes the second coming of Christ, and some describes what will transpire from the time of Christ's resurrection until his return. Other than verses 27, 28, for this sermon we will look only at the past.

I think what Jesus said in verses 15–28 and 32–35 has already happened in history. My defense for my view will come out clearly (and convincingly, I hope) as I answer three key questions. First, to whom is Jesus talking? Second, what is going to happen? Third, what are they (Jesus' first disciples) to do?

To Whom Is Jesus Talking?

The answer to the first question should be obvious. *To whom is Jesus talking?* He is talking to those who asked him the question in verse 3. He is talking to his first disciples and the Christians of their generation. We know this is the case for a number of reasons. Let me give you three.

First, there is the use of the pronoun "you." Throughout this passage that pronoun quite naturally refers to the disciples. For example, when Jesus says, at the beginning of verse 15, "*when you see* the abomination of desolation," he means *when the first disciples see* that event. The "you" is our first clue that Jesus is not talking to you or me but to them.

Besides that prominent pronoun, second, we also find specific details that make best sense in light of a specific first-century audience. For example, note the specific geography and topography mentioned at the end of verse 16.[3] It reads, "let those who are *in Judea* flee to the *mountains*." What possible meaning could that verse have to anyone who does not live in that region of the world? We can allegorize "Judea" (and also "flee" and "mountains" for that matter), but that only leaves us with 100,000 possibilities and perhaps 100,000 exegetical absurdities. It is most natural and reasonable to believe that Jesus is talking about some event that would *not* affect the whole world but only those who live in and around Jerusalem, only those who can flee to mountains. (I assure you, he is not talking to anyone who lives in Plainfield, Illinois or Wichita, Kansas.)

Third, look at what is specifically commanded in verses 17–20. Jesus says:

> Let the one who is *on the housetop* [the flat housetop, common in Judea] not go down to take what is in his house, and let the one who is in the field not turn back to take his *cloak*. And alas for women who are pregnant and for those who are nursing infants in those days! Pray that *your* flight may not be in winter or on a *Sabbath*.

Now think for a minute. Who would be worried about retrieving their necessities or valuables if it was the end of the world? You wouldn't need your gold watch or your wool mittens if the sun was to darken and the stars were to fall from the sky (v. 29), would you? And if this was the last day—the end of the world as we know it and as they know it—what difference would it make if this event happened in the winter or not or whether one was pregnant or not? And why would Jesus express sympathy for those attempting to flee that region? The second coming, as I read verse 31 and the book of Revelation, will be a good thing for the followers of Christ. All our labor pains—and those of these pregnant women—will be over. There will be no need to run if Jesus and his obvious and somehow universal presence is coming to town.

What Is Going to Happen?

Our second question is: *What is going to happen?* Verse 15 tells us that they were to expect "the abomination of desolation spoken of by the prophet Daniel, standing in the holy place."

The book of Daniel, as Jesus points out, forms much of the background of this phrase. That is why Matthew says, "let the reader understand." In other words, let the reader grasp that what Daniel said would happen is soon to happen.

During Israel's captivity Daniel prophesied that after the exile there would be seventy "weeks" (symbolic of groups of seven years), and then an "anointed one" (Daniel 9:25, presumably Christ) would be "cut off" (Daniel 9:26, presumably meaning his death on the cross). In the middle (not the end) of the last "week," an "abomination" would cause the temple to be deserted and the regular sacrifices to cease. In my mind it makes best sense to understand this "abomination of desolation" as referring to idolatrous Rome's absolute destruction of the temple in AD 70. I say *idolatrous* not only because the Romans worshipped the Emperor, but because their army carried images of such worship into the temple with them. In victory they placed their blasphemous banners upon holy ground and made sacrifices to their gods.[4] In this way it was an "appalling sacrilege" (24:15, AMPLIFIED), something both ordained by but also detestable to God.

I don't want to spend much time on this "abomination" or "sacrilege," for it is tricky business, and we have other important matters I want us to consider. I will, however, give briefly my top two reasons for my position that "the abomination of desolation" equals Rome's leveling of the temple.

First, this view fits well with the immediate context. Before Jesus predicts the destruction of the temple, he first speaks of its "house" (i.e., temple) as being "desolate" (23:38). It's the same Greek root word as used in 24:15. Remember also in Matthew's Gospel how Jesus used the barren or desolate fig tree to symbolize the judgment that would come upon Israel (21:19). And then, of course, we shouldn't forget that Jesus made a specific prediction regarding the temple. In 24:2 he said that that every stone from that temple would be "thrown down." And in verse 3 the disciples, with their questions, wanted to know when the temple would be destroyed. In verse 15 Jesus answers them, saying in essence, "It will be destroyed when you see these things happening" (cf. v. 34).

Second, and perhaps even more significant, if you look at Luke's Gospel he twice clarifies the ambiguity. In Luke 19:42–44, before Jesus cleanses the temple and after he weeps over Jerusalem he says:

> Would that you, even you, had known on this day the things that make for peace! But now they are hidden from your eyes. For the days will come upon you, when your enemies will set up a barricade around you and surround you and hem you in on every side and tear you down to the ground, you and your children within you. And they will not leave one stone upon another in you, because you did not know the time of your visitation.

Then in 21:20 Luke writes of Matthew's "abomination of desolation" in this manner: "[W]hen you see Jerusalem surrounded by *armies*, then know that its [i.e., Jerusalem's] desolation has come near." Here Jesus is not talking about spiritual armies any more than he is talking about spiritual rooftops. He is referring to the Roman "armies" who were responsible for the destruction of Jerusalem thirty-seven(?) years after Jesus spoke verses 2, 15, and 34.

Here is the history. In order to crush the Jewish Revolt in AD 66 the Roman General Titus worked his way south until he seized and conquered Jerusalem on the ninth of the month of Av (August 29) in AD 70. At first the temple was ordered to be preserved. But when it was later gutted by a fire set by one of the soldiers, the order came from Caesar to raze "the whole city and the temple . . . to the ground."[5] What happened next was quite remarkable. "Once the temple burned . . . the soldiers were so eager to retrieve the gold which melted and had flowed into the cracks between the stones that they overturned the huge stones of the burned-out building to retrieve the gold."[6] Therefore, precisely as Jesus had predicted, when they were finished, not one stone was left standing upon another.

Forty years after this event, the Jewish historian Josephus wrote, "All the rest of the wall encompassing the city was so completely leveled to the ground as to leave future visitors to the spot no ground for believing that it had ever been inhabited."[7] He also claimed that when the Romans sacked Jerusalem and devastated Judea, 97,000 Jews were enslaved, and another 1.1 million died by slaughter and starvation.[8]

Matthew 24:21 summarizes well the magnitude of this horrific event: "For then there will be great tribulation, such as has not been from the beginning of the world until now, no, and never will be." While this verse, along with verse 15, might have a double fulfillment—a future, final-days defilement related to the Antichrist ("the man of lawlessness," 2 Thessalonians 2:3, 4) and the beast (Revelation 14:9), who claim to be God and demand worship from the church—let's not forget that the terrors that came upon Jerusalem in AD 70 were the worst that city has ever experienced. They were greater than the destruction of the temple in 583 BC and greater than the desolation of it in 163 BC at the hands of Antiochus Epiphanes—when he erected a pagan statue in the Holy of Holies. The Romans destroyed the Holy of Holies and every holy building with it! And while today Jerusalem does experience much turmoil, no event we read of in the newspapers or watch on television comes close to reporting on the city's total destruction. What happened in AD 70 was truly "Israel's darkest hour," "a time of tribulation unsurpassed in Israel's history."[9]

What Are They to Do?

In verse 15 Jesus tells the first disciples what will happen: the temple will be destroyed. But how are they to respond? That's our third question. *What are they to do* during this time of great tribulation?

Jesus gives them three commands. Like the warning given to Lot before the fire dropped upon Sodom and Gomorrah (Genesis 19:17), they are first told to "flee to the mountains" (24:16) and to do it quickly (vv. 17, 18). As Blomberg summarizes: "They must interrupt whatever they are doing—whether relaxing, as customary on the flat rooftops of their homes, or working, as typically in the fields—and flee with the utmost of haste."[10]

This command to flee may seem out of place. Why did Jesus tell them in verses 9, 10 to expect persecution and then in verses 16–18 seemingly to escape from it? The answer is that here he is not telling them to flee suffering for the sake of the gospel. He is simply telling them to flee to avoid being slaughtered in a God-ordained military campaign ("The king was angry, and he sent *his troops* and destroyed those murderers and burned their city" [22:7]). They are to die for the gospel (if it comes to that), but not for the temple. So while at various times in its history Israel fled into the temple as a fortress of refuge, here Jesus counsels true Israel to fly away from it. This time the temple will offer no divine protection. Like a dead and withered fig tree, it is about to be pulled from the ground and burned.

The first command is to flee. Let me quickly run through the next two. Second, they are told to "pray" for the timing of this "abomination" (vv. 20, 15). With compassion for the least mobile among them (pregnant women and nursing mothers), they are told to pray specifically that it may not happen during a season or on a day when travel would be difficult—"in winter or on a Sabbath" (v. 20).

Third, they are commanded three different times not to be duped by false or fanatical teachers, who will come out of the woodwork, or better metaphorically-speaking, will arise from the ashes (vv. 23, 24). Because of the great troubles of those days Jesus warns them that they will be susceptible to impostors. They will so desire Christ's return and final vindication that they will be tempted to embrace whoever comes along with great signs and wonders, claiming to be just that. At that time, however, the "elect" (true believers) are not to "believe" such liars (vv. 22, 23). They are not to be led astray. The Son of Man is not returning at that time and in that way. When Jesus returns (don't worry about missing it) it will be as obvious as lightning flashing across a dark sky or a group of vultures gathering around a corpse (vv. 27, 28). Jesus uses such lovely illustrations! As Kim Riddlebarger states, "His coming will not be an isolated, secret, or local event but will be witnessed by the entire world. Every eye will see him."[11]

What Are We to Do with This Fulfilled Prophecy?

That is what Jesus said *to them*. What then does he say *to us*? What are we to do with this *fulfilled* prophecy? I've walked us through those verses on the past. I next want to use our text's eight imperatives to be our applications for the present: "flee" (v. 16), do "not go down" (v. 17), do "not turn back" (v. 18), "pray" (v. 20), "do not believe" (vv. 23, 26b), "do not go out" (v. 26a), and "learn" (v. 32). These eight can be grouped together into three groups—obedience, prayer, and discernment.

Obedience

First we have obedience. Under this group are all the imperatives, but here we will focus just on the admonishment to "flee" (v. 16) and two of the "you shall not" commandments—do "not go down" (v. 17) and do "not turn back" (v. 18). Those three imperatives focus on the disciples taking Jesus at his word—believing that what he said would happen will happen, and when it does happen to do precisely what he said.

You might think it would have been easy for the first Christians in Judea, when they saw the mighty Roman army march into town, to say (a) "Oh, Jesus was right. Here they are!" and (b) "Let's get to the mountains ASAP." But that is to underestimate the lure of Jewish nationalism and Christian triumphalism. Please understand that Jesus is commanding them to leave their city, their place of worship, and their people when the Gentile enemy of God's holy city, temple, and people come to town. That's not an easy command to keep.

Do you remember what Peter did when the soldiers came to arrest Jesus? He took out his sword and fought (26:51; cf. John 18:10). Peter and James and John and all those earliest Christians would be tempted when they saw Rome prance into town to pull out their swords and fight. They would be tempted to join the newest "resistance movement" and/or "to sign up to fight for a new Messiah."[12] Jesus tells them to fight off such temptations and natural tendencies and to "get out and run," not stay and fight.[13] And thankfully we know from the historian Eusebius that the church at Jerusalem did leave the city, relocating to the hill country, the same place where the Jews hid during the Maccabean revolt.[14] They did obey Jesus' commands and were saved! Soon after the desolation, the Romans left the region. The days had been "cut short," and "the elect" were saved or preserved (v. 22). You see, they were saved from their sins when Jesus died and rose again. But they were saved from death—being unnecessarily slaughtered—when they heeded Jesus' seemingly odd but certainly accurate words.

How about you? Do you trust Jesus' word? Do you think he knows what he's talking about? Do you believe that he has your best interest in mind?

These first disciples took Jesus at his word, and we should follow their example—in fact we have many more reasons to do so. Jesus' prophecy about his death and resurrection has come true. Jesus' prophecy about the destruction of the temple has come true. If Jesus said about 2,000 years ago that his *words* would "not pass away" (v. 35) and thus far he has been right, we have good reason to believe that what he said about love, divorce, adultery, prayer, fasting, vows, almsgiving, good works, lust, anger, anxiety, poverty of spirit, feeding the poor, materialism, idolatry, undue and ungrounded and unexamined criticism, humility, peace, pride, and the end of the world is also right. Right?

I wonder, in what areas of life are you most tempted not to take Jesus' word as true? Is it in the area of finances? Does money, "a root of all kinds of evils" (1 Timothy 6:10a), have its greedy claws in you? "O man of God, flee these things" (1 Timothy 6:11). Be content with what God gives—food and clothing (1 Timothy 6:6, 8). Look at and learn from the lilies. Seek first the kingdom of God and his righteousness—"Pursue righteousness, godliness, faith, love, steadfastness, gentleness" (1 Timothy 6:11b)—and all that you need will be added unto you (see 6:28, 29, 33).

I wonder, in what areas of life are you most tempted not to take Jesus' word as true? Is it in the area of idolatry? I don't mean the idols of Athens or the idols that the Romans brought into the temple. I mean all those little, medium, and large idols that these idol-making machines of ours (our brains) make on a daily basis. Do you make work an idol? Success? Grades? Food? Drink? Television? Computer games? Sports? Financial security? Beauty? Happiness? Reputation? Politics? Family? Marriage? Children? (Bad things and good things can be idols.) "[F]lee from idolatry," Paul exhorts *Christians* in 1 Corinthians 10:14. Jesus is to be first, and there are to be no other gods besides him.

I wonder, in what areas of life are you most tempted not to take Jesus' word as true? Is it in the area of sexuality? You know that Jesus says not to think this and not to do that. But you don't trust him, or you are tempted to not trust him. You know that the Word says to "[f]lee youthful passions" (2 Timothy 2:22) and to "flee from sexually immorality" (1 Corinthians 6:18), but the bed of the adulteress is too inviting, and the click of the computer button too easy and enticing, and the touch of the human hand seems so more real than the touch of God.

Do you know who the unhappiest person in the world is? I say it is the Christian who is living in disobedience to the word of Christ. Jesus saves, and Jesus wants to save you, Christian, from the dreadful, dangerous, potentially damning consequences of your sins.

In John 14:21a Jesus said, "Whoever has [i.e., knows] my commandments and keeps [i.e., obeys] them, he it is who loves me." Do you love Jesus? There is an easy litmus test. You know and keep his words (cf. John 14:24a). You trust and do what he says because you know that he knows what he is talking about. The Bible calls it *obedience*.

Prayer

First, we are to obey. Second, we are to pray. This imperative comes from verse 20 where Jesus tells that generation to "pray that your flight may not be in winter or on a Sabbath."

Until studying for this sermon, I have always pooh-poohed the travel-safety prayer. "Dear Lord, give us traveling mercies as we take a two-day drive down to Disney World." Part of the prayer that rubs me the wrong way is inconsistency: if we are going to pray when we take the 1,000-mile trek to visit Mickey, why don't we pray for the one-mile excursion to the grocery store? The other part of the prayer that rubs me the wrong way (or *did* rub me the wrong way) is the prayer for *safety*. Who says the Christian life is safe? Was it safe for Peter and Paul? Was it safe for Polycarp and Ignatius? Was it safe for Hus and Tyndale? Was it safe for Cranmer and Latimer?

But as I prepared this chapter, with verse 20 staring me in the eyes, I repented of my completely uncharitable thoughts toward the travel-safety prayer and other safety prayers like it. It's okay to pray, as our Lord taught us, "[D]eliver us from evil" (6:13)—from the evils of fallen people (wicked rulers, unfair judges, false teachers) and from the evils of this fallen world (famines, earthquakes, wars, and even car wrecks).

There is one other truth I have learned about this prayer-imperative that I think we can naturally and readily apply to ourselves. It has to do with the nature of prayer. If there is one thing that is clear in the Olivet Discourse, it is that God is sovereign over history. History is going somewhere, and he knows where it is going. So in light of that truth, it is not strange to read imperatives to us about readiness for the unexpected. What is strange (at least it was to me upon first reading) is that prophetically-accurate Jesus tells his follows to pray to an absolutely sovereign God.

We might think that if God has determined that Jerusalem will fall on a winter Sabbath; then God has determined it. Why would we bother him with our plea for safe travel? But that's not how God works. That's not how prayer works. Prayer is mysterious, as mysterious as the relationship between the sovereignty of God and the responsibility of man. We know that God is sovereign; we know that God hears our prayers. And we know that our prayers, in some way, affect God. Think about the prayers of Abraham or Moses. Think about the personal interaction they had with the Almighty. Prayer works; otherwise, Jesus wouldn't have commanded his followers here or elsewhere to pray. John Bengel summaries well the theology and *history* of verse 20: "Prayer helps; they prayed, and flight did not take place in winter."[15] It was August. Don't underestimate the power of *our* prayer to *the* sovereign God.

Discernment

Our final application to the eight imperatives involves discernment. The Olivet Discourse is a discourse on discernment—discerning what are signs and what are not signs, discerning what time it is and what time it is not, discerning which teacher is true and which is false. Here in verses 15–28 and 32–35, we find one imperative—"learn" (v. 32)—that is about discerning the times and another two imperatives—"do not believe" (vv. 23, 26b) and "do not go out" (v. 26a)—that are about discerning whose voice to heed.

Look with me now at verses 32–34. After Jesus has just spoken to all generations about how obvious his return would be—as obvious as "a loud trumpet call" (v. 31)—he says to that first generation:

> From the fig tree learn its lesson: as soon as its branch becomes tender and puts out its leaves, you know that summer is near. So also, when you see all these things, you know that he is near, at the very gates. Truly, I say to you, this generation will not pass away until all these things take place.

The lesson they are to learn is the same lesson we are to learn, and that lesson is: once Jerusalem has been seized and sacked, know that Jesus Christ can return at any time. In other words, the fall of the temple was the last sign before the final judgment.

Related to that lesson is the nearness of Christ's return. How near is the "near" of verse 33 or how immediate is the "immediately" of verse 29? *If* my reading is right (that's not a big if or a small if; it's a medium if), then "near" does not mean the year AD 71 or 1000 or 2000 or 2014. It does mean perhaps the day you are reading this. It means "soon and very soon, we are going to see the King." How soon? Soon and/or very soon. (More on that theme in the next chapter.)

Discernment involves learning. It also involves *listening*—listening to Jesus' word and not listening to the fanatics and/or the false teachers. In troubling times and in times of great tribulation, Christians are most susceptible to following the wrong crowd, and the wrong crowd is usually in, around, or at one time from the church.

One night over twenty years ago (when I had just become a new Christian), I was watching religious television. After the teacher had drawn me in through naming my particular trouble (I now realized he named quite a few troubles, the ones common to man), he asked if anyone wanted a miracle. I did! He first said to touch the screen as he prayed. I did. He next said to send a check to support his God-anointed faith-healing ministry. I didn't. But I would have if I wasn't dead broke.

I'm not alone in my past gullibility and present susceptibility. There is something about the fame, following, and even true miracles of these false teachers that can powerfully take our eyes and ears off Christ. There is something convincing about the charismatic leader who says, "If you want to know where and when to find Jesus, come on this special date to this secret location to get this exclusive information."

We live in an age of religious charlatans and skeptics. On one hand, or better *in one ear*, we have the charlatans—those who for the sake of money, fame, and admiration refuse to preach Christ and him crucified and refuse to preach the necessity of Christian cross-bearing. In the other ear we have the skeptics—those who for the sake of money, fame, and admiration deny Jesus' deity, the forgiving power of his death, and his resurrection. They deny everything (or nearly everything) about which Matthew is concerned. It is not just those false teachers who claim to know all the times, places, and people related to the end of the world that we are to watch out for, but it is also these charlatans, some of whom write the best-selling "Christian" books, and those skeptics, some of whom give very serious and scholarly interviews on the History Channel. It is imperative that we "do not believe" them (vv. 23, 26b) and that we "do not go out" (v. 26a) and follow them. You see, unbelief is sometimes necessary for believers, and disobedience is sometimes our duty.

So what are we to do with this fulfilled prophecy? We are to learn lessons about discernment, prayer, and obedience, as well as lessons about the person and power and everlasting authority of our Lord Jesus Christ.

God's Great Ordinance

I recently began reading through John Owen's classic *Of the Mortification of Sin in Believers* (first published in 1656). This book is a gold mine of practical Puritan theology at its best. There are nuggets like "Mortification from a self-strength, carried on by ways of self-invention, unto the end of a self-righteousness, is the soul and substance of all false religion in the world,"[16] and "be killing sin or it will be killing you,"[17] and "the life, vigour, and comfort of our spiritual life depend much on our mortification of sin,"[18] and "there is no death of sin without the death of Christ,"[19] and "a man may easier see without eyes, speak without a tongue, than truly mortify one sin without the Spirit,"[20] and "Set faith at work on Christ for the *killing* of thy sin. His blood is the great sovereign remedy for sin-sick souls. Live in this, and thou wilt die a conquerer; yea, thou wilt, through the good providence of God, live to see thy lust dead at thy feet."[21] Good stuff!

In the ninth chapter, Owen writes:

> Sometimes in reading the word God makes a man stay on something that cuts him to the heart, and shakes him as to his present condition. More frequently in the hearing of the word preached, his great ordinance for conviction, conversion, and edification, doth he meet with men. God often hews men by the sword of his word in that ordinance, strikes directly on their bosom-beloved lust, startles the sinner, makes him engage unto the mortification and relinquishment of the evil of his heart.[22]

I'm not sure how or if God has used the preaching of his Word in this sermon to convict or challenge you, or perhaps encourage or edify or enlighten you, but I would hope that this history lesson has taught you many practical lessons—lessons about discernment, prayer, and obedience, and lessons about the person and power and everlasting authority of our Lord Jesus Christ.

72

God Only Knows

MATTHEW 24:29–31, 36–51

A SECOND- AND THIRD-CENTURY Roman clergyman calculated that Jesus would return in AD 500. His prediction was based on the dimensions of Noah's Ark. Christ did not return at that time. On January 1, 1000 many Christians in Europe, as you can imagine, predicted the end of the world. Sadly, some Christians, if they can be called that, reacted to that millennial mark in a military fashion. As the first of the year approached, Christian armies traveled to some of the pagan countries in Northern Europe in order to make converts, by force if necessary, before Christ returned. Christ did not return then. In 1415 the Taborites, a group greatly influenced by the apocalyptic writings of Joachim of Fiore (ca. 1135–1202), thought that Christ would return once they shed "the blood of the enemies of Christ"—i.e., defeated their persecutors.[1] The group disbanded after they didn't fare so well against the German army. Christ did not return. Also in the Middle Ages, Pope Innocent III took the number 618 (the year Islam was founded) and added the number 666 (the number of the beast) to get 1284 as the year of Christ's final judgment. Christ did not return.

On February 14, 1835 Joseph Smith, the founder of The Church of the Latter Day Saints, called a meeting of Mormon leaders. He announced that Jesus would return within fifty-six years (*History of the Church*, 2:182). Earlier, in or around the year 1832, Smith wrote in *Doctrines and Covenants*, 130.17, "I prophesy in the name of the Lord God, and let it be written—the Son of Man will not come in the clouds till I am eighty-five years old." Smith would have been eighty-five in 1890. Unfortunately a mob murdered him before his thirty-ninth birthday. Christ did not return. William Miller, founder of a popular end-times movement that bore his name—"Millerism"—predicted that the second coming would occur sometime between 1843 and 1844. Christ did not return. In 1874 Charles Taze Russell, founder of what is now known as the Bible Student movement, from which came the Jehovah's Witnesses (Watchtower and Tract Society) and other organizations, predicted the rapture in 1910, followed by the end of the world and Christ's *invisible* return in 1914.[2] Christ did not return (or at least no one saw him).

In 1986 the group The Children of God predicted that Russia would defeat the United States and Israel, establishing a worldwide dictatorship. Then, in 1993, Christ would return. Christ did not return. In 1988 Whisenant Edgar wrote the book *88 Reasons Why the Rapture Is in 1988*, and Colin Deal wrote *Christ Returns by 1988*. Those books sold over four million copies. Christ did not return. Lee Jang Rim of the church Mission for the Coming Days prophesied that Jesus would return through the Sydney Harbor on October 28, 1992. Christ did not return (and sadly, Rim did not return as well, walking away with 4.4 million dollars from his followers' life savings). In 1998 a Taiwanese cult in Texas claimed that Christ would return and invite the faithful followers aboard a UFO. Christ did not return (and to my knowledge, no UFO was spotted). Also in 1998—a good year for such prophecies, as 666 times three equals 1998—psychic Edgar Cayce taught that a secret, underground chamber would be discovered between the paws of the Great Sphinx in Egypt. Within that chamber would be documents about the history of the lost city of Atlantis. This new revelation would activate the second coming of Christ. Christ did not return. In 2000 . . . well, the list of prophecies is too long. Each time Christ did not return.

To give one final example, Harold Camping (earlier in September 1994 and again 106 days ago before this sermon was preached) predicted the end of the world. He advertised on his fifty-five radio stations and on 6,000 billboards, "Judgment Day is coming/May 21, 2011. The Bible guarantees it!" You could even sign up for a live Twitter feed at Twitter.com/endofworldmay21. I doubt that Twitter feed is feeding anything now. Christ did not return.[3] Camping then, without apology for his earlier false prediction, named October 21, 2011 as the right date for Christ's return. Again Christ did not return.

We might laugh at some of these scenarios. But of course those false predictions are no laughing matter, for those who made such empty claims brought Christ and Christianity into disrepute. Those who made them were either ignorant of or disobedient to Jesus' clearest sentence in the often unclear Olivet Discourse: "But concerning that day and hour no one knows, not even the angels of heaven, nor the Son, but the Father only" (v. 36). Jesus is saying there, "Only God knows." Only God knows the timing of Christ's coming.

I'm certain that what R. T. France wrote about that verse is right: "In view of such plain statements as this, it is astonishing that some Christians can still attempt to work out the date of the parousia!"[4] And I'm not so sure that William Barclay's scolding is far off when he wrote, "Speculation regarding the time of the Second Coming is nothing less than blasphemy, for the man who so speculates is seeking to wrest from God secrets which belong to God alone."[5] Michael Green agrees. He also calls such prophecies "blasphemous" and adds a rabbinic maxim: "He who announces the messianic times based on calculations forfeits his share in the future."[6] Perhaps so.

What Is Not Known

Look with me now at the start of verse 36, which reads, "But concerning that day and hour . . ." The term "that day" and "[that] hour" are synonymous terms that refer to what the Old and New Testaments calls "the day of the Lord" or judgment day[7] and the New Testament calls "the *parousia*,"[8] the Greek word for "coming"—used in 24:39, 42, 43, 44, 46, 50; 25:10, 19, 27[9]—what Christian call the second coming.

Concerning *when* that time in history will be, Jesus says, "no one knows . . . but the Father only." "The angels of heaven" don't know. The Heaven-sent Son doesn't know. The highest heavenly created beings and the highest uncreated being don't know.[10] (And yet some Christians think they know. I don't get it.) God the Father alone has such knowledge.

That is clear enough. What is not so clear to us is why Jesus doesn't know. It's "unsettling" that the Son—who is so intimate with the Father throughout the Gospels—doesn't know something his Father does.[11] Or more to the theological point, how is it that the second person of the Trinity doesn't know something? Doesn't Jesus know everything?

The clearest explanation I found on this Christological complexity was that of Daniel Doriani. Why try to improve upon his fine work? I'll just quote him:

> Remember that Jesus chose to limit his divine powers when he became man (Phil. 2:6–8). God is omnipresent, omnipotent, and omniscient. Jesus possessed these powers, but chose not to exercise them at most points in his ministry.
>
> Jesus is omnipresent, yet he traveled from place to place by foot (typically) or by boat or donkey (occasionally). When Jesus wanted to go to Jerusalem, he *walked*. He didn't stand in Capernaum and tell the disciples "Since I am omnipresent, I am already in Jerusalem, so I'll stay here and see you there when you arrive!" When he walked, he laid aside his omnipresence.

> Jesus is omnipotent, yet unless he ate food he became hungry. Without sleep, he became tired. Eventually he slept—hard (Matt. 8:23–25). He did not draw on his omnipotence to fill his empty stomach or to refresh his weary body.
>
> Jesus is omniscient, yet he laid aside his knowledge too. Jesus asked genuine questions in the Gospels. In Mark 5:30–32, Jesus asked "Who touched me?" and "looked around" to see who it might be. In Mark 9:16, he asked the disciples, "What are you arguing about . . . ?" In John 5:6, he asked a man how long he had been sick. On other occasions, he asked visitors, "What do you want me to do for you?" (Matt. 20:32; cf. 20:21).
>
> Indeed, if Jesus had constantly exercised his divine attributes, he would not have led a genuine human life. If he endured no human limitations, his incarnation was a charade. If the crucifixion caused Jesus no pain, how could he suffer for us? If no bodily desires touched him, how can we say he was " in every respect . . . tempted" as we are (Heb. 4:15)?
>
> So Jesus truly did not know when he would return. He did not need to know, nor do we. He finished his work, so he is ready to return.[12]

I hope you find Doriani's explanation helpful as well as theologically satisfying. I do.

However, another question arose in my mind, that question being: does Jesus *now* know? That is, now that Jesus has returned to the glory that was his before the world began—in his post-incarnational state—does he now know the time of his return? I e-mailed my question to a world-class Gospels scholar, and he replied, "Wow, that is a good question. I just don't know if we can come up with an answer on that one."

At first I was unsettled by that answer or non-answer. (Don't such scholars get paid to answer such difficult questions?) But then I realized, as much as I assume Jesus, in his glorified state, knows more than he knew or now knows what he long ago knew—everything (cf. Revelation 2, 3)—I still don't know what he knows and doesn't know . . . and doggone it, that's okay. Some answers are for us and our children, and some are left only to the mind of God.

What Is Known

Having looked at what is not known concerning that day, we next look at what is known concerning that day. What is known is threefold: First, *it will be obvious*. Second, *it will be awesome*. Third, *it will be unexpected*.

First, *it will be obvious*. Let me point out what is obvious about this *obvious* point. Four illustrations are used. Two come from verses 27, 28, if you'll allow me to go back there. Jesus' return will be as obvious as lightning flashing from one end of the sky to the other and as obvious as a group of vultures gathering around a dead body. It will also be as obvious as those great lights created on day four of creation turning off—"the sun will be darkened, and the moon will not give its light, and the stars will fall from heaven" (v. 29). That darkness then is set in contrast to the heavenly "sign of the Son of Man" (v. 30).[13] We are told that Jesus will return in "great glory" and in such a way that "all the tribes of the earth . . . will *see*" him (v. 30; cf. Revelation 1:7). I surmise then that there will be some light about the Light of the World. Perhaps John's words—"They will need no light of lamp or sun, for the Lord God will be their light" (Revelation 22:5b)—sheds some light on this verse. Perhaps also Paul's phrase "in flaming fire" (2 Thessalonians 1:8) speaks to this. The reason everyone will see him is that he is the only light in the universe, if we are to take the words of verse 29 literally and not metaphorically (they can be either).[14]

The fourth and final illustration is that of the trumpet call.[15] Jesus has used our sense of sight—you will see this and see that. Next he uses our sense of sound. Just in case you miss seeing his return, you will hear it: "And he will send out his angels with a loud trumpet call" (v. 31).[16] How loud with this trumpet call be? I imagine it will be loud enough for the deaf to hear! The return of Christ will be loud, public, universal,[17] personal, and visible. In other words, it will be obvious.

Second, *it will be awesome.* Notice the title Jesus uses for himself in relation to his second coming. It is the title "Son of Man." He uses it four times in our text (vv. 30 [twice], 37, 39) and six times in chapter 24. That title does not have to do with Jesus' humanity but rather his divinely bestowed authority. It is used in Daniel 7:13, a passage in which we learn that "the Ancient of Days" (God Almighty) gave this Son of Man "dominion and glory and a kingdom, that all peoples, nations, and languages should serve him; his dominion is an everlasting dominion, which shall not pass away, and his kingdom one that shall not be destroyed" (Daniel 7:14). It's Daniel's version of Matthew's conclusion—"All authority in heaven and on earth has been given" to Jesus (28:18).

Other aspects of our text bring out what we can and should know about the awesomeness of Christ's return. In fact, every phrase of verses 29, 30, and 31 is brimming with Jesus' power and glory.

- Verse 29: He will appear with a heavenly light show. Whatever is described in that verse, it is an awesome cosmic upheaval. It will make the most incredible fireworks display look amateurish. It will make Halley's Comet look like two Boy Scouts rubbing sticks together to get a spark.
- Verse 30: Look at the phrases "all the tribes" and "the clouds of heaven" and "with power and great glory." For everyone to see Jesus coming from

Heaven—appearing or arriving (*parousia*) as the everlasting ruler of this earthly dominion—is another awesome image.

- Verse 31: Note Jesus' absolute authority—"he" and "his"—"And *he* will send out *his* angels . . . and they will gather *his* elect from the four winds, from one end of heaven to the other."[18] What *parousia* power! He has the whole world in his hands (v. 30), *and* he has the whole heavens in his hands too—"from one end of heaven to the other" (v. 31).

J. C. Ryle writes concerning this text (here's another long quote but a good one):

> The second personal coming of Christ will be as different as possible from the first. He came the first time as "a man of sorrows, and familiar with suffering" (Isaiah 53:3): he was born in the manger of Bethlehem, in lowliness and humiliation; he took the very nature of a servant, and was despised and not esteemed; he was betrayed into the hands of wicked men, condemned by an unjust judgment, mocked, flogged, crowned with thorns and at last crucified between two thieves. He will come the second time as the King of all the earth, with royal majesty: the princes and great men of this world will themselves stand before his throne to receive an eternal sentence: before him every mouth shall be silenced, and every knee bow, and every tongue shall confess that Jesus Christ is Lord.[19]

Third, *it will be unexpected.* This is the point of verses 37–44 along with verse 50 (cf. 25:13). Verse 50 tells us that "the master of that servant will come on a day *when he does not expect him* and at an hour he does not know." Then verse 44 summarizes the illustrations of Noah, the two men, and the two women by saying, "Therefore you also must be ready, for the Son of Man is coming at an hour *you do not expect.*"

What Then the Wise Person Does

This theme of unexpectedness is what Jesus emphasizes in verses 37–51, and he does so with four illustrations—the flood, the working men and women, the thief in the night, and the two servants or two types of servants. (If preachers ever needed a proof-text for the validity of illustrations, here it is). The point of Jesus' many illustrations on unexpectedness is to rouse unbelievers *and believers* to expectancy—that is, to stay awake (vv. 42, 43) or to be ready (v. 44) or, put differently and more completely, to be wise.

We turn now to what the wise person does. As at the end of the Sermon on the Mount, here at the end of chapter 24 Jesus contrasts the wise with the foolish. What then does the wise person do?

First, the wise person believes in Jesus and takes him at his word. This is not stated; it's implied. If you don't believe Jesus said what is written here or that he has both the power to save and to judge (and that he is actually coming someday to do so), then the call to expectancy falls on deaf ears.

Second, the wise person does good and not evil. To "stay awake" or to "be ready" is more than the *attitude* of attentiveness. It is also the *actions* of attentiveness. We are to wait expectantly as we work expectantly. Toward the end of John Calvin's life, when his friends wanted him to work less for the sake of his declining health, he would often reply to them, "Would you have my Master find me idle?"[20]

Every illustration Jesus uses involves people working. The least obvious is the one about the thief in the night.[21] So let me show you what I see. The idea is this: if you knew a thief was coming tonight, you would *do* something about it. You would perhaps secure the entranceways, set up a trap, call the authorities, or grab him before he grabs your stuff—you "would not have let [your] house be broken into" (v. 43).

Perhaps also less obvious is the illustration of Noah and the flood. Jesus gives the story from the perspective of those who were judged—"the careless (or clueless)."[22] But if you see (and of course we know) that story from Noah's perspective, we know that Noah worked and worked and worked on that big box of a boat. What a picture of expectancy! He had both the attitude (he had to have had it) and the actions of attentiveness. He thought, *Judgment is coming. I believe God's word. I'd better do what he says. I better get to work.*

Then we have the illustration of the four workers. Here the theme of work is evident. What is not obvious is what differentiates one worker from the other. Why is one taken and one not? And is "taken" a sign of being saved (cf. 1 Thessalonians 4:17) and "left" a sign of judgment?[23] It's not clear. However, based on the context of those in Noah's generation who were *taken* away by the waters of God's judgment, I think you may actually want to be "left behind."[24] Either way, the one who is saved is hard at work on his or her normal, everyday, God-given vocation—in the field or grinding at the mill.[25]

The final illustration is that of "the faithful and wise servant," who is contrasted with the "wicked servant." It is interesting to note that one is labeled "wise" and the other (or could it be the same person illustrating two ways to live?)[26] not "foolish" but "wicked." Look how verses 45, 46 read:

> Who then is the faithful and wise servant, whom his master has set over his household, to give them their food at the proper time? Blessed is that servant whom his master will find so *doing* when he comes.

Underline "doing." Doing "good" is implied. I say that based on the fact that this servant is doing what his master asked (and it fits the assumed parallel of v. 49), and we know what the Master or Lord Jesus asked of us—to *do* unto others as we would like to have done onto ourselves (7:12). We also know what he says about doing good to others in the Parable of the Sheep and the Goats. Moreover, we know what he says about working hard—using our talents—in the Parable of the Talents.

Jesus contrasts this expectant industrialism with different levels of unbelief or faithlessness. The first three illustrations involve people who don't listen and so don't care. This is the culture we live in, isn't it? People are so busy working ("grinding at the mill") and/or entertaining themselves ("eating and drinking" or perhaps better "wining and dining" or "gorging and guzzling")[27] that they think preachers like me who preach "repent, judgment is coming" are as crazy as an old man building an ark in the middle of the desert for 120 years (Genesis 6:13, 14; cf. 2 Peter 2:5).

The last illustration—that of the wicked servant—is of someone who does listen (he thinks the master will return) but thinks he has time to live lawlessly. This servant will be his own master, lording over others and loving self. He thinks to himself, "My master is delayed" (v. 48). His Lord is out of sight and thus out of mind (and out of heart?).[28] So what does he do? He doesn't do anything good. He "begins to beat his fellow servants [that's not very loving] and eats and drinks with drunkards [that's not very righteous]" (v. 49).[29] This man is harsh and godless because he believes in cheap grace: he thinks God is not looking and Jesus is not coming when he is sinning.

We all know people like this *outside* the church. But this man seems to be *inside* the church. (That's the convicting twist of this parable.) Notice that he is called a "servant," he has "fellow servants," and he calls Jesus "my master." He is a professing believer—that is how we would say it. He might even be a churchgoer. He might even be a church-doer—he works on various committees, helps serve Communion, and smiles when you come through the front door.

Perhaps if I was preaching this text to the secular world I'd focus on the flood: don't be caught unaware; indifference is a damnable offensive; Jesus is coming; repent; believe. But I'm preaching and writing this message to believers—the church—and so my focus will fall where Jesus' did—on the wicked servant. Thus my message to you is this: don't be caught unaware; indifference is a damnable offensive; Jesus is coming; repent; believe.

Wait! That's the same message. Yes, it is.

I know from experience that someone in this state of spiritual stupidity needs a loud wake-up call. The churchgoer/church-doer can be most deaf to the call of Christ. Jesus knows this as well. That is why he will give three parables on it in chapter 25 and also why he ends this short parable the way he does. His call comes in verses 50, 51. Tremble, if you must, at the sound of this trumpet. "The fear of the LORD is the beginning of wisdom" (Proverbs 9:10).

> But if that wicked servant says to himself, "My master is delayed," and begins to beat his fellow servants and eats and drinks with drunkards, the master of that servant will come on a day when he does not expect him and at an hour he does not know and will cut him in pieces and put him with the hypocrites. In that place there will be weeping and gnashing of teeth. (vv. 48–51)

The most neglected theme in the modern church is the theme of judgment. The second most neglected theme is the theme that the church shall be judged: "judgment [will] . . begin [with] the household of God" (1 Peter 4:17). The third most neglected theme is the theme that the individual Christian shall stand before the Judgment Seat of Christ to give an account for what he has done (16:27; cf. Romans 14:12).

Other than a few short lines in a few verses, the emphasis Jesus gives in our text to his second coming is not that of salvation but of judgment. Before Jesus goes to the cross (to take on the judgment of God on our behalf) in chapters 26, 27, he first judges the world and the church in chapters 23, 24, and 25.

Judgment is not a dirty word. It's not a bad word. It's not an old covenant word. It's a holy word. It's a good word. It's a new covenant word. It's a word from Jesus, the loving Lord of the universe. If your father or mother told you, "The stove is hot, don't touch it, you'll get burned," that's a warning that comes from love. If your Savior told you, "Unbelief and evil behavior is harmful, don't touch, you'll be damned," that's a warning that comes from love. The godless guru and the sentimental swami speak only of love but know nothing about love. If judgment is a reality, then love warns of judgment.[30] And here the Lord of love warns his church, especially those spiritually asleep within it, that "the wicked will not stand in the judgment" (Psalm 1:5). They will be cut to pieces (v. 51, a graphic image of divine retribution)[31] and assigned a place ("hell," as Jesus calls it elsewhere) where "there will be weeping and gnashing of teeth." That is another graphic image, this time an image of regret—"I knew better"—and sorrow and perhaps rage toward God.

The wise person believes in Jesus and takes him at his word. The wise person does good and not evil. And the wise person thinks and feels and acts those ways because the wise person believes that Jesus is coming soon to judge the living and the dead and that he brings with him punishment for the wicked (vv. 50, 51) and reward for the righteous (v. 47).

Jesus pulls and pushes us forward with his blessings—the Master will give the wise servant charge of "*all* his possessions" (v. 47) (wow!).[34] But he grabs us from the pit with his warnings. There are woos and woes of salvation. Those are the ways Christ helps us finish the race set before us.

Last Things First

In our day, as has been true throughout church history, Jesus' clear teaching on the end times has been ignored. We do not know the day or hour. Yet, what is also sadly ignored often in our circles is that the last things should be first. We don't know *when* Jesus will return, but we know for certain *that* he will.[35] And that should keep us busy building up and longing for the kingdom.

It was Martin Luther, I believe, who said that "Christians should live as if Jesus had died this morning, risen this afternoon, and was coming this evening."[36] And it was Jonathan Edwards, I'm certain, who wrote in his famous resolutions:

> 7. Resolved, never to do anything, which I should be afraid to do, if it were the last hour of my life. . . .
>
> 19. Resolved, never to do anything, which I should be afraid to do, if I expected it would not be above an hour, before I should hear the last trump.[37]

We need cool heads when the ecclesial oddballs give their strange speculations and when the evangelical eccentrics tell us the Bible can tell us all we need to know about modern science, American politics, and the end-of-the-world calendar. But we also need warm hearts,[38] hearts that resolve to live as though Jesus could return this moment, and hearts that cry out through all the false apocalyptic fervor with true apocalyptic fervor,[39] "Come, Lord Jesus!" (Revelation 22:20).

73

The Sad Story of Five Silly Girls

MATTHEW 25:1–13

AT THE LUNCH TABLE one Sunday afternoon, I asked my oldest daughter (whom shall remain nameless) what she thought of the sermon. She said, "It was medium boring." By that she meant half of it was interesting and half of it was boring. Well, I am glad to announce that this chapter is fully non-boring chapter. I say that with confidence because (a) our text is a story, (b) it is a very short story, (c) it is a very short story told by Jesus, an expert storyteller, and (d) it is a very short story told by Jesus about five silly girls and five smart ones.

But before we get to the five silly girls and the five smart ones, we start with a powerful king (this is a kingdom parable about the Son of Man) who is about to get married. This coming king Jesus calls "the bridegroom." We would simply call him the groom. But in Jesus' story no future wife is mentioned. The focus falls on the bridegroom and those who will help serve at his wedding, called "virgins." We would call them bridesmaids, young women (girls) who are not yet married.

Now "the bridegroom" could represent God, as it would be if we were reading the Old Testament (e.g., Isaiah 54:4–6). In the New Testament, however, the bridegroom represents Jesus (cf. 9:14, 15). Now my youngest daughter, Charlotte, would with Christological clarity say, "But, Daddy, Jesus is God." Precisely. While Jesus is not God the Father, he is God the Son. Jesus is fully God. He is the bridegroom.

This is a story about Jesus, the divine/human bridegroom, and the day or night or early, early morning of his wedding—a wedding at which some get in to celebrate with him and others don't. It's the happy story of five smart girls and the sad story of five silly girls.

The Bridegroom

As we study this parable, we will look at the three characters, learning a lesson from each. We begin with the bridegroom. By looking at the actions of the bridegroom in the story, Jesus tells about himself and his church, and we learn the first of our three lessons. The first lesson is this: *the bridegroom, with his unusually long delay and unexpected time of arrival, teaches us that predicting when Jesus will return is pointless.*

You might say, "Wasn't that the point of the previous sermon?" Yes, it was. But since Jesus took the time to go over it again, I will as well. It obviously is a point he thinks we might easily forget.

Let me explain the details, and then I'll drill home that familiar point even deeper. Let's read verses 1–6:

> Then the kingdom of heaven *will be* [at the future return and judgment][1] like ten virgins who took their lamps and went to meet the bridegroom. Five of them were foolish, and five were wise. For when the foolish took their lamps, they took no oil with them, but the wise took flasks of oil with their lamps. As the bridegroom was delayed, they all became drowsy and slept. But at midnight there was a cry, "Here is the bridegroom! Come out to meet him."

From what we know of first-century Jewish marriage customs, the groom would leave his house and journey to his bride's house. Usually the wedding ceremony was conducted there, sometimes (often?) at night.[2] After the wedding, everyone in the wedding party would return to the groom's home for a "marriage feast" (v. 10).

Concerning the details of this story, Jesus is simply sharing a scenario that would have been familiar to his original audience. The details, however, that stand out to all generations and cultures are (a) the unusually long delay and (b) the unexpected time of arrival. No one helping the wedding ceremony or celebration, like these ten girls were asked to do, would go to sleep unless the groom's delay was abnormally long, and since they all fell asleep they obviously didn't think (now that it was near midnight) that he would come at that late hour. The wedding would surely wait for the next evening. Who would get married past midnight?[3]

Those two different details reveal the lesson that I just stated—the bridegroom, with his unusually long delay and unexpected time of arrival, teaches us that predicting when Jesus will return is pointless. The preceding parables press this same point of pointlessness from different perspectives. Together they teach that Christ will return later than expected, sooner than expected, and at an unexpected time. "I think that covers all logical possibilities," Craig Blomberg summarizes, "and ought to put a stop to Christian guesswork about the timing of the end once and for all."[4]

But it doesn't, does it? Although Christian history is littered with strange speculations and false predictions, and although Jesus Christ twice made it absolutely clear that only God knows the timing of the second coming—24:36 ("But concerning that day and hour no one knows . . . but the Father only") and Acts 1:7 ("It is not for you to know times and seasons that the Father has fixed by his own authority")—it is still quite popular in this present age for Christians to claim end-times clarity on the day, time, and place.

But such "holy" horoscopes are unholy. The philosopher Sir Francis Bacon once wrote this simple but too-often forgettable truth:

> The desire of power in excess
> caused angels to fall;
> the desire of knowledge in excess
> caused man to fall.[5]

As fallen human beings we have an innate craving for the forbidden fruit that comes from "the tree of knowledge" (Genesis 2:9). "Whenever the Bible addresses the future of human history, and speaks somewhat cryptically of when and how it will unfold," we instinctively want to take a bite, to "unlock the mystery, decipher the symbols, and work out exactly what will happen and when."[6] But here in our text (once again) we are exhorted to abandon such appetites, for such information has been purposely withheld from us. We have been given neither the authority nor the ability to decipher the timing of Christ's coming. That is what the bridegroom, with his unusually long delay and unexpected time of arrival, teaches.

The Wise Virgins

Next we come to the five wise virgins. Let's discover who they are, what they did, and what they can teach us.

The wise virgins symbolize true Christians—the prepared and persevering saints. We are not to take their virginity literally, thus commending virginity to the truly holy or truly saved, as was sometimes done with this text in late antiquity. Christians aren't all virgins any more than they are all slaves or sheep.

That is who they are. Here is what they did. First, they "took their lamps and went to meet the bridegroom" (v. 1). This was obviously an act of obedience. They had a part to play in the wedding (likely providing light for the bridal party procession),[7] and they were ready to play that part when the groom arrived. Their lamps (think "torches" or "wind lanterns")[8] were in hand, oiled up if you will, and ready to go. Of course, all ten girls were equal in this task.[9] They all obeyed, and they all were ready. The difference between the two groups comes out in verses 3, 4. The difference is preparedness and lack of preparedness; more specifically, it is preparedness and lack of preparedness for the unexpected. We are told that "the wise took flasks of oil with their lamps" (v. 4), while the foolish "took their lamps," but they "took no [extra] oil with them" (v. 3).

The difference is the extra oil, not merely oil. All ten have oil. Thus, the original oil that runs out can't represent, as some argue, saving faith, good works, or the Holy Spirit, unless we believe that true Christians can lose their salvation, which doesn't fit well with the bridegroom's final words—"I do not know you" (v. 12); that is, "I never knew you," not "I once knew you but now I no longer know you."[10]

I think the oil is oil, and it simply symbolizes preparedness (cf. Luke 12:35, where "stay dressed for action" [i.e., be prepared] parallels "keep your lamps burning" [i.e., be prepared]). I know that takes the spiritual beauty out of it. I know an allegory about the extra oil representing the second blessing of the Holy Spirit would give you goose bumps. Sorry to be such a downer.

In fact, I think the oil is secondary to the oil-keeper. The focus falls not on the oil but on the person who has oil reserves. So, while I'm sympathetic to those who see the oil as "good works" (that reading fits Matthew, no doubt—especially the burning lamp being good works in 5:15, 16 and the emphasis of works in the rest of chapter 25) or short-term enthusiasm (like the seed sown upon the rocky soil in the Parable of the Soils, 13:20, 21)[11] or even "anything you please"[12] (the "open" interpretation—fill in whatever might be missing in your life), in the end I say that the oil is oil and the prepared person, not the lamp and oil within, is the emphasis.

To illustrate Jesus' oil illustration, think of two drivers with a pickup truck each. One driver has a filled gas can in the back of his pickup; the other driver does not. When the first driver runs out of gas on a deserted desert road, he can simply grab that can, fill up the tank, and keep going—because he is prepared to run out. The other driver, on the other hand, is stuck in a dangerous and potentially deadly situation.

The five wise virgins are like the driver with the extra can of gasoline.

How's that for bridging the cultural gap—five Middle Eastern girls driving a Ford pickup through an Arizona desert? How's that for not being boring?

Regarding these five smart girls, we have discovered who they are and what they did. Finally, we come to the main lesson they teach. The lesson is this: *the wise virgins teach us that preparedness for the parousia is rewarded with paradise*. Okay, I couldn't resist the alliteration, however slightly off the last word is. The other p-words (preparedness and *parousia*) work *p*erfectly. These five smart or sensible girls are prepared for the *parousia*—the coming of the bridegroom, and due to such preparedness, they are granted entrance into paradise, or here "the marriage feast." Their "obedience of faith" (Romans 1:5) is rewarded with the messianic banquet in the kingdom of heaven: "those who were ready went in with him [the groom] to the marriage feast" (v. 10).

If you find it difficult or dull to imagine Heaven as a perpetual choir rehearsal, imagine it instead as a wedding reception with fine filets and aged wine, good music and festive dancing. Those who have been "washed in the blood of atonement, clothed in Christ's righteousness, [and] renewed by the Spirit"[13] will eat and drink and sing and dance with the bridegroom—with him who loved us and gave himself for us (Galatians 2:20). The blessing or reward (I'm not afraid to use that word when preaching from Matthew's Gospel) is the wedding banquet *with* the bridegroom. It's not only quite the feast, but it's quite the feast *with Jesus*.

A number of colorful descriptions of Heaven and Hell in the New Testament make "vividly clear the glory and awfulness" of salvation and judgment, but perhaps the most powerful image of Heaven is "to be 'with the Lord for ever,' as Paul puts it in 1 Thessalonians 4:17 (cf. Phil. 1:23)," and the most powerful image of Hell is, "to quote Paul again, to be punished 'with everlasting destruction and shut out from the presence of the Lord and from the majesty of his power on the day he comes to be glorified in his holy people (2 Thessalonians 1:9–10)."[14]

Those wise young women were prepared in the present because they longed for the future feast with him—the bridegroom, the powerful but lowly and loving King of the kingdom of heaven!

The Foolish Virgins

The third and last lesson that we learn from the silly girls is this: *the foolish virgins teach us that too little preparation and too much presumption will result in rejection*.

To get to these themes of "too little preparation" and "too much presumption," we turn our attention to the two answers given to the fools from the two other characters. Do you see the word "answered" at the beginning of verse 9 and then verse 12? How the wise and how the groom answered those fools shows their folly.

We start with verse 9:

> As the bridegroom was delayed, they all became drowsy and slept. But at midnight there was a cry, "Here is the bridegroom! Come out to meet him." Then all those virgins rose and trimmed their lamps. And the foolish said to the wise, "Give us some of your oil, for our lamps are going out." *But the wise answered,* saying, "Since there will not be enough for us and for you, go rather to the dealers and buy for yourselves." (vv. 5–9)

At first reading you might be bothered at the apparent selfishness of the wise. Why didn't they share? True Christians are to love others. True Christians are to sacrifice. True Christians are to share with those in need. True. But they are also to be responsible for or obedient to the work the bridegroom has called them to do. Their ethical dilemma is not such a dilemma if we realize (a) obedience to the groom is their first priority, and (b) if they gave away their oil they would, as they said, all run out before their task of lighting the way was completed, and thus everyone would be in the dark and in danger. The wedding would be a disaster without their torchlight procession.

We might also add (this is a fitting place to do this) that this is a parable, and just as the one little piggy didn't really eat roast beef and the other one had none, not every detail in every parable is realistic, and not every detail in every parable teaches a moral.[15] Here, however, I do think there is a moral from a potential real-life scene, and the moral is that *too little preparation will result in rejection.*

The first rejection comes from the true Christians. The second comes from Christ himself, and this second rejection is far more serious. Look now at Jesus' answer in verses 10–12. So off the fools go . . .

> And while they were going to buy [oil], the bridegroom came, and those who were ready went in with him to the marriage feast, and the door was shut. Afterward the other virgins [the foolish] came also, saying, "Lord, lord, open to us." *But he answered*, "Truly, I say to you, I do not know you."

Now again, at first reading, just as you might have been bothered by the wise girls' apparent selfishness, here you might be bothered at the groom's apparent harshness. Why is the door shut? Why does the groom say to those *he asked* to be in *his* wedding that he doesn't even know them? And what did those silly girls do that was so sinful? Verses 10, 11 provide the picture of hurried activity. Those five fools aren't lazy fools (cf. 25:26).

They are told by the wise to go buy more oil, and off they go. They got the oil, lit up the lamps, and then hurried to the party. Sure, they were late, but they could have called it a day. They could have walked home and gone to bed. But they didn't. They went to the wedding, and they wanted to go in to the party. And then, at the shut door, they called out, "Lord, lord, open to us" (v. 11). Didn't they acknowledge Jesus as Lord (and yes, the double "Lord, Lord" is intended to remind of us of the end of the Sermon on the Mount and those lawless miracle-workers who don't get in [7:21])? And didn't Jesus teach his disciples to ask and they shall receive, and to knock and the door shall be opened (7:7)? So why then does this door stay shut? Why does their prayer go unanswered? Or I should say, why is it answered with an emphatic rejection—with Jesus' "I have no idea who you are"?

Alfred Lloyd Tennyson captured so well the ethical tension of verses 10–12, as well as this point of presumption, in his poem on this parable, entitled "Late, Late, So Late!"

> Late, late so late! and dark the night and chill!
> Late, late so late! *but we can enter still.*
> "Too late, too late! ye cannot enter now."
>
> No light had we; *for that we do repent;*
> And learning this, *the bridegroom will relent.*
> "Too late, too late! ye cannot enter now."
>
> No light: so late! and dark and chill the night!
> O let us in, that we may find the light!
> "Too late, too late: ye cannot enter now."
>
> *Have we not heard the bridegroom is so sweet?*
> O let us in, tho' late, to kiss his feet!
> "No, no; too late! ye cannot enter now." (emphasis mine)[16]

As Tennyson notes, these silly girls are not prepared, and yet they presume that if they go and get prepared minutes after the minutes they needed to be prepared, they "can enter still." And they presume that if they "do repent . . . the bridegroom will relent." They presume upon his kindness—"Have we not heard the bridegroom is so sweet?"

You see, these five very silly girls are irresponsibly secure. They think other Christians will surely help them get what is necessary to get in. "If and when the time comes, let's borrow from the prepared" is their attitude. Sure, we need church fellowship and more mature believers around us in order to persevere, but here Jesus places individual responsibility before us. As one scholar puts it, "Now, suddenly, everything is terrifyingly individual."[17] Don't count on other Christians' preparedness or righteousness. You're on your own before the judgment throne.[18]

These five very silly girls also think that if they can't get in on the backs of the saints, gentle Jesus will surely let them in. They might place the blame on him: "It's his fault, not mine. He came when I wasn't ready. He'd better let me in." Or they assume that the Jesus on Judgment Day is the Jesus of Christmas Day—little, harmless, non-threatening. Oh no. On that Day too late is too bad. Jesus will roar like a lion, not lie down like a lamb. The door will stay closed.

Listen, there is blessed assurance—prepared disciples can fall asleep each night without undue worry about Christ's judgment post-midnight. But there is also "*Un*blessed Assurance,"[19] when someone thinks that simply getting an invitation to the wedding and being asked to participate in it assures entrance to it. Haven't we already learned, in the Parables of the Hidden Treasure and the Pearl of Great Price (13:44–46), that it is "not enough just to '*find*' the treasure . . . one must also '*sell all*' to purchase the treasure if one wants to *have* it"?[20] This is not justification by works, but neither is it justification by dramatic conversion. The salvation equation is not faith plus works equals justification or teary-eyed profession of faith plus no works equals justification. Rather, the equation is faith plus nothing equals justification plus works, obedience, love, and eschatological readiness.

"Nothing in my hands I bring, simply to the cross I cling." Yes. True. Absolutely. But the cross of Christ is not a dead tree. It's a fruit tree. And for those who cling tight to it, they become one with it, producing the fruits of the Christian life.[21]

Ah, the sin of presumption! Do you presume upon the kindness of King Jesus? That's the somber question this sad ending throws in our faces. There is a time for everything under the sun—a time for mercy and a time for judgment, a time for late repentance (the thief on the cross) and a time for too late repentance (the five silly girls).

The celebrated Matthew scholars Davies and Allison summarize this point nearly perfectly when they write of the five fools, "[T]hey do not have enough time at this point because earlier they had too much time."[22] Only Jesus summarizes the point better: "Watch therefore, for you know neither the day nor the hour" (v. 13). Jesus says, "Let's reduce the whole story to one simple warning: 'Have your Christian life so in order that when you *are* surprised [by my return] you will be *ready*.'"[23]

His final point is most pointed! Jesus takes the points on the surprise of his return, the necessary preparation for it, and the danger of presumption and melds all those points into one big point, which points right to us—the readers: *You all* watch, for *you all* don't know when I'm returning.

Kneel among the Cotton

I began this chapter with a somewhat funny conversation I had with my oldest daughter. I'll end with a very serious but sweet song from an African-American slave. In the history of the world I don't know if there was a more prepared people. One slave sings:

> There's a king and a captain high,
> And he's coming by and by,
> And he'll find me hoeing cotton when he comes.
> You can hear his legions charging in the regions of the sky,
> And he'll find me hoeing cotton when he comes.
> There's a man they thrust aside,
> Who was tortured till he died,
> And he'll find me hoeing cotton when he comes.
> He was hated and rejected,
> He was scorned and crucified,
> And he'll find me hoeing cotton when he comes.
> When he comes! When he comes!
> He'll be crowned by saints and angels when he comes.
> They'll be shouting out Hosanna! to the man that men denied,
> And I'll kneel among my cotton when he comes.[24]

Too little preparation and too much presumption will result in rejection. But preparedness—working the cotton fields, waiting in the cotton fields—for the coming of Christ will result in freedom, joy, eternal life with Jesus Christ, a life in which you and the Bridegroom will live happily ever after. Amen.

74

From Vigilance to Diligence

MATTHEW 25:14–30

AFTER I PREACHED ON the end of Matthew 24, one person came up to me after the service and asked, "What does it mean to be ready for Jesus' return?" Then after I preached on Matthew 25:1–13—the Parable of the Ten Virgins—two people came up to me after the service, one after the other, with that same question. When I went to my Growth Group on that same Sunday night the question on everyone's mind was, "What does it mean to be ready?" When I received some feedback from other Growth Group leaders, I heard that the same question was raised in the other groups.

One group member, John Higgins, said that readiness for the second coming of Christ looks like readiness for the first coming of Christ. That's an excellent observation. I expect nothing less from John, my former intern extraordinaire. The question of readiness is not only raised but also answered in full in the three parables found in Matthew 25.

In the Parable of the Ten Virgins, readiness looks like *prepared waiting*—not just waiting but prepared waiting. All ten virgins are waiting for the bridegroom, but only the five wise ones are prepared in their waiting. They have brought extra oil for their lamps. In the Parable of the Sheep and the Goats, which we will explore in the next chapter, we are given another image of readiness. The image there is that of *loving the least.* The sheep demonstrate allegiance to Christ by loving the least even in some unlovely situations—sickness, imprisonment, and so on. Another picture of readiness is found in our current text. In the Parable of the Talents we will learn that readiness looks like *faithful working.* So we might say that readiness looks like hope (the Parable of the Virgins),[1] love (the Parable of the Sheep and the Goats), and faith (the Parable of the Talents). In this sermon our focus is on faith, more specifically on faithful working, or even more accurately a faithfulness that works.

J. C. Ryle, the nineteenth-century Bishop of Liverpool, summarizes today's parable by comparing and contrasting it with the previous parable. I haven't found a summary I agree with more than his. He writes:

> The parable of the talents is very like that of the ten virgins. Both direct our minds to the same important event: the second coming of Jesus Christ. [I agree.] Both bring before us the same people: the members of the professing church of Christ. [I also agree.] The virgins and the servants are one and the same people—but the same people regarded from a different point, and viewed on different sides. The practical lesson of each parable is the main point of difference: vigilance is the keynote of the first parable, diligence that of the second. The story of the virgins calls on the church to watch; the story of the talents calls on the church to work. [I couldn't agree more.][2]

The Parable of the Talents focuses on a faithfulness that works. It calls on the church to work. It calls on the church to be ready for Jesus' return by working between his resurrection and return with the gifts we have been given.

The Start of the Story

Let's get to work on this theme of work. Jesus' story is told in three scenes. Let's start with the two scenes found in verses 14–18.

> [Scene One] For it will be like a man going on a journey, who called his servants and entrusted to them his property. To one he gave five talents, to another two, to another one, to each according to his ability. Then he went away. [Scene Two] He who had received the five talents went at once and traded with them, and he made five talents more. So also he who had the two talents made two talents more. But he who had received the one talent went and dug in the ground and hid his master's money.

Note four things in these five verses. First, Jesus makes a number of contextual connections. For example, he starts with the words, "For it will be like. . . ." What is "it"? The answer is easily found in the preceding parable. "It" is "the kingdom of heaven" (v. 1).[3] "The kingdom of heaven will be like ten virgins" (v. 1), and the kingdom of heaven will also be like "a man going on a journey" (v. 14). That word "journey," along with the phrase "Now after a long time" in verse 19, also connects to the context. We are reminded that Jesus is still on the Mount of Olives (24:3), giving what has come to be known as the Olivet Discourse. He is foretelling the future (the fall of Jerusalem and his second coming), and he is forth-telling about the present and future (what his disciples then and now should do in light of such events).

The second thing to note is the identity of the "man" of verse 14, also called the "master" nine times throughout the rest of the parable. This "master" is Jesus. I say that because it is obvious, especially in light of the identity of the bridegroom in the previous parable (Jesus) and the king in the next parable (Jesus), but also because the word used here for "master" is the word "lord" (*kurios*), the title used throughout Matthew's Gospel for Jesus and used of him in verses 11, 37, and 44 of Matthew 25. So in this parable Jesus is the man, the master, the lord. He is the one who gives the talents to his servants, goes away, returns, and settles the accounts—he judges the workers' work or lack thereof.

The third thing to note is the talents. Verse 15 reads, "To one he gave five talents, to another two, to another one, to each according to his ability." That phrase "according to his ability" is used in the sense "according to his able-ness" ("power" [*dynamis*] is the actual word). In other words, if I know that Fred is *able* to lift heavy objects, I might *give* him heavy objects to lift. So the ability or able-ness preexists the talent. The talent is something above and beyond the ability. That is not to say that the ability is not also something given, for what do we have that is not a gift from Christ?

What then is the talent? The talent is money. Just look at the language. The final phrase of verse 14 is, "entrusted to them his property." Then verses 16, 17 talk about the first two servants making more of this property—e.g., "he made five talents more" (v. 16) and "made two talents more" (v. 17). Finally, verse 18 clarifies that this "property" is specifically "money"—"But he who had received the one *talent* went and dug in the ground and hid his *master's money*."

Now, of course, this fine deduction of mine would have been elementary for Jesus' original audience and Matthew's first readers. Everyone then knew that a talent was a unit of currency, a monetary weight. In our context a penny is the lowest currency and the hundred dollar bill the highest. In Jesus' context, we know that a denarius (a low unit of currency) was a day's wages for a common laborer (cf. 20:2) and that a talent (a high unit of currency) was worth six thousand denarii. Thus D. A. Carson equates one talent with "perhaps three hundred thousand dollars."[4] Grant Osborne, however, claims that one talent, due to the fluctuation in the value of silver or gold, is "worth $800,000 in today's money ($960,000 when gold is worth $600 an ounce)."[5] I'll let those two Trinity scholars duke it out. Either way, one talent is an enormous amount of money.

The amount is surprisingly high. And the shock of it is intended to compel us to think of Christ's generosity. It's intended to move us to worship. "Praise God from whom all blessings flow!" Jesus gives such great gifts to his church. The one, two, four, five, ten talents remind me of the ten thousand talents in the Parable of the Unforgiving Servant (18:24). Through Christ, God forgives our zillion-dollar debt ("Jesus paid it all"), and in Christ and with Christ he gives us at least three hundred thousand dollars to work with in service to him ("all to him I owe").

This "talent," of course, has an elastic quality to it. Let's remember that this is a parable, not a mathematical equation. So a talent can mean the gifts of knowledge, health, strength, time, intellect, advantages, opportunities, "various responsibilities"[6] (i.e., our jobs or vocations), perhaps people (a spouse, children, friend), and even further natural abilities (talents as we think of the word). A talent can also mean or include "spiritual gifts" as Peter and Paul called them,[7] such as the gifts of teaching, administration, mercy, healing, and so on.

The "talents" symbolize more than money, but not less than money. Listen, just because Jesus is not teaching economic theory here, don't think that he isn't teaching some economic truths. Money matters matter to Jesus, and it is the Master's money (quite plainly) we are dealing with here. While we "need not limit the application of this parable to money matters,"[8] let's not be so quick to expand "talents" to mean everything except our use of money. Wasn't it Jesus who said, "[W]here your treasure is, there your heart will be also" (6:21)? Might we not expand upon that thought, saying, "How your money/talents are used, there is your heart also"? To our Lord the link between a heart-check and a checkbook is a short, straight line. I'll spare you my sermon on "If only the majority of Western Christians tithed (gave 10 percent) of their income 'much of world poverty could be eradicated and millions more could hear the gospel.'"[9] Such a statistic while true (it is actually true) might be too convicting, and I'd hate for anyone to feel convicted about their use of money . . . I mean, talents.

Anyway, back to decoding some key symbols. The master symbolizes Jesus, the talents symbolize gifts/responsibilities/money, and the servants symbolize professing Christians, those who would call Jesus "Lord," are part of his household, and are called upon by him to do his will.

I must admit (as sort of a second aside) that being called a "servant" (or "slave" as the word can be rendered) is a bit hard on my healthy ego. Being called a "slave" is better than being called a "sheep" (stay tuned for 25:32, 33!), but a slave—even a slave who is entrusted with lots of money—is still a slave. Perhaps this humble title is an intentional heart-check for Christians. Are you okay with being a slave or servant to Jesus? Paul was—"Paul, a servant of Christ Jesus" (Romans 1:1a). Peter was—"Simon Peter, a bond-servant . . . of Jesus Christ" (2 Peter 1:1a, NASB).

The fourth thing to note is what each servant did with what he was given. The first two doubled their master's money. They also both got to work on their work immediately after the gift was given. Don't overlook the start of verses 16 and 17: "He who had received the five talents went at once" and got to work, and "So also" the next guy. We see then the opposite of industry and perhaps immediacy in the last guy. He eventually got around to doing something with the money. He dug a hole (did that take an hour or ten minutes to dig?) and buried the money in it. Note the contrast between the "aggressive . . . [and] recessive verbs"—instead of forward-moving verbs like "traded" and "made" used of the first two servants, the third servant "dug" and "hid."[10]

The Rewards of the Righteous

In verses 14–18 we get the start of the story: the setting is set, the characters introduced, the plot moves into motion. In verses 19–30 we get the end of the story, or Scene Three we can call it. Verse 19 reads, "Now after a long time the master of those servants came and settled accounts with them." The language of "after a long time" reminds us of the previous parable with the late-arriving bridegroom. The return of Christ may take a long time. The language of "settled accounts" reminds us that Jesus will return as a judge, as *the* judge of all people from every nation (25:32). Verses 20–30 then speak of the master's judgment of the faithful and the unfaithful. The faithful are rewarded (vv. 20–23) and the unfaithful punished (vv. 24–30). We'll look at the unfaithful and their crime and punishment soon. For now we turn our attention to more happy themes. Verses 20–23 are uplifting verses. Let them lift you up as you now read them again:

> And he who had received the five talents came forward, bringing five talents more, saying, "Master, you delivered to me five talents; here I have made five talents more." His master said to him, "Well done, good and faithful servant. You have been faithful over a little; I will set you over much. Enter into the joy of your master." And he also who had the two talents came forward, saying, "Master, you delivered to me two talents; here I have made two talents more." His master said to him, "Well done, good and faithful servant. You have been faithful over a little; I will set you over much. Enter into the joy of your master."

The extensive parallelisms are evident. The first and second servants both present their talents to the master, both present double what they were given, and both are rewarded equally. (That equality is important. As Meier notes, "that both servants receive the same reward shows that what is valued is not one's accomplishments in a quantitative sense but fidelity of one's commitment").[11] To both the Lord says, "Well done, good and faithful servant. You have been faithful over a little; I will set you over much. Enter into the joy of your master" (vv. 21, 23). The words are identical. The Lord Jesus equally rewards the two faithful servants' equal efforts.

The First Reward

Three rewards are given. First he gives praise-filled approval: "Well done, good and faithful servant."

I'm not someone who suffers from depression. I don't easily or often get depressed. I thank God for that. True depression can be so awful and debilitating. But I sometimes get discouraged, and perhaps you do as well.

I remember when I was in my early twenties and so excited about going into full-time Christian ministry when an old pastor (he has now been retired for many years—that's how old he was then) said that most pastors leave the ministry due to discouragement. When he said that, I internally rolled my eyes and thought, *What does this old stale Christian leader know about anything? Discouragement? Number one? No way!* Well, it turns out that that old bat batted a thousand. Discouragement is my number one nemesis, and it has been for a good decade now.

In fact, I recently told my wife, Emily, as we visited a church I helped plant ten years ago, that sometimes I feel with my current ministry like I'm flat on the ground with a huge stone on my back. I want to be free to jump and fly—to implement strategic ways to take the gospel to my city and the world, but sometimes I struggle to move forward even two steps. Discouragement—it's awful.

In Ohio recently, as I was teaching preachers how to preach, I gave an example sermon. Afterwards a pastor came up to me and said, "That was a work of art." What a first-class compliment! And with that compliment I felt the stone roll away. But it was only for a moment. You see, if I do the work I've been called to do for his approval or your approval (the praise of man), that stone of discouragement will always roll back onto my back. But if I recognize that I have only an audience of one—my Master, my Lord, my God—and if I am living for the final day and the one and only first-class compliment that matters, "Well done, my good and faithful servant," then I can stay the course, even working with the stone on my back if necessary, knowing that the road to the celestial city is rough and uphill and dangerous and full of seductive temptations and heavy discouragements.[12]

What is true for me I'm sure is true for you. So, when you are down, look up. When you are turning your attention to the present or the past, turn it to the future when Jesus will reward you with words—praise *for you* from the one to whom all praise is to be rendered.

The Second Reward

The second reward, which is just as counterintuitive as the first, is more responsibility. After Jesus says, "Well done, good and faithful servant," he says, "You have been faithful over a little; I will set you over much" (vv. 21, 23). In other words, "You have fulfilled this small work project; let me now give you a big one."

You see, the people ("servants" Jesus calls them—people who serve God and others) of the kingdom of heaven, on earth now and in Heaven later, are not passive. To enter into the kingdom through faith in Christ is to enter into his workforce, and it is to return in some sense to Eden, to pre-fall holiness, where work was given to man as a divine gift, not a curse. I'll put it this way: do your kingdom work well now, and you'll be rewarded with more work now and especially then. As one commentator put it, "Heavenly rewards are not beds of rest; they are posts of duty."[13] Or as another one put it, "Christ knows no idle life, not even in the kingdom of heaven."[14]

The Third Reward

The third reward is the Lord's joy. I say it that odd way because that's how Jesus says it. He doesn't say, "My good and faithful servant, enter into the joys of Heaven." Instead he says, "Enter into the joy of your master" (vv. 21, 23).

Listen, Jesus will do whatever it takes for you, dear Christian, to get you through the gates of the kingdom and to the final joy of the kingdom—that heavenly messianic feast *with him*, the ever-joyous Bridegroom. Sometimes he will use the motive of fear to warn you. (We'll get to that in a bit.) Other times (right here) he'll use the motive of relationship to woo you on your way.

1. The first reward is praise-filled approval.
2. The second reward is more responsibility.
3. The third reward (and I say that it is the greatest of the three) is that you and I will someday "enter into the joy" of our Lord and Savior and Friend and Brother and Betrothed.

I want you to take those three future rewards—stick them into your brain, sew them on each chamber of your heart, tattoo them on your hands if need be—and use them to motivate you to press on with your God-given unique and important kingdom work. For you see, what you do with your talents will matter on judgment day, so let them matter to you now.[15]

Crime and Punishment

I wish I could end here, for some of you, like me, just need to be encouraged to keep pressing on. But we are in the Olivet Discourse where the theme of judgment won't stay down no matter how hard modern Christians try to hammer it. It keeps rising above the surface because there are others in the church who need not to be wooed by Jesus but warned by him. So we come now to the end of the matter, the end of the parable, the end stress of all that comes before it.[16] "He who has ears, let him hear" (13:9):

> He also who had received the one talent came forward, saying, "Master, I knew you to be a hard man, reaping where you did not sow, and gathering where you scattered no seed, so I was afraid, and I went and hid your talent in the ground. Here you have what is yours." (vv. 24, 25)

Here we have a seemingly pious man. He acknowledges Jesus as "master" or "lord." (Oh, yes, he'll join that church camp who says, "Lord, Lord" on judgment day, 7:21, 22.) But he takes the Lord's name in vain. He sees Jesus as a hard or harsh or even mean, merciless, or cruel character who acts unjustly, demanding a harvest from a field where no seeds have been planted. His view of God, if you'll allow me, is so high it's too low: "Oh, Lord, you're such a sovereign master, an unmoved mover, that whatever I did with this talent wouldn't matter to you anyway, so I did nothing." He has cloaked his laziness behind his solemn God-talk excuses. He has a high view of God but a wrong view of God. He has a fear of God but an improper fear of God. And thus he has the audacity to blame generous Jesus for his own apathy and inactivity.

He reminds me a bit of Adam, who said, "The woman *whom you gave* to be with me, she gave me fruit of the tree, and I ate" (Genesis 3:12). He also reminds me of the church leaders who told the great missionary William Carey when he brought before them his idea of taking the gospel from England to India, "Sit down, young man; when God chooses to save the heathen he will do so without your help or ours!"[17] Really? Have you never read the end of Matthew's Gospel or that big book in our Bibles that we call the Acts of the Apostles, which talks about *the acts* of the apostles? Listen, in our parable don't the two good servants have the balance we all should have between God's grace and human work—"Master, *you gave* me five talents

[God's grace] . . . and here *I have made* five more [human work]"?[18] Jesus never belittles his servants' kingdom work, for he knows that he has saved us not only *from* our sins but *unto* his service. Jesus Christ "gave himself for us to redeem us from all lawlessness and to purify for himself a people for his own possession who are zealous for good works" (Titus 2:14).

So you see, this third servant's master isn't any different than the first and second servants' master. He is not cruel but generous, not unjust but fair. And it is this fairness that can seem cruel that we see next in our story. Look at verse 26. "But his master answered him . . ." Jesus will have none of this blame game. "You wicked and slothful servant! You *knew* that I reap where I have not sowed and gather where I scattered no seed?" Insert the phrase, "Read as sarcasm." "What do you *know* about me? Let's play your game—that I'm this cruel and unjust sovereign. Even if that's who I really am, that's still no excuse for not doing anything. 'Then you ought to have [at the very least] invested my money with the bankers,[19] and at my coming I should have received what was my own with interest' [v. 27]. In summary, any way you look at the situation, the issue is not my character flaw; it's yours."

This servant has rationalized his sin. His defense is as irrational as hiding a lamp under a bushel basket. The holy and just judge Jesus sees through the servant's illogical lawlessness, and thus he quickly but rightly renders his verdict:

> So take the talent from him and give it to him who has the ten talents. For to everyone who has will more be given, and he will have an abundance. But from the one who has not, even what he has will be taken away. And cast the worthless servant into the outer darkness. In that place there will be weeping and gnashing of teeth. (vv. 28–30)

The sin here is the sin of omission.[20] We all know that sins of commission—murder, adultery, stealing, and so on—are wrong and worthy of some kind of judgment. But what's so wicked about sloth? That's the sin here—sloth (not doing work). The good servants are called "good" and "faithful," while this last servant, who is no servant at all, is called "wicked" (the opposite of "good") and "slothful" (is that the opposite of "faithful"?—it is here to Jesus). Unfaithfulness is slothfulness, and slothfulness is a punishable offense.

The punishment is threefold. It's the opposite of the rewards for the righteous. This man receives no praise, no further work or responsibility (all is taken from him and is given to the first worker), and no joy in the master's presence. In fact, this now "worthless" man (v. 30; that's strong language) is "cast . . . into the outer darkness," in "that place [where] there will be weeping and gnashing of teeth" (that's strong imagery). Our final verse is a picture of Hell, where the emphasis is not on the pain of fire but the pain of separation—no one and nothing to see ("darkness") and nothing to do (eternally unemployed) but feel "forever the regrets of lost opportunities, misspent chances, stupid choices" ("weeping and gnashing of teeth").[21]

You don't want to go to Hell, Christian![22] That's what Jesus is getting at with his horror-story ending. So, don't be lazy with the gifts that you have been given. The point of the parable is that simple and that pointed. It's to hurt, if need be. It's to hurt now so it won't hurt later.

Six Months to Live

One recent summer I was having some heart issues—a tightness in my heart. When I called my doctor and told him the symptoms, he sent me to the emergency room immediately. As the hospital staff was running the first of five tests—an EKG—two thoughts came to my mind. The first was, *How much is all this going to cost me?* The second was, on a more serious and truthful note, *What if this is it?* That is, what if they say to me after four hours of tests, "We've found something. Your heart has this or that wrong with it. There is nothing we can do. You have six months, at best, to live." Now, I know little about the human heart, and I'm sure that my concerns were exaggerated. But I thought then what I thought. What would I do?

What would you do? We all have six months to live, or is it six days or six hours or sixty years? Do you know what I would do? Honestly, I would do what I'm doing. I would continue to preach as a dying man to dying men. When I first reflected on all this, I thought, Lord willing, I would finish the Gospel of Matthew and die the Sunday after Easter when I preach on the Great Commission. That would be a splendid way to go!

What that heart-check (a heart-check in two ways) did for me was (a) to let me know that I know what my Christ-given talents are (do you?), (b) to let me know I'm using them for his kingdom and his glory (are you?), and (c) to let me know that I'm looking forward to my Master's praise ("Well done") and to the additional work ("Thanks for doing a little, here's a lot") and to the eternal joy of being with Immanuel, "God with us" now and forever (are you?).

Listen, my beloved brothers and sisters, with the talents Christ has given you—whether it is something much esteemed in our society (the gift of being a heart specialist) or something little esteemed (the gift of children and raising children to know and love the Lord), please learn from this parable (if you learn anything) that you are to " be steadfast, immovable, always abounding in the work of the Lord, knowing that in the Lord your labor is not in vain" (1 Corinthians 15:58).

75

Jesus' Last Sermon

MATTHEW 25:31–46

AS CHRISTIANS WE ARE PEOPLE OF THE BOOK. That is, we recognize and appreciate that God has given us a sure revelation of himself and his will in the Bible. But it's one thing to believe that the Book is special—inspired, authoritative, sufficient, etc.—and it's another thing to know how to read it.

As people of the Book, how do we read the Bible? How especially do we read something complex such as the Olivet Discourse (Matthew 24, 25) or perhaps even more complex—a parable within the discourse itself? In this chapter I'm going to teach you how to read the Parable of the Sheep and the Goats, so that we might together think what we're to think, feel what we're to feel, and do what we are to do.

My strategy for this strange chapter of mine is simple and borrowed. There are a number of helpful methods for Bible reading. Perhaps you have heard of the method called COMA, which is not a method that is intended to put you into deep sleep but to wake you up to the life of the living Word. The C stands for context, the O for observation, the M for meaning, and the A for application. The method I want us to walk through is even simpler than COMA, and I hope even more lively! It is called the Swedish Method. It was named that by Ada Lum, a staff worker with the International Fellowship of Evangelical Students after she saw Swedish college students using it for their Bible study.

Here is how it works. After the group has read aloud the text to be studied, each person goes off on their own, looking for three things.

1. A Light Bulb: anything that shines out in the passage and draws attention. It can be something important or something that particularly strikes the reader.

2. A Question Mark: anything that is hard to understand; something that the reader would like to ask the author about.
3. An Arrow: anything that applies personally to the reader's life.[1]

Before the group reconvenes to share, each person must write down at least one and no more than three thoughts under each category. In this chapter I will stick to that rule for the Question Mark and the Arrow. I will ask and answer three questions and will supply you will three applications. With the lightbulbs, however, I found the limit of three too limiting. Thus, if you'll allow me (what choice do you have), I will share with you twenty more than allowed.

A Lightbulb

We'll begin with my long list of lightbulbs—details that I think are interesting and/or important.

1. This "parable" is technically not a parable. That is, unlike all the previous parables in Matthew we don't find terms like "like"—the kingdom of heaven is "like a grain of mustard seed" (13:31) or "like treasure hidden in a field" (13:44) or "like a master of a house who went out early in the morning" (20:1) or "like ten virgins" (25:1). Here Jesus gives a statement of fact: "When the Son of Man comes . . ." (25:31). The only parabolic elements are the simple similes of likening the righteous to sheep and the unrighteous to goats[2] and the structure—the use of parallels (e.g., hungry/hungry, food/no food) and a climactic end statement. So let's just call it "a revelatory discourse" or "a majestic vision" or "an apocalyptic prophecy" or a "two-verse analogy" with a thirteen-verse explanation.[3] Oh, shoot, let's just call this a parable.[4]

2. This parable is about the second coming of Christ. That first phrase—"When the Son of Man comes in his glory" (25:31) refers to his return. Let's remember we are in the Olivet Discourse, and a good half of it is about Jesus' *parousia*. Let us also remember that unlike his first coming in obscurity (a babe in a manager in a cave in Bethlehem) his second coming will be the most public event of all time.

3. As Jesus teaches here, and as we affirm in the Apostles' Creed, Jesus "shall come to judge." Here Jesus depicts himself as a shepherd king who like David (Ezekiel 34:23, 24) has come to bless God's people and punish his enemies. Yet, more than David, he has come to set all the nations aright (Psalm 2). The Olivet Discourse begins with the prophetic pronouncement of God's coming judgment upon Israel (the fall of Jerusalem), and it ends with Christ's coming judgment upon every nation. Human beings won't be judged before "the bar of history" but in the court of Christ.[5]

4. Jesus is more than the Davidic king (the Son of David); he is also the divine King (the Son of God). Paul writes of the kingdom of heaven as "the kingdom of his [i.e., God's] beloved Son" (Colossians 1:13). Here Jesus expresses his divine sonship in verse 34 when he says, "Come, you who are blessed by *my Father*."

5. Related to Jesus' divine sonship is his divine nature. Jesus applies to himself language and imagery used only of God in the Old Testament.[6] The most prominent examples come from Daniel 7 and Isaiah 66. Like "the Ancient of days" (God Almighty), Jesus claims that at his return he likewise will be enthroned as judge (Daniel 7:9), in the presence of angels (Daniel 7:10),[7] and as the one who will reward the righteous (Daniel 7:18) and punish the wicked (Daniel 7:26).[8] And like the Lord (Yahweh) in Isaiah 66:18, Jesus claims that he "is coming to gather all nations and tongues" so that "they shall come and shall see my glory" (cf. Joel 3:2).

6. In this same vein is the glory and authority associated with Jesus. This is a parable about the glorious and powerful second coming of Christ. The picture here of Jesus is awesome! God alone is glorious and powerful, and yet here what do we see? Jesus will come "in his [own] glory" and "sit [a position of authority] on [God's? no] *his* glorious throne" (v. 31).[9] He possesses his own glory; he possesses his own glorious throne.[10] And who will be with him? Some of the angels? No. "*All* the angels" (v. 31; cf. "*his* angels," 24:31). And who will stand before him? The Jews? The Gentiles? Some of the people of the world? No. "Before him will be gathered *all* the nations, and he will separate [insert—"all the"?] people . . ." (v. 32).[11] Do you see the picture? Jesus is the sole judge of the world, and absolutely every angel circles around him, and absolutely every person stands before him. What absolute glory and authority! Might we rightly say that Jesus' final sermon in Matthew's Gospel "ends where John's Gospel begins"?[12]

7. Need I go on? I will. Jesus is then called not "a king but "the King" (v. 34)—the divine King, also known as "the Son of Man" (v. 31). This "Son of Man" proceeds to judge the world based on people's relationship to his person and will. Note all the first-person personal pronouns in verses 35–46. I count the word "I" eleven times, "my" two times, and "me" fourteen times. If this reminds you of the end of the Sermon on the Mount when Judge Jesus said, "Not everyone who says to *me,* 'Lord, Lord,' will enter the kingdom of heaven, but the one who does the will of *my* Father who is in heaven" (7:21), good. It should.

8. Jesus' judgment involves gathering and separating. The language of gathering has a hopeful sound to true believers. The elect who have been scattered throughout the world are now gathered "from the four winds" (24:31)

for salvation. Their final salvation, however, comes by means of an "awful separation."[13] C. S. Lewis called it "the Great Divorce."

9. While Jesus separates people into two groups, the phrase "one from another" (v. 32) suggests the personal selection of every person from every nation, thus implying that we will all stand as individuals before the judgment seat.[14] That reading especially fits the Parable of the Talents with its stress of individual gifting, responsibility, and accountability. Related to this point of individual judgment is the individual judging. For Jesus to know who is a sheep and who is a goat requires not only a knowledge of human actions, but intimate knowledge of the motives of each human heart.

10. Jesus' judgment is based on works—on what one did or didn't do.[15] This is not an unfamiliar theme in Jesus' teaching. Earlier in 16:27 he said, "For the Son of Man is going to come with his angels in the glory of his Father, and then he will repay each person [No. 9] *according to what he has done* [No. 10]." We'll return to that theme later.

11. The works are works of love. Six basic physical and expected social works are mentioned. The only act on the list that jumps out to me is visiting those in prison. Are those in prison wicked or pious criminals? That is, are they lawless citizens who broke the law of the land or lawful Christians who broke the law of the land by preaching and/or living out the kingdom of God—people like Peter, John, and Paul mentioned in Acts and the Epistles (e.g., Colossians 4:18; Hebrews 10:34) or John the Baptist and Jesus mentioned in Matthew? When prison is mentioned in the New Testament, it is usually Christians behind bars being persecuted for righteousness' sake (5:10).

12. These works are illustrative, not exhaustive, and representative, not comprehensive. Even Jesus himself didn't act out all of these actions. He certainly fed the hungry (14:13–21; 15:32–39) and visited the sick (8:14–17). But we have no record of him welcoming a stranger into his home (he had no home per se in his adult ministry) or visiting the imprisoned. However, here we are not to ask the question, did Jesus do all six, and do you do all six? but rather to affirm the statement, "Jesus would do all six and six thousand more, and you and I should go and do likewise." We are always expanding upon ways to live out Jesus' ethics, thinking about how we can use medicine, economics, politics, education, etc., to help the needy of our cities, our country, and all over God's green and brown and blue earth.

13. These works of love are lowly, unspectacular, and seemingly nonreligious. Here Jesus doesn't say, "The one who worked for Caesar and influenced important political decisions gains approval." He doesn't say, "The one who visited the sick man and *healed* him gains approval." He doesn't say,

"The one who visited the imprisoned woman and *freed* her gains approval." And he doesn't say, "The one who prayed or fasted or attended church or tithed or preached a great sermon on this parable gains approval." In fact, there are no distinctly Jewish or Christian religious acts mentioned. Not even faith is mentioned. Here only love abides. Is this because miracles can be counterfeited and to speak in the tongues of angels can be self-serving? Or is it because only love is "the true test of faith"?[16] Maybe both.

14. These lowly, unspectacular, seemingly nonreligious works of love are thus democratic. That is, most people—unless there is a major physical or mental impairment—can feed the hungry, welcome the stranger, or visit the sick. The rich can; the poor can; the learned can; the unlearned can; men can; women can; Jews can; Gentiles can. It takes no special talent. It only takes willingness. It only takes a Spirit-wrought new heart.[17]

15. Those judged by Jesus meet opposite fates. The righteous "[c]ome" to Jesus (v. 34), and the unrighteous "[d]epart" from him (v. 41); the righteous are "blessed" (v. 34) and the unrighteous "cursed" (v. 41); the righteous are granted "eternal life" (v. 46b) and the unrighteous "eternal punishment" (v. 46a); the righteous "inherit . . . the kingdom" (v. 34) and the unrighteous "eternal fire" (v. 41).

16. Both types of people (there are only two types in the world according to this parable) have a place "prepared" for them (vv. 34, 41). Implied is that these places are prepared by God.[18] For the unrighteous, Hell has been "prepared for the devil and his angels" (v. 41) and those who act like them; for the righteous, the kingdom has been prepared for them ("for you") "from the foundation of the world" (v. 34). The phrase "foundation of the world" tells us that God had a grand plan in place either before he created everything or during the creation itself. God's kingdom for God's people was no afterthought.

17. There is a fearsome finality to Jesus' judgment. There are no second chances during the second coming. The too-late verdict of 25:11, 12 gives its haunting echo here. Those who had time to make wise decisions for themselves about the course of their lives will at the final judgment have a final decision about their final fate "made *for* them" with irresistible finality.[19]

18. Both the righteous and the unrighteous are surprised. Perhaps both are surprised because both are professing Christians. Like the two preceding parables, is this parable about judgment upon the church? When the righteous answer Jesus, they say, "Lord" (v. 37); when the unrighteous answer, that same confession is on their lips, "Lord" (v. 44; cf. 7:21, 22). Or is the second "Lord" on the lips of the unrighteous the acknowledgment that everyone will have when Jesus judges—"every knee [will] bow . . . and every tongue

confess that Jesus Christ is Lord" (Philippians 2:10, 11)? I think it's the latter. So the righteous weren't surprised that they were saved (they are not "anonymous Christians" as Karl Rahner called them),[20] but they were surprised that their little actions to the little people to whom they gave little thought were a big deal to Jesus.[21] Conversely, those on the left are surprised that their last-minute profession of faith is not enough and that their lack of little actions to the little people are a big deal to Jesus. Pascal in his *Pensées* phrased it perfectly: "The elect will be ignorant of their virtues, and the outcast[s] of the greatness of their sins."[22]

19. While the surprise of the right and the left surely surprised Jesus' original hearers, such surprises shouldn't surprise us now. That is, the moment after we read this parable we know what Jesus is looking for on judgment day. (I'll further apply that concept later.)

20. While Jesus is the glorious Son of Man, he identifies with the neediest people. Put differently, "The high Lord is found in the low human"—the widow and orphan, the needy and powerless.[23] Those who suffer a lack of basic needs—food, drink, clothing—he not only labels "the least of these *my* brothers" (v. 40), but he finds with them some sort of indefinable solidarity: what was done to them was done to him. The language "I was hungry" (v. 42) and "I was a stranger" (v. 43)—whatever the mystical or metaphorical or literal (!) connection—is an almost incomprehensible picture. The cosmic Lord of creation hungry, naked, sick? It's as incomprehensible as the incarnation, as Immanuel—"God with us." It's as incomprehensible as the crucifixion—the living God without life.

21. As it was in the Parable of the Talents, the sin of neglect leads to the damnation of the do-nothings.[24] Moreover, here the foundational idea is not merely that a life of service saves and a lack of service damns but that a life of service to others (that is, using your talents for the little people) is a life of service to Christ (little acts done in love are done unto the littlest ones' leader).

22. Typical of Jesus on the reality of Hell, he is pictorial. That is, he gives us graphic pictures of punishment—here "eternal fire" (v. 41), in the last text "outer darkness" (v. 30). So, is Hell literally fire or is it literally darkness? That's the wrong question. Jesus is not giving a realistic proposition but is picturing a reality—a reality of which you'd just as well not have a realistic view. "'Eternal fire' may indeed be metaphorical, but it is a metaphor for the awful."[25] It can mean either a qualitative awfulness (a fire that has eternal consequences) or quantitative (a fire that lasts for eternity). The natural reading—due to the antithetical parallelism ("eternal life"/"eternal punishment," v. 46)—is the latter. Either reading, however, pictures the awful.

23. Also typical of Jesus on the reality of Hell, he is neither sadistic nor sensationalistic. That is, he doesn't flesh out the fire metaphor like a medieval mosaic or like a turn-or-burn preacher. He doesn't say, "Have you ever touched a flame with the tip of your finger? Now imagine your whole body burning in Hell forever!" (Father Arnall's three fiery sermons on Hell in James Joyce's *A Portrait of the Artist as a Young Man* is the perfect example.[26]) Jesus gives just enough of a visual to make us step back and catch our breath, not enough to bend over and throw up. Jesus finds no delight in the judgment of the wicked.

A Question Mark

Those are the twenty-three lightbulbs that went off in my head. From all those observations there arose in my mind three key questions. The first question is: *Who are "the least of these"*?

There are two hotly debated options. The majority opinion of Bible commentators from the second century until the nineteenth century is that "the least" represent Christians, while the majority opinion of the nineteenth century onward take "the least" to represent "everyone in need, whether Christian or not."[27]

I think "the least" primarily refers to Christians. But I obviously don't think we can or should limit our application by neglecting to love our neighbors and the world's poor, thus following all that Jesus modeled and commanded elsewhere. So when we get to my three arrows, I will apply this passage accordingly.

I will, however, here and now give a brief defense for my view. This is not a mountain I'm willing to die on; it's a hill—a hill as high as Mount Olivet. I hold that "the least of these my brothers" (v. 40) are Christians for two reasons.

First, the word "brothers" (or "brethren" in the older translations) is used often throughout the New Testament for Christians. This is true of Matthew's Gospel as well. The two closest references to our text both use it that way. In 23:8 Jesus said to his disciples, "you have one teacher, and you are all *brothers*," and in 28:10 Jesus told the women at the tomb, "Do not be afraid; go and tell *my brothers* to go to Galilee." The "my" there and here seems to highlight this Christ-and-his-church connection (cf. 12:48, 49).[28] In fact, the phrase "my brothers" in the four Gospels is only used by Jesus for his followers. Paul will use that same phrase only for the church alone as well.[29] Moreover, the word "least" is the superlative form of the adjective "little,"[30] and Jesus called his disciples "little ones" in 10:42 and 18:6, 10, 14. In fact, the term was used in chapter 18 to refer specifically to those disciples who were often marginalized due to a lack of wealth, health, giftedness, or spiritual maturity.[31]

Second, in the Olivet Discourse Jesus is talking to the church. Matthew 24:3, 4 (cf. 26:2) records who the original hearers of Jesus' last sermon were—"the disciples [who] came to him privately." Also of importance is what Jesus said to them about what would happen to them. According to 24:14, as the first-generation believers testify to the nations about the gospel of the kingdom, they will be persecuted by the nations. "Then they will deliver you up to tribulation and put you to death, and you will be hated by all nations for my name's sake" (v. 9).

Isn't that a splendid short summary of early Christianity? The gospel went out, and God's messengers (whether they were officially commissioned witnesses like Paul or unofficial witnesses like those saints in Hebrews who lost their homes) suffered the persecutions of prison, poverty, homelessness, sickness, thirst, hunger, and inadequate clothing. So do you see how this reading of "the least of these my brothers" fits theologically with a passage like Paul's conversion—from persecuting Christians to proclaiming Christ? Listen afresh to the start of his story:

> Now as he went on his way, he approached Damascus, and suddenly a light from heaven shone around him. And falling to the ground he heard a voice saying to him, "Saul, Saul, why are you persecuting *me*?" And he said, "Who are you, Lord?" And he said, "I am *Jesus, whom you are persecuting*. (Acts 9:3–5)

D. A. Carson summarizes well where I stand:

> By far the best interpretation is that Jesus' "brothers" are his disciples. . . . The fate of the nations will be determined by how they respond to Jesus' followers, who, "missionaries" or not, are charged with spreading the gospel and do so in the face of hunger, thirst, illness, and imprisonment. Good deeds done to Jesus' followers, even the least of them, are not only works of compassion and morality but *reflect where people stand in relation to the kingdom and to Jesus himself*. Jesus identifies himself with the fate of his followers and makes compassion for them equivalent to compassion for himself.[32] (emphasis added)

The second question is this: *Does Jesus teach works-righteousness here*—that is, that we, through our meritorious works can earn our salvation? The answer is no. This concern is easily put to rest simply by pointing out the way the righteous replied. If they were trying to earn eternal life by feeding the hungry and so on, they wouldn't have been surprised when Jesus commended their good works. They would have said something like, "Lord, we knew that feeding-the-hungry thing was the ticket to Heaven. That's why we did it."

I also answer no to the allegation that this text teaches works-righteousness based on the context and the genre. I reminded you in the last chapter about the immediate context, showing you how the three parables in Matthew 25 answer the question of readiness for Christ's return. Note that the question raised then was not, how does one enter the kingdom? but rather, what does readiness for Jesus' return look like for those already in? Note also that each picture is important and inseparable. Readiness looks like hope (the Parable of the Ten Virgins), faith (the Parable of the Talents), and love (the Parable of the Sheep and the Goats).

Moving to the larger context—the whole of Matthew's Gospel—we move into this issue of genre. First, this is a parable, and no one parable contains within it a whole theological system. There is nothing comprehensive here about the Bible's theology of personal salvation. Second, this is a parable in one of the Gospels. In the Apostle Paul's letters he often gives us propositions—e.g., "Love is . . ."—and then provides a definition. In the Gospel genre, however, the writers provide us with pictures, not propositions. Matthew nowhere writes, "Faith is . . ." and then provides a definition. Rather, he shows us what faith looks like. It looks like a Gentile centurion coming to Jesus for a miracle on behalf of another. It looks like little children trustingly sitting on our Lord's lap for a blessing. It looks like welcoming other Christians in love and providing for their basic needs. That's faith in Jesus.

So, let's have some fun with this works-righteousness worry we might have, a worry that I think either stems from an insufficient attention to the words in our Bibles or a deficient view of the gospel itself.[33] Are you familiar with the famous Evangelism Explosion diagnostic question, "Why should God allow you into his Heaven?" Let's pretend Paul gets to the gates of Heaven and is asked that question. What would he say? I think Paul would answer, "The Apostle John once wrote, 'whoever believes in the Son has eternal life' (John 3:36a). I believe in Jesus! That's why you should let me in." Next, if Matthew came to the same gates and was asked the same question, what would he say? He would say, "The Apostle John once wrote, 'Whoever does not obey the Son shall not see life' (John 3:36b). I have obeyed Jesus! That's why you should let me in."[34] You see, John—in the very same verse—parallels the phrase "Whoever believes in the Son has eternal life" with "whoever does not obey the Son shall not see life," and none of the early Christians thought that was a typo. Pre-Reformation Christians, even the ones who wrote our Bibles, weren't suspicious about the conceptual connection between faith and works. They all believed that one cannot be a Christian and *not* be compassionate. Put positively, they all believed that faith, works, and love were lawfully wedded.

Even Luther himself had these shining moments, such as when he wrote in his "Preface to the Epistle of St. Paul to the Romans":

> O it is a living, busy, active, mighty thing, this faith. It is impossible for it not to be doing good works incessantly. It does not ask whether good works are to be done, but before the question is asked, it has already done them, and is constantly doing them. Whoever does not do such works, however, is an unbeliever.

The commentator from whom I got that Luther quote went on to say, "Isn't Luther's last sentence ("Whoever does not do such works, however, is an unbeliever") exactly the teaching of our parable—and of all three Parables of Judgment, and, indeed, of Matthew's whole Gospel?"[35]

The third question is: *Is the neglect of loving service to others so wicked that it deserves eternal fire?* The answer is yes.

In a work entitled "Temptation and Deliverance," Jonathan Edwards wrote, "Every sin naturally carries hell in it!" He went on to explain and exhort, "Let us then consider, that though the next voluntary act of known sin shall not necessarily and unavoidably *issue* in certain damnation, yet it will certainly *deserve* it."[36] Today the church is plagued with a high view of the goodness of man and a low view of the holiness of God. But Edwards's era didn't suffer from our disease, or at least not as much. To even ask the question, does this sin or that sin really deserve damnation? shows that the sinfulness of sin is not so sinful to us.

Let me add another answer to that first and foundational reply. If my reading of "the least of these my brothers" here refers to Christians, then a lack of loving service to the church demonstrates a lack of true saving faith. In a sense two sins of omission are seen here, one stated and the other implied. What is stated is a lack of loving service; what is implied is a lack of saving faith. People today can somewhat understand how a lack of love might be viewed as something wrong. There is something terribly wrong with a person if an orphan knocks on the front door in the dead of winter asking for some food, clothing, and shelter, and you turn her out. Such a sin of omission is an overtly sinful act. But according to Jesus, turning him out by not acknowledging him as Savior and Lord is a far deeper and more damnable sin. You see, just as we have a hard time getting into our heads that God is perfectly holy and every sin is thus damnable, we have an even harder time believing that trust in Jesus is all that will save us from the eternal wrath to come.

An Arrow

Having looked at twenty-three lightbulbs and having answered three question marks, finally we come to the arrows. I have three to stick in you. (I'll stick them in myself too.)

Our first application is a more generic one based on the end of the three parables in Matthew 25 and the whole tenor of the Olivet Discourse and most of Jesus' sermons in Matthew. Our first application is that we should be thankful for Jesus' clear teachings on the final judgment. We should be thankful because on that day finally the world will be set aright. Like a murder mystery—what Eugene Peterson labels "the cleanest, least ambiguous moral writing that we have"[37]—we know that by the end the murderer will be found out and captured. So much like the story line of the Bible itself, no matter how confused we are or misled by various clues and characters, justice shall prevail! When we think of all the evil and suffering and injustices in this world, we tend to ask God, "Why?" But the question more often posed by the people in the Bible is not "Why?" but "How long?"[38] The final judgment is final justice, that day when God's righteousness will finally flow like a river (Isaiah 48:18), and "the earth will be filled with the knowledge of the glory of the LORD as the waters cover the sea" (Habakkuk 2:14).

Moreover, we should be thankful for Jesus' teachings on judgment because such teachings are intended to create a discomfort that will keep us pressing on. Our Lord knows that we all want to sit down and relax on the comfortable couch of Christian commitment, and so he has placed these pointed prophetic rocks in the cushions to keep us up and to keep us going.

Another added value to Jesus' teaching on judgment is that it allows us to see the glory of God's grace and mercy and forgiveness upon the black backdrop of sin and death and Hell. One writer said it this way: "Our churches need the restoration of God's judgment message *for the sake of* the message of God's grace!"[39] I agree. Our churches need the full gospel. And isn't the full gospel summarized so well (of all places) in John 3:35, 36? I have quoted only the middle of it. Here is the whole picture John gives. It couldn't be a better summary of everything here in the Parable of the Sheep and the Goats.

> The Father loves the Son and has given all things into his hand. Whoever believes in the Son has eternal life; whoever does not obey the Son shall not see life, but the wrath of God remains on him.

Rescue from wrath through faith in Jesus as Lord is what makes grace so amazing.

Our second application I will say in two ways—one more theoretical, the other more practical. The theoretical is this: allegiance to Jesus is ecclesial. That is, how you treat other Christians (especially the little ones) demonstrates the nature of your relationship with Jesus. The even more practical way of saying that comes straight from the pen of Paul. In Galatians 6:10 he writes, "So then, as we have opportunity, let us do good to everyone, and especially to those who are of the household of faith."[40]

As followers of Jesus, this parable should motivate us to do good to everyone. We are to prepare for the *parousia*—that day when we will enter into his joy—by joyfully loving our neighbors, especially those in great need.

Thankfully, Christians have been, are now, and (Lord willing) will be on the front lines of every issue of social need and injustice. We couldn't count the number of children adopted and sponsored and mouths fed and homes built because of Christians motivated to act based on 25:40. That one verse has benefited the world's poor more than a million Marxist mantras, a thousand Socialist slogans, and a hundred welfare initiatives! Tolstoy said, "Where love is, there is God also." I say "Where love is, there are Christians also." The Red Cross, the YMCA, the Salvation Army, World Vision, Compassion International, Food for the Hungry, Tearfund, One Day's Wages, and Samaritan's Purse are but budding leaves from our compassionate Christ's mustard seed.

Furthermore, as followers of Jesus, this parable should motivate us to do good to Christians. We believe in the sacraments of baptism and the Lord's Supper—where the Lord is spiritually present to us in the elements of water, wine, and bread. We can add another sacrament, without being sacrilegious—the Sacrament of the Church, whereby we encounter the real presence of Christ in other Christians. Luther said, "He who wants to find Christ, must first find the church,"[41] and conversely I'd add, "He who finds the true church has truly found Christ." Allegiance to Jesus is ecclesial: we love the least of our brothers and sisters in this church because we love Jesus.

On this theme Tertullian's famous "peculiarities of the Christian society" is worth quoting, at least in part. Of the church in his day (late second century), he writes:

> We are a body knit together as such by a common religious profession, by unity of discipline, and by the bond of common hope. We meet together as an assembly and congregation, that offering a prayer to God as with united force, we may wrestle with Him in our supplications. . . . We pray, too, for the emperors, for their ministers, and for all in authority, for the welfare of the world, for the prevalence of peace, for the delay of the final

> consummation. . . . On the monthly day, if he likes, each puts in a small donation; but only if it be his pleasure, and only if he is able: for there is no compulsion; all is voluntary. These gifts are, as it were, piety's deposit fund. For they are not taken thence and spent on feasts, and drinking-bouts, and eating-houses, but to support and bury poor people, to supply the wants of boys and girls destitute of means and parent, and of old persons confined now to the house; such, too, as have suffered shipwreck; and if there happen to be any in the mines, or banished to the islands, or shut up in the prisons, for nothing but their fidelity to the cause of God's Church, they become the nurslings of their confessions. But it is mainly the deeds of a love so noble that lead many to put a brand upon us. *See,* they say, *how they love one another.*[42]

Our third application is to glory in the cross of Christ. Now you might say, "Preacher, where are you getting that theme from? There is no mention of the cross in this text." Correct. However, there is mention of it in chapters 26, 27, and 28. In the very next section—what we'll look at in the next sermon—we will see Jesus' body anointed, in his words, "for burial" (26:12). And we will witness in section after section—from that anointing until he hangs his lifeless head—Jesus suffering and dying. Matthew has already told us why Jesus came to earth—to "save his people from their sins" (1:21). He will put one huge exclamation point on that mission as we soon witness Jesus betrayed, denied, arrested, tried, falsely accused, convicted, spit on, flogged, crowned with thorns, mocked, pierced with nails, and hung on a Roman tree between two criminals for us and our salvation.

I say all that to remind you not merely of the fact of Jesus' death but to emphasize what Jesus is here emphasizing in his last sermon to his first disciples—that it is *the Son of Man*, the glorious divine King, who is going to the cross for us. Look at 26:2—Jesus' next words after his final sermon: "You know that after two days the Passover is coming, and *the Son of Man* will be delivered up to be crucified." This is not merely the post-transfiguration take two, but the post-transfiguration times ten. Jesus, the beloved Son of God, will come down from this final mountaintop—Mount Olivet—to mount a tree on a hill far, far away. You see, it is not just what Jesus did that matters but *who* did what.

If you didn't come to this text as a charismatic for Christ you'd best become one now. Shout "Amen." Raise your hands in adoration. All glory and honor and praise be to our Lord Jesus Christ! All glory and honor and praise be to the One who now reigns in his heavenly glory, who was crushed for our iniquities but who now sits upon the throne, who was then entombed for our sins but who now reigns over the righteous in his eternal kingdom, who gave his own life for us. You see, the one who will be mockingly charged as being "the King of Jews" is in fact the King of the Nations. The one whose death will bring the shadow of darkness over Jerusalem is the one who will come in the light of the glory of God to judge Jerusalem, Judea, Samaria, and all the ends of the earth.

76

The Passion of the Church and the Passion of the Christ

MATTHEW 26:1–16

NOT LONG AGO CHARLOTTE, my four-year old daughter, was sitting next to me on the couch. I was reading a book, and she was playing a game. I put my book down and turned to her. "Lotte," I asked, "do you know how much Daddy loves you?" I then opened the space between my pointer finger and thumb, saying, "This much?" She put down the game, leaped off the couch, stood in front of me, and said, "No, this much, this much, this much!" as she waved her arms wider and wider between each "this much." Then she paused and began to count as the arm-flailing restarted. "1, 2, 3, 4, 5, 6, 7, 100 this much!" she shouted.

What a sweet moment. What was especially sweet about it was that I have only done that "how much/this much love game" with her two or three times in her life. The last time I remember doing it was when she was three. Also, when I did it last, I only did three extremes—this much (showing her the space between two fingers), this much (half of the space of full hand extension), and this much (full extension). She added the arm-flapping and the counting to a hundred. Well, this exercise in love (and it was literally an exercise for her) showed me how much she thinks I love her. And yes, her estimation was right on target.

The text we will study now is about love. It's not about a father's love for his little girl or a little girl's love for her father. Rather, it's about a disciple's love for Jesus and his love for her. It's specifically about how she loved him and how he loved her.

A Spectacular Setting

Before we look at *how*, however, let's begin with *when* and *where*. That is, let's begin with the setting of our story.

> When Jesus had finished all these sayings, he said to his disciples, "You know that after two days the Passover is coming, and the Son of Man will be delivered up to be crucified." Then the chief priests and the elders of the people gathered in the palace of the high priest, whose name was Caiaphas, and plotted together in order to arrest Jesus by stealth and kill him. But they said, "Not during the feast, lest there be an uproar among the people." Now when Jesus was at Bethany in the house of Simon the leper. . . . (Matthew 26:1–6)

Notice four observations about the setting. First, with the start of verse 1, we are keyed into the fact that we have entered the fifth and final part of Matthew's Gospel. The phrase "When Jesus had finished all these sayings" or its equivalent is used five times in this Gospel (7:28; 11:1; 13:53; 19:1; 26:1), always ending a key teaching section and introducing the next narrative. The first time we saw this transition phrase was after the Sermon on the Mount. The last time we see it is here, after the Sermon on the other mount—Jesus' Olivet Discourse on the Mount of Olives.

Some scholars argue that these five sections are Matthew's way of pointing to the five-book structure of the Pentateuch or the five-discourse structure of Deuteronomy, part of the idea being that Jesus is a new Moses about to lead a new exodus.[1] Whatever Jesus' relation to Moses, Matthew certainly relates Jesus to Israel's exodus from Egypt. In 2:15, as the boy Jesus journeys from Egypt to Nazareth, Matthew quotes the final phrase of Hosea 11:1, "When Israel was a child, I loved him, and *out of Egypt I called my son*," and applies it to Jesus. In our text Matthew records that the week of Jesus' passion was the Passover, the yearly celebration of Israel's exodus.

That takes us to our second important observation. Let's call it Jesus' Passover prediction. In verse 2 Jesus prophesies to his disciples, "You know that after two days the Passover is coming, and [at that time] the Son of Man will be delivered up to be crucified." I will share more about the Passover in the next chapter. For now I simply want to remind you that the Passover—the final plague before the exodus—was when the angel of the Lord passed over the houses that had the blood of the Lamb on the doorposts but killed the firstborn sons of all the Egyptians (Exodus 12). Here in Jesus' own Passover story, God's people will be saved ironically when the Lord does *not* pass over his own firstborn Son. Jesus himself is the Lamb of God about to be sacrificed for the sins of the world (John 1:29).

Our third important observation is the Passover plot. While Jesus is openly expressing how he is about to freely give himself to be delivered over to death, the religious elite in town are plotting to beat him to the punch. As Jesus, the Great Prophet, gives his final prophecy about his great High Priesthood—the final mediation for sins through his death—Caiaphas, "the high priest" of Israel at the time (AD 18–36), has gathered representatives of the Sanhedrin—"the chief priests and the elders"—in order to secretly strategize the slaying of our Savior (vv. 3, 4). The irony is thick. Their plan is to have Jesus arrested quietly and secretly ("by stealth," v. 4) and do so *after* the Passover week ("[n]ot during the feast, lest there be an uproar among the people," v. 5). They're sneaky. They're smart. Jerusalem's history is filled with uprisings when messianic figures came along, especially during the Passover, when the city was mobbed with millions of pilgrims.

Whose will will win? we wonder. Will Jesus be killed during Passover, as he said? Or will Jesus be killed after the Passover, as they planned? The temple aristocracy is pitted against the incarnate Creator.[2] Let's see whose Passover plot prevails.

Our fourth important observation comes at the start of the second scene: it's *where* Jesus is. In scene one we can picture two places. There is Jesus in the open speaking openly to his disciples, and then there are the religious leaders plotting in the palace with the doors and windows closed. Then we come to scene two. In verse 6 we move from Jerusalem to "Bethany," from a palace to a "house," from Caiaphas the high priest to "Simon the leper." You see, *when* this woman shows her devotion to Jesus is nearly as significant as *where* she does it. Two days before the Passover (when) Jesus is in the house of "Simon the leper" (where). Matthew's artistry is magnificent.[3]

Do you know what those religious men in Caiaphas's palace would have been doing (besides plotting to kill Jesus)? They would have been preparing for the Passover by purifying themselves. In John 11:55, which comes right before John's record of this woman's anointing Jesus, we read, "Now the Passover of the Jews was at hand, and many went up from the country to Jerusalem before the Passover *to purify themselves*." So, as all the devout Jews in the land are busy cleaning their impure bodies, Jesus takes his pure body into the most impure setting imaginable—a leper's house!

Matthew further heightens the drama by leaving a few questions hanging above the readers' heads, the first being, who is this Simon the leper? The term "the leper" might just be to distinguish him from other Simons. Simon was the most popular name in Jesus' day. There are four other Simons mentioned in Matthew's Gospel alone. But that still doesn't tell us much about him. In fact, from that distinguishing and awkward title—"Simon *the leper*"—a further question arises: is this Simon still a leper? And if not, how did he get cured? Did Jesus cure him?[4] Is that his connection with Jesus? Or is he somehow connected to the woman mentioned, who we learn from John's Gospel is Mary, as in Mary, Martha, and Lazarus? Is Simon Mary's husband? Or is he perhaps her father? Who knows?

I think the vagueness is intentional. It makes perfect sense to say this Simon was presumably cured because if not, Jesus and his disciples were violating the law of Leviticus 13:45, 46, which forbade residing with lepers. It wouldn't be the first time, however, that this theme of Jesus trumping the Torah comes up. In fact, he will trump the Torah's whole sacrificial system on Good Friday. Why not start trumping it now?

Yes, this "leper" detail is very interesting. Jesus' first distinguishable miracle in Matthew, which comes right after the Sermon on the Mount, is his cleansing of a leper: "And Jesus stretched out his hand and touched him, saying, '. . . be clean.' And immediately the leprosy was cleansed" (8:3, 4).

Are we to make some sort of connection to Jesus' final act of public ministry, to Simon the leper? Did Jesus heal another leper here?[5] Does Jesus begin and end his healing ministry with the unclean, those he will ultimately "cleanse . . . from all sin" (1 John 1:7) by being "delivered up to be crucified" (26:2a)?

Perhaps I am reading too much into Matthew's magnificent artistry. To be safe I'll just stick with more certain connections of contrast—the contrast between the seemingly pure palace of Caiaphas and the seemingly unclean house of Simon and the contrast between the evil high priest who will soon no longer be able to offer any absolution of sin and the good High Priest who will sprinkle many nations through his own dead and buried body.

A More Spectacular Love Story

Those are my four observations about the spectacular setting. Now, if you think the setting is spectacular, we come next to the story itself. Set between two scenes of hatred—the plot of the priests (vv. 3–5) and Judas's betrayal (vv. 14–16)—is a love story. It is one of the greatest love stories in the Greatest Love Story ever told. It is short (told in two verses) but spectacular:

> Now when Jesus was at Bethany in the house of Simon the leper, a woman came up to him with an alabaster flask of very expensive ointment, and she poured it on his head as he reclined at table. (vv. 6, 7)

Again Matthew is vague. And again I think he is vague intentionally. Who is this woman? Was she rich or poor? Was this a small sacrifice or a huge one?

What were her motives? Was she a sinner, like that other woman in Luke's Gospel who did something like this (Luke 7:37, 38)? Was she in need of some miracle, like the great majority of women who approached Jesus in the Gospels? Or was she doing what she did for purely devotional reasons, like the magi who came bearing gifts to the newborn king? Our list of questions might go on.

What Matthew does here is simply communicate this woman's odd action and then in verses 8–16 give us three very different reactions to it. We'll look at those reactions in a moment, for they will interpret her action for us. For now I want us to focus on the woman herself. Put differently, we will soon look at *how* she loved Jesus, but first we will focus merely on *who* loved Jesus.

The *who* here is a her: "a woman" came up to Jesus (v. 7a). Here I think Matthew is setting up another ironic contrast. The contrast this time is between an unnamed woman and some of the named men. Jesus is named; so too are Caiaphas and Judas. Even Simon the leper is named! Many of the men have names; why not the woman? The Apostle John, in his Gospel, will name her "Mary," as I said. So why doesn't Matthew? It's not that Matthew is not into naming women. In his first chapter he lists five women in Jesus' genealogy, which was a rare thing to do in a Jewish genealogy.

I think the reason Matthew doesn't name this woman (I'm only speculating here, but I'm so good at speculating) is to set up two contrasts. First is the contrast between a lowly woman (someone so little esteemed in the first-century world) and Caiaphas, the high priest (about as important a man in that day as any). She shows love, he hatred. Second is the contrast between her and the apostles. She is a disciple of Jesus, but so are the Twelve. But in the scenes to follow we will see the man Judas betray his Lord and then the man Peter deny him, and then the ten men left standing will all fall when Jesus is raised up on the cross. In Matthew's Gospel as all the male disciples have scattered to their safe houses, faithful women stand beneath the cross (27:55, 56) and come the next day to the tomb (27:61).

There is a lesson in these peculiar historical facts. And the lesson is not that girls rule while boys drool. No, it's a theological, not a sociological lesson. The lesson is that all people can come to Jesus. Even the lowliest can love the Lord. Even the no-names can praise his name.

Near the prestigious Oriel College of Oxford University there is a pub called the Boar's Head. (The English have lovely titles for their taverns.) On the wall over the fireplace there is a collection of neckties tacked to the wall. The unstated rule and long-held tradition is that no ties are allowed in the establishment, and anyone walking in with one on will have it snipped off and tacked to the wall.[6] The snipping and tacking of ties is this pub's way of saying, "You may be an Oxford don, but when you enter this place everyone is equal."

A similar picture is given in our text. Matthew's unnamed woman is Jesus' invitation to all women, and men and children, to come to the table of Christian *koinonia*. If it's okay to use a pub analogy in this chapter (I hope so; forgive me if not so), the church is like the Boar's Head. There is no hierarchy of holiness upon entrance, and there is no pedigree and no degree requirement for entrance. The only prerequisite is faith in Jesus. All who have faith in Jesus can come for a meal.

How She Loves Jesus

Next we move from when and where and who to *how*. There are two ways to evaluate this woman's action. We can walk through the three reactions—from the disciples, Jesus, and Judas. Or we can, with those reactions guiding us, answer the question, how did she love Jesus? Let's take the second path, the path less traveled. I think it will make all the difference.

The First Characteristic

There are three characteristics of her love I want us to understand and apply. First, *she loved Jesus above all*. Take a look at verses 8–11.

> And when the disciples saw it [her pouring out the expensive ointment], they were indignant, saying, "Why this waste? For this could have been sold for a large sum and given to the poor." But Jesus, aware of this, said to them, "Why do you trouble the woman? For she has done a beautiful thing to me. For you always have the poor with you, but you will not always have me."

Here the disciples are partly right and partly wrong. They are right that this ointment "could have been sold for a large sum and given to the poor." Mark tells us that the ointment was made of "pure nard" (Mark 14:3; cf. John 12:3) and that it would have sold for "more than three hundred denarii" (Mark 14:5), a full year's wages for a common laborer (cf. 20:2).[7] That's a lot of money. She just poured out $30,000!

But they are wrong that what she did was wasteful. It was not wasteful, Jesus says, but "beautiful" (v. 10b). Why? Because it was done to Jesus: "For she has done a beautiful thing to me" (v. 10b). Underline "to me." Without the "to me" this is an absolute waste of money. Yes, it's a beautiful thing, Jesus continues, "For you always have the poor with you, but you will not always have me" in the flesh (v. 11). Again we find that word "me." We also have a striking antithetical parallelism. I'll reorder the sentence to show this parallelism better:

You	have always	the poor
You	will not have always	me

Here Jesus is claiming that her action is not objectionable because of love to him, but also not antithetical to love to others (remember the last parable we looked at). Jesus first, everything and everyone else second is how I've sometimes phrased it. Jesus put it this way: "Whoever loves father or mother more than me is not worthy of me, and whoever loves son or daughter more than me is not worthy of me" (10:37). Our unnamed woman demonstrates that radical commitment. She shows the church that Jesus must be first—above money and mother, above the home and even the homeless.

You see, the disciples' "poor theology," if you will, is poor (bad or wrong) because they have put our vertical relationship with Jesus as Lord on the same level as our horizontal relationship with others. Their mistake is natural, especially in view of Jesus' parable about loving the least being equal to loving him. But it's still a mistake. It's the same mistake Martha once made—shortsighted utilitarianism.[8] In some ways this is the story of Mary and Martha revisited, and once again Mary shows the better way (cf. Luke 10:42, NIV).

The better way is not to put off serving people. The better way is not to put off feeding the hungry. The better way is simply believing and demonstrating that Jesus deserves the highest outpouring of your love. Jesus taught a social gospel (love your neighbor, help the poor), but his social gospel is also the gospel of the Son of Man, in which our glorifying the glorious Lord always comes first.

The Second Characteristic

The second characteristic is that *she loved Jesus with costly love*.

In John's version of this event, while Jesus, Lazarus, and the apostles are reclining at table, Martha is serving them (John 12:2). Where's Mary? John doesn't tell us. Was she slaving away in the kitchen or serving alongside Martha? I doubt in that culture she was reclining with the men. Whatever she was up to, a spontaneous thought must have come over her. Instead of bringing in a pot of tea, she carried in an alabaster flask of perfume, perhaps a family heirloom. She broke the flask and began to pour it over Jesus' head. Can you picture that? How strangely extravagant and shockingly costly!

Now compare her action to Judas's. The "then" of verse 14—"Then one of the twelve, whose name was Judas Iscariot, went to the chief priests and said, 'What will you give me if I deliver him over to you?'" (v. 15)—has as diabolic a ring to it as the "then" of verses 3, 4—"Then the chief priests and the elders of the people gathered . . . and plotted together [to] . . . kill him." While one group of men plot, another man ("one of the twelve" no less) makes a part of that plot possible. Amazingly, after Judas has just seen this woman waste a year's salary on Jesus, he accepts about four months' wages for his Lord's life, "thirty pieces of silver" (v. 15), the price paid by the owners of an ox that gored a slave to death (Exodus 21:32). Is Jesus worth no more than a slave to him? Once again we have a remarkable contrast of characters and their character. While the woman gives generously, Judas seeks to gain greedily; "and whereas her sacrifice is costly, Judas settles his bargain for a relatively paltry sum."[9]

Earlier I quoted 10:37, where Jesus said, "Whoever loves father or mother more than me is not worthy of me, and whoever loves son or daughter more than me is not worthy of me." Look now at 10:38. Jesus continues, "And whoever does not take his cross and follow me is not worthy of me." Here this woman takes up her cross in the form of pouring out a bottle of costly perfume, and the church should follow her example.

You see, the question we are to ask ourselves as we witness afresh this odd act is not, how can I act more emotionally unstable in my relationship with Jesus? or how can I be more over the top in my giving money to the church?—although impulsive check-writing in access of $29,999 is always acceptable. Rather, the question is, are you willing to love Jesus with what is most valuable to you? Loving Christ is costly.

The Third Characteristic

The third characteristic is that *she loved Jesus for who he said he was*. Here is where verses 12, 13 come into play. Jesus teaches his disciples:

> In pouring this ointment on my body, she has done it to prepare me for burial. Truly, I say to you, wherever this gospel is proclaimed in the whole world, what she has done will also be told in memory of her.

One way to read verse 12 (I'll return to verse 13 later) is to say that while her actions indeed showed that she loved Jesus above all and in a costly fashion, she didn't necessarily get the symbolic value Jesus attaches to her actions. In reference to his burial, Jesus relates her action to the normal burial rite, in which a dead body would be drenched in perfume to cover the smell. In other words, she acts better than she knows. With the oil on his body, she unwittingly signifies his impending death, and perhaps with the oil going on his head (Matthew's emphasis) she unwittingly anoints him as King (cf. 1 Samuel 9:16).[10]

Another way to read verse 12 is not to say she acted better than she knew, but to say that while she knew little, she acted as best she could. This more positive reading would fit with the theme in Matthew's Gospel that the littlest people of the little people understand Jesus first. It would also fit with what we know about Mary. We know from John 11 that her family was very close to Jesus. We also know from that chapter that her sister Martha's theology was fairly well-informed and her mind teachable about new theological truths. We also know that Jesus gave four public predictions about his death (16:21; 17:22, 23; 20:17–19; 26:2), one of which Mary must have heard first- or secondhand.

So perhaps this woman (Mary of Bethany), who starts off the passion narrative, understood something of what was said to the first woman who starts off the birth narrative (Mary of Nazareth). Maybe she gets Matthew 1—that Jesus is King and Savior. Maybe the object of her love is Jesus as the Christ and as Christ crucified. Maybe contra to the Jewish leaders, those we met at the top and tail of our text, she believes that Jesus is the Son of Man (thus she christens him as the divine King of an everlasting kingdom) and believes that Jesus' coronation will somehow mysteriously come upon Calvary's cross.[11] Maybe she gets the crown and the cross. Maybe.

But whether I am reading too much or too little into her motives, our vision of Jesus today—post-crucifixion, burial, and resurrection—should be crystal clear. We are to take Matthew's Gospel as a discipleship manual, and her passion here is to be ours now. We are to love *Jesus above all* and *with costly love* and *for who he said he is* (the Son of Man who was delivered over to die and be buried for our sins).

The Passion of the Christ

Do you remember the story of when Jesus raised Lazarus from the dead? When Lazarus became very ill, Mary and Martha sent word to Jesus about their brother, saying, "Lord, he whom you love is ill" (John 11:3). Jesus *loved* Lazarus. Then when Jesus got the word, these words follow: "Now Jesus *loved* Martha and her sister and Lazarus" (John 11:5). Jesus loved that family.

I want to end by expanding upon that thought. We have looked at how Mary loved Jesus; let's next briefly see how Jesus loved her. There are three ways he showed his love.

First, he *defended* her. When the men were in a huff and puffed out, "Why this waste!" (v. 8). Jesus came to the rescue. He showed a simple but sadly rare male sensitivity.

Second, Jesus *praised* her. This was part of his defense. He didn't merely come to her rescue because the boys were being brutish, but rather because the boys got it wrong and the girl got it right. Jesus' "she has done a beautiful thing [or "good work," as it can be translated] to me" (v. 10) reminds us of our Lord's praised-filled approval in the Parable of the Talents, "Well done, good and faithful servant" (25:21). And Jesus' "Truly, I say to you, wherever this gospel is proclaimed in the whole world, what she has done will also be told in memory of her" (26:13) is as high a praise as Jesus gives anyone in any of the Gospels. And whether the phrase "this gospel" refers to the Gospel of Matthew (unlikely) or "the passion drama itself" (more likely)[12] or "the good news about the Messiah—news which must include this story and so his passion" (most likely),[13] her sweet perfume that filled this leper's house now fills the four corners and seven continents of the world.[14]

It's a rare day (don't you think?) when you can hear or read a sermon and learn that an actual Bible prophecy was fulfilled in your hearing or reading. But Jesus said that she would be remembered, and we are remembering her. As J. C. Ryle thoughtfully put it over a century ago:

> This prophecy of his about this woman is receiving a fulfillment every day before our eyes: wherever the Gospel of St. Matthew is read, her action is known. The deeds and titles of many a king and emperor and general are as completely forgotten as if written in the sand; but the grateful act of one humble Christian woman is recorded in 150 different languages [might we add 2,000 plus to Ryle's number, as the Gospel of Matthew has been translated into nearly 2,300 different languages], and is known all over the globe.[15]

So Jesus showed his love for her by defending her and praising her. But he also showed his love (third and finally and ultimately) by dying for her. There is her passion (devotional love) for him and his passion (suffering) for her. There is the passion of the Church and the passion of the Christ.

Matthew's Gospel has been called "a Passion Story with a long introduction."[17] That is true. For it is now in this Gospel that we come to the heart of the matter. As much as Jesus' birth matters, his miracles matter, his parables matter, his prophecies matter, his second coming matters, the matter that matters most is the cross of Christ. You see, as Jesus loved Lazarus and Martha and Mary, so he loves all who are his. He loves us—his church—with undying and *dying* love. He loves us with strangely extravagant and shockingly costly love. He loves us this much, this much, this much, 1, 2, 3, 4, 5, 6, 7, 100 this much!

77

The Paradoxes of the Last Passover

MATTHEW 26:17–30

WE COME NOW to one of the most famous passages in Matthew's Gospel and certainly the most infamous. It is infamous not only because there is a shadow of death and betrayal covering this otherwise lovely family meal, but also because these fourteen verses have lead to 14,000 divisions within the church and persecutions of the church by the church.

If you lived at the "wrong" time in church history, how you answered questions like, What did Jesus mean by "This is my body"? and How many elements should be consecrated? and Who should partake of the bread? were questions of life and death. Thankfully today, while we come with many of the same questions as our predecessors and many more of our own, we are safe to state what we believe about the Lord's Supper and, Lord willing, free enough to disagree on certain matters without the deacons tying you to the church stake (which we keep safely tucked behind the organ at my church) and the elders striking the deadly match.

A Sovereign Plan; A Responsible Man

What has often led to division, then as now, is an improper ordering of questions about the Lord's Supper. That is, making the questions that aren't answered directly by the text more central than those that are.

I want to begin with two questions raised and answered in the setting.

> Now on the first day of Unleavened Bread [a seven-day festival connected in Jesus' day to the Passover][1] the disciples came to Jesus, saying, "Where will you have us prepare for you to eat *the Passover*?" He said, "Go into

> the city to a certain man and say to him, 'The Teacher says, My time is at hand. I will keep *the Passover* at your house with my disciples.'" And the disciples did as Jesus had directed them, and they prepared *the Passover*. (vv. 17–19)

The first question we should ask is, when did the first Lord's Supper take place? The answer is at "the Passover." Matthew wants us to notice that detail, for he repeats it three times, once in every verse above. Passover. Passover. Passover. In these opening verses don't pass over the Passover!

Most commentators say that Jesus is celebrating some version of the Passover Seder, which took its present shape thirty years after the Lord's Supper (see Mishnah Tractate Pesahim, chapter 10), and they go into great detail about that meal.[2] Matthew, however, doesn't focus on the details of the meal. He focuses instead on *who* is serving (Jesus) and Jesus' surprising innovations to the Exodus feast.

Besides turning this family meal into a church community meal (that's innovative—who are his brothers and sisters but his disciples, 12:46–50), Jesus also turns the focus of the whole celebration on himself. Instead of focusing on the lamb—the focus of the Passover meal[3]—Jesus speaks of his body and blood: "my body" (v. 26) and "my blood" (v. 28). Your body? Your blood? What about the lamb and its body and blood? That lamb is nowhere on our Lord's lips and nowhere found in Matthew's account.[4]

What are we to do with this surprising omission and shift in focus? In Jesus' death is there some sort of new Passover and new exodus? Is Jesus a last and final Lamb of God and through his blood God's people are saved from death and freed from the slavery of sin, a far greater slavemaster than Pharaoh? In reading Matthew's focus on Jesus and his Passover innovations, are we to join with John the Baptist, saying, "Behold, the Lamb of God, who takes away the sin of the world!" (John 1:29, 36), and are we to soberly proclaim with Paul, "Christ, our Passover lamb, has been sacrificed" (1 Corinthians 5:7b)? Sure, why not? Or better, why of course!

The second question we should ask is, who's in charge? The answer is Jesus. This question might well be *the* question of Matthew's whole Gospel. In every chapter in this Gospel Jesus' divine authority is on display. Here it is on display in two ways—through Jesus' *spoken word* and through God's *written word*.

First we have Jesus' spoken word. Notice Jesus' authoritative command in verse 18: "Go into the city to a certain man and say to him, 'The Teacher says, My time is at hand. I will keep the Passover at your house with my disciples.'" Jesus essentially says to his disciples, "If you obey my word now, I'll guarantee that a mysterious 'certain man' will obey my word when you get there."[5] Well, well, doesn't Jesus sounds like a king? He sure speaks with the bold assumption that people will obey him and should obey him. Yes, he does sounds like a king or a "Lord," the title that eleven of the men will use for him in verse 22.[6] (Notice that only Judas calls him "Rabbi" and not "Lord.")[7]

Two other sentences are saturated with his sovereignty. Verse 21 features his favorite listen-to-me-now-for-what-I'm-about-to-say-is-really-important phrase, "Truly, I say to you." That's his personal version of "Thus says the Lord." Then there is what he calls himself twice in verse 24, "The Son of Man," that title from Daniel 7 for the divine king who will rule an everlasting kingdom.

Also under this category of Jesus' spoken word are his predictive prophecies. He predicts that someone will betray him (v. 21). He knows who that someone is (v. 25). He predicts his death and the timing of his death. It will occur during the Passover, as he stated back in verse 2 and reiterates with his language in verse 18, "My time is at hand."[8] He also and finally predicts his bodily resurrection and his disciples' bodily resurrections (v. 29). What else can he mean by "I tell you I will not drink again of this fruit of the vine until that day when I drink it new with you in my Father's kingdom"? One needs to be alive and have a body to drink wine.

Jesus' divine authority is on display through Jesus' *spoken word*. It is also on display through God's *written word*. Look at that phrase in verse 24, where Jesus says of himself, "The Son of Man goes [i.e., goes to be betrayed and killed] as it is written of him." Here our Lord has in mind not one Old Testament text but a compilation of texts, such as Isaiah 53:7–9 and Daniel 9:26, Scriptures that speak of this strange juxtaposition of a sovereign king but suffering servant.[9] And/or, Jesus might simply be referring to, as I noted earlier, the Passover lamb as a type. That is, take all those Passover texts together and those millions of lambs slain since Exodus 12,[10] and those shadows of the real thing come to a stop when Jesus' heart stops. They are fulfilled when the Son of Man is slain, "as it is written of him" (v. 24).

So Matthew's focus in these opening verses is on Jesus and his divine authority. And if we miss that focus, we'll misapply this meal.

I have titled this chapter "The Paradoxes of the Last Passover." It's titled that for two reasons. First, this is the *last* Passover meal. It is the last one because there is no need to celebrate the Passover now that the Lamb of God has shed his blood to free us from the slavery of sin. Second, there are *paradoxes* here. The first paradox I call "A Sovereign Plan; a Responsible Man." That responsible man, of course, is Judas. We've looked at Jesus' sovereignty; let's turn our attention next to Judas's responsibility.

> When it was evening, he reclined at table with the twelve. And as they were eating, he said, "Truly, I say to you, one of you will betray me." And they were very sorrowful and began to say to him one after another, "Is it I, Lord?" He answered, "He who has dipped his hand in the dish with me will betray me. The Son of Man goes as it is written of him, but woe to that man by whom the Son of Man is betrayed! It would have been better for that man if he had not been born." Judas, who would betray him, answered, "Is it I, Rabbi?" He said to him, "You have said so." (vv. 20–25)

Our Lord's language here is clear. Judas is held accountable for his actions. Jesus calls out his crime, and then he warns him of the woe to come. It's as if he said, "Judas, that 'woe' of judgment that came upon the unrepentant cities (11:21), on the person who leads the little ones into sin (18:7), and on the scribes and the Pharisees (Matthew 23) is about to come upon you."[11] One wonders if Jesus is wooing Judas with his woe: "Turn back, my friend. It's not too late to repent."[12] I don't know. Whatever Jesus is up to with this public announcement and denouncement, he is appealing to Judas's will and holding him responsible for the actions of that free will, free under God's sovereignty over all things, of course. Jesus is fully sovereign; Judas is fully responsible. There is mystery here, but not ambiguity. "This Jesus, delivered up according to the definite plan and foreknowledge of God [divine sovereignty], you crucified and killed by the hands of lawless men [human responsibility]" (Acts 2:23).

Now, just as our Lord's language on human responsibly is clear, so too are the warnings for us. The first warning is, "let anyone who thinks that he stands take heed lest he fall" (1 Corinthians 10:12).[13]

One of the first sermons I ever preached (I was twenty at the time) was on Judas's betrayal. I began that sermon with the provocative question, do you have a personal relationship with Jesus? Then I went on to point out how Judas had a very personal relationship with Jesus but was not saved. Whatever the phrase "It would have been better for that man if he had not been born" (v. 24) means, it does not mean Judas is in Heaven.[14] The shock factor of that old sermon was awesome. I had everyone quite concerned. But don't let my overdone point then distract you from the real point now.

> Judas Iscariot had the highest possible religious privileges. He was a chosen apostle and companion of Christ; he was an eyewitness of our Lord's miracles and a hearer of his sermons; he saw what Abraham and Moses

> never saw, and heard what David and Isaiah never heard; he lived in the society of the eleven apostles; he was a fellow-laborer with Peter, James and John: but for all this his heart was never changed.[15]

So don't you, O man, woman, child of religious privilege, be presumptuous in your personal relationship with Jesus. The eleven apostles asked, "Is it I, Lord?" and we must never grow old of asking that same question. In his "Saint Matthew's Passion," Bach has the congregation sing, after the words, "Is it I, Lord?" a confessional chorale: "I'm the one, I should repent."[16] Exactly!

Judas, this deepest and darkest character in the Gospels—in perhaps of all world literature[17]—is held up here as a mirror to us. We should repent. We should take heed lest we fall. That's the first warning.

The second warning is that the love of money strangles the soul. Or to use Paul's words again:

> But those who desire to be rich fall into temptation, into a snare, into many senseless and harmful desires that plunge people into ruin and destruction. For the love of money is a root of all kinds of evils. It is through this craving that some have wandered away from the faith and pierced themselves with many pangs. But as for you, O man of God, flee these things. (1 Timothy 6:9–11)

Many scholars today say that Judas's motive for betrayal is uncertain. Was it greed, disillusionment, or misguided zeal (Judas wanted to force Jesus' hand into acting like the Messiah should)? We don't know, they say. However, I say it's clear that Matthew links the motive to money.[18] Just follow the money. As we saw in verse 15, Judas's question to the Jewish leaders shows his hand (and heart): "What will you give me if I deliver him over to you?" Why ask for money if you want to force Jesus' hand or if you are seriously disillusioned? Just go and tell them where Jesus is and call it a day. Either way Judas would have done his part to save Israel. But instead he dismissed Jesus' teachings on money and this trusted treasurer allowed "the deceitfulness of riches" (13:22) to choke him.

My brothers and sisters, the love of money can tie a noose around our necks. We can give up all sorts of things for Christ, as Judas did, but if we do not give up covetousness, that one secret sin will choke all spiritual life out of us. Let Jesus' diagnostic question hang above us always: "For what does it profit a man to gain the whole world and forfeit his soul?" (Mark 8:36). May the penetrating prayer of Proverbs 30:7–9a be our persistent petition:

> Two things I ask of you; deny them not to me before I die: Remove far from me falsehood and lying; give me neither poverty nor riches; feed me with the food that is needful for me, lest I be full and deny you [or betray you?] and say, "Who is the LORD?"

A Little Ink Spilled; Enough Blood Shed

The second paradox is, a little ink spilled; enough blood shed. There is a double meaning to this paradox. The first meaning is this: since there is so little written in the New Testament on the Lord's Supper (i.e., a little ink spilled), the divisions and persecutions surrounding this meal should come to an end (i.e., there has been enough blood shed).

Let me flesh out this "little ink spilled" observation for you. Before we planted New Covenant Church in Naperville, Illinois, I did an extensive study on the doctrine of the church, limiting my study only to the New Testament. What I discovered anyone can discover and many others have discovered. Here is part of what I discovered and wrote back then:

> Considering the church's stress on the sacraments over the centuries, especially on the Lord's Supper, it is surprising how little this meal is mentioned in the New Testament. While "the breaking of bread" (likely but not certainly a reference to the supper)[19] is mentioned twice in the book of Acts (see 2:42 and 20:7), it is only mentioned once in each of the Synoptic Gospels, for a total of twenty-nine verses (Matthew 26:20–30; Mark 14:12–20; Luke 22:14–23) out of 3,639. In John's Gospel a "supper" is mentioned in 13:1–5 in the context of "the Feast of the Passover," but there is not a word about the acts or institution of that supper. Instead the focus falls on Jesus' washing of the disciples' feet and his words—his new commandment and high priestly prayer.[20]
>
> It is also surprising how little direct teaching we have on it. That is, unlike the Passover meal, mentioned in Exodus, Leviticus, Numbers, and Deuteronomy especially, we are given no directions in the Gospels on how we should celebrate this meal. And in Matthew, we don't even have Jesus' command, "Do this in remembrance of me" (cf. Luke 22:19). The closest directions we have are found in 1 Corinthians 10:14—11:34 (cf. 5:7–8), which is a rebuke more on what not to do than what to do.

That's what I wrote then, and here's what I say now. I know that "a little ink spilled" doesn't necessarily mean "of little importance." Just because there are only a few verses on the birth of Christ doesn't mean Christ's birth matters little. True enough. But I wonder if what is most important to the Christian life is what is most emphasized throughout the New Testament. In other words, Jesus' death, resurrection, and return can be found at the end of every Gospel and throughout every book that follows—from Acts to

Revelation; discipleship themes like repentance, faith, perseverance, holiness, forgiveness, and unity can be found on nearly every page of the New Testament.

In fact, I find it quite revealing that in 1 Corinthians 11 Paul is far more concerned with Christian unity, love, and holiness than the particular details of the Lord's Supper. He spills no ink on who should administer the sacrament or what kind of bread should be used or if the one cup they all shared should be wiped between sips. His focus is on remembering the death of Jesus and not receiving the sacrament "in an unworthy manner" (1 Corinthians 11:27). The unworthy manner is clear from the immediate context and the whole context of the epistle. Don't come to the table without love for and peace with your brother. Without brotherly love (1 Corinthians 13) and edifying prophecy (1 Corinthians 14) the Lord's Supper is *not* the Lord's Supper, and it would be far better if we all stayed at home. Paul puts it this way:

> But in the following instructions I do not commend you, because when you come together it is not for the better but for the worse. For, in the first place, when you come together as a church, I hear that there are divisions among you. And I believe it in part, for there must be factions among you in order that those who are genuine among you may be recognized. When you come together, it is not the Lord's supper that you eat. (1 Corinthians 11:17–20).

Wait. Can you have the Lord's Supper but it's not the Lord's Supper? I suppose so. Wait. Does that mean the meal itself is not efficacious? I suppose so. I think, I hope, I pray that Paul would agree with my first paradoxical point: enough disunity over this unifying meal! In his case some Christians were not waiting for others to arrive and were eating and drinking too much. In our case there are other issues. But in both cases if we don't want to heed all the ink spilled on themes like Christian love, sanctification, edification, and unity, then we will never correctly heed the little ink spilled on this sacrament. *Capiche*?

So the first meaning of our double-meaning paradox is that since there is so little written in the New Testament on the Lord's Supper (i.e., a little ink spilled), the divisions and persecutions surrounding this meal should come to an end (enough blood shed). The second meaning of the paradox stresses the significance of the Lord's Supper. It uses the word *enough* in the sense of sufficient and the word *blood* as being Jesus' blood. Thus the paradox is this: while there is so little said about the Lord's Supper, it is a meal of such great importance because it reminds us that Jesus' death is sufficient to save (enough blood shed to forgive many).

Now we come to the final section of our text:

> Now as they were eating, Jesus took bread, and after blessing it broke it and gave it to the disciples, and said, "Take, eat; this is my body." And he took a cup, and when he had given thanks [*eucharistēsas*] he gave it to them, saying, "Drink of it, all of you, for this is my blood of the covenant, which is poured out for many for the forgiveness of sins. I tell you I will not drink again of this fruit of the vine until that day when I drink it new with you in my Father's kingdom." And when they had sung a hymn, they went out to the Mount of Olives. (vv. 26–30)

With these final five verses, let's ask two interpretation questions and a few application questions. We'll start with the two interpretation questions.

First, what did Jesus mean by "this is my body"? He meant, quite simply, that "the bread symbolizes (represents, stands for, or points to) his crucifixion."[21] I don't think the Roman Catholic view of transubstantiation (the bread and wine become Christ's actual body and blood) or the Lutheran view of consubstantiation (Christ is really present "in, with, and under" the elements) does justice to the actual historical situation. When Jesus held up the bread and said, "This—my body" (there is no "is" in the Aramaic),[22] I can't imagine the Twelve thinking that the bread was a literal "extension of his flesh."[23] *Then* how could he be the one in the room handing them bread and be the bread itself, and *now* how can he be bodily present in Heaven and bodily present on earth? Let's be careful we don't dismiss Jesus' bodily ascension. He's up there, as Zwingli and Calvin rightly argued.

So here our Lord provides, with his typical figurative language ("I am the vine," "I am the door," etc.), yet another "vivid object lesson."[24] The bread is not literally his body any more than the cup is literally the covenant in his blood.

That is not to say I don't believe that Christ is spiritually present in the sacrament. Just because I don't believe in the real presence of Jesus in the Eucharist does not mean I believe in the real absence,[25] or that Immanuel is present spiritually with his church when we do church discipline (18:20) and discipleship (28:20) and at all times through his Spirit (John 14:23; 15:4–7) *except* during the Lord's Supper. I believe that "by faith" when we eat the bread and drink this cup we are "made partakers of his body and blood" and grow in grace through such spiritual nourishment.[26]

So what did Jesus mean by "this is my body"? He meant that the bread symbolizes his death on the cross. Second, what did Jesus mean by "this is my blood of the covenant"? He meant that through his sacrificial and substitutionary death, he promises the blessings of the new covenant upon his people (the "many").[27] I say the "many" are God's people because of the language of 1:21, "you shall call his name Jesus, for he will save *his people* from their sins," which picks up from the language of Isaiah 53, where the Servant "bore the sin of many" (Isaiah 53:12), who are earlier called "my people" (Isaiah 53:8, i.e., God's people). Compare also Luke's "poured out for you" in reference to Jesus' disciples (Luke 22:20).

What are the new covenant blessings bestowed on the "many"? Those blessings are total forgiveness of past, present, and future sins *and* eternal fellowship with God.[28] Here the blood covenant made by Moses at Mount Sinai (Exodus 24:7, 8) is renewed, embodied, fulfilled, and surpassed. It is a new and "better covenant" (Hebrews 7:22) because it is God's commitment—through Jesus' vicarious atonement—to "forgive" his people once and for all time "their iniquity" and "remember their sin no more" (Jeremiah 31:34).

This is sometimes why we say of this table, "We *celebrate* his *death*." What? Celebrate death? Yes, we celebrate *his* death because through it (and through it alone) we have the forgiveness of sins.

We also celebrate his death because it guarantees us eternal fellowship with God. Don't overlook our final two verses, where Jesus says, "I tell you I will not drink again of this fruit of the vine until that day when I drink it new with you in my Father's kingdom" (v. 29), and then after they sang "they went out to the Mount of Olives" (v. 30). Jesus has not left the Mount of Olives behind or the Olivet Discourse he gave on it. He lives and breathes eschatology. He's a mountain man forever. It's as if Jesus says to us, "Think of your future *with me*. Yes, every time you drink that wine, which symbolizes my blood poured out for you, let it remind you of the wedding banquet to come, where we will share that same drink forever at table together." Future fellowship! Forever fellowship! God with us, and someday soon we with God!

Why do we celebrate the Lord's Supper? Well, the two answers to our two interpretation questions provide us with the two main reasons: first, to "commemorate Jesus' redemptive death"; and second, to anticipate our future fellowship with him and "with all the redeemed."[29]

Finally, we come to a few application questions: should we have the Lord's Supper, as it is here, during the middle of a seemingly substantial meal? Should Jesus alone be allowed to break the bread and distribute it? Should only men be allowed to partake? Should only twelve men be allowed to partake? Should only twelve Jewish men be allowed to partake? Should known traitors be allowed to partake? Should we use only bread that can be easily broken—perhaps something flat and brittle like unleavened bread? Should we have only one loaf that all share, as seems to be the case here? Should we drink from one cup, which is certainly the case here?[30] Should we all dip our hands into one dish?[31] (Did the Lord of Creation not know about germs?) Should we use wine?[32] Should we only have this meal once a year, at the time of the Passover? Should we only eat it after sundown and in Jerusalem? Should we have this meal not in a church, synagogue, or temple but only in a house, as it is here and everywhere throughout the New Testament? Should we receive the elements as they did, reclining at a table—flat on our bellies with our bare feet sticking out? (Sorry, Leonardo Da Vinci.) Should we sing one hymn and only one at the very end of the service, and should that one "hymn" be one of the *Hallel* (Psalms 114—118, perhaps Psalm 118:22—"The stone that the builders rejected has become the cornerstone")?

What is descriptive here and what is prescriptive? That is, what of what they did should we do? How does our text answer that question? It doesn't. But if we assume that Matthew's Gospel was written to instruct the church, and then if we compile all the New Testament texts on the Lord's Supper (the few there are), we are given some guidelines. But guidelines are different than commands or laws or rules, right? So think Garden of Eden; think freedom within boundaries. Consider the seven freedom-within-boundaries guidelines I give below.

First: We should use unleavened bread and red wine. However, I think the case can be made that the church might use leavened bread symbolically to celebrate that Jesus has fulfilled the Passover. We might even say, he fulfilled it in his dying and *rising*! I also think the case can be made that grape juice qualifies as being "fruit of the vine," the only phrase we find here.

Second: It is more than appropriate to share this meal in a church building. The house churches of the New Testament were replaced by buildings from the third century on. With that said, it might be nice for us occasionally (once a year?) to be less formal and more family-like (as depicted here) and celebrate this meal as a full meal in a home.

Third: I see no definitive reason why any Christian cannot preside over the meal and serve it. However, it makes most sense to have the elders, as representatives of the church, preside over the meal (teaching and reminding you of what it is about) and then modeling servanthood to the church by distributing it to you. But a fine argument can be made for involving the congregation, especially in serving the elements. In fact, Wayne Grudem suggests that it is good to have men *and women* distribute the elements to show our unity and spiritual equality.[33]

Fourth: This is a meal for disciples only. In other words, non-Christians should not partake. However, since Jesus served Judas (knowing that he would betray him) and the eleven (knowing that they would all soon forsake him at his trial and death) we ought not to be more scrupulous than our Savior in fencing in the Table. Those who profess faith in Christ and have been baptized into Christ but live in unknown hypocrisy ultimately stand accountable before God. If such a believer eats and drinks, he "eats and drinks judgment on himself" (1 Corinthians 11:29).

Allow me another point on this fourth guideline. As we know from Exodus that children partook of the Passover meal—in fact, three times in the book of Exodus there is the emphasis on the father's responsibility to teach his children the story of the exodus from Egypt (Exodus 12:26; 13:8, 14), those children who are able, in Paul's language, to examine themselves and discern the body (1 Corinthians 11:28, 29) should also partake.

Fifth: A local church can distribute the elements however it would like. Perhaps a church, after weighing all the opinions, selects one tradition and sticks with it until the return of Christ. Or perhaps a church mixes things up a bit to remind people that how the elements are distributed matters little compared with Christian unity based on Christ and him crucified.

Sixth: We should celebrate this meal as often as we'd like or seems profitable. Paul writes, "For as often as you eat this bread and drink the cup . . ." (1 Corinthians 11:26a). If I understand that term "as often" correctly, it can mean once a year, once a month, once a Sunday, or once a day. We could follow the Passover tradition, thus celebrating once a year. Or we could follow the early church tradition, thus celebrating weekly ("On the first day of the week [Sunday], when we were *gathered together to break bread* . . . ," Acts 20:7) or daily ("And day by day, attending the temple together and *breaking bread* in their homes, they received their food with glad and generous hearts," Acts 2:46). One benefit of a more regular observance is that if the pastor fails to preach the gospel in the sermon, it is nearly impossible to fail to preach it in the Supper. Through this meal Jesus assures us that even the worst churches get to hear and apply the doctrine of the atonement. *Thank you, Jesus!*

Seventh: There are many reasons we should celebrate this meal, but the one certain reason we celebrate it is to preach to one another and to the world "the Lord's death until he comes" (1 Corinthians 11:26b). It has often been said that there is no Christianity without the cross, and the first person to say it was Jesus. To him the cross is at the center of the Christian faith. Now some might argue, "No, Jesus' birth or the resurrection is at the center." Or having being through most of Matthew now, I might argue that Jesus' teachings and miracles are at the center. But at the Last Supper Jesus bestows upon his church only one commemorative and recurring drama, and it centers on his cross, it focuses on his death. At the Last Supper Jesus said nothing about his birth (to remember it) or about his coming resurrection (to remember it) or about his glorious return (to remember it). He assumed we would, of course, remember all those great events, and two of them are hinted at here. But the one drama (yes, there is to be drama in the church) that he bestows upon his church is to remember his death by regularly having this tangible and movable feast.

Remembering One Remembrance

When I was in college a group of students from Wheaton College skipped church and headed out one hot September Sunday morning to the Indiana Dunes. When we got there, we changed into our swimsuits and spread out our blankets on the sandy shores. But just before we ran into the cool waters, Betsy, an Episcopalian, said to the group, "Shouldn't we at least celebrate the Lord's Supper? It's Sunday!" We all felt a bit guilty. Hearing no reply, she turned to me—the one Bible/Theology major among us (thus the most guilty of the group)—and asked or rather commanded, "Why don't you officiate."

Well, I did officiate. It was the first time I had ever officiated. I was an unordained, first-year Bible student breaking the Sabbath by saying the words of consecration in my swimming suit to my fellow Sabbath-breaking, scantily clad friends. And if that wasn't bad enough, we used hot dog buns for "the bread" and water (or was it Pepsi? God forbid) for "the cup."

Sometimes when I look back on that unique event, I cringe. How irreverent! How presumptuous! At other times, however, I look back on it and I think, *How beautiful! What a perfect display of Christian fellowship, freedom, and focus.* For you see, we stopped in the midst of our fun in the sun to remember the death of Jesus Christ. And we did so because Jesus' death mattered to us. We stopped to celebrate that day what we stop to celebrate every time we observe the Lord's Supper—that the Christ of the cross is the center of Christianity and that through Jesus' death our sins are forgiven. Do you believe that? And do you celebrate that, whether you're on the beach in Indiana or in the house of God in Jerusalem? If so, then feel free to whisper or shout out, "Amen."

78

Fearful Symmetry

MATTHEW 26:31–35, 69–75

Tyger! Tyger! burning bright
In the forests of the night,
What immortal hand or eye
Could frame thy fearful symmetry?[1]

The answer to William Blake's question as to who crafted the fearful symmetry of the tiger's eyes, shoulders, heart, claws, feet, and skin is, of course, God, the same immortal who crafted every event of world history, including the fearful symmetry of the greatest and truest moment of it—the passion of the Christ.

As we come now in our study of Matthew's Gospel to Jesus' sufferings and death, I want you to feel something of God's mysterious craftsmanship and also to notice that the action in the great drama of Jesus' incarnation has slowed down. It has slowed down enough for each and every reader of this Gospel to sense that something horrifically violent yet strikingly beautiful is set before our eyes. It's not a tiger lurking in the forest, but the Lion of Judah becoming the Lamb of God.

In 26:31–35, 69–75 we come to two scenes. One scene is set in the upper room at the Last Supper (vv. 31–35), and the other scene is set outside in the courtyard of Caiaphas's house (vv. 69–75). Both scenes feature two main characters—Peter and Jesus. The focus of our text falls on Peter and his denials. However, I want us, as we look at Peter, never to lose sight of the one who "calls himself a Lamb," as the poet Blake said in another of his famous poems.[2]

Marvel at the Plan of God in Christ

In this sermon there are two primary points of application. The first point is to *marvel at the plan of God in Christ*. I'll set the stage for the first scene.

The Last Supper has just been served and the Passover meal eaten when Jesus concludes the celebration with three prophecies, two of which are his own and two of which must have completely soured an already bitter dinner:

> Then Jesus said to them, "You will all fall away because of me this night. For it is written, 'I will strike the shepherd, and the sheep of the flock will be scattered.' But after I am raised up, I will go before you to Galilee." Peter answered him, "Though they all fall away because of you, I will never fall away." Jesus said to him, "Truly, I tell you, this very night, before the rooster crows, you will deny me three times." Peter said to him, "Even if I must die with you, I will not deny you!" And all the disciples said the same. (vv. 31–35)

We often miss marveling at the sovereign plan of God in the passion of the Christ. So marvel with me now as I point out part of that plan, revealed to us as three prophecies. The first prophecy comes in verse 31. Jesus predicts that twelve out of the Twelve will deny him. His language in verse 31 is, "You will *all* fall away"; then later in verse 34 he applies it to Peter specifically, "Truly, I tell you, this very night, before the rooster crows, *you* will deny me three times." Jesus predicts they will all apostatize. Put differently, they will each deny him, each in his own way.[3]

In verse 33 Peter protests against this prophecy. Peter is the church's first possibility thinker! He is the first to advocate the victorious Christian life without the victory of the death and resurrection of Christ. That is why he bets his house against Jesus' word. In verse 35 he even ups the ante by throwing in his favorite cloak, six children, and his grandfather's antique watch. He'll bet it all on his courageous faith. (He has such great faith in *his faith*.) But note that he is not alone. They all bet it all. Don't overlook that final sentence in verse 35: "And *all* the disciples said the same." They all echoed Peter's "Even if I must die with you, I will not deny you!" The exclamation point in the ESV is correct. They are all emphatic about the assurance of their allegiance.

We chuckle because we sometimes sound like them. We also chuckle—a sad, sorry chuckle, if there is such a thing—because we know how these favored ones fared. Will we see the Twelve holding hands in a circle beneath the cross singing, "Lift High the Cross"? No, we will not. Look at the end of verse 56: "Then *all* the disciples left him and fled." That's an awful inclusio to verse 31: "You will all fall away . . . *this night*," and *that very night* "all the disciples left him and fled."

All but one, of course—Peter must have fled but then circled back. After following "at a distance" (v. 58) Peter is "sitting outside in the courtyard"

(v. 69) of Caiaphas's courthouse or the house that was now serving as a courtroom for Jesus. Peter is still around, but not for long. Our text ends, saying of Peter, "And he *went out* [left Jesus] and wept bitterly" (v. 75).

That verse is the last word on Peter in the Gospel of Matthew. No more talking from Peter. No more great confessions. No more boasting. No more walking on water. No more drawing his sword.[4] There is only silence and the unmistakable noise of someone scampering in the dark and the faint sound of a once mighty man crying in the night. There is only silence until the resurrection and the Great Commission, when Peter will hear the words from Jesus, "I am with you always" (28:20).

Jesus' first prophecy is that all twelve would fall away. First Judas fell away, then ten more, and finally Peter.[5] The small rock (*petras*) had a great big fall! Jesus' second prophecy is about his resurrection. It's not all drab and dark in the upper room.[6] In verse 32 Jesus predicts, "But after I am raised up, I will go before you to Galilee." Jesus knows that he is going to suffer, die, rise, and meet up with them again. Whatever their falling away entailed, it would not last forever. He would meet up with them in Jerusalem first (as Luke and John point out) and eventually in Galilee (as Mark and Matthew point out). It is in "Galilee of the Gentiles" (4:15) no less that Jesus' Great Commission would be given—to "make disciples of all nations" (28:19a).

Sandwiched in between Jesus' two prophecies is Zechariah's prophecy. Jesus is as sure of *his* word as he is of Scripture. Or perhaps better phrased, he is sure of his word *because* he is sure of Scripture and his Christological reading of it. Jesus quotes Zechariah 13:7 in verse 31: "For it is written, 'I will strike the shepherd, and the sheep of the flock will be scattered.'" It would be fair to call this Old Testament quotation part of and the reason for the first prophecy about the apostles' apostasy: "Jesus said to them, 'You will all fall away because of me this night. *For* [or because] it is written, 'I will strike the shepherd, and the sheep of the flock will be scattered'" (v. 31). I have separated the two because the second part focuses specifically on another of Jesus' predictions—namely, of his own death.

The "scattered" part fits with Jesus' prophecy about the disciples all falling away. The "strike" part fits with Jesus' prophecy elsewhere in Matthew about his cross.[7] In 26:2b Jesus said of himself, "the Son of Man will be delivered up to be crucified." What is clarified in our text, with Jesus' quote and slight reworking of Zechariah 13:7,[8] is that God himself will strike the Shepherd (i.e., his Son).[9]

I want us to marvel at the plan of God in Christ. Part of that marveling involves seeing the sovereign hand of God in the death of his Son. "It is written"—in other words, it was planned in the mind of God long ago—that Jesus would die. How Jesus will die and why Jesus will die is about to unfold. For now we see the unfolding of the divine plan, a plan that is for us and our salvation, but is also a plan that is for God and his glory.

Boast in Nothing but the Cross of Christ

As we have settled our eyes on the cross of Christ, let's stay there for the rest of the chapter. We will now walk through the story of Peter's failure, but let's not remove Jesus' cross far from our vision. The whole point of Matthew's candid retelling of the chief apostle's apostasy is to show all disciples everywhere and at all times the absolute need for the atoning death of Jesus.

The first point is to *marvel at the plan of God in Christ*. The second point follows: *boast in nothing but the cross of Christ*. The language, I'll admit, is borrowed from Paul ("far be it from me to *boast except in the cross of our Lord Jesus Christ*," Galatians 6:14a), but that same idea is illustrated in the drama of Peter's denials.

However, before we turn our attention to verses 69–75, let's first return our attention to verses 33–35. I've pointed out a few of the details. Let me point out one more. Before the cock crows at the end of the story, Peter hollers like a high-pitched peacock at the start of it. Not only does Peter boast in his courageous faith, "Even if I must die with you, I will not deny you!" (v. 35), he builds himself up by cutting everyone else down: "Though *they* all fall away . . . *I* will never fall away." Peter says, "Jesus, I agree, you can't trust this lot. But you can trust me." And he says that with the other guys in the room. What bravado! Such machismo. *¡El stupido!* As Frederick Dale Bruner summarizes, "Peter's behavior fails . . . in three ways . . . : (1) in his *condescension* toward the *other* disciples, (2) in his *confidence* in *himself* as an exception, and (3) in his *contradiction* of his *Lord's* word."[10]

Let me hit a bit on that third failure. Peter *again* plays "you say, I say" with Jesus. The last time Peter contradicted Jesus' word was when Jesus first talked about going up to Jerusalem to die. We read about that in 16:22: "And Peter took him aside and began to rebuke him, saying, 'Far be it from you, Lord! This shall never happen to you.'" What Peter had then was what Luther called "a theology of glory." What he needed was what Luther called "a theology of the cross." That's why Jesus rebuked Peter, saying to him, "Get behind me, Satan! You are a hindrance to me. For you are not setting your mind on the things of God, but on the things of man" (16:23).

There is a similar issue here in chapter 26. However, here it is not that Peter disagrees that Jesus is going to the cross. That now seems to be a given.

Rather it is that Peter doesn't see his need for Jesus' cross. "Who needs the cross when you have unwavering faith like mine?" is perhaps what was running through Peter's hard head. When, at the meal, Jesus had raised a cup and said to them, "This is my blood of the covenant, which is poured out for many for the forgiveness of sin" (26:28), one wonders if Peter was thinking, *Forgiveness for what sin?* Ah, but Peter would learn (wouldn't he?) for what sin. He would learn through his three denials his three-hundredfold state of sin. They would all fall. But his fall would be so deep, nearly as deep as Judas's.[11]

Let's look next at the true state of Peter's unwavering commitment to Christ.

> Now Peter was sitting outside in the courtyard. And a servant girl came up to him and said, "You also were with Jesus the Galilean." But he denied it before them all, saying, "I do not know what you mean." And when he went out to the entrance, another servant girl saw him, and she said to the bystanders, "This man was with Jesus of Nazareth." And again he denied it with an oath: "I do not know the man." After a little while the bystanders came up and said to Peter, "Certainly you too are one of them, for your accent betrays you." Then he began to invoke a curse on himself and to swear, "I do not know the man." And immediately the rooster crowed. And Peter remembered the saying of Jesus, "Before the rooster crows, you will deny me three times." And he went out and wept bitterly. (vv. 69–75)

I began this chapter saying something about the mysterious and magnificent artistry of God in creation ("Tyger, Tyger burning bright") and in the passion narratives (that fearful symmetry of how salvation history unfolds). Here again there is artistry to be appreciated. Before we get to the theology of the cross, see something of the artistry of Matthew's record of Peter's denials.

Note the "now" in verses 59 and 69.[12] The first "now"—"Now the chief priests and the whole council were seeking false testimony against Jesus" (v. 59)—takes us into Jesus' trial. Jesus is *standing* on trial before the most powerful religious authorities in Jerusalem. The second "now"—"Now Peter was *sitting* outside. And a servant girl came up to him" (v. 69)—takes us outside to Peter's trial.[13] Inside, before powerful men Jesus fearlessly stands his ground. Outside, before powerless women (two *servant* girls), Peter fearfully falls on his face.[14] Somehow Peter, who in verse 51 drew his sword to fight a mob, now cowers under a few accusations from a few unarmed slaves. What happened? Was he not prepared for this—to so suddenly move "from spectator to participant, from observer to defendant"?[15] Was he ready to stand up for Jesus if he was formally brought on trial before the Sanhedrin or Pilate, but caught off guard by this unofficial venue and politically insignificant accusers? Did he not learn the lesson of Jesus' Gethsemane lecture—"Watch and pray that you may not enter into temptation. The spirit indeed is willing, but the flesh is weak" (v. 41)?[16]

Do you see the artistry here? We are to read the two trials as happening simultaneously—Peter's "trial of discipleship" and Jesus' "trial of messiahship," as Bruner labels the parallels[17]—and thus to see that as Jesus remains innocent of all charges brought against him, Peter grows in his guilt.

Peter's Trial of Discipleship

Peter's first denial is, "I do not know what you mean" (v. 70). To the first servant girl's accusation, "You also were with Jesus the Galilean" (v. 69), Peter gives this "mumbled protest of ignorance."[18] The sense of his sentence is, "I don't know what you're talking about" (so NIV and NLT). He sounds like one of our politicians, caught in a scandal, giving a press conference. The question is raised, "Do you or do you not know Miss Smith?" His reply is a weaseling of words. "Well, you know, there are a lot of Miss Smiths in the world, aren't there? So, which one are you talking about? I'm not sure I get your question." "I do not know what you mean" is how politician Peter puts it. And that's all he says. It's the end of the press conference, so he thinks. So he hopes.

He moves away from the microphone. Matthew says it this way: "And when he went out to the entrance . . ." (v. 71a). Note the body movement. "Peter's retreat ('he went out') tells in body language what is happening in soul language to Peter—he is getting farther and farther from Jesus."[19] He's looking for the closest exit. Ah, but it's too late. The sharks have smelled the blood in the water. Enter the second "witness," if you will.[20] We pick up the attack in verse 71: "Another servant girl saw him, and she said to the bystanders, 'This man was with Jesus of Nazareth.'"

Notice the phrase "with Jesus." It is used also in verse 69. When the Jewish Council in Acts 4:13 were astonished by the boldness and knowledge of Peter and John, Luke writes, "And they [the Council] recognized that they [Peter and John] had been *with Jesus*." In Acts Peter's face would be beaming to be accused of being "with Jesus." But here in Matthew, and also in Mark, Luke, and John—all four record for us his demise—the words "with Jesus" turn his face bright red, I imagine. He is terrified to be associated with Jesus, the guy being sentenced to death just a few feet away.

At this point Peter feels trapped. What should he say? What would you say? Have you ever been cornered by the watercooler—"Can you believe that anyone would believe what those out-of-date evangelicals have to say? You're not one of them, are you?" Well, with a solemn vow Peter gives his second denial: "I do not know the man" (v. 72). Here Peter takes some sort of oath—"I swear to God on the Bible that I'm not lying"—an action that is just dripping with irony. In the Sermon on the Mount Jesus warned about taking oaths to mask a lie (5:33–37); as Donald Senior notes, "From Matthew's point of view, Peter joins an unsavory set of characters whose oaths are signs of their undoing: Herod (14:7), the scribes and Pharisees (23:16–22), and Caiaphas (26:63)."[21] In Matthew, only the bad guys take oaths. A further irony is present here. Considering who Peter is and what he has previously confessed, this second denial is shocking. We want to jump into the pages of Scripture and say, "What! Weren't you, Peter, the one who answered Jesus' question, 'Who do you say that I am?' with an energetic public announcement, 'You are the Christ, the Son of the living God' (16:15, 16)? But now what are you doing? Who are you? You have moved from pretended ignorance to contemptuous refutation. What's next?"

What's next is his third denial. After Peter's "I do not know the man" in verse 72, there is a pregnant pause. We catch our breath. It feels all too familiar to us. Then comes verse 73: "After a little while the bystanders came up and said to Peter, 'Certainly you too are one of them, for your accent betrays you.'" Can you sense the increased intensity? First it was one woman one-on-one with Peter. Second it was another woman with a crowd present. Third it is the crowd ("the bystander*s*") with their irrefutable evidence—his accent.[22]

Peter's third denial is again "I do not know the man," preceded by his swearing and "invok[ing] a curse on himself" (v. 74). We wonder if Peter is calling down a curse on himself or on Jesus, for the word "himself" could refer to Jesus.[23] I think, however, the "himself" refers to Peter, the sense being, "Let me be damned if I'm lying." I say that because Peter intentionally never mentions Jesus' name. The girls say, "Jesus the Galilean" and "Jesus of Nazareth." But Peter does not say, "Oh no, it's Jesus *the Christ* or Jesus *the Son of Man*." He doesn't even say, "I do not know *Jesus*." Instead (twice), he says, "I do not know *the man*." Here Peter only had one salvation in mind—saving his own skin. Instead of losing his life for Christ's sake, he sought to save it (see 16:25).

Even if Peter felt safe at some point ("No, you've got me wrong. I'm just out here in the courtyard to have a smoke"), he must have felt dumb. He was from Galilee, not Jerusalem. His accent, as the bystanders pointed out in verse 73, *betrayed* him (I love the ESV's use of the word "betrays"). Jesus was the most popular guy in Galilee. It would be like saying that you live in Chicago and you have never heard of Oprah, Al Capone, Michael Jordan, or Mike Ditka. Peter says, "I don't know the man" in his distinct Galilean dialect.

Sure, you don't. Don't be dumb. Jesus is bigger than the Beatles in Galilee, and now he is the star of the show in Jerusalem. Everyone knows Jesus.

Whether Peter felt dumb with his final denial, we don't know for certain. What we do know for certain is as soon as that rooster crowed—it was morning now—a flood of guilt overwhelmed his dark soul. As that rooster sang its morning song, Peter remembered Jesus' seemingly impossible prediction, "Before the rooster crows, you will deny me three times" (v. 34; cf. v. 75). Once? Maybe. Twice? Unlikely. Three times? Never! But it was one, two, three . . . and down and "out" went Peter the Pretentious. Again notice the geographical shift. He moves farther and farther from Jesus. From sitting just outside in the courtyard (v. 69) to going out to the entrance (v. 71) and finally to moving beyond that entrance—out the door, into the wilderness, if you'll allow me (v. 75). Yes, as Peter's Lord and ours is being sentenced—"He deserves death," and then being spit upon, hit, slapped, and ridiculed, "Prophesy to us, you Christ! Who is it that struck you?" (26:66–68)—the fearful symmetry of Jesus' prophecy about Peter is fulfilled!

Perhaps Peter came that night to save the Savior. Instead he now knows that he will need this Savior to save him, for the curtain closes with humiliated and humbled Peter weeping "bitterly" (v. 75b). Are these tears of repentance? Yes, they are. It is the beginning of his repentance, a repentance that would lead to full restoration and a renewed call to mission. We know all that from the end of the story. So as Matthew Henry nicely phrased it, "The crowing of the cock is to Peter, instead of John the Baptist, the voice of one calling to repentance."[24]

Notice that Matthew, unlike John in his Gospel,[25] doesn't record Peter's restoration. The reason, I think, is because from here to the cross, "I don't think you can squeeze out one ounce of human virtue."[26] What's the reason for that? The reason is that there is this cosmic contrast at play: compare what all the fallen humans are doing—be it the high priest or the chief apostle—to what God is doing in his holy Son. And what God is doing in Jesus is bringing that Shepherd to be stricken, smitten, and afflicted. He is carrying his Son to Calvary where Jesus will die as the atonement for apostate apostles, blasphemous bystanders, taunting thieves, and even hate-spitting, flesh-whipping Roman soldiers. You see, the scene is spectacular, and the artistry is awesome. But more spectacular and the highest form of the highest art is the cross of Jesus Christ, that fearful symmetry of God's grand design.

Apostate Anonymous

Recently I was reading some of the original literature of Alcoholics Anonymous, and I came upon the first two "steps," as they are now called. Part of the first step is this: "An alcoholic must realize that he is an alcoholic, incurable from a medical viewpoint. . . ." The second step is this: "He must surrender himself absolutely to God, realizing that in himself there is no hope." This surrender, I read in another place, "involved the newcomer's confessing Jesus Christ as his personal Lord and Savior."[27]

I think it is fair and helpful perhaps to view our text in Matthew as another AA document that holds nearly identical values. In our case the AA stands for Apostate Anonymous. I say it that way because what we have here is Peter's confession to someone in the church (Mark and then to Matthew, Luke, and John?) of his greatest sin. We have the story of Peter's denial because Peter shared the story with others. In turn those others, namely and especially the Gospel writers, far from suppressing the scandal, made it a part of their Gospel—their good news! What refreshing honesty and humility.

But why did Peter share his fall, and why did Matthew record it? They did it to teach us "the deceitfulness of human nature,"[28] the necessity of humility before God and charity toward other fallen Christians,[29] the danger of presumption, pride, and trusting in one's own strength,[30] the expected trials of those who would seek to faithfully follow the Son of Man,[31] the reality of past, present, and *future* forgiveness in the blood of the covenant, the promise of complete restoration for the truly repentant, the hope of "future victory over our weaknesses,"[32] and "the glory of the forgiving love and cleansing power of Jesus Christ."[33] Put differently, to teach us to *boast in nothing but the cross of Christ*.[34]

Ah, holy Jesus, how hast Thou offended,
That man to judge Thee hath in haste pretended?
By foes derided, *by Thine own rejected*,
O most afflicted!

Who was the guilty? Who brought this upon Thee?
Alas, my treason, Jesus, hath undone Thee;
'Twas I, Lord Jesus, I it was denied Thee;
I crucified Thee.

For me, kind Jesus, was Thy incarnation,
Thy mortal sorrow, and Thy life's oblation;
Thy death of anguish and Thy bitter passion,
For my salvation.

Therefore, kind Jesus, since I cannot pay Thee,
I do adore Thee, and will ever pray Thee,
Think on Thy pity and Thy love unswerving,
Not my deserving.[35]

79

Drank Damnation Dry

MATTHEW 26:36–46

WHEN I WAS EIGHT, my father, older brother, and I traveled to Ireland, to the town where my father was born. There are two things I remember most about that trip. First, I remember that the food and drink were terrible. Eating soda bread and drinking warm, unpasteurized goat's milk for two weeks was more than my immature American taste buds could bear. I longed for the golden arches of the land of the free and the home of the brave, the country of salt and fat and grease! Second, I remember that the house my father grew up in—in the far western county of Connemara—was old and small but lots of fun to play in.

When I returned to Ireland with my son, Sean, when he was about eight, I had a very different view of my father's house and country. I then realized for the first time in my life how poor my father was. He grew up in Third-World poverty. He lived in a two-room house that had no electricity, no indoor plumbing, no running water, and a dirt floor. His father, like most of the men in those days, could only find work in England and thus left the family for months at a time simply to put bread on the table. Connemara is filled with rocks, which makes the stone walls built around each plot of land picturesque, but which should indicate to thoughtful visitors the sad reality that that picturesque land could not sustain most crops.

One recent Christmas my father, in a rare moment, got to talking about the poverty of his childhood. He shared about the time he stole two shillings from his father's wallet to buy apples from Mrs. McGillicuddy because his family rarely ate fruit. "Where did you get those apples?" my grandmother interrogated him. "Oh, Mrs. McGillicuddy is giving them away. She thought you'd like to make an apple pie," he replied. Well then, didn't my grandmother go to *thank* Mrs. McGillicuddy, and didn't she find out the truth, and meanwhile didn't my grandfather discover the missing money and didn't my father then get what was coming to him?

My father also shared how one Christmas Eve as a young boy he stayed up late because he was determined to see Santa Claus and more significantly to see what Santa would put in his stocking. All my dad would receive each Christmas was one gift in his stocking. That year he was hoping for a penny. Each hour he returned to where the stocking hung, looked for Santa, felt the stocking, and left if there was nothing in there. Finally he fell asleep. When he awoke, it was very early but not yet morning. He ran to the stocking and felt it again. Something was in it. He reached down and pulled out a penny. He looked up to Heaven and said, "Thank you, Santa!" My older brother then asked, "Dad, what would a penny buy?" "Oh," my father said with a big smile, "a candy." "*One* candy," I said. "Yes, one candy."

Twice in the text we will study now Jesus calls God his Father. Note the phrase "my Father" in verses 39 and 42. I make that simple observation not to make a thematic connection between my father and Jesus' Father, but rather to make a connection of perspective. Just as it took me a second visit to Ireland and two decades for progress in the obvious observations of life to recognize my father's poverty, when we start to grasp who Jesus is (the beloved Son of the Father) and where he comes from (his Father's eternal and glorious presence) we gain a better understanding and appreciation for the incarnation, the prayers of Gethsemane, and the hour of Christ's death.

To give us the proper perspective on Gethsemane, we'll walk through this text by asking and answering eight key questions. Each question will build upon the ones before it and will grow in complexity as well as importance. Thus the final two questions will be the most significant ones for us to wrap our heads and hearts around.

The First Question

The first question is, *where is Gethsemane?* Gethsemane is a place on the western slopes of the Mount of Olives, the hillside where Jesus had given his recent Olivet Discourse (Matthew 24, 25) and where he and his disciples climbed after they celebrated the Last Supper (26:30). Since the word *Gethsemane* means an olive press or oil press, the "place called Gethsemane" (v. 36) that Jesus went to was likely "an olive orchard on the Mount of Olives,"[1] or put differently a *garden* of olive trees. John calls it "a garden" (John 18:1). Mathew doesn't call it a garden, so I won't make some profound theological point about Jesus' relationship to Adam and the garden of Eden and how Adam failed to do God's will but Jesus here in the garden of Gethsemane perfectly submits to God's will. However, it's not a sin to think it if you are now thinking it.

The Second Question

The second question is, *who did Jesus take with him to Gethsemane?* Verses 36, 37a provide us with the answer.

> Then Jesus went with them to a place called Gethsemane, and he said to his disciples, "Sit here, while I go over there and pray." And taking with him Peter and the two sons of Zebedee . . .

Jesus took "his disciples," which is a reference not to all his followers but those most recently with him in the upper room. At this point that would be the Twelve minus Judas. Judas must have sneaked out at some point during the meal because he arrives with his evil entourage in verse 47. But of the eleven disciples who came with Jesus to Gethsemane, Jesus singled out Peter, James, and John.

Why? Was it because they were night owls? Was it because they were the most fearless? We don't know for certain. The only sure contextual connections we can make are: (a) these three most recently boasted about their courageous faith, and thus perhaps Jesus wanted to teach these sleepy souls a lesson, and (b) these three were the only three to witness the glory of the transfiguration, and thus perhaps Jesus wanted to show them—as official witnesses again—his less than glorious humanity in light of the weight of the cross. Whatever the reason, they alone can sing with historical accuracy those lines from "O Sacred Head, Now Wounded": "with grief and shame weighed down . . . . How art Thou pale with anguish." They witnessed Jesus' glory when the heavenly Father's voice proclaimed, "This is my beloved Son" (17:5), and they witnessed in part (they slept through most of it) his sorrow when our Lord cried out in distressful prayer, "My Father . . . My Father . . . My Father" (vv. 39, 42; cf. 44) and there was no audible answer from Heaven. Where was the Father's reassuring voice? Where was the Spirit's peaceful presence? Was God silent?

The Third Question

The third question is, *what did Jesus go to Gethsemane to do?* He went there to pray. The verbs "pray" and "prayed" are the most obvious actions in our text. "Sit here," Jesus said to his disciples, "while I go over there and *pray*"

(v. 36b). "And going a little farther he fell on his face and *prayed*" (v. 39). "Again, for the second time, he went away and *prayed*" (v. 42). "So leaving them again, he went away and *prayed* for the third time" (v. 44). And between the four times prayer is mentioned in reference to Jesus praying, we find in the middle of our text—that is, with five verses before it and five after it—Jesus' admonition to the tired trio, "Watch and *pray*" (v. 41).

The Fourth Question

The fourth question is, *how did the church's first prayer meeting go?* Well, there was a better turnout than usual. Four people were present. And there was a much better turnout from the one gender that almost never comes to prayer meetings—men! Four men were there. However, like the Parable of the Soils, only one was any good. Only Jesus prayed at the church's first prayer meeting. And while we might think that that's all the church will ever need—one perfect praying God-man interceding continually for the church (see, e.g., John 17)—Jesus here lets none of "*the* disciples" off the hook.[2] Sure, it was late. Sure, everyone was physically and emotional exhausted ("sleeping for sorrow," Luke 22:45). But Jesus gave an order: "Remain here, and watch with me" (v. 38b). It's hard to know what he meant by "watch." I think he might have meant, "stay awake *and* pray,"[3] because that's basically what he rebukes them for not doing in verse 40. Whatever Jesus meant by "watch," it did not mean "sleep." Perhaps that night Peter, instead of sleeping, should have been praying, "O God, please give me the strength so I will not deny Jesus in the next six hours."

Besides the command, Jesus also wanted companionship as well as human sympathy. It was "not good" that the God-man should be "alone" (Genesis 2:18); "a threefold cord is not quickly broken" (Ecclesiastes 4:12). He let them in on his *depression*.[4] I don't know of a better word for what he said in 26:38, "My soul is very sorrowful, even to death." Luke's version gives a graphic picture of his emotional state: "And being in agony he prayed more earnestly; and his sweat became like great drops of blood falling down to the ground" (Luke 22:44). The disciples should have stayed awake because Jesus asked them to stay awake! Also they should have stayed awake to pray because Jesus wanted their companionship and their prayers. Like any human being facing "dreadful things"[5]—sickness, torture, death—Jesus desired for them "to watch and pray alongside" him.[6]

Today while Jesus doesn't need our prayers for him, it is good for us to stop in the middle of this chapter as Jesus did in the middle of his praying to learn some lessons from Jesus on prayer. We should learn that as our Savior agonized, wrestled, lamented, groaned, and persevered in prayer to the Father at Gethsemane, so we can and should come to the Father in our hour of need and temptation. Moreover, as Jesus pleaded boldly for what he wanted, so we "should feel free also to unload our deepest desires before God."[7] We should learn, as the author of Hebrews puts it in one place, that we have now in Jesus a high priest who is able to "sympathize with our weaknesses" because "in every respect" he was "tempted as we are" (Hebrews 4:15), and in another place, "because he himself has suffered when tempted, he is able to help those who are being tempted" (Hebrews 2:18). N. T. Wright summarizes those thoughts well when he writes, "[W]hen we ourselves find the ground giving way beneath our feet, as sooner or later we shall, Gethsemane is where to go. That is where we find that the Lord of the world, the one to whom is now committed all authority (28:18), has been there before us."[8]

The Fifth Question

The fifth question is, *why did Jesus pray?* Does it ever strike you as odd to so often find in the Gospels the second person of the Trinity praying? Jesus prayed because he was/is fully human[9] and because he felt, at this crucial point in his earthly ministry, that he needed to pray.

One summer my family spent a week in Clear Lake, Iowa. Half of our time we spent in the water—whether in the lake or the pool. One morning I swam with the kids while Emily took a break. In the afternoon Emily swam with the kids while I took a break. So that afternoon I was poolside, but in regular clothes, reading a book in the shade. Charlotte, then four years old, was swimming in the shallow end. She was throwing one of those floating noodles in front of her and then swimming toward it. Suddenly I noticed that she stopped swimming. She somehow couldn't reach the noodle and now was nearly motionless in the pool. She was in an upright position, simply moving her hands slowly, and she had this look in her eyes of utter despair. She was about to give up and go under the water. She felt helpless. Well, I jumped in, scooped her up, and brought her to safety.

Here in Gethsemane, while it is perhaps difficult for us to imagine, Jesus felt as vulnerable as my little girl, so he cried out to his Father to rescue him. That is difficult for us to imagine because this is the same man who stood up against the religious rulers, made bold claims about himself, miraculously healed and fed multitudes, cast out demons, raised the dead, and taught with such great authority. But here Jesus seems like Superman with kryptonite tied around his neck. The mighty man is so weak. Ah, but that's just it. Jesus is not a superman. He is a man. And the moment we forget the full humanity of

Jesus is the moment we Christians embrace the spirit of antichrist. In 1 John 4:2, 3 John says bluntly, "By this you know the Spirit of God: every spirit that confesses that Jesus Christ has come in the flesh [a real human] is from God, and every spirit that does not confess Jesus is not from God. This is the spirit of the antichrist."

It is difficult for us to imagine Jesus depressed and weak because we have seen his power and authority. But I fear it is also difficult for us because we undervalue his true and full humanity, to accept that "Jesus' divinity chose to share humanity *completely*."[10] In Gethsemane there is no diluting his humanness. And thank God for that because Jesus' humanness is essential to our salvation. "What was not assumed was not redeemed" is how the Cappadocian father Gregory of Nazianzum worded it.[11] The argument is: if Jesus was not truly and fully human—in body, mind, emotions, etc.—then he could not stand in our place as our substitute for sin and as our representative before the Father. How true. Jesus' true humanity is something for us to truly ponder and appreciate.

The Sixth Question

The sixth question is, *how did Jesus pray?* First, note his posture. Verse 39 says that "he fell on his face and prayed." That is a posture of submission. It is not how I pray most often or very often. Yet now, with Jesus lying facedown before me in this text, I wonder if I sometimes should. Hebrews 5:7, 8 records, "In the days of his flesh, Jesus offered up prayers and supplications, with loud cries and tears, to him who was able to save him from death, and he was heard because of his reverence. Although he was a son, he learned obedience through what he suffered." I wonder if we should learn such obedience and reverence for God through suffering, the kind of suffering that affects the posture of our praying. Jesus prayed face flat down.

Second, note his petitions. All three prayers begin with the words, "My Father." I say all three because in 26:44 we are told that Jesus prayed "the same words again." All three prayers are the same petitions with slight progress in them.[12] By progress I mean that Jesus moves in the first petition from "if it be possible, let this cup pass from me; nevertheless, not as I will, but as you will" (v. 39) to "if this cannot pass unless I drink it, your will be done" (v. 42). He moves from a near meltdown to a firm resolution. In both petitions Jesus never questions God or God's will—why this plan, why me, why now? Instead he becomes an embodiment of much of what he taught his disciples to pray: "Our Father in heaven, hallowed be your name. Your kingdom come, your will be done . . ." (6:9, 10b). This is not a Stoic's prayer but a Son's prayer. Jesus was "no Socrates [*Phaedo* 58E], drinking the poison and telling his friends to stop crying because he was going to a much better life."[13] Jesus' disposition is that of the refrain of Psalms 42, 43, "Why are you cast down, O my soul, and why are you in turmoil within me?" (42:5, 11, 43:5), but his actual prayer is the Lord's Prayer. Yes, the Lord Jesus prays the Lord's Prayer, minus the part about seeking forgiveness of debts. He had no debts, trespasses, or sins (cf. Hebrews 4:15).

Third, note the period of prayer. After Jesus found the three sleeping after his first session of prayer, he rebuked them all through Peter (v. 40; note that), saying, "So, could you not watch with me one hour?" From Jesus' rebuke we learn that praying for "one hour"—whether it referred to sixty minutes or simply a period of time that lasted about an hour—was "not a long time" by his standards.[14] Since Jesus prayed three times and three times returned to sleepy disciples, it is safe to say he prayed a long time—more than an hour for sure, likely two or three hours.

Again Jesus models the praying life to his disciples both then and now: he prayed standing and on his face; he prayed short and long prayers; he prayed during the day and at night; he prayed alone and with others; he prayed his set daily prayers, and he prayed off the cuff when he was depressed and desperate; he prayed with reverence and yet with childlike trust in God's will for his life; and he prayed by pouring out his petition and then accepting God's "no" without grumbling and complaining. Let us imitate the Christ.

The Seventh Question

The seventh question is, *what is the cup?* If you are sleeping, now is the time to wake up. Wake up. Watch. Pray. Listen. When Jesus prayed for those hours, he prayed about the removal of some cup. The cup is stated explicitly in verse 39 ("My Father, if it be possible, let this cup pass from me") and implicitly in verse 42 ("My Father, if this cannot pass unless I drink it, your will be done"). The cup refers to his awful sufferings and death.[15] He knows he has to die and how he will die, and he fears dying by crucifixion.[16] But there is more to it than that. It's the kind of death he will die that has him sweating. In verse 45 Jesus says of himself that he is "betrayed into the hands of sinners." Also he speaks in that same verse of his hour—"the hour"—having arrived. "The hour" he refers to is broadly speaking "the last part of Jesus' ministry,"[17] but more narrowly the climax of that ministry ("the most decisive moment in human history")—his death on the cross.[18]

In 27:46 we read, "And about the ninth hour Jesus cried out with a loud voice, saying, 'Eli, Eli, lema sabachthani?' that is, 'My God, my God, why have you forsaken me?'" Here is the theological connection from Gethsemane to Golgotha: in Gethsemane what Jesus fears more than anything is the silence of God and the separation from God his Father. How can there be silence? How can there be separation? The answer is hinted at in 8:17, where Matthew quotes Isaiah 53:4, "He took our illnesses and bore our diseases," more directly stated by Jesus in 20:28: "the Son of Man came . . . to give his life as a ransom for many," in other words, to pour out his blood "for many for the forgiveness of sins" (26:28). How are sins forgiven? Jesus became sin for us, and in Jesus' becoming sin there was some inexplicable yet unavoidable silence and separation from the Father. Why? Because Jesus, in drinking the cup, became on our behalf the object of God's judgment for sin.

There is great mystery here as well as irony. In Isaiah 51 "the cup" represents the cup of God's wrath (Isaiah 51:17, 22). Likewise in Jeremiah 25, the cup is "the wine of [God's] wrath" (see Jeremiah 25:15–28). In the prophets the evil nations—Edom, Babylonia, etc.—drink the cup due to their sin.[19] But here it is holy Jesus who drinks the cup *for the nations*. Another mysterious irony relates to the title "Son of Man" (v. 45). In Daniel the Son of Man is a future figure who is supposed to come to judge sinners.[20] But here Jesus, as the self-professed Son of Man, has come to be judged by sinners. It's all very inexplicable, ironic, interesting. Breathtaking!

Why is Jesus so sorrowful and troubled? Why is he on his face? Why is he crying out for hours? Why is the one who came into the world to die so fearful of his death? The colossal burden that "bowed down the heart of Jesus was the weight of the sin of the world." The Greek Litany calls it the "unknown sufferings of Christ." And that's right. His sufferings at Gethsemane and Golgotha are unknown to us. We cannot conceive "the degree of suffering, both mentally and bodily, which an entirely sinless person like our Lord would endure in bearing the sin of all mankind," having "our guilt imputed to him," becoming a curse for us, "delivered up for our trespasses" (Romans 4:25).[21] *Ecce homo*—"Behold the man!" (John 19:5); *Ecce agnus Dei qui tollit peccatum mundi*—"Behold, the Lamb of God, who takes away the sin of the world!" (John 1:29).

In his book *King Solomon*, Phil Ryken recounts a story by Robert Coleman:

> It is the story of a little boy whose sister needed a blood transfusion. She was suffering from the same disease that the boy himself had survived two years earlier. The doctor explained that her only chance of recovery was to receive a blood transfusion from someone else who had conquered the same disease. Since the two children shared the same rare blood type, her brother was the ideal donor.

> "Would you give your blood to Mary?" the doctor asked. Johnny hesitated at first, but with his lower lip trembling he finally said, "Sure, for my sister."
>
> Soon the children were wheeled into the hospital room—Mary, pale and thin; Johnny, robust and healthy. Neither one of them spoke, but when their eyes met, Johnny grinned. His smile faded as the nurse inserted the needle into his arm and he watched the blood flow through the tube. When the ordeal was almost over, Johnny's shaky voice broke the silence. "Doctor," he said, "when do I die?"
>
> Only then did the doctor realize why Johnny had hesitated and why his lip had trembled when he agreed to donate his blood: he thought the doctor was asking for all of it! Yet out of love for his sister, he was willing to give it.

Now there is a subtle but significant difference between Johnny and Jesus. The boy was willing to die but didn't understand what was happening. Jesus was willing to die but fully understood what was about to happen.[22] He was about to drink damnation dry. As Charles Spurgeon said:

> The whole of the punishment of his people was distilled into one cup; no [mere] mortal lip might give it so much as a solitary sip. When he put it to his own lips, it was so bitter, he well nigh spurned it: "Let this cup pass from me." But his love for his people was so strong [and I'll add: his commitment to the Father's will was so steadfast], that he took the cup in both his hands, and
>
> "At one tremendous draught of love,
> He drank damnation dry."[23]

That was the cup, and that is what Jesus did for God's sake and ours.

The Eighth Question

There is a final question, one that returns us to the start of the sermon and the theme of perception. The eighth question is, *who drank the cup?* Jesus, of course, drank the cup. But who is Jesus? We have already hit on his humanity. Jesus is a through and through human with flesh and blood and pain and tears like you and me. Let's finish by diving into his divinity. I'm not providing this balance so you will remain orthodox in your Chalcedonian Christology, convinced that "our Lord Jesus Christ" is "at once complete in Godhead and complete in manhood, truly God and truly man,"[24] or to use Paul's statement of Christology, "For in him the whole fullness of deity dwells bodily" (Colossians 2:9). Rather, I finish with this point because Jesus finishes with it: "See, the hour is at hand, and the Son of Man is betrayed into the hands of sinners"

(26:45). Jesus calls himself "the Son of Man," a title that becomes Jesus' favorite title to bestow upon himself the closer and closer he gets to Calvary. What's with the title? What does it mean? At first reading you might think "Son of Man" refers to Jesus' humanity. He is the son of humans, we might say. But that is not what "Son of Man" means here. I've said this before but I shall say it again and again. With the title "Son of Man" Jesus is connecting himself to this divine king of Daniel 7:13, 14 who has an everlasting kingdom, who comes with the clouds of Heaven, and who presents himself before "the Ancient of Days" (God Almighty).

So, who drank the cup? The Son of Man drank it. Jesus highlights his divinity. He further highlights his divinity and his unique and intimate relationship with God with his language, "My Father."[25] He is the only, the unique, and the obedient Son of the Father. That is why he prays, "My Father." He teaches the church to pray, "Our Father," and he himself prays, "My Father." Fifty-three times in Matthew's Gospel (compared to only six times in Mark), Jesus calls God his "Father."[26] He is God's Son.

Who drank the cup? I summarize it this way: Jesus, the Son of Man and the Son of God. And to that theological truth—that realest of realities, I could call it—what should be our response? How do we respond to Gethsemane? Praise! Adoration! Glory! Honor! The closing words to the hymn "Fairest Lord Jesus" come to mind and should stick in our minds:

> Beautiful Savior! Lord of the nations!
> *Son of God and Son of Man!*
> Glory and honor, praise, adoration,
> Now and forevermore be Thine.

80

A Sovereign Scriptural Plan

MATTHEW 26:47–56

HAVE YOU EVER RECEIVED an encouraging note from a friend that is so uplifting that it's humbling? I received such a note one October for pastor's appreciation month. Below is a portion of it:

> My heart really *overflows* with appreciation when I think of you. In your vision casting for New Covenant . . . my love for the church was rekindled. In your consistent pointing to Jesus and marveling at Him in each sermon, my apathetic thought that "my best years with the Lord were behind me" has been drowned by ever increasing love for my Lord! When I think back to the hunger in my soul during college to hear more about Jesus in church, and then I think about how I have been fed on three years of Christ-exalting preaching under your pulpit—I AM THANKFUL!
>
> I come on Sundays filled with anticipation for understanding the Word better and loving Jesus more. I am grateful for how well you know the passage you preach and the people you are preaching to! You anticipate our questions and confusions, and trace out how we can apply it. I am grateful for the clarity and beauty you preach with—no jargon, no tactics, no posturing. You hold out the Word to us in a way that unveils its truth and beauty and power. I always feel a sinking feeling inside me when I realize you are wrapping up. I am never ready for you to end. I thank God for calling and equipping you—and for building us up through you![1]

What is the purpose of a Sunday morning sermon? My philosophy is simple. It is to *declare the excellencies of Jesus Christ*. The language is borrowed from the Apostle Peter, whom both the Apostle Matthew and I have been hard on in the past few chapters, and we will be hard on him in this sermon as well. In 1 Peter 2:9, fully restored and Spirit-inspired Peter writes to the church, "But you are a chosen race, a royal priesthood, a holy nation, a people for his own possession, that you may proclaim the excellencies of him who called you out of darkness into his marvelous light."

Throughout the Gospel of Matthew we have seen Jesus as a heroic figure. However, in the previous chapter, as the tragedy of Golgotha came into better focus in Gethsemane, we saw Jesus as both the hero and the victim, or more accurately phrased, the hero by becoming the victim. In what Dorothy Sayers called "the greatest drama ever staged,"[2] we see a hero unlike any hero and yet so likable. He is so fascinating, captivating, and even alluring. He is someone I find easy to marvel at in each sermon.

I invite you to join me in my marveling at him. For that's what Matthew (again and always) wants us to do. In this text he highlights the light of Jesus Christ by contrasting him with the darkness of old and new Israel. By "old Israel" I mean the religious rulers ("the chief priests and the elders of the people" mentioned in verse 47 and "the high priest" referenced via his servant in verse 51) and the crowd, those "with swords and clubs" (v. 47) who come to arrest Jesus. By "new Israel" I mean the church, embryonic in the Twelve, and thus including "all the disciples" mentioned in verse 56 as well as Peter and Judas singled out in verses 51 and 48, 49 respectfully (or not so respectfully). There are six characters in this drama—(1) the chief priest and elders, (2) the crowd, (3) Judas, (4) Peter, (5) all the disciples, and (6) Jesus—and only one looks like "the light of the world" (John 8:12; 9:5; cf. Matthew 5:14). Other than Jesus, a great darkness covers the characters. Set against the black failure of old Israel (the Jews) and new Israel (the church), the white light of true Israel (Jesus) shines.

Failure of Old Israel (Jews) and New Israel (Church)

Before we get to that light, let's first look at the darkness of old and new Israel. As was just noted, the character of Christ is set apart by contrasting him with the other characters. The first contrast is that of the Jews. Representative of the whole people is the "great crowd" sent "from the chief priests and the elders *of the people*." The crowd comes out at night to arrest Jesus. Behind it all, however, is the religious establishment, the highest-ranking member being the high priest. As noted earlier, the high priest's servant is there. He is the chap who has some cosmetic surgery done to him in verse 51. He is there because his boss sent him. We learn this boss's name in verse 57—Caiaphas. Jesus will soon stand on trial before him. After our Lord will talk about "the Son of Man [being] seated at the right hand of Power and coming on the clouds of heaven"

(v. 64), Caiaphas will tear his robe, cry out "blasphemy," and call for a specific verdict, which he gets—"They answered, 'He deserves death'" (vv. 65, 66).

Jesus "came to his own, and his own people did not receive him" (John 1:11). That is the dark reality we see in our text and the next and the next and the next. It is the crowd, with the prodding of their leaders, that will cry out "Let him be crucified!" (27:22, 23). And here it is the crowd with their swords and clubs—expecting a fight from the temple table turner?—who are there to do the will of the cowardly clergy. One wonders what happened to the crowd. The people had been as pro-Jesus as we are pro-life. What turned their vote in the opposite direction? Last time I looked in Matthew "the crowd" was "astonished at his teaching" (22:33) and spreading "their cloaks on the road" when Jesus rode into town (21:8). Now they are armed "with swords and clubs," treating him like he is an insurrectionist or terrorist. It makes no sense to Jesus: "Have you come out as against a robber, with swords and clubs to capture me? Day after day I sat in the temple teaching [unarmed in broad daylight in a sedentary position for days], and you did not seize me" (v. 55). It should make no sense to us. Sin so often is senseless.

Old Israel rejects their Messiah. But so does new Israel—the twelve apostles. Verse 56 ends the scene with this dark drapery pulled across the stage: "Then all the disciples left him and fled." At "the *beginning* of the Gospel . . . [they] 'left' (*aphienai*) their nets to follow Jesus (4:20); now near the *end* they 'leave' (*aphienai,* the same verb) to find safety."[3] Jesus is forsaken by his fleeing followers. "Like the scapegoat on the Day of Atonement, Jesus will have to go to his destiny alone."[4] The solitude of Jesus in Gethsemane somehow gets more solitary.

The Lost Sheep

But before all the sheep scatter, Matthew's camera lens closes in on two significant sheep—a lost one (Peter) and a black one (Judas). We'll leave Judas for last, for in this case the last shall be last. First look with me at Peter. I say "Peter" based on John's version of the story. I know that Matthew might be up to something important by not telling us the name of the man who "drew his sword and struck the servant of the high priest and cut off his ear" (v. 51), but it is not realistic for those who have four Gospels before them to pretend that we don't know that Peter was the swordsman and Malchus was the slave. John's record—"Then Simon Peter, having a sword, drew it and struck the high priest's servant and cut off his right ear. (The servant's name was Malchus)" (John 18:10)—makes that difficult to do. Luke adds that Jesus healed the man's ear (Luke 22:51). I'll leave that detail alone. We'll leave the ear on the ground as Matthew does. No need to borrow all our information from other Gospels.

So Peter was the swordsman. Okay then, first things first: what was Peter doing with a sword in the first place? It is "unexpected and unexplained."[5] Perhaps it was for self-defense.[6] Perhaps it was normal (cf. Luke 22:36–38). Maybe the rough-and-tumble fishermen of Galilee were always packing heat. Who knows? I don't. I also don't know why—viewing the odds—Peter would have raised his sword in the first place. Did he really expect to win the battle? Perhaps he was simply keeping his word, "Even if I must die with you, I will not deny you!" (26:35). Or perhaps he thought Jesus would be forced—like Jesus was when Peter began into sink the water—to lend a supernatural hand.

Now before we lower Jesus' hammer on Peter's sword, let's at least note that Peter was one brave soldier. We are not told that Andrew or Thomas or Bartholomew drew their weapons, or that Philip or Matthew or Thaddaeus tried to shield Jesus. What were they all doing? Shaking in their boots? Lacing up their running shoes? I like to imagine the sons of thunder (James and John) saying, "Lord, shall we strike with the sword?" (Luke 22:49) ten seconds before they are hiding behind the biggest olive tree. In Matthew's Gospel, Peter alone was courageous. He was always the most courageous. He was the only one to get out of the boat to walk on water. He was the only one to boldly confess Jesus as the Christ. And he was the only one to enter into the courtyard of Caiaphas's house. That took courage! The Caiaphas's courtyard bit especially took courage, for don't you think Malchus might be there? He works there. And don't you think Malchus might like a chance to go toe-to-toe with Peter without Jesus around to stop the fight?

Peter's courage aside, Jesus isn't so pleased with courageous Cephas. Our Lord's last pre-Easter teaching in Matthew is reserved for Peter, and it is not a pat on the back but a sword to the heart (cf. Revelation 2:12, 16). It's a sharp rebuke.

> Then Jesus said to him, "Put your sword back into its place. For all who take the sword will perish by the sword. Do you think that I cannot appeal to my Father, and he will at once send me more than twelve legions of angels?" (vv. 52, 53)

Matthew vaguely describes the swordsman as "one of those who were *with Jesus*" (v. 51), but Jesus is saying that the one who is really *with me* is not for this. Jesus' sword has two edges. First, Peter either underestimates or seeks to misappropriate Jesus' power, for our Lord says to him, "Do you think that I cannot appeal to my Father, and he will at once send me more than twelve legions of angels?" (v. 53). Does Jesus believe in angels? Oh yes. Does Jesus believe in his own guardian angel? Oh no. Rather, he believes in his own guardian *angels*! In the first century the Roman army had about twenty-five legions. A legion was comprised of 5,600 soldiers.[7] Jesus claimed that he had immediate access ("at once") to "more than twelve legions of angels" (v. 53). That is an enormous angelic army!

And when you think "angels" don't think of the cute Precious Moments version. Rather think about the angel who was sent to lead the Israelites out of Egypt (Numbers 20:16), and the angel who helped "blot . . . out . . . the Amorites and the Hittites and the Perizzites and the Canaanites, the Hivites and the Jebusites" (Exodus 23:23), and the angel who "struck down 185,000 in the camp of the Assyrians" (2 Kings 19:35), and the angel who protected Shadrach, Meshach, and Abednego in the fiery furnace (Daniel 3:28), and the angel who saved Daniel by shutting "the lions' mouths" (Daniel 6:22), and the angel who "seized the dragon, that ancient serpent, who is the devil and Satan, and bound him for a thousand years, and threw him into the pit, and shut it and sealed it over him" (Revelation 20:1–3). Those are just six angels in Jesus' arsenal. Think what 70,000–72,000 angels like that might do to a mob of mere mortals! Oh, Jesus has the power. He makes that quite clear. Who needs Peter's sword when you have the angels from the Lord, or, to paraphrase Jerome, "Who needs defense from twelve apostles on earth when one has twelve legions of angels in heaven?"[8]

First, Peter underestimates Jesus' power, or at the very least he misunderstands the timing of that power. Second, Peter still(!) misunderstands the mission and thus the means of the mission, for our Lord said to him, "Put your sword back into its place. For all who take the sword will perish by the sword" (v. 52). If you want to know what Jesus thinks about Christians bombing abortion clinics or crusading against the Muslims, wonder no more. Perhaps there is even something symbolic about the servant's *ear* being cut off,[9] for where Christians have used violence to promote (or protect?) Christianity, those regions of the world are somehow least receptive to the gospel. Having no ears, they cannot hear!

So here it is as if Jesus says, "Listen, Peter, I don't care if the servant of the high priest in Jerusalem uses a sword to do his master's will. The servants of this high priest in Heaven will not use such means." It is not that Jesus is merely advocating again his own law of nonresistance—"do not resist the one who is evil" (5:39). That is an under-reading of the text. And it is not that Jesus is advocating pacifism. That is an over-reading of the text. Jesus is pro-government—"render to Caesar the things that are

Caesar's" (22:21)—and one of the things that is Caesar's is the wielding of the sword for the promotion of peace and justice, for the punishment of wrongdoing, and for the prevention of riots, lootings, and anarchy. Read Romans 13:1–7 (cf. 1 Peter 2:13–17). Note also here in Matthew that Jesus doesn't say, "What's with the sword? Throw that weapon away! Christians aren't part of the NRA!" Instead he tells him to "put [his] sword back into its place" (v. 52). There is a place for the sword. That place is self-defense. That place is just war. That place is in the hands of a legitimate and properly functioning government with its legitimate and properly functioning armed forces and police force.

Jesus' mission is at the center of his rebuke. His mission is the cross. "Peter, stop resisting the cross of Christ. Put down your sword." Perhaps Peter is not personally named by Matthew because the evangelist wants all disciples of Jesus—then and now and forever—to heed Jesus' warning. If the message is the cross, the means ought never to be the sword. "Sword" and "swords" is used six times in our text, but Jesus desires that his church use it zero times. The sword is never to be used in propagating the gospel. Never. A violent church is a dead church. A cutting-off-the-ears church is a stabbed-in-the-heart church.

The Black Sheep

Finally we come to Judas. I wish we could color this page black for effect. For Judas, you see and you already know, is one black sheep. But he is a cool cat, too. He somehow got a hearing with the top dogs of the day and then actually got them to give him some cash for one kiss. Now, it's the kiss itself that makes Judas's pitch-black heart somehow blacker. Look with me again at verses 47–50 and tremble before this darkness:

> While he [Jesus] was still speaking, Judas came, one of the twelve, and with him a great crowd with swords and clubs, from the chief priests and the elders of the people. Now the betrayer had given them a sign, saying, "The one I will kiss is the man; seize him." And he came up to Jesus at once and said, "Greetings, Rabbi!" And he kissed him. Jesus said to him, "Friend, do what you came to do." Then they came up and laid hands on Jesus and seized him.

Notice that Judas is called "one of the twelve" in verse 47 and yet "the betrayer" in verse 48. Those two titles are there to heighten the irony and showcase the diabolic nature of his crime. We are to say with our arms raised in shock and protest, "One of the Twelve betrayed him?"

Next notice what Judas says and does to Jesus. He *says*, "Greetings, Rabbi!" (v. 49). Why not point to Jesus from a safe distance and whisper to the guard next to him, "Yeah, that's the guy"? But to come face-to-face with Jesus and then say to him, "Greetings, Rabbi!" which can also be translated, "Hello there, Rabbi!" or worse "Rejoice, Rabbi" or even "*Shalom*, Rabbi"[10] while two seconds before you have said to the crowd, "The one I kiss is the man; grab him!" (v. 48, Bruner's translation)[11] is just plain wicked. The "rabbi" bit is bad enough. Jesus is *not* his teacher anymore. Whatever Judas learned from Jesus—about money, honesty, etc.—he has unlearned.[12]

If the false greeting is not enough, what Judas *does* to Jesus is doubly wicked. "Judas twists a greeting of friendship . . . into a death sign."[13] He gives Jesus a kiss.[14] Was it a kiss on the forehead, like a mother would give a sick child? Was it a kiss on the cheek like men in many parts of the world then and today give as a sign of comradeship, peace, well-being, even safety? Or was it a kiss on the lips, also a traditional sign of friendship, but certainly a more intimate one? In Giotto's famous fresco of the scene, Judas kisses Jesus on the lips with his arms around Jesus' shoulders. It's a very intimate pose. In that painting, circling Jesus and Judas a violent battle is brewing. The artist depicts all this motion and commotion. Meanwhile, at the center there is this still life. Giotto has somehow painted a pause in the action for us to see Judas's affectionate evil, his unholy kiss of death.[15]

In Luke's version, after Judas kisses Jesus, Jesus says, "Judas, would you betray the Son of Man with a kiss?" (Luke 22:48). There is a sense of surprise in his voice. And there should be a sense of surprise also in our eyes. A kiss, Judas? Really? How insincere! What wickedness, "inner decadence,"[16] and "false friendship."[17] Hypocrite of hypocrites! It may have been dark, and Judas somehow needed to signal to the armed crowd the marked man, but a kiss? This is the darkest darkness!

But then there is Jesus. What does Jesus say to all this? It is the shortest speech he will give: "Friend, do what you came to do" (v. 50). By calling him "friend" is Jesus mocking him? He might be.[18] Jesus is not opposed to egging on his enemies. But here I don't think that is the case. Rather I think the word "friend" is sincere and sad, as in the sense, "Do you really want to go through with this after all we have been through together?"[19] Jesus still loves this "one of the twelve" he handpicked. Jesus must and does love his enemy. Does he wish that he like the father of the prodigal son might embrace Judas with the kiss of forgiveness, reconciliation, love? Yes. But Judas's kiss lingers on our Lord's lips reminding him of all the betrayals and infidelities he has come to give his life for, even our betrayals and infidelities.

We All like Sheep

Total depravity is what is depicted here. I have said before that the Gospels, as a genre, don't define or explain a doctrine; they show it to us. For example, in Matthew's Gospel *faith* looks like the Roman centurion coming to Jesus, believing that Jesus can cure his servant from a distance and with a word. What then does the doctrine of *total depravity* look like? Or, less Calvinistic but no less Pauline, what does Paul's indictment—"'None is righteous, no, not one' . . . for all have sinned and fall short of the glory of God" (Romans 3:10, 23)—look like? It looks like our text. Whether we call it "total depravity" or "total undependability,"[20] what is clearly illustrated in our text is sheep after sheep going astray while the Lamb of God is led away to the slaughter (Isaiah 53:6, 7). God is about to place the "iniquity of us all . . . on him" (Isaiah 53:6b). *All* have gone astray . . . *all* our sin was laid on him. *Thank you, Jesus!*

From the trial scenes to the crucifixion itself, don't miss that everybody (but Jesus) sins and falls short of the glory of God—Jews, Gentiles, and even inner-circle disciples.[21] There are the "big and little disciples (Peter and Judas), big and little Israel (Sanhedrin and people), and big and little Rome (Pilate and the soldiers)," and at the cross itself again Gentiles and Jews (the disciples still hiding) stroll by to shake their heads at Jesus, the colossal failure of a Christ.[22] Ah, but then as it is now "against this awful backdrop of infidelity, Jesus' fidelity looms high and lonely, and that is the point: amid all human failure, there is one who is *totally dependable*."[23]

Fulfillment by True Israel (Jesus)

The portrait Matthew has painted for us is that of darkness and light. We have looked into the darkness—the picture of the failure of old Israel (the Jews) and new Israel (the church). Next we look into the light—the picture of the fulfillment of true Israel (Jesus).

Each week I'm indebted to Bible commentators. Studying the Bible on my own has much benefit. Studying the Bible in community, however, has a far greater benefit. Reading alongside and interacting with commentators is the ultimate Bible study. I'm especially grateful to William Barclay for his two points on this passage. The two points are as follows:

1. Jesus' death was *by his own choice*.
2. Jesus chose to die because he knew that it was *the purpose of God*.[24]

That second point hits on the theme of the fulfillment of Scripture, which is the more obvious theme. The first point, however, hits on this less obvious but no less important theme of Jesus' authority throughout his betrayal. Let us examine this first point first.

By His Own Choice

To find this theme of Jesus' authority, it is helpful to read through the whole passage again, with the question in mind, who's in charge? The answer that comes to the surface again and again is Jesus. Let me show you what I have seen and what you too should see.

Look again and more carefully this time at verse 47: "While he [Jesus] was still speaking, Judas came . . ." Stop there. That's an interesting way to start a scene and phrase a sentence. Another commentator, one of my best commentator friends—Bruner, not Barclay—quotes one of his best commentator friends—Gnilka (we are all in this together) saying, "The power of Jesus' Word is pictured here: it is 'as though Judas was *drawn* here by the speech of Jesus.'"[25]

Well, I don't know if I fully agree with that observation. But I also don't fully disagree. Perhaps that's right. What is certainly right is that the power of Jesus' word is on display throughout our text. Other than a few words from Judas—only two to Jesus (v. 49)—the rest of the time it is Jesus who doles out the commands and corrections—Jesus to Judas, "Friend, do what you came to do" (v. 50); Jesus to Peter, "Put your sword back into its place" (v. 52); and Jesus to the crowd, "Have you come out as against a robber, with swords and clubs to capture me?" (v. 55a). If you just look at Jesus' short speeches here and ask the question, who's in charge? the answer is obvious. Jesus is in charge.

Now come again to verses 48–50 and see three signs of Jesus' authority demonstrated in his intentional inactivity. First, notice that Jesus didn't resist the kiss. He submitted himself to that shameless act.[26] He could have recoiled and stepped back, but he didn't. Second, notice that Jesus didn't resist arrest. The end of verse 50 reads, "Then they [the crowd] came up and laid hands on Jesus and seized him." Throughout this Gospel only Jesus laid his hands on others—to heal them. But here he allows the sick in soul to lay their hands on him. Why? Well, to heal them in a far different way. Lo, he goes "into the hands of sinners" (cf. 17:22; 26:45) to open wide his hands for the salvation of sinners. Jesus has the power to fight. He couldn't make that point clearer than in verse 53. With one whistle the heavenly hosts are at his disposal. But he stops the angels' surge just as he stops Peter's sword because he is here using his power and authority to freely and willingly give up his power and authority.

Jesus never needed to journey to Jerusalem for the Passover. Having come, he could have played by the religious leaders' rules. What's with "his deliberate policy of magnificent defiance"?[27] He could have gone easy on the table turning, easy on the Son of Man language, easy on the Christ claims, and easy on riding into town like King David! Even here in Gethsemane, why not slip away into the dark or literally run for the hills when you first see an army of torches and lanterns marching up the hill? You see, on this Good Friday (it is after midnight now) Jesus has chosen to give the world its greatest good. Every step of the way to Calvary the light gets brighter and brighter and clearer and clearer. "Jesus died, not because men killed him, but because he chose to die."[28]

The Purpose of God

Jesus' death was *by his own choice*. That is our first sub-point. Our second is: Jesus chose to die because he knew that it was *the purpose of God*. Barclay writes, "He took this way [that is, not the way of violent revolt, but the way of sacrificial love] because it was the very thing that had been foretold by the prophets."[29] In verses 52–54 Jesus said,

> Put your sword back into its place. For all who take the sword will perish by the sword. Do you think that I cannot appeal to my Father, and he will at once send me more than twelve legions of angels? But how then should *the Scriptures be fulfilled*, that it must be so?

Jesus reiterates that point of purpose in verses 55, 56:

> At that hour Jesus said to the crowds, "Have you come out as against a robber, with swords and clubs to capture me? Day after day I sat in the temple teaching, and you did not seize me. But all this has taken place that *the Scriptures of the prophets might be fulfilled*."

As we come now to the end of Matthew's Gospel we are reminded of how it began. In chapters 1—4 we heard that familiar phrase, "this took place to fulfill what the Lord had spoken by the prophet. . . ." There Matthew tells us of the fulfillments; here Jesus does. There from Jesus' birth (1:21) to his baptism (3:15) the Scriptures cited are specific; here there is this broadening inclusiveness. It's as if Jesus says, "Take all that the prophets wrote—converge all their sayings together—and you have me and my passion narrative."[30] What Jesus said in 5:17—"Do not think that I have come to abolish the Law or the Prophets; I have not come to abolish them but to fulfill them"—he is now acting out. What Paul would write later about Jesus, Jesus would have applauded: "all the promises of God find their Yes in him" (2 Corinthians 1:20a). The Son of Man of Daniel (Daniel 7:13, 14)? Yes. The new covenant of Jeremiah (Jeremiah 31:31)? Yes. The Suffering Servant of Isaiah (Isaiah 52:13—53:12)? Yes. The forsaken and mocked king of Psalm 22? Yes.

Jesus resolves to go to the cross because he knows it is the will of God. He knows it is the will of God because he knows his Bible. And his Bible speaks of him—the Messiah—and his sufferings as the climax of the script.[31]

That's a Lot of Information

At a staff meeting, my church's pastoral staff was discussing the length of sermons related to the average attention span. (We determined that we are all very proud of our congregation.) My associate Andrew asked me if I ever had someone tell me that my sermons were too long. I said, "Yes, I have." At the first church I pastored full-time, after a forty-minute sermon a slick businessman told me, "If you can't say it in twenty minutes, then you don't know what you're selling," or something to that effect. I also had an older gentleman sometimes come up to me afterwards with a bewildered look on his face and say, "Thank you, Pastor, for that sermon." Then he would pause and give his kind rebuke. "That . . . was a lot of information."

This chapter shared a lot of information. What should we do with all this information? Let's marvel at Jesus—that's always a good application. Let's love Jesus more—that's always another good application. But the one application I want you to get from this chapter has to do with seeing the story of Scripture unfold in the person of Jesus. Too often we remove the story from the Bible and collapse "the gospel . . . into the abstract, de-storified points in the Plan of Salvation."[32] *God is holy. You are a sinner. God loved you so much he sent Jesus. Believe.* That's true, but that's not how the Gospels present the gospel or how Jesus shares it. Jesus roots his whole ministry in the whole story of Israel—its prophets, priests, and kings, its saints and sinners and Scriptures. As Scot McKnight notes, "The Story of Jesus Christ, then, isn't a story that came out of nowhere like the Book of Mormon, and it isn't a timeless set of ideas, as with Plato's philosophical writings. The story of Jesus Christ is locked into one people, one history, and one Scripture: it makes sense only as it follows and completes the Story of Israel."[33]

So, can we share the gospel without sharing the story of Scripture? How would Jesus answer that question? I think he would say, "No." How would Paul? "No" likewise. In what is the clearest definition of the gospel in the New Testament (cf. Romans 1:1–5),[34] he writes:

> Now I would remind you, brothers, of *the gospel* I preached to you, which you received, in which you stand, and by which you are being saved, if you hold fast to the word I preached to you—unless you believed in vain. For I delivered to you as of first importance what I also received: that Christ died for our sins *in accordance with the Scriptures*, that he was buried, that he was raised on the third day *in accordance with the Scriptures*, and that he appeared to Cephas, then to the twelve. (1 Corinthians 15:1–5)[35]

To Paul, as it was to Jesus, the question, how important is our knowledge of the Old Testament? is as important a question as, how important is evangelism? Without Jesus there is no gospel. Without the Old Testament there is no gospel. Without Jesus fulfilling the Old Testament there is no gospel. What good news do we herald? What light do we bring to the dark world? That Jesus died for our sins, rose again from the dead to grant us eternal life, and will come again in power to make everything right . . . *just like the Hebrew Bible said.* Our gospel is "the saving Story of Israel . . . lived out by [true Israel,] Jesus, who lived, died, was buried, and was exalted to God's right hand" and who will soon come in glory to establish his forever kingdom.[36] So, in light of that Light, repent, believe, be baptized, and receive the forgiveness of sins, the Holy Spirit, and life everlasting. That is our application for today. That is our application for every day because that is the good news of Jesus Christ.

I don't know if I preach with clarity and beauty, as one person once claimed not so long ago. If so, I'll let God get all the glory for the gift. What I do know is that I tried, Sunday after Sunday, to gospel the Gospel of Matthew, knowing that the more people who understand the full story, the more likely they are to marvel, as I do, at Jesus.

81

What Jesus Deserves

MATTHEW 26:57–68

ONE OF THE MOST ENJOYABLE BOOKS I read last year was Carolyn Weber's memoir, *Surprised by Oxford*. It's the story of her conversion to Christ while at Oxford University pursuing her doctorate in Romantic Literature. Shortly before she was converted she began to read the Bible for the first time. Because she was too cheap to buy her own Bible and because she didn't want to be seen with one, she would enter a nearby church, sit in the back, and read the pew Bible. She recalls her findings:

> In this back pew I read the Bible steadily on borrowed pages. I devoured it, just as a best-selling book (which, coincidentally, it always has been). Even the long, monotonous lists. Even the really weird stuff, most of it so unbelievable as to only be true. I have to say I found it the most compelling piece of creative non-fiction I had ever read. If I sat around for thousands of years, I could never come up with what it proposes, let alone how intricately Genesis unfolds toward Revelation. That the supposed Creator of the *entire universe* became a vulnerable baby, born in straw, to a poor girl who claimed to be a virgin and who was betrothed to a guy probably scared out of his wits, but who stood by her anyway. It unwinds and recasts the world and our perception of it: that the Holy Grail is more likely to be the wooden cup of a carpenter than the golden chalice of kings.
>
> *No wonder this stuff causes war,* I thought as I read, *between nations and within each of us*.[1]

In this chapter, as we try to deal seriously and personally with his claims in 26:57–68, I want to discuss the "war" that Christ causes within each of us. However, first I want us to walk through the war of two worldviews that clash in Jesus' trial before the Jewish leadership.

Jesus' trial is ironic. The word *ironic* means something that happens "in the opposite way to what is expected," and this literary device is often used in literature and drama to cause "wry amusement," as the Oxford Dictionary has it, because of these unexpected twists.[2] Well, in Jesus' trial—which begins in verse 59 with the Council gathering in order to find a way to put Jesus "to death" and ends with their verdict in verse 66, "He deserves death"—there is nothing remotely amusing about this miscarriage of justice. That doesn't mean, however, that the whole scene isn't infused with irony.

> The Deliverer in bonds; the Judge attainted; the Prince of Glory scorned; the Holy One condemned for sin; the Son of God as a blasphemer; the Resurrection and the Life sentenced to die![3]

Irony of ironies. It's all irony.

In fact, I find this whole scene so ironic, I've decided to structure my teaching on this text by showing you four ironies.[4]

The First Irony

Before we explore the first irony, let me first explain who Jesus is up against. In verse 57 we are introduced to "Caiaphas the high priest," as well as "the scribes and the elders." Then verse 59 mentions "the chief priests and the whole Council." This "Council" was called the Sanhedrin. You can think of the Sanhedrin as the Jewish "supreme court" over Judea.[5] It was comprised of seventy-one members who were priests, scribes, and elders. The high priest presided over the group. Matthew says that "the whole council" (v. 59) was gathered. He either means all seventy-one, or more likely the quorum needed for a capital punishment trial, which was twenty-three (*m. Sanh.* 7:1). The gathering itself may have merely been an initial hearing or "unofficial interrogation,"[6] with the official trial being held in the temple in the morning (27:1).[7]

When you hear that the Council was comprised of the high priest, chief priests, scribes, and elders, you might think, "Oh, this is a very devout religious group Jesus is up against." Sure, they were all religious, but for many of them, think "religious" in the political sense. The nearest example I find is the clergy of post-Reformation England, where some priests and bishops in the English Church buddied up to the powers that be in order to get powerful posts. Other than the scribes (the Bible experts who were serious about the study of Scripture), the elders were lay leaders who were "mainly rich landowners,"[8] and the priests, including the high priest ("the dominant group" according to Luz),[9] were often from aristocratic families. Josephus, for example, claims that Caiaphas bought the high priesthood from Herod.[10] In other words, he came from money and used that money to buy power.

However Matthew doesn't give us background checks on each of the seventy-one, instead, he only focuses on their corporate falsehood amid the appearance of legality.

> Now the chief priests and the whole council were seeking false testimony against Jesus that they might put him to death, but they found none, though many false witnesses came forward. At last two came forward and said, "This man said, 'I am able to destroy the temple of God, and to rebuild it in three days.'" And the high priest stood up and said, "Have you no answer to make? What is it that these men testify against you?" But Jesus remained silent. And the high priest said to him, "I adjure you by the living God, tell us if you are the Christ, the Son of God." Jesus said to him, "You have said so." (vv. 59–64a)

There are two ironies here. The first irony is: *the Sanhedrin breaks God's Law while Jesus keeps it*. Based on a later Jewish document called the Mishnah (*Sanh.*), we have information on the Sanhedrin's rules for trials. One scholar summarizes:

> All criminal cases must be tried during the daytime and must be completed during the daytime. Criminal cases could not be transacted during the Passover season at all. Only if the verdict was Not Guilty could a case be finished on the day it was begun; otherwise a night must elapse before the pronouncement of the verdict, so that feelings of mercy might have time to arise. Further, no decision of the Sanhedrin was valid unless it met in its own meeting place, the Hall of Hewn Stone in the Temple precincts. All evidence had to be guaranteed by two witnesses separately examined and having no contact with each other. And false witness was punishable by death. . . . Still further, in any trial the process began by the laying before the court of all the evidence of the *innocence* of the accused, before the evidence for his guilt was adduced.[11]

It is difficult to know whether or not these rules were in place during the time of Jesus. If so, it certainly adds to the irony: "in their eagerness to get rid of Jesus," the Sanhedrin broke just about all of their own rules.[12]

However, Matthew's overall focus is on how the Jewish religious leaders "neglected the weightier matters of the law: justice and mercy and faithfulness" (23:23) and how they failed to uphold the ninth commandment, "You shall not bear false witness" (Exodus 20:16). Matthew contrasts the false testimony of the witnesses and the false findings of the court with Jesus' refusal to take an oath and his true confession.

We will come to Christ's confession in a moment. Let me first explain what I mean by Jesus' refusal to take an oath. We are familiar in our system of law of taking an oath before we take the stand. We place our hand on the Bible and answer the question, "Do you promise to tell the whole truth and nothing but the truth, so help you God?" by saying, "I do." Ironically Caiaphas, who paraded false witnesses and true witnesses who don't know what they are talking about before his judicial bench until he heard what he wanted to hear (or at least enough evidence to present a valid case to Rome), asks the only truth-teller in the room—Jesus—to swear by an oath. He pleads with Jesus, "I adjure you *by the living God*, tell us if you are the Christ, the Son of God" (v. 63b). "I adjure you by the living God" is the oath part. The irony is this: Jesus needs no oath to tell the truth. Oaths are only for liars or potential liars (cf. 5:33–37; 23:16–22). Jesus is the perfectly obedient Son of the living God! He was the only obedient Israelite ever. Of all people, Judas has it right when he confesses in 27:4, "I have sinned by betraying innocent blood." Jesus' blood is more innocent than Judas and Caiaphas could have imagined.

Here is where the second irony comes in.

The Second Irony

The second irony is: *the false witnesses who accuse Jesus of claiming that he will destroy the temple and rebuild it in three days provide a true testimony about Jesus' death and resurrection.*[13] Put differently, their accusation, and the Sanhedrin's acceptance of it as a crime, makes Jesus' temple prediction possible. If Jesus isn't sentenced to death, his body as "temple" cannot be destroyed and in three days rebuilt via resurrection!

Until the very last words Jesus says in this trial about the Son of Man—which are quite clear to the Council—it is as though Jesus and those against Jesus are speaking two different languages.[14] I twice traveled to Cuba, and on one of those trips I sat at a dinner party with a man who knew no English. I knew only enough Spanish to make what must have been an interesting conversation to overhear. I couldn't ask for the salt because I didn't know how to in Spanish, but I could say, "It is hot. My name is Douglas." Similarly, it was as though the two witnesses who came forward to accuse Jesus of saying, "I am able to destroy the temple of God, and to rebuild it in three days" (v. 61) were speaking a different language than Jesus. Perhaps these two witnesses saw Jesus overturn the tables in the temple (21:12, 13) and heard him say, "Destroy this temple, and in three days I will raise it up" (John 2:19). They took that to mean that Jesus was seeking to somehow knock down the stones and pillars of

Herod's Temple. Jesus, on the other hand, "was speaking about the temple of his body" (John 2:21). They were talking two different languages.

To Rome the Sanhedrin's charge of blasphemy held no weight, but a charge of desecrating a holy place would have been viewed as a capital offense.[15] Moreover, any action smelling of sedition was enough for Rome's judicial tail to wag. To Pontus Pilate Jesus' crime would be the political threat of claiming to be a king when under Roman jurisdiction only Caesar is Lord. Thus, this temple testimony against him was grounds enough to kill him. So can we say that Jesus was killed for a misunderstood metaphor? I suppose we could say it that way. But of course we know it was more than a metaphor when Rome itself destroyed the temple in AD 70 and when Jesus likewise allowed the Romans to destroy his temple, his body. And we know it is more than a metaphor when that truest tabernacle of God rose again on the third day!

The Third Irony

The third irony is: *the Sanhedrin mocks Jesus' claim to be the Christ—King David's King, if I can put it that way, while their violent actions begin to fulfill in Jesus Isaiah's prophecies about the Suffering Servant.*[16]

Let's return to Jesus' silence and his confession. In verse 63a, after Jesus has been accused of seeking to destroy the old temple and rebuild a new one, we read, "But Jesus remained silent." Why? Perhaps he was silent because he didn't want to consent to their misunderstanding of his claim about the temple or, related to that, because he had "contempt for the hostile proceedings."[17] Perhaps he was silent because "in many situations silence is a wise man's best defense."[18] Perhaps he was silent because "as a righteous man he is accountable only to God, not to his enemies."[19] Perhaps he was silent because at this time in his ministry there was no need to defend himself; just as he didn't defend himself physically in Gethsemane, he did not defend himself here legally.[20] Perhaps he was silent because he again was counting the cost, for if he says no he walks away a free man, but if he says yes he signs his own death warrant.[21] In his silence, was it Gethsemane take two? Was he silently praying, "Father, take this cup from me"?

Or perhaps this silence is merely but importantly an allusion to Isaiah 53:7: "He was oppressed, and he was afflicted, yet *he opened not his mouth*; like a lamb that is led to the slaughter, and like a sheep that before its shearers *is silent*, so *he opened not his mouth*." That allusion to Isaiah certainly fits (a) Jesus' statement in 26:56 about fulfilling the prophets, (b) what has just occurred at Jesus' arrest—the sheep have scattered as the Lamb of God is led to the slaughter, and (c) the physical sufferings Jesus endures, beginning in 26:67 when he is spit upon and ending in 27:50 when he suffocates on the cross.

Whatever the purpose of Jesus' "sovereign silence,"[22] it forces Caiaphas to break the silence: "And the high priest said to him, 'I adjure you by the living God, tell us if you are the Christ, the Son of God'" (v. 63b). In chapter 16 Jesus asked his disciples, "[W]ho do you say that I am?" (16:15) and Peter replied, "You are the Christ, the Son of the living God" (16:16). Now Jesus must answer his own question put to him by the high priest. He answers in the affirmative: "You have said so" (v. 64). That's an odd and guarded way to phrase it. Why not answer the question directly, "Yes, I am the Messiah"? What's with the "as you have said" or "that is your way of putting it"?[23] I think Jesus answers this way because his view of the Messiah and the high priest's are not quite identical.

The two titles in Caiaphas's question—"the Christ" and "the Son of God"—in Caiaphas's mind are synonymous. They both refer to Israel's coming King, the Messiah. In Jesus' mind, however, the title "the Son of God" is messianic but not merely messianic.[24] For example, in Gethsemane four times Jesus, as a son, referenced God by saying, "My Father" (26:39, 42, 44b, 53). Earlier in 11:27 Jesus spoke also of this unique relationship as the *Son* of God: "All things have been handed over to me by my Father, and no one knows the Son except the Father, and no one knows the Father except the Son and anyone to whom the Son chooses to reveal him." Furthermore, with Jesus' "Son of Man" language in verse 64 he moves as close as one can move to equating himself with God. So Jesus is not less than the Messiah, but he is more than the Messiah. He is, as one commentator comments, "the eternal, real Son of God" in "the metaphysical, ultimate, and full sense."[25]

Also different in the minds of Caiaphas and Jesus is the mission of Messiah. Caiaphas, likely embracing the popular concept of the day, thought of the Messiah as a nationalistic military liberator: Christ = Victorious War Hero. And perhaps giving Jesus a beating, and Jesus taking it without a fight, merely confirmed his suspicions that Jesus couldn't possibly be the Messiah. The Christ would fight back *and win*. Jesus' view of the Messiah, needless to say, was different. For now his Christ equation was: Christ = Suffering Servant.

Here is where the violent mockery captured in the final two verses of this passage ironically fits with Jesus' view, which fits with Isaiah's view. Our scene closes with this horrific image:

> Then they spit in his face and struck him. And some slapped him, saying, "Prophesy to us, you Christ! Who is it that struck you?" (vv. 67, 68)

They mock him as the Messiah; they say to him, "you Christ." They poke fun at his prophetic powers—"Prophesy to us . . . . Who . . . struck you?" They physically abuse him—spitting, striking, slapping (cf. Isaiah 50:6). This is contemptuous! This trial is out of order! But in God's plan all is in order. The promises to David and the prophecies of Isaiah rise together as the Suffering Servant is crowned with spit and slaps and strikes, as "the iniquity of us all" starts to be "laid on him" (Isaiah 53:6b). This is "a very great glory . . . that the Lord of the universe should endure such things for us," as Chrysostom summarizes.[26] Indeed. This is one of history's greatest ironies turned into history's greatest truth and need. This "most solemn face-off" between Israel's high priest and the world's High Priest is won by Jesus.[27] But it is won by Jesus seemingly losing face.

The Fourth Irony

The fourth irony is: *the members of the Sanhedrin "pass judgment on the one who will some day pass judgment on them."*[28] Here is the heart of the passage.

> Jesus said to him, "You have said so. But I tell you, from now on you will see the Son of Man seated at the right hand of Power and coming on the clouds of heaven." Then the high priest [as a symbol of his outrage, cf. 2 Kings 18:37] tore his robes and said, "He has uttered blasphemy. What further witnesses do we need? You have now heard his blasphemy. What is your judgment?" They answered, "He deserves death." (vv. 64–66)

What did Jesus say that would evoke such a response—the tearing of robes and the prompt deliberation of the death penalty?[29] He claimed to be the Son of Man. This is the first time Jesus used that title of himself openly to outsiders (non-disciples), and to Caiaphas it is an "extravagantly wild" statement.[30] Now remember, that title is not about Jesus' humanity. Rather it is about his divinity and more specifically about his divine power to judge.[31]

This scene is spectacular. I know I say this often, but it's true here again. There are two high priests in the room (Caiaphas and Jesus). There are two men who thus sit in judgment as judges (Caiaphas who then judges Jesus, and Jesus who will someday judge Caiaphas).

In verse 64 we have one of Jesus' fullest revelations of his identity and authority, and thus it is only proper that we dissect every phrase of this verse. First, there is Jesus' "You have said so." I just love that. To me it is the first edition of Philippians 2:11—every tongue will confess that Jesus Christ is Lord. Caiaphas doesn't mean it, but the words to Jesus, "you are the Christ, the Son of God" are on his lips (26:63). Next Jesus uses that favorite authority phrase of his, "But I tell you . . ." In the Sermon on the Mount he says six times, "You have heard that it was said . . . . But I say to you." Throughout Matthew when he is about to make a statement of great importance and with great authority, he says, "But I tell you" or "I say to you" or most commonly "Truly, I say to you." Here we find it again in his final words to the highest authority in Judaism. Don't miss or underestimate its importance!

Finally, we have the claim itself: "from now on you [plural] will see the Son of Man seated at the right hand of Power and coming on the clouds of heaven" (v. 64). The image here is that of awesome authority. This Jesus—who now *stands* before them with his arms bound as a prisoner, his head about to be slapped and spit upon, and his hands and feet to be pierced through on a piece of dead wood—claims that the next time his judges see him he will be *seated* on the divine throne of glory that is somehow moving from Heaven to earth to render them guilty![32] He claims to be the "undisputed King Messiah and sovereign Judge" of the world,[33] and thus the One to whom this Council will give an account for every reckless word, violent action, and foolish decision. He claims that his weakness will be turned into strength, his humiliation to exaltation, his shame to glory, and his subjection to power, that the "judged would become judge, and the conquered would conquer."[34]

What the Sanhedrin declares to be blasphemy, Jesus declares to be true.[35] Jesus is the Christ and the Son of God who, in accordance with 2 Samuel 7:13, builds the temple. Jesus is the king of Psalm 110:1 who sits at God's right hand. Jesus is the Suffering Servant of Isaiah 50:6 whose face is spat upon. Jesus is the Son of Man of Daniel 7:13 who will come on the clouds of heaven.[36] That's who Jesus is. Could he make his identity any clearer to Caiaphas?

Applying the Ironies

With all that said, what is Jesus saying here to us?[37] How shall we apply his last (and "single most important"?) short sermon to us?[38] More broadly, how shall we apply all four ironies? I'll give my best shot at it.

I spend a lot of time trying to get just the right sermon title because I want it to be interesting enough that my congregation longs for the sermon the moment they open the bulletin, but also comprehensive enough to capture in a few words the main theme or application of the text. So for this text titles that came to mind were "Two Seats of Power," "Victim and Victor," "Triumph through Humiliation," "The Condemned(!) Son of Man," and "Identity and Authority." In the end I went with "What Jesus Deserves." The reason I did so was in order to now (at the end of the sermon) contrast what the Sanhedrin thought Jesus deserved and what we think he deserves.

They thought he deserved death. They thought he was blaspheming, that he was insulting God's majesty by "claiming to be God's Son, to have a heavenly throne, and to be the exalted figure of Daniel 7:13."[39] And according to Leviticus 24:16 the punishment for that crime was death. But they were blind. Thus they were cruel and violent, the way so often false religion is cruel and violent.

What does Jesus deserve? He either deserves death (the Sanhedrin got it right), or he deserves adoration and allegiance (the early church got it right). I advocate the second option, and I want to end now by pressing you toward that goal. Those are the two applications to these four ironies.

First, he deserves our adoration. Look again at verses 57, 58:

> Then those who had seized Jesus led him to Caiaphas the high priest, where the scribes and the elders had gathered. And *Peter* was following him at a distance, as far as the courtyard of the high priest, and going inside he sat with the guards to see the end.

Why is Peter mentioned? Perhaps he is mentioned because it is just a historical detail in his story and reminds us to keep an eye on him as his own "trial" in the courtyard is soon to begin. Or perhaps he is there as an official apostolic eyewitness (or ear-witness) to the legal proceedings. Or, theologically-speaking perhaps he is there as our representative. What I mean is, he represents all that disciples are. We follow the Lord, sometimes closely and sometimes "at a distance," sometimes with courageous love, other times with cowardly fear, but however closely or bravely we follow Christ, we, like Peter, sin and fall short of the glory of God. And it is Peter's sin, as much as it is Caiaphas's sin, *as much as it is our sin*, that nailed Jesus to the cross.

> Who was the guilty? Who brought this upon Thee?
> Alas, my treason, Jesus, hath undone Thee;
> I crucified Thee.[40]

Jesus deserves adoration because he is the Son of Man. He deserves adoration because he is the Son of God. But he also deserves adoration because he is Christ crucified for *our sin*.

I recently read through the New Testament, studying and scribbling down all the prayers in it. In the book of Revelation, what amazes me is how and for what Jesus is praised. It is a blend of the theology of the cross (glorying in Jesus' sufferings) and the theology of glory (glorying in Jesus' power).

Revelation opens with a marvelous description of Jesus' person and work and a vision of his awesome authority. John sees Jesus as "the firstborn of the dead, and the ruler of kings on earth" (Revelation 1:5), the one "who loves us and has freed us from our sins by his blood and made us a kingdom" (Revelation 1:5, 6a), the one who died and yet lives forevermore (Revelation 1:18), and thus the one who deserves all "glory and dominion forever and ever" (Revelation 1:6).

In chapter 5 a new song arises to Jesus: "Worthy are you to take the scroll and to open its seals, for you were slain, and by your blood you ransomed people for God from every tribe and language and people and nation" (Revelation 5:9). Jesus alone is worthy to render God's justice to the nations because he alone is without spot or blemish. Jesus alone is worthy of our adoration because he, as the spotless Lamb of God, died for our sins. In Revelation, as it is in 26:64–68, Jesus' sufferings and Jesus' power blend into the church's worship—the glory of the cross of Christ, the glory of the coming Son of Man. "To . . . the Lamb be blessing and honor and glory and might forever and ever!" (Revelation 5:13). Let us join the four living creatures ("Amen") and the elders (who "fell down and worshiped," Revelation 5:14).

First, Jesus deserves our adoration. Second, he deserves our allegiance. Of course the two applications are closely related, for if you love him you will keep his commandments, and if you adore him you will show your allegiance to him. And in this passage our allegiance is to *this* Jesus. Not the social activist Jesus, the merely-a-prophet Jesus, the great teacher Jesus, the religious genius Jesus, the pacifist Jesus, the rebel Jesus, the Republican or Democratic Jesus, the Marxist Jesus, the vegetarian Jesus.[41] The list of Jesuses goes on and on! The Jesus we follow, however, is the one Peter preached at Pentecost: " Let all the house of Israel therefore know for certain that God has made him both Lord and Christ, *this Jesus* whom you crucified" (Acts 2:36).

Allegiance to this Jesus means bowing before his Lordship and walking the way of the cross and the crown. It means silently suffering for righteousness's sake (the cross), and it means crying out in faith for the coming, vindicating King (the crown). It means descending into hells of earthly suffering so that we might rise with him to the glory of heavenly power.

The ministry of Jesus was, in Jerome's words, "a good war . . . sent to break a bad peace."[42] Jesus doesn't allow us some safe middle ground. He came with a spiritual sword. He came to cause a war within each of us. So are you friend or foe? Do you love him or hate him? Do you desire to submit to him or seek to destroy him? No one who realizes who Jesus is and what he demands can possibly remain neutral.[43]

In the book I mentioned earlier—Carolyn Weber's *Surprised by Oxford*—she shares the following dialogue between her friends:

> "If you want to tick people off, just bring up the word *Jesus*." Rachel looked at each of us around the table. . . .
>
> "I know what Rachel's saying," Mark grinned. "Years after my conversion, I still get a kick out of the inevitable reaction. Say *Jesus* and people either get happy, or they get mad. They either smile, or a cloud comes over their faces. They are either elated or irritated. Embarrassed, they try to change the subject or walk away. No other name has such potency."[44]

Indeed.

82

Innocent Blood

MATTHEW 27:1–10

IS YOUR NAME Peter, Andrew, Thomas, Matthew, Philip, James, or John? I surmise that half of my male readers are nodding yes. Do any of you have any children, relatives, or friends who go by one of those apostolic names? Sure, we all do. But what about the name Judas—are any of you named after him? Does anyone plan on naming their firstborn son after him? Do any of you know anyone called by that name? You might know of someone called Jude or Judah, which is very similar, but I doubt anyone knows anyone named Judas.

In Jesus' day the name Judas, among Jewish males, was nearly as popular as the most popular name, Simon.[1] That's why four of the twelve apostles were named Simon or Judas. There were two Simons, and there were two Judases (Luke 6:16; John 14:22). The Judas we know as Judas Iscariot is the most infamous person in history. We don't name children, churches, colleges, hospitals, day cares, laundromats, casinos, or anything but heavy metal rock bands after him because he is, as pointed out in verse 3 and elsewhere (cf. 10:4; 26:25, 46, 48), the man who *betrayed* Jesus. In fact, when the name Judas is mentioned today it is often substituted for the term traitor or worse. No one wants to be associated with *a* Judas because of *the* Judas.

Christian literature has played its part in our perception of Judas. According to the Gospel of Bartholomew or Questions of Bartholomew, a second- to sixth-century Gnostic writing, after Jesus' descent into Hell only Cain, Herod, and Judas are left there. In Dante's *Divine Comedy* Judas is found in the lowest level of Hell, sharing with but surpassing the pain of two other traitors—Brutus and Cassius. Lines 61–63 of Canto XXXIV of the *Inferno* depicts Judas's head stuffed into the mouth of "Satan, Emperor of the Universe of

Pain" who is busy chewing his body with his sharp teeth.[2] In the medieval legend of St. Brendan the Navigator, the Irish abbot journeys from Ireland to the new world where, on his way, he encounters Judas sitting on a rock in the middle of the sea. Hail beats on Judas's head. Fire leaps from his body. However, this is not a description of Hell. Rather, Judas is getting a break from the torments of Hell because it is Sunday. Monday through Saturday he "burns day and night like molten lead in a pot," but on Sundays and other holy days "he finds respite."[3]

More recently, Judas has gained a more complete respite. (Modern authors are seemingly more merciful than medieval ones.) In Nikos Kazantzakis's *The Last Temptation of Christ*, Judas comes off as a hero who does God's will by keeping Jesus on the cross when Jesus is tempted to come down from it in order to start a family and work a regular day job as a farmer.[4] Similarly, in Leonid Andreyev's *Judas Iscariot and Others* Judas gets another sympathetic reading. Torn between the will to power and a love for Jesus, Judas commits suicide in order to finally be right with Jesus. His suicide is described as "a passion . . . that justified him."[5]

Matthew's portrait of Judas is notably different. To him, Judas is neither a straw man who is quickly set on fire and engulfed in flames, nor is he some kind of embodied personality disorder that is eventually cut down from the noose and set before us to serve as a noble example of something. Rather, his Judas looks a bit like you and me—a guilt-ridden sinner in need of serious help. He serves as a mirror in which we can and should look into our own souls to see if our dark sides resemble his and to see if there is any traitorous inclination that would lead us to "leave the God [we] love."[6]

The Tragedy of Israel's Condemnation of the Christ

Our text—27:1–10—is a tragedy. It is a tragedy in three parts that features three characters. Judas is the most apparent character and Jesus the most important. However, it is the chief priests and the elders of the people who are the prime protagonists. Most of the verbs relate to their actions. They took counsel, bound Jesus, delivered him over to Pilate, replied to Judas, took counsel again, bought a field,[7] and in and through it all somehow fulfilled Scripture.

Let's begin with them and what I'll call "The Tragedy of Israel's Condemnation of the Christ." In 23:23a Jesus said:

> Woe to you, scribes and Pharisees, hypocrites! For you tithe mint and dill and cumin, and have neglected the weightier matters of the law: justice and mercy and faithfulness.

Here in chapter 27 we can almost hear the echo of those words to the scribes and Pharisees bounce off the chief priests and the elders. Their actions in our text are (1) unjust, (2) unmerciful, and (3) ironic in their unfaithfulness to the ways of God even while they are faithful to the sovereign script of Scripture.

First, their actions are unjust to Jesus. Look with me at verses 1, 2:

> When morning came, all the chief priests and the elders of the people took counsel against Jesus to put him to death. And they bound him and led him away and delivered him over to Pilate the governor.

Every morning I read a Psalm to begin the day. Psalm 2 begins:

> Why do the nations rage
> and the peoples plot in vain?
> The kings of the earth set themselves,
> and the rulers take counsel together,
> against the LORD and against his Anointed [Christ], saying,
> "Let us burst their bonds apart
> and cast away their cords from us." (Psalm 2:1–3)

In Matthew it is the Jewish, not Gentile, rulers who rage, plot, and take counsel against the Christ, and they do so by binding him and handing him over to the Gentiles. Again it's ironic but also unjust. They should be kissing or doing homage to the Son, as that Psalm warns (Psalm 2:12). Instead, they hand over an innocent man to die.

Second, their actions are unmerciful to Judas. Look with me at verses 3–8:

> Then when Judas, his betrayer, saw that Jesus was condemned, he changed his mind [or "repented"] and brought back the thirty pieces of silver to the chief priests and the elders, saying, "I have sinned by betraying innocent blood." They said, "What is that to us? See to it yourself." And throwing down the pieces of silver into the temple, he departed, and he went and hanged himself. But the chief priests, taking the pieces of silver, said, "It is not lawful to put them into the treasury, since it is blood money." So they took counsel and bought with them the potter's field as a burial place for strangers. Therefore that field has been called the Field of Blood to this day.

I'll come back to Judas's actions in verses 3 and 5 in a moment. For now we are focusing on the chief priests and the elders, especially the priests. If I were to use one word to describe the role of the priests under the Levitical system, it would be the word mercy. Through sacrifices they mediated God's mercy to sinners. So here comes a self-professed sinner—Judas—who tries to return the blood money and says to them, "I have sinned by betraying innocent blood" (v. 4a). Betraying innocent blood is an awful crime according to the Old Testament (cf. Deuteronomy 27:25). Judas knows that. They know that. Yet how do these senior pastors counsel this suffering sinner? They say, "What is that to us? See to it yourself." Put differently, "What do we care? That's your problem" (v. 4, NLT). Hey, the guy wants to atone for his sin. Let him. At least be nice to him.

We almost wish Judas would have answered their question—"What is that to us?"—by saying, "Everything in the world. You are the chief priests! You have the power to reconvene the Sanhedrin, retry Jesus, let me testify that I was wrong, and then allow me into the temple to make a sin offering to atone for my sin."[8] God's people—let alone God's priests—are to "love mercy" (Micah 6:8, NIV). These men hate it.

Their contempt for mercy is further shown in their second reply to Judas. Judas throws the silver into the temple and throws a noose around his own neck. He kills himself. The four verbs here—"throwing down," "departed," "went," and "hanged"—paint a picture of hasty desperation.[9] It's as if he did all that in ten seconds. And what do the priests do? They do what religious people too often do. First, they hold another council. Second, at that council they draw up a major treatise on a minor doctrine. They are more concerned with what to do with Judas's blood money than what to do with Judas's dead body. They call their official decree "How to Create an Unclean Cemetery for Unclean People with Unclean Money."[10] Jesus would have labeled it "How to Strain a Gnat and Swallow a Camel." Whether Judas's sin is forgiven or not, they care not. Whether Jesus is guilty or innocent, they care not. Sticking to the letter of their own law they kill the spirit of God's Law.[11]

Judas is not a good guy. He is a hardened sinner somewhat softened by his horrific sin. But these men are calloused head to toe. They completely rebuff Judas, but not his claim that he has betrayed innocent blood. Do they too think Jesus is innocent? They don't think he is innocent of blasphemy, but they likely do know he is innocent of sedition or some other crime against Rome with which they will peg him. What they certainly don't think, however, is that *they* are guilty. To Matthew, however, they "bear the major responsibility for Jesus' impending death."[12] Their hands are no less clean than Pilate's after he washes or Judas's after he confesses. In fact, that flood of blood cries out like the blood of Abel "as a lasting memorial to their own guilt."[13]

> Make them bear their guilt, O God;
>   let them fall by their own counsels;

> because of the abundance of their transgressions cast them out,
> for they have rebelled against you. (Psalm 5:10)

Here we have the tragedy of Israel's condemnation of the Christ.[14] The chief priests and elders of the people—representative of unbelieving Israel (cf. 27:22, 25)—act unjustly, unmercifully, and unfaithfully. Yet, ironically in their lack of faithfulness to the moral will of God they fulfill the prophetic will of God. Our text ends:

> Then was *fulfilled* what had been spoken by the prophet Jeremiah, saying, "And they took the thirty pieces of silver, the price of him on whom a price had been set by some of the sons of Israel, and they gave them for the potter's field, as the Lord directed me." (vv. 9, 10)

Here in the last word on fulfillment in Matthew, we have another seemingly odd fulfillment scheme.[15] It is seemingly odd because it is not something that Jesus as Messiah fulfills. Rather, it is a prophecy about some potter's field. It is also seemingly odd because Matthew claims that the prophecy was "spoken by the prophet *Jeremiah*" though it sounds more like a prophecy from Zechariah. Zechariah 11:12, 13 reads:

> Then I said to them, "If it seems good to you, give me my wages; but if not, keep them." And they weighed out as my wages thirty pieces of silver. Then the LORD said to me, "Throw it to the potter"—the lordly price at which I was priced by them. So I took the thirty pieces of silver and threw them into the house of the LORD, to the potter.

For this reason Jerome says, "This testimony is not found in Jeremiah . . . [however] something similar is found in Zechariah."[16] Calvin goes so far as to state there was some mistake here: "How the name of Jeremiah crept in I cannot confess to know nor do I make much of it: obviously Jeremiah's name is put in error for Zechariah. Nothing of this sort is said in Jeremiah, or anything like it."[17] With little or less Christian conviction about Scripture's authority than Jerome and Calvin, some modern scholars have been far less charitable to Matthew. For example, Hyam Maccoby called Matthew's citation "a hotch-potch of misquotation and irrelevance."[18] Francis Wright Beare wrote, "This is surely the most extravagant example of Matthew's handling of scriptures as proof texts. . . . However he arrived at what he wrote, it must be agreed that he has botched it badly."[19]

Are these Bible scholars right? Did Matthew's memory fail him and thus he mistakenly wrote "Jeremiah" when he meant "Zechariah"? Or did some later scribe's hand unintentionally slip or intentionally change what Matthew originally and correctly wrote? And whatever the case, was Matthew merely using his apostolic authority mixed with his overly zealous imagination to rework the Old Testament to fit the events surrounding the passion of the Christ?[20] An easier-than-you-might-think solution is at hand as to why the words are mostly Zechariah's but Jeremiah is named.

When I don't know what to do with a difficult prophecy from Jeremiah, I invite to my office one of today's most component Jeremiah scholars. I suggest we all do this when stuck. Find a Jeremiah scholar and befriend him. That scholar is Dr. Michael Graves.[21] We meet every week to read the Greek of my preaching text. He reads and translates it extremely well. I stumble through it. When I asked him about the Jeremiah dilemma in verses 9, 10, he gave a very simple but satisfactory answer. I'll walk you through what he walked me through. He had me turn to Mark 1:2, 3, which reads:

> As it is written in Isaiah the prophet,
>
> "Behold, I send my messenger before your face,
> who will prepare your way,
> the voice of one crying in the wilderness:
> 'Prepare the way of the Lord,
> make his paths straight.'"

Mark weaves together Malachi and Isaiah but credits only Isaiah. Why? Mike went on to explain how this was a typical way of doing it. If an ancient author weaves together two quotes from two prophets, it was acceptable to name only the more famous of the two.[22] Thus, because Isaiah is more famous than Malachi, Mark used his name. Similarly, because Jeremiah is more famous than Zechariah, Matthew uses his name. The quote is 80 percent Zechariah and 20 percent Jeremiah, but Jeremiah gets the shout-out, if you will. The 20 percent relates to various texts in Jeremiah, specifically the allegory of the potter in Jeremiah 18, 19 and the purchase of a field with silver in Jeremiah 32. Davies and Allison also include texts in Jeremiah about "a purchase (19.1), the Valley Hinnom (where the Field of Blood is traditionally located, 19.2), 'innocent blood' (19.4), and the renaming of the place for burial (19.6, 11)."[23]

In summary: Matthew combines some words from Zechariah and themes from Jeremiah to show how the chief priest and elders' actions "fulfill" this pattern or typological parallel found in the prophets and played out in the drama of Jesus, the drama of God's people rejecting the Lord.[24]

The Tragedy of Half-Repentance

This text is a tragedy in three parts. We have looked at "The Tragedy of Israel's Condemnation of the Christ." Next let's turn to the tragedy of Judas, what I'll call "The Tragedy of Half-Repentance." Turn again to verses 3–5. Here we will focus on (1) what Judas did right and what he did wrong and (2) what we can learn from what he did right and what he did wrong.

First, note what he did right and wrong. Verse 3, 4a reads, "Then when Judas . . . saw that Jesus was condemned, he changed his mind and brought back the thirty pieces of silver to the chief priests and the elders, saying, 'I have sinned by betraying innocent blood.'" Judas really repented.[25] That's what he did right. Some say he was merely remorseful and not really repentant. But I say he was really repentant, but half-repentant. Perhaps the famous repentance train analogy will help. By acknowledging his sin and seeking to make amends, Judas got off the train going the wrong way. But that was all he did. He next needed to get on another train going the right way. That right way was back to Jesus for forgiveness. He went to the chief priests in the temple but not to the true High Priest who is the temple. Judas should have gone to Jesus who is sympathetic to our weaknesses and ready to forgive *all* our transgressions. He should have run to the tree of Calvary for life. Instead he ran to another tree for death.[26] Matthew describes this in this way: "And throwing down the pieces of silver into the temple, he departed, and he went [departed] and hanged himself [departed *from life*]" (v. 5). That's what he did wrong—he killed himself. He compounded his crime of betrayal with his sin of suicide.

Suicide is not the unpardonable sin—we must take into account mental illnesses (chemical imbalances), perceived military necessities (Saul's suicide in 1 Samuel 31:4, 5) and heroic self-sacrifices (Samson's suicide in Judges 16:28–30). However, suicide is always sinful. It breaks the sixth commandment—"You shall not murder" (Exodus 20:13). Although Judas finds some sympathetic scholars such as Karl Barth who taught that God's all-powerful grace outshined Judas's dark rejection,[27] there is no reason for such sentimentality. Matthew certainly doesn't portray Judas's final act as noble or heroic.[28] And Jesus himself seems to echo and expand upon the words of Deuteronomy 21:23—"for a hanged man is cursed by God"—when, at the Last Supper, he says of Judas, "*woe* to that man by whom the Son of Man is betrayed! It would have been better for that man if he had not been born" (26:24). If Judas is now in Heaven, Jesus' woe was wrong. But it was not wrong. Judas may not be in the lowest deeps of Dante's *Inferno*, but he is somewhere in God's Hell. We are to see Judas's death as "a most disgraceful death"[29] and to tremble and cry at the sad, sad sight.

There is despair, damnable despair. Damnable despair turns away from Jesus. Judas not only lost all hope; he lost all hope *in Jesus*. He doubted God's mercy through Jesus. He believed Jesus was an innocent man, but he should have added that Jesus was the innocent Son of Man who came to shed his innocent blood for less-than-innocent sinners.

Second, what are we to learn from what Judas did right and wrong? From what Judas did *right*, we should follow him in acknowledging our sin and seeking to confess it. We should also follow him in acknowledging Jesus' innocence. From what Judas did *wrong* we are to learn not to despair over our sin but to fully repent of it.

The easiest and perhaps best way to demonstrate that lesson is through the restoration of Peter. It is intentional that there are many parallels between Peter and Judas in chapter 26 and that their stories of betrayal are told side by side. Both Judas's betrayal and Peter's denial were equally condemnable. The main difference between the two is what they did after their great sins. When Paul wrote 2 Corinthians 7:10, I can't imagine he didn't have the difference between Peter and Judas in mind: "For godly grief produces a repentance *that leads to salvation* without regret [Peter], whereas worldly grief produces death [Judas]." Judas went to the chief priests; Peter went to Jesus (implied in Matthew and spelled out in John). Judas couldn't get his sin atoned for in the temple, so he took it upon himself to sentence himself to death. However, Peter got his sin atoned for through Jesus, who took it upon himself to sentence himself to death. Peter's shed tears of repentance led him to Jesus' shed blood for his sins.

The Divine Tragicomedy

Here is where this whole chapter is going—to the cross. Let me expand on this application of what Judas did wrong, or we might say, what Peter did right.

Earlier I pointed out that this text is a tragedy in three parts that features three characters. We have looked at the chief priests and elders as well as Judas. Finally we will look at (and to) Jesus.

What the religious leaders do is tragic. What Judas does is tragic. And what is done to Jesus is tragic. I say "done to" because you'll notice here that Jesus says or does nothing. Put differently, he does not act but is acted upon. That detail should leap off the page because in this Gospel Jesus is always doing or saying something. Throughout chapter 26 Jesus is in charge. He is "the active protagonist."[30] However, with the start of chapter 27, "Jesus becomes the passive victim,"[31] who in God's providence is *delivered up* first by Judas, second by the Jewish leaders, third by Pontus Pilate, but finally or ultimately *by God*. As Romans 8:32 (NKJV) puts it, "He who did not spare His own Son . . . *delivered Him up* for us all," and as Romans 4:25 clarifies the nature of this delivering up, Jesus was "*delivered up* for our trespasses."

Do you have any trespasses? Think about your little ones—a white lie, a stolen coin, a lustful glance, etc. Think about your big ones—betrayal, slander, false testimony, blasphemy, adultery, etc. What are you going to do about all those sins? If you don't think you have to do something about them, you're not thinking! What I suggest you do about them is come to Jesus.

In my church's hymnal the first hymn in the section entitled "His Suffering and Death" is "Lead Me to Calvary." The refrain goes:

Lest I forget Gethsemane;
Lest I forget Thine agony;
Lest I forget Thy love for me,
Lead me to Calvary.[32]

Let me lead you there. Listen, everyone is guilty. The Jews are guilty. The Gentiles are guilty. Judas and Peter are guilty. You and I are guilty. There is only one man who is "innocent" (27:4)—the one who was lifted up so that he might draw all men to himself (John 12:32).

My friends, there is no sin you have committed that cannot be forgiven. And there is no other place to have that sin (all our sins) forgiven than the cross of Christ.

What can wash away my sin?
Nothing but the blood of Jesus.
What can make me whole again?
Nothing but the blood of Jesus.

It is innocent blood shed for guilty sinners.

Oh! precious is the flow
That makes me white as snow;
No other fount I know,
Nothing but the blood of Jesus.[33]

In medieval literature, a comedy is a drama that ends happily. The divine comedy of Jesus—or tragicomedy to be more precise[34]—ends happily after great tragedy. That is, Jesus dies and rises again. And our own Christian comedy ends happily after great tragedy. That is, we recognize our sin as awful and offensive to God, we confess that sin to him, we turn away from it, and we turn to Jesus for salvation. Here is how Hebrews summarizes this theme:

> The former priests were many in number, because they were prevented by death from continuing in office, but he [Jesus—"a priest forever, after the order of Melchizedek," Romans 7:17; cf. v. 22] holds his priesthood permanently, because he continues forever. Consequently, he is able to save to the uttermost those who draw near to God through him, since he always lives to make intercession for them. For it was indeed fitting that we should have such a high priest, holy, *innocent*, unstained, separated from sinners, and exalted above the heavens. He has no need, like those high priests, to offer sacrifices daily, first for his own sins and then for those of the people, since he did this once for all when he offered up himself. (Hebrews 7:23–27)

Despair not. I bring you this day a message of great hope. Acknowledge your sin. Confess your sin. Repent of your sin. Cling to the cross of Christ. Draw near to God through the innocent blood of Jesus Christ shed for you.

83

Why?

MATTHEW 27:11–26

THEN HE RELEASED FOR THEM *Barabbas*" (27:26a). Why release Barabbas? Matthew calls him "a notorious prisoner" (v. 16). Mark labeled him a rebel "who had committed murder in the insurrection" (Mark 15:7). Luke confirms Mark's claim, saying that Barabbas was "a man who had been thrown into prison for an insurrection started in the city and for murder" (Luke 23:19).[1] Why release guilty Barabbas instead of innocent Jesus? Why?

"Then he released for them Barabbas, *and having scourged Jesus . . .*" (v. 26ab). Why scourge Jesus? Do you know what scourging was? Matthew refrains from giving us the "grisly particulars."[2] However I will share some of those particulars only to get you on the same page as Matthew's original readers. After a criminal was sentenced to death by crucifixion, Roman soldiers would tie that criminal to a post and repeatedly beat him with a whip that had a series of long leather straps, some of which contained pieces of metal or bone that tore into the skin, muscles, and tendons.[3] That's scourging. This beating was so horrendous it often proved fatal. Why was Jesus scourged? Why?

"Then he released for them Barabbas, and having scourged Jesus, *delivered him to be crucified*" (v. 26). Why deliver Jesus to be crucified? Why would he receive the supreme Roman penalty reserved for the worst criminals?[4] Why not imprison him for life or give him painless poison to drink? Crucifixion was "the worst form of death."[5] It was embarrassing: a man would hang naked on a wooden cross usually set in a prominent place—"at crossroads, in the theatre, on high ground, at the place of his crime"[6]—for all to see and jeer, and it was ex*cruc*iating.[7] Ancient writers are unanimous in stating that "crucifixion was a horrific, disgusting business,"[8] the cruelest "instrument of execution."[9] Pseudo-Manetho writes, "Punished with limbs outstretched

. . . they are fastened (and) nailed to it [the stake or cross] in the most bitter torment, evil food for birds of prey and grim pickings for dogs."[10] Seneca says:

> Can anyone be found who would prefer wasting away in pain dying limb by limb, or letting out his life drop by drop, rather than expiring once for all? Can any man be found willing to be fastened to the accursed tree, long, sickly, already deformed, swelling with ugly weals [welts?] on shoulders and chest [likely from the scourging], and drawing the breath of life amid long-drawn-out agony? He would have many excuses for dying even before mounting the cross.[11]

What had Jesus done to deserve that type of death? Why crucifixion? Why?

Why release guilty Barabbas instead of innocent Jesus? (It's so unjust.) Why have Jesus scourged? (It's so inhumane.) And why have Jesus delivered to be crucified? (It's so embarrassing and excruciating.) Why? Why? Why? Let's find out why. And let's find out why with "a bowed head and broken spirit," not a cool and reserved academic detachment,[12] and with a conscience gripped by our own guilt as well as pierced to the heart by Jesus' deep, deep love for us.

Themes, Style, and Structure

In 27:11–26 we have two familiar themes in Matthew's Gospel—kingship and culpability. It is obvious who is culpable for Jesus' death: "Pilate," mentioned in nearly every verse, as well as (and again) "the chief priests and the elders" (mentioned in vv. 12, 18, 20) along with "the crowd" or "all the people" (mentioned in vv. 15, 17, 20–25). It is also obvious who is called "king." The Roman "governor" Pilate has the language of Jesus' kingship on his lips. In verse 11 Pilate asks Jesus, "Are you the King of the Jews?" In verses 17 and 22 he labels Jesus as the one "who is called *Christ*," another word for "king." Then, in what follows our text but is simply the aftermath of the trial, the Roman soldiers mockingly dress Jesus up as a king—with a scarlet robe, a crown of thorns, and a reed in his right hand—and then kneel before him and with sardonic adoration say, "Hail, King of the Jews!" (vv. 28, 29). Those same soldiers or another set of them would add to that mockery by nailing Jesus' crime above his head: "This is Jesus, the King of the Jews" (v. 37).

The main themes are Jesus' kingship and human culpability. The literary method is, once again, irony. In an old German passion play Jesus was called "a man who turns the world upside down,"[13] and Matthew the Evangelist here shows that turning the world upside down by at least five ironic twists: (1) Jesus, the judge of the world, *stands* before Pilate, who *sits* in judgment on him (John 19:13; cf. Matthew 25:31). (2) While the Jewish leaders do everything in their power to get Pilate to sentence Jesus to death, a Gentile woman (Pilate's wife no less) does her best to have him released. (3) The crowd chooses Barabbas—the man's name means "son [bar] of a father [abbas]"—over Jesus, the self-attested Son of the heavenly Father (cf. 11:27; 24:36).[14] (4) Pilate's washing of his hands only confirms the verdict that he has governed unjustly. And (5) the crowd, who willingly takes responsibility—"His blood be on us and on our children!" (v. 25)—unwittingly prophesies their own destruction, as Rome massacred thousands from that generation during the revolt of AD 66–70.[15]

The main themes are kingship and culpability. The literary method is irony. And the literary structure follows Pilate's seven sentences, six of which are questions (vv. 11, 13, 17, 21, 22, 23). Even the seventh sentence is treated by the people as a question, for in verse 25 we read that they "answered." That seven-question structure will serve as this chapter's structure.

First and Second Questions

For the sake of time and ease of understanding, I'll pair the first question with the second, the third with the fourth, and the fifth with the sixth. The seventh sentence shall stand on its own.

Pilate's first two questions come in verse 11–14:

> Now Jesus stood before the governor, and the governor asked him, *"Are you the King of the Jews?"* Jesus said, "You have said so." But when he was accused by the chief priests and elders, he gave no answer. Then Pilate said to him, *"Do you not hear how many things they testify against you?"* But he gave him no answer, not even to a single charge, so that the governor was greatly amazed.

Pilate is a character who comes out of nowhere. There is no mention of him in Matthew until this chapter. We know from other sources, however, that from AD 26–36/7 Pontius Pilate was the prefect of Judea. This wasn't the easiest assignment. It was as if Tiberius Caesar assigned Pilate to be Governor of the Gaza Strip, for Judea was known as a "somewhat remote and rebellious" region of the Roman Empire.[16] Yet whatever Pilate's status in the Roman establishment, Matthew equates him as the symbol of Roman authority. He does this by the title "governor," used five times in our text and two more times in chapter 27 (27:2, 27). Thus Jesus' trial *before Pilate* symbolizes a showdown between Christ and Caesar.

But this historic showdown of powers is an odd one. Jesus makes it odd by the ways he answers Pilate's two questions. To the first question, "Are you the King of the Jews?" Jesus replies with those enigmatic words, "You have said so" (v. 11; cf. 26:25, 64), and to the second question, "Do you not hear how many things they testify against you?" Jesus pleads the Fifth (vv. 13, 14). He is silent. With the first reply Jesus ambiguously acknowledges that he is a king (made very clear in John 18:33–37)—"Pilate has unwittingly spoken the truth"[17]—and thus that the charge of sedition can stick. With his second reply or lack thereof, he decries the ill will of the Jewish religious leaders even while he fulfills the good will of God. He is once again fulfilling Scripture in that his silence symbolizes Isaiah's suffering servant:[18] "He was oppressed, and he was afflicted, yet he opened not his mouth; like a lamb that is led to the slaughter, and like a sheep that before its shearers is silent, so he opened not his mouth." I know Isaiah 53:7 isn't quoted here, but if you scrape the surface of any part of Matthew's passion narrative, Daniel's Son of Man, the Psalms' righteous man, Isaiah's Suffering Servant, or all three together rise above the text. Let it rise above here.

Pilate was "greatly amazed" (v. 14) because Jesus offered no defense. He surely wondered, *Why would a teacher so awe-invoking with words refrain from defending himself?* and *Who, when unjustly accused of a crime and about to be sentenced to scourging and crucifixion, doesn't fight to be free?* We should be greatly amazed too. We should be amazed that Jesus kept quiet then so that we might shout "Hallelujah!" now. Yes, hallelujah that though Jesus "had a just defense to offer," he was quiet at the judgment-seat of Pilate because, as Calvin claimed, he had become "answerable for *our* guilt."[19] As Calvin stated elsewhere, "God's Son stood trial before a mortal man and suffered accusation and condemnation that we might stand without fear in the presence of God."[20] And in another place Calvin writes, "Christ kept silence [then] to be our spokesman now."[21] Three cheers for Calvin; 3,000 cheers for Christ! His silence = our salvation. Let us break his silence with our roar of adoration!

Third and Fourth Questions

Next look with me at the third and fourth questions, found in verses 15–21:

> Now at the feast [Passover] the governor was accustomed to release for the crowd any one prisoner whom they wanted. And they had then a notorious prisoner called Barabbas. So when they had gathered, Pilate said to them, "Whom do you want me to release for you: Barabbas, or Jesus who is called Christ?" For he knew that it was out of envy that they had delivered him up. Besides, while he was sitting on the judgment seat, his wife sent

> word to him, "Have nothing to do with that righteous man, for I have suffered much because of him today in a dream." Now the chief priests and the elders persuaded the crowd to ask for Barabbas and destroy Jesus. The governor again said to them, "Which of the two do you want me to release for you?" And they said, "Barabbas."

I will turn two key observations about these verses directly into two applications. First, *just as first-century Israel chose the wrong Jesus to be their Savior, so too we can choose the wrong one to be ours.*

Obviously the two questions above are similar (vv. 17b, 21a). They are both about the choice between Jesus Barabbas and Jesus Christ. I say "Jesus Barabbas" because in one group of early manuscripts of the New Testament we have the first name "Jesus" before the surname "Barabbas." I surmise the name "Jesus Barabbas" was in the original manuscript (when have I ever been wrong on my reading of textual variants?) for a number of reasons, only two of which I will share with you.[22] Adding the name "Jesus" before the name "Barabbas" in verses 16, 17 fits well with how Pilate phrases his next question in verse 22: "Then what shall I do with Jesus who is called Christ?" I'll call that internal evidence. Externally, out of "reverence for Jesus the Messiah," it wouldn't be without precedence for a pious copyist to remove the name "Jesus" before Barabbas in order to distance our Lord from that villain.[23]

Whether it is a choice between two Jesuses or not, it is certainly a choice between types of Saviors. Do you want this "son of a father" (Barabbas) or that Son of the Father (Jesus)?[24] Do you want a man of violent insurrection *now* or a man of peaceful justice *then*? Do you want the man of the sword or the man of the cross? Do you want tall and mighty King Saul or the little shepherd boy David? The Jerusalem Jews chose Barabbas, who, I need not tell you, was not a man after God's own heart.

Today we have that same choice before us. In fact, our choice is far more expansive. Only two Jesuses were put before them then. We have at least two dozen Jesuses to select from now. Which Jesus do you want? We have the Jesus of our popular "Jesus" authors—do you want the Jesus of Marcus Borg, Anne Rice, Dan Brown, or Bishop John Shelby Spong? We have the Jesuses of the world religions—do you want the Jesus of Muhammad, Gandhi, or the Dalai Lama? We have the Jesuses of the cults and occult—do you want the Jesus of Deepak Chopra, Joseph Smith, Mary Baker Eddy, Edger Cayce, or David Koresh? We have the Jesuses of pop culture—do you want the Jesus of *The Simpsons* and *South Park*, the sports star ("I'd like to thank the Big Guy upstairs"), or Pamela Anderson (sporting across her chest "Jesus is my homeboy")? In this supermarket of spirituality, which Jesus shall we choose? That's *the* pressing question of our day.[25]

May I suggest (no, let me plead with you) not to follow today's accepted voices but rather the old apostolic testimony. The clear choice is the canonical Jesus. The New Testament canon is the only sure standard. It is the only authorized portrait of the true Jesus.

Here is the dilemma today's church faces. Because we don't go to this canon to help us choose the correct Jesus, our lack of clarity (who is Jesus?) has led to a lack of conviction (should I wholeheartedly follow Jesus?), which in turn leads to a lack of confidence (since I'm not so sure which Jesus is the right Jesus, I'm not so sure I can give the non-Christian a clear choice).

A few years ago when my family had just moved into our new home, a neighbor was talking with my wife about religion. She knew that Emily was a pastor's wife, so she assumed it was okay to talk religion and to bemoan some of the religious doctrines being taught to her son at her local Catholic church. Doctrines like Hell and anything touching on the exclusivity of Christ were at the top of her complaints list. After she registered her grievances, she gave one of those "You know what I mean?" questions. Emily disagreed. And she did so by kindly saying, "I don't think I can just make up any kind of Jesus I want to. I follow the Jesus of the Bible. If Jesus talked about Hell as real or himself as the only way, I don't think I have the right, as *his* follower, to disagree." I sat on the park bench adjacent to this conversation, shouting under my breath, "You go, girl! Preach it. Preach it. Preeeeach it!"

If we want to have conviction about our faith and courage to share our faith, we must be clear on the canonical Jesus. We must chose him if we are to live for him.

So, my first key observation/application from verses 15–21 involves this choice. My second involves Pilate's wife, and that observation/application is this: *We have a surer testimony of Jesus than Pilate's wife that should inform us that this righteous Jesus is right for the nations.*

On the day of Jesus' trial, this woman has a dream—"today in a dream" (v. 19). In antiquity dreams held greater authority than they do now, and in Matthew every dream mentioned is from God (think back to the warnings to Joseph and the magi in 1:20; 2:12, 13, 19, 22). Whether her dream constitutes divine revelation or just common sense matters little; what matters is that she alone in the two trial scenes gives a true testimony. She thinks Jesus is not merely innocent but "righteous" (v. 19; Isaiah 53:11). While the blind are leading the blind, she alone sees.

She tells her husband to open his eyes, but he hushes her due to that loud crowd. She is not like Eve, tempting her husband to dismiss God. She is not like Mrs. Job, nagging her husband to curse God. Whatever she is (a good wife, a true helpmate), she is indeed a "bright foil"[26] to all the dark men—her husband, the soldiers, the Jewish leaders, and the crowd. However, she is more than that. She is also a bright foreshadowing. The Coptic Church claims she became a Christian and canonized her as a saint. I won't go that far. But I will go far enough to say that Matthew certainly emphasizes and thus strategically places—with the Gentile wise men in chapter 2 who worship the baby Jesus and this Gentile wise woman in chapter 27 who acknowledges the man Jesus as "righteous" (v. 19; cf. 3:15)[27]—that this Jesus is "a light for revelation to the Gentiles" (Luke 2:32a). Can Gentiles be saved by Israel's Messiah? Our text leans in that direction. It leans toward the climax of Matthew's Gospel—"Go therefore and make disciples of *all nations*" (28:19a) as well as the second half of our New Testament where the apostle to the Gentiles—that former Pharisee of Pharisees, Paul—writes of salvation being first for the Jews and then for the Gentiles (see Romans 1:16).

She had a dream. I have a dream. Yes, I have a dream that one day men and women, Jews and Gentiles, servants and masters from the red hills of Georgia to the rolling hills of Rome will all sit down at the table of brotherhood and join hands under one creed, acknowledging that Jesus Christ is Lord of all.[28]

> Every valley shall be lifted up, and every mountain and hill be made low; the uneven ground shall become level, and the rough places a plain. And the glory of the LORD shall be revealed, and all flesh shall see it together, for the mouth of the LORD has spoken. (Isaiah 40:4, 5)

Let's not be afraid to whisper that dream into the ears of the nations. With clarity, conviction, and confidence, let's shout it from the rooftops!

Fifth and Sixth Questions

Having looked at questions one through four, next let's turn our attention to questions five and six, found in verses 22, 23:

> Pilate said to them, "Then what shall I do with Jesus who is called Christ?" They all said, "Let him be crucified!" And he said, "Why, what evil has he done?" But they shouted all the more, "Let him be crucified!"

In trying to release Jesus, Pilate has tied his own hands. He knows that Jesus is innocent of the fabricated charges brought against him (v. 12a): Jesus was not evading taxes, inciting a revolt, or claiming to be Israel's newly elected military king (see Luke 23:2; cf. John 19:12, 15). Jesus has not broken any Roman law. Yet there is the cry of the crowd. It's not *peer* pressure but *people* pressure. Shall Pilate fulfill his rightful duty as just judge (and listen to his wife's wise counsel), or shall he let the chant of the bullying crowd prevail? We know what happens. The weak-willed, insecure, cowardly governor is ruled by the people's court.

The crowd's double verdict—"Let him be crucified"—is striking (v. 23). It is striking in light of the crowd's previous chant of "Hosanna" (21:9, 15). It is also striking in light of Jesus' teachings on turning the other cheek and loving one's enemy, teachings that awed the crowds at one point in Jesus' ministry.[29] Furthermore, the crowd's verdict is striking in its sadistic tone. What is with these people? To Pilate's question, "Then what shall I do with Jesus?" (v. 22), why not act indifferently and say something like, "Forget about him" or "do whatever you want with him"?[30] But to order a Roman governor to crucify a fellow Jew is incredibly awful. We don't know what evil Jesus has done (none actually), but we do know what evil the people have done. They have begged for Jesus' blood. Here again in Matthew's passion narrative there is a contrast of characters and their character. Jesus turns the other cheek to his enemies; the crowd wants an innocent man brutally tortured and killed. Jesus is silent; the crowd thunders their horrific verdict: "Let him be crucified!"

Seventh Statement

Finally we come to Pilate's seventh sentence. Concerning Pilate, C. S. Lewis wrote that he "was merciful until it became risky."[31] Precisely. Look at our final verses:

> So when Pilate saw that he was gaining nothing, but rather that a riot was beginning, he took water and washed his hands before the crowd, saying, "I am innocent of this man's blood; see to it yourselves." And all the people answered, "His blood be on us and on our children!" Then he released for them Barabbas, and having scourged Jesus, delivered him to be crucified. (vv. 24–26)

Pilate's external ritual cleansing and confident declaration of innocence is ironic.[32] Pilate comes off guiltier *after* he washes his hands than before. This gesture is as futile as the Ku Klux Clan hiding their crimes behind white sheets. Barclay informs us that "legend has it that to this day there are times when Pilate's shade emerges from its tomb and goes through the action of the hand-washing once again."[33] I like to imagine him each time muttering under his breath that classic line from Lady Macbeth, "Out, damned spot."[34] "Washing hands does not cleanse the defiled soul."[35] "All the water in the world cannot wash blood from a guilty person's hands."[36] "Only blood removes blood."[37] Only Jesus' innocent blood removes sin's stain.

Pilate washes his hands, but the crowd willingly dirties theirs. Blame, like a hot potato, is being tossed from Judas to the Sanhedrin to the governor, until finally "all the people" (v. 25)—i.e., "God's people, Israel"[38]—grab hold of the guilt collectively. This is the climax of our text. However, this high point in the narrative is the lowest point in Israel's history.

Verse 25—"And all the people answered, 'His blood be on us and on our children!'"—is the lowest and perhaps saddest verse in the Bible. It is sad because, in a historically limited way, their self-curse came true. The generation that chose Barabbas in AD 33 (or thereabouts) thirty-three years later followed other Barabbas-like rebels into war against Rome, and in doing so they dug their own graves, tore down their own temple, leveled their own city walls,[39] and sacrificed their own children. It is also sad because too many Christians for too many generations used this self-curse as God's eternal curse on the Jews. In the fourth century Jerome wrote that "this imprecation upon the Jews continues until the present day."[40] And from the medieval crusades to Nazi Germany Matthew 27:25 was used like a satanic sword to advocate and justify the slaughter of millions of Jewish men, women, and children. How awful when God's merciful Word is used for murderous purposes! The church is at its best when armed with love and pointing the finger of accusation inward:

> Mine, mine was the transgression.[41]

This verse is sad. But that sad story is not all sorrows. This verse is not all tears. For Jesus knew that his people knew not what they did. On the cross he declared, "Father, forgive them, for they know not what they do" (Luke 23:34). This "Jesus" died to "save his people from their sins" (1:21). His blood was upon them. (True enough.) But his blood is saving blood. It is blood that made "a great many of the priests . . . obedient to the faith" (Acts 6:7), and it is also blood that covered persecutors like Saul/Paul who became God's "chosen instrument" to carry the gospel to "the Gentiles . . . and the children of Israel" (Acts 9:15). "Christ redeemed us [and them—believing Jews] from the curse of the law by becoming a curse for us" (Galatians 3:13a).

No more let sins and sorrows grow,
Nor thorns infest the ground;
He comes to make His blessings flow
Far as the curse is found,
Far as the curse is found,
Far as, far as the curse is found.[42]

Here's Why!

In the western lectern of the cathedral in Naumburg, Germany there is a carving of this trial.[43] All the characters are busy doing something. For example, angry Caiaphas is handing Jesus over to Pilate, while fearful Pilate is beginning to wash his hands. Jesus alone stares out into the congregation below the preacher. That is all that he is doing. He has a sad, almost confused expression on his face. It's as if he has the question, "Why?" coming from his calm and reassuring eyes. But, of course, he knows why Barabbas was released and he was scourged and crucified.

But do you know why? Let me summarize.

Jesus was scourged and crucified—"despised . . . rejected . . . stricken, smitten . . . afflicted . . . pierced . . . crushed . . . chastise[d] . . . oppressed" (Isaiah 53:3–10). Why? ". . . for our transgressions . . . for our iniquities" (Isaiah 53:5). The scourging brought us healing; the chastisement of the cross "brought us peace" (Isaiah 53:5). Guilty Barabbas was released, and innocent Jesus was convicted to symbolize theologically that God's judgment for sinners fell on Jesus: "the LORD has laid on him the iniquity of us all" (Isaiah 53:6; cf. vv. 11, 12). Call it penal substitutionary atonement. Call it the great exchange. Call it the joyous exchange. Call it whatever you like so long as you recognize it as the greatest good news the world has ever known (this is "a far, far better thing" to do than anyone has ever done)[44] and so long as you see that *that* substitution was necessary for your sins to be forgiven.

Barabbas was a notorious murderer and insurrectionist. He was likely the leader of those two "robbers" (27:38)—the word Josephus uses for "freedom fighters" and the word we'd use for terrorists—crucified next to Jesus.[45] There were three crosses placed on Golgotha, and the one in the middle was for Barabbas. Isn't that right? We should be taken aback when we grasp that "Jesus was nailed to a cross originally intended for Barabbas."[46] This is the story of our salvation (cf. Romans 5:6–8):

> The wrong Jesus was released, the wrong Jesus scourged, the wrong Jesus crucified, but God used all these wrongs to make *everything* right. "He who

> did nothing wrong was condemned for everything so that we who have done everything wrong would be condemned for nothing."[47]

This is the Passover Amnesty! God's people are freed (free at last) from the bondage of sin so that they might now worship the true and only and scandalously beautiful Son of the Father—Jesus the King. Let us join the loud choir of Heaven, singing, "Worthy is the Lamb who was slain, to receive power and wealth and wisdom and might and honor and glory and blessing . . . forever and ever!" (Revelation 5:12, 13).

84

Behold Your King!

MATTHEW 27:27–32

ONE OF THE MOST renowned religious paintings of the twentieth century is Salvador Dali's *Christ of St. John of the Cross*, painted in 1951. I have seen it in print and online. Perhaps some of you have seen it in person.[1] If you haven't seen it in any form, let me briefly describe it. Set in a darkened sky, Dali depicts Jesus on the cross hovering above the earth and leaning down toward it. The most unique feature is how Jesus seems to be bursting forth from the canvas at the observer. The intent, and certainly the effect, is that our Lord is seen as "close yet transcendent, suffering yet somehow triumphant."[2] It is as if this dying man has mysteriously reclaimed the world for God.

In his book *The Message of the Cross*, Derek Tidball tells of the time when the National Gallery in London hosted a exhibition entitled "The Image of Christ," and Dali's painting was featured toward the end of it. While the average art critic wasn't thrilled with the work, the average person was intrigued by it. Within the first two months, 50,000 people lined up to see it. And what happened to different groups of people was unexpected and unusual. At the time the *Scottish Art Review* reported, "Men entering the room where the picture is hung instinctively take off their hats. Crowds of chattering, high-spirited school children are hushed into awed silence when they see it."[3]

On that phenomenon, Tidball comments:

> Before the cross of Christ countless men and women of every generation and culture have stood in adoring wonder and humble penitence. The cross stands at the very heart of the Christian faith, manifesting the love of God,

> effecting salvation from sin, conquering the hostile forces of evil and inviting reconciliation with God.[4]

Since Jesus first predicted his death (16:21), we have been walking in the shadow of that cross—coming closer and closer to the foot of it. In chapter 26 we saw Judas's betrayal, Peter's denial, and Jesus' unjust trial before the Sanhedrin. In chapter 27 we saw Jesus' unjust trial before Pilate. Now in 27:27–32, as we stand so near the foot of the cross, let us once again gaze upon the man "born that man no more may die."[5] As we *hear* the Roman soldiers mock the Messiah and *feel* the prick of thorns upon our Savior's sacred head,[6] let us take off our hats in respect and come again with hushed awe before the dying king who indeed—in his sufferings—reclaimed the world for God.

Acknowledge Him

Since the last few chapters have had a ton of information and over-lengthy points of application (forgive me), in this one I wanted to slow down a bit, tackle a mere six verses, and give you three simply-phrased applications.

There is precedent for slowing down. All the Gospel writers slow down when they come to their respective passion narratives. Mark's Gospel makes this shift in speed most obvious. Almost half of his Gospel focuses on Jesus' final week, and for that reason his Gospel has been called a passion story with an extended introduction. Yet even that introduction gets us moving rapidly to the cross. In chapters 1—11 thirty-three times Mark uses the word "immediately." That word moves the reader to read faster. "On to the next thing"—that is the sense of it. The word "immediately," however, is used only twice in chapters 12—16, and that is because Mark has brought us to the focus of his Gospel—the cross! Just as Mark can't wait to get to the cross, the same can be said of Matthew. And as Matthew followed Mark's lead, so I will follow his. I will slow us down in order that we might see what we are to see and to do what we are to do with the sufferings of our Lord.

With that said, our first point of application is: *acknowledge him.* We are to acknowledge Jesus as a paradoxical suffering sovereign or crucified king.

Being the literary genius he was, Matthew gives us that point of application with literary flair. As is pointed out by likely the two greatest Matthew scholars—Ulrich Luz and Dale Allison—verses 27–31 is a chiasm.[7] Rather than merely explain to you what a chiasm or chiasmus is, you can look at one below:

27 Then the soldiers of the governor took Jesus into the governor's headquarters,
and they gathered the whole battalion before him.
28 And they stripped him and put a scarlet robe on him,
29a and twisting together a crown of thorns, they put it on his head and put a reed in his right hand.
29b And kneeling before him, they mocked him, saying, "Hail, King of the Jews!"
30 And they spit on him and took the reed and struck him on the head.
31a And when they had mocked him, they stripped him of the robe and put his own clothes on him
31b and led him away to crucify him.

Do you see how Matthew takes several similar words and actions, and starting from both ends, works his way to the center? In verses 27 and 31b the soldiers *lead* Jesus somewhere; in verses 28 and 31a they put on and take off a *cloak*; in verses 29a and 30 they do something to Jesus' *head* (note also the repetition of the word *reed*). But then, as we finally arrive at the center there is no parallel because we have arrived at the point, poetically and thematically. The point is that these soldiers pay homage to Jesus as king (v. 29b), but mockingly so.

Let's find out the likely intent behind Matthew's structure. Of all the historical details surrounding the sufferings of Jesus, Matthew focuses on mockery, and he employs irony to help us rightly apply the many mockeries. You see, here in verses 27–31 we are given none of the physical, emotional, or spiritual sufferings of Christ. We are not told that "Jesus cried out in pain" or that he prayed in anguish to the Father—"Enough with this mockery! I'm your beloved Son. Do something. Save me." Instead Jesus is once again silent. We hear only the voice of the mockers. Their words—such "instruments of torture"—must have pierced our Savior's soul.[8] But they are recorded here, and recorded the way they are recorded—as a chiasm—to ironically teach us what to call Jesus. We are to acknowledge him as the crucified king. We are to acknowledge him as the sovereign who, by means of his sufferings, reigns over Heaven and earth. Here we see more clearly than before that the King of kings is the King of Pain and that that King will soon rule from a wooden cross, not a golden throne.

This closing scene of Jesus' two terrible trials foreshadows the closing, triumphant scene of the Gospel. To the one to whom has been granted "[a]ll authority in heaven and on earth" (28:18; cf. 26:64), we are to say, "Hail, King of the Jews! Hail, King of the Gentiles! Hail, King of the Heavens and the Earth!" As much as the cross of Christ casts a shadow on the whole of Jesus' life, so too does the crown of Christ cast a brilliant light over all the darkness of his sufferings. The soldiers' adoration and enthronement is a farce; yet if we remove their appalling attitudes from their actions—take away the parody of the wreath of thorns as golden garland, a soldier's cloak as royal robe, a reed as scepter, and the adulation due Caesar conferred upon Christ—we have the truth set before us. As these joking Gentiles bow before Jesus (cf. 2:11; 15:22), so all the nations are to give to the true King of the kingdom of God the veneration due his majestic name. Put simply, their scorn is our call to worship.

This week I have been reading my youngest son, Simeon, from Geraldine McCaughrean's retelling of John Bunyan's *A Pilgrim's Progress*. On Tuesday I read chapter 4, "The Hill." It was so good that I reread it on Thursday, with his sister Evelyn joining us and helping me with the hard words. When Christian gets to the top of the hill, he sees three ancient and abandoned wooden crosses. The author describes the scene:

> Each [cross] was sunk into the ground and here and there rusty nails stuck out at haphazard angles. The wood around the nails was stained with blood. To the top of the middle cross, a notice had been nailed which seemed to read *King of the Jews*. No, now he looked at it squarely, it said nothing of the kind. It said *Light of the World*—or was it *The Truth and the Way*, or was it simply *The Door*? As clouds scrolled by and the sunbeams caught it from different angles, the words changed, though the cross remained all too horribly the same. There was no mistaking it for anything other than it was—a brutal instrument of torture and execution on which a man had been nailed up to die of thirst and suffocation. Christian's throat turned dry at the thought of it, his lungs too cramped to breathe. What if he had been there that day? What if he had seen it, that murderous cruelty, that unrightable wrong, that ghastly injustice committed under a hot afternoon sun? The thought was too much to hold in his head—like trying to hold hot metal between bare hands. It brought him to his knees.[9]

In Matthew's Gospel the escalating mockery of the "whole battalion"—picture 600 men kneeling before Jesus—is the ironic image of what the 7,000,000,000 men, women, and children of the world today should do: acknowledge Jesus as their crucified king.

Thank Him

As we move next to our second point, we pause to gaze—on your knees if able—at Jesus with gratitude. *Thank him* is our second application. Our third application will be to *imitate him*. These two final points are both responses to our acknowledgment of Jesus as king. In other words, they are two answers to the question, what does it mean to acknowledge Jesus as king? What it first means is to thank him for his sufferings. What it second means is to imitate him in his sufferings.

First, let's thank him.

One week after church I was handed a sealed, blank white envelope. The man who handed it to me assured me that he was serving merely as a carrier pigeon. Inside that envelope were ten one-hundred-dollar bills. That's $1,000 for those bad at math. I'm not the most perceptive man in the world, but I'm perceptive enough to know that at least one person in my church is my generous patron. I didn't ask him/her to stand up when I preached on this text, and I didn't send out my own people to draw him/her out. But what I did was stop mid-sermon to say, "Thank you." That's the least I can do.

Listen, we know who Jesus is and what he did for us. He gave us not a few hundreds but everything—he gave his life as a ransom for our sins (20:28). So how wretched it would be for us not to pause from time to time to publicly thank him, to sing:

> My heart is filled with *thankfulness* to Him who bore my pain;
> Who plumbed the depths of my disgrace and gave me life again;
> Who crushed my curse of sinfulness and clothed me in His light
> And wrote His law of righteousness with power upon my heart.[10]

Now, did you notice in those lyrics how Jesus' sacrifice exposes our sin? We sing of our "sinfulness" and the "depths of [our] disgrace." An older hymn of the faith makes this point even more pointedly.

> Ye who think of sin but lightly,
> Nor suppose the evil great,
> Here may view its nature rightly,
> Here its guilt may estimate.
> Mark the Sacrifice appointed!
> See who bears the awful load!
> 'Tis the Word, the Lord's Anointed,
> Son of Man, and Son of God.[11]

Such a proper self-evaluation in light of such a Sacrifice is precisely what happened to me as I prepared this chapter. As I meditated on the unimaginable sufferings of Christ, I saw something of the sinfulness of sin.

While Jesus here once again embodies the Sermon on the Mount in a number of ways, the Roman soldiers embody the world at its worse—unleashed anger, bullying brutality, cruel mockery, and senseless violence.[12]

Islam makes sure that Jesus is not seen suffering. The Quran teaches that it is "inappropriate that a major prophet of God should come to such an ignominious end,"[13] and thus "Allah took [Jesus] up to himself"[14]—i.e., saved him "from the shame of crucifixion."[15] Christianity, however, throws Jesus right into the cesspool of sin and says, "Now here's a Savior for sinners! Here's a God-man sent to save godless men. Here's a real for-the-sins-of-the-world Messiah." From the inhumane torture of American POWs by the Japanese in World War II to the junior high jokester poking fun at the fat kid on the playground, Jesus is sympathetic to our weaknesses because he is Savior of those sins and a zillion more.

For the sin of lying to your mother about what happened to your report card, "Behold, the Lamb of God, who takes away the sin of the world!" (John 1:29). Thank you, Jesus. For the sin of cheating on last year's taxes, "Behold, the Lamb of God, who takes away the sin of the world!" Thank you, Jesus. For the sin of lusting after your neighbor's spouse, "Behold, the Lamb of God, who takes away the sin of the world!" Thank you, Jesus. For the sin of spending too much on yourself to the neglect of your brothers and sisters in Christ, "Behold, the Lamb of God, who takes away the sin of the world!" Thank you, Jesus. For the sin of drinking too much rum and Coke at your brother's wedding, "Behold, the Lamb of God, who takes away the sin of the world!" Thank you, Jesus. For the sin of thinking too highly of yourself while you preach on the sufferings of Jesus, "Behold, the Lamb of God, who takes away the sin of the world!" Thank you, Jesus.

For the sins of abortion, adultery, anxiety, arrogance, backbiting, bearing false witness, bitterness, blasphemy, boasting, bribery, complaining, coveting, contention, coarse joking, deceit, defrauding others, despising the poor, dishonoring the government, disregarding the Lord's people on the Lord's Day, disrespecting your parents and elders, envy, evil thoughts, fornication, fortune-telling, fraud, gambling, giving grudgingly (or not giving at all), gluttony, gossip, greed, harsh words, hating your brother, holding a grudge, idleness, idolatry, immodesty, losing your temper, lust, lying, malice, murder, prayerlessness, racism, rage, rape, resisting the Holy Spirit, returning insult for insult, rioting, scoffing, selfish ambition, showing favoritism, slander, sloth, speaking idle words, stealing, unlawful divorce, violence, witchcraft, and loving the world, loving yourself, not loving your neighbor or enemy or fellow Christian or God . . . to name a few sins. For all those and more, Behold your crucified king! Give thanks to him. Give thanks. Give thanks. Give thanks.

Just imagine what the weight of the sins of the world felt like. Just imagine the one man "who knew no sin" being "made . . . to be sin . . . so that in him we might become the righteousness of God" (2 Corinthians 5:21). It is one thing to have a thorn pushing into your skull when a Roman soldier hits you in the head;[16] it is quite another thing—an unfathomable thing—for God the Father to charge/impute/bestow upon his only Son all of our sins.

You see, nothing reveals the weight of our sins like the sufferings of Jesus. Nothing reveals the mercy of God like the sufferings of Jesus. Nothing reveals our absolute inability to save ourselves like the sufferings of Jesus. And thus something of our heartfelt thanks offered up to him is more than appropriate, don't you think?

Imitate Him

We should acknowledge Jesus as King. And what it means to acknowledge him is first to thank him and second to imitate him.

As I showed you, verses 27–31 are a tight structural unit. Then there is verse 32: "As they went out, they [the soldiers] found a man of Cyrene, Simon by name. They compelled this man to carry his [Jesus'] cross." This verse seemingly stands on its own. It doesn't fit with the chiasmus of verses 27–31, and it doesn't fit neatly with verses 33–44 because those verses shift the scene to Golgotha and the focus back to Jesus. What then is with this slight and swift shift in Matthew's camera lens? Why is this detail about Simon carrying Jesus' cross mentioned? I'll come back to that question in a moment. First, let's ask another more basic question: who was this Simon?

Was Simon the Cyrene a Jew or a Gentile? His name is Jewish, but he is from a mostly Gentile region of North Africa, present-day Libya. However, Josephus informs us that a fourth of the population of Cyrene was Jewish.[17] Therefore, Simon (such a Jewish name!) was likely a Diaspora Jew in Jerusalem on pilgrimage for the Passover.

Was he a disciple of Jesus? Is that why he was chosen to carry the cross? Matthew tells us he was "compelled . . . to carry" Jesus' cross (v. 32). Luke uses stronger language. He says "they seized" him (Luke 23:26). That, of course, doesn't mean he wasn't a disciple, for who would want to carry a heavy, bloodstained horizontal crossbeam a few paces, let alone a few miles? Mark tells us that he was merely "a passerby" (Mark 15:21) and implies that he had just arrived in town. He also tells us, moreover, that he was "the father of Alexander and Rufus," two men who became well enough known Christians in the early church to have their names recorded forever in the Scriptures. Alexander is mentioned in Acts 19:33 and Rufus in Romans 16:13. How did these boys become Christians, and did their dad join them in the faith?

There is not much we know, but in Acts 2:10 we read that people from "parts of Libya belonging to Cyrene" were among the crowd amazed, astounded, and converted to Christ after Peter's Pentecost sermon. Thus, by natural deduction mixed with a bit of sanctified speculation, I surmise that Simon here in Matthew was just an innocent Jewish spectator pulled from the crowd the day he carried Jesus' cross, but after Pentecost he became a follower of Jesus.

Whatever the case may be, he is a bit of a foil to that other Simon we call Peter who vowed to die with Christ if necessary. The Twelve have all scattered. Jesus is alone. But here is this new Simon,[18] compelled to carry that old rugged cross that would soon save him the trip back to the temple next year and save him from the financial burden of regular animal sacrifices *and* save him (hallelujah!) from all his sins.

Let's return to that other question I raised earlier: why is this detail about Simon carrying Jesus' cross mentioned? Perhaps it is mentioned merely for historical reasons. The apostles are very concerned to give an accurate historical record. Certainly this detail shows how brutally Jesus was beaten. At some point he was unable to carry his own cross. But I wonder if there is also some symbolic value here. I'm not talking about odd allegories—that the red cloak is the "blood of the world,"[19] and "the sharp points of the thorns aptly pertain to the sins from which a crown of victory is woven for Christ," and "the reed symbolizes the emptiness and weakness of all those Gentiles, which is held firm in his grasp."[20] I'm talking about sensible symbolism. Matthew is not opposed to sensible symbolism. He sees patterns in Old Testament narratives as representative of what is occurring in Jesus' life. And he sees Jesus' mockery as a coronation.

Moreover, he is certainly happy to employ artistry whenever possible or needed. He loves irony. He delights in paradox. At times he is a structure fanatic. Why not a dash of symbolism? Could it be that Simon shows us that following Jesus involves suffering? Could it be that Simon's sharing in the sufferings of Christ teaches us to expect the same? Could it be, as Luther suggests, that Simon here is "an image of all Christians"?[21] To be honest, I'm not sure. But I am sure just how seriously that point is stressed elsewhere in Scripture, and even (and especially?) in Matthew.

My friend Jason Hood is writing a book on the theme of imitation.[22] He gave me a rough draft of a section on "Imitating Jesus" in the Gospel of Matthew. I found that his insights provide support for my application on imitation. He points out, for example, that as Jesus was meek (21:5) we are to be meek (5:5); as he was merciful and humble (9:27; 11:29) we are to be merciful and humble (23:12); as he was baptized with the Father, Son (himself), and Spirit present (3:16, 17) we are to baptize in the name of the Father, Son, and Holy Spirit (28:19); as he was a servant to God and others (4:10; particularly by coming "to serve" through his death, 20:28), we are to serve as well (20:26, 27); as he prayed (14:23) we are to pray (6:5–15); as he rejected the allure of earthly wealth (8:20) we are to serve God and not money (6:19–24); as he was ultimately rewarded after the resurrection (28:18), we shall be, on the last day, victoriously vindicated and rewarded as well (19:27–30).[23]

Jason goes on to list a number of other ways that Jesus teaches his followers that they are to imitate him (cf. 1 Corinthians 11:1). And he argues that Matthew urges his readers to become "apprentices of the Master" and that all those attributes above can be summarized as "facets of self-denial and the cross." He calls Matthew's emphasis of imitation "cross-shaped." Others have called it "Cruciformity."[24] That is, as Jesus was "persecuted for righteousness' sake" (26:57–68; 27:1, 2, 11–50) we are to suffer for such. As Jesus had his cross (27:37–50), so we have ours: "If anyone would come after me, let him deny himself and take up his cross and follow me" (16:24).

So, are we to imitate Simon the Cyrene as he imitated Christ? My answer is yes.

In saying that we should carry Christ's cross, I am in no way denying the sufficiency of the atonement—"Jesus paid it all, all to him I owe"[25]—nor am I denying Jesus' hope-filled teachings on how we share in his glorification and enthronement. (A slave is not above the master, but we are like the Master [cf. 10:24]. In his likeness we shall reign forever and ever.) But what I am saying is, cross now, crown then. What I am saying is that we should not see sufferings as strange and without God's supernatural joy and blessing attached to them. In 1 Peter 4:12–14 the old Simon Peter, newly restored, writes:

> Beloved, do not be surprised at the fiery trial when it comes upon you to test you, as though something strange were happening to you. But rejoice insofar as *you share Christ's sufferings*, that you may also rejoice and be glad when his glory is revealed. If you are insulted for the name of Christ, you are blessed, because the Spirit of glory and of God rests upon you.

Here Peter is not denying the sufficiency of the cross, for earlier he wrote of Jesus that "Christ also suffered once for sins, the righteous for the unrighteous, that he might bring us to God" (1 Peter 3:18), and "[h]e himself bore our sins in his body on the tree" (1 Peter 2:24a). But for Peter that atonement leads to ethics: "He himself bore our sins in his body on the tree, *that* we might die to sin and live to righteousness" (1 Peter 2:24).[26]

How can Peter talk like that? Or how can Paul write crazy things about rejoicing in his sufferings (Colossians 1:24) or boasting that he shares the brand-marks of Christ (see Galatians 6:17)? They can do so because they understand that our imitation of Christ is cross-shaped. As Jesus "endured the cross . . . for the joy that was set before him" (Hebrews 12:2), so we, who "have not yet resisted [as he did] to the point of shedding . . . blood" (Hebrews 12:4), struggle in this world—against sin, sickness, trials, and persecutions. And we do so because we grasp that it is cross now and crown then. So we don't think suffering strange. In fact, when suffering dishonor for Christ we *rejoice*, as the first Christians did, that we "were counted worthy to suffer dishonor for the name" (Acts 5:41).

I know that we all want to live in Leisureville. But Jesus has called us now to reside in Cross Town, where our currency has the head of our king crowned with thorns in the center circle and "In God We Trust and In Christ We Suffer" printed on both sides, and where our military dons the crest of the cross with the insignia *Abora Sicut Bonus Miles Christi Iesu* ("Share in suffering as a good solider of Christ Jesus," 2 Timothy 2:3), and where our constitution has Four Articles of Imitation that every good citizen has memorized:

> Article 1: "We suffer with him in order that we may also be glorified with him" (Romans 8:17).
>
> Article 2: "So Jesus also suffered outside the gate in order to sanctify the people through his own blood. Therefore let us go to him outside the camp and bear the reproach he endured" (Hebrews 13:12, 13).
>
> Article 3: "For it has been granted to you that for the sake of Christ you should not only believe in him but also suffer for his sake" (Philippians 1:29).
>
> Article 4: "For to this you have been called, because Christ also suffered for you, leaving you an example, so that you might follow in his steps" (1 Peter 2:21).

Our stadiums sport four banners of hope, hanging on the northern, southern, eastern, and western walls.

> As we share abundantly in Christ's sufferings, so through Christ we share abundantly in comfort too. (2 Corinthians 1:5)
>
> We rejoice in our sufferings. (Romans 5:3a)
>
> [We] consider that the sufferings of this present time are not worth comparing with the glory that is to be revealed to us. (Romans 8:18)

> After [we] have suffered a little while, the God of all grace, who has called [us] to his eternal glory in Christ, will himself restore, confirm, strengthen, and establish [us]. (1 Peter 5:10)

I know that we all want to live in Leisureville. But we now live in Cross Town. It will be the Celestial City later, but it's Cross Town now. You can flee to Leisureville to find your temporal escape or to get your worldly fix. Or you can be more pious about it and flee from the life of cruciformity into the high mysteries of the sacraments or the enthusiastic life of the Spirit,[27] forgetting that the sacraments of Christ focus on his sufferings, and the Spirit-filled life is filled with sufferings. We are to imitate Simon the Cyrene as he imitates Jesus the Christ. We too are to carry Christ's cross.

Acknowledge Jesus as the crucified king. Acknowledge him by thanking him and imitating him. It's that simple. It's that difficult.

85

The Power of the Cross

MATTHEW 27:33–44

ONE OF MY CREATIVE DAUGHTERS is working on what I assume will amount to her first great novel, *Boys vs. Girls*. She showed me a draft of the first chapter, entitled "The Powers." It begins like this:

> Now, before I tell you about everyone's supernatural powers, I must tell you this. The fourth grade boys and girls have been fighting for months! Okay, now I can tell you. Girls first. Lily can shoot spikes that are poison. Juliana can cure any sickness. Sarah can do many impossible gymnastics. Haley can grow as tall as twenty feet. Lauren P. can turn invisible. Lauren O. can run 100 mph. Rachel can turn into anything she wants. Katie can make people look really pretty. Naomi can shrink into a tiny person. Laura can jump up to fifty feet. That's it for the girls!
>
> The boys' powers are . . . Zachary can get any weapon. J. D.'s freckles can turn into bombs. Vince can shoot grenades out of his hands. Philip can remember anything. Brian can shoot books out of his hands. And Roman controls the weather.

When we think of power we often think of the Super Friends' powers—the strength of Superman, the bulletproof bracelets of Wonder Woman, the malleability of Plastic Man, the underwater adaptability of Aquaman, the supernatural speed of The Flash.

In 1 Corinthians 1:17–31 Paul summarizes a similar worldly perspective on power. After he writes about the potential of emptying "the cross of Christ . . . of its power" (v. 17), he says, "For the word of the cross is folly to those who are perishing, but to us who are being saved it is the power of God" (v. 18). He continues a few verses later:

> For Jews demand signs and Greeks seek wisdom, but we preach Christ crucified, a stumbling block to Jews and folly to Gentiles, but to those who are called, both Jews and Greeks, Christ the power of God and the wisdom of God. (vv. 22–24)

It is that theology of the cross that is played out here in Matthew's narrative of the cross. Already in Matthew 27, at the end of the two kangaroo court trials, we have seen both the Jews and the Gentiles separately mock Jesus. Here in 27:33–44, as Jesus hangs on the cross, those two voices join together in their summary mockeries of the Messiah. To the Gentiles—the Roman soldiers—this king on a cross is a joke. This is the height of foolishness. To the Jews—the common folk, the religious leaders, and the criminals—this Son of God on a cross is inconceivable. It's the height of weakness, not power. But to those who are being saved—Jews and Gentiles, Matthew's church and ours—Christ crucified is where "God made foolish the wisdom of the world" (1 Corinthians 1:20c). The cross is where Jesus magnified "the power of God and the wisdom of God" (1 Corinthians 1:24).

In our last few studies we considered Matthew's use of irony. Here again Matthew employs this literary device to help us apply the mockeries. We learn about this silent sufferer, Jesus (note again that Jesus doesn't say a word, and the only action he does is to taste but not drink the wine in v. 34), through the voices of those who think he's the world's biggest failure and fool. Put differently, Jesus' enemies unwittingly teach us about the meaning of the cross. Their putting Jesus to open shame—by crucifying, mocking, and disregarding him—shows us how, in allowing his Son to be nailed to the cross, God "disarmed the rulers and authorities and put them to open shame, by triumphing over them in him" (Colossians 2:15).

Jesus Reigns as King on the Cross (vv. 33–38)

There are three ironic instructions from Jesus' opposition. First, Jesus reigns as king *on* the cross. We learn this lesson in verses 33–38 where the focus falls on the Roman soldiers' obvious but evil actions toward Jesus.

> And when they came to a place called Golgotha (which means Place of a Skull), they offered him wine to drink, mixed with gall, but when he tasted it, he would not drink it. And when they had crucified him, they divided his garments among them by casting lots. Then they sat down and kept watch over him there. And over his head they put the charge against him, which read, "This is Jesus, the King of the Jews." Then two robbers were crucified with him, one on the right and one on the left.

The best baseball players are those who take seriously a return to the basics during spring training. Likewise, the good communicator returns to the basics on a regular basis. I recently read the first few chapters of Stanley Fish's book, *How to Write a Sentence and How to Read One*. A sentence has verbs in it, the most necessary component of a sentence. If we simply find and follow the verbs in verses 33–38, six or perhaps seven ironic mockeries come to light.[1]

The "perhaps" relates to the soldiers taking Jesus to "a place called Golgotha" (v. 33). I don't think they are intentionally mocking him. They are just doing their job—taking a convicted criminal to the place *outside* the city (cf. 21:39; Hebrews 13:12) for capital punishment. We call Death Row Death Row because that's where inmates who are to receive the death penalty are housed. "Golgotha" (which became *Calvarium* in Latin, thus Calvary in English) got the nickname "Place of a Skull" (v. 33) likely because the hill resembled a human skull but also because it was the hill where men went to die. Anyway, the irony might be (if the church fathers are to be believed; I believe them 51 percent of the time) that the mention of "a skull" refers to Adam's skull. This is the place where Adam was buried. (You will see this often in medieval paintings of the crucifixion—Adam's skull is beneath the cross.)[2] Now that's fairly cool: the second Adam through his death would bring physical and spiritual life to the first Adam and the sons of Adam. It's cool, but likely not correct. What is correct is the theology that in Jesus' death ironically the curse of the place of the skull in the life of man is buried forever.

The other six ironic mockeries are easy to see. I won't go through each in turn. Instead I'll group many of them together. However, we will start with the next one on its own. After the soldiers took Jesus to Calvary, "they offered him wine to drink, mixed with gall" (v. 34a). Once Jesus tasted what it was, he refused to drink it (v. 34b). That reaction tells us that the drink was either a cruel joke (like someone offering you lemonade but intentionally giving you lemon juice) or a drug to deaden the pain (an ancient anesthetic)[3] or to assist death (a suicide solution). If it's the latter, then Jesus' refusal is all the more admirable. He refused to give up control of his conscious choice of death by crucifixion. "He was determined to accept death at its bitterest and grimmest."[4] Either way, our Lord's refusal to drink from that cup shows us that he is still willing to drink the cup of God's wrath for us. He will neither take "a shortcut to death," nor will he allow their "malicious mockery" to drift him off course.[5]

Next we read in verse 34 that the soldiers crucified him and divvied up his garments by gambling for them. This verse is an odd verse. It's odd in that Matthew describes the chief event of the Christian faith with a single Greek participle, *staurōsantes.*[6] The language is as humble as the death. In verses 51–53 (part of our next text) we will see the supernatural fireworks that Jesus' crucifixion sets off. But here there is a seemingly greater emphasis placed on what happens to Jesus' garments than on what is happening to his dying body. The main truth of Christianity is "Jesus Christ and him crucified" (1 Corinthians 2:2), but the main verb of this sentence is "they divided his garments" (v. 35).

So while Mel Gibson, for example, in his movie *The Passion of the Christ*, focuses on the physical violence (what Mel Gibson movie doesn't focus on physical violence?), Matthew gives us none of the gory details. He doesn't mention that the cross was seven feet tall, just long enough to make sure that no man could touch the ground to hold himself up. He doesn't mention the hammer and the nails. He doesn't even mention blood, which Matthew has mentioned five times earlier in chapter 27 (vv. 4, 6, 8, 24, 25). Instead he highlights the mockeries—the soldiers' ironic insensitivity not only to human suffering but to the one human whose sufferings brings salvation to the world. While Jesus suffers without clothing (he is either naked or has a loincloth on), at the foot of the cross there's a casino—four soldiers gambling for Jesus' garments.

One of the earliest Christian hymns to Christ sings of this strange disgrace:

> He who hung the earth hangs there, he who fixed the heavens is fixed there, he who made all things fast is made fast upon the tree, the Master has been insulted, God has been murdered. . . . O strange murder, strange crime! The Master has been treated in unseemly fashion, his body naked, and not even deemed worthy of covering. . . . [7]

In verses 36–38 the soldiers' mockery intensifies. There is this contrast of control. While Jesus helplessly hangs, they are sitting. While he is above them dying, they are watching over him. While the innocent Christ is being crucified, they add to his indignity by placing him in between two insurrectionists and placing above his head, "This is Jesus, the King of the Jews" (v. 37). They watch him give his State of the Union speechless speech between two transgressors—one on his right, the other on his left (v. 38; cf. Isaiah 53:12).

What a picture of powerlessness! How can the power of God be displayed in this way? How does King Jesus reign crucified on a cross? There is no way for us to see Jesus' power unless we see it through the lens of Scripture. Psalm 22, which will soon be on Jesus' lips in verse 46, is already mixed into the ink of Matthew's pen. Soon we will hear the allusion to Psalm 22:7—the wagging of their heads (v. 39). Here it is the allusion to Psalm 22:18, "they divide my garments among them, and for my clothing they cast lots."[8] While the world sees failure, we are to see fulfillment. This must be the powerless Son of David, who through sufferings gains power, as the Psalm says toward its end:

> All the ends of the earth shall remember
> and turn to the LORD,
> and all the families of the nations
> shall worship before you.
> For kingship belongs to the LORD,
> and he rules over the nations. (Psalm 22:27, 28)

What the Romans hang mockingly above Jesus as his "crime," Matthew sees as a coronation. He turns their accusation into the church's proclamation—"*This is* Jesus, the King. . . ." (v. 37).[9] They might be sitting and laughing at the foot of the cross, but it is "He who sits in the heavens [that] laughs." Yahweh laughs "in derision" as through the cross he has set up his "King on Zion," on his "holy hill" (Psalm 2:4, 6).

Jesus' Death Destroys the Temple (Vv. 39, 40)

The second ironic instruction is that Jesus' death "destroys" the temple. We find such temple-talk in verses 39, 40:

> And those who passed by derided him, wagging their heads and saying, "You who would destroy the temple and rebuild it in three days, save yourself! If you are the Son of God, come down from the cross."

In verses 33–38 the Gentiles mock Jesus. Here in verses 39, 40, as well as in verses 41–44, the Jews mock Jesus. As there will be three groups of confessors right after Jesus' death—the soldiers, the women, and Joseph of Arimathea—here there are three groups of Jewish scoffers right before Jesus' death—the passersby, the religious leaders, and the co-crucified.[10]

First are the passersby.[11] We might also call them the curious crowd. Those who recently shouted, "Let him be crucified!" (27:22, 23) have come to see the scandalous spectacle. Perhaps they have come to see some shock and awe. Will this Jesus pull off the greatest miracle of all—will he fly from the cross, kill the Roman soldiers, tear down Pilate's palace, and set up David's eternal kingdom? However, when they walk by Jesus they shake their heads and jeer, "Hey, Temple-Basher and Three-Day Builder![12] Look at you now!"

In the trial before the Sanhedrin (26:61–65) Jesus was accused of being anti-God (because of his "blasphemy" of calling himself the Son of God and Son of Man) and anti-temple (because of his prediction of the temple's doom). In light of his power claims, especially his claim to destroy and rebuild the temple—a claim of incomprehensible power—the sight of him on the cross was pathetic to them. They looked at Jerusalem, and there was the temple still standing in its majestic beauty. They looked at Golgotha, and there was this Jesus still hanging in abject powerlessness, with no majestic beauty whatsoever.

They add to their head-shaking and temple-claim mockery the accusation and devilish temptation, "If you are the Son of God, come down from the cross" (v. 40b). Put differently, "If you, O Son of God, have come down all the way from Heaven, why not come down a foot or two off that cross. That is assuming, of course, that you are the Son of God" (cf. 26:64). "If you are the Son of God . . ." That's a big if. We remember hearing that phrase "If you are the Son of God" earlier in Matthew. It came from Satan when he tempted Jesus in the wilderness (4:3, 6; cf. 26:63).[13] "Here truly is Jesus' last great temptation."[14] How will he use his power—for himself or for others? Will he turn a stone into bread? Will he grasp for the kingdoms of the world? Will he worship Satan? Will he fly from the cross or stay on it?

When I was a boy, each Holy Week NBC showed the television miniseries *Jesus of Nazareth*. I must have watched that series at least five years in a row before they took it off the air. Each time it came to this scene where Jesus is asked to prove himself, I pleaded with him to do so. I wanted him to show those jeering jerks his power. I wanted him to recover like Superman from this kryptonite moment, push the nails out from his hands and feet, whisk away the wicked to the Hall of Justice, and recue the weeping women.

But it wasn't until much later in my life that I grasped that Jesus played the role of the true Super Man by being the Suffering Man and that in the temple of his body (see John 2:19–22)—through his sacrificial death and then glorious resurrection and eternal enthronement—he destroyed the need for a man-made temple. Matthew 27:51a illustrates the point: "And behold, the curtain of the temple was torn in two, from top to bottom." Hebrews 9:24–26 summarizes this:

> For Christ has entered, not into holy places made with hands, which are copies of the true things, but into heaven itself, now to appear in the presence of God on our behalf. Nor was it to offer himself repeatedly, as the high priest enters the holy places every year with blood not his own, for then he would have had to suffer repeatedly since the foundation of the world. But as it is, he has appeared once for all at the end of the ages to put away sin by the sacrifice of himself.

By the sacrifice of himself! Who would do such a thing—stay on that cross? What obedience to the Father's will held him there! What love for us held him there! Craig Blomberg writes, "It is difficult to study the crucifixion sensitively and sympathetically and not break down in tears." He goes on to add a few ecclesial applications to that emotional one:

> It is almost inconceivable that believers who frequently meditate on Jesus' suffering on their behalf could exalt themselves or quarrel with each other (hence 1 Cor 1:18–2:5 as Paul's response to the problems of 1 Cor 1:10–17). The ground is indeed level at the foot of the cross. That God should send his Son to die for us was the scandal of the Christian message in the first century (1 Cor 1:23) and remains so for many today.[15]

Last year during Holy Week someone at Yale University affixed a cross on campus with the inscription ROFL instead of INRI.[16] INRI stands for the Latin inscription *Iesvs Nazarenvs Rex Ivdaeorvm*, "Jesus of Nazarene, King of the Jews." ROFL is an Internet acronym for Rolling on the Floor Laughing. That modern mockery is not far removed from a second- or third-century one. On the Palatine Hill in Rome there is carved graffito of a crucified man with the head of a donkey. Next to Christ there is a Christian with a hand lifted in prayer. Beneath the picture is the inscription, ΑΛΕΞΑΜΕΝΟΣ ΣΕΒΕΤΕ ΘΕΟΝ ("Alexamenos venerates God").[17] It's a crude cartoon about the craziness of Christianity.

To claim, as Christians do, "that God himself accepted death in the form of a crucified Jewish manual worker from Galilee in order to break the power of death and bring salvation to all men" is uttermost madness to most men.[18] And to claim, as I am doing in this section, that Jesus destroyed the need of a man-made temple through his death turns all perceptions of power upside down. That magnificent building that took decades to build and shines brilliantly in the sun surely must be what God uses to save people from sin, not some suffering, dying, convicted criminal on a cursed tree. Ah, but that's the irony! In the temple of Jesus' suffering, dying, dead body God's presence and salvation come to us (1:21–23).

The world thinks the cross is crazy. It always has. It always will. But to those of us who believe it is our only hope for true sanity. It was a great miracle that Jesus walked on water. It was a great miracle that Jesus feed the 5,000. It was a great miracle that Jesus opened the eyes of the blind. It was a great miracle that Jesus raised the dead. It was a great miracle that Jesus himself rose from the dead. But perhaps the greatest miracle of all was his miraculous non-miracle—staying on the cross for our salvation. He did not call out for twelve legions of angels to rescue him. Instead he took in all our twenty-billion demons and crushed the greatest demon—death—with his bloody heel.

The Jews demand a sign—come down from the cross. But no sign will be given except the sign of Jonah (12:39; cf. 16:4)—that is, Jesus' death and resurrection. And no other sign will be given to us. The cross and the empty tomb—those are the two sure signs of our salvation. Those are the two signs that Jesus is now the temple we go to in order to enter into the presence of God and to stay in a right relationship with God (cf. 1 Timothy 2:5).

Jesus' Death Saves Believers (vv. 41–44)

In this chapter we are looking at the power of a participle—"And when they had crucified him . . ." (v. 35a). More straightforwardly, we are looking at the power of a person—Jesus, our Savior. We have looked at how Jesus reigns as king from the cross and how his sufficient sacrificial death destroys the need for a man-made temple. Finally, we will look at how Jesus' death saves believers. We learn this lesson from the second and third set of Jewish mockers. In verses 41–44 Jesus again is challenged to avoid crucifixion.

> So also the chief priests, with the scribes and elders, mocked him, saying, "He saved others; he cannot save himself. He is the King of Israel; let him come down now from the cross, and we will believe in him. He trusts in God; let God deliver him now, if he desires him. For he said, 'I am the Son of God.'" And the robbers who were crucified with him also reviled him in the same way.

Luke tells us that one of the "robbers" (better translated "terrorists" or "insurrectionists") had a change of mind (Luke 23:40–43). He repented and responded to Jesus. Matthew leaves out that detail. Perhaps he does so to show the loneliness of our Lord. Soon Jesus will cry out, "My God, my God, why have you forsaken me?" (27:46). Here he is forsaken by the Twelve. Here he is forsaken by the Jews—from their highest leaders to the lowest criminals. No one from all Israel and no one from the whole church of Christ wanted to attend this worship service. Jesus suffers and dies alone. His only companions are his enemies, who mock and revile him.

At the heart of their scorn are his claims to be King of Israel and the Son of God. They cannot fathom how God's anointed could be annihilated, the mighty Messiah murdered, the conquering Christ crucified. They stumbled over this stumbling stone. They failed to see that by losing his life, Jesus saves ours (cf. 16:25). But we should not fail to see this. He is the King of Israel.

He is the Son of God. He does trust in God, and God will vindicate him. He is now saving others. Every jest they say is true. The greatest truths of the gospel come from the mouths of these fools!

The Japanese-American artist Makoto Fujimura recently painted illustrated Gospels, entitled *The Four Holy Gospels*. For the text of Matthew 27 he painted a line of blood-red paint slowly moving from the bottom of one page to the top of the next, then slightly blending into a speckled gold streak that goes from the top of the page to the bottom.[19] What a simple but perfect illustration of what is happening on the cross. It is not the case that Jesus can't save himself, but he won't save himself. He has indeed saved others (see 8:25, 9:21, 22, 27; 14:39). He thus *can* save himself. He has the power to do so. Yet he understands that "[r]eal power is the control of power, the rejection of power, the willingness to express power in weak-seeming ways."[20] And if we haven't learned that lesson already from the Sermon on the Mount, perhaps now we shall learn it from the Sermon on the Cross.[21]

Jesus' death saves. It's ironic. It's the most beautiful and glorious irony in history. Jesus' death saves *believers*. I chose the word *believers* instead of something more generic like *sinners* or *the world* to play off the words from both Jewish religious leaders and criminals. They all reviled Jesus "in the same way" (v. 44). Thus both sets of people claimed that if Jesus came down from the cross, they would then "believe in him" (v. 42).[22] That's natural enough because their perception of power is worldly. The sense could include things people say today. "I will believe in Jesus if he cures me of cancer . . . if he writes his name in the clouds . . . if he stops all these terrible tornadoes . . . if he does whatever I ask of him *right now*." But as General William Booth, the founder of the Salvation Army, once said, "It is precisely because he would not come down that we believe in him."[23] We believe in Jesus as Savior because he stayed up there to die, came down only to be buried, and rose up again three days later. Jesus' death saves believers.

> Where is the one who is wise? Where is the scribe? Where is the debater of this age? Has not God made foolish the wisdom of the world? For since, in the wisdom of God, the world did not know God through wisdom, it pleased God through the folly of what we preach *to save those who believe*. For Jews demand signs and Greeks seek wisdom, but we preach Christ crucified, a stumbling block to Jews and folly to Gentiles, but to those who are called, both Jews and Greeks, Christ the power of God and the wisdom of God. (1 Corinthians 1:20–24)

Not a Mickey Mouse Religion

In 1998 when a little girl in Mablethorpe, England died of Batten's disease her graveside was marked by a simple cross. Soon afterward the local authorities asked her family to remove it due to a new local ordinance that stated "Crosses are discouraged, as excessive use of the supreme Christian symbol is undesirable." In lieu of the cross, the family was allowed to erect a headstone with Mickey Mouse on it.[24] No joke.

The cross will always be an offense to the world. But let's not change the symbol from a cross to the head of a harmless make-believe mouse. Mickey Mouse couldn't save a fly or hurt one. But Jesus will come again in *power* to judge the living and the dead, and his judgment will be based on what you thought of this scene in Matthew. Is Christ crucified a stumbling block for you, or is Christ crucified your only hope of salvation? I pray that "that old rugged cross, so despised by the world" would have "a wondrous attraction" for you.[25]

86

The Death of Death in the Death of Christ

MATTHEW 27:45–53

SOME CHRISTIANS, upon meditating upon the cross of Christ, are left speechless. Others can't say enough. There have likely been more sentences written on the cross of Christ than any other subject in world history. Here are just a few. John Stott calls the cross of Christ the "greatest and most glorious of all subjects" and says "there is . . . no Christianity without the cross."[1] Charles Spurgeon said, "The cross is the centre of our system."[2] J. I. Packer says that the cross "takes us to the very heart of the Christian gospel."[3] P. T. Forsyth claimed, "You do not understand Christ till you understand his cross."[4] G. Campbell Morgan said that "every living experience of Christianity begins at the cross."[5] And John Calvin said that "in the cross of Christ, as in a splendid theatre, the incomparable goodness of God is set before the whole world. The glory of God shines, indeed, in all creatures on high and below, but never more brightly than in the cross. . . ."[6]

What I have to say about the cross is simply what I believe Matthew is saying. Matthew doesn't explain to us in propositional language his doctrine of the atonement. He doesn't, as Paul does for example, say "Christ died for our sins" (1 Corinthians 15:3), or as Peter does, "For Christ also suffered once for sins, the righteous for the unrighteous, that he might bring us to God" (1 Peter 3:18), or as John does, "He is the propitiation for our sins" (1 John 2:2a), or as the author of Hebrews does, "we have been sanctified through the offering of the body of Jesus Christ once for all" (Hebrews 10:10). Rather, he *shows us* his crucifixion theology through Jesus' last two cries from the cross and God's four supernatural signs before and after Jesus' death.

The First Supernatural Sign and the Last Two Cries

We'll start with the first supernatural sign and Jesus' last two cries.[7] The first supernatural sign is recorded in verse 45: "Now from the sixth hour there was darkness over all the land until the ninth hour."

"The sixth hour" is high noon. High noon, as you know, is when the sun is at its zenith. However, here and now and for three hours the sun hides its face. Why? Is it because, as Matthew Henry said, "[The] sun never saw such wickedness as this before, and therefore withdrew"?[8] Or is it because, as Jerome cleverly commented, that the sun "retracted its rays lest it might seem to be weighing down the Lord"?[9] More likely the sun's eclipse symbolizes a mix of God's judgment—like the plague of darkness that was over all the land of Egypt (Exodus 10:22)—and God's mourning over the great evil of his Son's sufferings. Whatever the precise meaning of the sun putting on its widow's garb, the mood of this most decisive moment in world history is painted black.[10] And Matthew has painted it black by dipping his pen in the ink of the apocalyptic upheaval language of Amos 8:9, 10:[11]

> "And on that day," declares the Lord GOD,
>   "*I will make the sun go down at noon*
>   and darken the earth in broad daylight. . . .
> I will make it *like the mourning for an only son. . . .*"

Darkness is the first supernatural sign. Now, the world's outer darkness corresponds to Jesus' inner darkness: "And about the ninth hour Jesus cried out with a loud voice, saying, 'Eli, Eli, lema sabachthani?' that is, 'My God, my God, why have you forsaken me?'" (v. 46). After three hours of darkness (and silence?)[12]—it is now "about the ninth hour" (three o'clock, the time the lamb was brought into the temple)[13]—the Light of the World opens his mouth. But unlike the moment of the creation of the world, where he said, "Let there be light" (Genesis 1:3), here his voice joins the darkness as he echoes the cry of Psalm 22:1a.

Matthew gives us the Aramaic, "Eli, Eli, lema sabachthani" (v. 46). It is the only time he lets us hear how Jesus would have sounded on a day-to-day basis. Jesus spoke in Aramaic. And with the Aramaic, Matthew is highlighting something significant. The Aramaic in the raw not only makes sense of the confusion to come—why the people would hear "Elijah" when Jesus said "Eli"—but it also reveals something of the rawness of Jesus' cry. His "My God, my God, why have you forsaken me?" has a fingernails-on-the-chalkboard feel to it.

Why did Jesus cry out the first sentence of Psalm 22? Why didn't Jesus cry out its last three victorious verses—"All the prosperous of the earth eat and worship; before him shall bow all who go down to the dust, even the one who could not keep himself alive. Posterity shall serve him; it shall be told of the Lord to the coming generation; they shall come and proclaim his righteousness to a people yet unborn, that he has done it" (Psalm 22:29–31)? Or why not recite the first verses from Psalm 23—"The Lord is my shepherd; I shall not want. He makes me lie down in green pastures. He leads me beside still waters. He restores my soul" (Psalm 23:1–3a)—or the start of Psalm 21?

> O Lord, in your strength the king rejoices,
> and in your salvation how greatly he exults!
> You have given him his heart's desire
> and have not withheld the request of his lips. *Selah.*
> For you meet him with rich blessings;
> you set a crown of fine gold upon his head.
> He asked life of you; you gave it to him,
> length of days forever and ever.
> His glory is great through your salvation;
> splendor and majesty you bestow on him.
> For you make him most blessed forever;
> you make him glad with the joy of your presence. (Psalm 21:1–6)

Why Psalm 22:1? Also, why a question and not an affirmation on his lips?[14] Wouldn't something like "God loves all of you" be more soothing, or wouldn't "Let there be peace on earth" be less melodramatic? Why a question? And why a question *to God* about where God is when Jesus needs him most? While it is Scripture he quotes (Jesus' last words are God's Word), the cry of Psalm 22:1 sounds too normal, too human, too unsanctified to come from the fully sanctified Son of God.

Why such a dark cry at such a dark hour? Well, the voice fits the setting—a dark cry for a dark hour. Furthermore and more importantly, the verb of Jesus' question provides us with Jesus' theology of the cross—"forsaken." The world's greatest religion of the time—Judaism—has forsaken him. The world's strongest and seemingly most civilized empire—Rome—has forsaken him. His own apostles have forsaken him. And now has his Father forsaken him? Jesus feels that he has, if we are to take his words at face value, and I find absolutely no reason why we shouldn't.

But, of course, it is one thing to feel forsaken; it is another thing to actually be forsaken. Was there somehow a severing of Trinitarian fellowship? The Trinity cannot be broken, can it? Was there a divine divorce? How could there be? Did God really forsake his Son on the cross? And, if so, what was the nature and purpose of this God-forsakenness? Matthew doesn't directly tell us. (The mystery of the atonement might just be as mysterious as the mystery of the incarnation itself!) But he does record the darkness and the dark cry of dereliction to move us in a direction; and that direction, I'm convinced, is to what Paul would later summarize in 2 Corinthians 5:18–21, which I summarize as follows: God made sinless Jesus "to be sin" so that we might be forgiven of our sins (v. 21). That theory fits the verses in Matthew that teach that Jesus' death was the atonement for sins: Jesus saved his people from their sins (1:21) by giving his life as a ransom (20:28), by pouring out his blood for many for the forgiveness of sins (26:27, 28).

So perhaps Matthew's mysterious lack of explanation should be left alone by the preacher. Or perhaps it is the preacher's job to interpret Scripture by Scripture and to say, as Charles Cranfield said, that Jesus experienced "not merely a felt, but a real, abandonment by his Father," and "the paradox [is] that, while this God-forsakenness was utterly real, the unity of the Blessed Trinity was even then unbroken."[15] Either way the forsakenness of Jesus—whatever its true nature—should cause us to pause and to stand there in the darkness with him, to wonder what that "awful verb"[16] *forsaken* meant to him and should mean to us, and then to join Paul's spontaneous summary doxology in Romans 11, after he has explained in detail the mercies of God in Christ:

> Oh, the depth of the riches and wisdom and knowledge of God! How unsearchable are his judgments and how inscrutable his ways!
>
> "For who has known the mind of the Lord,
> or who has been his counselor?"
> "Or who has given a gift to him
> that he might be repaid?"
>
> For from him and through him and to him are all things. To him be glory forever. Amen. (Romans 11:33–36)

His Final Cry

Next let's turn our attention to Jesus' second and final cry on the cross. "And Jesus cried out again with a loud voice and yielded up his spirit" (v. 50). That verse is prefaced by the confusion about Elijah.

> And some of the bystanders, hearing it, said, "This man is calling Elijah." And one of them at once ran and took a sponge, filled it with sour wine, and put it on a reed and gave it to him to drink. But the others said, "Wait, let us see whether Elijah will come to save him." (vv. 47–49)

To be honest, I wondered why Matthew would spend three verses on this Elijah excursus. Or at least it seems like an excursus to me. The bystanders misunderstand Jesus' "Eli, Eli," which could sound like the name "Elijah" or a shortened form of it, especially coming from a dying man. People tend to hear what they want to hear anyway. The Jews of that time had a heightened expectation that Elijah would return "before the great and awesome day of the Lord comes" (Malachi 4:5). They also viewed him "as a kind of 'patron saint' of lost causes"[17]—the ancient version of St. Christopher. So they wondered, would Elijah who went up to Heaven in a whirlwind (2 Kings 2:11) come down in one and rescue this Jesus as he once rescued a widow and her son (1 Kings 17)? The reader of Matthew's Gospel knows that Elijah won't come, for he has already come at the transfiguration and symbolically in the figure of John the Baptist (17:1–13). The reader also knows that Jesus can save himself and is not expecting or panting for another savior.

So perhaps Matthew records their misunderstanding of "Eli" to highlight one last time that the Jews of Jesus' day completely misunderstood their Messiah. Or perhaps it is to highlight what Matthew has been highlighting in nearly the whole of chapter 27, the mockery Jesus endured. Certainly the last words our Lord hears are either misunderstanding or mockery. Verse 49 can be said with eager and sincere messianic expectation or with utter disbelief at this messianic pretender. I think mockery remains a theme, and thus even the man with the sponge is teasing and "tormenting Jesus."[18] I would read the first and last parts of verse 48 as an act of mercy—"And one of them at once ran and took a sponge . . . and put it on a reed and gave it to him to drink"—if not for the middle of that verse, which informs us that the sponge was "filled . . . with *sour* wine" (cf. Psalm 69:20, 21, "*Reproaches* have broken my heart . . . and for my thirst they gave me *sour* wine to drink"). Here mockery again wins over mercy. But whatever the case may be, the last crucifixion snapshot is colored by scorn and confusion. The dark day grows even darker.

Finally, for the first half of our text, we come to verse 50. Jesus, who has been so silent throughout chapter 27, breaks the silence with a loud cry: "And Jesus cried out again with a loud voice and yielded up his spirit." Note that the language—he "yielded up his spirit"—portrays Jesus as once again sovereign over his sufferings. It's as if the fully obedient Son—the moment his heart is to rupture or his lungs asphyxiate or he lose too much blood to live (whatever physical ailment finally did him in)[19]—hands his Father his last breath as a gift (cf. Luke 23:46).

However, before that we hear his last cry. Because John tells us the content of this final cry, "It is finished" (John 19:30), we should read it as a divine victory proclamation. "Jesus dies a victor with a shout of triumph on his lips."[20] Yet since Matthew is silent on the content of Jesus' final words, we should then also read them in light of Psalm 22:1, again the raw cry of human agony and death. The Son of God's final moment is his most human one, if I can phrase it in a slightly unorthodox way. God dies like a man.

Three Supernatural Signs

Whatever is the mysterious meaning of Jesus' final cry, there is no mystery as to what happened after that cry. God answered Jesus' prayer. "Why have I forsaken you? Here's why!" God gives the world three supernatural signs to reveal the mystery of the meaning of his Son's death.

After Jesus gives up "his spirit," the Spirit of God goes to work on the world (v. 50). Heaven showers down its signs of vindication and victory. The justification of God outshouts the voice of scorn and confusion. The Father has not abandoned his righteous suffering Son, and he gives an earthshaking, tomb-breaking, curtain-tearing ceremony to celebrate! He unmistakably affirms that Jesus' sacrifice was accepted.[21]

Let me read the three thunderous signs together for greater effect on your affections, and then I will divide them to hopefully have greater effect on your intellects (while still maintaining a high enough effect on your affections). *Hear* and *see* and *feel* now the divine fireworks set off by Jesus' death:

> *And* behold [take a look at this!], the curtain of the temple was torn in two, from top to bottom. *And* the earth shook, *and* the rocks were split. *And* the tombs were opened.[22] *And* many bodies of the saints who had fallen asleep were raised, *and* coming out of the tombs after his resurrection they went into the holy city and appeared to many. (vv. 51–53 AT)

The First Sign

The first post-crucifixion supernatural sign is the rending of the temple's veil. We know it is supernatural because huge, handwoven tapestries aren't usually "torn *in two*" and "*from top to bottom*" (v. 51).[23] What we don't know is to which veil Matthew is referring. Is it the inside veil that separates the Holy Place from the Most Holy Place or the Holy of Holies (the sanctuary where the Ark of the Covenant was kept and where only the high priest could enter only once a year on the Day of Atonement), or is it the outside veil that would have hung at the gate dividing the Court of the Jews from the Court of the Gentiles? If it is the outside veil it is a more dramatic and public spectacle, as that veil was eighty feet high and visible to all. If it is the veil to the entrance of the Holy of Holies it is less public but no less dramatic or theologically rich. Can you imagine Caiaphas's face?

So which veil is it? I'm so postmodern that I like the ambiguity. Which one? I don't know. Who can know? In the end what does it matter? Three decades after this moment in Matthew the temple was completely flattened to the ground. There wasn't even a stone left unturned, not to mention any tapestry hanging overhead.

What then does this veil-tearing signify? "The split veil of the temple says two truths about the temple: (1) judgment ('it is all over!') and (2) salvation ('it is all open!')."[24] The moment after Jesus breathes his last breath, the temple in Jerusalem becomes a desolate house (cf. 23:38). Once "the true High Priest had at length appeared; the true Lamb of God had been slain; the true mercy-seat was at length revealed," there is "no more need of an earthly high priest, a mercy-seat, a sprinkling of blood, an offering of incense and a day of atonement."[25] Jesus' death brings final judgment to the temple. It's all over!

However, while closing one door Jesus' death opens another. Now, through Jesus and him alone, the whole world is invited into the presence of God. It's all open! Both the demanding restrictions on access to God and the distinction between Jew and Gentile have been abolished. Those "who once were far off have been brought near by the blood of Christ" (Ephesians 2:13). Now it is not merely the high priest and him alone who can enter into the Holy of Holies and lay his hands upon the head of the innocent lamb to find forgiveness for the people. Now all the people—Jews and Gentiles, clergy and laity, old and young, male and female—can obtain direct access to God by faith (Romans 5:2). Hebrews 10:19–22 says it this way:

> Therefore, brothers, since we have confidence to enter the holy places by the blood of Jesus, by the new and living way that he opened for us through the curtain, that is, through his flesh, and since we have a great priest over the house of God, let us draw near with a true heart in full assurance of faith, with our hearts sprinkled clean from an evil conscience and our bodies washed with pure water.

"The whole of the Epistle to the Hebrews is commentary on the split veil."[26] Read through it today. Let that Scripture soak into your soul. We can enter into the Most Holy Place, behind the first and second curtains, because Jesus, through his atoning death, grants us all new access to God (see Hebrews 4:16; 6:19). Bruner says it this way:

> Jesus' death is as effective BC as it was AD; Jesus' death is as retroactive into the past as it is proactive into the future. . . . Thus Christ's death is as cosmic in *time* (BC, AD; past, future) as it is cosmic in *space* (the split veil giving the whole cosmos access to God). The death of Jesus reaches out as far horizontally into history as it reaches up vertically into eternity.[27]

The irony is that through Jesus' momentary separation from the Father—"My God, my God, why have you forsaken me?" (v. 46)—the world has been granted, through faith in Jesus, eternal access to God—"Our Father in heaven" (6:9). That's the beautiful lesson of the supernaturally split veil.

The Second and Third Signs

The second supernatural sign is the earthquake. God gives us an eye-opening earthly *inclusio* right before and after Jesus' death. Before Jesus dies, the earth turns black. After Jesus dies, the earth shakes. The earth is telling earthlings that something *seismic* is happening. The sun hides its face, and the earth shakes its feet to teach us to see and hear that a new earthly era has dawned in the death of Christ.

The crescendo of the cataclysmic signs, however, is not the ground shaking or rocks breaking. Rather it is the tombs opening and real resurrected human beings (not disembodied souls) walking about Jerusalem. This is the third supernatural sign. Like one of Jesus' parables, verses 51, 52 are structured with extensive parallelism as well as an end stress.

And	the curtain	was torn
And	the earth	was shaken [shook, ESV]
And	the rocks	were split
[And]	the tombs	were opened
And	many bodies	were raised[28]

The final line is the climax. And that climax continues into verse 53: "*and* coming out of the tombs after his resurrection they went into the holy city and appeared to many." Note that the actual event happens after Jesus' resurrection, not after his death. Yet Matthew places it here to open our eyes to the resurrection power of Jesus' death.

The language and picture that Matthew uses might remind you of Daniel 12:2, "And many of those who sleep in the dust of the earth shall awake," or of Zechariah 14:4, 5, "On that day his feet shall stand on the Mount of Olives that lies before Jerusalem on the east, and the Mount of Olives shall be split in two from east to west by a very wide valley. . . . And you shall flee as you fled from the earthquake in the days of Uzziah king of Judah. Then the LORD my God will come, and all the holy ones with him," or of Ezekiel 37:1–14 where the breath of God raises to life the valley of dry bones:

> And as I prophesied, there was a sound, and behold, a rattling, and the bones came together, bone to its bone. And I looked, and behold, there were sinews on them, and flesh had come upon them, and skin had covered them . . . and the breath came into them, and they lived and stood on their feet, an exceedingly great army. . . . "Thus says the Lord GOD: Behold, I will open your graves and raise you from your graves, O my people. And I will bring you into the land of Israel." (Ezekiel 37:7b–10, 12)

Matthew's post-crucifixion scene is as spectacular (more spectacular?) as Ezekiel's rising and marching bones. The holy ones in the holy city after the holiest event in the whole of history—that is wholly awesome! Matthew believes in the resurrection of the body! He can't even wait until Easter to tell us about it.

Recently I had a deep sorrow weighing down my soul. My wife told me to take a walk. So I obeyed. I walked through my neighborhood until I arrived at the local cemetery. That's how depressed I was. As I came to the tombstones of children who had died and were buried, I wept.

I also wondered.

I wondered about the power of the resurrection, and I thanked God that such power exists and that we know such power exists because of what we read in Matthew 28 ("And behold, there was a great earthquake, for an angel of the Lord descended from heaven and came and rolled back the stone," v. 2; cf. v. 9) as well as in Matthew 27 ("And behold. . . . The tombs . . . were opened. And many bodies of the saints who had fallen asleep were raised," vv. 51, 52). "Jesus' death is a resurrecting death: the dead are revived by his dying. As he passes from life to death they pass from death to life."[29] That's the point of these resurrected people.

We might want to know, how many people were raised? Were there ten or 10,000? We might want to know, who were these people? Were they Israel's old saints like Moses or David or Christianity's new ones like Joseph or John the Baptist? Were they "celebrity" saints or common ones? The New Testament never uses the word "saint" (singular). It is always "saints" (plural)—as in the saints Paul writes to in Corinth, those who are not always acting quite saintly. We might want to know, how old were these people? Did they rise to the age of their last breath or the moment of their greatest bodily strength? We might want to know, who did they talk to and what did they say? We might want to know, what happened to them after this resurrection? Did they die soon after? Did they go on living for another two decades? Did they ascend into Heaven with Jesus?

Matthew fails to satisfy our curiosities. And he does so, as I've said, because there is only one point he wants us to know. (He says more by saying less.) He does not so much want us to know everything we can know about these people but one significant something about Jesus. That significant something is captured in this sermon's title, borrowed from the Puritan John Owen, "The Death of Death in the Death of Christ." That is, Jesus' death defeated death, or as Augustine nicely phrased it, "His death . . . kill[ed] death."[30] So "Not only is Jesus' death strong enough to split the veil of the Holy of Holies and so cancel *sin*; it is also strong enough to open tombs and so cancel *death*. Sin and death are humanity's two greatest problems, and Jesus' death conquers both."[31] You see, the cross is not a cursed tree but a fruit tree. It produces "the firstfruits of those who have fallen asleep" (1 Corinthians 15:20).

Shaped Like a "V"

In the last sermon I described how the artist Makoto Fujimura illustrated the text of Matthew 27 by painting a straight slanted line of red paint from the bottom of one page to the top of the next, then slightly blending that line into a gold streak that also slants down from the top of the page to the bottom. If you turned those two pages upside down it would form a V for victory (*nika* in Greek; the letter η looking a bit like that Nike swoosh). I don't know if he intended for me to turn it upside down or not. But if so, he would be joining other less modern Christian artists who have depicted this V by representing Jesus on the cross with his arms above his head in the precise shape of a V.[32] Henry Clarke's magnificent stained-glass masterpiece, *The Adoration of the Cross* in St. Joseph's Church, Dublin, is an example of this.[33] Other artists have shaped the cross itself like a V.[34]

Those simple artistic illustrations of a suffering man whose cross or arms or both shows victory through suffering is the perfect illustration of what Matthew says happened on the cross. After all Jesus' sufferings—physical (the scourging, the crown of thorns, the weight of his own body on the cross, the thirst, the loss of blood), mental (the mockeries and desertion of his followers), and spiritual (the "desertion" of the Father)—Jesus' dies victorious. *Nika*. He conquers. Christ conquers the world (the darkness and the earthquake). Christ conquers sin (the torn veil). Christ conquers death (the resurrected bodies). That is the cross of Christ to Matthew, and that is to be the cross of Christ to us.

87

Things into Which Angels Long to Look

MATTHEW 27:54–61

AFTER COLLEGE I WAS PART OF A Christian basketball team that twice traveled to Cuba to play against the Cuban national team. My team had players from a number of schools around the country, most of them playing, as I did, for Division III programs. We had two Division I players. The last U.S. team the Cubans had played against was the Dream Team, which featured the greatest basketball players ever, including Michael Jordan, Scottie Pippen, and a few others who played on teams other than the Bulls. In their Tournament of the Americas matchup, the Dream Team destroyed the Cubans. The score was 136–57. In turn, the Cubans were happy to go against my less-than-dreamy team as they destroyed us game after game. We must have played ten times on our two-week tour. I won't give you the scores.

I was matched up against Juan Leopold Vazquez. Juan was stronger and could jump higher, run faster, and shoot better and was far meaner than I am or ever was. He never smiled. He was so serious. He looked so mad. It was the Cold War, basketball edition. I felt like he wanted to kill me. I was not merely his competition but his enemy.

However, when you play toe to toe with someone day after day you begin to get to know him, even if he speaks another language. Toward the end of the trip, and especially after a meal the two teams had together, Juan's heart somehow softened toward me. He now smiled at me after he made three-pointers over me. Quite seriously, some sort of heart-change was happening.

One day when I got to the gym, he came up to me and asked me for my shoes. All of the American players had at least two pairs of shoes with them.

He was asking me for my backup pair, the ones I wore to the gym but not during the game. I couldn't believe that he wanted my old shoes. But that is indeed what he wanted. I then noticed how the Cuban players only had one pair of shoes and that my old pair was better than his game pair. (Let's not become Communists anytime soon.) I agreed to give him the shoes. He thanked me. He told me, however, that he would get in a lot of trouble if the coach saw me give them to him. So we worked around the system. After the game, as planned, I left my bag with the shoes in it. He walked by, took the bag, went into the locker room, removed the shoes, and brought the bag back. He also told me that he would give me a gift in my bag but that I wasn't to open it until I left the country. I told him that a memento wasn't necessary. But he insisted.

The gift he gave me was his national team jersey!

Years later Juan defected to Canada. He escaped when his team came to play a game in Toronto. He now lives in Oshawa, Ontario. I visited him a few years ago. We went to see a Toronto Raptors basketball game. We sat together and enjoyed the game and a meal afterwards as good friends.

The Roman Soldiers Confessed Jesus

A change of heart is a beautiful thing to witness. In our text we witness such a change of heart take place in the Roman soldiers beneath the foot of the cross. Look at that remarkable verse 54: "When the centurion and those who were with him, keeping watch over Jesus, saw the earthquake and what took place, they were filled with awe and said, 'Truly this was the Son of God!'"

There are at least three details about this change-of-heart verse that are remarkable—who confesses, why they confess, and what they confess. Let's start backwards by answering the what question first. "Truly this was the Son of God!" is *what* was said the moment after Jesus died (v. 54). Now we can debate whether their confession was precisely orthodox. Shouldn't they have said, "Jesus *is* [not *was*] the Son of God"? We can also debate if their confession was a momentary mouthing of the truth—that is, if their confession was "only a sudden and passing impulse," as Calvin viewed it,[1] or if it was a lasting, lived-out conviction. However, what we should not debate is their sincerity, a sincerity that is pitted against the mocking insults hurled at Jesus just hours before—"If you are *the Son of God*, come down from the cross" (v. 40b) and "He trusts in God; let God deliver him now, if he desires him. For he said, 'I am *the Son of God*'" (v. 43).

These soldiers might have had imperfect faith in Jesus, but even imperfect faith in Jesus is faith in Jesus! Better to have mustard-seed faith than no faith. Better to have a missing-the-definite-article faith than a missing-the-direct-object faith. What they confessed was good enough for God. It was good enough for Matthew. It should be good enough for us. Echoing the Father's voice at Jesus' baptism and transfiguration—"This is my beloved Son" (3:17; 17:5) and Peter's great confession at Caesarea—"You are the Christ, the Son of the living God" (16:16), these soldiers voice what all Christians are to voice: Jesus is the divine Son of God. They answer in the affirmative Caiaphas's adjuration to Jesus: "I adjure you by the living God, tell us if you are the Christ, the Son of God" (26:63). They somehow (by God's transforming grace) see Jesus now as more than a common Jewish criminal whose pain they ignored and whose clothing they indifferently rolled the dice for, as well as more than (if at all) a "Greco-Roman 'divine man' (a great human hero deified upon his death)."[2] To Matthew, they mouthed what every post-crucifixion Christian must mouth: Jesus is "the unique Son of God" (cf. 1 John 5:5).[3]

The second remarkable detail about verse 54 answers the question, why did they confess? Matthew touches on *what they saw* and *how they felt*. When they "saw the earthquake and what took place, they were filled with awe" (v. 54). Matthew links their confession with the divine fireworks of verses 51–53, where God gave the world three supernatural signs—his earthshaking, tomb-breaking, curtain-tearing vindication celebration. Miraculously the temple veil is torn from top to bottom. Miraculously the earth shakes, and the rocks break. Miraculously the dead are raised to life again. And (miraculously?), witnessing some of this—certainly the odd earthquake as well as the strange darkness (v. 45)—these soldiers were "filled with awe" (or holy terror—the fear of the Lord) and filled with faith—"Truly this was the Son of God!" (v. 54). You see, following the earth's response to Jesus' death (the sun covers its eyes, and the earth shakes its feet) there comes the earthlings' response (the dead are raised to life, and the true identity of Jesus is announced).

It is announced by Roman soldiers. That's the answer to our who question. The first post-crucifixion Christian confession does not come from St. Peter or Mother Mary or any of Jesus' close friends or holy family. It doesn't come from the high priest or one of the elders of Israel. Rather, it comes from a high-ranking centurion and the soldiers who were with him. In Mark's account we hear only the voice of the centurion (Mark 15:39). In Matthew it's a choral confession, which is far more dramatic. Must Matthew always outdo Mark? I suppose he must. We wonder, did the centurion first say, "Truly this was the Son of God!" and the eight to a hundred men under him all joined in? Or did they all say spontaneously and in unison, "Truly this was the Son of God!"? We don't know. I like the latter. I'm with Matthew—the more dramatic the better.

While these soldiers likely didn't witness the veil-tearing in the temple, they nevertheless acted out the theology of it. They are Gentiles. They are Roman Gentiles. They are Roman soldier Gentiles. They are Gentile *sinners*. Whether they were the same soldiers involved in the brutal scourging, stripping, and spitting mockery of 27:26–30 we don't know. But we do know that they nailed Jesus to the cross. Also we do know that moments earlier they showed no respect for him as a fellow human being. And yet here there was "a fundamental reformation of opinion,"[4] or put more piously, "a conversion to Jesus as Christ." Luther says it this way: "The blood of Christ not only wakens dead bodies, but also sinners' souls."[5] Amen to that. These enemies of God come near to God through the blood of Jesus (cf. Romans 5:10) and the power of God.

Thus, this is the lesson for us: how these soldiers reacted to Jesus is how true disciples should react. In chapter 14 when Jesus walked on the water, the disciples were "terrified" (v. 26), and then that fear of God turned into a confession of Christ: "Truly you are the Son of God" (v. 33). Likewise, here these soldiers who were first filled with fear were then filled with faith: "Truly this was the Son of God!" (v. 54). They respond in faith to the cross of Christ. Psalm 22:27 prophesied that the nations would worship the righteous suffering King, and here is such worship. As Frederick Dale Bruner says, "*The New Temple of the people of God is beginning its first worship service right here*."[6] The soldiers' voices join the voices of the wise men of 2:1–12, the centurion of 8:5–13, and the Canaanite woman of 15:21–28 and anticipate the resounding chorus to come when all nations (28:19) shall sing to Jesus as King of kings and Lord of lords, and he shall reign forever! Let us join in singing that song today. Let us confess the soldiers' choral confession.

Joseph of Arimathea Buried Jesus

The Roman soldiers are the first of three characters we are considering in this sermon. We have looked at their confession. The other two characters are Joseph of Arimathea and the women. Let's next look at and learn from Joseph and his burial of Jesus.

> When it was evening, there came a rich man from Arimathea, named Joseph, who also was a disciple of Jesus. He went to Pilate and asked for the body of Jesus. Then Pilate ordered it to be given to him. And Joseph took the body and wrapped it in a clean linen shroud and laid it in his own new tomb, which he had cut in the rock. And he rolled a great stone to the entrance of the tomb and went away. (vv. 57–60)

Here are three key observations about Joseph. First, he was Jewish. We know that fact from his Jewish name (Joseph) and his Jewish hometown (Arimathea). Some scholars identify Arimathea as "Ramathaim-zophim of the hill country of Ephraim," the town where Samuel was born (1 Samuel 1:1), others as being "Ramah" where Jeremiah prophesied (see 2:18). Furthermore, we know from Luke 23:50 that he was a member of the Sanhedrin ("a respected member of the Council," Mark 15:43) and also that he did not consent with the Council's condemnation of Jesus (Luke 23:51).

I bring out the fact that Joseph was Jewish to say that in the death of Jesus, God has not completely rejected his people Israel. Immediately following Jesus' death, Gentiles enter the kingdom of heaven, and Jews (represented by Joseph and the women as well) anticipate something of the kingdom of heaven still being at hand (see Mark 14:43; Luke 23:51), even in a dead Messiah. Joseph was Jewish, but he was a Jewish "disciple of Jesus" (v. 57). This Jew followed Jesus.

Second, Joseph was "rich" (v. 57). Why does Matthew mention that detail? There is perhaps a theological reason—namely, even rich men can be faithful followers of Jesus. There is a place for rich men in the church, men who put Jesus before money by putting their money to work for Jesus. This is the first time in Matthew that wealth takes on a positive connotation. Abraham was a wealthy man. Job was a wealthy man. Solomon was a wealthy man. Scripture is not silent on the fear of the Lord being found in frightfully rich men. But in Matthew, Jesus teaches his followers, most of whom are poor, to consider the lilies and to ask for daily bread. And in Matthew that last rich man we encountered was the rich young ruler, who walked away from Jesus "sorrowful, for he had great possessions" (19:22), or because great possessions had him. So, can a rich man enter the kingdom of heaven? Yes. Okay then, how does a rich man enter the kingdom of heaven? The same way anyone does—through God's saving grace. "With man [such salvation] is impossible, but with God all things [even squeezing a fat camel through the eye of a needle] are possible" (see 19:26, 24). Grace is truly amazing.

Moreover, Matthew mentions Joseph's wealth for historical reasons. Only a rich (and politically connected) man could gain access to Pilate and actually be granted his request. And only a rich man would be able to afford "a clean linen shroud" (v. 59), a "new tomb" that was likely cut into a limestone hillside-cave (v. 60), and "a great stone" that was rolled in front of the tomb (v. 60). Poor men were buried in mass paupers' graves. Joseph's tomb had no other bodies in it; it was brand-new; it was above, not below, ground; and it had the expensive, state-of-the-art, rolling-stone feature. Most tombs had small square stones just to keep out animals and thieves. This tomb was the deluxe edition. It had all the bells and whistles.

In giving all this information, I don't intend to make light of the death and especially the burial of our Lord. But I want you to see that Joseph's procuring Jesus' body, covering it the way he did, and laying that dead body in such a tomb is filled with historical significance (and prophetic significance; see Isaiah 53:9). Jesus had to be really dead for Joseph to go to Pilate in the first place. Pilate had to agree that Jesus was really dead to give the body to Joseph.[7] Jesus had to be really dead for his face to be covered with a shroud. He wasn't breathing, and Joseph witnessed that firsthand.

The details of the tomb—above ground, in a known and visible place, a large circular stone, no other bodies in it—brings greater credence to the testimony of Jesus' resurrection. The women didn't mistakenly go to the wrong tomb. Joseph and Pilate could have easily checked. Unlike Moses ("no one knows the place of his burial to this day," Deuteronomy 34:6), the location of Jesus' tomb was well-known by a number of witnesses—the guards, the women, Joseph, Pilate, and likely others.

My third observation about Joseph was that he demonstrated courageous love for Christ. In Matthew's Gospel, Joseph makes a short cameo appearance. His scene is short but sweet. He arrives as quickly as he departs. He reminds us of the earlier Joseph in Matthew 1, 2,[8] as both Josephs are quiet (not a word of theirs is recorded for us) and both men's deeds speak more loudly than their words.

Perhaps this second Joseph is not mentioned earlier in Matthew because he was a coward. John tells us as much, for he writes that Joseph "was a disciple of Jesus, but secretly *for fear of the Jews*" (John 19:38). Well, after Jesus' courageous death it appears that Joseph had a conversion from bashful to brave. This coward became courageous. He is the *only* male disciple of Jesus to step forward in chapter 27. All the apostles are absent. It took great courage for a highly distinguished member of the Sanhedrin to go by himself to Pilate in order to ask for the body of a convicted and crucified criminal. What would the other members of the Council think about this? Would they resent him? Would they kick him out of the club? And what would Pilate think of such a politically-charged request? Pilate could have said no and ordered Jesus' body to remain on the cross to rot in the sun the next day, be picked apart by birds, and then torn apart by scavenger dogs. That would be quite the warning to anyone aspiring to insurrection! (And that was done in those days.) Or he could have ordered that Jesus' body be thrown into a mass grave with other criminals and no names. Or Pilate could have charged Joseph with siding with the enemy. Joseph was very bold here. By going to Pilate, he risked his reputation and perhaps even his life.

Along with being a courageous man, Joseph was a loving man. Rich men don't usually do slave's work. But here we see a rich man prepare Jesus' body for a proper and honorable burial. He dirtied his clean hands, during Passover no less, by touching Jesus' unclean body (thus, ironically, obeying the Law [Deuteronomy 21:22, 23]). He served the Servant of Servants, the one who came to serve and lay down his life for others. Joseph, who *took, wrapped, laid, cut, rolled,* and *went away* (note the six verbs),[9] embodied Jesus' John 13 foot-washing model. He loved the greatest man ever to live in the least great moment of that man's life. Joseph's kind action echoes the anonymous woman who anointed Jesus' body for burial (26:6–13). She anoints him for burial; Joseph prepares the body. Both are tender gestures. And both are now part of the Gospel story we tell (they have been rewarded for their good deeds). As the soldiers show us what Christian faith confesses, Joseph shows us how Christian faith works. Our faith is to be a courageous, loving, doing faith.

Aside from the person of Joseph, let's not miss the person of Jesus—the man whom Joseph buries—and how much that burial matters. Just because Jesus isn't doing anything in our text doesn't mean what he has done is not of greatest significance. Often the burial of Christ gets little mention when compared to the cross of Christ. But the whole of Jesus' humiliation is necessary for our salvation—his being born of a woman, born under the Law, born in a low condition, undergoing the normal miseries of human life, bearing the scorn of man and the wrath of God on the cross, and then dying and remaining dead and buried for a few days.[10]

Much can be said about the significance of Jesus' burial. Herman Ridderbos provides an excellent summary of what I would say if I were as smart as he. Ridderbos writes:

> Although the account of Jesus' burial is extremely terse and sober, we must never forget that here, as through the whole gospel, the Evangelist is telling the story of the Christ. The absence of biographical details focuses all attention on the main point, namely, that the path of humiliation walked by God's Anointed descended all the way to the grave, the place where death reigns supreme and mercilessly imposes its curse (see Gen. 3:19). Christ was dragged down to the place of deepest human humiliation and defilement and imprisoned behind a heavy stone. Even His closest friends thought He was gone for good, a figure from the past who now would be forgotten. Thus Jesus endured not only pain and suffering and the curse of death but even the terror of the grave, so that He could save His people from this forever.[11]

Jesus' burial is an essential part of the Christian creed. So let's confess, "He suffered under Pontus Pilate, was crucified, died, and was buried . . ." and let us do so with clear confidence and humble gratitude.

The Women Witnessed to Jesus

Jesus said, "And I, if I be lifted up from the earth, will draw all men unto me" (John 12:32 KJV). We have seen the Jewish man, Joseph, and the Gentile men, the Roman soldiers, drawn to Jesus after he was raised up on the cross. But Jesus' death draws "many women" as well. In 27:55, 56, 61 we read about them. Pre-burial, we are told that "[t]here were also many women there, looking on from a distance, who had followed Jesus from Galilee, ministering to him, among whom were Mary Magdalene and Mary the mother of James and Joseph and the mother of the sons of Zebedee" (vv. 55, 56). Then, post-burial, we are told that "Mary Magdalene and the other Mary [i.e., the mother of James and Joseph or Joses, cf. Mark 15:40, 47] were there, sitting opposite the tomb" (27:61).

There are three important observations to make about these women. First, there were "many" (v. 55). That detail is in contrast again with the twelve apostles, of whom none were there. While the women are eying the cross "from a distance"—perhaps due to "timidity or modesty"[12]—they are nonetheless *there*. It is especially interesting to note that "the mother of the sons of Zebedee" (v. 56), in contrast with her "sons of thunder," is present. "Her presence . . . serves as a foil for her sons' cowardly absence," and if she hadn't yet learned Jesus' lesson on kingdom greatness, perhaps witnessing his great death taught her "the true meaning of being on [his] . . . left and right."[13] Just as Mary Magdalene had seven demons cast out of her (Luke 8:2), this woman must have had those demons of her own pride cast out by Jesus' seemingly inglorious and powerless yet truly glorious and powerful death.

Again, like the Roman soldiers and Joseph of Arimathea, the faith of these women might be inadequate, but it's faith. Fearful faith is better than no faith. Faithful-till-the-end-on-the-hill-of-Golgotha faith is better than hiding-under-the-table-in-the-upper-room faith. But their faith might also be exemplary. I say that based on how Matthew describes them. They "followed Jesus from Galilee" (v. 55). The word "follow" is a favorite of Jesus. It's a good, healthy, noble word. To come near him for the 100 miles or more from Galilee to Jerusalem is a good, healthy, noble action. Then to further describe them as "ministering to him" (v. 55) has a nice serve-Jesus-serve-people ring to it.

Second, the women are women! Yes, the extra X chromosome matters. Ever since Eve's universally disastrous slipup, women have received bad press.[14] In the Gospels, however, women make the front page for their heroic deeds. That's not an exaggeration. Other than the two bad apples in Herod's sordid family, the mother of Jesus' momentary lapse of faith, and the mother of the sons of Zebedee's misunderstanding of kingdom power, the women in Matthew are just marvelous, especially when it counts most (at the end). Christianity didn't offer marginalized women feminism, but it did offer marginalized women freedom, the freedom that comes to both men and women, and that freedom comes through serving God and others. These women do both.

How do they serve both? They serve God as his witnesses to the crucifixion, burial, and resurrection. In our text many women were at the cross, and two women were at the tomb. Not a large funeral, but large enough to establish the Law's requirement of two witnesses (Deuteronomy 19:15). Thus they serve the church and the world as official eyewitnesses to the greatest events of history. I'll put it this strongly, in case that last sentence wasn't strong enough: without the women's witness, the church has no testimony. While women were not viewed as creditable witnesses in that culture,[15] God used them as his key witnesses, lending their "credibility . . . to the kerygmatic triad: Jesus died, was buried, was raised."[16] You see, the role of women in the Gospel of Matthew may be to teach the church that God uses the weaker things (or what the world considers the weaker things) to confound the wise. That fits gospel logic. But more certainly, God uses faithful people—men or women—as his faithful witnesses.

I like to imagine, one day after Jesus' ascension, Matthew sitting down with Mary Magdalene and the other Mary and taking notes about the events of Good Friday, Holy Saturday, and Easter (28:1–10).[17] "Now, Mary, tell me again about the tomb. It had a rolling stone? Really! And that bit about the angel after the stone was rolled away . . . say that over again. I need to make sure that I get all this down."

Don't underestimate the girls in the Gospels. Without the girls there are no Gospels, at least no good news ending to the Gospels.

The Beginning of the End

Many years after the drafting of the Declaration of Independence, Thomas Jefferson authored *The Life and Morals of Jesus of Nazareth: Extracted Textually from the Gospels in Greek, Latin, French, and English*, now commonly referred to as the Jefferson Bible (c. 1820). This Bible was Jefferson's private declaration of independence, we might say, from historic Christian theology, for he edited out (with a razor blade no less) all the parts of the Gospels that didn't fit his deistic theology. Using his naturalistic and rationalistic grid, he removed all supernaturalism, including references to the Trinity as well as to the divinity, miracles, and resurrection of Jesus. His Bible begins with the birth narrative, minus mention of angels and prophecy, and it concludes with the cross and the tomb (but not an empty one): "There laid they Jesus. And rolled a great stone to the door of the sepulchre, and departed."[18] That's Jefferson's version of Matthew 27:60. To Jefferson, Jesus died and was buried—period, end of story.

But, of course, to end where Jefferson ended is an "inadequate ending to a 'Gospel'!"[19] Gospel means "good news." To cut out 27:62—28:20 is to miss the whole point of 27:54–61! This transitional text is in our Bibles not as a conclusion but as the bridge to a new beginning. We will walk with the women over that bridge in the next chapter. The story isn't over. The best is yet to come. Will the stone stay still? Will the tomb be empty? Will the women's tears be wiped away by fear and joy and eyewitness astonishment? Will Jesus rise from the dead? Will this two-woman church grow into a billion men and women and children and counting? We shall see. We shall *see*.

88

Behold Him That *Was* Crucified

MATTHEW 27:62—28:15

This chapter was originally preached as a sermon on Easter 2012.

I AM A SINNER. YOU ARE A SINNER. Together we are sinners.

Perhaps this is not the normal way to start a Happy Easter sermon. But I'm not normal, and Matthew's view of Easter is not the norm today. To him Easter is not at all associated with that candy-addicted bunny and those pastel-colored plastic eggs he hides in shoes, drawers, and other odd places. Rather, Easter is associated solely with Jesus, who died and rose for our justification—that is, to make us right with God and to save us from all our sins and what those sins deserve.

So then, if you think it is a sin to say the word *sin*, let alone acknowledge your sin-sickness, you are a long way from cracking the riddle of self, let alone the mystery of God's salvation offered in a crucified and risen Christ. Or if you acknowledge some sins in your life (you might prefer to call them slipups and character flaws), and you think you have an infallible alibi before the judgment seat of God (if such a thing even exists), that you can blame it on your brain, your genes, some hormonal imbalance, an inherited temperament, your parents' failure to parent well, your awful education, or the neighborhood kids you grew up with, think again.[1] There is "false guilt" (feeling bad about some sin you have not done) and there is "false innocence" (thinking you are forgiven because the peace-peace prophets of our day say that you are forgiven or that you have nothing you need to be forgiven of).[2] We live in a world of "faulty diagnosis" of the human condition and thus "superficial remedies."[3]

Moreover, we live in a church culture today in which inadequate doctrines of the atonement are formulated to fit our inadequate doctrines of God and man.[4] What H. Richard Niebuhr said of the social gospel of the early last century can still be sadly said too often today: the gospel of the therapeutic, entertainment, consumerist church has become "A God without wrath [who] brought men without sin into a kingdom without judgment through the ministrations of a Christ without a cross."[5] Ah, but this Easter we must gird up our loins and speak the true good news: a wrathful God brought people with sin into a kingdom through Christ crucified and raised again (Romans 4:25; 8:34). Jesus took "the most ugly, wicked, defiled, evil, corrupt, rebellious, and hideous" crimes in all creation—our addictions, idolatries, vain ambitions, superficialities, lies, deceits, greed, self-righteousness (the list is longer than we have time for)—and descended into the hell of God-forsakenness, the place of punishment for our sins, and rose again for our justification.[6]

The Unbelievable Disbelief

In case you missed that fact in Matthew's retelling of the passion narrative—where we witnessed Jesus being scourged and mocked and crying out and dying and buried—today's text jogs our memories, for it starts and stops with the startling sadness of human sin. Yes, it is human sin that sandwiches the good news of Jesus' resurrection. In 27:62–66 and 28:11–15 we have what I'll call *the unbelievable disbelief* of the Jewish leaders.

I give this section an ironic title because their actions here are all ironic evils. A number of ironic evils are given in 27:62–66. Let's look there first. For example, why would the Jewish religious leaders gather before the Roman governor (Pilate) on the Sabbath—"after the day of Preparation" (v. 62; cf. "Now after the Sabbath" of 28:1)? Shouldn't devout Jews gather before God and with his people in the synagogue on the Sabbath? I hope they aren't skipping synagogue to assemble with the godless enemy—Rome. And why when they assemble with Pilate do they call him *kyrie*, translated "Sir" in the ESV and most other translations? The word in Greek can merely be a submissive and respectful title, like what we would call a high-ranking military officer. In Matthew, however, until this occasion "only Jesus, God, or figures in parables who stand for Jesus or God" are called *kyrie* or *kurios*,"[7] which is translated "Lord." So is there some ironic twist here, namely that the believers in Matthew's Gospel call Jesus "Lord" while the unbelievers call Pilate "Lord"? Is there some meat put on the bone of the cry that followed

"Let him be crucified!" (27:22, 23)—"We have no king but Caesar" (cf. John 19:15)? Has Caesar become their "Führer"[8]—to throw in that German word for "Lord" that makes most of us familiar with World War II cringe? Hail Caesar!

Furthermore, what's with all the worry? Every line in verses 63–66 is filled with worrywarts:

> "Sir [or Lord], we remember how that impostor said, while he was still alive, 'After three days I will rise.' Therefore order the tomb to be made secure until the third day, lest his disciples go and steal him away and tell the people, 'He has risen from the dead,' and the last fraud will be worse than the first." Pilate said to them, "You have a guard of soldiers ["take a guard of Roman soldiers" makes best sense of the fear of Pilate that comes into play in 28:14]. Go, make it as secure as you can." So they went and made the tomb secure by sealing the stone and setting a guard.

It is difficult to know if they are merely worried about what the disciples might do. Sure, the disciples might try to steal the body and then claim "He is alive!" But surely they noticed, as we have, that the apostolic band hasn't played a tune lately. Where have God's terrific twelve gone? In Matthew 27 the Twelve's treasurer betrayed Jesus, the apostles' leader denied him, and the rest fled. The irony here, as Donald Hagner points out, is that Jesus' "opponents took Jesus' words about rising from the dead more seriously than did the disciples."[9] The Jewish leaders remembered Jesus' word while the apostles apparently forgot it.

Now, if those leaders are not truly worried about the men (or the women for that matter),[10] that causes me to wonder if their worry centers on Jesus. I wonder if they wonder what this wonder-worker Jesus can really do. They have seen, or at least heard about, his powers. He has cured leprosy. He has walked on water. He has raised Lazarus from the dead. And he has claimed that he would rise from the dead. If those are their worries, then isn't it ironic that they think a few guards will hold back Jesus? If Jesus can rise from the dead, he can certainly move a stone, overpower guards, and so on. He can do just about whatever he wants to do.

Whatever the root of their worries, we know, and they shall soon learn, that their security measures (note the word "secure" in vv. 64, 65, 66) all prove ineffective, as ineffective as Daniel being "sealed" in the lions' den (Daniel 6:17). All they had to do was make sure that one tomb was secure for three days. Just three days and then the thought and threat of Jesus would forever be buried in the annals of history. But it all backfired. God broke in! The Roman and religious powers could not overpower the resurrection power of God! Indeed, "all the power[s] of earth and hell combined" could not "keep Christ a prisoner."[11] John Chrysostom says it this way: "*Behold* . . . a seal, a stone, and a watch, and they were not able to *hold* Him."[12]

When they questioned Jesus about giving them a sign, he told them that he would give them one sure sign—"the sign of the prophet Jonah" (12:38–40), namely his death and resurrection. Here is that sign, and yet they don't believe. At the foot of the cross, some of these same leaders mocked Jesus, saying, "[L]et him come down now from the cross, and we will believe in him" (27:42). Sure you will. He has come down, and he rose up again, and yet you still refuse to hear and see—to hear the guards' testimony and to see for yourself the Resurrected One! These "men of God" have missed "the supreme miracle"—"the supreme intervention of God in human existence."[13] These Bible people have missed "the most spectacular of all the biblical miracles,"[14] in fact, the central event of Biblical revelation and world history.

Anyway, that is what happens right before the resurrection. What transpires after the resurrection only adds further ironic evils. In 27:63 the Jewish leaders call Jesus "that impostor" or "deceiver," and yet 28:11–15 lays out *their* deceptions, one after another. Listen to the lies:

> While they were going, behold, some of the guard went into the city and told the chief priests all that had taken place. And when they had assembled with the elders and taken counsel, they gave a sufficient sum of money to the soldiers and said, "Tell people, 'His disciples came by night and stole him away while we were asleep.' And if this comes to the governor's ears, we will satisfy him and keep you out of trouble." So they took the money and did as they were directed. And this story has been spread among the Jews to this day.

This text records the second assembly in two days. It's the Second Council of Deceit. In 27:62 the Jewish leaders assembled before Pilate. Now they assemble with "the elders" (likely the Sanhedrin; v. 12). This Council is convened because someone told the truth. Parenthetically, that is too often why church councils are convened—to deal with truth-tellers who are spoiling some sacred tradition. Religious prigs are always keeping watch for wild boars who might knock to the floor encased relics in the glass cathedrals of Christendom.

Some of the soldiers came into Jerusalem to tell the chief priests what occurred—about the earthquake, their panic, the angel, and perhaps the angelic announcement, "Jesus who was crucified. . . . has risen" (28:5, 6). Thus the chief priests and the elders are the first people in the history of the world to hear the good news of Easter. However, to them it is the worst news. Their worst fears have been realized. By taking such high security measures, they only added to the validity of Jesus' resurrection. If they left the tomb alone, it would have been easier and more reasonable to say that the disciples stole the body. That now becomes a very sketchy stretch. What are they to do? Well, it's what they don't do that surprises me. They don't cross-examine the guards. There are no curious questions like "What did you see? Did you all really see an angel? Did you all really see that huge stone rolled back? Did any of you actually see Jesus? Were any of those blasted apostles around to blame? What *do you* think happened to the body?" Instead they are as pragmatic about the whole situation as election officials in Florida hand-counting hanging chads.

In his witty poem "The True Born Englishman," Daniel Defoe writes:

> Wherever God erects a house of prayer,
> The Devil always builds a chapel there.

Here the religious have assembled to contrive a devilish lie. This is quite the *holy* week they are keeping. The lie is the very thing they tried to prevent—having the disciples steal the body. Again, what incredible irony! Doriani calls it "a delicious irony" that by the authorities trying to "cover up the resurrection" they only help to further "*spread* the story of the empty tomb."[15]

They'll spread that story by stuffing the soldiers' pockets. Once again they put magical money to work for them. It has worked in the past with Judas. Judas is paid to share what he knows; the guards are paid to not share what they know.[16] We know that "the love of money is a root of all kinds of evils" (1 Timothy 6:10). They saw money as the solution to all sorts of problems. This Jesus-resurrection business can be laid to rest (pun intended) with a sly wink and a few stuffed wallets. So they think. Wink. Wink.

Now, bribery always involves two parties. The guards had a decision to make, and it appears that "a sufficient sum of money" (28:12) helped make up their mind. (Fear of death from the hands of Pilate might also have been on their minds, but it is the money that Matthew follows.) That term "sufficient sum" is intriguing to me. It seems to imply that some bartering was going on. I imagine this:

The leaders say, "We'll give you thirty pieces of silver."

"Oh no" is the reply, "Make it a hundred . . . a hundred each!"

"No way! Fifty each."

"Seventy."

"Sixty."

"Sixty-seven."

"Sixty-five."

"Sixty-sixty point seven."

"Sixty-sixty point five."

"Sixty-sixty point six."

"Deal."

"Deal."

66.6, it is. The devilish deal is this: the guards lie about the whereabouts and how-about of Jesus' body while the leaders pay them off and keep them "out of trouble" with Pilate (v. 14). The Great Commission is soon to come. Here is the Great Cover-up Commission. The disciples of Jesus will tell the truth to the world; the disciples of the evil authorities will tell a lie to the world. They will attempt to bury the resurrection under a shroud of see-through fibs.[17] If they can't stop Jesus from rising from the dead, perhaps they will have some success with their scam of hiding that truth. Some success! The Great Commission is called great because it is engulfs the whole of the nations. Might it also be called "great" because God has been greatly successful? The resurrection of Jesus Christ is being preached every Sunday in Caracas and Cairo, Moscow and Madrid, Dakar and Dublin, Buenos Aires and Baghdad, Santiago de Cuba and Seoul, Melbourne and Montreal, Bangalore and Belgrade, Reno and Rio de Janeiro. *Magna est veritas et praevalebit* (great is the truth, and it will prevail)![18]

"So they took the money and did as they were directed. And this story has been spread among the Jews to this day" (28:15). Here the phrase "this day" refers to the time and place Matthew wrote his Gospel—perhaps Antioch in the 60s. "This day," however, has an elastic quality to it, as does this tall tale. Most lies stretch well, don't they? The disciples-theft theory stretched into the middle of the second century, when the church leader Justin Martyr wrote against it (*Dialogue* 108), and also into the so-called Enlightenment and post-Enlightenment eras when it found its fullest life, so to speak, in the writings of Reimarus in the eighteenth century. Still today, from time to time this theory is "resurrected" (pun again intended) in various forms.[19]

However, that view, and others like it,[20] fails to answer the key questions. First, regarding the false testimony itself, how could the guards possibly know who stole the body *if they were asleep*?[21] Sleeping people aren't the most reliable eyewitnesses. And don't you think at least one of these trained guards—trained to stay awake upon penalty of death—would have awakened at the tremor of the earthquake or the sound of a huge stone being rolled away?

Further and more substantial questions that arise are: if Jesus died and was buried, why hasn't anyone ancient or modern produced the rotted corpse, bones, or some evidence of a *not* empty tomb? Blomberg notes that "no early writer—Jew, Greek, or Roman—ever identifies a tomb in which Jesus' body remained."[22] And how realistic is it to believe that the disciples of Jesus, if they indeed stole the body, would violate both the moral teachings of Jesus (which so attracted them and nearly everyone to him)[23] and their own consciences? Men might die because they are brainwashed or fooled. We can think of Japanese kamikaze pilots or Islamic terrorists sacrificing their lives for honor or reward. But men usually don't die for something they are certain is a lie. If the disciples knew where the body of Jesus was, what could possibly be the motive for preaching the resurrection? Could it be money? No. There wasn't any money in that message. Ask Paul. How about the motive of reputation? No again. That message cost Jesus' followers the loss of their reputation within their own religion (Judaism) and culture (Hellenism), and for some it cost them family ties, and for others it cost them their very lives. N. T. Wright states that "it was three centuries before anyone gained anything except insults, danger, torture and death by believing in the resurrection."[24]

Moreover, and related to that last thought, what turned the cowards we see in Matthew 27 into the courageous men we find in the Acts of the Apostles? If the Twelve didn't have enough courage to stick with Jesus until the cross, where did this courage come from after Jesus' burial? Their boldness has only one sensible explanation: they beheld the resurrected body of Jesus, as they themselves said and wrote. Something historical happened. Jesus' resurrection has a concreteness to it! To say that the early church embraced a spiritual resurrection—that Jesus arose in their hearts while his body sadly stayed in some grave or tomb—is to say something . . . how shall I say it? . . . *stupid*. "When you have eliminated the impossible," Sherlock Holmes once deduced, "whatever remains, *however improbable*, must be the truth."[25] The proof of the resurrection is that elementary, my dear friends.

Christians shouldn't be on trial to prove the resurrection, but non-Christians do have to disprove it. Sit down and please explain away to us, O skeptics, the accuracy of Jesus' predictions of his resurrection, the congruity of the resurrection with the Old Testament Scriptures, the empty tomb, the appearances of Jesus after his death witnessed by over 500 people, the existence of the church, the worship of Jesus as God by people coming from a monotheistic religion,[26] and the testimony of radically changed lives.[27] Explain also how the idea of a resurrection is even possible when both Jews and Gentiles in the first-century Mediterranean world were more skeptical about someone rising bodily from the dead than most modern Americans.[28] "Everybody in the ancient world, just like everybody in the modern world, knew perfectly well that dead people don't get resurrected."[29] There is no record from the Jewish literature of this time of people having visions of someone raised to life or of messianic movements claiming that their Messiah was alive bodily (or spiritually for that matter) after his death. If the apostles made up the notion of a resurrected man, it was quite the Copernican revolution! Innovative ideas or new worldviews aren't often (ever?) formed over three days. So explain to me how Christianity sprang up seemingly as fast as . . . I don't know, let's say . . . as Jesus rose up.

I think Paul was quite right when he said that Christians are "most to be pitied" if Jesus did not rise from the dead (1 Corinthians 15:19). But what are non-Christians to be if he did? Pitied? Yes. Persuaded? May it be so today. May they (may you) know the resurrection power of faith in Jesus. May you know that terror and delight we Christians call Easter! May you know the thrill of this sin-death-and-hell-pounded-into-the-ground holiday (holy day).

The Creditable Incredible

Finally, let's move from this *inclusio* of unbelief or sandwich of sin (27:62–66/28:11–15) in order to *behold* the first celebration of the risen Son.

I use the word "behold" because Matthew uses it four times in 28:1–10.[30] "And behold, there was a great earthquake" (v. 2); "and behold, he [Jesus] is going before you to Galilee; there you will see him. See [literally, 'behold'], I have told you" (v. 7); "And behold, Jesus met them [the women]" (v. 9).

In the last chapter I loosely translated "behold" as "Take a look at this!" I'll stick with that translation here.[31] Take a look at the earthquake and the angel. Then take a look at the angelic announcement. And then take a look at Jesus himself! Take a look at *the creditable incredible*. That's what I'll call this second and final section of the chapter. The first section was "The Unbelievable Disbelief"—how can anyone not believe that something supernatural has happened to Jesus' body as testified by those eyewitnesses whose one job it was to make sure no one tampered with the tomb? That's unbelievable! But now there is also something seemingly unbelievable, in the positive sense. It is incredible if not for the creditable witnesses. It's creditably incredible.

When I say "creditably" or "creditable" I am not referring to rationalistic proofs or tested deductions formed by the scientific method. There are other ways, sometimes even more reliable ways, to arrive at truth. Matthew's method is eyewitness testimony,[32] which is still the most valid way in our legal system of determining the whole truth or at least enough of the truth to render a verdict. But there is more than eyewitness testimony. There is also what George Eldon Ladd called "an inner quality of the gospel."[33] The authority and inspiration of the Bible makes more and more sense the more you understand the whole of the Bible (Genesis to Revelation) as well as the center of the canon (the death and resurrection of Jesus). Moreover, the full story of Scripture makes better sense only after you believe in Jesus. Faith precedes understanding. Faith doesn't precede all understanding. Christians don't leap over science and history to jump into the arms of Jesus. But once in the arms of Jesus through faith, the facts begin to open up like flower buds on an early April day.

We have looked at the downside of Easter—the scamming, bribing, and lying about the truth. Finally, we come to the upside—the hearing, seeing, touching, worshipping, and obeying of the truth. Happy days are here again. Look with me at 28:1–10.

We'll start with verse 1, which reads, "Now after the Sabbath, toward the dawn of the first day of the week, Mary Magdalene and the other Mary went to see the tomb." This setting is significant in that it provides historical details. Matthew provides us with a real day in history and two real people in history. The day is Sunday, that is, the day "after the Sabbath . . . the first day of the week" (v. 1). How interesting that God didn't select the Sabbath (Israel's holy day) as the resurrection day. Instead he chose the next day to be the new holy day. He chose Sunday to be the day we worship his Son (the Lord's Day). Perhaps he chose a new day because a new era was breaking into world history; a permanent cavity was torn in the cosmos to create an eternal eighth day of rest and rejoicing for all who rest and rejoice in Christ.

The day was Sunday, and the two people were the two faithful Marys. They were there on Friday for the burial, and they have now returned on Sunday for the surprise of their lives. As I noted in the last chapter, it is of historical consequence that it was two women who first witnessed the empty tomb and the risen Jesus. In the ancient world women were so marginalized that their testimony was not valid in a court of law. So if the Gospel writers were making up the resurrection story (all four mention the women—see also Mark 16:1–8; Luke 24:1–12; John 20:1–18), they would not have included women as witnesses.[34] But here those "daughters of Eve," to borrow from C. S. Lewis, witness the Lion of Judah's overturning of the deception of Eve and the first fatal sin of Adam. They have seen Jesus buried; they shall soon see him alive again.

Two cheers for the two ladies.
Three cheers for the one true God!

And Behold . . . an Angel

Now as the women "went to *see* the tomb," we are to join them in their looking (v. 1). (I have italicized all the seeing verbs to help you see the significance of seeing here).

> And *behold,* there was a great earthquake, for an angel of the Lord descended from heaven and came and rolled back the stone and sat on it. His appearance was like lightning, and his clothing white as snow. And for fear of him the guards trembled and became like dead men. But the angel said to the women, "Do not be afraid, for I know that you seek Jesus who was crucified. He is not here, for he has risen, as he said. Come, *see* the place where he lay. Then go quickly and tell his disciples that he has risen from the dead, and *behold*, he is going before you to Galilee; there you will *see* him. *See*, I have told you." So they departed quickly from the tomb with fear and great joy, and ran to tell his disciples. (vv. 2–8)

The focus of these verses falls on the angel, an "angel of the Lord" (v. 2). It was due to his presence that "there was a great earthquake" (v. 2). And his awesome appearance (he looked as bright as Jesus did at the transfiguration—"his clothing [as] white as snow" and "his appearance . . . like lighting," v. 3) and his awesome actions (descending from Heaven to earth,[35] rolling back the stone, sitting victoriously upon it) not only made the earth quake but also the guards shake. Jesus was supposed to be dead in the tomb, but the only "dead men" we read about are these guards who "trembled and became like dead men" (v. 4). I imagine that they are pale, frozen in place, and perhaps lying with face flat on the dirt. They need some rejuvenation.

However, the angel doesn't give them CPR. He doesn't even acknowledge them. He is only there to share with the women, to revive their faith. And his message to them is threefold: fear not, come and see, go and tell.

In the Bible every time a human encounters an angel he or she fears. That is why in nearly every angelic encounter, an angel first has to say, "Fear not" or "Do not be afraid." If the angel doesn't say that, you would keep shaking in your boots because God's wrath is on its way. Here, however, the angel has good news to announce to these good women, and so he starts with a word of comfort and courage. Then he moves on to their mission—to tell Jesus' disciples. In order to move them on to that mission, he invites them into the tomb.

> But the angel said to the women, "Do not be afraid, for I know that you seek Jesus who was crucified. He is not here, for he has risen, as he said. Come, see the place where he lay." (vv. 5, 6)

Note that we are given no eyewitness details about the actual resurrection—i.e., that Jesus' body began to glow, the shroud around his limbs burst apart, he stood up, stretched, and walked through the rock. Instead the resurrection story we have is the story of the "clear, visible, and traceable consequences" or effects of the resurrection.[36] The first effect is the empty tomb. The empty tomb is not the only or surest sign Jesus is alive, but it is a good start.

Note a few details here. First note that the stone was not rolled aside to let Jesus out but to let the women in.[37] How Jesus escaped we don't know. Matthew doesn't know. As I said, no one was let in to see the seemingly indescribable resurrection. But we all are let into the tomb, following the women's lead. And following them we are to see with them that the "Jesus who was crucified" (v. 5) is no longer dead. While Jesus remains, in a sense, the crucified one in the church's preaching of the saving effects of the cross (see 1 Corinthians 1:23; 2:2; Galatians 3:1), he does not remain in that tomb. "He is not here, for he has risen" (28:6a).

In Greek "he has risen" or "he has been raised" is one word (*ēgerthē*), a word in which "the whole of gospel truth rests like an inverted pyramid," as Bruner has said.[38] That same word will be used again in verse 7b, "[G]o quickly and tell his disciples that *he has risen* from the dead." When one word like that one is said twice in two verses, we should double underline it in our Bibles and in our brains.

"He has risen, *as he said*" (v. 6). The angel's words remind us of Jesus' own words. Our Lord predicted his death and resurrection six times in Matthew![39] That one word may be the tip of the triangle, but it is as sure and strong as all the prophetic words of Jesus, such as "Heaven and earth will pass away, but my words will not pass away" (24:35). Jesus was right that his words would stick around awhile, and he was right about his resurrection as well.

Note also that the angel's invitation is an invitation to what we would call "scientific research."[40] The angel doesn't say, "The stone may be rolled away, but there is no need to check inside the tomb. Just take it on faith that Jesus is gone." Rather he invites them to use their senses to make sense of what's going on. The angel also doesn't say, "There is no need to look in here or anywhere for Jesus because he is now spiritually raised. Look for him in your souls. Look for him anywhere and everywhere in nature. Check for his resurrected love under the shrub. Feel his pure presence in the warm wind. Rub the belly of your beloved canine and you've touched the happy heart of the Lord." No, the two Marys will *see* and *touch* Jesus—they will behold him in the flesh by holding on to his flesh—in real time and at real places, near the tomb (v. 9) and soon again in Galilee (vv. 7, 10). The resurrection calls for the renewal of our minds, not a lobotomy.[41] By following the women into the tomb, we are to open our ears and eyes—our minds—as they did.

And Behold . . . Jesus

Then the ladies are given their great commission, and off they go running to tell the others.

I love that Matthew records their mixed emotions of "fear and great joy" (v. 8). At least it wasn't great fear and some joy. Whatever fear they had (who wouldn't have some fear after seeing what they saw?), their great joy pushed them on their mission. Fear and joy are emotions that sometimes go together in Scripture (e.g., Psalm 2:11) because they are emotions that sometimes go together in real life. How else would you describe your own wedding day?

I also love that Matthew says "they departed quickly . . . and ran." The picture of pious Jewish women running with the good news of the resurrection is a beautiful sight. "How beautiful are the feet of those who [run to] preach the good news!" (Romans 10:15).

However, midstride Matthew strikes us and them with another "And behold" (28:9). This time it is not an angel of God but the Son of God. We move from "an angelology to a theophany."[42] "And behold, Jesus met them and said, 'Greetings!'" (v. 9a).

I love (obviously I love a lot about this text) that Jesus decides to honor these two faithful women as his first witnesses. I would have gone straight to Pilate or Peter, or even Caiaphas or Caesar. Jesus appears first to Mary Magdalene and . . . what's her name? . . ."the other Mary." It's so marvelous. It's so Jesus, isn't it?

I also love that his first post-resurrection words are not "Tah dah!" or "Told you so!" but rather "Greetings!" or "Hello," which has such a humanness to it, a common, cheerful earthiness to it.[43]

What happens next continues on this earthiness plane and yet also moves us up to Heaven. Look at their reaction to Jesus in verse 9b: "And they came up and took hold of his feet and worshiped him." I don't know if Matthew has in mind the church's doctrine of the two natures of Jesus—"And they . . . took hold of his feet [he is a man] and worshiped him [he is God],"[44] but that thought made its way into my mind, and now likely into yours. Let it stay there, for I think it fits. It fits the divine authority that comes from Jesus' lips in 28:18 as well as the divine action of the resurrection itself. It also fits the language and posture of worship—the worship of Jesus—throughout Matthew's Gospel. Ten times in Matthew Jesus is "worshiped" (2:2, 8, 11; 8:2; 9:18; 14:33; 15:25; 20:20; 28:9, 17),[45] twice after the resurrection (28:9, 17), and such worship always involves adoration.[46] Think of the magi bowing before him (2:11).

I love the heavenliness of Jesus, and I love the earthiness as well. I have highlighted some of Jesus' earthiness; here is more. Note here that Jesus is not a spirit. He is not a ghost. Have you ever noticed that ghosts are usually depicted without feet?[47] (Think of Casper the Friendly Ghost if you need help picturing perceptions of ghosts in history.) Jesus has resurrected feet, two feet to which two worshippers cling. You see, Christianity is a touchy-feely religion. It's a creed with ten toes! It's a *that which we have heard with our ears, that which we have seen with our eyes, and that which we have touched with our hands* faith (1 John 1:1; cf. 2 Peter 1:16).[48] Our two highest holidays are as tangible as human skin—a baby in a manger and a man with feet. As Bruner beautifully said, the beautiful thing is this:

> God did not "need" a fetus for the incarnation, water for his Son's baptism, a cross for his Son's death, or a cadaver for his Son's bodily resurrection—God can squeeze water from a stone. But God *used* all these lowly realities to do the great work of world salvation.[49]

This Easter let us behold our own sin and the sins of humankind. But also let us behold the earthquake and the angel, behold the angelic gospel announcement—he has risen, behold Jesus—hold on to his human feet, and bow down before our incarnate King.

89

Operation Immanuel

MATTHEW 28:16–20

IN HIS BOOK *If I Should Die Before I Live*, Joe LoMusio writes, "If I were to ask you to describe Easter without using any words, you could only use punctuation marks, which punctuation mark would you choose to describe this Easter for yourself?" He goes on to say how some might view Easter as a comma—"it makes you stop, pause, think and listen," but that's all it does for you. Others might view Easter as "a big bold period." That is, "You thought you'd feel excited" about it, but Easter felt empty again. LoMusio then describes Jesus' first disciples and how they moved from a period (Jesus was dead and buried, ending all their expectations) to a question mark (with the news of the empty tomb) and finally to "one massive exclamation point!" (as they beheld him with their own eyes).[1]

Indeed the resurrection is one massive exclamation point. But it's also four immense arrows. I know that arrows aren't punctuation marks, but they are on my computer keyboard, so that counts for something. What I mean is that the resurrection is an arrow that points upward to Jesus' universal power and downward to Jesus' ecclesial presence. It is also an arrow that points inward—calling for worshipful allegiance to the resurrected Christ. But also, or in turn, it is an arrow that points outward—commissioning Jesus' disciples to move out in order to bring others in.

The Inward Arrow

With that arrow analogy in place, let's start, as Matthew does, with the inward arrow first.

In the last chapter I attempted to cover 27:62—28:15. Of those twenty verses, at least one was neglected (28:10)—Jesus' final word to the two women.

He said to them, "Do not be afraid; go and tell *my brothers* to go to Galilee, and there they will see me" (v. 10). Note that he doesn't call the eleven apostles and those hiding with them "those wimps" or worse "those traitors." He could have called them both. Instead he calls them "my brothers." He calls them his accepted, forgiven, restored family members, his coworkers in the mission of world restoration.

It is from that good commission of the forgiveness of sins offered to the first church that we move into Jesus' Great Commission of the forgiveness of sins offered to the whole world.[2] The good news of Easter must extend over all the earth. All nations must hear and see and touch Jesus, if you will, and in doing so worship and obey him. Yes, all creation must *behold him that was crucified*!

But for that to happen something first has to happen to the apostles. Their allegiance to Jesus is crucial to the success of the operation. Look with me at verses 16, 17 and let's see how they respond to the Resurrected One:

> Now the eleven disciples went to Galilee, to the mountain to which Jesus had directed them. And when they saw him they worshiped him, but some doubted.

If we ask the question "why?" to five words, we'll get a good feel for this first arrow. First, *why eleven*? Eleven is an imperfect number, Biblically-speaking. Jesus chose twelve men because he was boldly rejecting apostate Israel (i.e., the twelve tribes) and reconstituting God's people around himself. Of course, we know why there are only eleven here. Judas has hanged himself. But why didn't the eleven add one more? They would eventually do that. In Acts 1:15–26 Matthias replaces Judas. Everything gets back into Biblical balance: having twelve does matter. But here they stayed eleven. Why? Perhaps it was because they thought the Jesus-as-Messiah train ride had stopped for good at the cross. They all got off at Golgotha. To change the analogy, they thought, *Why should we add another member to the board if the company has just closed its doors?*

We don't know the apostles' motive for staying eleven. We also don't know why Jesus didn't immediately add one more member before he gave the Great Commission. It would make better symbolic sense for verse 16 to start, "Now Jesus added a man named Matthias to the eleven. Then the *twelve* disciples went to Galilee," and on the story goes. Perhaps one reason eleven is mentioned relates back to verse 10—the term "my brothers" and the theme of God forgiving, restoring, and reestablishing sinful men as the leaders of his imperfect church.

Yes, it might be that the lesson of the eleven is that "[t]he church that Jesus sends into the world is 'elevenish,' imperfect, fallible. Yet Jesus uses this imperfect church to do his perfect work."[3] Knowing what I know of the New Testament (think of imperfect Peter in Acts 10 or in Galatians 2:11–14) and what I know of my church (think of me), I surmise it is.

Next let's look at *why Galilee* and why a *mountain* in Galilee. Here I promise I will leave aside *most* of my theological speculation. Galilee is about a hundred miles from Jerusalem. Why this walk? Perhaps it is a faith walk, reminiscent of Abraham's faith walk.[4] Jesus directed the two women, who in turned directed the eleven men to take a hike up to Galilee and then up a mountain. Such a walk takes some kind of trust. Don't underestimate what faith it must have taken to do that "which Jesus had directed them" (v. 16b).

But still, why go to Galilee and why up a mountain? The reason is that location is strategic to God's plan of salvation. The last time in Matthew where "Galilee" and "mountain" met up was in 4:12—5:1. In 4:12 Jesus began his earthly adult ministry in Galilee, "Galilee of the Gentiles" (4:15, quoting Isaiah 9:1, 2).[5] The theme of "all nations" (28:19) peeks its head out here first. Jesus began his earthly ministry as he would end it—with a focus on bringing the light of the gospel to both Jews *and Gentiles*.[6] At the end of chapter 4 Jesus calls his first apostles and then proclaims and shows the healing power of the kingdom "throughout all Galilee" (4:23). Then Jesus goes up on a mountain and gives the Sermon on the Mount (5:1ff.).

Jesus' first great speech will be on a mountain in Galilee as will his last. There are too many links between the two talks to share them in one chapter. Three will have to suffice. (It is good to keep your mouths watering for more of the Word than you'll get from me.) One link of continuity is that of authority. The Sermon on the Mount ends with this note of authority: "And when Jesus finished these sayings, the crowds were astonished at his teaching, for he was teaching them as one who had authority" (7:28, 29a), and the Great Commission begins with Jesus saying of himself, "All authority in heaven and on earth has been given to me" (28:18b). A link of discontinuity (divinely ordained discontinuity) is that of mission. The Sermon on the Mount focuses more inwardly: We are to be made disciples by obeying Jesus' commands. The Great Commission focuses more outwardly: we are to make disciples by teaching others to obey Jesus' commands. A final link is that of underlying ethics. That is, the move-out mission of the Great Commission is a mission of humility and love of neighbor. Put differently, the ethics of the Sermon on the Mount are the basis for the attitudes and actions Christians are to have in fulfilling the Great Commission.

So, why Galilee and why a mountain in Galilee? Those are some of my reasons for this.[7]

The final two whys are attached to the words "worshiped" and "doubted" (v. 17). Here we focus on the disciples' reactions to the resurrected Christ. When they finally get to the said location of disclosure, they do indeed see Jesus. Other Gospel writers tell us that the apostles saw Jesus before they went to Galilee. However, Matthew only gives us the Galilee viewing. And he does so, I believe, because he is moving the church out on mission. Jerusalem is behind us. To Galilee and beyond!

But before we, with Matthew, move on to the mission, let's first meet Jesus on the mountain. As the women showed mixed emotions—"fear and great joy" (28:8)—so the men also show mixed reactions. We read in verse 17, "when they saw him they worshiped him, but some doubted."

"They worshiped" is the same reaction that the two Marys had when they first beheld Jesus alive (28:9). Here, as there, we are to see such worship as a very positive and right reaction. When I talked about the women's reaction to Jesus in the last chapter, I mentioned the church's doctrine of the two natures of Jesus—"And they . . . took hold of his feet [he is a man] and worshipped him [he is God]" (28:9). There I focused more on Jesus' humanity. Here I want us to pause and ponder Jesus' divinity.

If some individuals knock on your front door and claim they are witnessing on behalf of Jehovah or claim to be part of the church of Jesus Christ that has latter-day saints, let them in and turn with them to 28:16–20 or to the opening of John's Gospel. Both are equally important on this crucial matter. If you go with Matthew, questions to ask your heretical visitors might include the following. Work your way backwards in 28:16–20. Starting with verse 20 ask, "Why does Jesus use the phrase 'I am' (*ego eimi*) of himself? Do you think he is intentionally relating himself to the God of the burning bush, 'I AM WHO I AM' (Exodus 3:14)? I'm just curious—what do you think?" If they say, "I don't know. I haven't thought about it," you can say, "I don't know either. I just found it a curious way for Jesus to talk. Maybe it's nothing. One of my favorite authors has a problem with overanalyzing texts. I might have got that from him."

"Okay, but what about," continue the conversation, "Jesus' claiming to be with his disciples always? Do you think Jesus is claiming to be omnipresent? Only God can be everywhere at all times, right? Even if Jesus is claiming to be present *only with his followers* at all times, that still has a dash of divinity to it, don't you think?"

After they have thought about that for a bit, attack posthaste with verses

19, 20, the Great Commission itself. Here are some zingers to zap them with: "Why are Christians to be baptized into the name of the Father *and the Son and the Holy Spirit*? An equality of persons—between the Father, Son, and Spirit—seems to be inferred there. Am I reading that wrong? What do you think?" Take a dramatic pause. Wipe your brow, then continue, "And why would and how could Jesus say that his disciples are to disciple others by 'teaching them to observe all' that he has commanded? What's with the first-person personal pronoun 'I': 'observe all that I have commanded you'? Shouldn't they be taught to obey God and God's commands, not Jesus and Jesus' commands?" Related to that, move them a step back to verse 18 and ask, "Again, what's with the personal pronoun 'me' attached to that all inclusive adjective 'all'? How can Jesus claim that all authority over all creation has been granted to him? To be honest, I can't think of a bolder claim in the history of the world. It makes silly bumper stickers like *Jesus is my copilot* and *My boss is a Jewish carpenter* look . . . well, silly."

Finally, if they haven't left the house yet, take them to that lovely verb in verse 17, "worshiped" and ask them, "What's with the worship here?" If they say that the word "worshiped" can also be translated "fell down" (NJB) or "bowed" (YLT), then reply, "Okay, what's with the bowing and/or falling on their faces before him?" When John, in Revelation 22:8, 9, fell facedown at the feet of the angel who showed him the visions, the angel replied, "You must not do that! I am a fellow servant with you. . . . Worship God." Why was John rebuked? Because no matter how awesome angels might appear, human beings are not to bow before them. The same is true of mere mortal men (think of Paul and Barnabas in Acts 14:14, 15). But here in Matthew they are bowing to Jesus, and there is no protest from anyone, not even (and not especially) Jesus. Here Jesus accepts their worship just as the Lamb of God in Revelation does: "Worthy is the Lamb who was slain, to receive power and wealth and wisdom and might and honor and glory and blessing!" (Revelation 5:12).

Therefore, don't you think, in light of all that I said above, that it is only appropriate that we now join "every creature in heaven and on earth and under the earth and in the sea, and all that is in them, saying, 'To him who sits on the throne [God the Father] and to the Lamb [Jesus] be blessing and honor and glory and might forever and ever!" (Revelation 5:13)? Don't you think we should join the four living creatures who shout "Amen" and the elders who fall down and worship Jesus Christ (Revelation 5:14)? Don't think too hard. The answer to those questions is an obvious yes.

Now before we completely station our heads in the heavens (I haven't even come to the upward arrow yet), let's remain with two feet on earth, as

Matthew does in sharing with us that unexpected phrase, "but some doubted" (v. 17b). Really? How many doubted? Two? Four? Six? Eight? Who are we not to appreciate? And who doubted? Thomas, sure. But who else? Give us names. And what did they doubt? And were these doubts ever resolved? Well, I doubt we will ever know the answers to all those questions.

What we do know, however, is that the word for doubt (*distazo*) can also mean "hesitate." So the sense could be that everyone first worshipped, but then some hesitated. That is, they "doubted" that the man they'd just worshipped was actually Jesus (maybe his appearance—his resurrected body—was altered in some way), or they "doubted" if it was right, as good Jewish monotheists who held to the creed that there is *one* true God, that it was proper to worship the man Jesus.[8] Or perhaps the nature of their doubt was initial unbelief because it was all so unbelievable. Some reacted, in other words, like a son would react after being reunited with his dad who had reportedly died in a covert combat mission ten years earlier. "I can't believe you're alive! I can't believe it's you!"

Or, on a more negative note, their doubt can be doubt in the sense that we usually think of the word—a lack of faith or too little faith. The only other time this word "doubt" is used in Matthew is when Jesus reached out his hand to save Peter who was sinking in the water after walking on it. Jesus said to Peter, "O you of little faith, why did you *doubt*?" (14:31b). There "doubt" is synonymous with "little faith."[9] So does "doubt" in 28:17 means "little faith"? I think it does in some sense.

Staying with the correlations between Matthew 28 and 14, I found another interesting connection between our text and that text: in that text there is doubt and then worship (when Jesus gets on the boat we read, "And those in the boat worshiped him, saying 'Truly you are the Son of God,'" 14:33); in our current text there is worship and then doubt. To me that seems anticlimactic. (Jesus just rose from the dead! That's even better than walking on water.) And yet for me, and perhaps the same can be said of you, the realism actually helps rather than hinders my faith. I'm encouraged by Matthew's truthfulness (he didn't have to record "and some doubted"), and my faith is strengthened ironically by these apostolic shortcomings. It's back to that theme of *eleven* apostles. God loves imperfect people into his perfect kingdom, and God uses imperfect people for his perfect plans. He uses bipolar disciples—don't we go all back and forth from worship to doubt?[10]—to make the world whole again. It's just lovely, isn't it?

What is also lovely is that doubt (if you struggle with it) is perhaps best overcome by following Jesus where he takes us next—to his exaltation and his commission. In other words, moving from an inward reaction to Jesus to upward and outward ones moves us farther and farther away from debilitating doubt. Look up to Jesus, look out to the fields white for harvest, and look where doubt has gone. You might be surprised that only worship is left.

The Upward Arrow

Next let's touch the tip of the upward arrow.

In my excursus on the deity of Jesus earlier I touched on much of this upward arrow. Let me simply add a brief exposition of verse 18, "And Jesus came and said to them, 'All authority in heaven and on earth has been given to me.'"

Recently a friend told me about The Improvised Shakespeare Company that performs Friday nights at Chicago's iO, the club self-touted as "Chicago's Best Improv Comedy." That theatre company performs two ninety-minute Shakespeare plays without a script, but not without a rich knowledge of Shakespeare. The cast asks the audience for a title of a Shakespeare play, and from there, using iambic pentameter, rhyming couplets, and authentically Shakespearian vocabulary, character development, and plot, the casts makes up a completely new script.[11] Each show is unrehearsed and unrepeatable.[12]

While 28:16–20 is not Matthew improvising per se, he is, nevertheless, tying together many of the main themes of his Gospel in these final five dense verses.[13] He is creating something new out of themes he has brought to the surface time and again in his Gospel. Jesus' authority, for example, is a key theme found throughout Matthew's Gospel.[14] Our Lord has demonstrated the authority to heal, the authority to cast out demons, the authority to judge, and the authority to forgive sins. Now he adds one small but super-significant word before all his previous authoritative assertions and acts—"all." He says, "All authority in heaven and on earth has been given to me." This is not necessarily "a new authority," but it is apparently "a new level of authority," the highest level possible.[15] It is "an all-embracing authority."[16] He is in a position of power up there (in the heavens) and down here (on the earth). That just about covers it.

From 1:18 ("Now the birth of Jesus Christ took place in this way . . .") until 27:50 ("Jesus cried out again with a loud voice and yielded up his spirit"), there has been, in a sense, a veil covering Jesus' face. But as the stone is rolled away and Jesus emerges alive from the tomb, that veil is torn in two. Now we see "the light of . . . the glory of God in the face of Jesus Christ" (2 Corinthians 4:6). Now we see the "absolute and all-encompassing" authority of the Son of Man:[17]

I saw in the night visions,

and behold, with the clouds of heaven
  there came one like a son of man,
and he came to the Ancient of Days
  and was presented before him.
And to him was given dominion
  and glory and a kingdom,
that all peoples, nations, and languages
  should serve him;
his dominion is an everlasting dominion,
  which shall not pass away,
and his kingdom one
  that shall not be destroyed. (Daniel 7:13, 14)

The Ancient of Days (the Father) has handed over absolute authority and everlasting dominion to his earthly but now exalted Son (cf. 11:27; 26:64). Jesus has been enthroned as King of the World (cf. Revelation 1:5), not merely King of the Jews (cf. 2:1).

As Christians living centuries removed from the claim of verse 18, we are not surprised when we read in Paul's letters that God

> worked in Christ when he raised him from the dead and seated him at his right hand in the heavenly places, far above all rule and authority and power and dominion, and above every name that is named, not only in this age but also in the one to come. And he put all things under his feet and gave him as head over all things to the church, which is his body, the fullness of him who fills all in all. (Ephesians 1:20–23)

or

> Therefore God has highly exalted him and bestowed on him the name that is above every name, so that at the name of Jesus every knee should bow, in heaven and on earth and under the earth, and every tongue confess that Jesus Christ is Lord, to the glory of God the Father. (Philippians 2:9–11)

or

> And [Jesus] is before all things, and in him all things hold together. And he is the head of the body, the church. He is the beginning, the firstborn from the dead, that in everything he might be preeminent. For in him all the fullness of God was pleased to dwell, and through him to reconcile to himself all things, whether on earth or in heaven, making peace by the blood of his cross. (Colossians 1:17–20)

The cosmic authority of Jesus is second nature to us. We can casually sing, clapping in beat, "He's got the whole world in his hands" without stopping mid-beat to ponder that we just sang the loftiest claim in world history!

I want you to stop now and think afresh about this cosmos-shaking claim. Verse 18 is indeed "the highest Christology to be found in the Bible."[18] How can Jesus say, "All authority . . . has been given *to me*" (v. 18) when the Lord God in Isaiah 42:8 says, "I am the LORD; that is my name; my glory I give to no other . . ."? Let's face it: Jesus is claiming here that he shares the glorious authority that "Israel's God has said he will not share with another."[19] Let's face it: Jesus is claiming that he is distinct from the Father and yet is in charge of creation just as God is. The Trinity is soon to be named in verse 19. We are baptized into only *one name* that strangely has three names—"Father . . . Son and . . . Spirit." Here the doctrine of the Trinity trickles into our ears for the first time in our New Testaments.[20] It's mysterious. It's marvelous. Jesus claims to have been granted the same power as God. Truly marvelous!

The Outward Arrow

Verse 18 is the key verse of Matthew's Gospel. If you memorize any verse, memorize this one. But don't merely memorize it, apply it! How? Worship Jesus. But also live out the Great Commission. Let's look there next. Verse 19 begins, "Go therefore . . ." That is, in light of Jesus' omnipotence let's do all that he says. What does he say? We come now to the outward arrow. He says:

> Go therefore and make disciples of all nations, baptizing them in the name of the Father and of the Son and of the Holy Spirit, teaching them to observe all that I have commanded you. (vv. 19, 20)

There are four verbs here: "Go," "make disciples," "baptizing," and "teaching." The first verb—"go"—is tightly connected to the second one—"make disciples." There is no debate grammatically as to which verb is the dominant imperative ("make disciples" is the main verb), but there is some debate on how much stress should be placed on the "go" or "going" or "as you go." However, the verbs—"baptizing" and "teaching"—are certainly subservient to the verb "make disciples." In other words, what is involved in making disciples? Baptizing them and teaching them Jesus' teachings.

We'll start with the verb "go" and find out just where it should go in the verb pecking order. I like what Sinclair Ferguson once said: "Being the church is doing evangelism." I also like what Douglas Wilson has said about worship "as a form of cultural conquest":

> As we gather in the presence of the living God on the Lord's Day, He is pleased to use our right worship of Him as a battering ram to bring down all the citadels of unbelief in our communities. Just as the walls of Jericho fell before the worship and service of God, so unbelievers tremble when Christians gather in their communities to worship the living God rightly.[21]

However, let's be careful to hold high and hold out the Great Commission's "go." There must be some movement to our mission. And the movement in our text is not the movement from sitting in our pews to standing to sing. Neither is the movement from the sanctuary to the fellowship hall. Rather, it is the movement out the front door to take the gospel to lost people.

This going (how can I say this strongly?) is why the church exists.[22] Is that strong enough? The verb "go" is a subordinate verb (a circumstantial participle) to the main aorist imperative "make disciples." However, poor "go" has become overly subordinated today. A return to the missions movement of the nineteenth century, where "go" was made the main command, might be just the corrective the contemporary church needs. Either way, you can't make disciples unless you go (move out to mission), and you can't go unless you know why you are going. "Go" and "make" go together.

So, we are to "go." But what are we to do? Jesus tells us that we have one primary task before us, and that is to "make disciples of all nations" (v. 19a). Fair enough. But what does Jesus mean by "all nations"? In the words of Revelation, he means "every tribe and language and people and nation" (Revelation 5:9). And in the words of Acts 1:8, he means moving out from "Jerusalem . . . to the end of the earth." The "eternal gospel" is to be proclaimed to all "those who dwell on earth" (Revelation 14:6).

Again, what an extraordinary claim! What "audacious internationalism."[23] What a monumental mission. Why didn't Jesus limit the scope to "all Palestine" or "the eastern Mediterranean countries"?[24] Or Chicago or the American Southwest? "[A]ll nations" is a bit too ambitious and unrealistic (v. 19). If I was on that mountain in Galilee on that day, I would have had a hard time believing him. But I wasn't on that mountain. I was conceived in the year of our Lord 1971. So I don't have a hard time believing him. In the small church I pastor we have people from every continent but two (Australia and Antarctica). Jesus predicted that Christianity would be a world religion, and it is. Jesus has indeed made the world his parish.

But listen, the job is not done. The world will not merely come to us, as the magi came to Jesus (2:1–12). We are to take Jesus' mission beyond the Roman centurion (8:5–13) and Canaanite woman (15:21–28) to all men and women and children of the world. Here the Son of David and the Son of Abraham (1:1) commissions his little church to fulfill the big Abrahamic covenant (Genesis 12:3; 18:18; 22:18), to bring in "all the families of the earth" under the Davidic kingdom of the Lord Jesus Christ. Any church worth its "salt" . . . and "light" (5:13–16) is a missions-giving, missions-sending, missions-praying, and "O for a Thousand Tongues to Sing" singing church.

We are to "make disciples of all nations" (v. 19). But what is a disciple? According to 12:46–50, a disciple is someone who hears, understands, and obeys Jesus' word.[25] So to "make disciples" is a broader concept than simply "to make a convert"—evangelizing a stranger in five minutes. The word "disciple" is a "slow, corporate, and earthy" word, as are "baptizing and teaching."[26] It is an educational term. We are to enroll people in the school of Christ and tutor them therein, meticulously mentoring them month by month, helping them mature in Christ.

We are striving not merely for a lost soul to make a decision about Christ, but we are striving for a lost soul to make a dramatic and permanent change of "personal allegiance."[27] So, following the example of Jesus in the Gospels and the apostles in the book of Acts, we are to make relationships with others to the extent that they, by God's grace, accept the message of the gospel and seek to grow in their knowledge of and devotion to God.

To "further specify what is involved in discipleship," Jesus mentions in verses 19, 20 baptism and teaching.[28] "Baptism and teaching," as Carson points out, "are not the means of making disciples,"[29] but they well characterize discipleship. Someone who is a genuine disciple of Christ will desire to be baptized into the one God and to learn about the teachings of our "one teacher" (23:8), Christ. (Note the dramatic shift from circumcision to baptism and from the Torah to Jesus' teachings.)

Regarding baptism, it is important for us to recognize that "the NT can scarcely conceive of a disciple" who was not baptized.[30] Throughout the book of Acts, as demonstrated in the aftermath of Peter's Pentecost sermon,[31] the conclusion of the Ethiopian eunuch's confession of faith, and following the dramatic conversion of Saul, "baptism was performed in the closest possible association with conversion."[32]

While it is proper to emphasize the internal baptism of the Holy Spirit (regeneration), it is improper to do so to the neglect of external baptism (water baptism), which is a sign of "both entrance into the Messiah's covenant community and of pledged submission of his lordship."[33] For as Jesus teaches here, one is to be baptized *in* or *into* "the name [the one name of God] of the Father and of the Son and of the Holy Spirit" (v. 19). When someone is baptized, he is publicly and visibly plunged into communion with the Triune God of our salvation. He is "brought into fellowship with and under the authority" of the Trinity.[34] He is "marked out, branded almost, with the holy 'name.'"[35]

Thus, in light of a proper understanding of baptism and in light of the fact that baptism, within the context of the Great Commission, "is synonymous with becoming a disciple,"[36] it ought not be a matter of indifference to us whether a Christian is baptized or not. "Baptism is not an optional extra for followers of Jesus."[37]

I'm not a big fan of large crusades or "revival" meetings, but if these events are to continue, I wish at the end of such services that the preacher would call forth all who want to receive Christ and exhort them not to merely fill out a card and to talk with a counselor but to be baptized into the name of their Savior. Baptism gives more of an edge to the commitment they are supposedly making, the kind of edge I think God intended. Baptism makes one think twice about the giving of one's whole body, one's whole self, to Christ. Baptism makes one think twice about diving into this new religion and into this new relationship. Don't undervalue what God has ordained! I agree with John MacArthur that "the person who is unwilling to be baptized is at best a disobedient believer. . . . If he is unwilling to comply with the simple act of obedience in the presence of fellow believers, he will hardly be willing to stand for Christ before the unbelieving world."[38]

Beyond baptizing, the apostles (and the church after them—the Great Commission is naturally self-perpetuating) are commanded to "teach" these new converts "to observe all" of Christ's commandments (v. 20).

I usually complain about red-letter editions of the Bible that highlight Jesus' words to the exclusion of all the other words of Scripture. I complain because these editions in some sense make an improper hierarchy of importance, as if Jesus' words were somehow more God-breathed than the rest of Holy Scripture. Yet, with that disclaimer made, I must also say that I like red-letter Bibles because they highlight, as Jesus does here, the teachings of Jesus.

If you have ever carefully read through all the red, you realize that "Christ's teachings cover a vast amount of topics—God and man, life and death, true religion and false religion, happiness and sadness, wealth and poverty, time and eternity, heaven and hell, righteousness and unrighteousness," to name a few.[39] Christ's teachings also cover not merely the imperatives ("lay up for yourselves treasures in heaven," 6:20) but "also proverbs, blessings, parables, and prophecies."[40] I also think it is fair to include under the broad umbrella of Christ's commands what Jesus teaches here (that he is the all-powerful and ever-present Lord and that the church has a commission), as well as what Jesus did in chapters 27, 28 (he died and rose again).[41] Furthermore, it is reasonable to include the Old Testament commands as fulfilled in Jesus (5:17–20), as well as the apostolic commands as extensions of Jesus' will (put differently, as "further explanation of the significance of Christ and his teachings"[42]). I'll put it this way: *we are to preach Christ from all the Scriptures*.

Jesus' teaching ministry is to be our teaching ministry. Christian churches are only Christian if they center on Christ's commands. Our mission is not to make Buddhists better Buddhists or Muslims better Muslims or atheists better atheists or witches better witches, but rather to invite all people from all other "faiths" into the one true faith under the commandments of the one true Lord. The Great Commission is exclusively inclusive—it is one Lord for all nations! So I ask you, do you know all that the Lord has commanded? Don't you think that should be the first priority of a disciple? We are not to listen for what Christ will command (as he mystically whispers in our ears) but to what he has commanded (past tense), what we have in the Spirit-breathed Word.[43] How often do we teach and preach about the commandments of Jesus? How often do we teach them to our children? How often do we employ them in evangelism? The vast and varied teachings should be upheld each and every Sunday morning and each and every second of the week by each and every Christian.

When I was a child, the church I attended had the wonderful weekly practice of having the minister process from the back to the front of the church holding a large Bible in front of and above his head. When he arrived at the altar, he placed the sacred Word upon it, genuflected before it, and kissed it. Now, unfortunately, like the church I grew up in, most churches today might every Sunday put on this drama of adoration toward the Word of God, but that is all it is, a drama, a mere performance, a show of lip service! Few churches in America (even some of the most liberal denominations) would dare claim that the Bible and the teachings of Christ are not important to the Christian faith, and yet it remains a sad reality that rarely is the Word of God opened and exposited in most churches on most Sunday mornings.

In many houses originally built for the purpose of filling our minds with the mind of Christ, God's Word is left sitting on the altar collecting dust, while God's people are left sitting in the pews collecting the rubbish that comes from the mind of man or woman.

> When you come to church, you may find compassion, you may find soup kitchens, you may find entertainment, you may find beautiful music, you may find friends, you may find all sorts of things when you come to church

> in the twenty-first century, but if you do not find the unique treasure of Christ's teaching then the church has sold you short.[44]

Christian churches and Christian people really need to shape up here! When we fail to teach the teachings of Christ, we fail to obey the Great Commission!

The Downward Arrow

We need to recognize that the Great Commission Jesus gave his church is very difficult, and that's why he gives us the second half of verse 20. He gives us himself! Just as Jesus gave this commission to his followers based on the reality of his universal sovereignty, so also he gives it based on the reality of his universal presence. Those two pillars—Jesus' power and presence—hold up the church and mobilize her. We can "go" and "make disciples" because Jesus has "all authority" and because Jesus promises to be with us.[45]

In the first chapter of Matthew's Gospel, we were introduced to baby Jesus under the name "'Immanuel' (which means, God with us)" (1:23).[46] Now in the last chapter of Matthew's Gospel we are given the confirmation of this *withness* promise in Christ's final climactic words:[47] "And behold, I am with you always, to the end of the age" (v. 20b).

Every phrase of this final sentence is significant. "And behold": in Matthew 28 this is the fifth and final "take a look at this," or here the sense is, "Now listen up!" What are we to hear? We are to hear that Jesus—not just his teachings or his Spirit in his people, but the resurrected, living, and eternal Lord himself—is the one who promises to be with us "always." This word "always" is the fourth and final time the word "all" in some form is used in our text—*all* (*pasa*) authority, *all* (*panta*) nations, *all* (*panta*) that he commanded, and now "with you *all* (*pasas*) the days." I almost entitled this chapter "Four Alls for Ye All." But I refrained for obvious reasons. Immanuel will mobilize his church for mission every day, all of the day, and for all the days—"to the end of the age," that is, until he returns (v. 20).

We are to look upward because Jesus has promised to work downward—to help from above. He will give us the courage. He will give us the wisdom. He will give us the harvest. He will give us the strength:

> Fear not, I am with you, O be not dismayed;
> For I am thy God and will still give thee aid;
> I'll strengthen thee, help thee, and cause thee to stand,
> Upheld by my righteous, omnipotent hand.[48]

You might think of our whole text in this way: Jesus' "first-person-pronoun assurances"—"I have all authority, and I am with you always"—enables us to keep his "second-person-pronoun commands": you go, you make disciples, you baptize, and you teach.[49]

Retractions

The Russian American novelist Vladimir Nabokov said the only way to write a novel is on three-by-five note cards and you must use a pencil.

Why a pencil, his interviewer wondered.

Nabokov said with Slavic emphasis, "So one can *errrase.*"[50]

Good writing requires meticulous editing, as does good preaching. One has to discern what should be left in and what should be tossed out. I preached these eighty-nine sermons on the Gospel of Matthew. If I were to preach them all again, I would erase a line or paragraph here or there. But I hope I have made clear throughout each of those chapters what I have attempted to make clear in this final chapter. Whether you remember the significance of Galilee or the symbolic value of mountains in Matthew, I hope you remember that Jesus is Lord.[51] I hope you love that reality. And I hope you live by that reality. May it be so for the glory of God, the good of his church, and the salvation of the world!

Soli Deo gloria!

Notes

Preface

1. It was common in the early church to interpret the four beasts in Ezekiel (see Ezekiel 1:10; 10:14; cf. Revelation 4:7) as the four Gospels (e.g., Irenaeus, *Against Heresies*, 3:11:8; and Jerome, in St. Thomas Aquinas, *Catena Aurea*, vol. 1, Part I: The Gospel of St. Matthew, trans. John Henry Newman [New York: Cosimo Classics, 2007], p. 9).

2. Similarly, D. Martyn Lloyd-Jones wrote,

> I am not decrying the value of a careful discussion and study of the Scriptures in that way; but I do feel constantly the need to warn myself and everybody else against becoming so immersed in the mechanics of Scripture that we miss its *message*. While we should be concerned about the harmony of the Gospels and similar problems, God forbid, I say, that we should regard the four Gospels as some kind of intellectual puzzle. The Gospels are not here for us to try to draw out our perfect schemes and classifications; they are here for us to read in order that we may apply them, that we may live them and practise them. (*Studies in the Sermon on the Mount*, 2nd ed. [Grand Rapids, MI: Eerdmans, 1976], p. 15.)

3. J. C. Ryle, *Matthew: Expository Thoughts on the Gospels*, Crossway Classic Commentaries (Wheaton, IL: Crossway, 1993), p. xvi.

Chapter One: The Melodic Line of Matthew

1. I allude here to the tradition that Peter is the source of Mark's Gospel: "Mark, the disciple and interpreter of Peter, himself also handed down to us in writing what was preached by Peter" (Irenaeus, *Against Heresies*, 3.1; cf. 3.10.6).

2. See Martyn Lloyd-Jones, *Preaching and Preachers* (Grand Rapids, MI: Zondervan, 1972), chapter 16.

3. John Stott, *Why I Am a Christian* (Downers Grove, IL: InterVarsity Press, 2003), p. 44.

4. Ibid., pp. 45, 46.

5. This theme of authority is found throughout Matthew. Eight examples should suffice. First, in his teachings Jesus often employs terms like King, Lord, and Master in reference to himself, as well as phrases like "kingdom of heaven" and "kingdom of God" (cf. his two kingdoms language in relationship to demonic activity, as well as his authority over demons [e.g., 12:26], and his language in relation to other kings [4:18–22; 9:9]). Second, he claims to be greater than the great King Solomon (12:42; cf. his relationship with David and actions that claim Davidic authority, e.g., 12:3, 4). Third, twenty-eight times he uses the authoritative Old Testament title "Son of Man"

of himself. Fourth, he claims knowledge of the future judgment and authoritative role in the judgment. Fifth, he declares who gets into the kingdom and who doesn't (e.g., 25:31–34, 41). Sixth, he gives many God-like authority claims (5:11, 17, 18, 21, 28, 32, 34, 39, 44; 7:21–27, 29; 9:1–8; 10:22, 32–42; 11:27–30; 12:30–32, 36; 16:24; 18:5, 6, 20; 19:28, 29; 20:23; 23:34–39; 24:9, 35; 25:1, 35ff. Seventh, in the recognition of his divine authority, he is worshipped (2:11; 8:2; 14:33; 28:9, 17). Eighth, the religious and political authorities notice and question Jesus' authority (see 21:23–27; 22:16; 26:53).

6. Timothy Keller, *The Reason for God: Belief in an Age of Skepticism* (New York: Dutton, 2008), pp. 40, 41. Also John Stott notes, "Nearly 80 percent of the world's Christians today are non-white and non-Western. Christianity is emphatically not a white man's religion" (*Through the Bible, Through the Year* [Grand Rapids, MI: Baker, 2006], p. 152).

Chapter Two: Perfect Aim

1. For the importance of genealogies to Jews, see Michael Green, *The Message of Matthew*, The Bible Speaks Today (Downers Grove, IL: InterVarsity Press, 2000), p. 57.

2. Craig L. Blomberg, *Matthew*, New American Commentary (Nashville: Broadman, 1992), p. 56.

3. John Nolland, *The Gospel of Matthew*, New International Greek Testament Commentary (Grand Rapids, MI: Eerdmans, 2005), pp. 101, 102.

4. See Ulrich Luz, *Matthew 1–7*, Hermenia (Minneapolis: Fortress Press, 2007), pp. 96, 97.

5. C. H. Spurgeon, *The Gospel of the Kingdom* (Pasadena, TX: Pilgrim Publications, repr. 1996), p. 1.

6. Charles Wesley, "Hark! the Herald Angels Sing" (1739).

7. Frederick Dale Bruner, *The Christbook: Matthew 1–12*, 2nd and rev. ed. (Grand Rapids, MI: Eerdmans, 2004), p. 14.

8. Spurgeon, *The Gospel of the Kingdom*, p. 3.

9. Ibid., p. 9.

10. Luz, *Matthew 1–7*, p. 83.

11. "Since it was quite usual for people to marry within their clan, it can be concluded that Mary belonged to the house of David. Several early Fathers of the church testify to this—Ignatius of Antioch, Irenaeus, Justin and Tertullian, who base their testimony on an unbroken oral tradition" (see *The Navarre Bible: Standard Edition, Saint Matthew's Gospel* [Dublin: Four Courts Press, 1999], p. 260).

12. These men were David's advisors, and Giloh was located in the mountains of Judah.

13. This "irregular element" prepares us for "the miracle of the virginal conception of Jesus." Rudolf Schnackenburg, *The Gospel of Matthew*, trans. Robert R. Barr (Grand Rapids, MI: Eerdmans, 2002), p. 17. Cf. Donald Senior, *The Passion of Jesus in the Gospel of Matthew* (Collegeville, MN: Liturgical Press, 1985), p. 20.

14. Michael Wilkins, *Matthew*, NIV Application Commentary (Grand Rapids, MI: Zondervan, 2004), p. 61.

15. Herbert McCabe, *God Matters* (London: Chapman, 1987), p. 249, quoted in Stanley Hauerwas, *Matthew*, Brazos Theological Commentary on the Bible

(Grand Rapids, MI: Brazos, 2006), p. 33. I took the liberty of correcting the spelling of murderers, which I'm assuming the editor missed. In Hauerwas it is "murders."

16. Ibid.

17. Luz, *Matthew 1–7*, p. 69.

18. Bruner, *The Christbook*, p. 10.

19. Julie H. Johnston, "Grace Greater Than Our Sin" (1911).

Chapter Three: Conceiving Christ

1. Simeon turned eight on May 19, 2012.

2. William Barclay, *The Gospel of Matthew*, vol. 1, rev. ed. (Philadelphia: Westminster, 1975), p. 18.

3. Ibid.

4. I take the "patiently" from J. C. Ryle. Ryle says, "He saw the 'appearance of evil' in the one who was to be his wife. But he did nothing rashly. He waited patiently to have the line of duty made clear" (*Matthew: Expository Thoughts on the Gospels*, Crossway Classic Commentaries [Wheaton, IL: Crossway, 1993], p. 4).

5. Wolfhart Pannenburg, *Systematic Theology*, 2:32, quoted in Frederick Dale Bruner, *The Christbook: Matthew 1–12*, 2nd and rev. ed. (Grand Rapids, MI: Eerdmans, 2004), p. 28.

6. Theologian Stanley Hauerwas says it this way: "For Matthew, the work of the Spirit is to point to the humanity of Christ" (*Matthew*, Brazos Theological Commentary on the Bible [Grand Rapids, MI: Brazos, 2006], p. 33).

7. Frederick Dale Bruner, *The Holy Spirit: Shy Member of the Trinity* (Eugene, OR: Wipf & Stock, 2001).

8. Bruner, *The Christbook,* p. 27.

9. So many of the epistles speak of the Spirit's work but so very few benedictions, doxologies, and greetings address him directly. In these texts it is usually just the Father (Colossians 1:2) or the Son (1 Corinthians 16:24; Galatians 6:18; Philippians 4:23; 2 Timothy 4:22; Philemon 25; 1 Peter 5:14; 2 Peter 3:18) or the Father and the Son (Romans 1:7; 16:27; 1 Corinthians 1:3; 2 Corinthians 1:2; Galatians 1:3; Ephesians 1:2; 6:23; Philippians 1:2; 1 Timothy 1:2; 2 Timothy 1:2; Titus 1:4; Hebrews 13:20, 21; James 1:1; 2 Peter 1:1; 2 John 1:3) who are mentioned. Only twice do we find all three members of the Trinity (2 Corinthians 13:14; 1 Peter 1:1, 2).

10. I use the term "father" with some reservation, as only God is called Jesus' "Father" in Matthew (cf. how "father" is used in 1:1–16: Joseph is not called the father of Jesus, but the husband of Mary, of whom Jesus was born).

11. Bruner, *The Christbook*, p. 47.

12. Cf. John Calvin, *Commentary on a Harmony of the Evangelists, Matthew, Mark, and Luke*, trans. William Pringle (Grand Rapids, MI: Baker, repr. 1993), p. 95.

13. Calvin comments, "When he heard the name of *David*, from whom he was descended, Joseph ought to have remembered that remarkable promise of God which related to the establishment of the kingdom, so as to acknowledge that there was nothing new in what was now told him" (ibid., p. 97).

14. While Luke focuses more on Mary than Matthew does, Joseph still remains the focus for both Gospel writers in regard to Davidic lineage. It may be assumed that Mary is from David's line; however, it is never stated. This omission is important. Compare such silence to what is said of Joseph: "In the sixth month the angel

Gabriel was sent from God to a city of Galilee named Nazareth, to a virgin betrothed to a man whose name was Joseph, *of the house of David*" (Luke 1:26, 27); "And Joseph also went up from Galilee, from the town of Nazareth, to Judea, to the city of David, which is called Bethlehem, because *he* was of *the house and lineage of David*, to be registered with Mary, his betrothed, who was with child" (Luke 2:4, 5).

15. Leon Morris, *The Gospel according to Matthew* (Grand Rapids, MI: Eerdmans, repr. 1995), p. 29.

16. Daniel J. Harrington, *The Gospel of Matthew*, Sacra Pagina (Collegeville, MN: Liturgical Press, 1991), p. 40.

17. Charlotte turned six on April 21, 2012.

Chapter Four: Fulfillments and Fulfillment

1. There are five Old Testament quotes in 1:18—2:23; six if 3:3 is added.

2. Schnackenburg says,

> The awaiting of a future, ideal ruler was widespread in antiquity; still the expectation of the astrologers from the East more likely refers to the oracle of Balaam (Numbers 22–24). The Gentile seer from the Euphrates (Num. 22:5) must bless Israel instead of cursing it (Num. 23:7–8), and says, "A star shall come out of Jacob, and a scepter shall rise out of Israel" (Num. 24:17). (*The Gospel of Matthew*, trans. Robert R. Barr [Grand Rapids, MI: Eerdmans, 2002], p. 22.)

3. You might be skeptical and say, "Wait a minute, Matthew wrote this Gospel at least twenty years after Jesus' death, so he's just making things up. He says Mary was a virgin, but she's wasn't. How could she be? And he says Jesus came from Bethlehem, but he's just doing some creative editing, placing Jesus' birth in that town to convince the gullible." Such critiques would be credible if there weren't witnesses. Mary and Joseph were witnesses to the virgin conception and birth, as was, I suppose, the angel Gabriel and the Holy Spirit. We don't know what happened to Joseph. But we know from Acts that Mary, our Lord's mother, was a member of the early church. So the question is, would she live a lie? She could. But as men and women begin to sacrifice their livelihoods and lives for the sake of the gospel, such a possibility becomes less and less likely. Some believe the Church was built on a bunch of lies, but I can't believe it, as truth-telling has always been esteemed one of the highest virtues of Christianity. Now, the case for Jesus being born in Bethlehem is even tighter. For you see, the first readers of Matthew's Gospel, if they were curious enough, could have checked the facts. Jesus was born in Bethlehem. Go check the Roman records. See what the census says. Sometimes I think we forget Matthew is writing about real events at a real time in history when real people could have validated or invalidated his claims. If someone claimed that JFK was born in Brookline, Massachusetts on May 29, 1917—that's nearly a hundred years ago—do you think we would be able to see if that's right or not? Sure, we would. I know that the evidence Matthew presents thus far is not yet enough to demand a verdict. Ah, but don't worry, he's just getting started with his case for Christ. This is just the second chapter. By the last chapter if you are not prostrate on the ground, like these wise men, you are not wise at all. The case is not yet closed. It's just opening, as should be your mind.

4. William Barclay, *The Gospel of Matthew*, vol. 1, rev. ed. (Philadelphia: Westminster, 1975), p. 38.

5. Ulrich Luz, *Matthew 1–7*, Hermeneia (Minneapolis: Fortress, 2007), p. 98.

6. Schnackenburg, *The Gospel of Matthew*, p. 27.

7. John Stott, *Through the Bible, Through the Year* (Grand Rapids, MI: Baker, 2006), p. 154.

8. Michael Green, *The Message of Matthew*, The Bible Speaks Today (Downers Grove, IL: InterVarsity Press, 2000), p. 73.

9. D. A. Carson, "Matthew," in *The Expositor's Bible Commentary*, vol. 8 (Grand Rapids, MI: Zondervan, 1984), p. 99.

10. Theodore Baker, trans., "Lo, How A Rose E'er Blooming" (1894).

11. See Michael Wilkins, *Matthew*, NIV Application Commentary (Grand Rapids, MI: Zondervan, 2004), pp. 116, 117.

12. The word "worship," which is not used often in the New Testament, is used three times here (cf. 14:33; 28:9, 17), once sarcastically by Herod but twice genuinely by the wise men and Matthew.

13. I borrow this line from the title of James Montgomery Boice's sermon in *The Gospel of Matthew*, vol. 1 (Grand Rapids, MI: Baker, 2001), p. 29.

Chapter Five: We *Two* Kings

1. See Rudolf Schnackenburg, *The Gospel of Matthew*, trans. Robert R. Barr (Grand Rapids, MI: Eerdmans, 2002), p. 22.

2. Also fitting this theme, we have in verse eleven the three gifts. We learn from other passages of Scripture (see Psalm 72:10, 11, 15; Isaiah 60:6) that the gift of gold was a treasure given especially and almost exclusively to kings.

3. See Josephus, *Antiquities*, 15–17. For much of the wording, see Michael Green, *The Message of Matthew,* The Bible Speaks Today (Downers Grove, IL: InterVarsity Press, 2000), p. 71. Cf. William Barclay, *The Gospel of Matthew*, vol. 1, rev. ed. (Philadelphia: Westminster, 1975), pp. 28, 29.

4. Barclay and other commentators use these three categories, which are quite obvious and good. See Barclay, *The Gospel of Matthew*, p. 30.

5. From John H. Hopkins, "We Three Kings" (1857).

6. Christopher Hitchens, *god Is Not Great: How Religion Poisons Everything* (New York: Twelve, 2007), p. 111.

7. Ibid., p. 123.

8. Lawrence W. Farris, "Year A: First Sunday after Christmas," *The Lectionary Commentary: Theological Exegesis for Sunday's Texts; The Third Readings: The Gospels*, ed. Roger E. Van Harn (Grand Rapids, MI: Eerdmans, 2001), p. 10.

9. Read Dinesh D'Sousa's excellent chapter on this issue, "Opiate of the Morally Corrupt: Why Unbelief is So Appealing," in *What's So Great About Christianity* (Wheaton, IL: Tyndale, 2008), pp. 265–283. He argues that most atheists (based on their own admissions) confine their rebellion more narrowly than we might imagine. D'Sousa summarizes, "It is, one may say, a pelvic revolt against God" (p. 273).

10. To be clear, Jesus has come to bring peace to those on whom God's favor rests or "with whom he is pleased" (Luke 2:14b), which is very different from the nebulous "world peace" everyone has been talking about since the stupid sixties.

11. From Hopkins, "We Three Kings."

12. J. C. Ryle, *Matthew: Expository Thoughts on the Gospels*, Crossway Classic Commentaries (Wheaton, IL: Crossway), p. 9.

13. From T. S. Eliot's famous poem, "Journey of the Magi."

14. "The 'homage' done the child fits his royal station and, according to Eastern custom, is accompanied by full prostration. In Greek Matthew's verb also suggests adoration, the reverence due to God (cf. Matt. 4:9–10; 14:33; 28:9, 17)" (Schnackenburg , *The Gospel of Matthew*, p. 24). "If this is not the Messiah, if this is not the one born to be king, if this is not the Son of God, then what these wise men do is idolatry" (Stanley Hauerwas, *Matthew*, Brazos Theological Commentary on the Bible [Grand Rapids, MI: Brazos, 2006], p. 40). Cf. the worship of God in the book of Revelation and note the posture—see 4:10; 5:14b; 7:11; 11:16; 19:4, 10; 22:8, 9.

15. I side with Joel B. Green's reading that Luke's "for all the people" should be viewed "in a universalistic way" (*The Gospel of Luke*, New International Commentary on the New Testament [Grand Rapids, MI: Eerdmans, 1997], pp. 133, 134, see especially n. 54).

16. Scott Hoezee, "Years A, B, C: Epiphany of the Lord," in *The Lectionary Commentary*, p. 6.

17. In William Hendriksen, *Matthew* (Grand Rapids, MI: Baker, 2002), p. 151.

18. Hoezee, "Years A, B, C: Epiphany of the Lord," p. 7.

19. See ibid.

20. Langston Hughes, "Shepherd's Song at Christmas."

Chapter Six: Baptism of Repentance

1. For some interesting and important Trinitarian observations and applications, see St. Jerome, *Commentary on Matthew*, Fathers of the Church, vol. 117, trans. Thomas P. Scheck (Washington, DC: Catholic University of America, 2008), pp. 70, 71. I especially like J. C. Ryle's comment: "It was the whole Trinity which, at the beginning of creation, said, 'Let us make man' (Genesis 1:26); it was the whole Trinity again which, at the beginning of the Gospel, seemed to say, 'Let us save man'" (*Matthew: Expository Thoughts on the Gospels*, Crossway Classic Commentaries [Wheaton, IL: Crossway, 1993], p. 17).

2. See Nicholas Perrin, *Jesus the Temple* (Grand Rapids, MI: Baker, 2010), pp. 40, 41.

3. The time between the arrival of Jesus and Malachi, the last prophet of the Old Testament, is called the Intertestamental Period. John's baptism is, if you will, an intertestamental baptism. It relates somewhat to the baptism of a Gentile proselyte when he became a convert to Judaism (and also somewhat to Christian baptism). See Michael Green, *The Message of Matthew*, The Bible Speaks Today (Downers Grove, IL: InterVarsity Press, 2000), p. 77.

4. That is, baptism in the Holy Spirit means repenting from sin and coming to trust in Christ. It does not mean an extra experience, blessing, or empowerment of the Spirit that only some believers receive, as taught in traditional Pentecostal theology. See Wayne Grudem's excellent chapter on this, "Baptism in and Filling with the Holy Spirit," in *Systematic Theology: An Introduction to Biblical Doctrine* (Grand Rapids, MI: Zondervan, 1994), pp. 763–787.

5. Examine the full context of that statement, and note that Paul makes no connection to "water" but rather to "spirit" or "the Spirit." Paul writes,

> I . . . urge you to walk in a manner worthy of the calling to which you have been called, with all humility and gentleness, with patience, bearing with one another in love, eager to maintain the unity of *the Spirit* in the bond of peace. There is one body and *one Spirit*—just as you were called to the one hope that belongs to your call—one Lord, one faith, one baptism, one God and Father of all, who is over all and through all and in all. (Ephesians 4:1–6)

6. William Barclay, *The Gospel of Matthew*, vol. 1, rev. ed. (Philadelphia: Westminster, 1975), p. 47.

7. Ibid.

8. What does John mean by saying that we need to "bear fruit in keeping with repentance" (3:8)? In Luke's retelling of this event, we are provided with specific examples that relate to loving God and others in accordance with God's word: "And the crowds asked him, 'What then shall we do?' And he answered them, 'Whoever has two tunics is to share with him who has none, and whoever has food is to do likewise.' Tax collectors also came to be baptized and said to him, 'Teacher, what shall we do?' And he said to them, 'Collect no more than you are authorized to do.' Soldiers also asked him, 'And we, what shall we do?' And he said to them, 'Do not extort money from anyone by threats or by false accusation, and be content with your wages'" (Luke 3:10–14). The Westminster Larger Catechism gives a marvelous answer to the question, "What is repentance unto life?" (Q. 76). Answer: "Repentance unto life is a saving grace, wrought in the heart of a sinner by the Spirit and word of God, whereby out of the sight and sense, not only of the danger, but also of the filthiness and odiousness of his sins, and upon the apprehension of God's mercy in Christ to such as are penitent, he so grieves for and hates his sins, as that he turns from them all to God, purposing and endeavouring constantly to walk with him in all the ways of new obedience."

9. The ESV's translation of *ginomai* as "prove" in John 15:8 is a fitting translation of that elastic verb.

10. The prophets promised that when God poured out his Spirit upon and within God's people (Ezekiel 39:29; Isaiah 44:3; Joel 2:28), he would "cause [them] to walk in my statutes and . . . obey my rules" (Ezekiel 36:27).

Chapter Seven: The Tempted Son

1. From Dick Lucas, "The Holy Spirit and Christian Warfare" (sermon on Luke 4:1–13), p. 1; http://www.proctrust.org.uk/dls/sermons/0001b.pdf; accessed on January 23, 2009.

2. For a discussion on Jesus' human nature, see Craig L. Blomberg, Matthew, New American Commentary (Nashville: Broadman, 1992), pp. 86, 87. I take Blomberg's position that "Jesus could have sinned but never did and that like Adam and Eve before the fall he had a sinless human nature" (p. 86).

3. Blomberg notes, "By this phrasing, Matthew warns against two common errors—blaming God for temptation and crediting the devil with power to act independently of God" (ibid., p. 83).

4. Cited in Lucas, "The Holy Spirit and Christian Warfare," p. 2.

5. Pablo Neruda, *Odes to Opposites* (New York: Bulfinch, 2008), p. 101.

6. For a description of this desolate wilderness, see William Barclay, *The Gospel of Matthew*, vol. 1, rev. ed. (Philadelphia: Westminster, 1975), p. 63.

7. James Montgomery Boice, *The Gospel of Matthew*, vol. 1 (Grand Rapids, MI: Baker, 2001), p. 55.

8. For some of the parallels with Israel, see Donald A. Hagner, *Matthew 1–13*, Word Biblical Commentary, vol. 33a (Nashville: Thomas Nelson, 1993), pp. 61, 62. Cf. James R. Edwards, *The Gospel According to Mark*, Pillar New Testament Commentary (Grand Rapids, MI: Eerdmans, 2002), p. 40. Edwards calls Jesus "Israel-reduced-to-one."

9. Boice, *The Gospel of Matthew*, vol. 1, p. 55.

10. Here the devil does not doubt that Jesus is truly God's Son. If demons understand his identity (e.g., 8:29), then surely Satan does (cf. James 2:19). Rather, as Blomberg suggests, "what is in doubt is what type of Son Jesus will be" (*Matthew*, p. 84).

11. This last line is a quote from "The Grand Inquisitor," in Fyodor Dostoevsky's *Brothers Karamazov*, cited in Stanley Hauerwas, *Matthew*, Brazos Theological Commentary on the Bible (Grand Rapids, MI: Brazos Press, 2006), p. 53.

12. Barclay, *The Gospel of Matthew*, vol. 1, p. 68.

13. F. Dean Lueking, "First Sunday in Lent, Year A," in Roger E. Van Harn, ed., *The Lectionary Commentary: Theological Exegesis for Sunday's Texts; The Third Readings: The Gospels* (Grand Rapids, MI: Eerdmans, 2001), p. 21.

14. Ibid., pp. 20, 21.

15. St. Jerome, *Commentary on Matthew*, Fathers of the Church, vol. 117, trans. Thomas P. Scheck (Washington, DC: Catholic University of America, 2008), p. 73.

16. Jerome summarizes this well: "The devil . . . interprets the Scriptures badly" (ibid., p. 73). I add that the bad interpretation is intentional.

17. See Lueking, "First Sunday in Lent, Year A," p. 21.

18. On "angels," see Hebrews 1:6. Perhaps the fact that the angels served Jesus (in 4:11) foreshadows the theology of Hebrews—namely, that Jesus is greater than the angels.

Chapter Eight: A Great Light in Galilee

1. W. D. Davies and Dale C. Allison Jr., *A Critical and Exegetical Commentary on the Gospel according to Saint Matthew*, International Critical Commentary, vol. 3 (Edinburgh: T&T Clark, 1988–1997), p. 420.

2. For the first two terms see Daniel J. Harrington, *The Gospel of Matthew*, Sacra Pagina (Collegeville, MN: Liturgical Press, 1991), p. 74.

3. David L. Turner, *The Gospel of Matthew*, Cornerstone Biblical Commentary (Wheaton, IL: Tyndale, 2005), p. 71. According to N. T. France, this mention of Galilee of the Gentiles "reflects the region's greater openness to surrounding Gentile populations, and perhaps especially Isaiah's Judean awareness of the deportation of Israelites from Galilee by the Assyrians both before (2 Kgs 15:29) and after the Assyrian conquest (2 Kgs 17:24–34), to be replaced by foreign populations. By NT times southern Jews were suspicious of Galilee's mixed population; indeed, by the Maccabean period the region had become so paganized that its remaining Jewish population was evacuated to Judea (1 Macc 5:14–23) . . . ." (*The Gospel of Matthew*, New International Commentary on the New Testament [Grand Rapids, MI:

Eerdmans, 2007], pp. 142, 143). Cf. Leon Morris, *The Gospel According to Matthew* (Grand Rapids, MI: Eerdmans, repr. 1995), pp. 81, 82.

4. Harrington believes that Matthew gives a "rather loose adaptation of the Septuagint text" (*The Gospel of Matthew*, p. 71).

5. John Nolland writes, "Light is . . . a universally recognized image of salvation" (*The Gospel of Matthew*, New International Greek Testament Commentary [Grand Rapids: Eerdmans, 2005], p. 174).

6. The seventh (and yes, most perfect, so to speak) of the fulfillment formulas comes in 5:17: "Do not think that I have come to abolish the Law or the Prophets; I have not come to abolish them but to fulfill them."

7. For the theme of Gentiles in this Gospel, see 1:3, 5, 6; 2:1; 8:10–12; 15:22–28; 21:43; 22:9; 24:14.

8. Turner, *The Gospel of Matthew*, p. 71.

9. According to Luke 5, this mending was due to their miraculous catch of fish. See my *excursus* sermon on this in the next chapter.

10. Turner, *The Gospel of Matthew*, p. 71.

11. Based on texts like Philippians 1:29 and Ephesians 2:8, 9, perhaps it is best to call our responsibility "our God-gifted responsibility," for repentance and faith are indeed gifts of God.

12. See especially 10:21, 22, 34–37; cf. 8:18–22; 12:46–50.

13. Turner, *The Gospel of Matthew*, p. 74.

14. See Nolland, *The Gospel of Matthew*, p. 179.

15. See Morris, *The Gospel according to Matthew*, p. 88.

16. Frederick Dale Bruner, *The Christbook: Matthew 1–12*, 2nd and rev. ed. (Grand Rapids, MI: Eerdmans, 2004), p. 145.

17. We know this from Luke's account. Just before Luke describes these four fishermen leaving everything and following Jesus, he records the miracle of the great catch. Peter and the boys had had a bad night of fishing. Jesus said, "Get back out there and put down your nets just one more time." They argued a bit at first but finally complied. And then what happened? They caught so many fish their nets were breaking. In fact, they had to signal to others to come and help. Two boats—each likely over seven feet wide and twenty-seven feet long, filled to the gunwales—began to sink from the excessive weight of the fish. Needless to say, witnessing such supernatural spectacles aided their faith in Jesus: "And when they had brought their boats to land, they left everything and followed him" (Luke 5:11).

Chapter Nine: A Sermon on *the* Sermon

1. That is no doubt true, as Frederick Dale Bruner notes: "Matthew is the moral evangelist. He sees Jesus experienced not only through mystical communion with Jesus' person but especially by moral obedience to Jesus' commands. In his commands the then-earthly and now-risen Jesus is especially alive" (*The Christbook: Matthew 1–12*, 2nd and rev. ed. [Grand Rapids, MI: Eerdmans, 2004], p. 150). Yet Matthew is more concerned, I'm arguing, with Jesus' authority first, then morality.

2. Daniel M. Doriani, *The Sermon on the Mount: The Character of a Disciple* (Phillipsburg, NJ: P&R, 2006), p. 5.

3. The first sentence in Augustine's commentary highlights that the Sermon is a sermon to the Christian about the Christian life: "If a person will devoutly and

calmly consider the sermon which our Lord Jesus Christ spoke on the mount, as we read it in the Gospel according to Matthew, I think he will find in it, as measured by the highest norms of morality, the perfect pattern of the Christian life." St. Augustine, *The Lord's Sermon on the Mount*, Ancient Christian Writers, vol. 5, trans. John J. Jepson (New York: Paulist, 1948), p. 11.

4. John R. W. Stott says, "The ultimate issue posed by the whole Sermon concerns the authority of the preacher" (*The Message of the Sermon on the Mount*, The Bible Speaks Today [Downers Grove, IL: InterVarsity Press, 1978], p. 26). James Montgomery Boice adds, "The preacher of the Sermon on the Mount is the Sermon on the Mount, and we are constantly brought into the most intimate contact with him" (*The Sermon on the Mount: Matthew 5–7* [Grand Rapids, MI: Baker, repr. 2004], p. 11).

5. In 5:21–48 we have six juxtapositions between, "It was said" and "But I say to you" (5:21–22, 27, 28, 31, 32, 33, 34, 38, 39, 43, 44), where Jesus claims authority over the Jewish teachers and traditions and even the Torah.

6. Quoting from Augustine, Robert Louis Wilken notes how God in the past spoke through the prophets, "but now through his Son he opens 'his own mouth.'" See "Augustine," in *The Sermon on the Mount through the Centuries: From the Early Church to John Paul II*, ed. Jeffrey P. Greenman, et al. (Grand Rapids, MI: Brazos, 2007), p. 44.

7. See Hans Dieter Betz, *The Sermon on the Mount*, Hermeneia (Minneapolis: Fortress, 1995), p. 34.

8. For this idea, see John Stott, *Why I Am a Christian* (Downers Grove, IL: InterVarsity Press, 2003), p. 33.

9. For Wesley's emphasis on faith in the Sermon on the Mount, see Mark Noll, "John Wesley," in *The Sermon on the Mount through the Centuries*, p. 173.

10. C. S. Lewis, *Surprised by Joy: The Shape of My Early Life*, rev. ed. (New York: Houghton Mifflin Harcourt, 1995), p. 111.

11. C. S. Lewis, *Mere Christianity* (New York: Macmillan, 1952), p. 56.

Chapter Ten: A Broken Blessedness

1. See Daniel M. Doriani, *The Sermon on the Mount: The Character of a Disciple* (Phillipsburg, NJ: P&R, 2006), p. 13.

2. Some of these are taken from ibid., p. 13. Of this kind of "blessedness" Martin Luther says, "In short, this is the greatest and most universal religion on earth" (*The Sermon on the Mount and the Magnificat*, Luther's Works, vol. 21, ed. Jaroslav Pelikan (St. Louis: Concordia, 1956), p. 12.

3. Cited in John R. W. Stott, *The Message of the Sermon on the Mount*, The Bible Speaks Today (Downers Grove, IL: InterVarsity Press, 1978), pp. 54, 55.

4. D. A. Carson, quoted in R. Kent Hughes, *The Sermon on the Mount: The Message of the Kingdom*, Preaching the Word (Wheaton, IL: Crossway, 2001), p. 19.

5. Ibid., p. 25.

6. See Doriani, *The Sermon on the Mount*, pp. 18, 19. Ambrose of Milan speaks of weeping for past sins, our own sins, and the sins of others (quoted in St. Thomas Aquinas, *Catena Aurea*, vol. 1, Part I: The Gospel of St. Matthew, trans. John Henry Newman [New York: Cosimo Classics, 2007], p. 150).

7. Doriani, *The Sermon on the Mount*, pp. 18, 19.

8. "Righteousness" here more likely refers to sanctification than justification. Even Luther acknowledges that "righteousness" here "must not be taken in the sense of that principal Christian righteousness by which a person becomes pious and acceptable to God. I have said before that these eight items are nothing but instruction about the fruits and good works of a Christian" (*The Sermon on the Mount and the Magnificat*, vol. 21, p. 26). For a "multifaceted" view, see Sinclair B. Ferguson, *The Sermon on the Mount: Kingdom Life in a Fallen World* (Carlisle, PA: Banner of Truth, 1997), p. 27. "Salvation is by faith alone . . . but poverty of spirit is the posture of faith" (Hughes, *The Sermon on the Mount*, p. 21); cf. D. Martyn Lloyd-Jones, *Studies in the Sermon on the Mount*, 2nd ed. (Grand Rapids, MI: Eerdmans, 1976), pp. 33, 34:

> If you prefer me to put it in a more theological and doctrinal form, I would say that there is no more perfect statement of the doctrine of justification by faith only than this Beatitude: "Blessed are the poor in spirit: for theirs (and their only!) is the kingdom of heaven."

9. Lloyd-Jones, *Studies in the Sermon on the Mount*, pp. 35, 36.

10. I found this famous A. M. Toplady hymn, "Rock of Ages," quoted in many commentaries.

11. President Bill Clinton told the grand jury (according to footnote 1,128 in Kenneth Starr's report):

> It depends on what the meaning of the word "is" is. If the—if he—if "is" means is and never has been, that is not—that is one thing. If it means there is none, that was a completely true statement. . . . Now, if someone had asked me on that day, are you having any kind of sexual relations with Ms. Lewinsky, that is, asked me a question in the present tense, I would have said no. And it would have been completely true.

12. So the Beatitudes, at least the first and last ones, speak of the present reality of the kingdom of heaven for those on earth who have entered the kingdom through poverty of spirit (utter reliance upon God, not self) and who so live out that faith that it costs them (e.g., they are slandered, mocked, and even beaten or killed).

13. The Scriptures teach that when we trust in Jesus (the King of this heavenly kingdom) we enter spiritually into all the benefits of that kingdom. Believers have "every spiritual blessing in the heavenly places" (Ephesians 1:3), yet we still long for the time when "The King Shall Come" (to borrow from an old hymn title) and when "the kingdom of the world" will become "the kingdom of our Lord and of his Christ" (Revelation 11:15)—a time when God's name will be universally honored and his will is done on earth as it is in Heaven (6:9, 10).

14. Rudolf Schnackenburg argues that the Beatitudes are "apocalyptic" in that they "direct our gaze toward the future" (*The Gospel of Matthew*, trans. Robert R. Barr [Grand Rapids, MI: Eerdmans, 2002], p. 46). Ronald J. Allen adds, "Matthew's beatitudes are eschatological, as Matthew joins other witnesses in widening 'blessing' to include participation in the divine rule in the new world (e.g., Dan. 12:12; 4 Macc. 17:18; 18:19; Rev. 1:3; 14:13; 16:15; 19:9; 22:7, 14)" (in "Fourth Sunday after the Epiphany, Year A," in *The Lectionary Commentary: Theological Exegesis*

for Sunday's Texts; The Third Readings: The Gospels, ed. Roger E. Van Harn [Grand Rapids, MI: Eerdmans, 2001], p. 27).

15. Note that "heaven" is used three times!

16. This dialogue is found on a number of Internet sites about Thoreau and/or his last words, e.g., http://www.nairaland.com/296450/last-words-famous-people-alexander.

17. Doriani, *The Sermon on the Mount*, p. 17.

18. Ibid.

19. John Calvin, *Institutes of the Christian Religion*, Library of Christian Classics, ed. John T. McNeill, trans. Ford Lewis Battles (Philadelphia: Westminster, 1960).

20. Augustine said, "A single heart is the same as is here called the pure heart" (quoted in Aquinas, *Catena Aurea*, p. 153).

21. In the context of the Bible, "the peacemakers" are not those who bring a false peace through their rhetoric of peace (cf. Ezekiel 13:10; Jeremiah 6:14) or "a cessation of hostilities among the nations" through political or military means, but those who bring the gospel of peace, the message of the Prince of Peace (cf. Isaiah 9:6; 52:7–10), who will "one day bring world peace only when evil is eradicated, but now brings, through faith, a cessation of hostility between man and God" (cf. Colossians 3:15) (see Ferguson, *The Sermon on the Mount*, p. 39). Cf. Schnackenburg, *The Gospel of Matthew*, p. 49.

22. I agree with Stott, who summarizes well Protestant teaching on this when he says:

> The beatitudes set forth the balanced and variegated character of Christian people. These are not eight separate and distinct groups of disciples . . . rather eight qualities of the same group. . . . Further, the group exhibiting these marks is not an elitist set. (*The Message of the Sermon on the Mount*, p. 31.)

Chapter Eleven: Unworldly for the World

1. D. Martyn Lloyd-Jones, *Studies in the Sermon on the Mount*, 2nd ed. (Grand Rapids, MI: Eerdmans, 1976), p. 28.

2. W. D. Davies and Dale C. Allison Jr., *A Critical and Exegetical Commentary on the Gospel according to Saint Matthew*, International Critical Commentary, vol. 1 (Edinburgh: T&T Clark, 1988), pp. 472, 473.

3. John R. W. Stott, *The Message of the Sermon on the Mount*, The Bible Speaks Today (Downers Grove, IL: InterVarsity Press, 1978), p. 60.

4. See Davies and Allison Jr., *A Critical and Exegetical Commentary*, vol. 1, pp. 471, 472.

5. That is implicit here but not so elsewhere, e.g., John 1:9–11; 3:19, 20.

6. Davies and Allison Jr., *A Critical and Exegetical Commentary*, vol. 1, p. 476.

7. We certainly are to witness in words (this is implied in vv. 9, 11). Paul also speaks of our speech being seasoned with salt (Colossians 4:6; Romans 10). However, the emphasis here is not on words but on works—Christian living, not talking!

8. Contra Jerome, Augustine, and Luther. Jerome wrote, "He is teaching about courage in preaching" (*Commentary on Matthew*, Fathers of the Church, vol. 117, trans. Thomas P. Scheck [Washington, DC: Catholic University of America, 2008], p. 77). Augustine wrote, "Therefore a person puts his candle under a bushel when he

dims and hides in temporal concerns the light of good teaching" (*The Lord's Sermon on the Mount*, Ancient Christian Writers, vol. 5, trans. John J. Jepson [New York: Paulist Press, 1948], p. 26). Luther wrote, "The real salt is the true exposition of Scripture" (*The Sermon on the Mount and the Magnificat*, Luther's Works, vol. 21, ed. Jaroslav Pelikan [St. Louis: Concordia, 1956], p. 59).

9. See the Westminster Confession of Faith, 16.

10. Cf. Luther, *The Sermon on the Mount and the Magnificat*, vol. 21, p. 65.

11. For the connection between 5:16 and 2 Peter 2:11, 12, as well as the view that glorifying the Father is representative of conversion, as I'm calling it—"those who, through their response to Jesus' message, have become subjects of his kingdom," as France puts it—see R. T. France, *The Gospel of Matthew*, New International Commentary on the New Testament (Grand Rapids, MI: Eerdmans, 2007), p. 177. On the phrase "glorify God" in 1 Peter 2:12, Thomas R. Schreiner notes: "The reference to glorifying God suggests that the salvation of Gentiles is in view. Typically in the New Testament people glorify God or give him glory by believing . . ." (*1, 2 Peter, Jude*, New American Commentary [Nashville: Broadman, 2003], p. 124).

12. This is why, I think, we find in the New Testament hardly any commands such as, "Open your mouth and preach the gospel!" (The closest references would be Matthew 28:18–20; Luke 9:60; 10:1ff.; Acts 8:4; 1 Peter 2:9.) Instead we find multiple exhortations to obey the ethics of the kingdom (e.g., Romans 8:4; Ephesians 5:8; Colossians 3:12–14; 1 Timothy 2:1–4; Titus 2:1–14; James 1:22; 1 Peter 3:13–22; 2 John 6).

13. William Barclay, *The Gospel of Matthew*, vol. 1, rev. ed. (Philadelphia: Westminster, 1975), p. 123.

14. Davies and Allison Jr., *A Critical and Exegetical Commentary*, vol. 1, p. 478.

15. See Lloyd-Jones, *Studies in the Sermon on the Mount*, pp. 112–115.

16. Thomas Aquinas notes, "He invites them to patience not only by the prospect of reward, but by example" (*Catena Aurea*, vol. 1, Part I: The Gospel of St. Matthew, trans. John Henry Newman [New York: Cosimo Classics, 2007], p. 159).

Chapter Twelve: "I Say to You," Part 1

1. Donald A. Hagner, *Matthew 1–13*, Word Biblical Commentary, vol. 33a (Nashville: Thomas Nelson, 1993), p. 116.

2. Ibid., p. 103.

3. Doriani quotes twice from the great Jewish rabbis: "He that talks much with womankind brings evil upon himself and neglects the study of the law and at the last will inherit Gehenna," and "Keep thee far from an evil neighbour and consort not with the wicked" (Aboth 1:5, 7, in *The Mishnah*, trans. Herbert Danby [New York: Oxford University Press, 1933], p. 446, quoted in Daniel M. Doriani, *Matthew*, Reformed Expository Commentary, vol. 1 [Phillipsburg, NJ: P&R, 2008], p. 140).

4. D. Martyn Lloyd-Jones, *Studies in the Sermon on the Mount*, 2nd ed. (Grand Rapids, MI: Eerdmans, 1976), p. 163. Lloyd-Jones says, "It is the most stupendous claim that He ever made."

5. Jacob Neusner, *A Rabbi Talks with Jesus: An Intermillennial, Interfaith Exchange* (New York: Doubleday, 1993), p. 1.

6. See ibid., pp. 30, 31; cf. pp. 3, 50, 95, 96.

7. Ibid., p. 111; cf. p. 115.

8. This term is taken from Timothy Keller, *The Reason for God: Belief in an Age of Skepticism* (New York: Dutton, 2008), p. 144.

9. Craig L. Blomberg, *Matthew*, New American Commentary (Nashville: Broadman, 1992), p. 105.

10. See Jeffrey P. Greenman, Timothy Larsen, and Stephen R. Spencer, eds., *The Sermon on the Mount through the Centuries: From the Early Church to John Paul II* (Grand Rapids, MI: Brazos, 2007), p. 111.

11. Deuteronomy 18:13 reads: "You shall be blameless before the LORD [YHWH] your God." The contexts of both texts are interestingly similar. In Deuteronomy 18:9–14, God's people are commanded to be different than the nations around them when they enter the land. In Matthew 5:43–47, God's people are to love differently than the unbelievers around them. This is also the context where Moses prophesies that YHWH will raise up another prophet who will instruct God's people: "it is to him you shall listen" (Deuteronomy 18:15).

12. In Matthew 5:17, as Jesus begins what is often called "the body" of the Sermon on the Mount, he speaks of the Law and the Prophets. He also speaks of them when he ends in 7:12. In the latter verse we find a summary of all that came before. There we find the Golden Rule: "So whatever you wish that others would do to you, do also to them, for this is the Law and the Prophets." The love of others—that is kingdom righteousness.

Chapter Thirteen: "I Say *To You*," Part 2

1. Jacob Neusner, *A Rabbi Talks with Jesus: An Intermillennial, Interfaith Exchange* (New York: Doubleday, 1993), pp. 95, 96.

2. John Nolland, *The Gospel of Matthew*, New International Greek Testament Commentary (Grand Rapids, MI: Eerdmans, 2005), p. 229.

3. Michael Green, *The Message of Matthew*, The Bible Speaks Today (Downers Grove, IL: InterVarsity Press, 2000), p. 95.

4. Ibid., p. 96.

5. On rabbinic casuistry in the matter of taking oaths, see Donald A. Hagner, *Matthew 1–13*, Word Biblical Commentary, vol. 33a (Nashville: Thomas Nelson, 1993), pp. 127, 128.

6. Green, *The Message of Matthew*, p. 96.

7. At times people rejoice (and rightly so) when God judges their enemies for acting wickedly, just as the Jews of Nazi Germany rejoiced when the Allied troops came into town to rescue them from concentration camps. Perhaps Psalm 139:22 is an example of such.

8. Perhaps the thought behind Jesus' statement is: if he is merely a man (thus a sinner like all men), why would this young man call him "good" (as God alone is)?

Chapter Fourteen: God-Rewarded Righteousness

1. See Christopher Hitchens, *god Is Not Great: How Religion Poisons Everything* (New York: Twelve, 2007), p. 46. The information about Saddam was taken from pages 25, 26.

2. A. B. Bruce said that we are to "show when tempted to hide" and "hide when tempted to show." Quoted in Daniel M. Doriani, *Matthew*, Reformed Expository Commentary, vol. 1 (Phillipsburg, NJ: P&R, 2008), p. 202.

3. D. Martyn Lloyd-Jones, *Studies in the Sermon on the Mount*, 2nd ed. (Grand Rapids, MI: Eerdmans, 1976), pp. 294, 295.

4. Exodus 23:10, 11; 30:15; Leviticus 19:10; Deuteronomy 15:7–14.

5. Jeremiah 22:16; Daniel 4:27; Amos 2:6, 7.

6. Matthew 6:2–4; Luke 6:34.

7. 2 Corinthians 9:7–15; Galatians 2:10.

8. John MacArthur, *Matthew 1–7* (Chicago: Moody, 1985), p. 355.

9. C. H. Spurgeon, *The Gospel of the Kingdom* (Pasadena, TX: Pilgrim Publications, repr. 1996), p. 33.

10. Lloyd-Jones, *Studies in the Sermon on the Mount*, p. 298.

11. R. Kent Hughes, *The Sermon on the Mount: The Message of the Kingdom*, Preaching the Word (Wheaton, IL: Crossway, 2001), p. 147.

12. The idea for these illustrations is taken from Doriani, *Matthew*, vol. 1, p. 201.

13. See Dietrich Bonhoeffer, quoted in Stanley Hauerwas, *Matthew*, Brazos Theological Commentary on the Bible (Grand Rapids, MI: Brazos, 2006), p. 74.

14. William Barclay, *The Gospel of Matthew*, vol. 1, rev. ed. (Philadelphia: Westminster, 1975), p. 187.

15. Martin Luther, *The Sermon on the Mount and the Magnificat*, Luther's Works, vol. 21, ed. Jaroslav Pelikan (St. Louis: Concordia, 1956), p. 162.

16. Ibid., p. 159.

17. See Doriani, *Matthew*, p. 237.

18. From John Piper, *A Hunger for God* (Wheaton, IL: Crossway, 1997), p. 14, quoted in Doriani, Matthew, pp. 236, 237.

19. Piper's summary, as phrased in Daniel M. Doriani, *The Sermon on the Mount: The Character of a Disciple* (Phillipsburg, NJ: P&R, 2006), p. 148.

20. Spurgeon, *The Gospel of the Kingdom*, p. 36.

21. MacArthur, *Matthew*, p. 352.

22. Ibid.

Chapter Fifteen: How *Not* to Pray

1. "In the Old Testament, then, prayer is not treated as a part of the law, as a duty imposed upon men. Rather, prayer arises spontaneously from the man who is conscious of his need and of God's power and goodness." Wayne R. Spear, *The Theology of Prayer: A Systematic Study of the Biblical Teaching on Prayer* (Grand Rapids, MI: Baker, 1979), pp. 11, 12.

2. Cf. Hebrews 5:7.

3. Prayer is commanded. For example, we are told to devote ourselves to prayer (Colossians 4:2), pray on all occasions (Ephesians 6:18), and pray continually (1 Thessalonians 5:17; cf. Luke 18:1; Romans 12:12).

4. R. A. Torrey gives eleven reasons why prayer is important (in James Montgomery Boice, *Foundations of the Christian Faith: A Comprehensive and Readable Theology* [Downers Grove, IL: InterVarsity Press, 1986), pp. 482, 483). Cf. Wayne Grudem's section "Why Does God Want Us to Pray?" in *Systematic Theology: An Introduction to Biblical Doctrine* (Grand Rapids, MI: Zondervan, 1994), pp. 376, 377.

5. Cf. 6:1, "Beware of practicing your righteousness before other people in order to be seen by them."

6. See W. D. Davies and Dale C. Allison Jr., *A Critical and Exegetical Commentary on the Gospel according to Saint Matthew*, International Critical Commentary, vol. 3 (Edinburgh: T&T Clark, 1988-1997), p. 585.

7. See Walter A. Elwell, *Topical Analysis of the Bible* (Grand Rapids, MI: Baker, 1995), pp. 622–624.

8. See D. A. Carson, "Matthew," in *The Expositor's Bible Commentary*, vol. 8 (Grand Rapids, MI: Zondervan, 1984), p. 140.

9. One of the earliest commentaries (by Theophylact) on this section of Scripture says, "What matters is 'not the place (*topos*), but the manner (*tropos*) and the aim (*skopos*)'" (quoted in Frederick Dale Bruner, *The Christbook: Matthew 1–12*, 2nd and rev. ed. [Grand Rapids, MI: Eerdmans, 2004], p. 287).

10. R. A. Torrey, *The Power of Prayer*, p. 76; Boice, *Foundations of the Christian Faith*, p. 486.

11. Bruner, *The Christbook*, p. 287.

12. Ibid., p. 288.

13. John MacArthur, *Matthew 1–7* (Chicago: Moody, 1985), p. 364.

14. "Since the presence of other people can so easily compromise the purity of this motive, prayer should always be as inconspicuous as possible" (Herman Ridderbos, quoted in Craig L. Blomberg, *Matthew*, New American Commentary [Nashville: Broadman, 1992], p. 117).

15. Matthew Henry, *Matthew Henry's Commentary on the Whole Bible*, vol. 5 (McLean, VA: MacDonald, repr. 1985), p. 71.

16. John Calvin, *Commentary on a Harmony of the Evangelists, Matthew, Mark, and Luke*, trans. William Pringle (Grand Rapids, MI: Baker, repr. 1993), p. 312.

17. Luther, quoted in Bruner, *The Christbook*, p. 289.

18. "The paradox of prayer is that only when it is relieved of the *necessity of* much will people experience the *freedom for* much. When disciples know they don't have to pray *much*, they will, surprisingly, desire to pray more" (Bruner, *The Christbook*, p. 289).

19. For the examples of "brief and pithy" prayers in Scripture, see William Hendriksen, *Exposition of the Gospel According to Matthew* (Grand Rapids, MI: Baker, 2002), p. 324.

20. In Bruner, *The Christbook*, p. 290.

21. MacArthur, *Matthew 1–7*, p. 366.

22. Bruner, *The Christbook*, p. 291.

23. Non-Christian religion often involves clearing the mind when praying or meditating. Christianity is the opposite. When Christians pray or meditate, they fill their minds (e.g., Psalm 1:2).

24. MacArthur, *Matthew 1–7*, p. 369.

25. "Let us not then make our prayer by the gesture of our body, nor by the loudness of our voice, but by the earnestness of our mind; neither with noise and clamour and for display, so as even to disturb those that are near us, but with all modesty, and with contrition in the mind, and with inward tears" (John Chrysostom, *Homilies on the Gospel of Saint Matthew*, Nicene and Post-Nicene Fathers, vol. 10 [Peabody, MA: Hendrickson, repr. 1999], p. 133).

26. Luther, quoted in Bruner, *The Christbook*, p. 291.

27. Ibid.

28. Ibid., p. 289.

29. Calvin, *Commentary on a Harmony of the Evangelists*, pp. 313, 314.

30. Blomberg, *Matthew*, p. 118.

Chapter Sixteen: How to Pray

1. M. E. Boring, quoted in Frederick Dale Bruner, *The Christbook: Matthew 1–12*, 2nd and rev. ed. (Grand Rapids, MI: Eerdmans, 2004), p. 292.

2. See ibid., p. 293.

3. Ibid., p. 294. Cf. Donald Senior, *The Passion of Jesus in the Gospel of Matthew* (Collegeville, MN: Liturgical Press, 1985), pp. 79, 80, 97.

4. "For he who calls God Father, by him both remission of sins, and taking away for punishment, and righteousness, and sanctification, and redemption, and adoption, and inheritance, and brotherhood with the Only-Begotten, and the supply of the Spirit, are acknowledged in this single title" (John Chrysostom, *Homilies on the Gospel of Saint Matthew*, Nicene and Post-Nicene Fathers, vol. 10 [Peabody, MA: Hendrickson, repr. 1999], p. 134).

5. "The point was . . . embodied in the Lord's Prayer, where the twin truths that God is 'Father' but 'in heaven' guard against craven fear on the one hand and flippancy on the other." Michael A. Eaton, *Ecclesiastes*, Tyndale Old Testament Commentaries (Downers Grove, IL: InterVarsity Press, 1983), p. 99.

6. Ulrich Luz, *Matthew 1–7*, Hermeneia (Minneapolis: Fortress, 2007), p. 316.

7. On 5:48, Donald A. Hagner comments: "As the kingdom Jesus brings is 'of heaven' (see on 3:2), so also the Father in Matthew is *οὐράνιος*, 'heavenly,' i.e., transcendent. . . . The expression [heavenly Father] beautifully combines God's divine transcendence ('heavenly') with his immanence in love and grace, which can only be described adequately in the intimate term 'Father'" (*Matthew 1–13*, Word Biblical Commentary, vol. 33a [Nashville: Thomas Nelson, 1993], pp. 135, 136).

8. Bruner, *The Christbook*, p. 297.

9. It is not that God needs our help in making his name more holy than it is. His holiness cannot be added to or diminished. God's name is holy in and of itself. Yet we ought to pray, as Luther's *Small Catechism* (1529) puts it, that God's name "may also be holy for us" (Theodore G. Tappert, ed., *The Book of Concord* [Minneapolis: Fortress, 1989], p. 346).

10. N. T. Wright, *The Lord and His Prayer* (Grand Rapids, MI: Eerdmans, 1997), pp. 24, 25.

11. From William Barclay, in R. Kent Hughes, *The Sermon on the Mount: The Message of the Kingdom*, Preaching the Word (Wheaton, IL: Crossway, 2001), p. 177.

12. There will be a time, when Christ returns and reigns in power, when the absolute will of God will be heeded by all always (see 1 Corinthians 15:24, 50; 2 Timothy 4:1,18; esp. Revelation 11:15).

13. Augustine, quoted in D. A. Carson, "Matthew," in *The Expositor's Bible Commentary*, vol. 8 (Grand Rapids, MI: Zondervan, 1984), p. 146.

14. Calvin's words, in John Calvin, *Commentary on a Harmony of the Evangelists, Matthew, Mark, and Luke*, trans. William Pringle (Grand Rapids, MI: Baker, repr. 1993), p. 322.

15. Bruner, *The Christbook*, p. 306.

16. Chrysostom, *Homilies on the Gospel of Saint Matthew*, p. 135.

17. On this petition, Luther said that we pray for "everything necessary for the preservation of this life, like food, a healthy body, good weather, house, home, wife, children, good government, and peace—and that [God] may preserve us from all sorts of calamities, sicknesses, hard times, war, revolution, and the like" (quoted in Bruner, *The Christbook*, p. 306).

18. See Bruner, *The Christbook*, p. 307.

19. The word for "trespasses or "transgressions" is used in 6:14, 15.

20. "Debt is also an image for sin in Matthew 18:23–35; Luke 7:41–43." John Nolland, *The Gospel of Matthew*, New International Greek Testament Commentary [Grand Rapids, MI: Eerdmans, 2005], p. 290).

21. Luther, quoted in Bruner, *The Christbook*, p. 308.

22. In Hughes, *The Sermon on the Mount*, p. 189.

23. In ibid. For proof against Pelagius and "complete sanctification," see Bruner, *The Christbook*, p. 308.

24. "There is no serious prayer for forgiveness except on the lips of a forgiver; this is no contradiction of justification by faith: as if a revenge-seeking heart could be said to believe in God's forgiveness of sins!" (Schlatter, quoted in Bruner, *The Christbook*, p. 310).

25. Craig L. Blomberg, *Matthew*, New American Commentary (Nashville: Broadman, 1992), p. 120.

26. Ibid.

27. From Charles Spurgeon, in Hughes, *The Sermon on the Mount*, p. 196.

28. See Bruner, *The Christbook*, p. 314.

29. Gnilka, quoted in ibid., p. 315.

Chapter Seventeen: Treasure and Trust

1. Contra Hans Dieter Betz, *The Sermon on the Mount*, Hermeneia (Minneapolis: Fortress, 1995), p. 423. Betz writes, "Indeed the shift from the cultic instruction to the new section could not be harsher." As I presented in this introduction, I see the thematic transition to be quite natural and smooth. See Rudolf Schnackenburg, *The Gospel of Matthew*, trans. Robert R. Barr (Grand Rapids, MI: Eerdmans, 2002), p. 70 and John R. W. Stott, *The Message of the Sermon on the Mount*, The Bible Speaks Today (Downers Grove, IL: InterVarsity Press, 1978), p. 170. Stott notes, "This is no more than an elaboration of the teaching implicit in the Lord's Prayer."

2. Jerome notes:

> Let the greedy hear this, let him hear that the one who is enrolled by the name of Christian cannot serve Christ and riches at the same time. And yet, he did not say: he who has riches, but: he who serves riches. For he who is a slave of riches guards his riches, like a slave; but the one who has shaken off the yoke of slavery distributes them, like a master. (*Commentary on Matthew*, Fathers of the Church, vol. 117, trans. Thomas P. Scheck [Washington, DC: Catholic University of America, 2008], p. 90.)

Cf. Martin Luther, *The Sermon on the Mount and the Magnificat*, Luther's Works, vol. 21, ed. Jaroslav Pelikan (St. Louis: Concordia, 1956), p. 122.

3. Mary E. Byrne, trans., "Be Thou My Vision" (1905).

4. R. H. Mounce says, "Worry is practical atheism and an affront to God," quoted in Michael Green, *The Message of Matthew*, The Bible Speaks Today (Downers Grove, IL: InterVarsity Press, 2000), p. 104.

5. I am indebted to John Stott for mention (but oddly, not exposition) of these three categories. See *The Message of the Sermon on the Mount*, p. 161.

6. See Sinclair B. Ferguson, *The Sermon on the Mount: Kingdom Life in a Fallen World* (Carlisle, PA: Banner of Truth, 1997), p. 146.

7. From Helmut Thielicke's post-World War II sermon in Stuttgart, Germany, cited in Stott, *The Message of the Sermon on the Mount*, p. 168.

8. Green, *The Message of Matthew*, p. 104.

9. Luther, *The Sermon on the Mount and the Magnificat*, p. 173.

10. R. Kent Hughes, *The Sermon on the Mount: The Message of the Kingdom*, Preaching the Word (Wheaton, IL: Crossway, 2001), p. 224.

11. Stott, *The Message of the Sermon on the Mount*, p. 170.

12. For some of these questions, see Hughes, *The Sermon on the Mount*, p. 209.

Chapter Eighteen: The Loving Art of Speck Removal

1. David L. Turner notes:

> Discipleship inevitably requires discerning "judgments" about individuals and their teachings (e.g., 3:7; 5:20; 6:24; 7:6, 16, 20; 10:13–17). Jesus himself made such judgments (see 4:10; 6:2, 5, 16; 7:21–23; 8:10–12; 13:10–13; 15:14). Therefore, Jesus did not forbid here what he has commanded and exemplified elsewhere. (*The Gospel of Matthew*, Cornerstone Biblical Commentary [Wheaton, IL: Tyndale, 2005], p. 111.)

2. John R. W. Stott, *The Message of the Sermon on the Mount*, The Bible Speaks Today (Downers Grove, IL: InterVarsity Press, 1978), p. 174.

3. Sinclair B. Ferguson notes: "Chapter seven emphasizes the judgment of God, and the impact this makes on the way we live" (*The Sermon on the Mount: Kingdom Life in a Fallen World* [Carlisle, PA: Banner of Truth, repr. 1997], p. 149).

4. Daniel M. Doriani, *The Sermon on the Mount: The Character of a Disciple* (Phillipsburg, NJ: P&R, 2006), p. 190.

5. I am aware that this story in John 8 is textually specious.

6. See J. C. Ryle, *Matthew: Expository Thoughts on the Gospels*, Crossway Classic Commentaries (Wheaton, IL: Crossway, 1993), p. 48.

7. See John MacArthur, *Matthew 1–7* (Chicago: Moody, 1985), pp. 437, 438.

8. Michael Green references how some have viewed it as "unpractical idealism" and how Leo Tolstoy, for example, thought of it as "a blueprint for Utopia" (*The Message of Matthew*, The Bible Speaks Today [Downers Grove, IL: InterVarsity Press, 2000], p. 111).

9. See http://www.fpcjackson.org/resources/sermons/matthew/matthew_vol_3-4/14bMatt.htm.

10. In Stott, *The Message of the Sermon on the Mount*, p. 180.

Chapter Nineteen: The Narrow Gate to Life

1. Frederick Dale Bruner, *The Christbook: Matthew 1–12*, 2nd and rev. ed. (Grand Rapids, MI: Eerdmans, 2004), p. 350.

2. Paul "frequently stressed the necessity (not the option) of perseverance and good works (e.g., Rom 2:13; 3:8; 11:22; 13:14; Gal 5:6; Eph 2:10; Col 1:23; Titus 2:7, 14; 3:8, 14)" (David L. Turner, *The Gospel of Matthew*, Cornerstone Biblical Commentary [Wheaton, IL: Tyndale, 2005], p. 120).

3. For Matthew, one's actions, not words, determine one's spiritual identity because what one does inexorably reveals one's heart. See ibid., p. 116.

4. One might say that the Sermon begins with "being" and ends with "doing."

5. See Philip Melanchthon, "Loci 1: God," in *Loci Communes (1543)*, trans. J. A. O. Preus (St. Louis: Concordia, 1992).

6. In R. Kent Hughes, *The Sermon on the Mount: The Message of the Kingdom*, Preaching the Word (Wheaton, IL: Crossway, 2001), p. 145.

7. This idea of ease comes out in the parable at the end of our text. Two guys are building two identical houses. One builds it, painstakingly I would imagine, on a slab of rock. The other drills down into a foundation of sand and says, "Oh, this thing will be built in a jiffy." He takes the easy way out. Like many buildings that crumble to the ground in our world, he neglects the hard work of finding the proper place and building upon the proper foundation.

8. Bruner, *The Christbook*, p. 357.

9. This is N. Richard Niebuhr's famous critique of the social gospel of his day (*The Kingdom of God in America*, 1956, p. 193), quoted in ibid., p. 354.

10. The ultimate issue of the Sermon is the authority and identity of the preacher. See Michael Green, *The Message of Matthew*, The Bible Speaks Today (Downers Grove, IL: InterVarsity Press, 2000), p. 107.

11. The scribes wouldn't speak without quoting some authority for credence and support. Jesus not only didn't quote anyone to support his claims, he quoted them and then taught against them. Thus he "stood forth as a legislator, not as a commentator, and commanded and prohibited, and repealed, and promised, on his own bare word" (Plummer, quoted in John R. W. Stott, *The Message of the Sermon on the Mount*, The Bible Speaks Today [Downers Grove, IL: InterVarsity Press, 1978], p. 215).

12. Ibid. In verse 21 Jesus claims that only those who do the will of his Father will enter the kingdom. In verse 24 he claims that everyone who practices his words will stand firm during the storm of the final judgment. Isn't he in essence saying that whatever he speaks *is* the will of the Father?

13. Ibid., p. 219.

14. For an excellent sermon on this topic and the particular point of this sentence, see G. Campbell Morgan, "The Authority of Jesus," *The Westminster Pulpit*, vol. 1 (Grand Rapids, MI: Baker, 2006). See especially pp. 77, 78.

15. Jesus ends his sermon—his exposition of the Law, if you will—as Moses did, with a warning and an invitation. "Choose life" is how Moses puts it in Deuteronomy 30:19. "Enter by the narrow gate . . . walk down the hard path . . . that leads to life," is how Jesus essentially says it. "Choose life—enter this gate, not that one." That is the gracious invitation of our Lord.

Chapter Twenty: Pictures of Power

1. What N. T. Wright says of 12:15–21 is fitting for this text as well:

> Matthew looks back over the ministry of Jesus, knowing where it would lead. He sees Jesus as the Servant, not only when he dies a cruel death,

wounded for our transgressions and bruised for our iniquities, but also in the style of what he was already doing in Galilee. He was going about bringing God's restoration wherever it was needed, not by making a fuss, but by gently leading people into God's healing love. (*Matthew for Everyone*, vol. 1 [Louisville: Westminster John Knox, 2002], p. 143.)

2. D. A. Carson comments that Isaiah is thinking of the servant's

taking the diseases of others upon himself through his suffering and death for their sin (Gundry, *Use of OT*, p. 230). . . . If the Davidic Messiah of Jewish expectation (Pss Sol 17:6) purifies his people by annihilating sinners, Matthew's Davidic Messiah-Suffering Servant purifies his people with his death, takes on himself their diseases, and opens fellowship to sinners (cf. Hummel, pp. 124–25). (*The Expositor's Bible Commentary*, vol. 8 [Grand Rapids, MI: Zondervan, 1984], pp. 205, 206.)

In verse 17 Matthew does not restrict the prophecy of Isaiah to purely spiritual maladies. Yet the One who carries infirmities (Isa. 53:4) bears iniquities too (53:5–6); Jesus' healing of diseases cannot be separated from his forgiveness of sins (9:1–8) or from the death that secures forgiveness (26:28). (J. Knox Chamblin, "Matthew," in *Evangelical Commentary on the Bible*, ed. Walter A. Elwell [Grand Rapids, MI: Baker, 1996], p. 732.)

3. "Then a leper comes to Jesus, falls at his feet, and addresses him with the majestic title 'Lord' (κύριε). In 7:21, 22 Matthew applied this title for the first time to Jesus as the lord of judgment. He is consistent in his use of the title. The disciples address Jesus this way (8:25; 14:28, 30; 16:22; 17:4; 18:21) as do the sick who come to the Lord for help (8:2, 6, 8; 9:28; 15:22, 25, 27; 17:15; 20:30, 31, 33). The title does not appear on the lips of outsiders and is not simply polite speech. From the perspective of this Christological dimension the expression 'if you will' becomes understandable. Everything depends on the sovereign will of Jesus who himself appears as the Lord who has his authority from God" (Ulrich Luz, *Matthew 8–20*, Hermeneia [Minneapolis: Fortress, 2001], pp. 5, 6). On the importance of this title in Matthew, cf. Donald Senior, *The Passion of Jesus in the Gospel of Matthew* (Collegeville, MN: Liturgical Press, 1985), p. 62.

4. "Lohmeyer, 155, points out that a significant historical side effect of this story has been that Christianity is the only world religion that has everywhere accepted lepers" (in Frederick Dale Bruner, *The Christbook: Matthew 1–12*, 2nd and rev. ed. [Grand Rapids, MI: Eerdmans, 2004], p. 375).

5. "The gospel is in that grasp" (ibid., p. 374).

6. As Carson notes, "at Jesus' touch nothing remains defiled" ("Matthew," p. 198).

7. Bruner, *The Christbook*, p. 377.

8. John MacArthur, *Matthew 8–15* (Chicago: Moody, 1987), p. 12.

9. Ibid., pp. 12, 13.

10. Ibid., p. 13.

11. Luz, *Matthew 8–20*, p. 10.

12. MacArthur, *Matthew 8–15*, p. 14.

13. Since C. H. Dodd, *According to the Scriptures: The Sub-structure of New Testament Theology* (London: Fontana, 1952), many scholars argue that if a New Testament author quotes an Old Testament text, the whole context of section of Scripture should come to mind.

14. "We see here that a married man was called by Christ as an apostle. . . . Jerome concedes that all apostles were married except for John. Why then is it that the Roman popes took away the wives from the bishops and the other servants of the church?" (Bullinger, quoted in Luz, *Matthew 8–20*, p. 14).

15. The serving part is not some first-century, sexist tack-on. It merely shows, like Lazarus walking out of the tomb, that this woman was truly healed and, like the leper and the servant, healed instantaneously. Moreover, as Blomberg notes, "Her action need imply nothing more than proper etiquette as a hostess" (Craig L. Blomberg, *Matthew*, New American Commentary [Nashville: Broadman, 1992], p. 143).

16. "Matthew having in the leper shewn the healing of the whole human race, and in the centurion's servant that of the Gentiles, now figures the healing of the synagogue in Peter's mother-in-law" (Anselm, quoted in St. Thomas Aquinas, *Catena Aurea*, vol. 1, Part I: The Gospel of St. Matthew, trans. John Henry Newman [New York: Cosimo Classics, 2007], p. 311).

17. Bruner, *The Christbook*, p. 385.

18. See Carson, "Matthew," p. 204; cf. Bruner, *The Christbook*, p. 386.

19. This means that for Matthew, Jesus' healing miracles pointed beyond themselves to the cross.

Chapter Twenty-one: Even the Wind Obeys Him

1. The title "teacher" was often used as a title of respect in Jesus' day, but as David L. Turner notes, "Those who call Jesus 'teacher' in Matthew are not believers in him (cf. 8:19; 9:11; 17:24; 22:16, 36)" (*The Gospel of Matthew*, Cornerstone Biblical Commentary [Wheaton, IL: Tyndale, 2005], p. 176).

2. The leper talks about Jesus; the centurion talks about his servant.

3. On the title "Son of Man," see Frederick Dale Bruner, *The Christbook: Matthew 1–12*, 2nd and rev. ed. (Grand Rapids, MI: Eerdmans, 2004), p. 395. Cf. Donald Senior, *The Passion of Jesus in the Gospel of Matthew* (Collegeville, MN: Liturgical Press, 1985), p. 98.

4. See Bruner, *The Christbook*, pp. 393, 395.

5. Ibid., p. 395.

6. See N. T. Wright, *Matthew for Everyone*, vol. 1 (Louisville: Westminster John Knox, 2002), p. 86; cf. Rudolf Schnackenburg, *The Gospel of Matthew*, trans. Robert R. Barr (Grand Rapids, MI: Eerdmans, 2002), p. 84.

7. "This saying does not condemn natural affection to our parents, but shews that nothing ought to be more binding on us than the business of heaven; that to this we ought to apply ourselves with all our endeavours, and not to be slack, however necessary or urgent are the things that draw us aside" (Chrysostom, cited in St. Thomas Aquinas, *Catena Aurea*, vol. 1, Part I: The Gospel of St. Matthew, trans. John Henry Newman [New York: Cosimo Classics, 2007], p. 318).

8. James Montgomery Boice, *The Gospel of Matthew*, vol. 1 (Grand Rapids, MI: Baker, 2001), p. 132.

9. Ibid.

10. Ibid.

11. Augustine, quoted in Ulrich Luz, *Matthew 8–20*, Hermeneia (Minneapolis: Fortress, 2001), p. 18.

12. Interestingly both Mark and Luke place this story after the Parable of the Soils.

13. R. T. France, *The Gospel of Matthew*, New International Commentary on the New Testament (Grand Rapids, MI: Eerdmans, 2007), p. 329.

14. See John MacArthur, *Matthew 8–15* (Chicago: Moody, 1987), pp. 24, 25.

15. C. H. Spurgeon, *The Gospel of the Kingdom* (Pasadena, TX: Pilgrim Publications, repr. 1996), p. 51.

16. Boice, *The Gospel of Matthew*, p. 132.

17. I imagine him walking away sad, though, not mad like the locals are (v. 34), who don't walk away from Jesus but tell Jesus to walk away—"to leave their region" because he is bad for their economy.

18. Spurgeon summarizes it well: "He spoke to the men first, for they were the most difficult to deal with: wind and sea could be rebuked afterwards" (*The Gospel of the Kingdom*, p. 52).

19. Bruner, *The Christbook*, p. 399.

20. Ibid., p. 398.

21. For the third to last sentence, see ibid., p. 400.

22. Stier in *Bengel*, 1:44, quoted in ibid., p. 400; second quote from ibid., p. 400.

23. Ibid.

24. Ibid., p. 401.

25. Ibid., p. 398.

26. Ibid.

27. See http://www.people.westminstercollege.edu/faculty/mmarkowski/Hall/Perpetua-text.htm; accessed on September 24, 2009.

Chapter Twenty-two: *Christus Victor*

1. Michelle A. Vu, "Screwtape Demon Captures Hearts of Theatergoers," *The Christian Post Review*, April 22, 2008.

2. Frederick Dale Bruner, *The Christbook: Matthew 1–12*, 2nd and rev. ed. (Grand Rapids, MI: Eerdmans, 2004), p. 402.

3. Craig L. Blomberg, *Matthew*, New American Commentary (Nashville: Broadman, 1992), p. 149.

4. Ibid.

5. John MacArthur, *Matthew 8–15* (Chicago: Moody, 1987), p. 33.

6. See Leviticus 11:7; Deuteronomy 14:8; cf. Luke 15:15.

7. "Why did Jesus allow the demons to go into the pigs and let the pigs perish? Some have complained that Jesus was inconsiderate in regard to those who owned the pigs. Others say the pigs were probably owned by Jews and that Jesus was punishing them for raising these forbidden animals. The actual reason is probably the same as the reason Jesus healed the paralyzed man in the next story, that is, as a visible proof of what had happened" (James Montgomery Boice, *The Gospel of Matthew*, vol. 1 [Grand Rapids, MI: Baker, 2001], p. 143). "The destruction of the herd of pigs served as a graphic assurance to the men in question that they really were free at last and that the evil spirits would never return" (Michael Green, The

Message of Matthew, The Bible Speaks Today [Downers Grove, IL: InterVarsity Press, 2000], p. 121).

8. On "one" man in Mark and Luke and "two" in Matthew, see W. D. Davies and Dale C. Allison Jr., *A Critical and Exegetical Commentary on the Gospel according to Saint Matthew*, International Critical Commentary, vol. 2 (Edinburgh: T&T Clark, 1988-1997), p. 80.

9. "Does the fact that Matthew (with Mark) uses the same verb—begged—to describe both the demons' request for the pigs' company and the city's request for Jesus' departure indicate that the evangelists see the city, too, as under demonic influence? (In the city's case perhaps, of the demon Mammon?) If the evangelist does intend this, he does not press it. We are to ask whether the city values property more than persons, economics more than human beings, their pigs more than the rehabilitation of their townsmen" (Bruner, *The Christbook*, p. 406).

10. Ibid.

11. "Even in Scripture itself, there is some reason to believe that demon possession is not very common. There is just one case of demon possession in the OT (Saul, in 1 Samuel 16). After the Gospels it becomes rare again (only Acts 16:16–18). It seems, then, that when Christ came to claim his kingdom, the kingdom of Satan rose up to resist, so there was great upsurge of evil. Still, sane, credible pastors have encountered cases of demon possession in America. Missionaries report demonic activity in lands that give themselves over to the worship of evil spirits" (Daniel M. Doriani, *Matthew*, Reformed Expository Commentary, vol. 1 [Phillipsburg, NJ: P&R, 2008], pp. 357, 358).

12. Douglas R. A. Hare, *Matthew*, Interpretation (Louisville: John Knox, 1993), p. 98.

13. Note the text starts with "a crowd" (v. 18) and ends with "they begged him to leave" (v. 34).

14. "Readers concerned about the destruction of animal life and the loss of the farmers' livelihood exhibit a contemporary sentimentality not shared by a Jewish audience who knew these pig farmers should not have been raising animals whose meat was forbidden to eat" (Blomberg, *Matthew*, p. 152).

15. Doriani, *Matthew*, vol. 1, p. 362.

16. Mark and Luke give some focus to the restored man. Matthew focuses on Jesus' person and power.

17. The disciples are likely on the boat with Jesus in 9:1, but Matthew uses "he" referring to Jesus.

18. As readers we know Jesus' identity first through the testimony of the angel (1:23) and of God the Father (3:17).

19. Theophylact, cited in Broadus, in D. A. Carson, "Matthew," in *The Expositor's Bible Commentary*, vol. 8 (Grand Rapids, MI: Zondervan, 1984), p. 218. Cf. Chrysostom, cited in Aquinas: "Because there were who thought Christ to be a man, therefore the dæmons came to proclaim His divinity, that they who had not seen the sea raging and again still, might dear the dæmons crying" (St. Thomas Aquinas, *Catena Aurea*, vol. 1, Part I: The Gospel of St. Matthew, trans. John Henry Newman [New York: Cosimo Classics, 2007], p. 324).

20. Mark and Luke include their precise title, "Jesus, Son of the Most High God" (Mark 5:7; Luke 8:28; cf. Luke 1:32).

21. MacArthur, *Matthew 8–15*, p. 43.

22. Bruner, *The Christbook*, p. 398.

23. Gnilka, quoted in Davies and Allison Jr., *A Critical and Exegetical Commentary on the Gospel according to Saint Matthew*, vol. 2, p. 72.

24. "The second question shows that there will be a time for demonic hosts to be tortured and rejected forever (cf. Jude 6; Rev 20:10; cf. 1 Enoch 16:1; Jub 10:8–9; T Levi 18:12; IQS 3:24–25; 4:18–20)" (Carson, "Matthew," p. 218).

25. The demons prefer the pigs to the abyss, but when the pigs rush into the lake, it becomes their abyss (Doriani, *Matthew*, vol. 1, p. 360).

26. Martin Luther, "A Mighty Fortress Is Our God" (1529).

27. "He can save from *anything*. Henry, 111, is right: 'The scope of this chapter is to show the divine power of Christ, by the instances of his dominion over bodily diseases, which to us are irresistible; over winds and waves, which to us are yet more uncontrollable; and lastly, over devils, which to us are most formidable of all. Christ has not only *all power in heaven and earth* and all deep places, but has the keys to hell too'" (Bruner, *The Christbook*, p. 407).

Chapter Twenty-three: Authority to Forgive

1. See F. L. Cross and E. A. Livingstone, eds., *The Oxford Dictionary of the Christian Church*, 3rd edition (New York: Oxford University Press, 1998), p. 256.

2. As James R. Edwards points out, "The Gospels preserve several instances of Jesus fulfilling the petition of one party on behalf of another" (*The Gospel According to Mark*, Pillar New Testament Commentary [Grand Rapids, MI: Eerdmans, 2002], p. 76). So R. T. France may be right when he says, "Faith is apparently exercised on behalf of another, while the patient himself remains inactive until v. 12, and is silent throughout" (The Gospel of Mark, New International Greek Testament Commentary [Grand Rapids, MI: Eerdmans, 2002], p. 124). But I agree more with Calvin, who wrote,

> With regard to the present passage, though Christ is said to have been moved by the faith of others, yet the *paralytic* could not have obtained *the forgiveness of sins*, if he had had no faith of his own. Unworthy persons were often restored by Christ to health of body, as God daily *maketh his sun to rise on the evil and the good*, (Matth. v. 45) but there is no other way in which he is reconciled to us than by faith. There is a *synecdoche*, therefore, in the word *their*, when it is said that *Jesus saw THEIR faith*: for Christ not only looked at those who brought the paralytic, but looked also at *his* faith. (John Calvin, *Commentary on a Harmony of the Evangelists, Matthew, Mark, and Luke*, trans. William Pringle [Grand Rapids, MI: Baker, repr. 1993], pp. 393, 394.)

3. It is significant that "faith" defined here reflects well what is said in Hebrews 11:1: "Now faith is the assurance of things hoped for, the conviction of things not seen," as well as what is said in James 2, where faith expresses itself through love and good deeds on behalf of others.

4. "Along with great love, his friends had great faith. There was no way they would have gone to such outrageous extremes of action if they did not implicitly believe that Christ could and would heal their friend. A wavering faith would have

demurred when they began hoisting the stretcher up to the roof or would have bolted when they began digging. 'Hey, guys, this is embarrassing. You'll have to finish it yourselves.' But the four truly believed! This kind of faith invites the Lord's miraculous power" (R. Kent Hughes, *Mark: Jesus, Servant and Savior*, Preaching the Word, vol. 1 [Wheaton, IL: Crossway, 2001], p. 63).

5. Ibid., vol. 1, p. 65.

6. It is probably right to say, as Eduard Schweizer did,

> It is not as if this sick man were unusually sinful, but his case makes the universal separation of man from God more conspicuous and illustrates the truth which is proclaimed over and over in the Old Testament, that all suffering is rooted in man's separation from God. For this reason, Jesus must call attention here to man's deepest need; otherwise the testimony of this healing would remain nothing more than the story of a remarkable miracle. (*The Good News According to Mark* [Richmond, VA: John Knox, 1970], p. 61.)

7. These scribes, who Luke tells us in his account came from "every village of Galilee and Judea and from Jerusalem" (Luke 5:17), traveled this distance motivated by more than a sense of curiosity. They were sitting there in the midst of the crowd, seemingly sitting in judgment upon Jesus' teaching. "Who is this Jesus, and what is the content of his message?" They honestly wanted to know. I'll put it this way: they were there for inquiry, but not yet for inquisition; note here that we only have their thoughts, or perhaps their whispers to one another. No concerns or accusations are expressed publicly. The scribes remained silent and likely would have remained silent if not for Christ exposing their thoughts.

8. E.g., Exodus 34:6, 7; Isaiah 1:18; 43:25; 44:22; Psalm 103:3, 10, 12; Daniel 9:9; Micah 7:18.

9. Daniel J. Harrington, "The Gospel According to Mark," in *The New Jerome Biblical Commentary* (Englewood Cliffs, NJ: Prentice Hall, 1990), p. 602.

10. "Jesus is the only one on the earth with the power and right to forgive sins. On this interpretation Jesus has replaced the temple in Jerusalem and its priests. 'A greater than the temple is here'" (W. D. Davies and Dale C. Allison Jr., *A Critical and Exegetical Commentary on the Gospel according to Saint Matthew*, International Critical Commentary, vol. 2 [Edinburgh: T&T Clark, 1988-1997], p. 93).

11. Robert Lowry, "What Can Wash Away My Sin?" (1876).

12. Hughes, *Mark*, vol. 1, p. 65.

Chapter Twenty-four: Supper with Sinners

1. And what happened after Christ's ascension? According to Acts, his apostles preached the message of forgiveness throughout the known world. In Jerusalem Peter said to the Jews, "Repent and be baptized every one of you in the name of Jesus Christ for the forgiveness of your sins" (Acts 2:38). Later Peter preached the same message to the Gentiles: "To him [Christ] all the prophets bear witness that everyone who believes in him receives forgiveness of sins through his name" (Acts 10:43). Moreover, after Paul's remarkable experience of forgiveness, he also proclaimed the good news of forgiveness. For example, in Acts 13:38, 39 he preached, "Let it be known to you therefore, brothers, that through this man [Jesus] forgiveness of sins

is proclaimed to you." And in Colossians 1:13, 14 he wrote, "[God] has delivered us from the domain of darkness and transferred us to the kingdom of his beloved Son, in whom we have redemption, the forgiveness of sins."

2. "There was a tax or toll station at Capernaum, at the frontier of Herod Antipas's region (see 8:5)" (Rudolf Schnackenburg, *The Gospel of Matthew*, trans. Robert R. Barr [Grand Rapids, MI: Eerdmans, 2002], p. 88).

3. I disagree with Chrysostom who wrote: "Therefore he did not call them all together at the beginning, when Matthew was still in a hardened condition. Rather, only after countless miracles, after his fame was spread abroad, did he call Matthew. He knew Matthew had been softened for full responsiveness" ("The Gospel of Matthew" [Homily 30.1], quoted in *Matthew 1–13*, ed. Manlio Simonetti, Ancient Christian Commentary on Scripture, NT Ia [Downers Grove, IL: InterVarsity Press, 2001], pp. 176, 177).

4. Jonathan Edwards, *The Works of Jonathan Edwards*, ed. Edward Hickman, vol. 1 (Carlisle, PA: Banner of Truth, repr. 1992), p. 379.

5. W. D. Davies and Dale C. Allison Jr. are slightly too strong: "Jesus, it should be underlined, is the one in command. Matthew does not choose Jesus. Jesus chooses Matthew" (*A Critical and Exegetical Commentary on the Gospel According to Saint Matthew*, International Critical Commentary, vol. 2 [Edinburgh: T&T Clark, 1988-1997], p. 99).

6. "The word for 'follow' is used in the Gospels only of Jesus' disciples, never of those who oppose him. Occurring nineteen times in Mark, 'following' is a load-bearing term that describes the proper response of faith (10:52!), and is indeed practically synonymous with faith. 'Following' is an act that involves risk and cost; it is something one does, not simply what one thinks or believes" (James R. Edwards, *The Gospel According to Mark*, Pillar New Testament Commentary [Grand Rapids, MI: Eerdmans, 2002], pp. 81, 82).

7. William L. Lane, *The Gospel of Mark*, New International Commentary on the New Testament (Grand Rapids, MI: Eerdmans, 1974), pp. 101, 102.

8. John Calvin, *Commentary on a Harmony of the Evangelists, Matthew, Mark, and Luke*, trans. William Pringle (Grand Rapids, MI: Baker, repr. 1993), pp. 398, 389.

9. R. Kent Hughes, *Mark: Jesus, Servant and Savior*, Preaching the Word, vol. 1 (Wheaton, IL: Crossway, 2001), p. 68.

10. Lane, *Mark*, p. 101.

11. Edwards, *Mark*, p. 83.

12. For more on tax collectors, see what Alfred Edersheim says (quoted in John MacArthur, *Matthew 8–15* [Chicago: Moody, 1987], pp. 60, 61).

13. "Matthew is doing in his narrative what the great Dutch painter Rembrandt van Rijn did in one of his most famous paintings of the crucifixion. He portrayed all the characters one would expect in such a scene: Jesus, the two thieves, the soldiers, and a large crowd of onlookers. But down in the corner of the painting, as one who shared in the guilt of the crucifixion and is not afraid to admit it, Rembrandt has painted a portrait of himself. Thus, as Matthew, he has testified to the fact that he too was a sinner and that he trusted in Jesus as the one who died to save him from his sin" (James Montgomery Boice, *The Gospel of Matthew*, vol. 1 [Grand Rapids, MI: Baker, 2001], p. 149).

> He wrote a book which is known all over the earth. He became a blessing to others as well as blessed in his own soul. He left a name behind him which is better known than the names of princes and kings. The richest man of the world is soon forgotten when he dies; but as long as the world stands millions will know the name of Matthew the tax collector. (J. C. Ryle, *Matthew: Expository Thoughts on the Gospels*, Crossway Classic Commentaries [Wheaton, IL: Crossway, 1993], p. 64.)

14. This idea is taken from a Dick Lucas sermon.
15. C. T. Studd, quoted in William Barclay, *Letters to Timothy, Titus, and Philemon* (Louisville: Westminster John Knox, repr. 2003), p. 62.
16. See J. Knox Chamblin, "Matthew," in *Evangelical Commentary on the Bible*, ed. Walter A. Elwell (Grand Rapids, MI: Baker, 1996), p. 733. Cf. Davies and Allison Jr., *A Critical and Exegetical Commentary on the Gospel according to Saint Matthew*, vol. 2, p. 101.
17. Edwards, *Mark*, p. 84.
18. Lane, *Mark*, pp. 106, 107.
19. See "Apostles' Creed," in F. L. Cross and E. A. Livingstone, eds., *Oxford Dictionary of the Christian Church* (New York: Oxford University Press, 2005), p. 90.

Chapter Twenty-five: A Critique of "Pure" Religion

1. Sam Harris, *The End of Faith: Religion, Terror, and the Future of Reason* (New York: W. W. Norton, 2005), p. 29.
2. Dinesh D'Souza, *What's So Great About Christianity* (Wheaton, IL: Tyndale, 2007), p. 172.
3. Ibid., p. 173.
4. Ibid.
5. See D. A. Carson, "Matthew," in *The Expositor's Bible Commentary*, vol. 8 (Grand Rapids, MI: Zondervan, 1984), p. 227.
6. John MacArthur, *Matthew 8–15* (Chicago: Moody, 1987), p. 70.
7. "Marcion understands the text to describe the relationship between the Old Testament and the gospel, the *Gospel of Thomas* (logion 47), the impossibility of serving two masters. Augustine interprets it to refer to the fleshly senses and the new person, Origen to law and grace, Chromatius to the church and the perfidy of the 'old' synagogue, Luther to the righteousness of the law and of faith" (Ulrich Luz, *Matthew 8–20*, Hermeneia [Minneapolis: Fortress, 2001], p. 38).

> The cloth of the new garment and the new wine should be understood as the Gospel precepts which the Jews cannot endure, lest a greater tear is made. Even the Galatians were desiring to do something similar, when they wanted to intermingle precepts of the Law with the Gospel and "put new wine into old wineskins." (St. Jerome, *Commentary on Matthew*, Fathers of the Church, vol. 117, trans. Thomas P. Scheck [Washington, DC: Catholic University of America, 2008], p. 110.)

8. Donald A. Hagner, *Matthew 1–13*, Word Biblical Commentary, vol. 33a (Nashville: Thomas Nelson, 1993), p. 244.

9. See W. D. Davies and Dale C. Allison Jr., *A Critical and Exegetical Commentary on the Gospel according to Saint Matthew*, International Critical Commentary, vol. 2 (Edinburgh: T&T Clark, 1988-1997), p. 114.

10. See Proverbs 1:8–19; 12:26; 13:20; 14:7; 16:29; 17:12; 22:24, 25; 23:20, 21; 24:1, 2; 27:17.

11. "Why do the disciples of the one who preaches repentance (4:17) not display acts of repentance?" (Davies and Allison Jr., *A Critical and Exegetical Commentary on the Gospel according to Saint Matthew*, vol. 2, p. 107).

12. While I don't intend to make a firm connection between the practices of the Pharisees and John's disciples, there is a textual connection here: "Then the disciples of John came to him, saying: 'Why do *we and the Pharisees* fast [often], but your disciples do not fast" (Hagner's translation of 9:14, emphasis mine). Of further significance, see Hagner's note (note a) on the critical Greek text on the word "often" (*Matthew 1–13*, p. 241).

13. Frederick Dale Bruner, *The Christbook: Matthew 1–12*, 2nd and rev. ed. (Grand Rapids, MI: Eerdmans, 2004), pp. 424, 425.

14. "For Matthew's readers the bridegroom is, of course, Christ (cf. 22:1–14; 25:1–13)" (Luz, Matthew 8–20, p. 37).

15. Beare, p. 229, quoted in Bruner, *The Christbook*, p. 425.

16. Timothy F. Lull, ed., "The Freedom of a Christian," in *Martin Luther's Basic Theological Writings* (Minneapolis: Fortress, 1989), p. 596.

17. Cf. Colossians 2:16–23.

Chapter Twenty-six: Two Touches

1. R. Kent Hughes, *Mark: Jesus, Servant and Savior*, Preaching the Word, vol. 1 (Wheaton, IL: Crossway, 2001), p. 127.

2. John Calvin, *Commentary on a Harmony of the Evangelists, Matthew, Mark, and Luke*, trans. William Pringle (Grand Rapids, MI: Baker, repr. 1993), pp. 410, 411.

3. Rudolf Schnackenburg, *The Gospel of Matthew*, trans. Robert R. Barr (Grand Rapids, MI: Eerdmans, 2002), p. 90.

4. See 1 Kings 17:21; 2 Kings 4:34.

5. Through faith is this daughter of Abraham now a daughter of God? Cf. 12:48–50.

6. "Sadly, her bleeding would have destroyed her chances for marriage, or, if she were married, it would have precluded all sexual relations with her husband. She must have been very, very, lonely" (James Montgomery Boice, *The Gospel of Matthew*, vol. 1 [Grand Rapids, MI: Baker, 2001], p. 156).

7. Hughes, *Mark*, vol. 1, p. 126.

8. D. A. Carson, "Matthew," in *The Expositor's Bible Commentary*, vol. 8 (Grand Rapids, MI: Zondervan, 1984), p. 230.

9. I say this because Matthew shortens the dialogue between Jesus and his disciples and then the woman. In other words, Matthew's Jesus gets right to commending her faith.

10. Calvin, *Commentary on a Harmony of the Evangelists, Matthew, Mark, and Luke*, p. 411.

11. Jerome, "Homily 33," quoted in *Mark*, eds. Thomas C. Oden and Christopher A. Hall, Ancient Christian Commentary on Scripture, NT II (Downers Grove, IL: InterVarsity Press, 1998), pp. 73, 74.

12. In James A. Brooks, *Mark*, New American Commentary (Nashville: Broadman, 1991), p. 94.

13. Calvin, *Commentary on a Harmony of the Evangelists, Matthew, Mark, and Luke*, p. 416.

14. I agree with N. T. Wright's assessment of Jesus being doubly unclean—a touch from a bleeding woman and his touching of the dead body (*Matthew for Everyone*, vol. 1 [Louisville: Westminster John Knox, 2002], pp. 104, 105). But unlike Wright, I see it only as a subplot.

15. I paraphrased David E. Garland, *Mark*, The NIV Application Commentary (Grand Rapids, MI: Zondervan, 1996), p. 229.

16. Timothy George, *Theology of the Reformers* (Nashville: Broadman, 1988), p. 105, quoted in ibid.

17. "Viewed from Matthew's perspective, the christological scope is primary. Just as saving the hemorrhaging woman is more than simply healing her (although the latter is part of the former), so the resurrection story points to Christ's all-encompassing power to give life—a power that transcends the one-time event of the miracle" (Ulrich Luz, *Matthew 8–20*, Hermeneia [Minneapolis: Fortress, 2001], p. 44).

18. Horatio Spafford, "It Is Well with My Soul," 1873.

Chapter Twenty-seven: Too Blind Men

1. See Dinesh D'Souza, *What's So Great About Christianity* (Wheaton, IL: Tyndale, 2007), p. 183.

2. The miracles narrative in Matthew 8, 9 "underlines the theme of faith; see 8.10, 26; 9.22, 28" (W. D. Davies and Dale C. Allison Jr., *A Critical and Exegetical Commentary on the Gospel according to Saint Matthew*, International Critical Commentary, vol. 2 [Edinburgh: T&T Clark, 1988-1997], p. 140).

3. "On the other hand, it has been noticed that in Mark 10:47–48, and then especially in Matthew, 'Son of David' is used by the sick, primarily by the blind, to address the miracle worker, Jesus (Mark 10:47, 48; Matt 9:27; 20:30, 31, cf. 12:23; 15:22; 21:15)" (Ulrich Luz, *Matthew 8–20*, Hermeneia [Minneapolis: Fortress, 2001], p. 47).

4. John MacArthur, *Matthew 8–15* (Chicago: Moody, 1987), p. 90.

5. Frederick Dale Bruner, *The Christbook: Matthew 1–12*, 2nd and rev. ed. (Grand Rapids, MI: Eerdmans, 2004), p. 441.

6. Ibid., pp. 441, 442.

7. "This rather violent verb reveals Jesus' intense desire to avoid a falsely based and ill-conceived acclaim that would not only impede but also endanger his true mission (see on 8:4)" (D. A. Carson, "Matthew," in *The Expositor's Bible Commentary*, vol. 8 [Grand Rapids, MI: Zondervan, 1984], p. 233).

8. On the "messianic secret," see C. M. Tuckett, ed., *The Messianic Secret* (London: SPCK, 1983).

9. Davies and Allison Jr., *A Critical and Exegetical Commentary on the Gospel according to Saint Matthew*, vol. 2, p. 135.

10. Cf. Isaiah 29:18; 42:7, 16 (in ibid.).

11. Craig L. Blomberg, *Matthew*, New American Commentary (Nashville: Broadman, 1992), p. 162.

Chapter Twenty-eight: The Motive and Means of Misison

1. "Especially noteworthy is the fact that 4.23 and 9.35 are nearly identical and form an important *inclusio*. . . . 9.35–10.4 is a door that closes off one room and opens another. . . . So it is no surprise that while 9.35–10.4 resembles another introduction to a major discourse it also recalls the conclusion of another miracle triad" (W. D. Davies and Dale C. Allison Jr., *A Critical and Exegetical Commentary on the Gospel according to Saint Matthew*, International Critical Commentary, vol. 2 [Edinburgh: T&T Clark, 1988-1997], p. 143).

2. Donald A. Hagner said it well:

> What causes Jesus' deep compassion at this point is not the abundance of sickness he has seen but rather the great spiritual need of the people, whose lives have no center, whose existence seems aimless, whose experience is one of futility. The whole Gospel is a response to just this universal human need. (*Matthew 1–13*, Word Biblical Commentary, vol. 33a [Nashville: Thomas Nelson, 1993], p. 260.)

3. On this theme, Frederick Dale Bruner writes:

> Why is there mission? First of all, quite simply, because Jesus' heart goes out to people. . . . The first reason for Christian mission is the fellow feeling of Jesus, which we can formally call Jesus' compassion. . . . Jesus feels for people. That is principle one of mission. (*The Christbook: Matthew 1–12*, 2nd and rev. ed. [Grand Rapids, MI: Eerdmans, 2004], pp. 447, 448.)

4. Found at http://www.hcs.harvard.edu/~gsascf/shield.html; accessed on January 3, 2010.

5. "They thus bridge the times, establishing continuity between Jesus and his church" (Davies and Allison Jr., *A Critical and Exegetical Commentary on the Gospel according to Saint Matthew*, vol. 2, p. 151).

6. John Chrysostom, "The Gospel of Matthew" (Homily 32:1–2), quoted in *Matthew 1–13*, ed. Manlio Simonetti, Ancient Christian Commentary on Scripture, NT Ia (Downers Grove, IL: InterVarsity Press, 2001), pp. 190, 191.

7. Contra Davies and Allison Jr., *A Critical and Exegetical Commentary on the Gospel according to Saint Matthew*, who assert (without any defense for their position), "The Lord of the Harvest is clearly, God, not Jesus" (vol. 2, p. 149).

8. John Stott, *The Spirit, the Church, and the World: The Message of Acts* (Downers Grove, IL: InterVarsity Press, 1990), p. 34.

9. See Pelikan's universalism, in Frederick Dale Bruner, *The Christbook: Matthew 1–12*, 2nd and rev. ed. (Grand Rapids, MI: Eerdmans, 2004), p. 450.

Chapter Twenty-nine: Jesus' Sermon on Suffering Mission

1. Victor Kuligin, *Ten Things I Wish Jesus Never Said* (Wheaton, IL: Crossway, 2006), pp. 11, 12.

2. Ulrich Luz, *Matthew 8–20*, Hermeneia (Minneapolis: Fortress, 2001), p. 125.

3. D. A. Carson notes, "Moreover Jesus is envisaging a time before the absolute separation of church and synagogue has taken place, for synagogue floggings (cf. 23:34; Mark 13:9; Acts 22:19; cf. 2 Cor 11:24–25) were most easily inflicted on synagogue members" ("Matthew," in *The Expositor's Bible Commentary*, vol. 8 [Grand Rapids, MI: Zondervan, 1984], p. 248).

4. Frederick Dale Bruner, *The Christbook: Matthew 1–12*, 2nd and rev. ed. (Grand Rapids, MI: Eerdmans, 2004), p. 445.

5. Because of this, Luz calls it the "disciples discourse" (*Matthew 8–20*, p. 63).

6. See Matthew 10:5; 20:17; 26:14, 20, 47; see esp. 19:28; cf. Acts 6:2; 1 Corinthians 15:5; Revelation 21:14.

7. Concerning the number twelve, W. D. Davies and Dale C. Allison Jr. speak of Jesus creating a "prophetic symbol" (*A Critical and Exegetical Commentary on the Gospel according to Saint Matthew*, International Critical Commentary, vol. 2 [Edinburgh: T&T Clark, 1988-1997], p. 152).

8. Jerome uses the language, "Strictly to them was it said" (*Commentary on Matthew*, Fathers of the Church, vol. 117, trans. Thomas P. Scheck [Washington, DC: Catholic University of America, 2008], p. 121).

9. Daniel M. Doriani provides a good summary

> There are a number of views regarding the meaning of "before the Son of Man comes." Some critics assert that Jesus was simply mistaken. He wrongly believed he would come in his glory within weeks or months. Some evangelicals believe Jesus "comes" in judgment in AD 70, when the Romans obliterated Jerusalem, thereby fulfilling his prophecies of judgment on the unbelieving people. Others believe Jesus "comes" in the complex of events that led to his coronation as Lord. The events include his death, resurrection, and ascension, and the gift of the Spirit. (*Matthew*, Reformed Expository Commentary, vol. 1 [Phillipsburg, NJ: P&R, 2008], p. 432.)

N. T Wright comments

> The phrase echoes Daniel 7.13, where the "coming" of "the son of man" is not his coming from heaven to earth, but his coming from earth to heaven: exalted, after suffering, to be the judge and ruler of the world, and particularly of the "beasts" that have opposed "the people of the saints of the most high." (*Matthew for Everyone*, vol. 1 [Louisville: Westminster John Knox, 2002], p. 116.)

10. For various texts on being brought before Gentiles, see Acts 4:1–22; 5:17–41; 6:12; 12:1–3; 16:19–21; 21:27; Philippians 1:12–18; for Spirit-filled responses, see Acts 4:8ff., 31; 5:32; 6:5, 10; 7:55; 13:9.

11. St. Jerome, "Homily 14," *Homilies 1–59 on the Psalms*, Fathers of the Church (Washington, DC: Catholic University of America, repr. 2001), p. 109.

12. Bruner, *The Christbook,* p. 466.

13. Ibid., p. 465.

14. Stanley Hauerwas, *Matthew*, Brazos Theological Commentary on the Bible (Grand Rapids, MI: Brazos Press, 2006), p. 106.

15. The idea for the animal coat-of-arms comes from Bruner, *The Christbook*, pp. 471–475.

16. Craig L. Blomberg, *Matthew*, New American Commentary (Nashville: Broadman, 1992), p. 174.

17. Dietrich Bonhoeffer, *The Cost of Discipleship*, trans. Barbara Green and Reinhard Krauss (Minneapolis: Fortress), p. 197.

18. See T. David Gordon's foreword to my book, *God's Lyrics: Rediscovering Worship through Old Testament Songs* (Phillipsburg, NJ: P&R, 2010).

19. J. C. Ryle, *Matthew: Expository Thoughts on the Gospels*, Crossway Classic Commentaries (Wheaton, IL: Crossway, 1993), p. 75.

20. David L. Turner, *The Gospel of Matthew*, Cornerstone Biblical Commentary (Wheaton, IL: Tyndale, 2005), p. 155.

21. J. Knox Chamblin, "Matthew," in *Evangelical Commentary on the Bible*, ed. Walter A. Elwell (Grand Rapids, MI: Baker, 1996), p. 734; cf. Blomberg, *Matthew*, p. 175.

Chapter Thirty: His Mighty Works

1. Daniel M. Doriani, *Matthew*, Reformed Expository Commentary, vol. 1 (Phillipsburg, NJ: P&R, 2008), p. 459.

2. Josephus claims Herod imprisoned John in the fortress of Machaerus, east of the Dead Sea (*Antiquities*, 18.5.2).

3. N. T. Wright, *Matthew for Everyone*, vol. 1 (Louisville: Westminster John Knox, 2002), p. 132.

4. Frederick Dale Bruner, *The Christbook: Matthew 1–12,* 2nd and rev. ed. (Grand Rapids, MI: Eerdmans, 2004), p. 505.

5. The Old Testament records only two cases of someone raising the dead (1 Kings 17:7–24; 2 Kings 4:8–37).

6. See Craig S. Keener, *Matthew*, IVP New Testament Commentary Series (Downers Grove, IL: InterVarsity Press, 1997), p. 220.

7. Craig L. Blomberg, *Matthew*, New American Commentary (Nashville: Broadman, 1992), p. 191.

8. Stanley Hauerwas, *Matthew*, Brazos Theological Commentary on the Bible (Grand Rapids, MI: Brazos Press, 2006), p. 115.

9. James Montgomery Boice, *The Gospel of Matthew*, vol. 1 (Grand Rapids, MI: Baker, 2001), p. 197.

10. Bruner, *The Christbook*, p. 510.

11. The thought and some of the language is taken from Bruner (ibid., p. 512).

12. Keener, *Matthew*, p. 215. Keener cites S. L. Edgar, "The New Testament and Rabbinic Messianic Interpretation," *New Testament Studies* 5 (1958), p. 48 and T. W. Manson, *The Saying of Jesus* (Grand Rapids, MI: Eerdmans, 1979), p. 214.

13. See Bruner, *The Christbook*, p. 513.

14. Ibid., p. 512.

Chapter Thirty-one: Resting in the Son

1. My slight rewording of "You cannot have God for your Father if you have not the Church for your mother" (St. Cyprian, *The Lapsed; the Unity of the Catholic*

Church, Ancient Christian Writers, vol. 25, trans. Maurice Bévenot [New York: Paulist Press, 1956], pp. 48, 49).

2. The second title comes from Frederick Dale Bruner, *The Christbook: Matthew 1–12*, 2nd and rev. ed. (Grand Rapids, MI: Eerdmans, 2004), p. 525.

3. D. A. Carson, "Matthew," in *The Expositor's Bible Commentary*, vol. 8 (Grand Rapids, MI: Zondervan, 1984), p. 275.

4. Ulrich Luz, *Matthew 8–20*, Hermeneia (Minneapolis: Fortress, 2001), p. 162.

5. See John 3:3–8; cf. 1:13.

6. See Luz, *Matthew 8–20*, p. 166.

7. "Torah is seen as but one expression of God's larger Wisdom, and not the final or definitive one. Jesus' person, life, and teaching are seen as the climactic expression of God's wisdom and will." Ben Witherington III, *Matthew*, Smyth & Helwys Bible Commentary (Macon, GA: Smyth & Helwys, 2006), p. 239.

8. Jesus' use of the term "Father" for God—especially his expression "my Father"—was understood (rightly so!) by his enemies as claiming equality with God (see John 5:18).

9. On "Son" being a reference to "Son of God," see Luz, *Matthew 8–20*, p. 169.

10. The thought of this paragraph (and a few other lines) were triggered by Ravi Zacharias, *Jesus Among Other Gods: The Absolute Claims of the Christian Message* (Nashville: Word, 2000), pp. 4, 5.

11. Quoted in Bruner, *The Christbook*, pp. 530, 531.

12. William Hendriksen, *Matthew*, 13th ed. (Grand Rapids, MI: Baker, 2002), p. 497.

13. Craig Blomberg notes,

> The language of these verses ("hidden," "revealed," "your good pleasure") is incontrovertibly predestinarian in nature, but the language of free will appears equally clearly in vv. 20–24, in which people are judged for their rejection of Jesus, and in vv. 28–30, in which Jesus offers salvation to those who will respond more positively. Scripture in fact regularly and without sense of contradiction juxtaposes the themes of divine sovereignty and human responsibility (e.g., Gen 50:19–20; Lev 20:7–8; Jer 29:10–14; Joel 2:32; Phil 2:12–13). (*Matthew*, New American Commentary [Nashville: Broadman, 1992], p. 192.)

I add also the language of Romans 9–11. Note especially how strongly Paul stresses human responsibility in Romans 10, 11 (see esp. 10:3b, 21; 11:12, 15, 20, 23, 30).

14. On this issue of antinomy, see J. I. Packer, *Evangelism and the Sovereignty of God* (Downers Grove, IL: InterVarsity Press, 1991), pp. 18–21.

15. "He imposes no hard conditions; he does not say anything about work to be done first, or establishing whether we deserve his gifts: he only asks us to come to him just as we are, with all our sins, and to submit ourselves like little children to his teaching." J. C. Ryle, *Matthew: Expository Thoughts on the Gospels*, Crossway Classic Commentaries (Wheaton, IL: Crossway, 1993), p. 88.

16. Adapted from Emma Lazarus, "A New Colossus."

17. See Hendriksen, *Matthew*, p. 505. I borrow much of his language in this sentence and the one before it.

18. W. D. Davies and Dale C. Allison Jr., *A Critical and Exegetical Commentary on the Gospel according to Saint Matthew*, International Critical Commentary, vol. 2 (Edinburgh: T&T Clark, 1988-1997), p. 291.

19. Bruner, *The Christbook*, p. 538.

20. Ibid., p. 539.

21. Michael Green writes, "[Jesus] offers 'rest,' not cessation from toil, but peace and fulfillment and a sense of being put right. We have only to come, to entrust ourselves to him, and we shall find rest" (*Message of Matthew*, The Bible Speaks Today [Downers Grove, IL: InterVarsity Press, 2000], p. 143).

22. On this image, see Bruner, *The Christbook*, p. 541.

23. Rudolf Schnackenburg notes that "find rest for your souls" means "not peace of mind but, using biblical speech (Isa. 28:12; Jer. 6:16), the satisfaction of the salvific longing of the entire human being (cf. 1 Peter 1:9; Heb. 3:11–4:11). Wisdom's invitation is transferred to Jesus" (*Gospel of Matthew*, trans. Robert R. Barr [Grand Rapids, MI: Eerdmans, 2002], p. 111). Cf. M. Jack Suggs, *Wisdom, Christology, and Law in Matthew's Gospel* (Cambridge, MA: Harvard University Press, 1970), p. 130.

24. This phrase comes from Davies and Allison Jr., their sixth and final possible alternative for understanding how Jesus' yoke can be considered comfortable and his burden light (*A Critical and Exegetical Commentary on the Gospel according to Saint Matthew*, vol. 2, p. 291).

Chapter Thirty-two: Lord of the Sabbath

1. William Barclay, *The Gospel of Mark*, rev. ed. (Philadelphia: Westminster, 1975), p. 63.

2. James R. Edwards, *The Gospel According to Mark*, Pillar New Testament Commentary (Grand Rapids, MI: Eerdmans, 2002), p. 93.

3. Ibid.

4. C. H. Spurgeon, *The Gospel of the Kingdom* (Pasadena, TX: Pilgrim Publications, repr. 1996), p. 85.

5. Alan Cole, "Mark," in *New Bible Commentary*, eds. G. J. Wenham, et al., 4th ed. (Downers Grove, IL: InterVarsity Press, 1994), p. 955.

6. The idea for this paragraph comes from Frederick Dale Bruner, *The Christbook: Matthew 1–12*, 2nd and rev. ed. (Grand Rapids, MI: Eerdmans, 2004), pp. 547, 548, and the last sentence from p. 548.

7. D. A. Carson, "Matthew," in *The Expositor's Bible Commentary*, vol. 8 (Grand Rapids, MI: Zondervan, 1984), p. 281.

8. Craig L. Blomberg notes, "As for the Sabbath commands, believers fulfill them when they heed Matt 11:28–30 and rest daily in the Lord (cf. Heb 4:9–11, in which 'Sabbath-rest' is equated with becoming a believer)" (*Matthew*, New American Commentary [Nashville: Broadman, 1992], p. 199).

9. See Edwards, *The Gospel According to Mark*, p. 97; James A. Brooks, *Mark*, New American Commentary (Nashville: Broadman), p. 67.

10. J. C. Ryle, *Mark: Expository Thoughts on the Gospels*, Crossway Classic Commentaries (Wheaton, IL: Crossway, 1993), p. 31; David E. Garland, *Mark*, The NIV Application Commentary (Grand Rapids, MI: Zondervan, 1996), p. 107.

Chapter Thirty-three: Lord of Mercy and Justice

1. Jennifer Speake and John Simpson, eds., *The Oxford Dictionary of Proverbs* (New York: Oxford University Press, 2008), p. 255.

2. See James R. Edwards, *The Gospel According to Mark*, Pillar New Testament Commentary (Grand Rapids, MI: Eerdmans, 2002), p. 99. For other examples, see William Barclay, *The Gospel of Mark*, rev. ed. (Philadelphia: Westminster, 1975), p. 67.

3. Perhaps Jesus also has in mind Proverbs 12:10 and Deuteronomy 22:4.

4. I like what C. H. Spurgeon says on this verse: "One wonders that anybody ever thought otherwise. But zeal for externals, and hatred of spiritual religion, when united, create a narrow bigotry as cruel as it is ridiculous" (*The Gospel of the Kingdom* [Pasadena, TX: Pilgrim Publications, repr. 1996], p. 86).

5. It is only five words in Greek.

6. With this said, in this miracle we need to recognize that Jesus sought to provoke his opponents because he sought to die on the cross for the sins of the world. So in a sense while it looks like Jesus is falling into their trap, in reality it is the Pharisees who are falling into his.

7. J. Alec Motyer, *Isaiah*, Tyndale Old Testament Commentaries (Downers Grove, IL: InterVarsity Press, 1999), p. 260.

8. Frederick Dale Bruner, *The Christbook: Matthew 1–12*, 2nd and rev. ed. (Grand Rapids, MI: Eerdmans, 2004), p. 557.

9. Following the Sabbath texts, it is ironic that it is the Gentiles who will hope in Jesus (cf. John 1:11–13; Romans 9—11).

10. Bruner, *The Christbook*, p. 558.

11. See ibid., p. 557.

12. Julia Howe, "Battle Hymn of the Republic," 1861.

13. Ibid., p. 558.

14. Pascal, quoted in David Tracy, (Chicago: University of Chicago Press, 1994), p. 86.

15. This is all true. Yet the Pharisees' apparently rash decision to seek the death penalty "is not the result of a single incident; it is the response to an accumulation of incidents" (Williams L. Lane, *The Gospel of Mark*, New International Commentary on the New Testament [Grand Rapids, MI: Eerdmans, 1974], p. 122). To them, "the evidence against Jesus has been compounding: Sabbath violations (Mark 1:21–25; 2:23–28), fraternizing with sinners (1:40; 2:13–17), disregarding rabbinic custom[s] (2:18–22), [the] presumption to forgive sins (2:10–11)" (Edwards, *The Gospel According to Mark*, p. 101), and also the vain audacity to call himself "the Son of Man" and "the Lord of the Sabbath." The Pharisees had their reasons for wanting to "destroy" Jesus.

16. See W. D. Davies and Dale C. Allison Jr., *A Critical and Exegetical Commentary on the Gospel according to Saint Matthew*, International Critical Commentary, vol. 2 (Edinburgh: T&T Clark, 1988-1997), p. 326.

17. From Charles Wesley, "Hark! the Herald Angels Sing" (1739).

Chapter Thirty-four: Two Kingdoms, One Choice

1. Frederick Dale Bruner, *The Christbook: Matthew 1–12*, 2nd and rev. ed. (Grand Rapids, MI: Eerdmans, 2004), p. 564.

2. D. A. Carson, "Matthew," in *The Expositor's Bible Commentary*, vol. 8 (Grand Rapids, MI: Zondervan, 1984), p. 287.

3. N. T. Wright, *Matthew for Everyone*, vol. 1 (Louisville: Westminster John Knox, 2002), p. 147.

4. Ibid., p. 146.

5. This is not to deny that false prophets can perform miracles (7:21–23; 24:24; 2 Thessalonians 2:9, 10; Revelation 13:13, 14). However, their powers center on "false signs and wonders" (2 Thessalonians 2:9), not on exorcising demons.

6. Some scholars think of it as three, and that is fine. See W. D. Davies and Dale C. Allison Jr., *A Critical and Exegetical Commentary on the Gospel according to Saint Matthew*, International Critical Commentary, vol. 2 (Edinburgh: T&T Clark, 1988-1997), pp. 334, 341.

7. Martin Luther, "A Mighty Fortress Is Our God" (1529).

8. Davies and Allison Jr., *A Critical and Exegetical Commentary on the Gospel according to Saint Matthew*, vol. 2, p. 341.

9. Bruner, *The Christbook*, p. 565.

10. J. F. Walvoord's definition, as quoted in Craig L. Blomberg, *Matthew*, New American Commentary (Nashville: Broadman, 1992), p. 203.

11. J. C. Ryle, *Matthew: Expository Thoughts on the Gospels*, Crossway Classic Commentaries (Wheaton, IL: Crossway, 1993), p. 97.

12. Henry, quoted in Bruner, *The Christbook*, p. 567.

13. Wright, *Matthew for Everyone*, vol. 1, p. 151.

Chapter Thirty-five: Easter and the Evil Generation

1. This is recorded in Eusebius's *Life of Constantine*. I was reminded of it by reading through James T. Brezke, *Consecrated Phrases: A Latin Theological Dictionary* (Collegeville, MN: Liturgical Press, 1998), p. 63.

2. Note that the prepositional phrase "from heaven" modifies *semeion* in the Synoptics in other passages (e.g., 16:1; Mark 8:11; Luke 11:16; 21:11).

3. D. A. Carson notes that adultery was "frequently used by OT prophets to describe the spiritual prostitution and wanton apostasy of Israel (Isa 50:1; 57:3; Jer 3:8; 13:27; 31:32; Ezek 16:15, 32, 35–42; Hos 2:1–7; 3:1 et al.) ("Matthew," in *The Expositor's Bible Commentary*, vol. 8 [Grand Rapids, MI: Zondervan, 1984], p. 295).

4. "Matthew's text seems to make explicit what is implicit in the speeches in Acts, namely, that the resurrection is God's one great sign to Israel (cf. Acts 2:24, 32, 36; 3:15; etc.)." W. D. Davies and Dale C. Allison Jr., *A Critical and Exegetical Commentary on the Gospel according to Saint Matthew*, International Critical Commentary, vol. 2 (Edinburgh: T&T Clark, 1988-1997), p. 355.

5. See Genesis 40:13; 1 Kings 20:29; 2 Chronicles 10:5, 12; Esther 4:16—5:1; Hosea 6:2.

6. As usual, Frederick Dale Bruner is helpful here:

> If one is eager for a perfect match between Jesus' prophecy and actual events in order to get the "three *nights*," an eagerness too close for comfort to the demand for a sign itself, one can refer to the "night" from noon to three on Friday afternoon (27:45), and then to the subsequent Friday and Saturday nights. But surely such harmonizing is unworthy. (*The Christ-*

book: Matthew 1–12, 2nd and rev. ed. [Grand Rapids, MI: Eerdmans, 2004], p. 574.)

7. Taylor, quoted in Frederick Dale Bruner, *The Churchbook: Matthew 13–28*, 2nd and rev. ed. (Grand Rapids, MI: Eerdmans, 2004), p. 682.

8. Bruner, *The Christbook*, p. 574.

9. Ibid., p. 575.

10. Dinesh D'Sousa, *What's So Great About Christianity* (Wheaton, IL: Tyndale, 2007), p. 201.

11. Blaise Pascal, *Pensées* (New York: Oxford University Press, 1999), p. 163.

12. Pascal, quoted in Timothy Keller, *The Reason for God: Belief in an Age of Skepticism* (New York: Dutton), p. 210. I am indebted to Keller's excellent chapter "The Reality of the Resurrection," pp. 201–212.

13. David L. Turner's comment on miracles is helpful:

> No amount of further signs would avail for such people, not even the resurrection of Jesus from the dead (12:40; cf. 28:11–15; Luke 16:27–31; 1 Cor 1:22). This passage also illustrates why Jesus did miracles. Miracles were deeds of power done with compassion for those in need, not spectacular feats designed to convince those already hardened in skepticism. For hearts not hardened in rebellion, comparatively little evidence was needed, as in the case of Nineveh and the queen of Sheba. (*The Gospel of Matthew*, Cornerstone Biblical Commentary [Wheaton, IL: Tyndale, 2005], p. 177.)

14. As Craig S. Keener notes,

> The images of the Ninevites and the queen of Sheba condemning Jesus' generation in Israel at the judgment would have horrified Jesus' hearers, many of whom expected Israel's final vindication against the nations on judgment day (compare Amos 5:18). (*Matthew*, IVP New Testament Commentary Series [Downers Grove, IL: InterVarsity Press, 1997], p. 233.)

15. See John Calvin, *Institutes of the Christian Religion*, Library of Christian Classics, ed. John T. McNeill, trans. Ford Lewis Battles (Philadelphia: Westminster, 1960), II.xv.

Chapter Thirty-six: Focus on the Family

1. "There are in existence over 5,000 Greek manuscripts of the New Testament in whole or in part." F. F. Bruce, *The New Testament Documents: Are They Reliable?* 5th revised ed. (Downers Grove, IL: InterVarsity Press, repr. 1990), p. 16.

2. On textual variants, see Bruce M. Metzger and Bart D. Ehrman, *The Text of the New Testament: Its Transmission, Corruption, and Restoration*, 4th ed. (New York: Oxford University Press, 2005).

3. See Matthew 5:22–24, 47; 7:3–5; 18:15, 21, 35; 23:8; 25:40; 28:10.

4. Matthew 1:11; 4:18, 21; 10:2, 21; 13:55; 14:3 (note "brothers" in 13:55, then "brother" in 14:3); 17:1; 19:29; 20:24; 22:24, 25.

5. I agree with D. A. Carson:

> The most natural way to understand "brothers" (v. 46) is that the term refers to sons of Mary and Joseph and thus to brothers of Jesus on his

mother's side. To support the dogma of Mary's perpetual virginity, a notion foreign to the NT and to the earliest church fathers, Roman Catholic scholars have suggested that "brothers" can have a wider meaning than male relatives (Acts 22:1). Yet it is very doubtful whether such a meaning is valid here, for it raises insuperable problems. For instance, if "brothers" refers to Joseph's sons by an earlier marriage, not Jesus but Joseph's firstborn would have been legal heir to David's throne. The second theory—that "brothers" refers to sons of a sister of Mary also named "Mary"—faces the unlikelihood of two sisters having the same name. All things considered, the attempts to extend the meaning of "brothers" in this pericope, despite McHugh's best efforts, are nothing less than farfetched exegesis in support of a dogma that originated much later than the NT (see on 1:25; Luke 2:7; cf. Broadus on 13:55-56). ("Matthew," in *The Expositor's Bible Commentary*, vol. 8 [Grand Rapids, MI: Zondervan, 1984], p. 299.)

6. Daniel J. Harrington, *The Gospel of Matthew*, Sacra Pagina (Collegeville, MN: Liturgical Press, 1991), p. 191. Rudolf Schnackenburg notes, "Even some more recent Catholic exegetes incline toward the prevailing Protestant view that tradition spoke of Jesus' actual brothers and sisters" (*The Gospel of Matthew*, trans. Robert R. Barr [Grand Rapids, MI: Eerdmans, 2002], p. 138).

7. David L. Turner, *The Gospel of Matthew*, Cornerstone Biblical Commentary (Wheaton, IL: Tyndale, 2005), p. 178.

8. Here to read "brothers" as "cousins" makes little literary sense. If "brothers" means "cousins" the ironic edge is dulled.

9. On the authorship of James, see Douglas J. Moo, *The Letter of James*, Pillar New Testament Commentary (Grand Rapids, MI: Eerdmans, 2000), pp. 20–22.

10. "Prayer to Our Lady, Assumed into Heaven" is another example:

> Immaculate Virgin, Mother of Jesus and our Mother, we believe in your triumphant assumption into heaven where the angels and saints acclaim you as Queen. We join them in praising you and bless the Lord who raised you above all creatures. With them we offer you our devotion and love. We are confident that you watch over our daily efforts and needs, and we take comfort from our faith in the coming resurrection. We look to you, our life, our sweetness, and our hope. After this earthly life, show us Jesus, the blest fruit of your womb, O kind, O loving, O Sweet Virgin Mary. Amen.

11. Ironically a book that was written to defend Roman Catholic doctrine cites many of the key texts that show that the Protestant position is more catholic or universally accepted (Luigi Gambero, *Mary and the Fathers of the Church: The Blessed Virgin Mary in Patristic Thought* [San Francisco: Ignatius, 1999]).

12. Michael Green, *The Message of Matthew*, The Bible Speaks Today (Downers Grove, IL: InterVarsity Press, 2000), p. 151.

13. Bonnard, quoted in Frederick Dale Bruner, *The Christbook: Matthew 1–12*, 2nd and rev. ed. (Grand Rapids, MI: Eerdmans, 2004), pp. 582, 583.

Chapter Thirty-seven: The Purpose of Parables

1. Blomberg notes, "The farmer's practice sounds strange to us. But in Jesus' world it seems to have reflected standard procedure for broadcast sowing." For more on this, see Craig L. Blomberg, *Preaching the Parables: From Responsible Interpretation to Powerful Proclamation* (Grand Rapids, MI: Baker, 2004), p. 106.

2. According to W. D. Davies and Dale C. Allison Jr., "Their effect—illuminates or darkens—depends upon the status of the hearer. Knowledge is rewarded with knowledge, ignorance with ignorance" (*A Critical and Exegetical Commentary on the Gospel according to Saint Matthew*, International Critical Commentary, vol. 2 (Edinburgh: T&T Clark, 1988-1997), p. 391). On the element of knowing see also p. 389.

3. Note how the purpose of revealing truth gets more attention or at least more lines. D. A. Carson notes that the latter two sections of the text "are a well-ordered chiasm whose inversion echoes OT form (e.g., Ps 89:28–37) and emphasizes the climax of judgment and mercy (so K. E. Bailey, *Poet and Peasant* [Grand Rapids: Eerdmans, 1976], pp. 61f.)" ("Matthew," in *The Expositor's Bible Commentary*, vol. 8 [Grand Rapids, MI: Zondervan, 1984], p. 306). However, see how judgment, not mercy, is at the center! Below is Bailey's structural outline:

Therefore I speak to them in parables,

1 because seeing *they see not* and hearing *they hear not,* nor understand.
2 And *it is fulfilled to them* the *prophecy* of Isaiah which says,
3 "Hearing you shall hear and shall not understand,
4 and seeing you *shall see* and shall *not perceive*.
5 For this people's *heart* is become dull
6 and the *ears* are dull of hearing
7 and their *eyes* they have closed,
7' lest they should perceive with the *eyes*
6' and hear with the *ear*
5' and understand with the *heart*, and should turn again and I should heal them."
4' But blessed are *your eyes*, for they see,
3' and your *ears*, for they *hear*.
2' For truly I *say unto you* that many *prophets* and righteous men
1' desired to see what *you see*, and *did not see*, and to hear what *you hear,* and *did not hear*.

4. While the Parable of the Good Samaritan does fit this theory, that parable is the exception rather than the rule. It illustrates and answers the question, "Who is my neighbor?" According to the passage we have before us, the rule is that parables are not clever short stories designed to attract the attention of sluggish minds or merely visual aids designed to illustrate a simple point.

5. Francis J. Moloney, *The Gospel of Mark: A Commentary* (Peabody, MA: Hendrickson, 2002), p. 90.

6. Davies and Allison Jr. note:

> Matthew's [*oti*] makes the parables a response to unbelief: they are uttered because people see and do not see, because they hear and do not hear. This puts the emphasis unambiguously on human responsibility. More particularly, it makes the parables a consequence of the unbelief that has withstood Jesus' gracious teaching and salvific ministry (see Mt 8–12). For Matthew, Jesus did not speak in parables to outsiders until hostility raised its ugly head. (*A Critical and Exegetical Commentary on the Gospel according to Saint Matthew*, vol. 2, p. 392.)

7. Donald English, *The Message of Mark*, The Bible Speaks Today (Downers Grove, IL: InterVarsity Press, 1992), p. 94.

8. Blomberg, *Preaching the Parables*, p. 110. See also Frederick Dale Bruner, *The Churchbook: Matthew 13–28*, 2nd and rev. ed. (Grand Rapids, MI: Eerdmans, 2004), p. 12, where he writes, "Augustine somewhere told the story of two men in church: one stood and accepted the message; the other remained seated and rejected it. And Augustine concluded: 'Let him who stands give glory to God; let him who remained seated blame himself.'"

9. Blomberg, *Preaching the Parables*, p. 110.

10. David E. Garland, *Mark*, The NIV Application Commentary (Grand Rapids, MI: Zondervan, 1996), p. 158.

11. Ibid.

12. See James R. Edwards, *The Gospel According to Mark*, Pillar New Testament Commentary (Grand Rapids, MI: Eerdmans, 2002), p. 133.

13. See Luther on this tough issue (in Bruner, *The Churchbook*, p. 15).

14. Bruner comments:

> This admonition fits the call to be fishers of men (4:17) as well as salt and light to the earth (5:13–14). Calvin (2:84) notes of Christ, "His work in teaching them was not only aimed at making them wise for themselves but that they might impart to others what had been deposited to them." (in Ibid., p. 55.)

Chapter Thirty-eight: Three Ways of Disaster, Three Grades of Glory

1. See Elizabeth Barrett Browning, "Aurora Leigh" (1857), Book VII, l, pp. 812–826. Browning called it "a novel in verse."

2. Craig L. Blomberg calls it the "climactic focus" (*Matthew*, New American Commentary [Nashville: Broadman, 1992], p. 215).

3. Cyril of Alexandria, quoted in *Mark*, eds. Thomas C. Oden and Christopher A. Hall, Ancient Christian Commentary on Scripture, NT II (Downers Grove, IL: InterVarsity Press, 1998), p. 53.

4. Donald English, *The Message of Mark*, The Bible Speaks Today (Downers Grove, IL: InterVarsity Press, 1992), p. 94.

5. James Montgomery Boice, T*he Gospel of Matthew*, vol. 1 (Grand Rapids, MI: Baker, 2001), p. 235.

6. Jesus' rejection in Nazareth foreshadows his rejection in Jerusalem.

7. Craig L. Blomberg, *Preaching the Parables: From Responsible Interpretation to Power Proclamation* (Grand Rapids, MI: Baker, 2004), p. 112.

8. "There is no trace in Matthew of any doctrine that we can have instant salvation apart from constant perseverance." Michael Green, *The Message of Matthew*, The Bible Speaks Today (Downers Grove, IL: InterVarsity Press, 2000), p. 160.

9. Marty, quoted in Boice, *The Gospel of Matthew*, p. 243.

10. I like very much what John Chrysostom said of these verses: Jesus "warned not of 'the world' but of the 'care of the world; not 'riches' as such but the 'deceitfulness of riches.' Let us not place the blame on what we possess, but on our own corrupt mind. For it is possible to be rich and not be deceived. It is possible to be in this world, and not be choked with its cares" ("The Gospel of Matthew," Homily 44.6, quoted in *Mark*, eds. Thomas C. Oden and Christopher A. Hall, Ancient Christian Commentary on Scripture, NT II [Downers Grove, IL: InterVarsity Press, 1998], p. 53).

11. James A. Brooks, *Mark*, New American Commentary (Nashville: Broadman, 1991), p. 79.

12. Ibid., p. 80.

13. Robert Gundry's terms (*Mark: A Commentary on His Apology for the Cross* [Grand Rapids, MI: Eerdmans, 1993], p. 206), used in David E. Garland, *Mark*, The NIV Application Commentary (Grand Rapids, MI: Zondervan, 1996), p. 164.

Chapter Thirty-nine: Seven Parables; Three Themes

1. Note the numerology—the perfect number seven conquering the imperfect number thirteen.

2. "The image recalls OT passages that picture a great kingdom as a large tree with birds flocking to its branches (Judg 9:15; Ezek 17:22–24; 31:3–14; Dan 4:7–23)." D. A. Carson, "Matthew," in *The Expositor's Bible Commentary*, vol. 8 (Grand Rapids, MI: Zondervan, 1984), p. 317.

3. Michael Green, *The Message of Matthew*, The Bible Speaks Today (Downers Grove, IL: InterVarsity Press, 2000), p. 158.

4. "The net here is not the small one used by modern anglers to bring individual fish into a boat, but a large net or seine with weights on the bottom and floats on the top that encircles many fish." David L. Turner, *The Gospel of Matthew*, Cornerstone Biblical Commentary (Wheaton, IL: Tyndale, 2005), p. 193.

5. Craig L. Blomberg, *Matthew*, New American Commentary (Nashville: Broadman, 1992), p. 220.

6. For this paragraph, see Green, *The Message of Matthew*, p. 158.

7. Carson writes,

> On "Son of Man," see on 8:20. The title recurs at v. 41: Jesus is the one who both sows the good seed (v. 37) and directs the harvest. One of the most significant details in Jesus' parables is the way key images that in the OT apply exclusively to God, or occasionally to God's Messiah, now stand for Jesus himself. These images include sower, director of the harvest, rock, shepherd, bridegroom, father, giver of forgiveness, vineyard owner, lord, and king (cf. Philip B. Payne, "Jesus' Implicit Claim to Deity in His Parables," *Trinity Journal* [1981]: 3–23). ("Matthew," p. 325.)

8. Scholars today debate whether Jesus is speaking of the church or the world, especially with the Parable of the Weeds. I think his language is intentionally elusive.

For example, in verse 38 Jesus says, "The field is the world," and "the weeds are the sons of the evil one," but then in verse 41 he speaks of the angels gathering the weeds "out of his kingdom" on behalf of the Son of Man. The Parable of the Wedding Feast (22:2–14) is perhaps the best cross-reference in making sense of the Parable of the Weeds. There we have three groups of people: (1) those invited who refused to come, (2) those invited (the called) who came but were not properly dressed for a wedding—the lawless within the church (cf. 7:22, 23; 25:10–12, 24–30, 41–46), and (3) those invited (the chosen) and properly dressed.

9. You want God to judge all evil right now, but are you ready for him to judge you? According to my count, judgment is talked about in twenty-four different sections in Matthew (3:7–12; 5:21–30; 7:13–27; 8:11, 12; 8:28–32; 10:12–15; 10:28–33; 11:22–24; 12:36; 12:41–45; 13:4–16; 13:30, 40–42; 13:48–50; 16:27; 18:8, 9; 18:34; 21:12, 13, 18–20; 21:40–45; 22:2–14; 23:33; 24:30; 24:37–41; 24:48–51; 25:1–46; cf. 22:44; 23:16, 38; 24:2, 14; 26:64), and Jesus is the speaker in all but one of those sections. In 3:7–12 John the Baptist speaks of judgment (that's the one exception). But even he ends that section, saying of Jesus, "His winnowing fork is in his hand, and he will clear his threshing floor and gather his wheat into the barn, but the chaff he will burn with unquenchable fire" (v. 12). So I guess it is really twenty-four out of twenty-four! Jesus talks about judgment. And I contend that every instance is a gracious invitation.

10. Quoted without reference by J. C. Ryle, *Matthew: Expository Thoughts on the Gospels*, Crossway Classic Commentaries (Wheaton, IL: Crossway, 1993), p. 107.

11. Carson comments:

> Derrett (*Law*, pp. 1–16) has pointed out that under rabbinic law if a workman came on a treasure in a field and lifted it out, it would belong to his master, the field's owner; but here the man is careful not to lift the treasure out till he has bought the field. So the parable deals with neither the legality nor the morality of the situation (as with the parable of the thief in the night) but with the value of the treasure, which is worth every sacrifice. When the man buys the field at such sacrifice, he possesses far more than the price paid (cf. 10:39). ("Matthew," p. 328.)

Blomberg is likewise helpful:

> One should not worry about the man's ethics in hiding the treasure. We need neither justify his behavior nor imitate it. This is simply part of the story line that helps to make sense of the plot. Jesus frequently tells parables in which unscrupulous characters nevertheless display some virtue from which Christians can learn (cf. esp. Luke 16:1–8; 18:1–8). (*Matthew*, p. 223.)

12. Blomberg, *Matthew*, p. 223.

13. Carson, "*Matthew*," p. 328.

Chapter Forty: The Headless Prophet and the Heartless King, Part 1

1. Boring notes that this is the only story in either Matthew or Mark "not directly concerned with Jesus" (p. 139), as quoted in Frederick Dale Bruner, *The Churchbook: Matthew 13–28*, 2nd and rev. ed. (Grand Rapids, MI: Eerdmans, 2004), p. 63.

2. Ibid. W. D. Davies and Dale C. Allison Jr. list six parallels between John's passion and Jesus' (*A Critical and Exegetical Commentary on the Gospel according to Saint Matthew*, International Critical Commentary, vol. 2 [Edinburgh: T&T Clark, 1988-1997], p. 476).

3. "Unbelief begets not only misunderstanding (vv. 1–2) but also violent opposition to Jesus and those on his side (vv. 3–13; cf. also 13:53–8)" (Davies and Allison Jr., *A Critical and Exegetical Commentary on the Gospel according to Saint Matthew*, vol. 2, p. 465).

4. In William Barclay, *The Gospel of Mark*, rev. ed. (Philadelphia: Westminster, 1975), p. 149.

5. The territory of the Nabatean kingdom would be located in present-day Jordan, southern Syria, southern Israel, and northwestern Saudi Arabia. Hoehner (pp. 136–146) speaks of how Herod Antipas, due to his divorce, found himself at war with his first father-in-law (see Davies and Allison Jr., *A Critical and Exegetical Commentary on the Gospel according to Saint Matthew*, vol. 2, pp. 470, 471, n. 34).

6. Josephus, *Jewish War* I, 14.4.

7. See Davies and Allison Jr., *A Critical and Exegetical Commentary on the Gospel according to Saint Matthew*, vol. 2, p. 469.

8. ". . . (cf. m. *'Adob. Zar.* 1.3; SB 1, pp. 680-1; Origen, *Comm. On Mt.* 10:22.)" In ibid., p. 472.

9. Josephus, *Antiquities*, XVIII, v. 4.

10. "What sort of dance was performed? Was it lewd or unseemly? And what about Antipas' character? Were his scruples such that he would have been troubled by an indecent spectacle? Or should we hesitate to put anything past a man whose father and example was Herod the Great?" (Davies and Allison Jr., *A Critical and Exegetical Commentary on the Gospel according to Saint Matthew*, vol. 2, p. 472).

11. Ahasuerus, the King of Persia, said to Esther (three times), "What is it, Queen Esther? What is your request? It shall be given you, even to the half of my kingdom" (see Esther 5:3, 6; 7:2).

12. John Nolland, *The Gospel of Matthew*, New International Greek Testament Commentary (Grand Rapids, MI: Eerdmans, 2005), p. 579.

13. On foolish oaths in the Bible, see Judges 11:30; 1 Samuel 14:24, 45.

14. Then Freud could say that the solution is for Herod first to become conscious of these unresolved conflicts buried in the deep recesses of his unconscious mind and then to channel his pent-up past (and sexual energy) into positive social, artistic, or political achievements.

15. Bruner comments:

> Herod is undone by his own sensuality. Overwhelmed by the sensual in the first place, he seduces his brother's wife. Now amid the sensual pleasures of a party, overcome again by a pleasurable woman—this time the dancing daughter of his illegally gotten wife—he plunges again into excess. (*The Churchbook*, p. 64.)

16. R. Kent Hughes and Bryan Chapell, *1–2 Timothy and Titus*, Preaching the Word (Wheaton, IL: Crossway, 2000), p. 53.

17. Cranmer, quoted in ibid., p. 54.

18. Barclay, *The Gospel of Mark*, p. 147.

19. From Sir Walter Scott, "Canto XVII," *Marmion: A Tale of Flodden Field in Six Cantos.*

20. See Mark Connelly's sermon at http://www.sermoncentral.com/sermons/oh-what-a-tangled-web-we-weave-mark-connelly-sermon-on-sin-general-60590.asp; accessed on April 15, 2010.

21. See ibid.

Chapter Forty-one: The Headless Prophet and the Heartless King, Part 2

1. Quoted in William Barclay, *The Gospel of Mark*, rev. ed. (Philadelphia: Westminster, 1975), p. 152.

2. John Nolland comments: "John was critical of the new marriage as violating OT law. It was not just the fact of divorce, but that the specific provisions of Lv. 18:16; 20:21 were being violated. What Herod had done was considered to be a form of incest within the family" (*The Gospel of Matthew*, New International Greek Testament Commentary [Grand Rapids, MI: Eerdmans, 2005], p. 582). Josephus speaks of Herodias as "parted from a living husband" to marry "her husband's brother" and says this was to "flout the way of our fathers" (*Antiquities* 18.136).

3. See W. D. Davies and Dale C. Allison Jr., *A Critical and Exegetical Commentary on the Gospel according to Saint Matthew*, International Critical Commentary, vol. 2 (Edinburgh: T&T Clark, 1988-1997), p. 470.

4. James R. Edwards, *The Gospel According to Mark*, Pillar New Testament Commentary (Grand Rapids, MI: Eerdmans, 2002), p. 188.

5. J. C. Ryle, *Mark: Expository Thoughts on the Gospels*, Crossway Classic Commentaries (Wheaton, IL: Crossway, 1993), pp. 87, 88.

6. C. H. Spurgeon, *The Gospel of the Kingdom* (Pasadena, TX: Pilgrim Publications, repr. 1996), p. 112.

7. Edwards, *The Gospel According to Mark*, p. 189.

8. See Davies and Allison Jr., *A Critical and Exegetical Commentary on the Gospel according to Saint Matthew*, vol. 2, p. 476; cf. Dale C. Allison Jr., "Foreshadowing the Passion," *Studies in Matthew: Interpretation Past and Present* (Grand Rapids, MI: Baker, 2005), pp. 225, 226.

9. Translators phrase it various ways. See, for example, "The ofterner we are mown down by you, the more in number we grow; *the blood of Christians is seed*" (Tertullian, *Apology*, Ante-Nicene Fathers, vol. 3 [Peabody, MA: Hendrickson, repr. 1999], p. 55).

10. Kierkegaard, quoted in David E. Garland, *Mark*, The NIV Application Commentary (Grand Rapids, MI: Zondervan, 1996), p. 249.

Chapter Forty-two: Contemplation and Compassion

1. He was like us in every respect (i.e., he had a human body, heart, mind, will, emotions, etc.)—except for sin (see Hebrews 2:17; 4:15).

2. Donald A. Hagner, *Matthew 14–28*, Word Biblical Commentary, vol. 33b (Nashville: Thomas Nelson, 1993), p. 422.

3. "Jesus' intended goal is to isolate himself for a period." John Nolland, *The Gospel of Matthew*, New International Greek Testament Commentary (Grand Rapids, MI: Eerdmans, 2005), p. 589.

4. A number of notable commentators, such as Ulrich Luz, surmise that "Jesus withdraws because of the threat from Israel's leaders" (Luz, *Matthew 8–20*, Hermeneia [Minneapolis: Fortress, 2001], p. 313). However, I favor Hagner's reading. Hagner begins,

> Presumably Jesus had gone . . . "privately to a deserted place," in order to pray, the death of John perhaps turning his mind to his own approaching passion (cf. v 23). There is no indication at all that Jesus is attempting to flee from Herod Antipas (or, indeed, that Jesus was now newly threatened by the latter), despite the assumption of many commentators. (*Matthew 14–28,* p. 417.)

Later he continues,

> The solitude of Jesus is the important motif for Matthew at this point. The other references to Jesus praying . . . in Matthew are in 26:36, 39, 42, 44 (cf. Luke 9:28), all in connection with his own imminent suffering and death. In the present instance, the same thoughts may be presumed to be in Jesus' mind, prompted perhaps by the report of John the Baptist's death. (Ibid., p. 422.)

While R. T. France and John Nolland agree with Luz (see France, *The Gospel of Matthew*, New International Commentary on the New Testament [Grand Rapids, MI: Eerdmans, 2007], p. 560; Nolland, *The Gospel of Matthew*, p. 588), nevertheless, they make interesting (supporting Hagner?) observations. For example, France notes that this is "indeed the only place after the initial period in the wilderness (4:1–11) where Matthew specifically mentions that Jesus chose to be truly alone" (pp. 568, 569). Based on this observation, before he dismisses the notion as an argument from silence, France admits, "It would be possible therefore to read this unusual note as indicating a particular crisis at this point in Jesus' ministry" (p. 569). I'll insert here that one doesn't have to take it necessarily as "a crisis," but it could be a time of serious contemplation on the cross. Nolland's insights are as follows. After noting that the only other place Jesus prays alone (though not intentionally, however) is Gethsemane, he asks, "Is the substance of Jesus' prayer introduced as a puzzle here, to be clarified in his coming Passion? The christological focus of the material from 13:54 to 16:20 prepares for the beginning of the Passion predictions in 16:21 (note already the intimations of the Passion in 13:54–58 and 14:1–12)" (p. 599). Again, I find these key observations to be additional support for Hagner's argument.

5. "Jesus is hurt by the news of John the Baptist's death and wants to get away by himself." Frederick Dale Bruner, *The Churchbook: Matthew 13–28*, 2nd and rev. ed. (Grand Rapids, MI: Eerdmans, 2004), p. 67.

6. *m. Ber.* 6:1.

7. Ulrich Luz, *Matthew 8–20*, Hermeneia (Minneapolis: Fortress, 2001), p. 397.

8. Also note the possible allusion in 14:21 to Exodus 12:37.

9. Another possible connection with Moses is Jesus alone on the mountain (compare Exodus 24:2).

10. The first to point out the connection to this text was Tertullian (see *Adv. Marc.* 4:21, as noted in W. D. Davies and Dale C. Allison Jr., *A Critical and Exegeti-*

cal Commentary on the Gospel according to Saint Matthew, International Critical Commentary, vol. 2 (Edinburgh: T&T Clark, 1988-1997), p. 482.

11. Frederick Dale Bruner, *The Churchbook: Matthew 13–28*, 2nd and rev. ed. (Grand Rapids, MI: Eerdmans, 2004), p. 68.

Chapter Forty-three: It Is I AM

1. If it is not obvious from our text in Matthew, John notes that the wind was "strong" (John 6:18).

2. Frederick Dale Bruner notes:

> Jesus' "*I am*" (*ego eimi*) is not just an everyday self-identification formula ("I am he"); it is a divine Self-Revelation along the lines of Isa 43:1–4 (cf. Schnackenburg, 1:138; Gundry, 299). . . . See the other great "I Am's" in ancient Scripture: Deut 32:39; Isa 41:4; 43:10; 45:18–19; 48:12; 51:12. Especially in combination with the "Fear not," the "I am" has the aura of God's ancient comforting of his people: "Fear not, for I am . . ." (Gen 15:1 . . . 28:13; 46:3; Isa 41:13; Luz, 2:408). (*The Churchbook: Matthew 13–28*, 2nd and rev. ed. [Grand Rapids, MI: Eerdmans, 2004], p. 75.)

3. Ibid., p. 73.

4. W. D. Davies and Dale C. Allison Jr. point out, "Clearly the theophanic action of Yahweh has become the epiphanic action of Jesus (cf. Heil, pp. 56–7). The powers of the deity have become incarnate in God's Son" (*A Critical and Exegetical Commentary on the Gospel according to Saint Matthew,* International Critical Commentary, vol. 2 [Edinburgh: T&T Clark, 1988-1997], p. 504). Furthermore, "What matters is not that Jesus has done the seemingly impossible but that he has performed action which the Old Testament associates with Yahweh alone" (p. 510).

5. Ibid., vol. 2, pp. 512, 513.

6. J. C. Ryle, *Matthew: Expository Thoughts on the Gospels*, Crossway Classic Commentaries (Wheaton, IL: Crossway, 1993), p. 121.

7. Bruner, *The Churchbook*, p. 78.

8. John Calvin, in ibid., p. 77.

9. Matthew Henry, in Bruner, *The Churchbook*, p. 76.

10. Davies and Allison Jr., *A Critical and Exegetical Commentary on the Gospel according to Saint Matthew*, vol. 2, pp. 513, 514.

11. A wonderful example of Peter's courage is found in Acts 4:18–24. In verse 24, note the similar themes of prayer and "the sea":

> So they called them and charged them not to speak or teach at all in the name of Jesus. But *Peter* and John answered them, "Whether it is right in the sight of God to listen to you rather than to God, you must judge, for we cannot but speak of what we have seen and heard." And when they had further threatened them, they let them go, finding no way to punish them, because of the people, for all were praising God for what had happened. For the man on whom this sign of healing was performed was more than forty years old. When they were released, they went to their friends and reported what the chief priests and the elders had said to them. And when they heard

it, *they lifted their voices together to God* and said, "Sovereign Lord, who made the heaven and the earth and *the sea* and everything in them . . ."

12. Cf. 6:25–34.

13. On the topic of faith, James Montgomery Boice writes:

> What is faith? Faith is not merely knowing that Jesus is the Son of God and believing that he can save us from sin but actually committing ourselves to him. I have often highlighted the three essential elements of faith by using the Latin words for them: *notitia*, *assensus*, and *fiducia*. *Notitia* refers to faith's content. It concerns understanding the doctrines of the gospel, particularly who Jesus claimed to be and what he accomplished on the cross. *Assensus* means agreement, assenting to the doctrines that are taught. It is like saying, "I understand what the Bible teaches about Jesus, and I believe it. I believe that Jesus is the Son of God and that his death was a true atoning death for human sin." *Notitia* and *assensus* are two necessary parts of faith, but they are not yet saving faith in the full biblical sense. True faith also involves *fiducia*, which is an actual trust in Jesus as the Son of God and Savior. It means that a person actually commits himself or herself to Jesus. To use the image of the story, it means stepping out toward him in faith. (*The Gospel of Matthew*, vol. 2 [Grand Rapids, MI: Baker, 2001], p. 274.)

Chapter Forty-four: The Damning Effects of Spiritual Blindness

1. I'm not claiming that the scribes and Pharisees were there to witness either of those miracles. However, I am making a reasonable assumption that news of those miracles reached their ears, and that is why, or one of the reasons why, they traveled from Jerusalem (see 15:1), to see for themselves what this man could do.

2. See Exodus 30:17–21; 40:13; cf. Leviticus 22:1–6.

3. See *m. Ned.* 1:2-4; 9:7, as cited in Craig L. Blomberg, *Matthew*, New American Commentary (Nashville: Broadman, 1992), p. 238.

4. Slight rephrase of Douglas Wilson, *Mother Kirk: Essays and Forays in Practical Ecclesiology* (Moscow, ID: Canon, 2001), p. 61.

5. David E. Garland, *Mark*, The NIV Application Commentary (Grand Rapids, MI: Zondervan, 1996), p. 277.

6. Frederick Dale Bruner, *The Churchbook: Matthew 13–28*, 2nd and rev. ed. (Grand Rapids, MI: Eerdmans, 2004), p. 95.

7. Bengel, quoted in ibid.

8. Bruner, *The Churchbook: Matthew 13–28*, p. 94.

9. Ibid., p. 93.

10. See J. C. Ryle, *Matthew: Expository Thoughts on the Gospels*, Crossway Classic Commentaries (Wheaton, IL: Crossway, 1993), p. 126.

11. Bengel, quoted in Bruner, *The Churchbook*, p. 95.

Chapter Forty-five: Feeding the "Dogs"

1. See Grant R. Osborne, *Matthew*, Exegetical Commentary on the New Testament (Grand Rapids, MI: Zondervan, 2010), pp. 1092–1095.

2. Ibid., pp. 1096–1099.

3. Speaking on John's Gospel, Craig Blomberg spoke of "Jesus' shockingly gracious overtures to the outcasts, so characteristic of the Synoptics." "Jesus as Purifier: *Das Plausibilitätskriterium and the Fourth Gospel,*" ETS, November 16, 2011.

4. Frederick Dale Bruner, *The Churchbook: Matthew 13–28*, 2nd and rev. ed. (Grand Rapids, MI: Eerdmans, 2004), p. 97.

5. Craig L. Blomberg, *Matthew*, New American Commentary (Nashville: Broadman, 1992), p. 242.

6. Ibid., p. 244.

7. See Bruner, *The Churchbook*, p. 102.

8. James A. Brooks, *Mark*, New American Commentary (Nashville: Broadman, 1991), p. 125.

9. Ibid.

10. Ibid.

11. Cf. Francis J. Moloney, *The Gospel of Mark: A Commentary* (Peabody, MA: Hendrickson, 2002), p. 155.

12. James R. Edwards, *The Gospel According to Mark*, Pillar New Testament Commentary (Grand Rapids, MI: Eerdmans, 2002), p. 231.

13. "It is fascinating and perhaps highly symbolic that whereas twelve basketfuls were taken up after the feeding of the five thousand (twelve is highly appropriate in this Jewish feeding of the twelve tribes of Israel), seven basketfuls were taken up after this Gentile feeding of the four thousand—and seven is the number of completeness. It may fittingly symbolize meeting the needs of the entire world: *all ate and were satisfied*." Michael Green, *The Message of Matthew*, The Bible Speaks Today (Downers Grove, IL: InterVarsity Press, 2000), p. 174, n. 19.

14. Sand, quoted in Bruner, *The Churchbook*, p. 106.

15. Paul E. Miller, *A Praying Life: Connecting with God in a Distracting World* (Colorado Springs: NavPress, 2009), p. 190.

16. N. T. Wright, *Matthew for Everyone*, vol. 1 (Louisville: Westminster John Knox, 2002), p. 201.

17. In *Auslegungen der Reformatoren*, ed. G. Friedrich et al., p. 81, quoted in Bruner, *The Churchbook*, p. 103.

18. See "The Doctrine of Catholic-Evangelical Faith (Catholic Evangelicalism)," in Bruner, *The Churchbook*, p. 82.

Chapter Forty-six: Dual Dangers

1. For this idea I am indebted to Frederick Dale Bruner, *The Churchbook: Matthew 13–28*, 2nd and rev. ed. (Grand Rapids, MI: Eerdmans, 2004), p. 115.

2. Douglas Sean O'Donnell, *God's Lyrics: Rediscovering Worship Through Old Testament Songs* (Phillipsburg, NJ: P&R, 2010).

3. W. D. Davies and Dale C. Allison Jr., *A Critical and Exegetical Commentary on the Gospel according to Saint Matthew*, International Critical Commentary, vol. 2 (Edinburgh: T&T Clark, 1988-1997), p. 579.

4. Madeleine L'Engle, "The Irrational Season," *The Birth of Wonder* (New York: HarperCollins, 1977), p. 21.

5. On this point see James Montgomery Boice, *The Gospel of Matthew*, vol. 1 (Grand Rapids, MI: Baker, 2001), p. 297.

6. For more on the sign of Jonah, see Chapter 35 of this book.

7. J. C. Ryle, *Matthew: Expository Thoughts on the Gospels*, Crossway Classic Commentaries (Wheaton, IL: Crossway, 1993), p. 138.

8. Bruner, *The Churchbook*, p. 115.

9. Ibid., p. 114

10. Ibid.

Chapter Forty-seven: The Great Confession

1. Frederick Dale Bruner, *The Churchbook: Matthew 13–28*, 2nd and rev. ed. (Grand Rapids, MI: Eerdmans, 2004), p. 120.

2. See Raymond E. Brown, *The Death of the Messiah*, vol. 2 (New York: Doubleday, 1994), pp. 473–480.

3. On the importance of the definite article, see Cyril of Alexandria, "Fragment 190," quoted in *Matthew 14–28*, ed. Manlio Simonetti, Ancient Christian Commentary on Scripture, NT Ib (Downers Grove, IL: InterVarsity Press, 2001), p. 45.

4. Bruner, *The Churchbook*, p. 126.

5. Jonathan Edwards, *The Works of Jonathan Edwards*, ed. Edward Hickman, vol. 1 (Carlisle, PA: Banner of Truth, repr.1992), p. 581.

6. Ibid., vol. 1, p. 379.

7. Bruner, *The Churchbook*, p. 125.

8. On the history of interpretation, see Ulrich Luz, *Matthew 8–20*, Hermeneia (Minneapolis: Fortress, 2001), pp. 472–480.

9. To name a few, this view was held by Gregory of Nyssa, Isidore of Pelusium, Hilary, Theodoret, Theophances, Theophylact, John Chrysostom, Origen, Eusebius, Ambrose, Theodore of Mopusuestia, and John of Damascus.

10. See Bruner, *The Churchbook*, p. 129.

11. It is interesting that Jesus' "rock" talk is only found in Matthew's Gospel. Also of interest is that Matthew does not record, as John does, Peter going to the tomb.

12. Note that throughout Matthew, Simon Peter is almost always called "Peter." Thus I don't view this as a naming ceremony.

13. A possible exception is Ezekiel 26:4, 14.

14. Cf. Deuteronomy 32:3, 4; 1 Samuel 2:1, 2; 2 Samuel 22:1–3; 23:3; Psalm 78:35; 95:1; Isaiah 26:4.

15. Compare Heidelberg Catechism (Q 84): "How is the kingdom of heaven opened and shut by the preaching of the gospel?" Answer: "By proclaiming and openly witnessing, according to the command of Christ, to believers, one and all, that, whenever they receive the promise of the gospel by a true faith, all their sins are really forgiven them of God for the sake of Christ's merits; and on the contrary, by proclaiming and witnessing to all unbelievers and such as do not sincerely repent that the wrath of God and eternal condemnation abide on them so long as they are not converted."

16. J. C. Ryle, *Matthew: Expository Thoughts on the Gospels*, Crossway Classic Commentaries (Wheaton, IL: Crossway, 1993), p. 140. Cf. Michael Green, *The Message of Matthew*, The Bible Speaks Today (Downers Grove, IL: InterVarsity Press, 2000), p. 181.

17. Green, *The Message of Matthew*, p. 177.

Chapter Forty-eight: No Cross; No Crown

1. I did read the book the week I preached this, but I am indebted to N. T Wright's use of Carroll's work as an introduction to his commentary on this section of Matthew (*Matthew for Everyone*, vol. 2 [Louisville: Westminster John Knox, 2002], pp. 9, 10).

2. Jesus would teach them this same message about ten more times; see 17:9, 22, 23; 20:17–19, 28; 26:2, 12, 20–32; cf. 17:12; 26:54.

3. Frederick Dale Bruner, *The Churchbook: Matthew 13–28*, 2nd and rev. ed. (Grand Rapids, MI: Eerdmans, 2004), p. 141.

4. George Bennard, "The Old Rugged Cross" (1913).

5. David L. Turner, *The Gospel of Matthew*, Cornerstone Biblical Commentary (Wheaton, IL: Tyndale, 2005), p. 224.

6. This idea is taken from Bruner, *The Churchbook*, p. 145.

7. See ibid., p. 144.

8. See Bengel, quoted in ibid., p. 146.

9. John Wesley, quoted in Amy A. Kass, *Giving Well, Doing Good: Readings for Thoughtful Philanthropists* (Bloomington, IN: Indiana University Press, 2008), p. 426.

10. Bruner, *The Churchbook*, pp. 119, 138.

11. Dietrich Bonhoeffer, *The Cost of Discipleship* (New York: Touchstone, repr. 1995), p. 89.

12. John Calvin, *Institutes of the Christian Religion*, Library of Christian Classics, ed. John T. McNeill, trans. Ford Lewis Battles (Philadelphia: Westminster, 1960), 3.VII.

13. James Montgomery Boice, *The Gospel of Matthew*, vol. 1 (Grand Rapids, MI: Baker, 2001), p. 315.

14. Ibid.

15. Bruner, *The Churchbook*, p. 148.

16. See W. D. Davies and Dale C. Allison Jr., *A Critical and Exegetical Commentary on the Gospel according to Saint Matthew*, International Critical Commentary, vol. 2 (Edinburgh: T&T Clark, 1988-1997), p. 679. D. A. Carson notes:

> It seems best to take 16:28 as having a more general reference—viz., not referring simply to the Resurrection, to Pentecost, or the like, but to the manifestation of Christ's kingly reign exhibited after the Resurrection in a host of ways, not the least of them being the rapid multiplication of disciples and the mission to the Gentiles. ("Matthew," in *The Expositor's Bible Commentary*, vol. 8 [Grand Rapids, MI: Zondervan, 1984], p. 382.)

17. See Carson, "Matthew," p. 380; Leon Morris, *The Gospel According to Matthew* (Grand Rapids, MI: Eerdmans, repr. 1995), pp. 434, 435.

18. See Bruner, *The Churchbook*, p. 156.

19. "In Matthew, ortho*praxis* is the main way to be ortho*dox*. And it is this orthopraxis that will be judged and that will determine the reality of claims to orthodoxy" (ibid., p. 160).

20. This is a quote from Bruner (ibid., p. 157). I am indebted to him for much of the language of this paragraph. See pp. 156, 157.

21. Lewis Carroll, *Alice's Adventures in Wonderland; and Through the Looking Glass*, Everyman's Library Children's Classics (New York: Knopf, 1992), p. 328.

Chapter Forty-nine: This High Mountain . . . That Lowly Hill

1. Commenting on 17:9, W. D. Davies and Dale C. Allison Jr. speak of Peter, James, and John as "authoritative bearers of the tradition about Jesus" (*A Critical and Exegetical Commentary on the Gospel according to Saint Matthew*, International Critical Commentary, vol. 2 [Edinburgh: T&T Clark, 1988-1997], p. 711).

2. This is Davies and Allison Jr.'s summary of "the most common interpretation in Christian history" (ibid., vol. 2, p. 684).

3. How did Peter, James, and John recognize Moses and Elijah? We don't know. My guess (and it is only that—a guess) is that there was some symbol (a writing on the wall or name tags on the chest, if you will) that made it obvious. Was Moses holding the tablets? Was Elijah surrounded by a mini-whirlwind?

4. With John the Baptist in mind (17:9–13), perhaps Luke 16:16 serves as a helpful cross-reference: "The Law and the Prophets were until John; since then the good news of the kingdom of God is preached, and everyone forces his way into it."

5. Frederick Dale Bruner, *The Churchbook: Matthew 13–28*, 2nd and rev. ed. (Grand Rapids, MI: Eerdmans, 2004), p. 166.

6. John Calvin, *Commentary on a Harmony of the Evangelists, Matthew, Mark, and Luke*, trans. William Pringle (Grand Rapids, MI: Baker, repr. 1993), p. 312.

7. On the possible chiastic structure, see Davies and Allison Jr., *A Critical and Exegetical Commentary on the Gospel according to Saint Matthew*, vol. 2, p. 684.

8. This is what is taught in Luke's Gospel about the transfiguration, where we read that Moses and Elijah spoke with Jesus about his "departure" (9:31), which I take to mean Jesus' death (cf. 2 Peter 1:15).

9. It remains popular, as many Jews still save a seat and open the door for Elijah after the fourth cup of wine at the Passover Seder meal. They still eagerly await his return.

10. Much of the language here is taken from Davies and Allison Jr., *A Critical and Exegetical Commentary on the Gospel according to Saint Matthew*, vol. 2, p. 706 (see also and notably their helpful table on p. 707).

11. N. T. Wright says it this way:

> Here, on a mountain, is Jesus, revealed in glory; there, on a hill outside Jerusalem, is Jesus, revealed in shame. Here his clothes are shining white; there, they have been stripped off, and soldiers have gambled for them. Here he is flanked by Moses and Elijah, two of Israel's greatest heroes, representing the law and the prophets; there, he is flanked by two brigands, representing the level to which Israel had sunk in rebellion against God. Here, a bright cloud overshadows the scene; there, darkness comes upon the land. Here Peter blurts out how wonderful it all is; there, he is hiding in shame after denying he even knows Jesus. Here a voice from God himself declares that this is his wonderful son; there, a pagan soldier declares, in surprise, that this really was God's son. (*Matthew for Everyone*, vol. 2 [Louisville: Westminster John Knox, 2002], p. 14.)

12. Chrysostom, "The Gospel of Matthew" (Homily 56.3), quoted in *Matthew 14–28*, ed. Manlio Simonetti, Ancient Christian Commentary on Scripture, NT Ib (Downers Grove, IL: InterVarsity Press, 2001), p. 54. Ulrich Luz says it this way: "Easter includes the way to the passion. That the Son of Man is the Son of God in

the glory that was revealed on the mountain is only right and true when the Son of God as Son of Man in humiliation has gone the way of suffering" (*Matthew 8–20*, Hermeneia [Minneapolis: Fortress, 2001], p. 399).

13. Wright, *Matthew for Everyone*, vol. 2, p. 15.

Chapter Fifty: Visualize Mustard-Seed Faith

1. C. S. Lewis, *Screwtape Letters* (New York: MacMillan, 1948), pp. 39, 40.

2. The father uses the word *selēniazetai* (literally, "he is moonstruck," from which we derive *luna*tic, *luna* being Latin for moon).

3. Douglas R. A. Hare, *Matthew*, Interpretation (Louisville: John Knox, 1993), p. 201.

4. For example, my reading differs from W. D. Davies and Dale C. Allison Jr. who write, "The focus—in complete contrast to Luke's presentation—is not on Christology, that is, on Jesus as healer or any other christological theme, but on discipleship and faith. In Matthew the lesson is not what Jesus can do but what his followers can do" (*A Critical and Exegetical Commentary on the Gospel according to Saint Matthew*, International Critical Commentary, vol. 2 [Edinburgh: T&T Clark, 1988-1997], p. 720). Also Frederick Dale Bruner writes of this passage: "This is not so much a healing story as it is a story instructing disciples in the ability to heal" (*The Churchbook: Matthew 13–28*, 2nd and rev. ed. [Grand Rapids, MI: Eerdmans, 2004], p. 186). Bruner cites others who take this reading, including Bultmann, Held, and Harrington.

5. Martin Luther, "A Mighty Fortress Is Our God" (1529).

6. G. Walter Hansen, "The Emotions of Jesus and Why We Need to Experience Them," *Christianity Today* (February 3, 1997), pp. 43–46. Cf. B. B. Warfield, "On the Emotional Life of Our Lord," in *The Person and Work of Christ* (Nutley, NJ: Presbyterian and Reformed, 1970), pp. 93–145.

7. Daniel M. Doriani, *Matthew*, Reformed Expository Commentary, vol. 2 (Phillipsburg, NJ: P&R, 2008), p. 119.

8. Bruner, *The Churchbook*, p. 188.

9. As Bruner explores this idea of Jesus' divinity in Jesus' emotions, he points out this verse (ibid.).

10. These texts are cited in Hare, *Matthew*, p. 201.

11. D. A. Carson, "Matthew," in *The Expositor's Bible Commentary*, vol. 8 (Grand Rapids, MI: Zondervan, 1984), p. 391.

12. Thankfully after the death, resurrection, and ascension of Jesus these early disciples finally learned this lesson. If we look at their acts in the Acts of the Apostles, we see that they indeed got their act together. The early church under their leadership was devoted to prayer (cf. Acts 2:42). Moreover, we have recorded also in Acts the role of prayer in many of the apostolic miracles. In Acts 9:40, for example, we read of Peter's actions before restoring Tabitha to life: "But Peter put them all outside, and knelt down and *prayed*; and [then] turning to the [dead] body he said, 'Tabitha, arise.' And she opened her eyes."

13. Craig L. Blomberg, *Matthew*, New American Commentary (Nashville: Broadman, 1992), p. 266.

14. Bruner, *The Churchbook*, p. 191.

15. Bloomberg clarifies:

> "*Nothing* will be impossible for you" must thus be interpreted as *nothing Jesus has given you the authority to do*, such as this exorcism. Obviously, many other things are impossible for believers—based on the limitations of their humanity and of God's will. As v. 22 immediately makes plain, even Jesus' own miracle-working abilities did not permit him to escape the cross despite repeated temptation to do precisely that. See 1 Cor. 6:12; Phil. 4:12–13 for other important limitations on the permissibility and possibility of Christians doing "all things." Verse 20 nevertheless provides a precious promise we dare not ignore. Much is not accomplished for the kingdom because we simply do not believe God will adequately empower us or else because we undertake various activities in our own strength rather than God's. Yet we must recognize the limitations of this promise, in light of other Scriptures, and not use it to foist a guilt trip on ourselves or others when faith does not eliminate every calamity from our lives. (*Matthew*, p. 268)

16. Story taken from John R. W. Stott, *Understanding Christ: An Enquiry into the Theology of Prepositions* (Grand Rapids, MI: Zondervan, 1981), p. 39.

17. David E. Garland, *Mark*, NIV Application Commentary (Grand Rapids, MI: Zondervan, 1996), p. 364.

18. James R. Edwards, *The Gospel According to Mark*, Pillar New Testament Commentary (Grand Rapids, MI: Eerdmans, 2002), p. 280.

19. Ibid.

Chapter Fifty-one: Death and Taxes

1. "[T]he miracle of the fish almost certainly belongs to folklore." W. D. Davies and Dale C. Allison Jr., *A Critical and Exegetical Commentary on the Gospel according to Saint Matthew*, International Critical Commentary, vol. 2 (Edinburgh: T&T Clark, 1988-1997), p. 741.

2. I find William Barclay's rejection of and solution to "bald and crude literalism"—that this miracle occurred as outlined in verse 27—a good example of an anti-supernatural exegetical method: "Jesus was saying, 'Back to your job, Peter; that's the way to pay your debts.' . . . He was telling him that in his day's work he would get what he needed to pay his way" (*The Gospel of Matthew*, vol. 2, rev. ed. [Philadelphia: Westminster, 1975], p. 171).

3. C. H. Spurgeon, *The Gospel of the Kingdom* (Pasadena, TX: Pilgrim Publications, repr. 1996), p. 147.

4. Chrysostom, "The Gospel of Matthew, Homily 58.2," quoted in *Matthew 14–28*, ed. Manlio Simonetti, Ancient Christian Commentary on Scripture, NT Ib (Downers Grove, IL: InterVarsity Press, 2001) pp. 65, 66.

5. This theme of Jesus' foreknowledge fits with the context—his foreknowledge of the fact and timing of his death and resurrection in 16:21; 17:9b, 22, 23 (cf. 26:1, 2) and his foreknowledge of the donkey in Bethphage (21:2) and the room in Jerusalem (26:18).

6. Jerome says, "In this passage I not know what I should admire first, the foreknowledge or the greatness of the Savior" (*Commentary on Matthew*, Fathers of the Church, vol. 117, trans. Thomas P. Scheck [Washington, DC: Catholic University of America, 2008], p. 205).

7. See also Exodus 38:26; 2 Chronicles 24:6, 9 (cf. Nehemiah 10:32, 33).

8. Craig L. Blomberg, *Matthew*, New American Commentary (Nashville: Broadman, 1992), p. 269.

9. On the significance of the temple in Jesus' day, see Nicholas Perrin, *Jesus the Temple* (Grand Rapids, MI: Baker Academic, 2010), especially the final sentence on p. 14, which serves as an apt summary.

10. Frederick Dale Bruner, *The Churchbook: Matthew 13–28*, 2nd and rev. ed. (Grand Rapids, MI: Eerdmans, 2004), p. 202.

11. Elvina Mable Reynolds Hall, "Jesus Paid It All" (1865).

12. Bruner, *The Churchbook*, p. 202.

13. Donald A. Hagner offers a good summary: "Jesus would pay the temple tax once more before he accomplished in his death on the cross the unique sacrifice that would make the temple superfluous" (*Matthew 14–28*, Word Biblical Commentary, vol. 33b [Nashville: Thomas Nelson, 1993], p. 513).

14. What J. C. Ryle writes on rights is worth heeding:

> We should never give up God's rights, but we may sometimes safely give up our own. It may sound very fine and seem very heroic to be always standing out tenaciously for our rights! But it may well be doubted, with such a passage as this, whether such tenacity is always wise, and shows the mind of Christ. There are occasions when it shows more grace in the Christian to submit than to resist. (*Matthew: Expository Thoughts on the Gospels*, Crossway Classic Commentaries [Wheaton, IL: Crossway], p. 156.)

15. Martin Luther, "The Freedom of a Christian," in *Martin Luther's Basic Theological Writings*, ed. Timothy F. Lull (Minneapolis: Fortress, 1989), p. 596.

16. Ibid., p. 620.

17. Bruner, *The Churchbook*, p. 206.

18. Douglas R. A. Hare, *Matthew*, Interpretation (Louisville: John Knox, 1993), p. 207.

Chapter Fifty-two: Little Ones

1. Douglas Sean O'Donnell, *God's Lyrics: Rediscovering Worship Through Old Testament Song* (Phillipsburg, NJ: P&R, 2010), p. 78.

2. To be fair there is something commendable about their question. They believe in "the kingdom of heaven"—what Jesus has been teaching about himself, his coming reign, and the community that will exist under his Lordship. They don't perfectly understand the concept, as shown in their question, but they do think Jesus is the coming King (Messiah), and they do think his vision of this kingdom will succeed. Thus, vying for their place in the hierarchy before the restoration of "the kingdom to Israel," as they would wrongly phrase it in Acts 1:6, makes sense.

3. Frederick Dale Bruner, *The Churchbook: Matthew 13–28*, 2nd and rev. ed. (Grand Rapids, MI: Eerdmans, 2004), p. 208.

4. "The apostles were converted in one sense, but even they needed a further conversion. They needed to *be converted* from self-seeking to humbleness and content. A little child has no ambitious dreams; he is satisfied with little things; he trusts; he aims not at greatness; he yields to command." C. H. Spurgeon, *The Gospel of the Kingdom* (Pasadena, TX: Pilgrim Publications, repr. 1996), p. 148.

5. See Bruner, *The Churchbook*, p. 209.

6. Included in "trust" I see a lack of self-righteousness. Thus Spurgeon's observation: "The little child receives Christ humbly, for he never dreams of merit or purchase. I do not recollect ever having met with a child who had to battle with self-righteousness in coming to Christ" (*Come Ye Children: Practical Help Telling Children About Jesus* [Fearn, Ross-shire, UK: Christian Focus, repr. 2003], p. 41).

7. On 18:15, W. D. Davies and Dale C. Allison Jr. comment that "he hears" (ESV, "he listens") equals "he heeds" or obeys (*A Critical and Exegetical Commentary on the Gospel according to Saint Matthew*, International Critical Commentary, vol. 2 [Edinburgh: T&T Clark, 1988-1997], p. 783). I find a similar idea being acted out in 18:2 in reference to "listen to him" (17:5).

8. Adolf von Harnack, *What Is Christianity?*, p. 73, quoted in Bruner, *The Churchbook*, p. 212.

9. This broader definition is supported by (a) the content of what our Lord says in verses 5–14, (b) the content of what immediately follows in the rest of chapter 18 (which is about church life—adults especially included), (c) the exclusive use of "little ones" throughout the rest of our text (Jesus never returns to the words "child" or "children" again), and (d) the natural way Jesus moves from "these little ones" in verse 14 to "your brother" in verse 15.

10. In Matthew, Jesus balances his warnings of Hell to disciples (5:22, 29, 30; 10:28; 18:9) and non-disciples (13:42, 50; 23:15, 33) alike.

11. Davies and Allison Jr., *A Critical and Exegetical Commentary on the Gospel according to Saint Matthew*, vol. 2, p. 763.

12. John Milton, *Paradise Lost*, 1:405.

13. John Owen, *The Mortification of Sin in Believers* (London: The Religious Tract Society, 1799), p. 9.

14. W. A. Strange, *Children in the Early Church: Children in the Ancient World, the New Testament and the Early Church* (Carlisle, UK: Paternoster, 1996), p. 58.

15. I think the shepherd is "Jesus" rather than "the Father" because the language here relating to God the Father is distant—"the will of my Father *who is in heaven*" (18:14).

16. Jesus is called a shepherd in the Gospels (see John 10:1-18; cf. Matthew 2:6 [quoting Micah 5:2]; 26:31 [quoting Zechariah 13:7]) and in the epistles (see Hebrews 13:20; 1 Peter 5:4). Jesus also calls his disciples "little flock" (Luke 12:32). These references and others are likely an allusion to the Lord as shepherd in Ezekiel 34, which adds additional support for my view of the high Christology of Matthew 17, 18.

17. Bruner, *The Churchbook*, p. 220.

18. Verses 10–14 certainly contain an inclusio and possibly is a chiasm. See P. Gaechter's arrangement below. Note the word "one" at the top, tail, and center!

10a one of these little ones
10b   my Father who is in heaven
12b   has gone astray
12c   the ninety-nine
12c   the one that went astray
13b   the ninety-nine
13b   went astray
14   your (or: my) Father who is in heaven
14 one of these little ones

Gaechter, *Die literarische Kunst im Mattäus-Evangelium*, Stuttgarter Bibelstudien Band 7 (Stuttgart: Verlag Katholisches Bibelwerk, 1968), pp. 50ff., quoted in Davies and Allison Jr., *A Critical and Exegetical Commentary on the Gospel according to Saint Matthew*, vol. 2, p. 768.

19. Bruner, *The Churchbook*, p. 219.

20. Matthew Henry, quoted in ibid., p. 218.

Chapter Fifty-three: Immanuel's *Ecclesia*

1. I added the word "church" to Frederick Dale Bruner's "Our text is the Magna Carta of confrontation" (*The Churchbook: Matthew 13–28*, 2nd and rev. ed. [Grand Rapids, MI: Eerdmans, 2004], p. 22).

2. If you wish to explore further the relationship between Christ's command in 18:15–20 and his seemingly contradictory commands in 7:1–5 and 13:24–30, 36–43, see ibid., pp. 225, 226, 233.

3. W. D. Davies and Dale C. Allison Jr., *A Critical and Exegetical Commentary on the Gospel according to Saint Matthew*, International Critical Commentary, vol. 2 (Edinburgh: T&T Clark, 1988-1997), p. 791.

4. On favoring the inclusion of "against you," see Knox Chamblin, *Matthew*, A Mentor Commentary, vol. 2 (Fearn, Ross-shire, UK: Mentor, 2010), p. 892.

5. Bruner, *The Churchbook*, p. 223.

6. I borrowed a few of my ideas in this paragraph from Daniel M. Doriani, *Matthew*, Reformed Expository Commentary, vol. 2 (Phillipsburg, NJ: P&R, 2008), p. 151.

7. Dietrich Bonhoeffer, *Life Together* (New York: Harper & Row, 1954), pp. 112, 113.

8. For Jesus' interaction with Gentiles, see 8:5–13; 15:21–28, and with tax collectors, see 9:9–13.

9. Craig L. Blomberg, *Matthew*, New American Commentary (Nashville: Broadman, 1992), pp. 279, 280.

10. Davies and Allison Jr., *A Critical and Exegetical Commentary on the Gospel according to Saint Matthew*, vol. 2, p. 785.

11. *Ecclesia* can just mean an assembly, gathering, congregation, or even town meeting. Yet, because of Jesus' use of the term in 16:18, where he speaks of building "my church," I think he refers here to the universal Christian community—those gathered in his name—locally assembled to worship or, as in this context, to judge.

12. When Jesus says "my name" it is shocking. For with the immediate reference to his "Father in heaven" we might expect Jesus to continue in verse 20 speaking about God—to gather in God's name. Instead it is in Jesus' name!

Chapter Fifty-four: The Heart of Perfect Forgiveness

1. In Tractate *Joma*, Rabbi Jose ben Judah (c. AD 180) says, "If a brother sins against you once, forgive him; a second time, forgive him; a third time, forgive him; but a fourth time, do not forgive him."

2. As pointed out by W. D. Davies and Dale C. Allison Jr., Peter may also have in mind the following Old Testament references: "Gen 4.15 (sevenfold vengeance upon Cain's murderer); Lev 16 (there is a sevenfold sprinkling of blood for the sins of the people); Lev 26.18 ('I will chastise you again sevenfold for your sins'; cf. vv. 21, 24)" (*A Critical and Exegetical Commentary on the Gospel according to Saint

Matthew, International Critical Commentary, vol. 2 [Edinburgh: T&T Clark, 1988-1997], p. 792).

3. The first version of the ESV went with "seventy times seven," the current edition with "seventy-seven times." While the manuscript evidence slightly favors the latter reading, I think the earlier one fits better with Jesus' teaching theme. However, either reading gives the same idea.

4. Daniel M. Doriani adds this interesting insight:

> We can count up to three offenses and think: I forgive you once, twice, three times . . . and now vengeance is mine! We can even count to seven sins: One, two, three, four, five, six, seven!—and now you're mine, you fool! But no one can count sins and hold their rage until seventy-seven. Forgiveness either becomes a way of life or we blow up. (*Matthew*, Reformed Expository Commentary, vol. 2 [Phillipsburg, NJ: P&R, 2008], p. 162.)

5. See Davies and Allison Jr., *A Critical and Exegetical Commentary on the Gospel according to Saint Matthew*, vol. 2, p. 793. Cf. John Calvin, *Commentary on a Harmony of the Evangelists, Matthew, Mark, and Luke*, trans. William Pringle (Grand Rapids, MI: Baker, repr. 1993), p. 364.

6. In his helpful article "'Where Two or Three Are Convened in My Name . . .': A Sad Misunderstanding," J. D. M. Derrett writes, "The positive obligation to forgive is not absolute and invariable, since that would destroy discipline" (*Expository Times*, 91 [1979-1980], p. 84).

7. Note the inclusio of the verb "forgive" in 18:21 and 18:35.

8. Matthew 18:15–20 is about the procedure of forgiveness and restoration; 18:21–35 is about the attitude.

9. "In Jewish law, the sale of an Israelite as a slave was permitted only in a case of theft, that of his spouse never (Billerbeck, *Kommentar zum Neuen Testament,* 1:798)." Rudolf Schnackenburg, *The Gospel of Matthew*, trans. Robert R. Barr (Grand Rapids, MI: Eerdmans, 2002), p. 181.

10. Robert H. Gundry, *Matthew: A Commentary on His Literary and Theological Art* (Grand Rapids, MI: Eerdmans, 1982), pp. 373, 374.

11. Frederick Dale Bruner, *The Churchbook: Matthew 13–28*, 2nd and rev. ed. (Grand Rapids, MI: Eerdmans, 2004), p. 237.

12. Ibid., p. 238.

13. See Craig L. Blomberg, *Matthew*, New American Commentary (Nashville: Broadman, 1992), p. 283.

14. Bruner, *The Churchbook*, p. 238.

15. On Lamech's violent vengeance—"Lamech said to his wives: 'Adah and Zillah, hear my voice; you wives of Lamech, listen to what I say: I have killed a man for wounding me, a young man for striking me. If Cain's revenge is sevenfold, then Lamech's is seventy-sevenfold" (Genesis 4:23, 24)—A. H. M'Neile writes, "The unlimited revenge of primitive man has given place to the unlimited forgiveness of Christians" (*The Gospel according to St. Matthew* [London: Macmillan, 1915], p. 268).

16. Those adjectives are used by the following commentators: Blomberg, *Matthew*, p. 282; David Jackman and William Philip, *Teaching Matthew: Unlocking the Gospel of Matthew for the Expositor* (Fearn, Ross-shire, UK: Christian Focus, 2003),

p. 162; Knox Chamblin, *Matthew*, A Mentor Commentary, vol. 2 (Fearn, Ross-shire, UK: Mentor, 2010), p. 911; Daniel J. Harrington, *The Gospel of Matthew*, Sacra Pagina (Collegeville, MN: Liturgical Press, 1991), p. 270.

17. This idea was borrowed from N. T. Wright, *Matthew for Everyone*, vol. 2 (Louisville: Westminster John Knox, 2002), p. 39.

18. "Matthew points to the 'heart' (cf. 6:21; 11:29; 12:34; 15:8) since true forgiveness may not simply hang from the lips" (Schnackenburg, *The Gospel of Matthew*, p. 181).

19. Douglas R. A. Hare, *Matthew*, Interpretation (Louisville: John Knox, 1993), p. 218.

20. D. A. Carson summarized the point well:

> Jesus sees no incongruity in the actions of a heavenly Father who forgives so bountifully and punishes so ruthlessly, and neither should we. Indeed, it is precisely because he is a God of such compassion and mercy that he cannot possibly accept as his those devoid of compassion and mercy. ("Matthew," in *The Expositor's Bible Commentary*, vol. 8 [Grand Rapids, MI: Zondervan, 1984], p. 407.)

21. Blomberg summarizes my view precisely:

> The subordinate details of the parable should not be pressed. Verse 34 does not promulgate any doctrine of purgatory. Even when one allegorizes the prison, torturers, and repayment, one winds up with a picture of hell, not purgatory, since this man could almost certainly never repay his debt or escape. (*Matthew*, p. 285.)

Calvin adds his usual flair: "The Papists are very ridiculous in endeavoring to light the fire of purgatory by the word *till*; for it is certain that Christ here points out not temporal death, by which the judgment of God may be satisfied, but eternal death" (*Commentary on a Harmony of the Evangelists, Matthew, Mark, and Luke*, p. 368).

22. This is the scholarly consensus. Davies and Allison Jr. summarize:

> As the parable now stands, with the debt amounting to 10,000 talents, the punishment must be perpetual, for the debt so immense could never be repaid. Thus the situation is a transparent symbol of eschatological judgment. (*A Critical and Exegetical Commentary on the Gospel according to Saint Matthew*, vol. 2, p. 803.)

23. Cf. Chapter 52, n. 10.

24. On this theme, see Thomas R. Schreiner and Ardel B. Caneday, *The Race Set Before Us: A Biblical Theology of Perseverance and Assurance* (Downers Grove, IL: InterVarsity Press, 2001). For a shorter version of their thesis, see Thomas R. Schreiner, *Run to Win the Prize: Perseverance in the New Testament* (Wheaton, IL: Crossway, 2010).

25. Bruner, *The Churchbook*, p. 240.

26. J. C. Ryle, *Matthew: Expository Thoughts on the Gospels*, Crossway Classic Commentaries (Wheaton, IL: Crossway), p. 166.

27. I borrow the phrase "persistent power" from Herman Ridderbos's excellent summary: "Whoever tries to separate man's forgiveness from God's will no

longer be able to count on God's mercy. In so doing he not merely forfeits it, like the servant in the parable. Rather he shows that he never had a part in it. God's mercy is not something cut and dried that is only received once. It is a persistent power that pervades all of life. If it does not become manifest as such a power, then it was never received at all" (*Matthew*, Bible Student's Commentary [Grand Rapids, MI: Zondervan, 1987], p. 346).

Chapter Fifty-five: The Beginning and End of Marriage

1. For a helpful chart on the different views, see Andreas Köstenberger, *God, Marriage, and Family: Rebuilding the Biblical Foundation* (Wheaton, IL: Crossway, 2004) p. 235.

2. See *m. Git.* 9:10, in *The Mishnah*, trans. Herbert Danby (New York: Oxford University Press, 1933), p. 321.

3. On this theme Paul R. House writes:

> Permanence is inherent in the canon's statements about marriage. Only death separates Sarah from Abraham (Gen 23:2), Jacob from Rachel (Gen 35:19) or Ezekiel from his wife (Ezek 24:15–18). . . . Proverbs 5:15–23 at the least implies that the joy one takes in the spouse of one's youth is to last a lifetime, or as long as both lives last. (*Old Testament Theology* [Downers Grove, IL: InterVarsity Press, 1998], p. 468.)

4. W. D. Davies and Dale C. Allison Jr. (with G. J. Wenham) are helpful here:

> As in Genesis, the meaning of "one flesh," is not perfectly clear; but perhaps the best guess is that in both places the phrase "does not denote merely the sexual union that follows marriage, or the children conceived in marriage, or even the spiritual and emotional relationship that it involves, though all are involved. . . . Rather it affirms that just as blood relations are one's flesh and bone . . . so marriage creates a similar kinship between man and wife." (Wenham, *Genesis 1–15* [Waco, TX: Word, 1987), p. 71, quoted in *A Critical and Exegetical Commentary on the Gospel according to Saint Matthew*, International Critical Commentary, vol. 3 [Edinburgh: T&T Clark, 1988-1997], pp. 12, 13.)

5. N. T. Wright, *Matthew for Everyone*, vol. 2 (Louisville: Westminster John Knox, 2002), p. 42.

6. "In the case of adultery after marriage, it is lawful for the innocent party to sue out a divorce: and, after the divorce, to marry another, as if the offending party were dead" (*Westminster Confession of Faith*, 24.5).

7. I. Howard Marshall, *The Gospel of Luke*, New International Greek Testament Commentary (Grand Rapids, MI: Eerdmans, 1978), pp. 371, 372.

Chapter Fifty-six: The Impossibility of Salvation

1. Nicholas Perrin, *Jesus the Temple* (Grand Rapids, MI: Baker Academic, 2010), p. 122.

2. James R. Edwards, *The Gospel According to Mark*, Pillar New Testament Commentary (Grand Rapids, MI: Eerdmans, 2002), p. 309.

3. W. D. Davies and Dale C. Allison Jr., *A Critical and Exegetical Commentary on the Gospel according to Saint Matthew*, International Critical Commentary, vol. 3 (Edinburgh: T&T Clark, 1988-1997), p. 46.

4. Taken from the Roman satirist Juvenal, quoted in David E. Garland, *Mark*, The NIV Application Commentary (Grand Rapids, MI: Zondervan, 1996), p. 406.

5. Therefore, by his refusal to obey Christ's command, he clearly demonstrated that he not only failed to obey the Tenth Commandment, but he failed to obey the First Commandment, and in fact all of the commandments of the Law. For as James rightly says, "whoever keeps the whole law but fails in one point has become accountable for all of it" (James 2:10).

6. Much of the paragraph is taken from Garland, *Mark*, p. 408.

7. Mark Twain, quoted in *The Wit and Wisdom of Mark Twain* (New York: Harper Perennial, 2005), p. 24.

8. Garland, *Mark*, p. 401.

9. E.g., Matthew 6:19–34; 13:22; Mark 4:19; Luke 12:13–34; 16:1–9, 19–31; 19:1–10.

10. Garland, *Mark*, p. 402.

11. Ibid., p. 403.

12. Ibid., p. 399.

13. J. C. Ryle, *Mark: Expository Thoughts on the Gospels*, Crossway Classic Commentaries (Wheaton, IL: Crossway, 1993), p. 153. See also point 1 on pp. 173, 174, "The danger riches bring to the soul," in J. C. Ryle, *Matthew: Expository Thoughts on the Gospels*, Crossway Classic Commentaries (Wheaton, IL: Crossway, 1993).

14. William Hendriksen, *Exposition of the Gospel According to Mark* (Grand Rapids, MI: Baker, 2002), p. 400. In his Matthew commentary, Hendriksen says it this way: "At every point, beginning, middle, end, man is completely dependent on God for salvation" (*Exposition of the Gospel According to Matthew* [Grand Rapids, MI: Baker, 2002], p. 728).

15. Jonathan Edwards, *The Works of Jonathan Edwards*, ed. Edward Hickman, vol. 1 (Carlisle, PA: Banner of Truth, repr. 1992), p. 581.

Chapter Fifty-seven: The "Injustice" of a Generous God

1. This story is told in Kevin Leman, *Adolescence Isn't Terminal* (Wheaton, IL: Tyndale, 2002), pp. 30, 31.

2. The key issue is this: I take Jesus' parable as a continuation of his encouragement to Peter and the Twelve (see 19:28–30) rather than a rebuke for Peter's seemingly self-focused concern—"What then will we have?" (19:27).

3. Exodus 15—17; Numbers 14—17; cf. 1 Corinthians 10:10.

4. E.g., Luke 5:30; John 6:41; Jude 16.

5. W. D. Davies and Dale C. Allison Jr., *A Critical and Exegetical Commentary on the Gospel according to Saint Matthew*, International Critical Commentary, vol. 3 (Edinburgh: T&T Clark, 1988-1997), p. 74.

6. R. T. France, *The Gospel according to Matthew*, Tyndale New Testament Commentaries (Grand Rapids, MI: Eerdmans, 1985), p. 289.

7. Daniel M. Doriani, *Matthew*, Reformed Expository Commentary, vol. 2 (Phillipsburg, NJ: P&R, 2008), pp. 216, 217.

8. Davies and Allison Jr. label the parable "The Generous Employer" (*A Critical and Exegetical Commentary on the Gospel according to Saint Matthew*, vol. 3, p. 66). R. Hoppe calls it "The Parable of the Generous Householder" (quoted in Rudolf Schnackenburg, *The Gospel of Matthew*, trans. Robert R. Barr [Grand Rapids, MI: Eerdmans, 2002], p. 192).

9. C. L. Blomberg, "Degrees of Reward in the Kingdom of Heaven?" *Journal of the Evangelical Theological Society* 35 (1992): pp. 159–172.

10. One notable example is given by Frederick Dale Bruner:

> The difference between Jesus' gospel and most others' can be seen most clearly by contrasting Jesus' parable with a strikingly comparable rabbinic parable in the Jerusalem Talmud, *Berakot* 2:5c:15 (emphasis added): "When Rabbi Bun bar Chija was asleep, Rabbi Sera went up to him and spake: . . . A king . . . hired many laborers, one of whom so distinguished himself by industry and skill that the king took him by the hand and walked up and down with him. In the evening the laborers came, and the skillful one among them, to receive their pay. The king gave them all the same pay. Wherefore those who had worked the whole day murmured, and spake: We have worked the whole day, and this man only two hours, and yet he also has received his whole pay. The king answered: *This man has wrought more in two hours than you in a whole day*. Even so hath Rabbi Bun bar Chija in twenty-eight years wrought more in the Law than many studious scholars in a hundred years." (*The Churchbook: Matthew 13–28*, 2nd and rev. ed. [Grand Rapids, MI: Eerdmans, 2004], p. 323.)

Chapter Fifty-eight: The Greatness of Going Up to Jerusalem

1. This essay first appeared in *Literary Cavalcade* (May 1990). I found it in Constance Hale, *Sin and Syntax: How to Craft Wickedly Effective Prose* (New York: Broadway, 1999), pp. 52–54.

2. It may also be, as Craig L. Blomberg observes, that there is a link in the disciples' minds from their question of the "kingdom" and Jesus' talk about the behavior of "kings" in 17:25. See *Matthew*, New American Commentary (Nashville: Broadman, 1992), p. 272.

3. In his article on "Church," I. Howard Marshall writes:

> The concept of the kingdom of God implies a community. While it has been emphasized almost *ad nauseam* that the primary concept is that of sovereignty, or kingship, or actual rule of God, and not of a territory ruled by a king, it must also be emphasized that kingship cannot by exercised in the abstract, but only over a people. The concept of the kingship of God implies both the existence of a group of people who own him as king, and the establishment of a realm of people within which his gracious power is manifested. (in *Dictionary of Jesus and the Gospels*, eds. J. B. Green, Scot McKnight, and I. Howard Marshall [Downers Grove, IL: InterVarsity Press, 1992], p. 123.)

4. C. H. Spurgeon, *The Gospel of the Kingdom* (Pasadena, TX: Pilgrim Publications, repr. 1996), p. 171.

5. I agree with J. D. Kingsbury who argues that the ten are upset "not because their motives are purer, but because they covet these same positions of honor" (*Matthew as Story* [Philadelphia: Fortress, 1986], p. 116).

6. It should be noted that synonymous parallelisms are "very seldom precisely synonymous"; that is, the second line "does not simply repeat what has been said, but enriches it, deepens it, transforms it by adding fresh nuances and bringing in new elements," which in turn "renders it more concrete and vivid and telling." James Muilenburg, quoted in Greidanus, *The Modern Preacher and the Ancient Text: Interpreting and Preaching Biblical Literature* (Grand Rapids, MI: Eerdmans, 1988), p. 62. Robert Alter calls this "focusing" (*Art of Biblical Poetry* [New York: Basic, 1987], pp. 2–26, 62–84. Others call it "climactic" parallelism.

7. W. D. Davies and Dale C. Allison Jr., *A Critical and Exegetical Commentary on the Gospel according to Saint Matthew*, International Critical Commentary, vol. 3 (Edinburgh: T&T Clark, 1988–1997), pp. 93, 94.

8. Douglas R. A. Hare, *Matthew*, Interpretation (Louisville: John Knox, 1993), p. 234.

9. Part of this paragraph comes from Fredrick Dale Bruner, *The Churchbook: Matthew 13–28*, 2nd and rev. ed. (Grand Rapids, MI: Eerdmans, 2004), p. 333.

10. Of interest and importance, Bruner notes: "There is a noteworthy configuration in the three passion predictions, observable strikingly in Mark and only a little less sharply in Matthew:

> 1. *Jesus* takes his disciples *down* three times into the valley of his suffering Messiahship, teaching them that his death must precede his resurrection (Mark 8:31; 9:30–32; 10:32–34; Matt 16:21; 17:22, 23; 20:17–19).
> 2. Right afterwards, in all three predictions, *disciples* take Jesus and themselves back *up* a mountain of glory, hoping that Messiahship means their victory, not their defeat (Mark 8:32; Matt 16:22), greatness not obscurity (Mark 9:33, 34; Matt 18:1), and power, not servitude (Mark 10:35–37; Matt 20:20, 21).
> 3. And three more times *Jesus* must take his disciples back *down* into the valley and teach them afresh that the way up is down (Mark 8:33–39:1; 9:35–37; 10:38–45; Matt 16:23–28; 18:2–5; 20:22–28)." (Ibid., p. 326.)

11. See ibid., p. 329.

12. "During his incarnation, the Son of God remained functionally subordinate to the Father, despite their equality in essence. All authority will be delegated to Christ after his resurrection (28:18), but for now Jesus has voluntarily relinquished some of that authority (Phil. 2:6–8)" (Blomberg, *Matthew*, p. 307).

13. Bruce B. Barton, et al., *Matthew*, Life Application Bible Commentary (Wheaton, IL: Tyndale, 1996), p. 396.

14. Blomberg is strong but accurate when he writes:

> Jesus himself provides the perfect example of servant leadership (v. 28a; cf. esp. John 13:1–17). Few models are more desperately needed in an age of celebrity Christianity, high-tech evangelism and worship, and widespread abuses of ecclesiastical power for self-aggrandizement or, more insidious-

ly, in the name of "attracting" more people to the gospel—a "gospel" that is thereby badly truncated. (*Matthew*, p. 308.)

15. From Brother Lawrence, *The Practice of the Presence of God,* quoted in James Montgomery Boice, *The Gospel of Matthew*, vol. 2 (Grand Rapids, MI: Baker, 2001), p. 425. I'll add Dabney's famous statement:

> The education of children for God is the most important business done on earth. . . . To it all politics, all war, all literature, all money-making, ought to be subordinated; and every parent especially ought to feel, every hour of the day, that, next to making [their] own calling and election sure, this is the end for which [they are] kept alive by God—this is [their] task on earth. (Quoted in R. Kent Hughes and Barbara Hughes, *Disciplines of a Godly Family* [Wheaton, IL: Crossway, 2007], p. 16.)

16. Blomberg, *Matthew*, p. 306.
17. Hare, *Matthew*, p. 232.
18. William Barclay, *The Gospel of Matthew*, vol. 2, rev. ed. (Philadelphia: Westminster, 1975), p. 228.
19. Cf. 16:27; 19:28.
20. See Duane Litfin, *Word Versus Deed: Resetting the Scales to a Biblical Balance* (Wheaton, IL: Crossway, 2012).
21. Donald A. Hagner, *Matthew 14–28*, Word Biblical Commentary, vol. 33b (Nashville: Thomas Nelson, 1993), p. 583.
22. A. Sand, *Das Evangelium nach Matthäus*, Regensburger Neues Testament (Regensburg: Pustet, 1986), p. 405, in Bruner, *The Churchbook,* p. 335.
23. For a list of Bible texts, see Walter A. Elwell, *Topical Analysis of the Bible* (Grand Rapids, MI: Baker, 1995), p. 466.
24. Davies and Allison Jr., *A Critical and Exegetical Commentary on the Gospel according to Saint Matthew*, vol. 3, p. 90.
25. Rudolf Schnackenburg, *The Gospel of Matthew*, trans. Robert R. Barr (Grand Rapids, MI: Eerdmans, 2002), p. 195.
26. On first-century thought on the term "many" referring to the elect, see Craig Keener, *A Commentary of the Gospel of Matthew* (Grand Rapids, MI: Eerdmans, 1999), pp. 487, 488.
27. Cf. Ulrich Luz, *Matthew 8–20*, vol. 2, Hermeneia (Minneapolis: Fortress, 2001), p. 546, n. 42.
28. Blomberg, *Matthew*, p. 308.
29. See Luz, *Matthew 8–20*, vol. 2, p. 546. The first definition is from Spicq, *Lexicon*, 2.426–427.
30. Fred R. Shapiro and Joseph Epstein, *The Yale Book of Quotations* (New Haven: Yale University Press, 2006), p. 231.

Chapter Fifty-nine: Seeing with the Blind

1. U2, "Mysterious Ways," *Achtung Baby* (Island Records, 1991).
2. Cf. 2 Corinthians 4:3, 4; Isaiah 6:9, 10.
3. For this paragraph, see Frederick Dale Bruner, *The Churchbook: Matthew 13–28*, 2nd and rev. ed. (Grand Rapids, MI: Eerdmans, 2004), p. 349.

4. Matthew is building on the expectations of Old Testament texts, such as Psalm 89:3, 4, 29; Isaiah 9:6, 7; 11; Jeremiah 23:5, 6; 33:15, 16.

5. Exodus 4:11; Psalm 146:8, 9.

6. Isaiah 29:18; 35:5 (cf. Matthew 11:3–5); 42:7.

7. In 2 Kings 6:18–20 Elisha prayed that God would blind the Arameans, and he brought them into Samaria and then prayed that God would restore their sight. This is still technically YHWH taking away and giving sight.

8. Bruner, *The Churchbook*, p. 348.

9. Daniel M. Doriani, *Matthew*, Reformed Expository Commentary, vol. 2 (Phillipsburg, NJ: P&R, 2008), p. 238.

10. Bruner, *The Churchbook*, p. 349.

11. Ibid., pp. 351, 352.

12. John R. W. Stott writes of crucifixion:

> It is probably the most cruel method of execution ever practised, for it deliberately delayed death until maximum torture had been inflicted. . . . Cicero in one of his speeches condemned it as *crudelissimum taeterrimumque supplicium,* "a most cruel and disgusting punishment" [*Against Verres* II.v.64, para. 165]. (*Cross of Christ* [Downers Grove, IL: InterVarsity Press, 1986], pp. 23, 24.)

Cf. Martin Hengel, *Crucifixion in the Ancient World and the Folly of the Message of the Cross* (Philadelphia: Fortress, 1977).

13. Doriani, *Matthew*, vol. 2, p. 241.

14. J. D. Kingsbury, *Matthew as Story* (Philadelphia: Fortress, 1986), p. 54.

15. There is an interesting contrast here to the first healing of the two blind men. In 9:30, 31, the men disobey Jesus' clear command (v. 30) and walk away (v. 31). In 20:34 they walked after him.

16. Rudolf Schnackenburg, *The Gospel of Matthew*, trans. Robert R. Barr (Grand Rapids, MI: Eerdmans, 2002), p. 198.

Chapter Sixty: The Son of God on a Child of a Donkey

1. C. F. Keil, "The Minor Prophets," in C. F. Keil and F. Delitzsch, *Commentary on the Old Testament*, vol. 10 (Peabody, MA: Hendrickson, repr. 2006), p. 577. Here Keil quotes Hengstenberg without reference.

2. D. A. Carson, "Matthew," in *The Expositor's Bible Commentary*, vol. 8 (Grand Rapids, MI: Zondervan, 1984), p. 438. Cf. Rudolf Schnackenburg, *The Gospel of Matthew*, trans. Robert R. Barr (Grand Rapids, MI: Eerdmans, 2002), p. 200.

3. D. A. Carson, "Matthew," p. 438.

4. John Stott, *Why I Am a Christian* (Downers Grove, IL: InterVarsity Press, 2003), p. 35.

5. Ibid., p. 44.

6. Ibid., p. 45.

7. Ibid., p. 38.

8. Frederick Dale Bruner, *The Churchbook: Matthew 13–28*, 2nd and rev. ed. (Grand Rapids, MI: Eerdmans, 2004), p. 357.

9. Ibid., pp. 353, 355.

Chapter Sixty-one: A Withered Temple

1. R. Kent Hughes, *Mark: Jesus, Servant and Savior*, Preaching the Word, vol. 2 (Wheaton, IL: Crossway, 2001), p. 87.

2. Ibid.

3. Rudolf Schnackenburg, *The Gospel of Matthew*, trans. Robert R. Barr (Grand Rapids, MI: Eerdmans, 2002), p. 203.

4. There is a memorable passage in C. S. Lewis's *Voyage of the Dawn Treader* where Edmund and Lucy come upon a pure, white, and gentle lamb who during their conversation miraculously transforms into a grand and powerful lion (see *The Voyage of the Dawn Treader* [New York: HarperCollins, 1994], p. 269).

5. Bertrand Russell, *Why I Am Not a Christian, and Other Essays on Religion and Related Subjects* (New York: Carion Books, Simon and Schuster, 1957), pp. 17–19.

6. The words, not the sentiment, are Hughes's (*Mark*, vol. 2, p. 85).

7. R. T. France, *The Gospel of Matthew*, New International Commentary on the New Testament (Grand Rapids, MI: Eerdmans, 2007), p. 792, n. 11. Cf. Donald A. Hagner, *Matthew 14–28*, Word Biblical Commentary, vol. 33b (Nashville: Thomas Nelson, 1993), p. 605.

8. Cf. Luke 13:6–9.

9. James R. Edwards, *The Gospel According to Mark*, Pillar New Testament Commentary (Grand Rapids, MI: Eerdmans, 2002), pp. 343, 344.

10. Ibid.

11. Ibid.

12. For a brief and excellent summary of thoughts on Jesus' temple action, see the first paragraph of Nicholas Perrin, *Jesus the Temple* (Grand Rapids, MI: Baker Academic, 2010), p. 80.

13. Quote found in Tyron Edwards, *A Dictionary of Thoughts* (Detroit: F. B. Dickerson Co., 1908), p. 50.

14. W. R. Telford, *The Barren Temple and the Withered Tree* (Sheffield, UK: JSOT, 1980), pp. 238, 239.

Chapter Sixty-two: What Authority? What Authority!

1. James Joyce, *A Portrait of the Artist as a Young Man* (Norwalk, CT: Easton, 1977), pp. 8, 9.

2. See F. Stagg, "Matthew," in *The Broadman Bible Commentary*, vol. 8, ed. C. J. Allen (Nashville: Broadman, 1969), p. 201.

3. Frederick Dale Bruner, *The Churchbook: Matthew 13–28*, 2nd and rev. ed. (Grand Rapids, MI: Eerdmans, 2004), p. 372.

4. See David Jackman and William Philip, *Teaching Matthew: Unlocking the Gospel of Matthew for the Expositor* (Fearn, Ross-shire, UK: Christian Focus, 2003), p. 177.

5. See Isaiah 5:1, 2; cf. Psalm 80:8–10; Jeremiah 2:21; Ezekiel 19:10.

6. Donald A. Hagner, *Matthew 14–28*, Word Biblical Commentary, vol. 33b (Nashville: Thomas Nelson, 1993), p. 621.

7. Douglas R. A. Hare, *Matthew*, Interpretation (Louisville: John Knox, 1993), p. 249.

8. John Chrysostom, "The Gospel of Matthew" (Homily 68.1), quoted in *Matthew 14–28*, ed. Manlio Simonetti, Ancient Christian Commentary on Scripture, NT Ib (Downers Grove, IL: InterVarsity Press, 2001), pp. 139, 140.

9. Craig L. Blomberg, *Matthew*, New American Commentary (Nashville: Broadman, 1992), p. 325.

10. Rudolf Schnackenburg provides an excellent summary of this section:

> A new beginning follows, with a Christological continuation originating with the primitive church. The quotation concerning the stone that the builders rejected, made by God the cornerstone (hardly the keystone), is taken literally from Psalm 118:22–23 in the Greek, an important Christological testimonial for the primitive church (Acts 4:11; 1 Peter 2:7; cf. Eph. 2:20). Jesus, executed on the cross by human beings, attains a unique significance by being raised by God. Upon him is founded the new community of salvation (the church), to which even the erstwhile heathen belong (cf. 1 Peter 2:9–10). He alone is the source of redemption and salvation for all human beings (Acts 4:12). After the murder of the son in the parable, the primitive church wished to introduce the concept of Jesus' resurrection. Jesus' way does not end in a catastrophe, but is rendered consummately meaningful by God—an astonishing, wondrous event. Other 'stone' passages (the chosen, precious cornerstone, Isa. 28:16; the stone that for the contemptuous becomes the stone of scandal and fall, Isa. 8:14–15) were seen as connected with this one, as 1 Peter 2:6–8 shows. For Matthew, whose thinking is in the context of the church, the most important thing is the formation of a new people of God. In the *logion* of verse 43, which reveals his overarching concern, the key concepts are the 'kingdom of God,' the 'people'—here not the ancient people of God (*laos*) but the new people (*ethnos*), one that includes the Gentile peoples (Matt. 12:18–21; 28:19)—and the 'fruits' that this new people is to produce. In the Matthean view, Jesus' cross and resurrection accomplish the transition from the ancient people of God to the new. Israel is not denied the Reign of God for its time; but now, after the crucifixion of its Messiah, that Reign is taken from it and—after the raising of the crucified one—given to another people. At the same time we are aware of the pervasive Matthean concern that this new people yield the corresponding moral fruits (7:21–23; 13:41–43; 25:31–46; 28:20). (*The Gospel of Matthew*, trans. Robert R. Barr [Grand Rapids, MI: Eerdmans, 2002], p. 212.)

11. For a good summary of this notion, see 2 Chronicles 36:15, 16.

12. Bruner, *The Churchbook*, p. 377.

13. Ibid., p. 378.

14. Ibid., p. 384.

Chapter Sixty-three: A Peculiar Parable with a Poignant Point

1. "The reader naturally identifies the son with Jesus, this because (i) the son of the previous parable is obviously Jesus, (ii) in 9.15 and 25.1 Jesus is the bridegroom, (iii) God is often the king in Matthew (cf. 5.35 and 'kingdom of God'), and (iv) other early Christian texts speak of the eschatological wedding feast of Jesus Messiah (e.g., Rev 19.7, 9)." W. D. Davies and Dale C. Allison Jr., *A Critical and Exegetical*

Commentary on the Gospel according to Saint Matthew, International Critical Commentary, vol. 3 (Edinburgh: T&T Clark, 1988-1997), pp. 198, 199.

2. E.g., see 6:9; 16:27; 28:19.

3. "Observe that the whole sequence is dominated by the direct speech of the king (vv. 4, 8–9, 11–12, 13); no one else says anything. This underlines the authority of the king and the fact that everything revolves around his words." Davies and Allison Jr., *A Critical and Exegetical Commentary on the Gospel according to Saint Matthew*, vol. 3, p. 194.

4. For a clear example of this concept, read Isaiah 10:5, 6. Scripture clearly testifies that God used pagan rulers like Nebuchadnezzar (Jeremiah 27:5–8; 28:14) and Cyrus (Isaiah 41:2–4; 44:28; 45:1) for his divine purposes.

5. I am indebted to Frederick Dale Bruner, *The Churchbook: Matthew 13–28*, 2nd and rev. ed. (Grand Rapids, MI: Eerdmans, 2004), p. 387.

6. Commenting on 26:57–68, Davies and Allison Jr. write:

> In Matthew Jesus is neither the victim of tragic, impersonal circumstances nor the casualty of the ordinary machinery of justice. He is rather done in by wicked people. Jesus' adversaries speak falsehoods (vv. 59–60), accuse him of blasphemy (v. 65), condemn him to death (v. 66), and viciously hit and mock him (vv. 67–8). In the midst of this sinful folly Jesus' identity become more visible. (*A Critical and Exegetical Commentary on the Gospel according to Saint Matthew*, vol. 3, p. 520.)

7. Rudolf Schnackenburg summarizes the scholarly consensus: "There can be no missing Matthew's allusion to Jerusalem and its destruction in AD 70" (*The Gospel of Matthew*, trans. Robert R. Barr [Grand Rapids, MI: Eerdmans, 2002], p. 215.)

8. C. S. Lewis, *The Problem of Pain* (New York: Macmillan, 1962), p. 35.

9. Bruner again, and as usual, is marvelous. He writes,

> Jesus' audacity is his implying divine Sonship. The person of Jesus is the mysterious center of this entire set of stories (20:29–22:14); indeed, properly studied, there is hardly a paragraph in the Gospel that does not raise the question of Jesus' person—the question of his "authority." One remarkable feature in all three Polemical Parables, binding them together as a unit, is that the Father-Son relationship is at the center of each (Boring, 417). (*The Churchbook*, p. 386.)

10. Robert H. Gundry, *Matthew: A Commentary on His Literary and Theological Art* (Grand Rapids, MI: Eerdmans, 1982), p. 440.

11. C. H. Spurgeon, *The Gospel of the Kingdom* (Pasadena, TX: Pilgrim Publications, repr. 1996), p. 192.

12. Davies and Allison Jr., *A Critical and Exegetical Commentary on the Gospel according to Saint Matthew*, vol. 3, p. 203.

13. "When Israel rejected its Messiah a disaster occurred, to be sure, but not only a disaster; a universal mission opened up as well: Israel's Messiah became the world's Savior (cf. 21:43; Rom 11:1b–32)." Bruner, *The Churchbook*, p. 389.

14. *Gospel of Thomas*, 64.

15. For the same or similar imagery, see 8:12; 13:42, 50; 24:51; 25:30.

16. Augustine, "Sermon 90.6," in *Matthew 14–28,* ed. Manlio Simonetti, Ancient Christian Commentary on Scripture, NT Ib (Downers Grove, IL: InterVarsity Press, 2001), p. 147.

17. So Gundry, *Matthew*, p. 439.

18. Luther, quoted in Bruner, *The Churchbook*, p. 390.

19. G. K. Beale, *The Book of Revelation*, New International Greek Testament Commentary (Grand Rapids, MI: Eerdmans, 1999), p. 438.

20. Calvin, quoted in Bruner, *The Churchbook*, p. 390.

21. Cf. Bruner, *The Churchbook*, p. 390.

22. What Matthew Henry called "salvation by sanctification of the Spirit." Bruner, ibid., quotes Henry later on p. 393.

23. Ibid., p. 391.

24. Ibid., p. 392.

25. See Craig L. Blomberg, *Matthew*, New American Commentary (Nashville: Broadman, 1992), p. 329.

26. Schweizer, quoted in Bruner, *The Churchbook*, p. 392.

27. To be fair, Paul is not afraid to give similar warnings—read 1 Corinthian 10 or Galatians 5:19–23. He also does use the terms as Jesus did: "I am astonished that you are so quickly deserting him who *called* you in the grace of Christ and are turning [to their destruction] to a different gospel" (Galatians 1:6).

28. Bruner, *The Churchbook*, p. 392.

29. Gundry, quoted in ibid.

30. Schnackenburg, *The Gospel of Matthew*, p. 215.

31. As G. Barth points out, cited in Bruner, *The Churchbook*, p. 289.

32. Ibid., p. 390.

33. Douglas R. A. Hare, *Matthew*, Interpretation (Louisville: John Knox, 1993), p. 252.

Chapter Sixty-four: Give Back to God

1. Plato, *Republic*, trans. G. M. A. Grube, revised by C. D. C. Reeve (Indianapolis: Hackett, 1992), 1:514–515.

2. According to H. W. Hoehner, the Herodians "are not portrayed [in the Gospels] as either domestic servants or officers of Herod but as influential people whose outlook was friendly to the Herodian rule and consequently to the Roman rule upon which it rested" (in Craig A. Evans and Stanley E. Porter, eds., *Dictionary of New Testament Background* [Downers Grove, IL: InterVarsity Press, 2000], p. 493).

3. *NIV Study Bible* (Grand Rapids, MI: Zondervan, 1985), p. 1876.

4. "Jesus dies with 'the king of the Jews' over his head. Here the words convey that Jesus' claim to be the Christ (cf. 26.64) involves kingship (cf. 21.5; 25.34, 40) and so means political sedition: there can be no king but Caesar (cf. Jn 19.12, 15)." W. D. Davies and Dale C. Allison Jr., *A Critical and Exegetical Commentary on the Gospel according to Saint Matthew*, International Critical Commentary, vol. 3 (Edinburgh: T&T Clark, 1988-1997), p. 581.

5. Ibid., vol. 3, p. 213.

6. Frederick Dale Bruner, *The Churchbook: Matthew 13–28*, 2nd and rev. ed. (Grand Rapids, MI: Eerdmans, 2004), p. 398.

7. Davies and Allison Jr. point out that "according to Hippolytus, *Ref. omn. haer.* 9.26, the Essenes refused to use the denarius, 'saying that they ought not either to carry, or behold, or fashion an image'" (*A Critical and Exegetical Commentary on the Gospel according to Saint Matthew*, vol. 3, p. 216).

8. We know this from the famous dig at Mount Carmel in 1960.

9. As Davies and Allison Jr. have it (*A Critical and Exegetical Commentary on the Gospel according to Saint Matthew*, vol. 3, p. 216).

10. So Bruner, *The Churchbook*, p. 398.

11. Davies and Allison Jr., *A Critical and Exegetical Commentary on the Gospel according to Saint Matthew*, vol. 3, p. 216.

12. Craig L. Blomberg has *Divus et Pontifex Maximus* (*Matthew*, New American Commentary [Nashville: Broadman, 1992], p. 331).

13. McNeile, cited by Bruner, *The Churchbook*, p. 399.

14. As pointed out by Bruner, ibid.

15. For a moving depiction of this, read José Saramago, *The Gospel According to Jesus Christ* (New York: Harcourt Brace & Company, 1994). Saramago's novel depicts Joseph, Mary's husband, as one who was innocently killed in this Roman revenge.

16. Blomberg, *Matthew*, p. 331.

17. Bruner, *The Churchbook*, p. 399.

18. J. C. Ryle, *Matthew: Expository Thoughts on the Gospels*, Crossway Classic Commentaries (Wheaton, IL: Crossway, 1993), p. 207.

19. Douglas R. A. Hare, *Matthew*, Interpretation (Louisville: John Knox, 1993), p. 253.

20. "Whether one considers Jesus' answer to his opponents to be clever or profound or (as we think) both, the performance is impressive and unforgettable. Jesus not only avoids a well-conceived trap but additionally communicates his own teaching. . . . The reader of 22.15–22 not only feels admiration but also knows that here is a teacher without peer and that feeling and knowledge in turn reinforce our Gospel's portrait of Jesus as the great *didaskaios* whose teachings are to be observed until the end of the age." Davies and Allison Jr., *A Critical and Exegetical Commentary on the Gospel according to Saint Matthew*, vol. 3, p. 219.

Chapter Sixty-five: Like Angels in Heaven

1. As Rudolf Schnackenburg notes:

> The case history of the seven brothers is intended to show that a belief in the resurrection, which the Sadducees, unlike the Pharisees, rejected (cf. Acts 23:7–8; Josephus, *Antiquities* 18.16), is untenable. Fictitious narratives like this one served for purposes of disputation. Although it is a matter of a "mocking question," it is intended not to make belief in the resurrection actually laughable but simply to reduce it *ad absurdum*. (*The Gospel of Matthew*, trans. Robert R. Barr [Grand Rapids, MI: Eerdmans, 2002], p. 200.)

2. W. D. Davies and Dale C. Allison Jr., *A Critical and Exegetical Commentary on the Gospel according to Saint Matthew*, International Critical Commentary, vol. 3 (Edinburgh: T&T Clark, 1988-1997), p. 227.

3. Knox Chamblin, *Matthew*, A Mentor Commentary, vol. 2 (Fearn, Ross-shire, UK: Mentor, 2010), p. 1505; cf. Josephus, *Antiquities*, 13.10.6 and 18.1.4.

4. J. Knox Chamblin, "Matthew," in *Evangelical Commentary on the Bible*, ed. Walter A. Elwell (Grand Rapids, MI: Baker, 1996), p. 749. Perhaps Mike Mason is onto something:

> Considering the rich imagery of weddings and marriage throughout the Bible, it seems more probable that far from there being *no* marriage in Heaven, what Jesus must really have been getting at is that Heaven will be *all* marriage. Indeed, in earthly marriage we may detect the sign and promise that in eternity everyone is to be married to everyone else in some transcendent and unimaginable union, and everyone will love everyone else with an intensity akin to that which now is called "being in love," and which impels individual couples to spend their whole lives together. In this way Christian marital love is (or should be) as close as we are likely to experience to being "a piece of Heaven on earth," for it is a true leftover from Paradise. (*The Mystery of Marriage: Meditations on the Miracle* (Sisters, OR: Multnomah, 1985), p. 86.)

5. D. A. Carson, "Matthew," in *The Expositor's Bible Commentary*, vol. 8 (Grand Rapids, MI: Zondervan, 1984), p. 461.

6. On his deathbed Jonathan Edwards's final words to his youngest daughter, Lucy, are well worth considering: "Give my kindest love to my dear Wife, and tell her that the uncommon union which as so long subsisted between us had been of such a nature as I trust is spiritual and therefore will continue forever." Quoted in George M. Marsden, *Jonathan Edwards: A Life* (New Haven, CT: Yale University, 2003), p. 494.

7. Douglas Sean O'Donnell, *The Song of Solomon: An Invitation to Intimacy*, Preaching the Word (Wheaton, IL: Crossway, 2012).

8. See J. C. Ryle, *Matthew: Expository Thoughts on the Gospels*, Crossway Classic Commentaries (Wheaton, IL: Crossway, 1993), p. 210; cf. William L. Lane, *The Gospel of Mark*, New International Commentary on the New Testament (Grand Rapids, MI: Eerdmans, 1974), p. 428.

9. In *Against Heresies*, 1.9.4 Irenaeus employed an analogy for heretics' treatment of Scripture. Daniel B. Clendenin summarizes: "Heretics are also like people who arbitrarily rearrange the poetry of Homer so that, while the verses themselves are original, the meaning has been grossly distorted. In other words, it is one thing to have at one's disposal the original material of Scripture, and quite another to use it properly" (*Eastern Orthodox Christianity: A Western Perspective* [Grand Rapids, MI: Baker, 1994], p. 113).

10. Chamblin, "Matthew," p. 750.

11. William L. Lane, *The Gospel of Mark*, New International Commentary on the New Testament (Grand Rapids, MI: Eerdmans, 1974), p. 430.

Chapter Sixty-six: Out of the Eater Came Something to Eat

1. Rudolf Schnackenburg, *The Gospel of Matthew*, trans. Robert R. Barr (Grand Rapids, MI: Eerdmans, 2002), p. 223.

2. David E. Garland, *Mark*, The NIV Application Commentary (Grand Rapids, MI: Zondervan, 1996), p. 476.

3. Ibid.

4. Rabbi Hillel, quoted in William Barclay, *The Gospel of Mark*, rev. ed. (Philadelphia: Westminster, 1975), pp. 293–295.

5. William Hendriksen, *Exposition of the Gospel According to Matthew* (Grand Rapids, MI: Baker, 2002), p. 810.

6. Frederick Dale Bruner, *The Churchbook: Matthew 13–28*, 2nd and rev. ed. (Grand Rapids, MI: Eerdmans, 2004), p. 418.

7. Ibid.

8. Ibid.

9. Barclay, *The Gospel of Mark*, p. 295.

10. D. A. Carson, "Matthew," in *The Expositor's Bible Commentary*, vol. 9, rev. ed. (Grand Rapids, MI: Zondervan, 2010), p. 523.

11. See Hendriksen, *Exposition of the Gospel According to Matthew*, p. 809.

12. James R. Edwards, *The Gospel According to Mark*, Pillar New Testament Commentary (Grand Rapids, MI: Eerdmans, 2002), p. 371.

13. Hendriksen, *Exposition of the Gospel According to Matthew*, p. 809.

14. W. D. Davies and Dale C. Allison Jr., *A Critical and Exegetical Commentary on the Gospel according to Saint Matthew*, International Critical Commentary, vol. 3 (Edinburgh: T&T Clark, 1988-1997), p. 241.

15. Paul uses this language in reference to the command to love others. See Romans 13:8, 10; Galatians 5:14; 6:2. James also uses it (James 2:8).

16. Augustine, *Confessions*, X.29. This famous phrase is rendered various ways. For example, consider R. S. Pine-Coffin's translation, "Give me the grace to do as you command, and command me to do what you will!" (*Confessions* [New York: Penguin, 1961], p. 233).

17. E.g., The Belgic Confession, Article 29; Heidelberg Catechism, Q. 86; Westminster Confession of Faith, chapters 13–16.

18. Bruner, *The Churchbook*, p. 409.

19. Schnackenburg, *The Gospel of Matthew*, p. 223.

20. Edwards, *The Gospel According to Mark*, pp. 372, 373.

21. Ibid.

22. Ibid.

23. See Palladius, *The Lausiac History*, Ancient Christian Writers, vol. 34, trans. Robert T. Meyer (New York: Paulist, 1964), pp. 52–54.

24. For other similarities between this text and the Sermon on the Mount, see Davies and Allison Jr., *A Critical and Exegetical Commentary on the Gospel according to Saint Matthew*, vol. 3, p. 247.

25. Barbara De Angelis, *Real Moments for Lovers: The Enlightened Guide for Discovering Total Passion and True Intimacy* (New York: Dell, 1997), end of chapter 2.

26. I refer to Augustine's hermeneutical maxim of selecting the interpretation that most fosters the love of God and neighbor. E.g., "Whoever, therefore, thinks that he understands the divine Scriptures or any part of them so that it does not build the double love of God and our neighbor does not understand it at all" (*On Christian Doctrine*, trans. D. W. Robertson Jr. [New York: Macmillan, 1958], XXXVI.40).

27. Todd Wilson, "Encountering Christ from the Pulpit," February 28, 2010, Calvary Memorial Church, Oak Park, Illinois.

Chapter Sixty-seven: Answering to Jesus

1. For this opening illustration and keen exegetical insights, I am indebted to Michael Lefebvre, *Singing the Songs of Jesus: Revisiting the Psalms* (Fearn, Ross-shire, UK: Christian Focus, 2010), pp. 59, 60.

2. Swete says it sweetly: "He had answered all their questions; a single instance was enough to show that they could not answer His" (p. 287). Quoted in W. D. Davies and Dale C. Allison Jr., *A Critical and Exegetical Commentary on the Gospel according to Saint Matthew*, International Critical Commentary, vol. 3 (Edinburgh: T&T Clark, 1988-1997), p. 256.

3. Other than 2 Samuel 7, see Isaiah 11:1–10 and Jeremiah 23:5.

4. Davies and Allison Jr., *A Critical and Exegetical Commentary on the Gospel according to Saint Matthew*, vol. 3, p. 250.

5. Cf. 1:1; 9:27; 15:22; 20:30, 31; 21:9.

6. Cf. 2:15; 3:17; 4:3, 6; 8:29; 14:33; 16:16; 26:63, 64; 27:43, 54.

7. C. H. Spurgeon, *The Gospel of the Kingdom* (Pasadena, TX: Pilgrim Publications, repr. 1996), p. 203.

8. Joseph Fitzmyer notes that to Matthew's church Jesus "was somehow on par with Yahweh of the OT." Fitzmyer, quoted in Donald A. Hagner, *Matthew 14–28*, Word Biblical Commentary, vol. 33b (Nashville: Thomas Nelson, 1993), p. 617.

9. The ESV footnotes "besides" as an alternate translation of "before."

10. Frederick Dale Bruner, *The Churchbook: Matthew 13–28*, 2nd and rev. ed. (Grand Rapids, MI: Eerdmans, 2004), p. 242.

11. Ibid., p. 425.

12. D. A. Carson labels this reality "dual paternity" ("Matthew," in *The Expositor's Bible Commentary*, vol. 8 [Grand Rapids, MI: Zondervan, 1984], p. 468).

13. John Chrysostom, "The Gospel of Matthew" (Homily 71.2), quoted in *Matthew 14–28*, ed. Manlio Simonetti, Ancient Christian Commentary on Scripture, NT Ib (Downers Grove, IL: InterVarsity Press, 2001), p. 159.

14. N. T. Wright, *Matthew for Everyone, vol.* 2 (Louisville: Westminster John Knox, 2002), p. 93.

15. I follow Luz's lead that the title "Son of God" in Matthew is primarily a Christological title (see Ulrich Luz, *Studies in Matthew* [Grand Rapids, MI: Eerdmans, 2005], p. 88). Also on this theme in Matthew, I. Howard Marshall notes:

> Perhaps we are to see some developments in the Gospel. At the outset Jesus is principally the messianic Son of David, thus emphasizing his role in relation to Israel, and his divine origin is stressed rather than his sonship. By the end of the Gospel, he is named in a Trinitarian formula as the Son of God, thus emphasizing his cosmic status for the world after the resurrection. (*New Testament Theology: Many Witnesses, One Gospel* [Downers Grove, IL: InterVarsity Press, 2004], pp. 113, 114.)

16. Cf. 2 Timothy 2:8.

17. Régis Debray, *The New Testament Through 100 Masterpieces of Art* (New York: Merrell, 2004), p. 18. On this Jesse Tree tradition, Debray quotes Victor Hugo:

"A lineage rose up along it like a long chain; below a king was singing [David], on high a God was dying [Jesus]."

18. James Montgomery Boice, *The Gospel of Matthew*, vol. 2 (Grand Rapids, MI: Baker, 2001), p. 486.

19. Ibid.

20. Boring (p. 426), in Bruner, *The Churchbook*, p. 425.

21. Grant R. Osborne, *Matthew*, Exegetical Commentary on the New Testament (Grand Rapids, MI: Zondervan, 2010), p. 830.

22. John Bunyan, *The Pilgrim's Progress*, World's Classics (Oxford: Oxford University Press, 1984), p. 63.

23. Ibid., two quotes from two different sections on page 64.

24. Ibid., p. 65.

25. Ibid., p. 68.

26. What Robert H. Gundry says of Jesus in John's Gospel is true here in Matthew as well: "Jesus is what *is* spoken even as he *does* the speaking" (*Jesus the Word According to John the Sectarian: A Paleofundamentalist Manifesto for Contemporary Evangelicalism, Especially Its Elites, in North America* [Grand Rapids, MI: Eerdmans, 2002], p. 49).

27. Bruner, *The Churchbook*, p. 599.

28. Osborne, *Matthew*, p. 953.

Chapter Sixty-eight: The Exaltation of Humility

1. The word *iūstitia* and the name *Eustace* don't mean the same thing, but their similar sound got my mind running from one word to the other.

2. James I. Packer, "Still Surprised by Lewis," *Christianity Today*, vol. 42, Issue 10, September 1998.

3. C. S. Lewis, *The Voyage of the Dawn Treader* (New York: HarperCollins, 1994), p. 91.

4. Ibid., p. 248.

5. Manson, *Sayings*, p. 228, in W. D. Davies and Dale C. Allison Jr., *A Critical and Exegetical Commentary on the Gospel according to Saint Matthew*, International Critical Commentary, vol. 3 (Edinburgh: T&T Clark, 1988-1997), p. 267.

6. Adolf Schlatter, *Der Evangelist*, p. 670; *Das Evangelium*, p. 343, in Frederick Dale Bruner, *The Churchbook: Matthew 13–28*, 2nd and rev. ed. (Grand Rapids, MI: Eerdmans, 2004), p. 436.

7. I side with Plummer, Gundry, and others that the disciples are to heed the teaching of the scribes and Pharisees only insofar as they truly teach Moses. See A. Plummer, *An Exegetical Commentary on the Gospel according to S. Matthew* (London: E Stock, 1909), p. 314; Robert H. Gundry, *Matthew: A Commentary on His Literary and Theological Art* (Grand Rapids, MI: Eerdmans, 1982), p. 455.

8. Cf. Exodus 13:1–10; 13:11–16; Deuteronomy 6:4–9; 11:13–21.

9. For a parody and picture of this reality, see Jonathan Acuff, *Stuff Christians Like* (Grand Rapids, MI: Zondervan, 2010), p. 83.

10. For a full official description of this "spectacle of glory and magnificence which has no parallel," read "The Coronation of Pope Leo XII on March 3, 1878," *Catholic World*, March 20, 1879, pp. 280–285. Also found at www.traditio.com/tradlib/coron.txt. It's unbelievable!

11. Bruner, *The Churchbook*, p. 435.

12. Is this a "general prohibition against all ecclesiastical titles"? So Davies and Allison Jr., *A Critical and Exegetical Commentary on the Gospel according to Saint Matthew*, vol. 3, p. 278.

13. Calvin, *Institutes*, IV.viii.1, in Bruner, *The Churchbook*, p. 437.

14. Calvin, 3:50, in ibid., p. 438.

15. Cf. Ignatius, *Epistle to the Magnesians*, 9.1.

16. Bruner, *The Churchbook*, p. 437. Bruner also lists Kingsbury, *Story*, p. 46.

17. Craig L. Blomberg provides a helpful summary:

> As with many of Jesus' teachings in the Sermon on the Mount, texts elsewhere in the New Testament make it clear that he is not promulgating absolute commands. People are properly called teachers in Acts 13:1; 1 Tim 2:7; and Heb 5:12. Paul will even refer to a spiritual gift that enables some people to be so identified (Eph 4:11; 1 Cor 12:28–29; cf. Jas 3:1). It remains appropriate to call a biological parent one's father, and even one's spiritual parent may be addressed with this term (1 Cor 4:15; cf. also 1 John 2:13; Acts 22:1). So the point of vv. 8–12 must be that such titles are not to be used to confer privilege or status. (*Matthew*, New American Commentary [Nashville: Broadman, 1992], pp. 342, 343.)

J. C. Ryle adds, "The rule here laid down must be interpreted with proper scriptural qualification. We are not forbidden to esteem ministers very highly in love for their work's sake (1 Thessalonians 5:13)" (*Matthew: Expository Thoughts on the Gospels*, Crossway Classic Commentaries [Wheaton, IL: Crossway, 1993], p. 216).

18. The Roman Catholic priest and exegete John P. Meier, in his Matthew commentary (1980) comments on this verse: "The Catholic Church in particular must reflect on whether these inspired words call it to forsake the ecclesiastical titles which have proliferated in its midst. . . ." (quoted in Bruner, *The Churchbook,* p. 439).

19. John Chrysostom, "The Gospel of Matthew" (Homily 72.3), quoted in *Matthew 14–28,* ed. Manlio Simonetti, Ancient Christian Commentary on Scripture, NT Ib (Downers Grove, IL: InterVarsity Press, 2001) p. 168.

20. Donald A. Hagner, *Matthew 14–28,* Word Biblical Commentary, vol. 33b (Nashville: Thomas Nelson, 1993), p. 661.

21. Bruner, *The Churchbook*, p. 441.

22. Lewis *The Voyage of the Dawn Treader*, p. 108.

23. Ibid., p. 109.

Chapter Sixty-nine: "Is He Quite Safe?"

1. C. S. Lewis, *The Lion, the Witch and the Wardrobe* (New York: HarperCollins, 1994), pp. 79, 80.

2. Robertson and Plummer, quoted in William Barclay, *The Gospel of Matthew*, vol. 2, rev. ed. (Philadelphia: Westminster, 1975), p. 288.

3. For a good summary of the Jewish religious authorities, see Knox Chamblin, *Matthew*, A Mentor Commentary, vol. 2 (Fearn, Ross-shire, UK: Mentor, 2010), pp. 1502–1517.

4. In verses 37–39 the "you" expands to represent all of God's people (i.e., Jews) who rejected Jesus.

5. Norman H. Baynes, *The Speeches of Adolf Hitler, April 1922–August 1939*, vol. 1 (Oxford: Oxford University Press, 1942), pp. 19, 20. I am grateful to Eric Bargerhuff for this reference.

6. E.g., Isaiah 5:8–24; Amos 5:18–20; Micah 2:1–4; Habakkuk 2:6–20.

7. W. D. Davies and Dale C. Allison Jr., *A Critical and Exegetical Commentary on the Gospel according to Saint Matthew*, International Critical Commentary, vol. 3 (Edinburgh: T&T Clark, 1988-1997), p. 286.

8. Barclay, *The Gospel of Matthew*, vol. 2, p. 294.

9. Ibid.

10. "The sin is not observance of the small but disregard of the large." Davies and Allison Jr., *A Critical and Exegetical Commentary on the Gospel according to Saint Matthew*, vol. 3, p. 296.

11. In the ESV the word "hypocrite" is used twice, "hypocrisy" four times, and "hypocritically" once. In the Greek the word is used in various forms seven times.

12. This definition is a slight rewording of Grant R. Osborne's definition (*Matthew*, Exegetical Commentary on the New Testament [Grand Rapids, MI: Zondervan, 2010], p. 847). On character formation, Kevin J. Vanhoozer refers to Constantin Stanislavski's method of convincing acting. Vanhoozer writes, "Actors who exploit the theater are 'the deadliest enemies of art' [Stankislavski, *An Actor Prepares* (New York: Routledge), 1964, p. 31], just as those who exploit the church [i.e., hypocrites] are the deadliest enemies of faith" (*The Drama of Doctrine: A Canonical Linguistic Approach to Christian Theology* [Louisville: Westminster John Knox, 2005], p. 370).

13. So Rudolf Schnackenburg, *The Gospel of Matthew*, trans. Robert R. Barr (Grand Rapids, MI: Eerdmans, 2002), p. 232.

14. Davies and Allison Jr., *A Critical and Exegetical Commentary on the Gospel according to Saint Matthew*, vol. 3, p. 285.

15. "The passage refers to the murders of the righteous from Genesis 4 (the first murder in the Hebrew Bible) to 2 Chronicles 24 (the last murder in the Hebrew Bible) [literarily, not chronologically]; in other words, Abel and Zechariah are the first and last in a series" (ibid., vol. 3, p. 319).

16. Some of the language for this sentence is taken from Merrill C. Tenney, *The Genius of the Gospels* (Grand Rapids, MI: Eerdmans, 1951), p. 118.

17. Ibid., pp. 118, 119.

Chapter Seventy: Our Heads inside the Heavens

1. J. C. Ryle, *Matthew: Expository Thoughts on the Gospels*, Crossway Classic Commentaries (Wheaton, IL: Crossway, 1993), p. 225.

2. See Ulrich Luz, *Matthew 21–28*, Hermeneia (Minneapolis: Fortress, 2005), pp. 184–189; cf. pp. 209, 213, 214. D. A. Carson calls the history of interpretation "immensely complex" ("Matthew," in *The Expositor's Bible Commentary*, vol. 8 [Grand Rapids, MI: Zondervan, 1984], p. 488).

3. W. D. Davies and Dale C. Allison Jr., *A Critical and Exegetical Commentary on the Gospel according to Saint Matthew*, International Critical Commentary, vol. 3 (Edinburgh: T&T Clark, 1988-1997), p. 369.

4. R. T. France argues that only the fall of Jerusalem is in view in 24:1–35 (*The Gospel According to Matthew*, Tyndale New Testament Commentaries (Grand Rapids, MI: Eerdmans, 1985), pp. 333–336.

5. Kim Riddlebarger, *A Case for Amillennialism: Understanding the End Times* (Grand Rapids, MI: Baker, 2003), p. 161.

6. Based on the thought that "neither an exclusively historical nor an exclusively eschatological interpretation is satisfactory," C. E. B. Cranfield concludes, "We must allow for a double reference, for a mingling of historical and eschatological" (*The Gospel According to St. Mark*, The Cambridge Greek Testament [New York: Cambridge University Press, 1983], pp. 401, 402).

7. Daniel M. Doriani, *Matthew*, Reformed Expository Commentary, vol. 2 (Phillipsburg, NJ: P&R, 2008), pp. 353, 354.

8. David Jackman and William Philip, *Teaching Matthew: Unlocking the Gospel of Matthew for the Expositor* (Fearn, Ross-shire, UK: Christian Focus, 2003).

9. For example, David Jackman and William Philip write:

> We can understand this in terms of looking at a mountain range. From a distance, mountains which may be very many miles apart seem to be close together; but as you get nearer to them, so your perspective changes and you begin to see the real distances which separate peak from peak. That is what often happens in Old Testament prophecy. Take, for example, the classic example of Isaiah. He sees the destruction of Babylon and the final day of the Lord as if it was one day of divine judgment. The same pattern emerges in both, but we now know that there are many centuries between those two events, that the two peaks, as it were, have a huge distance separating them. But because of their similarities, they are both called 'the day of the Lord' in the closing chapters of Isaiah's prophecy. (*Teaching Matthew: Unlocking the Gospel of Matthew for the Expositor* [Fearn, Ross-shire, UK: Christian Focus, 2003], p. 203.)

10. See Michael Wilkins, *Matthew*, The NIV Application Commentary (Grand Rapids, MI: Zondervan, 2004), p. 790.

11. Frederick Dale Bruner, *The Churchbook: Matthew 13–28,* 2nd and rev. ed. (Grand Rapids, MI: Eerdmans, 2004), p. 470.

12. George R. Beasley-Murray, *Jesus and the Last Days: The Interpretation of the Olivet Discourse* (Peabody, MA: Hendrickson, 1993), p. 383. Of the Second Temple, Josephus wrote,

> The exterior of the building wanted nothing that could astound either mind or eye. For, being covered on all sides with massive plates of gold, the sun was no sooner up than it radiated so fiery a flash that persons straining to look at it were compelled to avert their eyes, as from the solar rays. To approaching strangers it appeared from a distance like a snow-clad mountain; for all that was not overlaid with gold was of purest white. Some of the stones in the building [he goes on to say they were huge, they] were forty-five cubits in length, five in height and six in breadth. (*Bell* 5.184-226.)

Cf. Josephus, *Antiquities*, 15.391-402; *Jewish War*, 5.190-277.

13. Josephus writes that the temple was "built of hard, white stones, each of which was about 25 cubits [35 feet] in length, 8 in height [11 feet] and 12 in width [17 feet]." Quoted in William Lane, *The Gospel According to Mark*, New International Commentary on the New Testament (Grand Rapids, MI: Eerdmans, 1982), p. 451.

14. See David L. Turner, *Matthew*, Baker Exegetical Commentary on the New Testament (Grand Rapids, MI: Baker, 2008), p. 566.

15. "There is no other sign of the *parousia* than the Son of Man himself." Rudolf Schnackenburg, *The Gospel of Matthew*, trans. Robert R. Barr (Grand Rapids, MI: Eerdmans, 2002), p. 244.

16. James R. Edwards, *The Gospel According to Mark*, Pillar New Testament Commentary (Grand Rapids, MI: Eerdmans, 2002), p. 368.

17. Will and Ariel Durant, *The Lessons of History* (New York: Simon & Schuster, 1968), p. 81.

18. Davies and Allison Jr., *A Critical and Exegetical Commentary on the Gospel according to Saint Matthew*, vol. 3, p. 341, n. 87.

19. Edwards, *The Gospel According to Mark*, p. 368.

20. Wilkins, *Matthew*, p. 775.

21. Craig L. Blomberg, *Matthew*, New American Commentary (Nashville: Broadman, 1992), p. 356.

22. Tertullian, *Apology* 50, quoted in Everett Ferguson, *Church History, Volume One: From Christ to Pre-Reformation: The Rise and Growth of the Church in Its Cultural, Intellectual, and Political Context* (Grand Rapids, MI: Zondervan, 2005), p. 127.

23. Bruner, *The Churchbook*, p. 490.

24. Ibid.

25. Ibid., p. 491.

26. Ibid.

27. My question is a borrowed from two separate sentences in ibid., p. 492.

28. George W. Kitchin (1887) and Michael R. Newbolt (1916, alt.), "Lift High the Cross."

29. G. K. Chesterton, quoted in R. Kent Hughes, *Luke: That You May Know the Truth*, Preaching the Word, vol. 2 (Wheaton, IL: Crossway, 1998), p. 295.

30. David E. Garland, *Mark*, The NIV Application Commentary (Grand Rapids, MI: Zondervan, 1996), p. 491.

Chapter Seventy-one: Apocalypse Then

1. This story was shared by Rev. Zdzislaw Tawlik of Poland at Whitworth College in 1984, recorded in Frederick Dale Bruner, *The Churchbook: Matthew 13–28*, 2nd and rev. ed. (Grand Rapids, MI: Eerdmans, 2004), p. 521. I have borrowed some of Bruner's language.

2. "This was perhaps our Lord's strongest assertion of deity yet. His words will never pass away, though the heavens and earth will. The reason Jesus can speak of the future with such certainty is because his words are the words of God" (Kim Riddlebarger, *A Case for Amillennialism: Understanding the End Times* [Grand Rapids, MI: Baker, 2003], p. 177).

3. D. A. Carson speaks of the details here being too limited "geographically and culturally" to point beyond AD 70 ("Matthew," in *The Expositor's Bible Commentary*, vol. 9, rev. ed. [Grand Rapids, MI: Zondervan, 2010], p. 561).

4. See John Nolland, *The Gospel of Matthew*, New International Greek Testament Commentary (Grand Rapids, MI: Eerdmans, 2005), p. 971.

5. Josephus, *Bell*, 7.1.

6. Riddlebarger, *A Case for Amillennialism*, p. 171.

7. Josephus, *Jewish War*, V. 12, 4.

8. Josephus, *Bell*, 6.420-421.

9. Riddlebarger, *A Case for Amillennialism*, pp. 171, 178.

10. Craig L. Blomberg, *Matthew*, New American Commentary (Nashville: Broadman, 1992), p. 358.

11. Riddlebarger, *A Case for Amillennialism*, p. 173.

12. N. T. Wright, *Matthew for Everyone*, vol. 2 (Louisville: Westminster John Knox, 2002), pp. 118, 119.

13. Ibid.

14. Eusebius, *Ecclesiastical History*, trans. Christian Cruse (Grand Rapids, MI: Baker, 1955), pp. 86, 87.

15. Bengel, 1:272, quoted in Bruner, *The Churchbook*, p. 500. I credit Bruner with bringing this prayer-application to my attention.

16. John Owen, *The Works of John Owen*, ed. William H. Goold, vol. 6 (Carlisle, PA: Banner of Truth, 1987), p. 7.

17. Ibid., vol. 6, p. 9.

18. Ibid., vol. 6, p. 21.

19. Ibid., vol. 6, p. 33.

20. Ibid., vol. 6, p. 34.

21. Ibid., vol. 6, p. 79.

22. Ibid., vol. 6, p. 49.

Chapter Seventy-two: God Only Knows

1. See Paul Boyer, *When Time Shall Be No More: Prophecy Belief in Modern American Culture* (Cambridge, MA: Harvard University Press, 1992), pp. 53–55.

2. This was the most famous of the nine false Jehovah Witness's doomsday prophecies—1874, 1878, 1881, 1910, 1914, 1918, 1925, 1975, and 1984.

3. The source I used for many of the dates above was www.bible.ca/pre-date-setters .htm; accessed on September 26, 2011.

4. France, *Matthew*, p. 349, quoted in Craig L. Blomberg, *Matthew*, New American Commentary (Nashville: Broadman, 1992), p. 367.

5. William Barclay, *The Gospel of Matthew*, vol. 2, rev. ed. (Philadelphia: Westminster, 1975), p. 315.

6. Michael Green, *Matthew for Today* (Dallas: Word, 1989), pp. 233, 235, quoted in Blomberg, *Matthew*, p. 367.

7. See 2 Thessalonians 2:2; 2 Peter 3:10.

8. W. D. Davies and Dale C. Allison Jr., *A Critical and Exegetical Commentary on the Gospel according to Saint Matthew*, International Critical Commentary, vol. 3 (Edinburgh: T&T Clark, 1988-1997), p. 378.

9. See Davies and Allison's helpful chart in ibid., p. 337.

10. Pesch, *Marcus*, p. 310, adds another thought: "Even the angels do not know, although they have a part in the End events; even the Son does not know, the Son of Man himself whose Day it is!" Quoted in Frederick Dale Bruner, *The Churchbook: Matthew 13–28*, 2nd and rev. ed. (Grand Rapids, MI: Eerdmans, 2004), p. 521.

11. Rudolf Schnackenburg, *The Gospel of Matthew*, trans. Robert R. Barr (Grand Rapids, MI: Eerdmans, 2002), p. 246.

12. Daniel M. Doriani, *Matthew*, Reformed Expository Commentary, vol. 2 (Phillipsburg, NJ: P&R, 2008), pp. 381, 382. Blomberg is also helpful on this "most astonishing and significant of all of Jesus' sayings both for eschatology and Christology" (*Matthew*, p. 364) when he comments: "Christians who balk at the implications of this verse reflect their own docetism (the early Christian heresy of not accepting the full humanity of Jesus) and lack a full appreciation for the extent of God's condescension in the incarnation and in the various human limitations he took upon himself" (p. 365). The *ESV Study Bible* also gives a very helpful note on this verse.

13. "The supernatural darkness of the consummation is richly symbolic. Not only does it belong to the correlation of beginning and end, but it is a sign of both divine judgment and mourning and becomes the velvet background for the Son of man's splendor (24.27, 30). Moreover, on the literary level it foreshadows the darkness of Jesus' death (27.45) while that darkness in turn presages the world's assize." Davies and Allison Jr., *A Critical and Exegetical Commentary on the Gospel according to Saint Matthew*, vol. 3, p. 358.

14. Blomberg takes them as metaphors: "He does not intend his language to be taken as a literal, scientific description of events but as a vivid metaphor, much as we speak of earth-shaking developments" (*Matthew*, p. 362). So also N. T. Wright, *Matthew for Everyone*, vol. 2 (Louisville: Westminster John Knox, 2002), pp. 122, 123 and Schnackenburg, *The Gospel of Matthew*, pp. 243, 244. While the prophets use the same language that Jesus uses as metaphors, I'm not convinced that Jesus is speaking in metaphors. Might not he usher in the new creation with some cosmic connection to the first creation?

15. Perhaps Jesus gives five illustrations. The fifth would be the flood (vv. 37–39), which was not only universal but obvious to the whole world. No one missed seeing and experiencing it.

16. Paul adds more sound to the second coming: "For the Lord himself will descend from heaven with *a cry of command,* with *the voice of an archangel,* and with *the sound of the trumpet* of God" (1 Thessalonians 4:16; cf. 1 Corinthians 15:52).

17. On the theme "universal," note the language—"all the tribes of the earth" (v. 30) and "the four winds" (v. 31). We might even say "universal" and "cosmic" based on the phrase "from one end of heaven to the other" (v. 31).

18. Meier notes, in *Matthew*, pp. 287, 288, "Compared with 16.27, what is striking here is the total absence of God the Father. The Son of Man acts completely on his own authority, sending out *his* angels to gather in from all the earth *his* elect. . . . Mt raises the divine majesty of the Son of Man to the greatest heights possible" (Meier, quoted in Davies and Allison Jr., *A Critical and Exegetical Commentary on the Gospel according to Saint Matthew*, vol. 3, p. 362).

19. J. C. Ryle, *Matthew: Expository Thoughts on the Gospels*, Crossway Classic Commentaries (Wheaton, IL: Crossway, 1993), p. 232.

20. Calvin, quoted in J. C. Ryle, *Mark: Expository Thoughts on the Gospels*, Crossway Classic Commentaries (Wheaton, IL: Crossway, 1993), p. 216.

21. Used later in the New Testament for Jesus' return (1 Thessalonians 5:2; 2 Peter 3:10; Revelation 3:3).

22. Bruner, *The Churchbook*, p. 524.

23. They are left because they are not prepared. So claims Davies and Allison Jr., *A Critical and Exegetical Commentary on the Gospel according to Saint Matthew*, vol. 3, p. 383.

24. See Doriani's helpful translation and explanation in *Matthew*, pp. 382, 383. Cf. Blomberg, *Matthew*, p. 366.

25. "People who seem so similar at work will be shown dramatically dissimilar at the Judgment." Bruner, *The Churchbook*, p. 527.

26. Is it "that" one servant who is either wise or wicked? I'm not convinced. Based on the context, I favor two different people—like the two working the mill and the sheep and the goats. Our text is filled with and surrounded by the contrast between two people or groups. If this is an exception, it is the only one.

27. Bruner, *The Churchbook*, p. 525.

28. Bruner captures this well: "A distant Lord is no longer Lord" (ibid., p. 539).

29. Noah's generation was drinking; this man is drinking with others *and beating* others! They got water; he'll get fire!

30. Bruner, *The Churchbook*, p. 526.

31. Or is this cutting to pieces an allusion to the line from the warning song of Moses, symbolizing God's removing them from memory (cf. 25:12)? Thus the parallelism:

> I will cut them to pieces;
> I will wipe them from human memory. (Deuteronomy 32:26)

32. Davies and Allison Jr. note that the "reward is more responsibility, not (as one might expect for a slave) freedom" (*A Critical and Exegetical Commentary on the Gospel according to Saint Matthew*, vol. 3, p. 388). True. However, I'll add, isn't service to Christ true freedom?

33. See Bruner, *The Churchbook*, pp. 523, 525.

34. See ibid., p. 523.

35. Jonathan Edwards, *The Works of Jonathan Edwards*, ed. Edward Hickman, vol. 1 (Carlisle, PA: Banner of Truth, repr. 1992), pp. xx, xxi.

36. David Jackman and William Philip, *Teaching Matthew: Unlocking the Gospel of Matthew for the Expositor* (Fearn, Ross-shire, UK: Christian Focus, 2003), p. 213.

37. "Eschatological agnosticism" (Bruner, *The Churchbook*, p. 522) does not mean there is not "eschatological vigilance" (Davies and Allison Jr., *A Critical and Exegetical Commentary on the Gospel according to Saint Matthew*, vol. 3, p. 374).

Chapter Seventy-three: The Sad Story of Five Silly Girls

1. In 9:15 Jesus speaks of his present ministry using nuptial imagery. Here Jesus compares his future kingdom to a wedding. This is not a contradiction. The kingdom is already and not yet. In the first coming of Christ the kingdom has already arrived, but it has not yet been culminated. That is, we will enter into the kingdom through faith in Christ, and yet as kingdom people we pray, "Your kingdom come."

2. See note on 25:1 in *ESV Study Bible*.

3. This late hour—"at midnight"—Augustine calls "the moment of least expectation" and "complete unawareness" ("Sermon 93.7," quoted in *Matthew 14–28*,

ed. Manlio Simonetti, Ancient Christian Commentary on Scripture, NT Ib [Downers Grove, IL: InterVarsity Press, 2001], pp. 217, 218).

4. Craig L. Blomberg, *Preaching the Parables: From Responsible Interpretation to Power Proclamation* (Grand Rapids, MI: Baker, 2004), p. 196.

5. Brian Vickers, ed., *Francis Bacon: The Major Works*, Oxford World's Classics (New York: Oxford, 2008), pp. xxxiii, xxxiv.

6. Peter Bolt and Tony Payne, *Mark: The Beginning of the Gospel*, Faith Walk Bible Studies (Wheaton, IL: Crossway, 2000), p. 55.

7. David Wenham, *The Parables of Jesus* (Downers Grove, IL: IVP Academic, 1989), p. 80.

8. Rudolf Schnackenburg, *The Gospel of Matthew*, trans. Robert R. Barr (Grand Rapids, MI: Eerdmans, 2002), p. 250.

9. "Jesus probably chose the number 'ten' because of its biblical implications as a symbol of fullness or completeness (ten commandments, ten plagues, ten percent tithe . . .)." Grant R. Osborne, *Matthew*, Exegetical Commentary on the New Testament (Grand Rapids, MI: Zondervan, 2010), p. 915.

10. Craig L. Blomberg, *Matthew*, New American Commentary (Nashville: Broadman, 1992), p. 371. Also, "The OT speaks of God 'knowing' his chosen people (Jer. 1:5; Hos. 13:5; Amos 3:2). The same theme continues in the NT, where it describes a saving relationship with God through Jesus Christ (cf. Gal. 4:8–9; 2 Tim. 2:19)," *ESV Study Bible* on 25:11, 12.

11. So Calvin, in W. D. Davies and Dale C. Allison Jr., *A Critical and Exegetical Commentary on the Gospel according to Saint Matthew*, International Critical Commentary, vol. 3 (Edinburgh: T&T Clark, 1988-1997), p. 397, n. 159.

12. A. B. Bruce's reading, see ibid.

13. J. C. Ryle, *Matthew: Expository Thoughts on the Gospels*, Crossway Classic Commentaries (Wheaton, IL: Crossway, 1993), p. 241.

14. Wenham, *The Parables of Jesus*, p. 81.

15. Were the wise virgins selfish? No. As Garland notes: "[T]he parable is an allegory about spiritual preparedness, not a lesson on the golden rule" (Garland, Matthew, quoted in Davies and Allison Jr., *A Critical and Exegetical Commentary on the Gospel according to Saint Matthew*, p. 399).

16. Tennyson, quoted in Philip Schaff, *Christ in Song: Hymns of Immanuel Selected from all Ages* (Vestavia Hills, AL: Solid Ground Christian Books, repr. 2003), p. 307.

17. Frederick Dale Bruner, *The Churchbook: Matthew 13–28*, 2nd and rev. ed. (Grand Rapids, MI: Eerdmans, 2004), p. 548.

18. In some evangelical circles it is popular to talk about salvation in corporate terms—i.e., we are saved as or with the church and there is nothing or little to nothing that is individualistic about salvation. Well, Jesus didn't get the memo. Each illustration he uses in these five or six parables are about an individual and his or her right or wrong stand with God at Jesus' second coming.

19. Bruner, *The Churchbook*, p. 545.

20. Ibid.

21. For this idea, see ibid., p. 547.

22. Davies and Allison Jr., *A Critical and Exegetical Commentary on the Gospel according to Saint Matthew*, vol. 3, p. 398.

23. Bruner, *The Churchbook*, p. 529.

24. Found in William Barclay, *The Gospel of Matthew*, vol. 2, rev. ed. (Philadelphia: Westminster, 1975), p. 318.

Chapter Seventy-four: From Vigilance to Diligence

1. On the Parable of the Ten Virgins, Hilary of Poitiers writes,

> The whole story is about the great day of the Lord, when those things concealed from the human mind will be revealed through our understanding of divine judgment. Then the faith true to the Lord's coming will win the just reward for *unwavering hope*. ("On Matthew, 27.3," quoted in Matthew 14–28, ed. Manlio Simonetti, Ancient Christian Commentary on Scripture, NT Ib [Downers Grove, IL: InterVarsity Press, 2001], p. 215, emphasis mine.)

2. J. C. Ryle, *Matthew: Expository Thoughts on the Gospels*, Crossway Classic Commentaries (Wheaton, IL: Crossway, 1993), p. 242.

3. Ben Witherington calls the Parable of the Talents a "twin parable" with the Parable of the Ten Virgins (Matthew, p. 459, in David Wenham, *The Parables of Jesus* [Downers Grove, IL: IVP Academic, 1989], p. 459).

4. D. A. Carson, "Matthew," in *The Expositor's Bible Commentary*, vol. 9, rev. ed. (Grand Rapids, MI: Zondervan, 2010), p. 579.

5. Grant R. Osborne, *Matthew*, Exegetical Commentary on the New Testament (Grand Rapids, MI: Zondervan, 2010), p. 924.

6. W. D. Davies and Dale C. Allison Jr., *A Critical and Exegetical Commentary on the Gospel according to Saint Matthew*, International Critical Commentary, vol. 3 (Edinburgh: T&T Clark, 1988-1997), p. 402. Cf. R. T. France, *The Gospel of Matthew*, New International Commentary on the New Testament (Grand Rapids, MI: Eerdmans, 2007), p. 951.

7. Romans 12:3–8; 1 Corinthians 12; Ephesians 4:7, 8; 1 Peter 4:10.

8. Craig L. Blomberg, *Matthew*, New American Commentary (Nashville: Broadman, 1992), p. 375.

9. Ibid.

10. Frederick Dale Bruner, *The Churchbook: Matthew 13–28*, 2nd and rev. ed. (Grand Rapids, MI: Eerdmans, 2004), pp. 554, 556.

11. Meier, Matthew, p. 299, quoted in Davies and Allison Jr., *A Critical and Exegetical Commentary on the Gospel according to Saint Matthew*, vol. 3, p. 408.

12. "Human beings have been created to be goal- and praise-oriented. The single great goal of Christians can be to hear their Lord's 'Wonderful!' spoken to their life work at the Judgment. We cannot live without laying up treasures somewhere—so we can lay them up in heaven, as Jesus commanded, by doing all with an eye to divine approval at the Judgment—'for your eyes only' (cf. 6:19–21). This is Matthew's version of faith." Bruner, *The Churchbook*, p. 557.

13. Ibid., p. 558.

14. Schlatter, *Das Evangelium*, p. 372, in ibid., p. 558.

15. "One speaks of the future judgment for the sake of the present." Ulrich Luz, *Matthew 21–28*, Hermeneia (Minneapolis: Fortress, 2005), p. 258.

16. "That the three scenes and the entire story end by referring to the wicked and slothful slave shows where the emphasis lies, as does the extra space given to his

punishment: the parable is more warning than encouragement." Davies and Allison Jr., *A Critical and Exegetical Commentary on the Gospel according to Saint Matthew*, vol. 3, pp. 401, 402.

17. See Bruner, *The Churchbook*, p. 560.

18. "Shouldn't the servant have been more modest or Christ-centered and have said something like, 'Look what *you* did through me,' instead of 'Look! *I made . . . ?*' But in the first part of his little speech the servant already honored grace ("Lord, you *gave me*") as the source of his work (cf. Marguerat, 559). When Christians acknowledge the priority of God's work, they may rejoice in the posteriority of their work. Here is a joy in work that should not be depressed by a heavy-handed spirituality. Jesus wants disciples to feel good about their work. There is a naturalness about the moralism of the Gospel of Matthew that is sometimes evangelically freeing" (ibid., p. 557).

19. Carson is helpful in sorting through the potential Old Testament ethical issues related to Jesus' banking illustration (see "Matthew," p. 581).

20. "Do you see how sins of omission also are met with extreme rejection? It is not only the covetous, the active doer of evil things and the adulterer, but also the one who fails to do good." Chrysostom, "The Gospel of Matthew" (Homily 78.3), quoted in *Matthew 14–28*, ed. Manlio Simonetti, p. 229.

21. Bruner, *The Churchbook*, p. 563.

22. Contra Jeremias, *Parables of Jesus*, trans. S. H. Hooke (London: SCM Press, 1971), p. 62, William Barclay, The Gospel of Matthew, vol. 2, rev. ed. (Philadelphia: Westminster, 1975), pp. 322, 323), and N. T. Wright, *Matthew for Everyone*, vol. 2 (Louisville: Westminster John Knox, 2002), pp. 137, 138, I agree with Davies and Allison that "Jesus spoke the parable not to [or about] outsiders [e.g., the scribes and Pharisees] but to insiders, to emphasize responsibility" (*A Critical and Exegetical Commentary on the Gospel according to Saint Matthew*, vol. 3, p. 403).

Chapter Seventy-five: Jesus' Last Sermon

1. David Helm, *One to One Bible Reading: A Simple Guide for Every Christian* (Kingsford, NSW, Australia: Matthias Media, 2011), pp. 44, 45.

2. "Some suggest that sheep and goats were separated each night because goats were more vulnerable to the cold and would need more protection. This explanation has been repeated often because of Jeremiah's influence, but is without basis. Klaus Wengst shows that this theory is based on a misunderstanding of a comment from G. Dalman and is not supportable from early Palestine. He suggests that the division took place to separate young males for slaughter. Others suggest that it is the separation of the ewes for milking. It is not even certain that 'goats' are in view, for the word so translated, *eriphos*, refers to a young male kid. In the end, no reason is given for the separation, and the text does not say that such a separation takes place each night. The reason for the separation does not impact interpretation. Goats, if that is the right translation, do not carry a negative connotation in ancient Palestine; both sheep and goats were valued and were pastured together. The analogy is built on the separation of right and left, not on the character or valuation of goats, even if sheep would have been valued more highly. Nothing cultural prepares the reader for the strong condemnation of the goats." Klyne R. Snodgrass, *Stories with Intent: A Comprehensive Guide to the Parables of Jesus* (Grand Rapids, MI: Eerdmans, 2008), pp. 550, 551.

3. Rudolf Schnackenburg says, "It is not a parable but a revelatory discourse with a graphic portrayal, a painting with shining colors and moving themes" (*The Gospel of Matthew*, trans. Robert R. Barr [Grand Rapids, MI: Eerdmans, 2002], p. 255). Ben Witherington III calls it "an apocalyptic prophecy with some parabolic elements" (*Matthew*, Smith & Helwys Bible Commentary [Macon, GA: Smith & Helwys, 2006], p. 465). R. T. France believes it is closer to "the majestic visions of divine judgment in the Book of Revelation" than to the parables (*The Gospel of Matthew*, New International Commentary on the New Testament [Grand Rapids, MI: Eerdmans, 2007], p. 960). Snodgrass calls it "a two-verse analogy" with the rest being "explanation" (*Stories with Intent*, p. 543).

4. "Strictly speaking, this text is not a parable. . . . The passage is often treated in a study of Christ's parables, however, because of its similarity in structure, theme, and use of figures of speech to the other stories of Jesus that clearly fall into that category" (Craig L. Blomberg, *Preaching the Parables: From Responsible Interpretation to Power Proclamation* [Grand Rapids, MI: Baker, 2004], p. 206).

5. See Frederick Dale Bruner, *The Churchbook: Matthew 13–28*, 2nd and rev. ed. (Grand Rapids, MI: Eerdmans, 2004), p. 568.

6. "What is spoken of Yahweh in the OT belongs to Christ" (Grant R. Osborne, *Matthew*, Exegetical Commentary on the New Testament [Grand Rapids, MI: Zondervan, 2010], p. 933).

7. "Jesus' coming 'with the angels' refers to the host of heaven who at the eschaton will be the eschatological agents of resurrection and judgment (cf. Zech 14:5; Matt 13:41, 49; 16:27; 24:31; 1 Thess 4:15; 2 Thess 1:7; Jude 14)" (ibid.).

8. See the chart in W. D. Davies and Dale C. Allison Jr., *A Critical and Exegetical Commentary on the Gospel according to Saint Matthew*, International Critical Commentary, vol. 3 (Edinburgh: T&T Clark, 1988-1997), p. 419. They also list the similarities in Revelation 20:11–15.

9. "In Revelation 4 God is the one on the throne; in Revelation 5:6 the Lamb stands between the throne and the four living beings, and judgment is reserved to God (Rev. 20:11–15)" (Schnackenburg, *The Gospel of Matthew*, p. 256).

10. Bruner writes, "Matthew uses the word 'glory' twice in one sentence as if to say, 'You want glory?—The Return of the Son of Man for Judgment, there's glory!'" (*The Churchbook*, p. 565).

11. "As always, meaning can only be determined in context. In Matthew *ethne* is used of Gentile nations (e.g., 10:5) and presumably of all nations, including the Jews (20:25)" (Snodgrass, *Stories with Intent*, p. 554).

12. Bruner, *The Churchbook*, p. 565.

13. Ibid., p. 566.

14. Schnackenburg, The Gospel of Matthew, p. 257.

15. Cf. Romans 14:10; 1 Corinthians 3:10–15; 2 Corinthians 5:10.

16. Davies and Allison Jr., *A Critical and Exegetical Commentary on the Gospel according to Saint Matthew*, vol. 3, p. 433.

17. God the Son is both the ultimate recipient and the only origin of such love.

18. "But concerning the fire, he does not say this but 'prepared for the devil.' I prepared the kingdom for you, he says, but the fire I did not prepare for you but 'for the devil and his angels.' But you have cast yourselves in it. You have imputed it to yourselves" (Chrysostom, "The Gospel of Matthew" (Homily 79.2), quoted in

Matthew 14–28, ed. Manlio Simonetti, Ancient Christian Commentary on Scripture, NT Ib [Downers Grove, IL: InterVarsity Press, 2001], p. 234). Perhaps this is valid.

19. Bruner, *The Churchbook*, p. 566.

20. Craig L. Blomberg, *Matthew*, New American Commentary (Nashville: Broadman, 1992), p. 377.

21. Those on the right embody what Jesus taught in 6:3 in that their left hand never knew what their right hand did. They didn't think twice about helping others.

22. Pascal, *Pensées*, 514, quoted in Bruner, The Churchbook, pp. 571, 572.

23. Bruner, *The Churchbook*, p. 581.

24. See ibid., p. 580.

25. Ibid., p. 579.

26. See my short summary of *A Portrait of the Artist as a Young Man*, in Leland Ryken, Philip Graham Ryken, Todd A. Wilson, eds., *Pastors in the Classics: Timeless Lessons on Life and Ministry from World Literature* (Grand Rapids, MI: Baker, 2012), p. 165.

27. Davies and Allison Jr., *A Critical and Exegetical Commentary on the Gospel according to Saint Matthew*, vol. 3, p. 428.

28. Other texts on this theme of Christ's oneness with his disciples include John 6:56; 15:4–7; 1 John 2:24; 3:24; 4:15.

29. E.g., Romans 7:4; 1 Corinthians 11:33; Philippians 4:1.

30. Blomberg, *Preaching the Parables*, p. 207.

31. By "little one" in Matthew 18 Jesus could mean everyone in the kingdom of heaven regardless of age, or he could mean, as I think he means, "the least of these my brothers" (25:40). This broader definition is supported by (a) the content of what our Lord says in 18:5–14, (b) the content of what immediately follows in the rest of chapter 18 (which is about church life—adults especially included), (c) the exclusive use of "little ones" throughout the rest of that text (Jesus never returns to the words "child" or "children" again), and (d) the natural way Jesus moves from "these little ones" in verse 14 to "if your brother" in verse 15.

32. D. A. Carson, "Matthew," in *The Expositor's Bible Commentary*, vol. 9, rev. ed. (Grand Rapids, MI: Zondervan, 2010), p. 583. On pp. 583, 584 Carson lists scholarly studies that side with his position. Cf. Blomberg, *Preaching the Parables*, p. 213, n. 6.

33. Carson, "Matthew," p. 558.

34. Paul also is not opposed to using the concepts of faith and obedience in the same thought. See, for example, his use of the term "obedience of faith" in Romans 1:5; 16:26 and his speaking of Christ's judging in such terms ("when the Lord Jesus is revealed from heaven with his mighty angels in flaming fire, inflicting vengeance on those who do not know God and on *those who do not obey the gospel* of our Lord Jesus," 2 Thessalonians 1:7, 8).

35. Bruner, *The Churchbook*, p. 545. In his essay "The Shy Member of the Trinity: Expository Preaching Gives the Filling of the Holy Spirit," Bruner also summarizes well Gerhard Ebeling's lectures on Luther given at the University of Zürich. Ebeling was asked "how it happened, historically, that Luther's Reformation, in contrast to the many prior attempts at church reformation in the Middle Ages, became a reformation in deed and not just in words; that is, how it became a world-changing reformation. Ebeling's reply is paradoxical and deep. Luther's Reformation, he

writes, became a reformation in deed, not just in words because Luther trusted only in the Word and not at all in deeds" (Frederick Dale Bruner and William Hordern, *The Holy Spirit: Shy Member of the Trinity* [Eugene, OR: Wipf & Stock, repr. 2001], p. 29). Bruner's source was Ebeling, *Luther: Einführung in sein Denken* (Tübingen: J. C. B. Mohr [Paul Siebeck], 1964), p. 60.

36. Jonathan Edwards, *The Works of Jonathan Edwards*, ed. Edward Hickman, vol. 2 (Carlisle, PA: Banner of Truth, repr. 1992), p. 228.

37. Eugene H. Peterson, *The Pastor: A Memoir* (New York: HarperOne, 2011), p. 250.

38. Christopher J. H. Wright, *The God I Don't Understand: Reflections on Tough Questions of Faith* (Grand Rapids, MI: Zondervan, 2008), p. 27.

39. Bruner, *The Churchbook*, p. 534.

40. A fuller context from that quote is appropriate for the themes of Matthew 25:

> Do not be deceived: God is not mocked, for whatever one sows, that will he also reap. For the one who sows to his own flesh will from the flesh reap corruption, but the one who sows to the Spirit will from the Spirit reap eternal life. And let us not grow weary of doing good, for in due season we will reap, if we do not give up. So then, as we have opportunity, let us do good to everyone, and especially to those who are of the household of faith. (Galatians 6:7–10)

41. Luther, quoted in Bernard Lohse, *Martin Luther: An Introduction to His Life and Work*, trans. Robert C. Schultz (Minneapolis: Fortress, 1986), p. 180, n. 112.

42. Tertullian, cited in Blomberg, *Preaching the Parables*, pp. 209, 210.

Chapter Seventy-six:
The Passion of the Church and the Passion of the Christ

1. See especially Dale C. Allison Jr., *The New Moses: A Matthean Typology* (Minneapolis: Fortress, 1994).

2. The absence of the Pharisees (found in no part of what follows) and the scribes (mentioned only in 26:57 and 27:41) is likely due to the fact that we are now in Jerusalem, where the Sanhedrin holds the religious power.

3. As Donald A. Hagner comments, "The passion narrative is a literary masterpiece" (*Matthew 14–28*, Word Biblical Commentary, vol. 33b [Nashville: Thomas Nelson, 1993], p. 749).

4. So thinks Jerome, "Commentary on Matthew" (4.26.6), quoted in *Matthew 14–28*, ed. Manlio Simonetti, Ancient Christian Commentary on Scripture, NT Ib (Downers Grove, IL: InterVarsity Press, 2001) p. 240.

5. According to John 11:54a, Jesus could no longer appear in public. Thus if Jesus was in hiding (as likely Lazarus was, 12:10), perhaps he entered a hideout that no one would expect—the house of a leper.

6. As described by Carolyn Weber, *Surprised by Oxford: A Memoir* (Nashville: Thomas Nelson, 2011), pp. 183, 184.

7. To give you another picture of this ointment's worth, in Mark 6 Philip thinks it would take 200 denarii (v. 37) to fed the 5,000 men (v. 44), perhaps 20,000 people.

8. Swete, Mark, p. 323, in W. D. Davies and Dale C. Allison Jr., *A Critical and Exegetical Commentary on the Gospel according to Saint Matthew*, International Critical Commentary, vol. 3 (Edinburgh: T&T Clark, 1988-1997), p. 445.

9. Ibid., vol. 3, p. 450.

10. It is perhaps significant that Matthew omits Jesus' burial anointing and speaks only of the woman pouring the ointment on Jesus' head.

11. I appreciate Frederick Dale Bruner's "cross-coronation" (*The Churchbook: Matthew 13–28*, 2nd and rev. ed. [Grand Rapids, MI: Eerdmans, 2004], p. 601). C. H. Dodd wrote of Jesus as "the messianic King whose throne is a cross" (*Tradition*, p. 173, cited in Davies and Allison Jr., *A Critical and Exegetical Commentary on the Gospel according to Saint Matthew*, vol. 3, p. 448).

12. Donald Senior, *The Passion of Jesus in the Gospel of Matthew* (Collegeville, MN: Liturgical Press, 1985), p. 55.

13. Davies and Allison Jr., *A Critical and Exegetical Commentary on the Gospel according to Saint Matthew*, vol. 3, p. 448.

14. "Jesus did foresee Gentiles entering the kingdom (8:11) in response to his disciples' preaching, and that the word of God would be preached in the world (13:37; 24:14). Thus the groundwork has already been laid for this saying and also for the Great Commission (28:18–20)." D. A. Carson, "Matthew," in *The Expositor's Bible Commentary*, vol. 9, rev. ed. (Grand Rapids, MI: Zondervan, 2010), pp. 591, 592.

15. J. C. Ryle, *Matthew: Expository Thoughts on the Gospels*, Crossway Classic Commentaries (Wheaton, IL: Crossway, 1993), p. 251. Ryle continues:

> On that great day [judgment day] no honor done to Christ on earth will be found to have been forgotten. The speeches of parliamentary orators, the exploits of warriors, the works of poets and painters, will not be mentioned on that day; but the least work that the weakest Christian woman has done for Christ, or his members, will be found written in the book of everlasting remembrance. Not a single kind word or deed, not a cup of cold water, or a jar of perfume, will be omitted from the record. Silver and gold she may not have had; rank, power and influence she may not have possessed; but if she loved Christ, confessed Christ and worked for Christ her memorial will be found on high: she will be commended before assembled worlds. (pp. 251, 252)

16. Martin Kähler, quoted in Bruner, *The Churchbook*, p. 586.

Chapter Seventy-seven: The Paradoxes of the Last Passover

1. On the Feast of Unleavened Bread, see especially Exodus 12:14–27, Leviticus 23:4–6, and Deuteronomy 16:3, 4. Craig L. Blomberg notes:

> Here begins the first day of the Passover, also known as the Feast of the Unleavened Bread because nothing with yeast could be eaten or even left in the homes of faithful Jews (v. 17a). We have not actually begun the Passover day itself (which started Thursday at sundown). Technically the Passover was a one-day feast, while the Feast of the Unleavened Bread had evolved from a seven- to an eight-day-long festival beginning the day before Passover, but in popular language and thinking the two holidays

had coalesced. So this period of the afternoon preparations for the evening meal was loosely referred to as the first day of the festival. (*Matthew*, New American Commentary [Nashville: Broadman, 1992], p. 387.)

2. D. A. Carson, "Matthew," in *The Expositor's Bible Commentary*, vol. 9, rev. ed. (Grand Rapids, MI: Zondervan, 2010), pp. 597, 598 and William L. Lane, The *Gospel of Mark*, New International Commentary on the New Testament (Grand Rapids, MI: Eerdmans, 1974), p. 501 provide good summaries of the Seder meal. Lane's description is below, as summarized by Grant R. Osborne, *Matthew*, Exegetical Commentary on the New Testament (Grand Rapids, MI: Zondervan, 2010), p. 964:

1. The festival and the wine is blessed, followed by the first cup.
2. The food is then brought in—unleavened bread, bitter herbs, greens, stewed fruit, roast lamb.
3. The son asks why this night is distinguished from others; the family head answers with the exodus story, followed by praise to God for past and future redemption from the first part of the Hallel (Pss 113—114/15).
4. The second cup of wine is drunk.
5. The unleavened bread is blessed, broken, and distributed; then it is eaten with the herbs and fruit, as the father explains the meaning of the bread.
6. This is followed by the meal proper, which was not to extend beyond midnight.
7. At the consummation of the meal, the head blesses a third cup, followed by singing the second part of the Hallel (Pss 115/16—118).
8. A fourth cup concludes the meal.

3. See Exodus 12:3–11, 21–23, 43–49 and Deuteronomy 16:2, 5–7.

4. "Jeremias (Eucharistic Words, 222ff.) theorizes that the reason no mention is made of the Passover lamb in our accounts is that Jesus had already identified himself as the Lamb. This is possible because the failure to mention the lamb in any of the Synoptics is startling. But like most arguments from silence, it falls short of proof. Yet the allusions to the Passover—not least being the timing of the Last Supper—are cumulatively compelling" (Carson, "Matthew," p. 603).

5. As usual, Frederick Dale Bruner provides thought-provoking insights:

> This nameless man in Jerusalem complements the nameless woman in Bethany; both provided hospitality for Jesus: the woman preparing him for his burial; the man preparing him for the sacrament of death (Cf. Heil, 30-31). . . . Together, Judas' Plot and Passover Preparation teach us that while Jesus had a secret enemy among his friends he also has a secret friend among his enemies (cf. Bengel). There are wolves among the sheep, but there are also sheep among the wolves (Augustine). (*The Churchbook: Matthew 13–28*, 2nd and rev. ed. [Grand Rapids, MI: Eerdmans, 2004], p. 617.)

6. "The title occurs 79 times in the Gospel of Matthew (compared to 17 occurrences in Mark and Luke respectively). In many instances it is applied to Jesus in

contexts asserting his authority and power. On this cf. F. Hahn, *The Titles of Jesus in Christology* (London: Lutterworth Press, 1969), 68–128; R. Fuller, *The Foundations of New Testament Christology* (New York: Scribner, 1965), 184–185." Donald Senior, *The Passion of Jesus in the Gospel of Matthew* (Collegeville, MN: Liturgical Press, 1985), p. 62, n. 19.

7. "By addressing Jesus as 'Rabbi' Matthew indicates that Judas speaks as do the enemies of Jesus, failing to perceive his master's true identity. His failure is not only a result of avarice but stems from broken faith" (Senior, *The Passion of Jesus in the Gospel of Matthew*, p. 64).

8. I like what Senior says on Matthew's use of "time" here. He says it relates to Jesus' death being "the turning point of history, the breakthrough of the New Age of salvation" (ibid., p. 61).

9. On this phrase Osborne notes, "Here the passion is the fulfillment of Scripture, not any single passage but all those used throughout the Passion Narrative (cf. 26:54, 56; eg., Zech 13:7 in 26:31; Zech 11:12, 13 in 27:9–10; Ps 22:1 in 27:46; cf. Ps 22:18 in 27:35) as well as the suffering Servant of Isa 52–53" (Matthew, p. 965). Bruner comments that

> The Son of Man's going back "*exactly as it stands written of him*" may refer to Jesus' creative conviction that the Danielic Son of Man is the Isaian Suffering Servant as well as the Psalms' Innocent Sufferer. For Jesus, Dan 7 coalesced with Ps 22 and Isa 53. Perhaps Jesus was able to bear the cross, in part, because he was convinced that he was Dan 7, Ps 22, and Isa 53, altogether. (*The Churchbook*, p. 617.)

Could this fulfillment also include Judas's betrayal (see Acts 1:16–20, quoting Psalm 69:25 and 109:8)?

10. On the number of lambs slain during Passover, see William Barclay, *The Gospel of Matthew*, vol. 2, rev. ed. (Philadelphia: Westminster, 1975), pp. 327, 328.

11. Osborne, *Matthew*, p. 965.

12. Chrysostom thinks so: "See how he spares the traitor. He did not say, 'Judas, you will betray me,' but only 'one of you will betray me.' This was again to offer time for repentance by keeping his identity concealed. He was willing to allow all the others to be alarmed, just for the sake of redeeming this one" ("Gospel of Matthew" [Homily 81.1], quoted in *Matthew 14–28*, ed. Manlio Simonetti, Ancient Christian Commentary on Scripture, NT Ib [Downers Grove, IL: InterVarsity Press, 2001], p. 246).

13. That warning is especially applicable because it is given in the context of the Corinthians' abuse of the Lord's Supper.

14. I agree with Blomberg that "some kind of conscious punishment in the life to come is again implied here" and that "Annihiliationists cannot say that 'it would be better for him if he had not been born' since a person who is totally destroyed simply reverts back to a state of non-existence as before conception" (*Matthew*, p. 389). Cf. Osborne's insight:

> In 18:6 Jesus says it would be preferable to be thrown into the sea with a large millstone around the neck than to face God's judgment. This passage is even more serious, for now it "would be better" to have never been born than to face such terrible judgment (cf. 1 En. 38:2; 2 Ban 10:6). For such

horrible apostasy and betrayal the eternal punishment predicted in 25:46 must await. (*Matthew*, pp. 965, 966.)

15. J. C. Ryle, *Matthew: Expository Thoughts on the Gospels*, Crossway Classic Commentaries (Wheaton, IL: Crossway, 1993), p. 252.

16. Bruner, *The Churchbook*, p. 613.

17. N. T. Wright, Matthew for Everyone, vol. 2 (Louisville: Westminster John Knox, 2002), p. 150.

18. W. D. Davies and Dale C. Allison Jr., *A Critical and Exegetical Commentary on the Gospel according to Saint Matthew*, International Critical Commentary, vol. 3 (Edinburgh: T&T Clark, 1988-1997), p. 452.

19. I say that "the breaking of bread" is a likely but not certain reference to the Lord's Supper because similar language is used in Acts for common meals (Acts 20:11), including meals with non-Christians (Acts 27:35, 36). Another possible reference to the supper is Luke 24:30–35. Perhaps shedding further light on the supper (but not the supper itself), see Jesus' similar actions of blessing bread in the miracle feedings in Mark 6:41 and 8:6; Luke 9:15, 16 and also his words in John 21:13; 27:35. In *Didache* 14:1, the term "break bread" is used for the Lord's Supper.

20. The metaphorical language of John 6 is likely not referring to the Lord's Supper. This is so for three reasons: (1) because of all the language of belief in that chapter, (2) because of Jesus' other "I am" statements, (3) because John often in his Gospel explains difficult statements or tells how the present church (John's church) understood them, e.g., John 7:39. He does not do that in John 6.

21. Blomberg, *Matthew*, p. 390.

22. Ben Witherington III, *Matthew*, Smith & Helwys Bible Commentary (Macon, GA: Smith & Helwys, 2006), p. 484.

23. Blomberg, *Matthew*, p. 390.

24. Ibid.

25. "Out of a zeal to avoid the conception that Jesus is present in some sort of magical way, certain Baptists among others have sometimes gone to such extremes as to give the impression that the one place where Jesus most assuredly is not to be found is the Lord's Supper. This is what one Baptist leader termed 'the doctrine of the real absence' of Jesus Christ." Millard J. Erickson, *Christian Theology* (Grand Rapids, MI: Baker, 1994), p. 1123.

26. Westminster Shorter Catechism, A. 96; cf. John Calvin, *Institutes of the Christian Religion*, Library of Christian Classics, ed. John T. McNeill, trans. Ford Lewis Battles (Philadelphia: Westminster, 1960), IV.xvii.10.

27. "Luke and Paul use the adjective 'new' before covenant and thus allude to Jeremiah 31:31–34 . . . the passage from Jeremiah was almost certainly in Jesus' mind, as Matthew reports him, because 'for the forgiveness of sins' reflects Jeremiah 31:4. Matthew has already shown his grasp of the significance of Jesus' allusion to covenant terminology in general and to the 'new covenant' in particular; in 2:18 . . . he cites Jeremiah 31 so as to show that he interprets the coming of Jesus as the real end of the exile and the inauguration of the new covenant" (Carson, "Matthew," p. 602). Blomberg comments, "Here's the inauguration of Jeremiah's new covenant (Jer 31:31–34). 'New' does not appear in many of the best manuscripts of Matthew but does in Luke 22:20, from which it was probably borrowed by later copyists and inserted here. Nevertheless, the newness is clear from the Old Testament allusions" (*Matthew*, p. 391).

28. "Reconciliation and forgiveness become the hallmark of the Matthean Jesus (see, for example, 5:23–24; 6:12, 14–15; 18:21–35)" (Senior, *The Passion of Jesus in the Gospel of Matthew*, p. 69).

29. Blomberg, *Matthew*, p. 392. Robert Stein concludes, "Clearly, Jesus does not see his passion as a tragedy or error, but the crowning act of his ministry in which he pours out his blood as the once-for-all sacrifice which secures redemption 'for many' and insures a glorious consummation in the future" ("Last Supper," DJG, p. 449, quoted in Osborne, *Matthew*, p. 969).

30. "Mark says, 'All of them drank from *it*.' . . . Both formulations testify that it was a *community cup*. At the Jewish Passover meal, each participant probably had his own drinking cup" (Rudolf Schnackenburg, *The Gospel of Matthew*, trans. Robert R. Barr [Grand Rapids, MI: Eerdmans, 2002], p. 268, emphasis mine).

31. "This likely refers to dipping the bread in a bowl that contained herbs and a fruit puree" (Carson, "Matthew," p. 599). "Perhaps we should think of the bowl in which the bitter herbs were dipped, the bowl of harost, a sauce made of fruit, nuts, ginger or cinnamon, and wine or vinegar" (Davies and Allison Jr., *A Critical and Exegetical Commentary on the Gospel according to Saint Matthew*, vol. 3, p. 462).

32. Paul's accusation that some Christians are getting drunk at the Lord's Supper answers that question (1 Corinthians 11:21).

33. Wayne Grudem, *Systematic Theology* (Leicester, UK: Inter-Varsity Press, 1994), p. 998.

Chapter Seventy-eight: Fearful Symmetry

1. William Blake, "The Tyger," in *Songs of Innocence and Experience* (London, 1794).

2. "The Lamb," in ibid.

3. "Sinful people are within this complete control of God, otherwise sin would be a marvelous achievement, if by it we could remove ourselves from God's sovereign and absolute power" (D. Broughton Knox, "The Everlasting God," in *Selected Works, Volume I: The Doctrine of God*, ed. Tony Payne [Kingsford, NSW, Australia: Matthias Media, 2000], p. 56).

4. According to John (John 18:10, 26), it was Peter who "struck the servant of the high priest and cut off his ear" (26:51).

5. "At the supper Jesus spoke of betrayal by one disciple (vv. 21–25); now he speaks of desertion by all of them, and of denial by Peter. There is thus a sequence of predictions of the failure of disciples (Judas, vv. 21–25; the Twelve, v. 31; Peter, v. 34), which will all be fulfilled in the same sequence in the following narrative (Judas, vv. 47–50; the Twelve, v. 56; Peter, vv. 69–75)" (R. T. France, *The Gospel of Matthew*, New International Commentary on the New Testament [Grand Rapids, MI: Eerdmans, 2007], p. 997).

6. I like how Chrysostom sees this positive element. He writes of Jesus,

> He was urging them to be attentive to what has been prophetically predicted of his death and resurrection, and at the same time he wanted to make it plain that he was indeed crucified according to God's purpose. All of this was to show that he was no alien from the old covenant or from the God who preached it. . . . All the prophets proclaimed all things beforehand from the beginning that are included in this salvation event. All this

was to increase faith. ("The Gospel of Matthew" [Homily 82.2], quoted in *Matthew 14–28*, ed. Manlio Simonetti, Ancient Christian Commentary on Scripture, NT Ib [Downers Grove, IL: InterVarsity Press, 2001], p. 251.)

7. On Zechariah 13:7 functioning "as a superscription to the passion events—the fleeing of the disciples (scattering of the sheep), the arrest of Jesus (Matt 26:50), and the smiting of the shepherd," Grant R. Osborne (*Matthew*, Exegetical Commentary on the New Testament [Grand Rapids, MI: Zondervan, 2010], p. 967) points to Douglas J. Moo, "The Use of the Old Testament in the Passion Texts of the Gospels" (PhD dissertation, University of St. Andrews, 1979), p. 186. See also W. D. Davies and Dale C. Allison Jr., *A Critical and Exegetical Commentary on the Gospel according to Saint Matthew*, International Critical Commentary, vol. 3 (Edinburgh: T&T Clark, 1988-1997), p. 548. They write, "26.30–35 is almost an outline of the remainder of the Gospel. It foretells that the disciples will forsake Jesus (26.56), that Peter will deny his Lord (26.69-75), that Jesus will be killed ('I will smite'; 27.32-56), that he will be raised from the dead (28.14-10), and that he will appear to his disciples in Galilee (28.16-20)."

8. "Matthew's Jesus quotes a form of the LXX in which second-person plural imperatives ('strike the shepherd' and 'scatter the sheep') are changed into first-person singular and third-person plural indicative, respectively ('I will strike the shepherd,' and 'the sheep . . . will be scattered'). The implied subject of both verbs is God. The action God commands (LXX), even when carried out by others (Matthew), is thus derivatively his action too" (Craig L. Blomberg, *Matthew*, New American Commentary [Nashville: Broadman, 1992], pp. 392, 393).

9. Cf. John 10:11, 14.

10. Frederick Dale Bruner, *The Churchbook: Matthew 13–28,* 2nd and rev. ed. (Grand Rapids, MI: Eerdmans, 2004), p. 642.

11. Peter's crime is appalling because "repetition reflects resolution" (Davies and Allison Jr., *A Critical and Exegetical Commentary on the Gospel according to Saint Matthew*, vol. 3, p. 549). However, Judas's premeditation makes his crime more appalling.

12. *Hoi de* (v. 59) and *Ho de* (v. 69), rendered "now" by the ESV, NRSV, and NKJV.

13. On the postures in the passion narrative, Davies and Allison Jr. observe that "the disciples sit in Gethsemane (v. 36), the guards (and evidently the high priest) sit at the trial (cf. vv. 58, 62), Pilate sits when interrogating Jesus (27.19), and the soldiers at the cross likewise sit (27.36). All this contrasts with earlier chapters, in which it is Jesus who sits, that is, takes the position of authority and rest (5.1; 13.2; 15.29; 21.7; 24.3; 25.31). But after the last supper he no longer sits or reclines. He instead stands (27.11), falls to the ground (26.39), and hangs from a cross (27.35). His posture during the passion reflects his temporary renunciation of authority (cf. 26.53) and the lack of all comfort" (ibid., vol. 3, pp. 444, 445).

14. "Three times *Jesus* is confronted by verbal threats (false witnesses, valid witnesses, Caiaphas); three times *Peter* is similarly tested (two servant girls and the bystanders)" (Douglas R. A. Hare, *Matthew*, Interpretation [Louisville: John Knox, 1993], p. 310).

15. Bruner, *The Churchbook*, p. 695.

16. Peter did eventually learn Jesus' lesson, for in 1 Peter 5:5b–9a he combines the themes of humility and alertness, admonishing the church, "Clothe yourselves,

all of you, with humility toward one another, for 'God opposes the proud but gives grace to the humble.' Humble yourselves, therefore, under the mighty hand of God so that at the proper time he may exalt you. . . . Be sober-minded; be watchful. Your adversary the devil prowls around like a roaring lion, seeking someone to devour. Resist him, firm in your faith."

17. Bruner, *The Churchbook*, p. 694.

18. Donald Senior, *The Passion of Jesus in the Gospel of Matthew* (Collegeville, MN: Liturgical Press, 1985), p. 102.

19. Bruner, *The Churchbook*, p. 696; cf. Senior, *The Passion of Jesus in the Gospel of Matthew*, p. 101.

20. If we view this as Peter's "trial," then the Law's legal demand for two witnesses (Numbers 35:30; Deuteronomy 17:6) is met in the second servant.

21. Senior, *The Passion of Jesus in the Gospel of Matthew*, p. 101.

22. A number of commentators cite the example in the book of Judges 12:6 of the Ephraimites being unable to pronounce "Shibboleth." Perhaps the first commentator was Jerome. See Jerome, "Commentary on Matthew" (4.26.72-75), quoted in *Matthew 14–28*, p. 270.

23. As argued by Davies and Allison Jr., *A Critical and Exegetical Commentary on the Gospel according to Saint Matthew*, vol. 3, pp. 448, 449.

24. Henry, quoted in Bruner, *The Churchbook*, p. 699.

25. For John's threefold reinstatement scene, read John 21:15–19.

26. The quote is from my former intern, Rhett Austin.

27. Information taken from http://www.dickb.com; accessed on November 3, 2011.

28. Origen, "Commentary on Matthew 88," quoted in *Matthew 14–28*, p. 252.

29. J. C. Ryle, *Matthew: Expository Thoughts on the Gospels*, Crossway Classic Commentaries (Wheaton, IL: Crossway, 1993), p. 269.

30. Rudolf Schnackenburg, *The Gospel of Matthew*, trans. Robert R. Barr (Grand Rapids, MI: Eerdmans, 2002), p. 279.

31. What Scot McKnight said of the Last Supper can be applied to our application of 26:69–75: "If the bread is connected to the cup, and the cup to sacrificial death, then the bread of affliction Jesus shares is participation in his death. This can only mean that the bread, now identified with Jesus, is given to the followers in order that they share in the death of Jesus in order to accrue its benefits" (*Jesus and His Death: Historiography, the Historical Jesus, and Atonement Theory* [Waco, TX: Baylor University Press, 2005], p. 281).

32. Osborne, *Matthew*, p. 1004.

33. William Barclay, *The Gospel of Matthew*, vol. 2, rev. ed. (Philadelphia: Westminster, 1975), p. 345.

34. At a later date Peter put it this way: "Christ . . . suffered once for sins, the righteous for the unrighteous, that he might bring us to God" (1 Peter 3:18). Cf. 1 Peter 2:21–25. Note especially Peter's use of the shepherd imagery: "For you were straying like sheep, but have now returned to the Shepherd and Overseer of your souls" (1 Peter 2:25).

35. Robert Bridges, trans., "Ah, Holy Jesus, How Hast Thou Offended" (1899).

Chapter Seventy-nine: Drank Damnation Dry

1. W. D. Davies and Dale C. Allison Jr., *A Critical and Exegetical Commentary on the Gospel according to Saint Matthew*, International Critical Commentary, vol. 3 (Edinburgh: T&T Clark, 1988-1997), p. 493.

2. "In Gethsemane Matthew explicitly refers to '*the* disciples' three times (vv. 36, 40, 45), not, more intimately, to *his* disciples. It is almost as if in Gethsemane they are hardly *his* anymore. The cold neutrality of the threefold 'the,' 'the,' 'the,' could suggest that sometimes disciples have only the name." Frederick Dale Bruner, *The Churchbook: Matthew 13–28*, 2nd and rev. ed. (Grand Rapids, MI: Eerdmans, 2004), p. 662.

3. "Watching and praying, a constant staying awake for prayer, is often enjoined on Christians (Luke 21:36; Eph. 6:18; Col. 4:2; 1 Pet. 4:7; cf. with 5:8)." Rudolf Schnackenburg, *The Gospel of Matthew*, trans. Robert R. Barr (Grand Rapids, MI: Eerdmans, 2002), p. 271.

4. Bruner, *The Churchbook,* p. 649. For example, he writes, "Jesus depressed? Isn't that wrong? This text is the Magna Carta of depression."

5. "Dreadful things" is Rev. John Ames's phrase for such sufferings in Marilynne Robinson's novel, *Gilead* (New York: Farrar, Straus, and Giroux, 2004), p. 16.

6. N. T. Wright, *Matthew for Everyone*, vol. 2 (Louisville: Westminster John Knox, 2002), p. 161.

7. Craig L. Blomberg, *Matthew*, New American Commentary (Nashville: Broadman, 1992), p. 395.

8. Ibid.

9. Citing 26:38, Irenaeus names Jesus' soul being exceedingly sorrowful as one of the "tokens of the flesh" (*Against Heresies*, 3:22.2).

10. Bruner, *The Churchbook*, p. 648.

11. See Edward R. Hardy, ed., *Christology of the Later Fathers*, Library of Christian Classics (Louisville: Westminster John Knox, 1954), p. 31.

12. Besides the *three* disciples accompanying Jesus in Gethsemane—Peter, James, and John (26:37), "the alternating series of triads" of Jesus praying (vv. 39, 42, 44) and the disciples sleeping (vv. 40, 43, 45) (see Davies and Allison Jr., *A Critical and Exegetical Commentary on the Gospel according to Saint Matthew*, vol. 3, p. 490), we find in the two final sections in chapter 26 three questions put to Jesus during and after his trial (vv. 57–68) and Peter's three denials (vv. 69–75). Bruner points out

> other threes in this Gospel: three generations of fourteen (chap. 1); three temptations (chap. 4); two sets of three commands, social and political (chap. 5); three Devotions and two sets of three petitions in the Lord's Prayer (chap. 6); three Warnings (chap. 7); three sets of three miracles (chaps. 8–9); three controversy stories (chap. 12); three People-of-God parables (chap. 21); three People-of-God questions (chap. 22); three Judgment Parables (chap. 25); and three Peter denials (chap. 26). (*The Churchbook*, p. 662.)

What is the significance of these triads? I'll let you decide.

13. Wright, *Matthew for Everyone*, vol. 2, p. 160.

14. Blomberg, *Matthew*, pp. 395, 396.

15. Cf. 20:22, 23. John and James would likewise suffer for the gospel.

16. To say of Jesus, as Jerome did, that "he felt sorrowful not because he feared the suffering that lay ahead" is at best exegetically ungrounded and at worst theologically heretical ("Commentary on Matthew," 4.26.37, quoted in *Matthew 14–28*, ed. Manlio Simonetti, Ancient Christian Commentary on Scripture, NT Ib [Downers Grove, IL: InterVarsity Press, 2001], p. 255).

17. Davies and Allison Jr., *A Critical and Exegetical Commentary on the Gospel according to Saint Matthew*, vol. 3, p. 501.

18. The quote comes from Grant R. Osborne, *Matthew*, Exegetical Commentary on the New Testament (Grand Rapids, MI: Zondervan, 2010), p. 982.

19. Cf. Revelation 14:10; 16:19.

20. See Daniel 7:13, 14, 26, 27; cf. Matthew 13:41; 24:30–51; 26:64.

21. For the quotes as well as much of the language and thought of this paragraph, see J. C. Ryle, *Matthew: Expository Thoughts on the Gospels*, Crossway Classic Commentaries (Wheaton, IL: Crossway, 1993), pp. 260, 261.

22. Philip Graham Ryken, *King Solomon: The Temptations of Money, Sex, and Power* (Wheaton, IL: Crossway, 2011), p. 122. The story comes from Robert Coleman, *Written in Blood*, as summarized in *750 Engaging Illustrations for Preachers, Teachers, and Writers*, ed. Craig Brian Larsen (Grand Rapids, MI: Baker, 2002), p. 74.

23. Charles Haddon Spurgeon, *Sermons of the Rev. C. H. Spurgeon of London*, third series (New York: Sheldon, Blakeman, & Company. 1858), p. 298.

24. Here is more of the language of the Council of Chalcedon (AD 451): "Our Lord Jesus Christ" is

> at once complete in Godhead and complete in manhood, truly God and truly man, consisting also of a reasonable soul and body; of one substance with the Father as regards his Godhead, and at the same time of one substance with us as regards his manhood; like us in all respects, apart from sin . . . recognized in two natures, without confusion, without change, without division, without separation; the distinction of natures being in no way annulled by the union, but rather the characteristics of each nature being preserved and coming together to form one person and subsistence, not as parted or separated into two persons, but one and the same Son and Only-begotten God the Word, Lord Jesus Christ. . . .

25. About the title, "My Father," Osborne says that it "is found often in Matthew (7:21; 11:25–27; 12:50; 16:17; 25:34) as a title of intimacy" (*Matthew*, p. 979).

26. Donald Senior, *The Passion of Jesus in the Gospel of Matthew* (Collegeville, MN: Liturgical Press, 1985), pp. 79, 80.

Chapter Eighty: A Sovereign Scriptural Plan

1. This wonderful letter came from Moriah Sharp, October 30, 2011.

2. Dorothy Sayers, *Creed or Chaos?* (New York: Harcourt, Brace, and Co., 1949), p. 5. The hero/victim imagery is also hers.

3. Frederick Dale Bruner, *The Churchbook: Matthew 13–28*, 2nd and rev. ed. (Grand Rapids, MI: Eerdmans, 2004), p. 677. Bruner cites Raymond E. Brown, *The Death of the Messiah: From Gethsemane to the Grave; A Commentary on the Passion Narratives in the Four Gospels*, vol. 1 (New York: Doubleday, 1994), p. 287.

4. Grant R. Osborne, *Matthew*, Exegetical Commentary on the New Testament (Grand Rapids, MI: Zondervan, 2010), p. 987.

5. W. D. Davies and Dale C. Allison Jr., *A Critical and Exegetical Commentary on the Gospel according to Saint Matthew*, International Critical Commentary, vol. 3 (Edinburgh: T&T Clark, 1988-1997), p. 511.

6. Brown, *The Death of the Messiah*, vol. 1, pp. 268, 269.

7. Ulrich Luz, *Matthew 21–28*, Hermeneia, vol. 4 (Minneapolis: Fortress, 2005), p. 420. Other commentators understand a legion to be comprised of 6,000 men.

8. St. Jerome, *Commentary on Matthew*, Fathers of the Church, vol. 117, trans. Thomas P. Scheck (Washington, DC: Catholic University of America, 2008), p. 304.

9. Bruner, *The Churchbook*, p. 671.

10. See ibid., p. 669.

11. Ibid., p. 668.

12. As Davies and Allison Jr. note, not only is Jesus "forsaken and left alone, but his teaching seems without effect: betrayal, violence, and cowardice characterize those who have paid him most heed" (*A Critical and Exegetical Commentary on the Gospel according to Saint Matthew*, vol. 3, p. 517).

13. Donald Senior, *The Passion of Jesus in the Gospel of Matthew* (Collegeville, MN: Liturgical Press, 1985), p. 84.

14. This was a kiss like Joab's kiss of Amasa; 2 Samuel 20:9, 10 tells us,

> And Joab said to Amasa, "Is it well with you, my brother?" And Joab took Amasa by the beard with his right hand to kiss him. But Amasa did not observe the sword that was in Joab's hand. So Joab struck him with it in the stomach and spilled his entrails to the ground without striking a second blow, and he died.

15. The commentary is mine. The painting is found in Luz, *Matthew 21–28*, vol. 4, p. 415 (Figure 28).

16. Bruner, *The Churchbook*, pp. 668, 669.

17. Origen, "Commentary on Matthew 101," quoted in *Matthew 14–28*, ed. Manlio Simonetti, Ancient Christian Commentary on Scripture, NT Ib (Downers Grove, IL: InterVarsity Press, 2001), p. 261.

18. "Matthew has already used it [the word "friend"] in 20:13 and 22:12, in the first text as a distancing, condescending address, in the second with a threatening undertone" (Luz, *Matthew 21–28*, vol. 3, p. 418).

19. N. T. Wright, *Matthew for Everyone*, vol. 2 (Louisville: Westminster John Knox, 2002), p. 164. The first half of the sentence is Wright's; the second half is mine.

20. Bruner, *The Churchbook*, p. 665.

21. "For the crucifixion to have taken place, the cooperation of three simultaneous forces was needed . . . the treachery of Judas, who was a Christian; the hatred of Annas, who was a Jew; and the indifference of Pilate, who was a Gentile." Dominic M. Crossan, "Anti-Semitism and the Gospel," *Theological Studies* 26 (1965): 189, quoted in Bruner, *The Churchbook*, pp. 665, 666.

22. Bruner, *The Churchbook*, p. 666. Bruner summarizes: "One of the purposes of the Trial Stories in the Passion Narrative is to teach the sinfulness of *all* strata of the human race" (p. 668).

23. Ibid., p. 666.

24. William Barclay, *The Gospel of Matthew*, vol. 2, rev. ed. (Philadelphia: Westminster, 1975), p. 351.

25. Gnilka, vol. 2, p. 417, emphasis added and quoted in Bruner, *The Churchbook*, p. 667.

26. Chrysostom, "The Gospel of Matthew" (Homily 83.2), quoted in *Matthew 14–28*, p. 260.

27. Barclay, *The Gospel of Matthew*, vol. 2, p. 351.

28. Ibid.

29. Ibid.

30. On Matthew's "fulfillment formula" and its relation to the prophets, see Senior, *The Passion of Jesus in the Gospel of Matthew*, p. 88, n. 61.

31. "Jesus believed in a special form of the Bible—a crucio-christocentric Bible," or "passio-christocentric, a Suffering-Christ-Centered Bible" (Bruner, *The Churchbook*, pp. 674, 675).

32. Scot McKnight, *The King Jesus Gospel: The Original Good News Revisited* (Grand Rapids, MI: Zondervan, 2011), p. 51.

33. Ibid., p. 50.

34. See McKnight's excellent summary of Romans 1:1–5 (Ibid., p. 60). Cf. John Chapman, *Know and Tell the Gospel: Help for the Reluctant Evangelist* (London: St. Matthias, 1981), pp. 18–28; John Stott, *Romans: God's Good News for the World* (Downers Grove, IL: InterVarsity Press, 1994), pp. 46–54.

35. Cf. these words from the Nicene Creed:

> . . . who, for us men and for our salvation, came down from heaven, and was incarnate by the Holy Spirit of the virgin Mary, and was made man; and was crucified also for us under Pontius Pilate; He suffered and was buried; and the third day He rose again, *according to the Scriptures* . . .

as well as those earlier (AD 190) from Ignatius:

> this faith: in one God . . . in one Christ Jesus . . . and in the Holy Spirit, *who made known through the prophets the plan of salvation*, and the coming, and the birth from a virgin, and the passion, and the resurrection from the dead, and the bodily ascension into heaven of the beloved Christ Jesus, our Lord, and his future appearing from heaven in the glory of the Father to sum up all things and to raise anew all flesh of the whole human race. (*Against Heresies*, 1.10.1, emphasis mine, quoted in McKnight, *The King Jesus Gospel*, p. 66.)

36. Ibid., p. 160.

Chapter Eighty-one: What Jesus Deserves

1. Carolyn Weber, *Surprised by Oxford: A Memoir* (Nashville: Thomas Nelson, 2011), p. 103.

2. *Concise Oxford English Dictionary*, 11th ed. (New York: Oxford University Press, 2004), p. 750.

3. Stier, quoted in Bengel, vol. 1, p. 298, in Frederick Dale Bruner, *The Churchbook: Matthew 13–28*, 2nd and rev. ed. (Grand Rapids, MI: Eerdmans, 2004), p. 691.

4. I'm indebted to W. D. Davies and Dale C. Allison Jr., *A Critical and Exegetical Commentary on the Gospel according to Saint Matthew*, International Critical Commentary, vol. 3 (Edinburgh: T&T Clark, 1988-1997), p. 537. They point out five ironies. I used most of their categories and some of their wording.

5. Rome recognized the Sanhedrin "as a self-governing body with judicial authority" (ibid., vol. 3, p. 524).

6. Grant R. Osborne, *Matthew*, Exegetical Commentary on the New Testament (Grand Rapids, MI: Zondervan, 2010), p. 995. Donald Senior calls it "a strategy session" (*The Passion of Jesus in the Gospel of Matthew* [Collegeville, MN: Liturgical Press, 1985], p. 91). Matthew seems to take it more seriously than that.

7. "Thus what is meant is that at the end of its session, when it was morning, the Sanhedrin formally condemns Jesus to death" (Ulrich Luz, *Matthew 21–28*, Hermeneia [Minneapolis: Fortress, 2005], p. 426). For a helpful harmonization of the Gospels' accounts of the Jewish and Roman trials, see D. A. Carson, "Matthew," in *The Expositor's Bible Commentary*, vol. 9, rev. ed. (Grand Rapids, MI: Zondervan, 2010), pp. 617, 618.

8. Bruner, *The Churchbook*, p. 681.

9. Luz, *Matthew 21–28*, p. 426.

10. Josephus, *Antiquities* 18.2.2, 4.3, referenced by St. Jerome, *Commentary on Matthew*, Fathers of the Church, vol. 117, trans. Thomas P. Scheck (Washington, DC: Catholic University of America, 2008), p. 305. Jerome adds, "It is no wonder, then, if an unjust high priest judges unjustly." Moreover, Osborne claims, "The Romans appointed the high priests, so Caiaphas owed his job to Rome" (*Matthew*, p. 1010).

11. William Barclay, *The Gospel of Matthew*, vol. 2, rev. ed. (Philadelphia: Westminster, 1975), pp. 353, 354.

12. Ibid., p. 354.

13. Davies and Allison Jr., *A Critical and Exegetical Commentary on the Gospel according to Saint Matthew*, vol. 3, p. 537.

14. N. T. Wright, *Matthew for Everyone*, vol. 2 (Louisville: Westminster John Knox, 2002), pp. 166, 167.

15. D. A. Carson, "Matthew," p. 620.

16. Davies and Allison Jr., *A Critical and Exegetical Commentary on the Gospel according to Saint Matthew*, vol. 3, p. 537.

17. Raymond E. Brown, *The Death of the Messiah: From Gethsemane to the Grave; A Commentary on the Passion Narratives in the Four Gospels*, vol. 1 (New York: Doubleday, 1994), p. 464.

18. Luz, *Matthew 21–28*, p. 428.

19. Ibid. Luz cites Psalms 38:14, 15 and 39:10 as well as Matthew 12:19.

20. Craig L. Blomberg, *Matthew*, New American Commentary (Nashville: Broadman, 1992), p. 402.

21. Barclay, *The Gospel of Matthew*, vol. 2, p. 355.

22. Donald A. Hagner, *Matthew 14–28*, Word Biblical Commentary, vol. 33b (Nashville: Thomas Nelson, 1993), p. 799.

23. See Blomberg, *Matthew*, p. 403.

24. As Osborne notes: "By 'Son of God' the high priest was simply using another term for Messiah (in the OT the divine sonship of the Messiah is stated in 2

Sam 7:14; Ps 2:7; 89:26–27), but in Matthew Son of God goes beyond that (see 2:15; 3:17; 4:3, 6; 8:29; 14:33; 16:16; 17:5; 27:40, 43, 54)" (*Matthew*, p. 997).

25. Bruner, *The Churchbook*, p. 685.

26. Chrysostom, "The Gospel of Matthew" (Homily 85.1), quoted in *Matthew 14–28*, ed. Manlio Simonetti, Ancient Christian Commentary on Scripture, NT Ib (Downers Grove, IL: InterVarsity Press, 2001), p. 267.

27. Bruner, *The Churchbook*, p. 683.

28. Davies and Allison Jr., *A Critical and Exegetical Commentary on the Gospel according to Saint Matthew*, vol. 3, p. 537. Other commentators phrase the irony as follows: "Jesus then will judge those who now judge him" (Blomberg, *Matthew*, p. 403). "Now as the accused he reveals to his judges his future as the World Judge" (Luz, *Matthew 21–28*, p. 430). "Jesus places his judges under the judgment of God, a judgment soon to descend upon them and entrusted to himself (cf. Matt. 23:39)" (Rudolf Schnackenburg, *The Gospel of Matthew*, trans. Robert R. Barr [Grand Rapids, MI: Eerdmans, 2002], p. 277).

29. Was the rending of these priestly garments (likely top down) a foreshadowing of the temple curtain being torn in two (27:51)?

30. Luz, *Matthew 21–28*, pp. 429, 430.

31. "The 'Son of Man' has nowhere to lay his head (8:20) and will suffer rejection and death (11:19; 12:40; 17:12, 22–23; 20:18). The very mission of the Son of Man is 'not to be served but to serve, to give his life as ransom for the many' (20:28). Yet this same Son of Man, Matthew's Gospel insists, is the one who will come in triumph at the end of the world, gathering together his elect and presiding over the judgment of all humanity (10:23; 13:41; 16:27–28; 24:27, 30, 37, 39, 44; 25:31)" (Senior, *The Passion of Jesus in the Gospel of Matthew*, p. 98).

32. In light of Matthew 19:28, 25:31, and 26:64, I take *the sitting and coming* to reference Jesus' *parousia*. For this position see Davies and Allison Jr., *A Critical and Exegetical Commentary on the Gospel according to Saint Matthew*, vol. 3, pp. 531, 532. See Bruner for the full scholarly options (*The Churchbook*, pp. 687–689). I do not deny that there is an immediate exaltation in Matthew (28:18), and thus Jesus' "from now on you will see" could in part refer to that. Osborne's summary of the issue is helpful: "There is an imminent and yet inaugurated (speaking of what will continue in the future) thrust, as it means Jesus will take his seat with God immediately at his death and resurrection, and in his resurrection his vindication will be immediately visible to all; yet at the same time he will be in the seat of 'power' from his resurrection to the parousia and beyond (so Gundry, Brown, Hagner)" (*Matthew*, p. 997).

33. D. A. Carson, "Matthew," p. 621.

34. Osborne, *Matthew*, p. 1003.

35. Luz, *Matthew 21–28*, p. 436.

36. Most of the words in this sentence are from Davies and Allison Jr. They add an excellent summary: "Obviously the passage is, like 16.13–20, a climactic confluence of the main christological streams which run throughout the text" (*A Critical and Exegetical Commentary on the Gospel according to Saint Matthew*, vol. 3, p. 520).

37. "Matthew writes the *praesens historicum* 'says' (not 'said') because what Jesus *says* here is of permanent significance—he is *still* saying it (cf. Sand, 539)" (Bruner, *The Churchbook*, p. 685).

38. Ibid.

39. Davies and Allison Jr., *A Critical and Exegetical Commentary on the Gospel according to Saint Matthew*, vol. 3, p. 533.

40. Robert Bridges, trans., "Ah, Holy Jesus, How Hast Thou Offended" (1899).

41. See Scot McKnight, *The King Jesus Gospel: The Original Good News Revisited* (Grand Rapids, MI: Zondervan, 2011), p. 122.

42. Jerome, quoted, in Weber, *Surprised by Oxford*, p. 169.

43. See Barclay, *The Gospel of Matthew*, vol. 2, p. 356.

44. Weber, *Surprised by Oxford*, pp. 87, 88.

Chapter Eighty-two: Innocent Blood

1. See Table 6 in Richard Bauckham, *Jesus and the Eyewitnesses: The Gospels as Eyewitness Testimony* (Grand Rapids, MI: Eerdmans, 2006), p. 85. The name Simon ranked first and Judas fourth among the most popular male names among Palestinian Jews AD 330–200 BC.

2. Dante Alighieri, *The Divine Comedy,* Everyman's Library, trans. Allen Mandelbaum (New York: Knopf, 1995), p. 211. For a visual of this, see Giovanni's painting of it.

3. These examples are used in Ulrich Luz, *Matthew 21–28*, Hermeneia (Minneapolis: Fortress, 2005), pp. 481, 482.

4. Nikos Kazantzakis, *The Last Temptation of Christ*, trans. P.A. Bien (New York: Simon & Schuster, 1960), pp. 490, 491, cited in Luz, *Matthew 21–28,* p. 488.

5. Luz, *Matthew 21–28*, p. 486. This is not merely a modern opinion, for as Luz writes on p. 470 Origen held a similar view: "He killed himself in order to be in hell before Christ so that there he could ask him for forgiveness."

6. Robert Robinson, "Come Thou Fount" (1758).

7. Many commentators point out the apparent discrepancies with Acts 1:18. However, Grant R. Osborne explains: "There [in Acts] Judas buys the field, while here [in Matthew] the priests buy it. Yet this can be easily harmonized: they purchased the field in his name and with his money" (*Matthew*, Exegetical Commentary on the New Testament [Grand Rapids, MI: Zondervan, 2010], p. 1013). I'm fine with this explanation. Why must modern commentators be so snarky!

8. This idea, as well as some of the language, is borrowed from Frederick Dale Bruner, *The Churchbook: Matthew 13–28*, 2nd and rev. ed. (Grand Rapids, MI: Eerdmans, 2004), p. 706.

9. Ibid., p. 707.

10. See Osborne, *Matthew*, p. 1012.

11. Perhaps they had Deuteronomy 23:18 in mind. However, more likely it was their own oral tradition upon which they based their decision.

12. Luz, *Matthew 21–28*, p. 471.

13. Walker, *Heilsgeschichte*, 72, quoted in ibid., p. 474.

14. This burden of responsibility has shifted since the Holocaust from the Jewish religious leaders to the Roman political leaders. Knowing what I know of the Holocaust, I'm sympathetic to this shift. However, it is not a historically accurate

one. It's easy to blame ancient Rome alone for the injustice of Jesus' sufferings and death. But ancient Rome isn't here to stand up and defend itself!

15. G. K. Beale and D. A. Carson label it "perhaps the strangest fulfillment quotation in all of Matthew" (*Commentary on the New Testament Use of the Old Testament* [Grand Rapids, MI; Baker, 2007], p. 95).

16. St. Jerome, *Commentary on Matthew*, Fathers of the Church, vol. 117, trans. Thomas P. Scheck (Washington, DC: Catholic University of America, 2008), p. 310.

17. Calvin, 3:177, quoted in Bruner, *The Churchbook*, p. 710.

18. Maccoby (v, p. 45), quoted in W. D. Davies and Dale C. Allison Jr., *A Critical and Exegetical Commentary on the Gospel according to Saint Matthew*, International Critical Commentary, vol. 3 (Edinburgh: T&T Clark, 1988-1997), p. 570.

19. Beare (pp. 527ff.), quoted in Bruner, *The Churchbook*, p. 710.

20. So Rudolf Schnackenburg: "It is at most a piece of evidence for the zeal of primitive Christian 'scribes' in searching for instances of fulfillment of Scripture" (*The Gospel of Matthew*, trans. Robert R. Barr [Grand Rapids, MI: Eerdmans, 2002], p. 281).

21. See Michael Graves, trans., *Commentary on Jeremiah (Jerome)*, Ancient Christian Texts (Downers Grove, IL: IVP Academic, 2012) and Michael Graves, *Jerome's Hebrew Philology: A Study Based on His Commentary on Jeremiah*, Supplements to Vigiliae Christianae 90 (Leiden/Boston: Brill, 2007), as well as his forthcoming Jeremiah commentary in the International Theological Commentary series (T & T Clark/Continuum).

22. To support this "mixed citation" theory, see Raymond E. Brown, *The Death of the Messiah: From Gethsemane to the Grave; A Commentary on the Passion Narratives in the Four Gospels*, vol. 1 (New York: Doubleday, 1994), p. 651. Also Davies and Allison Jr., who write:

> We accept solution (x [see Brown above]), for not only was it common practice to substitute part of one verse for part of another, that is, to create conflated citation, but, in early Christian circles, such citations were sometimes attributed to one rather than two sources. Mk 1.2 attributes Mal 3.1 + Isa 40.3 to Isaiah. Rom 9.27 assigns Hos 2.1 + Isa 10.22 to the same prophet. Mt 2.5–6 attributes to "the prophet" a quotation from Mic 5.2 + 2 Sam 5.2 = 1 Chr 11.2, and 21.5 prefaces its conflation of Isa 62.11 and Zech 9.9 with "the word through the prophet saying." Mt 27.9–10 is one more example of this phenomenon. That Jeremiah is named rather than Zechariah (who is never assigned a quotation in the NT despite several citations) may be due to the prominence of the former or to his reputation as the prophet of doom or to Matthew's desire to call attention to what might otherwise be missed (whereas the use of Zechariah is obvious; cf. Senior). The effect in any event is to prod us to read Zech 11.13 in the light of Jer 18.1ff. (the allegory of the potter) and 32.6–9 (Jeremiah's purchase of a field with silver). (*A Critical and Exegetical Commentary on the Gospel according to Saint Matthew*, vol. 3, p. 569.)

23. Davies and Allison Jr., *A Critical and Exegetical Commentary on the Gospel according to Saint Matthew*, vol. 3, pp. 568, 569.

24. For further study on this text, see D. J. Moo, "Tradition and Old Testament in Matt 27:3–10," in *Gospel Perspectives*, vol. 3, ed. R. T. France and D. Wenham (Sheffield: JSOT, 1983), pp. 157–175. On Matthew's use of the Old Testament in the passion narratives, see Douglas J. Moo, *The Old Testament in the Gospel Passion Narratives* (Sheffield: Almond, 1983).

25. I side with Luz over Senior. Senior writes, "Matthew's choice of words is deliberate: Judas is described as 'having remorse.' This is not the word usually used for 'repentance' in the Gospels" (Donald Senior, *The Passion of Jesus in the Gospel of Matthew* [Collegeville, MN: Liturgical Press, 1985], p. 105). Luz says, "There is little difference between *metamelhqei.j* and *metanoe/w*, the words for 'repent'" (Luz, *Matthew 21–28*, p. 470). Bruner adds further evidence for this position: "While the word for 'changed his mind' is not *ordinarily* used for 'repent' in the Gospel, the word *is* used twice favorably in the Parable of the Two Sons (21:29)" (*The Churchbook*, p. 705).

26. Bruner notes: "Judas's death is an ominous mirror image of Jesus' death" (*The Churchbook*, p. 703). Later, on p. 707, he adds: "Death by hanging was considered 'unclean death' in Israel (Lohmeyer, 376). Thus an unclean death at the beginning of the chapter prepares grotesquely, heartbreakingly for a cleansing death at the end."

27. Luz quotes Barth and then adds his agreement: "It may have been more in keeping with the gospel (not with Judas's deed) if his story had ended differently, so that greedy devils would not be carrying his soul to hell as in medieval pictures, but rejoicing angels would carry it to heaven" (Luz, *Matthew 21–28*, p. 477). To that I say, "Rubbish!" The text, not today's most prominent Matthean scholar, is king. Is gospel antithetical to judgment?

28. While we can't be certain if Matthew has in mind the suicide of Ahithophel, betrayer of King David (2 Samuel 17:23; cf. Psalm 41:9, cited in Mark 14:18 and John 13:18), what his depiction of Judas's suicide shows, nevertheless, is a correlation. The betrayer of the Son of David likewise kills himself.

29. Chrysostom, "The Gospel of Matthew" (Homily 85.2), quoted in *Matthew 14–28*, ed. Manlio Simonetti, Ancient Christian Commentary on Scripture, NT Ib (Downers Grove, IL: InterVarsity Press, 2001), p. 272.

30. Davies and Allison Jr., *A Critical and Exegetical Commentary on the Gospel according to Saint Matthew*, vol. 3, p. 556.

31. Ibid.

32. Jennie Evelyn Hussey, "Lead Me to Calvary" (1921).

33. Robert Lowry, "Nothing But the Blood" (1876).

34. Bruner calls it a "Tragi-Comedy" (*Churchbook*, p. 681).

Chapter Eighty-three: Why?

1. John calls Barabbas "a robber" (John 18:40b). However, don't take "robber" to mean "thief," for as Rudolf Schnackenburg notes, "the Greek word for 'robber' is also used by Flavius Josephus to denote . . . a freedom fighter" (*The Gospel of Matthew*, trans. Robert R. Barr [Grand Rapids, MI: Eerdmans, 2002], p. 283). Think terrorist.

2. W. D. Davies and Dale C. Allison Jr., *A Critical and Exegetical Commentary on the Gospel according to Saint Matthew*, International Critical Commentary,

vol. 3 (Edinburgh: T&T Clark, 1988-1997), p. 593. Others in church history are not so reserved. For example, according to Réau, *Iconographie* 2/2.453, St. Bridget of Sweden claims that Jesus was given 5,475 lashes (in Ulrich Luz, *Matthew 21–28*, Hermeneia [Minneapolis: Fortress, 2005], p. 519)!

3. Mark Driscoll and Gerry Breshears, *Vintage Jesus: Timeless Answers to Timely Questions* (Wheaton, IL: Crossway, 2007), p. 108.

4. According to ancient Greco-Roman writers, those crucified included "murderers, robbers, mischief-makers . . . and deceivers" (Martin Hengel, *Crucifixion in the Ancient World and the Folly of the Message of the Cross* [Philadelphia: Fortress, 1977], p. 9) as well as those guilty of "desertion to the enemy, the betraying of secrets, incitement to rebellion, murder, prophecy about the welfare of rulers (*de salute dominorum*), nocturnal impiety (*sacra impia nocturna*), magic (*ars magica*), serious cases of the falsification of wills, etc." (ibid., pp. 33, 34).

5. Ibid., p. 5. Cf. Josephus, *Jewish War*, 57.203.

6. Hengel, *Crucifixion in the Ancient World and the Folly of the Message of the Cross*, p. 87.

7. "The pain of crucifixion is so horrendous that a word was invented to explain it: *excruciating* literally means 'from the cross'" (Driscoll and Breshears, *Vintage Jesus*, p. 108).

8. Hengel, *Crucifixion*, p. 37.

9. Ibid., p. 89.

10. Ibid., p. 9.

11. Seneca, quoted in ibid., pp. 30, 31. John R. W. Stott adds:

> Cicero in one of his speeches condemned it as *crudelissimum tueterrimumque supplicium*, "a most cruel and disgusting punishment." A little later he declared: 'To bind a Roman citizen is a crime, to flog him is an abomination, to kill him is almost an act of murder: to crucify him is—What? There is no fitting word that can possibly describe so horrible a deed." (*The Cross of Christ* [Downers Grove, IL: InterVarsity Press, 1996], p. 24.)

12. Stott, *The Cross of Christ*, p. 12.

13. Anonymous, *"Christi Leiden in einer Vision geschaut*," quoted in Luz, *Matthew 21–28*, p. 433.

14. Note Matthew's interest in the meaning of names (cf. 1:21; 16:17), as pointed out by Davies and Allison, *A Critical and Exegetical Commentary on the Gospel according to Saint Matthew*, vol. 3, p. 585.

15. I am indebted to Davies and Allison's observations of these ironies (ibid., vol. 3, pp. 593, 594). I have phrased them in my own way.

16. Craig L. Blomberg, *Matthew,* New American Commentary (Nashville: Broadman, 1992), p. 406.

17. Davies and Allison Jr., *A Critical and Exegetical Commentary on the Gospel according to Saint Matthew*, vol. 3, p. 581. Donald Senior elucidates the irony further:

> Similar to Jesus' response to Judas at the Last Supper (see 26:25) this phrase affirms that the questioner himself has stated the truth in the very question posed. Pilate has not asked "Who are you?" but "Are you the king

> of the Jews?" Jesus' answer has the touch of irony that runs through the passion story: Jesus' opponents often stumble onto an ironic truth apparent to the reader but hidden from them. (*The Passion of Jesus in the Gospel of Matthew* [Collegeville, MN: Liturgical Press, 1985], p. 111.)

18. As Senior notes: "The evangelist does not explicitly quote from the Suffering Servant song of Isaiah but clearly wraps the figure of Jesus in the mantle of that mysterious Israelite who bore abuse in silence and atoned for the sins of the people" (*The Passion of Jesus in the Gospel of Matthew*, p. 111). Cf. Douglas J. Moo, *The Old Testament in the Gospel Passion Narratives* (Sheffield: Almond, 1983), pp. 148–151.

19. Calvin, *Isaiah*, 8.119, quoted in Michael LeFebvre, *Singing the Songs of Jesus: Revisiting the Psalms* (Fearn, Ross-shire, UK: Christian Focus, 2010), p. 83.

20. Calvin, 3:179, quoted in Frederick Dale Bruner, *The Churchbook: Matthew 13–28*, 2nd and rev. ed. (Grand Rapids, MI: Eerdmans, 2004), p. 712. Bruner also cites Matthew Henry: "He was arraigned that we might be discharged."

21. Calvin, 3:180, quoted in ibid., p. 714.

22. Bruner notes that "most commentators believe that it ["Jesus" before "Barabbas"] was in the originals" (ibid., p. 717). He lists nine of today's top Gospel scholars.

23. Schnackenburg, *The Gospel of Matthew*, p. 283. Blomberg comments:

> Several important manuscripts and versions (Θ, f^1, 700, Syriac, Armenian, Georgian, Origen), and only in Matthew, add in both vv. 16 and 17 that Barabbas's forename was "Jesus." Although the external evidence for accepting these readings as original is relatively weak, it is hard to imagine anyone creating this potentially embarrassing parallel if it were not true (whether or not Matthew actually wrote it in his autograph). . . . Certainly, having both characters named Jesus tightens the parallelism and makes the irony of the crowd's response all the greater. (Blomberg, *Matthew*, p. 411.)

24. The fivefold repetition of Jesus' and Barabbas's names seems to emphasize this reading of contrast.

25. For many of the thoughts in this paragraph I am indebted to chapter 1 of Mark Driscoll and Gerry Breshears, *Vintage Jesus*, as well as Pastor Todd Wilson's sermon "This Jesus," at http://www.calvarymemorial.com/sermons/this-jesus/; accessed February 16, 2012.

26. Trilling, *Israel*, p. 68, quoted in Luz, *Matthew 21–28*, p. 498.

27. "Throughout this story it is the women who speak or act truly: the unnamed woman who anointed Jesus, the servant-girls who challenge Peter's concealment, the women at the cross and beside the tomb." N. T. Wright, *Matthew for Everyone,* vol. 2 (Louisville: Westminster John Knox, 2002), p. 179.

28. These are direct statements or obvious allusions to Martin Luther King Jr.'s famous speech delivered August 28, 1963 at the Lincoln Memorial in Washington, DC.

29. On the "good crowds" in Matthew, see Senior, *The Passion of Jesus in the Gospel of Matthew*, pp. 115, 116.

30. Bruner, *The Churchbook*, p. 720.

31. C. S. Lewis, *Screwtape Letters* (New York: Macmillan, 1948), p. 149.

32. On hand washing as a gesture of removing guilt, see Deuteronomy 21:1–9. Ironically Pilate comes off worse than Judas, who confessed and repented of his sin of handing over an innocent man.

33. William Barclay, *The Gospel of Matthew*, vol. 2, rev. ed. (Philadelphia: Westminster, 1975), p. 362.

34. Shakespeare, *Macbeth*, Act 5, Scene 1.

35. Leo the Great, quoted in Luz, *Matthew 21–28*, p. 506.

36. Bruner, *The Churchbook*, p. 722.

37. Ibid.

38. Luz, *Matthew 21–28*, p. 501.

39. See Bruner, *The Churchbook*, p. 725.

40. St. Jerome, *Commentary on Matthew*, Fathers of the Church, vol. 117, trans. Thomas P. Scheck (Washington, DC: Catholic University of America, 2008), p. 313.

41. "O Sacred Head, Now Wounded" is based on a medieval Latin poem ascribed to Bernard of Clairvaux and translated into German by Paul Gerhardt (1656) and into English by James W. Alexander (1830).

42. Isaac Watts, "Joy to the World" (1719).

43. See Figure 40, in Luz, *Matthew 21–28*, p. 505.

44. From Charles Dickens, *A Tale of Two Cities,* referenced in Wright, *Matthew for Everyone*, vol. 2, pp. 177, 178.

45. See endnote 1. As Daniel M. Doriani notes, "Rebellion was punishable with crucifixion, but robbery was not" (*Matthew*, Reformed Expository Commentary, vol. 2 [Phillipsburg, NJ: P&R, 2008], p. 121, n. 8).

46. Davies and Allison Jr., *A Critical and Exegetical Commentary on the Gospel according to Saint Matthew*, vol. 3, p. 585.

47. Bruner uses quotation marks in the second sentence without reference, in *The Churchbook*, p. 726.

Chapter Eighty-four: Behold Your King!

1. It is now on display at Kelvingrove Art Gallery and Museum, Glasgow, Scotland. Dali named the painting after a drawing of St. John of the Cross, the sixteenth-century mystic, on which he based some of the dimensions—most notably the extreme angle of the forward-leaning Jesus.

2. Derek Tidball, *The Message of the Cross*, The Bible Speaks Today (Downers Grove, IL: InterVarsity Press, 2001), p. 319.

3. Quoted in ibid., p. 20.

4. Ibid.

5. Charles Wesley, "Hark! the Herald Angels Sing" (1739).

6. See the first half of Jesus' third prediction in 20:18, 19.

7. W. D. Davies and Dale C. Allison Jr., *A Critical and Exegetical Commentary on the Gospel according to Saint Matthew*, International Critical Commentary, vol. 3 (Edinburgh: T&T Clark, 1988-1997), p. 597; Ulrich Luz, *Matthew 21–28*, Hermeneia (Minneapolis: Fortress, 2005), p. 512.

8. Frederick Dale Bruner, *The Churchbook: Matthew 13–28*, 2nd and rev. ed. (Grand Rapids, MI: Eerdmans, 2004), p. 727.

9. *John Bunyan's A Pilgrim's Progress*, retold by Geraldine McCaughrean, illustrated by Jason Cockcroft (New York: Overlook Press, 2005), pp. 35, 36.

10. Keith Getty and Stuart Townend, "My Heart Is Filled with Thankfulness" (Thankyou Music, EMI Christian Music Publishing, 2003).

11. Thomas Kelly, "Stricken, Smitten, and Afflicted" (1804).

12. N. T. Wright, *Matthew for Everyone*, vol. 2 (Louisville: Westminster John Knox, 2002), p. 183. On the Sermon on the Mount Wright comments:

> Notice how, in this passage, parts of the Sermon on the Mount come back into play. Jesus himself, at last, is struck about the face by the soldiers, and doesn't retaliate (Matthew 5:39). They take off his outer and inner garments, leaving him naked (Matthew 5:40). As he is going out to be crucified, the soldiers use their "right" under Roman law to compel someone to carry a burden for them, just as in Matthew 5:41; only this time the burden in question is the heavy crossbeam on which Jesus will be hung. The point of it all is this: Jesus is leading the way he has spoken of from the beginning, the way of being God's true Israel, the light of the world. He himself is set on a hill, unable now to remain hidden (5:14).

13. As summarized by John R. W. Stott, *The Cross of Christ* (Downers Grove, IL: InterVarsity Press, 1996), p. 40.

14. Quran 4:157–158. I used *The Qur'an: The First American Version*, trans. T. B. Irving (Brattleboro, VT: Amana, 1985), pp. 50, 51.

15. As summarized by Daniel M. Doriani, *Matthew*, Reformed Expository Commentary, vol. 2 (Phillipsburg, NJ: P&R, 2008), p. 495.

16. "Then the soldiers take the reed and repeatedly . . . hit Jesus on the head. Since that is where the crown of thorns is, it does not require much imagination on the part of the readers to figure out that such blows are especially painful" (Luz, *Matthew 21–28*, p. 515).

17. Josephus, *Antiquities*, 14.115.

18. R. T. France, *The Gospel of Matthew*, New International Commentary on the New Testament (Grand Rapids, MI: Eerdmans, 2007), p. 1065.

19. So Origen, as noted in Luz, *Matthew 21–28*, p. 516.

20. Hilary of Poitier, "On Matthew" (33:3), quoted in *Matthew 14–28*, ed. Manlio Simonetti, Ancient Christian Commentary on Scripture, NT Ib (Downers Grove, IL: InterVarsity Press, 2001), p. 284.

21. Luther, quoted in Luz, *Matthew 21–28*, p. 530.

22. Much of the information on imitation in Matthew is from an e-mail Jason Hood sent me on June 13, 2011. The title of his book is *Imitating God in Christ: Recapturing a Biblical Pattern* (Downers Grove, IL: IVP Academic, 2013).

23. Hood provides a number of references from Matthew. I limited the texts to one each.

24. For example, Michael J. Gorman, *Cruciformity: Paul's Narrative Spirituality of the Cross* (Grand Rapids, MI: Eerdmans, 2001).

25. Elvina M. Hall, "Jesus Paid It All," 1865; cf. Hebrews 9:23–26.

26. The sacrifice of Jesus' body for us is perfect. However, we are called on the basis of his sufferings to likewise offer our living sacrifices (Romans 12:1). As Leon Morris summarizes: "If Christ died for us, we are to live for him" (*The Atonement: Its Meaning and Significance* [Downers Grove, IL: IVP Academic, 1983], p. 204).

27. See Martin Hengel, *Crucifixion in the Ancient World and the Folly of the Message of the Cross* (Philadelphia: Fortress, 1977), p. 18.

Chapter Eighty-five: The Power of the Cross

1. Bengel notes that as there are the seven last words by Jesus on the cross, so there are "seven scoffs" by his enemies below the cross (Bengel, 1:305, in Frederick Dale Bruner, *The Churchbook: Matthew 13–28*, 2nd and rev. ed. [Grand Rapids, MI: Eerdmans, 2004], p. 736).

2. For example, see Régis Debray, *The New Testament Through 100 Masterpieces of Art* (New York: Merrell, 2004), pp. 173, 175, 177.

3. See Proverbs 31:6; cf. *Sanh.* 43a.

4. William Barclay, *The Gospel of Matthew*, vol. 2, rev. ed. (Philadelphia: Westminster, 1975), p. 366.

5. W. D. Davies and Dale C. Allison Jr., *A Critical and Exegetical Commentary on the Gospel according to Saint Matthew*, International Critical Commentary, vol. 3 (Edinburgh: T&T Clark, 1988-1997), p. 613.

6. Bruner, *The Churchbook*, p. 733. Ulrich Luz remarks, "Strangely reserved and frugal is this text that tells of the crucifixion of Jesus—what one might call the most sacred part of the Christian faith" (*Matthew 21–28*, Hermeneia [Minneapolis: Fortress, 2005], p. 535). Similarly, Raymond E. Brown asks, "In all comparable literature, has so crucial a moment ever been phrased so briefly and uninformatively?" (*The Death of the Messiah: From Gethsemane to the Grave; A Commentary on the Passion Narratives in the Four Gospels*, vol. 2 [New York: Doubleday, 1994], p. 945).

7. From Melito's *Homily on the Passion*, quoted in Martin Hengel, *Crucifixion in the Ancient World and the Folly of the Message of the Cross* (Philadelphia: Fortress, 1977), p. 21.

8. This reference is made explicit in John's Gospel (John 19:23, 24).

9. Bruner notes the different *tituli* used by the four Gospel writers and points out how Matthew's addition of "this is" turns the *titulus* from "an accusation to a proclamation, from a charge to a claim" (Bruner, *The Churchbook*, p. 735).

10. Ibid., p. 736; cf. Davies and Dale C. Allison Jr., *A Critical and Exegetical Commentary on the Gospel according to Saint Matthew*, vol. 3, p. 617, n. 43.

11. I say that "those who passed by" (v. 39) are Jews because of the substance of their scorn (the "temple" and "Son of God" (v. 40) language) as well as their grasp (mistaken as it was) of Jesus' cry in 27:47.

12. Bruner, *The Churchbook*, p. 737.

13. Donald Senior notes the irony that "the very opponents who had accused Jesus of being in league with Satan (cf. 9:34; 12:24) themselves parrot the demon's proposals" (*The Passion of Jesus in the Gospel of Matthew* [Collegeville, MN: Liturgical Press, 1985], p. 132).

14. Craig L. Blomberg, *Matthew*, New American Commentary (Nashville: Broadman, 1992), p. 418.

15. Ibid., pp. 417, 418.

16. See the articles by Jordan Walker at http://yaledailynews.com/blog/2011/04/21/walker-an-insulting-prank-and-hypocritical-response/ and Garrett Fiddler at http://yaledailynews.com/blog/2011/04/21/fiddler-good-friday-and-the-rofl-cross/; accessed on January 17, 2013.

17. See Luz, *Matthew 21–28*, p. 537, Figure 51.

18. Hengel, *Crucifixion*, p. 89.

19. Makoto Fujimura, *The Four Holy Gospels* (Wheaton, IL: Crossway, 2011), pp. 38, 39.

20. Bruner, *The Churchbook*, pp. 738, 739.

21. Ibid., p. 739.

22. Grant R. Osborne notes that this is the only the second time in the Gospels that the verb "believe in" is used (cf. Luke 24:25) (*Matthew,* Exegetical Commentary on the New Testament [Grand Rapids, MI: Zondervan, 2010], p. 1036).

23. Booth, quoted in Barclay, *The Gospel of Matthew*, vol. 2, p. 367.

24. *The Times*, September 6, 1998. This story is told in Derek Tidball, *The Message of the Cross*, The Bible Speaks Today (Downers Grove, IL: InterVarsity Press, 2001), p. 200.

25. George Bennard, "The Old Rugged Cross" (1913).

Chapter Eighty-six: The Death of Death in the Death of Christ

1. John R. W. Stott, *The Cross of Christ* (Downers Grove, IL: InterVarsity Press, 1996), pp. 7, 68.

2. Spurgeon, quoted in Derek Tidball, *The Message of the Cross*, The Bible Speaks Today (Downers Grove, IL: InterVarsity Press, 2001), p. 22.

3. J. I. Packer, quoted in Stott, *The Cross of Christ,* p. 7.

4. Forsyth, quoted in Tidball, *The Message of the Cross*, p. 135.

5. Campbell, quoted in ibid., p. 22.

6. Calvin, quoted in Stott, *The Cross of Christ*, p. 206.

7. Because the three signs following Jesus' death are best understood as divine interventions, I take this darkness to be a divine intervention as well. Furthermore, as Grant R. Osborne points out, this reading fits "with Matthew's predilection for divine intervention (cf. 1:18, 20–21; 2:12, 13, 19–20; 27:51–53; 28:2–3)" (*Matthew*, Exegetical Commentary on the New Testament [Grand Rapids, MI: Zondervan, 2010], pp. 1036, 1037). Cf. Origen, "Commentary on Matthew 134," quoted in *Matthew 14–28*, ed. Manlio Simonetti, Ancient Christian Commentary on Scripture, NT Ib (Downers Grove, IL: InterVarsity Press, 2001), p. 293.

8. Matthew Henry, quoted in Frederick Dale Bruner, *The Churchbook: Matthew 13–28*, 2nd and rev. ed. (Grand Rapids, MI: Eerdmans, 2004), p. 745. I have slightly reordered Henry's sentence.

9. Jerome, quoted in ibid., p. 746.

10. By saying that Matthew has painted the scene black, I'm in no way denying the historical facts of this whole scene—from darkness to resurrected bodies. Perhaps what Paul N. Anderson said of John's Gospel might also be applied here to Matthew's—that the Gospel of Matthew is *history dramatized*, not drama historicized. See his *Fourth Gospel and the Quest for Jesus: Modern Foundations Reconsidered*, Library of New Testament Studies (New York: T&T Clark/Continuum, 2006), p. 32.

11. "The end of Jesus is the end of the world in miniature." W. D. Davies and Dale C. Allison Jr., *A Critical and Exegetical Commentary on the Gospel according to Saint Matthew*, International Critical Commentary, vol. 3 (Edinburgh: T&T Clark, 1988-1997), p. 639.

12. Davies and Allison Jr. believe that silence is implied by verse 46 (ibid., vol. 3, p. 622).

13. Schlatter, *Der Evangelist*, pp. 782, 783, in Bruner, *The Churchbook*, p. 746.

14. Bruner, *The Churchbook*, p. 746.

15. Cranfield, quoted in Stott, *The Cross of Christ*, p. 82.

16. Bruner, *The Churchbook*, p. 748.

17. Donald Senior, *The Passion of Jesus in the Gospel of Matthew* (Collegeville, MN: Liturgical Press, 1985), p. 137.

18. Ulrich Luz, *Matthew 21–28*, Hermeneia (Minneapolis: Fortress, 2005), p. 552.

19. Brown surveys the possible medical reasons for Jesus' death. See Raymond E. Brown, *The Death of the Messiah: From Gethsemane to the Grave; A Commentary on the Passion Narratives in the Four Gospels*, vol. 2 (New York: Doubleday, 1994), pp. 1088–1092.

20. William Barclay, *The Gospel of Matthew*, vol. 2, rev. ed. (Philadelphia: Westminster, 1975), p. 370.

21. Tidball, *The Message of the Cross*, p. 131.

22. The ESV renders it "The tombs *also* were opened" (v. 52). That misses the important rhythm of the repeated *kai*.

23. The passive verb "was torn" (v. 51), as Luz notes, "suggests an act of God (*passivum divinum*)" (*Matthew 21–28*, p. 566). Luz also notes that Matthew speaks in the *passivum divinum* for each of the three signs (pp. 566, 567).

24. Bruner, *The Churchbook*, p. 757.

25. J. C. Ryle, *Matthew: Expository Thoughts on the Gospels*, Crossway Classic Commentaries (Wheaton, IL: Crossway, 1993), p. 284.

26. Bruner, *The Churchbook*, p. 759.

27. Ibid., p. 763.

28. Davies and Allison Jr., *A Critical and Exegetical Commentary on the Gospel according to Saint Matthew*, vol. 3, p. 628.

29. Ibid., vol. 3, p. 633.

30. Augustine, quoted in Bruner, *The Churchbook*, p. 760.

31. Ibid.

32. Régis Debray notes that the seventeenth-century Jansenists characteristically did this (*The New Testament Through 100 Masterpieces of Art* [New York: Merrell, 2004], p. 171).

33. See Peter Harbison, *The Crucifixion in Irish Art* (Harrisburg, PA: Morehouse, 2000), pp. 84, 85. For other examples in Irish Art of the V-shaped Christ, see pp. 38, 45, 62, 74, 89, 94.

34. See Imogen Stuart's large bronze crucifix at St. Patrick's Cathedral, Armagh, pictured in ibid., p. 97.

Chapter Eighty-seven: Things into Which Angels Long to Look

1. Calvin, quoted in Frederick Dale Bruner, *The Churchbook: Matthew 13–28*, 2nd and rev. ed. (Grand Rapids, MI: Eerdmans, 2004), p. 766.

2. Craig L. Blomberg, *Matthew*, New American Commentary (Nashville: Broadman, 1992), p. 422.

3. Ibid.

4. W. D. Davies and Dale C. Allison Jr., *A Critical and Exegetical Commentary on the Gospel according to Saint Matthew*, International Critical Commentary, vol. 3 (Edinburgh: T&T Clark, 1988-1997), p. 635.

5. Luther, quoted in Bruner, *The Churchbook*, p. 764.

6. Ibid., p. 766, emphasis his.

7. "The fact that Joseph requested Jesus' body from Pilate, and that Pilate granted the request, shows well enough that Jesus was indeed dead. Roman soldiers and governors didn't go in for half-measures when it came to carrying out capital sentences. Any possibility that they had let a condemned rebel leader escape death can be left out of the question. Likewise, the fact that Jesus' main disciples had nothing to do with the whole procedure, but were in hiding, indicates well enough that they wouldn't have been in a position to steal the body" (N. T. Wright, *Matthew for Everyone*, vol. 2 [Louisville: Westminster John Knox, 2002], pp. 195, 196).

8. "While we do not draw a parallel between the new tomb and Mary's virgin womb, we do see similarities between 27.57–66 and the Gospel's opening. Both sections tell of the pious actions of a Joseph on behalf of a helpless Jesus. Neither Joseph says anything. And in both instances Jewish leaders gather to the secular authority to oppose Jesus and his cause. These agreements produce aesthetic satisfaction: beginning and end mirror each other. They also teach a theological lesson: despite all that happens between the birth and death of Jesus, unbelief stands fast, hostility endures. The wicked stay set in their ways" (Davies and Allison Jr., *A Critical and Exegetical Commentary on the Gospel according to Saint Matthew*, vol. 3, p. 656). On that same page they also quote, as other commentators do, Richard Crashaw's poem:

> How Life and Death in Thee
> Agree!
> Thou had'st a virgin wombe
> And Tombe
> A Joseph did betroth
> Them both.

9. Bruner, *The Churchbook*, p. 772.

10. See Westminster Shorter Catechism 1:27; cf. Westminster Confession of Faith 8.4.

11. H. N. Ridderbos, *Matthew*, Bible Student's Commentary (Grand Rapids, MI: Zondervan, 1987), pp. 540, 541.

12. D. A. Carson, "Matthew," in *The Expositor's Bible Commentary*, vol. 9, rev. ed. (Grand Rapids, MI: Zondervan, 2010), p. 652.

13. Davies and Allison Jr., *A Critical and Exegetical Commentary on the Gospel according to Saint Matthew*, vol. 3, p. 648.

14. Bruner, *The Churchbook*, p. 766.

15. See *m. Roš Haš.* 1:8; Josephus, *Antiquities* 4.219.

16. Davies and Allison Jr., *A Critical and Exegetical Commentary on the Gospel according to Saint Matthew*, vol. 3, p. 637.

17. As Calvin said,

> Not without reason do the Evangelists give first place to the women, as worthy to be put before the men. In my judgment the tacit contrast is serious criticism of the apostles. . . . In their later publication of the Gospel they must have borrowed from the women the chief part of the story. (Quoted in Bruner, *The Churchbook*, p. 767.)

18. Taken from Douglas Sean O'Donnell, *God's Lyrics: Rediscovering Worship Through Old Testament Songs* (Phillipsburg, NJ: P&R, 2010), pp. 3, 4.

19. Bruner also uses the Jefferson Bible illustration and gives this helpful summary statement (*The Churchbook*, p. 773).

Chapter Eighty-eight: Behold Him That *Was* Crucified

1. See John R. W. Stott, *The Cross of Christ* (Downers Grove, IL: InterVarsity Press, 1996), p. 91.
2. See ibid., pp. 98, 99.
3. Ibid., p. 99.
4. See ibid., p. 109.
5. H. Richard Niebuhr, *The Kingdom of God in America* (Chicago: Willett, Clark, 1937), p. 193.
6. Mark Driscoll and Gerry Breshears, *Vintage Jesus: Timeless Answers to Timely Questions* (Wheaton, IL: Crossway, 2007), p. 114.
7. Frederick Dale Bruner, *The Churchbook: Matthew 13–28*, 2nd and rev. ed. (Grand Rapids, MI: Eerdmans, 2004), p. 774.
8. Ibid., p. 775.
9. Donald A. Hagner, *Matthew 14–28*, Word Biblical Commentary, vol. 33b (Nashville: Thomas Nelson, 1993), p. 864.
10. Perhaps the Jewish leaders paid no attention to the "many women" at the crucifixion and the two who came to the tomb because they couldn't imagine women rolling back a stone or the testimony of women being believed.
11. Henry, quoted in Bruner, *The Churchbook*, p. 777.
12. Chrysostom, 89:2:526, quoted in Bruner, *The Churchbook*, p. 777, emphasis mine.
13. R. E. Brown, "The Resurrection of Jesus," in *The New Jerome Biblical Commentary* (Englewood Cliffs, NJ: Prentice Hall, 1990), p. 1373.
14. Craig L. Blomberg, *Matthew*, New American Commentary (Nashville: Broadman, 1992), p. 425.
15. Daniel M. Doriani, *Matthew*, Reformed Expository Commentary, vol. 2 (Phillipsburg, NJ: P&R, 2008), p. 517.
16. John Nolland, *The Gospel of Matthew*, New International Greek Testament Commentary (Grand Rapids, MI: Eerdmans, 2005), p. 1256.
17. H. N. Ridderbos, *Matthew*, Bible Student's Commentary (Grand Rapids, MI: Zondervan, 1987), p. 552.
18. This Roman proverb is quoted in William Barclay, *The Gospel of Matthew*, vol. 2, rev. ed. (Philadelphia: Westminster, 1975), p. 377.
19. Bruner, *The Churchbook*, p. 775.
20. Other views that are "alive" today include (a) the women went to the wrong tomb, (b) Jesus never really died on the cross, and (c) someone other than the disciples stole the body.

21. So Calvin, in Bruner, *The Churchbook*, p. 801.

22. Blomberg, *Matthew*, p. 424.

23. "What do you say, chief priest? Do you really think that Christ said to his men 'after three days I will rise again' and then secretly commanded them to steal his body during the night and to tell everyone that he had risen from the dead after three days? Yet it is manifestly incredible that after giving such great moral instruction to all peoples and after demonstrating such great power throughout all of Judea, he would then turn and deceive his disciples." Origen, "Commentary on Matthew 145," quoted in *Matthew 14–28*, ed. Manlio Simonetti, Ancient Christian Commentary on Scripture, NT Ib (Downers Grove, IL: InterVarsity Press, 2001), p. 302.

24. N. T. Wright, *Matthew for Everyone*, vol. 2 (Louisville: Westminster John Knox, 2002), p. 204.

25. Arthur Conan Doyle, *The Sign of the Four*, quoted in Paul Beasley-Murray, *The Message of the Resurrection*, The Bible Speaks Today (Downers Grove, IL: InterVarsity Press, 2000), p. 51.

26. "How could this remarkable transformation in the perceived status of Jesus have come about if he had remained dead? He died as a common criminal, perhaps even a prophet, or maybe a martyr—but the most this would merit would be veneration of his tomb (see 23:29). Why did the early Christians start talking about a dead rabbi as if he were God? And, perhaps even more intriguing, why did they start talking about him as if he were alive, praying to him and worshipping him?" Alister McGrath, *Doubting: Growing Through the Uncertainties of Faith* (Downers Grove, IL: InterVarsity Press, 2006), p. 99.

27. These are George Beasley-Murray's six facts pointing to the resurrection, as summarized by his son, Paul Beasley-Murray, *The Message of the Resurrection*, p. 246. Some of the wording is mine.

28. For an extensive study on the Jewish backgrounds related to the resurrection of Jesus, see N. T. Wright, *The Resurrection of the Son of God* (Minneapolis: Fortress, 2003), pp. 85–206.

29. Wright, *Matthew for Everyone*, vol. 2, p. 202.

30. "Gnilka [*Matthäusevangelium,* 2:490] notes the centrality of verbs for 'seeing' in this final section (28:1, 6, 7, 17, plus the six uses of 'look' . . . in the chapter) and concludes that Matthew stresses what one can see with the eyes as interpreted through the Word. Matthew clearly believes that Jesus actually appeared and was 'seen' by the disciples." Grant R. Osborne, *Matthew*, Exegetical Commentary on the New Testament (Grand Rapids, MI: Zondervan, 2010), p. 1056. Cf. W. D. Davies and Dale C. Allison Jr., *A Critical and Exegetical Commentary on the Gospel according to Saint Matthew*, International Critical Commentary, vol. 3 (Edinburgh: T&T Clark, 1988-1997), p. 659.

31. Wright states that a colloquial equivalent of *idou* would be "Guess what!" (*The Resurrection of the Son of God*, p. 640).

32. In 1 Corinthians 15:3–6 Paul writes of Jesus being "raised on the third day" and appearing "to Cephas [Peter], then to the twelve . . . [and then] to more than five hundred brothers at one time, most of whom are still alive." Timothy Keller comments, "Here Paul not only speaks of the empty tomb and resurrection on the 'third day' (showing he is talking of a historical event, not a symbol or metaphor) but he also list the eyewitnesses. Paul indicates that the risen Jesus not only appeared to

individuals and small groups, but he also appeared to five hundred people at once, most of whom were still alive at the time of his writing and could be consulted for corroboration. Paul's letter was to a church, and therefore it was a public document, written to be read aloud. Paul was inviting anyone who doubted that Jesus had appeared to people after his death to go and talk to the eyewitnesses if they wished" (*The Reason for God: Belief in an Age of Skepticism* [New York: Dutton], p. 204).

33. George Eldon Ladd, *I Believe in the Resurrection* (London: Hodder & Stoughton, 1975), p. 140.

34. "In a purely fictional narrative one would have avoided making women the crown witnesses of the resurrection since they were considered in rabbinic Judaism as incapable of giving valid testimony. . . . The circumstance that the same women wanted to anoint the dead Jesus right after his burial, as Jewish custom demanded, proves that basically none of the disciples nor the women themselves . . . expected the resurrection." Pinchas Lapide, *The Resurrection of Jesus: A Jewish Perspective*, quoted in Beasley-Murray, *The Message of the Resurrection*, pp. 250, 251.

35. Comparing the angel in Matthew 28 with the one in Matthew 1, 2, Luz and others point out the significance of this second angel not coming indirectly through dreams but bodily and directly from Heaven. See Ulrich Luz, *Matthew 21–28*, Hermeneia (Minneapolis: Fortress, 2005), p. 595.

36. Ibid.

37. "An angel descended and rolled back the stone. He did not roll back the stone to provide a way of escape for the Lord but to show the world that the Lord had already risen. He rolled back the stone to help his fellow servants believe, not to help the Lord rise from the dead. He rolled back the stone for the sake of faith, because it had been rolled over the tomb for the sake of unbelief." Chrysologus, "Sermons 75.4," quoted in *Matthew 14–28*, p. 306.

38. Bruner, *The Churchbook*, p. 789.

39. See 12:40; 16:21; 17:9, 23; 20:19; 26:32, as noted by a number of commentators.

40. Bruner, *The Churchbook*, p. 789.

41. The lobotomy bit comes from ibid., p. 790.

42. Osborne, *Matthew*, p. 1069.

43. Bruner, *The Churchbook*, pp. 795, 796.

44. Ibid., p. 796.

45. As pointed out by Bultmann; see ibid., p. 797.

46. Rudolf Schnackenburg, *The Gospel of Matthew*, trans. Robert R. Barr (Grand Rapids, MI: Eerdmans, 2002), p. 296. As David L. Turner states, "the women's worship is indicative of Matthew's high Christology" (*The Gospel of Matthew*, Cornerstone Biblical Commentary [Wheaton, IL: Tyndale, 2005], p. 371).

47. Davies and Allison Jr., *A Critical and Exegetical Commentary on the Gospel according to Saint Matthew*, vol. 3, p. 699.

48. See John 20:8, 11–18, 19–23, 24–29; 21:4–14.

49. Bruner, *The Churchbook*, p. 788.

Chapter Eighty-nine: Operation Immanuel

1. Joe LoMusio, *If I Should Die Before I Live* (Chino, CA: R. C Law & Co., 1989). I am thankful to Sparky Pritchard for this reference.

2. I say "forgiveness of sins" because that is part of Jesus' teachings (Matthew 6:12, 14, 15; 9:1–8; 12:31, 32; 18:15–35; 26:28) and what the apostles preached in Acts (Acts 2:38; 5:31; 8:22; 10:43; 13:38; 26:18). Furthermore, Ulrich Luz notes that "the promise of the forgiveness of sins is also associated with baptism" (*Matthew 21–28*, Hermeneia [Minneapolis: Fortress, 2005], p. 632). Baptism is the outward sign of God's full forgiveness.

3. Frederick Dale Bruner, *The Churchbook: Matthew 13–28*, 2nd and rev. ed. (Grand Rapids, MI: Eerdmans, 2004), p. 806.

4. Ibid., pp. 793, 806.

5. Other key Isaiah texts on "the nations" include Isaiah 42:6, 49:6, and 54:2, 3.

6. Building on D. A. Carson, Grant R. Osborne notes: "'Galilee of the Gentiles' (4:15) is a major theme of the great commission (28:19) and sums up the Gentile mission in Matthew (see 1:5, 6; 2:1–12; 4:14–16, 25; 8:5–13, 28–34; 10:18; 12:21, 42; 13:38; 15:21–28, 29–31; 24:14, 31; 25:31–46; 28:10, 19)" (*Matthew*, Exegetical Commentary on the New Testament [Grand Rapids, MI: Zondervan, 2010], p. 1069).

7. As Craig L. Blomberg points out, we should remember that in Matthew mountains or "the mountain" is viewed "as a place of revelation and communion with God . . . (cf. 4:8; 14:23; 15:29; 17:1; 24:3; 26:30)" (*Matthew*, New American Commentary [Nashville: Broadman, 1992], p. 430).

8. N. T. Wright, *Matthew for Everyone*, vol. 2 (Louisville: Westminster John Knox, 2002), p. 206.

9. See 21:21 for an antithetical parallel with a different word for "doubt."

10. Bruner, *The Churchbook*, p. 810.

11. See http://ioimprov.com/chicago/io/shows/improvised-shakespeare; accessed April 9, 2012.

12. From Matthew Mason's paper, "Training Drama Queens and Raising Pumpkin Patch Kids: Theodramatic Catechesis in the Local Church." Read in June 2011 at the annual meeting of SAET (The Society for the Advancement of Ecclesial Theology).

13. Osborne states that Otto Michel was "the first to call this passage the conclusion and recapitulation of Matthew's major themes." Michel, "The Conclusion of Matthew's Gospel," in *The Interpretation of Matthew*, ed. G. Stanton (Edinburgh: T & T Clark, 1995, originally 1950), pp. 39–51, in Osborne, *Matthew*, p. 1076. Most commentators agree. "This short account contains the culmination and combination of all of Matthew's central themes" (Blomberg, *Matthew*, p. 429). Luz calls it "the 'summa' of the Gospel" (*Matthew 21–28*, p. 636). "The Great Commission is nothing less than a summary of the whole Gospel of Matthew" (Bornkamm, "Auferstandene," 173, from B. J. Hubbard, *The Matthean Redaction of a Primitive Apostolic Commissioning* [1974], p. 98), in Bruner, *The Churchbook*, p. 806. I must include Adolf Harnack's famous praise: "The formulation of the *Manifesto* Matthew 28:18ff. . . . is a masterpiece. . . . One cannot say anything greater or more in forty words" (in Bruner, *The Churchbook*, p. 812).

14. See 7:29; 8:8, 9; 10:1; 21:23, 24, 27.

15. Osborne, *Matthew*, p. 1079.

16. Rudolf Schnackenburg, *The Gospel of Matthew*, trans. Robert R. Barr (Grand Rapids, MI: Eerdmans, 2002), p. 298.

17. H. N. Ridderbos, *Matthew*, Bible Student's Commentary (Grand Rapids, MI: Zondervan, 1987), p. 552.

18. Osborne, *Matthew*, p. 1083. Osborne adds, "As God himself, Jesus has power over all the forces of heaven and over his creation, earth (John 1:3–4; 1 Cor 8:6; Col 1:16; Heb 1:3). Everything said of Yahweh in the creation theology of the OT (e.g. Job 38–41; Ps 89:11–13; Isa 40:26, 28; 42:5) applies to Jesus in his cosmic authority."

19. N. T. Wright, *The Resurrection of the Son of God* (Minneapolis: Fortress, 2003), p. 644.

20. Osborne comments:

> Most doubt the Trinitarian emphasis because of the absence of any such theology in Matthew. For instance, Luz says, "Of course, the triadic baptismal command does not yet imply the much later dogma of the Trinity, although later it was thusly interpreted" [*Matthew 21–28*, p. 632]. Certainly this is not the Nicene Creed, but there is a Trinitarian theology in the NT, seen in 1 Cor 12:4–6; 2 Cor 13:14; Eph 4:4–6; 2 Thess 2:13–14; 1 Pet 1:2; Jude 20–21; Rev 1:4–5; and this is in line with the early beliefs in the deity of each member of the Godhead, the personhood of each member, and the fact that there is one God. We must speak of at least an incipient Trinitarian theology, and that this passage states that conversion and baptism bring us into a unity and community with that threefold Godhead. . . . Moreover, Jesus is still bringing together his many statements on his Father (5:48; 6:1, 4; 11:25–27; 24:36), himself as the Son (16:27; 24:36), and the Holy Spirit (12:18, 28, 32); and Matthew is once again (as in all the discourses) abbreviating a lengthy teaching of Jesus on the mountain of revelation. (*Matthew*, p. 1081.)

Blomberg is also helpful. He writes:

> Here is the clearest Trinitarian "formula" anywhere in the Gospels, and it is therefore often accused of being a very late development and not at all something Jesus himself could have imagined. But this view misjudges both the speed of the development of New Testament theology (cf. Jesus as God already in Acts 3:14–15—unless by circular reasoning this passage is also dismissed as late because of its high Christology), as well as how technical a formula this is. Acts 2:38 demonstrates that other baptismal formulae were also used in the earliest stages of Christianity. Jesus has already spoken of God as his Father (Matt 11:27; 24:36), of himself as the Son (11:27; 16:27; 24:36), and of blasphemy against God's work in himself as against the Spirit (12:28). Mounce states, "That Jesus should gather together into summary form his own references . . . in his final charge to the disciples seems quite natural" [*Matthew*, p. 227]. On the other hand, it is not inconceivable that Matthew distilled the essence of Jesus' more detailed parting instructions for the Eleven into concise language using the terminology developed later in the early church's baptismal services. (*Matthew*, p. 432.)

21. Douglas Wilson, *A Primer on Worship and Reformation: Recovering the High Church Puritan* (Moscow, ID: Canon, 2008), p. 32.

22. To this point John MacArthur wisely notes,

> If God's primary purpose for the saved were loving fellowship, He would take believers immediately to heaven, where spiritual fellowship is perfect, unhindered by sin, disharmony, or loneliness. If His primary purpose for the saved were the learning of His Word, He would also take believers immediately to heaven, where His Word is perfectly known and understood. And if God's primary purpose for the saved were to give Him praise, He would, again take believers immediately to heaven, where praise is perfect and unending. There is only one reason the Lord allows His church to remain on earth: to seek and to save the lost. (*Matthew 24–28* [Chicago: Moody, 1989], p. 333.)

23. Bruner, *The Churchbook*, p. 815.
24. Ibid., p. 816.
25. See D. A. Carson, "Matthew," in *The Expositor's Bible Commentary*, vol. 8 (Grand Rapids, MI: Zondervan, 1984), p. 596.
26. Bruner, *The Churchbook*, p. 824.
27. R. T. France, *The Gospel according to Matthew*, Tyndale New Testament Commentaries (Grand Rapids, MI: Eerdmans, 1985), p. 414. "Most evangelism today is obsessed with getting someone to make a *decision*; the apostles, however, were obsessed with making *disciples*" (Scot McKnight, *The King Jesus Gospel: The Original Good News Revisited* [Grand Rapids, MI: Zondervan, 2011], p. 18).
28. France, *The Gospel according to Matthew*, p. 414.
29. Carson, "Matthew," p. 597.
30. Ibid.
31. Cf. Peter's sermon in Acts 10:34–48, where he hits on nearly every theme in Matthew 28:16–20.
32. MacArthur, *Matthew 24–28*, p. 344.
33. Ibid.
34. Ridderbos, *Matthew*, p. 555.
35. Wright, *Matthew for Everyone*, vol. 2, p. 208.
36. MacArthur, *Matthew 24–28*, p. 344.
37. Wright, *Matthew for Everyone*, vol. 2, p. 208.
38. MacArthur, *Matthew 24–28*, p. 344.
39. From Dick Lucas's sermon "Christ's Teaching on Christ's Teaching," available at http://www.audiop.org.uk/search/series/156.
40. W. D. Davies and Dale C. Allison Jr., *A Critical and Exegetical Commentary on the Gospel according to Saint Matthew*, International Critical Commentary, vol. 3 (Edinburgh: T&T Clark, 1988-1997), p. 686.
41. "Christ did not explicitly tell His apostles on this occasion that they also had to proclaim His cross and resurrection, but their early preaching makes it obvious that they understood this (see Acts 2, 3, 10)" (Ridderbos, *Matthew*, p. 556).
42. Blomberg, *Matthew*, p. 433.
43. "The past tense '*commanded you*,' rather than a future tense '*shall* command you,' nails disciples down to the teaching of the *pre*-Easter *historical* Jesus rather than to a *post*-Easter *mystical* Christ." Bruner, *The Churchbook*, p. 827.
44. Ibid.

45. Cf. Acts 18:10; Hebrews 13:5.

46. Luz notes:

> This "being-with-us" of God in the Immanuel Jesus has proven to be a basic note sounding throughout the entire Gospel (9:15; 17:17; 18:20), but with special intensity in the passion narrative (cf. 26:11, 18, 20, 23, 29, 36, 38, 40, 51, 69, 71). The evangelist repeatedly tells stories about Jesus' helping presence among his disciples (e.g., 8:23–27; 14:13–21, 22–33; 15:29–39; 17:1–8; 26:26–29). (*Matthew 21–28*, p. 634.)

47. France, *The Gospel according to Matthew*, p. 411.

48. John Rippon, "How Firm a Foundation," in Rippon's *Selection of Hymns* (1787).

49. Bruner, *The Churchbook*, p. 830.

50. The Nabokov interview was recounted in Larry Woiwode, *A Step From Death: A Memoir* (Berkeley, CA: Counterpoint, 2008), p. 37.

51. I hope your life begins where Matthew's Gospel ends—Christ-centered, focusing on Jesus's divine attributes more than on our missional actions.

Scripture Index

General Index

Index of Sermon Illustrations

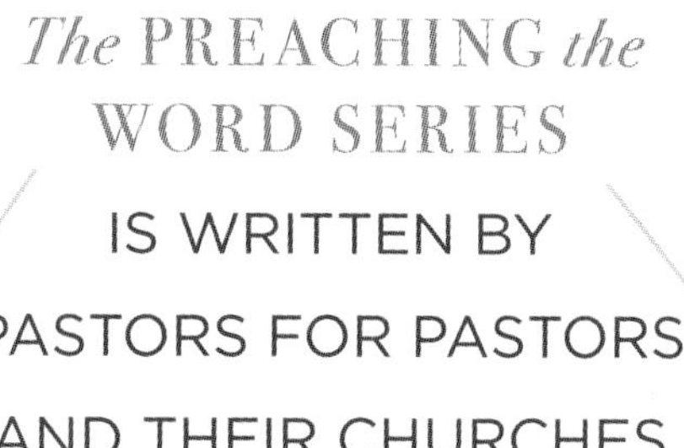

The PREACHING *the* WORD SERIES
IS WRITTEN BY
PASTORS FOR PASTORS
AND THEIR CHURCHES